Parenting with Intimacy Workbook

Dr. David & Teresa Ferguson
Dr. Paul & Vicky Warren
& Terri Ferguson

All Scripture is from the *New American Standard Bible,* © the Lockman Foundation 1960, 1962, 1963, 1968, 1971, 1972, 1973, 1975, 1977.

Editor: Barbara Williams

Design: Scott Rattray

ISBN: 1-56476-523-7

1 2 3 4 5 6 7 8 9 10 Printing/Year 99 98 97 96 95

Contents

Introduction **7**

1 Let the Journey Begin **17**

Part One Know Your Child

2 Unwrapping God's Gifts **29**

3 Understanding Your Child's Needs **47**

4 Understanding Your Child's Fallenness **71**

Part Two Knowing Your Child's Parents

5 Finish Growing Up **93**

6 Provide the Security of a Committed Marriage **121**

7 Live in the Present . . . for Eternity **148**

Part Three Let Your Child Know You

8 Revealing Hope through Your Humanity **185**

9 Revealing Care through Your Discipleship **215**

10 Revealing Truth through Your Testimony **246**

Part Four Becoming Caringly Involved

11 Becoming Caringly Involved to Communicate Worth **285**

12 Becoming Caringly Involved to Build Belonging **309**

13 Becoming Caringly Involved to Instill Competence **330**

Appendices **357**

About the Authors **385**

Acknowledgments

The Parenting with Intimacy Workbook has been a labor of love, and our hearts are filled with gratitude as we pause to reflect on those who labored with us.

First and foremost, thanks be to God who loves us with an everlasting love and forgives us when we falter—which is often! Thank You, Lord, that You're not looking for perfect parents—only faithful ones. "The Lord's loving-kindnesses indeed never cease, for His compassions never fail. They are new every morning; great is Thy faithfulness" (Lam. 3:22-23).

To our son Matthew—the joy of our lives—for his loving heart, patience, and forgiving spirit. We know you've made many sacrifices in order for this project to become a reality—you've been a minister of grace and love to us. We love you!

To our families and friends for their love, support, and sustaining prayers.

To David and Teresa Ferguson, our friends and coauthors, for their love and support, for their example, and for allowing us the joy of ministering with them as part of the Intimate Life team.

To Terri Ferguson—for her friendship, creativity, sense of humor, and love for kids.

To Betty Zamorsky for her patience, graciousness, and servant's heart.

To Bill Anderson for his typesetting and layout contributions—and his lightning speed!

To Barb Williams for her editorial expertise and commitment to seeing this project come to fruition.

And, finally, to David Horton and Victor Books—Thank you for catching the Intimate Life vision and for believing in this project.

—Paul and Vicky Warren

I feel blessed to be a part of the *Parenting with Intimacy Workbook* and pray that your family will be blessed by the challenges within. I am grateful for those who have traveled this writing journey along with me.

To my parents, it has been a great privilege to be called a "fellow-author."

To Paul and Vicky, thank you for your willingness to serve the Lord on behalf of families and children.

To Bill Anderson, I appreciate your tireless efforts to make our "writing dreams" come true.

To Betty Zamorsky, we could never say enough "thank you's."

I am also grateful for the godly individuals who have supported and sustained me with their love, friendship, and prayers.

To Cyndi, thank you for the inspiration of your life and the passion of your heart.

To Lorri, God has used you mightily in my life. You bring authenticity to everyone you touch.

To Debbie, with each day that passes, I am more grateful for our friendship. It's one of a kind.

To Jeff, thank you for allowing me to see your loving heart and brilliant sense of humor.

—Terri Ferguson

Introduction

CONGRATULATIONS! YOU'VE MADE an important decision that will have far-reaching, may we be so bold as to say even life-changing, ramifications. With all the other pulls and demands on your time, you've demonstrated by your willingness to tackle a "workbook" on parenting with intimacy that you've made family a priority. Our hats are off to you! We realize that this will require an investment of your time that could be spent on other more personally pleasurable activities such as pursuing a hobby, putting your feet up in a hammock, piloting through cyberspace, or perfecting your armchair quarterbacking skills. We promise to make it worth your while. It's a decision you won't regret!

Parents, like children, come in all sizes, shapes, and ages. Whether you entered parenthood in your teens or in your forties, have one child or a houseful, are facing the challenges of parenthood with a partner or alone, God has called you to be a wise steward of what and who He has entrusted to you. Your children, in fact, are your dearest disciples. An awesome reality—and responsibility. But there is far more to making disciples than discipline. In fact, if you purchased this workbook thinking you were getting a discipline manual, you may want to revisit the bookstore and request a refund. While discipline is without question a vital aspect of parenting, it's not the number-one issue. What is? Knowing your child, allowing him to know you, and then seeking to become caringly involved in one another's lives.

It's one thing to know something "about" someone. It's quite another to really "know" that person. This workbook is dedicated to exploring this crucial concept of "knowing." Our goal is not to give you something more to read or to simply fill your head with more knowledge about parenting so you can put another notch in your "good parent" belt. Rather, we want to challenge you to think and, most importantly, to take action. Love is more than just a feeling—it's an action. Unconditional love in action, committed to doing whatever is in the best interest of your child, whatever the cost, has the power to change lives. As you discover, explore, and implement this adventure we call "parenting with intimacy," lives will be transformed—yours, your child's, your family's. We can state this confidently not because of any pearls of wisdom we might impart but because these intimacy principles are God's principles—based on His Word—and we know that God is pro-parent, pro-child, and pro-family.

Our enemy, on the other hand, seeks to steal, kill, and destroy (John 10:10). Today's family is under attack. We're in a battle. The Bible speaks of our adversary prowling around like a roaring lion (1 Peter 5:8). It's a jungle out there! But not to worry. We're promised that *"greater is He who is in you than he who is in the world"* (1 John 4:4). Ephesians 6:11 admonishes us to put on the full armor of God that we may be able to stand firm against the schemes of the devil. As you and your family stand to fight this enemy who would seek to destroy you, we want to challenge you to add these intimacy principles to your arsenal as well.

Intimacy is God's idea. Proverbs 3:32 and Genesis 2:18 state clearly our need to relate to our Creator and to meaningful others—*"God is intimate with the upright." "It is not good for man to be alone."* We all long to experience close, warm, "intimate" relationships. Several Old Testament words are used descriptively of this need for intimacy. Reviewing these passages provides valuable insights into this key aspect of human "longing" and motivation.

Intimacy means you know me.

"My intimate friends have forgotten me" (Job 19:14).

This Hebrew word (transliterated—YADA) is from the root word "to know" and speaks of deep personal awareness and understanding. Surely it is God who knew us first. He knew us from our mother's wombs, and it is God who knows us best. He's acquainted with our every thought, emotion, and motivation. It's this deep inner "knowing" of one's heart, thought, and intention that goes well beyond the mere sharing of facts, ideas, and opinions.

It's this "knowing" of one's spouse that gives marriage special meaning and separates it from other human relationships as the "two become one flesh."

This "knowing" of our children is a key challenge of parenting. Parents have received *"gifts of the Lord"* (Ps. 127:3) and the challenge is to "unwrap" them as we enter into each child's world and truly know her. It's this "knowing" and "being known" that denotes true fellowship within the body of Christ. We are truly known by our Creator and have the privilege of knowing Him. Because of our intimacy with God we can truly know others and be known by them.

Intimacy means you care about me.

"Thou . . . art intimately acquainted with all my ways" (Ps. 139:3).

This particular Old Testament word (transliterated—SAKAN) speaks of "beneficial or caring involvement." In many ways this aspect of intimacy speaks to the motivation behind the "knowing." Why is it that God puts a priority on "knowing" me? It's so He can express His very nature of loving care.

Notice also the breadth of this caring involvement: in ALL my ways! He knows me. He knows all the failures, faults, and shortcomings and yet still cares! *"While I was yet a sinner, Christ died for me."*

This word for intimacy beautifully portrays the liberating motivation for marriage and family life. Why is it that I seek to enter into my partner's or child's world? Why prioritize time for these relationships? Why give sacrificially to my children's needs? It's because I care! It's not mere duty or obligation. I don't give as a manipulative tactic to have my own needs met. This selfless, giving motive, however, is not natural. It's supernatural.

Intimacy means I can know you.

"But He is intimate with the upright" (Prov. 3:32).

This reference to "intimacy" is even more startling as the word (transliterated—SOD) speaks of God disclosing Himself; the Creator reveals His "secret counsel" to us, the created. We find the ultimate revelation of this self-disclosure in Christ as *"the Word became flesh and dwelt among us."*

In His High Priestly Prayer of John 17, Jesus speaks to the eternal significance of this intimate "knowing" when He boldly declares *"And this is eternal life, that they may KNOW Thee, the only true God, and Jesus Christ whom Thou has sent"* (John 17:3).

"Freely you have received, freely give" (Matt. 10:8). Having received abundantly of the Heavenly Father's divine caring involvement produces a grateful heart that overflows in selfless giving. It's this moment by moment gratefulness, the awe and wonder that my Creator, my Savior is caringly involved in all my ways that prompts me to give. It's this unbounded grace that empowers my intimate caring toward others. It also prompts my openness and longing to truly and intimately know this One who would love me.

It's this longing of the heart that the psalmist declares in Psalm 42:1, *"As the deer pants for the water brooks, so my soul pants for Thee, O God."* It's this intimate "knowing" that became the passion of the Apostle Paul's life: *"I count all things to be loss in view of the surpassing value of knowing Christ Jesus my Lord"* (Phil. 3:8). It's the intimacy of knowing this One that brings forth the chorus of praise and worship in Revelation 4 and 5.

"Worthy art Thou, our Lord and our God, to receive glory and honor, and power" (Rev. 4:11). *"Worthy is the Lamb that was slain"* (5:12). It's this life of intimate knowing and humble worship that then manifests His love to others as the *"Love of Christ controls us"* (2 Cor. 5:14) to love a spouse, children, and others. Intimate love becomes contagious!

Marriage Staff Meetings

Developing and maintaining marriage and family intimacy requires that husbands and wives spend quality, consistent time together. The external stresses of work, carpools, child-rearing, and checkbooks need not take their toll on marital "oneness." Couples will need to take the time to manage family events before they are managed *by* them! During His public ministry, even Jesus found it necessary to consistently withdraw from the crowds and spend time with His disciples. He needed special times of sharing and encouragement.

Here are some characteristics of a successful marriage staff meeting.

Schedule a time—don't leave it to chance! Preferably, the staff meeting should be a standing appointment, occurring the same time and place each week. You might have lunch every Thursday, meet Tuesday nights after the children are asleep, or during Saturday morning breakfast. Some couples' schedule is such that the time has to change each week. If so, at least have a standard day and time that you schedule the staff meeting for the coming week. You might set aside a few minutes each Sunday evening in order to plan the next week's staff meeting.

Couples will need to take the time to manage family events before they are managed* by *them!

Prioritize the time—honor your commitment. Once the time is scheduled, protect it! Treat the appointment like it's the most important item on your schedule. Prioritizing the marriage staff meeting will produce a renewed sense of closeness. This may mean turning down a golf game or rescheduling the appointment at the hair salon, but it will be worth the effort.

Protect the time—from interruptions and distractions. Find a quiet place at home or, if necessary, meet away from the home and office. Avoid phone calls or visitors if possible. A fearful thought for many couples would be, "What in the world would we talk about?" A productive staff meeting might have this agenda.

Consider calendar coordination—for the coming week. What's planned? What's the children's schedule for the week? Who's working late? What social activities are scheduled? (Operate from a principle of agreeing on time commitments which affect the entire family before making these commitments.) Plan your next "date" and your next family outing. You'll even find that there's often great value in calendaring some of your lovemaking times!

Listen to one another—one spouse may just need to talk. When listening, establish eye contact and give undivided attention. Be quick to offer comfort, encouragement, and support. Avoid advice-giving, arguing, belittling, teaching, or lecturing. Be open to share hopes and dreams, feelings, and insights about recent moodiness, and concerns and fears about the marriage, kids, money, and the future. The power of giving undivided attention allows you to enter into another person's "world" and really get to know them.

Discuss family goals—and monitor their progress. As marriage communication deepens, written annual goals need to be developed for the family and broken down into quarterly/monthly target dates. Goals and plans could be developed in these areas: marriage, social, financial, personal, family, educational, spiritual, and professional.

1. Does the budget look "tight" this coming week and, if so, how can we all help?
2. What's our next major household expenditure and how could we all "contribute" to bring it about?
3. Have we scheduled our family vacation? Reservations made? Itinerary set?
4. Have we decided on some new couples we want to get to know this year?
5. How are our personal goals progressing . . . reading, diet, exercise, hobby . . . and how can we encourage/support one another?
6. What aspects of church life do we want to be involved in this next quarter?
7. What's the next fun marriage "getaway" we have planned?

Discuss parenting plans—if you don't become united on parenting issues, the kids will "divide and conquer"!

1. Discuss significant discipline issues; what seems to be working and what doesn't.

2. Plan family times together plus "quality times" with each child (a shopping trip for Mom and daughter, a fishing trip for Dad and son).
3. Discuss and agree upon parenting responsibilities and schedules for the next week. Who's needing help? Who's needing a "break" without the kids?
4. What goals seem reasonable for our children this quarter in the areas of behavior, attitude, and responsibilities, and how can we work together to achieve them?

Practice vulnerability—lovingly share areas of irritation, hurt, and disappointment. In an intimate relationship, there will be the freedom to *"[Speak] the truth in love"* (Eph. 4:15). A marriage staff meeting provides a "neutral" setting in which "touchy issues" can be honestly shared in an atmosphere of acceptance and openness.

For instance, you might need to share:

"I sure miss being alone with you. Could we plan a 'date' together?"

"It would mean a lot to me if we could remain in agreement in front of the kids . . . and discuss any differences privately."

"Sometimes it seems your initial response to situations is negative. Could we talk about why that is and discuss how I could be helpful in encouraging optimism?"

"Last Tuesday I felt embarrassed when. . . . Could we talk about it?"

Share words of appreciation—for who your spouse is and what he/she has done. Use your weekly "staff meeting" as a reminder that your spouse is a blessing to you! He does have good qualities!

For instance, you might share:

"Thanks for your help this week with the kids."

"I was reminded this week of how much I appreciate your diligence in seeing that things get done around the house."

"You are a very giving person, and it really showed this week when you. . . ."

"I love you, just for who you are."

Establishing and maintaining a meaningful, weekly marriage "staff meeting" will be one of the most important steps you make in pursuing wholesome and intimate marriage and family relationships. Conflicts, hurts, and misunderstandings will be resolved, and a oneness will develop, allowing you to experience the joy of "walking together" according to Amos 3:3. (For additional Marriage Staff Meeting ideas, see the "Intimate Life Newsletter.")

Family Nights Help Develop Family Intimacy

"Spend quality time with your family!" We know we're supposed to. We know it would help. We know we'd enjoy it. Why don't we spend quality time with our family? Perhaps it's because although we know what to do, we often don't know *how* to do it. Here are some practical suggestions on how to develop intimacy among family members.

Why don't we spend quality time with our family? Perhaps it's because although we know what to do, we often don't know* how *to do it.

Start with a schedule. Schedule an evening when all the family can be together and then protect the evening from conflicts and distractions. Keeping the same night each week would be recommended, but the main thing will be to have one each week. Don't turn on the TV, watch a movie, or anything else that would minimize conversation. Devote an entire evening to family activities such as:

Have dinner together. Instead of eating out, cook at home. Take turns choosing the menu and cooking. Teach the children to cook; let everyone have their "specialty" dish they prepare. Occasionally, decorate for special occasions and highlight birthdays and holiday themes. Plan to involve the whole family in cleanup.

Talk together. During dinner, involve everyone in both fun and vulnerable types of conversation. Begin by having everyone respond to "fun" questions such as, "What would you do if you inherited a million dollars?" or, "What would be your ideal vacation?" Then progress to more serious topics such as, "What would you like to be doing five years from now?" or, "When do you feel most loved?"

Communicate appreciation for one another. Put each person in the "spotlight" and ask every family member to share what they appreciate most about that person. Further affirm the person by showing loving affection for her while saying, "I love you."

Allow everyone to share how they're "feeling." Create a loving environment in which disappointments, hurts, fears, and other sensitive feelings can be shared. In responding to expressed feelings, avoid instructing, preaching, and criticism; instead, "rejoice with those who rejoice" and "weep with those who weep."

Play together. After everyone helps with the dishes, engage in interactive games and activities such as board games, Ping-Pong, charades, cards, and sports activities.

Plan family "fun" projects. Take turns letting each family member choose a "fun" project to do. Go horseback riding, fly kites, play tennis, camp out, search for a "special" antique, go fishing, plant a garden, visit a museum, or build something.

During the project, the focus should be on having fun together, not on "getting something done." If a project doesn't work out as planned, that's OK.

Try to keep a "souvenir" from your time together—a physical item that can serve as a future reminder of good memories.

Go horseback riding, fly kites, play tennis, camp out, search for a "special" antique, go fishing, plant a garden, visit a museum, or build something.

Maintain Disciplines That Build Character and Deepen Spiritual Commitment

Journal of gratefulness. On a regular basis, spend time adding to and reflecting on a *journal of gratefulness* in which family members can record blessings, answers to prayer, or anything else for which they're grateful. This journal will help cultivate and maintain a spirit of gratefulness in the family and will serve to strengthen faith in God's future provision.

Scripture memory. As a family, memorize select Scripture verses, perhaps beginning with one per month. Periodically "check" each other on current and past verses. During family nights, discuss personal reflections on each verse.

Character studies. As a family, study key biblical characters and modern-day men and women of God, looking for important character strengths and spiritual principles that guided their lives. Discuss how these principles could be applied to family members' lives. (You might want to begin with Moses, Sarah, Abraham, David, Ruth, Peter, Mary, or Paul.)

Praying together. On a regular basis, share prayer requests and then pray together. A good time to do this is around the dinner table before the meal. Expand the normal "prayer of thanks" into a two to three minute prayer time, allowing time for every person to pray. Be sure to also share answers to prayer.

Intimate relationships never just "happen"; they must be cultivated and developed.

Knowing what to do is not enough.
Knowing how to do it is not enough.
You have to *do* it!

Here are some steps of action. Make specific plans for at least one of these:

- Our next family night is scheduled for ___________ (*date*).
- Our next Scripture verse to memorize is ___________ (*verse*).
- We're going to begin a character study on ______________ (*Bible character*).
- ___________ (*family member*) is in charge of our next "family fun project," and it's scheduled for ___________ (*date*).
- The menu for our next dinner together will be ______________ ____ (*menu*).

CHAPTER 1

Let the Journey Begin

A CLASSIC STUDY in 1939 identified **rapid change** and **fast-paced society** as elements which tended to produce emotional distance in families and increase parent-child conflicts! It seemed that such rapid change and fast-paced living tended to foster **insecurity,** reduce important **family time** together, and heighten differences between generations (Davis, 1939). How much more of an issue does this promise to be as we enter the twenty-first century!

Knowing Someone Takes Time

It takes time to build close relationships, and the more relationships involved, the more challenging it becomes. With three, five, or more family members, it requires planning and commitment to consistently have everyone at a meal together. As children get older the challenge to find family time becomes even greater.

In today's typical family, there are late nights of work, committee meetings, social activities, church activities, P.T.A., children's sports, tutoring, studies, gymnastics, etc. Feeling the pressure "not to miss out," families are being torn apart by the tyranny to stay busy. Out of **false guilt** parents often press their children to do more than they got to do as children. Characteristic of their age-group, older children and teenagers may succumb to the pressure of overinvolvement, seeking to belong to every important peer group. All of these contribute to the family's lack of intimacy.

Making a Living Rather Than Sharing a Life

Another family time pressure relates to parental emphasis on making a living. We undoubtedly need to provide for our family, but where do we draw the line between making a living and never having enough? Family "success" must be measured by things other than numbers of bedrooms, bathrooms, or the size of one's backyard! This pressure may needlessly send mothers back to work and fathers sacrificing relationships for status, success, or financial security. Many an adult-child has been asked by a pastor, youth worker, or counselor: "How did you know that your parents loved you?" The response many times is, "My parents worked hard. They provided for us. We had everything we needed." The hollow emotional depths from which this response comes speaks volumes concerning the pain and loneliness of financially driven families.

Feeling the pressure "not to miss out," families are being torn apart by the tyranny to stay busy.

The One-eyed "Monster"

National studies estimate that American children are watching thirty-plus hours of TV per week. This is often more time than they spend in a classroom! The TV has been blasted for its violence, sex, and moral corruption, but possibly even more devastating is the subtle influence it has in destroying family closeness. It serves as a third-party detractor that allows family members to occupy the same room, be entertained or amused, but never get to know one another.

A New Parenting Goal: A Heritage of Intimacy!

As a parent, why not begin the journey toward a new goal? Leave behind the goal of busyness. Turn off the television and reevaluate the emphasis placed on acquiring more. Begin the journey toward a new goal. Let's begin to share our life with family members. Let's begin a heritage of intimacy. Dream of your children being able to respond—"I know my parents loved me . . ."

- through the undivided attention they gave me.

- through their patient listening to my hurts and fears.
- through their example of faith, conviction, and prayerful walk.
- through their empathy and openness as we shared feelings.
- through their valuing my thoughts and opinions.
- through their trust of my decisions and plans.
- through the common interests and fun we shared.
- through their verbalized appreciation and love.
- through their openness to touch, hug, and reassure just with their presence.
- through their example of a grateful, worship-filled heart.
- through their priority of God, His Word, and people.

Parenting with Intimacy—It's Worth the Journey!

As we begin the journey, we must first consider where we are.

Priorities. Everyone has them. Regardless of whether you've written yours down or even thought about them, you're living out what's important to you.

Most Christian parents, when asked to list their priorities, know some version of a correct answer: (1) God, (2) Family, (3) Ministry, (4) Work. We may score well on this written exam, but how are we doing on the living exam?

Continually ask yourself, "What's going to really matter ten years from now?"

The following self-assessment will help you assess the true status of your priorities. If you have to hedge on a lot of your answers or if you simply respond with a lot of no's, you probably need to do some restructuring in priorities. Continually ask yourself, "What's going to really matter ten years from now?" and, "What are the most important things in this life?" From God's eternal perspective, few things really matter: God, His Word, and people.

Parenting with Intimacy Self-Assessment Inventory

Yes *No*

☐ ☐ 1. I spend regular, quality, uninterrupted time alone with my spouse at least once a week (if married).

- ☐ ☐ 2. I spend regular, quality, uninterrupted time with my children at least once a week.
- ☐ ☐ 3. I know who my children's friends are, what they're doing in school, and the stresses they're under.
- ☐ ☐ 4. My spouse and children truly know me. I share with them my feelings and concerns.
- ☐ ☐ 5. I'm approachable to my spouse and family. They're not hesitant to vulnerably share their feelings or to approach me when I've offended them.
- ☐ ☐ 6. I keep up with and give priority to family birthdays and other special occasions.
- ☐ ☐ 7. I spend regular, quality time deepening my intimate walk with God and becoming equipped in His Word.
- ☐ ☐ 8. I seek to share Christ with others in word and by example. I start by sharing Christ with my family.
- ☐ ☐ 9. My checkbook, ministry commitments, TV, and reading habits reflect my love for God and devotion to my family.
- ☐ ☐ 10. I often use my discretionary time to "enter into my family's world" and do what they want to do.

Review the ten questions above and reflect on possible changes:

As part of establishing an Intimacy Heritage in my family, it will be important for me to give additional time and attention to:

____

____

____

Pause now and reflect on these desired changes. In a prayer, ask God for His guidance and strength. Write your thoughts and prayers to God here:

____

____

____

Let's get serious about these changes!

"He who began a good work in you will perfect it until the day of Christ Jesus" Philippians 1:6.

Intimacy Disciplines—
Marriage Staff Meetings and Family Nights

Time is much like money. It requires that we budget. Each month there's a financial allocation for a roof over our heads. We all have rent or house payments. Next comes the bill for water and lights. You'll need food to fill the refrigerator, gas for the car, money for the doctor, and clothing. As soon as the money runs out each month, there's usually a few, or several things still on our list! There may be a trip we'd like to take, dental work that we need done, or home repairs we've put off again. What has just taken place is a lesson in priorities. Whoever or whatever gets our money first is a priority, and the rest will have to wait! It's the same way with time and parenting. We had better plan time for God, spouse, and family, or it just won't happen. After prioritizing personal time to deepen our intimacy with God, two significant blocks of relational time are recommended. We recommend you allocate time for two important disciplines. Marriage Staff Meetings and Family Nights help build an Intimacy Heritage.

Scripture Journaling—1 Thessalonians 2:8

"Having thus a fond affection for you, we were well pleased to impart to you not only the Gospel of God but also our own lives, because you had become very dear to us."

In this passage, the Apostle Paul puts an emphasis on "imparting our own life" to those dear to us, those for whom we have great affection.

Spend time reflecting on the "dearness" and great affection you have for your family. Write a few thoughts of grateful appreciation to the Heavenly Father as the Giver of these good gifts:

Second, allow this grateful appreciation to prompt a renewed desire and commitment to "impart your life" to your family. How might you share a relationship with each family member? Share your thoughts and prayers here:

Marriage Staff Meeting

Set aside at least an hour of quiet time together with your spouse. Spend this time discussing only the issues related to this workbook; save discussions about work pressures, finances, or household concerns for a later time.

We suggest the husband take the initiative and begin sharing his reflections first. He shares his questions, insights, or summary statements about the exercises. The wife then shares her information. Each partner also shares from their Scripture Journaling; (1) reflections on grateful appreciation, and (2) reflections on renewed commitments. Be sure to let each partner share his or her responses without interruption or comments.

Make this first session a positive and hopeful session. Listen attentively to your spouse. Make eye contact and be sure your mind is free from distractions. End your time together by holding hands, thanking each other for having the courage to vulnerably share responses and, if you feel comfortable, say a silent prayer, thanking God for your family and asking for His guidance.

Here are some examples of what you might communicate to your spouse:

"I was reminded of how grateful I am for your love and support . . . and how blessed I am with our children. I'm looking forward to making you and the kids a renewed priority."

"I was convicted about my lack of spiritual example to the family. I committed to see that change as God leads us through this study."

"I'm not even sure how to "impart my life" to you and the kids but I want to learn . . . because I love you."

Family Night Activity—Have Fun This Week!

During your Marriage Staff Meeting, review your family's quality time together. Review your Family Time commitments and schedule a "Family Night." Such a night might include the following:

- the calendar cleared of all conflicts
- take turns choosing a fun family activity . . . include all ages
- children's homework is completed before dinner
- each family member committed to be on time for dinner together
- no friends over, no phone calls, and no interruptions
- dinner conversation positive and appreciative (no "rules," criticism, or conflicts)
- one thirty-minute family TV program or video
- then, spend the next one-and-a-half hours having fun! Pick one or two of these age-appropriate activities and enjoy an evening together.

    1. Visit a park; climb/swing; throw balls and Frisbees.
    2. Have a card, checker, or chess tournament.
    3. Play charades (kids love to see parents act silly).
    4. Play Pictionary, Trivial Pursuit, or Bible Trivia.
    5. Color, draw, or paint.
    6. Play with blocks, cars, and army men.
    7. Play house, army, or cowboys and Indians.
    8. Try cooking a new recipe together.
    9. Build or repair something together.
    10. Play hide-and-seek or similar games.
    11. Go for a family walk or bike trip.
    12. Make a playhouse, tent, or tree house.
    13. Visit an airport and watch the planes take off and land, or go to a lake and watch the boats.

14. Go on a picnic. How about a picnic breakfast?
15. Make popcorn, maybe even caramel corn if you're more adventurous.
16. Enjoy the snow together by building a snowman, making a snow fort, or throwing snowballs. How about some snow ice cream?
17. Go swimming or water-skiing.
18. Plan a scavenger hunt. Try to find something in the house for every letter of the alphabet.
19. Read a good book aloud. (C.S. Lewis' *Chronicles of Narnia* series appeals to children and adults alike.)
20. Look through photo albums or view family slides or movies.
21. Play miniature golf or croquet.
22. Make a tape recording of the most recent family "news," and send it to a close friend or relative whom you seldom see.
23. Go fishing.
24. Play a board game that all can enjoy—Yahtzee, Sorry, Monopoly.
25. Sing favorite songs, nursery rhymes, or hymns around the piano.
26. Make a collage using seeds, rice, cereal, old buttons, and sewing scraps.
27. Do needlework: cross-stitch, crewel, candlewicking, rug-hooking.
28. String popcorn and place on a tree for the birds.
29. Make puppets out of lunch bags, old socks, felt, wooden clothespins. Put on a puppet show.
30. Have a bonfire and roast hot dogs or marshmallows.
31. Go to your nearest hospital and look at the babies in the maternity nursery. (Visiting hours only!)
32. Visit a shut-in or an elderly friend or relative.
33. Pick wildflowers. (You might want to press them.)
34. Read a psalm together. Then write a psalm of praise for your own family.
35. Play "I think you're nice because . . ." Someone thinks of a quality he likes in the person who's "it."

36. Listen to a tape recording of a Bible story (many come with read-along books for little children).
37. Share prayer requests that affect and concern the whole family. Then pray together.
38. Encourage little ones to color a picture to send to grandparents.
39. Play badminton, volleyball, tennis, or yard darts.
40. Take the kids on a tour of where Dad or Mom works.
41. Draw a family tree on paper and complete it as a family. Add old photographs if available.
42. Give each person a large piece of paper and take turns tracing the outlines of their bodies on it. Color in the outlines to look like you.
43. Go to the library. Check out books, records, and art reproductions.
44. Gather a variety of leaves and identify them.
45. Write a letter to a missionary family.
46. Take a walk through your neighborhood.
47. Put together a scrapbook describing a favorite vacation or any special event (pictures, photos, writing, souvenirs).
48. Write and act out a pantomime or play centered on a specific holiday, a Bible story, or a character quality.
49. Make snowflakes out of lightweight white paper and hang from ceiling with thread.
50. Go to a ball game, or play one—football, kickball, softball, baseball, basketball, soccer.

For Group Discussion

Discuss the three Hebrew words often translated "intimacy" and develop your own working definition. Share it with the group and discuss how it relates to parenting, your marriage, and your involvement with others. Encourage all parents who have completed chapter 1 to answer the following:

After reviewing the ingredients in the Intimacy Heritage on pages 18–19, reflections I had were:

After completing the Parenting with Intimacy Self-Assessment Inventory, the thing I realized about myself was:

After our first Marriage Staff Meeting, one positive impression I had was:

After our first Family Night, one positive impression I had was:

Part One

Know Your Child

"Behold, children are a gift of the Lord."

PSALM 127:3

CHAPTER 2

Unwrapping God's Gifts

IMAGINE BEING PRESENTED with an exquisitely wrapped package. You receive it graciously and proceed to carefully place it on the shelf. Six months later the giver returns to your home and is disheartened to observe that the gift has remained unopened all that time. What would be the logical conclusion? You're uninterested and unappreciative. You've taken the gift and the giver for granted. You've also missed a tremendous blessing. What a waste!

An integral part of "parenting with intimacy" is taking your child (your gift), and untying the bow, undoing the wrapping, and enjoying and getting to know this child deeply and intimately.

One of the most important investments a parent can make in the life of a child is to know him. An integral part of "parenting with intimacy" is taking your child (your gift), untying the bow, undoing the wrapping, then enjoying and getting to know this child deeply and intimately. Unwrap your gift carefully, with a sense of awe. Appreciate each stage of the unveiling because each layer is important and reveals clues about the treasure that lies within.

One significant place to begin in "unwrapping your gift" is to review the developmental challenges each child goes through. Regardless of how many children you have or which stages they've already passed through, you'll learn much about each child as you consider their developmental journey.

As you review each of the six stages that follow, reflect on each of your children's journeys—along with your **remembrances, regrets,**

opportunities, and **dreams.** As you then write about your reflections, consider the special uniqueness of each of God's special gifts to you.

The Infancy Stage: 0–18 months

Key Developmental Issues . . .

- Limited motor activity but very active senses . . . especially hearing, touch, and sight
- Judgments made as to the world being safe or unsafe, especially in relationships
- Judgments made are primarily related to whether basic needs for food, comfort, and nurturance are met
- Judgments are at an emotional level prior to verbal/cognitive processing
- Judgments made of caregivers as loving, comforting, caring, nurturing, rejecting, punitive, uncaring, or hurtful
- Judgments made result in close emotional bonding (trust) . . . or emotional distancing (mistrust)

Practical Suggestions for Parents

- Provide visual stimulation, soothing talk, and music
- Nurture! Nurture! Nurture with touch, talk, and holding
- Lovingly and consistently meet basic needs with gentleness rather than anger
- Express joy; smile and laugh around your infant; pray "over" child
- Avoid raised voices, angry tones, and overprotectiveness
- Remove a child from problem areas rather than discipline
- Allow child to have a favorite toy, blanket, or pillow; they may need their thumb or pacifier for security as well
- Begin to take short times away from the child; expect crying; give reassurance as you leave and comfort when you return

Nurture! Nurture! Nurture with touch, talk, and holding.

Now consider each of your children as they passed through this stage or are currently in this stage. Write about your:

Remembrances (For instance: I remember Eric's favorite pillow; I remember rocking Amy in my arms most every evening. I prayed and thanked God for her.)

Regrets (For instance: I regret being overprotective and at times impatient with Sarah; I wish I had been more available to hold, hug, and care for Matt.)

Opportunities (For instance: I'm going to start hugging my children more! Even though Melanie cries when we leave, her mother and I need more couple dates to rekindle our love.)

Dreams (For instance: I dream about watching Vicky take her first steps; I dream about taking Aaron on his first fishing trip.)

The Early Childhood Stage: 18 months–3 years

Key Developmental Issues

- Rapid development of motor, verbal, and language skills
- Autonomy needed in feeding and potty training
- Approval of parents and significant others very important
- Differentiating between acceptable/unacceptable behavior begins
- Exploring/experimenting are essential to test limits and survive mistakes
- Freedom to explore and receive positive reenforcement says "I'm OK"
- Freedom to make mistakes and yet receive acceptance says "I'm OK"
- "I'm not OK" comes from overprotective, critical, demanding, permissive, neglectful, punitive environments

Practical Suggestions for Parents

- Stimulate motor development in walking, running, throwing, climbing, etc.
- Read! Read to your child. Read Bible stories and nursery rhymes. Sing songs together
- Provide a safe environment in which to explore and express curiosity
- Minimize "don't," "quit," "stop," "no" messages (some are essential)
- Praise and encourage every success; pray with your child
- Teach, train, warn, discipline, and reassure
- Discipline rebellion and not childish acts; use firm, but gentle words and not a voice of anger
- Distract a child from problem areas rather than overdiscipline

Read! Read to your child. Read Bible stories and nursery rhymes. Sing songs together.

Now consider each of your children as they passed through this stage, are currently in this stage, or will soon pass through this stage. Write about your:

Remembrances (For instance: I remember the day Britney said her first complete sentence. I remember Nathan's favorite bedtime story.)

____

____

____

____

____

Regrets (For instance: I wish I had let Anna express her curiosity as a two-year-old. I told her no too often. I regret the harsh way I disciplined Steven.)

____

____

____

____

____

Opportunities (For instance: I'm going to give Andrew more opportunities to play hard and expend energy. I'm going to start getting Haley ready for bed a few minutes earlier. We'll read together before she goes to sleep.)

____

____

____

____

____

Dreams (For instance: I dream about the time when Jennifer learns to read. I'm looking forward to the time when Philip and I can take swimming lessons.)

____

____

____

____

The Middle Childhood Stage: 3–5 years

Key Developmental Issues

- Sense of competence comes out of freedom to undertake personally meaningful activities
- Develops conscience and awareness of others' feelings
- Desires to differentiate from others. May use "me" and "mine" often
- Initiative which is squelched by control or lack of opportunity produces guilt
- Often inquisitive; likes world of fantasy and pretend
- Encouraging the freedom of choice is significant

Practical Suggestions for Parents

- Encourage and praise favorite activities and interests the child enjoys; experience Bible songs, videos, games
- Talk about feelings as you see sadness, frustration, fear, rejection; assist in the development of a feeling vocabulary
- Encourage social interactions with other children at home, church, and preschool
- Give choices about clothes, play activities, snacks, etc.
- Apologize and request forgiveness for your temper, broken promises, etc.

Apologize and request forgiveness for your temper, broken promises, etc.

Now consider each of your children as they passed through this stage, are currently in this stage, or will soon pass through this stage. Write about your:

Remembrances (For instance: I remember the anatomy question Elizabeth decided to ask when we were in line at the grocery store. Jonathan loved to pretend like he was Superman. He had a special T-shirt and cape.)

____

____

____

____

Regrets (For instance: I regret the power struggles between Amanda and me. She needed more opportunities to choose. I regret losing my temper with Erin. She was showing frustration and I saw it as disrespect.)

____

____

____

____

____

Opportunities (For instance: I'm going to give Misty choices about the friends who come over to play. I am going to make any necessary apologies before Matthew goes to sleep.)

____

____

____

____

____

____

Dreams (For instance: I dream about shooting baskets or playing catch with Katy. I dream about taking Mark to the beach.)

The Late Childhood Stage: 6–12 years

Key Developmental Issues

- Need to set and attain personal goals
- Social skills have heightened importance in rules, roles, sharing, and sexual differences
- Capacity to reason develops as does a desire to be helpful
- Sexual awareness grows and instruction is needed
- Acceptance from parents, peer group, and other significant adults is important
- Lack of acceptance/encouragement develops a sense of inadequacy/inferiority

Practical Suggestions for Parents

- Find families with children the age of yours; initiate positive family friendships
- Explore and encourage hobbies, abilities, and talents
- Identify and praise personal responsibility and unique character qualities
- Special talks and experiences to teach social skills; i.e., instruction needed for table manners, phone etiquette, and social settings
- Continued affection from both parents; verbal affection and touch are important
- Begin open dialogue between mother and daughter, father and son on sex roles and differences
- Share feelings; heal hurts; teach biblical principles such as sovereignty, decision-making, avoiding evil, etc.

Share feelings; heal hurts; teach biblical principles such as sovereignty, decision-making, avoiding evil, etc.

Now consider each of your children as they passed through this stage, are currently in this stage, or will soon pass through this stage. Write about your:

Remembrances (For instance: I remember how excited Josh was about his soccer trophy. I remember how important it was for Tiffany to get lots of affection from her dad.)

____

____

____

____

Regrets (For instance: I regret not being at Julie's dance recitals. I know she was disappointed each time I couldn't make it. I regret not having a talk with Brandon about sex and about relationships.)

____

____

____

____

____

Opportunities (For instance: I am going to set aside one day a week to have lunch with Susan. I'm going to invite Bobby to go with us on a "date." We'll treat Mom to a special evening together.)

____

____

____

____

____

Dreams (For instance: I dream about watching Corey graduate from high school. I dream about the day when Courtney will realize her gifts and use them to honor Christ.)

____

____

The Adolescence Stage: 13–18 years

Key Developmental Issues

- Dramatic physical growth; increased mental capacities; explosive feelings and hormones!
- Body image, sexual identity, and social acceptance important
- Needs to assert independence; questions authority and tests limits
- Peer/parent conflicts are common
- Needs guidance in interpersonal relationship skills; chosen peer group and life direction help give identity
- Continual emphasis on competence; goals in real life issues are important

Practical Suggestions for Parents

- Look for hidden needs and fears beneath problematic behaviors; admit your failures and share your own childhood struggles
- Let natural consequences be a key discipline tool; give freedom to fail
- Continue positive family friendships with positive peer influences
- Ask open-ended questions rather than yes/no questions. For example: "Tell me something interesting about your day."
- Have special mother-daughter and father-son times; take trips, share projects, set goals for learning life skills
- Focus on the "big" issues; don't sweat the small stuff

Ask open-ended questions rather than yes/no questions. For example: "Tell me something interesting about your day."

Now consider each of your children as they passed through this stage, are currently in this stage, or will soon pass through this stage. Write about your:

Remembrances (For instance: I remember the time Travis shaved his head just to impress a girl. I remember how many "best friends" Angela had during her freshman year.)

____

____

____

____

Regrets (For instance: I wish I had spent more time talking **with** Brian and less time lecturing him. I regret the harsh judgments I made about Debbie's friends.)

____

____

____

____

____

Opportunities (For instance: I'm going to set limits for Melissa, but I'm going to give her a chance to give input about those limits. I'm going to teach Joel how to balance a checkbook and work out a budget.)

____

____

____

____

____

Dreams (For instance: I dream about watching Hannah make confident choices about her future. I dream about the day when Philip takes initiative in looking for a part-time job.)

____

____

The Young Adulthood Stage: 19–30 years

Key Developmental Issues

- Experiencing intimacy with friends of both sexes is a crucial task
- Social relationships like courtship, marriage, and parenting are paramount
- Career, social, and civic direction is needed
- Establishing a clear sense of personal identity facilitates intimacy development

Accept friends; offer protection and a "sounding board" about relationships.

Practical Suggestions for Parents

- Let your guidance sound like suggestions from a friend rather than rules from a parent
- Discuss your failures and regrets openly; seek forgiveness as necessary
- Seek their input and advice in areas of strength
- Continue training in real-world issues: finances, relationships, goals, and biblical wisdom
- Listen more; give fewer corrections
- Dream together about the future
- Accept friends; offer protection and a "sounding board" about relationships

Now consider each of your children as they passed through this stage, are currently in this stage or will soon pass through this stage. Write about your:

Remembrances (For instance: I remember when Jason made his decision about joining the Marines. You couldn't help but notice his sense of purpose. I remember the day Jaime announced her engagement. Her relationship with Peter has always been such a blessing.)

Regrets (For instance: I regret that I discouraged Michelle from following her dreams. I wish that I hadn't been so intrusive with Patrick. He's needed my acceptance of his female friends.)

Opportunities (For instance: I'm going to give Cathey a call. I want to let her know that I'm here to listen. I'm going to ask Eddie's advice about some money market accounts.)

Dreams (For instance: I dream about the day when Leslie has a family of her own. I dream about the time when Jimmy resolves the conflict with his stepbrother.)

As you have reflected on each of your children's journeys through these stages, take time now to summarize some of the key things you've learned about each child:

Child's Name	*Reflections on Their Developmental Journey* (For instance: I've realized that I've been very critical of Lisa as she's grown up. She's needed my unconditional acceptance. I missed countless opportunities to show Jake that he is important to me. Even though he's in junior high, I can still give my time and individual attention.)

Research Reflection: Children who feel connected to their parents and who report spending quality time with their families, show significantly lower levels of delinquency when compared with children whose ties to parents are weak and quality family time lacking ("Sibling Resemblance in Juvenile Delinquency: Findings from the National Youth Survey," *Criminology* 31 [1993] 387–406).

Children who feel connected to their parents and who report spending quality time with their families, show significantly lower levels of delinquency when compared with children whose ties to parents are weak and quality family time lacking.

Take a few minutes to write about each of your children's connectedness with the family and ideas you have on how to improve it through quality time investments:

Child's Name	*Reflections on "Connectedness" and Quality Time* (For instance: Tyler spends a great deal of time alone in his room. I'm going to ask him to teach me how to play his video games. Courtney seems to "get lost" in our family. Her quiet temperament is overshadowed by other family members. I'll ask her to choose the activity for our next family night.)
________	________________________
	________________________
	________________________
	________________________
________	________________________
	________________________
	________________________
	________________________
	________________________

Scripture Journaling—2 Corinthians 6:1

"Receive [not the gifts] of God in vain."

In this passage, the Apostle Paul admonishes the reader to never "take for granted" God's gifts.

Reflect on your children as gifts from the Lord and then write a prayer of thanksgiving and renewed commitment. Share your thoughts with God here:

Marriage Staff Meeting

Set aside time this week to reflect with your spouse on your children's developmental journey. Begin by sharing some of your fond

remembrances concerning each child. Pause after this sharing for a quiet, reflective prayer of gratefulness.

Next, spend time vulnerably sharing some of your **regrets.** Be sensitive and comforting of one another during this time. Be careful not to blame or attack one another. Instead, give reassurance: *"Neither of us has been the perfect parent. God will be pleased as we admit our regrets. Admitting our regrets will prompt us to be even better parents."* Thank God for His forgiveness when we fail and His strength to change us when we cooperate.

Spend time vulnerably sharing some of your regrets. Be sensitive and comforting of one another during this time.

Finally, discuss the present **opportunities** and **dreams** you have for each child. How might you be able to incorporate some of these opportunities into your family night activities or daily schedule?

Family Night Activity—Focus on Character Qualities

Spend an evening focusing on character qualities. Place a piece of poster board on a table so that everyone can see it. Take ten to fifteen minutes to brainstorm different character qualities and have each family member write his/her ideas on the board. Your list might include traits like: sensitivity, diligence, compassion, honesty, creativity, helpfulness, etc. Younger children may want to find pictures in magazines that show others being kind, helpful, honest, brave, and hardworking.

Next, take turns verbalizing appreciation to the person on your left. Give an example of how this person demonstrates one of the qualities in her daily life. For example: *"Sarah, I really appreciate your helpfulness, like when you walk Andy to his class."* or *"Thanks, Eric, for picking up your room. You've become very diligent and supportive this year."* Reverse directions and share about the person on your right. Make sure each member has received two appreciations.

You may want to repeat this activity periodically. It might become an annual event or an activity for special holidays like Thanksgiving, New Year's, or birthdays. It helps keep a focus on the positive and an emphasis on verbalizing appreciation.

For Group Discussion

As you have reflected on the development of each child, you've undoubtedly recounted their individuality. Each child brings a different challenge and uniqueness to the family. As a group, discuss how you've coped with these differences. How well have you honored and accepted the uniqueness of each child? Tell the group one positive quality that describes each child.

Please share your responses to these statements after looking at your child's development:

I am glad that I . . .

____

____

____

It was hard to admit the regrets because . . .

____

____

____

I'm looking forward to God making these changes in me as a parent . . .

____

____

____

____

Share reflections on your Marriage Staff Meeting and Family Night activity. Have these times together become a "habit"? Are you anticipating your Staff Meetings? Take turns sharing creative ways you're making them enjoyable. Are family members beginning to look forward to Family Nights? Take turns sharing how you're making them fun. Learn from one another! We're all in this together . . . and no one has all the answers!

CHAPTER 3

Understanding Your Child's Needs

"*MY GOD SHALL supply all your needs according to His riches in glory in Christ Jesus*"—Philippians 4:19.

The obvious premise of this verse is that we all have needs. If we didn't have needs, why would God promise to meet them?

No one teaches children to need attention, affection, or approval. They instinctively reach out for these needs.

Evidently, Adam had been created with certain needs which God intended to be met in the context of human relationships.

We discover the birth of intimacy through man's neediness in Genesis 2. God placed Adam in a perfect environment with abundant provision. Although Adam's physiological and spiritual needs were being met by his Creator, God pronounced, "It is not good for the man to be alone" (v. 18). Evidently, Adam had been created with certain needs which God intended to be met in the context of human relationships. Apparently, God desired not only for Adam to be the recipient of His divine acceptance, affection, and encouragement, but also for him to receive them from meaningful human relationships. God therefore established marriage (v. 24), the family (4:1; Ps. 127:3), and the church (Matt. 16:16-19; 1 Cor. 12:27) as divine relationships through which He wants to bless us abundantly.

Reflect a few moments on the power and potential of these thoughts. In your own words describe what life was like for Adam in Genesis 2. Before sin had entered the world, what kind of life did Adam enjoy? Write your thoughts here:

____

____

____

____

Even though Adam enjoyed a relationship with God as they walked and talked together in the Garden, Genesis 2:18 describes a particular dilemma. What does God say about Adam's condition? How does this relate to you and your family? Write your thoughts here:

____

____

____

____

There must be nothing wrong with having needs. The problems come in how we go about having our needs met. We find disappointment if we expect from others rather than having confident faith in God's provision. Our demanding and manipulating tactics will bring pain. To admit that we have needs is not wrong or a sign of sin, it's an acknowledgment of our humanity and our poverty of spirit (Matt. 5:3). To admit that I have needs also helps resist the extremes of selfishness and self-reliance.

There must be nothing wrong with having needs. The problems come in how we go about having our needs met.

Finally, the acceptance of my neediness prevents a self-condemning attitude and the feelings of false guilt associated with having needs. In the Bible, God is portrayed as a God who delights to give good gifts (James 1:17), and who demonstrated His commitment to meet our needs (Rom. 5:8). As a sovereign God, free to act without the confinement of human wisdom, God may choose to meet our needs directly or through His three divine relationships: marriage, family, and the church. For instance, the church is called upon to accept one another (Rom. 15:7), comfort one another (2 Cor. 1:3-4), love one another (John 13:35), and forgive one another (Eph. 4:31-32).

Interestingly, several secular researchers have addressed this connection between relatedness, intimacy, and human need. For example, Clinebell and Clinebell (1970) actually defined intimacy as "the degree of mutual need-satisfaction within relationships." Fairbairn (1952) and Winnicott (1988), in their work in object-relations theory, describe the basic human motivation as "intimacy seeking."

As a parent, you can lovingly give to your children's intimacy needs.

Carefully conducted research can, at best, only observe the truth of God's Word: "It is not good for man to be alone" and, "[God] is intimate with the upright" (Gen. 2:18; Prov. 3:32).

Reflect on your role of removing your child's "aloneness." As a parent, you can lovingly give to your children's intimacy needs. Contrast this concept of parenting with the view of just making a living or giving out discipline when they "mess up." Write your thoughts here:

____

____

____

____

Characteristics of Intimacy Needs

Needs are cross-cultural. African-Americans have the same physical, emotional, and spiritual needs as Anglos. Orientals' and Latin Americans' needs transcend cultural differences. It doesn't matter if:

- your skin is black or yellow.
- you live in a mud hut or a brick house.
- you eat tortillas or crepes.
- you drive a car or push a ricksha.

Needs are the same in all generations. Adam, Abraham, Pilate, Tertullius, Mozart, Lincoln, and Churchill all shared one thing in common. They all had needs; they had the same needs as you and me. Needs are not a twentieth-century phenomenon. Every person who has ever lived or will live has needs.

Needs are lifelong and continuous. Have you ever noticed that all young children share the same inherent needs? When you bring a baby home from the hospital she exhibits a need for:

Attention—Even when her diaper is dry, her tummy's full, and she's had plenty of sleep, she's likely to cry just because she wants attention.

Comfort—Many times when a child falls down, he looks around to see if anyone has noticed. If no one is watching, the child may pick himself up and continue to play. But if he realizes that someone saw his accident he may begin to cry. This child knows instinctively that he needs comfort.

Affection—When children are around people they trust, they'll often reach out to be held, embraced, and hugged. They want affection.

Approval—Why do children always want you to notice the picture they've just drawn, their expertise on the basketball court, or the song they've just learned on the piano? They have a need for approval.

Adults do have the same needs as children. An eighty-year-old grandfather has the same need for attention and comfort as a four-year-old child.

Are these simply needs of childhood? Do you grow out of these needs as you mature? Can these needs be met once for all? If needs are met early in life, can you scratch them off the list and go on to something else?

The answer to all these questions is an emphatic "No!"

Adults do have the same needs as children. An eighty-year-old grandfather has the same need for attention and comfort as a four-year-old child.

Your needs must be continually met; they cannot be met "once and for all." You *do* have a distinct need for attention; but like your need for air, food, and water, it must be constantly replenished.

You Can't Meet Your Own Needs!

The next time you have a hard day, wrap your arms around your chest, and gently pat yourself on your back. Tell yourself, "I'm so sorry you've had a hard day. Tell me all about it. I hurt for you." It just doesn't work. You can't meet your own need for comfort.

How about your need for attention? You could stare at yourself in the mirror for an hour and say things like, "How are you doing? You really look nice today. Tell me the latest news about your job. Wanna go to lunch?" But your need for attention will not be satiated.

Intimacy needs cannot be satisfied by **things.**

A car is not a substitute for *affection.*

A house cannot meet your need for *love.*

Degrees and diplomas will not satisfy your need for *respect.*

A position of authority is not an alternative for *comfort.*

Successful projects will not produce *peace.*

Because we all have needs, we need each other!

Intimacy needs can only be met by emotional and spiritual "commodities."

Only *love* can satisfy your need for *love.*

Only *affection* will meet your need for *affection.*

Empathy is a source of *comfort.*

Forgiveness produces *peace.*

And these emotional and spiritual commodities can only be ours as part of *"God's grace in its various forms"* (see 1 Peter 4:10) as administered by Him and as He ministers to us through others around us.

Because we all have needs, we need each other! If we didn't have needs, we'd be like computerized robots on an assembly line—doing our own thing with no regard for others.

Pause to reflect on **your** being "needy" of attention, affection, approval, and comfort. Write about a time when God met one of these needs "directly" and then write about a time when He met one of those needs through your spouse or a friend. Write your reflections here:

____

____

____

____

____

Consider Matthew 10:8, *"Freely you have received, freely give"* and describe in your own words God's plan for intimacy and how this plan keeps His love, comfort, acceptance, forgiveness, etc. in circulation! Share your thoughts here.

____

____

____

____

Consider Hebrews 12:6, *"Those whom the Lord loves He disciplines,"* and reflect on the order of **first** He loves as He meets our needs, and **second** He disciplines. How might this order of "meeting needs, then disciplining" relate to our role in "parenting with intimacy"? Write your thoughts here:

____

____

____

____

Consider Ephesians 6:4, *"Provoke [not] your children to anger."* Reflect on this premise: One of the quickest ways we provoke a child to anger is to discipline a child whom we don't intimately "know." Share your reflections here:

____

____

____

The Priority of Needs Is Different for Every Individual

While we all seem to have the same needs, the *priority* of those needs is different for each person. Your greatest need may be for *affection,* while your partner's greatest need may be *security.* One child may have an acute need for *comfort,* but her sibling's greatest need may be *approval. Appreciation* may be at the top of the list for your son, while your daughter needs *encouragement* more than anything else.

If we're not careful, we'll treat everyone as if they all have the same priority of needs. We might also try to meet other people's needs based on our own priority. For instance, if your greatest need is for affection, you may gallantly and sincerely inundate your partner with affection without realizing that it may be at the bottom of his/her list of needs. You might become somewhat indignant if your partner isn't overwhelmed with gratefulness for your affectionate giving. It would be an innocent, well-meaning mistake, but a mistake nevertheless.

An important aspect of learning to love individuals, particularly our spouse and children, is taking the time to know them and to discover their unique priority of needs. This is perhaps part of what Peter meant when he admonished husbands to, *"Live with your wives in an understanding way"* (1 Peter 3:7). It may also be a part of how a woman, *"Looks well to the ways of her household"* (Prov. 31:27). With adults, it's not uncommon to discover that their most important individual needs are those which were either unmet in childhood or those which were generously and sufficiently met. In other words, if I had little security growing up, I may need a lot of it as an adult. However, if I had plenty of security growing up, I might also need a lot of it as an adult, simply because I was accustomed to receiving it and I enjoy feeling secure.

God's plan for our lives involves a connectedness with one another. We need to relate to each other in a close and loving way. Instead of our relationships being distant, aloof, indifferent, formal, removed, limited, and superficial, they can be close, personal, deep, caring, affectionate, and warm. They can be *intimate*.

We need to relate to each other in a close and loving way.

How is intimacy spawned? How is it deepened and maintained? When two people lovingly draw upon God's unlimited resources and meet one another's needs, the result is intimacy. Needs, therefore, are the catalyst for intimacy.

Intimacy is the by-product of needs being met.

Let's explore this idea of uniqueness as it relates to marriage. Review the list of Top 10 Intimacy Needs below. Indicate which of these you would most enjoy receiving from your spouse (pick three of the ten during your Marriage Staff Meeting). Compare your two lists. How many of the three were the same for both you and your spouse? Most couples will find that their spouse picked intimacy needs significantly different from their own. We've discovered that 80 percent of couples will have none or only one intimacy need in common. This simple exercise can be a powerful reenforcement of our God-created uniqueness. You'll see the same uniqueness in your children.

Top 10 Intimacy Needs

Attention	Acceptance
Appreciation	Support
Encouragement	Affection
Respect	Security
Comfort	Approval

Next, write down the names of your children, indicating your "guess" at their top three intimacy needs. From your subsequent Family Night activities, you'll be able to return and update this list with your child's opinion. Write your ideas using the Top 10 Intimacy Needs list:

Child's Name	*My Guess of Top 3 Needs*		
Andrew	attention	comfort	approval

Child's Name	*Partner's Guess of Top 3 Needs*		

Child's Name	*Child's Opinion of Top 3 Needs*		

Needs Affect Our Thinking, Feeling, and Behavior

To understand the impact that needs have on our lives, let's consider the **needs principle.**

A simple version of this principle is:

Needs met = satisfaction, contentment, feelings of being loved and cared for → Intimacy

Needs unmet = frustration, anxiety, dissatisfaction → Pain

To illustrate the validity of this principle, consider some of your physical needs. You have a need for sleep, and after a good night's sleep you feel satisfied and contented. But if you go for several days without sleep, you begin to feel edgy, irritable, and frustrated. The same applies to your need for food. Following a good meal you feel gratified and fulfilled, but if you go for an extended period of time without eating, you might feel discontented, touchy, and frustrated.

If this principle applies to physical needs, do you think it would also apply to emotional and spiritual needs? The answer to that is a resounding yes! If our needs for attention, approval, and appreciation are neglected, negative results are produced. If these needs are met, the outcome is positive.

As our needs are met or unmet, we tend to unknowingly progress through a process which involves how we think, how we feel, and eventually how we behave.

The process goes like this:

Needs met = Healthy Thinking → Positive Emotions → Productive Behavior

Needs unmet = Unhealthy Thinking → Painful Emotions → Negative Behavior

Our God-given needs are so strong and persistent, they will eventually affect our behavior.

The diagram on page 58 illustrates in more detail the progression from needs to behavior.

Let's look at two case studies and see how these principles might work.

Sally is a twelve-year-old who rides the bus home from school each day, and arrives at an empty house. Mom is busy with civic responsibilities, community service, and church committees. Dad works sixty- to seventy-hour weeks trying to get ahead, and on weekends has to have "his" time for TV, golf, and sporting events. Sally struggles with making friends and is feeling the torment of dealing with peer pressure alone. She longs for Dad's verbalized love and praise. She wishes Mom would have time for "girl talk," or just window-shopping with her at the mall.

A conflict soon develops at home as a sixteen-year-old boy begins paying attention to Sally, calling the house, and walking her home. She experiences her first of many "groundings" as angry words fill the air at home. She spends more time withdrawn in her room, hurting alone. It's not long until she is sneaking out at night. She begins lying about her activities and friends.

When Sally's needs were not met at home, she slowly digressed through this process:

Needs Unmet—"I need attention, approval, respect, affection, and encouragement from my family, but I'm not getting it.

Unhealthy Thinking—"What's wrong with me? I must be unimportant. I don't matter. I'll try harder. Nothing will ever change."

Painful Emotions—"I feel hurt, bitter, anxious, insecure, and lonely."

Unproductive Behavior—Denial, acting-out, manipulative games, seeking for needs to be met in inappropriate ways.

Painful Outcomes—Depression, outbursts of anger, "shutting down" of emotions, moral compromise.

Sally's wrong responses and her pain were important to God. Her loneliness and pain never justify her wrong responses, but God cares about both her sinfulness and her loneliness.

Understanding Intimacy Needs

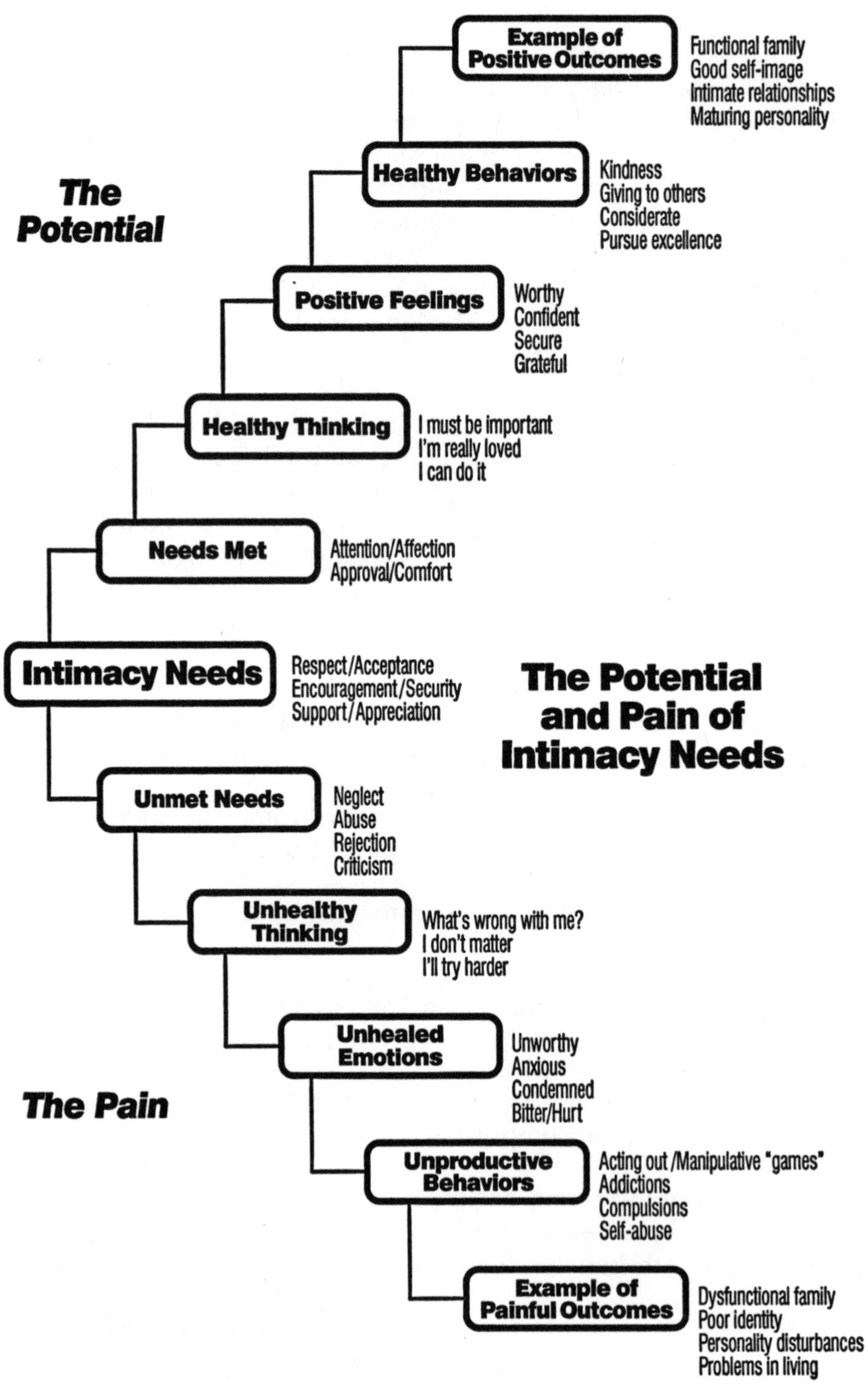

Example of Positive Outcomes
Functional family
Good self-image
Intimate relationships
Maturing personality
Healthy Behaviors
Kindness
Giving to others
Considerate
Pursue excellence
The Potential
Positive Feelings
Worthy
Confident
Secure
Grateful
Healthy Thinking
I must be important
I'm really loved
I can do it
Needs Met
Attention/Affection
Approval/Comfort
Intimacy Needs
Respect/Acceptance
Encouragement/Security
Support/Appreciation
The Potential and Pain of Intimacy Needs
Unmet Needs
Neglect
Abuse
Rejection
Criticism
Unhealthy Thinking
What's wrong with me?
I don't matter
I'll try harder
Unhealed Emotions
Unworthy
Anxious
Condemned
Bitter/Hurt
The Pain
Unproductive Behaviors
Acting out /Manipulative "games"
Addictions
Compulsions
Self-abuse
Example of Painful Outcomes
Dysfunctional family
Poor identity
Personality disturbances
Problems in living

To illustrate how the process can progress from met needs to positive outcomes, let's consider another case study.

Dave has a ten-year-old son named Jeffrey. Although Dave is a busy executive, every week he takes the initiative to give priority to spending time with his son. And instead of spending time doing "guy things," they do "kid's stuff." Dave often takes Jeffrey to the video arcade shop, looking for baseball cards, or to eat at—where else—McDonald's.

Every kid has a need for attention, and Jeffrey's need is regularly met by his loving and caring father.

As Jeffrey's need for attention is lovingly and consistently met, he will tend to progress through this process.

Needs Met—"Spending time with me is more important to Dad than his busy schedule. He often stops doing other things in order to give me attention and approval."

"I must be important. I'm really loved. I can do it! My father loves and cares for me."

Healthy Thinking—"I must be important. I'm really loved. I can do it! My father loves and cares for me."

Positive Emotions—"I feel secure, confident, worthy, and grateful."

Positive Behaviors—Kindness, giving to others, demonstration of positive character, gratitude, meeting other people's needs.

Positive Outcomes—Obedience, loyalty, productive work, good sense of identity, ability to develop intimate relationships, maturing personality.

Implications for Childhood

Personality development is "intense" during the first six years of a child's life as the child moves through this complex maze of personal needs (Paul Meier reports the personality 85 percent developed by age six; Meier, 1977).

Unmet needs are inevitable as we grow up in an imperfect world—as imperfect children—in imperfect families; we were all "undernourished" in some areas of need; **Healthy/Functional** families deal with the hurt of unmet needs as they go along; **Dysfunctional** families may deny the hurts, ignore the needs, and/or blame the child for having needs!

Children don't fully comprehend their needs so it's incumbent on parents to understand their needs, validate their importance, and focus on "giving" to the child.

Implications for Parenting

Unmet needs underlie a great deal of a child's acting-out behavior; lack of attention might bring **anger;** missing **appreciation** and acceptance might bring **withdrawal**; successful parents address inappropriate behaviors as well as explore unmet needs; this requires awareness of a parent's needs, openness about feelings, and a Christ-centered identity on the part of the parent (Narramore, 1987).

Need frustration is seen as a factor to "Problems in Living" (i.e., labeled "pathology" by many. Unmet needs contribute to lack of identity and worth; self-defeating attitudes or behaviors may develop; discouragement, insecurity, and loneliness might develop; abusive or addictive patterns might arise, harming oneself or others (Smith, 1990).

Reflect for a few minutes on the "Pain and Potential" diagram on page 58. Consider some of your intimacy needs and whether they were met or unmet, and how they may impact your thinking, feeling, and behavior. Recall your top three intimacy needs. What happens when one of these three needs goes unmet? What are your thoughts and feelings? What does your behavior look like?

___

___

___

Reflect on this parenting implication: As parents we often concentrate on a child's unproductive behavior. In doing so, we miss opportunities to give to their underlying intimacy need. Regrettably, our focus can become exclusively centered on correcting their behavior rather than meeting their needs. Consider for a moment each of your children and write any reflections you have here:

___

___

___

___

___

We recently met with a fourth-grade boy who was exhibiting behavioral problems at school. Andrew had never been in trouble before, but he suddenly started talking-out in class and disrupting other students. His punishment was simple. Andrew had to stay after school, alone with his teacher.

Andrew's mother brought him in for counseling. After visiting with Andrew about his hobbies and interests, we asked this question: "When do you feel most loved and cared for?" His immediate response was, "When my teacher spends time with just me. She talks with me after school and she's not getting paid for it."

Andrew had an acute need for attention which was being neglected, so he decided to do something about it.

We soon discovered that Andrew's mother was working a 3 to 11 P.M. shift. She wasn't able to spend a lot of time with her son. Andrew had an acute need for attention which was being neglected, so he decided to do something about it. He discovered that he could act up in school and get some personal attention from someone whom he loved and respected—his teacher.

One approach to solving this problem would have been to focus only on his behavior. We might have tried to change Andrew's behavior by separating him from his classmates, taking away privileges, or giving him a lecture about the woes of misbehavior and rebellion. Andrew's behavior would likely not have changed. An alternate approach would simply be for Andrew's parents to make arrangements to meet his need for attention. They might adjust work schedules or alternate times home after school. Which strategy do you think would work best?

The Zaccheus Principle

Let's take a moment to consider Christ's strategy with a tax-collector named Zaccheus, and a Samaritan woman at Jacob's well.

Read Luke 19:1-10 and John 4:7-26. Christ ministered to many individuals across the pages of Scripture. He met people where they **hurt,** physically, emotionally, and spiritually. He was to them the Great Physician. He met people at their point of **need,** physically, emotionally, and spiritually. He was to them, the Great Provider. Christ could **accept** and minister to the sinner while not condoning wrong behavior. Christ demonstrated **unconditional** love as He viewed a person's **worth** as separate from their **behavior.** *"But God demonstrates His own love toward us [declaring our worth], in that while we were yet sinners"* Romans 5:8.

Consider this first-century tax collector:

- **His Behavior**—likely included stealing, deceit, lying, etc.
- **His Feelings**—possibly lonely, rejected, guilty, fearful, insecure.
- **His Thoughts**—possibly "no one cares"; "nothing will ever change."
- **His Needs**—noticeably he needed **acceptance, understanding,** etc.

How did Christ minister?

"Zaccheus, hurry and come down, for today I must stay at your house"—Luke 19:5.

He ministered to needs—acceptance, attention, and understanding. Jesus initiated fellowship with this unpopular man and *Zaccheus experienced* ***different feelings*** *and* ***changed behavior!***

"He hurried and . . . received Him gladly"—Luke 19:6.

"Behold, Lord, half of my possessions I will give to the poor, and if I have defrauded anyone of anything, I will give back four times as much" —Luke 19:8.

Consider this **outcast** Samaritan:

- **Her Behavior**—adultery, immorality, etc.
- **Her Feelings**—possibly guilty, insignificant, outcast, lonely.
- **Her Thoughts**—possibly "What's wrong with me"; "I'm such a failure."
- **Her Needs**—noticeably she needed attention, acceptance, forgiveness, etc.

How did Christ minister?

"Give Me a drink"—John 4:7 . . . breaking all social custom by giving her **attention!**

"Whoever drinks of the water that I shall give . . . shall never thirst"—John 4:14 . . . **accepting** her by offering the gift of Himself before she changed her behavior!

We have been declared by Him as having a worth that is incomprehensible.

The Samaritan woman must have experienced a life-changing encounter as *"many of the Samaritans believed in Him because of the word of the woman who testified"*—John 4:39.

Look beyond Others' Faults and See Their Need!

"Accept one another just as Christ also accepted us"—Romans 15:7.

Acceptance doesn't mean condoning sin but rather to look deeper—just as Christ saw my sin and looked deeper, Christ declared that "You and I sin" but we are more than our sin. We have been declared by Him as having a **worth** that is incomprehensible.

He allowed His Son to die for me. The inexpressible joy and wonder of that truth prompts and empowers changed behavior in me.

So it is with others as they look toward me to be a **good steward** of this amazing grace! This "secret" of ministry is clearly evident in the life of Christ, the Apostle Paul, and other messengers of God.

This "secret" will powerfully impact your marriage and family with deepened insight and heightened sensitivity.

Reflect on Christ's ministry to Zaccheus, the Samaritan woman, and to you and me. Write about how He *"looked beyond my faults and saw my needs."*

It is the grateful wonder and appreciation I experience as He meets my needs that prompts and empowers changes within me. *"The love of Christ constrains me."*

Write about how this gratefulness has brought changes in your life.

Intimacy Needs... Met or Unmet?

Listed below are the Top Ten Intimacy Needs. We've given some possible outcomes if these needs are met or not met. You'll notice that the outcomes may be extremely different. For instance, when people's need for attention is not met, some may become boisterous and extroverted. By their behavior they demand attention. Others may become reclusive and introverted when their need for attention goes unmet. They may choose to withdraw instead of facing more pain.

Attention—*Met*—good sense of identity, confident, feelings of "I'm important," secure, willing to be a servant; attentive to others' needs.
Unmet—promiscuous, boisterous, poor identity, feelings of being worthless, delinquency, shy and withdrawn, concentration on appearance and pleasing others.

Acceptance—*Met*—secure, confident, feelings of worth, relaxed, peaceful.
Unmet—performance-oriented, workaholic, poor identity, insecure; defensive.

Appreciation—*Met*—positive and optimistic, good work ethic, grateful, encouraging to others.
Unmet—easily discouraged and pessimistic, performance-oriented, insecure, self-doubt.

Support—*Met*—encouraged, grateful, feelings of being loved, hope, sensitive to "giving" opportunities.
Unmet—discouraged, weariness toward life, fear of failure, timidity.

Encouragement—*Met*—"Can do" attitude, positive and optimistic, creative, productive.
Unmet—lack of confidence, failure complex, defeatist attitude, pessimistic, frustrated, withdrawn, negative.

Affection—*Met*—secure, free to give, feelings of being loved and comforted; healthy boundaries with the opposite sex.
Unmet—aloof and distant, uncomfortable being physically close to people, cold and unfeeling, promiscuous, flirting, clinging to others of the opposite sex.

Approval—*Met*—productive, confident, good sense of identity.
Unmet—search for approval, performance-oriented, workaholic, "self-made," lack of self-confidence, insecure, confused, fearful.

Security—*Met*—full of faith, confident, giving, grateful, positive, adaptable, flexible.
Unmet—fearful, insecure, controlling, possessive, anxious, worrier, negative, rigid, self-reliant.

Comfort—*Met*—caring, compassionate, positive, giving, sensitive, self-confident, loving.
Unmet—unable to comfort others, feelings of being alone and empty, volatile, promiscuous, avoidance of emotions, emphasis on "fixing" situations and people, obsessive-compulsive orientation.

Respect—*Met*—respectful of others, freedom to "grow up," giving, sensitive, loving, positively assertive.
Unmet—feelings of worthlessness and inferiority, insecure, demanding, intolerant, "victim" mind-set.

Needs (*met or unmet*) do affect our thinking, emotions, and ultimately our behavior.

Identifying the Relationship between Unproductive Behavior and Unmet Needs

Also, as we have seen, in many cases, unproductive behavior is the result of unmet needs. An infant may cry, seeking affection. A child may color on the wall, wanting attention. A teenager may pursue unwholesome relationships, when needing approval. A businessman may become a workaholic, trying to gain respect.

In our attempt to correct the situation, we often focus only on the wrong behavior. We ignore a critical underlying issue: the unmet needs. A more productive approach would be to see a correlation between behavior and unmet needs, and then begin meeting these needs while at the same time addressing wrong behavior.

Write down the names of each of your children. List some of their behavior problems, and then try to establish a link to unmet needs.

Name ____

Unproductive behavior ____________________________

____

Needs possibly related to this conduct ________________

____

Name ____

Unproductive behavior ______________________________

____

Needs possibly related to this conduct __________________

____

Name ____

Unproductive behavior ______________________________

____

Needs possibly related to this conduct __________________

____

Scripture Journaling—1 Peter 4:10

Reflect on the "manifold" (many-sided) nature of God's grace as He lovingly extends His affection, comfort, acceptance, and forgiveness. Now consider how a parent is to be a "good steward" in sharing this many-sided grace with each child. Write a prayer of thanksgiving for how God has blessed you and then mention to God specific aspects of His grace you want to share with each child. (For instance: *"God, I want to show Peter the same forgiveness that You have shown me. You don't remind me of all the times I've messed up. I want to give him that gift as well."* Or *"God, thank You for the way You accepted me. While I was still a sinner, You gave Your Son to die for me. When Melissa and I disagree about privileges, help me to show her acceptance that's not based on her behavior."*)

Write your prayer here: ______________________________

____

____

____

Marriage Staff Meeting

Begin this discussion by comparing your list of Top 10 Intimacy Needs. Identify the three that you would most like to receive from your spouse. Note the uniqueness of the two lists. In order to deepen your marriage intimacy, make note of your partner's top three needs. Ask him/her how you could best meet this need, then focus on mutually giving to one another.

Compare your lists on page 55 where you've guessed each child's top three needs. Depending on the ages of your children, you can ask them directly about their priority of needs. Older children and teens can easily pick three from the Top 10 List. Preschool and young children could more easily complete this statement: "I feel loved when ____________________."

Discuss the "Zaccheus Principle" of looking for needs beneath the deeds. How do you see it working in your own life? Do unmet needs come out in irritation, withdrawing, or escaping?

Review the *Characteristics of Intimacy Needs . . . Met or Unmet* on pages 64–66. In which needs might *you* have been "undernourished" as you grew up? What symptoms did it produce? What symptoms do you see in each child that might indicate an undernourished need? Pray together, asking God to give insight into each child's needs and to prompt your caring involvement from a grateful heart.

Top Ten Need of the Week—Attention

Attention—taking thought of one another, entering into one another's world.

Look for opportunities this week to meet the need for attention in each child. Noted below are several ideas for meeting the need of attention. This might sound like:

- "Johnny, I'd like to go to your baseball game tonight."
- "Jill, let's spend the day together on Saturday. We'll do anything you'd like to do. You plan out the day and I'll tag along."
- "Christi, tell me about the science fair that's coming up. I'd like to hear your ideas."

- "Jessica, after dinner I'd like to play with you."

Family Night Activity—"I feel loved when . . ."

Take turns around the dinner table or after a Family Night activity to finish the following sentence:

"I feel loved by you when ______________________________."

This activity helps open communication and identify specific needs. Dad and Mom should give their answers first. They might share about one aspect of their relationship:

"I feel Dad's love when he comes outside to sit with me and quietly talk." (attention)

"I feel Mom's love when she greets me with a kiss at the door." (affection)

Next, Dad and Mom share with each child:

"I feel Robin's love when she gives me a hug after a fun shopping trip." (affection/appreciation)

"I feel Eric's love when he invites me to watch football with him." (acceptance/attention)

"I feel Terri's love when she tells me she's proud of my teaching." (approval)

Finally, have children share with parents and with one another.

Additional activity for older children and teens—using copies of the list of Top 10 Intimacy Needs, have each family member pick three they would most enjoy receiving from the family. Give each family member an opportunity to share their lists, telling **why** these are important and how family members could meet them.

For Group Discussion

Ask each group member to share their top three intimacy needs. Then invite everyone to share a time when one of those needs went unmet. What were your thoughts and feelings? What did your behavior look like? What were the needs beneath your deeds?

Think about the needs beneath your children's deeds. Share one example that illustrates the relationship between your child's unmet need and their behavior. How might you begin meeting this need in order to help prevent misbehavior? How might you handle a similar situation in the future?

Invite parents who have completed the Marriage Staff Meeting and Family Night activity to share about their experiences. What intimacy need(s) might have gone "undernourished" as you grew up? Were there any surprises? What new insights did you gain? Were there any difficulties or challenges associated with this activity?

Did you gain a new appreciation for the way God "parents" us? As you realized that He not only addresses our behaviors but also seeks to meet our needs, what feelings does that promote? How do these feelings, stirred up by the Holy Spirit within, prompt changes in our behavior?

CHAPTER 4

Understanding Your Child's Fallenness

"BLESSED ARE THE poor in spirit [the needy], for theirs is the kingdom of heaven"—Matthew 5:3.

It's obvious that we have needs built into our physical, emotional, and spiritual DNA. But the question is . . . Why? Why did God create us with a need for sleep? Why do we need air? And why do we all yearn for comfort, attention, and security? Do these needs represent flaws in God's design? Why did God create us with needs? How does our neediness relate to our "fallenness"?

Unfortunately, in our society we seem to have established a mentality that says: "If you're mature, then you've grown out of these needs. Or in the male psyche, if you're tough, you don't admit to having needs in the first place."

If you need comforting, there's something wrong with you.

If you need appreciation, you're insecure.

If you need support, you're weak.

If you need security, you lack faith.

If you need acceptance, you have a poor self-image.

But to admit that we have needs is not an admission of *our fallenness,* it's a confession of *our humanity.* We all have needs;

that's the way God made us. And to admit that we have needs is not only truthful, it's beneficial.

Unfortunately, this reluctance to admit that we have needs is often conveyed most frequently in **Christian circles.** We often succumb to a subtle but erroneous teaching that the more mature we become in Christ, the fewer needs we have and the less we need each other.

This reluctance to admit that we have needs is often conveyed most frequently in Christian circles.

The truth is, God has created us with needs so that we might constantly look to Him. We allow Him to minister to us Himself and through others. Then we can devote ourselves to unselfishly meeting other people's needs. This truth will produce a humble, unselfish, spiritual brother or sister, whose heart is full of gratitude. Out of this gratefulness they can focus on lovingly meeting the needs of family and friends. This person is grateful that God is meeting their needs, often through other people.

It seems clear that we're all needy, and it's not sinful or wrong to be needy. The issue of our sinfulness or fallenness comes in how we deal with our neediness. God's plan for our neediness is that we might:

- **express humility**—*"God is opposed to the proud, but gives grace to the humble"*—James 4:6.
- **exercise faith**—*"My God shall supply all your needs according to His riches in glory in Christ Jesus"*—Philippians 4:19. God is free to involve people in order to minister His provision. He involved the Philippians to provide for Paul's need in this passage.
- **experience intimacy**—*"[God] is intimate with the upright"* —Proverbs 3:32; *"I have called you friends, for all that I have heard from My Father I have made known to you"*—John 15:15.

Parenting as God intended helps impart these ingredients into a child's life. A parent/child relationship can validate the humility of neediness, shape a child's faith, and role model the potential of intimate relationships. Therefore, one of our most sobering challenges as parents is to help prepare a child to walk uprightly and intimately with his God in these three ways.

Pause now and reflect on how God might intend for parents to role model these three ingredients. Write your thoughts below:

- express humility ______________________________

____

- exercise faith ________________________________

____

- experience intimacy ___________________________

____

As parents role model these three attributes, they serve as a challenge for their children to do the same.

As parents role model these three attributes, they serve as a challenge for their children to do the same.

As we embark on this challenging journey, we must address a fuller understanding of a child's "fallenness" (and thus our own). The Bible is clear that sin entered the world through Adam and that through him all have sinned (Rom. 5:12). It's also clear that we live out this sinfulness as we each *"have gone astray, each . . . to his own way"* (Isa. 53:6). No works of righteousness or goodness on our part will help us (Titus 3:5); they are but *"filthy rags"* (Isa. 64:6). Our only hope is *"by grace through faith"* (Eph. 2:8-9) in the provision the Father has made for us through His Son (John 3:16). The Bible also speaks of every man, woman and child walking according to the *"course of this world, according to the prince of the power of the air, of the spirit that is now working in the sons of disobedience. Among them we too all formerly lived in the lusts of our flesh"* (Eph. 2:2-3).

Notice the completeness of this Fall: following the world, fulfilling the flesh, empowered by the evil one. Theologians might then say that we each enter this world depraved, by nature children of wrath (v. 3), fallen and apart from God. Hopefully, as parents, we have been brought near to God by personally receiving the gift of Christ, no longer strangers and foreigners, but fellow citizens with the saints and of the household of God (vv. 13, 19).

Only in this new state as new creations in Christ (Rom. 5:17) will we ever be to our children all our Creator and our children need us to be.

Reflect on how you came to receive the provision of God for your fallenness. Think about how Christ has created in you a new creation, a new husband, wife, mother, and father. And if this gift of God to you has yet to be received, receive it from Him now.

Take a minute to write a note of gratefulness to God for offering His Son Jesus in your behalf. Write your prayer of gratefulness here:

____

____

____

____

"Freely you received, freely give"—Matthew 10:8.

Just as we have received of the Father's abundant provision, out of a grateful heart come rivers of living water to touch and change our children. But what does this ministry to my child's fallenness look like? Let's consider more of the specifics underlying our fallenness, along with our "Parenting with Intimacy" response:

First, parents help replace a child's fear with faith (trust).

Every "needy" child enters this world fearful. God has not given us a spirit of fear so it must have come from the "other guy" . . . as we enter this world, walking according to the prince of the power of the air. Underlying each fear is a lie from the father of all lies; and there may be no greater lie than the one that says **"you must selfishly take, or your needs will go unmet."** Think back on your newborn child . . . needy and demanding; needy and selfishly taking; and she enters a world that says "life is for the taking." "You only go around once, so get all the gusto you can get." Painful reminders of the Genesis 3 fall, *"and the woman took of the fruit"* (see v. 6).

Notice from the chart on page 75 that each child begins his journey on the left . . . selfishly, fearfully taking. God's plan is for two parents walking intimately with Him to give from a grateful heart to the intimacy needs of each child. Having freely received of His perfect love, we freely give. But how do we know He loves us?—**He took initiative to meet our needs!**

The chart below highlights this parenting with intimacy challenge:

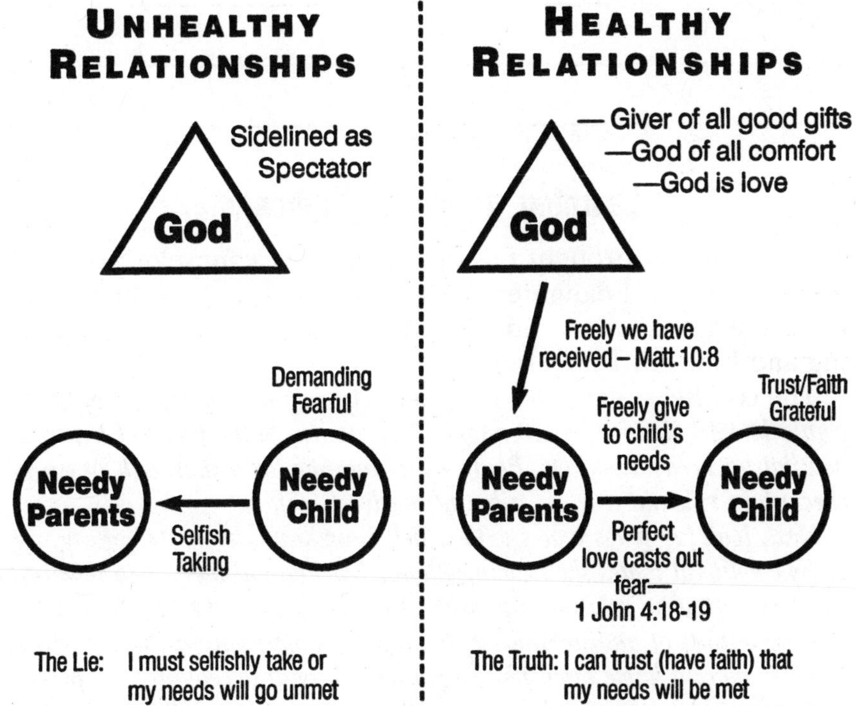

We needed acceptance, forgiveness, comfort, security, and the list goes on and on. It's this same "taking initiative to meet needs" that begins to drive out a child's fear and begins to turn their impressionable hearts toward God. Thus unconditional giving toward their needs removes their aloneness and begins to stir within them a grateful heart that begins to ponder the question, "Who is it out there who has given my parents such a great love for me?"

How could you initiate giving to each child this week?

(For instance: Rebecca—I can give her acceptance. I'll initiate conversations and ask her about her classes. I'll show interest in the things that interest her.)

Child's Name	*Loving Initiative to Give*
________	______________________________________
________	______________________________________
________	______________________________________
________	______________________________________

Learning from Life Applications

A mom recently brought this question to the counselor's office: My fourteen-year-old daughter is a well-adjusted teenager but sometimes she gets anxious and starts to hyperventilate. What's happening and how can I help her?

The counselor gave this response: *Anxiety over a myriad of things would be typical for many teenagers, but anxiety to the point of hyperventilating needs attention. Begin by taking her for a thorough physical checkup to rule out any contributing medical factors.*

Next, look for stress issues with which your daughter is struggling, especially emotional issues she's facing alone. The key will then be to remove her aloneness. Review relationship issues, beginning with the family and home. Are there times of quality talking, spontaneous affirmations, and verbalized love? Is there a home atmosphere of unconditional acceptance, or pressure to perform? After parental review of these issues, begin setting aside time to visit with your daughter, focusing on stress issues in her life. Begin with home/family relationships, boyfriends, peers, and teachers. Look for "pressure to perform" issues like grades, athletics, and peer acceptance.

As relationships and issues of stress are identified, provide reassurance, encouragement, and particularly empathy ("It saddens me that you're feeling such pressure to perform at school. I really hurt for you because I love you.") As a parent, you may not be able to remove the stress (and at times you shouldn't remove legitimate stress), but you can remove the aloneness.

Reflect on any anxieties, insecurities, or uncertainties that you see in your children. These are all fears which could benefit from your initiative in sharing God's perfect love. Note these issues and plans for your initiative.

(For instance: Michael seems to be afraid that I love his baby sister more than him. If he acts out when I'm holding the baby, I'll ask him if he needs a hug. When Allison goes down for a nap, Michael and I can read together.)

Child's Name	*Loving Initiative to Give*
________	______________________________
________	______________________________
________	______________________________
________	______________________________

The following exercise will assist you in listening beyond your children's words to discern their needs. As noted in this section, fear often prompts our temptation to "take" in order to get our needs met. Learning to minister to needs beneath the fear will drive out the fear and allow trust to grow.

Learning to Identify Intimacy Needs: Listen to What They Say

We all have important intimacy needs. They serve as a catalyst for motivation, and they strongly affect behavior. Even if we acknowledge our neediness, we often forget to properly express our needs to our loved ones.

Listed below are some phrases you might hear from your children, your spouse, or friend. Beside each phrase, write down the need that's being expressed. Possible needs are: acceptance, approval, security, respect, encouragement, attention, support, comfort, affection, and appreciation.

1. "You're too busy." ______________________
2. "Look what I did." ______________________
3. "Do you mind asking my opinion?" ______________
4. "Will you always love me?" _________________
5. "I just can't do this." ____________________

6. "I feel out of place." ____________________

7. "I've had a bad day." ____________________

8. "I feel like a failure." ____________________

9. "Could we spend more time together?" ____________________

10. "I'm really upset!" ____________________

11. "Hold me." ____________________

12. "Would you help me?" ____________________

13. "I have a big nose." ____________________

14. "What do you think of what I've done?" ____________________

15. "I can't do anything right!" ____________________

16. "I've had it!" ____________________

17. "You're always making all the decisions." ____________________

18. "I just want a place we can call home." ____________________

Second, parents help redirect a child's expectations toward God.

These "needy" children (and adults), longing for more than air, food, and water, enter life with their **expectations** directed only one direction—toward others, beginning with Mom and Dad. A newborn instinctively looks to Mom for milk and soon learns to cry out to be held, hugged, and rocked when hearing a familiar voice. Here again, we begin to uncover one of the lies associated with our fallenness. **"Others exist in order to meet my needs."**

In contrast, God's truth will be, "He is here to meet our needs (often involving others) in order that we might then give to others."

Parenting with intimacy will involve redirecting your children's expectations toward the true source of provision. The chart on page 79 highlights this parenting with intimacy challenge.

Each child begins her journey on the left side of the diagram. She is totally focused on expecting others to meet her needs. God's plan is for parents to be a living epistle. Parents lovingly redirect these expectations toward Jehovah Jirah, the true provider. It's this parental testimony that shapes a child's expectations into hope,

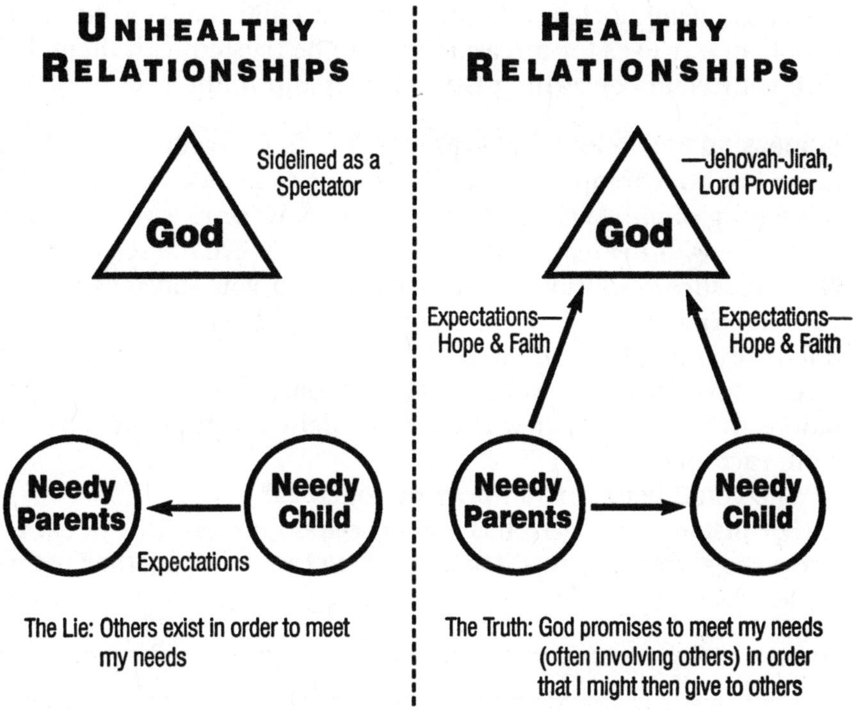

UNHEALTHY RELATIONSHIPS

God

Sidelined as a Spectator

Needy Parents

Needy Child

Expectations

The Lie: Others exist in order to meet my needs

HEALTHY RELATIONSHIPS

God

—Jehovah-Jirah, Lord Provider

Expectations—Hope & Faith

Expectations—Hope & Faith

Needy Parents

Needy Child

The Truth: God promises to meet my needs (often involving others) in order that I might then give to others

giving rise to faith as the *"assurance of things hoped for"* (Heb. 11:1).

Practically, this redirecting might include the following:

Pray with your children—Mealtimes and bedtimes provide obvious opportunities. Take opportunities throughout the day to say, "Let's just stop now and pray about it." This models for children the availability and interest of a Heavenly Father. He desires for us to talk with Him.

Journal of gratefulness—*"Forget none of His benefits"* (Ps. 103:2). Regularly involve family members in a "blessing search." Each family member names a recent blessing and expresses gratefulness. Writing down the blessing helps confirm the blessing and deepens faith.

Trust God with other people—It takes a great faith to trust God with other people, such as teachers, coworkers, playmates, and bullies in the neighborhood. Model for your child that God has put people in our lives for a reason. He can be trusted with them. Pray with your child concerning God's leadership in the lives of others.

Confession and vulnerable prayer—You may have broken a promise or lost your temper. Your child needs to hear an apology. "It was wrong of me. Will you forgive me?" Now pray with your child. "Help me with my temper, God. Change me. Give me self-control." Now reassure your child: "I want to remind you and reassure you that there's Someone who never lets us down. He never disappoints us. That Someone is God."

After reviewing these practical applications to help redirect expectations to God, consider who in your family could possibly benefit from each one.

Who could benefit from **praying together?**

(For instance: Rebecca has a dentist appointment this week. I know she's dreading it. I'll ask her if we can pray together before we leave.)

____

____

____

Who could benefit from a **journal of gratefulness?**

(For instance: Stacey and I need to sit down and write about the gifts and talents God has given her. She could use a boost of self-confidence.)

____

____

____

Who could benefit from **trusting God with other people?**

(For instance: Before Anthony goes to bed tonight, I'll pray with him about the situation at school. We'll ask God to help him know how to respond when the other boy picks on him. And we'll ask God to intervene in any way He thinks is best.)

____

____

Who could benefit from **confession and vulnerable prayer?** (For instance: Ashley needs to hear an apology from me. I know that I embarrassed her yesterday in front of her friends. I'm going to let her hear my prayer for patience and sensitivity.)

Learning from Life's Applications

One morning, Sarah's dad feels a tinge of guilt after yelling at her the previous evening. His outburst of anger was uncalled for. He needs to say something to his daughter, but he's not sure what to say. "After all," he rationalizes to himself, "rules are rules, and Sarah was on the phone after hours."

Let's freeze the picture frame and analyze this situation. It's obvious that Dad owes his daughter an apology. He needs to confess. Regardless of whether or not she should have been on the phone, his angry, unloving response was unwarranted. In fact, it's very likely that one of the ways Sarah will learn to take more responsibility for her actions is to see her parents take responsibility for theirs.

It's very likely that one of the ways Sarah will learn to take more responsibility for her actions is to see her parents take responsibility for theirs.

Since this particular vignette is fiction, let's create several different options for Dad's confession and analyze each one.

Option #1

"Sarah, I realize we had a little misunderstanding last night. I had a terrible day at the office and I guess I just brought that frustration home with me. [Dad is attempting to blame others. He's passing the buck.]

Option #2
"Sarah, I realize we had a little misunderstanding last night. You know I love you; let's forget it and go on." [Dad is denying his guilt. He's trying to ignore the problem.]

Option #3
"Sarah, I realize we had a little misunderstanding last night, but I've told you many times not to talk on the phone after 9." [Dad is trying to rationalize his sin. He's highlighting Sarah's fault in order to avoid his own.]

Option #4
"Sarah, I realize we had a little misunderstanding last night. If I hurt you by what I did, I'm sorry." [Dad is offering a flippant confession. The phrase, "if I hurt you," indicates lack of conviction of having done wrong.]

Option #5
"Sarah, I realize we had a little misunderstanding last night. I don't want what happened last night to ruin our day today. Let's talk about it." [Dad is making an attempt at confession, but only to avoid further confrontation and trouble.]

Option #6
"Sarah, I realize we had a problem last night. It's important for you to realize some things. The rules of the house are for everyone's good and they need to be obeyed and enforced." [Dad is making excuses for his behavior.]

Option #7
"Sarah, I realize that what I did last night was wrong. I got angry and said things I shouldn't have said and did things I shouldn't have done. I know I hurt you. I was also wrong in not asking your forgiveness last night. I realize that has deepened your pain. Would you forgive me?" [A true confession includes humble acknowledgment of specific wrong, without explanation or justification.]

"Confess your sins to one another, and pray for one another, so that you may be healed"—James 5:16.

Review the first six options above. Which of these six sound most like you? What response do you usually give, rather than a genuine confession? Write about your reflections here: (For instance: I usually try to avoid the issue. I don't like confrontation and I sure don't like admitting that I'm wrong.)

____

____

____

Write a short prayer asking God to prompt your vulnerable confession in accordance with James 5:16. Write your prayer here:

____

____

____

The chart below highlights this aspect of the parenting with intimacy challenge:

UNHEALTHY RELATIONSHIPS

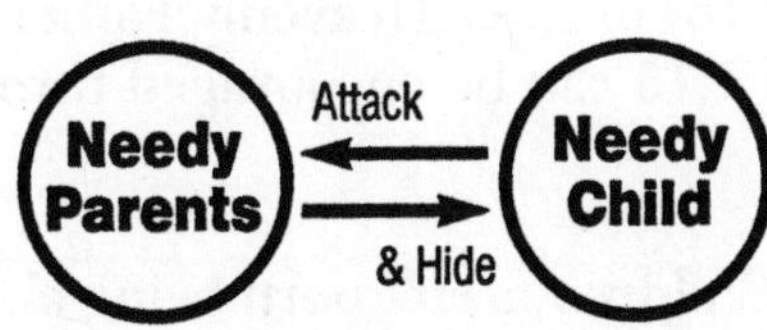

The Lie: No one really wants to know my needs; it's not safe to share them; I must either "hide" my needs or "attack" others to have them met

HEALTHY RELATIONSHIPS

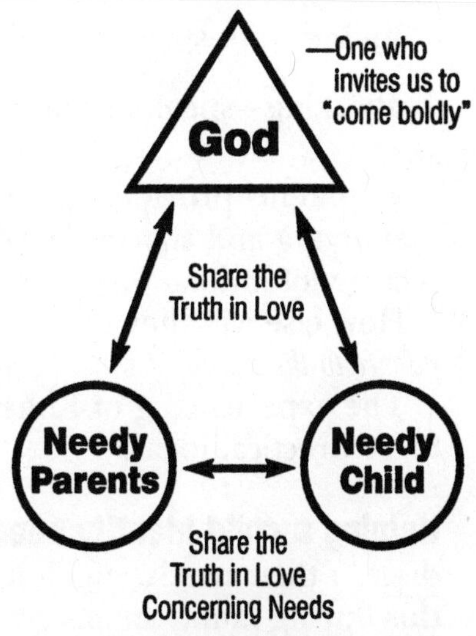

The Truth: Both my parents and God want to know my needs; they're approachable; it's safe to be vulnerable

Finally, parents role model vulnerability and approachability concerning need.

Every child comes into this world with a tendency to both "attack" and "hide" concerning their needs. Just watch a young child spot her favorite toy in the hands of a rival playmate! We wouldn't expect her to *"share the truth in love"*—Ephesians 4:15. Or watch a child hide when he needs a diaper changed, when it's bedtime, or when he just broke your favorite dish. Since our fallenness has its roots in the Garden of Eden, it's not surprising that when God went looking for Adam and Eve after their sin, they **hid** from Him. And when finally confronted, they resorted to **attacking** and **blaming** one another.

Children begin their journey on the left side of the diagram (p. 83). They enter into an uncertain world, not understanding their own needs. They tend to believe the lie that, "No one really wants to know my needs. It's not safe to share them. I must either hide them or attack." God's plan is for parents to help make a child's world a safe place to discover and express needs. Ephesians 4:15 speaks of *"speaking the truth in love"* as God's solution to:

hiding—not speaking the truth, or

attacking—speaking the truth, but not in love

As parents provide a home environment which is conducive to identifying and sharing needs and hurts, children experience the security of intimacy and an affirmed worth that someone cares.

How else will they one day learn how to come *"near with confidence to the throne of grace"* (Heb. 4:16) of their Heavenly Father?

The experiencing of Ephesians 4:15 can be encouraged through these practical ideas:

Helping a child identify needs—Children aren't born being able to discern their needs, much less have names for them. Encourage this during family nights or around the dinner table. "I feel loved by Mom/Dad when ____________________." Have each family member answer this question and then discuss what intimacy need the answer seems to meet. Do I need appreciation, attention, support, encouragement, or affection? You might also use the exercise on pages 77–78 to identify needs from what people say.

Practice the Zaccheus principle—You notice four-year-old Susie's irritability from a long day of play. She picks a fight with her brother and then begins to torment the cat. You look beyond her deeds and see her needs, "It looks and sounds like you might be needing some laptime, and maybe a hug?" A smile crosses her face as she jumps into Mommy's lap. Susie is learning that at the end of a busy day, she is tired. She needs comfort, and it's safe to ask! Maybe next time we'll hear these words before Susie torments the cat: "Mommy, can I sit in your lap? I'm tired."

Practice confession concerning unmet needs—"I really apologize for being insensitive when you struck out in the game. You needed encouragement and support, not advice. That was wrong. Will you forgive me?"

Announce your availability and invite sharing of needs—"Sandy, let's plan to spend Saturday afternoon together, just the two of us. You can share with me how I can be helpful and supportive as you start your new school year."

After reviewing these practical applications to help encourage vulnerability in an approachable, secure environment, consider who in your family could possibly benefit from each one.

Who could benefit from **help in identifying needs?**

(For instance: "Heather, I want you to know how much I love you. Would you like to: wrestle on the floor, play with Play-Doh, or sit in my lap to read?")

____

____

____

____

Who could benefit from the **Zaccheus Principle?**
(For instance: Six-year-old Jeremy has suddenly developed a stomachache. "Jeremy, I know you might be nervous about flying on the airplane. It sounds like you might need to hold on to my hand until we take off. Let's meet the flight attendant and see if she'll bring us a glass of Sprite.")

____

____

____

____

Who could benefit from a **confession concerning unmet needs?**
(For instance: "Ryan, I know you needed my support during your final exams. I gave you lectures instead. It was wrong of me to add more pressure. Will you forgive me?")

____

____

____

____

Who could benefit from **your availability and sharing of needs?**
(For instance: "Madison, let's go swimming this afternoon. We can have a picnic at the pool. I want to hear about the fun things you'd like to do this summer.")

____

____

____

____

In summary, parents can play a vital role in preparing their children for an intimate relationship with Jesus Christ. As you purposefully address the issues of fallenness, your children will develop eternal relationship skills.

- Expectations are redirected toward God. Hope develops into trusting faith.
- Fear is replaced with faith. Trust develops in a safe environment.
- Vulnerability and approachability are role modeled. Children learn that God is available and approachable. He cares about and wants to hear of my needs.

This child is growing in the freedom of God's intended plan as

- humility is expressed
- faith is exercised
- intimacy is experienced.

Scripture Journaling—1 Corinthians 13:11

"When I was a child, I used to speak as a child, think as a child, reason as a child; when I became a man, I did away with childish things"—1 Corinthians 13:11.

Having reviewed these three significant aspects of our fallen condition and their roots in childhood expression, it might be important to make sure we've *"put away childish things"* (see v. 11).

In summary, parents can play a vital role in preparing their children for an intimate relationship with Jesus Christ.

Reflect on the three lies identified. Use your own words to write about God's truth.

1. The lie is: I must selfishly take or my needs will go unmet.

   The truth is ____

   ____

2. The lie is: Others exist to meet my needs.

   The truth is ____

   ____

3. The lie is: No one really wants to know my needs; it's not safe to share them. I must either "hide" them or "attack."

The truth is ____

____

Pause and write a short prayer, asking God to help you put away childish things. Write your prayer here:

____

____

____

____

Marriage Staff Meeting

Set aside at least one hour this week for your staff meeting. Take turns sharing your reflections and remembrances on how you became a Christian. How has God begun His work in you as a new creation? Discuss how our **need** of Him is related to our (1) expressing humility, (2) exercising faith, and (3) experiencing intimacy. Next, discuss three of the key aspects of "fallenness" covered in this chapter and where you see each child in the battle to "put away" the three childish lies. Discuss your plans of ministry to each child. What childish things did you see in yourself? Take time to pray together, thanking God for His plans for your freedom and your children's.

Pray together, thanking God for His plans for your freedom and your children's.

Top Ten Need of the Week—Acceptance

Acceptance—deliberate and ready reception with a favorable response.

This week, put particular emphasis on communicating acceptance to each child. Example sentences follow:

- "Tracy, I love you. Regardless of what you do or don't do, or how you act, I'll always love you."

- "I don't know if I've told you lately, but God created you as a very special person. You're special to Him and to me."
- "Patrick, I love you just the way you are. Don't ever think you have to change in order for me to love you."

Family Night Activity—Identify Feelings

Explore the connection between feelings and needs. Indicate that one of the reasons God gave us "painful" feelings is to help us discern our needs! God gave us families as a safe place where we can share our feelings and needs. This gives us confidence that both God and our family CARE about us!

During one of your family nights or around the dinner table, use some poster board to begin a "Feeling Chart." Divide the poster into two columns: for "positive" and "painful" feelings. Take turns naming as many feelings as you can. Even four- and five-year-olds can participate with feelings like happy, sad, mad, and afraid.

Make a special point to explain that "painful" feelings are not necessarily wrong. It's how we handle our painful emotions that is important. After a few nights of developing a feeling vocabulary you're ready to move on to the next step: Share your feelings with one another.

> ***"Painful" feelings are not necessarily wrong.***

Take turns sharing an event that happened during the day and then share how it made you feel. You might start with each family member sharing a positive event/feeling and then a painful event/feeling. What did the painful feelings indicate you might be needing? This project can help family members develop a vocabulary of feelings and help identify needs. It will also validate the fact that it's OK to have feelings and needs, and to talk about them!

Imagine the positive impact on a child when he or she hears that Dad felt lonely or sad today. This communicates to the child that if Dad felt that way, it must be all right for me to feel that way. Second, this gives a child hope that if Dad made it through his loneliness or sadness, then I can too! If Dad needs comfort then it must be OK for me to need comfort!

For Group Discussion

Think about our society's resistance to admit neediness. At the beginning of this chapter, we pointed out a mentality that says, "I am tough and/or mature. I don't have needs." We've all succumbed to this mentality to some degree. How has the resistance shown itself in your life? Have you struggled with admitting a need for comfort, acceptance, security, or support? How might this resistance affect a marriage or a family?

Review the activity on pages 77–78. Compare your answers with other group members. How easy or difficult was it to identify the needs associated with each statement?

All of us have at least one "favorite" lie that was described in this chapter. We may decide to take from others in order to get our needs met. We may falsely believe that others exist to meet our needs or that others don't really care about our needs. Share which of the lies is your "favorite" and how it shows itself in your relationships.

Ask parents who have completed the Family Night Activity to share about their experiences. How well developed is your feeling vocabulary? Tell about the time spent sharing feelings. How comfortable were you admitting feelings and needs? What impact did it make on your kids?

Part Two

Knowing Your Child's Parents

"It was for freedom that Christ set us free."

GALATIANS 5:1

CHAPTER 5

Finish Growing Up

IN ONE SENSE, we never "leave" our childhood. Childhood memories, sibling relationships, friends, parental influence, hometown environment—all leave an indelible impact on our lives. They significantly impact who we are. It's important to remember that these events are unchangeable. We often had little control over parts of our past and our childhood; that's why it's important to trust our all-knowing, always-loving God and believe that He will cause *"all things to work together for good."*

However, God doesn't want us to continue in bondage to hurts and fears. He doesn't want us to remain paralyzed by rejections and losses from the past. His desire is that we be free from past emotional pain. Continuing in this process of growing up will be critical to establishing an intimate marriage, experiencing intimacy with children, and even serving with maturity and wisdom in roles God may call us to within the church.

Childhood memories . . . significantly impact who we are.

Gaining freedom from childhood hurts strongly relates to our ability to experience a happy marriage. An important part of God's plan for a healthy marriage is that *"a man shall leave his father and his mother, and shall cleave to his wife; and they shall become one flesh"* (Gen. 2:24). The prescription is: leave, cleave, then become one. The order of these three principles is important. You can't "become one" until you're "united," and unity isn't possible until you've "left" your childhood. As long as we're carrying emotional baggage from our childhood, "leaving father and mother" will be difficult, if not impossible.

Pause and consider the order of the Genesis 2:24 admonition: (1) **leave** father and mother, (2) **cleave** unto your spouse (become **united** with) and then, (3) **become one.** Reflect in your own words on how "becoming one" in marriage might be hindered if you haven't finished leaving and cleaving. Write your thoughts below: (For instance: I can see how it would be difficult to be joined with your spouse if you're always looking back to your childhood home for approval or comfort.)

____

____

____

How has your "becoming one" in marriage been impacted by this principle? (Single parents and blended families should explore the relevance of this principle to your previous marriage relationship). Write your thoughts below: (For instance: I know my relationship with my mom has always caused problems between Jill and me. I just can't seem to stop taking care of her. I'm sure that my relationship with Bobby has been affected by my first marriage. It's always been hard for me to trust men. I don't really tell my husband how I feel.)

After "leaving father and mother," becoming united with your spouse, and establishing oneness in your marriage, it's then time to consider having children!

____

____

____

"Adam had relations with . . . Eve, and she gave birth to Cain and . . . Abel"—Genesis 4:1-2.

The intended biblical order seems clear: After "leaving father and mother," becoming united with your spouse, and establishing oneness in your marriage, it's then time to consider having children! Many of us have reversed the order. You're already a parent, but you may not have finished leaving. There may be some things left unresolved from your own growing up experience that are impacting your ability to parent. As a parent, you are challenged to give your child attention and enter into his world. But what if Mom and Dad were too busy to enter into your world? What if the person who really knew you was the baby-sitter? Every day after school you'd sit and talk to her while she ironed and cooked. She was the only one who ever really listened to you. Or maybe that one person who really cared about you was a teacher or a high school coach.

Your child desperately craves approval, but if you never received it then you won't be sure how to give it. You may not know what appreciation looks or sounds like. When you're called upon to comfort your child through the inevitable disappointments of life, you may come to grips with an important fact. As you were growing up, you hurt alone. What now? You cannot give to your children what you do not possess.

Pause and reflect on how raising children might be hindered if this process of leaving-cleaving-becoming one has not been completed. Write your thoughts below: (For instance: I can see how raising children would be more difficult if you haven't completely grown up yourself. Raising kids takes so much unselfishness and wisdom.)

____

____

____

____

How might the unfinished aspects of leaving-cleaving-becoming one possibly impact your children and your parenting? Write your thoughts below:

____

____

____

Unfinished "leaving" (For instance: I know that the constant tension between Dad and me affects my family. I can't be an attentive mother if I'm always worried about what he'll do next.)

____

____

____

____

Unfinished "cleaving" (For instance: I know that my hesitancy to get emotionally close to Susan affects the family. If I can't have an intimate relationship with my wife, it will be even more difficult with the kids.)

____

____

____

____

Unfinished "becoming one" (For instance: When Brad and I aren't in agreement or are having problems communicating, it affects the way I deal with the children.)

____

____

____

____

"[An elder] . . . manages his own household well"—1 Timothy 3:4.

The New Testament spells out the criteria for effective leadership and ministry within the church. Scripture seems to point out that our effectiveness as leaders in the church is directly related to our maturity at home.

Therefore we might find significant church pain when leaders seek to lead even though they've not completed the growing-up process of leaving-cleaving-becoming one—and managing your own household well.

Reflect, in your own words, on how church ministry can be hindered when this divine plan for growing up is not followed. Write your thoughts below: (For instance: Church conflicts sometimes occur with leaders who don't seem to have "oneness" at home.)

____

____

____

____

How have some unfinished aspects of this growing-up process hindered your church involvement, ministry, and leadership? Write your thoughts below: (For instance: I've tried to run things at church when at times I wasn't able to lead my own family. I've withdrawn at times from active church involvement as my teenagers began to "act out.")

____

____

____

____

My Childhood Isn't Over?

In our heart-of-hearts, we can all say, "I've been there!" The hurt, the fear, the circumstance will vary, but most of us have been hindered in our parenting journey by unresolved childhood issues. Although we don't claim to be psychic, we are confident we can tell you three things about yourself:

- As you were growing up, you were an imperfect person
- You grew up in an imperfect environment
- You had imperfect people around you

We know, beyond a shadow of a doubt, that these things are true because you're human. All human beings are imperfect, no exceptions! A natural consequence of the interaction of these three truths is that you have experienced dimensions of hurt. Before you get defensive ("But my parents did the best they could!"), we need to separate our motives and methods. A parent can have great motives, "I love you. I care about you. I want what's best for you," but at the same time employ methods that are hurtful. If someone accidentally drops a heavy rock on your foot, it still hurts even though it was unintentional. Acknowledging pain doesn't translate into assigning blame. We must come to see that it involves the pursuit of truth.

Tragically, many individuals must face the truth that their parents' motives were wrong, as well as their methods. In the case of abuse, incest, and related traumas the motive and method are terribly wrong. This dual pain of both motives and methods will require additional grief as covered in this chapter.

The question is not, "Have you experienced hurt?" That's a foregone conclusion. We've all been undernourished in some areas of need, and the result is hurt. The question is, "Has the hurt been faced? Has it been healed?" Facing hurt head-on leads to opportunities for growth. Denial, on the other hand, stunts our growth as an adult, spouse, and parent.

As we begin this journey into freedom from the past, write about your feelings. Look back at how you might have been hurt or what you might have missed. Write your feelings below:

As I think about looking back to my own growing up, I feel . . .

____

____

____

____

____

____

When I think about exploring what I might have missed or how I might have been hurt, I feel . . .

___

___

___

___

Tell God about these feelings. Ask Him to give guidance, peace, healing, and freedom. Write your prayer here:

___

___

___

___

Why Look Back?

"It was for freedom that Christ set us free"—Galatians 5:1.

Why can't we just "press on to what lies ahead" you may ask? The answer is simple: freedom **from** the past . . . not denial of it, is what enables us to move forward. Although the "events" may be years or decades in the past, the pain of hurt, bitterness, fear, and guilt may still be very real—right now in the present. So, let's explore several significant benefits to looking back at our own growing up:

Truth sets free—"No, I never heard my parents tell me they were proud of me, but it's no big deal."

"No, I never heard my dad actually say he loved me, but that's just the way he was. It didn't really hurt me."

"I'm not sure I could honestly say anyone knew me—not really deep-down. But hey, I did OK without it."

This may sound harsh, but those statements just cannot be true. They represent emotional bondage. John 8:32 says, *"You shall know the truth, and the truth shall make you free."* If you're going to find freedom and help your children find it, you're going to have to confront and deal with the truth about your own childhood.

Honor father and mother—Truly honoring your father and mother means recognizing the pain that was also present in their lives. This pain may have hindered them in their ability to meet some of your needs. You honor them as you allow them to come down off a pedestal that keeps them out of reach. You honor them as you allow them to be human beings who made (and make!) mistakes. You can only honor a "real" person, not an "imaginary" one. You can't really come to a full appreciation of the blessings you received from your parents without also acknowledging the hurts. In essence, blockading the hurts blockades the blessings as well.

Truly honoring your father and mother means recognizing the pain that was present in their lives.

Sensitive giving to your children's needs—Without one resolution of your own pain, giving sensitively to your own children is much more difficult. Two different reactions are commonplace. A parent may be intolerant or insensitive to a child's needs. "I didn't get a lot of approving words, so why should you?" "When I was upset, I got lectures. Why should you need comfort?" Adults can also go overboard in their efforts not to repeat the steps of their own parents. "At all costs, I'm going to give you the attention I missed." "You're going to become the athlete I wanted to be." As well intended as this is, it is not true giving. It's as much for the parent as it is for the child!

Free to admit being an imperfect parent yourself—An integral part of every child's developmental journey is coming to grips with the fact that her parents were not (and are not) perfect. If you're unwilling to wrestle with that truth and its implications, you're destined to be on a never-ending, unachievable personal quest to be a perfect parent yourself. And your children will suffer because of it.

Without this resolution, parents may find it hard to apologize and admit wrong to their children. Children then lose their model of vulnerability and forgiveness that comes with making amends. Children could lack the freedom to bring up their own disappointments and hurts for fear of their parents' reaction.

Blessed are those who mourn—One of the most important benefits of bringing resolution to past pain is God's promised blessing of comfort. Looking back at unmet needs is painful, but these represent losses to be "mourned." Matthew 5:4 actually speaks of great **blessing** that comes to those who mourn!

Review the five benefits noted above. Which one of these benefits seems most important to you? Write about it below: (For instance: I need to be free from my anger at Dad. Whatever it takes I want to learn how to give true comfort and attention to my children.)

____

____

____

____

Tell God about these benefits. Tell Him your desire and need for them. He's a good God who gives good gifts. Thank Him in advance for blessing you in this growing-up journey. Write your prayer here:

____

____

____

____

God Doesn't Want Us to Hurt Alone

Not only is God committed to be a comforting Father to us, but He also desires to channel some of His comfort through others (2 Cor.

1:2-4). Much of life's pain has come our way through people. Perhaps 2 Corinthians 1:2-4 is part of God's wisdom in knowing that we could benefit from some of His comfort coming our way through people too. The depth of His care and love for us is thus confirmed through the testimony of two witnesses . . . our Heavenly Father and His appointed "journeymates."

The blessing of a journeymate—Life is full of hurtful times. It always hurts to hurt. That's intrinsic. But to hurt alone is insufferable.

Why would anyone ever hurt alone? We might not have anyone who will hurt with us. That's why it's important, even necessary, to have a "journeymate" in life. We need someone with whom we can share, cry, laugh, and hurt. This is part of God's plan for marriage, family, and the church.

A journeymate is someone whom you can trust . . . who is available.

A journeymate is someone *who cares for you.* You're not going to share your hurt with someone unless you're convinced of that person's care for you. You need someone who will stay close enough to know what you're going through and someone who will always be available to help. You must sense that he cares for you just because of who you are, not because of what you do. It's good to know that in addition to God, there is at least one other human who really cares for you.

A journeymate is someone *whom you can trust.* You'll also be reluctant to vulnerably share your hurt with someone unless you know you can trust him/her. A trustworthy journeymate must: be confidential about any sensitive information you may share, respond with compassion and acceptance to your hurts and pain, not use any information shared in confidence against you, and not allow any embarrassing information you share to adversely affect the relationship.

A journeymate is someone *who is available.* You may have a friend who cares about you and is trustworthy, but if he's not available when you need him, you'll still hurt alone. This is one of those times when availability is infinitely more important than ability. This highlights the need for Marriage Staff Meetings, periodic dates, and Family Nights.

Do you have a caring, trustworthy, and available journeymate? If not, developing such a friend should be an important priority in life. Your marriage partner can become your "best friend"; for single parents, friendships can be developed in the church to meet your needs for companionship and comfort.

Reflect on this journeymate role in your life. First consider how you fulfill this role for your spouse. Be prepared to set aside time to share this reassurance and question: "I'm wanting to be everything God wants me to be as your "journeymate"; would you share with me:

How can I better communicate that I care about you? (Write his response here)

____

____

____

____

How can I deepen your trust of me? (Write her response here)

____

____

____

____

How can I be more available to you as the friend God wants me to be? (Write his response here)

____

____

____

____

Now reflect on your need for a journeymate as you consider these questions.

I would feel cared about by my spouse/journeymate through their . . . (For instance: acceptance of my feelings. I would like to be able to share feelings without a fear of criticism or a lecture.)

____

____

____

____

It would deepen my trust of my spouse/journeymate if . . . (For instance: I was sure that my wife wouldn't share my struggles with her friends.)

____

____

____

____

I could benefit from my spouse/journeymate being more available to . . . (For instance: hear my feelings in an unhurried way. It would mean a lot to me if we could have portions of uninterrupted time together.)

____

____

____

____

Avoid Self-Reliance

Some people may have a sensitive journeymate, but they still hurt alone because they're unwilling to express their hurt. Our society, and often even the teachings of the church, presents a subtle message that, "It's a sign of weakness to grieve or mourn," or "The more spiritual you become, the less you should feel hurt or loss. If you do, you certainly shouldn't share it." And yet the Bible declares that:

"Blessed are those who mourn, for they shall be comforted" (Matt. 5:4).

"Blessed are the poor in spirit, for theirs is the kingdom of heaven" (Matt. 5:3).

"[Jesus'] power is perfected in weakness" (2 Cor. 12:8).

And, as if we needed more evidence that mourning is all right, Jesus, the God/man, often shared His hurts and disappointments:

"My soul is deeply grieved to the point of death" (Mark 14:34).

"You will all fall away" (Mark 14:27).

"Jesus wept" (John 11:35)

If it was all right for Jesus to express hurt and mourn, it's certainly all right for us to.

Reflect on the Scripture passages above. Write about God's view of your admitting your needs or hurts. Write your thoughts here:

____

____

____

____

____

Consider Christ admitting His needs, hurts, and sadness. Seeing Christ's example can give us reassurance that it's appropriate to express our hurt. God longs to hear from our heart. Write your prayer here. Express your gratitude for Christ's example:

____

____

____

Learn How to Comfort

A third reason why we often hurt alone is that our journeymate might not know how to properly respond to our mourning. When emotion is expressed (and mourning is an emotion), an emotional response must be given in return (Matt. 5:4). But quite often, we offer one of these four unproductive responses: logic or reasoning, criticism, complaining, or neglect. Here's how these might sound in a real-life situation. Perhaps you've just lost a loved one in death and you're mourning your loss. A journeymate might inappropriately respond with:

Logic or reasoning—"Don't be sad; you know she's better off in heaven," or "It's appointed unto man once to die."

Criticism—"Don't be so emotional; everyone goes through rough times."

Complaints—"Well, you know, I'm also hurt. He was my friend too, and no one told me about his death until yesterday."

Neglect—"Don't focus on this one tragedy. Life's full of happy, positive events. Let's talk about some of those."

The only proper response to mourning is comfort.

Comfort includes understanding, empathy, gentleness, and affection. Here are some examples of what comfort might sound like:

"I can really see you're hurting."

"It saddens me that you are hurting."

"I'm committed to go through this with you."

"I'm sorry you hurt; I hurt for you."

"I want to do whatever I can to help, because I care about you."

If we share our hurt with a caring, trusting, available journeymate, and receive comfort, we will feel blessed (Matt. 5:4).

Do you ever hurt alone? Set aside time to be real and vulnerable with someone who cares.

Are you sensitive to others who may be suffering by themselves? Try to find someone around you who would be blessed by your caring attention.

> ***If we share our hurt with a caring, trusting, available journeymate, and receive comfort, we will feel blessed.***

God never intended for us to be alone (Gen. 2:18), particularly when we're hurting. Begin taking time to purposefully reach out to your spouse, family, and friends to develop meaningful relationships which will be a source of refuge and comfort during the hurtful times of life.

Consider the contrast of true comfort with logic, criticism, complaints, and neglect. When you observe someone close to you hurting, which of the four unproductive responses do you sometimes give? Write about it here:

____

____

____

Instead of giving comfort to my spouse's hurt, I often give . . .

____

____

____

to my children's hurt, I often give . . .

____

____

to my friend, I often give . . .

____

____

Review what comfort "sounds like" in the sentences above. Ask God to give you His comforting, compassionate heart. Write your prayer here:

____

____

____

____

Begin the Healing

Identify areas of unmet need—In chapter 2 we identified the Top 10 Intimacy Needs and asked you to do a needs assessment for each of your children. Now the focus is on you. Listed below are those 10 needs along with a number of others. With your renewed commitment to facing the truth, prioritize a quiet, reflective time to review this list. Mark the list as follows: If this need was met by your dad, give yourself a half-circle ["("]. If you received this from your mom, give yourself the other half-circle [")"]. If you received it from both of them, you'll have a full circle ["O"]. As you go through the list, you may find some that you missed altogether. Mark those with an "X."

Take your time. Try to remember, if possible, a specific time when this need was met, or a specific time when it was unmet. Try completing the exercises as you remember events associated with your childhood or preteen years. If you lack memory of these years, begin with years you do remember—preteen, teen, or young adult.

___ 1. **ACCEPTANCE**—deliberate and ready reception with favorable positive response—(Rom. 15:7)
___ 2. **ADMONITION**—constructive guidance in what to avoid; to warn—(Rom. 15:14)
___ 3. **AFFECTION**—to communicate care and closeness through physical touch and verbalized love—(Rom. 16:16)
___ 4. **APPRECIATION**—to communicate with words and feel personal gratefulness for another—(1 Cor. 11:2)

___ 5. **APPROVAL**—expressed commendation; to think and speak well of—(Rom. 14:18)

___ 6. **ATTENTION**—to take thought of another and convey appropriate interest, support, etc.; to enter into another's "world"—(1 Cor. 12:25)

___ 7. **COMFORT**—to come alongside with word, feeling, and touch; to give consolation with tenderness—(1 Thes. 4:18)

___ 8. **COMPASSION**—to suffer with and through another in trial/burden—(Heb. 10:34)

___ 9. **CONFESSION**—open acknowledgment of wrongs committed based upon inner conviction—(James 5:16)

___ 10. **DEFERENCE**—to yield or defer oneself to another for their benefit—(Eph. 5:21)

___ 11. **DEVOTION**—a firm and dependable foundation of committed care—(Rom. 12:10)

___ 12. **DISCIPLINE**—to reprove and correct when boundaries are crossed and limits exceeded—(Prov. 23:13; Rev. 3:19)

___ 13. **EDIFICATION**—to positively promote the growth and development of another—(Rom. 14:19)

___ 14. **ENCOURAGEMENT**—to urge forward and positively persuade toward a goal—(1 Thes. 5:11; Heb. 10:24)

___ 15. **FORGIVENESS**—to cancel out or "release" wrongs committed and bestow instead unconditional favor—(Eph. 4:32)

___ 16. **HARMONY**—an environment of pleasant acceptance and secure love—(1 Peter 3:8)

___ 17. **HOSPITALITY**—open reception of another with a loving heart—(1 Peter 4:9)

___ 18. **INTIMACY**—deep sharing and communion with another as lives are shared in "common"—(1 John 1:7)

___ 19. **KINDNESS**—pleasant and gracious servanthood—(Eph. 4:32)

___ 20. **LOVE**—seeking welfare of others and opportunity to do good; consistent with having first been loved by God and seeing His value of others, the characteristic Word of Christianity—(John 13:34)

___ 21. **PRAYER**—to entreat God's attention and favor upon another—(James 5:16)

___ 22. **RESPECT**—to value and regard highly; to convey great worth—(Rom. 12:10)

___ 23. **SECURITY**—confidence of "harmony" in relationship; free from fear and harm—(Mark 9:50)
___ 24. **SENSITIVE**—seeking to understand and accept another without judging—(Rom. 12:16)
___ 25. **SERVE**—giving up of oneself in caring ministry to another—(Gal. 5:13)
___ 26. **SUPPORT**—come alongside and gently help carry a load (problem, struggle)—(Gal. 6:2)
___ 27. **SYMPATHY**—to identify with another "emotionally" —(1 Peter 3:8)
___ 28. **TEACHING**—constructive and positive instruction in how to live—(Col. 3:16)
___ 29. **TRAINING**—journey to model God's way of facing life's issues—(Luke 6:40)
___ 30. **UNDERSTANDING**—patient endurance of another's humanness—(Eph. 4:2; Col. 3:13)

After you have completed this exercise, write about your reflections here. From my dad, I really missed . . . (For instance: Approval—I really needed to know that he was proud of me. Just once, I wish he would have told me what a good job I had done.)

___

___

___

___

From my mom, I really missed . . . (For instance: Attention—I needed her to spend time with me, come to my games, and ask about my boyfriend.)

___

___

___

___

Grieve the Loss

Allow yourself to grieve the "loss" associated with the pain. It will be helpful to remember specific hurts. Think about particular times when you needed comfort and missed it; you needed approval but no one noticed; you needed attention or affection and important people in your life did not provide it. To grieve is to focus on the emotions behind your loss—just as you would grieve over the loss of a loved one. Continue journaling your feelings. Can you identify that: "I felt" or "I feel" . . . lonely . . . sad . . . afraid . . . angry . . . disappointed . . . unloved . . . violated . . . or unimportant?

Allow yourself to grieve the "loss" associated with the pain.

Don't expect to move through this quickly. Grieving is a process, not a once-and-for-all exercise. As experiences and situations arise that bring to mind the hurt again, allow yourself to grieve.

Write about your reflections and feelings here:

I remember wishing . . .

____

____

____

and I ended up feeling . . .

____

____

____

It hurt so much when . . .

____

____

____

From some of my earliest memories, I often felt . . .

____

____

____

____

Receive Comfort

Blessed are those who mourn, for they shall be comforted—(Matt. 5:4).

God desires to comfort your grief and He often will involve other people. Identify a special "journeymate" to share in your grief. This might be a spouse, pastor, counselor, or a special friend within the body of Christ. If you're married, the most "blessed" comfort will come from your spouse. So, if at all possible, involve her/him. Allow this person to "journey" with you in sharing your grief and ministering comfort. You might want to read from your journal or talk about your feelings concerning what you missed and how you felt. Also share what you need from your journeymate, in terms of their response: "I have something I'd like to share with you about some of my hurts and feelings. As I do, I just need you to listen." Or, "I could sure use a hug right now." Allow them to feel sad about your hurt and to hurt with you. It will be important to genuinely receive God's comfort through your journeymate. You may feel awkward or unworthy in receiving comfort. You might want to verbalize your gratefulness as a testimony of your receiving God's provision. For example, say, "Thanks for caring," or "Thanks for hurting with me." As you are comforted, you will, in turn, be better able to minister comfort to others.

Scripture Journaling—2 Corinthians 1:3-4

"Blessed be the God and Father of our Lord Jesus Christ, the Father of mercies and God of all comfort; who comforts us in all our affliction so that we may be able to comfort those who are in any affliction with the comfort with which we ourselves are comforted by God."

Take your unmet needs to the great Comforter. Let God know the hurts that resulted from an imperfect world. Let Him know what you missed and how that felt. What do you need from God? Have you been still long enough to hear His loving response? Have you been honest with God about your feelings and experiences? Have you been receptive to His comfort? Will you allow Him to additionally provide His comfort through a journeymate who cares for you?

Write any thoughts or prayers here:

____

____

____

____

Special Thoughts for Single Parents

As a single parent, you will want to be careful to finish your own emotional grief work. Individuals who have gone through a divorce or death of a spouse have many grief issues. It will be important for you to identify any unresolved losses so that you will be free to respond adequately to your children. With a trusted friend, counselor, or journeymate work to identify your own feelings, hurts, and losses. Your sensitivity to your own struggles will increase your sensitivity to your children. If you minimize your own pain, you will tend to minimize the hurts of your child. If you get stuck in your own pain and don't move past it, your children may begin to feel responsible for your feelings or happiness.

If you minimize your own pain, you will tend to minimize the hurts of your child.

Special Thoughts for Blended Families

You and your spouse may find it necessary to spend some time grieving the loss of the "perfect family." You will then need to comfort one another. As with any family, the blended family must face the positive and negative experiences that go along with relationships. Don't deny the challenges of blending two families, but focus on the opportunities you have together.

Share Your Reflections

You and your partner may be reluctant to look back at the past hurts of childhood or previous relationships. There is a mistaken tendency to ignore the past and press on toward the future. But coming to terms with past hurts will allow you to bring resolution to that pain.

Tell God what you missed in your childhood or previous relationships and how you felt:

____

____

____

____

Ask God for His comfort and healing. Be still and quiet to receive it, then write a prayer of thanksgiving.

____

____

____

____

Tell God about your openness to receive more of His comfort through your spouse/journeymate.

____

____

____

____

Marriage Staff Meeting

It might be helpful this week to have two different meetings. One meeting will focus on the wife's sharing with the husband as the comforting journeymate. In the second meeting, the husband shares and his wife provides comfort.

You might begin with reflections on "leaving-cleaving-becoming one" in relation to marital oneness, parenting, church ministry, and church leadership. What feelings did you begin with as you entertained the idea of looking at unmet needs and childhood hurts? Ask one another your journeymate questions concerning care, trust, and availability on pages 103–4. Be sensitive in sharing your responses. Avoid criticizing and minimize use of the word "you." Your responses might sound like, "It would mean a lot to me if we could . . ."

Or, "I would enjoy it if we . . ."

Pause to give prayerful thanks for your journeymate.

After reviewing your half-circles, circles, and "X's" on pages 108–10, come prepared to answer the following questions related to your growing-up years (birth through sixteen).

Who really met your need for attention? (Who left their world, entered into yours, and did things with you that you liked to do?)

Who gave you affection? (Who communicated care and closeness through physical touch and verbalized love?)

___

___

___

Who gave you approval? (Who expressed affirmation and appreciation to you? Who said, "I'm proud of you"?)

___

___

___

Who gave you comfort? (Who expressed feelings of hurt and sadness when you hurt, instead of giving advice or pep talks?)

___

___

___

Set aside time to discuss your insights and feelings.

Then share your feeling responses on pages 107–8. As your partner shares, give undivided attention, eye contact, reassuring touch, and comforting words.

"It really saddens me that you missed . . ."

___

___

"It hurts me that you were hurt like that."

"I'm committed to be here for you."

Next, receive your partner's comfort and express gratefulness. "Thank you for caring; It's reassuring to have you hurt with me."

Now pray together, expressing gratefulness for the blessing of comfort and a journeymate who cares.

Top Ten Need of the Week—Comfort

Comfort—giving consolation with tenderness.

This week place a particular emphasis on sharing comfort. Avoid the responses of logic, criticism, complaints, or neglect. As you see family members discouraged, sad, or upset, give a comforting response. Example words might include:

- "Stacy, I know that phone call must have hurt. I'm really sorry."
- "It hurts me that you often sit by yourself at lunch."
- "It makes me sad that your boyfriend broke up with you."
- "I'm sorry you lost the match. I know it meant a lot to you to win the tournament."

Family Night Activity

Share thoughts on emotional responding—When emotion is shared, giving logic, reasons, and facts doesn't help. Emotional hurt is not healed with explanations, criticism, or reminding you of my hurt. Emotional openness needs to be reciprocated with emotion. As a vocabulary of emotions is developed by each spouse and then each family member, the next step is to learn to "answer" emotion with emotion.

Examples of Productive Emotional Responses:

"I can see that you are upset. I'd like to hear about it."

"I don't like to see you hurting."

"It makes me sad to see you get hurt."

"I really care about you and love you."

"I want you to know I'm here for you. We'll get through this together."

"I genuinely regret my part in hurting you."

"Can you share with me how I've hurt you and how it made you feel? I want to understand and make it right."

"I see now that I hurt you by my ____________________,
and that was wrong of me. Will you forgive me?"

Practical emotional responding—The Scene Junior high kids can be ruthless. In the course of struggling with their self-image, young teenagers will make fun of each other, belittle one another, and gang up on "weaker" members of the group.

On a particular day in this battle of survival, Cindy has been cruelly victimized. First, someone made fun of her complexion—in front of the boys. Next, she ended up sitting alone at lunch. After lunch was algebra. She was so upset about what happened in the morning and over lunch, she failed her algebra test. It was not the best of days.

Pretend that Cindy walks into the house. What could I say to offer comfort? Young children may answer: What could I say or do to make Cindy feel better? Take turns asking the family to give responses.

Give particular attention this week to increasing the level of emotional responding you do with family members.

Pray together asking God to make your home a place of comfort and refuge.

A Family Night Project

Experiencing 1 Corinthians 13 in family relationships

Love is patient, love is kind, and is not jealous; love does not brag and is not arrogant, does not act unbecomingly; it does not seek its own, is not provoked, does not take into account a wrong suffered, does not rejoice in unrighteousness, but rejoices with the truth; bears all things, believes all things, hopes all things, endures all things.

The following diagnostic questions will help put a practical perspective on what loving our family and friends might look like. There are many good answers to each question. As you consider various interpersonal relationships, personalize your answers to meet the needs of each individual. We've offered one possibility for each question, but they're not in order. Match the question on the left with the correct loving answer. You might also take turns sharing about a time when a family member showed this aspect of love.

1. How can I show you that I am patient?
2. How can I show you special kindness?
3. How can I show you that I am not envious?
4. How can I show you that I am not trying to impress you?
5. How can I show you that I am not proud?
6. How can I show you that you are more important to me than I am to myself?
7. How can I show you that I am not defensive?
8. How can I show you that I have erased the memory of an offense?
9. How can I show you that I am not delighting in your defeat?
10. How can I show you that I am happy when you make difficult but right decisions?

____ By not reminding you of your past failures.

____ By being helpful to you during sickness and disappointment.

____ By understanding the struggle and praising your wisdom.

____ By not sharing your defeats with others.

____ By not getting irritated when you don't understand me.

____ By not reacting when you show me that I am wrong.

____ By making your personal needs a priority in my schedule.

____ By treating you as I would want to be treated.

____ By telling others how God is working through you.

____ By not promoting my own skills or accomplishments, but praising the efforts of others.

For Group Discussion

1. Give each parent a piece of modeling clay. Ask each person to manipulate the clay so that it illustrates their degree of marriage

oneness. Have you left your childhood home? Are you united with your spouse? Are the two of you becoming one? Single parents will want to represent their previous relationship and how these issues revealed themselves.

It may be important to stipulate that only couples who have completed their Marriage Staff Meeting be allowed to participate. Sharing your view of marital oneness needs to be discussed between marriage partners before it is shared with the group.

Give each person an opportunity to tell what his clay represents. Also ask each person to share the hope he has for oneness and what that might look like.

2. Ask participants to share any reluctance they had about looking back to their childhood. What was difficult? How did you feel? Contrast these hesitancies with the benefits of looking back. How was it productive? What benefits can/could you see?

3. Finally, ask each person to share one specific time when a need went unmet. Tell about the event and what feelings you felt. Allow the group to share statements of comfort. Guard against the tendency to give responses which fall into the categories of logic, complaint, criticism, or neglect.

CHAPTER 6

Provide the Security of a Committed Marriage

MAID, TAXI DRIVER, tutor, nurse, or whatever it takes, Janet is determined to be all that her kids need. She genuinely loves her two children. She's completely devoted to them. Most of her time, energy, and emotional resources are focused on the well-being of her kids.

Paul is the most hardworking, dedicated father you could find. During the week, he's committed to making a good living for his kids. He also goes to the soccer games and attends the recitals on the weekend.

She's a great mother and he's a good father, but in their zeal to be "super mom and super dad," they're neglecting one another. Their relationship is beginning to suffer. They're aware of the problem but rationalize their neglect by thinking, "My partner's an adult, he/she can take care of him/herself. The children need me. If I have to choose between the two, my spouse can wait." They don't realize that the quickest way to damage the kids is to weaken the marriage relationship. One of the best ways they can love their kids is to love each other.

It is vitally important that children see Mom and Dad prioritize their marriage as the first of God's ordained human relationships.

It is vitally important that children see Mom and Dad prioritize their marriage as the first of God's ordained human relationships. Children feel secure when they see a strong level of intimacy between their parents. An intimate foundation in marriage also allows children the freedom to grow up. To have a healthy marriage and family, both the parents and children must sense that Mom and Dad love each other and are committed to one another. This principle is an especially critical factor in blended families. There's often an internal pressure for parents to attempt to make up for a broken home by prioritizing the children above the new marriage. Just the opposite is what is needed! Children from a broken home need to see an adult man and an adult woman live out Christlike committed love toward one another. This is exactly the gift a new marriage can give to children in the blended family!

To further explore the priority of your marriage, consider this question. If your spouse were to make a list of your top priorities, what would he/she say? Write down how you think your spouse would answer:

My partner would say that my top five priorities in life seem to be:

1. ______________________________
2. ______________________________
3. ______________________________
4. ______________________________
5. ______________________________

Based upon your responses above, are there particular changes in your priorities that you would like to make in order to better prioritize your marriage or family? Write about the priority changes you'd like to see made in your life: (For instance: I know that Heather would like for me to spend less time at the office and more with her and the kids. I will leave the office by 6 each evening.)

____

____

____

____

Key Ingredients in a Committed Marriage

Reservations, acknowledgments, and affirmations

Children are constantly "reading" their parents' marriage, looking for the evidence and security of committed love. We'll explore three significant ingredients of committed love: reservations, acknowledgments, and affirmations.

Let's look at how a couple **"reserves"** certain things for one another and their marriage:

- Reserve some *knowledge* that will be *private* among parents, such as: marriage goals, personal goals, educational plans, and ministry ideas.
- Reserve some *feelings* that will be *private* among parents, such as: unresolved negative feelings toward certain family members, coworkers, and others.
- Reserve some *topics* that will be *private* among parents, such as: sexual intimacy specifics, unhealed personal family history, financial business, and family status.
- Reserve some *times* to be *private* among parents, such as: weekly staff meetings, sexual intimacy times, date nights. Get a lock on your bedroom door. Children should knock before entering.

Reflect on this ingredient and write your thoughts here:

It would be helpful if my spouse and I reserved the following just for us: (For instance: I wish we could save our discussions about finances until the kids are not around. I would like to get a sitter at least once a month so that Kelly and I can have some time alone.)

____

____

____

Our next ingredient deals with important **acknowledgments** which help convey a depth of secure commitment.

- *Verbally acknowledge the oneness* of your relationship in front of others. You can: greet your spouse first when entering the house, use pet names for each other (Honey, Sweetie), and avoid calling each other "Mom" and "Dad."

Acknowledge the priority of your relationship as children see signs of caring.

- *Physically acknowledge the oneness* of your relationship in front of others. You can: greet each other with a kiss, allow the children to "catch" you hugging, stand or sit with each other during family outings and social gatherings, hold hands, sit together while watching TV.
- *Acknowledge the priority* of your relationship as children see signs of caring. They might notice things such as: the giving of small gifts, flowers, opening doors, serving each other, or doing chores for each other.
- *Acknowledge the romance* of your marriage as you go out on dates alone. At least twice a month, your children need to see you dress up and model for them proper dating habits and good manners.

Consider this ingredient. Write about other ways you could demonstrate your marriage commitment.

It would be important if my partner and I would acknowledge one another in the following ways: (For instance: I'd like for Karen and me to hold hands as we pray before the meal. I'd like for Jim and me to sit next to each other in church. Shelby and Shawn can sit on either side.)

____

____

____

____

Finally, marriage **"affirmations"** help communicate commitment to marriage:

- Affirm and support your spouse when he disciplines the children. You can confer together in private if you do not agree.
- Affirm your spouse's parenting policies when she is absent:
  - Support the rules that have already been set. If rules need to be changed, both parents should discuss the changes together and privately.
  - If a child asks you for something, make certain that the child has not already asked the other parent first.
- Affirm your spouse with praise and appreciation in front of the children; "You're the most sensitive husband anyone could ever have." Or "I'm sure blessed to have you as my wife."
- Make positive comments concerning the physical attractiveness of your spouse. Your children might hear statements like: "I love that dress on you, Honey." Or "You have such beautiful brown eyes."

Write about how your marriage could benefit from additional affirmations. Write your thoughts here. (For instance: I would like for Jay and me to decide upon bedtimes for the kids and stick to them.)

____

____

____

____

Life application from research—Research at the University of Tennessee studied stable marriages that lasted more than thirty years. Their findings underscore the importance of commitment and religious faith in marital success. Selected findings include the following:

- the couple held an "expectation that the marriage would endure."

- the couples viewed marriage as a permanent relationship which is not to be abandoned when difficulties emerge.
- for these couples "divorce was not an option."
- couples consistently recalled "times in which they had prayed or studied together."
- couples often referred to their "turning to their faith for moral guidance in dealing with decisions and conflict"

(Source: Linda C. Robinson and Priscilla W. Blanton, "Marital Strengths in Enduring Marriages," *Family Relations* 42 [1993]: 38–45).

Review the five key points noted above. On a scale of 0 to 5, indicate how many of these points would be true of you and your marriage. In which areas could you, your marriage, and your children benefit from changes or added emphasis? Write about these changes here: (For instance: Recommitting to pray together would please God and bless my spouse and family. More verbal reassurance of my commitment is needed; we need to ask our pastor to help us work on areas of insecurity.)

____

____

____

____

____

____

____

Note from the children: One of the most painful wounds children endure is to live in an environment lacking in the security of their parents' enduring love. If you have been involved in any way in threats to leave, separation, abusive attacks, or violence, then ask God to renew your commitment to marriage. If you've engaged in wars of silence or moved to separate bedrooms, ask God to speak to you concerning your need for confession, forgiveness, and restoration. Pause and ask God to begin a healing process in you, your partner, and your children. Write your prayer here.

____

____

____

____

____

____

____

____

____

Removing Hindrances to Marriage Intimacy

The adversary knows that one of the most important gifts you can give your children is your intimate marriage, so he seems to work overtime against it. Whether overtly through conflict or more subtly through busyness and boredom, our adversary uses many tools against us.

Pause and ask God to begin a healing process in you, your partner, and your children.

**Intimate relationships—
they must be developed and protected.**

Marriage intimacy doesn't just happen—it takes conscientious effort to develop a close, meaningful relationship. And once intimacy is established, it must be protected. This twofold emphasis is seen in John 10:10, *"The thief comes only to steal, and kill, and destroy* (Satan wants to destroy the closeness we have with God and others); *I came that they might have life, and might have it abundantly."* (One of the ways we experience a meaningful life is through intimacy with God and others.)

Marriage intimacy can be developed through:

- *Affectionate Caring*—"I care about you."
- *Vulnerable Communication*—"I trust you."
- *Joint Accomplishment*—"I need you."
- *Mutual Giving*—"I love you."

Marriage intimacy must be protected from:

- *Emotional Bondage* (hinders affectionate caring)
- *Fearful Self-Condemnation* (hinders vulnerable communication)
- *Prideful Self-Sufficiency* (hinders joint accomplishment)
- *Self-Centered Selfishness* (hinders mutual giving).

Let's take a closer look at these common hindrances to marriage intimacy.

Affectionate Caring Hindered by Emotional Bondage

"Let all bitterness and wrath and anger . . . be put away from you . . . be kind to one another . . . forgiving each other, just as God in Christ also has forgiven you"—Ephesians 4:31-32.

It's difficult to have a caring, loving spirit if you're filled with bitterness, guilt, rage, and anger. These emotions or sins will damage all your relationships, not just the ones to which the anger is directed. For instance, if your anger is not resolved with your boss, that anger will affect more than that one relationship. It will adversely affect your relationship with your spouse, children, and friends. Anger poisons the soul.

The guilt I feel over my un-Christlike actions can be resolved through proper confession.

Ephesians 4 teaches us that we must "get rid of" these vices (turn loose of, put away, empty out of us). This is done through forgiveness. Past hurts, even those suffered in childhood, must be properly dealt with in order to gain emotional freedom. Then we'll be free to be "kind and compassionate" and be able to engage in affectionate caring.

Likewise, the guilt I feel over my un-Christlike actions can be resolved through proper confession (James 5:16).

Pause and reflect on who you might need to forgive. Write your thoughts here. (For instance: My anger toward my brother is poisoning my relationships. My kids always ask me if I'm mad at them. My husband just keeps his distance.)

____

____

____

____

Meditate on Ephesians 4:31-32 above, being reminded of God's forgiveness of you. Remember that forgiveness is really a divine gift He gives to you so that you can then give to others. Write a prayer of gratefulness for your forgiveness and then an expression of your choice to give this gift to others. Write your prayer here.

____

____

____

____

____

Spend time thinking about who you may have offended. Who needs your confession? Pause to ask God's forgiveness and then write words that you will share. Remember, a good confession is specific, admits wrong, and offers no justification. Write your confessions below. (For instance: "James, my words and accusations were wrong. I was wrong to make such judgments. You must have felt hurt and betrayed. I'm sorry. Will you forgive me?")

____

____

____

Vulnerable Communication Hindered by Fearful Self-Condemnation

"There is no fear in love; but perfect love casts out fear"—1 John 4:18.

"There is therefore now no condemnation for those who are in Christ Jesus"—Romans 8:1.

Various manifestations of fear and self-condemnation will hinder vulnerable communication:

If I fear your criticism or doubt my worth to you, I'll hold back from sharing my feelings, hurts, or needs.

If I question my own adequacy, I'll hesitate to take initiative and avoid emotionally challenging conversations.

If I fear being hurt, disappointed, or used, I may seek to control all situations so as not to appear vulnerable or needy.

If I question your sincerity or my worthiness, I may demand to have it "proven" before I can accept it.

As we begin to understand and experience the perfect love of God, our personal fears are eliminated, our worth affirmed, and we're able to vulnerably relate to God. As we learn to apply His perfect love in human relationships, these relationships mature, trust develops, and vulnerability deepens.

What fears do you have about being vulnerable with your partner? Write about them here:

____

____

____

____

I sometimes fear that if, ____________________________

then ____________________________________

I sometimes fear my partner's ________________________

Stop and ask God to begin freeing you from fears. Claim His promise of 1 John 4:18. Write a short prayer asking God for this freedom. Ask Him to strengthen and prepare you to share these fears with your spouse during your Marriage Staff Meeting. Write your prayer here:

____

____

____

____

What doubts about your worth to God or your spouse sometimes prompt feelings of self-condemnation? Write about them here:

____

____

____

____

I sometimes don't share about my ____________________

because I doubt ______________________________

I sometimes avoid being vulnerable with my needs or hurts

because I question ____________________________

____

Pause to consider the promise of Romans 8:1 and then reflect on Romans 8:32, *"[Since God] did not spare His own Son . . . will He not also with Him, freely give us all things?"* What kind of God does this verse speak of—a generous one or a "stingy" one? If you have already received Christ, doesn't this same generous God want to give you all things? . . . Our generous God does want to provide you with a spouse who cares and gives to you. Write a prayer of thanksgiving and hope here:

Joint Accomplishment Hindered by Prideful Self-Sufficiency

"I am rich; and have become wealthy and have need of nothing" —Revelation 3:17.

"Apart from Me you can do nothing"—John 15:5.

A "Lone Ranger" mentality is damaging to any relationship, particularly marriage. This is the voice that says, "If I think I can make it on my own, why do I need you?"

> ***A "Lone Ranger" mentality is damaging to any relationship, particularly marriage.***

The truth is, we need each other! God created us to be mutually giving to each other. Practically speaking, no one person has all the gifts, talents, skills, and resources needed to get the job done.

Self-sufficiency often develops through prolonged periods of unmet needs. The associated hurt drives a person to deny their needs or to turn to self-nurturing ways to meet them (eating, fantasizing, achievement, perfectionism, and other forms of escape). Self-sufficiency is also reinforced by the "stoic, macho, hero" mentality which is often encouraged in our society.

To the contrary, we need to look to one another and say, "I need you; I can't do this without you." "As we each receive abundantly from God and then freely give to one another, we'll make it!" or "We did it together!" Then intimacy is deepened.

What self-nurturing patterns do you see in your life (i.e., eating, TV, sports, hobbies, spending, etc.)? Write about them here.

In what areas do you deny having needs? How does your "Lone Ranger mentality" come through? Write about them here.

____

____

____

____

Instead of self-sufficiency, write about the **truth** below:

I really do need __________________ from my spouse.

I'm looking forward to the time when we ______________

Mutual Giving Hindered by Selfishness

"Do nothing from selfishness or empty conceit, but with humility of mind let each of you regard one another as more important than himself" —Philippians 2:3.

Unfortunately, we often get so obsessed with our own needs that we neglect giving to the needs of others. We begin to take to have our needs met. Many marriage relationships can be characterized by a take/take mentality, but there's no satisfaction in taking to have our needs met. There's a big difference between taking a hug and being lovingly given one. A marriage characterized by taking will soon show signs of resentment, discouragement, and distance. A relationship characterized by mutual giving will be satisfying, abundant, and intimate.

I sometimes find myself trying to take ________ from my partner. (For instance: When Michael works too many weekends in a row, I start demanding that he spend more time at home. My nagging and complaining are my attempts to get attention.)

____

____

____

Some of the ways I might try to selfishly take include . . . (For instance: I find myself thinking of ways to convince Becky that we need more affection in our relationship. I'll sometimes use manipulation or even guilt tactics.)

____

____

____

> ***Because marital conflict is universal and inevitable, it is a factor in every child's life.***

After looking at the significant ingredients in marriage intimacy and the hindrances which often develop, we now turn our attention to another ingredient in every home. Conflict! Be prepared for a possibly sobering and even convicting look at how we handle conflict in marriage.

Inevitable Marriage Conflict—Impacting Your Child!

Because marital conflict is universal and inevitable, it is a factor in every child's life. When we remember that each of us comes to marriage with a set of expectations, goals, ideas, and plans, it is not surprising that conflict is a natural result. In the closeness of day-to-day living, the differences which attracted us to one another may become sources of discord. Each of us brings our own set of parental influences into our marriage relationship. These influences can affect us in two totally different ways. We may desire to make our home "just like my growing up" or "different at all costs." Both marriage partners bring to the altar their unconscious expectations, insecurities, and behavior patterns that can spark conflict that neither understands. The issue then is not *if* conflict will occur, but *when* conflict occurs, how will it be handled?

As a child progresses through his or her life stages, the contradictory and confusing messages from disagreeing parents stress the child's loyalties. These messages also complicate a child's attempts to discern order and predictability in the world. Thus, it is essential to study the various patterns of handling marital conflict. It's sometimes helpful to explore this topic of conflict using the four major styles noted below.

Open-Abusive Conflict

The open-abusive manner refers to a highly verbal and sometimes physical expression of resolving conflict. The atmosphere in these households is often characterized as tense, angry, and explosive. This produces an insecure and fearful environment for children.

Spousal abuse is an extreme example of the open-abusive manner. Other examples would include: In a misguided attempt to win a conflict, one spouse may verbally assault the worth and character of the other. This may fire a deep anger within the child as he is forced to take sides. If verbal abuse is directed toward the child himself, he may experience a sense of worthlessness and discouragement. Feelings of hopelessness and despair become firmly rooted as the child observes his parents' failure to resolve family issues.

As difficult as it may be to consider, reread the paragraph above and answer the following questions:

- We sometimes have the following aspects of open-abusive conflict in our home: (For instance: There are times when we do make verbal assaults. I never thought that the name calling and the cruel words between Jack and me might affect Timothy.)

____

____

____

____

- I sometimes contribute to this environment by my (For instance: When Carrie spills her juice or tips over her dinner plate, I don't always respond well. Words like, "You're so stupid" seem almost automatic.)

____

____

____

- Write about what feelings your children may have as they observe conflict handled in this way. (For instance: They probably feel scared when they hear us yelling. Jennifer gets sick of it. She goes to her room and slams the door.)

____

____

____

____

- Pause to ask God to allow you to sense His compassion, concern, and care for your children as they observe conflict handled in this way. Write your prayer below: (For instance: God, remind me of how damaging my words can be. Help me stop, cool off, and then talk calmly. Let me see my children's faces and remember their feelings.)

____

____

____

____

Open-Triangulated Conflict

The open-triangulated pattern is characterized by the involvement of another person, usually a child, in the conflict of the parents. A parent may demand that a child take his side in a disagreement, causing feelings of alienation, isolation, and a sense of "being used."

Triangulation may also be identified in a situation in which one or both parents may physically project their hostilities onto the child. This may occur when a parent who feels mistreated seeks out a target for his own frustration. Child abuse is frequently the unfortunate and traumatic result of triangulation.

A child who is raised in this environment can experience profound feelings of rejection and anger. Respect for authority is undermined. Nurturing and affection needs may go largely unmet or may be accompanied by the mixed messages of self-doubt and fear. A child must sort through confusing messages: Is Mom giving me a hug because she loves me or because she wants me on her side?

As difficult as it may be to consider, reread the paragraphs above and answer the following questions:

> ***Nurturing and affection needs may go largely unmet or may be accompanied by the mixed messages of self-doubt and fear.***

- We sometimes have the following aspects of open-triangulated conflict in our home: (For instance: It must hurt Lindsay when her dad and I talk to her about our marriage issues. I guess we're really trying to "win her over," when we involve her that way.)

____

____

____

____

- I sometimes contribute to this environment by my: (For instance: I get so angry with Stacy sometimes; but rather than talk to her, I'll come home and fuss at the kids. I take my anger out on them.)

____

____

____

- Write about what feelings your children may have as they observe conflict handled in this way. (For instance: They must feel confused and angry. We are involving our children in "adult only" issues. That's not fair. Our kids need the freedom just to be kids.)

____

____

____

- Pause to ask God to allow you to sense His compassion, concern, and care for your children as they observe conflict handled in this way. Write your prayer below: (For instance: God, help me talk to You and my husband about my feelings. Help me to remember my child's confusion when I attempt to win her alliance. Help me see her as my child. She is not our referee.)

____

____

____

Submerged Conflict

Those who choose the submerged style of conflict develop covert methods of dealing with marital tension. In this situation, an individual may throw himself into his work in order to maintain some control over his life. A woman may devote excessive attention to her children, developing an enmeshed or smothering relationship. The child then loses self-identity in this controlling atmosphere. Alcoholism may be a symptom of the submerged method, as the alcoholic attempts to control the family through his addiction.

These overt manifestations are merely symptoms of deeper unresolved issues and conflicts. When a submergent parent reacts by developing an enmeshed relationship with a child, the child loses her own identity as she becomes insecure, fearful, and dependent. Covert fighting is, by nature, less than truthful and founded on manipulation techniques. Children reared in this environment might be expected to have difficulty with honesty, show manipulation in relationships, and be reluctant to accept responsibility.

As difficult as it may be to consider, reread the paragraphs above and answer the following questions:

- We sometimes have the following aspects of submerged conflict in our home: (For instance: We don't yell at our house, but silence wars are just as severe. The atmosphere is always so tense. Dan and I are just civil to each other in front of the kids.)

- I sometimes contribute to this environment by my: (For instance: I know that I need to talk to Dan rather than talk around him. I need to be honest about my feelings, but kind in my approach.)

- Write about what feelings your children may have as they observe conflict handled in this way. (For instance: I know the kids must feel the tension too. It must be so hard for them to handle the pressure and constant strife. I know the pressure gets to Lisa, because she gets stomach ulcers so often.)

- Pause to ask God to allow you to sense His compassion, concern, and care for your children as they observe conflict handled in this way. Write your prayer on the next page. (For instance: God, give me the courage to admit my feelings and then share them with Wendy. Help me to remember the priority of my children. They need a home where it is safe to grow up.)

Balanced-Resolving Conflict

The balanced-resolving method of dealing with marital conflict is the positive, healthy way to manage conflict. A couple diffuses conflict through balancing personal accountability with the needs of the family unit as a whole. Rather than leaving emotional wounds untreated or simply ignored, the couple openly admits and resolves the hurt and conflict. They apply principles of godly sorrow (1 John 1:9; 2 Cor. 7:9-11) and confession to one another (James 5:16).

The balanced-resolving method of dealing with marital conflict is the positive, healthy way to manage conflict.

This balancing of personal and interpersonal needs requires give-and-take, open communication, and compromise. However, the effort required to achieve and maintain this balance reaps healthy rewards. In a balanced-resolving home, children develop respect and cooperation with others. The reduced tension resulting from the resolving factor in these relationships provides a generally secure, positive, and hopeful home atmosphere.

Reflect on balancing personal accountability with the needs of the family as a whole.

- Consider the admonition of Romans 14:12, *"Each one of us shall give account of himself to God"* and then write a brief accountability prayer to God.

  "Heavenly Father, It's my heartfelt desire to be accountable to You for my ______________________. Guide me, control me, change me as You may need."

- Consider the admonition of Philippians 2:3, *"Do nothing from selfishness . . . but with humility . . . let each of you regard one another as more important than himself"* and then write a brief servant's prayer to God. *"Heavenly Father, I want to be a Christlike servant to my partner and my family. Help me better serve my partner by*

  ____

  ____

  Help me better serve my children by ______________________

  ____

  Thank You, Lord, for serving me through Your Son; help me serve others in the same way."

- Consider the following scene: Would it be true that your children have witnessed the following powerful example? They've seen Dad apologize to Mom: "It was wrong of me to take my anger out on you. Will you forgive me?" Then Mom forgives: "Yes, I forgive you." They lovingly embrace and family life goes on, healed and renewed. They also see Mom apologize to Dad: "Forgive me for being critical. That was wrong." Dad forgives; they embrace, and family life goes on, healed and renewed. *"You are a living epistle known and read by all."*

Ask God to give you and your marriage this "living epistle." Write your prayer below: (For instance: God, I want this to be true in our family. Give me the courage to admit my wrongs and the grace to forgive. Help me to put my own pride or stubbornness aside.)

____

____

____

____

____

Romancing the Home

Children are constantly reading the level of romance in your marriage: How is it going?

Has the romance gone out of your marriage? Here are some pointers on how you can jump-start the creativity in your relationship.

- Write the story of how you met.
- List your spouse's best qualities in alphabetical order.
- Tour a museum or an art gallery.
- Notice the little changes your spouse makes in his/her appearance.
- Float on a raft together.
- Take a stroll around the block and hold hands as you walk.
- Stock the cupboards with food your spouse loves to eat.
- Give your spouse a back rub.
- Rent a classic love-story video and watch it while cuddling together.
- Build a fire in the fireplace, turn out the lights, and talk.
- Take a horse-drawn carriage ride.
- Go swimming in the middle of the night.
- Write a poem for your spouse.
- Stop in the middle of your busy day and talk to your spouse for fifteen minutes.
- Create your own special holiday.
- Watch the sunset together.
- Picnic by a pond.
- Give your mate a foot massage.
- Serve breakfast in bed.
- Brush his/her hair.
- Go kite flying.
- Reminisce about your first date.
- Attend a sporting event you've never been to together.
- Plant a tree together in honor of your marriage.

Even though some of these ideas might seem silly, this helps return to the joy of first love. Knowing your partner as only you do, write a short list of ideas that are sure to rekindle the romance. Write your list here:

____

____

____

- My partner might really enjoy ____________________

____

- My partner might like to receive __________________

____

- I could surprise my spouse with __________________

____

After reviewing these lists with one another during your Marriage Staff Meeting, begin giving to one another in some of these ways . . . and let your children "catch you" creatively communicating your love. The whole family will be blessed!

Children read Mom and Dad as a "living letter" long before they even know how to read God's love letter to them.

Scripture Journaling: 2 Corinthians 3:2

"You are our living letter . . . known and read by all."

Children read Mom and Dad as a "living letter" long before they even know how to read God's love letter to them (the Bible). As they begin to hear of God's Word, His plan, and His truth, they look for confirmation and consistency at home. It's the confirmation of God's Word and your example that helps solidify the foundation of truth in their hearts. Write about the kind of "living letter" you want yourself and your marriage to be. "Heavenly Father, I want my children to see . . ."

Marriage Staff Meeting

Spend one-and-one-half to two hours working together through this material. Your marriage and family are worth the effort! Discuss your inventory of acknowledgments and affirmations, giving particular attention to needed improvements. Share reflections you had from the research on long-lasting marriages. Pause to offer words of recommitment.

Work through the material on the four major hindrances to intimacy, one section at a time. Stop to discuss your reflections concerning emotional bondage, self-condemnation, self-sufficiency, and selfishness. Allow time for confessions and forgiveness. (For instance: I know that I've hurt you by distancing myself from you and the family. My withdrawal hurts you and the kids. Will you forgive me?) Share your fears and doubts, giving your partner opportunity to give reassurances.

- "I know you sometimes fear my criticism. I'm committed to allowing God to change me."
- "I want to reassure you that God will always love you and I will always love you too."
- "I want to know and understand your needs. I want to give to you in ways that you enjoy."

Stop to pray and thank God together for your marriage.

Take the material on handling conflict slowly. Be accountable for yourself and avoid blaming. Discuss the goal of children seeing confession and forgiveness in the balanced-resolving approach. Finally, discuss your romance ideas and lovingly embrace as you recommit to give your children this most precious gift—your marriage.

Top Ten Need of the Week—Affection

Affection—to communicate care and closeness through physical touch and loving words.

Place a particular emphasis on sharing affection this week. Demonstrate verbalized love and caring touch. Examples might include:

- "Come here, Sweetheart; let me give you a hug."
- "Lauren (kiss on the cheek), I know you're going to have a challenging day at school today. I'll be praying for you."
- "Mark (quick neck rub), thanks for helping with the yard today. I always enjoy spending time with you."
- "John (warm embrace), I love you."

Family Night Activities

Building a sense of belonging The need to belong is so strong that it will be met at any cost. Children will fulfill this need through relationships with parents or peers, by good influences or bad. Building a strong sense of family belonging is the best investment parents can make in protecting children/teenagers from the unhealthy influences of peer pressure.

Families who laugh together, vacation together, and work together help build belonging. Belonging is built through the closeness of hugs, verbalized love, and words of endearment. Family traditions at holidays, birthdays, and other special times build closeness. Family common interests, special memories, and fun times create an important bond.

> ***Families who laugh together, vacation together, and work together help build belonging.***

During your next Family Night, discuss these issues with your children.

- What fun activity would you like to see us do together?
- Do you have any ideas for our family vacation this summer?

- We're thinking of starting a family tradition of having Valentine's breakfast together. Do you have some ideas on what you would enjoy?
- What would you enjoy doing during some of our Family Nights together?

[Note: Don't be surprised if children or teens think such vulnerable questions and topics are "uncool." Persevere in your commitment to open sharing. Your kids need it even if they struggle with expressing it.]

How Do We Handle Conflict?

Discuss the inevitability of conflict within your family. Talk about how important it is to handle conflict properly.

Here are several practical thoughts to encourage a "balanced-resolving" approach to conflict:

- Resolve personal anger. Never take it out on others.
- When parental discipline is needed, discipline behavior. Never attack personal worth or character.
- Consider the needs and feelings of others. Never selfishly focus on your needs.
- Parents need to resolve parenting issues privately. Never force a child to take "sides."
- Apologize openly to one another. Adults and children should stop pretending to be perfect.
- Share your concerns and feelings directly. Never talk to one person about another (triangulating).
- Address hurts and problems openly. Never pretend they don't exist.
- Encourage personal responsibility/accountability. Never blame others for your inappropriate behavior.
- Parents implement consequences for a child's behavior, rather than attempting to control a child's behavior.
- Risk vulnerability with emotions and affection. Never use manipulations and guilt trips.
- Prioritize the people in your home—never the possessions or work that surround it. It's the "trappings" like toys, TV channels, and chores that seem to stir up conflict.

As you discuss each item, specific ones will give parents opportunity to share insights they've learned from this chapter. There will be excellent opportunities for parents to offer apologies. They can begin to role model their "living epistle."

Finally, talk about the balance of personal responsibility—Romans 14:12, and family needs—Philippians 2:3.

__ consider committing these verses to memory
__ pause for a family prayer time of commitment to responsibility and a servant's heart.

For Group Discussion

Ask each couple to share one area where they plan to make changes with regard to: Reserving time for one another, acknowledging one another, and affirming each other. Encourage couples to be specific in their sharing. Ask both partners to verbalize their own commitment to making these changes.

Ask each person to identify which hindrance to intimacy they most easily fall into. Are they prone to self-sufficiency, self-centeredness, self-condemnation, or bitterness and anger? As a group, discuss how each of these has robbed your marriage of intimacy.

Discuss the four patterns of dealing with conflict giving particular focus to balancing personal responsibility (Rom. 14:12) and a servant's heart for each family member (Phil. 2:3). Discuss your marriage as a "living letter" to your children.

Give each couple one sheet of paper. Invite the couples to write a prayer to God. As both partners give input, this prayer should reflect your hopes and expectations. Ask God for help in specific areas. Tell Him "thank You" for insights this week, and then verbalize your hope for what only He can do in your family.

Read the prayers aloud. This will encourage group members toward mutual accountability and solidify the prayers to the Lord.

CHAPTER 7

Live in the Present ...for Eternity

JESUS CHRIST IS the only one who has ever lived each day in the present. He never **woke up regretting anything about yesterday** or went to sleep **fearful about tomorrow.** He experienced His Father's abundance, one moment at a time, unhindered by past concerns or future worries. In this, He is our role model for parenting with intimacy. Only when parents find this same freedom can we truly live in the present—only then can we be available, attentive, and sensitive to our children and their needs.

"I came that they might have life, and might have it abundantly"—John 10:10b.

"The thief comes to steal, and kill, and destroy"—John 10:10a.

What were your first waking thoughts, impressions, and feelings this morning? What were the first stirrings of consciousness? Consider two possibilities:

Living in the present—A gratefulness stirs my heart over this day that He has made and is allowing me to share. There's an **expectancy** of His leadership and provision. There's a confident **hope** that He will involve me today fully in His purposes. There's an **indescribable awe and wonder** that I might with **love and sensitivity** serve others around me, imparting to them not only the

Gospel but my very life. This is the day He has made. I **rejoice** and am **glad!**

Living in the past/future—**Regrets** of yesterday may flood my mind. There are things I wanted to say or do but didn't. There were also things I didn't want to say or do but did. Sometimes I get **irritated and angry** over most anything: the car that didn't run, the child who didn't mind, the helpmate who didn't help, the pastor who didn't pastor, the leader who didn't lead, or the government that didn't govern. I find myself feeling **anxious and worried** over a seemingly endless list of things to do. There seem to be more obligations and duties than any one person could perform. I'm entering a new day where I'll be tossed by circumstances, used by people, and probably ignored by those I need.

> ***Living in the present is part of Christ's promise of abundance.... Living in the past/future is part of the thief's plan to steal, kill, and destroy.***

Living in the present is part of Christ's promise of abundance in John 10:10b. Living in the past/future is part of the thief's plan to steal, kill, and destroy in John 10:10a.

Personal Inventory: Let's pause and ask God to help review your life events over the last few days. Briefly note below thoughts that God brings back to your mind and heart. Ask God to guide you, tell Him of your openness, and then write your honest reflections.

- I regretted ____

____

____

- I became irritated over ______________________________

____

____

- I was angry about ___________________________________

____

____

Noted below in the graphic is a portrayal of this John 10:10 principle:

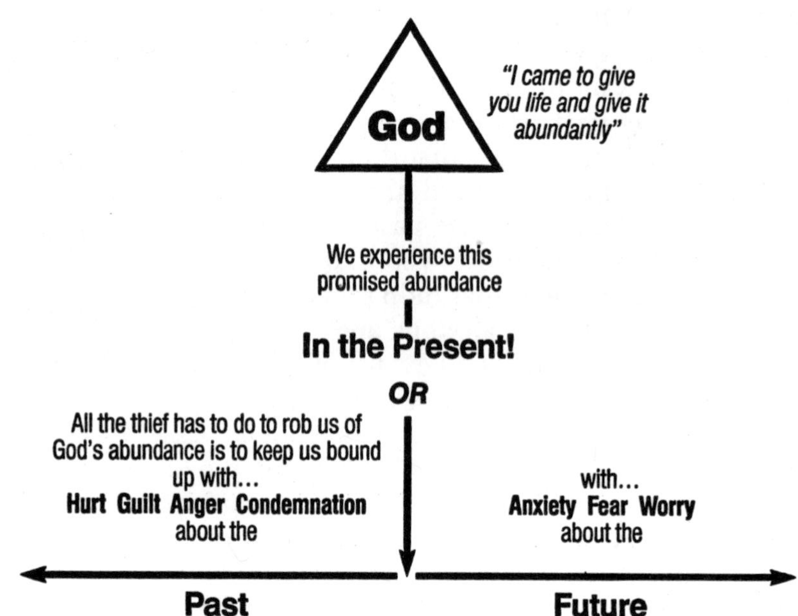

- I became anxious concerning ______________________________
____
____

- I was worried that ______________________________
____
____

Now in your own words describe how living emotionally in the **past** or **future** may have hindered God's abundance toward you in these same few days. Without these hindrances . . .

- I could have been more **grateful** for ______________________

____

____

____

- I could have been more **expectant** of God to ______________

____

____

____

- I could have had more **hope** that ______________________

____

____

____

- I could have experienced the **indescribable awe** and **wonder** that ______________________________________

____

____

- I could have demonstrated more **loving sensitivity** toward

____

____

Now stop and review the material above and compare:

- what the thief has done through regrets, irritations, anger, anxiety, and worry.

Contrast this with:

- what the Lord wants to give through gratefulness, expectancy, hope, and loving sensitivity.

Write a prayer, asking God to bring healing and freedom to your guilt, anger, condemnation, fear, and hurt. His healing will allow you to experience in this present moment all of His abundance for you. Write your prayer below: (For instance: God, I want You to bring peace instead of worry. I choose to accept Your forgiveness instead of guilt.)

____

____

____

____

____

____

What does living in the present have to do with parenting?

We're glad you asked! It's only as parents experience freedom to live in the present that they can:

- sensitively discern a child's needs.
- receive God's abundance in order to give.
- lovingly give, unhindered by their own painful emotions.

Let's consider each of these three challenges:

Living in the Present Allows for Sensitive Discernment

Children aren't born really knowing what they need. Beyond their physiological need for food, air, and water, children don't know what to call their need for comfort, or what it sounds like for a parent to mourn with them (Rom. 12:15): "It really makes me sad that you were called such terrible names. It hurts me to see you hurt because I love you." Remember four-year-old Amy in one of our previous chapters? She was tired from a long day of playing, became irritable with everyone around her, and then proceeded to torment the cat. Little did she know that what would really meet her need were those kind words from Mom: "Amy, I think you might need a hug and some of Mommy's lap time. Come let me rock you." Such transactions require parents who are unhindered by past pain or future worries. A parent must be able to discern present need in their children, spouse, and others.

A parent must be able to discern present need in their children, spouse, and others.

David and Teresa's son Eric, nineteen years old at the time, challenged them one Saturday evening with this needed sensitivity. They returned home about 8 P.M. after conducting an out-of-town seminar and headed toward the bedroom with the luggage. David found Eric sprawled out on the living room floor watching TV. "How was your day, Buddy?" "It was OK," responded Eric. The words were the right words, but David sensed something in the tone of voice. Everything wasn't OK. He paused, put the suitcase down on the couch, then walked over and sat down on the floor next to Eric. "It sounds like it might not have been such a great day. Do you want to talk?" There was a long, long silence. Then Eric began to share about a disappointing time with a close friend. Dad got to listen, comfort, and care. David would later comment, "I almost missed it. The day was long and tiring. The suitcases needed unpacking and Teresa and I were both starving. But God was faithful to give discernment. I know I've missed many opportunities in the past. I'm glad God's at work!"

Let's explore an interesting biblical portrayal of this insight from Jesus and His disciples as they encounter a woman in Mark 5. Recall the overwhelming need of this woman who had *"tried much at the hands of many physicians and spent all of her money and rather than be helped at all, she had grown worse."* Notice the striking contrast in the response of the disciples compared to the response of the Savior. Listen as the Scriptures tell the story:

And when Jesus had crossed over again in the boat to the other side, a great multitude gathered about Him; and He stayed by the seashore. And one of the synagogue officials named Jairus came up, and upon seeing Him, fell at His feet, and entreated Him earnestly, saying, "My little daughter is at the point of death; please come and lay Your hands on her, that she may get well and live." And He went off with him; and a great multitude was following Him and pressing in on Him. And a woman who had had a hemorrhage for twelve years, and had endured much at the hands of many physicians, and had spent all that she had and was not helped at all, but rather had grown worse, after hearing about Jesus, came up in the crowd behind Him, and touched His cloak, For she thought, "If I just touch His garments, I shall get well." And immediately the flow of her blood was dried up; and she felt in her body that she was healed of her affliction. And immediately Jesus, perceiving in Himself that the power proceeding from Him had gone forth, turned around in the crowd and said, "Who touched My garments?" And His disciples said to Him, "You see the multitude pressing in on You, and You say, 'Who touched Me?' " And He looked around to see the woman who had done this. But the woman fearing and trembling, aware of what had happened to her, came and fell down before Him, and told Him the whole truth. And He said to her, "Daughter, your faith has made you well; go in peace, and be healed of your affliction."—Mark 5:21-34

Now reflect on these questions:

- Who discerned her need? Who missed it?
- What were the disciples preoccupied with?
- Who was living in the present? Who was anxious to get on with the job at hand, fulfill today's obligations, and complete the things-to-do list?

In your own words, write a parenting lesson about discerning needs based on this passage and this principle. Write your thoughts here:

____

____

____

Living in the Present
Allows Me to Receive of God's Abundance

Intimacy with God: a prerequisite for intimacy with others

Consider these two important facts:

FACT #1—You can't give to others what you don't possess yourself.

FACT #2—There are certain divine commodities which have their origin in God alone. They are only available from Him.

When considered together, these thoughts produce a portentous truth: An intimate relationship with God is a prerequisite for intimate, healthy relationships with children, spouse, or anyone!

Here's how it works: Many of the ingredients that are crucial in our relationships with other people are only available from God. They are a part of His manifold (many-faceted) grace (1 Peter 4:10). Therefore, we can only minister them to others to the extent that we have received them from God. For instance, here are four of these divine commodities:

Love—*"Let us love one another, for love comes from God"* —1 John 4:7.

Comfort—*"The God of all comfort . . . comforts us . . . so that we may be able to comfort those who are in any affliction"* —2 Corinthians 1:3.

Forgiveness—*"Forgiv[e] each other, just as God in Christ [forgave] you"* —Ephesians 4:32.

Acceptance—*"Accept one another, just as Christ also accepted you"* —Romans 15:7.

It's hard to imagine having an intimate relationship with a spouse, child, or friend without giving them a steady dose of love, comfort, forgiveness, and acceptance. And since these qualities are only available from God, we must be constantly receiving from God if we hope to continually give to others.

"Freely you received, freely give"—Matthew 10:8.

Consider the insightful story from Mark 1:35-37 as Peter thinks Christ is missing out on the action!

"And in the early morning, while it was still dark, He arose and went out and departed to a lonely place, and was praying there. And Simon and his companions hunted for Him; and they found Him, and said to Him, 'Everyone is looking for You' "—Mark 1:35-37.

Now consider and reflect on these questions:

- Who was living in the present, receiving fellowship with His Father?

  ____

  ____

  ____

  ____

- Who was busy worrying about missing out on something?

  ____

  ____

  ____

  ____

- What do you sometimes fear you may "miss out on"?

  ____

  ____

  ____

  ____

  ____

- What distractions in your life keep you from receiving God's love, comfort, forgiveness, and acceptance?

____

____

____

____

- Stop now and call upon Him. Block out thoughts from yesterday or of tomorrow. Be still and know that He is God. Ask of Him as the Giver of all good gifts, then gratefully receive. Write your prayer here:

____

____

____

____

____

Living in the Present Frees Me to Lovingly Give

Well-meaning intentions are great, but they're just intentions. It's God's liberating grace that turns intentions into loving action. As parents we too often find ourselves in Paul's dilemma of Romans 7:

"The good that I wish I do not do; but practice the very evil that I do not wish"—Romans 7:19.

Experiencing freedom from pain in the past and fear of the future is often critical to turning intentions into loving care. It's a lack of freedom that would negatively impact giving in the following kinds of ways:

- A parent's **guilt** about past wrongs (temper outbursts, unkept promises, hurtful words, etc.) can produce "hiding" from my own children. We "hide" in relationships just as certainly as Adam and Eve hid from God!

When I don't heal my **guilt** through confession, I begin "hiding," avoiding, or escaping by: (For instance: When I'm feeling guilty about losing my temper with the kids, I just stay late at work for a few nights. If I'm gone for a few nights, maybe they'll forget the incident. Besides, I feel more guilty when I'm around them.)

____

____

____

____

- A parent's **anger** over past hurts (at work, in marriage, in my childhood, etc.) can be "displaced" onto children through impatience and a quick temper. Displacing anger prompts one of the most painful outcomes in the children. A child grows up **fearing** a dad or mom, rather than feeling secure in their love.

A parent's anger over past hurts can be "displaced" onto children through impatience and a quick temper.

Reflect on displaced anger and how it may have prompted **fear** in your family and other relationships.

Who may **fear** your anger or disapproval? The anger may have prompted **compliant behavior** and a desire to please you, but it is from fear and not loving gratefulness.

____

____

____

Who may fear your anger or disapproval? It may have prompted **defiant behavior** and a desire to get back at you.

____

____

____

What issues of hurt from your past may at times come out in **anger** toward those you love?

____

____

____

- Issues at work/church? I've been hurt by ______________

  ____

  ____

- Issues in marriage? I've been hurt by ______________

  ____

  ____

- Issues from childhood, siblings, family-of-origin? I've been hurt by

  ____

  ____

- Issues with children, friends, previous relationships, in-laws? I've been hurt by ______________

  ____

Stop and ask God to help you put away your anger as we work through biblical principles in this chapter. Express the desire that your displaced anger no longer prompt fear in those you love. Write your prayer here:

____

____

____

- A parent's **condemnation** about past wrongs or failures can render the parent ineffective and powerless. Condemnation comes from the accuser of the brethren. Our adversary brings thoughts like, "You're a terrible parent." "You're not a good Christian." "Why should God answer your prayers?" "Why should He help your family or bless your life?" "You don't deserve to experience abundance or a happy family." The Holy Spirit, however, convicts specifically concerning our guilt. The Spirit prompts us to look at our temper or unkept promises, but the accuser's condemnation or "false-guilt" attacks our worth to God and our adequacy as His children.

Condemnation can prompt parents to disengage and give up on certain challenges or issues. At times I find myself struggling not to give up on: (For instance: When I'm feeling guilty, I think I'm a terrible parent and a terrible person. Then I can't seem to motivate myself to provide the structure that Eric needs.)

____

____

____

____

Condemnation robs me of the joy of blessings and good things that come my way. It also prevents gratefulness, since the accuser tells me, "You're not **worth** receiving any blessings. They're not really for you!" I find it difficult to acknowledge blessings when: (For instance: I find it difficult to acknowledge blessings when I'm feeling bad about myself. I don't see the good about my life or the daily gifts God gives to me.)

____

____

____

____

Pause to reflect on the truth concerning God's declaration of your worth to Him.

"But God, being rich in mercy, because of His great love . . . made us alive together with Christ"—Ephesians 2:4-5.

Now reflect on the truth concerning God's declaration of your adequacy.

"I can do all things through Christ which strengthens me"—Philippians 4:13.

In your own words describe your worth to God and your adequacy in Him.

____

____

____

____

- A parent's **fear** concerning the future undermines faith and prompts fear in other family members.

When I attempt to **control** too many aspects of my children's life, my children don't learn to trust in God. Rather than trusting God to guide, direct, and protect my children, I find myself trying to control: (For instance: I'm so concerned that my kids will grow up feeling unprotected as I did. I sometimes go overboard in having to know where they are and what they're doing.)

____

____

____

____

____

When my children see me overly concerned about things no one can control, this undermines their security. I find myself exhibiting disproportionate anxiety and fear concerning: (For instance: I get too anxious about the possibility of the kids getting sick or injured in a game.)

____

____

____

Family fears often become generalized into an atmosphere of anxiety.

Family fears often become generalized into an atmosphere of anxiety. One family member may fear financial devastation. One person may fear rejection, and another may fear the dark or the dentist! Review your family fears and note them below.

Name	Seems to fear
______________	______________________
______________	______________________
______________	______________________
______________	______________________
______________	______________________
______________	______________________

Stop to reflect on this Scripture: *"God has not given us a spirit of [fear]"*—2 Timothy 1:7. Then answer these questions: If a spirit of fear didn't come from God, where does it come from? If God wanted us to have a spirit of fear, He would have given it, so what does He want to happen to it? Write a short prayer asking Him to take away the spirit of fear and replace it with His peace and love.

____

____

____

Before dealing more specifically with God's plan for freedom from the past and future, let's consider two common objections:

Are you saying: I'm not supposed to think about the past?

Absolutely not! We need to learn from the past **and** gain freedom from the painful emotions of guilt, anger, condemnation, and fear.

We must come to **intellectually** embrace the truth that God is at work to bring forth His goodness—Romans 8:28.

And we must come to **emotionally** embrace the truth that it is for freedom that Christ set us free—Galatians 5:1.

Are you saying: I'm not supposed to plan for the future?

Absolutely not! We need to plan for the future, and at the same time, guard our hearts from anxiety!

We must help establish a vision for our family's future, for without a vision, people perish—Proverbs 29:18.

And we must experience His perfect love which casts out all fear about the future—1 John 4:18-19.

Now we'll turn specifically to God's principles of freedom. Through these principles, we can live in the present for His glory and the good of our families.

"It was for freedom that Christ set us free"—Galatians 5:1.

It's exciting that God has not left us without instruction as to how we find healing and freedom from yesterday's pain and tomorrow's worries. Consider the following guidance and its application to your life:

Guilt Needs to Be Confessed—first to God

Write about your need of confession here:

- I have wronged God and my spouse by ____________________

____

____

- I have wronged God and my children by ______________________

____

- I have wronged God and the following people by ___________

____

____

- I have wronged God in the following ways: ______________

____

"If we confess our sins He is faithful and righteous to forgive us our sins and to cleanse us from all unrighteousness"—1 John 1:9.

Pause and ask God to sorrow your heart over these wrongs. Meditate on Isaiah 53:3-5, *"being reminded that it was for my wrongs that Christ died."*

To "confess" is to "agree with," or "say the same," and God's provision for my sin is that Christ had to die. To "confess" is to then experience the brokenness of heart that comes as I agree with God that I have been part of His death.

As you reflect on this truth that **my** wrongs are part of why Christ had to die, describe in your own words this *"godly sorrow that leads to repentance"*—2 Corinthians 7:11. Write about your sorrow here:

____

____

____

Now give thanks to the Father that He has "forgiven and cleansed us" just as He promised (1 John 1:9). Write your thanksgiving below: (For instance: God, thank You that I receive Your forgiveness when I confess.)

____

____

____

If this was truly the first time both your heart and mind connected Christ's death with your sin, and by faith you received His forgiveness and cleansing, you'll particularly want to write about this eternally significant day. Note today's date and your prayer of gratefulness that today you have come to know Him intimately.

Today ____________________ (date) I have received forgiveness of my sin and God's gift of eternal life. *"And this is eternal life, that they may know Thee . . . and Jesus Christ whom Thou hast sent"*—John 17:3.

Write about your gratefulness of establishing intimacy with Jesus Christ. (For instance: It's amazing to me that something so simple can be so significant. Establishing a relationship with Christ is going to make a real difference in my life.)

____

____

____

____

Plan to share the joy of this decision with your spouse and family soon, allowing them to rejoice with you and be challenged by your example.

- **Guilt** needs to be **confessed**—first to God; second, to those I've wronged.

Review your list of wrongs above plus the material on a genuine confession (pages 163–64) and write how you can express your sorrow to others below:

To your spouse: (For instance: Honey, I know that my critical words must have hurt you. I was wrong. Will you forgive me?)

____

____

____

____

To your children: (For instance: Shane, I was wrong to lose my temper today. I know that I scared you. Will you forgive me?)

____

____

____

____

To others: (For instance: Teresa, I apologize for "dropping the ball" on this project. My lack of responsibility has impacted everyone. Will you forgive me?)

____

____

____

____

- **Anger** needs to be **forgiven**

"Let all bitterness and wrath and anger . . . be put away from you, along with all malice. And be kind to one another, tender-hearted, forgiving each other, just as God in Christ also has forgiven you"—Ephesians 4:31-32.

As we begin this section, you might recall and recap the hurtful issues you noted previously from pages 159 where you identified:

- hurts from work/church, etc.

____

____

- hurts from marriage

____

____

- hurts from childhood, siblings, family-of-origin

____

____

- hurts from children, friends, previous relationships, in-laws, etc.

____

____

Now in reviewing the Ephesians 4:31-32 principles of forgiveness notice these ingredients:

To forgive is to drop it, turn it loose, lay it down, let it go.

First, forgiveness will be a choice to "put it away." Imagine each of the hurts above being held in your hand, just like you would a pen or pencil. To forgive is to drop it, turn it loose, lay it down, let it go. Pause and tell God if He gives you the power to forgive, to turn loose of your anger . . . then you will. Write your prayer here:

____

____

____

____

____

Second, forgiveness is prompted by the gratefulness that I've first been forgiven by God for my wrongs. This gratefulness is the power which prompts me to "turn loose" of my anger toward others.

It's helpful to meditate on this truth. Forgiveness is a gift I first receive from God and I can then give to others who have offended me. Forgiveness is not really mine. It's a gift I've been given. It's really God's gift and He allows me to be a good steward in giving it to others.

Prayerfully, one by one go back over your list of how you've been hurt by others.

- identify the hurt, imagine it's in your hand, reflect on the gratefulness of your forgiveness, and release the anger. Write about your choices below:

I choose now to forgive ______________ for ______________

I choose now to forgive ______________ for ______________

I choose now to forgive ______________ for ______________

Write a short reflection to God on the freedom you now have and the gratefulness you sense. Write it here: (For instance: I think that by withholding forgiveness, I've actually hurt myself. Unforgiveness seems to poison my joy. God, thank You for restoring my joy.)

____

____

____

Finally, the testimony of our forgiveness is evident through our kindness and tenderhearted compassion. Write about how you could demonstrate these toward those who have hurt you:

I could demonstrate kindness and tenderhearted compassion

toward ____________________ by ____________________

toward ____________________ by ____________________

toward ____________________ by ____________________

toward ____________________ by ____________________

(For instance: I could demonstrate kindness and tenderhearted compassion toward Jeff by not reminding him of his mistakes. I could demonstrate kindness and tenderhearted compassion toward Cynthia by including her in my weekend plans.)

- **Condemnation needs the freedom of grateful truth**

"There is therefore now no condemnation for those who are in Christ Jesus. For the law of the Spirit of life in Christ Jesus has set you free" —Romans 8:1-2.

Condemnation from our accuser seeks to **equate** our worth with our **behavior.**

"You're a bad Christian because you ______________________"
(behavior)

"You're a terrible parent because you ______________________"
(behavior)

"You're not a worthy person because you ____________________"
(behavior)

God's truth is that He has made us **worthy** in spite of our behavior.

"God demonstrates His own love . . . while we were yet sinners" —Romans 5:8.

Worth is determined by our Creator, and He chose to pay the ultimate price in the gift of His Son.

Pause and allow gratefulness to God to well up inside you. Never in any relationship have you been so perfectly loved and accepted. Never has anyone sacrificed like this for you. Recall the Apostle Paul's victory shout:

"Wretched man that I am! Who will set me free . . . thanks be to God through Jesus Christ our Lord"—Romans 7:24-25.

Write your own love letter to God expressing the awe and wonder of His love toward you. Share it with God here. Thanks be to God for . . .

____

____

____

- **Fear needs to be cast out by perfect love**

"Perfect love casts out fear"—1 John 4:18.

It's particularly helpful to try to trace the fears concerning significant relationships in your life. Begin with your relationship with God, then your spouse, and then children.

Concerning my relationship with God, I sometimes fear that . . . (For instance: Sometimes, I'm afraid that He's going to stop loving me. Because I have to ask forgiveness so often, I'm scared He's going to say, "Enough is enough!")

____

____

____

____

____

____

____

Now review His word concerning "truth" about these issues. You might start with passages such as: Numbers 14:17-18; 1 Samuel 15:29; John 3:16; Romans 8:37-39; 2:4; 2 Peter 3:8-9; and Luke 15:28.

Underneath each **fear** is a lie from the "father of all lies" (John 8:44). Embrace a specific truth from God's Word, hide it away in your heart, and meditate on it often. (Sharing this fear and God's truth with your spouse will allow him/her to join you in renewing the mind as His love brings freedom.)

Concerning my relationship with my spouse, I sometimes fear

that ______________________________________

____

and if that happened, I fear ______________________

____

and if that happened, I fear ______________________

____

and if that happened, I fear ______________________

____

and if that happened, I fear ______________________

____

and if that happened, I fear ______________________

____

(For instance: I sometimes fear that I can't do enough to please my spouse and then he/she might be unhappy. He/she might look elsewhere and then he/she might leave me. Then I'd be alone; I sometimes fear that I can't let my spouse see me weak and then I fear hurting alone. I fear we'll never become really "one.")

During your Marriage Staff Meeting, these fears will be vulnerably shared. Each spouse will be challenged to share some of God's perfect love as reassuring truth is offered.

Considering my relationship with my children, I sometimes fear

____

____

and if that happened, I fear ______________________

____

and if that happened, I fear ______________________

____

and if that happened, I fear ______________________

____

and if that happened, I fear ______________________________

____

and if that happened, I fear ______________________________

____

(For instance: I sometimes fear telling Eric no. If I did, I'd be afraid he wouldn't like me. Then I fear we'd never have the close relationship that I've always wanted with a son.

I sometimes fear that my kids won't forgive me for the times I've "blown it," and then I fear they'll leave home and we'll never be close.)

During a later Family Night Activity, you'll want to share some of these fears—on an age-appropriate basis—with your children. (We'll cover this aspect of parental self-disclosure in chap. 8.)

Finally,

- **Hurt needs to be comforted**

"Blessed are those who mourn, for they shall be comforted"—Matthew 5:4.

Dealing with this realm of mourning, grieving, and sadness . . . as difficult as it is to consider . . . is in many ways the most liberating. Our **hurt** has connections to all the other emotions we've addressed in this chapter: i.e.,

Underneath my **anger** is my sense of hurt and loss.

Underneath my **fear** is the desire not to hurt . . . again.

Underneath my **condemnation** is in some way hurt for which I blame myself.

Underneath my **guilt** is my sinful retaliation that I've also been hurt.

We've therefore come to a core issue of freedom and learning to "live in the present," because in this present world hurt is inevitable! The Bible promises "tribulation" (John 16:33) and it comes in all shapes and sizes. But interestingly enough, it's *not* hurt, sadness, or sorrow that rob us of present abundance. We only need to consider Jesus to know of this truth.

Tribulation comes in all shapes and sizes.

He was a man acquainted with sorrow and grief, despised and rejected . . . yet would always be able to say, *"I glorified Thee on earth, having accomplished the work which Thou hast given Me to do"*—John 17:4.

It's not our hurting that robs us of present abundance—it's our hurting alone!

Christ experienced hurt but never alone. Expressing humility and exercising faith, He would experience the intimacy of His Father's care.

Herein lies an oft-hidden secret of His life—He never hurt alone. He always counted on the God of all comfort and He was blessed by it (2 Cor. 1:2-4; Matt. 5:4).

In our lives

— it's hurting alone that deepens our **anger** into bitterness.

— it's hurting alone that magnifies our **fear** that we'll soon be hurt again.

— it's hurting alone that pulls the sinful trigger on the **guilt** of our retaliation.

— it's hurting alone that gives the accuser access to **condemn** us for hurting in the first place.

Pause and thank God for being the God of all comfort, being intimately acquainted with all your ways, and then being caringly involved in your times of pain. Write your thoughts to the God of all comfort here:

____

____

An additional blessing of His comforting provision to our pain is that He often shares His comfort through meaningful others in our life—like a spouse, family, and friends within the body of Christ.

With regard to marriage, remember from Genesis 2:18 God said, *"It is not good for the man to be alone; I will make him a helper suitable for him."*

During your Marriage Staff Meeting you'll want to share some of your hurt—giving your partner the opportunity to comfort. You'll also want to be prepared to offer comfort to your spouse.

In preparation for this time of mourning and comforting, complete the following sentences.

- I think I've often hurt alone over: (For instance: I've never really talked about the impact of my father's alcoholism.)

  ____

  ____

- Underneath some of my anger at times I think I'm hurting over: (For instance: I think my anger may be covering up my hurt over Daniel's death.)

  ____

  ____

- I'm fearful at times because I don't want to be hurt again like the time: (For instance: I'm afraid at times because I don't want to experience those same feelings of being abandoned and betrayed.)

  ____

  ____

- It would mean so much to me to have my spouse comfort me concerning: (For instance: It would mean so much to me if Mark could reassure me about his love. I'd like for him to verbalize understanding about my hurt and then reassure me that he's not going to leave.)

  ____

  ____

We can now portray this journey into freedom as follows:

God
"I came to give you life and give it abundantly"
• Having learned from the past
• Free from the guilt, anger, condemnation, and hurt
• With a vision for the future
• Free from anxiety and worry
Living in the Present!
• Free to discern others' needs
• Free to receive God's abundance
• Free to lovingly give to others

Pause and thank God for preparing you to comfort your spouse. Write your prayer here and then ask Him to prompt your openness and your partner's comfort during your sharing time. Write your request here:

____

____

____

Scripture Journaling—1 Peter 4:10

"As each one has received a special gift, employ it in serving one another, as good stewards of the manifold grace of God."

Reflect on some of the many-facets of God's grace . . . His love, comfort, forgiveness, etc. and see how many you can think of. List them here as a testimony of your gratefulness.

I'm grateful for God's ______________________________

____

______________________________________ toward me.

Now consider each of your family members by name. Select at least one of these aspects of God's grace that you want to be a good steward of.

To ______________ I want to gratefully give ____________
(spouse's name)

To ______________ I want to gratefully give ____________
(child's name)

To ______________ I want to gratefully give ____________
(child's name)

To ______________ I want to gratefully give ____________
(child's name)

To ______________ I want to gratefully give ____________
(child's name)

Pause to thank God for His plan for your freedom:

- freedom from the penalty and power of sin
- freedom one day from the presence of sin
- freedom also from anger, fear, condemnation, and guilt—to live abundantly in the present. Write your prayer here:

____

____

____

____

Marriage Staff Meeting

It might be helpful to schedule **two** different times for your sharing. You will need one meeting for the husband to share and then another for the wife.

Begin your time of sharing as you discuss your personal experience this week with John 10:10. How did the "thief" steal away abundance with regrets, irritations, anger, anxiety, and worry? Be specific in your sharing.

Discuss the woman with the issue of blood in Mark 5 and how this "discernment of need" relates to your marriage and your family. Like the disciples, what things are you hurriedly "off to" which can hinder your discernment and sensitivity? How do these things relate to your anxieties, fears, guilt, anger, obligations, and irritations? In what ways do you find yourself living in the past? What emotions get in your way of enjoying the present? In what ways do you find yourself living in the future? What emotions get in your way of enjoying the present?

What emotions get in your way of enjoying the present?

Discuss the exercises on freedom from guilt through confession to God. Were you able to sense a depth of godly sorrow? Talk about it. If this was the first time your heart and mind have connected your sin with Christ's death and you received Christ as the Father's gift to you, then share this with your spouse! Pause and pray together before proceeding, thanking God for His plan for freedom.

Next, vulnerably share items of guilt in which you've hurt your spouse, asking him for forgiveness (see pp. 163–64). (For instance: I know that I hurt you by withholding information about the kids. I was wrong to keep that information to myself. You must have felt left out and unimportant. Will you forgive me?)

As your partner shares, be reminded of God's forgiveness of you and from a grateful heart be a good steward of this forgiveness. Reach over and touch your partner, verbalizing your forgiveness. Discuss other confession and anger issues as necessary.

Be sure to cover the fear issues concerning your marriage relationship (pp. 170–72). Take turns sharing a fear and then your spouse offers reassuring truth. (Be careful not to consider your partner's fears silly or unimportant. They're real to him/her.)

(For instance: Fear—I sometimes fear that I won't be able to provide for you like you want. I'm afraid you'll be unhappy, and then you might leave.)

Reassuring Truth—I'm never going to leave you . . . no matter what we have or don't have. I'm committed to you and I love you.

Finally, discuss hurting alone and each of your reflections on your times of hurting. As your partner shares, be gentle and empathetic, offering words of tenderness and reassuring touch.

Top Ten Need of the Week—Security

Be observant this week of very practical times you might initiate sharing reassurance with your children . . . confirming to them the security of your care and commitment.

Example words might include the following:

- "Sheri, I want you to take the good car; I'll drive the klunker."
- "John, I want you to know that I love your mother dearly, and nothing will ever come between us."
- "Jim, I want you to know that I love you; I'll always love you, and I'll always be available to help you."
- "Susan, I want you to know that I'm saving for your college education and God can be counted upon to provide."

Family Night Activity

Family Drama—Prepare the family to act out the scene from Mark 5. Use props and costumes. Have someone play the woman . . . maybe your youngest, and someone to play Jesus and the rest of the disciples. Read the story together and then act it out. You might act it out a second time using a current day situation . . . the family (disciples) are busily on their way to go swimming or play ball when this lady "interrupts them."

Afterward, discuss how important it is that our homes be a "safe place" where people will notice when we're down, hurting, discouraged, or lonely. Have each family member discuss what well-meaning activities sometimes hinder them from seeing others' needs. Discuss also how our anger, guilt, and fear keep us from being sensitive to others. (Dad and Mom might vulnerably share first. This would also be an excellent setting for any confessions that need to be made from Dad and/or Mom. They may need to discuss unhealed hurts this chapter identified on p. 159.)

Discuss how Jesus was able to be sensitive to others as He remained dependent upon His Father. He trusted His Father to take care of Jairus' daughter while He stopped to heal the woman.

As we trust and depend on God to watch over us and change us as He desires, we'll also be sensitive to others around us. Hold hands for prayer giving each family member the opportunity to pray. Ask God to make you sensitive to one another's needs and make your home a safe place.

Building Family Memories

It's important to build a "treasure chest" of family memories. Here are some practical suggestions on ways to remember those special times together. Discuss these three ideas with your family. Choose or modify an idea that your family can begin as a new tradition.

Matchbook collection Whenever you eat out as a family or when you travel together, save the matchbook from the restaurant or hotel. Inside the front cover, write down where you were, the occasion, who was present, and something about the trip. Store all the matchbooks in a designated box or chest. During Family Nights, take turns letting each family member pick a matchbook at random, read what's inscribed on the inside, and reminisce about times spent together.

Photograph diaries On family outings (even on routine trips like shopping at the mall) take a pocket camera with you and take turns taking pictures. If there are four family members, each person takes every fourth picture. They can snap a shot of anything they want; but, preferably, a family member should be in every picture. Even let small children participate. Obviously, the purpose is not to take award-winning photographs, but to get the family involved in recording memories. It's important to get the film developed the same day and to spend time looking at the pictures. Store the photographs in a permanent album, not in a shoe box, and review the albums during Family Nights.

"Artifacts" display On family trips and vacations, involve everyone in selecting one "artifact" that will remind them of the trip. Preferably, it will be an unusual item you find or purchase, not a souvenir you buy in the tourist center. It could be a seashell, a menu, a book, a program, or something unusual that you find. Exhibit the "artifacts" in a china cabinet or display cabinet and periodically discuss the items as a way of reflecting back on times together.

Optional activity—for older children and teens The Declaration of Dependence on page 182 can serve as a family commitment to trusting and depending on God. Consider sharing it during Family Night. Give each family member an opportunity to offer a prayer of commitment and then sign it.

For families with home computers, feel free to retype it and change it as you may desire. Then share it, pray, sign, and frame it as a powerful family reminder of the true builder of our home!

Group Discussion

Begin your group by reading and discussing the "Declaration of Dependence" on page 182. Give group members a chance to share impressions or feedback. Then invite everyone to recount the circumstances of their salvation. Describe the process of how God took you "out of the darkness of mere existence into His marvelous light."

Next, ask group members to share ways that they sometimes live in the past. How do you at times live in the future? How have these tendencies impacted your life? Share blessings and gratefulness from your staff meeting time of finding freedom. Review key emotions which can hold us captive to the past along with biblical truth to be experienced for freedom. Review emotions which can hold us captive to the future along with God's biblical provision. What hope is renewed by the possibility of living in the present?

For the final activity, discuss the intimacy need of the week. How does the need for security demonstrate itself in your life? Your children's lives? Brainstorm practical ways to meet this need.

Declaration of Dependence

When in the course of human existence it becomes evident that mere man is totally incapable of pleasing his Creator and further when these mere men have acknowledged this inability and sought reconciliation with their Creator through the only available avenue, the shed blood of Jesus Christ, having received namely their Creator's gift of becoming true children of God, these new Children of Reconciliation seem compelled to declare their allegiance to and dependence upon this One who has brought them out of the darkness of mere existence into His marvelous light.

Be it therefore vowed before our Creator and acknowledged before all men that we the undersigned do hold these truths to be self-evident, from the most Holy Scriptures, that all men are created equal in needing a Savior, that they are endowed by their Creator with certain unexplainable, unmerited opportunities, that among these are new life, liberty from the curse of sin, and a joy inexpressible and full of glory. That to secure these opportunities of divine grace, man is called upon to exercise truth heart faith—reckoning them as so, even when they are not so, in order for them to be so. And that this initial appropriation of faith which has brought mere man into the spiritual family of the Creator, has also translated this new Child of God out of the realm of the mere seen, into the world of the unseen.

It is in this new world of the unseen that these children of the Most High God believe all things, hope all things and trust all things. It is in this world of the unseen that God's children can thus interpret mere existence in this world, which can be seen. For it is in this world of the seen that we are promised much tribulation, while from the realm of the unseen, we are encouraged to be of "good cheer," for Christ has overcome the world. It is in this world of the seen where we observe in this tribulation a "shaking" as in a removing from us of those things which can be shaken, as in worldly things, until only that which cannot be shaken, as of eternal things, shall remain. We, as Your children, have sensed Your divine "shaking" and we ask that You not stay Your hand until You have perfected Yourself Holy among us in the world's sight.

Signed ______________________ ______________________

______________________ ______________________

______________________ ______________________

this Day ____________ in the year A.D. ____________

Part Three

Let Your Child Know You

"You are our letter... known and read by all men."

2 CORINTHIANS 3:2

CHAPTER 8

Revealing Hope through Your Humanity

AS WE EMBARKED on our journey of parenting with intimacy, we encouraged you to see your child as a gift from God—one to be unwrapped, appreciated, and enjoyed. We're now about to head down a slightly different, albeit parallel, road. Have you ever considered that you are God's gift to your child? Chances are good that you've never heard such affirmation slip from your child's lips, but it's true nonetheless. Just as surely as God has entrusted your child to you as a gift to be nurtured and guided, He has given you to your child as a gift. You were hand-chosen by God to love and guide this precious child of His through the twists and turns of life. Just as your child is a gift that must be unwrapped, your life is a gift that must be unwrapped and revealed before your child. The parents' willingness to vulnerably disclose their lives appropriately to their child is perhaps the greatest gift they can give. Great hope is prompted by the disclosure of our humanity—as children hear and see of the Christ within us, having begun a good work, being faithful to complete it (Phil. 1:6).

Have you ever considered that you are God's gift to your child?

As we have addressed in previous chapters, you are disclosing a lot about yourself and your marriage whether you realize it or not. We might call this *passive disclosure.* Second Corinthians 3:3 says we are a living epistle, being known and read by all men. Your child is reading your actions, priorities, attitudes, and convictions. Your child can feel your emotions, your moods, your pain. You can walk into a room having successfully conned your coworkers, the checker at the grocery store, your friends at church, perhaps even your pastor into believing that you're doing fine . . . great . . . never better, but your child knows the truth. You can stay busy, do your household chores, and go about "business as usual," but your child knows where your heart is. So, rather than playing games, parenting with intimacy involves being real before your kids. That's what true intimacy is all about and it's what teaches your child how to be a real person in a world that screams at him to live life behind a mask and to wall himself off from all that truly satisfies relationships.

In contrast to this more "passive" disclosure of yourself to your children, we now turn to this "active" disclosure as parents take initiative to reveal themselves to their children. As noted in chapter 1, Proverbs 3:32 uses the word transliterated as *"sod"* which means *to reveal, to disclose* oneself. That passage of Scripture says that God is intimate with the upright. He *reveals* Himself. He *discloses* Himself to the upright. So, first He knows us (*yada*), and then He allows us to know Him (*sod*). This is part of what was going on in the Upper Room in John 15:15 when Jesus looked at His disciples one day and said, *"No longer do I call you slaves, for the slave does not know what his master is doing; but I have called you friends, for all things that I have heard from My Father I have made known to you."* He had disclosed His Father's will to them. It's the beauty of the Incarnation that He became flesh and dwelt among us, and we beheld Him . . . full of grace and truth. Part of parenting with intimacy is dwelling with your children vulnerably and transparently—allowing them to behold you, warts and all.

Pause and consider John 1:14—*"And the Word [Jesus] became flesh and dwelt among us, and we beheld His glory."* As you consider here the Father's initiative to let us truly know Him, answer the following questions in your own words:

1. Who takes the initiative in us being able to know the Father better? ____

____

2. Try giving an example from Scripture of when Christ revealed to us an example of:

   Being a servant to others ____________________

   Dealing with temptation ____________________

   Hurting with others when they hurt ____________________

   Calling upon the Heavenly Father for help ____________________

3. How does having the life of Christ revealed to you in Scripture provide you an example and encouragement?

   ____

   ____

4. Describe in your own words how this principle might apply to parenting with intimacy. ____________________

   ____

So, what's the key purpose in this "disclosing" of oneself?

Simply put, it helps remove aloneness! Your kids need you to be more than just leaders. They're traveling a long and arduous road to maturity. They need mentors and journeymates. They need more than just someone to point them in the right direction. They need someone to come alongside, share "war stories" about their own journey, and walk with them. Parental self-disclosure ministers to children's sense of aloneness and fear as they hurdle each developmental milestone on their way to maturity. It encourages and empowers their progress, catapulting them through difficult times. As they navigate the sometimes tumultuous and treacherous waters of separation and individuation, their parents' vulnerable self-disclosure serves as an anchor to keep them from capsizing.

Consider for a minute some of these "self-disclosures" from the Scriptures and then note how they help minister to "aloneness:"

"In the world you have tribulation, but take courage; I have overcome the world"—John 16:33.

This passage can help me not be *alone* when ________________

____

"All authority has been given to Me in heaven and on earth. . . . Lo, I am with you always even to the end of the age"—Matthew 28:18, 20.

This passage can help me not be *alone* when ________________

____

"Peace I leave with you; My peace I give to you; not as the world gives, do I give to you. Let not your heart be troubled, nor let it be fearful"—John 15:27.

This passage can help me not be *alone* when ________________

____

In this ministry to my aloneness, several blessings are experienced:

First, my *experience* is validated as real, significant, and purposeful.

Second, *hope* is engendered that another has already traveled this way.

Third, *trust* is deepened as vulnerable sharing allows intimates to "know" and "be known" by one another.

Finally, my *worth* is affirmed as I consider that I'm being valued as a companion and loved as a friend.

Consider now your children and these possible blessings. Who could benefit from *validation* of their experiences? *Hope* instead of fear? Deepened *trust* in relationships? An affirmation of their *worth?* Write your thoughts below:

Child	*Possible Benefits from Parents' Self-Disclosure*
________	______________________________
________	______________________________
________	______________________________

A Word of Caution and Encouragement!

As you share yourself appropriately with your child, it is very likely that some of your own pain—both childhood and adult—may resurface. Scripture calls us to maturity. This does not mean denying your pain, but it does mean having an adult perspective on it and not calling upon your child to carry your pain. If you find yourself needing someone to process this pain with you, find a journeymate other than your child—your spouse, a friend, a counselor, pastor, or support group. It's important for you to have someone to share with, but your goal in disclosing yourself to your child is not to weigh her down but to equip her for growth and forward motion. Remember our admonition in chapter 6 to "leave father and mother" and in chapter 7 to find freedom from living in the past or the future. It's time to live in the present! This is a new day, a new opportunity to break unhealthy patterns. *Carpe diem*—seize the day!

Parents are often hesitant to disclose themselves for a number of reasons. Perhaps the strongest reason is that they're not sure what or how much to share.

Parents are often hesitant to disclose themselves for a number of reasons. Perhaps the strongest reason is that they're not sure what or how much to share because they may have felt all alone themselves at these developmental stages. Their own parents were stuck in the trap of building walls around their lives and erecting fences to separate themselves emotionally from their children. Commit yourself to removing walls and tearing down fences. Let's begin our "disclosure journey."

When—and How Much Should I Share?

Just as growing up follows a predictable developmental progression, so does parental self-disclosure. Successful completion of earlier disclosure experiences is essential for later developmental success. After considering examples from the life of Christ, we'll approach each milestone, remind ourselves of the key developmental issues facing the child, and then look at the important aspects of parental disclosure for each particular stage.

Let's consider briefly this progressive self-disclosure of Christ to His disciples. During His rather short three-and-one-half years with them, notice how His sharing was progressively deeper, more personal, more vulnerable:

"I must preach the kingdom of God to the other cities also, for I was sent for this purpose"—Luke 4:43.

"Do not fear, from now on you will be catching men"—Luke 5:10.

"Why do you call Me, Lord, Lord, and do not do what I say?"—Luke 6:46

"My mothers and My brothers are these who hear the Word of God and do it"—Luke 8:21.

"The Son of Man must suffer many things, and be rejected . . . and be killed, and be raised up on the third day"—Luke 9:22.

Comment on *why* it was that Jesus progressively revealed or disclosed Himself to His disciples. Write your thoughts here:

___

___

How might this progressive self-disclosure apply to parenting with *intimacy?* Share your thoughts here:

___

___

God's plan for growing up is one of His most intricate creations—exciting and scary, exhilarating and tiring, rewarding and frustrating, all-too-short and endless—all at the same time. The developmental milestones, or watershed events, that need to occur at various ages along God's timetable are extremely important. Nobody ever grew up to be a healthy, mature adult by avoiding them. It's natural for parents to want to shield their child from some of the painful moments encountered along the way, but learning to negotiate the road blocks and detours is critical to the completion of the journey. If a child doesn't deal with the issues of being twelve when he's twelve, he'll

DEVELOPMENTAL ASSESSMENT		
Developmental Stage	**Key Life Issue**	**Contrasting Scriptural Assessment**—*which more accurately describes each child?*
1. Infancy *Ages 0–18 months*	Trust *vs.* Mistrust	*"Put your trust in the Lord . . . and you will be established"* —2 Chronicles 20:20. *"that you fear continually all day long"* —Isaiah 51:13.
2. Early Childhood *Ages 18–36 months*	Autonomy *vs.* Shame/ Doubt	*"in all these things we overwhelmingly conquer"*—Roman 8:37. *"The one who doubts is like the surf of the sea—driven and tossed by the wind"* —James 1:6.
3. Middle Childhood *Ages 3–5 years*	Initiative *vs.* Guilt	*"I can do all things through Christ"*—Philippians 4:13. *"he who doubts is condemned"* —Romans 14:23.
4. Late Childhood *Ages 6–12 years*	Motivation (Industry) *vs.* Inferiority	*"the love of Christ controls us"* —2 Corinthians 5:14. *"wretched man that I am"* —Romans 7:24.
5. Adolescence *Ages 13–18 years*	Identity *vs.* Role Confusion	*"We are His workmanship"* —Ephesians 2:10. *"who am I, that I should go?"* —Exodus 3:11
6. Young Adult *Ages 19–30 years*	Intimacy *vs.* Isolation	*"God is intimate with the upright"* —Proverbs 3:32. *"I was afraid . . . so I hid myself"* —Genesis 3:10.

have to deal with them later . . . at age twenty, twenty-five, thirty-five, forty-five. . . .

Remember . . . things take time. Growing up is no exception! Also remember that critical to relating intimately with your children is to truly know them and to let them *know* you. One of the ingredients in helping your child negotiate these developmental stages is your own self-disclosure! As caregivers vulnerably disclose themselves along this journey, a child finds validation of his experience, hope is engendered, trust is deepened, and their worth is affirmed. Their "aloneness" removed, fear diminishes and they move forward along their developmental journey, secure in their parents' companionship. Enjoy watching the panorama of your child's life as it unfolds frame-by-frame, according to God's timetable. God has created and ordained the process of growing up. Every moment of every day is incredibly important and brings an opportunity for building relationships. Gaining an understanding of this orderly progression of stages enables us to be more empathetic and equips us to help our children discover their uniqueness and God-given potential. Using the "Developmental Assessment" chart on page 191, let's review the six key developmental stages and one crucial life issue to be faced in each. As we do so, consider where each of your children may be along this journey.

Key uses for the developmental assessment include both *preparing* to help your newborn along each stage plus *ministry* to any child (or adult) regardless of age.

How to Use the Developmental Assessment and Intimacy Disclosures

Ideally, parents of newborns can incorporate these principles into their parenting plans from the outset. The key life issues and supporting Scriptures along with the intimacy disclosures which follow can guide parents in taking initiative in these areas. This material can serve as a lifelong agenda for father-son discussions, father-daughter "dates," mother-son sharing times, and mother-daughter visits. It also can provide significant guidance in family sharing times which move beyond "chit-chat" to true intimate sharing. Family Night sharing on this level will bring long-lasting impact and life-changing ministry.

Family Night sharing on this level will bring long-lasting impact and life-changing ministry.

Pause and consider each member of your family—beginning with yourself, then your spouse, then each child. Reflect on who exhibits the following developmental strengths: (Put an "X" in each column where this strength is exhibited.)

Developmental Strengths	Myself	Spouse	Child	Child	Child
			(Name)	(Name)	(Name)
Trust—*Who exhibits trust in relationships?*					
	______	______	______	______	______
Autonomy—*Who exhibits security in decisions?*					
	______	______	______	______	______
Initiative—*Who exhibits confident actions?*					
	______	______	______	______	______
Motivation (Industry)—*Who exhibits the internal promptings of gratefulness?*					
	______	______	______	______	______
Identity—*Who exhibits clarity of worth and purpose?*					
	______	______	______	______	______
Intimacy—*Who exhibits vulnerable sharing and sensitive caring?*					
	______	______	______	______	______

Completing this table will help identify where intimacy disclosures may be helpful. For example, couples might identify that a husband lacks *initiative* and a wife needs more *autonomy*. Additionally, each child will be "somewhere" along the developmental journey—needing encouragement toward the next stage or additional ministry to develop strength in a stage they've already passed through. (Specific intimacy disclosures to address each strength area will be discussed in the next sections.)

A second use for these principles is in ministry to children (or adults) of any age. Suppose your teenage daughter struggles with "trust" issues—finding it difficult to believe, "count on," and trust others. Then she likely could benefit from the *intimacy disclosures* noted in stage 1 of the following figure, namely *acceptance, care,* and *joy*. Imagine that your young adult son struggles with separating from peer pressure, seemingly unable to establish his own "*autonomy*" . . . he could likely benefit from the intimacy disclosures in stage 2, disclosures such as *approval, empathy,* and *faith.* Suppose your wife has difficulty truly "feeling" your love and thus uncertain of her *identity* as your helpmate. It's surely a paradox but she could likely benefit from intimacy disclosures in stage 5, namely a husband's *painful feelings* and his own *inadequacies.* Many a wife has begun to feel again her husband's love as she heard of his sadness and hurt. ("If I have hurt and disappointed him so deeply, he must really love me!") Other wives have experienced great closeness as they heard of their husband's "inadequacies," his needs. ("I have a great need for him to need me! . . . If he's not really a self-reliant superman, then I feel needed, important, and loved!")

Note below which particular developmental strength(s) could be the focus of ministry to each family member:

Family Member	**Developmental Strength Needing Emphasis**
Myself	____________________
Spouse	____________________
Child __________	____________________
Child __________	____________________

(For instance: I need to exhibit more *initiative;* my spouse could be more *trusting;* two-year-old Sandy is definitely working on her *autonomy!* Our twenty-four-year-old son Justin seems to have missed out on establishing his own *identity.*)

As material is presented in this chapter for each developmental stage, pay particular attention to the *intimacy disclosures* suggested. Couples can then focus on sharing with one another in these ways. Parents can then take specific initiative in sharing self-disclosures with each child.

The following figure provides a summary of key intimacy disclosures across the developmental stages. Remember it's the parents' intimacy disclosures at each developmental stage that helps the child grow and mature into the fullness of his God-intended potential.

INTIMACY DISCLOSURES

—Letting Your Child Know You—

Stages	*Disclosure at Each Stage*
1. **Infancy** 0–18 Months Trust vs. Mistrust	• Acceptance • Care • Joy —continue these disclosures, then share your
2. **Early Childhood** 18–36 Months Autonomy vs. Shame/Doubt	• Approval • Empathy • Faith • Protection —continue these disclosures, then share your
3. **Middle Childhood** 3–5 Years Initiative vs. Guilt	• Affirmation • Confession • Positive Remembrances —continue these disclosures, then share your
4. **Late Childhood** 6–12 Years Industry vs. Inferiority	• Dreams • Decision-making • Struggles • Hopes • Individuality • Remembrances of Same-sex Friends • Experiences of Delayed Gratification —continue these disclosures, then share your
5. **Adolescence** 13–18 Years Identity vs. Role Confusion	• Negative Feelings • Temptations • Dating Experiences • Inadequacies —continue these disclosures, then share your
6. **Young Adult** 19–30 Years Intimacy vs. Isolation	• Enjoyment of Common Interests • Painful Remembrances • Need for Mutual Giving • Confession

Now we'll focus on each of the six developmental stages highlighting areas of intimacy disclosure. As you review each stage and the practical disclosures, consider each family member and who might benefit.

Infancy (0–18 months)

"[I] proved to be gentle among you, as a nursing mother tenderly cares for her own children. . . . Pleased to impart to you not only the Gospel but [my very life], because you had become very dear to me"—1 Thessalonians 2:7-8.

As soon as baby makes his or her grand entrance into the world of bright lights and beeping delivery room monitors, he or she begins testing the waters to see if the world is a safe place. Looking for an answer to the fundamental question, *"Can relationships be trusted?"* baby sizes up the situation based on whether or not intimacy needs are met.

You may be asking yourself, "Well, how do I disclose myself to a baby who can't even talk yet?" Don't sell baby short. From his or her first waking moment, baby is making assessments about his world based primarily on his interactions with you. Your best line of communication is through *tactile/sensory* stimulation. Your God-given senses will enable you to connect with your baby as he begins to discover who you are and how important he or she is to you.

Parental self-disclosure at this crucial beginning stage should revolve around communicating the following:

Acceptance
"We accept you into our family. You belong." Gentle words and tender touch help welcome the child into your world. And most of us never grow out of needing these! Giving freedoms where safely possible communicates a secure world.

Gentle words and tender touch help "welcome" the child into your world.

Care
"We're going to pay attention to your needs because we love you. You're important to us." Thoughtful initiative to "check in" on this child communicates, "I was thinking

about you." Spontaneous loving touch says, "You can count on my presence."

Joy
"You bring joy to our lives. We're so glad God gave you to us!" Smile often and let laughter fill your home. Allow the gratefulness of His blessing to flood your heart and conversation with thanksgiving.

Reflect on these intimacy disclosures and consider which family members could benefit from receiving them. Write your thoughts here: (For instance: "I want to make a conscious effort to be more affectionate with Justin. My hugs and kisses will communicate that I care." Or, "I want to show acceptance to my new daughter-in-law. I'll make sure that I greet her with the same warmth as I give my son.")

____

____

____

Research Study—Your Child Is "Reading" Your Emotions

Children, even from early ages, are attentive to the *"emotional" atmosphere* at home. A recent study of nine-month-old infants monitored infants observing their mothers express *joy* or *sadness,* facially and verbally. The infants expressed more joy and looked longer at their mothers during the joy condition and they showed more sadness, anger, and avoidance during the sadness condition. The infants likewise engaged in more play behavior when mothers expressed joy rather than sadness (Termine, 1988).

A home's atmosphere is directly related to the *emotions* being expressed there—joy, encouragement, and hope *or* fear, anger, and blame.

Practical Suggestions

- *Take a Feeling Inventory*—List the most frequently shared emotions in your home—gratefulness, joy, hope or fear, anger, and worry.
- *Build a Feeling Vocabulary*—Talk about feelings by name; see how many the family can list; take turns sharing about an event and its associated feelings.

- *Openly Express Positive Emotions*—Verbalize your grateful appreciation, expectant joy, and confident security.
- *Validate and Learn from Painful Emotions*—Encourage constructive verbalizing of fear, anger, and hurt or they will come out destructively; learn to look behind the emotion to an unmet need for security, attention, affection, etc.

Early Childhood (18–36 months)

"Like newborn babes, long for the pure milk of the Word, that by it you may grow"—1 Peter 2:2.

As a child begins the task of learning to balance the teetertotter of *autonomy* and dependency while also resolving the issue of splitting (i.e., the Mommy/Daddy that loves me is the same Mommy/Daddy who sometimes has to tell me no or discipline me when I do things I shouldn't), it's important for your words as well as actions to model unconditional love. Parental self-disclosure should center around communicating:

Approval
Celebrate every little milestone. This conveys your approval of the way God has made this special person rather than the quality of the job. It is absolutely essential as they begin the process of separation and individuation that they feel your support of who they are, not what they do. "You are my beloved son (or daughter) in whom I'm well pleased."

Empathy
When you see her sad, disappointed, or hurt, resist giving advice, lectures, or pep talks. Share empathetic comfort from your heart: "I'm sad that you're hurting because I love you." This is a powerful ingredient in softening a child's heart to a God who cares!

Faith
It's important at this age for your children to see that you are looking to Someone outside yourself—to God—to help you. As you pray with your children at bedtime, let them hear you asking God to watch over them and to accomplish things in their lives. Let

your life speak of your gratefulness to Him for who He is, what He has provided, and your confidence that He will do what's in the best interest of you and your children.

Protection

Begin laying the groundwork for your child's understanding that the rules and consequences you have for them are for their benefit and protection—not to cheat them out of having fun. They are an expression of your love for them. At this age, "teachable moments" frequently present themselves when your child is reaping a painful consequence from disobedience of some kind. When your self-disclosure is clothed in a blanket of comfort, it will fall on a far more receptive heart. Take, for example, a toddler who has just burned his finger on a hot stove. Consider these two responses and what they disclose to the child.

"I told you not to touch the stove! That wouldn't have happened if you had obeyed me. Go to your room and stay there until it's time for dinner!"

Or, first bending down to get on his level, you kiss the hurt and then say, "I'm sorry you burned your finger. I know how much that hurts. Let's run some cold water on it to make it feel better. You know, Sweetie, when Daddy and I tell you not to do something, it's because we love you and don't want you to get hurt."

Reflect on these intimacy disclosures and consider which family members could benefit from receiving them. Write your thoughts here: (For instance: "I want to reestablish our bedtime prayers. Morgan needs to hear that we all have a God we can count on." Or, "Britney needs to hear my words of approval when she attempts certain tasks, not just when she succeeds. I need to thank her for taking turns and notice when she tries to make it to the potty.")

____

____

____

Middle Childhood (3–5 years)

"I had to be in My Father's house"—Luke 2:49.

As children take *initiative* to explore the world in earnest, making daily discoveries about who they are physically, cognitively, emotionally, and sexually, parental self-disclosure focuses on three key areas:

Affirmation
Affirm your children's uniqueness. "You're such a good helper." Share with them the specific character traits you admire about them and help them see their value and benefit to others. "I'm proud of you for being such a good friend to Jimmy." (See Appendix for list of Fifty Character Qualities.)

Confession
Model a willingness to admit mistakes and ask forgiveness. "It was wrong of me not to keep my promise. Will you forgive me?" As a child makes discoveries about herself and her world, she must have the security of knowing mistakes are allowed. Parents who are willing to model that by vulnerably confessing their own mistakes provide fertile soil for their child's continued growth.

Remembrance
As parents share positive memories of their early years, a child's sense of identity is enhanced, especially with the same-sex parent. "I remember when I turned four. Your grandmother gave me a Lone Ranger birthday party. . . . When I was five, my favorite TV show was . . . " [As an aside, this is an essential precursor to establishing same-sex peer relationships later.] It's critical at this age for a child to get an initial comprehension that their parents were once that age, and that someday they'll be adults too.

Reflect on these intimacy disclosures and consider which family members could benefit from receiving them. Write your thoughts here: (For instance: "I need to apologize to Ben for embarrassing him in front of his friends." Or "Katelyn would enjoy hearing about my first day in kindergarten.")

____

____

____

Late Childhood (6–12 years)

"Jesus kept increasing in wisdom and stature, and in favor with God and men"—Luke 2:52.

During these years your child is continuing to make discoveries about who he is and experiencing the *motivation* that comes from God's love for him. Faced with such weighty issues as sibling rivalry, competition, "fairness vs. justice," and his need to feel successful in the eyes of parents, peers, and other adults, it's clear that parental self-disclosure will play a pivotal role in helping stay the course as particular focus is given to:

Dreams/Aspirations
Share your own dreams and aspirations at this age. Did you want to be a professional baseball player? A jet pilot? A fireman? A movie star? A fashion designer? A beautician? A doctor? Challenge your child to view the possibilities as limitless and assure her of your support and encouragement. Dream with her. Now is not the time for cold realities and practicality. Encouraging dreams will stimulate the vision God has planned for each life (Prov. 29:18).

Decision-making
It's tragic that so many children enter their teenage years with no experience under their belt in making decisions. Their decisions—some good and some not so good—serve as "teachable moments" to help them learn to link consequences with choices—positive and negative. Parents have an opportunity to share their own experiences. "I remember when I chose to ______________________________ and experienced ________________" (pain). Or, "I remember when I made a wise choice to ______________ and ________________" (blessing). Sharing decision-making skills with your children and allowing them to make some decisions for themselves facilitates their growing sense of identity and responsibility . . . as they mature in *"giving an account of themselves to God"*—see Romans 14:12.

It's tragic that so many children enter their teenage years with no experience under their belt in making decisions.

Struggles and Resulting Success/Failure
A child this age often perceives his or her parents as always successful, invincible! Disclosing times when you've struggled, experienced failure, and experienced God's supportive love reflects to the child that it's possible to have those feelings and still grow up and have a meaningful life. It doesn't have to be the end of the world! "I remember when I struck out in the big game." "I remember how disappointed I was when I didn't ______________." Help him understand that experiencing failures is not the same as being a failure and that he could *never* be a failure to you or God. Sharing the testimony of your personal salvation experience will help put life into its eternal perspective. It's important for him to be challenged with life's eternal perspective and find the deep security of God's love before he reaches the storms of adolescence.

Hopes
With the doom and gloom that bombard children on a daily basis in the media, it's important for them to experience hope. Share times in your life when things have looked bleak and dismal but God met your need and caused *"things to work out for your good"* (Rom. 8:28). "I remember thinking that I'd never have a real friend but ______________."

Individuality
Share the things you did at this age that were uniquely you—hobbies, sports, etc. "I was really into roller-skating when I was your age . . . that was long before roller-blades!" Affirm your child in areas where she is different from you as well as where she shares similar strengths and interests. "You're really good at fixing things that break . . . much better than I'll ever be." It's important for her to realize that her identity is more than just being your child. Affirming a child's uniqueness prepares her to be *"the people of God"* (1 Peter 2:10).

Same-sex Friendships
By sharing experiences of same-sex friendships—memories from the past, best friends and what you did together—you encourage the same in your child. "Stanley and I used to ride bicycles in the

snow"; "When I was your age, I had a best girlfriend named Linda. We did everything together." This further facilitates identity, separation, individuation, and healthy opposite-sex friendships later. Looking at school pictures and old yearbooks together can be a fun way to share these days of yesteryear.

Delayed Gratification
Is it any wonder that children who have known a life of one-minute oatmeal, five-minute rice, and instant pudding—not to mention having information at their fingertips within minutes on the Internet—have difficulty with delayed gratification? And yet, it is important for them to learn that all important things take time. Neglecting to do so sets them up for a rude awakening when they're out on their own and things don't come quite so easily. "I remember saving from my allowance for six months to help buy my first bicycle." "It took three years of trying before I finally made the team."

Reflect on these intimacy disclosures and consider which family members could benefit from receiving them. Write your thoughts here: (For instance: "I think I'll share my basketball story with Philip. It might encourage him to know that I struggled with coordination too.")

____

____

____

____

Adolescence (13–18 years)

"When I was a child, I used to speak as a child . . . when I became a man, I did away with childish things"—1 Corinthians 13:11.

These years are ones of tremendous change. In early adolescence thoughts, feelings, and bodies are changing so fast they can hardly keep up with them, which at least partially explains their incredible disorganization and frequent bouts of aphasia. In later adolescence, they begin sorting through issues of sexuality and moving from depending on their peer group as a group to developing deeper one-on-one relationships. Separation and individuation are major forces as they move toward adulthood. These kids need parents and other adults who will be committed to genuineness and integrity, qualities that will equip them to face the future with confidence, secure in their *identity* as recipients of divine love. Parental self-disclosure should focus on:

Negative/Painful Feelings

It is imperative that your teenagers begin to realize that their behavior affects and influences others. One of the best ways to accomplish this is for the parent-child relationship to begin connecting on a deeper emotional level. As you, the parent, are willing to share painful feelings, your teenagers begin to see the impact of their words and actions as the Holy Spirit is freed to bring conviction and repentance (John 16:8; 2 Cor. 7:10).

Eric had a habit of throwing his clothes on the floor, even the clean ones. For years Teresa had been telling him, "I get so upset when you throw your clothes on the floor. When are you ever going to become more responsible?" Her focus was on his behavior. On one occasion she took a slightly different angle, sharing her true feelings. "I don't know if I've ever told you this, Eric, but when I go to your closet and see clean clothes on the floor, I feel so unappreciated." She was not judgmental but shared her own feelings of pain. Her need to be appreciated had not been met. It was the first time it had dawned on Eric that his behaviors had the potential of positively or negatively impacting people he cared about. Up until then, in his mind it had been an issue of, "Why is she in my room anyway?" Sharing at this level of feeling is not a power struggle. It's disarming . . . penetrating to the heart of the issue. Do I care about this person I've hurt? Eric was being called upon to practice empathy and true confession, and then his behavior began to change.

Temptations

Share with your teenagers times when you were tempted—times you "passed" and times you didn't. Sharing such memories strengthens their individuality and need for God and provides comfort as you minister to their aloneness. It's best to offer these disclosures when they're not struggling with that particular temptation. Otherwise, it comes across sounding like a "lecture." Family Nights would provide an appropriate arena for such dialogue. Offer some biblical examples of people who confronted temptations and discuss what can be learned from their experiences (i.e., David, Abraham, Tamar, Joseph, etc.).

Dating/Romance (Opposite-sex Friendships)
Share memories of your first date, and first girlfriend/boyfriend. This not only begins to reassure them that Mom and Dad are normal but also lets them see that the first person they date may or may not be the person they end up marrying! This can be liberating.

Parental Inadequacies/Admiration of Child's Gifts
Be willing to vulnerably share your own inadequacies and how you dealt with them. At the same time identify things that your child is better at than you are, in a spirit of affirmation. "Terri, you're really a creative decorator; we may get you to redo our whole house!" "Robin, you're so organized and responsible; I think we'll let you run our life!" "Eric, I wish I had the mechanical ability you have; we're going to hire you as our resident handyman." This will reinforce the legitimacy of their individuality and communicate that they are free to be their own person. It also models for them that they can be happy for a friend's achievements and abilities that exceed their own. This is hard for all of us to master. What better time to lay the groundwork.

Reflect on these intimacy disclosures and consider which family members could benefit from receiving them. Write your thoughts here: (For instance: "I plan to talk with Bryan about my temptations with alcohol. I want him to hear how my choices hurt me and others around me." Or, "Holly might benefit from hearing about my first date. I felt awkward too.")

____

____

Young Adult (19–30 years)

"Let a man regard us in this manner, as servants of Christ, and stewards of the mysteries of God"—1 Corinthians 4:1.

Your relationship with your child is entering a new phase. Now you are fellow adults. Although this is what you've been preparing them for, it's often difficult for parents to face once it arrives. It's only natural to grieve somewhat over things that will never be again, but embrace the new depth and breadth of communication that awaits you. As they leave home for school, careers, and marriage, your times of one-on-one dialogue will diminish, so afford yourself of the opportunities when they arise. Parental self-disclosure should revolve around the following:

Enjoyment of Common Interests
Acknowledge to your children that you recognize that you are now fellow adults, and that while you will always be available for imparting parental wisdom and counsel when they choose to seek it, you also look forward to expanding your relationship into new dimensions. "It's such a blessing just to enjoy our friendship together." "I'm looking forward to us exploring some fun common interests."

Painful Remembrances/Regrets
Share with your young adult things you wish you had done differently and why. "I deeply regret not being more involved in your school activities as you were growing up." This is a courageous move because all parents, for the most part, do the best they can; but we realize along the way that even though our motives were good, our methods may have been hurtful. "Thinking I was 'providing' for the family, I worked many more hours than I wish I had; I missed being with you more and I regret it." This demonstration of your commitment to truth will open doors of communication that might otherwise have remained shut and impeded your child's ability to develop vulnerable, intimate relationships with others.

"Thinking I was 'providing' for the family, I worked many more hours than I wish I had; I missed being with you more and I regret it."

Confession

The next step is to open up a whole new dimension of confession. After you have shared the areas you're aware of that are in need of confession and forgiveness, then acknowledge to your young adult that you realize there are surely others you're not aware of. Give them permission to share those in love, genuinely asking them to reveal to you areas where you may have unknowingly hurt them. "I know there have been times when I've disappointed you or let you down, and not even realized it. I'd really like, as the Lord brings them to your heart, for you to share them so we can visit about them and heal them. I want to hurt with you because I love you." This is a vulnerable, selfless move, calling for a servant's heart willing to go beyond the natural desire to defend oneself to responding compassionately and repentantly in order to achieve a higher good.

As you are willing to make yourself vulnerable in this way, the doors of communication swing open. A sense of security is produced that invites future dialogue and promises a deepening relationship as you relate adult-to-adult. What greater joy could any parent desire!

Need for Mutual Giving

Parents never outgrow their "need to be needed" by their children, and young adults have matured to the point where they can now give to the needs of their parents. The challenge comes in communicating and fulfilling this mutual giving within the confines of healthy, appropriate boundaries. A great deal of tension and conflict often arises between parents and their grown children out of this tremendous need to be needed. In fact, if adult children don't find their parents a need to meet, parents will choose their own! Then we find the adult child moaning, "My parents are still trying to control me!" Or, "My parents are always critical of me. They think I'm still a little kid."

This is an area that has great potential for misunderstanding as boundaries may be perceived as being encroached upon. However, if healthy self-disclosure has been taking place at the previous developmental stages, the groundwork has been laid for open, honest communication. Parents, don't be afraid to express your needs, speaking the truth in love, while at the same time acknowledging and affirming your adult child's need to be independent.

- Parent shares with young adult: "I really appreciated helping with your decorating ideas. It feels great to still be needed."
- Parents can also affirm the blessing of their young adults "giving" to their intimacy needs.
- Parent shares with young adult: "It really meant a lot to me last week when you called me, checking on the outcome of my important meeting! Thanks!"

These can be years of tremendous satisfaction and fulfillment as you watch your child spread his or her wings and fly like an eagle!

Reflect on these intimacy disclosures and consider which family members could benefit from receiving them. Write your thoughts here. (For instance: "I want to propose an area of common interest for Joni and me. Perhaps we can encourage each other in our exercise routine.")

____

____

Scripture Journaling—Isaiah 40:30-31

"Though youths grow weary and tired, and vigorous young men stumble badly, yet those who wait for the Lord will gain new strength; they will mount up with wings like eagles, they will run and not get tired, they will walk and not become weary."

Reflect on the Lord's promise of "new strength" at any time of life. As you have identified needed strength for yourself, your spouse, and your children, ask Him for it now. Write your thoughts below:

For myself, as spouse, parent, and Your child, I need

____

____

____

For my spouse, I ask for ______________________________

____

____

For my child ________, I ask for ______________________

____

____

For my child ________, I ask for ______________________

____

____

For my child ________, I ask for ______________________

____

____

(For instance: Lord, I need Your strength to share times of confession with my children. God, my children need Your strength to withstand the temptations of peer pressure.)

Now pause and thank Him by faith for His strength to each person, expressing your gratefulness that He attends to our needs. Write your prayer here:

____

____

____

Marriage Staff Meeting

Start with a discussion of Christ's progressive self-disclosure to His disciples. What was the purpose of this progression and how does it relate to "removing aloneness"? Apply this principle to Parenting with Intimacy and discuss how children can mature as they come to more deeply "know" their parents.

You'll want to continue this discussion on intimacy disclosures and developmental stages by focusing on your life and marriage. What needs for additional trust, autonomy, identity, etc. do you see in your life? Share these and then discuss how you could benefit from your spouse's intimacy disclosures from this stage. (For example: "To deepen trust, I could benefit from your initiative to check in on me during my day and maybe share gentle words and tender touch.") Pause and pray together asking the Lord to strengthen your mutual giving.

Now progress through each of the six stages highlighting needed intimacy disclosure from each parent to each child. Work together as you help one another complete the following material, i.e., reflecting on my disclosure to each child:

Child's Name

__________ could most benefit from my sharing of ________ (Write a sentence describing what this will "sound like" or "look like.")

____

____

__________ could most benefit from my sharing of ________ (Write a sentence describing what this will "sound like" or "look like.")

____

____

__________ could most benefit from my sharing of ________ (Write a sentence describing what this will "sound like" or "look like.")

____

____

(For instance: Tiffany could most benefit from my sharing of affirmation. I might say to her, "I'm proud of you for sharing with Haley.")

End with a time of prayer thanking God for each child and asking Him to prepare each one to receive your gift of yourself as you share your intimacy disclosures.

Top Ten Need of the Week—Respect

Respect—To value and regard highly; to convey great worth.

Respect is a key issue which frees your child to move through God's plan for maturity. Showing respect is critical to affirming worth, giving liberty, and encouraging autonomy. Look for opportunities this week to communicate respect.

- "Susan (knock on her bedroom door), may I come in?"
- "Johnny, we need to buy you some school clothes. What kind of clothes would you like?"
- "Where do you kids want to go on vacation?"
- "I realize you may need some time just by yourself tonight. If you need me, I'll be in the den."

Family Night Activity

Begin by reading John 15:15—*"No longer do I call you slaves; for the slave does not know what his master is doing; but I have called you friends, for all things that I have heard from My Father I have made known to you"*—noting the journey from servants to friends. Note that friendship involves disclosing oneself or "making things known."

Read the following passages of Scripture. These Scriptures are examples of Christ's increasing level of vulnerability. Next, look at the six disclosures. Match these disclosures with the appropriate Scripture example. For instance, which Scripture is an example of Christ communicating a belief? a positive emotion? a painful emotion? etc. As you rank the six disclosures, emphasize that Christ's sharing became deeper and deeper the longer He was with the disciples.

Instructions: Match one of the following disclosures with each of the verses. Write the appropriate disclosure in the blanks below. The six disclosures are—thought, belief, relational disclosure, observation, positive emotion, and painful emotion.

CHRONOLOGY	INCREASING VULNERABILITY	DISCLOSURES
Ministry Begins	*"And He found in the temple those who were selling oxen and sheep and doves, and the moneychangers seated."* —John 2:14	________
First Year of Ministry	*"And Jesus knowing their thoughts said, 'Why are you thinking evil in your hearts?'"*—Matthew 9:4	________
Second Year of Ministry	*"If anyone wishes to come after Me, let him deny himself, and take up his cross daily, and follow Me."*—Luke 9:23	________
	"At that very time He rejoiced greatly in the Holy Spirit, and said 'I praise Thee, O Father."—Luke 10:21	________
Third Year of Ministry	*"When Jesus therefore saw her weeping . . . He was deeply moved in spirit. . . . Jesus wept."*—John 11:33-35	________
Final Days	*"I have called you friends, for all things that I have heard from My Father I have made known to you"; "Simon, son of John, do you love Me?"*—John 15:15; 21:15	________

To apply the principle of progressive self-disclosure to family relationships play the Intimacy Ladder game. Take turns having each member answer each question beginning at the top of the ladder and then move "down" the ladder to the next question. Note this journey down the ladder is where families become and stay intimate friends.

INTIMACY LADDER

Begin at the Top

—each person shares a response

—then move down to the next question

—notice the deepened sharing

1. One observation I had today was that ______________________

2. A thought I had today was ______________________

3. A "belief" I consider very important is that ______________________

4. Recently, I found myself excited about ______________________

5. Recently, I found myself disappointed/sad about ______________________

6. I feel a great deal of love and appreciation for ______ (family member) because ______ (express gratitude)

Something to Think About

Here are some "conventional wisdom" sayings, along with corollary truths from the Bible. In your next Family Night, use these platitudes/Scriptures as a source of meaningful conversation. Share them one by one and then discuss the relevance of each of them with your family.

- Jesus can turn water into wine, but He can't turn your whining into anything. *"Do all things without grumbling or disputing"*—Philippians 2:14.

- A diamond is a chunk of coal that made good under pressure. *"Consider it all joy . . . when you encounter various trials, knowing that the testing of your faith produces endurance"* —James 1:2-3.

- What a big difference there is between giving advice and lending a hand. *"Little children, let us not love with word or with tongue but in deed and truth."*—1 John 3:18.

- Some people are always grumbling because roses have thorns; I am thankful that thorns have roses. *"Offer to God the sacrifice of thanksgiving"*—Psalm 50:14.

Group Discussion

1. Begin by discussing the connection between disclosure and aloneness. As you considered Christ's disclosures, what specific areas of aloneness were addressed? How does disclosure in this group setting eliminate aloneness? How do you see disclosure relieving aloneness in your family?
2. Look back over the stages of Developmental Assessment. What areas of development need to be strengthened in each child? Regardless of your child's age, do you see a need for developing trust, initiative, or motivation? For example, the teenager who finds it difficult to believe in or count on others is demonstrating a lack of trust. Share your observations and specific examples with the group. Parents will also likely find areas of development that need to be strengthened in their own lives.
3. Based on these observations, look carefully at the Disclosure Guidelines for this stage. How can your disclosure meet the identified need for each child? for your spouse? According to the Intimacy Disclosures Chart, if this teenage daughter lacks *trust,* she needs a parent who discloses acceptance, joy, and care. Strengthening an area that was missed may be a little tricky. Communicating the acceptance, care, and joy that was needed at eighteen months old may seem awkward as a child reaches eighteen years old. As a group, brainstorm together. How can we give age-appropriate disclosures that still meet the undernourished areas of development?
4. Discuss any areas of struggle that you encountered as a result of this material. Were there any particular areas of disclosure that were difficult? Discuss any blessings you received as you began to self-disclose. Were there any special moments of fulfillment?

CHAPTER 9

Revealing Care through Your Discipleship

CHILDREN ARE YOUR dearest *"disciples."* Paraphrasing a familiar Bible passage, *"what profit would it be if we gained the whole world"* . . . and lost our children? An alarming possibility but also a too common reality. In one of the largest research projects of church-attending youth ever undertaken, noted author and speaker Josh McDowell teamed up with researcher George Barna to conduct the extensive "Right from Wrong" campaign (McDowell, 1993). Over and over in issues such as lying, cheating, pornography, drugs, and premarital sex, parents were failing to pass on Bible-centered values to their children. The alarm was sounded for a multi-year campaign, enlisting thousands of churches and Christian ministries, and hundreds of thousands of parents to focus on one battle cry—Protect your child from being captured by the culture!

Protect your child from being captured by the culture!

Jesus Christ stands without comparison in countless ways—His virgin birth, sinless life, sacrificial death, and miraculous resurrection, just to name a few. But among the most practically relevant to parenting with intimacy is His uniqueness in propagating His message. Other so-called "religious leaders" might establish great schools or generate voluminous writings—but not Jesus! He simply trained disciples! He did not build great monuments, structures, or libraries—but transformed lives. This is still the secret of truly propagating the Gospel—as men and women become disciples of Christ and then are used by God to challenge others in discipleship. The essence of Christ's call to make disciples is found in this proverb: "I may impress people from a distance but I can only impact them up close!" Thus, parents are called to impart their very life to their children and, by doing so, impact them positively for Christ. This matter of true discipleship lies at the very heart of "success" in the Christian home. We merely "discipline" a child when we remove her from this larger framework of discipleship.

The Greek word for "disciple" simply means a "learner, one who is taught, a follower." It was Christ's goal that He impart His very life to His disciples. With this as His goal, He shared His conflicts, His joys, His prayer life, and His relationship with the Father. He thus became the "context" or setting for His own teaching. This is what discipleship is all about—as Paul shares with the Thessalonians—*"[imparting] not only the Gospel of God but also our own lives"*—1 Thessalonians 2:8.

What if fathers and mothers in "training up their children in the way they should go" saw as their priority the discipleship of their own children—modeling for them a life of Christlikeness and then spending the time and love necessary to see this Christlikeness reproduced in their children? After all, how difficult is it to lead a consistently Christlike life in front of someone you meet with once a week for an hour? In contrast, the challenge to live out your faith twenty-four-hours a day in front of your children is one guaranteed to keep your feet to the fire. This is the essence of parenting with intimacy!

Pause and reflect on how Christ propagated His message to a mere handful of disciples "up close." List some of the *methods* He used to impart His life to this few who, in turn, turned the world upside down. Write your list here: (For instance: He shared everyday life events with them; He shared His ideas, plans, and pain with them.)

____

____

____

____

Reflect on 2 Timothy 2:2—*"and the things which you have heard from me in the presence of many witnesses, these entrust to faithful men, who will be able to teach others also"* and in your own words write your thoughts on how this relates to parenting with intimacy.

____

____

____

Six Ingredients—Add just the right amount in just the right order!

It is toward this goal of Christlikeness that parents should view the issues of child discipline. Discipline is much more than correcting bad behavior. True discipline includes the six essential ingredients noted below, carefully shared by loving parents in just the right order. The process will model the Heavenly Father's plan that *"those whom the Lord loves He disciplines"*—Hebrews 12:6.

This ministry of unconditional love says, "I'm committed to doing whatever is in your best interest, whether you agree with me or not." Let's look at several key ingredients that build into this process of disciplining, i.e., the discipleship of your own children. After we consider each one, we'll take time to reflect on our parenting journey.

1. *Intimacy*—Establishing closeness is the fundamental ingredient in disciplining your child. Just as surely as bread without yeast will never rise, trying to discipline a child in an environment lacking intimacy will be disastrous. There must be a foundation of love and friendship and a proper balance of love and discipline. Remember the Heavenly Father's example: He provides intimate love first, then discipline.

It's quite possible that you may have been hurt and scarred because that balance was improper as you were growing up. In many homes, the philosophy of discipline goes something like this. "You *(mother)* give them the love; I'll *(father)* give them the discipline."

Wrong! Each parent must be involved in both love and discipline. The child must see that the same hand that disciplines him also loves and comforts him—just like the Heavenly Father.

When discipline is administered in an atmosphere in which there is no intimacy or too little intimacy, the child will often grow up to resent the discipline (and the discipliner) and a root of bitterness will begin to grow. The child can end up with a mind-set that says, "There is this stranger who seems to enter my life at the point when I'm doing something wrong and inflicts punishment on me, and I resent that." There's possibly no quicker way to "*provoke a child to wrath*" than to discipline without intimacy (Eph. 6:4).

Intimacy takes time. In contrast, you can quickly spank a child or send him to his room. Developing intimacy with your child requires an investment of time, but the yield on your investment will be higher than any interest-bearing account you could ever hope to open.

Reflect now on this ingredient in your children's discipleship. Which words would each child use to describe you? friend/stranger; close/distant; truly knows me/knows my problems.

Child	*Circle below how each might describe you:*		
________	Friend/Stranger	Close/Distant	Knows Me/ Knows My Problems
________	Friend/Stranger	Close/Distant	Knows Me/ Knows My Problems
________	Friend/Stranger	Close/Distant	Knows Me/ Knows My Problems
________	Friend/Stranger	Close/Distant	Knows Me/ Knows My Problems

Now write about what steps you could take to deepen intimacy with each child. Write about your reflections below: (For instance: "Lately, it seems to take a few hours for Timothy to warm up to me. My frequent business trips obviously affect our level of intimacy. I'll request trips that are in-state only.")

____

____

____

2. *Instruction*—Children need to be told what needs to be done. This too takes time. Parents need to sit down with their children and explain what they want them to do. Whenever possible, express your expectations in a positive form. For example, "Please take your clothes to the laundry room" will be more effective than "Quit leaving your clothes thrown everywhere!"

Also, don't expect them to read your mind. Rules and expectations must be clear and consistent. Help them understand the "big picture," that the goal is not just compliance on their part but helping them learn to be responsible for themselves. Focus on the positive. A special word of caution is warranted at this juncture. Be careful what expectations you convey to your children.

Parental messages to children can become painful prophecies if words and role modeling are not guarded carefully. Among these painful messages are these:

- *False or Impossible Goals*—"I must please everyone if I am to feel loved."
- *Denial of One's Basic Worth*—"I'm basically stupid (or unimportant), so why would anyone want anything to do with me?"
- *Faulty Values*—"Get to the top, regardless of who gets hurt in the process."

In addition, these statements are made by frustrated parents, "If you can't straighten yourself out, you're never going to amount to anything," or "Can't you do anything right?" It's eerie how often these prophetic statements come to fruition. Instead, instill confidence by saying things like, "Your mom and I know you can handle this." Reassure them that you'll be nearby if they need help, and that they can always come back to home plate for a visit with the umpires!

Reflect now on this ingredient in your children's discipleship. Which words would each child use to describe you: takes time to instruct/disciplines first, questions later; positive/critical; clear expectations/mind reading required; accepting/hard-to-please? Write about any changes you'd like to make: (For instance: I know Anna must think I'm on her case all the time. I'll give her short, positive instructions. I'll sound less critical and Anna will feel more success by completing more manageable tasks.)

____

____

____

3. *Training (in how to do it)*—All parents will agree (especially dads!) that the three most dreaded words on Christmas Eve are "Some Assembly Required." As you sit down with the box, you tip it upside down, dumping all 355 parts on the floor, and proceed to correctly put each piece in the proper place with no instructions—right? Hardly. Why, even with the instruction manual, it often requires several attempts before some semblance of victory can be claimed. Why, then, would we expect our children to know not only *what* they should do but *how* they should do it without help?

The best training is through your example! How you talk respectfully, how you help around the house, how you remain gentle when provoked. Many chores require hands-on training. For example, "Take out the trash" may sound simple to you but not to an eight-year-old. It often includes everything from: (1) find all the small trash containers hidden around the house; (2) empty them; (3) replace trash liners; (4) return trash containers to their previous locations. Show them how, then do it together, then turn them loose!

Why, then, would we expect our children to know not only what they should do but how they should do it without help?

Consider for a moment some of your common discipline/conflict issues with each child. As you consider each one, what "training" from you might be helpful—either better training through your improved example or "hands-on" training as you come alongside and show them how. Write your thoughts here: (For instance: "I need to show Alexis what I mean when I say, 'Please set the table.' That means: set out four placemats and napkins; put a fork and knife on each placemat, etc. We'll do it together two or three times, then I'll let her try on her own.")

____

____

____

4. *Warning* (the consequences): "You can ride your bike when your homework is finished." "You can borrow the car after the lawn is mowed." "We can keep playing with the blocks if you don't throw them." Be specific and positive. Have a repertoire of consequences that are age-appropriate and "fit the crime," keeping in mind that the consequences are always in the best interest of the child, not the parent. Giving warning before implementing consequences allows the child to grow up in a predictable, secure environment. When there's no warning, the home atmosphere is unpredictable and insecure, prompting anxiety and fear in the child.

   Some situations may be dealt with simply with *words* of correction and a call to accountability. At other times, you'll want to guide your child into seeing the natural and logical consequences of their actions. For example, "It's your choice whether you do your homework or not; but if you choose not to you must realize that you'll get a 'zero' on that assignment which will affect your grade in that class. And if you don't pass the class, you won't be able to play football" *(natural consequence).* Or, "If you choose not to do your chores, you won't be able to go out with your friends Saturday night" *(logical consequence).* Perhaps the most difficult (and humbling) of all consequences is having to make at least partial *restitution* for one's actions. For example, "If you wear your sister's nail polish again without her permission, you will have to buy her a new bottle with your allowance." We'll cover these and other "Methods of Correction" later in this chapter, but critical to this warning stage is to communicate the warning clearly, firmly but with gentleness, and then implement the consequences given as necessary. There's no second, third, or fourth chances: one warning, then consequences. Lack of parental follow-through helps contribute to *power struggles* between parent and child.

Reflect now on this ingredient in your children's discipleship. Which words would each child use to describe this ingredient in our home: clear warnings/unpredictable punishment; positive warnings/ negative threats; consistency/uncertainty; firm boundaries/walking on eggshells; secure respect/fearful anxiety? Write about any changes you'd like to see made. (For instance: "I need to stop making threats that I don't plan to carry out. When Britney acts up in McDonalds, I need to give her one positive warning. 'You can play on the playground as long as you get along with the other kids.' ")

____

____

____

Giving *positive* warnings can be a challenge. Review some of your children's typical "violations" and using the examples below as guidelines, write out examples of positive warnings.

Typical "Violations"	**Positively Worded Warning**
Damon throws his toys.	"You can keep playing with the toys if you don't throw them."
Eric doesn't make his bed.	"You can ride your bicycle after you make your bed."
____________	________________
____________	________________
____________	________________

5. *Correction (implement consequences)*—Correction (discipline) is based on what the child has been warned is going to happen. Correction is implemented with self-control and gentleness, without anger directed at the child. It's helpful to communicate sadness for the child's behavior as correction is given. The consequences are not capricious or arbitrary; they have already been well thought out, discussed, and agreed upon by Mom and Dad, and communicated to the child. No surprises. If you just start

pulling consequences out of the air for whatever seems to be the need of the moment, you'll end up with inconsistency, and sometimes irrationality if anger enters the picture. Then, feeling guilty for having overreacted, you won't follow through. This results, interestingly enough, in your child feeling insecure, living in an inconsistent environment in which he or she doesn't know what to expect next.

It's important to distinguish between discipline and punishment. The goal of discipline, or correction, is to help the child become responsible and to teach self-control as righteous living and convictions are internalized. The goal of punishment, on the other hand, is to extract retribution or inflict a penalty. It's possible to "punish" anyone who's smaller than you are. That's what empowers bullies to impose themselves on their victims. Discipline, however, has a much higher degree of accountability and purpose.

Review the chart contrasting discipline with punishment:

A Parenting Tip:
Discipline . . . Don't Punish

	DISCIPLINE	PUNISHMENT
Purpose	To train and mature	Retribution and penalty
Attitude	Parental concern with love	Parental frustration, hostility, or rejection
Emphasis	Future improved behavior and attitude	Past wrongs
Child's Emotional Response	Security and gratitude; Positive sense of worth	Anger, Condemnation, and Fear
Child's Concept of God	God loves and protects through discipline; He is available and worth knowing intimately	God seeks to punish and is therefore to be avoided

Reflect on your home environment and write about which elements of *true discipline* you see being lived out. Write your thoughts here:

___

___

___

You can only discipline someone you know, someone whose world you've entered for the purpose of developing an intimate relationship.

Write about any elements of punishment you see in your home and tell God what you'd like to see changed. (For instance: "God, I don't want to punish Kevin in anger. I know my frustration level is short these days, but I don't want to crush his spirit. Change my attitude and response.")

___

___

___

In summary, you can only discipline someone you know, someone whose world you've entered for the purpose of developing an intimate relationship. Proverbs 3:12 speaks powerfully to this: *"For whom the Lord loves He reproves, even as a father, the son in whom he delights."* Tell God about your "delight" in your child, expressing your gratefulness to Him. It's this delight that prompts us to truly know our children, and our gratefulness helps guard our hearts from punishing in anger freeing us to discipline with love. Write your prayer here:

___

___

___

___

It's now time for the final, but possibly most important, ingredient in your child's discipleship journey.

6. *Reassure*—Through touch, words, hugs, and other expressions of love, communicate acceptance and worth and give affection, affirmation, and encouragement. What you're communicating to the child at this point is, "I'm displeased with your behavior, but I'm separating your behavior from your worth as a person. I am committed to you and love you unconditionally. There's nothing you could ever *do* that would make me stop loving you." (It's this unconditional love which separates worth from behavior and role models the Heavenly Father's declaration of our worth to Him—*"Christ died for us,"* in spite of our behavior—*"while we were yet sinners"*—Rom. 5:8.)

It's right here in their journey that parents can give children the security of knowing that no matter what they *do* their parents will always love them. . . . And, as they filter their concept of God, their Heavenly Father, through the lens of how they see their earthly parents, the groundwork has been laid for them to live life resting securely in the arms of a God who loves them with a love that is perfect and complete. It is this "perfect love" that casts out fear (1 John 4:18-19). Do not minimize the impact of this step of reassurance. Your child will reap what you sow—now, and for generations to come.

Pause and consider how it is you give reassurance with affection, affirmation, and encouragement—after you discipline. Write about any needed changes below: (For instance: "I need to give reassurance to Melanie. She knows that lying about below her weekend plans was wrong, but I never reassured her of my love. I need to initiate a hug and an evening bike ride together.")

____

____

____

____

____

What If I've "Blown It"?—Beginning Over

There's no such thing as "perfect" parents or perfect children—so we've all "blown it"! The crucial issue is, how have I addressed my mistakes? Many a child's spirit has been wounded and remains closed to parents because hurts have gone unhealed. Parents must take the initiative in confession and requesting forgiveness. Parents should initiate dialogue over needed changes as the family system grows together.

Review the chart on common discipline mistakes and plan for any needed time of confession.

COMMON DISCIPLINE MISTAKES

"provoke not children to wrath"—Ephesians 6:4

Little Intimacy—being corrected by a parent who is basically a "stranger" to the child.

Negative Instruction—overattention to "don't," "stop," "quit," excessive rules, and much criticism.

Poor Training—do as I say and not as I do! Being a hypocritical example or neglecting to spend time training.

No Warning—rash "eruptions" and arbitrary discipline provokes insecurity and anger in the child.

Excessive Warning—too many warnings trains your child *not* to obey and undermines authority.

Correcting in Anger—wounds the child as he/she feels personally rejected by a parent's anger.

After reviewing your responses in this section and the common discipline mistakes, note below any needed confessions to your children:

Child	*Need Confession Concerning Discipline*

(For instance: "I need to apologize for yelling at Christopher. I was wrong to yell. I was also wrong to punish him for saying words that I use myself.")

Now that we've addressed some of the major ingredients in our children's discipleship, let's look in more detail at the following chart.

Common Methods of Child Correction

Communication—*"Speak the truth in love"* and decisively communicate rules, warnings, and consequences regardless of what other method of correction you may employ. Ultimately, as the child grows up, your hope and goal will be that he responds to your *words*—with no other consequences necessary.

"I would like you to clean your room today. That includes putting your clothes away, making your bed, and putting away your toys."

(After warning) "We'll need to put the blocks away since you threw another one of them."

Positive Reinforcement—*"Train up a child in the way he should go"* —Proverbs 22:6.

Put more emphasis on what your child does *right.* Reinforce good behavior with affirming words that are communicated both privately and publicly. Incorporate special rewards like fun activities, treats, and privileges.

Ignoring—*"Don't sweat the small stuff."*

This is sometimes called "extinction"—leave it alone and it will go away. Ignoring a behavior means giving no negative consequence for the poor behavior. You can't ignore some things but you can ignore many things!

"No clown will perform without an audience."

For example, often ignore whining, complaining, pleading, acting younger than one's age, arguing, making faces, etc. Say, "I will be able to listen to you when you're finished whining, complaining, etc."

Natural Consequences—*"Let nature take its course."*

Let the law of the harvest bring the consequences. *"Whatsoever a man sows, that he will also reap."*

Keep a toddler safe but "back off" occasionally and let him bump his head rather than always saying "no." He'll soon learn not to raise up while under a coffee table!

"Remember, if you don't turn that assignment in correctly, your grade will be affected. If you don't pass the class, you won't be able to play football."

"Tomorrow is Saturday and you open the store. If you stay out too late again tonight, you may oversleep in the morning and be late for work." (The boss calls Saturday morning and wakes them up with a frantic telephone call—the law of the harvest at work!)

Logical Consequences—Learn to "pair" daily responsibilities with a child's enjoyable activities. The child becomes in control of "if" or "when" he gets to participate:

"You can go out with your friends tonight after the lawn is mowed."
"After you make your bed you can play ball."
Other examples include:
Time-out—a "dull place" like the dining room corner would be appropriate; the child must be quiet, not playing, etc. (If these rules are violated the period of time-out is extended.)

Pay the Piper—bad behavior "costs" the children
"We'll need to put this toy away if you hit your sister with it."

Restitution—payback for inappropriate behavior
"If you use your sister's fingernail polish without asking, you'll have to use your own money to buy her more."

Spanking—should be reserved as a rare consequence for absolute defiant behavior in children under eight or nine years old.

The Scriptures warn us not to spare the rod, but remember, the shepherd used the rod primarily as a tool of leadership, direction, stability, and safety.

After reviewing these five general methods of correction, consider each child and ask yourself "what seems" to work and "what doesn't seem" to work. Write your reflections here:

Child	*Correction Method That Seems to Work Best*	*Correction Method That Seems Not to Work*
________	________	________
________	________	________
________	________	________
________	________	________
For instance: Matthew	Logical Consequences—He makes the connection between choices and consequences.	Ignoring—His frustration increases if I ignore him.

It's not uncommon to find that different children respond differently to each method of correction—it's part of their uniqueness! Now consider each child and your most common correction methods. What new methods of correction might each of your children benefit from?

Child	*New Correction Method to Be Tried*
________	________
________	________
________	________
________	________
For instance: Andrea	Restitution—If she borrows my clothes and does not return them in good condition, she pays for the dry cleaning with her allowance.

Dynamic Parenting—Understanding Your Child's Developmental Priorities

Time sure doesn't stand still and neither will your child's development. About the time you think you have your child figured out, she enters a new "phase" and wakes up a different person. If you have more than one child, you have discovered that what works with one child may or may not work with another! On top of all this, your child doesn't seem to fit the parenting books you read or respond like everyone says he/she should. Such is the parenting dilemma! But before you lose hope consider the issue of Dynamic Parenting—changing as your child changes.

Tremendous confusion can be eliminated as "Dynamic" parents come to view their child's journey through the grid of developmental priorities (see figure on p. 230). These five priorities portray a simple framework within which parents can focus their parenting activities and not be terrorized by every "urgent" demand.

These five priority areas can serve as the basis for parenting discussions at Marriage Staff Meetings and Family Nights. Specific goals can be developed for each child consistent with the child's age and the corresponding developmental priority.

If there's doubt concerning the importance of these five seemingly "simple" priorities, just look around and observe countless teenagers who lack "compliant behavior" and functioning adults who lack positive attitudes and daily responsibility.

DYNAMIC PARENTING: *Understanding Your Child's Developmental Priorities*

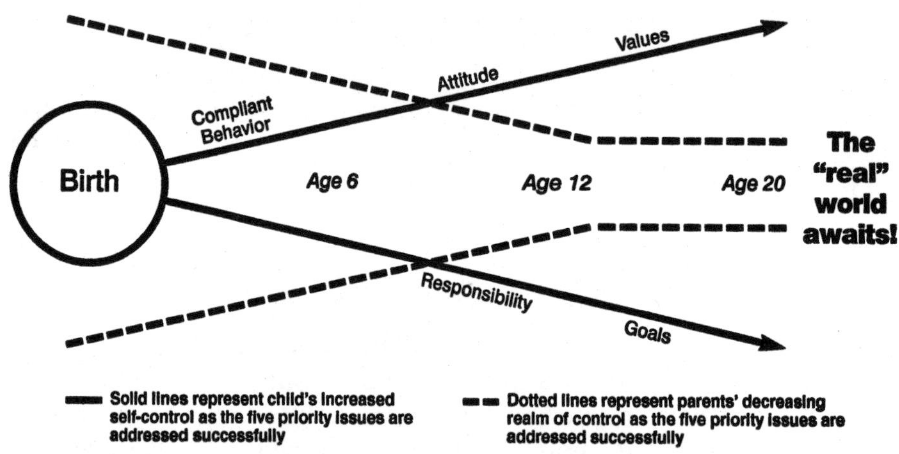

Preschool Age Compliant Behavior

Preschool Age—*Compliant Behavior*

One simple focus is addressed during this developmental phase and that is compliant behavior . . . doing that which is required/requested. *"Children, obey your parents"*—Ephesians 6:1. In an atmosphere of loving closeness, the child's "will" is shaped through consistent discipline from gentle and supportive parents.

A significant challenge is for parents to respond in firm but gentle ways to inevitable "wrath" from a child who is developing his or her own self-will (Prov. 15:1).

Goal: By age six, when the child is asked to do something—they do it! Pause and reflect on this goal for each child. Comment on your gratefulness or any needed attention in this area.

Child	*Compliant Behavior: Gratefulness or Needed Attention*
________	______________________________
________	______________________________
________	______________________________
________	______________________________
________	______________________________

School Age—*Attitude—Responsibility*

Now our priority becomes compliant behavior with a good attitude and responsibility. A child, for example, might complete his/her daily hygiene "routine" with a good attitude and at his/her own initiative . . . without having to be told!

Attitude development is stimulated as appreciation is given to inner character strengths rather than simply good grades or accomplished athletics.

Responsibility is fostered through parental example, positive reinforcement, and "backing off" to let a child experience the natural consequences of irresponsibility.

Goal: By age twelve, the child is carrying out daily responsibilities and requests with a good attitude, without having to be reminded. Comment on your gratefulness or any needed attention in this area.

Child	*Attitude/Responsibility: Gratefulness or Needed Attention*
________	______________________________
________	______________________________
________	______________________________
________	______________________________
________	______________________________

Adolescent Age—*Values—Goals*

During the teenage years, a young person should begin internalizing a set of values, beliefs, and convictions that will guide his/her life journey. Believing something just because parents do won't prepare them for life. Critical to this goal are parental discussions on healing inevitable family hurts.

A teenager should begin to dream his or her own dreams, develop and fulfill progressively challenging goals, and establish a sense of life vision and purpose.

Similarly, a teenager should begin to dream his or her own dreams, develop and fulfill progressively challenging goals, and establish a sense of life vision and purpose.

These objectives are encouraged by honest parental role modeling and vulnerable communication with much listening. The adolescent senses that he/she is able to question and try for themselves . . . without fear of rejection.

Goal: By age eighteen, family hurts are healed, biblical values internalized, and Spirit-led goals are in progress. Comment on your gratefulness or any needed attention in this area.

Child	*Values/Goals: Gratefulness or Needed Attention*
____________	____
____________	____
____________	____
____________	____

Important Reminders on "Why Children Misbehave" Needs beneath the Deeds

Your child needs your investment of time in trying to discern the reasons behind their misbehavior. It's very easy to walk in on a child, see him behaving incorrectly, and discipline him based only on what appears on the surface. That seldom tells the story, however. Realizing that your time's in short supply, we must implore you once again, however, to spend it wisely. No other pull on your time could be of greater importance than trying to discern the need beneath your child's deed. It is best to look beyond the misbehavior and try to understand what he is feeling. With an understanding of the feelings which led to misbehavior, you'll be able to guide and discipline him in the most effective and appropriate way.

God is concerned both about our wrong behaviors *and* our intimacy needs. Remember Adam's dilemma in Genesis 2 and 3 from chapter 2. God certainly addressed His sinful behavior (Gen. 3:17-24), and as parents so should we with our children! Additionally, however, God was concerned about Adam's "needs" (Gen. 2:18) and so should we with our children!

God has entrusted us with the care of His children. We have the opportunity to develop intimate relationships with children by meeting their God-given intimacy needs. As parents and other adults begin to focus upon meeting intimacy needs, many behavior problems can be prevented and many others quickly solved. Children need adults who are willing to see young people as having needs—not problems. Teenagers need adults who are committed to looking beyond behavior to unmet intimacy needs. Remember Christ's ministry to Zaccheus and the key message from a popular hymn: *"He looked beyond my faults and saw my needs."*

An Intimacy Plan for Resolving Misbehavior

By focusing on intimacy needs, adults can more quickly resolve misbehaviors and defuse potentially damaging situations. The steps for resolving misbehaviors by integrating intimacy principles are:

A. Identify the behavior.
As adults, we rarely have difficulty identifying unacceptable behavior. This is the easy part. But it is important to name the specific behavior—separate from the character of the child or teen. Identifying behavior means giving the behavior a label—not the child (lying, cheating, sneaking out of the house, etc. —not liar, cheater, deceiver).

B. Become aware of the relationships that surround the behavior.
Sensitivity about the relationships that surround behavior will give you insight into a child's point of need. Step inside the

child's "skin" and see the situation from his eyes, ears, and heart. Consider the relationship between the adults who care for the child, beginning with *your* relationship—what impact might these relationships be having on the child? It is important to notice whether misbehavior occurs in public or in private settings. Consider if the teenager is around parents, friends, or authority figures. Identify any promises that have been made or schedules that have been altered. Also, consider issues that represent the relationship the child has with himself/herself. Does the misbehavior have anything to do with grades, school performance, sports, the opposite sex?

C. Identify the feelings.

After acknowledging and paying close attention to the relationships that surround a behavior, identify how the child might be feeling. Is this child feeling disappointed? afraid? embarrassed? Does this teenager feel insecure? alone? hurt? A loving adult will be careful not to misinterpret a child's behavior or let the behavior overshadow a child's true feelings. A teenager who slams the bedroom door in anger may be hiding the disappointment he feels over an unkept promise. One of the most important ministries we can have in the life of our children is to discern feelings which then help us identify need.

D. Identify unmet needs.

A child's unmet intimacy needs will push her toward a wide range of misbehaviors. The youngest child knows instinctively when needs have gone unfulfilled. The drive to look for substitute fulfillment is just as instinctive. When children sense a lack of attention, they turn to attention-getting misbehavior. Since it is awful to feel insecure and out of control, children resort to aggressive or stubborn behaviors in order to reestablish some sense of security. When teenagers sense a lack of acceptance from the important adults in their lives,

When teenagers sense a lack of acceptance from the important adults in their lives, many find substitute fulfillment in peer relationships that result in unwanted pregnancy, chemical abuse, and criminal activity.

many find substitute fulfillment in peer relationships that result in unwanted pregnancy, chemical abuse, and criminal activity.

E. Find ways to meet the need.
God has put us in positions to meet the intimacy needs of children. It is our responsibility and our privilege as the adults in their lives. Meeting a child's need may be something as simple as acknowledging their feelings and then verbalizing support. Meeting the need for respect may come in the form of an apology. Communicating appreciation to a child might involve sending a card that says thank you for their kindness toward a sibling. Meeting the need for security may require readjusting circumstances so that the teenager knows no one is going to make fun of him.

F. Remind child of needing intimacy with God.
After all intimacy needs are met in the child's life on a "horizontal" level through God's gift of Mom and Dad, etc.—it will never be enough! The child personally will be challenged to live on a "vertical" level intimately with our Creator through His Son Jesus (Prov. 3:32). In fact, Dad and Mom's love and focus on giving to the child's needs are reminders and encouragements in this world of the child's need for an eternal relationship and a life empowered by the Holy Spirit.

Stop and review these six steps, being reminded that you "know" He loves you because He abundantly met your needs! Write about needs God has met in your life as evidence of His love. Write about them here: (For instance: "God meets my need for acceptance and forgiveness on a continual basis. Because He loves me, He looks past my deeds.")

____

____

____

____

____

Pause now to ask God to equip your heart to live out a role model of "those whom the Lord loves, He disciplines." Write your prayer here: (For instance: "God, give me a heart that sees needs as well as deeds. I want to *know* my children *as* I discipline.")

____

____

____

____

An Intimacy Plan for Avoiding Misbehaviors

By becoming aware of and remaining sensitive to a child's intimacy needs, adults can help prevent potential problems. An adult who is interested in an intimate relationship with a child will look ahead at situations and circumstances and how those might affect a child. Following these same steps will not only help prevent misbehavior, but you will find that the adult-child relationship will be enhanced and/or restored.

A. Stay aware of the relationships that surround the child.
Caring adults will want to be sensitive to a young person's relationships in order to maintain the intimacy between adult and child. Pay close attention to divorce, separation, or deaths that may affect a child. Adjusting to a new teacher, a best friend moving, or a conflicting relationship with a coach are all examples of relationship issues that will have some effect on children and teens.

B. Identify the feelings that might be produced.
Feelings are God-given, spontaneous, continual "thermometers" that tell us when something about our world is dangerous, painful, or pleasant. Relating to a child or teenager in an intimate way means addressing their feelings. Identifying what a child might be feeling does not mean identifying what you think they should be feeling or what an adult would be feeling in the same situation. Give the child permission to feel their own feelings.

C. Identify the needs that may occur.

Relating to a child or teenager in an intimate way means focusing on needs. Identifying what a child might be needing requires an adult who is willing to invest time, energy, and insight.

For example, if you know a child will be going into a new situation, identify what they might be *feeling* and *needing*.

"I know going into a new Sunday School class might be *scary* for you, but I want you to know that Miss Lancaster is a friend of mine and she will know how important it is for you to feel *safe*."

D. Plan ways to meet the needs so they don't go unmet.

Needs that go unmet produce negative feelings and behaviors, but needs that are met produce positive feelings and behaviors.

"I know going into a new Sunday School class might be scary for you, but I want you to know that Miss Lancaster is a friend of mine and she will know how important it is for you to feel safe. I will be just in the next building and I will be back to see you right after you have snack time. How does that sound?"

Comments like these acknowledge a child's feelings of apprehension and meet the need of security. This child will know that it is OK to feel afraid in this situation but that Mom understands the need and is not far away. This child has a meaningful time frame (after snack time) in which to plan for Mom's return.

Pause and consider what challenges your children might be facing that could benefit from ministry to "needs behind the deeds." Write your thoughts below and make note of how you might minister to needs:

Child	*How You Might Minister to Needs*
________	______________________________
________	______________________________
________	______________________________
________	______________________________

For instance: Nicole	Nicole's best friend got transferred out of her class. She might be feeling sad and scared. She might be needing reassurance and comfort. I can empathize with her sadness. Having lunch with her a couple of days may reassure her that school is a safe place to be.

The Appendix worksheet on "Needs beneath the Deeds" can be a helpful tool in devising your Parenting with Intimacy plan.

Healing a Wounded Heart— Resolving Hurt and Anger

Sometimes children feel so discouraged and hurt that they doubt that others love them. When this happens, they may hurt others as they feel they have been hurt. Parents should be aware that they aren't necessarily the "cause" of this kind of behavior . . . the hurt may have come from a friend or classmate. But home is often the safest place to vent the hurt.

The Appendix material on "Emotional Capacity" highlights how unresolved emotional pain can accumulate to the point that we see symptomatic behaviors like temper outbursts, escaping into other relationships, addictions, etc. (See Appendix, p. 362.)

The figure on page 239 gives the "Top 10 Signs of a Parent-Child Power Struggle." You'll want to review it as you give attention to eliminating such struggles and healing wounded hearts. If it is suspected that there is unresolved hurt/anger toward the parent it will be important to "heal" this hurt through sharing, understanding, empathizing, and oftentimes confession and forgiveness. (See Appendix, p. 366 on Healing Family Emotional Hurts.) If the hurt/anger is related to someone else, but is being dumped or "displaced" on the parent, the parent needs to respond with calm reassurance and avoid "personalizing" the hurtful words. After reassuring empathy has prompted calmness, discussion of the "real" hurt can be undertaken. (See Appendix, p. 368 on Emotional Responding.) Later, instructing and training the child in "sharing the truth in love" (Eph. 4:15) may be helpful in reducing "displaced" anger. (See Appendix, "Speaking Words that Edify," p. 369.)

Top 10 Signs of a Parent-Child Power Struggle

1. Your throat is sore at the end of the day from yelling.
2. Your most frequent form of discipline is spanking.
3. Attempting to enforce strict rules in virtually all normal day-to-day routines.
4. You tend to be more critical than complimentary.
5. You lack humor in your relationship with your child.
6. You offer little or no nurture in the way of physical contact. When you do offer affection and the child does not respond the way you expect, you become enraged.
7. When you discipline your child for disobedience you feel that it is "never enough." You are unable to clear the slate emotionally.
8. You have great difficulty confessing your own faults to your child. Letting your child see your faults may actually bring on a power struggle.
9. You feel that your child has the power to inflame your anger with the slightest of body language (eyes, shoulder, arm, feet movements, voice inflections, etc.).
10. You find yourself using shaming words about your child on a regular basis. (You always . . . You never . . . calling them stupid, idiot, good-for-nothing, Your brother never does that.)

Pause and review this list for any signs you see with any of your children. Make note of your reflections for each child below:

Child	*Power Struggle Signs*
__________	______________________________
__________	______________________________
__________	______________________________
__________	______________________________
For instance: Tracey	When she rolls her eyes and shrugs her shoulders, I can feel my blood pressure rise.

Now, write a prayer to "Abba" Father, asking Him to do everything He needs to do in you to bring freedom and liberty in your parenting. Write your prayer here:

____

____

____

____

Who do I see displaying symptoms of unresolved pain?

Second, although parents don't cause children to misbehave, problems can become worse if parents don't seek to understand their child's needs and feelings and respond as *adults!* As parents respond to the needs of a child, they role model Christ's love and point the child toward the "God who supplies all your needs" (Phil. 4:19)—preparing them to one day consider the eternal significance of needing to relate intimately to their Creator through His Son Jesus Christ.

Consider any "Wounded Hearts" in your family. First, who do I see displaying symptoms of unresolved pain? (See Appendix, p. 362 on Emotional Capacity.)

Name	*Symptoms*
________	________________________________
________	________________________________
________	________________________________
________	________________________________
For instance: Brandon	I sometimes wonder if Brandon's perfectionism and self-criticism are a result of hurts in his life.

Third, who do I need to apologize to for ways in which I have hurt them—allowing God to help us "put away anger—forgiving one another"? (Refer to Appendix on Healing Family Emotional Hurts, p. 366 for steps of healing.) Write your thoughts on the following page:

Name	*Wrongs I've Committed That Need My Confession*
____________	____
____________	____
____________	____
____________	____
For instance: Brandon	I need to ask Brandon's forgiveness for not paying enough attention to him. I need to tell him that it's not good grades or good track meets that make him important. He's important because he's my son.

Fourth, who in our family is hurting, down, and disappointed concerning events outside our family—but needs the comfort of my emotional responding?

"Rejoice with those who rejoice, and weep with those who weep" —Romans 12:15.

Write your thoughts and words you could share. (Refer to Appendix, p. 368 on Emotional Responding.)

Name	*Pain and Pressures from outside Our Family*
____________	____
____________	____
____________	____
____________	____
For instance: Brandon	I know you might feel discouraged and disappointed after the track meet. I want you to know that I love you and that it makes me sad to see you upset.

Finally, consider this promise and its application to you, your spouse, and your family.

Scripture Journaling

"Walk by the Spirit, and you will not carry out the desire of the flesh" —Galatians 5:16.

Reflect on the certainty of this promise and then consider who in your family needs prayer and encouragement in establishing and maintaining an intimate walk with Jesus Christ. Write a short prayer for each here:

Name	*Prayer for Intimacy with God*
___________	___________________________________
___________	___________________________________
___________	___________________________________
___________	___________________________________
___________	___________________________________

Marriage Staff Meeting

Begin your time with a discussion on how Christ's methods of discipleship might apply to your parenting. Describe His method of sharing His life "up close" with His disciples and then reflect on the six discipline ingredients: (1) intimacy, (2) instruction, (3) training, (4) warning, (5) correction, and (6) reassurance. Review the Common Discipline Mistakes and then share what changes would be helpful in your parenting (be specific with each child). "Jennifer needs more time with me to build intimacy. All the kids need warning and not my overreacting.")

Discuss the list of Common Methods of Child Correction and which new ones you might consider trying. Next, take time to help one another with positively worded warnings which could be helpful with each child. Review the material on Dynamic Parenting and highlight your areas of gratefulness and needed attention for each child.

Top Ten Need of the Week—Support

Support—Coming alongside and gently helping carry a burden.

Look for opportunities this week to show support. Ask family members how you can be of help. Offer your assistance, communicate your interest, then get involved.

- "Travis, I know your science fair project is due next Monday. I've reserved all day Saturday to help you finish it."

- "Janie, you'll be going to college next year. Why don't we start writing for information about various colleges? Let's do it together."

- "Mark, I know you're tired. Why don't you go on to bed? I'll finish cleaning the garage."

- "Let me know what needs to be done, and I'll help you."

Family Night Activity

Building Security through "Belonging"
Psalm 122:6 says, *"May they prosper who love You."* Make it a priority to provide security to each of your children. A child feels secure when he knows he belongs. Let your son or daughter know that he or she is an important part of your family. Here are some practical ideas:

- Make a special place for family photos and display individual as well as family snapshots.
- Take your children with you to the office one afternoon and show them the family mementos on your desk.
- Carve someone's initials on a tree in the backyard as a reminder of the family who lives there.
- Take turns fixing favorite meals—every family member gets to choose the dinner menu for Sunday nights.
- Encourage all family members to attend events that are important to individuals. It communicates a message of security when all siblings attend the grade schooler's choir performance—not just the parents.

Review together as a family the Top 10 Discipline Tips and have each family member pick one they'd like to see "more" of in your family.

Top 10 Discipline Tips

1. **Be Decisive.** Children's radar picks up the maybe in the no! State it assertively and decisively.
   "I would like you to clean your room tonight. That includes putting your clothes away, making your bed, and putting away your toys where they belong."
2. **Be Positive.** Direct attention away from what your child doesn't want to do, to what he does want to do.
   "As soon as you get out of the tub and brush your teeth we can read a story."
3. **Explain Yourself.** This promotes the child's reasoning skills. "Hold the knife carefully, cutting away from you, or you'll cut yourself."
4. **Make Rules Impersonal.** Make the conflict between child and rule instead of child and you.
   Change—"I don't want you to drink grape juice in the living room."
   To—"The rule is: food and drink in the kitchen only, please."
5. **Be Brief and Clear.** When disciplining a child it is not a time to give them a sermon on why you have come up with this philosophy on cleanliness, or table manners.
6. **Offer a Choice—Whenever Possible.**
   "You need to have your room picked up before you go to bed tonight. Do you want to do it now or after dinner?"
7. **Reward Good Behavior.** Give praise, prizes, and hugs for being "caught" doing good! Ask the child for ideas. This is an excellent way to prove you are interested and really listen.
8. **Know When Not to Get Involved.** This will be different for each family, but often it will include school issues and sibling issues. Let a child work out a conflict at school on his own, or resolve a conflict with a sibling without your help.
9. **Work Together.** The effective parent does not say, "Get going," but instead he says, "Let's go."
   a. State the problem areas.
   b. Ask for suggestions.
   c. Come up with a workable approach.
10. **Pick Your Battles.** Adjusting expectations may increase cooperation.
    a. Choose your issues. "Do I really want to set a limit here? Is it important for the child's growth or is it just a personal preference of mine that can be negotiated?"
    b. Is this request age-appropriate? (i.e., "Is it reasonable to ask a six-year-old to stop asking questions, or to ask a two-year-old to not request snacks between meals?")

Group Discussion

1. Take a look at the six ingredients for discipline. Which ingredient needs your attention—intimacy, instruction, training, warning, correction, or reassurance? Which of these ingredients seems to be lacking? What changes do you plan to make? What insights did you gain?
2. Think about your own parents' perspective on discipline. How might you be repeating their behaviors? How might you be reacting against your parents' methods? Discuss any feelings associated with these questions. Allow the group and/or your spouse to comfort any hurts.
3. What is the most challenging discipline issue you face right now? Share this struggle with the group and how you feel about the struggle. Be careful not to turn this into an advice-giving session. Share empathy with one another. Acknowledge one another's feelings and communicate your concern. Reassure one another that God gives generous amounts of wisdom to those who ask. End the discussion by praying for each parent and the wisdom needed for each child.

CHAPTER 10

Revealing Truth through Your Testimony

This is what was spoken of through the Prophet Joel—Acts 2:16.

WITH THESE FEW words the Apostle Peter addressed the crowd's question: "What do these things mean?" Jerusalem was filled on this day as it was every Jewish holiday with a huge international crowd—residents of Mesopotamia, Judea, Cappadocia, Pontus, Asia, Egypt, Libya, Cyrene, visitors from Rome, Cretans and Arabs (Acts 2:9-12).

But on this festive Day of Pentecost had come unusual events which startled the multitudes:

- a noise like a violent, rushing wind
- tongues of fire distributing themselves (upon the disciples)
- a filling with the Holy Spirit and speaking with other languages as the Spirit was giving utterance.

As the huge international crowd gathered, there was *"amazement and great perplexity . . . while others mocked"*—Acts 2:12-13. And then Peter stood to address their questioning.

"Men of Judea, and all you who live in Jerusalem, let this be known to you, and give heed to my words"—this is that which was written.

Peter's response is inspired, profound, and timeless—

this which you are seeing and experiencing is simply—
that which is written about in God's Word.

The people's response is in a similar way miraculous:

- so then those who had received the word were baptized and there were added that day about 3,000
- and everyone kept feeling a sense of awe and many wonders and signs were taking place
- and all those who had believed were together and had all things in common—Acts 2:41-43.

Maybe one of the most significant impact a parent can make is this profound testimony to a child: *"This* which you are seeing and experiencing in our home is *that* which is written about in this book . . . called the Bible." It's possible that this concept of *"truth being confirmed by two or more witnesses"* is a powerful missing ingredient today in families, homes, and even churches. Consider the following, for example:

"This which you are seeing and experiencing in our home is that which is written about in this book . . . called the Bible."

- Notice that it was *truth being experienced* that stirred hearts in Jerusalem.
- Peter and the disciples were then able to point them to the Scriptures and the Christ of the Scriptures.
- Could it be that our children need to see and *experience biblical truth* so that their hearts are stirred to ask, "What do these things mean?"
- Parents can then point them to the Scriptures and the Christ of the Scriptures.

It's possible the author had this in mind as he penned the poem that follows:

Sermons We See

A Special Encouragement to Parents

I'd rather see a sermon than hear one any day;
I'd rather one should walk with me than merely tell the way.
The eye's a better pupil and more willing than the ear,
Fine counsel is confusing, but example's always clear;
And the best of all the preachers are the men who live their creeds,
For to see God put in action is what everybody needs.

I soon can learn to do it if you'll let me see it done;
I can watch your hands in action, but your tongue too fast may run.
And the lecture you deliver may be very wise and true,
But I'd rather get my lessons by observing what you do.
For I might misunderstand you and the high advice you give,
But there's no misunderstanding how you act and how you live.

When I see a deed of kindness, I am eager to be kind.
When a weaker brother stumbles and a strong man stays behind
Just to see if he can help him, then the wish grows strong in me,
To become as big and thoughtful as I know that friend to be.
And all the travelers can witness that the best of guides today
Is not the one who tells them, but the one who shows the way.

One good man teaches many, men believe what they behold;
One deed of kindness noticed is worth forty that are told.
He who stands with men of honor learns to hold his honor dear,
For right living speaks a language which to everyone is clear.
Though an able speaker charms me with his eloquence, I say,

I'd rather see a sermon than to hear one, any day.

Author Unknown

Pause and reflect on this principle of *first* living or experiencing biblical truth and that this then prompts an openness and hunger for others (like children) to want to know the truth and the God of all truth. Write in your own words how this might relate to you and your children. Write your thoughts here. (For instance: "I've never realized that my behavior as an adult could be a tool that God might use to draw my children to Christ.")

A Parent's Testimony of Grace

Possibly no other word captures the essence of this parental testimony of biblical truth than the word "grace." Parents are to be a "living epistle" of divine grace—children being born into this world, fallen and in sin, but encountering in their parents living testimonies of divine grace, *not of this world.* It's in this contrast of environments that children come to ask, "What do these things mean?" having had their hearts prepared to be called out of darkness into His marvelous light (1 Peter 2:9).

Thus far we've defined intimacy as, "genuinely knowing another person, allowing them to know us in a similar way, and becoming caringly involved in one another's lives."

Additionally, we have identified various "intimacy needs" such as acceptance, attention, affection, appreciation, and comfort. Still there's a "power" outside ourselves that must enable the real experiencing of intimacy. The complexity and overwhelming "neediness" of our human condition means that relationships tend to move toward deterioration.

Our only hope is outside ourselves in this "closed system" of humanism. An unlimited source of love, acceptance, comfort, and forgiveness is needed to enable and sustain any intimate relationship. Such a source is available, and His name is Jesus. The Bible calls this divine contribution . . . grace!

Consider each of the Scriptures noted below and in your own words write about insights you gain into some of the characteristics of grace.

"And God is able to make all grace *abound to you, that always having all sufficiency in everything, you may have an abundance for every good deed"* —2 Corinthians 9:8.

Insights about grace: ______________________________

____

____

"Now may our Lord Jesus Christ Himself and God our Father, who has loved us and given us eternal comfort and good hope by grace, *comfort and strengthen your hearts in every good work and word"*
—2 Thessalonians 2:16-17.

Insights about grace: ______________________________

____

____

"Let us therefore draw near with confidence to the throne of grace, *that we may receive mercy and may find* grace *to help in time of need"*
—Hebrews 4:16.

Insights about grace: ______________________________

____

____

"God resists the proud but He gives grace *to the humble"*—James 4:16.

Insights about grace: ______________________________

____

____

Share a prayer of gratefulness concerning how God has blessed you with His grace. Write a short prayer of gratitude here:

____

____

____

Now consider 1 Peter 4:10 and its implications for parents being good stewards of divine grace toward their children. *"As each one has received a special gift, employ it in serving one another* as good stewards of the manifold grace of God."

Write about this stewardship responsibility in your own words. (For instance: "I realize that because of God's grace, I have strength, hope, confidence, and comfort. Because of God's grace, I have an abundance of these things. Since I have this 'surplus,' I am able to give my children strength, hope, confidence, and comfort.")

I realize that because of God's grace, I have strength, hope, confidence, and comfort.

____

____

____

____

Finally, consider a parent's role as a testimony or example of grace and write in your own words how you might practically live out an example of divine grace with each of your children.

Child	*My Testimony of Grace*
_______	_______________
_______	_______________
_______	_______________
_______	_______________
For instance: Kate	God has taken initiative to give to me. He moved first. I can make the first move toward Kate. She needs to experience grace after our conflict over curfew.
Or: Nathan	God says that He gives grace to the humble. I can demonstrate humility and grace as I apologize to Nathan.

In order to further explore the possibilities of a parental testimony of grace, we'll consider three significant aspects of this divine gift—the *initiative* of grace, the *liberty* of grace, and finally the *motivation* of grace. As we explore each one, we'll do so from the perspective that parents are God's living letter to their children.

A Parent's Testimony of Grace—Grace Initiates

"For by grace you have been saved"—Ephesians 2:8.

Divine grace initiates our intimate relationship with God. It was Christ who humbled Himself, took on the form of a servant, and became obedient to the point of death (Phil. 2:7-10) . . . that we might become a partaker of the divine nature (2 Peter 1:4). Noted Bible scholar Donald Grey Barnhouse speaks of our undeserved gift of grace in this way: "love that goes upward is worship; love that goes outward is affection; love that stoops is grace." Christ "stooped" from heaven, entered into my world, and gave Himself! What an example; having partaken of this divine initiative, one spouse initiates caring involvement in a partner's life and it's this initiative that genuinely communicates, "I was thinking of you," and "I care." In a similar way, parents take initiative to really know their children and enter into their world as good stewards of this divine grace.

Reflect on this concept of *initiative* . . . who moved first—God or you? The Bible speaks about *"none seeking after God"* but Christ coming to *"seek and save the lost."* It was Christ who left His world and entered into ours. Write about your testimony of initiative toward those you love; in what ways do you "move first"? In what ways do you leave your world and enter into your child's world? What additional initiatives might be needed? Share your reflections here. (For instance: "I need to 'enter into David's world of karate.' I pick him up from the class, but we're always in such a hurry to get to church that I don't really know how he's doing.")

____

____

____

We'll now focus on several "experiencing truth" principles and exercises which can powerfully communicate the *initiative* of grace. As you review each one, consider how God may challenge you with more initiative toward those you love.

Experience Acts 20:35—*"It is more blessed to give than to receive."*

With this in mind, review the list of intimacy needs . . . affection, appreciation, attention, respect, comfort, security, encouragement, approval, support, etc. What needs would each of your children most enjoy receiving? What about your spouse? Don't discuss it with them . . . just begin giving! Meet this need consistently and joyfully this week. See if your family notices this difference and then asks you, "What does this mean?" If they do notice your increased giving, simply tell them, "I was just reminded how much I love you and how much I enjoy giving to you." List each family member, which need you'll emphasize, and how you'll meet it.

Child	*Need*	*How to Meet the Need*
______	______	______
______	______	______
______	______	______
______	______	______
Spouse	______	______
For instance: Julie	Respect	I will ask Julie's permission before I tell stories about her in front of my friends

Experience 1 Thessalonians 5:17—*"Pray without ceasing."*

Prayer is an important part of family spiritual closeness. Prayer can come with gratefulness at times of joy. Prayer can come with burdens at times of pain. A special time of prayer comes after parental apologies . . . thanking God for His forgiveness and your child's forgiveness; then requesting His changes (this models the brokenness of personal responsibility).

Pray "over" your children—Parents, slip into your child's room and quietly pray together; begin this at an early age and continue it even as your children work through the "tough spots" of adolescence. Mention this to your children, conveying the care and burden you have for them. They'll feel special.

Pray "for" your children—Begin a prayer list of key issues for each child; pray for spiritual openness, decisions, and growth; pray for specific character quality development, freedom from specific struggles, and direction in ministry, career, and life mate.

Pray "with" your children—After bedtime reading and at meal times are good places to start; but keep these from just being "formalities." Seize other special times of great joy, struggle, and times of "parting"; encourage children to pray as they are comfortable.

Write about your thoughts on initiating more prayer toward your children. (For instance: "I want to set aside a few minutes of each Marriage Staff Meeting to pray for our children.")

____

____

____

____

____

Experience 1 Thessalonians 2:8—*"I was well pleased to impart my very life"* (paraphrased).

Does your child sense your interest in what's important to her? Does she have memories of times when you have played together? Does she only have memories of doing things the adults thought were fun? Is the only time spent together in discipline, chores, homework, or housework?

In the space below list each child's name. Next to their name list the child's hobbies or areas of interest. Now take out your calendar or appointment book and schedule play time with your children. Enter their world. Is your son interested in soccer, cars, baseball cards, Nintendo? Then find a place and a time when the two of you can play together. Let him teach you if your skill level or knowledge isn't up to par. Is your daughter interested in Girl Scouts, drill team, basketball, or art? Then enjoy these events together. Go with her to sell cookies, shoot baskets at the gym, or make chalk drawings on the sidewalk.

Child	*Hobby or Area of Interest*
____________	______________________________
____________	______________________________
____________	______________________________
____________	______________________________
____________	______________________________
For instance: Steve	Model cars—On Saturday, we'll go to a hobby store and purchase a model we can build together.

Experience Proverbs 29:18—*"Where there is no vision, the people are unrestrained."*

Parents need to give children "permission" to dream about their future. As they grow up, God will begin to channel these dreams into His vision for their life. Enter into your child's world this week and initiate "dreaming" together.

Carve out a few minutes with each child during the next few days and dream with them. What do they dream about? Becoming a professional baseball player? Going to Disneyland? Finding a hidden treasure? Take off your adult "hat" and adult practicalities and just dream. Listen carefully and rediscover the joy of dreaming. Pretend with your child. You may discover things you never knew. What do their dreams communicate? Can you tell what's important to them? What dreams make them happy? Does anything make them afraid?

As you complete this with each child, make note of some of their dreams. Pray with and for them that God will instill His vision as you and your child journey together with Him.

Child	*Dreams for the Future*
________	________________________
________	________________________
________	________________________
________	________________________
For instance: Justin	Wants to be a paleontologist. I definitely see his interest in science and curiosity about life.

Experience James 5:16—*"Confess your sins to one another, and pray for one another so that you may be healed."*

Who "moves first" to apologize in your home? Parents role model Christ's initiative when they demonstrate their accountability to God and vulnerability toward others through experiencing this verse. Confessing our wrongs to our children lets them know that we have a Father to whom we are accountable. He lets us know when we've sinned and then we take responsibility for agreeing with God about the wrong. It is the same God who graciously enables us to do what we do right as parents. It is through confession, forgiveness, and prayer together that our families are healed.

Confessing our wrongs to our children lets them know that we have a Father to whom we are accountable.

Make note of who might need the initiative of your confession.

Name	*Needed Confessions*
________	________________________
________	________________________
________	________________________

____________	____
____________	____
____________	____
For instance: Adam	I need to apologize for breaking my promise about going to play miniature golf.

Research Study—Your Child Is "Reading" Your Busy World

Sociological studies have frequently addressed the extraordinary amount of parent-adolescent conflict in our Western culture. Why does America have such major parent-teen struggles? A classic study of 1939 identified *rapid change* and *fast-paced society* as elements which tended to increase parent-youth conflicts. (How much more the 1990s!) Rapid change and fast-paced living tended to foster *insecurity,* reduce important *family time* together, and heighten *differences* between generations (Davis, 1939).

Practical Suggestions

- **Slow Down for Family Times**—Prioritize one night per week (or at least per month!) for Family Night activities.
- **Trim Schedules**—At least semiannually review all weekly schedules to trim activities done mostly out of obligation, pressure from others, or boredom; add freedom and fun!
- **Review Your Responses**—Minimize these common ones: I'm too busy, too tired, too hungry; not now; later; maybe tomorrow.
- **Be Available**—Physically and mentally: add some unscheduled quiet time just to "be available" in case a family member needs you!

A Parent's Testimony of Grace—Grace Liberates

"It was for freedom that Christ set us free"—Galatians 5:1.

It's grace that frees us from the penalty of sin and grants eternal life so that one day we will be free from the *presence* of sin (Titus

3:5). But "much more" than this, it's grace that can liberate us from the *power* of sin in this life.

- There's liberty from selfishness . . . freeing me to see and give to the needs of others.
- There's liberty from criticism . . . freeing me from judging others.

Just as Christ looked beyond my faults and saw my needs, I'm now free to look beyond others' faults and see their needs. Instead of judging another's behavior, we have the freedom to give unselfishly in meeting their intimacy needs (Phil. 2:3).

Reflect on your *life* and *home* as a testimony of liberty. What aspects of liberty do children see about your life? What bondage? Is there an environment of freedom in your home? . . . or the pressure to perform? Write your thoughts below. (For instance: "I think I am mostly 'liberated' from selfishness. I do see the kids' needs and give to them. But I know that I need to work on my criticism. I seem to always be 'on' the kids about something.")

____

____

____

____

____

We'll now focus on several "experiencing truth" principles and exercises which can powerfully communicate the *liberty* of grace. As you review each one, consider how God may challenge you with more liberty.

Experience Luke 2:52 – *"And Jesus kept increasing in wisdom and stature, and in favor with God and men."*

Much has been written in recent years about the short- and long-term effects of stress in the workplace. High blood pressure, fatigue, anxiety, heart problems, sleep problems, and digestive disorders are just a few of the ailments that have been linked to stress overload. Studies have been conducted and strategies implemented for providing a more stress-free environment in order to improve work conditions and, thereby, increase productivity.

Ever thought about the stress level in your child's work environment? To do so would first require answering the question, "What is the work of childhood?" Going to school? Doing homework? Taking out the trash and making their bed? Making sure they never drip ketchup on their shirt or belch in public? Going to church every Sunday? Making their parents look good? Sorry! All those things may be taking place, but the work of childhood is two simple but insightful words—two words, whose reality is elusive but to experience them is liberating. The two words? Succinctly put, the job of a child is to *grow up!* They may go out into the world laboratory for periods of time to execute responsibilities such as school, play, etc., but the real "work" is accomplished at home. The environment that greets them and sustains them at home will have a tremendous impact on whether they flourish or flounder.

Review some of the mixed messages that at times might be communicated that hinder liberty (i.e., your main job is to "mind me," keep your room clean, make good grades, help with chores). Think about this verse and this principle, then identify some of the mixed messages.

Take an inventory of each child and name the mixed messages that may be communicated within your household. List them below and schedule your talks.

Child	*Mixed Messages/False Assumptions*
______________	______________________________
______________	______________________________
______________	______________________________
______________	______________________________
For instance: Casey	She may think that her only "job" is to make good grades. We really put a lot of emphasis on academics.
Or: Dillan	He may think that his main job is to act calmly and keep himself quiet. The majority of our talks and interactions focus on getting him to settle down.

Experience 2 Corinthians 3:17—*"Where the Spirit of the Lord is, there is liberty."*

Home: A Place of Liberty or Bondage? As they're growing up, children are rapidly building their "belief system" about themselves and about life. They are "tape recording" and storing in their cognitive computer banks important parental messages received verbally and nonverbally. Positive and negative alike are cataloged as if they are true—whether they are or not.

We live in a world that operates on the premise of "doing" things in order to be "OK."

We live in a world that operates on the premise of "doing" things in order to be "OK." We work to keep jobs and work even harder to get raises. Performance = Worthiness. The emphasis is on what we *"do"* not on who we *"are."* God has a different set of criteria. Working hard can't make us "OK" with Him. *"He saved us, not on the basis of deeds which we have done in righteousness, but according to His mercy, by the washing of regeneration and renewing by the Holy Spirit"*—Titus 3:5.

A powerful ingredient in our liberty is that the Father has declared us worthy of His love—in spite of our performance! Liberty comes from knowing that since I could not and did not "earn," or "do" things to merit God's love—I can't "do" anything to lose it. So it should be in our homes.

Now get ready to declare this liberty for each child through the powerful declaration of God's grace. Review Matthew 3:13-17 as the Heavenly Father declares this loving affirmation of His Son, *"This is My beloved Son in whom I am well pleased"*—and it was on Christ's first day of ministry; He hadn't even preached a sermon or performed a miracle! He hadn't "done" anything to earn this loving affirmation.

This week, seek out each child one by one and give him or her this type of spontaneous affirmation. Interrupt them in their room, outside, in the kitchen or living room and then announce, "I was just reminded today how much I love you and how proud I am you're my son/daughter. I just needed to tell you that," then hug them and walk on; leave them standing in the awe and wonder of "what did I do to deserve that?" The answer is clear—they did nothing! That's grace, and it liberates. After you've shared this blessing with each child, record their subsequent reactions here:

Child	*Reaction to the Blessing*
______________	______________________________________
______________	______________________________________
______________	______________________________________
______________	______________________________________
______________	______________________________________
For instance: Melanie	Melanie looked at me with great suspicion and then returned to her homework. You could see her puzzled expression, but I knew she liked what she'd heard.

Experience Matthew 10:8—*"Freely you have received, therefore freely give."*

Since each of us is born with needs for acceptance, approval, and comfort, what must we "do" in order to receive them? Must they be earned through *acceptable performance* or can they be *freely received?* This probing question begs for an honest answer because these two paths are diametrically opposed to one another. One leads to bondage; the other to liberty. Jesus said we are to be in the world but not of the world. Choose to take the path that leads to liberty. Here are some road markers that will guide your way:

"Be" then "Do"—It's essential to keep the correct order. Intimate relationships are founded upon first *"being"* accepted, loved, and valued. A desire to *do* things consistent with this acceptance, love, and worth then follows. Why should one for whom Christ freely died have to earn my acceptance? What gives me the right to withhold that which I freely received in Christ? What did I (or you) do to receive His love, acceptance, kindness, forgiveness, or comfort? (Eph. 5:2; Rom. 15:7; Eph. 4:31-32; 2 Cor. 1:4) The answer is blatantly obvious—we did NOTHING to deserve these things. Christ set the precedent. He established the pattern. He gave freely; we received. Therefore, as we have freely received, we are to freely give.

Trying to live on the world's performance treadmill leads to nowhere and hinders relationships in the process. The broad path of performance is one that many families travel, but its end is destructive. The narrow path of unconditional giving is one that fewer families travel, but its end is greatly blessed.

Two practical challenges this week: (1) try telling your children fewer things "to do"—"put that down, pick that up, clean that up, don't do that, do what I said" and (2) instead, develop a plan for one specific "love gift" you'll give them this week. Enter your ideas here:

Child *Plan for Giving "Love Gifts"*

____________ Could benefit from my giving ____________

and being told less frequently ____________________

____________ Could benefit from my giving ____________

and being told less frequently ____________________

____________ Could benefit from my giving ____________

and being told less frequently ____________________

____________ Could benefit from my giving ____________

and being told less frequently ____________________

For instance: Brandy — Could benefit from my giving more appreciation for her contagious laughter and being told less frequently to clean up her room.

Experience Confession and Forgiveness

How approachable are you? If home is to be a place of liberty where grace is spoken, parents must demonstrate a willingness to be vulnerable and approachable. Do your children have the liberty to share with you when they feel hurt by you? Misunderstood? Dealt with unfairly? Would you respond defensively or in anger if your child pointed out a perceived inconsistency?

Healthy families deal with the reality of inevitable hurt. One of the most powerful ways to deal with the hurts that occur within the family is through confession and forgiveness. How long has it been since your children heard you genuinely apologize for some wrong on your part as a parent? If you are aware of ways you have hurt your spouse or your children, take the initiative to deal with God first and then with them. Hearing, "I was wrong, will you forgive me?" sends a powerful message to a child. It communicates a sense of value and gives them permission to make mistakes. "If Mom and Dad can admit their mistakes, that must mean I need to admit mine, also. And if Mom and Dad can be forgiven for their mistakes, so can I. What a relief!"

There will be other times when your child will experience disappointments, hurts, losses, or misunderstandings and you'll be unaware of it. What do you do about those? Do your children feel the freedom to approach you with their hurts? Providing an atmosphere of approachability that offers comfort, not lectures or blame, will cultivate closeness and intimacy.

Now for the hard part, schedule a time with each child (or share generally in Family Night and ask each child to share with you privately) to open up this avenue of approachability. You might say something like this, "When I realize I've hurt or disappointed you in some way I need to apologize. Hopefully you've noticed I've been doing more of this. There will also be times when I've hurt or disappointed you—and I don't even know it. At those times, I want you to feel safe to come and share your hurts with me. I need to know when I've hurt you and God will help me to hear your hurt and lovingly respond. As specific hurts may come to your heart and mind, please share them with me." As you visit privately with each child, make note of their vulnerability as a point of reference for your specific prayer for God's grace and change in your life.

Child	*Vulnerably Shared Hurt/Disappointment or Need*
______________	____
______________	____
______________	____

For instance: Evan — Evan reminded me that I told him to "shut up" the other day. I hurt him by my words, and I used the very words we've told him are not acceptable.

Experience 1 Thessalonians 5:14—*"And we urge you . . . admonish the unruly, encourage the fainthearted, help the weak, be patient with all men."*

This Scripture directs our response to certain behaviors. With a discerning heart this week, take a look at your child's behavior and the needs behind the behavior.

- We are to *admonish the unruly behavior*—or gently direct a child's disorderly behavior.
- We are to *encourage the fainthearted*—or to inspire confidence in our children through praise and affirmation when they feel "little spirited."
- We are to *help the weak*—give strength to our children through comfort and reassurance when they feel broken or fragile.
- Through all our encounters we are to *be patient*—calmly persevering through the challenges of childhood behavior.

You might keep a journal for one week. Keep track of the different moods and emotions that your child displays. Also keep track of your responses. Are you matching scriptural responses with their behavior? Are you admonishing when you should really be encouraging? How did you respond to normal childhood inquisitiveness, energy, and activity? A significant element in "liberty" at home is that children come to feel secure in a *balanced* environment of (1) admonition, (2) encouragement, (3) comfort, and (4) patience. Consider these four ingredients and write about the one you plan to put more emphasis on this week. Write your thoughts on the next page:

A significant element in "liberty" at home is that children come to feel secure in a* balanced *environment.

Experience Psalm 127:3—*"Behold, children are a gift of the Lord."*

All kids like a surprise gift! Try this activity at Christmas, Valentine's Day, birthdays, or a special Family Night:

- Locate individual pictures of each of your children and frame them.
- Wrap the pictures in festive paper with a bow and enclose this along with a special note on the inside: *"Behold, children are a gift of the Lord"*—Psalm 127:3.
- Let these gifts be "mystery" packages. Don't indicate who they're "from" or "to"—set them out early, where everyone can see.
- As the children's curiosity increases, gather the children close when it's time to open them and begin to unwrap the package announcing that the mystery gift is for Mom and Dad.

Your children will receive a special blessing as they finally realize that the gift is them! Then share with them: "One of the most special gifts we could ever receive, we have already received—as God has blessed us with you!"

Reflect on this question and answer. What signs of "perfectionism" do you see in your life and home? These can be a major hindrance to God's intended liberty. What connections do you see with "trying to play God"? "Worth = Performance?" "Insisting that others be perfect?" Write your reflections on the next page. (For instance: "When I insist that every toy be in place, and every room be spotless, I am insisting on perfection. My children may begin to wonder if my love for them is based on how clean their rooms are kept.")

Since You Asked . . .
Experiencing Biblical Truth in Perplexing Situations

Q: I seem to constantly struggle with insisting on things being perfect—at home, work, church, with my spouse and children. I'm making life miserable for myself and others. How did I get this way and how do I change?

A: The demand that people and things be perfect is quite common yet very destructive. Perfectionism can be caused by several things: conditional love from significant others, a "worth equals performance" society, and certain temperament characteristics. Overcoming perfectionism is difficult but begins with admitting that it is an effort to "play God" and that we were never intended to be all-knowing, all-powerful, and everywhere at once like God. Christ died for us because we could not be perfect. Out of gratefulness, we are to strive to become more and more like Christ while here on the earth, knowing that we will never be perfect. We are called to "press on to the mark," while still living under grace. In this life, we will never be totally Christlike, so we must not attack ourselves or others when this perfect Christlikeness is not achieved on a day-to-day basis.

As you may have experienced pain from conditional love and a "worth equals performance" environment, the sadness of this hurt can be mourned and comforted by a caring "journeymate" which will bring the promised blessing of Matthew 5:4.

The chart that follows summarizes key elements and outcomes in a home filled with the *liberty of grace* in contrast with relationships of this world—filled with conditions, performance, and pressure.

Unconditionally loving a child "frees" them from performing in order to please people. Having truly partaken of grace, they are genuinely free to give to others. Having received that which they could not earn and did not deserve (i.e., grace), they are therefore free from fear of never having it and the fear of ever losing it. *"Where the Spirit of the Lord is, there is liberty"*—2 Corinthians 3:17.

After reviewing this chart and the material in this section on grace, write about how your family could be more and more "not of this world" (John 17:15-16) as intimate relationships are deepened. Write your reflections below. (For instance:

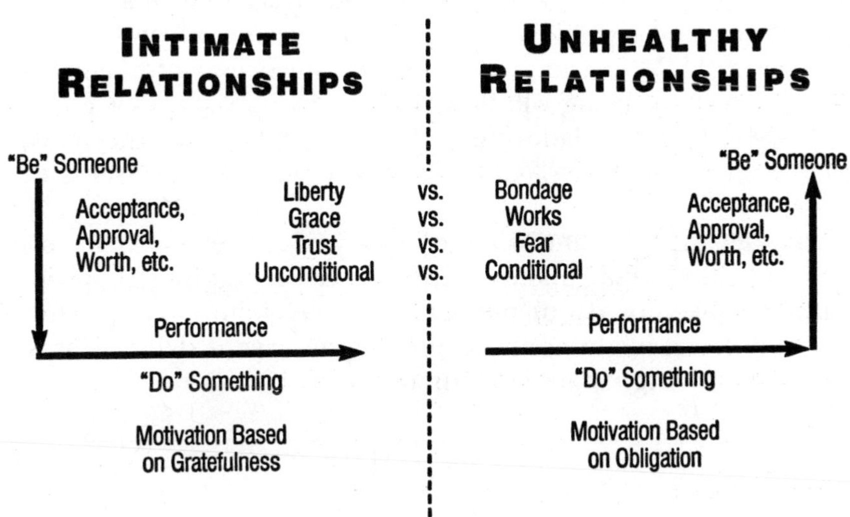

"We need to refocus our attentions toward 'who' the kids are, not just what they 'do.' We need to remind them and ourselves that there is nothing they can do to make us love them more. There is nothing they can do that will make us love them less.")

____

____

____

____

A Parent's Testimony of Grace—Grace Motivates

"As good stewards of the manifold grace of God"—1 Peter 4:10.

Living in the awe and wonder of all that we *have* and *are* in Christ motivates a stewardship of grace.

This life of intimacy with God and others is not lived out in obligation or duty. There wells up within the believer such a joyful gratefulness and humble appreciation that giving unconditionally to a spouse, child, friend, or even our enemy is uncontrollable! Out of our innermost being will flow rivers of living water that nourish intimacy in human relationships (John 7:38). Grace is infectious, contagious . . . the love of Christ is now *"constraining* us" (see 2 Cor. 5:14).

Consider the "awe and wonder" that you've been eternally loved by the Creator, made a joint-heir with Christ, and by His Spirit you've partaken of His divine nature. Write about your gratefulness and how it might motivate and empower your daily life as well as your parenting. Share your thoughts here:

____

____

____

____

____

Let's recall again the Gospel accounts of Jesus' first day of public ministry as we find Him going down to the River Jordan to submit Himself to John to be baptized. First, He hears the testimony of John—*"Behold, the Lamb of God who takes away the sin of the world!"* and then comes confirmation of even greater significance. When He comes up out of the water, the heavens open, the Spirit of God descends upon Him like a dove, and a voice speaks. *"This is My Beloved Son in whom I am well pleased."* Let's stop right there. You miss the whole import of this passage if you think that was said for the crowd's benefit. That was

He blessed Him because of who He was, not what He'd done.

the Heavenly Father affirming His Child. The beautiful part of this story is that Jesus hadn't yet preached a sermon or performed a miracle. And yet His Father affirmed Him. He blessed Him because of who He was, not what He'd done.

Scripture tells us that immediately thereafter Jesus spent forty days and forty nights in the wilderness where He was tempted by the devil. Can you imagine how His Father's blessing must have sustained Him! Could it be that part of what prompted, undergirded, and motivated the earthly ministry of Jesus was an overwhelming sense of gratefulness for that blessing? As He ministered during the ensuing three years of His life, He was intimately acquainted with sorrow and grief but always had those words locked in His heart and ringing in His ears: *"This is My Beloved Son in whom I am well pleased."*

Now we'll turn our attention to principles and experiences centered around this motivation of grace as God's gratefulness empowers our living.

Experience Psalms 103:2—*"Bless the Lord, O my soul, and forget none of His benefits."*

Journal of Gratefulness—Multiplied blessings are ours as we pause to *"forget none of His benefits"* toward us. Regularly involve family members in a "blessing search" as each member names a recent blessing and assumes responsibility for sharing appreciation. (A sample format for a family Journal of Gratefulness is included in the Appendix, p. 372.) Appreciation helps seal in one's heart the reality of the blessing as well as blessing and encouraging others. Appreciation could be shared privately, publicly, verbally, or in writing. A few of the many benefits of a grateful heart are:

- Guards us from a critical, negative attitude.
- Guards us from a judgmental spirit.
- When expressed to others, it can motivate them to continue in "good deeds."
- When acknowledged to God, it is an important element of worship.

Pause and reflect on recent blessings—loved ones you've been reminded of, answers to prayer, character qualities in family/friends, or often overlooked blessings like health, finances, the Scriptures, etc. Write a specific prayer of thanksgiving expressing your gratitude to God. Share your prayer here:

____

____

____

____

____

Now pause and reflect on the person and character of this One who would bless you abundantly in such ways. Write a short prayer of praise and adoration to this "giver of all good gifts." Write your prayer of praise here:

____

____

____

____

____

____

Research Study—Your Child Is "Reading" Your Priorities

"Not now"—"I'm busy"—"Later"

If these words sound all too frequent and familiar, they may be impacting your child.

An important research study focused on positive mother-child interactions such as play and conversation in conduct-problem children. A sample of preschool conduct-problem children was surveyed in both preschool and home environments. Findings support the notion that conduct-problem children may be missing out on certain forms of harmonious experience . . . like talk and play . . . with their parents! (Gardner, 1987)

A child's need for *attention* is so great that when not met through positive home interactions, a child often begins to "act out" through negative behaviors.

Practical Suggestions

- Remember: Intimacy Needs + Met = Fulfillment

  Intimacy Needs + Unmet = Frustration

  Learn to look past your child's "frustration" to any unmet intimacy need, i.e., attention, affection, approval, etc.

- **Plan Fun Times** with each child for individual attention; give the child several options and let him/her pick; plan ahead to enjoy the benefits of anticipation.

- **Bedtime Talking**—Read a few minutes with younger children and then talk; for older children ask open-ended questions like: "Share something exciting about your day," and then be quiet—listen!

- **Enter the Child's World**—Play dolls, school, army, etc.; get on the floor, make tents, or build a tree house—join them in their world.

Experience Psalm 139:14—*"I will give thanks to Thee, for I am fearfully and wonderfully made."* (And so are your children!)

God has made each of us uniquely different. Think about the way God has designed your child. What character strengths, gifts, talents, and interests are present? How are these the same or different from you? Your spouse? Other siblings? What challenges have resulted because of these differences? Are any of these challenges present because of an attempt to change God-given characteristics?

Be especially alert to any statements of comparison that may be a subtle attempt to change a child. Statements like, *Why can't you be more like* . . . communicate a lack of acceptance.

Pause and write about some of the "uniqueness" surrounding each of your children—some of the ways they've been fearfully and wonderfully made. (You may want to refer to the list of Fifty Character Qualities in the Appendix.) Write your thanksgiving here:

Child	*Unique Character Strengths, Gifts, Talents, and Interests*
________	________________________________
________	________________________________
________	________________________________
________	________________________________
For instance: Trent	Trent is forgiving, observant, responsible, and industrious.
Or:	
Trina	Trina is sensitive, takes initiative, is detail-oriented, and gifted in the arts.

Experience James 1:17—*"Every good thing bestowed and every perfect gift is from above, coming down from the Father."*

And remember . . . according to Psalm 127:3, our children are God's gifts to us. You might want to write a thank-You note this week. Tell God about your appreciation for the child He's given you. Mention the specific things you like about your "gift." What character traits do you find most precious? Let God know of your gratefulness for such a priceless gift. After the thank-You note is written, you will want to think of ways to communicate these same thoughts to your child. Mail a card, give a hug, then verbalize to your child your gratefulness. You might want to give him a copy of your letter to God. Write your note of thanksgiving here:

____

____

____

As you consider your note of thanksgiving, you might reflect on this one which Paul and Vicky Warren wrote and shared with their son, Matthew.

Dear Matthew,
We waited a long time for God to bring you into our lives. But you were worth the wait! Your name means "Gift of God" . . . and you truly are a precious gift.

When you were born one of the first things people commented about when they saw you was how big and beautiful your deep blue eyes were. The nurses at the hospital said that you didn't miss a thing then—and you still don't. Sometimes you amaze us at the observations you make and the insight God has given to you.

We've thought many times about how you remind us of Amy Grant's song, "My Father's Eyes." Not only has God given you beautiful eyes in the physical sense, but He has given you beautiful eyes in the sense that you have an unusual sensitivity to the needs and feelings of others.

Your laughter and sense of humor are contagious. Mom still chuckles to herself every time she remembers the day you announced to her when you were about five, "I can't help it, Mommy, God just made me funny." Thank you for helping us to not always take life so seriously, and for helping us rediscover our own childlike faith and spontaneity. Remember when Mom convinced you that you wanted to see Peter Pan, even though she was really the one who wanted to see it? Thanks for going with her!

When we come into your room at night after you're asleep to make sure you're tucked in and your stereo is turned off, we sometimes just stand by your bed and look into your sweet, peaceful face. In those quiet moments, we're reminded of the things that are of eternal value and our hearts are thankful to God for giving our family one more day together. We pray that we never take you, or those days, for granted. If we do, tell us!

We love you, Matthew!

Experience 2 Peter 3:11—*"Since all these things are to be destroyed . . . what sort of people ought you to be?"*

One of the counterfeits to God's grace in this world is materialism. It's tragic how much time, attention, and effort is directed toward "when will I ever get ____________________" and "why don't I have ________________________." Families can so easily become enslaved in the pursuit of "things" prompting either of two tragic results:

Either, "things" remain elusive—prompting the barrenness of a "busy" life plus fear that "I'll never have them" and/or anger that "I don't have them."

One of the counterfeits to God's grace . . . is materialism.

Or, "things" are obtained—prompting an emptiness and despair as I confront the probing question: "Is this all there is to life?"

Reflect on your family's battle with materialism. Is there inordinate time, discussion, and effort centered on gaining more "things"? Are there family members who can be distracted by the pressure of money and things? Write about any family challenges you see regarding materialism. (For instance: "Haley is never satisfied with enjoying family time together. She always wants a 'surprise' too. We may have established a precedent we don't want to continue.")

____

____

____

____

____

____

____

____

Experience 2 Corinthians 5:14—*"The love of Christ controls us."*

Adopt an attitude in your home that reflects *"in the world but not of the world"* (John 17:15-16). Affirm your children for just being your children. If you typically give incentives for grades or chores, give the same reward just because you love them—not tied to any grade or chore. They'll wonder what the surprise is for. When they ask, call it a "just because I love you surprise." Give hugs for no apparent reason. Praise the efforts of a child—don't just comment on

Since You Asked . . .
Experiencing Biblical Truth in Perplexing Situations

Q: My eight-year-old child is beginning to experience intense peer pressure in the area of materialism. How do I say no to these wants?

A: First, make sure *you* are properly dealing with materialistic temptations. It's amazing how much our children learn from us, just by observing our behavior and priorities.

It's important for all of us to know that our worth never comes from material possessions.

Our worth has been declared by God, and joy in life comes from sharing in intimate relationships with Him and meaningful others. Your relationship with your child is his or her opportunity to sense an affirmation of his/her worth to God and then he/she will be more free to enjoy material possessions as blessings from God. Here are some steps of action you can pursue:

- Empathize with your child, "I understand you would like to have ______________________."
- Set some limits, "But we can't afford ______________________," or simply say, "No."
- Comfort your child, "I know that may disappoint you, and I regret that it does because I love you."
- Use such times as "teachable moments" to share some of your own struggles in prioritizing God above material possessions (possibly sharing Scriptures).
- Then offer yourself, "I would really like to spend some time with you. How about this Saturday, just you and me? What would you enjoy doing?"

Deep down inside, we long to spend quality time with those we love. When we don't have meaningful relationships with God and others, our natural tendency is to substitute any number of things, material possessions being one of them.

success or failure. Go out of your way to verbalize love: "I was just reminded today how much I love you." Create a home environment that is characterized by grace, not by works. When your children inquire, "What's going on," share with them about the "constraining" love of Christ. "I just can't help myself . . . from showing love to you."

Write about your "constraining love plan" on the following page:

Child	*Blessing of Christ's Constraining Love*
______________	______________________________
______________	______________________________
______________	______________________________
______________	______________________________
For instance: Ian	I'll surprise Ian with a special card. He loves to get mail.
Or:	
Hillary	I'll bring a lunch and eat with Hillary at school.

Finally, in our testimony of grace . . .

Scripture Journaling

"Let us consider how to stimulate one another to love and good deeds, not forsaking our own assembling together, as is the habit of some, but encouraging one another; and all the more, as you see the day drawing near"— Hebrews 10:24-25.

- **Let us consider** . . . Take *initiative* rather than being reactive in parenting. The word "consider" implies pondering, thinking about, weighing the advantages and disadvantages of a decision, entering your child's world in order to assess his/her need.

- **How to stimulate** . . . Your goal is to move them toward growth, to prompt them to action, to excite them about *discovering who God has created them to be.*

- **One another** . . . Parenting with intimacy requires *leaving the Lone Ranger* lifestyle in the dust and riding the trail with the "pardners" God's entrusted to you.

- **To love and good deeds** . . . With the right kind of root stimulators, positive emotions and behavior will grow in fertile soil and will result in *an attitude of gratitude* as they try their wings and begin to fly.

- **Not forsaking our own assembling together as is the habit of some** . . . Have we relegated *"Family Time" to a back burner* in order to make time for the myriad of activities that crowd out time for meaningful relationship-building?

- **But encouraging one another** . . . Determine to make meeting one another's intimacy needs a priority. As you each step out the front door to face the world, what a fabulous feeling to know that you have a *cheering section* pulling for you!

- **And all the more as you see the day drawing near** . . . Children are bombarded with daily reminders that the world is an unsafe place. They see the faces of abducted children on milk cartons and grocery bags. As they flip through the newspaper on their way to the "funny papers" they pass story after story recounting incidents of kids killing kids and adults abusing kids that are sober reminders that the world in which they live is far from "funny." Radio, television, and movies add their gruesome contributions as well. Your grace-filled home will provide a *place of refuge* for your children.

Consider each of the key ingredients noted above and write out thoughts you have on taking action to be a living testimony to your kids. Write your comments on any of the items below, giving particular focus to ones you may need to emphasize or make changes in.

- initiative________________________________
- discovering who God created them to be ____________
- leaving the Lone Ranger lifestyle ________________
- attitude of gratitude________________________
- relegated "Family Time" _____________________
- cheering section ___________________________
- place of refuge____________________________

(For instance: "I am going to make a special effort to work on my temper outbursts. I want our children to think of their home as a safe place—not one where they might get yelled at.")

Share a brief prayer asking for God's gracious prompting and empowering in any of these areas. Write your prayer here:

____

____

____

____

____

Marriage Staff Meeting

Begin with a brief review of "this is what" (Acts 2:16) and how your home is to be a place where Bible verses come alive! Discuss how this might give home life and parenting a whole new meaning.

Share your reflections on "Grace Initiates" and discuss how your family might benefit from additional initiative on your part. Next, share your reflections concerning "Grace Liberates" giving particular attention to the diagram on page 267. What characteristics of intimate relationships do you see in each family member? (i.e., trust, gratefulness, liberty) What characteristics of unhealthy relationships do you see in family members? (i.e., fear, bondage, obligation, etc.)

Finally, discuss your reflections on "Grace Motivates" and express thanksgiving for blessings that God has reminded you of during this study. Discuss plans for Family Night activities and then pray together, asking God to make your home a place where *Bible verses come alive!*

Top Ten Need of the Week—Encouragement

Encouragement—Urging forward and positively persuading toward a goal.

This week puts particular emphasis on communicating encouragement to each child. Example sentences follow:

- "Steve, I know you can do it!"

- "I know you must be discouraged, but you're the right person for the job. I know it will work out alright."
- "Vicki, I just wanted to call and tell you that I'll be praying for you at work today. I know you're feeling bad. I'll be thinking about you."
- "If there's anything I can help you with, let me know. I know it looks overwhelming, but you will do great once things are broken into bite-sized pieces. You can do it!"

Family Night Activity

Share the Acts 2 story with your family—possibly involve family members in a dramatic presentation. Read the story up to the point of the crowd's crying out, "What do these things mean?" Then discuss the "this is that which was written" principle, focusing on the desire for your family to become a place where *Bible verses come alive!*

Review with the family specific verses from this chapter which can "come alive" tonight, for example:

Psalm 103:2	*"Forget none of His benefits"*	Journal of Gratefulness
James 1:17	*"Every good and perfect gift comes down from the Father"*	Letters to Your Kids
James 5:17	*"Confess your faults to one another"*	Apologies to Your Kids

First Thessalonians 5:11 says to *"Encourage one another, and build up one another."* Assign each family member a day of the week. On their assigned day, every other family member tells that person special qualities they appreciate about them. You may want to post the character qualities somewhere in the house where everyone can see them. (See Appendix for list of Fifty Selected Character Qualities.) Affirm their personhood, not their performance.

"Things" Dedication Day

In our society, one of the pressures most families face is materialism. Teenagers insist on wearing just the right labels on clothing. Kids throw temper tantrums over the latest toys, and adults yield to the pressure of "He who dies with the most toys wins."

In Genesis 2, Adam possessed everything—he had it all, and yet God said, *"It is not good."* Obviously, materialism is deceptive. We think all these "things" will make us happy, but they will not. How do you deal with materialism in your family? During your next Family Night, try this project:

- Over dinner, discuss the materialistic pressures that each family member faces.
- Discuss Adam's dilemma in Genesis 2. What was *"not good,"* even though Adam "had it all"? What relationships has God created to minister to our aloneness?
- Discuss the idea that people are more important than possessions; relationships are more important than things.
- Next, ask each family member to go get two of their favorite possessions (a child's favorite toy, stuffed animal, or game; a teenager's favorite CD, sweater, or his/her car keys; Mom's favorite necklace, antique, or fur coat; Dad's favorite remote control, golf club, or computer). When you're back together, read 2 Peter 3:10-12 and discuss the fact that all our favorite "things" will be gone someday. Reemphasize the "eternal" aspect of relationships as you consider the probing questions: "What sort of people should we be?" and "What should be the focus of our lives?" Close with prayer.

Group Discussion

1. Begin this group discussion by reflecting on the Scriptures related to grace. Look over your responses to pages 250–51. What areas of gratefulness did you find related to God's grace? Share specific examples of how God's grace has impacted your life. In what ways do you sense this abundant supply? Make a list of these individual responses. Then from the list, discuss how

these same areas of grace relate to parenting. How do we employ grace as we serve our children? (1 Peter 4:10)

2. Share ways that you plan to initiate demonstrations of grace. What plans have you made to give to a specific need, pray with your children, enter their world, or initiate confession? Give a detailed plan and the time frame in which it will be completed. Hold each other accountable for these steps of initiative. Ask about them at a later meeting.
3. Continue your group discussion by asking each parent to declare his or her "wish for freedom." What area of their family do they want to see liberated? You may want to focus on the diagram given on page 267.
4. Do you see conditional love but want unconditional love to describe your family? Do you sense fear or trust among family members? Do you notice a behavior that is motivated by obligation or gratefulness? Is performance derived from inner character or is performance an attempt to achieve approval, worth, and acceptance?
5. End this group discussion by asking each parent to pass around a picture of his or her child. As the picture is shown to group members, parents complete these sentences: "This is the 'gift' the Lord has given to me"; "He/she is precious because . . ." "I treasure this 'gift' because . . ." "This 'gift' means more to me each day because. . . ." Close the discussion by encouraging members to verbalize the thoughts to their children as well.

Part Four

Becoming Caringly Involved

"We were well-pleased to impart to you not only the Gospel of God but also our own lives."

1 THESSALONIANS 2:8

CHAPTER 11

Becoming Caringly Involved to Communicate Worth

MARK TWAIN ONCE shared his philosophy about how to raise teenagers: "When a kid turns thirteen, stick him in a barrel, nail the lid shut, and feed him through the knothole. When he turns sixteen, plug the hole."

For sure, raising kids can be a challenge; but it need not be as traumatic as Twain would suggest. Even the teenage years can be anticipated and enjoyed if we realize that children are indeed a gift from the Lord, that each child is unique, and that their lives can be positively impacted by lovingly meeting their intimacy needs.

In our parenting with intimacy journey, we've now come to an important juncture. Previously, we've focused on truly "knowing" our children, "knowing" ourselves, and allowing our children to "know" us. It's now time to channel these principles into caring involvement as we see God shape our children into all He desires. But where is He headed with them—what's the "target" or goal He has in mind? It's true for many parents that we've given birth to our children and desire to be good parents, but at the same time we're not quite sure what this "target" or goal is. By the time your children are "grown and gone," what do you hope to have seen accomplished?

By the time your children are "grown and gone," what do you hope to have seen accomplished?

First, let's consider two key declarations from Jesus as a beginning point of defining a significant aspect of this parenting goal:

"Take My yoke upon you, and learn from Me, for I am gentle and humble"—Matthew 11:29.

"[I came not] to be served, but to serve"—Matthew 20:28.

Consider that with these admonitions, Christ has revealed "where He's headed" with us and our children! Combine these verses into a description of what kind of person Christ is challenging us to be. Write your thoughts here:

____

____

____

____

Now consider that the characteristics above describe key aspects of our parenting "target" with our children. Imagine that they one day leave home as this type of person. Write about how these characteristics of a *humble, gentle servant* would positively impact their life as:

A witness for Christ ____________________________

A friend to others ______________________________

A spouse as God may lead ________________________

A parent as God may decide ______________________

(For instance: "My hope is for Jeremy to become a man of God. Humility would keep him teachable. Gentleness enables a strong relationship with a wife and kids. A servant's heart would be a constant testimony for Christ.")

Now let's pursue how we arrive at this destination. How do we hit this parenting target? What type of person serves God and others with humility and gentleness? We have no further to look than to again explore Christ's example:

Free to Serve

"Jesus, knowing that the Father had given all things into His hands, and that He had come forth from God, and was going back to God, rose from supper, and laid aside His garments . . . and began to wash the disciples' feet"—John 13:3-5.

There must have been other things on His mind, such as His impending death. Yet Jesus, while sharing the last Passover meal with His disciples, demonstrated to them that He had not come into the world to be served, but to serve. He washed His disciples' feet.

He even washed Judas' feet. Knowing that Judas had betrayed Him for a silver reward, Jesus gently caressed the dirty feet of the betrayer. It was love, forgiveness, and servanthood, wrapped together like a three-stranded cord.

But the washing of feet was to continue. It was not a single incident but an example to be followed, for Jesus said, *"You call Me Teacher and Lord; and you are right, for so I am. If I then, the Lord and the Teacher, washed your feet, you also ought to wash one another's feet."*

But Jesus not only showed us what to do, He told us the secret to His being able to wash dirty feet. The same knowledge that allowed Jesus to gird Himself with a towel and become a servant will give us the necessary confidence to do likewise. What did Jesus know? From what perspective did He serve?

According to John 13:3, Jesus knew who He was, where He had come from, and where He was going.

The key to servanthood is knowing who you are, where you came from, and where you're going.

If you are convinced that God loves you, that you are created in His image, that you have been forgiven and accepted, and that someday you will rule and reign with Him in the heavenlies—you won't have any trouble becoming a servant. In contrast, if you're intent on trying to prove to everyone that you're "somebody" or if you're trying to exert your "rights" or maintain a "position" . . . you'll have a hard time handling a bowl of water and a towel.

We need to learn who we are and focus on where we're going. The more we learn, the more comfortable we'll be in imitating Jesus—the Servant.

Families could benefit from reenacting this special time of ministry as they come together for a Family Night. Lessons in gentle servanthood can be learned as well as powerful lessons in humility as self-sufficiency gives way to "receiving" from others.

Reflect on this example and then consider each individual in your family beginning with yourself:

Who might we find "trying to prove I'm somebody"? ____________

Who might we find "exerting their rights"? ____________________

Who might we find "trying to maintain a position"? ____________

Who is "convinced that God loves them"? ____________________

Who is secure that they're "forgiven and accepted"? ____________

During the closing three chapters of this workbook, parents will be challenged with caring involvement in shaping and affirming the identity of each child. As a child comes to embrace his incalculable *worth to the Heavenly Father,* finds security in his *belonging as a joint-heir with Christ* and experiences the *competency of life in the Spirit* . . . he will enter adult life prepared and motivated to lead the servant's life God intends.

No single factor is more closely associated with successful growing up than one's sense of identity: "Who am I?"

"Identity" is sometimes thought of as a person's "internalized picture" of himself. Thus a person can like, dislike, or even hate himself. Additionally, most research indicates an individual's sense of identity is "formed" by adolescence. Thus, shaping a child's sense of identity is of major importance in the parenting priority. This sobering reality can stimulate parents to better understand the crucial dimensions that form a child's identity and the practical keys to building them into your children.

Children have an eternal significance to their Creator; they have a special identity to Him. *God the Father has declared them worth* the gift of His Son. *The Son longs for them to belong* to His family as joint-heirs with Him. *The Spirit seeks to fill and empower their competence* to do all things through Christ who strengthens them. Parents have

Dimensions of Affirmed-Identity with Top 10 Intimacy "Needs"

I'm **worth**...

Attention (care) as you enter "my world," get to know me, my character qualities, and my dreams

Respect (honor) of my decisions, "space," ideas, opinions, and feelings

Acceptance of me through your unconditional love, forgiveness, and patient care

I **belong** to a family who gives...

Affection...verbally and physically

Comfort through compassionate care when I'm hurt, lonely, afraid, disappointed, or rejected

Security through direction, limits, and discipline

Approve of me "just for who I am" apart from what I "do"

Appreciate me as you value my unique strengths and gifts

I feel **competent** when you...

Encourage me as we set goals and work together toward them

Support me as we "journey" together through life's issues

Worth Declared by the Father

Belonging as Joint-Heirs with the Son

Affirmed Identity

Competence Empowered by the Spirit

the privilege for a few short years to "affirm" this identity that the Father has declared. It's this "affirmed identity" that should be our "target," seeking to one day launch our children as humble, gentle servants.

First pause and reflect on *your* identity:

- How God the Father has declared your **worth**: *"The free gift of God is eternal life in Christ Jesus our Lord"* —Romans 6:23.
- How God the Son has given you **"belonging"** as a joint-heir: *"The Spirit Himself bears witness with our spirit that we are children of God . . . and fellow heirs with Christ"*—Romans 8:16-17.
- How God the Spirit empowers your **competence**: *"I can do all things through Him who strengthens me"* —Philippians 4:13.

In your own words, write about *who* God says you are: (For instance: "God says that I am worth the gift of His Son. I have become a child of God.")

____

____

____

____

____

Now express your gratitude to God in a short note of thanksgiving and praise. Write about your gratefulness here:

Dear Heavenly Father,

____

____

____

____

Experience 1 Thessalonians 3:6—*"But now that Timothy has come to us from you, and has brought us good news of your faith and love, and* *that you always think kindly of us, longing to see us just as we also long to see you."*

This passage tells us that Timothy brought the "good news of his faith" to the church of Thessalonica. Spend some time reflecting about the good news of your own faith. How have you changed because of your relationship with Christ? What "good" things are the result of your relationship with God? If there are no changes, or you aren't sure that you have a relationship with Christ, then find someone who can help. Talk with a trusted friend, minister, or family member about these important issues.

Spend some time reflecting about the good news of your own faith. How have you changed because of your relationship with Christ?

Share your testimony with your children. Let them know the circumstances that led to your salvation. Tell your kids about a time when God answered a prayer. Share a time when God protected you or a member of your family. Let them know about a time when you experienced God's forgiveness.

Write a brief testimony here which you can share with your children at Family Nights or individually. Write about the "good news of your faith" here: (For instance: "I felt very sad and alone before Christ came into my life. When I asked Jesus to live in my heart, He promised to never leave. He has taken away my fearful and anxious heart.")

____

____

____

____

Becoming Caringly Involved

"Behold, children are a gift of the Lord"—Psalm 127:3.

The Hebrew word translated "gift" (*nahal*) speaks of a heritage or inheritance—much like the Promised Land was a gift to Israel

(Ex. 15:17). The same word is used to describe Israel as God's "inheritance" or gift. In Exodus 34:9, Moses pleads with Jehovah that He might not reject Israel in the face of their rebellion, but instead take them as His inheritance/gift. Deuteronomy 32:8-14 describes God's loving care toward Israel—as they are the recipient of His initiative and attention, His special care and protection. Clearly, throughout the Old Testament, we see God's priority of His gift, the nation of Israel.

In a similar way, children are to be treated as gifts. Gifts are to be treasured, valued, studied, protected, and even "bragged upon"—not ridiculed, neglected, criticized, rejected, or "used." So it is with children as gifts from the Lord—*treasure* them with your affection and care; *study* them with your initiative, time, and listening; *protect* them with exhortation and discipline; "*brag upon*" them with praise and appreciation.

Reflect on this concept of "valuing" your children as gifts. Consider each of your family members beginning with your spouse and then each of your children:

- Who could benefit from being "*treasured*" with more verbalized love and affectionate touch? ________________
- Who could benefit from being "*studied*" by you with additional initiative, priority time, and listening? ____________
- Who could benefit from additional "*protection*" as you invest time to teach, train, exhort, and discipline as necessary?

  ____
- Who could benefit from being "*bragged on*" through private and public praise and appreciation? ________________

Schedule time and make plans now to address these needs. Write your plans here:

Family Member	*When*	*What I'll Do*
____________	____________	______________________
____________	____________	______________________
____________	____________	______________________

For Instance:	Each Afternoon Natalie	Natalie needs some extra time and individual attention. I'll "study" my gift in Natalie after I put the baby down for a nap.

Affirming Your Child's Worth

"Worth" is caught and not taught. Children "catch" how worthy they are as parents communicate to them a priority that is not

DIMENSIONS OF AFFIRMED-IDENTITY WITH TOP 10 INTIMACY "NEEDS"

I'm **worth**...

Attention (care) as you enter "my world," get to know me, my character qualities, and my dreams

Respect (honor) of my decisions, "space," ideas, opinions, and feelings

Acceptance of me through your unconditional love, forgiveness, and patient care

threatened by career, materialism, or personal indulgences. The paramount cost to parents is TIME! Time to be involved in children's activities and hobbies; time for family fun; time to listen and get to know your child; time to notice and praise your child's character strengths; time to offer explanations for decisions which affect your child. Without this sense of worth, a child often unknowingly embarks on a journey of "performing" and trying harder—in order to gain this elusive sense of worth. Your child is WORTH the investment!

Three key intimacy needs are highlighted as making significant contribution to a child's sense of worth. We'll explore each of these in some detail along with practical suggestions on meeting each need.

Attention

To take thought of another and convey appropriate care, interest, concern, and support; to enter into another's world.

"But that the members [of the body] should have the same care for one another"—1 Corinthians 12:25.

Jesus met our ultimate need for attention by leaving His environment (heaven) and entering into our world; He became like us in order to personally relate to us and us to Him. During His earthly ministry, Jesus didn't spend time with just the masses but invested much of His time with individuals (Zaccheus, Nicodemus, the Samaritan woman, the disciples).

God continues to meet our need for attention by providing us with the privilege of prayer, whereby we may receive His individual, undivided, and unlimited attention. Furthermore, we are convinced of the individual attention He gives us because the Bible says that He knows our thoughts (Ps. 139:2), counts the number of hairs on our head (Luke 12:7), knew us in our mother's womb (Ps. 139:13), and promises to provide for our every need (Matt. 6:25-34).

1. Spend time with your children. There's no substitute for spending time. They're especially blessed when they realize that we're taking time out of our busy schedule to spend time with just

them. Time is a valuable commodity; therefore, it's a wonderful expression of attention.

2. Spend *individual* time with your children. Don't just spend time with your family as a group, but arrange for private time. Our need for attention is not always met in groups. For instance, if you have three children, you need to spend private time with each child; start with a goal of two hours each month with each child.
3. Go where your children are—enter into *their* world. Have lunch with your child—at his school. When your child has a recital, concert, game, program, or awards ceremony—be there. This always requires the sacrifice of leaving *your* world—your agenda, priorities, and comfort zones.
4. Listen to your children. Don't dominate conversations but encourage others to talk—and to talk about themselves—their feelings, goals, and plans. Try to talk where there won't be any interruptions and concentrate on the conversation; don't daydream or succumb to distractions.

Review the practical suggestions on meeting this need and consider a plan of ministry to each family member:

Child	*Practical Steps I Could Take to Meet This Need*
____________	________________________________
____________	________________________________
____________	________________________________
____________	________________________________
____________	________________________________
For instance: Scott	I will listen to Scott as he tells me about his day. I will make eye contact and free my mind from distractions. I will not interrupt him when he's speaking.

Acceptance

Deliberate and ready reception with a favorable response; to receive willingly; to regard as good and proper.

"Wherefore, accept one another, just as Christ also accepted us to the glory of God"—Romans 15:7.

Jesus met our ultimate need for acceptance in that *"while we were yet sinners"* He died for us (5:8). He looked beyond our faults and saw and met our needs. During His earthly ministry, Jesus accepted people where they were regardless of background, race, or condition (the Samaritan woman, the thief on the cross, the Gentile centurion, the woman caught in adultery); helped them deal with their failures (Peter's denial, disciples' lack of faith); loved people with unconditional love; and forgave freely ("Father forgive them . . .").

He continues to provide us with acceptance in that if we *"confess our sins, He is faithful and righteous to forgive us our sins and to cleanse us from all unrighteousness"*—1 John 1:9.

1. Look beyond your children's faults and minister to their needs. The closer we get to someone, the more we notice their imperfections! Acceptance involves looking past these flaws and meeting their needs. (We can address the "flaws" later, one by one, as God burdens us and gives us wisdom.)
2. Quickly forgive your children when personally offended. Unforgiveness short-circuits acceptance. Don't pout, reject, or ignore them as punishment.
3. Help your children to properly deal with their failures and disappointments. Our need for acceptance is accentuated when we experience a failure or when we are unduly disappointed. We need to notice when loved ones experience a failure (real or perceived) or when they're disappointed (particularly in themselves) and minister to their need for acceptance. Acceptance is based upon a person's innate value to God as a person of special worth, and not on their performance or productivity. Give empathy; don't minimize, ignore, or ridicule your child's pain.
4. Love your children with God's unmerited, unconditional, and unlimited love. God's love for us is unmerited (we don't deserve it and can't earn it), unconditional (it's not based on what we do or don't do), and unlimited (it will never "run out" or be detained). We should accept and love others in like manner.

Review the practical suggestions on meeting this need and consider a plan of ministry to each family member:

Child	*Practical Steps I Could Take to Meet This Need*
______________	____
______________	____
______________	____
______________	____
For instance: Shaun	I will accept Shaun's apology without questioning his heart. I will move toward him in love and allow God to work in the heart of my teenager.

Respect

To value and regard highly; to convey great worth, to esteem.

"Show proper respect to everyone"—1 Peter 2:17 (NIV).

During His earthly ministry, Jesus ignored all the social prejudices of His society by showing respect to tax collectors, Samaritans, the poor, lepers, and women. He treated all people as equals.

God considers us to be of such great worth that He sacrificed His only Son that we might be redeemed. Furthermore, He respects our individuality and the sovereignty of our wills by not forcing Himself or His will upon us but by allowing each person to decide for himself whether or not he will receive what God has to offer.

1. A general guideline of respect is that before making any commitment that impacts another person's life, take time to fully discuss it with them. For instance, marriage partners should discuss business commitments, trips, houseguests, major financial outlays, and other decisions *before* commitments are made. Parents should discuss with their children issues such as household chores and discipline measures. As your child grows up you'll want to discuss family schedules, trips, and commitments beforehand.

2. Solicit and show deference to your children's opinions. Everyone is entitled to his or her opinion—regardless of maturity or age; and since opinions are so personal, the need for respect is satisfied when we ask people to share their opinions and particularly when we show deference to their opinions. For instance, instead of telling your family where they're going on vacation, ask them where they would like to go. Instead of handing down "orders" to do household chores, allow them to be involved in the decision-making process.
3. Respect your children's property, privacy, and personal preferences. Take proper care of objects that you borrow and property you share. Honor other people's right of privacy; knock before you enter your child's room; if your child wants to "be alone," honor his/her request. If your child wants the breakfast toast fixed a certain way, be flexible as you honor his/her preference.
4. Respect your children's time. When you've made a commitment of your time—keep it. Don't take advantage of your child being a child, communicating that you were busy with "important" things.

Review the practical suggestions on meeting this need and consider a plan of ministry to each family member:

Child	*Practical Steps I Could Take to Meet This Need*
______________	____
______________	____
______________	____
______________	____
______________	____
______________	____
For instance: Tara	I will allow Tara to choose the comforter she wants for her bed. I will give her a specific price range, but will respect her final opinion.

Since You Asked . . .
Experiencing Biblical Truth in Perplexing Situations

Q: My husband is obsessed with our only son. It's beginning to be unhealthy. He spends all his time with him (certainly more time than he spends with me) and is even getting jealous of our son's involvement in other healthy relationships—he even tries to control his friends. What's going on?

A: As with most situations, the problem could be complex. The problem your family's experiencing could stem from one or a combination of several issues. Here are a few possibilities.

There's always a reason behind unproductive/abnormal behavior and often it has to do with unmet needs. Our tendency is to focus on the behavior instead of on what's prompting the behavior; but until we look beyond this, it's doubtful that the behavior will change.

For instance, what was your husband's home life like growing up? Did he receive from his parents adequate attention, approval, and appreciation? If not, that could explain why he's overly obsessed with your son. He could be overcompensating for the loss he felt as a boy and even be trying to assuage some of his own pain and hurt by pouring his life into the boy. In a kind and unthreatening way, enourage your husband to discuss his own childhood. As hurts and pains are identified, encourage him to mourn those losses and then minister comfort to him. In time, help him to see the correlation between his past losses and his present relationship with his son.

Another thought is: How is your husband/wife relationship? If it is strained and unfulfilling this might cause a partner to "look elsewhere" for the things that we all need from close, intimate relationships. Of course, this is a major contributing factor to infidelity in marriages. If needs are not being met at home, we may seek to have them illegitimately met in other ways. Therefore, it's not unusual to see a husband or wife "pour themselves" into the lives of their children simply because there's a lot of pain and stress in the marriage relationship. Though this is unhealthy, it often happens.

The answer to this challenge, of course, is to deepen the love and intimacy in the marriage.

—*Beware of "Unhealthy" Attention*

Scripture Journaling—John 13:14

"If I then, the Lord . . . washed your feet, you also ought to wash one another's feet."

Serving others with sensitivity and initiative is critical to deepening relationships. Christ exemplifies this in His washing of the disciples' feet. First, He was sensitive to their need; He noticed others' needs around Him. Second, He took initiative to give to the needs. Jesus didn't wait for the disciples to ask.

Consider Christ's example of sensitivity and initiative. Write about how exhibiting these two ingredients can communicate "worth" to a loved one. (For instance: "When I take the initiative to settle a conflict with Jason, this validates his worth because I am concerned about our relationship. When I serve Bethany by helping her in the kitchen, it validates her worth because I notice her needs.")

____

____

____

____

____

Now pause to pray this request: *Heavenly Father, I want to be a better servant to my family. Help me this week; lift my focus beyond myself to notice the needs of others. Prompt and empower my initiative in giving to meet these needs.*

Marriage Staff Meeting

Discuss together the idea that an important goal of our parenting is to see children come to exhibit humility, gentleness, and a servant's heart. How does this goal parallel the life of Christ? In what ways is it contrary to the "world's" concept of parenting? Reflect on areas where you see signs of humility in your family . . . gentle caring for others . . . a servant's heart. How could we as parents better role model this "target" for our children?

Now discuss the major ingredients of worth, belonging, and competence as they relate to the Trinity—God the Father, Son, and Holy Spirit. Give particular emphasis from this chapter on how parents can help "affirm" to a child their significant worth to God. Review the Appendix material on affirming worth and discuss how meeting needs for attention, acceptance, and respect are practical ways parents can communicate a sense of worth. As you review each of these needs, be vulnerable in sharing some of your specific ideas and plans for better meeting some of these needs. (See Appendix pp. 379–80.)

Review the article below on family devotions and plan to begin including some of the ideas into your Family Night activities. The most significant way to affirm your children's sense of worth is to help acquaint them with God and His special love for them.

Family Devotions . . . Boredom or Blessing?

When you see the phrase "family devotions," what comes to mind? Here's one possibility:

The family sitting side by side on the couch, attentively anticipating the arrival of "preacher Dad"—who soon enters with a large family Bible under one arm and a Greek/Hebrew lexicon under the other. After an opening prayer, voiced by one of the "parishioners," Dad delivers his prepared lecture on the topic: "Eschatological implications of the second seal in the Book of Revelation." The audience is stunned by the scholarly treatment of such a difficult text. Later in the service, an altar call is given and the service ends with a sober call to repentance.

Here's another possibility:

It's Saturday morning and everyone's slept a little late. Dad makes waffles and the family enjoys a casual breakfast together. Everyone knows what to expect next because more times than not, on Saturday mornings, the family spends some time together talking about their spiritual lives.

It's sister's turn to select a Scripture verse to discuss. She chooses Matthew 6:33, *"But seek first His kingdom and His righteousness; and all these things shall be added to you."* They discuss the verse one word at a time. "But"—this word means that the verse is connected to the previous verses. What do those verses say? "Seek"—how do you seek Jesus' kingdom and righteousness; are we talking about a treasure hunt? "First"—this word implies priority. "His kingdom"—is there another kingdom besides the Lord's? What is His kingdom? Mom, Dad, sister, and even little brother—everyone shares his/her thoughts. Sure, not everything that's said is profound, or even on the subject, but nobody is "corrected" or "belittled" for what he or she shares.

Mom picks out a verse for the family to memorize during the coming week. She selects Proverbs 20:3, *"Keeping away from strife is an honor for a man."* Everyone writes it down on a small card which can be carried throughout the week.

Dad asks everyone to share how they're feeling. Any hurts, fears, or anxieties that are expressed are met with words of comfort and encouragement and then added to the prayer list. Any feelings of joy and happiness become the basis for gratitude and thanksgiving.

Any hurts, fears, or anxieties that are expressed are met with words of comfort and encouragement and then added to the prayer list.

The family keeps a "Journal of Gratefulness" as members make note of special blessings and how they can express appreciation. Dad then asks if there's anything happening in the coming week that needs prayer. Sister shares about a friendship that has turned sour, Mom's teaching a Bible study Wednesday night, brother has a T-ball game, Dad will be out of town at an important business meeting. They pray together as a family.

A family devotion need not be a highly organized, lengthy, stressful, or boring event. It can be relaxed, fun, interesting, and interactive. It may only last fifteen minutes, but if held once a week on a consistent basis, the time can have a profound impact on the health of your family. These devotions can: establish Christ as the center of the family, provide a basis for wholesome family communication, affirm Dad as the servant-leader of the family, provide a weekly update on how everyone is feeling, help unify the family schedule, and provide a systematic plan for Bible study and memorization. Family devotions—they're fun, productive, and worth the effort!

Top Ten Need of the Week—Approval

Approval—expressed commendation; thinking and speaking well of.

This week puts particular emphasis on sharing approval. Your statements of approval might sound like:

- "Son, thank you for being so diligent in your studies."
- "You're tops!"
- "If I had 'custom ordered' a child, I would have asked for someone just like you."
- "I was reminded again today of how proud I am that you're my son."

Family Night Activity

Consider beginning this time together centered around Christ's washing of His disciples' feet in John 13. You might read the story together and dramatically act it out. You might even go further with a family reenactment as you take turns washing one another's feet. (Mom and Dad will want to wash one another's feet and then wash each child's. Children are also given the opportunity to wash Mom and Dad's feet. Another approach for large families would be to draw names, use several pans of water, and let the washing begin!)

Close the time with John 13 and a discussion of serving one another in humility and gentleness. Point out how Christ's sensitive caring to meet the disciples' needs communicated how important the disciples were to Him . . . if they weren't valued by Him, He would not have served them. Serving others communicates "I care and you are valued by me."

Now discuss the following three intimacy needs and how we can serve one another in these ways:

Attention

Attention relates to your decision to leave your daily routine and become involved with a family member's interest and concern. Jesus set the standard. Philippians 2:5-8 describes how the Lord climbed down from His throne to assume the position of a slave. In so doing, He placed your interests and those of others above His own. We are encouraged to have the same selfless attitude Christ exhibited.

Brad sought to enter into his son's world. One day Nathan came into the kitchen and announced to his dad that it was his teddy bear's birthday. "Dad," said Nathan, "Andrew Bear is four months old today, and we need to make him a birthday cake." Brad got the Betty Crocker cookbook out of the kitchen drawer, blended together the ingredients for a chocolate cake, and celebrated the teddy bear's birthday with his son. On another occasion, Nathan requested, "Dad, let's go lizard huntin'." So Brad and Nathan "fixed up" a lizard cage and went on a lizard hunt. With a little luck they trapped one and Nathan was very excited.

Undoubtedly you long for members of your family to willingly enter your world and affirm your worth and value. How would you like a family member to meet your need for attention? Have each family member think about an answer and then share your responses. Write family family members' responses here:

____

____

____

Acceptance

Acceptance involves an intentional choice on your part to keep on receiving and loving each member of your family. The model of acceptance is Jesus Christ, who "accepted us" (Rom. 15:7). Christ received believers when they were not only "helpless" (5:6), but also "ungodly" (v. 6), "sinners" (v. 8), and "enemies" (v. 10).

Heather modeled this kind of acceptance toward her teenage son Levi by focusing on his needs rather than his faults. Levi had a few bad habits and some tastes which conflicted with hers. For example, he liked to wear his hair in a particular style that Heather really didn't like. She thought his haircut was "worldly." However, Heather ministered to Levi's need for acceptance and unconditional love. This allowed Levi the freedom to be himself and express his individuality without feeling judged or condemned. Heather wisely refused to forfeit the relationship with her son over something that really had no eternal significance. Heather's response was instrumental in Levi's decision to change some of his unproductive habits . . . and after only two weeks, he went back to a more traditional haircut!

One way to demonstrate acceptance to a family member is to look past his/her imperfections and meet his/her needs. In what ways can you show unconditional acceptance toward a member of your family? And in what ways can a family member demonstrate acceptance toward you? Think about your answers and then share your responses. "I feel accepted when . . ." Write family responses here:

____

____

____

Respect

You convey respect to a family member by valuing him/her and holding them in high regard. According to Philippians 2:28-30, the believers in Philippi were not to think incorrectly of Epaphroditus for coming home. Epaphroditus had not failed when Paul needed him most. Epaphroditus was to be welcomed and held "in high regard." Paul's desire here illustrates how we ought to relate toward those who may be misunderstood by others. Christian love is always desirable, for it defends others and overlooks their faults.

When Mark and Joy considered moving to a different city and state, they called a family meeting and discussed the idea with their children. They tried to address the concerns of each child and to value everyone's opinion. Consequently, the children felt included in a plan which ultimately changed the course of their entire lives.

How can family members address your need for respect? Think

about your answer and then share your responses. "I feel respected when . . ." Write family responses here:

____

____

____

Goal-setting Helps Communicate "Worth"

A special way to encourage "worth-building" is to discuss goal-setting with your child and then work together to see these goals fulfilled.

- What are some things you'd like to see done in your room? or with your wardrobe?
- Are there some friends you'd like to get to know better this year?
- Are there hobbies you'd like to learn or spend time on?
- What improvements would you like to see made this year on your bicycle, sound system, car, etc.?

Close by sharing Galatians 3:26—*"For you are all sons of God through faith in Christ Jesus."*

Take this opportunity to remind your children that they have an identity greater than being "your kids." They are loved intimately and abundantly by God, and they can be a part of His family. (If your children are developmentally ready, talk to them about how to have a personal relationship with Christ. Ask for the assistance of a church staff member if you don't feel completely equipped. If your child already has a personal relationship with Christ, remind them of the Heavenly Father who is available to help them.) Share your personal testimony of how you came to establish a personal relationship with Christ.

Family Devotional (for older children and teens)

Pass out Bibles, choose teams, and enlist the family in a Bible "race" to see which team can come up with the longest list of benefits of spending time in God's Word. You'll find these benefits in Psalm 119. (Noted below is a beginning list of 22 benefits!)

God's Word ...

1. Establishes my way (vv. 1-5)
2. Purifies my life (vv. 9-11)
3. Gives me counsel (v. 24)
4. Removes everything false in me (v. 29)
5. Produces reverence for God (v. 38)
6. Increases my courage (v. 46)
7. Comforts me in afflictions (v. 50)
8. Guards me from panic (vv. 61-62)
9. Teaches me discernment and knowledge (v. 66)
10. Makes me resourceful (v. 79)
11. Cultivates patience (v. 87)
12. Keeps me spiritually revived (v. 93)
13. Accelerates my understanding (vv. 98-100)
14. Creates a joyful heart (v. 111)
15. Sustains me when I feel helpless (v. 116)
16. Enables me to honor right and hate wrong (v. 128)
17. Causes me to walk in the truth (v. 133)
18. Surrounds me with delight, even in times of difficulty (v. 143)
19. Develops the discipline of prayer (v. 147)
20. Rescues me when I am defenseless (vv. 153-154)
21. Fills me with praise without and peace within (vv. 164–65)
22. God's Word draws me back when I stray (v. 176)

Close with this reminder:

As you get to know the Author, you'll see that nothing else can do these things for you! There's nothing magical about just reading the words on the page; the "magic" is in the relationship with Jesus Christ, the central theme of the entire Bible.

Group Discussion

Begin this discussion by reviewing this goal of parenting—to see our children develop humility, gentleness, and a servant's heart. How well do you model these qualities for your children? How well does this goal fit with your expectations for your daughter? Your son? What pressures from school, work, or society seem contrary to this goal of a gentle, humble servant? How can we as parents support one another in resisting these pressures?

What insights or reflections did you have as you thought about your own worth to the Father? Your place of belonging as joint-heir with Christ? Your guarantee of compliance as the Spirit of the Living God dwells inside your understanding of your identity?

Share the practical ways you plan to meet the need for attention, acceptance, and respect in your children. To emphasize the connection between these needs and the concept of worth, complete this sentence: "Because my child is worth the Heavenly Father's love, I will. . . ."

Close your time together by making "price tags" for each family member (don't forget to make one for yourself). Using blank printer labels and magic markers, make "price tags" that declare your and your child's worth. Your price tags might contain words like:

God says I'm worth—$ Christ's death on the cross
$ Undivided attention from those who love me
$ Receiving __________, __________, and __________

Be sure to wear your price tag home, then distribute the price tags to your children as well. Explain the meaning of the price tags and affirm your child's worth!

CHAPTER 12

Becoming Caringly Involved to Build Belonging

IT IS UNTHINKABLE that this could have happened to the Apostle Paul—but it did:

"At my first defense no one supported me, but all deserted me; may it not be counted against them"—2 Timothy 4:16.

During his time of greatest need, the esteemed apostle and leader of the first century church was deserted.

By contrast, we're commanded in Ephesians 6:2 to *"Bear one another's burdens, and thus fulfill the law of Christ."* Corrie ten Boom reminds us that, "God doesn't make any suggestions." Carrying another's burden isn't a suggestion. God comands it.

Succinctly stated, we have a biblical mandate to comfort those who need comforting, to stand with friends in times of distress, and to carry one another's burdens. This is a major part of following Christ and a prerequisite for experiencing the abundant Christian life.

Families have a specific calling to provide a "place of belonging" where each family member is confident and secure that they'll never be deserted!

God declares us fellow-heirs with Christ in Romans 8:17. The Bible tells us that we have been adopted into God's family and are His special children. We belong to Him. We are part of a spiritual family and are members of the body of Christ. We see these principles most dramatically portrayed when we meet followers of Christ from another community or culture. When you experience the instant bonding and sweet Christian fellowship with someone whom you've just met, you understand what it means to belong. All you know is that you and this "stranger" are both children of the same Heavenly Father.

All you know is that you and this "stranger" are both children of the same Heavenly Father.

And you experience the joy of knowing where you came from. You also experience the assurance that you're not alone on this spiritual journey.

Our mission as earthly parents is to create an environment within our family that produces these same assurances. Children need to know where they came from.

They need to sense a place of security, of refuge and connectedness. Children need to know that they are not alone on their journey toward adulthood.

God's Gifts Have a Purpose

"The fruit of the womb is a reward"—Psalm 127:3.

The Hebrew word translated here as "reward" (*sakar*) speaks of great benefit—typically coming as the result of work performed. The word is therefore used to describe hiring an army (2 Sam. 10:6; 2 Kings 7:6; 1 Chron. 19:6), skilled laborers (2 Chron. 24:12; Isa. 46:6), and counselors for advice (Ezra 4:5).

Uniquely, Psalm 127:3 speaks of children as "reward" with no mention of work performed—children as a "grace" from God, not a work to be "earned" by mere humans. Thus, children are an undeserved blessing (grace) with a divinely intended purpose.

Why are gifts given? What is their purpose? One purpose in "gift-giving" is to remind us of the giver. Gifts are often given, received, valued, and cherished as "reminders" of the one who gave the gift. Therefore, children serve as an ever-present reminder of Yahweh, the Creator behind the Creation.

Pause now and thank God for your "gifts" and then praise Him as the *"giver of all good gifts."*

I thank You, Father, for ______________________________

I praise You, Father, for ______________________________

Second, gifts encourage our stewardship and responsibility. Scripture is filled with admonitions that, "to whom much is given, much is required" (see Luke 12:48). So it is with parenting. Children call us to accountability and stewardship. Just as Jehovah responded responsibly to Israel, parents should provide example, security, and the commitment of unconditional love to their children.

Consider this concept of children challenging us to be good stewards of God's blessing. Meditate on the multitude of ways God has blessed you. List as many as you can below. (For instance: "God has blessed me with His love and forgiveness, His comfort, His daily provision, and His assurance of salvation.")

____

____

____

____

____

____

Build Belonging

The need to "belong" is so strong that it will be met . . . by parents or peers; by good influences or bad ones. Building a strong sense of family belonging is the best investment parents can make in protecting children/teenagers from unhealthy peer pressure influences. Families who laugh together, vacation together, and work together help build belonging. Belonging is built through the closeness of hugs, verbalized love, and words of endearment; family traditions at holidays, birthdays, and other times are important; family common interests, special memories, and fun times also help build belonging.

Since You Asked...
Experiencing Biblical Truth in Perplexing Situations

Q: I see so many kids who seem to idolize gangs and gang behavior. How can I protect my children from this?

A: Gang behavior is often symptomatic of deep unmet needs in children and teenagers. Needs such as acceptance, approval, and security are illegitimately and only temporarily met by being a member of a gang. To help protect your children from the temptations of being a part of a gang (or any socially unacceptable group), make sure their needs are being lovingly and adequately met within the sphere of your family and church friends. For instance, to affirm their importance to the family, share with them, "I really like having you in our family. You are a special gift to us. You really belong here!" Reinforce their positive character traits, "I appreciate your hard work. I admire your patience and kindness." Affirm their worth regardless of their performance, "Even when you make mistakes, I love you. I love you just the way you are." Help provide peer relationships by taking the initiative to cultivate family friendships where your children are frequently around peers with common convictions and values. Finally, on a regular basis, enter into your child's world in order to meet their need for attention, "Let's play together. Where would you like to go this Saturday?" If your children's needs are adequately met through wholesome relationships, they will be more resistant to having them met in the context of unwholesome ones.

—the need to "belong" is so strong, it will be met

Review again the chart that follows with a specific focus on building a sense of belonging through meeting the intimacy needs of affection, comfort, and security.

We'll review each of these key needs in significant detail with practical suggestions on how parents can become caringly involved.

Affection

To communicate care and closeness through physical touch and affirming words.

"Greet one another with a holy kiss"—Romans 16:16.

During His earthly ministry, Jesus was continually in physical contact with others. When Jesus healed, He often did so accompa-

DIMENSIONS OF AFFIRMED-IDENTITY WITH TOP 10 INTIMACY "NEEDS"

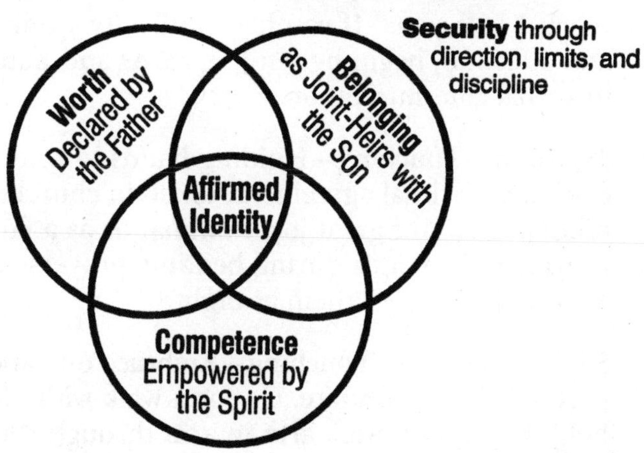
I **belong** to a family who gives...
Affection...verbally and physically
Comfort through compassionate care when I'm hurt, lonely, afraid, disappointed, or rejected
Security through direction, limits, and discipline
Worth
Declared by the Father
Belonging
as Joint-Heirs with the Son
Affirmed Identity
Competence
Empowered by the Spirit

nied by physical contact (Matt. 8:3, 15; 9:29); He consoled His disciples accompanied by physical contact (17:7); and He ministered to children through physical affection (Matt. 19:13; Mark 10:16).

1. Using discretion, become more physical in your relationships—beginning with your spouse and children. The appropriateness of certain gestures will be determined by the relationship:

Spouse—hold, caress, give back rubs, hold hands, kiss. It's important that these physical gestures be shared, not just as acts leading to sexual intimacy, but as expressions of emotional love and support. Kids feel great security as they see this affection.

Your own children—cuddle, kiss, hold hands, wrestle, hug, give back scratches, tickle.

Friends—shake hands, hug, give a pat on the back, embrace.

2. Verbalize your love: speak words of love, kindness, and affection. It's particularly encouraging to speak spontaneous expressions which are "unmerited." For instance, you might say, "I've been thinking today about how special you are to me and how much I love you." If you have difficulty speaking words of love and affection, begin by sending cards and notes, then progress to verbal communication.

3. "Spiritual" Touching—Holding hands to pray communicates common spiritual agreement; touch in church; embrace one another at times of great joy; hold hands as a family at the dinner prayer. Hold hands during bedtime prayers. Touch your child as you pray "over" them at night.

4. Soul (Friendship) Touching—Embrace one another as you depart and as you reunite. Go for a walk with your child as you hold their hand; walk arm in arm through the mall with your spouse; "claim" one another through your embrace when you're out in public!

Give "family group hugs" where the entire family participates. Even if hugs aren't reciprocated, keep giving them!

Parents should role model affectionate caring in the marriage relationship to convey the appropriateness of affection in adult, "real-world" relationships.

Give "family group hugs" where the entire family participates. Play family games like Twister or London Bridge that require touch. Resist "backing off" of affection as the child becomes a teenager. Even if hugs aren't reciprocated, keep giving them!

Research Study—Affection—We All Need It

"Everyone needs at least three hugs a day in order to be healthy," says Sidney Simon who teaches at the University of Massachusetts at Amherst.

The skin is the body's largest sense organ with millions of nerve endings. Without stimulation, humans often experience an ache or longing that the medical world labels "skin hunger." People with this condition find it more difficult to get and stay well.

Over the past decade, scientific evidence has been mounting on the favorable effects of touch on the human body.

- The heartbeats of many intensive care patients stabilize after their hands are held by nurses.
- Cerebral palsy victims move more normally after receiving sensory stimulation.
- Children with Down's syndrome walk earlier if they're hugged, touched, and stroked a great deal by their mothers.
- "Laying on of hands," an ancient religious healing practice, has now been found to have a scientific basis.
- Hemoglobin levels and brain waves respond to touch.
- Children with the highest grades get more hugs at home.

(From an article by Barbara Deane, *USA Today*.)

Review the practical suggestions on meeting this need for affection and consider a plan of ministry to each family member:

Child	*Practical Steps I Could Take to Meet This Need*
____________	____________________________
____________	____________________________
____________	____________________________
____________	____________________________
____________	____________________________
For instance: Courtney	She loves to get things in the mail. I'll send her a card once a week—just to tell her I love her.

Comfort

To give strength and hope; to ease the grief or pain; to console, cheer; to weep with those who weep, mourn with those who mourn.

"The God of all comfort; who comforts us in all our affliction so that we may be able to comfort those who are in any trouble"—2 Corinthians 1:3-4.

Jesus ministered comfort throughout His earthly ministry, often identifying with the hurts of others to the degree that He wept with them (John 11:35; Luke 19:41). Even on the eve of His death, Jesus comforted His disciples (John 14:1, 18; 16:33).

God is the "God of all comfort" (2 Cor. 1:3), and the Holy Spirit is often referred to as the "Comforter" (John 14:16, 26; 15:26; 16:7). The Greek word for comfort is "*parakaleo*" which means "to come to one's side, to one's aid" and suggests the ability to console and give help.

1. Learn to recognize times when your children have an increased need for comfort and be available and willing to minister to them. We have an acute need for comfort when: we've experienced rejection or disappointment; we're physically ill; under stress; a tragedy has occurred; we've experienced the trauma of a divorce or separation; or when our "comfort zone" is challenged or violated (a school change, move to another city).

2. When someone needs comforting, refrain from correcting them ("The reason this happened is . . ."), teaching them ("Next time . . ."), giving them a "pep-talk" ("Come on, cheer up! It's a beautiful day outside!"), or giving advice ("If I were you, I'd . . ."). Instead, learn to *empathize* with those who are hurting. Empathy involves identifying with the feelings of others—to hurt with those who hurt, to weep with those who weep. Comfort is an emotional need and cannot be met by intellectual instruction (such as correction, teaching, or giving advice).

3. Learn the "vocabulary of comfort"—phrases like, "I'm so sorry that you're hurting," "I hurt for you," "I love you, and I want

to pray for you right now," "I'm on your side, and I'm committed to help you through this." These phrases can be communicated verbally or in writing.

Since You Asked . . .
Experiencing Biblical Truth in Perplexing Situations

Q: I've just adopted a one-year-old boy who has been in an abusive situation. He seems fine now but we anticipate some challenges in the future. Is there anything special we should do?

A: First, your desire to be prepared for special ministry to your son is to be applauded. It surely must bless God as He sees parents preparing to more effectively care for their *"gift from the Lord"* (Ps. 127:3).

Anticipate the possibility of mood swings and "acting out behavior" later in childhood. Give lots of affection, affirmation, and reassurance. Provide consistent instruction and discipline but avoid displaying anger in discipline. Instead, be ready with gentle words and comforting touch as you see anger expressed (Prov. 15:1).

Don't expect that your affectionate nurturing by itself will take away the pain; the "great Physician" will be there for your son. Role model unconditional love and acceptance as a testimony of the Heavenly Father . . . speaking often of Him and His ministry of comfort and healing.

Later in adolescence, the pain of early neglect and abuse can be grieved as feelings of sadness, loneliness, and hurt are experienced. As caring parents, you can minister words of comfort to your son, "It grieves me deeply that you experienced such trauma early in life. My heart is broken for you . . . and I love you." It's often difficult for adoptive parents to express this type of empathy toward their child's pain of earlier rejection, thinking that to do so means that as adoptive parents you have not done everything you could to "make-up" for this earlier pain. Avoid this faulty thinking for these are two separate issues. You have been caring, nurturing adoptive parents; but your son experienced pain before you came into his life, and that early pain must be properly mourned and comforted.

—every adopted child can benefit from loving comfort

Review the practical suggestions on meeting this need for comfort and consider a plan of ministry to each family member:

Child	*Practical Steps I Could Take to Meet This Need*
______________	____
______________	____
______________	____
______________	____
______________	____
For instance: Benjamin	Ben's best friend just moved to another city. I'll talk to him tonight and let him know that it's OK to feel sad. I'll tell him that I love him and I know he misses his friend.

Security

Freedom from fear and danger; to put behind the danger of losing, want, or deprivation; confidence of "harmony" in relationships.

"May they prosper who love You"— Psalm 122:6.

During His earthly ministry, Jesus offered security to those who were close to Him by continually meeting their physical, emotional, and spiritual needs. At times He even performed a miracle to meet the physical need for food (feeding of the 5,000).

God meets our need for security by promising never to leave us or forsake us He promises to meet needs for food, clothing, and shelter

God meets our need for security by promising never to leave us or forsake us (Josh. 1:5). He promises to meet needs for food, clothing, and shelter (Matt. 6:25-32), and those who trust Jesus as Savior are eternally secure, *"I give eternal life to them, and they shall never perish; and no one shall snatch them out of My hand"*— John 10:28.

1. Provide "relational" security within each family relationship. For instance, a husband or wife should live in such a way that their spouse and children know they are committed to marital faithfulness. Children should feel secure in knowing that their parents will always care for them. They need reassurance that divorce is not an option for their parents. Or if a divorce has occurred, children need to know that the divorce was not their fault and that the parents' love for them remains intact.

2. Let your children know that you're aware of their physical, emotional, and spiritual needs and that you're committed to help meet those needs. We're "satisfied" or "blessed" when our needs are currently being met; we're "secure" when we know that our needs will be met in the future. For instance, relative to our need for food—we feel satisfied after consuming a delicious meal; we feel secure in knowing that we'll have food tomorrow and beyond. You can also minister security to others by verbally reassuring them of your love and attention, "I just want you to know how committed I am to meeting your needs and loving you as God has loved me."

3. Provide financial security for those to whom you're responsible. For instance, mothers and fathers should provide financial security for their families by: operating on a budget, adhering to scriptural principles of finances, having a good work ethic, developing marketable skills, producing adequate income, having a viable will, and providing a secure financial future.

4. Provide the security of your gentleness. Proverbs 15:1 says, "*A gentle answer turns away wrath [anger], but a harsh word stirs up anger.*" Many times the response of anger is a direct result of an emotional need going unmet. Your child may need acceptance from a friend, but receive rejection instead. Your child may express anger as a result of the rejection—perhaps toward a friend, a sibling, or you. A significant aspect of your child's security is whether he or she can "count on" your gentle answer to his or her expressions of anger.

Look sensitively at any outbursts of anger this week. Try to discern if an unmet need may have provoked the anger. Most of all, resist reacting with your own harsh words. Let your gentle answer turn away wrath. For example:

A child who needs big doses of security may respond in anger if left in the nursery or daycare. Let your words speak gently to their need. *I know you're going to miss Mommy while I'm in my class, and I will miss you too. Miss Karen will be here with you. I'll see you after snack time.*

Review the practical suggestions on meeting this need for security and consider a plan of ministry to each family member:

Child	*Practical Steps I Could Take to Meet This Need*
______________	____
______________	____
______________	____
For instance: Sarah	I'll initiate a conversation with Sarah and let her know that we're going to have to work out transportation for her. She needs to know that I recognize her effort in finding a job and that I'm committed to helping her fulfill her responsibilities.

A Child's Advice to His Parents

Give Me **Affection**	I am a special gift from God. Treasure me as God intended, stopping me occasionally just to say you love me; let me start and end each day with a hug.
Give Me **Comfort**	From time to time I'll need you to be sad with me when I'm hurting; please don't give me advice or "pep talks"—just hold me and comfort me. Your sadness with me reassures me it's OK to be sad.
Give Me **Security**	Please don't be afraid to leave for a weekend together. Kids need vacations from parents, just as parents need to get away occasionally. This is also a great way to make us feel secure that your marriage is very special.

What "advice" do you see here that could positively impact your relationship with your child? Write here about any thoughts God brings to mind:

____

____

____

____

Proven Ways to Produce "Problem" Children

Don't Provide **Affection**	When faced with a choice of whether to focus your time and attention on material pursuit or the "simplicity" of quiet talks, affirming words, and gentle touch—always choose material.
Don't Provide **Comfort**	Be too busy with business, ministry, civic, or social life to notice your child is worried, disappointed, or insecure; let him grow up hurting alone.
Don't Provide **Security**	Don't teach your child the security of God's Word and God's ways. Let him wait until he is old enough to decide right from wrong for himself.

Prayerfully consider each reflection above and ask God to show you additional dimensions of affection, comfort, and security that might be beneficial for your children. Write your thoughts here.

____

____

____

____

Scripture Journaling—1 Samuel 2:22-24

"Now Eli was very old; and he heard all that his sons were doing to all Israel . . . and he said to them, 'Why do you do such things, the evil things

that I hear from all these people? No, my sons; for the report is not good which I hear the Lord's people circulating.' "

Painfully, earlier in this chapter of 1 Samuel it is written, *"Now the sons of Eli were worthless men; they did not know the Lord"* (v. 12). Even though they were children of a religious leader, Eli's sons lacked this critical sense of "belonging."

Reflect on verses 22-24 above and consider these three key issues:

1. How did Eli learn of his sons' evil behavior? What does this say about the depth of intimacy in the relationships? Should our goal as parents be to so "know" our children that we "sense" their pain, guilt, and "evil" long before hearing it from others?

2. Consider Eli's "response": "Why do you do such things?" Doesn't asking "why" convey the message that "if I can rationalize a good enough reason . . . maybe I'll get out of trouble"? What would have been a more appropriate rebuke and discipline? (Notice 1 Sam. 3:13 speaks of God's judgment because Eli "did not rebuke" his sons.)

3. Reread verses 22-24 and consider these questions: What does Eli seem most concerned about as he discovers his sons' evil? Are there any references to his concern over God being displeased or grieved?

The Bible speaks of these things happening *"as an example, and they were written for our instruction"*—1 Corinthians 10:11.

Prayerfully consider and make note of God's impressions to you concerning:

Your need to truly "know" your children, sensing their needs, pain, and guilt:

____

____

____

Your need to reprove, exhort, rebuke in love, rather than offer or accept justifying, rationalizing, and blaming:

____

____

____

____

Your need to seek God's approval on your parenting, resisting the temptation to "parent" for the approval of others:

____

____

____

____

Marriage Staff Meeting

Begin this time together with a discussion on your home as a "place of belonging." Just as certainly as Christians have been made a part of Christ's body, His church—our homes are to provide a place of "sure connectedness." Our homes can provide this atmosphere of refuge as we minister to the key intimacy needs of *affection, comfort,* and *security.*

Review the Appendix material entitled "Build Belonging" as you reflect on your consideration of these three needs (see Appendix, p. 381). What additional displays of caring *affection* might be called for with your children? in your marriage? i.e., more spontaneous "I love you's," more hugs upon departing and reuniting? more tickling and wrestling? more holding hands to walk, to pray? What opportunities to share *comfort* do you see with each child? Practice with one another what comfort "sounds like." (Remember, it's not advice, lectures, or "pep talks.") What additional *security* could be added to your home? Do children sense the

> ***Just as certainly as Christians have been made a part of Christ's body, His church—our homes are to provide a place of "sure connectedness."***

unconditional commitment of a secure marriage? Do they enjoy the security of your gentle words in response to their occasional temper outbursts? (Prov. 15:1) Does your family enjoy the security of fun times sharing Bible stories and the eternal lessons conveyed?

Discuss Psalm 19:7-10 and the "testimonies of the Lord." Could your family benefit from a study of Joseph, Lot, or Tamar? Schedule these into your Family Night activities. As an idea to "kick-off" more opportunities of sharing the Bible with your family, review the Family Night activity entitled "Home Dedication" from 1 Kings 8 (on p. 329) and schedule it into an upcoming time with your family.

Top Ten Need of the Week—Appreciation

Appreciation—Communication of personal gratefulness for another.

Place a particular emphasis on sharing appreciation this week. Let your child know that you're grateful for who he is. Your responses might include:

- "Tanya, I admire the way you're always sensitive to new kids who enroll in your school."
- "Thanks for helping with the dishes."
- "John, I appreciate you watching your little brother while Mom and I went out last night."
- "Teresa, you're one of the finest workers I know. If I had a company and could hire a key employee, I'd hire you."

Family Night Activity

Review the "Since You Asked" question concerning "Why kids join gangs," page 312. For children ten and older, discuss this question as an opening to discuss "belonging." For younger children you might introduce the topic by cutting out a large house from a piece of poster board. Write every family member's name on the house in large letters. Cut the house into puzzle pieces. Let your children put the puzzle together and find their name on the puzzle. Discuss the importance of every family member. Complete this sentence: "You are an important part of our family because . . ."

Discuss how your family can be a "place of belonging" as affection, comfort, and security needs are met. We don't anticipate that the stranger on the street will care that we're sad—but we need our family to care enough to comfort us. We don't want just anyone giving us hugs, but it feels good when our family does.

Now share about *affection, security,* and *comfort* and discuss how we can build belonging through meeting these needs in our family.

Affection

Affection involves your willingness to communicate oneness and concern through gentle touch and tender words. A beautiful picture of affection can be seen in the relationship between Paul and the Christians at Thessalonica (1 Thes. 2:7-8). Paul and his companions cared for their converts as a *"nursing mother tenderly cares for her own children"* (v. 7). The gentleness and unselfishness of Paul as a spiritual caregiver shines through in this illustration. Paul's "fond affection" for the Thessalonians led him to impart not only the message of eternal salvation but also his own life (v. 8).

One way that Sam demonstrates affection to his daughter, Julie, is by tickling her at bedtime and in the mornings to wake her. Julie really feels loved when she is tickled. She likes her dad's playful affection. This provides Sam an avenue to express affectionate love to Julie.

Verbalize affection to a family member. Develop the discipline of speaking spontaneous words of kindness to your child for no apparent reason. For example, you might say, "I've been thinking today about how special you are to me and how much I love you." If you are uncomfortable expressing yourself verbally in that way, consider sending cards and notes, as you cultivate verbal communication.

In what ways can you express physical and verbal affection to a family member? How could a family member better meet your need for affection? Write everyone's name on a slip of paper and then draw names. Ask every family member to think of a time and a way that they can surprise this person with an "I love you." Set a deadline (for example: before bedtime tomorrow) and let each person plan their surprise affection. Write each family member's preference here. How can our family meet your need for affection:

____

____

Security

You can meet a family member's need for security by promoting harmony in the relationship. Peaceful conditions prevailed in the Thessalonian church, but they had to be maintained. Thus Paul exhorted his readers to "live in peace with one another" (1 Thes. 5:13).

Tony met his son's need for security by clearly defining behavioral expectations and consequences. Eric knew that if he washed the family car and refueled it after each use, he could drive it on weekly outings with his friends. However, if he failed in his responsibility, then he would lose his privilege.

Cindy feels secure when she sees her mom and dad hug and kiss, sensing their enduring commitment to one another.

What would cause you to feel more secure in the relationship with a family member? How could you increase harmony with family members? Share your responses. Write family member's responses here:

____

____

____

Comfort

Next, discuss the need for comfort by sharing Tom's story and the four responses we *don't* need when we're sad, upset, or disappointed.

"As an adolescent," Tom said, "I went through a 'chubby' stage. My peers at school called me such names as 'pound cake' and 'fatso.' Whenever I shared my hurt with others, I received one of our unproductive responses":

1. **Logic or reasoning**
   "Tommy, this is just a stage you're going through. You won't always be fat. Besides, kids will always find a reason to tease you."

2. **Criticism**
   "Tom, if you wouldn't eat so much you wouldn't be fat. If you just wouldn't put so much sugar in your tea . . ."

3. Complaints

"Tom, people have always made fun of me, especially my height. As a kid growing up, they called me 'stump,' 'shorty.' "

4. Neglect

"Tommy, just focus on something positive."

Do any of these four responses sound familiar? None of them will "connect" with your emotional need or that of a family member. What Tom needed was comfort. He needed for his parents and other family members to "feel into" his hurt, to "enter into" his suffering so that he would not have to endure it alone.

Practice with your family what comfort "sounds like." Give each family member opportunity to share what comforting words they would like to hear. Guide them to see the power of gentle, compassionate empathy.

Home Dedication

Finally, prepare your family for a special time of dedicating your home as a "place of refuge"—a place where each of you can retreat from this world's stress and pressure, confident that you'll find people who care.

Begin with a Bible reading of selected parts of 1 Kings 8 and then guide your family through the steps of Home Dedication at the end of this chapter. Pause to pray briefly after each dedication (perhaps taking turns, asking a different family member to pray each time).

For Group Discussion

1. Spend a few moments reflecting on your "status" as a fellow-heir with Christ. Think about what it means to be a member of Christ's family and to have the same access to the Father. Personalize these thoughts; make them real for you. What impact could this have on your life? Your family's life?

2. Practice comforting one another during this discussion. Divide into groups of two or three people. Ask each person to tell

about a current life situation in which they feel inadequate, worried, confused, or afraid. As each person shares their story, the other group members share words of empathy. Guard against the tendency to give logic, criticism, advice, or a pep talk. Meet emotion with emotion. Share words of comfort.

As you end this activity, discuss how difficult it can be to give true comfort. Our natural tendency is to give responses rather than empathy. But in order to communicate a sense of belonging to our children, we must override this tendency.

3. Share ways that you plan to increase the amount of affection in your home. Some parents may feel less comfortable expressing affection; talk about this hesitancy and the associated feelings. Discuss ways to continue to show affection to teenagers even when they resist.

4. Share reflections or plans concerning your Family Night Home Dedication. What impact did it have or do you hope it will have on your family?

5. Close your time together by discussing this question: "Since we belong to Christ's family, what resources do we have that will help us in our earthly family?" Remember we have the Perfect Parent living inside us. He's interested and available to help us with the smallest details of family life.

Home Dedication

<u>SCRIPTURE READING</u> – In I Kings 8:22-28, King Solomon seeks God's blessing on God's new "home" as the temple in Jerusalem is dedicated.

On this day our family joined together to dedicate our home to the Lord...seeking His presence, guidance and blessing.

In an attitude of prayer and gratefulness, take turns sharing these Scriptures and a short prayer of dedication after each: Solomon knelt before the Lord and you also might find this meaningful.

DEDICATION AS A <u>PLACE OF PRAYER</u> – *Read together I Kings 8:28-30. Might God often find us in prayer...individually and as a family...at mealtime and bedtime...in thanksgiving and intercession.*

DEDICATION AS A <u>PLACE OF FORGIVENESS</u> – *Read together I Kings 8:33-40. Might each of us quickly seek God's forgiveness as we find ourselves "defeated" because of occasional sin...and might we also quickly forgive one another, letting not the sun go down on our anger.*

DEDICATION AS A <u>PLACE OF MINISTRY</u> – *Read together I Kings 8:41-43. Father, might you often, through our invitation, bring people into this home who will sense that it is a special place...dedicated to You...a place of hospitality, peace and love.*

DEDICATION AS A <u>PLACE OF REFUGE</u> – *Read together I Kings 8:44-45. Father, as each of us is sent out daily by "whatever way you send us"...to work or to play... to school or to church...we will often return from these "battles" needing encouragement, support and love; might we each find this refuge in one another...in this place.*

DEDICATION AS A <u>PLACE OF WORSHIP</u> – *Read together I Kings 8:53-61. Lord, because we are your people and we have been blessed by your abundant provision...we choose to incline our hearts toward you that we might walk in your ways...that through our lives, our family and our home, people might come to know that <u>the Lord is God</u>!*

Acknowledged this day before the Lord, Who is Our God. Might His glory fill this place!

Family Member Signatures

__________________ __________________ __________________

__________________ __________________ __________________

Date __________________

"And it came about when the priests came from the holy place, that the cloud filled the house of the Lord so that the priests could not stand to minister because of the cloud, for the glory of the Lord filled the house of the Lord." I Kings 8:10-11.

CHAPTER 13

Becoming Caringly Involved to Instill Competence

THE CREED FOR the '60s was expressed in the lyrics of a popular song written by Simon and Garfunkel—"I am a rock, I am an island." The idea was: "Be self-sufficient, impregnable, self-confident—each man to his own."

It didn't work. In fact, the self-sufficient attitude of the '60s led to the morally corrupt and materialistic mentality of the '70s and '80s. The creed of the early church was quite different: "We are a body; we need each other; we have all things in common." We could call it the "one another" mentality of the early church.

A fundamental aspect of God's plan for His people and His families is revealed through Scripture and modeled by the early church: we need each other.

God has constructed His body in such a way that we are to be found mutually giving to "one another." Have you ever noticed how often "one another" is mentioned in the New Testament?

"Greet one another"	26 times
"Comfort one another"	6 times
"Love one another"	16 times
"Teach one another"	4 times
"Admonish one another"	2 times
"Serve one another"	4 times

"Honor one another"	2 times
"Be devoted to one another"	1 time
"Bear one another's burdens"	2 times
"Accept one another"	1 time
"Forgive one another"	3 times

To admit that we need each other is not a sign of weakness; it's a confirmation of our humanity. It's not indicative of spiritual immaturity; it's an integral aspect of how the body of Christ functions . . . and how He desires our families to work.

As families come together through their "one-another" giving, they experience another blessing—the blessing that I'm *not alone!* Recall again man's first dilemma from Genesis 2. *"It's not good to be alone"* (v. 18). It seems clear, in fact, that one of God's original burdens for us was to remove our "alone-ness." Through the provision of Himself and His ordained relationships . . . marriage, family, and the church . . . we need never be alone.

Pause and consider this contrast between the aloneness of self-sufficiency and the blessing of "one-another" giving (i.e., intimacy). List as many consequences of self-sufficiency as you can think of, followed by a list of blessings from the mutual giving of intimacy. Write your thoughts below.

Painful consequences of self-sufficiency: (For instance: "When I am self-sufficient, I keep the people I love at arm's length. I cut myself off from the joy of an intimate relationship.")

____

____

____

Blessings of intimate relationships: (For instance: "When I am involved in a mutually giving relationship, I experience the thrill of giving to another and the blessing of receiving. Both experiences produce humility.")

____

____

____

It would seem then a significant aspect of God's plan for families would be that through the impact of intimate relationships our aloneness might in some part be removed. We'll also explore how this removal of aloneness frees us to develop *competency*, becoming fully adequate for every undertaking God directs.

Family closeness is not automatic. It doesn't happen merely because we live in the same house or share the same last name. Neither is it guaranteed simply because we share in the same structured routine. Family intimacy cannot be "programmed" to happen but neither can it be expected to spontaneously "appear."

In contrast to this need for marital and family closeness is the issue of loneliness. Research findings and surveys consistently identify "*loneliness among children*" as a major underlying issue of widespread proportion. A picture often evolves from these studies which highlights the intergenerational transmission of loneliness to children. Parental loneliness is quite often lived out, not in withdrawal and isolation, but in the "barrenness" of an overly busy life . . . well-meaning activity, but little interpersonal closeness.

Parents play an obvious essential role in helping guide the family into deeper closeness. Beginning with a foundation of their own marital closeness, they are then free to prioritize family intimacy. Importantly, parents should place a *priority* on family closeness which will involve *time* together in an *atmosphere* characterized by a giving, accepting *attitude.*

Reflect on the ingredients of *prioritized time* and a *giving, accepting atmosphere.* In your own words, write about how your family home environment emphasizes these ingredients (hopefully in additional ways through this study together). Write your thoughts here.

- We prioritize time together as a family through ________

  ____

- Our home atmosphere is characterized by "giving" through

  ____

- Our home atmosphere is characterized by unconditional "acceptance" through ________________________

  ____

Intimacy Encounters Include Three Dimensions

Spirit, Soul, and Body

Family closeness needs a *spiritual dimension:* mealtime or bedtime prayers are shared, "blessings" are recounted, hurts are healed in confession/forgiveness, and common projects are undertaken. The *friendship dimension* (soul) in a family might involve Family Night games together, sharing appreciation, or supporting one another in personal goals. *Physical closeness* communicates positive caring through bedtime talking, affectionate embrace, or family fun times (wrestling, tickling, and family hugs).

Physical closeness communicates positive caring through bedtime talking, affectionate embrace, or family fun times (wrestling, tickling, and family hugs).

Research Study—Your Child Is "Reading" Your Relationships

Loneliness among children is growing in almost epidemic proportions. Loneliness is highly correlated with depression, substance abuse, acting out behaviors, and suicide. A recent study focused on the intergenerational transmission of loneliness . . . and found that daughter loneliness scores were highly correlated with their mother's loneliness (Lobdell, 1986).

What seems to be important in avoiding loneliness patterns is for adults to model healthy relational interactions within the family and practice positive conflict resolutions.

Practical Suggestions

- Ask "open-ended" questions to promote conversation: *"Tell me something about your day"* is much preferred over *"How was your day?"*
- Initiate family social times with other families for games, cards, contests, and activities which require communication.
- Use mealtimes for sharing of reflections on the day, feelings, and upcoming fun times (not teaching, nagging, or correction).

- Heal inevitable hurts between family members with genuine regret and apology followed by gentle reassurance and touch.

Consider the preceding research study and write about:

What practical steps might you take to help minister to your children's loneliness? (For instance: "Justin spends a few hours alone before I get home. I'll ask him if he'd like to invite one of the college students to shoot baskets with him until I get home. I want to reestablish the priority of family meals. We need to talk instead of just watching television.")

____

____

____

____

____

What practical steps might you take to help minister to your loneliness? (For instance: "I'll try out that support group that's been advertised at church." Or "I'll invite Jack to go hunting next weekend. We can talk on the way there.")

____

____

____

____

____

"Like arrows in the hand of a warrior, so are the children of one's youth" —Psalm 127:4.

Children are like "arrows" the psalmist says. They are to be formed, shaped, straightened, sharpened . . . and ultimately launched toward their target. It's hard to imagine when we first bring them home from the hospital that we're destined to turn them loose! When they're just taking their first steps it's hard to comprehend them being "launched" out into the cold, cruel world, but that's their destiny. The key remaining issue is "will they be ready when the launching comes?" Will they enter adulthood with a sense of bold competency and adequacy? It's this ministry of instilling competency that we'll now address, reminded that although it may be among our children's final challenges in their growing up journey, parents can never begin too soon.

From a child's earliest stages, a significant aspect of their identity is wrapped up in their sense of competency. "I can tie my shoes," "I can say my ABC's," "I can ride my bike without training wheels," "I can count to 100." The list is endless, and one's sense of adequacy is directly affected by the number of things a person feels competent to tackle. Feeling "unsure" of oneself and fighting self-doubt will undermine identity, stifle initiative, hinder motivation, and nourish despair.

The parental goal of instilling competence is not designed to build prideful self-centeredness but rather it's to impart the confident hope that *"I can do all things through Him"*—Philippians 4:13. As we will explore in this chapter, competency is developed as a child walks through a myriad of challenges and learning experiences; and, as they walk, they're *not alone!*

Consider briefly the following connections between my competency and my "aloneness":

- If I'm alone . . . I worry about failing . . . I need your *approval* of who I am.
- If I'm alone . . . I'm often afraid to try . . . I need your *support.*
- If I'm alone . . . I grow weary in trying . . . I need your *encouragement.*
- If I'm alone . . . I miss someone sharing in my victories . . . I need your *appreciation.*

Review these four connections between aloneness and competency and then reflect on:

- Who seems to worry about failing? (For instance: "Anna gets really anxious before every spelling test.")

____

____

- Who seems to be afraid to try? (For instance: "Lauren is afraid to try out the diving board, even if it means being left out of the fun.")

____

____

- Who seems to grow weary in trying? (For instance: "Nathan gets discouraged easily when he tries to tie his shoes.")

____

____

- Who seems to need someone to share in victories? (For instance: "Paul needs me to cheer for him during his soccer games.")

____

____

Using the chart on page 337 to highlight key intimacy needs related to competency, we'll now explore in detail giving our children *approval, support, encouragement,* and *appreciation.*

If I'm alone . . . I worry about failing . . . I need your approval of who I am.

Approval—to accept as satisfactory; to give formal or official sanction to; to have or express a favorable opinion; to affirm as valuable

"For he who in this way serves Christ is acceptable to God and approved by men"—Romans 14:18.

DIMENSIONS OF AFFIRMED-IDENTITY WITH TOP 10 INTIMACY "NEEDS"

Worth
Declared by the Father
Belonging
as Joint-Heirs with the Son
Affirmed Identity
Competence
Empowered by the Spirit
I feel **competent** when you...
Encourage me as we set goals and work together toward them
Support me as we "journey" together through life's issues
Approve of me "just for who I am" apart from what I "do"
Appreciate me as you value my unique strengths and gifts

God met our ultimate need for approval as the Bible affirms us as saints (Rom. 1:7), sons of the Most High (Eph. 1:5), joint-heirs with Christ (Rom. 8:17), royal priests, and people for God's own possession (1 Peter 2:9).

1. Affirm your children privately and publicly as of great value to you and to God:

   "I'm sure proud you're my daughter."
   "You're my beloved son in whom I'm well pleased!"
   "God could not have given me a more special son/daughter."

2. Acknowledge your children privately and publicly for *who* they are . . . more than for *what* they do; this is the difference between a human "being" and a human "doing." Children need to be affirmed for who they are more than for what they do.

"I'm really proud of your sensitivity to the new girl in your class."
"Sharing your toys says you have a caring heart. I'm proud of you."

3. Identify special character strengths of each child—verbalizing praise for their uniqueness. This helps free them from competing with siblings and others through external performance as they seek approval.

Identify special character strengths of each child—verbalizing praise for their uniqueness. This helps free them from competing with siblings and others through external performance as they seek approval.

As children grow in the security of parents' unique and unconditional approval, they experience freedom to grow in their competency without fear of failure. Review the practical suggestions noted above, and then write about specific follow-up plans for each child:

Child	*Plans for Sharing Additional Approval*
______________	____
______________	____
______________	____
______________	____
______________	____
______________	____
For Instance: Casey	I will send some balloons to Casey before she gives her speech at school. I want her to know that I'm proud of her, just because she's my daughter.

Review the list of "Fifty Selected Character Qualities" in the Appendix (pp. 363–65) and identify three unique *character strengths* for each of your children. Write your list here.

Child	*Three Character Strengths I Can Affirm*
______________	____
______________	____
______________	____
______________	____
______________	____
For Instance: Blake	I will notice when he is being sensitive to others' feelings and affirm him for it.

A fun activity to affirm the uniqueness of each family member is to complete a Family Care Inventory—identifying in very specific ways "How does each family member feel loved and cared for." Use the inventory on the next page during one of your Family Nights. The important tie to "approval" is in affirming how unique each family member is. By affirming that it's OK for you to most enjoy reading, board games, and going out to eat while I enjoy walking, nursing home visits, and pillow fights—I not only accept you, but I minister approval to you in that, "It's OK for you to be you!"

Family Care Inventory

Affirmation and approval—we all need a large, constant dose. How free are you in giving affirmation to family members?

One thing is certain: "Different strokes for different folks"—we all have our preferences relative to how we feel blessed and affirmed. Some people like physical expressions of care the most, like a pat on the back or a bear hug. Others like verbal expressions such as, "I love you" or, "You're very special to me." Some revel in appreciative expressions such as, "Your dinner was delicious" or "You do a great job cleaning your room."

Unfortunately, many individuals are not aware of their family members' favorite expressions of care. To help you better identify the types of care you and your family enjoy, check the items that seem to appeal to you. Also write the family member's name next to the item you think they would enjoy receiving from you. Pick your top three, then pick one or two that you think each family member might enjoy, then share your list.

Name of Family Member

____________ Visit an arcade

____________ Take a family walk

____________ Initiate a family hug

____________ Shop together

____________ Have a pillow fight

____________ Wash the family car

____________ Hearing "I love you"

____________ Go ice-skating

____________ Hearing "I appreciate you"

____________ Have a family wrestling match

____________ Cook together

____________ Spend a quiet evening together

____________ Have dinner with friends

____________ Go out for ice cream

____________ Read together

____________ Visit a nursing home

____________ Have a picnic in the park

___________ Work out in the yard

___________ Go out to eat

___________ Draw or color together

___________ Play board games

___________ Listen to music together

___________ Other ______________

After you and your family members complete this information, share your lists with one another. It's important for each person to understand, "How do I feel loved and cared for?" and then to lovingly express it! Focus on giving to each other this week in some of these ways.

If I'm alone—I'm afraid to try—and I need your support.

Support/Bear Burden

To come alongside and gently help carry a problem or struggle; to assist; to provide for.

"Bear one another's burdens, and thus fulfill the law of Christ" —Galatians 6:2.

God met our ultimate need for support by anticipating the great burden that we could not bear ourselves (the payment for our sins), and by committing His personal resources (His Son Jesus) to suffer and die on our behalf (He suffered in all ways and was tempted in all ways). During His earthly ministry Jesus invited the multitudes to *"Come to Me, all who are weary and heavy-laden, and I will give you rest"* (Matt. 11:28). When Jesus completed His earthly ministry, the Holy Spirit was given to believers as the Paraclete, the "One called alongside" who supports us as He teaches (John 16:12-15), comforts (Acts 9:31, John 14:16), assures (Rom. 8:16), guides (Rom. 8:14), and intercedes for us (Rom. 8:26).

1. Anticipate and notice periods of "high stress" in your child's life and be available to help. Times of high stress can be produced

by: busy schedules, new situations, changing environments, peer struggles, or pressures at school. These stressful times can produce more pressure than one person can bear, in which case the support of others is necessary.

2. Be willing to become personally involved and even to do "menial" tasks to help. Burden-bearing often requires that we do menial tasks which we normally don't have to do. We may need to: run errands, go to the library, help with a science project, shop for shoes, help with chores, or countless other "little" things.

3. On an age-appropriate basis, identify competency tasks for each child and come alongside to instruct, train, and encourage.

"Let's work on tying shoes together."
"Come join me in cooking dinner tonight."
"Let's sit down and write a letter to Grandma."

As a child senses the availability of support at times of anxiety and experiences the fun of learning together, he will show growing initiative in tackling new tasks and facing new challenges. Review the practical suggestions noted above and then write about specific follow-up plans for each child.

Child	*Plans for Sharing Additional Support*
____________	____________________________
____________	____________________________
____________	____________________________
____________	____________________________
For Instance: Derrick	I'll ask Derrick if I can make something for the bake sale. I want to support his leadership and participation in the student council.

Review the list of age-appropriate Life-Skill Ideas in the Appendix (pp. 373–75). Choose one or two life skills each child needs to develop. Plan your initiative in training and support. Share your thoughts here.

Child	*Life-Skills to Address in the Next Few Months*
______________	____
______________	____
______________	____
______________	____
For Instance: Tiffany	Tiffany and I need to work on loading and unloading the dishwasher.

A special ministry of support is needed as older children and teens begin to experience the pain of relationships. As they encounter rejection and disappointment, they need not only your empathetic comfort ("It really saddens me that you were treated like that . . . because I love you"), but they also need your supportive understanding. Key to this support is your vulnerable self-disclosure, allowing your child to know you as you share times of experiencing similar pain. An additional dimension of this support relates to how Christ is our "Great High Priest." Thus, parents are able to convey the life-changing message that: "When you're hurting, you have a friend named Jesus, who has suffered in every way you have, or will ever suffer."

Key to this support is your vulnerable self-disclosure, allowing your child to know you as you share times of experiencing similar pain.

Listed below are many of the hurts and sorrows that we inevitably encounter in life's journey. In the Gospel of Matthew we see how Jesus experienced every one of these emotions. That's why the writer of Hebrews says, *"Therefore, He had to be made like His brethren in all things, that He might become a merciful and faithful high priest. . . . For since He Himself was tempted . . . He is able to come to the aid of those who are tempted"*—Hebrews 2:17-18.

Rejected: Matthew 13:53-58—When Jesus entered His hometown, they questioned His integrity and *"took offense at Him."*

Disappointed: Matthew 26:40—Jesus, while in the Garden of Gethsemane, shares with His disciples that He is hurting and then asks them to pray with Him. Three times He returns to find them sleeping.

Sad: Matthew 14:13—After Jesus' childhood friend John the Baptist was beheaded, Jesus *"withdrew from there in a boat, to a lonely place by Himself."*

Threatened: Matthew 22:15—*"The Pharisees went out and counseled together how they might trap Him in what He said."*

Unappreciated: Matthew 26:6-13—When a woman anointed Jesus with very expensive perfume, the disciples' response was, *"What is the point of this waste?"*

Falsely accused: Matthew 26:59-60—*"The chief priests and the whole Council kept trying to obtain testimony against Jesus in order that they might put Him to death . . . Later on two came forward."*

Lonely: Matthew 26:40—Hours before His death, Jesus expressed His need for His disciples, *"You could not keep watch with Me for one hour."*

Misunderstood: Matthew 9:3—When Jesus healed a paralytic, some of the teachers of the Law accused Him of blasphemy.

Ridiculed—Laughed at: Matthew 9:24—When Jesus was about to heal a ruler's daughter, *"They were laughing at Him."*

Forsaken/Abandoned: Matthew 26:56—After Jesus was arrested, *"Then all the disciples left Him and fled."*

Matthew 27:46—*"On the cross, Jesus cried, "My God, My God, why hast Thou forsaken Me?"*

Pause and consider who might be experiencing some of these painful emotions and then write about a similar time in your life. Write your thoughts on the following page.

Child	*Pain*	*Personal Example I Could Share*
____________	____________	______________________________
____________	____________	______________________________
____________	____________	______________________________
____________	____________	______________________________
____________	____________	______________________________
For instance: Aaron	Disappoint-ment	I'll tell Aaron about the time I didn't make the basketball team.

If I'm alone . . . I grow weary trying . . . and I need your encouragement.

Encouragement

To urge forward and positively persuade toward a goal; to inspire with courage, spirit, or hope; to stimulate.

"Therefore encourage one another, and build one another up"
—1 Thessalonians 5:11.

God met our ultimate need for encouragement by providing us with an abundant life through Jesus (John 10:10), and by promising us that He will never leave us or forsake us (Heb. 13:5). During His earthly ministry, Jesus continually encouraged His disciples and those who were downcast and discouraged. The Pharisees even criticized Him because He regularly met with those who were spiritually and emotionally sick (Matt. 9:12-13). God continually encourages us through the ministry of His Word, the presence of His Spirit, and answered prayer.

1. Encourage your children to set goals and then help them to achieve their goals. Encourage your children, spouse, and friends to live productive lives by helping them develop God-given plans and goals and then become actively involved in helping them reach those goals. If they're already goal-oriented, learn what their goals are and encourage them to succeed.

2. Recognize when your children are discouraged and minister encouragement to them. Everyone goes through times of discouragement (we can even become "weary in well-doing"). When we do, we need to be encouraged through edifying words and caring concern. During times when a child seems "overwhelmed," treat her to a special snack or offer a fun "diversion."

3. Encouragement can be administered through a phone call, card or letter, visit, or an appropriate word. Surprise your kids with a phone call from work just to say, "I was thinking of you today." Every child likes to get mail . . . send a note of uplifting praise. Make it a habit to perform several encouraging gestures each day.

4. Let your children know you're praying for them. If they perceive that you are a person of prayer, they'll be encouraged to know that you're praying for them, even when you're not around! It's also very appropriate and effective to pray for your children "right on the spot" instead of just saying, "I'll be praying for you."

As children struggle with daily routines and face challenging tasks each day, they need to count on a home environment filled with encouragement. As they experience uplifting words and an atmosphere of hope, they'll *"press on toward the mark of their high calling."* Review the practical suggestions noted above and then write about specific follow-up plans for each child.

Child	*Plans for Sharing Additional Encouragement*
____________	____________________________
____________	____________________________
____________	____________________________
____________	____________________________
For instance: Erin	I will talk to Erin about her goal for selling Girl Scout cookies. We'll plan our strategy for selling all those boxes.

Goal-setting . . . Without a Vision, People (and Families) Perish—Proverbs 29:18

We don't seem to be getting anywhere! I don't think we're accomplishing anything! . . . These are often repeated family complaints. Such complaints usually can be traced to a deeper concern; namely, individuals, marriages, and families have no idea where they're going, so they don't have any idea if they've arrived! The Hebrew word for "perish" is also translated "go unrestrained . . . each to his own way."

Each to his own way! What a tragic but fitting description for many marriages and families—husband and wife each frantically pursuing their own overly full agenda. Children are left to develop their own agenda or, at the other extreme, are overinvolved in their own "busy but barren" existence. Meals together are a rarity. Family time consists of an occasional TV program or riding to church together. Conflicts become frequent over rules, responsibilities, resources, and roles. Fleeting thoughts occasionally arise to question the reasons for such vain emptiness. These are signs of a family "perishing!"

King Solomon, the writer of Proverbs, was indeed wise . . . what's needed is a vision . . . a sense of direction and destiny; a guiding framework around which we can make our decisions and distinct objectives toward which we can stretch. The contrast seems clear: perish or flourish; wander aimlessly or stretch forth purposefully.

Review the list of Family-Goal Ideas (located in the Appendix, pp. 376–77) and consider which two or three might be beneficial for each child. Write about these and keep them in mind when your family shares this exercise during Family Nights. Share your thoughts here.

Child	*Family-Goal Ideas to Consider and Discuss*
____________	______________________________
____________	______________________________
____________	______________________________
____________	______________________________
For instance: Gretchen	Establish the habit of bedtime prayers. Each evening we will pray together before Gretchen goes to sleep.

Three Key Ingredients in Goal-setting

A goal needs three elements in order to stir vision and give purposeful direction:

WHAT—do I want to see accomplished? Being as specific as possible makes a goal "measurable" and "observable" (i.e., "be more spiritual" is too vague and undefined; "establish a prayer time for family needs" is more defined).

HOW—will I go about accomplishing the "what?" This will be my plan or method. It gives additional definition to my goal so I know when I've accomplished it (i.e., weekday prayer using the *Intimate Family Moments* devotional guide).

WHEN—will this "how" be done? If it's a daily or weekly goal, time must be allocated in my schedule (i.e., prayer time using *Intimate Family Moments* devotional guide, Monday–Friday from 7–7:30 A.M.). If this is not a recurring goal, then a completion date will be needed as to when I will complete this task (i.e., complete children's wallpaper by March 1st).

If I'm alone . . . I miss someone sharing in my victories . . . so I need your appreciation.

Appreciation

To recognize with gratitude; to communicate with words and feelings personal gratefulness for another person; to praise.

"I praise You"—1 Corinthians 11:2.

During His earthly ministry, Jesus continually voiced appreciation to individuals: the Canaanite woman (Matt. 15:28), Mary of Bethany (Mark 14:6), a centurion (Luke 7:9), John the Baptist (Luke 7:28), and a poor widow (Luke 21:3). God has promised to affirm and appreciate those who are faithful (2 Tim. 4:8; Luke 6:35; Eph. 6:8).

1. Praise your children verbally and publicly. When your children demonstrate a positive attitude or character trait or perform a positive deed—praise them. Verbal praise is particularly effec-

tive when stated publicly. To praise your children when no one is around is great, but to praise them in front of other people may even be better.

2. Focus on what your children do that's right, not just what they do that's wrong. Some parents seem to have a "sin patrol" mentality—trying to catch their children doing something wrong, bring it to their attention (and others'), and then administer punishment or rebuke. Instead, try to catch your children doing something right, and then verbally and publicly praise them. Your children will be more motivated by positive reinforcement than by negative comments.

Focus on what your children do that's right, not just what they do that's wrong.

3. Generously give cards, trophies, ribbons, plaques, and special gifts. Small tokens of appreciation are very effective and usually long-lasting. The monetary value of a gift is relatively unimportant; it's the thought and effort that's important. "Special gifts" are particularly effective—become familiar with people's hobbies, what they collect, their favorite foods and drinks, and give them gifts that relate.

As children sense a home filled with "cheerleaders," they enjoy their journey and experience the blessing of shared joy—as even more important than the victory itself. Review the practical suggestions noted above and then write about specific follow-up plans for each child.

Child	*Plans for Sharing Additional Appreciation*
______________	______________________________
______________	______________________________
______________	______________________________
For instance: Kevin	I am going to look for times when Kevin is demonstrating responsibility. I'll notice when he takes his plate to the kitchen and picks his books up off the floor.

Review the list below and pick four or five new affirmations to add to your vocabulary!

101 Ways to Praise a Child

Wow
You're Special
Great
Well Done
I'm Proud of You
Nice Work
Beautiful
Now You've Got It
You're Fantastic
You're on Your Way
Good Job
Dynamite
Nothing Can Stop You
You're a Winner
Spectacular
You're Precious
You Figured It Out
Bingo
Terrific
You're Sensational
Super Job
You're a Real Trooper
You Learned It Right
You Are Fun
You Care
You're a Good Friend
You Mean a Lot to Me
You've Got a Friend
I Respect You
You're a Joy
You're Perfect
You're the Best
I Love You!

Way to Go
Outstanding
Good
Remarkable
Fantastic
Looking Good
Now You're Flying
You're Incredible
Hurray for You
How Nice
That's Incredible
You're Beautiful
Good for You
Remarkable Job
You're Spectacular
Great Discovery
Fantastic Job
Magnificent
You're Important
Super Work
Fantastic Job
You're Responsible
What an Imagination
You're Growing Up
Beautiful Sharing
I Trust You
You Make Me Happy
You Make Me Laugh
You're the Cat's Meow
You're a Treasure
Awesome
A Big Hug

Super
Excellent
Neat
I Knew You Could Do It
Super Star
You're on Top of It
You're Catching On
Bravo
You're on Target
How Smart
Hot Dog
You're Unique
I Like You
Beautiful Work
You're a Darling
You've Discovered the Secret
Hip, Hip, Hurray
Marvelous
Phenomenal
Creative Job
Exceptional Performance
You're Exciting
What a Good Listener
You Tried Hard
Outstanding Performance
You're Important
You Belong
You Brighten My Day
That's Correct
You're Wonderful
A+ Job
A Big Kiss

P.S. Remember, a smile is worth 1,000 words!

A powerful avenue to produce an "environment of appreciation" is to focus on the positive! Fill your home, your mealtimes, and your conversations with grateful, appreciative words. This is the power of keeping a Journal of Gratefulness (see Appendix, p. 372).

The Search for Blessings

Regularly share together in a "blessing search" as each of you names a recent blessing and assumes responsibility for sharing appreciation. You might want to look for blessings in these areas:

- Character qualities in your spouse and children which are a blessing.
- Often overlooked blessings of life, health, provision, creation.
- Specific answers to prayer.
- Spiritual realities like the Scriptures, salvation, Holy Spirit, etc.

The Expression of Appreciation

Appreciation helps seal in your heart the reality of the blessing. Appreciation blesses and encourages others. Appreciation can be shared:

- Verbally with a simple "thanks."
- In writing with a note of appreciation.
- Creatively with a special gift or other expression.
- Publicly as testimony is given of our genuine gratitude.

Stop and ask God to remind you of several blessings. Write about them here and be prepared to share appreciation during Family Night. (For instance: "I was reminded this week of Paula's forgiving spirit. She is always so tolerant even when I blow it. I am grateful for God's provision of health to our children.")

____

____

____

____

____

Scripture Journaling—Hebrews 4:15-16

"For we do not have a high priest who cannot sympathize with our weaknesses, but one who has been tempted in all things as we are, yet without sin. Let us therefore draw near with confidence to the throne of grace, that we may receive mercy and may find grace to help in time of need."

Reflect on the humanity of Jesus and how He was tempted as we are, was acquainted with sorrow and grief, was despised and rejected . . . yet He was found adequate in all things as He called upon His Father's provision. Write about an area of adequacy or competence that you sometimes struggle with.

(For instance: "I sometimes wonder if I respond appropriately to the kids' acting out. I don't feel confident in my ability to cope with their behavior.")

____

____

____

____

As you stop to ask God for His leading, strength, and grace, can you "approach the throne of grace with confidence," knowing that Christ understands and has gone before you in all things victorious? Write a "bold" prayer to God here.

(For instance: "God, You know how to respond in any situation. You lovingly discipline Your own children every day. I am asking for that same wisdom with my own children and I thank You in advance for how You will equip me in the days to come.")

____

____

____

____

Marriage Staff Meeting

Begin this time together reflecting on how your spouse is helping remove your "aloneness." Consider for example, "I felt really supported by you recently when ______________"; "It was very comforting to me recently when you ______________"; "I felt very appreciated by you when ______________."

As you share, express your gratefulness to one another and then pause to express gratefulness to the Father. Discuss the goal of your family relationships driving out aloneness: How is family closeness being deepened spiritually? through friendship? through physical affection? Visit about progress you've seen your family make during this study together.

Visit together about building competence through giving *approval,* thus freeing your children from seeking to earn it through performance. Review the Appendix material entitled "Instill Competence" and discuss plans for increasing ministry to these needs along with specific character strengths you see in each child (see Appendix, pp. 383–84). Discuss the importance of giving *support,* including which "life-skill" ideas you think each child might be challenged with (refer to your reflections on pages 340–41 and the Life-Skill Ideas in the Appendix, pp. 373–75).

> ***Involving your children in family goal-setting not only helps "shape" them now but also prepares them for the future as you help instill VISION.***

Discuss possible life-goals for each child and how they relate to ministering *encouragement.* Consider your home atmosphere and its level of *appreciation.* How could you increase the positiveness and hopefulness of home life?

Discuss your plans for Family Night and pray together for each child, asking God to make them *"adequate for every good work"* which He calls them to.

Family Night Activity

Goal-setting with Children Helps Build Competence

Involving your children in family goal-setting not only helps "shape" them now but also prepares them for the future as you help instill

VISION. Plan to use some Family Night time to enlist children's input regarding family goals. You'll often find that children's input on vacation ideas, hobbies, room improvements, or wardrobe is valuable. It's important for children to see that things just don't "happen" but must be planned. You will also affirm a family member's identity as children and teenagers become involved in goal-setting.

You might introduce this goal-setting topic with a scene from *Alice in Wonderland.* Alice is lost in the Enchanted Forest and encounters the Cheshire Cat, perched in his tree. Looking up, Alice asks of the cat, "Which way do I go?" to which the cat responds, "Where are you going?"

Looking puzzled Alice says, "I don't know." The cat replies, "Then I guess it really doesn't matter."

Use this scene to stimulate discussion on "Where are you going?" Discuss the need for a good goal to have a "what," "how," and "when." Using the Goal-setting Worksheet located in the Appendix (p. 378), write down one or two goals for each family member. Give each family member a copy of the worksheet, discuss them from time to time, and encourage one another along the journey.

I Feel Competent in My Abilities!

With each succeeding year, children need to grow in their sense of competence as new challenges are presented and "conquered." Competence means more than what is learned in school. "Real life" includes issues like tying shoes, cooking, washing clothes, and balancing checkbooks!

- Let's work on tying shoes and buttoning shirts.
- Can we work together on cooking desserts this month?
- Let's work on answering the telephone and mailing letters this summer.
- Next week during Family Night we're going to change a flat tire and check the oil in the car.
- Are there activities you'd like to work on which might help better prepare you for the "real world"?

Discuss the life-skill ideas for each child using material from the Appendix; brainstorm other ones and find at least one life-skill each child would like to "master" during the next few months. Add these to your Goal-setting Worksheet, entering "what" you want to accomplish, "how" you'll do it, and then "when" you'll do it TOGETHER!

Family "Trust" Fall . . . for Younger Children

A family trust fall requires at least four family members, but many more can play. (Involving other families is more safe and more fun.)

- Especially for children ages 3–8.
- Locate a ledge, platform, or table (usually outside) about 3 to 4 feet high where a child can stand.
- One child stands on the platform with back to other family members and eyes closed.
- Parents face one another and lock arms to catch the child; other family members can stand next to parents and lock arms or stand at the end and help catch the child's head.
- Child on platform "falls" backward into the locked arms of family members.
- Reminder—be safe; keep alert.
- Reluctant participants should not be forced or teased, but reassured and guided to make small steps of progress until they complete the "fall."

For Group Discussion

1. Begin your group discussion by sharing ideas about the blessings of mutual giving and the painful consequences of self-sufficiency. What are the risks involved with intimacy? Self-sufficiency? Can you see the wisdom of the "one-another" passages? Please explain.

2. Share one character strength that you see in each child. Give a specific example of how they exhibit this strength. Also share your plans for *how* you will communicate approval to each child.

3. Ask each couple or single parent to draw a picture that represents the supportive relationships within their family. You may want to use stick figures and draw them in a pyramid with God as the base. Tell about ways you support one another during stress

periods. Share examples of your willingness to be involved in "menial" tasks as you support one another.

4. Appreciate one another for the growth you've seen in fellow group members. Select one person at a time and allow group members to share words of appreciation. Say things you may admire about a group member. Praise one another for the courage to participate in a parenting group. Praise each other for honesty, vulnerability, and the diligence to keep on parenting!

5. Finally, as a group read Deuteronomy 26:1-19. Pause and consider the key points of this passage. Reflect on the kind of God we have who looks down from heaven and commands us to look toward heaven and ask that He bless us!

We have an awesome God! . . . who has blessed us with Himself and with one another.

Appendix A

Intimacy Principles

Key elements in the *Intimate Life* message include: our need for intimacy with both God and meaningful others, our fundamental need to experience biblical truth, and God's provision for both our "fallenness" and our aloneness.

1. Man is viewed from a Judeo-Christian worldview as being created in God's image and having existence in three dimensions–spirit, soul, and body. These dimensions give rise to various human functions, namely: the body functions through the five senses make us "world conscious"; the soul functions through our thoughts, feelings, and choices make us "self-conscious"; the spirit functions through conscience, intuition, and worship make us "God conscious."

2. Man is by nature "fallen," separated from God, and is motivated out of a need for intimacy with God and intimacy through meaningful relationships ordained by God, i.e., marriage, the family, and the church (the body of Christ).

3. Fulfillment and abundance in life are considered from a biblical perspective as coming by grace through faith in personal intimacy with Jesus Christ and in intimate relationships with meaningful others as ordained by Him.

4. Man's need to relate to Jesus Christ and meaningful others is viewed as a personal challenge to express humility, exercise faith, and experience intimacy. In contrast, man's fallen condition prompts a selfish, self-reliant, and self-condemning response to this neediness.

5. Individual problems in living and relational conflict are considered from an object-relations/developmental framework, in the context of unmet intimacy needs which result in unhealthy thinking, unhealed emotions, and unproductive behaviors. God's concern for both our

"fallenness" (Gen. 3) as well our neediness/aloneness (Gen. 2) is considered foundational.

6. This pattern of unmet needs, unhealthy thinking, unhealed emotions, and unproductive behaviors outlines the major hindrances to intimacy and thus the focus of the Spirit's sanctifying work. God is viewed as the ultimate provision for all human neediness and the Bible as giving complete and adequate instruction for mature living and fulfilling relationships.

7. A systems' perspective seeks to address the personal, relational, and intergenerational origins of the intimacy hindrances noted above. Thus, in marriage and family relationships, a premise of Genesis 2:24 would be to *"leave father and mother, cleave to one another, and the two shall become one flesh."* In other words, since "leaving" precedes "cleaving," one would expect intergenerational issues to hinder the relational issues involved in marital "cleaving" and these issues to directly impact parenting and family relationships.

8. Intimacy is enhanced through receiving of God's manifold grace. His grace is experienced as intimacy needs are met across the spectrum of four major ingredients or intimacy processes, namely: affectionate caring, vulnerable communication, joint accomplishment, and mutual giving. For intimacy to be maintained, these intimacy processes become linked to one another in a repeated spiral over the family life cycle.

9. The family life cycle is considered as bringing predictable challenges to relational intimacy, and thus the need to repeat the "spiral" of intimacy ingredients, beginning with affectionate caring. Thus, the marital stage of mutual giving is challenged by the addition of children to return to affectionate caring, followed by vulnerable communication, joint accomplishment, and again, mutual giving.

10. Intimacy is built upon man's need to experience biblical truth. The experience of biblical truth leads to emotionally focused freedom, cognitive renewal, and behavioral discipline. The "empathic comforting of identified hurts and needs" is a pivotal element in the affectionate-caring ingredient of intimacy. Because a fundamental breakdown or hindrance to intimacy results from a lack of empathic comfort, this connection serves as the beginning point of experienced intimacy.

11. A "staged" approach to address individual, marriage, and family issues seeks to address in Stage 1: Initial Assessment (or self-inventory) of the individuals, the marriage and family relationships and intergenerational dynamics; in Stage 2: Increased Stability of the individual and relationships as a basis for improved functioning and additional maturity; in Stage 3: the Leave-Cleave issues of intergenerational significance which contribute to personal problems in living and relational discord; in Stage 4: the Becoming One Disciplines with both God and others which help ensure relational intimacy, personal maturity, and life fulfillment.

12. A working definition and goal of intimacy in relationships draws upon the biblical model of God "knowing" us, allowing us to "know" Him and His caring involvement in our lives. Thus, mature personality development and fulfilling relationships are based upon this mutual "knowing" and caring involvement.

13. Significant ministry occurs as we serve a God-intended role within the body of Christ to assist and encourage others along a journey toward experiencing "life and life abundant" (John 10:10). Key elements in this ministry include imparting our very life to others (1 Thes. 2:8-9) along with encouraging them to encounter the working of God's Spirit at the point of His Word. Specifically, this ministry role is fivefold as a believer lives and shares biblical truth within the framework of eliminating hindrances and enhancing intimacy. He/she is to assist the individual, couple, or family in their need for intimacy with God and with others by:

	Eliminating Hindrances	**Enhancing Intimacy**
a.	Identifying and Interrupting Unproductive Behaviors	Modeling and Reinforcing Productive Behaviors
b.	Resolving Unhealed Emotions	Experiencing Positive Emotions
c.	Identifying and Countering Unhealthy Thinking	Internalizing Healthy Thinking
d.	Identifying Unmet Intimacy Needs	Modeling and Encouraging the Meeting of Intimacy Needs
e.	Exposing and Resisting Selfishness, Self-Reliance, and Self-Condemnation	Encouraging Expressions of Humility, Exhortation to Express Faith, and Rejoicing in Experienced Intimacy

Appendix B

Top 10 Intimacy Needs

Look over this list of ten intimacy needs. First, mark the three needs you consider the most important for you to receive from your partner. Next, mark the three needs you think your partner would consider most important to receive from you. Finally, identify needs you think each of your children would most enjoy receiving and write their names by each need.

Myself	Intimacy Needs	Partner	Child
☐	Acceptance—deliberate and ready reception with a favorable positive response (Rom. 15:7).	☐	________
☐	Affection—to communicate care and closeness through physical touch and verbalized love (Rom. 16:16).	☐	________
☐	Appreciation—to communicate with words and feelings a personal gratefulness for another (1 Cor. 11:2).	☐	________
☐	Approval—expressed commendation; to think and speak well of (Rom. 14:18).	☐	________
☐	Attention—to take thought of another and convey appropriate interest and support; to enter into another's "world" (1 Cor. 12:25).	☐	________
☐	Comfort (empathy)—to come alongside with word, feeling, and touch; to give consolation with tenderness (Rom. 12:15).	☐	________

- ☐ Encouragement—to urge forward and positively persuade toward a goal (1 Thes. 5:11; Heb. 10:24). ☐ ________
- ☐ Respect—to value and regard highly; to convey great worth (Rom. 12:10). ☐ ________
- ☐ Security—confidence of harmony in relationships; free from fear and harm (Rom. 12:16a; Mark 9:50). ☐ ________
- ☐ Support—come alongside and gently help carry a load (Gal. 6:2). ☐ ________

- Discuss with your partner why you chose the three you marked for yourself and for your partner.
- How close were you to selecting your partner's top three?
- Focus specifically on meeting one or two of your partner's top three needs.
- Use this worksheet as a Family Night Activity to explore intimacy needs, having each child pick his/her "top" three needs and then discuss.

Appendix C

Emotional Capacity

Symptoms of a "Full Cup"

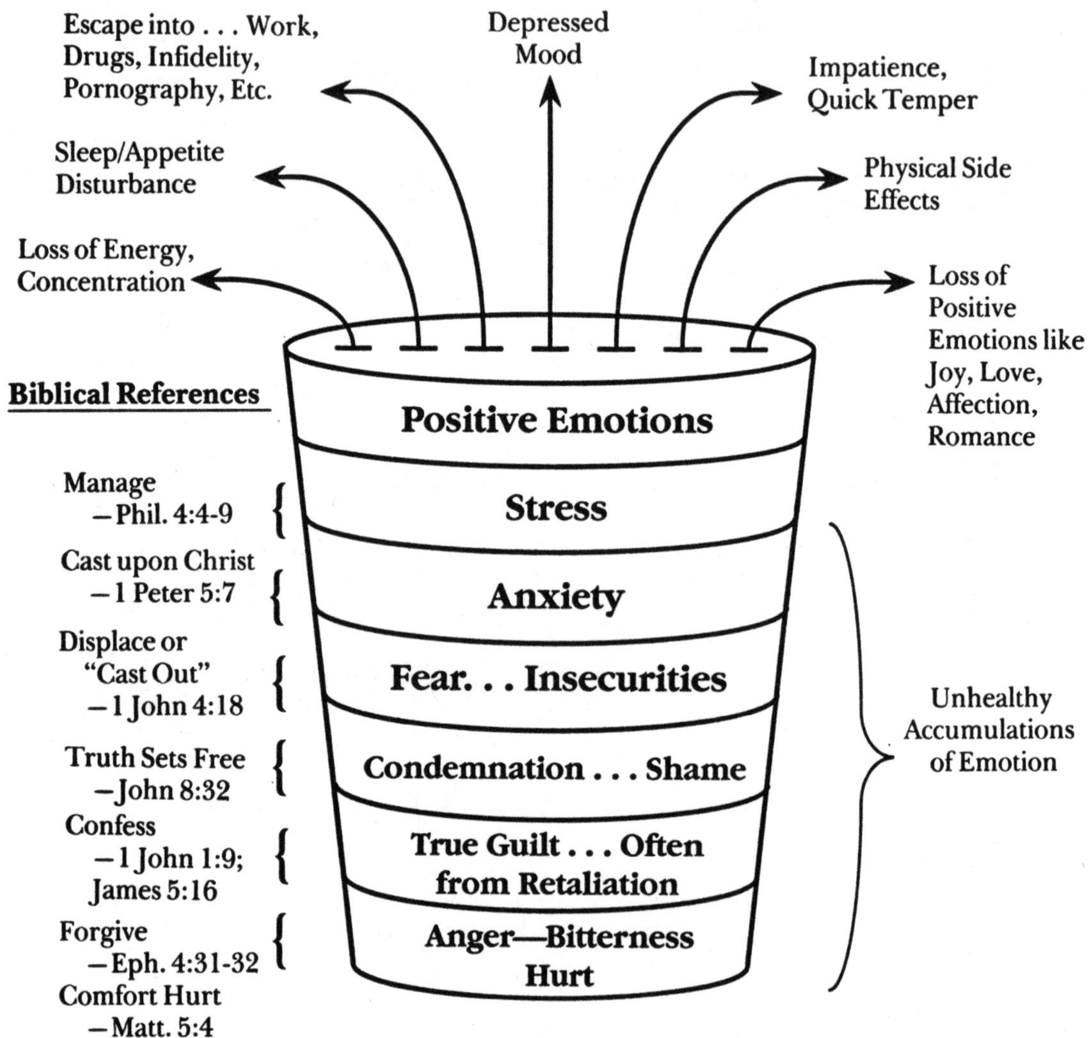

You Can Only Hold So Much Emotion

Appendix D

Fifty Selected Character Qualities

1. **Alertness**—Learning to pay attention to all the lessons God is teaching through authorities, friends, and experiences.
2. **Attentiveness**—Learning who to be attentive to, what to listen for, and who not to listen to.
3. **Availability**—Learning to reject distractions that hinder me from fulfilling my responsibilities.
4. **Boldness**—Demonstrating the confidence that following the principles of Scripture will bring ultimate victory regardless of present opposition.
5. **Cautiousness**—Gaining adequate counsel before making decisions. Recognizing temptations and fleeing them.
6. **Compassion**—Reliving the hurts of others and doing all that is possible to relieve them.
7. **Contentment**—Learning to enjoy present possessions rather than desiring new or additional ones.
8. **Creativity**—Finding ways to overcome seemingly impossible obstacles; discovering practical applications for spiritual principles.
9. **Decisiveness**—Learning to finalize difficult decisions on the basis of God's ways, Word, and will.
10. **Deference**—Limiting my freedom in order not to offend the personal tastes of those God has called me to serve.
11. **Dependability**—Learning to be true to my word even when it is difficult to carry out what I promised to do.
12. **Determination**—Learning to give whatever energy is necessary to complete a project.
13. **Diligence**—Seeing every task as an assignment from the Lord and applying energy and concentration to accomplish it.
14. **Discernment**—Knowing what to look for in evaluating people, problems, and things.
15. **Discretion**—Knowing what is appropriate and what is inappropriate. Seeing the consequences of words and actions down the road.
16. **Endurance**—Maintaining commitment to a goal during times of

pressure. Recognizing and laying aside hindrances.

17. **Enthusiasm**—Learning what actions and attitudes please God and becoming excited about them.
18. **Fairness**—Looking at a situation through the eyes of each one involved in it.
19. **Faith**—Developing an unshakable confidence in God and His Word. Identifying God's will and acting upon it.
20. **Flexibility**—Learning how to cheerfully change plans when unexpected conditions require it.
21. **Forgiveness**—Learning to demonstrate Christ's love toward others, remembering how much God has forgiven me.
22. **Generosity**—Recognizing that all possessions belong to God. Learning how to be a wise steward of time, money, and possessions.
23. **Gentleness**—Learning to respond to needs with kindness and love. Knowing what is appropriate for the emotional needs of others.
24. **Gratefulness**—Learning to recognize the benefits which God and others have provided; looking for appropriate ways to express genuine appreciation.
25. **Hospitality**—Learning how to provide an atmosphere which contributes to the physical and spiritual growth of those around us.
26. **Humility**—Recognizing my total inability to accomplish anything for God apart from His grace.
27. **Initiative**—Taking steps to seek after God with my whole heart. Assuming responsibility for the physical, emotional, and spiritual encouragement of those around me.
28. **Joyfulness**—Learning to be happy regardless of outside circumstances.
29. **Love**—Learning how to give to the basic needs of others without motive of personal reward; an unconditional commitment to an imperfect person.
30. **Loyalty**—Adopting as my own the wishes and goals of those I am serving.
31. **Meekness**—Learning how to yield rights and possessions to God. Learning to earn the right to be heard rather than demanding a hearing.
32. **Neatness**—Learning to organize and care for personal possessions.
33. **Obedience**—Yielding the right to have the final decision.
34. **Patience**—Learning to accept difficult situations as from God without giving Him a deadline to remove the problem.
35. **Persuasiveness**—Effectively presenting my case while demonstrating commitment to my convictions by the example of my life.

36. **Punctuality**—Showing esteem for other people and their time by not keeping them waiting.
37. **Resourcefulness**—Seeing value in that which others overlook. Learning to make wise use of things which others would discard.
38. **Responsibility**—Learning to establish personal restrictions and guidelines that are necessary to fulfill what I know I should do.
39. **Reverence**—Learning to respect the authority and position of God to others.
40. **Security**—Learning to exhibit a freedom from fear.
41. **Self-control**—Learning to quickly identify and obey the initial promptings of the Holy Spirit. Bringing my thoughts, words, and actions under the control of the Holy Spirit.
42. **Sensitivity**—Being alert to the promptings of the Holy Spirit. Avoiding danger by sensing wrong motives in others. Knowing how to give the right words at the right time.
43. **Sincerity**—Having motives that are transparent. Having a genuine concern to benefit the lives of others.
44. **Thoroughness**—Learning what details are important for the success of a project.
45. **Thriftiness**—Knowing how to accomplish the most with what's available.
46. **Tolerance**—Learning how to respond to the immaturity of others without accepting their standard of immaturity.
47. **Truthfulness**—Learning to share that which is right without misrepresenting the facts. Facing the consequences of a mistake.
48. **Understanding**—Viewing life from another's perspective; looking past life's obvious disappointments to find the comfort of God.
49. **Virtue**—Learning to build personal moral standards which will cause others to desire a more godly life.
50. **Wisdom**—Learning to see life from God's perspective. Learning how to apply principles of life in daily situations.

Appendix E

Healing Family Emotional Hurts

Put away all bitterness and anger . . . and be kind, tender-hearted, forgiving each other—Ephesians 4:31-32.

IDENTIFY HURT

I. ALONE list ways in which I have hurt my spouse and our marriage (or my parents/child).

Examples: selfish, critical/negative, insensitive, disrespectful, verbally abusive, unsupportive, ungrateful, unfaithful, wrong priorities, rejecting, unforgiving (specific hurtful events, fights, arguments, or "scenes" may need confession—use extra paper as needed!)

GAIN GOD'S FORGIVENESS

II. CONFESS to God and receive His forgiveness.

1 John 1:9 "If we confess our sins He [God] is faithful and just to forgive us and to cleanse us from all unrighteousness."

Example: God, I have deeply hurt You and my spouse (child or parent) by my ________________ (from Item I).

These are very wrong and I ask You to forgive me. Thank You for doing so and I ask You to change me into the kind of person I need to be.

CONFESS HURT

III. TOGETHER share your lists and request forgiveness.

James 5:16 "Confess your faults to one another and pray for one another that you may be healed."

Example: (At husband's or father's initiative) I've seen that I've hurt you deeply by being ________________ (from Item I).

I have been very wrong. Will you forgive me? ("Wrong" is much better than "sorry" since confess means "to agree with God" and God has said these things are wrong.)

CHOOSE TO FORGIVE

Response:	"I forgive you."
Remember:	Forgiveness is a *choice*, not primarily a feeling! The question is not "do you *feel* like forgiving, but *will* you?" Will you release (drop) the hurt? . . . and then new feelings will come!
Other:	It might be important to ask, "Are there other major hurts that I've not seen that need my apology? Please share them with me so I can confess them now and seek your forgiveness."
Next:	Wife shares her list (followed by children sharing theirs if this is a family session).

HEAL WITH NEW MEMORIES

IV. EXCHANGE LISTS and tear them up!

Philippians 3:13 "Forgetting what lies behind and pressing forward to what lies ahead."

Start the "forgetting" process with a focus on this new memory of forgiveness as lists are exchanged and destroyed. (Some people burn or bury them!)

Additional suggestion: Hold hands and pray (even silently), thanking God for His forgiving you, changing you, and healing your marriage and family.

CONTINUE

V. A NEW HABIT! "Let not the sun go down on your anger"—Ephesians 4:26.

Confession to God and others we hurt along with forgiving others who have hurt us must become a daily habit if intimacy is to be maintained; otherwise your "Emotional Capacity" begins to fill again with hurtful emotions.

Appendix F

Emotional Responding

Rejoice with those who rejoice, mourn with those who mourn–Romans 12:15.

Unproductive Responses

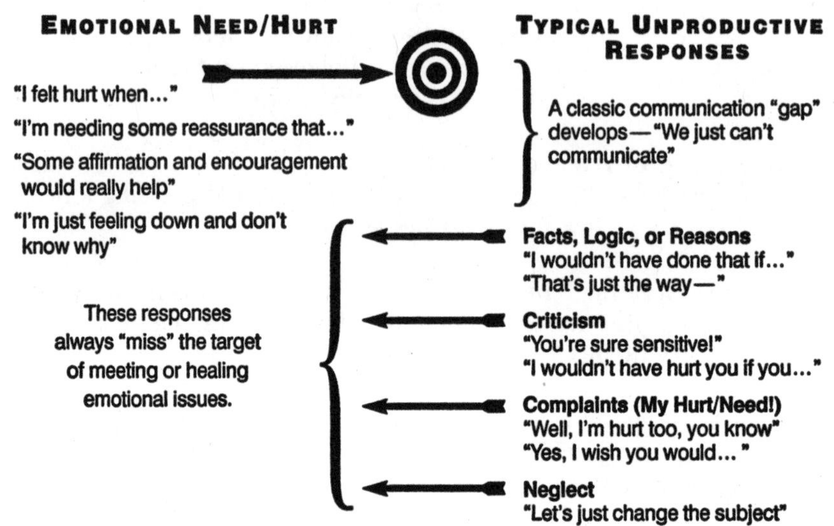
EMOTIONAL NEED/HURT
TYPICAL UNPRODUCTIVE RESPONSES
"I felt hurt when..."
"I'm needing some reassurance that..."
"Some affirmation and encouragement would really help"
"I'm just feeling down and don't know why"
A classic communication "gap" develops—"We just can't communicate"
These responses always "miss" the target of meeting or healing emotional issues.
Facts, Logic, or Reasons
"I wouldn't have done that if..."
"That's just the way—"
Criticism
"You're sure sensitive!"
"I wouldn't have hurt you if you..."
Complaints (My Hurt/Need!)
"Well, I'm hurt too, you know"
"Yes, I wish you would... "
Neglect
"Let's just change the subject"

Emotional Responding

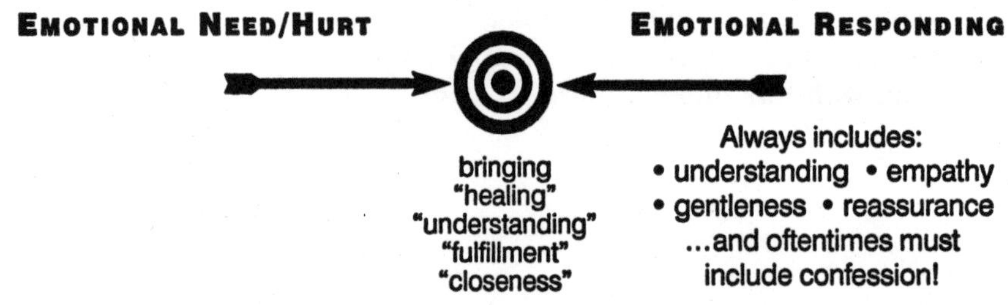
EMOTIONAL NEED/HURT
EMOTIONAL RESPONDING
bringing
"healing"
"understanding"
"fulfillment"
"closeness"
Always includes:
• understanding • empathy
• gentleness • reassurance
...and oftentimes must include confession!

Examples of Productive Emotional Responses

"I can really see that you're hurting (or_____)."

"I don't like to see you hurting."

"It saddens me to see you so fearful (or_____)."

"I deeply care about you and love you."

"I'm committed to go through this with you."

"I genuinely regret my part in hurting you."

"Can you share with me how I've hurt you?...And how it made you feel? I want to understand and make it right."

"I now see that I hurt you by my _______ and that was wrong of me...will you forgive me?"

Appendix G

Speaking Words that Edify

Learning to share the truth in love—Ephesians 4:15, 29.

A "bridled" tongue, the Bible says, is a sign of maturity (James 3:2) and when it comes to sharing hurts and needs there's not a more difficult area of communication to "bridle." "Wholesome" words, the Bible says, are those that "edify," build up, and encourage (Eph. 4:29). Miraculously even sharing my pain has the power to edify if I learn the three principles below of taking negative thoughts "captive" and rewording them **before** I speak.

Steps	Examples	
I. Identify Your Negative/General Complaints You never care what I think! You always forget what's important to me! You're just selfish!	You're a jerk for ignoring me.	You seem to care more about work than you do me.
Write recent complaints you've had:		
II. Rethink What Your Specific Concerns/Needs Are I just need undivided attention occasionally. I miss hearing from her that she loves me. I'm feeling a little left out and need some quality time.	I'm really missing spending fun time together.	One way I feel loved is through affection and I'm feeling rejected without it.
Rewrite your complaints from Step 1 into specific needs you have:		

III. Reword into Positive/Vulnerable Sharing

I've really missed our having some time alone; could we look at our schedules tonight and plan some? I really miss you.

It would really mean a lot to me if we could visit soon about some discipline guidelines for the kids; I'm really needing your input.

What can I do to help free some of your time so we could plan some fun together? I really enjoy being with you.

I'm really looking forward to some more hugs and verbalized love. That means so much to me. I love you.

Reword your needs from Step 2 into positive/vulnerable expressions of your needs:

Appendix H

Finding the Needs Beneath the Deeds

1. Identify the behaviors.

4. What behaviors might be prevented as I focus on intimacy needs?

2. Become aware of the relationships that surround the behavior. What might your child be feeling?

3. What changes in feeling may occur if emotional needs are met?

3. What might your child be thinking?

2. What changes in thought might take place as these needs are met?

4. What needs may be going unmet?

1. Take specific steps to meet the needs of your child. Anticipate needs that may surface.

Appendix I

Journal of Gratefulness

Praise the Lord, O my soul, and forget none of His benefits—Psalm 103:2.

The Benefits of Gratefulness

Multiplied blessings are ours as we pause to "forget none of His benefits" toward us (Ps. 103:2). Among the numerous benefits of a grateful heart are the following:

- Gratefulness guards us from a critical, negative attitude.
- Gratefulness guards us from a judgmental spirit.
- Gratefulness, when expressed to others, can motivate them to continue in "good deeds."
- Gratefulness, when acknowledged to God, is an important element of worship.

The Search for Blessings

Involve family members in a blessing search. Each member names a recent blessing and assumes responsibility for sharing appreciation. Where to "look":

- Loved ones, whom you've recently been reminded of in a special way.
- Special character qualities in family or friends.
- Often overlooked blessings of life, health, provision, creation.
- Specific answers to prayer.
- Spiritual realities like the Scriptures, salvation, Holy Spirit, etc.

The Expression of Appreciation

Appreciation helps seal in my heart the reality of the blessing as well as bless and encourage others. Appreciation can be shared:

- Verbally with a simple "thanks."
- In writing, with a note of appreciation.
- Publicly as testimony is given of our genuine gratitude.

Note: Especially as God has blessed us, our verbal thanks and testimony to others are of major importance.

Date	Family Member	How We Have Been Blessed	How We Shared Our Appreciation

Appendix J

Life-Skill Ideas

You began the parenting journey by teaching your child to feed himself, dress himself, and helped him learn his colors. You taught your child to count, ride a bicycle, and helped with her ABC's. Continue this process during the critical school-age and adolescent years. Incorporate these and other ideas into your family nights. Make them fun!

Life Skills for the School-Age Child (Ages 6–12)

Give your school-age child these experiences:

- swim, dive, fish, bowl, ski, play tennis or golf
- write and mail letters
- practice using the phone, learn proper manners and message taking
- learn how to dial long distance and make collect calls
- learn emergency procedures—fire, crime, weather, accidents, and learn to dial 911
- learn about cars—pump gas, check oil and water, put air in the tires, learn to pack the car
- learn about computers through games, educational software, and word processing
- discuss rules and terminology concerning various sports and politics
- establish wise financial habits; learn about money—saving, tithing, value shopping
- help with household chores—dishwasher, disposal, washer, dryer, microwave, vacuum
- experience a musical, play, opera, or ballet together
- visit museums, art exhibits, historic sites, government facilities
- travel together by boat, train, airplane, subway, bus
- read weather maps, road signs, newspaper articles, magazines, dictionaries, encyclopedias
- attend a parade, sporting event, court, legislative assembly, city council meeting

- play musical instruments together
- learn to pray together, memorize Scripture, share your faith
- learn how to handle "strangers," unwanted attention, and improper affection
- experience food, language, dress, and customs of a different culture
- attend a fair, rodeo, family reunion, and trial
- help, minister, and share with those less fortunate
- visit a hospital, police stations, fire station, nursing home
- read about Bible heroes, history, and Christian leaders
- help with recipes, sewing, lawn care, preparing meals, setting the table
- learn medical procedures for cuts, burns, bites, poisons, CPR
- study geography, family genealogy, government, current affairs
- practice asking directions, help find merchandise in a store
- begin father-daughter talks about boys, social etiquette, and love
- begin father-son talks on modesty, hygiene, sex (by age 10 or 11), respect, being a gentleman
- begin mother-daughter talks on modesty, hygiene, sex (by age 10 or 11), respect, being a lady
- begin mother-son talks on girls, being a gentleman, emotionality

Life Skills for the Adolescent (Ages 13–18)

Give your adolescent these experiences:

- try canoeing, camping, hunting, rafting, scuba, snorkeling, surfing
- write and mail a "thank-you" note, write and mail invitations, order from catalogue
- write a letter to the editor or political leader
- learn about cars—how to use jumper cables, change a tire, drive, check the oil, check hoses, belts
- learn about computers—networks, E-mail, home applications, school applications
- learn about money—saving and/or checking accounts, budget, investments
- help with chores—cooking, meal planning, recipes, plumbing, fire alarms, security systems
- travel together—navigate trips by car, navigate in airports, make reservations for hotel, airfare
- read bank statements, maps, schedules for airlines or subways, stock quotes

- learn phone skills—reservations for dinner, third party billing, message taking, office etiquette
- practice asking for assistance in a store, how to return merchandise for a refund or return
- learn how to ask for advice from a friend, get support from a friend
- learn about famous poets, musicians, statesmen, historians, political leaders
- experience the classics in music, art, architecture, theater, movies, and comedy
- father-daughter "dates" to role model etiquette and manners, talks about understanding men
- father-son times of recreation, sports, hobbies, talks about how to treat girls
- mother-daughter times of cooking, shopping, common interests, talks about how to treat boys
- mother-son times for domestic competencies, talks about understanding girls
- co-lead a Bible study, take a missions trip, learn how to share your faith
- plan a party, trip, a family ministry project, a personal weekly calendar
- learn how to use all household equipment—VCRs, blenders, lawn mowers, battery chargers
- study Bible commentaries, Bible concordance, Bible dictionary
- start a devotional journal/diary, Scripture memory program
- learn how to use ATM machines, postage machine, FAX machine, learn about parking garages
- talk about tipping—at restaurants, airports, hotel service personnel
- learn hotel etiquette and procedures – signing for room service, credit cards, billing
- take pictures, plant a garden, take a taxi
- order flowers by phone
- learn about different kinds of people; work with children, older adults, disabled, homeless
- volunteer at a hospital, daycare, hospice program, nursing home, or medical clinic

Appendix K

Family Goals Ideas

Without a vision, people perish—Proverbs 29:18.

Spiritual
Read through a children's Bible in a year
Begin a weekly family devotional
Weekly involvement in church worship services
Read a biography of a missionary to your children
Pray together before each meal; pray together at bedtime

Family
Establish monthly contact with a "distant" relative
Begin weekly family nights—just have fun together
Plan and save for a family vacation
Plan a father/daughter "date"; plan a father/son camping trip Plan a mother/daughter craft project; plan a day for mother/son cooking

Financial
Read two books on Christian financial principles
Make sure each family member has something for the church offering
Discuss the way we worship through tithing
Establish a savings account or college fund for each child
Eliminate all credit card debt by the year's end
Complete work on the family will

Personal/Social
Develop friendships with two new families; look for families that have children the same age as yours
Learn a new hobby or skill; take up tennis, fishing, needlepoint, or rollerblading
Join the YMCA for recreation and family oriented activities
Read five nonfiction books this year; read five new books out loud to your children

Initiate two get-togethers with friends at church, work, or neighborhood

Marriage

Establish weekly times for Marriage Staff Meetings

Schedule times to get away for the weekend without the kids

Schedule at least two "dates" together per month

Identify hobbies or areas of interest that the two of you can do together

Participate in a marriage enrichment seminar and/or read a marriage book together

Household

Clean out and organize the garage, closets, or attic

Put a lock on parent's bedroom door for privacy

Ask for each child's input as you update their room to fit their growth and needs

Establish a specific set of age-appropriate responsibilities around the house; Who sets the table? Who takes out the trash? Who clears the table after the meal?

Make a plan for the yardwork that needs to be done; Set up a schedule for completing it; Assign each family member a job, and work together to accomplish the goal

Career

Join a professional organization within your field

Bring your children to your office; let them see where Mom or Dad works

Reorganize office or work space for maximum efficiency

Don't bring work home

Spend time with colleagues in your profession; attend job-related seminar or workshop

Ministry

Volunteer as a Sunday School teacher in your child's class; get to know his friends

Host a backyard Bible club in your neighborhood

Spend a week of vacation doing missions work

Start a Christmas "praise" letter in which every family writes a sentence or paragraph

Volunteer as a family at a homeless shelter – serving food or leading Bible studies for the children

Appendix L

Goal-setting Worksheet

Where there is no vision, people perish—Proverbs 29:19 (KJV).

Period covered __________ to__________ Prepared by __________

Goal-setting Areas	What (Obejectives)	How (Plan)	When (Schedule)
Spiritual			
Marriage			
Family			
Household			
Financial			
Career			
Personal/Social			
Ministry			

Appendix M

Affirming Worth

Through Attention, Respect, and Acceptance

Infancy 0–18 months

- Smile at me, coo, make silly faces
- Hold me, rock me, sing to me
- Accept my uniqueness—I may have a different energy level, feeding or sleeping schedule than you or my sister/brother
- Respect my sensitivity and feelings—use a gentle tone of voice around me and handle me with patient care

Early Childhood 18 months–3 years

- Play with me—slide with me, swing with me—it's not enough to be in the same room with me
- Accept my need to be separate from you—handle my temper tantrums with firmness and gentleness—let me handle the jobs that I am equipped to handle

Middle Childhood 3 years–5 years

- Play with me, read to me, sing with me, act silly, and participate in lots of moving activities with me
- Accept my curiosity, answer my questions with patience
- Respect me and my feelings; apologize when you're wrong

Late Childhood 6 years–12 years

- Show interest in my activities and pursuits; come to my school nights, attend my concerts and games
- Show me respect by asking about my preferences and giving me choices; tell me about schedules ahead of time and give explanation for rules
- Accept my changing interests

Adolescence 13 years–18 years

- Show interest in my activities and relationships; come to school events, invite me to do things with you, find common interests
- Show me respect by listening to what I say before formulating a response; never roll your eyes or dismiss my thoughts as unimportant; ask for my opinion
- Accept my mood swings and reluctance to talk; sometimes talk to me on the telephone, write me notes, or talk while we're driving; take some of the pressure off

Young Adult 19 years–30 years

- Ask about my friends and show interest in their lives; keep track of which friends are most important to me
- Respect my decisions and wishes; ask before you make decisions that affect me
- Accept my uniqueness—my choice of career, dreams, and aspirations

Appendix N

Build Belonging

Through Affection, Comfort, and Security

Infancy 0–18 months

- Hold me, pat my back, tell me you're glad to have me; talk soothingly
- Comfort me when I'm sick or when I hurt myself; I'll need lots of hugs and kisses as I learn to walk
- Be attentive to my needs; lovingly rather than grudgingly make sure that I am fed, changed, and held

Early Childhood 18 months–36 months

- Tickle me; hold me when I want to be held; cuddle with me when we read; kiss me goodnight; hold hands and pray with me
- Kiss my hurts when I bring them to you or call them to your attention
- Tell me that the rules are to keep me safe; use a firm, but gentle voice, not an angry voice when you have to discipline me

Middle Childhood 3 years–5 years

- Hold me when I want to be held, wrestle with me, tickle me, cuddle with me when we read
- Honor my feelings when they get hurt, tell me it's OK to feel sad or mad or afraid
- Explain the reasons for the rules—tell me that the rules are to keep me safe and because you want what's best for me; define the limits but remember I need to explore

Late Childhood 6 years–12 years

- Give me hugs, hold my hand when you pray with me, send me mail—I'll enjoy the chance to read your words of affection
- Be sensitive to times when my feelings are hurt
- Give me the security of knowing that I will not be compared to anyone else; take disagreements between adults to a place where I cannot hear; hearing conflict makes me afraid

Adolescence 13 years–18 years

- Give me hugs, put your arm around me, put your hand on my shoulder, put a note in my backpack telling me you love me; write "I love you" on the bathroom mirror since I spend a lot of time there
- Don't make fun of my vacillating emotions—take me seriously
- Be patient with my anger or irritation; sometimes when I'm angry it means that I am hurt inside and don't know how to tell you
- Let me know that I can depend on you to be there if I need to talk; be available

Young Adult 19 years–30 years

- Give me hugs, walk with me arm and arm, write me a letter telling me that you love me, send me care packages with my "favorites" inside
- Empathize with my hurts, avoid lecturing or "I told you so's"
- Let me know that I am free to become the adult God intended, but that your welcome mat is always at the door

Appendix O

Instill Competence

Through Encouragement, Approval, Appreciation, and Support

Infancy 0–18 months

- Hold me so that I feel safe but let me explore; encourage me to take my first steps
- Tell me that I'm special just because I'm Mommy's and/or Daddy's child
- Clap for me when I drink from a cup and say my first words
- Stay near to me and let me know that you're close; I feel supported when you do things *with* me rather than *for* me

Early Childhood 18 months–36 months

- Urge me to think and discover; talk "with" me not "at" me—this helps me develop vocabulary; patiently remind me about my potty training because I want to do the things that big boys and girls do
- Show enthusiasm when I show you my accomplishments; show enthusiasm when you've been gone, let me know that you've missed me
- Praise my efforts as well as the completed tasks; thank me for trying to put on my clothes by myself, even if I don't get it just right
- Give me instructions a little at a time, show me, and then let me try myself

Middle Childhood 3 years–5 years

- Talk to me about your positive experiences that match my stage of life; tell me that I can make it because you did too!
- Notice when I share with others; comment on my helpfulness
- Tell me I am diligent when I finish my chores; tell me I am sensitive when I notice other's feelings; I feel important when I hear those big words
- Reassure me of your presence but let me see what I can or cannot do without your help

Adolescence 13 years–18 years

- Encourage me to try new things and pursue my interests; help me define who I am
- Surprise me with your words of approval; tell me that you're glad I'm your child—not just when I've done something right
- Acknowledge your inadequacies and tell me about the things that I can do better than you—this helps me balance my strengths and weaknesses
- Ask me for ways that you might show your support; this lets me know you're interested and available yet I still get to be "me"

Young Adult 19 years–30 years

- Encourage me to pursue "my" best not "the" best
- Let me know that I am wanted at family gatherings—just because you love me and I am an important part of the family
- Invite me to go to dinner to celebrate my victories, ask me to help you or give advice in my areas of expertise
- Become my comrade and my confidante; let me know you're there if I need you; show interest in what interests me

About the Authors

Dr. David and Teresa Ferguson serve as Directors of Intimate Life Ministries and Professional Associates with the Center for Marriage and Family Intimacy. David's doctoral work at Oxford Graduate School focused on the development of Intimacy Therapy, a biblically centered counseling approach.

David and Teresa appear regularly on the Intimate Life radio program and have coauthored several books including *The Pursuit of Intimacy, Intimate Moments*, and *Intimate Encounters.* Married for thirty-two years, they are the parents of three children—Terri, Robin, and Eric.

Dr. Paul Warren is the Medical Director of the Child and Adolescent Division of the Minirth-Meier New Life Clinic in Richardson, Texas as well as a Professional Associate of the Center for Marriage and Family Intimacy. He is the coauthor of several books including *Kids Who Carry Our Pain, Things That Go Bump in the Night,* and *The Father Book.*

Vicky Warren, a graduate of UCLA, has held staff positions with Campus Crusade for Christ, Minirth-Meier Clinics, and *Today's Better Life* magazine before joining the Center for Marriage and Family Intimacy.

Paul and Vicky have been married for fifteen years and have a son, Matthew.

Terri Ferguson is a certified teacher and has taught children of all ages in both church and academic settings. While pursuing an M.A. in counseling, Terri develops curriculum for the Center for Marriage and Family Intimacy and serves as a seminar speaker.

Introduction to Sociology

THIRD EDITION

Laurence A. Basirico
Elon University

Barbara G. Cashion
Shippensburg University of Pennsylvania

J. Ross Eshleman
Wayne State University

BEST VALUE TEXTBOOKS

Text Design and Composition: Archetype Book Composition

Managing Editor: Dr. William E. Kimberlin, Bowling Green State University/Firelands

Project Editor: Suzanne Morse

Editor: Nandi Crosby

Cover Design and Production Coordinator: Jenifer Meda

ISBN: 1-932856-67-6

Table of Contents

PART ONE
SOCIOLOGY: PERSPECTIVES AND METHODS 1

CHAPTER 1
THE NATURE AND USES OF SOCIOLOGY 3

What is Sociology? 6
The Sociological Perspective 7
Sociology and Popular Wisdom 8
Sociology and the Other Social Sciences 11
HOW TO READ A TABLE 12
Occupational and Personal Uses of Sociology 15
Academic Sociologist 15
Professional Sociologists in the Workplace 16
SOCIOLOGY AT WORK 18
Fostering Civic Responsibility 18
Nonsociologists in the Workplace 19
Nonsociologists in Society and Other Social Environments 22
Summary 23
Key Terms 24
Discussion Questions 25

CHAPTER 2
THE DEVELOPMENT OF SOCIOLOGY 27

The Development of Sociology in Europe 29
Auguste Comte 30
Herbert Spencer 32
Karl Marx 34
SOCIOLOGY AT WORK 34
Helping Migrant Farmworkers 34
Emile Durkheim 37
Max Weber 39
The Development of Sociology in America 40
The Chicago School 41
The Shift of Influence to the East 42
The Major Theoretical Perspectives in Society 42
Structural Functional Theory 43
Conflict Theory 46
POLICY DEBATE 48
Prayer in Schools 48
Symbolic Interaction Theory 51
Exchange Theory 53
Evolutionary Theory 55
Additional Theoretical Perspectives 57
Summary 58
Key Terms 60
Discussion Questions 61

CHAPTER 3
METHODS OF STUDYING SOCIETY 63

Is Sociology a Science? 66
The Components of Scientific Theory 67
Concepts and Variables 67
Propositions and Hypotheses 67
Theory 68
The Standards of Scientific Inquiry 68
Objectivity 68
Replication 69
Precision of Measurement 69
Sociology and Science 70
Types of Sociological Research 70
Descriptive Research 70
Explanatory Research 72
Evaluation Research 74
Sociological Research Methods 77
Observation Studies 78
Survey Research 79
Experimental Designs 82
SOCIOLOGY AT WORK 82
Research Analyst 82
Secondary Analysis 85
The Research Process 85
Summary 89
Key Terms 90
Discussion Questions 92

PART TWO
INDIVIDUALS WITHIN SOCIETY 93

CHAPTER 4

CULTURE AND SOCIETY 95

Elements of Culture 98
Symbols 98
Language 99
SOCIOLOGY AT WORK 100
Training Teachers in Cape Verde 100
Values 102
Norms 104
Technology and Material Culture 106
Cultural Lag 107
Interpreting Culture: Our Own and Others 108
Ethnocentrism 108
Xenocentrism 109
Temporocentrism 109
Cultural Relativism 110
Cultural Complexity and Diversity 111
Subcultures 111
POLICY DEBATE 112
Bilingual Education 112
Countercultures 114
Idiocultures 114
Ideal and Real Culture 115
Social Institutions 116
Summary 116
Key Terms 118
Discussion Questions 119

CHAPTER 5

SOCIAL STRUCTURE, SOCIAL GROUPS, AND SOCIAL ORGANIZATIONS 121

Social Statuses 123
Social Roles 123
Social Groups 126
Types of Social Groups 128
Primary and Secondary Groups 128
In-Groups and Out-Groups 130
Peer Groups 131
Reference Groups 132
Small Groups and Large Groups 133
SOCIOLOGY AT WORK 136
Developing Products and Enhancing the Features of Bank Credit Card Services 136
Social Networks 137
Formal Organizations 138
POLICY DEBATE 140
Employee Drug Testing 140
The Importance of Formal Organizations 142
The Goals of Formal Organizations 142
Bureaucracy 143
Bureaucracy As an Ideal Type and Its Functions 143
Dysfunctions of Bureaucracies 144
Must Bureaucracies Be Dehumanizing and Impersonal? The Case of Japan 145
Voluntary Associations 146
Summary 147
Key Terms 149
Discussion Questions 150

CHAPTER 6

SOCIALIZATION AND SOCIAL INTERACTION 151

What is Socialization? 153
Is Human Interaction Necessary? 154
Children in Institutions 154
Isolated and Feral Children 154
Sociobiology and the Nature–Nurture Debate 155
Symbolic Interaction 157
George Herbert Mead: Mind, Self, and Society 157
Charles Horton Cooley: The Looking-Glass Self 159
Erving Goffman: The Presentation of Self 160
Maintaining the Self 162
Agencies of Socialization 163
The Family 163
The Schools 164
Peer Groups 164
The Mass Media 165
Socialization of Gender Roles 165
Infant and Childhood Experiences 166
Gender-Role Socialization in Schools 166
Gender-Role Socialization in Peer Groups 167

Mass Media and Socialization of Gender Roles 168
Socialization in Adulthood 169
Types of Adult Socialization 169
Resocialization 170
Summary 171
Key Terms 172
Discussion Questions 173

CHAPTER 7

DEVIANCE AND SOCIAL CONTROL 175

What is Deviance? 177
Traditional Views of Deviance and of Deviants 178
The Absolutist and Moral Views 178
The Medical and Social-Pathological Views 178
The Statistical View 178
The Relative Nature of Deviance 178
Variation by Time 179
Variation by Place 180
Variation by Situation 181
Variation by Social Status 181
Theories Explaining Deviance 183
Biological Theories of Deviance 183
Psychological Theories of Deviance 184
Sociological Theories Explaining Deviance 185
Strain and Anomie Theory 185
SOCIOLOGY AT WORK 186
Redirecting Juvenile Offenders 186
Conflict Theory 188
Sociocultural Learning Theories 189
Labeling Theory 191
The Social Consequences of Deviance 193
Social Functions of Deviance 193
Social Dysfunctions of Deviance 194
Deviance and Crime 195
Deviance and Social Control 197
Internal Controls of Deviance 197
External Controls of Deviance 198
Summary 199
Key Terms 201
Discussion Questions 202

PART THREE
SOCIAL INEQUALITY 203

CHAPTER 8

SOCIAL DIFFERENTIATION AND STRATIFICATION 205

Social Stratification 207
Types of Societies and Social differentiation 208
Types of Stratification 209
Sources of Power In a Class System 210
Social Class 210
Social Status 210
Parties 210
Socioeconomic Status 211
Theories of Social Stratification 212
SOCIOLOGY AT WORK 212
Helping Disabled Drug Addicts 212
Structural Functional Theory 213
Conflict Theory 214
Attempts at Synthesis 214
Inequality in the United States 215
The Distribution of Income 215
The Distribution of Wealth 215
Social Status in American Society 216
Class Consciousness 216
Poverty 217
Inequality and Life Chances 218
Occupations 218
Housing and Lifestyle 218
Education 219
Medical Care 219
Social Mobility in the United States 221
Structural Characteristics of Mobility in the United States 222
Individual Characteristics and Upward Mobility 222
Summary 223
Key Terms 224
Discussion Questions 225

CHAPTER 9

RACIAL AND ETHNIC DIFFERENTIATION 227

Racial, Ethnic, and Minority Groups 230

Racial Groups 231
Ethnic Groups 232
Minority Groups 232
Attitudes, Behaviors, and Their Influence 233
Prejudice 233
Discrimination 236
Racism 237
Patterns of Group Interaction 239
Ethnic Stratification: Inequality and Interaction 239
Ethnic Antagonism 241
Integration and Assimilation 242
Segregation 243
Pluralism 244
Major Racial, Ethnic, and Other Minority Groups in the United States 245
Hispanic-Americans 246
African-Americans 247
Asian-Americans 249
Native Americans 250
WASPs and White Ethnic Americans 251
Jewish-Americans 252
The Future 252
Summary 254
Key Terms 255
Discussion Questions 257

CHAPTER 10

GENDER DIFFERENTIATION 259

Sex and Gender Differentiation 261
Biological Bases of Gender Differentiation 261
Social Bases of Gender Differentiation 261
Adult Sex Differentiation 262
Cross-Cultural Gender Differentiation 263
Theories of Gender Differentiation 263
Structural Functional Theory 263
Conflict Theory 264
Gender Differentiation and The Workplace 265
Women in the Workplace 265
Income 266
The Split Labor Market 266
Comparable Worth 267
Upward Mobility 267
Women's Work in the Family 268
The Women's Movement 269
The Women's Movement in the United States 269
The Women's Movement in Europe 269
The Consequences of Inequality 270
Gender and Poverty 270
Women's Self-Esteem 271
Medical Care 271
Sexual Harassment 272
Family Violence 273
Rape 273
The Future of Gender Inequality 274
Summary 274
Key Terms 275
Discussion Questions 276

CHAPTER 11

AGE DIFFERENTIATION AND THE AGED 277

Age, Aging, and the Aged 280
Myths about Old Age 282
Demographic Aspects of Aging 285
Numbers of the Elderly: The Graying of America 285
Life Expectancy 286
Social Characteristics of the Elderly 287
Theories of Aging and of Age Differentiation 289
Structural Functional Theory 289
Symbolic Interaction Theory 291
Social Exchange Theory 292
Conflict Theory 292
Problems of the Aged 293
Retirement 293
Lifestyles and Income 295
Health 297
SOCIOLOGY AT WORK 298
Using Sociology in Nursing Care of the Elderly 298
Abuse 300
Death and Dying 301
Summary 303
Key Terms 304
Discussion Questions 305

PART FOUR
SOCIAL INSTITUTIONS 307

CHAPTER 12

FAMILY GROUPS AND SYSTEMS 309

What is Family? 311
Variation in Kinship and Family Organization 314
Marriage and Number of Spouses 314
Norms of Residence 316
Norms of Descent and Inheritance 316
Norms of Authority 317
Norms for Choice of Marriage Partner 317
A Functionalist Perspective on the Family 318
Socialization 318
Affection and Emotional Support 319
Sexual Regulation 319
Reproduction 319
Social Placement 320
A Conflict Perspective On the Family 320
Other Perspectives On the Family 322
An Exchange Perspective 322
An Interactionist Perspective 323
A Developmental Perspective 324
The American Family System 326
Marriage Rates and Age at Marriage 328
Family Size 329
Divorce 331
SOCIOLOGY AT WORK 332
Family Counseling 332
Nontraditional Marital and Family Lifestyles 334
Nonmarital Cohabitation 335
Childless Marriage 335
One-Parent Families 336
Dual-Career Marriages 338
Summary 339
Key Terms 341
Discussion Questions 342

CHAPTER 13

RELIGIOUS GROUPS AND SYSTEMS 345

A Sociological Approach to Religion 348
What Is Religion? 348
The Organization of Religion 349
Churches, Sects, and Cults 350
Theories of Religion 353
A Functionalist Approach 353
A Conflict Approach 356
Religions of the World 357
Christianity and Judaism 357
Islam 359
Hinduism 360
Buddhism 361
Confucianism 361
Religion in the United States 362
The Development of Religious Movements 363
SOCIOLOGY AT WORK 364
Helping Religious Refugees Readjust 364
Current Trends in Religion 365
Secularization 366
Religiosity and Church Attendance 367
The Electronic Church 367
POLICY DEBATE 368
Should Corporal Punishment of Children Be Allowed? 368
Ecumenism 371
A New Religious Consciousness 371
Religion and Other Institutions 372
Summary 373
Key Terms 374
Discussion Questions 376

CHAPTER 14

EDUCATIONAL GROUPS AND SYSTEMS 377

Structural Functional Theory of Education 379
The Manifest Functions of Education 379
The Latent Functions of Education 380
Conflict Theory of Education 382
The Hidden Curriculum 382
The Teaching of Values 382
The Learning of Norms 383
Credentialism 383
Historical Perspectives on Education 384
Occupational Training 384

Beliefs About Children 385
Who Rules the Schools? 386
Stratification in the School System 387
School Boards 387
Faculty 387
Students 388
Biased Intelligence Tests 388
American Private Schools 389
Parochial Schools 389
Private Preparatory Schools 390
Selective Private Colleges 390
The Failure of American Schools 391
Why Students Do Not Learn 391
Financial Problems 391
School Facilities 392
Inadequate Curricula 393
The Self-Fulfilling Prophecy 394
High Dropout Rate 394
Improving the Schools 394
Magnet Schools 394
Decentralized Bureaucracies 395
Vouchers 395
New Management 395
Creating Future Goals 396
SOCIOLOGY AT WORK 396
Developing Strategies in the Classroom 396
Contest and Sponsored Mobility 398
Is All This Education Necessary? 398
Summary 400
Key Terms 401
Discussion Questions 401

CHAPTER 15
POLITICAL GROUPS AND SYSTEMS 403

Types of Power 405
The Development of Political Systems 407
Structural Functional Theory 408
Conflict Theory 408
Political Structures in Modern Societies 409
The Democratic State 409
The Totalitarian State 410
Political Parties 410
The Political System in the United States 412
The Power Elite 413
Political Pluralism 413
Political Action Committees (PACs) 413
Lobbies 414
The Role of the Individual 416
Political Socialization 416
Political Socialization in the Mass Media 417
POLICY DEBATE 418
Should Former Members of Congress or Congressional Staff Be Restricted from Lobbying? 418
Political Participation 420
SOCIOLOGY AT WORK 422
Sociology and Municipal Politics 422
Summary 424
Key Terms 425
Discussion Questions 426

CHAPTER 16
ECONOMIC GROUPS AND SYSTEMS 429

Types of Economic Systems 431
Capitalism 432
Socialism 432
Welfare Capitalism 432
Communism—A Utopian Idea 433
Theories of Economic Development 434
Structural Functional Theory 434
Conflict Theory 436
The American Economic System 436
The Growth of Large Corporations 437
Multinational Corporations 439
The Changing Nature of Work 440
Factory Work and Alienation 440
Scientific Management 440
The Human Relations School 441
Modern Trends in Management 442
Unionization 443
Service Work 444
Professions 445
Politics and the Distribution of Wealth 446
Welfare 446
Welfare for the Well-Off 447
The Chinese System: An Example of Socialism 447

SOCIOLOGY AT WORK 448
Counseling Investors: Sociology and the Stock Market 448
Summary 451
Key Terms 452
Discussion Questions 453

CHAPTER 17
HEALTH-CARE GROUPS AND SYSTEMS 455

The Social Nature of Health and Illness 457
Theoretical Perspectives On Illness 458
A Functional Explanation of Illness 458
The Conflict Perspective of Illness 460
Symbolic Interaction and Illness Behavior 461
The Change in Illness Over Time 462
The Age of Infectious Diseases 462
Current Causes of Death 463
Alcoholism: Moral Failure or Major Disease? 464
The American Health-Care System 465
The Social Model of Illness 465
The Medical Model of Illness 465
The Profession of Medicine 465
Hospitals 467
Nurses 468
Other Health-Care Workers 469
Paying For Medical Care 470
Health Insurance 470
Prepaid Health Care 472
Health Movements 472
Health and the Second Great Awakening 472
Alcoholics Anonymous (AA) 473
Modern Concerns About Diet and Exercise 473
Health Care in Other Countries 474
SOCIOLOGY AT WORK 474
Monitoring Medical Billing Practices 474
The British Health-Care System 475
Health Care in the People's Republic of China 476
The Herbalist in Underdeveloped Nations 477
Summary 479
Key Terms 480
Discussion Questions 481

PART FIVE
HUMAN ECOLOGY AND CHANGE 483

CHAPTER 18
COLLECTIVE BEHAVIORS AND SOCIAL MOVEMENTS 485

What is Collective Behavior? 487
Precondition of Collective Behavior 488
Spatially Proximate Collective Behaviors: Crowds 492
Characteristics of Crowds 492
Types of Crowds 493
Theories of Acting-Crowd Behavior 494
The Classical Perspective 495
The Interactionist Perspective 495
The Emergent-Norm Perspective 496
The Game Perspective 497
Spatially Diffuse Collective Behaviors 498
Masses and Mass Behavior 499
SOCIOLOGY AT WORK 500
Market Research 500
Publics and Public Opinion 502
Social Movements 504
Types of Social Movements 504
The Development and Life Cycle of Social Movements 504
Summary 506
Key Terms 507
Discussion Questions 509

CHAPTER 19
POPULATION AND ECOLOGY 511

Demography and the Study of Population 515
Collecting the Data 515
Fertility 516
Mortality 517
Migration 519
Population Trends and Life Experiences 521
The World Population Explosion and the Demographic Transition 523

Population Density 525
Population and Ecology 526
Malthus's Theory of Population 526
World Food Distribution Today 527
Population and Other Natural Resources 527
SOCIOLOGY AT WORK 528
Monitoring Population Trends 528
POLICY DEBATE 530
Should Stricter Environmental Protection Measures Be Enacted? 530
Political Policies Regarding Population 532
Zero Population Growth 532
Summary 533
Key Terms 534
Discussion Questions 535

CHAPTER 20
THE CHANGING COMMUNITY 537

The Origin and Development of Communities 539
Early Community and Urban Development 539
Preindustrial Urban Communities 540
Community Development in the Industrial Era 540
Third World Urbanization 541
Urbanization in The United States 543
Population Trends 543
The Metropolitan Community 544
Urban Ecology 546
Urban Processes 546
Urban Structure 547
Life in Cities and Suburbs 548
City Life 549
Suburban Life 551
Urban Problems 552
Urban Rejuvenation: Problems and Prospects 555
Downtown Revitalization 555
Urban Renewal 556
Urban Planning 557
Diversity of Values 558
Summary 560
Key Terms 562
Discussion Questions 563

CHAPTER 21
THE NATURE OF SOCIAL CHANGE 565

Theories of Social Change 567
Evolutionary Theory of Change 567
Conflict Theory of Social Change 568
Cyclical Theories of Change 568
Structural Functionalism and Social Change 568
Social Change Theory: A Synthesis 569
What Causes Social Change? 569
Population, Geography, and Political Power 569
Changing Ideology 570
Discoveries and Inventions 571
Diffusion 571
The Automobile: Impact of an Innovation 572
The Automobile and Economic Growth 572
The Automobile and the Environment 573
Social Change in Underdeveloped Nations 573
Modernization in Underdeveloped Nations 573
Dependency or World Systems Theory 574
Social Change and the Individual 575
SOCIOLOGY AT WORK 576
Societal Analysis in the Auto Industry 576
Summary 580
Key Terms 581
Discussion Questions 582

GLOSSARY 583

REFERENCES 605

INDEX 623

Preface

Our purpose in writing this text is to convey both the excitement of sociology and its relevance to our lives. The excitement of sociology comes from what it studies: social life and social organization. Sociology encompasses all aspects of society: family life, community change, individual development, group differences, and gender inequality, to name a few. It involves a unique way of looking at the world in which we live, forcing us to question the obvious and understand how society and behavior are patterned and organized. People are discovering that sociology provides them with unique skills and abilities in research methods, in applying social theory in the working world, and in using their understanding of social processes, organization, and change.

SUPPLEMENTS

We have assembled the following supplements to support *Introduction to Sociology*.

1. *Study Guide.* Kathryn Mueller of Baylor University has prepared a thorough and practical student study guide that includes learning objectives, chapter outlines, questions, and ideas that help the student review the material presented in this text. Also included are student activities and projects designed to enhance the practical application of sociological concepts.

2. *Instructor's Manual.* A comprehensive manual provides a wealth of teaching suggestions, objectives and resources, outside activities stressing the importance of sociology to personal lives, suggested readings from short stories and novels, a guide to films, and much more. The *Instructor's Manual* was written by Kathryn Mueller of Baylor University.

3. *Test Bank.* An extensive test bank of 2,100 questions is available to instructors in both hard copy and electronic forms. All questions have been written by the authors. Each chapter consists of two sets of 30 multiple-choice questions, 15 true-false questions, and 5 short essay questions. The test bank is in two parts (test A and test B), permitting differently worded but similar questions to be given to different classes. Each question is referenced to the appropriate text page to make verification quick and easy.

4. *Transparencies.* A set of acetate transparencies is available to adopters. The set includes charts, tables, and graphs from the text and additional charts and graphs from other sources.

ACKNOWLEDGMENTS

As in the previous editions of this text, we wish to acknowledge the input and contributions of many people. How do we express an intellectual debt to the scholars, researchers, teachers, and students who provided the ideas, data, and findings used here? Obviously, that is impossible. We can, however, acknowledge specific individuals who had a role or made a contribution to the preparation of this book. For the three of us, this includes many people.

We thank, of course, our own personal groups-our families and friends who have supported our efforts as we have studied and worked in our chosen field. Special thanks to our children Jill, Sid, Janet, Libby, Jonathan, and Bridget, who have taught us as much as we have taught them. We also thank our teachers, those people who have sparked our interest in sociology and helped us develop our ability to think through the issues of the discipline.

We extend our thanks to our colleagues at Appalachian State University, Elon University, Shippensburg University, and Wayne State University who support us in our daily activities. Certain professors and professional colleagues have been especially influential: Thomas Arcaro, Anne Bolin, Muriel Canter, Deborah Cassidy, Edward Dager, Marilyn Daniels, A. M. Denton, Thomas Henricks, Larry Keeter, the late Leonard Kercher, Fei Lin, A. R. Mangus, Greg Nagy, Howard Nixon, Joyce Rhymer, George Taylor, John Turner, Leon Warshay, the late Eugene A. Weinstein, and Rudy Zarzar. Special recognition and thanks are due to several people who provided valuable assistance in very specific ways: Joe Therrien and Joe Sloan at Wayne State with computers, Sara Nixon at Appalachian State with library resources, and the library staff at Elon University and administrators there who approved a sabbatical leave.

We want to thank the many instructors who used a previous edition of our text and provided us with valuable feedback. We are especially grateful for the comments and suggestions offered during preparation of this third edition. In particular we wish to thank the following scholars:

David A. Gay
University of Central Florida

Lee F. Hamilton
Montana State University

Gary D. Hartley
Simpson College

Harlowe Hatle
University of South Dakota

A. C. Higgins
SUNY Albany

Tim Johnson
Central College

Tye Craig Johnson
University of South Carolina

Cheryl A. Joseph
College of Notre Dame

Barbara Karcher
Kennesaw State College

James H. Leiding
East Stroudsburg University

Martin L. Levin
Emory University

Jerry Lewis
Kent State University

Margarite Martin
Gonzago University

Barbara McCoy
Northeast Mississippi Community College

Richard B. Miller
Missouri Southern State College

Man J. Molseed
University of Michigan, Flint

Kay Mueller
Baylor University

Donna Phillips
San Bernardino Valley College

William G. Roy
University of California, Los Angeles

William A. Schwab
University of Arkansas

Dwayne M. Smith
Tulane University

Thomas Sparhawk
Georgia Southern College

James Sutton
Chattanooga State Technical Community College

Nancy Terjesen
Kent State University

Kathleen A. Tiemann
University of North Dakota

Steven Vassar
Mankato State University

Richard Veach
Whatian Community College

Robert Wooley
Mansfield University

PART ONE

Sociology: Perspectives and Methods

People who like to avoid shocking discoveries, who prefer to believe that society is just what they were taught in Sunday School, who like the safety of the rules … should stay away from sociology.

PETER BERGER

The Nature and Uses of Sociology

The Resurgence of Public Sociologies

In 1972, a mining company dam burst and created a flood that devastated the area. Believing that the mining company was at fault, the 650 survivors filed legal charges against them. Kai Erikson, a sociologist, was called in by the survivors' attorneys to help determine whether the mining company's practices might have precipitated the flood and to evaluate the personal and social impact of the flood. Erikson notes, "My assignment on Buffalo Creek … was to sift through the store of available sociological knowledge to see what light it might shed on a single human event" (Erikson, 1976, p. 12). Along with lawyers, legal assistants, psychiatrists, and insurance representatives, Erikson played an instrumental part in winning $13.5 million from the coal company for the survivors.

In 2003, the space shuttle Columbia tragically disintegrated upon reentry. Diane Vaughan, a sociologist who had studied the causes of the 1986 Challenger disaster, worked with the Columbia Accident Investigation Board to examine the causes of that shuttle's disaster. The head of the board, Admiral Harold Gehman, invited Vaughan to join the investigation because he was persuaded of the relevance of the sociological perspective and analysis for Columbia. Her role was to help examine the human factors that may have played a part in the accident (Vaughan, 2003).

Work such as Erikson's and Vaughan's calls attention to an important issue that has long confronted social scientists: What is the primary purpose of the social sciences and social scientists? Is it to gain basic knowledge in order to achieve a fundamental understanding of social life, or is it to develop practical solutions to personal, organizational, and social problems? It could be argued that these are both noble purposes for social science and scientists to pursue. While these objectives are neither mutually exclusive nor polar opposites, each requires different kinds of professional commitments and responsibilities. Discussions about whether the work of social scientists should be oriented toward practical needs usually referred to as "applied sociology" or "sociological practice") or toward the development of a theoretical knowledge of social life (traditionally referred to as "pure," "basic," or "academic" sociology) or toward both have been particularly evident in the field of sociology. However, in recent years, sociologists have been turning their attention to melding these two approaches and their reciprocal importance is increasingly valued and recognized in an area of sociology known as "public sociologies." In fact, "Public Sociologies" was the central theme of the American Sociological Association's Annual Meetings in 2004.

Howard Freeman and Peter Rossi (1984), two sociologists who have written extensively about this issue, feel that while academic sociology and applied sociology share common research methods and theoretical perspectives, there are many differences. A few of the differences between these approaches are as follows (Larson, 1990):

1. *Choice of study topic*—Academic sociologists and applied sociologists have different ways of deciding what to study. Academic sociologists choose their research topics according to their own interests. Although what they choose to study is influenced somewhat by the availability of funding sources (such as grants) and the interests and requirements of publishers, the problems and issues that academic sociologists study are usually related to a topic in which they are particularly interested. The problems and issues that applied sociologists study are usually selected by the clients for whom they work, such as the attorneys Kai Erikson worked for in helping to sort out the Buffalo Creek disaster and the Columbia Accident Investigation Board for which Diane Vaughan served as a consultant.

2. *Evaluation of work*—The work of academic sociologists is evaluated by other academic sociologists, whereas applied sociological work is evaluated by the clients for whom the work is done.

3. *Standards governing the work*—Academic sociologists must conform to rigid standards of scholarship, whereas applied sociologists must comply with the practical needs of the clients for whom they work.

4. *Goal of the work*—The primary goal of academic sociologists is to develop theories and to increase the body of sociological knowledge.

Applied sociologists are primarily interested in finding solutions to problems and providing their clients with information that will improve their ability to make decisions and establish policies.

The differences between academic and applied science raise important questions for social scientists and for the future of the social sciences. Should there be different reward structures for different types of scientific activity? Who should get the highest rewards? Who determines the value of different types of scientific activity? If there is a limited amount of private and government funding for the social sciences, what types of work should have priority? Which objective should be emphasized in higher education for social scientists? Although questions such as these may seem more relevant to professional sociologists than to students, it is nevertheless worthwhile for you to consider how the various sciences can be used. Many of these questions are relevant to the natural sciences, as well. Throughout this book, you will be introduced to many uses of sociology and the ways in which it can serve the needs of individuals and society.

Our lives are governed by the society in which we live. Social rules and conventions influence every aspect of our daily lives. We begin to learn them before we can talk, and they are reinforced, altered, or contradicted every time we enter a social situation, whether new or familiar. By the time we reach college age, these rules are such a part of us that we obey them without thinking. This, however, does not diminish their importance or pervasiveness.

The answers to many of the questions we wonder about have at least some social components. Why, for example, do roommate situations with three people almost always have more problems than those with two? Do sororities or fraternities serve any real purpose? Why do they choose to admit some people but not others? Have you had an argument with anyone lately? If you have, the chances are that it arose at least in part from having different perceptions about how people should behave—perceptions influenced by social surroundings. The people employed in the housing offices of most schools are aware of this important sociological fact and try to place people from similar backgrounds as roommates. Why do most of us feel uncomfortable with a group of people we do not know? Part of the reason is that we do not know how to behave—our social behavior is determined by a constant exchange of social cues, and these cues may differ from group to group. Indeed, why are you attending college, taking this course, and reading this book right now? (Rates of college attendance differ dramatically from one social group to another.)

The list could be extended indefinitely, but our point should be clear: Whether or not we like it or are even aware of it, the social fabric that surrounds us dictates many aspects of how we live. One of the pleasures of studying sociology is that it not only has scientific applications, but also personal and occupational applications. Sociology attempts to explain not only the factors that draw group members together, but also why we may feel uncomfortable talking to most athletes and yet feel very comfortable talking to most members of the drama club (or vice versa). Although we may not recognize them, there are reasons for our social behavior, and a knowledge of these reasons is useful in our personal lives, in our occupations, and in understanding trends in the world around us. At its best, an understanding of sociology can bring to light an entire new dimension of social forces that influence us constantly.

WHAT IS SOCIOLOGY?

What is **sociology**? There are several ways to answer this question. The dictionary will tell you that it is the study of social relationships, social institutions, and society. The term itself, often credited to Auguste Comte (1798–1857), the founder of sociology, is derived from two root words: *socius*, which means "companion" or "associate," and *logos*, which means "word." At its most basic, then, it means "words about human associations or society."

Another way to find out what sociology is would be to observe some sociologists at work. Some might spend most of their time poring over volumes from the census bureau or traveling to northern Alaska every year to talk to Eskimos about their hunting practices. Some might use a survey to investigate sexual behavior or might study kinship systems (i.e., family relationship patterns) among natives of the South Pacific. Others might look into how college students perceive their professors or how television has influenced family life in the United States.

If you pursued all these approaches, you would probably find yourself with a bewildering variety of ideas about what sociology is. What do they have in common? They all suggest that sociology is concerned with every aspect of the self in relationships with others and every aspect of the social world that affects a person's thoughts or actions. As stated by the American Sociological Association in a booklet called "Careers in Sociology" (2002), sociology is the study of social life and the social causes and consequences of human behavior. The term *social life* encompasses all interpersonal relationships, all groups or collections of persons, and all types of social organizations. The "causes and consequences of human behavior" encompass how these relationships, groups, and organizations are interrelated; how they influence personal and interpersonal behavior; how they affect and are affected by the larger society; how they change or why they remain static; and what the consequences are of these factors. This definition reflects the belief that people can be understood only in the context of their contacts, associations, and communications with other people. The very heart of sociology, then—its concern with the complexities and subtleties of human social life—makes it a discipline that is highly relevant not only to professional sociologists, but also to people in virtually every line of work and at every level.

Thus, sociology may consider a wide range of general questions such as the following:

1. How do groups influence individual human behavior?
2. What are the causes and consequences of a particular system of social order?
3. What social factors contribute to a particular social change?
4. What purpose is served by a particular social organization?
5. What are the causes and consequences of a particular social system?

Sociologists then use these general questions to help in identifying and responding to more specific questions. In the case of question 5, for example, a sociologist might further inquire about a particular social system by asking such questions as, How do the patterns of social interaction in a small village differ from those in a large city? How do city planners help ensure social tranquility in rural areas undergoing rapid economic growth and development?

Other areas investigated by sociologists include racial and ethnic relationships, prejudice and discrimination, power and politics, jobs and income, families and family life, school systems and the educational process, social control, organizations, bureaucracies, groups and group dynamics, leisure, health-care systems, military systems, women's movements, and labor movements. The stratification of people by wealth, education, power, and such differences as gender or age may also be examined. As you can see, sociology is an extremely broad field. It provides knowledge that directly applies to occupations that involve evaluation, planning, research, analysis, counseling, and problem solving. In its most comprehensive sense, sociology can be regarded as including every aspect of social life—its causes, its forms and structures, its effects, and its changes and transformations.

The Sociological Perspective

In addition to its specific content areas, sociology is also a perspective, a way of looking at society and social behavior. Like the blind men who described the elephant differently, depending on whether they felt its trunk, tail, ear, body, or leg, everyone regards the world from his or her own point of view. A school building may be seen as a place of work by a teacher, as a place of study by a student, as a tax liability by a homeowner, as a fire hazard by a firefighter, and as a particular structural design by a builder. In the same way, sociologists consider the social world from their own unique perspective.

What is the **sociological perspective**? It is a conscious effort to question the obvious, and to remove ourselves from familiar experiences and examine them critically and objectively. This sort of *empirical* (based on observation or experiment) investigation enables us to determine whether our generalizations about society are accurate. These investigations could involve asking questions about poverty in a wealthy nation, about the social forces leading to unionization, or about the effects of divorce on family life and on children.

This perspective also entails efforts to see beyond individual experiences. The sociologist tries to interpret patterns—the regular, recurrent aspects of social life. An awareness of interaction patterns and group processes can help us to understand the relationship between our personal experiences and the society we live in.

Human behavior is, to a large extent, shaped by the groups to which people belong, by social interactions, and by the surrounding social and cultural context. Apart from the social and cultural context, for example, it may be extremely difficult to understand the spontaneous, simultaneous, and collective shout that occurs when a person with a wooden stick hits a round object over the head of a person wearing a thick leather glove on one hand but not on the other. It may be difficult to understand the anger of people in a neighborhood when children are bused to a school in a different neighborhood. Behaviors such as these reflect the group, the institution, and the society in which they occur. Because individual behavior can be understood only in its social and cultural context, the sociological perspective considers the individual as part of the larger society. It notes how the society is reflected in individuals and attempts to discover patterns in behaviors and regularity in events.

The sociological perspective operates at two levels, which sociologists term *macro* and *micro*. The difference relates to the size of the unit of analysis. **Macrosociology** deals with large-scale structures and processes: broad social categories, institutions, and social systems, such as war, unemployment, and divorce. Solutions to these problems are sought at the structural or organizational level.

Microsociology, on the other hand, is concerned with how individuals behave in social situations. The social problems of a veteran, an unemployed worker, or a divorcée would be subjects for microsociological research. Solutions would be sought at the personal or interpersonal level. The sociological perspective involves investigations of problems on both scales.

Perhaps the distinction between macrosociology and microsociology can be clarified by elaborating on the issue of divorce. At a *micro* level, we can observe husbands and wives in interaction and note that divorce is more likely to occur if the persons involved cannot agree on important issues, if one person takes a rigid or inflexible stance, or if the personalities of the persons involved are incompatible. At a *macro* level, we can observe how divorce rates vary cross-culturally by degree of societal modernization or how divorce rates are related to various systems of mate selection, lineage, or place of residence.

At micro levels, the unit of analysis is the person or persons in interaction; thus, the micro-level solutions to divorce may entail personal counseling, marital education programs, or small-group workshops. At macro levels, the unit of analysis is the organization, institution, or system; macro-level solutions to divorce may by related to decreasing "free choice" of mates in favor of "parental choice," moving to a single (patrilineal or matrilineal) lineage system rather than a bilateral or multilineal one, or living with the kin group rather than in a separate residence or locale. At a micro level, we may try to change the person, the behavior, or the interaction pattern. At the macro level, we may attempt to change the structure, the organization, or the social system. Sociologists study and analyze society and social life at both levels.

Thinking Sociologically

1. It was suggested that human behavior is, to a large extent, shaped through our social interactions and cultural contexts. Discuss ways in which members of our communities influence our everyday choices. More personally, to what extent are you alone responsible for your own condition or destiny?
2. In regard to a particular social issue (e.g., abortion, death penalty, single parenting), what different questions might be raised at the macrosociological level, in contrast to the microsociological level? What different suggestions or solutions might each propose?

Sociology and Popular Wisdom

It is widely assumed, sometimes accurately so, that research findings tend to support what we already know. We all have some idea as to why people act the way they do and how society works. As social beings, most of us were raised in families and communities. Everyone has learned to obey traffic signals and danger signs. We have all heard the debate and rhetoric of presidential and local political campaigns. We have all read newspapers and heard television reports that remind us continually of crime, racial conflicts, poverty, inflation, pollution, AIDS, and teenage pregnancies. We all understand social life—our own experiences make us experts in human behavior and in the nature of society. Let us examine a few examples to prove our point. Aren't the following statements obviously true?

1. With divorce at an all-time high, the institution of marriage is breaking down, and the number of families is decreasing drastically.
2. Midlife divorces are usually initiated by men who leave their wives for younger women.
3. Because capital punishment leads people to give serious thought to the consequences before committing crimes, crime rates are

much lower in states that have capital punishment than in those that do not.

4. Because blacks in the United States are "the last to be hired and the first to be fired," have lower average levels of education, are disproportionately represented below the poverty level, and are discriminated against in most areas of social life, blacks more than whites experience low self-esteem and, consequently, have much higher suicide rates than whites. Also, suicide rates for blacks or whites are higher for women than for men because women in most societies are confined to the home, receive relatively low pay, and are dependent and oppressed compared with men.
5. Because we all know that death is approaching as we grow older, a fear of dying increases with age.

Many other examples could be given, but these common-sense ideas should illustrate our point. Although you may agree with all of them, research findings indicate that all of these statements are false. Divorce rates are actually lower than they were in the 1980s. The decrease in rates is partially due to an aging population and alternative family forms, neither of which decry the value of the family. Also, marriage is not breaking down. While the marriage rate has decreased somewhat since 1970, it is not a drastic decrease (see Table 1-1). Further, most people who divorce remarry. Although people are tending to marry at a later age (an increasing number of young people are choosing to remain single longer), most people eventually marry. When we also recognize that the number of persons in society is increasing, neither the number of marriages nor the rate of marriages per thousand people is changing very dramatically (see Table 1-1).

The second statement in our list of popular wisdom suggests that men, perhaps as a result of their midlife crises, leave their wives for younger women. A study conducted for the American Association of Retired People found that the majority of midlife divorces are initiated by women. In the AARP survey, 66 percent of women reported that they asked for the divorce, compared with 41 percent of men. Women tend to recognize the danger signs of a problem marriage earlier than men do, according to Howard Markman, codirector of the Center for

TABLE 1-1: MARRIAGE AND DIVORCE RATES, 1970 TO 2005 (RATES PER 1,000 POPULATION)

Year	Marriage Rates	Divorce Rates
1970	10.6	3.5
1975	10.0	4.8
1980	10.6	5.2
1984	10.5	5.0
1985	10.1	5.0
1986	10.0	4.9
1987	9.9	4.8
1988	9.8	4.8
1989	9.7	4.7
1990	9.8	4.7
1991	9.4	4.7
1992	9.3	4.8
1993	9.0	4.6
1994	9.1	4.6
1995	8.9	4.4
1996	8.8	4.3
1997	8.9	4.3
1998	8.3	4.2
1999	8.6	4.1
2000	8.5	4.2
2001	8.4	4.0
2002	7.8	4.0
2003	7.7	3.8
2004	7.8	3.7
2005	7.5	3.6

Source: July 21, 2006 U.S. National Center for Health Statistics, *Vital Statistics of the United States; National Vital Statistics Reports;* and unpublished data.

Marital and Family Studies at the University of Denver (Enright, 2004).

The third statement suggests that crime rates are lower in states that have capital punishment than in states that do not. The evidence, however, suggests that there is very little relationship between the rate of murder and other crimes and the use of capital punishment. The murder rates in states that have the death penalty are not consistently lower than the rates in states that do not have it. In general, the death penalty is not a deterrent to murder or other crimes. Even imprisonment does not seem to be a major deterrent, as is evident from the *recidivism* (relapse into repeating criminal behavior) rate of people who have been in prison. Rather than changing people's attitudes, punishment may make them more cautious and promote extra efforts to avoid apprehension.

The fourth statement suggests that because blacks are socially and economically oppressed, have lower levels of training and skills, and are frequent victims of racism, they have lower levels of self-esteem than non-blacks. Studies (Russell, 2002; Abood & Chandler, 1997) consistently call into question the prevailing view that blacks have negative self-evaluations, however. Suicide rates are much lower among blacks than among whites, as well as much lower for females than for males (see Table 1-2). In 2003, only 1.9 black females per 100,000 population committed suicide, compared to 4.6 white females. The comparable figures for black males and white males are 9.2 and 19.6, respectively. Disparities between these groups have been consistent since the 1950s.

The fifth statement suggests that because the likelihood of death increases with age, a fear of dying increases as well. A Gallup Poll survey (January 1991) revealed that the fear of death actually diminishes, rather than increases, with age. About one-third (33 percent) of Americans ages 18 to 29 years old said that they fear death, compared to one-fourth (25 percent) of those ages 30 to 49, and only one-sixth (16 percent) of those age 50 and older. Interestingly, the survey revealed that being religious, irrespective of age, did not make much difference in fearing death; in fact, those who claimed to have no religion at all were the least likely to fear death.

TABLE 1-2 DEATH RATES FROM SUICIDE BY SEX AND RACE, 1950–2003 (RATES PER 100,000 POPULATION)

	1950	1960	1970	1980	1990	2000	2001	2002	2003
White males	22.3	21.1	20.8	20.9	22.8	19.1	19.6	20.0	19.6
Black males	7.5	8.4	10.0	11.4	12.8	10.0	9.8	9.8	9.2
White females	6.0	5.9	7.9	6.1	5.2	4.3	4.5	4.7	4.6
Black females	1.8	2.0	2.9	2.4	2.4	1.8	1.8	1.6	1.9

Source: U.S. National Center for Health Statistics, *Vital Statistics of the United States; National Vital Statistics Reports;* and unpublished data.

These examples illustrate that although some popular observations may be true, many others are not supported by empirical data. Without social research, it is extremely difficult to distinguish what is actually true from what our common sense tells us should be true. Many people have suffered enormous losses in personal relationships and business deals because they acted on the basis of what they considered "common sense" about what they believed was "the truth." We believe that the knowledge you gain from sociology will help to improve the quality of your personal and professional life. Even if this is the only sociology course you ever take, we hope that after completing it you will have a far greater understanding of yourself, of your society, and of human behavior, as well as an increased ability to question many of the popular observations widely accepted as truth by the press and by our fellow citizens.

Sociology and the Other Social Sciences

All branches of science attempt to discover general truths, propositions, or laws through methods based on observation and experimentation. Science is often divided into two categories: the social sciences and what are often referred to as the natural sciences. The natural sciences include (a) the *biological sciences*—biology, eugenics, botany, bacteriology, and so forth, which deal with living organisms, both human and nonhuman; and (b) the *physical sciences*—physics, chemistry, astronomy, geology, and so on, which deal with the nonliving physical world. The word natural must be applied to these sciences with caution, however. The **social sciences** are just as natural as those that the natural sciences embrace. The organization of cities, the collective action of a football team, and the patterns of interaction in a family system are just as natural as electricity, magnetism, and the behavior of insects.

Sociology is a social science, but it is important to realize that a complete understanding of a society or of social relationships would be impossible without an understanding of the physical world in which societies exist and an understanding of the biological factors that affect humans. Like the other social sciences—psychology, anthropology, economics, and political science—sociology deals with human relationships, social systems, and societies. Although the boundaries among the various social sciences are sometimes hazy, each tends to focus on a particular aspect of the world and tries to understand it. Scientists who devote their lives to the study of rocks, birds, plants, child rearing, or poverty do not deny the importance of other aspects of the world. Rather, they find that the area they have chosen to study requires their full concentration.

Each social science focuses on selected aspects of social relationships or social systems. Scientists in each field generally devote their attention to "what is" rather than "what should be." The social sciences are also likely to have as a goal the acquisition of knowledge rather than the direct utilization of that knowledge. Each scientist is likely to seek general laws or principles instead of isolated descriptions of particular cases or events. Thus, they differ little in their focus on social phenomena, in their methods, and in their goals, but they do differ in their particular focus of attention. Also, it is not unusual for the social sciences to overlap somewhat. People living in poverty, for example, may be of equal interest to the sociologist, the demographer, and the historian. Each of these social scientists, however, would concentrate on a different aspect of the situation. As a result, an introductory course in sociology is very different from an introductory course in economics, political science, anthropology, or psychology. A brief description of the other social sciences may help us understand the nature of social science in general and of sociology in particular.

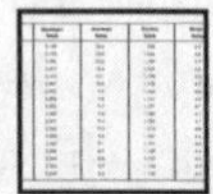

How to Read a Table

Sociologists make frequent use of tables to present the findings of their own research, to provide numerical evidence to support or reject statements they make, or to show comparisons among social groups, categories, or events, or across different points in time. Numerous tables are presented throughout this text, not so much to present our own research findings as to lend numerical support to substantive content and to show comparisons among groups or periods of time. You will be able to understand the contents of a table more easily if you follow a systematic procedure. The first table in this text is used as a model (Table 1-1) in leading you through the steps to follow in reading a table.

1. *Examine the title.* At the top of a good table is a title that tells precisely what the table contains. The title in Table 1-1 informs us that this table includes information about marriage and divorce rates for the selected years 1970 through 2005.

2. *Check the source.* The source of the information presented usually appears at the bottom of the table. Unless the table presents original data, it probably includes a source note listing the research journal or other publication that contains the original information. The source note tells where the data comes from and where we can go to locate the data; it helps us judge how reliable the information is. In Table 1-1, the data come from U.S National Center for Health Statistics, as published in the *Vital Statistics of the United States.*

3. *Look for any headnotes or footnotes.* Headnotes generally appear below the title; footnotes are likely to appear below the table but above the source note. Headnotes or footnotes may tell how the data were collected, how a question was asked, why some information is lacking, which statistical measure was used, or why the data were presented as they were. Table 1-1 has neither, but if you look ahead to Table 12-1, you will see several footnotes. The second footnote indicates that for the year 1970, percentages also include 14-year-olds. It is important to know what the figures actually indicate, or if there are any exceptions to the rest of the data in the table.

Economics is the study of how goods, services, and wealth are produced, consumed, and distributed within societies. Figures about the gross national product, balance of payments deficits, or per-capita income may seem to belong more to the realm of statistics or mathematics than to social science, but these statistics reflect individual behavior, the relationships among groups, and the functioning of society. The effects of supply and demand on prices and the distribution and consumption of material goods serve as indicators of social exchange. Although sociologists also study factors such as these, they devote their attention to different aspects of them. Unlike sociologists, few economists pay much attention to actual behavior or attitudes, to business enterprises as social organizations, or to the impact of religion or education on levels of productivity or consumption. Economists may provide us with import and export figures, ratios of savings to investment, and information about the rate at which money changes hands, but they would be unlikely to interpret these factors as being the result of people

How to Read a Table, *continued*

4. *Read the column and row headings.* Tables contain two important types of headings. The column headings appear at the top and tell what appears below them. The row headings appear on the left and describe the information to the right of them across the table. Referring again to Table 12-1, you will see several levels of headings. The top heading tells you which data occurred in March 2005. The information within March 2005 is further divided into numbers and percentages. The last column is data for 1970. The first column (Characteristics) explains what is in the row headings below. Keep both the column and the row headings in mind as you look at the table to make comparisons.

5. *Make comparisons.* Now that we know what the figures mean (numbers and rates), what the column headings refer to (marriages and divorces), and what the row indicates (year), we are ready to read the table and to make comparisons. Looking back at Table 1-1, by looking at the vertical column we see that the general pattern was a decrease in the marriage rate from 1970 to 2005. Looking at the horizontal row, we can compare the marriage rates with the divorce rates, and so forth. Comparing columns and rows, we can note similarities, differences, or trends. By doing this, we are ready for the final and highly important step: drawing conclusions.

6. *Draw conclusions.* What can we conclude from the material presented? Has the marriage rate increased, decreased, or done both at different times? What about the rate of divorce? How might we explain increases or decreases in specific years? Do these data support the popular wisdom mentioned in the text that the institution of marriage is breaking down drastically?

Tables will vary considerably in format and complexity, but following these six steps should assist you in understanding and grasping the information presented in any table you encounter. You will not only read tables when studying sociology, but you will also often use the ability to read and interpret tables in your personal and professional life.

buying new cars to gain prestige or of their starting new businesses because they are frustrated with their jobs or their bosses.

Political science studies power, governments, and political processes. Political scientists study different kinds of governments, as well as interpersonal processes and means through which power is exercised, focusing on both abstract theory and the actual operation of government. During elections, it is political scientists who provide us with information about voting patterns, changes from previous elections, and the characteristics of voters. Traditionally, political scientists have been interested primarily in political theory and government administration. More recently, however, they have begun to devote more attention to matters of interest to the sociologist, such as the acquisition of political beliefs, the social backgrounds of political activists, and the role of women and of ethnic, racial, and other minorities in political outcomes.

Anthropology, like sociology, is a broad and varied discipline. It includes physical anthropology, archaeology, cultural history, social linguistics, and social and cultural anthropology. *Physical anthropologists* attempt to understand both primitive and modern cultures by studying physical traits such as the shape and size of skulls, artifacts such as pottery and weapons, and genetic mutations of both human and nonhuman forms of life. The work of *cultural* or *social anthropologists*, on the other hand, is very similar to that of sociologists. Like sociologists, they are concerned with social institutions, patterns of organization, and other aspects of society. There are differences in the two fields, however. Anthropologists generally study a society as a whole, whereas sociologists are likely to concentrate on one aspect of a society. Also, anthropologists often live in the culture or community they are studying so that they can observe behavior directly. Sociologists are more likely to rely on statistics, questionnaires, or secondary data; they are frequently interested in comparing information about the social processes and structures across different cultures, whereas anthropologists often study cultures or communities individually.

Psychology is concerned primarily with human mental processes and individual human behavior. Frequent areas of study include learning, human development, behavior disorders, perception, emotion, motivation, creativity, personality, and a wide range of other mental and behavioral processes. In addition to being studied by psychologists, some of these areas are also studied by sociologists and by members of a field known as **social psychology**. These three branches of social science have different emphases, however. *Psychology* is concerned with individuals. *Social psychology* is the study of how an individual influences his or her social interactions with other individuals or with groups, and of how social behavior influences the individual. *Sociology* deals primarily with groups and social systems. Much of the material covered in sociology textbooks technically is considered to be social psychology.

History is considered either a social science or one of the humanities and provides a chronological record of past events. Sociology is an analytical discipline that tries to derive general truths about society. History, on the other hand, is basically descriptive; historians traditionally consider every event to be unique, assuming that attempts at classification or generalization may impair their ability to understand exactly what happened. For example, a sociologist studying the Bolshevik revolution might therefore try to determine whether revolutions evolve through a standard series of stages or whether particular social situations are common to most prerevolutionary societies. A historian studying the same revolution would be more interested in discovering the exact sequence of the events that actually occurred, particularly as described in documents written by persons who experienced those events.

Increasingly, however, many historians are becoming more sociological in their orientation. Instead of concentrating exclusively on events—names, dates, successions of kings, details of battles—they are analyzing broad social movements and general social patterns. Many are turning to sociological methods of analysis to determine what social forces influenced specific historical events.

Geography, often considered a natural science, is concerned with the physical environment and the distribution of plants and animals, including humans. Geographers may study such things as why a particular trade route evolved or how the formation of nations is influenced by the physical landscape. The *physical geographer* investigates climate, agriculture, the distribution of plant species, and oceanography. *Social* and *cultural geographers*, like sociologists, may be interested in how the distribution of people in a particular area influences social relationships. Sometimes, urban geographers and urban sociologists work together on such problems as how various types of housing affect family life and how a given transportation system affects employment and productivity. Although physical geography usually is not considered a social science, social geography clearly shares many areas of interest with the other social sciences.

Is **social work** a social science? Technically, it is not. Social work is the field in which the principles of the social sciences, especially sociology, are applied to actual social problems in the same way that the principles of physiology are applied in medicine and the principles of economics are applied in business. The **applied sciences**—those that directly use these principles—are often considered distinct from the **pure sciences**—those that seek knowledge for its own sake; but the two actually can be considered to occupy different points on the same continuum. At one end of the continuum would be the disciplines that use knowledge to solve actual problems. A social worker might, for example, use information obtained from family research to try to place children in foster homes or to establish centers for abused spouses. At the other end of the continuum would be the disciplines involved in research—not to solve a specific problem, but simply to increase our understanding of the world. A researcher of this sort might study child rearing or spouse abuse as a function of income or education levels. Nevertheless, few social scientists do only pure research, and few social workers do only applied science. Social workers, for example, devise their own research and techniques to help people solve personal and group problems, and the resulting applications contribute to our existing body of knowledge. For their part, sociologists have always been involved in both applied and pure research. Thus, sociologists and social workers do share some common tasks, but it is a mistake (albeit a common one) to regard sociology as equivalent to social work or social welfare. Likewise, it is a common mistake to assume that social work is the only way to apply sociology.

Thinking Sociologically

1. The education of children and youth is a topic of widespread concern within most countries of the world. How would each of the social sciences described in this chapter address this topic?
2. Are sociologists social workers? Are social workers sociologists? Explain your answers.

OCCUPATIONAL AND PERSONAL USES OF SOCIOLOGY

Sociology is not only for sociologists. Although sociology is used professionally in academic ("basic" or "pure" sociology) and nonacademic ("applied" or "practical" sociology) careers and occupations, sociological skills and knowledge are used in many jobs, by many different types of people, and also in our personal lives. One of the fascinating and exciting things about sociology is its diversity of applications.

Beginning students of sociology often ask a number of related questions. Some of the more common ones are: (a) "Why should I take sociology? If I'm not interested in a sociological career, what use will it be to me?" (b) "What is the value of sociology to society? Why should this field be supported?" (c) "What do sociologists do? If I decided to become one, what career options would be open to me?" These are important questions that we continue to address throughout this book. One of our goals for this book is to demonstrate how the subject matter in each chapter can be used in occupations and in daily personal life. For now, though, we look briefly at four applications of sociology: (1) academic sociologists, (2) professional sociologists in the workplace (nonacademic), (3) nonsociologists in the workplace, and (4) nonsociologists in society and other social environments.

Academic Sociologist

More sociologists are employed as teachers than in any other capacity. There are more than 15,000 sociologists in the United States today, and at least two-thirds of them consider teaching to be their primary responsibility. Most teaching sociologists also serve other functions—researcher, administrator, or social critic, for example. Most teaching positions are found in liberal arts colleges or colleges of arts and sciences, in departments devoted to sociology exclusively, or to some combination of sociology, anthropology, and social work. Increasingly, sociologists are being hired in the professional schools of such fields as medicine, nursing, law, social work, business administration, theology, and education.

In addition to teaching, most academic sociologists do research. The research function is often regarded as contributing to the society at large by providing new knowledge about society. Most researchers engage in basic or pure research—the acquisition of knowledge for its own sake, with little thought about how the results will be used. For example, the basic researcher may seek information about the causes of crime, its prevalence, and its distribution by age, gender, or geography, but not be overly concerned with how this knowledge will be used.

Professional Sociologists in the Workplace

Peter H. Rossi and William Foote Whyte (1983), two prominent applied sociologists, suggest that sociology can be applied to the workplace in three major ways: through applied social research, social engineering, and clinical sociology. Collectively, this type of work is referred to as applied sociology, practical sociology, or sociological practice. As suggested in the opening vignette to this chapter, public sociologies are the concern of many sociologists.

Applied Social Research. Many companies, government agencies, and other groups employ professional sociologists to collect and interpret research data on a variety of social issues or problems that the group may face. **Applied social research** is the use of sociological knowledge and research skills to obtain information for groups and organizations, such as banks, insurance companies, public utilities, retail stores, government agencies, schools, community service organizations, child-care centers, hospitals, and mental health centers, among others. An insurance company, for example, might employ sociologists to find out who the company's prospective customers are, as well as the types of insurance the prospective customers will need, their income levels and lifestyles, their values and beliefs, and the ways in which they determine which types of insurance they need.

A state government might request the services of a sociologist to evaluate the impact of a proposed law before it actually goes into effect: Will the new law have the desired consequences? How will the law be enforced? What will be the increased cost to taxpayers to ensure that the law is enforced? Will people comply with the law? Will failure to comply overburden the courts and impede the system of justice?

The questions that organizations need to have answered by sociologists are endless. There are many types of applied social research that it would not be practical to try to discuss all of them here. There are, however, three broad categories that encompass most of the specific types: (1) descriptive studies, (2) analytical or explanatory studies, and (3) evaluative studies. These are described briefly here and are discussed in more detail when we turn to research methodology later on.

Descriptive studies are used primarily to obtain information about a particular social problem, event, or population. For example, a college administrator may need to know how many freshmen fail out of American colleges each year, as well as these freshmen's ages, genders, and races, and the types of extracurricular activities in which they were involved. Although this type of research is often a first step in arriving at cause–effect relationships and explanations, its main goal is to describe what is occurring rather than to explain why it occurs.

Analytical (or **explanatory**) **studies** are used in various careers and occupations to help explain what causes (or what is related to) some specific events or problems. Is there a relationship between a state's legal minimum drinking age and the dropout rate of students attending college in that state? Do colleges that allow freshmen to pledge to fraternities and sororities have a higher dropout rate than colleges that do not allow freshmen to pledge? Whereas descriptive studies are used mainly to obtain information about what is occurring, analytical studies focus on why events take place. Like descriptive studies, analytical studies are needed in most occupations. Sociologists doing this kind of research tend to look for social factors that precede or result from the event or problem in question.

Evaluative studies are among the most widespread forms of applied sociological research. They are used to estimate the effects of specific social programs or policies. Will a policy that prohibits freshmen from pledging to fraternities and sororities lower the dropout rate, or will it lead freshmen to engage in behavior that would increase their rate of failure? What will be the impact on a college's enrollment if sororities and fraternities are prohibited? Simply put, evaluative studies find out how well a program, policy, or project works or is likely to work.

Thinking Sociologically

Sociologists often study phenomena that have a strong ideological basis. That is, some areas of sociological investigation—such as political or religious groups and social movements—are connected with very strong and influential belief systems.

1. What might sociologists want to know about cults, gangs, or popular media?
2. Is it possible to investigate phenomena related to ideologies such as Nazism or Christianity without making value judgments—that is, without praise or condemnation?
3. If it is possible to be objective, should sociologists refrain from making judgments on groups that they have found to be blatantly beneficial or destructive? Why or why not?

Clinical Sociology. *Clinical sociology* is the use of sociological perspectives, theories, concepts, research, and methods for consulting and providing technical assistance to individuals, groups, or organizations. The Sociological Practice Association (which changed its name from the Clinical Sociology Association) defines clinical sociology as sociological intervention—using sociology to help in specific situations.

Clinical sociology is similar to another area of sociology, **social engineering**, which is attempting to change the way a society, organization, institution, or group is arranged so that a particular goal may be achieved. Both have to do with social intervention, and it is sometimes difficult to see the difference between them. Social engineering is concerned with large-scale social planning, whereas clinical sociology is concerned more with advising on specific social settings and situations. Social engineering is likely to be involved with designing policies, laws, programs, and projects, whereas clinical sociology involves consultation, counseling, therapy, and conflict mediation. It is social engineering, for example, to develop a statewide basic education program to improve the quality of education that students receive; it is clinical sociology to counsel teachers in a particular high school about how to communicate better with students in the classroom. It is social engineering to create a nationwide project that would encourage corporations to offer on-site child care for working

SOCIOLOGY AT WORK

Fostering Civic Responsibility

"May we all continue the struggle to create a more just world" is the slogan that Tom Arcaro uses as a signature for his e-mail and on his Web site. Arcaro is professor of sociology at Elon University in North Carolina and director of Elon's chapter of Project Pericles. Project Pericles is an excellent example of public sociology, described in the opening vignette to this chapter. An initiative sponsored by the Eugene Lang Foundation, Project Pericles has challenged ten colleges and universities to provide a learning experience that will "instill in students an abiding and active sense of social responsibility and civic concern." Under the guidance of Arcaro, Elon University has accepted the challenge, which fits with the university's stated mission to prepare students to be global citizens and informed leaders and to foster an ethic of work and service.

Project Pericles has enabled Elon to rise to this student challenge. Building on Elon's commitment to student engagement and community service, Arcaro has formulated the following objectives for Project Pericles:

- foster a conversation in the community about ways in which Elon can better partner with local organizations
- be more deliberate about embedding civic engagement and social responsibility in the curriculum
- invite all constituencies of the university to integrate Periclean values into all dimensions of the institution
- implement a systematic program for highly motivated students designed to enhance their awareness of civic responsibility and provide them with skills to be proactive members of society

A few of Arcaro's most notable successes for Project Pericles, thus far, include:

- hosting a highly successful Summit for Civic Engagement, bringing faculty, students and local community leaders together to discuss ways that Elon can better partner with local agencies

parents; it is clinical sociology to offer group therapy to working parents to help them overcome their conflicting loyalties, anxieties, and everyday problems.

Like many other areas of applied and basic sociology, clinical sociology and social engineering often overlap. According to Rossi and Whyte (1983), "The clinician will often encounter structural factors that must be changed before the clinical treatment can produce the hoped-for results. Similarly, the social engineer must recognize that the implementation of a major structural change in an organization may be effectively facilitated by a skillful clinician" (p. 12).

Clinical sociologists are engaged in careers such as legislative consultation, law and criminal justice, corporate marketing, social work, psychiatric health care, community health care, child guidance, student counseling, and family therapy. They are often sought out by governments, businesses, and communities to offer suggestions or advice. Their services have been requested in court decisions on busing, in neighborhood programs for crime prevention, in the development of personnel policies for insurance companies, in discrimination cases involving automotive companies, and in the creation of community

Fostering Civic Responsibility, *continued*

- distributing $40,000 worth of course enhancements grants of up to $1,000 each to support those ideas, and encouraging faculty to join forces to sponsor larger projects
- funding course projects such as a building a playground in an Aboriginal neighborhood in a studies abroad course in Australia; an education class comparing schools in wealthy and poor districts; and a ceramic art project to benefit Crossroads Sexual Assault Response and Resource Center of Alamance County in North Carolina

One of Arcaro's most significant projects involves student Periclean Scholars is an HIV/AIDS awareness program designed educate groups both here and in Africa about the complex issues surrounding this devastating pandemic. The students in the Periclean Scholars program come from all majors across the campus, and Arcaro's grasp of cultural and sociological perspectives allows him to communicate the deeper issues associated with HIV/AIDS. Activities such as these, embedded in academic classes, open students' eyes to the needs of the world and our obligation as citizens to become engaged to alleviate these needs.

Arcaro states: "My background as a sociologist has helped me to formulate my vision and approach to Project Pericles on our campus, especially the Periclean Scholars program. My job as director of Project Pericles can accurately be described as applied sociology. Through this role I am able to share this perspective with students in all my classes." Arcaro's career-long commitment to humanist sociology combined with his passion for sociological theory has helped him forge a link with the earliest sociologists who had interests in social justice and social reform. "Being a sociologist has helped me to imagine how to best communicate the objectives and goals of Project Pericles to my colleagues all around our campus and to lead the Periclean Scholars toward a greater understanding of what it takes to make a positive impact on our world."

mental health centers. Sociologists seldom work as full-time consultants, however. They are used in specific situations, such as offering methodological advice to groups doing evaluation studies, assisting in data analysis, or explaining the probable consequences of a set of alternative courses of action.

Thinking Sociologically

Select a social phenomenon about which you are curious—such as a specific group, organization, or activity—and use as much information in this chapter as possible to discuss how you might investigate it from a sociological perspective. What would you focus on? What types of questions would you want to answer? What types of explanations would you expect to discover? How could the results of your study be useful professionally and personally?

Nonsociologists in the Workplace

Although it is usually necessary to have a graduate degree (M.A. or Ph.D.) to be employed as a professional sociologist, sociology offers knowledge and skills that can be used by nonsociologists in a multitude of careers and occupations. Even if you are not interested in a career in sociology, the study of sociology offers valuable preparation for other types of careers. You do not even have to major in sociology to take advantage of its applications within most occupations. For example, if your interests lie in business, law, education, medicine, architecture, politics, or any profession dealing with people, social life, or social organization, sociology can be useful because it provides a wealth of knowledge that can be applied to any of these fields. Besides the specific theories, concepts, and perspectives that can be useful in and of themselves in occupational settings, sociology students develop research skills, critical-thinking and problem-solving skills, interpersonal skills, and communication skills. In recent years, several studies have found that these skills are necessary for success in many careers and occupations.

Research Skills. *Research skills* involve basic investigative capabilities. Essentially, they include *quantitative* (numerical) and *qualitative* (nonnumerical) data-collection methods. The sociology student may develop skills in survey techniques (in-depth interviews and questionnaire construction), empirical observation, participant observation, experimentation, and library research. These skills are used by lawyers, physicians, advertisers, market analysts, clerks, administrative assistants, publishers, and many others.

In business, information must often be gathered quickly. A newly employed investment banker must be able to find out very quickly who may be potential clients in a particular region. The manager of a retail store either could go with a hunch that a costly investment will pay off or could conduct a consumer survey to reduce the probability of making a financial blunder. Because research is basic to sociology, even a brief introduction to the field will acquaint you with a range of research techniques and methods you can use. Whether we use simple observation, formal structured interviews, content analysis, experimental designs, or elaborate statistical computations, an understanding of the variety of research techniques should be useful in many occupational settings and situations.

Critical-Thinking and Problem-Solving Skills. Research skills and knowledge of sociological theories and concepts can add to your critical-thinking and problem-solving skills. To possess critical-thinking skills means to have the ability both to analyze a situation or information and to arrive at careful, precise judgments. With theory and research, you can investigate and carefully arrive at some solutions to problems faced in many occupations. For example, a physician who is having personnel problems with office staff might attribute the conflict to clashes in personalities. A knowledge of small-group processes, along with the ability to find and analyze models of successful organizational or personnel relationships, would be more useful than continually hiring and firing staff members. A lawyer must be able to critically evaluate the terms of a settlement and to find solutions to problematic areas in that settlement to ensure the protection of the client's interests. Two young chiropractors may need to figure out how to establish their practice and develop clientele in a city where they have no existing personal connections or other patient referrals.

The ways in which sociology must be learned, which determine the nature of most sociology textbooks, facilitate the development of critical-thinking and problem-solving skills. The key to understanding sociological theories and concepts is not memorization but rather involves carefully analyzing the meanings and implications of these abstractions and trying to come up with concrete examples. Most sociology textbooks, particularly at the advanced levels, do not merely present theories but usually evaluate the merit of those theories as compared to other ones. This type of learning forces the student to think critically. The assignment of term papers in which sociological theories and concepts must be applied to particular situations or events helps students to sharpen their problem-solving skills. Sociology students also learn other analytical skills, such as constructing and testing hypotheses, discovering explanatory factors, and reading tables. It would be hard to think of an occupation in which the ability to think critically and solve problems is not needed.

Interpersonal Skills. Interpersonal skills are techniques that help you to efficiently manage yourself and others within an organization or in other interaction settings. These skills include management, leadership, interaction, diplomatic skills, and the ability to facilitate and coordinate group activities. Competence in setting goals, the ability to plan projects, and knowledge of how organizations work are also important interpersonal skills. Unclear objectives or poorly designed work programs could result in poor team work performance. For example, the business manager who is unable to coordinate the goals of the product-development staff (which stresses innovation at any cost) with the goals of the accounting department (which values cutting expenses wherever possible) is bound to have problems.

Interpersonal skills can be developed through an understanding of sociological theories and concepts that focus on interpersonal and group relationships. Some of these theories and concepts concern culture, race and ethnic relations, gender relations, social stratification, socialization, social interaction, and social organization. For example, suppose that you are an elementary school teacher who wishes to increase the involvement of your Hispanic students' parents in your school. You might choose to do this by organizing a special club for Hispanic students' parents. The knowledge that child rearing is traditionally the primary responsibility of mothers in Hispanic cultures might help give you some ideas for bringing such a group together. Health professionals might find it useful to know that people from different cultures respond to pain and symptoms in very different ways and, thus, might develop different ways of dealing with them. Both the factory managers and the workers' union managers would be interested in knowing which aspects of the work environment different types of factory workers consider to be most important. The list goes on and on. For almost every job, knowledge of sociology would be a valuable tool that could be used to enhance interpersonal skills.

Communication Skills. Perhaps the most important skill you need to have is the ability to communicate well. Without this ability, your other skills may not be apparent. As a student of sociology, you will have to develop both oral and written skills. Most assignments in sociology, written or oral, are concerned not only with giving correct answers, but also with developing and presenting the argument in order to get your point across. It is necessary not only to think clearly, but also to express yourself clearly so that your argument can be understood. The perpetual interplay of ideas between students and professor—via class discussions and critical analyses—provides practical experience with thinking "on your feet" and with communicating your thoughts and ideas to others. Again, this is a skill that must be developed to be a success in any career.

Sociological insight plays an important role in effective communication. Sociology tells us, for example, that people from different cultures and social groups interpret language and other symbols in different ways, and that language influences a person's perception of a given situation. With this in mind, middle-aged professors would find it useful to know the jargon of the various student groups at a college (jocks, punks, preppies, honors students, etc.) to reach each of them emotionally and intellectually.

Advertisers and salespeople would benefit if they could quickly find out the needs and wants of their clients through the subtle messages found in their conversations. The transplanted New Yorker who is recruited to be the director of a child-care center in North Carolina needs to understand why Southern parents might not trust "fast-talkin' Yankees." There are hundreds of other examples of how sociology can help us in our day-to-day communication problems. By now, you have probably thought of some examples of your own.

Nonsociologists in Society and Other Social Environments

Because it is concerned with every aspect of social life, sociology should interest every social being. Just as we should have an understanding of sickness without having to be physicians and an understanding of money without having to be economists, an understanding of sociological principles can be useful in our daily lives because they are concerned with an enormous range of events. Sociologists may study topics as diverse as the intimacy between husband and wife and the dynamics of mob violence. Violent crime may be the subject of one study, the communion of persons in a religious institution the subject of another. One investigator may be concerned with the inequities of race, age, and gender, while another may investigate the shared beliefs of common culture. Sociology is interested in both the typical or normal and the unusual or bizarre.

Sociology can teach us to consider perspectives other than our own and to look beyond the individual in our efforts to understand individual behavior. It encourages us to look not merely at how people and events are unique and different, but at how people share perceptions and how events occur in patterns. It familiarizes us with a range of theoretical explanations of how people think and act, of how societies' structures change, and of how society operates.

Perhaps most important, though, is that sociology can help us to understand ourselves. Humans are social animals, and people can understand themselves only in the context of the society in which they live. A knowledge of the social constraints that bind us can be frustrating—we may feel trapped, angry about our inability to control our lives, and disappointed at the social inequities that surround us. Only through understanding our society, however, can we truly understand ourselves.

C. Wright Mills (1959) wrote that the "sociological imagination" enables us to distinguish between "personal troubles" and "public issues." By understanding how societies and groups are organized, we may well come to realize that problems that we thought we had caused ourselves might in fact be problems that result from social forces. Think of all the times you came down hard on yourself—or someone else—because of a problem you faced. If you knew how the problem was generated by social forces, you might be better able to deal with it. This one sociological idea alone—and there are hundreds of others—has implications for many of your social relationships. Consider, for example, how parents might handle a problem with their child if they could understand the cultural, structural, institutional, and group forces acting on the child instead of focusing solely on the child's problematic behavior.

Sociology is useful for more than just helping us with our problems. It also can help us with most of our important personal decisions, such as whether to get married, how many children to have, whether to buy a home, how much education to get, what kind of career to pursue, and when to retire.

Although "personal uses of sociology" have been discussed last, this is perhaps the most important section of the chapter for many of you. The author of College: The Undergraduate Experience in America, a report issued by the Carnegie Foundation for the Advancement of Teaching, states, "We found on most campuses a disturbing gap between the college and the larger world. ... We feel compelled to ask: How can the undergraduate college help students gain perspective and prepare them to meet their civic and social obligations in the neighborhood, the nation, and the world?" (Boyer, 1986, p. 16). This report is as relevant in 2005 as it was in 1986.

Sociology has always been one of the disciplines best able to help meet such a challenge. In light of the Carnegie Foundation's recent findings, sociology is now more relevant to a college education than ever before. This book introduces you not just to sociology as a science, but also to sociology as a tool for improving the quality of your life and the lives of those around you.

Thinking Sociologically

Review ways in which sociology may be of professional or personal use to you.

SUMMARY

1. *Sociology* is the study of society, social life, and the causes and consequences of human social behavior. The terms society and social life encompass interpersonal relations within and among social groups and social systems.

2. Sociology is concerned with all aspects of the social world. Concerns and topics of study range from small groups, such as the family, sibling rivalry, and small-group dynamics, to large ones, such as international conflict, organizational processes, and bureaucracies as immense as the federal government.

3. In their efforts to understand social life, sociologists question the obvious, seek patterns and regularities, and look beyond individuals to social interactions and group processes. They try to assess individual behavior in the context of the larger society.

4. This perspective is applied both to *microsociology*, which considers problems at the level of interpersonal and small-group processes, and to *macrosociology*, which considers large-scale problems, structures, social organizations, and social systems.

5. Although many people believe that the structure and workings of society are a matter of common knowledge, countless sociological findings disprove popular conceptions and provide surprising insights.

6. Sociology is one of the *social sciences*, which are disciplines that try to systematically and objectively understand social life and predict how various influences will affect it. Each social science attempts to accumulate a body of knowledge about a particular aspect of society and the social world.

7. *Economics* deals with the production, consumption, and distribution of goods and services. *Political science* deals with power, governments, and political processes. *Anthropology* deals with the social and physical aspects of both primitive and contemporary cultures.

8. *Psychology* is concerned with the bases of individual human behavior and with mental processes (feelings and thoughts). History explores past events, and *geography* investigates

the relationship between people and their physical environment.

9. Strictly speaking, *social work* is not a social science—it is not concerned chiefly with accumulating a body of basic knowledge. Rather, it is considered an applied discipline that uses the knowledge of the social scientist to improve social life.

10. At the end of this chapter, we raised and answered three questions about sociology: (1) What do sociologists do, and what career options are available to them? (2) Why should students who are not interested in sociology as a career take it as a course? (3) What is the value of sociology to society? In answering these questions, we noted that most sociologists are employed as teachers, researchers, administrators, consultants, or in some combination of these roles.

11. Sociology is valuable even to people uninterested in making it their career because it (a) provides a basic understanding of social life, (b) is a useful preparation for other careers, (c) broadens the range of perspectives from which we try to understand the social world, (d) provides an orientation toward the use of research techniques applicable in a wide variety of contexts, and (e) helps us to understand ourselves and our positions in society.

KEY TERMS

analytical or explanatory studies The studies used to help explain what causes certain events or problems.

anthropology The study of the physical, biological, social, and cultural development of humans, often on a comparative basis.

applied science The area of science in which the knowledge gained from the "pure" sciences is put into practice.

applied social research The use of sociological knowledge and research skills to obtain information for groups and organizations.

clinical sociology The use of sociological perspectives, theories, concepts, research, and methods for consulting and providing technical assistance to individuals or organizations.

descriptive studies Studies used primarily to obtain information about a particular social problem, event, or population.

economics The study of how goods, services, and wealth are produced, consumed, and distributed.

evaluative studies Studies used to estimate the effects of specific social programs or policies.

geography The study of the physical environment and the distribution of plants and animals, including humans.

history The study of the past; social history is concerned with past human social events.

macrosociology A level of sociological analysis concerned with large-scale units such as institutions, social categories, and social systems.

microsociology The level of sociological analysis concerned with small-scale units such as individuals in small group interactions.

political science The study of power, government, and the political process.

psychology The study of human mental processes and individual human behavior.

pure science The area of science in which knowledge is sought for its own sake with little emphasis on how the knowledge might be applied.

social engineering Attempting to change the way a society, community, organization, institution, or group is arranged so that a particular goal may be achieved.

social psychology The study of how individuals interact with other individuals or groups and how groups influence the individual.

social science A science that has as its subject matter human behavior, social organizations, or society.

social work The field in which the principles of the social sciences are applied to actual social problems.

sociological perspective A way of looking at society and social behavior that involves questioning the obvious, seeking patterns, and looking beyond the individual in an attempt to discern social processes.

sociology The study of human society and social life and the social causes and consequences of human behavior.

DISCUSSION QUESTIONS

1. What types of questions might be of interest to sociologists? Are all of these topics "social problems"? Discuss the differences or similarities between a sociological problem and a social problem.
2. Reference is made to a "sociological perspective." Explain and give examples of this.
3. What is the difference between macrosociology and microsociology? Use an example other than the one cited in this chapter (divorce) to illustrate.
4. Four so-called common-sense examples of false statements were given in this chapter. Can you think of others? How might we explain the frequent acceptance of ideas that are not true?
5. Discuss what the social sciences have in common. How is each unique or different from the others?
6. Can you distinguish among descriptive, analytical, and evaluative studies? Give examples of each.
7. Should sociology be a required college course? Why or why not?
8. What are some relevant areas for "public sociologies" to be concerned with today, and how could they be useful?

The Development of Sociology

How Theory Affects Social Policies and Solutions to Social Problems

How did human life originate? Creationism holds that human beings came into existence according to the literal biblical account of creation as told in the Book of Genesis. That is, God created the world in six days, the sixth day being the day on which human life began. Evolutionism—the theory presented by Charles Darwin in *The Origin of the Species*—holds that humans evolved from lower forms of life over a period of tens of millions of years through a process of natural selection and organic evolution. The publication of Darwin's book in 1859 fueled a controversy between those who believed in the divine creation of life (creationists) and those who believed in a natural origin of life (evolutionists). National attention focused on this controversy in the summer of 1925, when John Scopes, a high school biology teacher in Dayton, Tennessee, was put on trial for breaking a state law that prohibited the teaching of evolution. Although John Scopes was being tried for violating a state law, the "Scopes trial"—or "monkey trial" as it is often called—became a battle about the right to hold and profess particular ideas.

William Jennings Bryan—the prosecuting attorney in the case and a Democratic nominee for president in 1896, 1904, and 1908—tried to make his case against Scopes by appealing to the religious convictions of the jury and by promoting the sanctity of the Bible. Clarence Darrow—one of Scopes's defense lawyers and an attorney of great national prominence at the time—argued that Scopes's academic freedom and his constitutional rights (specifically, freedom of speech and the guarantee of separation between church and state) had been violated. Nevertheless, Scopes had broken a state law and was therefore convicted. In order to defuse the controversy somewhat, the trial judge fined Scopes only $100 and gave no prison sentence. Later, the conviction was appealed and overturned on a technicality. The significance of the Scopes trial is not so much in its outcome as in the intensity of passions that it aroused in the adherents of creationist and evolutionist views on life. It clearly demonstrated that the theories that people hold about matters of great import—such as the origin of life or the nature of social reality—often dictate their views on practical matters.

Even though most theologians have reconciled the evolutionist views with their religious views, the evolutionist–creationist controversy still exists, especially when matters of policy are concerned. Both of these theories have implications for the ways in which social policies are enacted. Creationism suggests that because humans were created by God, specific values and morals are also provided by God and are absolute. On the other hand, evolutionism implies that because human life evolved over millions of years, specific values and morals have also evolved, to serve the best interests of humankind.

Thus, these two different views require very different approaches to policy decisions. For example, policies that support a woman's right to have an abortion would be seen by creationists as unacceptable under any circumstances because of the view that God alone is responsible for decisions regarding life. Policies that benefit homosexuals would be seen by creationists as unacceptable because sexual mores prohibiting homosexuality are contained within the Bible. Policies that give rights to unmarried heterosexual couples or unwed mothers would be seen by creationists as unacceptable because of biblical constraints against sex outside of marriage. Evolutionists might or might not find such policies unacceptable—or any policies related to moral views expressed in the Bible—depending on their interpretations of natural or social scientific ideas. Evolutionists would make their determinations based on what they see as the positive or negative value of such policies for individuals and society, not based on what they believe that God has determined.

The sociological significance of the creationism versus evolutionism controversy goes far beyond specific issues and policy discussions. The controversy is important because it illustrates the influence of theories in determining people's perspectives on social issues and solutions to social problems. Further, it demonstrates the central sociological idea that social reality is subjective and open to interpretation. Nevertheless, once social reality is interpreted in a particular way—that is, once a theoretical viewpoint is accepted—it is acted on as if that interpretation is the reality. This chapter introduces you to some of the most widely used theoretical perspectives in sociology today.

It is important not only to understand these theories, but also to understand that many different interpretations of social life exist and that each interpretation carries with it implicit assumptions for dealing with social issues, problems, and policies.

THE DEVELOPMENT OF SOCIOLOGY IN EUROPE

The study of sociology is a recent development in social history. Philosophers such as Aristotle and Plato had much to say about society and human relationships, but until the late nineteenth century, no writer we know of could appropriately be considered a sociologist. In fact, the label *sociologist* was not applied to the early practitioners of the field in their own time; they have been identified as such only in retrospect.

Most early writers were interdisciplinary in orientation, drawing their ideas from philosophy and from the physical and biological sciences. Actually, as a result of developments in the natural sciences, much of the early writing in sociology was based on the assumption that laws of human behavior could be discovered in the same way that laws of nature had been discovered by astronomers, physicists, and other natural scientists. These early writers also had great faith in the power of reason, assuming that it could be used to formulate laws that could be applied to improve social life and to eliminate or diminish social problems.

These assumptions were rapidly put to a test as the Industrial Revolution presented new challenges and social problems. People began to migrate to towns and cities for factory jobs. With many of these jobs came low wages, long working hours, harsh child labor practices, housing and sanitation problems, social alienation, social conflict, encounters with crime, and a variety of other social problems that provided an abundance of conditions for concern, study, and solution. The Industrial Revolution that began in England, the social revolution in France under Napoleon, and the political upheavals throughout Europe provide the backdrop for the emergence of the discipline known today as sociology.

Sociology originally developed as a practical discipline intended to address social problems and social reform. Turner and Turner say that

> by 1880 … the label "sociology" embraced such activities as philanthropic and reform efforts to help the "dependent classes," public edification on the need for social reform, attempts at making the church more effective in the social arena, arguments bolstering the intellectual authority of the cooperative movement, and programs for collecting statistics on the laboring classes. Each of these associations was embodied in some form of work, ranging from reformist activity and government research to college teaching and literary writings. (1990, p. 12)

We can begin to understand this discipline, now less than 200 years old, by briefly examining a few of the early writers who were influential in its development. All knowledge, all societies, all institutions have a social history. We can examine selected aspects of this historical development by focusing on five European theorists: Comte, Spencer, Marx,

Durkheim, and Weber. These sociologists all lived in the nineteenth century, and their ideas stemmed from their personal circumstances and social settings. Certainly, these are not the only important European thinkers who helped shape sociology. However, their work was seminal in shaping the foundations of the discipline.

Auguste Comte

Auguste Comte (1798–1857) was born in southern France, the son of a minor government official. Educated in Paris, his studies were concentrated in mathematics and the natural sciences. Before completing his schooling, he was expelled for participating in a student insurrection against the school's administration. He then became secretary to Henri Saint-Simon, an influential political leader and advocate of a pre-Marxist version of socialism—a system in which the means of production (e.g., industry) are owned by the people. Comte was greatly influenced by Saint-Simon, but their relationship ended when Comte was accused of plagiarism, a charge he denied. He held another job in Paris for approximately 12 years but was again dismissed. He had made too many enemies and too few friends.

Comte is usually credited with being the "father of sociology" because he coined the term *sociology*. He first called this new social science "social physics" because he believed that society must be studied in the same scientific manner as the world of the natural sciences. Like the natural sciences, Comte said, sociology would use empirical methods to discover basic laws of society, which would benefit humankind by playing a major part in the improvement of the human condition.

Comte is best known for his **law of human progress**, which states that each of our leading conceptions, each branch of our knowledge, all human intellectual development, passes successively through three different theoretical conditions: (1) the theological, or fictitious; (2) the metaphysical, or abstract; and (3) the scientific, or positive. In addition, each mental age of humankind is accompanied by a specific type of social organization and political dominance. In the first stage, the theological, everything is explained and understood through the supernatural. The family is the prototypical social unit (the model or standard to which others conform), and political dominance is held by priests and military personnel. In the second stage, the metaphysical, abstract forces are assumed to be the source of explanation and understanding. The state replaces the family as the prototypical social unit and, as in the Middle Ages and the Renaissance, the political dominance is held by the clergy and lawyers. In the third and highest stage, the scientific, the laws of the universe are studied through observation, experimentation, and comparison. The whole human race replaces the state as the operative social unit, and the political dominance is held by industrial administrators and scientific moral guides. It was Comte's assertion that the scientific stage of human knowledge and intellectual development was just beginning in his day. According to Comte, sociology, like the natural sciences, could henceforth draw on the methods of science to explain and understand the laws of progress and the social order.

A related concept originated by Comte was the view that society was a type of "organism." Like plants and animals, society had a structure consisting of many interrelated parts, and it evolved from simpler to more complex forms. Using this organic model as a base, he reasoned that sociology should focus on **social statics**, the structure of the organism, and on **social dynamics**, the organism's processes and forms of change. Comte believed that sociology was the means by which a more just and rational social order could be achieved.

APPLYING COMTE

Auguste Comte was primarily interested in applying scientific principles of social life to affect social situations. That social actions are governed by laws and principles—just as physical actions are—is a significant fact that is useful to others besides academic social scientists. Whether in our personal lives or in our occupations, if we believe that individual personalities alone or fate alone can explain why problems occur, we might look in the wrong places for solutions or become powerless to solve them. In a discussion about Comte's ideas, social theorist Lewis Coser (1977) states, "As long as (people) believed that social actions followed no law and were, in fact, arbitrary and fortuitous, they could take no concerted action to ameliorate them" (p. 4).

Although Comte wrote primarily for intellectual social leaders of his day, his ideas were useful to many people. His belief that society should be studied scientifically is the basis for all sociological research—academic and applied (hence his title, "father of sociology"). Sociologists do not merely speculate, philosophize, or use opinions to formulate theories about social behavior; rather, they rely heavily on the scientific principles emphasized by Comte: observation, experimentation, and comparison. To explain the high rate of divorce in the United States, for example, a sociologist might first formulate hypotheses to test. Perhaps the researcher believes that the rate of divorce has something to do with the changing roles of men and women in our society. The sociologist might then collect data that would enable him or her to compare the rates of divorce in traditional marriages (those in which the husband is the primary breadwinner and the wife is the homemaker) with nontraditional marriages (those in which there is greater equality between husband and wife).

You can use Comte's prescription for scientific analysis in many ways in your professional and personal lives. Instead of quickly making decisions based on gut feelings, you may be better off systematically collecting as much information as possible on the situation before you act. Think, for a moment, how you will go about deciding on a career and looking for a job. Very often, college graduates and others looking for jobs do what they think is the right thing—such as look at the classified ads and pray. If you are a little more scientific in your approach, however, you can significantly increase your chances of getting a satisfying and highly rewarding job—possibly even the one that you want.

For example, suppose that you are interested in computer programming and you want to work for Microsoft. You could collect data regarding Microsoft personnel:

How do they expect people to dress?
What types of personalities are they looking for?
Do they expect people to relocate?
What are their long-term goals?
From what geographical areas are they most likely to recruit people?
Where do they currently advertise their job openings?
How do they expect you to act during interviews?
What do they look for on a résumé?
Most of all, what is the precise nature of the job for which you are applying?

If you take this more scientific approach to finding a job, you will have a better chance of getting the one you want sooner than if you leave it up to chance alone.

Herbert Spencer

Herbert Spencer (1820–1903) was born in England, the son of a schoolteacher. Like Comte, he received considerable training in mathematics and the natural sciences but little in history and none in English. Feeling unfit for a university career, he worked as a railway engineer, a draftsperson, and finally as a journalist and writer.

One of Spencer's major concerns was with the evolutionary nature of changes in social structure and social institutions. He believed that human societies pass through an evolutionary process similar to the process Darwin explained in his theory of natural selection. It was Spencer who coined the phrase "survival of the fittest," and he was the first to believe that human societies evolved according to the principles of natural laws. Just as natural selection favors particular organisms and permits them to survive and multiply, societies that have adapted to their surroundings and can compete will survive. Those that have not adapted and cannot compete will encounter difficulties and eventually die.

Spencer's theory paralleled Darwin's theory of biological evolution in other ways. He believed that societies evolved from relative homogeneity and simplicity to heterogeneity and complexity. As simple societies progress, they become increasingly complex and differentiated. Spencer viewed societies not simply as collections of individuals, but as organisms with a life and vitality of their own.

In sharp contrast to Comte, the idea of survival of the fittest led Spencer to argue for a policy of noninterference in human affairs and society. He opposed legislation designed to solve social problems, believing it would interfere with the natural selection process. He also opposed free public education, assuming that those who really wanted to learn would find the means. Just as societies that could not adapt would die out, Spencer contended, individuals who could not fit in did not deserve to flourish.

As you can imagine, Spencer's ideas had the support of people of wealth and power. His theories strengthened the position of those who wanted to keep the majority of the population impoverished and minimally educated. His ideas also tended to support a discriminatory policy: Was it not a natural evolutionary law that kept people unequal? Spencer thought that conflict and change were necessary parts of the evolutionary process (like Marx, discussed in the next section). Unlike Marx, however, he believed that planned change would disrupt the orderly evolution of society, which he thought would eventually improve the social order. (His goals are a radical departure from those of Marx in other respects, too, of course.)

Spencer was one of the earlier writers to be concerned with the special problems of objectivity in the social sciences. Comte never seemed concerned with potential conflicts among his personal views, his religious mission, and his analysis of society. Marx denied that objective social science was possible, believing that theory was inseparable from socialist practice. Spencer, however, devoted attention specifically to the problem of bias and other difficulties that sociologists face in their work.

Those familiar with contemporary politics in the United States will recognize a resurgence of ideas similar to those espoused by Spencer, but today, few sociologists accept his ultraconservative theory of noninterference in social change. There is, however, widespread acceptance of the idea that societies grow progressively more complex as they evolve and an increasing recognition that evolutionary processes seem to operate in areas such as population changes or the selection by the stratification system of the "socially most fit" for particular types of education and positions.

APPLYING SPENCER

Although few contemporary sociologists accept Spencer's policy of noninterference in social problems, knowledge of his ideas is useful in helping us understand some present-day politics. By analyzing Spencer's theory of noninterference, for example, how could a politician, a political science major, or a citizen gain insight for interpreting some policies implemented under some conservative political administrations? For example, Ronald Reagan, who became president of the United States in 1980, and who recently died in 2004, will be remembered largely for the dictum of "getting government off the backs of the people." This dictum was manifested in policies that led to lower taxes, less government regulation of environmental pollution, cutbacks in federal aid for college loans and to colleges in general, reduction in aid for social service programs, and deregulation of many industries. Americans were told that the rationale for such noninterference was to give people more freedom, and this would, theoretically, stimulate the economy. This policy was reinforced again under the administration of George W. Bush. Is it possible that the "survival of the fittest" idea is well and alive in the United States today?

If you analyze Spencer's ideas concerning noninterference and see who really benefits from them, however, you may begin to understand the implications of such a policy for Americans today. You may come to see that it does not necessarily lead to increased freedom and benefits for the majority, but rather for those who are already wealthy and powerful.

To illustrate this idea, suppose that your teacher placed 100 five-dollar bills on the floor at the front of the classroom. The money is available for everyone to take. All you need to do is to get to it before someone else does. The teacher will not interfere in any way whatsoever. If you are sitting in the front of the classroom, how do you feel about the teacher's policy of noninterference? Being in a position of advantage, you would probably praise the teacher for such an enlightened idea that gives you so much freedom. However, suppose now that you were sitting anywhere from the middle to the back of the classroom. Now how would you see the policy of noninterference? Would you be as "free" to get the money as the people in the front? Does the teacher's policy of noninterference give you more freedom or less? Would some sort of regulation or intervention about how much money the people in the front could take actually increase the freedom of those in the middle and back of the room?

It is important for all of us to understand that some political viewpoints give the appearance of improved social conditions for everyone, but as we look a little deeper, we see that they may really benefit only a select few. We are told, for example, that a decrease in taxes that go toward social services will provide us with more individual money. However, who really benefits from a decrease in taxes—the wealthy or the middle class—if that decrease also leads to cutbacks in

SOCIOLOGY AT WORK

Helping Migrant Farmworkers

Sandy Smith-Nonini is a former journalist, turned anthropologist. She earned her Ph.D. in anthropology from the University of North Carolina at Chapel Hill and is in the Department of Sociology and Anthropology at Elon University in North Carolina. Smith-Nonini's work is an example of how Marx's theories can be used to explain the origins of inequities in the workplace.

Smith-Nonini has been studying migrant farmworkers and meat packers in North Carolina and working with advocacy groups defending their labor rights. These workplaces, which now depend heavily on immigrants, have unusually high rates of injuries and even deaths. Yet many citizens have little knowledge of new immigrants, much less the working conditions of companies that stock the counters of our grocery stores. For this reason, Smith-Nonini has worked with a Unitarian-Universalist committee on a documentary project on farmworker conditions. The goal of her research and documentary is to raise awareness of the general public and of the farmworkers themselves, many of whom are not aware that they have rights to fair labor conditions.

In 2004, when President Bush proposed a new legal status for immigrant workers, Smith-Nonini noted that many hoped for an end to the Administration's "close the border" mentality. However, when she looked closer at the new proposals, Smith-Nonini became concerned. Under the plan, Mexican workers would be granted temporary visas to work in a specific job for an employer who participates in a "guestworker" program. The visas would be for three-year periods, and could be renewed with the same employer. Having studied the existing federal guestworker program, known as H2A, Smith-Nonini realized that the new proposal was likely

services that the middle class needs, such as the availability of federal loans to college students?

Karl Marx

Karl Marx (1818–1883) was born in Germany. His father, a lawyer, and his mother were both descended from long lines of rabbis. Marx attended college, planning to practice law, but after becoming involved with a radical antireligious group he decided to devote his life to philosophy. Unable to get a university position, he became a writer for a radical publication and wrote a series of articles on various inhumane social conditions. His articles attracted the attention of government officials who opposed his views, and he lost his job. Shortly thereafter, he moved to Paris and met the leading intellectuals of the radical movements of Europe, completing his conversion to socialism. He began his lifelong friendship with Friedrich Engels, with whom he wrote the now-famous Communist Manifesto (1847). Having joined the Communist League in Brussels, he returned to Germany. He was again pressured to leave the country for his activities. He moved to London where—with his friend Engels—he continued to promote his views until his death in 1883.

The theme common to all the writings of Marx and Engels was a profound sense of moral outrage at

Helping Migrant Farmworkers, *continued*

to replicate some of the worst abuses now affecting H2A workers. In a news article criticizing the Bush plan, she noted that the problems "derive from the fact that the employer is also the de facto immigration officer, with the power to deport those who grumble about work conditions or pay." From a Marxian perspective, the employers are clearly the owners of the means of production able to create working conditions that the farmworkers have no choice but to accept.

"For example," Smith-Nonini states, "farmworkers employed by the North Carolina Growers Association (NCGA), the largest H2A farm labor brokerage in the country, routinely complain that workers who leave their assigned farm or who anger their farmer employer end up on a blacklist maintained by the NCGA." These workers, then, are not rehired. Smith-Nonini continues: "Abuses such as the blacklist, long contract period, and the inability of workers to change employers are possible only in a dual-labor market of the kind that is created by guestworker programs, where a class of workers lacks full citizenship and labor rights. If employers had to compete in the general market for workers, they would be forced to improve conditions to attract workers."

Migrant workers play a role in strengthening the economy in many areas of the United States. One study, at North Carolina State University, estimated that each farmworker's labor contributed $12,000 to the state's agricultural profits. Smith-Nonini's research and advocacy raise the question of whether it's fair for the larger community to benefit so handsomely from this cheap labor, when the workers themselves are not reaping a fair share of the rewards, and are often suffering grave injustices in the process.

---

the misery produced in the lower classes by the new industrial social order. Marx concluded that political revolution was a vital necessity in the evolutionary process of society and that it was the only means by which the improvement of social conditions could be achieved.

Marx was a major social theorist and contributor to economic and philosophical thought. He believed that **social conflict**—struggle and strife—was at the core of society, the source of all social change. He asserted that all history was marked by **economic determinism**—the idea that all change, social conditions, and even society itself are based on economic factors and that economic inequality results in class struggles between the **bourgeoisie** (the owners and rulers) and the **proletariat** (the industrial workers). These conflicts between the rich and the poor, the owners and the workers lead to feelings of alienation, a feeling of frustration and disconnection from work and life, among the workers. The recognition among workers that society is stratified and that they share the same plight is known as **class consciousness**, which, according to Marx, leads ultimately to revolution. It was Marx's belief that conflict, revolution, and the overthrow of capitalism were inevitable.

Today, regardless of whether they agree or disagree with Marx's ideas, few sociologists deny the importance of the contributions he made. Sociologists are still trying to understand the influence of economic determinism, social conflict, social structure, social class, and social change on society.

APPLYING MARX

Karl Marx's ideas are used in practically every area of sociology. To simplify one of Marx's tenets that is used by academic sociologists, there is a fundamental inequality in all social relationships between those who have assets (land, money, jobs, equipment, prestige, etc.) that provide them with power, and those who do not. This inequality of power allows those who have it to dominate and exploit those who do not. Thus, all social relationships contain the elements of conflict between "haves" and "have-nots."

Many academic sociologists use this idea as a premise for interpreting a variety of social relationships regarding gender and race relations, marriage, economics, politics, employment, education, religion, justice, and other matters. In developing theories about the family, for example, a Marxian analyst may focus on the conflict within it—say, between husband (in many cases, the one who controls the money) and wife, or between parents (the ones who control everything) and children. In trying to explain education, the focus might be on the inherent conflict between faculty (the ones who control the grades) and students, or administration (the ones who control jobs and salaries) and faculty.

It may surprise you that Marx's ideas are used also by some clinical sociologists. Marx-oriented therapists, for example, can be of immediate use to their clients who have capital-related problems such as depression over failure to achieve quick financial success, frustration over being powerless at work, overwhelming fear of not being able to pay one's bills, and other problems related to money. Much suffering can be relieved by helping the clients realize that their problems are not isolated, individual ones but rather a societal matter that appears in many forms in different social classes and groups. For example, if a client experiences problems in her marriage because she's anxious and frustrated by the way she's treated by the supervisors at her job, a Marxist therapist can help her realize that her anger is rooted in the structure of capitalism and help her to defuse it. When some clients un,ate psychological stress and that other people are affected with similar problems, the pain of alienation often subsides.

Smith-Nonini (2002) is a journalist turned anthropologist who has used insights developed from Marxian theory to help call attention to and eradicate the plight of Latino migrant farmworkers and workers in meat-packing plants in North Carolina. Contrary to popular ideas, the immigrant population in many areas of the United States stimulates the economy, rather than takes away from it. The Bryan School of Business and Economics for the Center for New North Carolinians, highlights how entrepreneurial activity picks up in areas with large immigrant populations and the vast majority of immigrants do not take away jobs from native-born Americans (Hummel, 2004). Through her efforts (highlighted in this chapter's "Sociology at Work" box), Smith-Nonini has helped create awareness of injustices toward this group of people.

Many nonsociologists also benefit from Marx's ideas. Armed with the knowledge of how the powerful (say, factory owners) may exploit the powerless (the workers), labor leaders could convey to union members how they are being taken advantage of. This may help to promote "class consciousness" and solidarity among the members and thus increase the union's bargaining power.

Finally, Marx's ideas are useful for you personally. Your knowledge that the powerful members of society seek to maintain their power may help you think more critically about issues when it comes time for you to vote in elections. When new tax laws are proposed that supposedly are designed to benefit the whole population, for example, you may find cause to question whether the wealthy and powerful will benefit more than the middle and lower classes. You may use Marxian ideas to understand your intimate relationships better. A spouse who has chosen not to be employed may realize that he or she lacks equal say in important marital decisions (such as what car to buy, where to go on vacation, or where to live) because the working partner has more resources (namely, control of the money). Realizing this, the unemployed spouse may seek employment to create more equality in the relationship.

Emile Durkheim

Emile Durkheim (1858–1917) can be considered the first French academic sociologist. Before Durkheim, sociology was not a part of the French education system, although such related fields as education, social philosophy, and psychology were studied. In 1892, the University of Paris granted him its first doctor's degree in sociology. Six years later he became the first French scholar to hold a chair in sociology (i.e., to be given an honorary position). In addition to teaching, Durkheim wrote critical reviews and published important papers and books. His best known books include *The Division of Labor in Society*, *The Rules of Sociological Method*, *Suicide*, and *The Elementary Forms of Religious Life*.

Durkheim is responsible for several important ideas. For one, he refused to explain social events by assuming that they operated according to the same rules as biology or psychology. To Durkheim, social phenomena are **social facts** that have distinctive social characteristics and determinants. He defined social facts as "every way of acting, fixed or not, capable of exercising on the individual an external constraint" (1933, p. 13). Because these facts are external to the individual, they outlive individuals and endure over time. They include such things as customs, laws, and the general rules of behavior that people accept without question. Stopping at traffic lights, wearing shirts, and combing one's hair are behaviors most people perform without dissent. In short, individuals are more the products of society than the creators of it.

Although an individual can come to know and be a part of society, society itself is external to the individual. For this reason, Durkheim concentrated on examining characteristics of groups and structures rather than individual attributes. Instead of looking at the personal traits of religious believers, for example, he focused on the cohesion or lack of cohesion of specific religious groups. He was not so concerned with the religious experience of individuals but rather with the communal activity and the communal bonds that develop from religious participation (Coser, 1977).

Such communal interaction gives rise to what Durkheim called a **collective conscience**—a common psyche (spirit) that results from the blending together of many individual mentalities yet exists over and above any individual. Although the collective conscience is socially created, it is a powerful reality that comes to control us and cannot be denied. From this perspective, for example, whether God exists as a supernatural being is secondary to the fact that God exists as a result of people sharing and demonstrating their belief in God. To those sharing that belief, God is unquestionably and undeniably real, and thus an inescapable force. It is no longer a matter of a personal belief, but is now a belief in something outside of any one of us.

Durkheim's work *Suicide* deserves special attention for several reasons. It established a unique model for social research, and it clearly demonstrated that human behavior, although it may seem very individual, can be understood only by investigating the social context in which the behavior takes place. After looking at numerous statistics on different countries and different groups of people, Durkheim concluded that suicide was a *social* phenomenon, related somehow to the individual's involvement in group life and the extent to which he or she was part of some cohesive social unit. Durkheim's central thesis was that the more a person is integrated into intimate social groups, the less likely he or she is to commit suicide. Thus, people who have a low level of social integration and group involvement, such as the unmarried and those without strong religious convictions, would be expected to have higher suicide rates. Durkheim found that this was true.

He believed that social integration was achieved through people's mutual dependence and acceptance of a system of common beliefs. An important element in the system of beliefs was religion, the ceremonies of which become common experiences, symbols shared by the association of a group of people and thus a significant part of the collective conscience.

Durkheim played a key role in the founding of sociology. Although Comte, Spencer, and Marx introduced new ideas about society and helped convince the public that sociology and the other social sciences deserved a hearing, it was Durkheim who made sociology a legitimate academic enterprise.

APPLYING DURKHEIM

Like Comte's emphasis on the scientific method, Durkheim's concept of social facts is central to every form of sociological investigation. Virtually every theory or concept developed by academic sociologists is rooted in the idea that human social behavior is affected by forces external to the individual. Sociologists do not, for example, explain divorce in terms of individual psychological makeup. Rather, they look to social factors external to the individual, such as the economy, income, education, religion, age, or occupation. Is divorce more likely to occur when the economy is doing well or in trouble? Do people in lower or upper income groups have higher divorce rates? Are highly educated people more likely to divorce than people with less education? When the answers to these and other questions are found, sociologists can begin to analyze how certain types of social conditions (the state of the economy, degree of education, level of income, etc.) account for divorce instead of just looking at individuals. Durkheim's ideas about social facts and the collective conscience have important applications that are indispensable in clinical settings. It is important to keep in mind that although sociologists often work in clinical settings, Durkheim's ideas benefit anyone intervening in social problems. To help people deal with a particular problem—whether it involves helping parents to deal with a child's poor performance in school, counseling a suicidal person, or counseling a politician on strategies for getting elected, the clinician cannot adequately understand the situation solely on the basis of individual personalities or psychological characteristics. Rather, the social world of these people—the relevant social facts and collective conscience—must be analyzed. People usually do not explore the social processes that underlie situations or their decisions and tend to look exclusively at psychological processes.

Suppose, for example, that a high school guidance counselor notices that a student getting ready to apply for college suffers a sharp decline in grade point average (GPA) two semesters in a row. Rather than assume that the student is lazy or anxious about being rejected by colleges, how could knowledge of the student's social environment—say, that her parents are getting divorced—help the counselor deal with this student's situation? Knowing that social facts and a collective conscience exist, we can better look behind the scenes to help ourselves and others and deal with most situations.

Max Weber

Max Weber (1864–1920) was born in Germany, the son of a wealthy German politician. He was trained in law and economics, receiving his doctorate from the University of Heidelberg at the age of 25. For the next several years, he taught economics, but he soon succumbed to a severe mental illness that kept him an invalid and recluse for much of his life. Despite this condition, Weber was a prolific writer. His best-known works in sociology include *The Protestant Ethic and the Spirit of Capitalism*, *The Sociology of Hinduism and Buddhism*, *Theory of Social and Economic Organization*, and *Methodology of the Social Sciences*.

Weber's mixed feelings toward authority, whether familial or political, are reflected in his writings on the topic of power and authority. Weber discussed why men claim authority and expect their wishes to be obeyed. (Typically for his period, women were not considered.) His approach to sociology, however, has probably been as influential as his ideas. His predecessors considered societies in terms of their large social structures, social divisions, and social movements. Spencer based his studies on the belief that societies evolved like organisms; Marx considered society in terms of class conflicts; and Durkheim was concerned with the institutional arrangements that maintain the cohesion of social structures. These theorists assumed that society, although composed of individuals, existed apart from them.

In Weber's work, however, the *subjective* meanings (the personal beliefs, feelings, and perceptions) that humans attach to their interactions with other humans played a much greater role. Weber believed that sociologists must study not just social facts and social structures, but *social actions*, the external objective behaviors as well as the internalized values, motives, and subjective meanings that individuals attach to their own behavior and to the behavior of others. He also contended that social actions should be studied through qualitative, subjective methods as well as objective and quantitative techniques. The goal, Weber believed, was to achieve a "sympathetic understanding" of the minds of others. He called this approach **verstehen**: understanding human action by examining the subjective meanings that people attach to their own behavior and to the behavior of others. Once values, motives, and intentions were identified, Weber contended, sociologists could treat them objectively and scientifically.

This approach is evident in Weber's interpretation of social class. Whereas Marx saw class as rooted in economic determinism, particularly as related to property ownership, Weber argued that social class involves subjective perceptions of power, wealth, ownership, and social prestige, as well as the objective aspects of these factors.

APPLYING WEBER

Weber's concept of verstehen is a vital tool for academic and applied social researchers. As mentioned, Weber explained social class not just in terms of how much power, wealth, and prestige people have, but in terms of how they see and feel about their power, wealth, and prestige. So, for example, in conducting research on inequality between upper-class and middle-class groups, academic researchers need to find out not only what differences exist due to power and wealth, but also how people in each group feel about their own self-worth and the worth of others.

Verstehen is helpful to clinical sociologists working with clients. Consider a situation in which a counselor is called in to help with an interpersonal conflict among employees: An owner of an auto dealership is having a problem with conflict among the salespeople. It appears that in their struggle to acquire sales, the work environment has become the equivalent of a battlefield. Remember that for Weber, subjective meanings guide people's behavior; therefore, the clinician must try to identify with the people and their motives and try to see their actions from the involved persons' perspectives. How do the salespeople perceive their jobs? By trying to identify with them, the clinician may find out that (a) the salespeople feel threatened by one another; (b) they are uncomfortable with the close supervision of the manager; (c) they are convinced that if they do not sell enough, they will be fired; and (d) they think that aggressively competing with the others is smiled upon by management. In helping the clients (in this case, the manager) deal with their problem, they can be taught the techniques of verstehen to help them come to an understanding of the situation from each other's perspectives.

This technique is not only essential for clinical sociologists, but it also can be used in almost any situation—personal or occupational. Certainly, a professor could teach more effectively if she were to put herself in the minds of her students. Also, the students would fare better if they would try to see where the teacher was coming from in her lectures or assignments. A salesman would also benefit from applying verstehen; he would gain more if he looked at his sales approach from the customer's perspective rather than trying to direct hard sell.

Besides the scholars just discussed, other European thinkers (Georg Simmel, Harriet Martineau, Henri de Saint-Simon, Vilfredo Pareto, Ferdinand Tönnies, Karl Mannheim) made important contributions to sociology. With rare exceptions, they viewed society as a social unit that transcended the individual or was greater than the sum of individuals. It was for this reason, in part, that they did not investigate the means by which individual humans come to accept and reflect the fundamental conditions and structures of their societies—a question that was an important concern of some early American sociologists.

Thinking Sociologically

1. Describe and contrast the major contributions made to sociology by Comte, Spencer, Marx, Durkheim, and Weber.

2. Consider the political assumptions and orientations of different political parties or of differing world leaders. How are their ideas consistent with or different from those of Spencer, Marx, or Weber?

THE DEVELOPMENT OF SOCIOLOGY IN AMERICA

The earliest sociologists were Europeans, but much of the development of sociology took place in the United States. The first department of sociology was established in 1893 at the University of Chicago, and many important early figures of the discipline were associated with that institution. Sociology is such a young discipline that some of your instructors may have met or studied with many of the leading early sociologists. Most of the earlier American sociologists shared with their European forerunners an interest in social problems and social reform, in part because of the rapid social change that had been taking place in this country. These scholars focused on urbanization and urban problems—ghettos, prostitution, drug addiction, juvenile delinquency, immigration, and race relations.

The Chicago School

Until the 1940s, the University of Chicago was the leading sociological training and research center in America. Seven of the first 27 presidents of the American Sociological Association (ASA) taught or were educated at that institution. The city of Chicago served as a living laboratory for the study of many early social problems.

One leading figure in this group was Robert E. Park (1864–1944), who studied in Germany with a sociologist named Georg Simmel. Before beginning his work at the university in 1914, Park had worked as a secretary to Booker T. Washington and also as a journalist. He was the author of several important books. With another writer, he wrote an early textbook in sociology (1921) and a book titled The City (1925), which showed how urban communities are areas of both cooperation and competition, much like ecological habitats that occur in nature. The multidisciplinary approach he established became known as "social ecology."

After World War I, a group of scholars at the University of Chicago developed an approach to social psychology known today simply as the **Chicago School**. Previously, human behavior had been explained primarily in terms of instincts, drives, unconscious processes, and other innate characteristics. The Chicago School, the members of which included Charles Horton Cooley, George Herbert Mead, and W. I. Thomas, emphasized instead the importance of social interactions in the development of human thought and action. Mead was the chief advocate of the view that (a) humans respond to symbolic and abstract meanings, as well as to concrete experiences; and (b) self and society are one and the same, in that individuals *internalize* (take into their minds) social role expectations, social values, and norms. Humans are both actors and reactors; they are self-stimulating, and they can produce their own actions, responses, and definitions. To most members of society, for example, the act of burning a flag implies more than a desire for heat. People have learned to attach a special significance and meaning to a flag and respond with agreement or anger over a particular symbolic act. They might turn to others to ask why this is happening or to tell others what to do. This ability to internalize norms, share meanings, and anticipate responses is what makes social order and social systems possible. These ideas are basic to what was later called the "symbolic interactionist perspective," which is explained in more detail in this chapter and in those that follow.

The 1930s was a period of rapid change in American sociology. It was during this time that the field developed its service relationship to national public policy, its theoretical focus on macro-level systems, and its methods of large-scale quantification. In the words of Lengermann (1979, p. 196), "The societal crisis of the thirties raised new empirical and theoretical questions for sociologists, brought new demands from public and state to bear on the professional community, opened up new sources of employment and research support, created career anxiety for many sociologists and helped produce the regional associations." Lengermann claims, however, that the Great Depression of the 1930s was not the cause of changes in sociology during this decade because the methodological, theoretical, and professional transformation was in process prior to 1929. Rather, the changes were brought about by factors such as the growth and differentiation of the profession, by emerging elitist coalitions, and by the loss of momentum of the Chicago scholars.

The Shift of Influence to the East

In the 1940s, the center of sociological research shifted from Chicago to schools such as Harvard and Columbia. Talcott Parsons (1902–1979), who was affiliated with Harvard, rapidly became the leading social theorist in America, if not the world. Drawing heavily on the work of European thinkers such as Weber and Durkheim, he developed a very broad "general theory of action" (Parsons and Shils, 1951).

Robert K. Merton (1910–2003), a student of Parsons's, began his teaching career at Harvard. Since 1941, however, Merton had been affiliated with Columbia University. Although his general orientation was similar to Parsons's, Merton was much less abstract and much more concerned with linking general theory to empirical testing. This approach came to be known as the **middle-range theory**. His contributions to our understanding of such concepts as social structures, self-fulfilling prophecies, deviance, and bureaucracies place him among the leading American social theorists.

C. Wright Mills, Peter Blau, W.E.B. DuBois, Jane Addams, Erving Goffman, Herbert Blumer, Ralf Dahrendorf, Randall Collins, and Jessie Bernard were other scholars who greatly contributed to sociology's development in reaching its present state. These contributions included the following sociological theories: neofunctionalism and neo-Marxism, the development of phenomenology, ethnomethodology, rational choice, humanistic and feminist theory, as well as the major theories addressed in the next section. These are just a few of the many influential persons whose ideas are mentioned throughout this book; although major attention is given to the major theories, most of these others are briefly examined.

Research on traditional subjects such as the family, urban sociology, race relations, and criminology continues to be funded and studied, and much new work on the elderly, gender roles, popular culture, globalization, and peace studies is being undertaken. Most colleges and universities have departments of sociology, and sociologists are increasingly found in nonacademic settings. Outstanding theorists, researchers, and practitioners can be found from California, New York, and Texas to Michigan, North Carolina, and Florida. The number of professional sociologists in the United States alone is estimated to approach 15,000. In addition, the methodological tools and procedures and the range of theories to explain social phenomena are more diverse today than ever before. These major social theories and theoretical orientations are discussed in the next section.

THE MAJOR THEORETICAL PERSPECTIVES IN SOCIETY

Theories are explanations offered to account for a set of phenomena. *Social theories* are explanations of social phenomena—why people choose to marry as they do or why people behave differently in different social situations. We all develop theories (to use the term in its broadest sense) to help us explain and predict a wide variety of events. Even when the explanations are wrong, they may help us develop guidelines for behavior and hypotheses that can be tested.

Suppose, for example, that several sociologists are trying to determine why the rate of armed robbery has risen in Metropolis in the past ten years. One sociologist might suggest the proposition that it was due to the increase in unemployment, which forced people to rob to get money for food. Another might hypothesize that the crime rate is largely the result of the increased cost of heroin—addicts are robbing more to get money for a fix. A third might suggest that armed robbery is related to the incidence of divorce—children from broken homes are spending too much time on the street and are getting into trouble.

After they develop their hypotheses, the sociologists would begin to test them. They could examine statistics, interview parents, check police records, and use other means to acquire information. In this greatly oversimplified example, let us assume that the sociologist with the "broken home" idea discovers that most of the robbers who have been caught are in their 20s and 30s. This conclusion argues against his theory—the robbers would probably have been living away from their families. Is it possible, though, that the robbers are alienated and incapable of holding jobs because of experiences they had as children? (This is an example of a theory leading to new avenues of exploration even though it appears to be wrong.) The sociologist, upon further investigation, determines that the divorce rate in Metropolis underwent a sharp decline in the 1960s and 1970s, contrary to the national trend. This assumption means that his secondary theory—that the robbers are the victims of homes disrupted by divorce when they were children—is also wrong.

Let us assume, however, that the other propositions are supported by the information discovered. The robbery rate began to climb shortly after the local air conditioner factory closed, and it jumped dramatically at about the time the police say that heroin became more readily available for sale on the street.

Does the fact that both of these theories received support from research mean that one of them is wrong? Not necessarily. Sociology offers multiple explanations of most phenomena. Explanations can be different without being incompatible, and even those that seem unlikely or illogical should be evaluated in the context of the events they were designed to explain.

In the preceding example, the term theory is used rather broadly. To be more precise, **a theory** is a set of interrelated statements or propositions intended to explain a given phenomenon. It is based on a set of assumptions and self-evident truths, includes definitions, and describes the conditions in which the phenomenon exists.

Although sociological theories exist to explain everything from childrearing to automobile sales, a small number of basic theories predominate in the field. These are explained next. Each theory is followed by a brief discussion of how it can be applied in work settings and in your personal life. They are also described in more detail and applied to specific settings throughout this book.

Structural Functional Theory

Structural functionalism has its roots in the work of the early sociologists, especially Durkheim and Weber. Among contemporary scholars, it is most closely associated with the work of Parsons and Merton. Many would argue that structural functionalism is the dominant theoretical view in sociology today. It is sometimes referred to as "social systems theory," "equilibrium theory," or simply "functionalism."

The terms structure and function refer to two separate but closely related concepts. Structures can be compared to the organs or parts of the body of an animal, and functions can be compared with the purposes of these structures. The stomach is a structure; digestion is its function. In the same way, health care organizations and the military are social structures (or social systems), and caring for the sick and defending governmental interests are their functions. Like a biological structure, a social system is composed of many interrelated and interdependent parts or structures.

Social structures include any component or part of society: clubs, families, nations, groups, and so forth. Central to an understanding of social structures are the concepts of status and role. Simply defined, a status is a socially defined position: female, student, lawyer, or Catholic. Some of these are **ascribed statuses**—that is, given to us at birth (e.g., age, sex, race), whereas others are **achieved statuses** (e.g., college graduate, father, teacher). Sets of interrelated statuses or positions are **social systems**. The interrelated statuses of mother, father, and children, for example, constitute a family system. The interrelated statuses of teachers, students, and school administrators constitute an educational system.

Each social system performs specific functions that make it possible for society and the people who comprise that society to exist. Each serves a function that leads to the maintenance or stability of the larger society. The educational system is intended to provide literary and technical skills, the religious system is intended to provide emotional support and to answer questions about the unknown, families are intended to socialize infants and children, and so on. The functionalist perspective assumes that these social systems have an underlying tendency to be in equilibrium or balance; any system that fails to fulfill its functions will result in an imbalance or disequilibrium. In extreme cases, the entire system can break down when a change or failure in any one part of the system affects its interrelated parts.

A social system can be regarded as having two types of functions: (1) the immediate purpose of what the system does and (2) the broader, less immediate consequences that result from a particular type of structure or organization. For example, in a biological system, the immediate function of the eyes is to obtain information about the environment. This function more broadly enables the viewer to seek food and shelter and to avoid danger. In a social system, one function of government might be to maintain order. An advantage of this function is that people can carry on their affairs—running businesses, raising families—without having their lives disrupted.

According to Merton, a social system can have both **manifest functions** and **latent functions.** Manifest functions are intended and recognized; latent functions are neither intended nor recognized. One manifest function of education systems is to teach literary and technical skills. They also perform the latent functions of providing supervision for children while parents work and of providing contacts for dating and even for marriage. Correctional institutions have the manifest functions of punishment and removing criminals from social interaction with the larger society. They may also perform the latent functions of providing advanced training in breaking and entering and other criminal endeavors.

Merton recognized that not all consequences of systems are functional—that is, they do not all lead to the maintenance of the system. Some lead to instability or the breakdown of a system. He termed these consequences **dysfunctions.** Families have a manifest function of rearing children. The intensity of family interactions, however, can lead to the dysfunction, or negative consequence, of domestic violence and child abuse. This dysfunction may lead to the disruption of relationships within the family system or even to the total breakdown of the system.

Sociologists who adhere to the functionalist perspective examine the parts of a given system and try to determine how they are related to one another and to the whole. They observe the results of a given cluster or arrangement of parts, attempting to discover both the intended (manifest) and the unintended (latent) functions of these parts. In addition, they analyze which of these consequences contribute to the maintenance of a given system and which lead to the breakdown of the system. It should be noted that what may be functional in one system may be dysfunctional in another. A function that is good for corporate profits may not be good for family solidarity, or one that is good for religious unity may not be good for ethnic integration.

According to the functionalist perspective, social systems exist because they fulfill some function for the society. Functionalists focus on order and stability, which has led some critics to argue that it supports the status quo. With the emphasis on equilibrium and the maintenance of the system, the process of change, critics say, receives little attention.

APPLYING STRUCTURAL FUNCTIONAL THEORY

Even though it has its critics, structural functional theory is one of the most generally applicable perspectives in social science. It is used by academic sociologists to study and analyze every form of social system, including families, prisons, governments, communities, schools, sports teams, and many others.

Just as structural functionalism is broadly applicable to problems of interest to academic sociologists, so is it a useful tool for almost every type of applied sociological problem. It can be particularly useful as a means of identifying and analyzing the components and goals of a system and of ensuring that those goals are met. When we try to solve problems in any type of social system—whether it is a society, a corporation, a family, a sorority, or a sports team—we must answer some central questions: What are the parts of the system? What functions do the parts actually serve? What functions are they intended to serve? How do the parts influence each other?

Consider how a clinical sociologist or a faculty advisor might use structural functional analysis to help a fraternity that is in jeopardy of having its charter revoked because of the low overall GPA of its members. Two important parts of the fraternity are the current members and the *pledges* (candidates for initiation). One of the intended (manifest) functions of the current members is to test the loyalty of the pledges so that when they are initiated into the brotherhood, the trust and solidarity characteristic of fraternities will remain intact. One way of testing that loyalty is through having pledges go through rigorous and mindless antics (such as hazing) that consume hours of time. The manifest function is that the pledges' dedication will be proven. A latent function of pledging, however, is low grades because of the enormous amount of time it takes the candidates to prove themselves sufficiently loyal. In reality, the latent dysfunction of pledging may be the demise of the fraternity—the very opposite of the intended function.

Robert Merton's theory of **functional alternatives** provides one way to avoid dysfunctions such as the destruction of the fraternity. Functional alternatives are other ways to achieve the intended goal. Perhaps the fraternity brothers could have the pledges demonstrate their loyalty and sincerity to the fraternity by requiring pledges to achieve a 3.5 GPA. Putting in countless hours to achieve a 3.5 GPA is more grueling and demands more loyalty than toilet-papering the college president's house at 3 in the morning. This functional alternative would promote loyalty and would provide the reputation necessary for the college administration's approval.

The functional perspective can also be applied to tensions among the various parts of a system. The expectations or actions of the different parts of a system may fail to mesh. A lumberyard that sells a variety of construction supplies, for example, may have some employees who receive commissions from in-store sales and others who receive commissions from outside sales. Suppose that you are hired as an outside sales representative and you develop a large clientele of building contractors through contacts made while on the road. However, when one of those customers decides to purchase material directly from the store, an inside salesperson takes credit for the sale. Who should get the commission for the sale? The conflict arises not because of poor performance on the part of the salespeople but because of a systemic dysfunction. This lack of clarity and confusion over the store's specific goals and the goals of each of its parts can cause serious personnel conflicts that could undermine the business. In this situation, some type of explicit goal-setting or value-clarification process would be appropriate. These examples demonstrate that by focusing on the functions of the parts of a system, we might be able to discover solutions to a problem.

Conflict Theory

Conflict theory also had its origins in early sociology, especially in the work of Marx; among its more recent proponents are C. Wright Mills, Lewis Coser, Ralph Dahrendorf, and others. These sociologists share the view that society is best understood and analyzed in terms of conflict and power.

Karl Marx began with a very simple assumption: The structure of society is determined by its economic organization, particularly the ownership of property. Religious dogmas, cultural values, personal beliefs, institutional arrangements, class structures—all are basically reflections of the economic organization of a society. According to Marx, inherent in any economic system that supports inequality are forces that generate revolutionary class conflict. The exploited classes eventually recognize their submissive and inferior status and revolt against the dominant class of property owners and employers. The story of history, then, is the story of class struggle between the owners and the workers, the dominators and the dominated, the powerful and the powerless.

Contemporary conflict theorists assume that conflict is a permanent feature of social life and that, as a result, societies are in a state of constant change. Unlike Marx, however, these theorists rarely assume that conflict is always based on class or that it always reflects economic organization and ownership. Conflicts are assumed to involve a broad range of groups or interests: young against old, male against female, or one racial group against another, as well as workers against employers. These conflicts result because such things as power, wealth, and prestige are not available to everyone; they are limited commodities, and the demand exceeds the supply. Conflict theory also assumes that those who have or control desirable goods, services, and other resources will defend and protect their own interests at the expense of others.

In this view, *conflict* does not mean the sort of event that makes headlines, such as war, violence, or open hostility. It is instead regarded as the struggle that occurs day after day as people try to maintain and improve their positions in life. Neither should conflict be regarded as a destructive process that leads to disorder and the breakdown of society. Theorists such as Dahrendorf and Coser have focused on the integrative nature of conflict, its value as a force that contributes to order and stability. How can conflict be a constructive force? Basically, the answer is that people with common interests join together to seek gains that will benefit all of those sharing these common interests. By the same token, conflict among groups focuses attention on inequalities and social problems that might never be resolved without conflict. Racial conflicts, for example, may serve to bind people with common interests together and may also lead to constructive social change that may actually lessen the current conflict among groups.

There is an obvious contrast between the views of the functionalists, who regard society as balanced and in a state of equilibrium, and the views of conflict theorists, who assume that society is an arena of constant competition and change. Functionalists believe that the social process is a continual effort to maintain harmony; conflict theorists believe that it is a continual struggle to "get ahead." Functionalists view society as basically consensual, integrated, and static; conflict theorists believe that it is characterized by constraint, conflict, and change. Whereas functionalists have been criticized for focusing on stability and the status quo, conflict theorists have been criticized for overlooking the less controversial and more orderly aspects of society.

APPLYING CONFLICT THEORY

Like structural functionalism, conflict theory is used by sociologists to explain the relationship between the parts of a social system and the inequalities that exist among these parts. By recognizing that conflict is a permanent feature of the life of any social system, conflict theory can be used to discover and explain the sources of the conflict. In addition to discovering and explaining the sources of conflict, conflict theory may be used to help create techniques to deal with conflict or to use it constructively in the workplace and in your personal life. Sociologists working as group therapists or marriage counselors recognize that if conflict in relationships does not surface or is repressed, individuals may encounter problems that may have a worse impact on a relationship than if the conflict is recognized and handled.

In dealing with any situation, whether it is running a business, coaching a basketball team, teaching a class, presiding over a group, maintaining a family, or organizing a labor union, conflict theory tells us to look for the hidden strains and frustrations, particularly between those in power who make the decisions (bosses, managers, owners) and those who carry out these decisions (workers, players). Even when those involved do not express dissatisfaction, there may still be conflict. Conflict in relationships is not always explicit, nor is it always expressed by individuals. Nonetheless, some clues might help you to recognize conflict.

When sociologists or counselors are looking for clues to conflict, they often look to clues that indicate inequalities in positions between husbands and wives, or between managers and workers. Some of these clues, or expressions of power differentials may include covert signs of anger (e.g., overeating, boredom, depression, illness, gossip), *passive aggression* (sarcasm, nitpicking, chronic criticism), *sabotage* (spoiling or undermining an activity another person has planned), *displacement* (directing anger at people or things another person cherishes), devitalization of the relationship (a relationship that has become lifeless, equivalent to "emotional divorce"), or violence (resulting from unreleased pressures and tensions) (Lamanna and Riedmann, 2003). These same consequences are likely to occur in families or in any other relationship in which conflict is denied. Realizing this, a sociologist, or anyone working with a group, might try to build into the group's activities some ways of airing conflicts among members in a way that is approved and expected. Perhaps a basketball coach would initiate weekly "gripe sessions" when each member of the team is expected to discuss things that bother him or her about other players or about the coaches.

Another sign that there may be an unexpressed conflict is low morale. Imagine that you are the manager of an insurance company with a large pool of clerical workers whom the company has always promoted exclusively on the basis of seniority. To improve efficiency, you decide to change the policy and promote on the basis of merit, not number of years employed. This might cause some discontent among the clerks, especially those who have been with the company for a number of years. Suddenly, you notice a change in the secretaries' behavior: reduced work effectiveness, poor attitudes, higher rates of absence due to "illness," and a general lack of camaraderie. Understanding conflict theory, you might realize that the abnormal behavior is probably a result of some form of conflict among the employees rather than a sudden

POLICY DEBATE

Prayer in Schools

The First Amendment to the U.S. Constitution provides that "Congress shall make no law respecting an establishment of religion, or prohibiting the free exercise thereof." In various court cases in the early 1960s, the Supreme Court—based on its interpretation of the First Amendment—ruled that government may not advance religion in the public schools, sponsor or prescribe devotional exercises such as prayer and Bible reading as a regular part of the school day, teach or instill the precepts or prohibitions of any religion in the school curriculum, permit private groups the use of school premises for the purpose of giving religious instruction during the school day, post religious texts such as the Ten Commandments on classroom walls, and permit the distribution in public school of religious literature such as the Gideons' Bible. These prohibitions apply to state governments as well as to the federal government. In spite of the Supreme Court's rulings, a controversial debate about whether prayer should be allowed in schools continues.

Clearly, whether prayer and other religious activities should be allowed in the public schools and other public spaces (such as a plaza in front of a federal court) and in national documents (such as "The Pledge of Allegiance") is ultimately a constitutional question—one based primarily on the interpretation of the "establishment" and "free exercise" clauses of the First Amendment (Provenzo, 1990). However, it is important to recognize that underlying the opposing views in this and other policy debates, even though this is a constitutional matter, are the theoretical perspectives (not necessarily sociological) that people hold. While the underlying theoretical perspectives and beliefs of policy disagreements do not always emerge among the populace, they are, nevertheless, usually at the root of such debates. To illustrate this point, the school prayer debate is discussed here in terms of its relationship to theoretical perspectives and beliefs rather than in terms of its constitutionality. Although there may be other relevant perspectives relevant to this debate, this discussion looks at how the competing arguments are tied to evolutionist and creationist views of human life, and the sociological perspectives of functionalism and conflict theory.

First, it is important to recognize who in the populace is taking sides in the controversy. This should provide us with insights about the underlying beliefs and perspectives used. Proponents of school prayer are largely members of conservative fundamentalist and evangelist religious groups, collectively known as the Religious Right (Marshall, 2001). These groups are quite clear and vocal in their support of what they call "creationist science" (i.e., creationism) and in their opposition to what they call "secular humanism" and other views that are rooted in an evolutionist explanation of the origin of life. Opponents of school prayer come from many members of Protestant and Jewish organizations, the American Civil Liberties Union (ACLU), People for the American Way, and Americans United for the Separation of Church and State. While these people do not necessarily deny biblical accounts of creation and sectarian morality, they believe that biblical and scientific accounts are and should be open to interpretation.

Creationists are likely to support school prayer because of the belief in the absolute sanctity of the Bible as a prescription for living. Consider, for example, the longstanding role of schools to instill morals and build character. Boardman W. Kathan, archivist of the Religious Education Association, notes that moral education and character building have always been tasks assigned to the schools. All parties agree about this point. However, they disagree about the source of morality. Propo-

Prayer in Schools, *continued*

nents of school prayer feel that there is a relationship between morality and school prayer. According to Ed McAteer, president of the Religious Roundtable, a political fundamentalist group, "If we are to stem the tide of lawlessness, drug addiction, and sexual perversion which adversely affect academic performance, we must start with putting God back into our school systems" (in Provenzo, 1990, p. 75). Other religious leaders, such as televangelist James Robison, have blamed the Supreme Court's ban on mandatory school prayer for assassinations, war, crime, the disintegration of families, racial conflict, teenage pregnancies, and sexually transmitted diseases (Provenzo, 1990. p. 76).

While "the Moral Majority would like us to believe that no morality can be taught without a religious framework," according to Cynthia Stokes Brown, opponents of school prayer believe that morality can stem from sources other than religion. Brown states her opinion:

> Unlike them, I suggest that morality does not require God, that moral virtues can be taught in public schools without adding the religious dimension of some form of higher being. This dimension can be provided by families and by religious institutions, for the schools' instruction in humanistic morality can be accomplished without interfering with the religious option. (Brown, 1988, p. 43)

For opponents of school prayer, humanistic morality, not religious morality, is appropriate for schools to teach. Humanistic morality is grounded in the idea of the kinship of humanity. The underlying assumption is that every human being has certain rights by virtue of being human. The notion that morality is based on human agreements seems to underlie the opponents' reasoning here.

While the two opposing views about the sources of morality, and thus the propriety of school prayer, appear to be rooted in the creationist–evolutionist controversy, we can also take a more sociological approach and use functionalism and conflict theory—especially these theories' treatment of religion—to examine the sides of the debate. For example, Emile Durkheim, whose ideas lie at the heart of functionalism, theorized that common belief systems such as religion function to preserve and solidify society and help to establish a collective conscience. Thus, from the functionalist view, religion serves as a source of integration, solidarity, consensus, and social control.

Consider sociologist Robert Bellah's notion that "there actually exists alongside of and rather clearly differentiated from the churches an elaborate and well-institutionalized civil religion in America" (Bellah, 1967, in Kathan, 1989, p. 235). This includes creeds, dogmas, rituals, symbols, saints, holy days, and scriptures that Americans heed and observe. Proponents of school prayer thus argue that there is a need for school prayer because the public school has been perceived as the primary institution for the practice and inculcation of this civil religion. However, Kathan notes that in the same court decisions in which organized religious practices were banned from schools, the justices recommended the use of documents, addresses, anthems, and other literature in American history in which faith in God is expressed. Opponents of school prayer maintain that these items adequately serve the inculcation of our "civil religion" and enable it to serve its social functions.

Conflict theory can also be used to gain insight into the school prayer debate. For example, Karl Marx, whose ideas helped form conflict theory, wrote that religion "is

(continues)

Prayer in Schools, *continued*

the opiate of the masses because it pacifies them and distracts them from finding solutions to their problems. More generally, conflict theorists see religion as a source of conflict between groups competing for ideological and political power rather than as a source of social consensus. Along these lines of thinking, many opponents of prayer in schools feel that it is an attempt at a "quick fix" for larger educational and cultural problems (e.g., Brown, 1988; Farmer, 1984), and a way for ultraconservatives to push their total political agenda. Kathan feels that the attempt to override the Supreme Court ban on school prayer represents a struggle for ideological control of the public schools. Specifically, proponents of school prayer, Kathan feels, are eager to bring God and religion back to the classroom in order to rid the schools of secular humanism and to reaffirm creationism. They feel that mandated or organized prayer is one way to achieve this (Kathan, 1989). Opponents of this view feel that school prayer is a means of advocating a religious point of view that may not be shared by all citizens in our pluralistic society (Farmer, 1984, p. 248).

Clearly, this brief discussion is not a comprehensive analysis of the school prayer debate. There are many other factors to consider in the debate, both in terms of constitutionality and theoretical perspectives. This discussion merely demonstrates how theoretical perspectives and belief systems lie at the root of many policy debates.

unexplained incompetence. The employees might not openly express their discontent because they may feel that they are powerless to change the situation. In fact, many sociologists and social psychologists have suggested that people fail to express dissatisfaction not because conflict does not exist, but because (a) they feel powerless to change things, (b) they may not be aware that things could be better than they are, or (c) they are resigned to the situation (Johnson, 1986).

Conflict theory helps us realize that because conflict is normal and usually inevitable, it is okay to express it. In fact, some clinicians go so far as to recommend to their clients—whether they are married couples, occupational groups, or sports teams—that they periodically engage in conflict to release tensions and initiate emotional interactions. This is not meant to prescribe all-out war within groups but is meant to encourage people with conflicts to develop explicit procedures to deal with differences in a rational and constructive way rather than pretend that they do not exist or that they will disappear.

Thinking Sociologically

1. Explain why structural functional theories are often portrayed as conservative and conflict theories as radical.
2. To what extent is conflict inherent in all social situations? Is conflict detrimental to maintaining order? To initiating change? To justice? To personal well-being?

Symbolic Interaction Theory

Symbolic interaction theory, although influenced somewhat by early European sociologists, was developed largely through the efforts of George Herbert Mead, W. I. Thomas, and Charles Horton Cooley, who belonged to the Chicago School. The key difference between this perspective and those discussed earlier revolves around the size of the units used in investigation and analysis. *Macrosociological orientations*—the evolutionary, structural functional, and conflict theories—interpret society in terms of its large structures: organizations, institutions, social classes, communities, and nations. *Microsociological orientations*, such as symbolic interaction theory, on the other hand, study individuals in society and their definitions of situations, meanings, roles, interaction patterns, and the like. Although these levels of analysis overlap considerably, they operate from different assumptions and premises.

The question of how individuals influence society and how society influences individuals is central to sociology. As you recall, early sociologists (Spencer, Durkheim, and Marx, for example) regarded society as an entity existing apart from the individual. Symbolic interactionists, however, assume that society exists within every socialized individual and that its external forms and structures arise through the social interactions taking place among individuals at the symbolic level.

What does "symbolic level" mean? It can be explained this way: Suppose that you are driving down the road in your car, and you see that a brick wall closes off the entire road. You stop, of course, because you have learned that you cannot pass through a physical object. If, however, you are riding down the same road and you come to a stoplight, once again, you stop—but why? No physical object prevents you from progressing. Your reason for stopping is that you have learned that the red light is a *symbol* that means "stop." The world around us can be said to consist of these two elements: physical objects and abstract symbols. Language is a system of symbols. It represents physical objects or concepts that can be used to communicate.

According to George Herbert Mead, who played an important role in the development of symbolic interactionism, it is the ability of humans to use symbols that sets us apart from animals and that allows us to create social institutions, societies, and cultures. People in a society share an understanding of particular symbols (the stoplight, for example). Social learning takes place at both symbolic and nonsymbolic levels. In interaction with others, we internalize social expectations, a specific language, and social values. In interaction with others, we learn to share meanings and to communicate symbolically through words and gestures. As humans, we can interact at both a physical (e.g., a slap) and a symbolic (e.g., showing a fist or making a verbal threat) level. Because we can relate symbolically, we can carry on conversations with ourselves. We can also imagine the effects of different courses of action. We can imagine what would happen if we were to throw a rotten tomato in the face of a police officer. By thinking through alternative courses of action, we can choose those we believe to be the most appropriate for a given situation. The fact that others share similar expectations makes life patterned and relatively predictable. Those who fail to recognize that red traffic lights mean stop will have trouble getting any place safely in their cars.

The interactionist perspective examines patterns and processes of everyday life that are generally ignored by many other perspectives. It raises questions about the self, the self in relationships with others, and the self and others in the wider social context. Why do some of us have negative feelings about ourselves? Why can we relate more easily with some persons than with others? Why do we feel more comfortable around friends than among strangers? How is it possible to interact with complete strangers or to know what to do in new situations? How are decisions made in families? Symbolic interactionists try to answer such questions by examining the individual in a social context. The starting point of this examination is the social setting in which an individual is born and the interactions he or she has with parents, siblings, teachers, neighbors, or others. From these interactions, we learn what is proper or improper, whether we are "good" or "bad," who is important, and so forth. A more complete explanation of this perspective is given in other sections throughout the book.

APPLYING SYMBOLIC INTERACTION THEORY

The symbolic interactionist perspective emphasizes that people act on the basis of their interpretation of the language and symbols in a situation and not the situation in and of itself. This perspective is useful, in that it points to the necessity of having people achieve at least a minimal agreement about the definition or meaning of a situation. One problem that can develop in any relationship—whether on the job or in the home—is the lack of consensus in people's definitions of a situation. The lack of consensus may be the result of a disagreement or a misunderstanding. The confusion may be about the roles individuals develop for themselves, the goals they think should be pursued collectively, or the ways in which resources (such as money or power) should be distributed. This could lead to a breakdown of a relationship altogether or, at the very least, to confusion, tension, strife, and general unhappiness within the relationship or social system. Some examples may show how the definition of a situation can be at the core of some interpersonal problems and how symbolic interaction theory can be used.

Imagine that you are the manager of a retail jewelry store, and you hire two salespeople. The salespeople are told that their salaries will be partly straight pay and partly commission generated by their sales. Person A defines the situation as one in which potential customers should be divided equally between the two employees because they both work in the same place. Person B sees the situation as one of competition among the employees for sales. Both interpretations are possible and quite feasible. As a result, Person A sees Person B as aggressive, money-hungry, and cutthroat. Person B sees Person A as uncompetitive, complacent, and not sales oriented. The tension mounts, and each salesperson thinks the other has a personality problem. The problem, though, may not be due to personalities but to a lack of clarity about how each person defines what he or she has been employed to do. As the manager, how could your knowledge of symbolic interaction theory help you to resolve this problem? Symbolic interaction theory alerts us to the importance of effective communication among people so that they can understand each other's perspectives. If this occurs, they may be able to coordinate their actions better. According to Johnson (1986), "the ultimate outcome is not only reinforcement of appropriate role performance but also the creation of a more supportive and satisfying atmosphere" (p. 60).

It is also important to understand that individuals' definitions of a situation are related to their definition of what constitutes a problem. What one person considers a problem may not be seen as a problem by another person. A male boss who continuously flirts with his female secretary through physical contact (arm touching, back rubbing, and so on) or sexually suggestive comments may think that he is creating a friendly, supportive work atmosphere. He may be unaware that the secretary sees his actions as sexual overtures and feels harassed and exploited by his "friendliness."

In both of these examples, open communication is needed so that the definition of the situation can be clarified. Often, a mediator—perhaps a sociologist, but not necessarily—is needed to help explain each side to the other, in the hope of helping the parties to achieve at least a minimal agreement about the definition of the situation.

Thinking Sociologically

Explore the significance of "symbolic" in symbolic interaction theory. What does it mean that meanings are not inherent in acts or objects?

Exchange Theory

Although symbolic interaction theory is the most widely used and recognized interaction perspective, exchange theory also falls within this general orientation. **Exchange theory** has a diverse intellectual heritage, drawing from sources in economics, anthropology, and psychology, as well as sociology. This perspective is based on the belief that life is a series of exchanges involving rewards and costs. In economic exchanges, people exchange money, goods, and services, hoping to profit or at least break even in the exchange. In anthropological, psychological, and sociological exchanges, the items of exchange include social and psychic factors, as well: In return for your companionship, I'll invite you to my house; in return for your positive teacher evaluation, I'll work extra hard to be a good instructor. Work, gifts, money, affection, ideas—all are offered in the hope of getting something in return.

Social exchange theory seeks to explain why behavioral outcomes such as marriage, employment, and religious involvement occur, given a set of structural conditions (age, race, gender, class) and interactional possibilities. Women, for example, marry men of a higher social status more frequently than men marry women of a higher social status. Exchange theorists would attempt to explain this finding by examining the desirable qualities that men and women have to exchange. In the United States, for men to have money or a good job is viewed as desirable; for women to be physically attractive is viewed as desirable. Thus, we might expect that very attractive lower-status women could exchange their beauty for men of a higher economic and occupational status, which seems to be what happens.

Exchange theory assumes that people seek rewarding statuses, relationships, and experiences, and they try to avoid costs, pain, and punishments. Given a set of alternatives, individuals choose those from which they expect the most profit, rewards, or satisfaction, and they avoid those that are not profitable, rewarding, or satisfying. When the costs exceed the rewards, people are likely to feel angry and dissatisfied. When the rewards exceed the costs, they are likely to feel that they got a good deal (unless they got it through exploitation or dishonesty, in which case, they may feel guilty and choose to avoid further interactions). Both parties are more likely to be satisfied with the interaction if there is perceived equity in the exchange, a feeling on the part of both that the rewards were worth the costs.

Although people may work selflessly for others with no thought of reward, it is quite unusual. The social exchange perspective assumes that voluntary social interactions are contingent on rewarding reactions from others. When rewarding reactions cease, either the actions end or dissatisfaction results.

There are two different schools of thought in the exchange theory perspective. George Homans, the theorist responsible for originating exchange theory, represents a perspective consistent with that of behavioral psychologists, who believe that behavior can be explained in terms of rewards and punishments. Behaviorists focus their attention on actual behavior, not on processes that can be inferred from behavior but cannot be observed. In exchange theory, the rewards and punishments are the behavior of other people, and those involved in exchanges assume that their rewards will be proportional to their costs.

Peter Blau is the advocate of a different school of exchange theory, one that is consistent with symbolic interactionism. Blau does not attempt to explain all exchanges in terms of observable behavior. He argues that the exchange is more subjective and interpretive and that the exchanges occur on the symbolic level. As a result, money may be a just reward only if it is defined by the receiver as such, and psychic rewards of satisfaction with doing a good job or of pleasing someone may be as important as money, gifts, or outward responses of praise.

Both Homans and Blau agree that what is important is that each party in the exchange must receive something perceived as equivalent to that which is given (to Homans, "distributive justice"; to Blau, "fair exchange"). All exchange involves a mutually held expectation that reciprocation will occur. If resources or exchange criteria are unequal, one person is at a distinct disadvantage, and the other has power over and controls the relationship. As a result, in marriage, unequal exchanges between husband and wife are likely to result in dominance of one over the other or may even end the relationship. In employment, if employee and employer do not recognize a fair exchange of rewards and costs, dissatisfaction may result, and the employee may quit, or the employer may dismiss the employee.

In exchange theory, then, social life is viewed as a process of bargaining or negotiation, and social relationships are based on trust and mutual interests. In recent years, some sociologists have criticized exchange theory as overly adhering to economic and mathematical models that do not put enough emphasis on the human elements or content of a situation (Zafirovski, 2003).

APPLYING EXCHANGE THEORY

Although most of us probably do not like the idea that we rationally calculate relationships in terms of rewards and costs, exchange theory is supported by much research concerning family relationships, dating, and the workplace (see, for example, Rubin, 1973; Blau, 1964; and Homans, 1974). An exemplary application of exchange theory is found in Blau's (1964) study of relationships between supervisors and workers in complex organizations such as hospitals, factories, and corporations. Blau found that supervisors often reward workers with special favors in exchange for positive evaluations. Such favors include services (such as being paid on time and taking coffee breaks), nonenforcement of some of management's rules, or the development of comradeship with the workers. In exchange for these favors, the workers express their loyalty.

Because the demand for fair exchange seems to be a fact of most social relationships, we might use this knowledge to ensure that cost–reward outcomes are fair and, more important, are perceived as fair by the people involved. Dissatisfaction in marriage and occupations, for example, often results from the belief that there is an imbalanced give-and-take in the relationship. What sometimes needs to be done in such troubled situations is to help the individuals or parties involved evaluate rationally the costs and rewards of the relationship. What may be perceived as an imbalanced exchange may actually not be as unfair as it seems. If this is the case, helping each party understand that there is a balanced exchange could salvage the relationship. However, if there is indeed an imbalance of rewards and costs to one or all of the parties, then there must be some form of negotiation to restore the necessary balance of exchange.

If you were a marriage counselor, how could you use exchange theory to help a troubled relationship? Suppose that a couple comes to you in which the husband is employed outside the home and the wife works taking care of the house and the children. The husband may feel that because he is out working for pay all day, when he comes home, he deserves to be demanding, to be free of household chores, to spend little time caring for the children, and so forth. In terms of exchange theory, he may feel that his cost (being employed) deserves a reward (freedom from housework). At the same time, the wife may resent her husband's lack of participation in family chores. After all, she too has worked all day (albeit not for pay). Thus, she may perceive that she is putting more into the relationship than she is getting in return. In this case, you might help the husband see that even though his wife is staying home during the day, she is working just as hard as he is to meet the needs of the family. Perhaps he would then see that the leisure time (the rewards) should be divided more equally between them.

Exchange theory can also be used for other than troubled relationships. Rewards can be used to induce people to give more of themselves (a cost). These rewards are not necessarily material and may also be psychological. Think of how you could use this knowledge to enhance your interpersonal skills in your job. Imagine that you are a bank manager in a large branch. You need a way to induce the head teller to come in early every day for two weeks to train some new tellers who have been hired. Instead of merely giving her the assignment, you might also mention to her that besides paying her overtime, you are going to make a note in her personnel file about her dedication to the bank. You might also express your praise openly to her so that the president of the bank happens to overhear it. In this case, recognition is being exchanged for time spent. Similarly, an automobile dealership may buy newspaper space each month to give credit to the top salesperson for that period, as an inducement for the salespeople to do extra work for the company.

Thinking Sociologically

1. Select a group or organization in which you are involved, and explore it in terms of structural functionalism, conflict theory, symbolic interactionism, and exchange theory. What types of things would each perspective be interested in finding out? What types of answers might each perspective reach?

2. Select a controversial policy debate that exists today, other than the one discussed in this chapter (school prayer) and examine how various theoretical perspectives in sociology can be used to explain the opposing views in the debate.

Evolutionary Theory

The evolutionary approach is associated with biological concepts and concerned with long-term change. **Evolutionary theory** suggests that societies, like biological organisms, progress through stages of increasing complexity. Like ecologists, evolutionists suggest that societies, also like organisms, are interdependent with their environments.

Most of the early sociologists and some recent ones adhere to an evolutionary view. Early sociologists often equated evolution with progress and improvement, believing that natural selection would eliminate weak societies and those that could not adapt. The strong societies, they believed, deserved to survive because they were better. It was for this reason that early theorists such as Spencer opposed any sort of interference that would protect the weak and interfere with natural evolutionary processes.

Contemporary evolutionists, on the other hand, rarely oppose all types of intervention. They tend to view evolution as a process that results in change, but they do not assume that the changes are necessarily for the better. Almost all would agree that society is becoming more complex, for example, but they might argue that the complexity brings about bad things as well as good. The telephone is a good illustration of a technological improvement that makes our lives more complex. Surely it is an improvement—it permits us to be in contact with the whole world without stirring from our homes—but a contemporary evolutionist might point out that a phone can also be an annoyance, as students trying to study and harried office workers can attest. Early evolutionists, on the other hand, would have been more likely to regard the telephone as a sign of progress and hence an unmixed blessing.

Evolutionary theory provides us with a historical and cross-cultural perspective from which to judge a wide range of social influences. If its basic premises of directional change and increasing complexity are valid, it should provide better comprehension of current trends and even help us to predict the future.

APPLYING EVOLUTIONARY THEORY

Although evolutionary theory is concerned mostly with long-term macro change, it applies to short-term sociological phenomena as well. For example, to a professional sociologist, city planning is not merely a matter of creating space to accommodate more people but also entails the organization of buildings and space so that the evolving needs of the population will be met as society grows more complex. Evolutionary theory can be used by sociologists in the workplace, then, to make sure that there is a balance between the relative complexity of the parts of a system and the complexity of the system itself. The city planner, for example, must make sure that the number, size, and arrangement of buildings, schools, parks, and malls are in line with the needs of the entire city. It would not make sense to plan for the construction of new housing developments without also planning for the construction of additional educational facilities to accommodate the increased number of children.

For helping a small business, how could sociologists apply the basic premises of evolutionary theory that (a) over time, social systems become more complex in their diversity, specialization, and interdependence of parts; and (b) the most fit survive? Consider the emergence of many craft businesses (such as pottery, stained glass) entered into by baby-boomers, and jewelry-making that became popular during the 1970s and early 1980s. Many of these small businesses were started by craftspeople who shared an intense interest in making a living by producing a particular craft.

One sociologist (Basirico, 1983, 1986) notes that a typical pattern is followed by contemporary stained-glass artisans. A group of like-minded craftspeople would get together for the purpose of producing and selling stained-glass creations. Often, this took place in out-of-the-way, low-rent locations with little overhead. The common interest and activities and the simple lifestyle associated with the craft were often the basis for starting the business. In time, however, some businesses could not compete and failed, while other artisans' business affairs often became more complex: new locations, larger workplaces, higher rent and overhead, advertising costs, tax bills, different types of clientele with varied needs, and diversification of the business into areas such as selling supplies and giving lessons. As they grew more complex, many of these small businesses also began to experience difficulties, and most closed down after a few years.

Had the artisans used an evolutionary perspective, some of their businesses may have been saved. Remember that evolutionary theory states that systems and the parts of systems become more complex over time. If we look at some of these craft businesses, we see some significant growth in their complexity. However, the roles of the craftspeople themselves did not change that much. In other words, there was no balance between the level of complexity of the business (the system) and the level of complexity of the artisans' roles (the parts of the system). They kept to their simple, undifferentiated, independent tasks, whereas the business—in order to survive—evolved into a system that demanded a specialization of tasks and interdependence among the artisans.

Knowledge of evolutionary theory might also be a useful perspective in your personal life. How, for example, would the theory that social systems move from simple to complex influence your decision about buying or building a house for your family? Often home owners find that the home they bought simply for its attractiveness and decor no longer fits the needs of their family. You might save money and headaches if you realize that families are social systems that evolve and become more complicated over time. Successful architects who design homes (and office buildings) consider more than just their clients' present needs; they also consider the evolving nature of the group for which they are designing.

Although each of the theoretical perspectives has been discussed separately with regard to how they can be applied, it is important to note that in most cases, more than one can be used, and some may even be used in conjunction with each other. It should also be noted that even though some of the applications discussed might not be exactly what the people who originally devised the theories had in mind, this does not lessen the validity of these applications. On the contrary, using scientific theories in ways that extend beyond their original purpose demonstrates the significance of the theories. A number of additional theoretical orientations are discussed briefly to conclude this section.

Additional Theoretical Perspectives

The reader should not be led to think that the structural functional, conflict, symbolic interaction, exchange, and evolutionary theories compose all of the theories or theoretical perspectives in sociology. In fact, Ritzer (1999) sees this as a time of theoretical synthesis: an integration of micro and macro ideas, an integration of Marx's ideas into structural functionalism, a joining of exchange and structural theories into a new network theory, and so forth. Ritzer's argument is that many sociological theories are borrowing heavily from one another, with the result that traditionally clear theoretical boundaries are growing increasingly blurred and porous.

Perhaps an example of an older interdisciplinary theoretical linkage can be seen in *sociobiological* orientations. You may have noted that Spencer's ideas of the survival of the fittest, described earlier in this chapter, had a biological base. Today, sociobiological theories link social behavior (crime, drinking, aggression, and so forth) to genetic or biological factors. For example, a sociobiologist would probably explain male sexual dominance or female nurturance by the differing genetic makeup of the sexes. If male–female differences are biologically determined, it could be expected that social influences would not greatly modify behavior. It could also lead to justifying sexual and racial inequalities because "that's the way things are," and little can be done to change them. Yet sociologists note that in spite of biological predispositions toward a particular behavior pattern, wide variations exist in sexual domination, nurturance, and other behaviors generally assigned to one sex or the other. Beliefs that human behaviors can be changed led to other theoretical linkages, such as the two examples that follow: humanistic and feminist theories.

Humanistic theories, consistent with ideas expressed by Marx, reject the positivist position that social science can or should be value free. This perspective is based on the following beliefs and practices: Sociologists or other social scientists should be actively involved in social change; efforts should be made toward achieving social justice and equity for everyone irrespective of gender or race; the mind has "free will"; and humans are in charge of controlling their own destiny. Secular humanism (the solving of problems by humans through their own efforts) disputes the religious focus on a god or on supernatural powers. Sociologists often take a humanistic perspective with a goal of using the knowledge, skills, and tools of sociology to improve social conditions and the lives of those less fortunate.

Feminist theories and perspectives hold the belief that gender is basic to all social structure and organization. The impetus for contemporary feminist theory is a simple question, What about the idea that women interpret and experience the world different from men? Answers to this question are based on beliefs that gender should not be the basis of social inequality, nor should men be more valued in the political arena (as more effective leaders of the country), in the home (as heads of the house), or in the workplace (where they sometimes make more money than women). Early waves of the feminist movement focused on equal rights. Contemporary feminist perspectives include multicultural, liberal, and socialist perspectives, and examine the interlocking systems of racism, sexism, and classism. This "third wave" movement is marked by a desire for personal empowerment.

Other perspectives, such as network theory, existentialism, and phenomenology are generally closely linked to one or more of the perspectives discussed in this chapter. Numerous variations of the major theories are presented throughout the text.

Thinking Sociologically

Discuss the humanists' idea that sociologists should use their knowledge and skills to improve social conditions and the feminists' idea that gender is basic to all social organization and interaction.

SUMMARY

1. Compared with the other sciences, sociology is of recent origin. Not until the 1880s was a scientific methodology applied to social phenomena. The Industrial Revolution and political upheavals in Europe encouraged various scholars to try to explain social change and the social order. Five theorists who had an especially important influence on the development of sociology are Comte, Spencer, Marx, Durkheim, and Weber.

2. Auguste Comte is credited with being the father of sociology. He first called it "social

physics" because he believed that society must be studied in the same scientific manner as the natural sciences. He believed that human progress evolved through three stages: the theological, the metaphysical, and the scientific.

3. Karl Marx, one of the most radical thinkers of his time, made major contributions to our understanding of social conflict. He believed that all history was based on economic determinism, which resulted in class struggles between the rich and powerful bourgeoisie and the working-class proletariat.

4. Emile Durkheim made major contributions to our understanding of social facts. He rejected explanations of social events that assumed that society operated in a fashion parallel to biology. In a classic study, he demonstrated that suicide was related to the degree of involvement in a cohesive group or social unit.

5. Max Weber focused his writings on a new methodology for studying social life. He emphasized the need to focus on subjective meanings—verstehen—in studying human interaction and social systems.

6. The development of sociology in America drew heavily from European writers, especially at the macrosociological level, but America was also very influential in the development of microsociology. Important contributions were made by such sociologists as Cooley, Mead, and Thomas, who stressed the importance of social interaction and the influence of society on human thought and action.

7. Not until the 1930s did sociology shift from the University of Chicago to other major educational institutions. In the eastern United States, Parsons, Merton, Mills, Coser, Homans, and Blau were influential in the development of social theory.

8. A *social theory* is a systematically interrelated proposition that seeks to explain a process or phenomena. Five major theories—three at the macro level and two at the micro level—have had an important influence on contemporary sociology: structural functional theory, conflict theory, symbolic interactional theory, exchange theory, and evolutionary–ecological theory.

9. *Structural functional* theory focuses on the parts of a system, the relationships among these parts, and the functions or consequences of social structures. These functions can be either intended and recognized (*manifest*) or unintended and unrecognized (*latent*). Some consequences are dysfunctional, in that they lead to the instability and breakdown of the system. Structural functional theories assume that systems have a tendency toward equilibrium and balance.

10. *Conflict theory* assumes that conflict is a permanent feature of social life and a key source of change. The Marxist orientation toward conflict assumes that it is rooted in a class struggle between the employers and the workers or between the powerful and the powerless. Many conflict theorists assume that conflict serves an integrative function and acts as a source of constructive change.

11. *Symbolic interactionism*, a micro-level theory, emphasizes relationships among individuals and between individuals and society. According to this theory, society is based on shared meanings, language, social interaction, and symbolic processes. It is the mind that differentiates

humans from nonhumans and permits people to develop a social self, to assume the roles of others, and to imaginatively consider alternative courses of action.

12. *Exchange theory* assumes that social life involves a series of reciprocal exchanges consisting of rewards and costs. Exchange theories endeavor to explain why particular behavioral outcomes result from a given set of structural conditions and interactional possibilities.
13. *Evolutionary theory* suggests that societies, like biological organisms, go through transitions or stages and are interdependent with the environment or world about them.
14. Other theoretical perspectives or orientations include sociobiology, humanism, and feminism. The latter two both reject a positivist notion of total objectivity and noninvolvement and stress instead the need for active involvement in social change.
15. Upon completion of this first part of the book, you will have a clearer understanding of sociology and of the close relationship between theory and research.

KEY TERMS

achieved status A social position, such as teacher, graduate, or wife, obtained through one's own efforts.

ascribed status A social position assigned to a person on the basis of a characteristic over which he or she has no control, such as age, sex, or race.

bourgeoisie The class of people who own the means of production.

Chicago School An approach developed by Cooley, Mead, Thomas, and others in the 1920s that emphasized the importance of social interactions in the development of human thought and action.

class consciousness Awareness among members of a society that the society is stratified.

collective conscience A collective psyche that results from the blending of many individual mentalities, but exists above any one individual.

conflict theory A social theory that views conflict as inevitable and natural and as a significant cause of social change.

dysfunction In structural functional theory, factors that lead to the disruption or breakdown of the social system.

economic determinism The idea that economic factors are responsible for most social change and for the nature of social conditions, activities, and institutions.

evolutionary theory A theory of social development that suggests that societies, like biological organisms, progress through stages of increasing complexity.

exchange theory A theory of interaction that attempts to explain social behavior in terms of reciprocity of costs and rewards.

functional alternatives Alternate ways to achieve an intended goal in order to avoid dysfunctions.

latent functions The unintended consequences of a social system.

law of human progress Comte's notion that all knowledge passes through three successive theoretical conditions: the theological, the metaphysical, and the scientific.

manifest functions The intended consequences of a social system.

middle-range theory A set of propositions designed to link abstract propositions with empirical testing.

proletariat The group in capitalist societies that does not own the means of production and has only labor to sell.

social conflict A view of Karl Marx that social conflict—class struggle due to economic inequality—is at the core of society and the key source of social change.

social dynamics Comte's term for social processes and forms of change.

social facts Reliable and valid items of information about society.

social statics Comte's term for the stable structure of a society.

social system A set of interrelated social statuses and the expectations that accompany them.

structural functionalism The theory that societies contain certain interdependent structures, each of which performs certain functions for the maintenance of society.

symbolic interaction theory The social theory stressing interactions between people and the social processes that occur within the individual that are made possible by language and internalized meanings.

theory A set of logically and systematically interrelated propositions that explain a particular process or phenomenon.

verstehen Understanding human action by examining the subjective meanings that people attach to their own behavior and the behavior of others.

DISCUSSION QUESTIONS

1. Why did early sociologists use natural science terms and methods to describe society? Discuss some shortcomings in following this approach.
2. Spencer's idea of survival of the fittest led to his belief in noninterference in human affairs. Are such hands-off policies appropriate today, in terms of the poor and disadvantaged?
3. Provide some examples of "social facts." How are they separate or different from personal characteristics?
4. Durkheim concluded that suicide was a social phenomenon. Explain.
5. What is your perception of societies "evolving"? Do they always become more complex? Do they always "improve"?
6. Make a list of your ascribed and achieved statuses. Select two, and show how your behavior would differ if your status were different—such as male instead of female or single instead of married.
7. Explore some manifest and latent functions of this sociology course. Do dysfunctional aspects exist as well?
8. How might conflict theory apply to black–white, male–female, or management–labor relationships? Explain, and give examples.
9. Many people get disturbed if someone burns a flag or burns two pieces of wood in the form of a cross on someone's lawn. Why? Consider the

significance of symbols and their meanings in your response.

10. Apply social exchange theory to the interaction between you and your parents or your best friend. What do you offer to them and receive from them? What happens when the social exchanges are not defined as equitable?

11. Discuss how the five theoretical perspectives in this chapter are rooted in the ideas of specific social theorists.

12. Compare how each of the five theoretical perspectives discussed in this chapter would examine the institution of the family.

13. Use Karl Marx's idea of "economic determinism" to compare social life in the United States with social life in a communist country.

14. Discuss aspects of American society that contribute to what Emile Durkheim called a "collective conscience." To what extent does a collective conscience exist in the United States? Discuss how a collective conscience has come to exist in a community, organization, or group to which you belong.

Methods of Studying Society

Ethics in Research and the Role of Institutional Review Boards

Institutional Review Boards (IRBs) are present in almost every college, university, and organization that conducts research on human subjects. The role of an IRB is to oversee research projects in order to protect human subjects from potential harm. In recent years, as the presence and scope of IRBs has increased in academia and other research organizations, there has been much debate about their usefulness and functions, and about the extent to which they help or hinder scientific research (for example, Colombo, 1995; Marshall, 2003; Platter, 2003; Singer and Levine, 2003). Consider the following example and think about the potential consequences, positive or negative, that might have resulted if IRBs had played more of a part at the time the research was conducted.

Philip G. Zimbardo was interested in exploring how the social structure of prisons psychologically affects prison guards and prisoners. He felt that there might be something about the way that relationships are structured within prisons that leads to violence and brutality. In order to find out, he selected two dozen young men to participate as subjects in a study in which a mock prison was set up. According to Zimbardo, "they were mature, emotionally stable, normal, intelligent college students from middle class homes throughout the United States and Canada. They appeared to represent the cream of the crop of [their] generation." Half of the students were assigned to play the role of guard, and half were assigned to play the role of inmate in the mock prison. The experiment was supposed to last for two weeks but was stopped prematurely after only six days because of what was occurring. States Zimbardo,

> The majority had indeed become prisoners or guards, no longer able to clearly differentiate between role playing and self. There were dramatic changes in virtually every aspect of behavior, thinking and feeling. ... We were horrified because we saw some boys (guards) treat others as if they were despicable animals, taking pleasure in cruelty while other boys (prisoners) became servile, dehumanized robots who thought only of escape, of their own individual survival and of their mounting hatred for the guards. (Zimbardo, 1972)

Apparently, Zimbardo was very successful in simulating a prison situation—a situation that was dehumanizing and individually demeaning. From his success, we learn a great deal about the impact of *total institutions*—institutions such as prisons that control every aspect of an individual's life—on individuals. However, the gains from his research were achieved at the psychological expense of the subjects that participated in the study. Research such as this raises a very important issue for social scientists. When and how should social scientists limit their research when developing systematic, verifiable knowledge—knowledge that may ultimately benefit humanity?

A number of ethical issues in research concern social scientists. First are issues related to the use of human subjects. In Zimbardo's research, his goal was to learn more about the way that prisons dehumanize and demean their inhabitants. His goal was certainly worthwhile: In addition to advancing our knowledge of human behavior, such knowledge offers foreseeable practical benefits. For example, this type of knowledge could help us to create corrective institutions that are more likely to rehabilitate prisoners. However, in research that requires the use of human subjects—such as Zimbardo's—scientists must ask whether the purpose of science justifies the research methods that may be involved. Fred Leavitt (1991) poses four important questions related to the use of human subjects: (1) Is it ever appropriate to harm anybody for the advancement of science? (2) Is it ever proper to deceive anybody in the interests of research? (3) Do researchers have the right to invade the privacy of others? (4) Must informed consent of subjects be a prerequisite to research?

A second major category of ethical issues is whether research should be conducted if the knowledge it leads to has the potential for harm or misuse. For example, much sociological research has been conducted about collective behavior and social movements. Much of that research deals with learning about how crowds, mobs, and riots develop and how organized movements for social change come about. While the results of such research adds to our basic understanding of social behavior and could potentially be useful in helping to avoid disaster, it also provides knowledge that potentially could be used to place limits on individual freedom.

A third area of ethical concerns is whether the results of research should be suppressed if publication of the results potentially could be harmful to people. For example, Leavitt (1991, p. 120) comments on how studies of racial differences on intelligence test scores have painfully shaken many people's self concept and had adverse effects on race relations. While such studies could be used to expose cultural and racial biases of intelligence tests, the potential for harm to racial minorities nevertheless exists as the research results become public.

Unfortunately, ethical issues such as the ones raised here cannot be resolved unequivocally. Professional social science organizations—such as the American Sociological Association (ASA), the American Psychological Association, the American Anthropological Association, and others—publish ethical guidelines, and most colleges and universities have IRBs to help social scientists make decisions about their research. A question that remains is: to what extent should final decisions about the well-being of human subjects be left up to individual scientists?

People arrive at their opinions and beliefs through a number of different routes, and notions about reality vary greatly. Some people believe that politicians are crooked, others that they are dedicated public servants. Some believe that hard work will lead to success, others that it is a waste of time and that for them, failure is inevitable.

We get ideas such as these from a number of different sources. We derive some from *everyday experiences* and *common sense:* Our past experiences and personal observations convince us that certain things are true. We see blondes having a good time and are convinced that blondes have more fun. We talk to women who want children and assume that a desire for children is instinctive in women. Experience and common sense may lead others to different conclusions, however.

We get other ideas from *authorities*, people assumed to be knowledgeable because of their experience or position. We may consider the Pope, the President of the United States, our personal physician, our professor, or our parents to be authority figures. We seldom bother to investigate the source of their expertise or the information they used to reach their conclusions because we feel that their information is not subject to question. Like ideas derived from common sense, however, the opinions of authorities may differ. The conclusions of one physician are not always identical to those of another. Even our parents sometimes disagree with each other and often disagree with other parents.

A third source of ideas or knowledge is *revelation*. Revelation may be thought to result from divine experiences, prayer, or magic. Knowledge acquired through revelation is often considered sacred and absolute, so it is not subject to question. Some people, for example, believe that wives should submit to their husbands' authority because the Bible says that they should do so.

A fourth source of ideas is *tradition*. The wisdom of previous generations is passed on and accepted as accurate. We may plant corn by the phase of the moon and take a sip of brandy to cure a chest cold. Why? Because that's the way it's always been done.

A fifth source of knowledge is *research* that uses empirical methods. Some sociologists do not reject personal experience, common sense, authority, revelation, and tradition as sources of knowledge, but most rely heavily on methods considered empirical or scientific. Empirical methods focus on observable phenomena, which means that others should be able to observe the same phenomena and check our observations for accuracy. Unlike the common-sense observations made as part of our daily experience, however, researchers using empirical methods strive to be objective. In this chapter, we consider the use of scientific methods in sociology. We also examine standards of scientific inquiry, types of sociological research, research methods, and the process of research.

Many students are apprehensive about studying research methods, for a few reasons. First, they often equate research methods with advanced mathematics and statistics. In reality, much advanced sociological analysis does employ statistics, but most sociological research and analysis is accomplished with only an elementary knowledge of statistics, and some uses no statistics at all.

A second reason students give for not wanting to study research methods is the belief that these methods are relevant only to sociologists. This is simply not true. All persons in society are affected by their knowledge (or lack of it) of basic principles of research methods. To know nothing about the scientific method is to be a victim of false claims about products and ideas when being exposed to advertising in newspapers, on TV, or from any source. It is also important to know where and how to gain access to legitimate research results when making personal decisions and choices.

We hope that after reading this chapter, you will see the relevance of research methods in all areas of your life and that you will at least begin to sense some of the exciting discoveries and insights that sociological research has to offer.

Thinking Sociologically

Of the five sources from which we gain our ideas, which would you say were most influential in what you know about (a) human sexuality, (b) life after death, and (c) communism? Why are the sources likely to be different? Which are likely to be the most correct?

IS SOCIOLOGY A SCIENCE?

Comte, Spencer, and other early sociologists regarded their new discipline as a science. The natural sciences had successfully formulated laws, principles, and theories about the physical world through the use of the **scientific method**, a procedure that involved systematically formulating problems, collecting data through observation and experiment, and devising and testing hypotheses. Early social theorists believed that the same method could be used to develop laws, principles, and theories about the social world. There was also a practical reason for adopting science as the model of inquiry. The Western world, particularly the United States, has regarded science as almost sacred. Sociologists seeking legitimacy for their new discipline wished to convey to a skeptical world that they too could be objective, systematic, precise, and predictive in their field of study. They also hoped to develop a social technology that could be used to direct change and resolve social problems.

Not everyone regards sociology as a science, however. Some contend that, defined strictly, science does not include the descriptions, hunches, opinions, and statistical tendencies of sociology. It has also been argued that human behavior is too complex and unpredictable to be studied scientifically and that sociology is too young a discipline to have developed a body of laws and principles like those found in the natural sciences. An additional criticism is that sociologists are part of the societies they observe, which makes it extremely difficult for them to prevent bias from affecting their perceptions.

Defenders of sociology as a science assert that any subject may seem complex to an untrained observer and that people have been engaging in the study and practice of sociology on an informal basis for thousands of years. In response to the criticism that sociologists must be biased because of their closeness to their subject matter, it can be argued that they can be objective by separating themselves from the subject, by repeating studies using multiple observers, and by making cross-cultural and historical comparisons. Thus, although one can argue correctly that many sociologists are biased, naive, simplistic, limited in cultural perspective, and bound by the present, this type of argument tells us little about whether sociology can be considered a science.

How then does one proceed? To determine whether sociology is a science, we have to rephrase the question, asking what distinguishes the scientific mode of inquiry from nonscientific modes of inquiry. Can sociology and the other social sciences follow the scientific mode? To answer this question, we consider the nature of scientific theories and standards of scientific inquiry.

THE COMPONENTS OF SCIENTIFIC THEORY

Theories are attempts to find patterns and consistencies in seemingly idiosyncratic and inconsistent events. Good theories are a key source of ideas for researchers to test; the information they discover through testing may be used in turn to modify and refine the theory. The building blocks of theories are concepts and variables, conceptual frameworks, and propositions and hypotheses.

Concepts and Variables

A **concept** is an abstract system of meaning that enables us to perceive a phenomenon in a particular way. This may sound complex and difficult, but it really is not. Concepts are simply tools that permit us to share meanings. Most of the terms in the glossary are sociological concepts: norm, status, stratification, group, mob, folkway, and so on. The concept of "stratification," for example, represents a particular type of inequality that exists in society; developing the concept made it possible for people to think and communicate about the social differentiation of people by wealth, gender, age, social position, and other characteristics.

When concepts can have two or more degrees or values, they are referred to as **variables**. For example, *husband* is a concept, and *years married* is a variable. *Dollar* is a concept; *level of income* is a variable. Years of marriage and level of income can both vary, but the meanings of the words *husband* and *dollar* remain constant.

Propositions and Hypotheses

A **proposition** is a statement about the nature of some phenomenon. It generally consists of a statement about the relationship between two or more variables. The statement "Social activity is related to student grades" would be a proposition. If this proposition is formulated so that it can be tested, it is considered a **hypothesis**. A testable hypothesis would be "Students who attend more than one social activity per week have higher grade point averages than those who do not." Thus, hypotheses are a type of proposition that indicate how the stated relations can be tested.

Frequently, as in the preceding example, a hypothesis states that if one variable changes in some regular fashion, a predictable change will occur. Thus, as social activity goes up, grade point averages are proposed to go up. This is known as a **direct relationship. Inverse relationships** are also possible—for example, "As social activity goes up, grade point averages go down." Hypotheses that involve direct or inverse relationships are *directional hypotheses. Null hypotheses*, which state that there is no relationship between the variables of interest, can also be formulated: "There is no relationship between social activity and grade point averages."

Theory

A **theory** is a set of logically interrelated propositions that explains some process or set of phenomena in a testable fashion. A good theory should be stated in abstract terms and should allow predictions to be made. Theories also serve as important sources of new hypotheses.

There are many theories to explain crime, for example. Early explanations were based on biological theories, and propositions were established that attempted to relate crime to the shape of the head, the size of the body, or chromosome abnormalities. Some psychological theories of crime led to propositions linking criminal activity to emotional immaturity, a particular personality type, or a mental defect or illness. Sociologists have developed theories of crime based on social and cultural factors. These theories have led to propositions and testable hypotheses linking crime with social inequality, socialization or learning experiences, disorganization in the social order, and lack of effective societal controls. All these theories are sets of interrelated propositions that attempt to explain crime or some criminal activity. A theory provides direction in what we study and enables us to develop hypotheses that we can test.

The formulation of theories is just one aspect of the scientific method. Measured against this standard alone, sociology would certainly be considered a science. Most sociologists are keenly aware of the importance of organizing concepts, testing hypotheses, and developing theories. In addition to using this framework for their investigations, however, scientists adhere to a number of widely accepted standards of inquiry.

THE STANDARDS OF SCIENTIFIC INQUIRY

Objectivity

The scientific standard of objectivity asserts that in the study of any phenomenon—social or nonsocial—the personal biases and values of the people doing the research must never influence the data reported or the interpretation of results. The political, religious, racial, or other beliefs of the investigators should in no way determine the findings of a study. Two independent researchers who study the same phenomenon should produce identical results regardless of their differences in status, belief, or personal behavior.

Whether totally objective research, social or nonsocial, is possible has been seriously questioned. Even in the "hard" sciences, such as physics and biology, what is studied and the interpretation of data have been shown to be influenced by subjective factors. In the social sciences, the literature from social psychology shows that people's interests and perceptions are influenced by their social background, social class, level of education, and numerous other factors. It also indicates that they are selective in what they perceive, remember, and report. Male and female researchers studying marriage often report different perceptions of the same married couple. Sociologists studying race relations have found that a journalistic account of an event by a black writer differs from an account of the same event by a white writer. It is argued that human beings cannot be totally objective.

If absolute objectivity is to be regarded as a requirement, then most disciplines, including sociology, can be dismissed from the realm of scientific inquiry. There are, however, many procedures for minimizing the level of subjectivity. One procedure is to recognize the influence of existing biases and assumptions and to strive to eliminate the influence of those we can control. Another procedure is to base research on a particular theory and to test it by seeking evidence that could either support or reject it. Other methods of minimizing the level of bias and subjectivity are discussed in the following sections on the other standards of science and the scientific method.

Replication

The scientific standard of replication asserts that research should be conducted and reported in such a way that someone else can duplicate it. The use of similar subjects and measuring procedures under similar conditions should produce results virtually identical to those of the original study. Thus, another way to reduce investigator bias is to have identical or similar studies undertaken by people who have differing biases and personal values.

In the physical sciences, replication of studies under identical conditions is often easier than it is in the social sciences, but even in the physical sciences, it is sometimes impossible to recreate identical conditions. A California earthquake or a space shuttle explosion cannot be duplicated. In the social sciences, the problems of replication are compounded by human factors. Some studies may be impossible to duplicate because of the nature of the problems studied. It would not be possible, for example, to duplicate studies of the reactions of East and West Germans on the day the Berlin Wall was opened and came down, or to duplicate studies of the residents of a particular town destroyed by flood or fire. It is possible, however, to perform studies on the residents of other communities or on other citizens who are granted freedom from a particular type of governmental or social repression and to note patterns of psychological adjustment, points of greatest stress, changes in kin and child relationships, or other conditions. The principle of replication of studies is based on the conviction that similar conditions and circumstances should produce highly similar results.

Precision of Measurement

The scientific standard of precision of measurement asserts that the phenomenon being studied should be measured in precise, reliable, and valid ways. The more accurate our measurements, the better we are able to test our ideas about the social world. An ability to test or study anything, whether it be height, a religious practice, or a theory, is in large part dependent on the ability to measure it accurately. Theories could be debated endlessly without progress if no one determined how to observe and measure the ideas or concepts central to them. For example, no one has developed a precise, reliable, or valid measurement of the influence of angels, so there is no way to prove or disprove their existence.

Some concepts or variables are much easier to measure than others. We may all agree on how to measure the number of males and females in a room, because we know how to measure quantities of people and how to determine gender, but how would we proceed with a study of the relationship between gender and happiness? *Happiness* is an abstract term that means different things to different people, and opinions would vary on how to measure it. In general, the more abstract a variable is and the further it is removed from direct observation, the more difficult it is to reach a consensus on how it should be measured. This is not to say that the variable *happiness* cannot be measured—it can.

The process of arriving at a means of measuring a concept or variable is referred to as *operationalization*. In this procedure, the sociologist selects quantitative indicators of an abstract concept, determining what will be observed and how it will be measured. In the preceding example, this would involve determining some criteria for assessing happiness. We might decide that happiness is whatever the individuals themselves think it is and simply ask them whether they are happy or not, or ask them to rate their own happiness on a five-point scale. On the other hand, we might decide that factors such as absence of depression, high levels of self-esteem, or the ability to function successfully are indicators of happiness and attempt to measure those. Although opinions may differ on whether the criteria selected actually reflect happiness, the operationalization of the definition ensures that we understand the term *happiness* and thus know what it is that we are measuring. An **operational definition**, then, is a definition of a concept or variable such that it can be measured during research. Operationalization makes an abstract variable measurable and observable and permits another researcher to objectively replicate our study. This process also improves the precision of our measurements.

SOCIOLOGY AND SCIENCE

Now that we have discussed some of the methods and attributes of scientific inquiry, we can return to our original question. Should sociology be considered a science? Like many questions, this one cannot be answered with a simple yes or no. The issue is not so much whether sociology is a science, but to what extent it is pursued with scientific modes of inquiry. According to the criteria we have discussed, some sociological studies would certainly be regarded as scientific. A sociologist studying the correlation between age at marriage and divorce rates would develop operational definitions and precise measurements to objectively examine the marriage and divorce phenomena in a replicable study. Studying a problem such as the relationship between gender and happiness might have to use methods that, strictly speaking, would not be considered scientific. In short, the techniques used by sociologists range from those that meet the strictest standards of scientific inquiry to those that, although still useful, fall short of that standard.

Now that we have discussed the basic procedures of science and sociology, we can turn our attention more specifically to research methods and the logic of proof.

TYPES OF SOCIOLOGICAL RESEARCH

The distinction between scientific and unscientific sociology can be clarified by examining the methods used to prove a hypothesis. One criterion that social scientists use to evaluate theories and propositions is the extent to which they can be empirically researched. This research is of three basic types: descriptive, explanatory, and evaluative.

Descriptive Research

Descriptive research describes social reality or provides facts about the social world. A descriptive study would be undertaken to determine whether people who have served time in prison have more trouble finding jobs than people who have not been in prison, or to determine what percentage of college students use various forms of drugs and how frequently.

All descriptive studies share the goal of providing data on *social facts*, which are reliable and valid items of information about society. A *fact* could be a *behavior* (John scored three touchdowns), an *attitude* (women want equal pay for equal work), a *law* (the speed limit is 55), or even a *statistic* (the median married couple income in 2001 was $30,116). The information must be reliable and valid. **Reliability** is the extent to which repeated observations of the same phenomenon yield similar results. **Validity** is the extent to which observations actually yield measures of what they are supposed to measure. For example, if a bathroom scale registers different weights each time you step on it, it is not reliable. If it gives the same weight each time but it is not an accurate measure, the bathroom scale may be *reliable* (same results each time) but not *valid* (inaccurate weight). A common problem with research validity is that critics question whether the measurement instrument actually measures what it is supposed to measure. For example, on the bathroom scale, if the scale reliably and accurately determined your height, it would not be valid as a measurement of your weight. For a measure of your weight to be considered a fact, the scales must be both reliable (consistent) and valid (accurate measure of the factor or characteristic). A key goal of descriptive research is to provide an accurate view of social reality by providing social facts that are both valid and reliable.

One particular type of descriptive research that is growing in popularity among social scientists is called **ethnography**. Ethnography has always been the primary form of investigation in anthropological research and has always been a valued method of research for sociologists as well. Indeed, Max Weber's notion of *verstehen*, sympathetic understanding (discussed in Chapter 2), is testimony to the value that sociologists have placed on ethnographic research since the earliest days of the discipline. Ethnography is a method of studying the social and cultural dimensions of human interaction. It is a form of research focusing on the sociology of meaning through close observation of sociocultural phenomena. Its goal is to understand communities and cultures from an insider's perspective, and then translate that understanding to outsiders. Ethnography focuses on what people do in face-to-face interactions and depends heavily on participation, observation, and interviewing. This methodology is grounded in the same principles behind experiential learning—that we can learn and interpret the world as much by doing as by rational analysis. Typically, ethnographers select informants (or "consultants") who are known to have an overview of the activities of the communities they are studying. Ethnography is as useful for studying local communities as it is for "exotic" foreign ones. It can also usefully be applied to assessing and addressing problems and needs in particular cultures. With ethnography, one might study the stereotypes of tattoo parlors, unsafe working conditions among Latino farmworkers, economic dependency in Belize's tourist trade, or the world of professional bodybuilders. Ethnography employs multiple methods such as interviewing, observation, and participant observation in order to obtain clarification and deeper understanding of what it means to be a member of the community or culture that is being studied (Goodall, 2000; Marshall and Roshmann, 1999).

APPLYING DESCRIPTIVE RESEARCH

There are many different types of descriptive studies, which cover many different topics and are used in many different ways. However, all of them answer questions regarding who, what, where, when, how often, and how many. Who is victimized by particular types of crimes or wrongdoing? What are the needs of a particular community for a new park? Where do people prefer to shop? When are people most likely to watch TV? How often do people buy a new car? How many people favor a particular presidential candidate? What is the level of morale of employees in an organization? To clarify these potential applications, we take an example of a descriptive study and look at how it can be used.

One study was done to determine how often and how seriously airline flight attendants are physically or verbally assaulted on routine air travel (Salinger et al., 1985). The researchers found not only that the problem is widespread but also that it occurs most during weekends in December. How is this particular research useful? First, academic sociologists might use it to develop theories and explanations about social behavior in general. What does the information found in this study tell sociologists about crowd behavior? How does time of year affect social behavior? What is the impact of fear (such as fear of flying) on human behavior? How does being in a confined area (an airplane) affect relationships? One study alone cannot lead to such generalities, but it could be used to support other theories or as a starting point for new ones.

Second, professional sociologists employed by a specific airline (say, "Friendly Sky Airways") might use the findings of that study to help plan administrative policies that would improve efficiency or would minimize assault, or they might conduct similar studies to find out how much assault occurs in "Friendly Sky Airways." Are there other forms of victimization in "Friendly Sky Airways" that management should know about? When, for example, is passenger luggage most likely to be reported lost? Are there times when passengers themselves might be at greater risk of crime (for example, victims of pickpocketing) in the airport terminal? Sociologists could use this and other information to make recommendations that would help airlines improve their services in the highly competitive air travel industry.

Third, the study could be used by many nonsociologists working in air travel. Travel agents could use it to minimize discomfort for their clients (and thus increase their business) by booking flights during more peaceful hours. Airport security could use it to determine the amount of police protection needed at various times. Flight attendants could use it to be aware of the periods when passengers are more irritable and to be more sensitive to them during those times. Finally, in making your own travel plans, knowing when these kinds of assaults or other types of annoying situations (lost luggage, etc.) are likely to occur could be useful to you personally.

Explanatory Research

Explanatory research attempts to explain why things do or do not happen. Why do people with prison records have trouble finding jobs? What factors are related to students using drugs? Questions such as these are concerned with the problem of causation. What factors make a designated phenomenon happen or change? What is the cause of a given effect?

In all scientific studies, the variable that is presumed to cause an effect is known as the independent variable. The variable that is presumed to be affected by the **independent variable** is the **dependent variable**. In a study of child abuse, the abuse itself would be the dependent variable, the effect; the causes of child abuse—perhaps such factors as stress and the parents' own childhood experiences of having been abused—would be the independent variables. In a medical study, lung cancer (effect) could be the dependent variable and smoking (cause) the independent variable.

The same variable may be independent in one context and dependent in another. In a study of the causes of divorce, for example, divorce would be considered the dependent variable (effect), and the causes of divorce, the independent variable. In a study of factors that influence job performance, however, divorce might be found to be an independent variable (a cause), and job performance (the effect) the dependent variable.

Sometimes, the independent variables are known, and the investigator focuses on dependent variables. A study of this sort was undertaken to determine whether soldiers exposed to atomic fallout during nuclear tests suffered any ill effects. The cause, or independent variable (nuclear radiation), was known, and the effect, or dependent variable, was being investigated: Did these soldiers develop health problems?

In other cases, dependent variables are known, and investigators focus on independent variables. Studies of this sort were undertaken at various sites in Michigan, New York, and other states. The investigators knew that farm animals were dying, that meat was being contaminated, and that people in particular areas were suffering from a number of health problems; that is, they knew the effect, the dependent variable. They had to search for the independent variable, the cause of the health problems. They found that the farms and homes in these areas were located near waste disposal dumps in which toxic substances had been discarded and that the residue was causing serious health problems.

When a clear relationship in time exists between an independent and dependent variable, they are easy to distinguish. The independent variable (cause) must precede the dependent variable (effect). Lung cancer does not cause smoking. In the social sciences, however, cause and effect are sometimes hard to distinguish clearly. Do sexual problems cause marital problems, for example, or do marital problems cause sexual problems?

To establish a cause–effect relationship, researchers must establish an association between two variables. Variables that are not associated cannot be causally related. The age of one's grandparents is not related to one's driving ability—obviously, neither one causes the other. Even when two variables can be associated, however, it is not safe to assume that one causes the other. Hours of daylight begin to increase at the same time that the rate of drowning begins to increase, but it would be absurd to argue that one causes the other. Thus, we can see that there must also be a logical rationale for relating two variables before they can be considered to have a cause–effect relationship.

APPLYING EXPLANATORY RESEARCH

Explanatory (or analytical) studies and descriptive studies are similar, in that they both provide useful information about social reality. The primary difference between them is that explanatory studies are also concerned with answering the question "Why?" Explanatory research answers the question "Why?" by discovering the independent variable (the cause or event that precedes the behavior in question). It may be true that assault against airline attendants is higher on weekends in December, but what are the conditions that precede or lead to this kind of behavior (that is, what are the independent variables associated with assault)? Is it because flights are overbooked more often during those times? Or is it because younger people are more likely to travel then? Are the people that drink alcohol during the flight more likely to commit assault or less likely? Does assault occur more often on longer or on shorter flights? Does it occur more often in first class or in coach? In other words, what causes the behavior—in this case, the assault?

Like descriptive studies, explanatory studies are the essential material out of which academic sociologists construct their theories. Suppose that explanatory research was conducted to find out the socioeconomic position of people who supported a particular presidential candidate. This information could help academic sociologists to construct general theories and explanations about the relationship between social class and voting behavior in general. However, this information is also useful for those involved in planning political campaigns. Does this mean that applied social research (research studies conducted by professional sociologists in the workplace) and academic ("basic") research are exactly the same? At times, yes, the same studies could be used in different ways. However, a major difference between academic (basic) research and applied research is that sociologists doing research in the workplace are focusing on variables that are of specific interest to specific clients. The primary goal of professional sociologists in the workplace is to help a particular client find out what leads to or what is the result of particular actions or situations.

Knowing what precedes (or causes) a particular type of behavior is important for two major reasons: It helps us to predict behavior, and it helps us to control behavior. Think of the power that kind of knowledge can give you! As a manager, you may be able to control the rate of personnel turnover by finding out what causes employee dissatisfaction. By discovering what leads to higher worker morale you might be able to stimulate greater employee production of goods and services. By knowing what attracts people to a product, you might be able to create better marketing devices. Advertising and marketing rely heavily on these kinds of studies. Most TV commercials provide very little product information, if any. Rather, they appeal to particular types of people who will use specific types of products under given types of circumstances. By finding out, for example, that most people who drink beer do so at the end of a day or after long arduous tasks (except college students, of course), the advertisers for the Miller Brewing Company created "Miller Time." Thus, many people at the end of "a long hard day" may drink Miller not because they have any idea whatsoever about the quality of the beer, but merely because it is "Miller Time."

There are many types of descriptive and explanatory studies. Although it is not very likely that most of you will become sociologists, it is very likely that most of you will do or use descriptive and explanatory research as part of your job or in your personal life. As a sales representative for a beverage distributor, you will need to know where to find the highest rates of soft-drink consumption. As a display manager in a department store, you will need to find out what stimulates customers to remain in a store. As a physician opening up a new practice, you will have to find the locations that have the highest rates of illness in your specialty, and to discover what makes people feel at ease in a medical office.

A third kind of sociological research that has come to be known more for its applications in the workplace than for its use in academic sociology is evaluation research.

Evaluation Research

Evaluation research measures how well a program or project works in relation to its goals. It determines the extent to which the intended goals are being met and provides a basis for deciding to continue, alter, or eliminate a program. Does the mandatory seat-belt law actually save lives? Does the law that requires a minimum legal drinking age of 21 years reduce drunk driving? Does a mandatory class-attendance policy lead to better grades? Some researchers feel that evaluation research "is the bread and butter of applied social science" (Finsterbusch and Mars, 1980, p. 119). It is one of the most widely used types of research in the workplace.

Evaluation research includes two types of studies: outcome evaluations and field experiments.

Outcome evaluations assess the effects of an organization's existing policies, programs, or projects. Administrators of a project, program, or policy that is already set in motion may need to know how successful it is and whether it is achieving the intended goals. For example, do social programs such as the Personal Responsibility and Work Opportunity Reconciliation Act, formally Aid to Families with Dependent Children (AFDC) actually help poor people improve their situation, or do they create a cycle of dependency, keeping people down? Conversely, evaluation studies may precede the implementation of a program, project, or policy to help determine whether it will produce the intended results. *Field experiments* are test situations created to include the actual conditions proposed by a policy, program, or project. The purpose of these test situations is to determine the effects of a new or proposed policy, program, or project. Before passing a law that would require corporations to provide child care for the children of working parents, this policy might be tried in a few corporations to evaluate the cost of such a policy and its effects on worker performance.

Evaluation research is one of many ways in which people engage in evaluation. Politicians, journalists, concerned citizens, and others often try to evaluate the worth of a program informally and subjectively. *Evaluation research* describes only systematic and objective methods of data collection and analysis. It uses the same methodological techniques of descriptive and explanatory research and often utilizes the findings of descriptive and explanatory studies to make its recommendations. If the results of descriptive research tell you that the number of drunk drivers is greater now than before the new minimum age law went into effect, for example, what does that tell you about the effectiveness of the law itself?

There are four steps involved in systematic evaluation research: specification, measurement, analysis, and recommendation (Gones, 1984). Specification is the first and most important step. It means defining or identifying the goals to be met by the program, policy, or project. The goal of sex-education programs, for example, may be to reduce teen pregnancies. If that is the goal of sex education, then the basis for evaluating these programs must be the degree to which the programs reduce the rate of teen pregnancies. The program should *not* be judged on the basis of whether teens continue to engage in premarital sex. Clearly, it is imperative that the goal of the program being evaluated be fully understood before going any further in the research.

The *measurement* is the way in which the researchers collect the information needed to evaluate the specified goal. This can be done through surveys, interviews, observation, secondary analysis, or experimentation. (These techniques are described later in this chapter, in the section on sociological research methods.) To measure the rates of teen pregnancies, a researcher might compare city hospital records on this subject for the years before and after a citywide sex-education program went into effect. Perhaps a survey of teens that asks them whether they regularly use birth control could be done to compare high schools with sex-education programs and those without them.

Analysis, the third step in evaluation research, is the use of the information collected in the measurement stage to draw conclusions. Methods of analysis range from very complex to very simple. That is, sometimes, analysis may involve sophisticated statistical analysis of the data collected, and at other times, it may involve a simple interpretation of descriptive findings, depending on the specific research involved. Suppose that, in our evaluation of sex-education programs, we found that teen pregnancies in some participating schools increased, and in some schools, they decreased. A simple interpretation of the data here would not work. It would probably be necessary to determine whether there were other variables that account for the teen pregnancy rate, such as age of students in the school, socioeconomic status, or religion. However, if it turned out that the number of teen pregnancies declined in every school that had a sex-education program and went up in every school that did not have such a program, without doing any complex statistical analysis, it would be fairly safe to assume that the program works.

Recommendation is the final stage of evaluation research. This refers to the advice that is given, based on the analysis, regarding what should be done. Should the program continue as is, are there particular changes that should be made, or should the program be eliminated altogether? An analysis of the sex-education program might find that teen pregnancies are reduced most when birth control devices are actually brought into class and students are instructed in how to use them, but that in programs where such devices are merely discussed or described, there is no change in the number of pregnancies. In this case, the researcher might recommend that all sex-education courses include exposure to actual birth control devices and specific instructions on how to use them.

APPLYING EVALUATION RESEARCH

Evaluation research can be used to determine the effectiveness of any purposeful activity. Practically all of the human and public service fields regularly use evaluation research. It is primarily done by professional sociologists and other social scientists for social service organizations, government agencies, politicians, city planning departments, schools, hospitals, and other such organizations. However, the results of the research are used also by many nonsociologists, such as college administrators, politicians, social workers, hospital administrators, and teachers.

Another use of evaluation research is in the commercial world. An advertising company needs to know whether its campaigns are attracting the clientele they are after. Grocery stores may need to know whether their policy to stay open 24 hours a day is increasing profits. More customers may be shopping there, but perhaps not enough to cover the increased costs of remaining open.

Although evaluation research is done primarily by professional sociologists and other social scientists, it is likely that at some point you will conduct some evaluation research of your own in your occupation. As a teacher, you may need to assess whether your innovative techniques are actually attracting students to your courses and holding students' attention more or whether these techniques are frightening students away and distracting them in class. As a dentist, you might want to determine whether your informal attire in the office makes your younger patients more comfortable, or whether it is perceived as a lack of professionalism and a lack of caring. As an automobile sales representative, you may need to find out whether your friendly, personal approach with customers puts them at ease or makes them distrust you. Very often, finding out the answers to these questions before you actually implement your plan can save you much time, trouble, and money.

Evaluation research might also benefit you in your personal life. Although this would not be as formal or as methodologically sophisticated as that done by professional sociologists or by someone as part of his or her job, you will still probably need to do it at some point. You may do it to evaluate your educational plans, career plans, investment strategies, or even the way you are raising your children. Will getting your M.B.A. or Ph.D. actually improve your chances of getting a better job and a higher salary? Upon carefully evaluating the situation, you might find that further education could actually hurt your chances of getting an entry-level position. Will the jobs that require these degrees be available when you complete your education? Does the particular employer you would like to work for really want someone with an M.B.A., or will this degree overqualify you for the job you want? Would you be better off starting work right after college? Will the money lost due to time not working and the cost of tuition be balanced out by any income that you might make after you receive your degree? How long will it take you to make up the difference?

You might ask similar questions regarding your personal investments. It may seem, for example, that putting money in the bank every month increases your savings. However, are you spending more on interest in credit card payments than the interest you are getting in the bank? In childrearing, will your strict rules regarding what your children can and cannot do lead them to become mature, independent people, or will they make them dependent, rebellious, and uncreative? Clearly, there are many ways that you will use evaluation research in your personal life. You may have thought of many others already.

How do sociologists go about their research, whether it be descriptive, explanatory, or evaluative? How do they determine facts, associations, cause–effect relationships, or the effectiveness of programs? What procedures do they use to observe and generalize in a scientific manner? Some of the methods used in sociological research are reviewed in the following section.

Thinking Sociologically

1. Should the social sciences be held to the same standards of scientific inquiry as the biological and physical sciences? Why or why not?
2. Select a topic for study, such as cohabitation, female employment, or busing. What types of questions could be answered with descriptive, explanatory, and evaluation research?

SOCIOLOGICAL RESEARCH METHODS

Sociological research involves two types of methods: qualitative and quantitative. **Qualitative methods** are used to determine the essential characteristics, properties, or processes of something or someone. Rather than desiring to count how many, how much, or how often, qualitative researchers may attempt to study conditions or processes such as how police make a decision to arrest someone, the reactions or responses of a spouse or parent to the loss of a loved one, or the processes used in obtaining illegal drugs. This type of research often involves *case studies* (detailed studies of individuals or of small groups of individuals, such as a family) and *participant observation*, in which the observer takes part in the activity being observed.

Quantitative methods are designed to obtain numbers or amounts of something: the median age at marriage, the range of incomes, or crime rates, for example. To quantify is to count, to determine frequencies, to measure amounts, or to state something in mathematical or statistical terms. This type of research often involves surveys or experiments.

Today, both qualitative and quantitative research are widely used, with both recognized within the discipline as legitimate methods of social research. However, many sociologists demand "hard" facts and rigorously gathered data and consider only these data to be what they regard as "real science"; they question the validity of impressions, interpretive descriptions, or "soft" data. On the other hand, many feminists would argue that numbers and hard data are viewed as masculine and that masculinity means power and superiority. Verbal descriptions, relational and emotional skills, and soft data are seen as feminine, and femininity is viewed as weak and inferior. One consequence of such a view is reflected (quantitatively) in the greater difficulty of getting qualitative research published in the leading sociological and social science journals (Bakanic et al., 1987; Grant et al., 1987).

Ideas such as these should not blind us to the benefits gained from both qualitative and quantitative research. Throughout the research process, careful consideration must be given to the range of alternative methods or procedures that might meet one's objectives, and a variety of suitable procedures and methods do exist. Expense, facilities, access to people with computer and statistical skills, time, research objectives, and other factors will influence the choices made. By carefully choosing a research design and methods, a great deal of time and money can be saved, and the research can be conducted more efficiently. Observation studies, survey research, experimental designs, and secondary analysis are the research options considered most often.

Observation Studies

One qualitative method of obtaining information about social processes is through **observational research**. The researcher or research team watches what is happening and makes no attempt to control, modify, or influence the ongoing activity. The researcher systematically observes what is happening, and the focus is specifically on the variables or dimensions defined by the hypotheses, propositions, or theory.

Systematic observations may take several forms. One type is the *laboratory observation*, in which the sociologist controls the environment in which a particular activity takes place. Sometimes one-way windows are used to reduce the chances that the activity will be influenced by the researcher. This technique might be employed to study how aggression in children's play is influenced by their watching violence on television or to explore interactions between men and women in a small group. Laboratory observations are most likely to be confined to the work of academic sociologists for the purpose of developing theories or explanations of particular types of behavior.

A second type of observation takes place in a natural setting rather than in a laboratory. Often termed *field observation*, this type is done by the researcher "on location." For example, the researcher might observe student behavior in a classroom or the interactions between salespeople and customers at a store.

Observation as a research technique is used by sociologists doing both descriptive and explanatory research. To better understand how the judicial system works in our country, for example, a sociologist might observe proceedings in traffic court. By observing this natural setting in a systematic way, the sociologist might collect data to describe how many people are tried on a typical day, the number of males and females, the ages of the defendants, and the types of punishments received. With these data, the sociologist might try to explain the relationship between particular variables—say, age of defendants and severity of punishment. Is there a relationship between how old a person is and the type of punishment he or she receives?

It is likely that you will have reason to use various observation techniques at different times in your life. Imagine, for example, that you decide to open a restaurant near a college. Before you make any major decisions about how you are going to run or design the restaurant, you might spend some time observing similar types of restaurants in other college towns, or you might spend time on a college campus observing what students like or dislike. This could help you make decisions on the kind of decor to use, the type of music to play, the type of food to serve, and the type of clothing the food servers should wear.

You may even use observation in your personal life. As a new parent, you may learn a great deal from observing how other parents deal with their infants. As a new student entering college, you probably learned quite a bit about how you are supposed to act, speak, think, feel, eat, and drink by observing sophomores, juniors, and seniors.

A third observation technique is *participant observation*, in which the researcher is an active participant in the event being studied. Anthropologists frequently use this method to study a particular community or subculture. Sociologists have been participant observers in studies of nudist camps, bars, prisons, the drug trade, and entire communities. Unlike laboratory or field observers, the researchers become directly involved in the group or community activities. As participants, they may learn about some of the subtleties involved in personal interactions. The researcher may therefore acquire a deeper understanding of the emotions and beliefs that bind the group together than would be possible if observations were made by a person not participating in the group. That kind of information is essential to many sociologists attempting to develop theories about particular types of groups or relationships.

Participant observation is something that you will probably use often in your life, personally and professionally. The restaurant example may help to show this. Rather than merely observing similar restaurants that cater to students, you might become employed as a food server for a while at such a restaurant. As a participant observer, you would be able to get more of a "feel" for what does or does not work in that type of restaurant. On the personal level, the parent-to-be might consider doing some weekend baby-sitting for a relative to get a "feel" for ways of taking care of children. Many colleges offer cooperative education experiences (gaining college credit for work experience), for which you would probably be asked to record and reflect on your experiences as a participant observer. For example, if you worked for an insurance company part time or during summer months, you would gain much more insight about the insurance field than having someone tell you about it.

Most participant observation research takes the form of a *case study*, in which an individual person, group, community, or activity is observed. The use of participant observation for case studies offers numerous advantages and positive outcomes. Often, such studies are sources that generate new insights and hypotheses. Sometimes, one or two carefully selected case studies provide information that cannot be seen or could not be determined through quantitative analysis. Some case studies are believed to have universal application. For some sociologists, an in-depth examination of one or a few select cases is the only way to uncover the full breadth and depth of the actual experiences of the subjects.

This is not to say that case study researchers do not have their critics. Some argue that generalization is impossible because a single case may be the exception and can prove or illustrate anything. Others argue that a researcher who is also a participant can have difficulty remaining objective and making unbiased observations. One possible consequence is that the observers may see only what they want to see. Still others suggest that the researcher may be an intruder or an outsider, and her or his very presence could affect what takes place (this is described later in this chapter, in regard to the Hawthorne effect).

Survey Research

The procedure used most frequently to obtain information about the social world is **survey research**. This quantitative technique involves systematically asking people about their attitudes, feelings, ideas, opinions, behaviors, or anything else. Usually, the researcher uses a questionnaire to guide the questioning. You may have participated in a survey at some point, either an informal survey in a magazine—"Should college athletes be subject to drug tests?"—or a formal survey of your attitudes toward birth control or some other issue.

You may have cause to conduct survey research of your own someday in your job. As the manager of a restaurant, you might want to find out what your customers like best and least about the food and service you offer. You do not necessarily have to be a sociologist or to employ a sociologist to conduct the survey. Perhaps you could have customers fill out a card with a short list of questions when they receive the bill. In any line of work you may choose, conducting a survey may help you find out what your customers or clients need, which can be a very effective way of improving your business.

Surveys have a number of advantages over many other data-gathering procedures. They are usually easy to administer and often permit researchers to gather data on identical variables from many people simultaneously. Unlike most participant observation studies, which may take months or years, surveys provide a lot of information within periods ranging from a few minutes to several weeks. When highly structured, survey responses are uniformly categorized, which makes tabulation easier. Finally, the precise categorical data provided by surveys is highly amenable to quantitative statistical analysis.

There are problems with surveys too, of course. First, if questions concern personal information about age, income, sex life, or criminal activities, for example, the respondents may not answer honestly. Second, if the questions or responses are highly structured, the results of the survey may not reflect the actual beliefs of the people being questioned but rather the researcher's conceptions of how the questions should be asked and what people's answers are likely to be. To give an exaggerated example, a survey question about attitudes toward abortion would not yield valid information if it listed as the only possible answers either "I think abortion should not be allowed under any circumstances" or "I think abortion is permissible in situations involving rape or danger to mother's health." Third, do surveys assess only the most superficial aspects of social life or cover only a limited part of the respondents' thoughts on a subject? Surveys may fail to assess areas that are difficult to examine, and people's beliefs may be far more complex than a survey indicates.

Despite problems such as these, survey research has gained increasing methodological sophistication and is widely used by social scientists. Public opinion pollsters use surveys to gather information about the popularity of politicians. Market researchers employ them to discover why people use a particular product. Census takers use them to learn the characteristics and size of the population. They are helpful to sociologists in getting information on a great variety of factors and in testing hypotheses.

One major problem in research is identifying a group of people to be studied. The group might be doctors, students, taxpayers, voters in a given election, or any selected group that can provide the information needed to prove or disprove the hypotheses. This group is usually called the "population." Because we can rarely study all doctors, students, or taxpayers due to such factors as cost and time, we must pick an appropriate sample. A **sample** is a group of people chosen from the population who are thought to represent the population. The sample is questioned, and their answers are expected to reflect the beliefs of the population as a whole.

Samples are chosen by a variety of methods. A **random sample** is chosen by chance, so that every member of a group has an equal chance of being selected. Because it is usually impossible to place all names in a hat, as is often done at prize drawings, sociologists often assign a number to each name and use a table of random numbers to select which persons should be included. They may also use a method known as **systematic sampling**, in which a specific pattern of selection is followed, such as selecting every twentieth name. A third method is **stratified sampling**, in which the population is divided into groups and then chosen at random from within those groups. If our population were students, we might stratify them by class rank, sex, or race and then randomly select from each of these groups.

Regardless of how the sample is chosen, if every person has an equal chance of being chosen, it should be representative—it should reflect the attitudes of the total population. A small representative sample is likely to provide far more accurate data about a population than a large nonrepresentative one. If you as a restaurant manager decide to conduct a survey of your clientele, you will get a more accurate picture of how all customers feel if you conduct a survey of a few people at various times of the day than if you survey many people only at breakfast. There are obvious benefits in being able to study a few hundred people and make accurate generalizations about an entire population on the basis of the findings. These procedures are used daily in the ratings of television programs, by market researchers of consumer purchasing patterns, and by sociologists testing hypotheses.

The ability to study a representative sample is a necessary skill in many professional fields. As one clinical sociologist comments about health professions,

> It has become obvious even to many psychologists and psychiatrists that their training is inadequate to diagnose and treat problems rooted in a social context. ... Because the majority of psychiatrists do not receive any sociological theory or sociological methods during their training, they usually commit the particularistic fallacy by generalizing about problems they confront from particular cases, not having any real understanding of the role of sampling in creating knowledge about human social behavior in group life. (Swan, 1984, pp. 11–12)

Likewise, we have to be careful in our personal and professional lives not to commit the "particularistic fallacy" of generalizing about problems, situations, and events from experience with only one or a few. It might prove disastrous to our restaurant business to assume, for example, that all customers like to hear loud rock music with meals simply because the first few said they loved the music. It would be a mistake for us, as parents, to assume that all child-care centers are inadequate because we had one bad experience; it would also be a mistake to assume that all are good based on one good experience.

The survey is not completed with the selection of a sample, of course. Once the sample subjects are chosen, it is necessary to administer our tests or to ask our questions. The questions themselves must be formulated according to the principles of scientific inquiry, which were discussed earlier. Our questions must be carefully worded, precise, operationally defined, free from investigator bias, valid, reliable, and so forth. Imagine how the responses might be influenced if we were to ask a question such as this: "Do you agree with the view of all patriotic Americans that an increase in the military budget is vital to our national defense?" As you can see, it is important to ask questions that are not slanted toward a particular type of response or are unclear. Care should be taken to ensure a complete set of possible response choices. The use of improper questions, regardless of the representativeness of the sample, will yield data that cannot be used to prove or disprove a hypothesis or to adequately complete the research process.

SOCIOLOGY AT WORK

Research Analyst

Jean Brittain Leslie is a research analyst at the Center for Creative Leadership in Greensboro, North Carolina. Prior to her current position, she was a research project manager at the *Greensboro News and Record*, a major daily newspaper in North Carolina. She received her B.A. in sociology from Elon College and her M.A. in sociology at the University of North Carolina at Greensboro.

Jean Leslie is one of those people who happened to stumble into sociology and fall in love with it. "I would like to say that I aspired to become a 'sociologist' but that is not the case. I, like many students, did not know what I wanted to do when I 'grew up' so I took many introductory courses. Sociology was one of them. Needless to say, I enjoyed it so much that I decided to major in it. In retrospect, sociology as compared to other majors most closely fits my personal orientation toward the world. A sociology degree ... offers an intellectually stimulating framework to address the world." She says that sociology encourages her to objectively approach her work "or at least be aware of how my own values infiltrate my perspectives. Sociology has taught me to question what appears to be reality and to not take for granted shared meanings." Besides obviously benefiting from an understanding of symbolic interactionism and knowledge about how different cultures operate, Jean feels that the macro-level perspective that sociology offers is invaluable to her when studying organizations.

Jean credits her degree in sociology to helping her obtain her current position at the Center for Creative Leadership. "I am a researcher by occupation. My employer was looking for someone with skills similar to the ones I acquired through studying sociology." She says that courses such as research methods, statistics, sociological

Thinking Sociologically

1. The July issue of a popular magazine included a perforated page with questions about marital violence. The readers were invited to complete the questions and mail them in by September 1. The results were to be published in the November issue. What are the strengths and weaknesses of this type of research?

2. Why must those who conduct research (e.g., sociologists) and those who read about it (e.g., consumers) be conscious of and cautious about the research results and statistics they use and see?

Experimental Designs

A third procedure for obtaining information about the social world is through the **experimental design**, a classic scientific procedure used to determine cause–effect relationships in carefully controlled situations. In an ideal experiment, it is possible to control all relevant factors and to manipulate, statistically or in the society itself, one variable to determine its effect.

Research Analyst, *continued*

theory, and cultural anthropology provided her with a basic understanding of human behavior that is pertinent to her job. "I am working for an organization that studies managers and leaders from diverse organizations and cultural regions. Every time I go into a new project, I must read literature from other academic disciplines (for example, business, psychology, counseling)." Jean notes that she often finds sociological perspectives in works from other disciplines. "It is not uncommon to find popular sociologists cited in non-sociological journals or presentations at Academy of Management meetings. Having attended both business and sociological professional conferences, I can tell you that both disciplines are facing similar quality research issues.

When thinking about a career, Jean thinks that there are some skills that all employers would prefer their employees have, which you can gain from sociology courses. "Writing abilities are a premium, the ability to communicate with others is another plus, and above all one must learn how to survive in a world where norms are often implicit. These things can be exercised through sociology if the student believes them to be important." Additionally, she feels that the perspective that sociology teaches is not duplicated in other academic disciplines. "Sociology offers a unique analytical approach to the world that can be applied in any career and organizational setting. … The most obvious difference between sociology and other academic disciplines is the macro orientation. The unit of measurement for most of my coworkers is the individual. Because of my sociological orientation, I am able to bring a much more global perspective to our work. I do quite a bit of cross-cultural research in which sociology (as opposed to other disciplines) has the opportunity to shine."

To carry out an experiment, two matched groups of subjects are selected. In the **experimental group**, an independent variable is introduced, and it is the effect of this variable that is tested. The **control group** is identical to the experimental group in every respect, except that the variable is not introduced to this group. If we were studying the effects of dim lighting on social interaction, for example, we might randomly choose two groups of students. The experimental group would be placed in a dimly lit room, whereas the control group would be in a normally lit room. All other aspects of these settings would be identical (e.g., furnishings, size, time of day). The researcher would note differences in the behavior of the two groups: frequency of interaction, level of noise, number of subgroups formed, and other behaviors considered germane. Differences in the social behavior of the two groups would presumably be due to the influence of the independent variable, dim lighting.

Experiments are most frequently done in a laboratory setting where it is easier to control conditions than it is in a natural or field (nonlaboratory) setting. It has been argued, however, that laboratory settings are artificial and yield distorted results.

Among the social sciences, the experimental design is used most often in psychology, and extensive experimental work has been done in the study of learning, perception, attachment, frustration, and similar behaviors. Students often ask how it is possible to conduct experiments with humans in either a laboratory or nonlaboratory setting. Can we lock people in rooms, withhold food, punish them, or remove them from friends and family? We cannot, of course, because such research would be highly unethical. However, scientists can study circumstances that already exist in the social world: populations of starving people, families who do abuse their children, jobs that provide little variation in activity, neighborhoods destroyed by floods or fire, hospitals that isolate people from their loved ones, and prisons that put people in solitary confinement. The social world also contains populations of well-fed people, families that do not abuse their children, and so forth. It is often possible to find existing experimental and control groups that have all characteristics in common except the independent variable chosen for observation.

For example, suppose that we wish to find out whether playing music to workers in a factory influences their productivity. We could design an experiment in which music was played to one group (the experimental group) and withheld from another group. An alternative method would be to find existing settings in which music was provided or not provided and to compare the workers' productivity. A third method would be to statistically compare two groups in which the selected variables could be controlled. Sociologists have used each of these procedures. As you can see, a variety of alternatives are available with an experimental type of design.

You also may have the opportunity or the need to conduct some experiments. In the hypothetical restaurant that you recently opened, you might want to find out whether people order more drinks when served by a waiter or by a waitress. In this case you might have two rooms with identical decor, lighting, and music and have the only difference be the presence of waiters or waitresses. If everything else remains the same and people order more drinks in the room with waitresses, this would tell you that you might be able to increase your business if you had all waitresses instead of waiters. As a waiter or waitress, what kind of experiment do you think you could devise to find out what leads to bigger tips?

One of the best-known experiments in sociology resulted in what is widely referred to as the "Hawthorne effect." Before World War II, at the Hawthorne plant of Western Electric, Elton Mayo separated a group of women (the experimental group) from the other workers and systematically varied their lighting, coffee breaks, lunch hours, and other environmental factors (Roethlisberger and Dickson, 1939). In the control group, work conditions went on as usual. Much to the amazement of the researchers, the productivity of the experimental group (the dependent variable) increased regardless of the variables that were introduced, including returning the workers to their original conditions. Obviously, the desired result, increased productivity, was not being caused by a specific independent variable. On the one hand, the experiment seemed to be a success—the experimental group differed from the control group when independent variables such as lighting and coffee breaks were introduced. The experiment appeared to be a failure, however, in that one independent variable seemed to have as much influence as another. The researchers concluded that the women were trying to please the researchers and enjoyed the attention they were getting. The very presence of the researchers contaminated the experiment to the point that they became a significant independent variable and caused a change in the dependent variable—work productivity. The Hawthorne effect can be a potential problem whenever an experiment is conducted. On the other hand, knowledge of the Hawthorne effect might be effectively used by management to increase productivity.

Secondary Analysis

Observation studies, survey research, and experimental designs are three frequently used methods of gathering information and of doing sociological research, but other procedures and ways of obtaining data for analysis are used as well. One example is the common use of **secondary analysis**, which refers to the use of existing information that was gathered by others or that exists independently of your research.

Secondary materials may include *personal documents*, such as letters, diaries, autobiographies and speeches; *public records*, such as health, school, police, marriage, death, and divorce; *news sources*, such as radio, TV, newspapers, magazines, books, professional journals, and reference materials available in most libraries; and *actual research data* gathered from other studies and available in existing data banks, such as at the National Opinion Research Center (NORC) in Chicago or the Roper Public Opinion Research Center in Massachusetts.

In deciding where to open a new restaurant, you might use secondary sources—for example, a comparison of the 1990 and 2000 census—to track population growth in a selected area. If you are a sales representative in a computer store, you might read competitors' advertisements to get ideas on how to price your equipment. We use secondary sources much of the time in our daily lives to make important decisions. When moving to a new town, you might scan the real estate section of the newspaper to get an idea of the value of neighborhoods you are considering. You might also check the police reports in the local newspaper for the past few months to get some sense of the crime rate in that area. For help in personal investments, many people read Money magazine to get the advice of professional investors and to see what other people are investing in. Before you buy that new stereo or new car, you may check *Consumer Reports*, to get a review of what some experts say about a particular product.

One researcher may use secondary sources to analyze the average age at marriage based on government marriage-license records. Another researcher may do a **content analysis** of letters to the editor of the local newspaper to determine what community problems were written about over a selected time period. *Content analysis* refers to the procedure of systematically extracting thematic data from a wide range of communications—for example, how the roles of women were portrayed by Shakespeare, or how conservative versus liberal news sources describe or report the same speech or event.

The use of secondary sources may save the cost and time of gathering original data, may enable the gathering of data from the past or from sources that are not otherwise available, or may permit trend studies covering years or decades of time. However, secondary sources also have potential weaknesses. The exact information we want may not be available, the data that does exist may be out of date or incomplete, and the material may not have been gathered systematically, accurately, or completely. In brief, it may be neither valid nor reliable. A summary comparison of the four research methods just described can be seen in Table 3-1.

The Research Process

Most research proceeds in accordance with a sequence of rules and procedures basic to the scientific method:

1. Formulate the problem
2. Review the literature
3. Develop hypotheses
4. Choose a research design

TABLE 3-1 FOUR RESEARCH METHODS: A SUMMARY COMPARISON

Method	Application	Advantages	Disadvantages
Observation studies • Laboratory observation • Natural field observation • Participant observation	• Case studies • Group behaviors • Community activities • Other cultures • Explanatory, descriptive, and evaluative	• Generates qualitative data • Generates new insights and hypotheses • Can take place in natural setting	• Generalization difficult • Observer (researcher) may influence outcome • Roles of participant and researcher may be difficult to separate • May be very time consuming
Survey research • Questionnaires • Interview schedules	• Study of the nonobservable (opinions, attitudes, values) • Public opinion polls • Market research • Census taking • Cross-national studies • Explanatory, descriptive, and evaluative	• Generates easily quantifiable data • Can be used on large populations • Permits standardized questioning • Easily administered • Requires only a short time frame for gathering data	• Sampling difficulties • Exclusion of nonrespondents • Honesty of responses to personal/sensitive questions not known • Difficulty of question construction: clear, nonambiguous, nonloaded • Omission of relevant questions
Experimental designs • Experimental and control groups • Laboratory or field setting	• Comparison of two groups of workers, students, or children • Explanatory, descriptive, and evaluative	• Controls the specific conditions • Often permits replication of experiment • Specifies cause-effect relationships	• Artificiality of laboratory, "nonnatural" setting • Cannot always control all variables • Hawthorne effect
Secondary analysis • Historical records • Official data • Public records • Mass media • Data banks	• Historical study • Permits the analysis of the content of communications • Allows observation of trends and changes • Explanatory, descriptive, and evaluative	• Data already gathered or available • Inexpensive • Sources from past or otherwise not available	• Desired variables or materials missing or omitted • Out-of-date or incomplete data • Nonsystematic, inaccurate records • No control over possible bias in data

5. Collect the data
6. Analyze the results
7. Interpret the findings, and draw conclusions in relation to the hypothesis
8. Disseminate the results

The first step is to formulate the problem, but sociologists using scientific methods can choose only those problems that are amenable to observation and testing, and the problem must be articulated such that the researchers know exactly what they are trying to determine. Let us suppose that we choose to do a quantitative study, and the problem we want to investigate concerns the effects of age at marriage on the number of children a couple has.

Having decided what to research, the next step is to review the literature. Examining texts and articles in periodicals will tell us what is already known, where there are gaps in our existing knowledge, and more specifically what we should investigate. In our example, we may suppose that our review indicates that little work has been done in this area.

The third step is to develop hypotheses for testing. As mentioned previously, *hypotheses* are statements of relationships between two or more variables that can be empirically proved or disproved. We might state our hypothesis as follows: "Age at marriage is negatively related to family size." Unlike the concept of happiness discussed earlier, these variables are easy to define operationally.

The fourth step is to choose a research design, which is the process of establishing procedures to gather the evidence that will be used to support or reject the hypothesis. These procedures include the methods to be used to gather the data (observation, survey, experiment, secondary analysis), the sample to be selected and the means of selecting them, the types of questions to be asked, and the general plan to make it possible to collect and analyze the data. Many factors must be considered, including the time and money available, the reliability and validity of various designs, and so on. It is important to keep in mind that aspects of the design may have to be changed once the process is begun. For our example, we might choose to mail a questionnaire to a representative sample of 1000 married couples, to search public documents and link marriage and birth records, or to seek the information from U.S. Census Bureau material.

The next step in the research process is to collect the data, as described in the research design. In this case, we could note each person's date of birth, marital status, date of marriage, and number of children. To check the validity of the data, we should gather it from several different sources.

When the data are collected, they must be assembled, organized, and classified so that the hypotheses can be tested. This is the stage in which we analyze the results. In most cases, it is necessary to arrange the data in a manageable form. With our example, it might be desirable to organize age information into different categories, such as five-year intervals. It would then be a simple matter to make a graph or table of results that could easily be interpreted.

In addition, we might want to include some descriptive data about each of the variables. The **mode** is the most frequent response. We might discover that the mode of male age at marriage was 22 years; that is, more males married at age 22 than at any other age. The **median** is the midpoint, above which are one-half of the respondents, and below which are one-half. We might discover that half the women were married before age 20 and half after age 20. The **mean** is the average, the sum of the age at marriage divided by the number of people involved. Suppose, for example, that the first seven people in our study were married at ages 40, 26, 20, 18, 16, 16, and 16. The most frequent age at marriage (*mode*) is 16. The age half are below and half are above (*median*) is 18. The average age (*mean*) is 21.7—the sum of the ages divided by seven. These *figures are measures of central tendency.*

We may wish to discover the range of a variable, the distance between the largest and the smallest amounts. Suppose that the youngest person in our study was 15 and the oldest was 75, giving us an age range of 60 years. For the variable age at marriage, we might discover that the 15-year-old had married at that age, and the 75-year-old also had just married. The range for age at marriage, therefore, also would be 60 years.

Variance is a related concept. In descriptive research, the variance tells us how the data are spread over the range. Three groups could all have an age range from 15 to 75, for example, but the distribution of the age of those married in the three groups could differ.

In Figure 3-1, all three bar graphs have an age range of 60 years, yet the example on the left shows no variance in the age at marriage—everyone who married did so at age 45. The middle example shows a normal variation, with the most people marrying at age 45 and fewer marrying at older and younger ages. The example on the right illustrates maximum variance, with half the group marrying at age 15 and half at age 75.

After analyzing the data, we begin the final activities of the research process. We interpret our findings; draw our conclusions; and confirm, reject, or reformulate our original hypothesis, proposition, and theory. We then disseminate the results. These final activities can be very difficult, however. Suppose we found that people who married at a young age did have larger families but that they were only slightly larger than the families of those who married when they were older. If people who married before age 20 had an average of 1.9 children and those who married after age 20 had an average of 1.8

FIGURE 3-1 VARIABILITY OF AGE AT MARRIAGE: THREE EXAMPLES

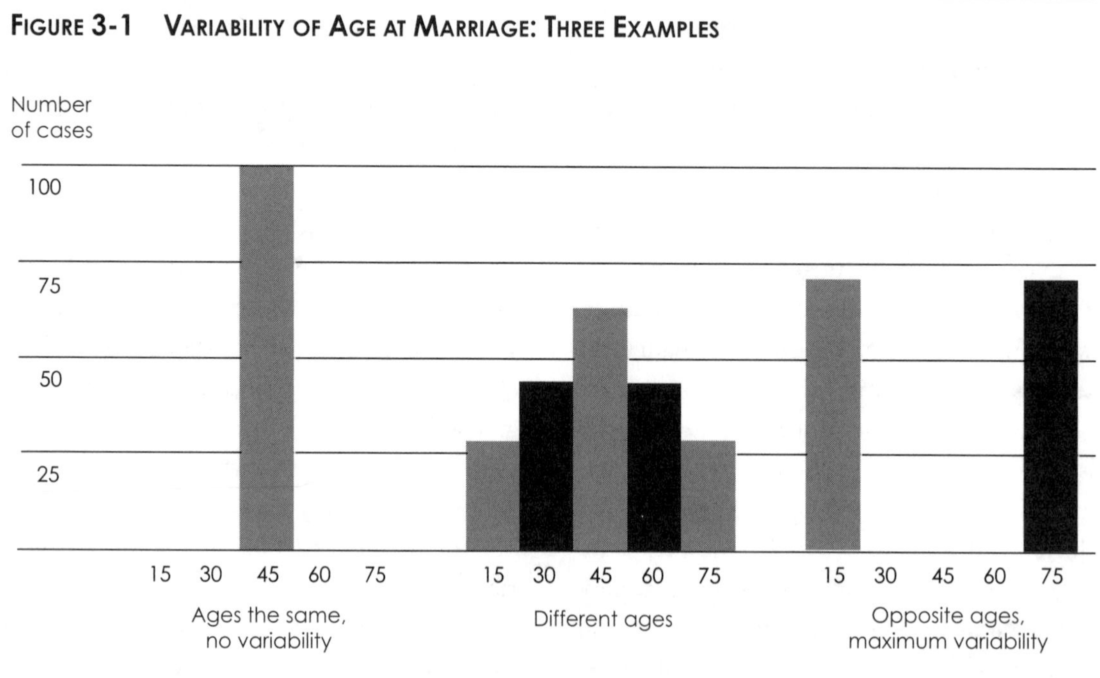

children, should we accept our hypothesis? Would this finding be significant, or could the difference be the result of chance or a bias in the sample we investigated? Interpretations must take into account any factor in the research process that could have influenced our results.

By reporting our findings and conclusions, we make them subject to public review, criticism, and application. Sociologists frequently publish their results in professional journals, where they are reviewed by other sociologists. Sometimes, the results are published in books, monographs, or popular magazines. When the results have been disseminated, the research process is complete.

Thinking Sociologically

1. Formulate a quantitative research study. Following the research process described, provide an outline for each step.
2. Formulate a qualitative research study. Can these same steps be followed? Why or why not? Discuss.

SUMMARY

1. Although we also learn about society from everyday experiences, common sense, authority, revelation, and tradition, sociology depends heavily on empirical research that uses the scientific method.
2. Is sociology a science? Some argue that it is, some that it is not. It may be more constructive to note what distinguishes scientific modes of inquiry from nonscientific modes of inquiry and then to consider whether sociology can follow a scientific mode.
3. There are certain standards of inquiry basic to science. Objectivity involves excluding personal values, beliefs, and biases from the research process, findings, and interpretations. The standard of replication requires that research be undertaken and reported such that someone else can replicate it. The standard regarding precision in measurement requires that whatever is studied be measurable and that measurements be precise, reliable, and valid.
4. Sociological research is of three basic types: descriptive, explanatory, and evaluative. *Descriptive research* provides reliable, valid data on social facts. *Explanatory research* goes beyond description to determine why a particular social situation occurs and to discover cause–effect relationships. *Dependent variables* in explanatory research are those the investigator wants to explain; they depend on or are determined by other variables. *Independent variables* are those that cause the variations in the dependent variable. *Evaluative research* measures how well a program or project works in relation to its goals.
5. Sociological methods are often categorized into two types: qualitative and quantitative. *Qualitative methods* are used to determine the essential characteristics, properties, or processes of something or someone. These methods often include case studies, laboratory observations, field observations, and participatory observations.
6. *Quantitative methods* are designed to determine the amounts or numbers of something: how

many, how often, how statistically significant, and so forth. Experimental research and surveys are generally quantitative methods.

7. *Surveys*, the most frequently used method of sociological research, involve systematically asking people about their attitudes or behaviors, which is usually accomplished with the use of questionnaires. Choosing an appropriate sample and wording questions carefully are crucial parts of the survey method.

8. The *experimental method* involves the use of two or more similar groups. An independent variable is introduced into the experimental group but withheld from the control group.

9. Valuable data are often found in public records and secondary sources. Content analysis is one procedure used to critically examine this material.

10. Research generally involves a sequence of tasks, including the following: formulating the problem, reviewing the literature, developing hypotheses for testing, choosing a research design, collecting data, analyzing the findings, drawing conclusions, and disseminating the results.

11. There are often many different ways to categorize the data, to formulate tables, and to use statistical measures such as the mode, median, mean, range, and variance. When the data analysis is finished, conclusions are drawn and the results are made available to the public.

12. Research methods are not only important and useful for sociologists but also an integral part of many occupations and used often in our daily lives.

KEY TERMS

concept An abstract system of meaning that enables us to perceive a phenomenon in a certain way.

content analysis The procedure of systematically extracting thematic data from a wide range of communications.

control group In an experiment, the group not exposed to the independent variable that is introduced to the experimental group.

dependent variable A variable that is changed or influenced by another variable.

descriptive research Research that describes social reality or provides facts about the social world.

direct relationship A relationship between two variables in which an increase in one variable is accompanied by an increase in the other; compare with inverse relationship.

ethnographic research A form of descriptive research focusing on the sociology of meaning through close observation of sociocultural phenomena.

evaluation research Research that measures how well a program or project works in relation to its goals.

experimental design A scientific procedure in which at least two matched groups, differing only in the variable being studied, are used to collect and compare data.

experimental group In an experiment, the group to which an independent variable is introduced; this variable is not introduced in the control group.

explanatory research Research that attempts to explain why things do or do not happen by examining the relationship between social variables.

hypothesis A statement about the relationship between variables that can be put to an empirical test.

independent variable A variable that causes a change or variation in a dependent variable.

Institutional Review Boards (IRBs) Committees on college/university campuses and in research organizations that provide oversight of research that is conducted on human subjects.

inverse relationship A relationship between two variables such that an increase in one variable is accompanied by a decrease in the other; compare with direct relationship.

mean A measure of central tendency computed by adding the figures and dividing by the number of figures; also known as the average.

median A measure of central tendency in which half the figures fall above and half the figures fall below; also known as the midpoint.

mode The most frequent response in a body of data.

observational research Research in which the researcher watches what is happening and makes no attempt to control or modify the activity being observed.

operational definition A definition of a concept or variable such that it can be measured.

proposition A statement of the relationship between two or more concepts or variables.

qualitative methods The gathering and reporting of non-numerical data used to determine the essential characteristics, properties, or processes of something or someone.

quantitative methods The gathering and reporting of data based on numbers or amounts of something.

random sample A sample selected in such a way that every member of a population has an equal chance of being chosen.

range The span between the largest and smallest amount of a variable.

reliability The extent to which repeated observations of the same phenomena yield similar results.

sample A number of individuals or cases drawn from a larger population.

scientific method A procedure that involves systematically formulating problems, collecting data through observation and experiment, and devising and testing hypotheses.

secondary analysis The use of existing information that was gathered or exists independently of one's own research.

stratified sampling Sampling in which a population is divided into groups and then subjects are chosen at random from within those groups.

survey research A quantitative research technique that involves asking people questions about the subject being surveyed.

systematic sampling Obtaining a sample from a population by following a specific pattern of selection, such as choosing every tenth person.

theory A set of logically and systematically interrelated propositions that explain a particular process or phenomenon.

validity The extent to which observations actually measure what they are supposed to measure.

variable A characteristic such as age, class, or income that can vary from one person to another; a concept that can have two or more values.

variance A descriptive statistic that tells how the data are spread over the range.

DISCUSSION QUESTIONS

1. Are music and art sciences? Are physics and biology sciences? Is any social science discipline (including sociology) a science? Why or why not?
2. Formulate two general propositions. Can you operationalize them—that is, reformulate them in terms of testable hypotheses?
3. Why are reliability and validity important in social research? Give examples to illustrate each.
4. Compare and contrast the advantages and disadvantages of qualitative and quantitative research. Give examples of where each type (a) could be used and (b) could be more appropriate than the other.
5. What do you think of the idea that quantitative research represents masculine characteristics and qualitative research represents feminine characteristics?
6. List examples where observation research would be appropriate. What are its strengths and weaknesses?
7. Can sociologists conduct experimental designs? Give examples.
8. After reading about the Hawthorne effect, illustrate how researchers themselves might influence or contaminate the results.
9. Suppose that you want to study police brutality. What methods could you use? What are some ethical and political issues that you should consider? Should unpopular or undesirable results or findings not be made public?
10. An instructor says that she is going to grade on a curve. She returns your exam results with a score of 50. What types of additional data do you need to know to assess whether 50 is a good or a poor grade?

PART TWO

Individuals Within Society

Then I began to think, that it is very true which is commonly said, that the one-half of the world knoweth not how the other half liveth.

FRANÇOIS RABELAIS

Culture and Society

Bilingualism

Picture a colorful, thoughtfully designed mural in East Los Angeles containing depictions of Superman, a wired fence, clenched fists, the Statue of Liberty, and protesters carrying flags. At the bottom is the caption: "El presente es de lucha el futuro es nuestro," which means, "The present is to fight; the future belongs to us." It is significant that the Spanish language is juxtaposed with symbols that represent the culture of the United States, such as the Statue of Liberty. The combative nature of the mural seems to represent the artist's view that Hispanic-Americans are not receiving their fair share of the benefits and equality for which these American symbols stand. The artist's view is especially meaningful in light of the fact that the proportion of Hispanic and nonwhite Americans in the United States is rapidly increasing.

The 2000 U.S. census revealed that one American in four defined himself or herself as Hispanic or nonwhite. If current trends in immigration and birth rates continue, half of all Americans will identify with a racial or ethnic group other than white by the year 2050 (U.S. Census). The rapidly changing ratio of white to nonwhite Americans has led to a resurgence of interest in issues that have faced the United States since its birth—issues related to bilingualism. *Bilingualism* can be loosely defined as the use of two or more languages. While on the surface, issues of bilingualism seem to be about language, ultimately they reflect much deeper concerns. As this chapter shows, language is not simply a means of communicating. It is also a symbol of a group's identity and its entire way of life. According to Hakuta (1986, p. 9),

"Bilingualism, in addition to being a linguistic concept, refers to a constellation of tensions having to do with a multitude of psychological, societal, and political realities." Because language is also a representation of a group's identity and way of life, it follows that issues related to bilingualism often generate intense emotional reactions from all of those who may be affected by bilingualism. Even though the acceptance or rejection of bilingualism is not necessarily the result of valuing one culture over another, it can be perceived that way.

One important bilingual issue—one that highlights the significance of language as part of culture—is the long-standing debate as to whether the United States should adopt an official language. Obviously, English is the dominant language in the United States. Nonetheless, contrary to popular belief, English is not the official language of the United States. Although the Constitution of the United States was written in English, there is no provision designating any language as the official language of the United States. "In fact," Hakuta (1986, p. 165) points out, "John Adams' proposal to set up a national language academy, which would give English the official stamp of approval and prescribe its 'proper' usage, was debated by the founding fathers and rejected. The proposal was deemed incompatible with the spirit of freedom in the United States." Evidently, the Founding Fathers understood the full implications of language as being much more than a means of communication.

Still, the debate is far from over. It has been raised most recently by U.S. English, Inc. (U.S.E), an organization that is dedicated to the belief that English is, and should remain, the only official language of the people of the United States (Schaefer, 2002). Besides advocating a constitutional amendment to make English the official language of the United States, the group wants to restrict bilingual-education programs, eliminate non-English voting ballots, and tighten language-proficiency standards for prospective citizens. They contend that, with the increasing number of immigrants in recent years, the primacy of English has been threatened. However, U.S.E. does not pretend that the issue is only one of language. In 2003, Mauro E. Mujica, the director of U.S.E. said, "The whole notion of a melting pot culture is threatened if immigrants aren't encouraged to adopt the common language of this country" (www.us-english.org). The group's ultimate concern is that the American culture is at risk of undergoing a radical change. Opponents of U.S. English, Inc. say that the movement is nothing more than racism and a cover for bigotry directed at America's newest immigrants—especially Hispanics and Asians (Schaefer, 2002). They feel that English-only laws not only would deny people the right to maintain their cultural heritage, but also would hinder people's access to the government to which they pay their taxes (Time, February 19, 1990).

This controversy highlights the fact that language is a very important part of society. Society is characterized by possession of a common culture, and language is both an important determinant and a result of that culture. The growing realization that language and culture are inseparable is leading to greater tensions over issues of bilingualism in American society. This chapter shows why bilingualism is such an important topic and describes what culture means, as culture both shapes and is shaped by all the subtleties and complexities of people's lives.

The term *culture* means different things to different people. In the minds of many people, it is associated with such activities as attending the opera, listening to classical music, and going to art museums. This perspective links culture to the wealthy, affluent, or upper classes and is referred to by some sociologists as **elite culture**. Thus, according to this definition, relatively few of us have culture. If you wanted to become part of this culture, you might begin by studying Mozart, Rembrandt, and Chaucer.

In contrast to the elite culture of the upper classes, frequent reference is made in the social sciences and humanities to popular culture: music, art, dance, radio, linguistic trends, and literature produced and consumed by members of lower and middle classes. Examples of **popular culture** include: soap operas, rap music, wrestling matches and baseball games, slang, Playboy and Playgirl magazines, and Miller or Bud Light beer. In this case, culture, in contrast to being created by and for the elite, is constructed by and shared among common persons such as you and me.

Sociologists and cultural anthropologists do not deny that there are cultural differences among differing social classes or that culture includes both opera and baseball games. To a sociologist, however, a **culture** is a system of ideas, values, beliefs, knowledge, norms, customs, and technology shared by almost everyone in a particular society. A **society** is a group of interacting persons who live in a specific geographical area, who are organized in a cooperative manner, and who share a common culture. A culture is a society's system of common heritage. Each of us has a culture because we were all raised in a society. We express our culture continuously in our dress, food, work, language, recreation, and other activities. We learn our culture from our forebears and contemporaries and then we pass it on to future generations.

In general terms, a culture can be said to include all the human phenomena in a society that are not the products of biological inheritance. Culture includes all learned behavior, not just the behavior of the wealthy or the highly educated. It consists of both the nonmaterial aspects of a society, such as language, ideas, and values, and the material aspects, such as houses, clothes, and tools. Both the skills needed to make a product and the product itself are parts of culture. Sociologists do not judge culture on the basis of the taste or refinement of the society of which it is a part. Bowling and fox hunting, rock groups and symphony orchestras, wood carvings and museum paintings—all are human products, and all reflect culture.

Culture is one of the most complex sociological and anthropological concepts and one of the most central concepts to understanding human behavior. As such, a comprehension of the elements of culture is vitally important to all interpersonal relationships, from personal life to occupation. Indeed, a time-honored anthropological axiom is that "in order to work with a people it is essential to understand their culture" (Foster, 1952). Throughout this chapter, we provide some examples of how the elements of culture can be translated into ideas that might be useful for you.

ELEMENTS OF CULTURE

In most discussions of culture, it is assumed that the various groups of people within a society share some expectations about how it works and how its members should behave. In America, people live in houses or apartments. We buy food in a supermarket or grow it ourselves, we have jobs, and we generally expect our spouses to be sexually faithful to us. In traditional Eskimo culture, by contrast, people lived for part of the year in houses made of snow. They hunted for food because no one had "jobs" in our sense of the word. In some circumstances, sexual infidelity was not merely tolerated, but it was even encouraged through a practice of "wife lending." Because behaviors of these types vary from one group or society to another, they are viewed as products of culture rather than as basic aspects of human nature. In other words, these behaviors are not programmed genetically, as in most animal life—they are determined by the culture. Humans are not born knowing which beliefs and behaviors are appropriate. These must be learned.

Symbols

The existence of culture depends on people's ability to create and understand symbols. A **symbol** is something that is used to represent something else. Words, numbers, flags, crosses, and kisses are symbols. During World War II, raising the middle and index fingers of one hand was the symbol "V" for victory. During the 1960s, the same gesture came to symbolize "peace." Raising the middle finger, or putting thumbs up or thumbs down, or spreading one's thumb and little finger ("hang loose" in Hawaii) all convey particular meanings. In the same way, a stop sign is a symbol meaning "halt" and a cross is a symbol of Christianity.

Symbols are arbitrary designations. There is no necessary connection between a symbol and what it represents. There is nothing inherent in the act of holding one's thumb up that indicates we approve of something. Neither is there anything inherent in an "A-Okay" gesture, signaled by forming a circle with the thumb and forefinger and holding up the other three fingers. Many people in the United States use it to signify that "all is fine." However, to use that same symbol in France and Belgium would convey a message that you are of little or no worth. In Greece and Turkey, it would suggest an insulting sexual invitation. In parts of Italy, it would be an offensive reference to one part of the female anatomy. It's no wonder that interpersonal relationships among people from different cultures are influenced by an awareness of the meanings attached to symbols.

It is important to realize that symbols are collective creations. They are not only products of group experiences and needs, but they also shape a group's experiences and future needs. Astute entrepreneurs—restaurateurs, physicians, retail store managers, and so forth—often use their insights about the clientele they are trying to attract by displaying symbols that are meaningful to their target groups (for example, yuppies, born-again Christians, Italians, or liberals). A dentist in a college town who is trying to build a clientele of students might be better off having the office radio tuned to rock music rather than to Mozart, having copies of *Rolling Stone* magazine available rather than *U.S. News and World Report*, and dressing casually rather than wearing a pin-striped suit. Many advertising agencies realize the importance of cultural symbols and distinguish between *general marketing*, aimed at the total population, and segmented marketing, aimed at specific ethnic, racial, or other groups. *Segmented marketing* uses symbols such as speech patterns (accents, slang), music, clothing, objects, hand signals, and other symbolic elements that are thought to be characteristic of the group the advertisers are trying to attract.

Only humans can assign symbols to represent the objects around them, which is one of the things that makes humans different from animals and enables us to create cultures. The difference is not one of degree. It is not that humans have better reasoning ability than animals. Rather, it is a fundamental difference in kind. Most sociologists assume that the ability to use symbols is uniquely human and that animals do not communicate symbolically or deal with abstractions. Unlike animals, human beings can use symbols to understand reality, to transmit messages, to store complex information, and to deal with an abstract symbolic world. Our success or failure in many relationships, from personal to professional, often depends on our ability to communicate symbolically.

Language

The most important set of symbols is **language**. Language, among humans, is the systematized usage of speech and hearing to convey or express feelings and ideas. It is through language that our ideas, values, beliefs, and knowledge are transmitted, expressed, and shared. Other media, such as music, art, and dance, are also important means of communication; but language is uniquely flexible and precise. It permits us to share our experiences in the past and present, to convey our hopes for the future, and to describe dreams and fantasies that may bear little resemblance to reality. Some scientists have questioned whether thought is even possible without language. Although language can be used imprecisely and can seem hard to understand, it is the chief factor in our ability to transmit culture.

All human societies have languages. Although there are thousands of different languages in the world, linguistic behavior as such is universal. Some societies cannot read or write their language, but they all have a spoken language. Like symbols, language is uniquely human, which is one of the basic distinctions between human beings and other forms of life. Like the use of symbols, the difference between humans and animals is a difference in *kind*, not merely in *degree*.

Note, for example, the difference between a human being and a chimpanzee, believed to be one of the most intelligent animals. Numerous experiments (Hayes, 1951; Kellogg and Kellogg, 1933) over the past 60 years by psychologists who reared both infants and chimpanzees lead most sociologists to conclude that language is the key to understanding differences between the two forms of life. Chimpanzees lack the neural equipment to either generate speech or comprehend language. Although chimps emit sounds and respond to commands, their sounds do not constitute a system of symbols and their responses do not involve a system of shared definitions and meanings. Chimpanzees also lack the type of pharynx found in humans, whose size, shape, and mobility are crucial to the production of speech.

Epstein (2000) sees the inability of chimpanzees to develop language as a critique of the Animal Rights movement's attempt to grant rights to prevent the capture and exploitation of chimpanzees and bonobos. One important question that this raises is whether or not language as we know it (that is, verbal communication) is the only form of language.

Language is so basic to culture and essential for human interaction and social organization that it is often taken for granted, but we can only speculate as to its origins. Did it begin with the imitation of sounds of nature, such as running water or wind in the trees? Did it start with the utterance of grunts, sighs, coughs, and groans? Did it originate in calls and sounds that came to be shared by group members and later expanded to include new experiences

SOCIOLOGY AT WORK

Training Teachers in Cape Verde

Cape Verde is a group of islands in the North Atlantic off the coast of Senegal. Katherine Carter has her B.A. in sociology from Elon University and an M.A. in sociology and certificate in English Language Studies from The University of North Carolina, Charlotte. She currently works for the Institute of Superior Education in Cape Verde as a teacher trainer. Carter prepares future high school English teachers with courses in methodology, linguistics, literature, and culture.

Carter recognizes the important part that sociology plays in her work as a teacher of teachers. "Sociology has helped me understand that we see the world and interact with others based on our personal expectations and underlying values. By teaching English abroad, these have become even more clear to me. I have found my habits of getting right to the point, getting down to business, arriving on time, being methodologically organized, and my independent behavior has been truly offensive to other teachers or students in a place where indirectness and subtlety, pleasure before business, being organized naturally, collective work and group ties, and a more flexible view of time are all valued. In the classroom, I found that culture is part of the interaction between language and thought. Cultural patterns and rituals are expressed in language. For example, in remote parts

and objects? We do not know, but there do seem to be attributes shared by many of the world's languages. Regularities of words over time and place, and the widespread use of certain words, indicate that language is an integral and universal part of culture. Linguistic symbols are learned and shared just like other cultural elements.

Cultures develop not only a verbal and written language but also a nonverbal language of gestures, expressions, mannerisms, and even the use of space. Latin American and North American (Canada and the United States) cultures, for example, use space between people differently during conversation. For Spanish speakers, standing close conveys cordiality and sincerity, whereas for English speakers it conveys pushiness. The distance that English speakers see as proper for conversations Spanish speakers see as cold. Knowledge of another culture's nonverbal or "silent" language is invaluable for any type of interaction that involves people from different cultures, such as international businesspeople, lawyers, politicians, or diplomats. Business deals and international agreements often rely heavily on the private interaction of a few high-powered individuals. A deal might easily be soured if one party interprets the other's normal speaking distance as pushy or standoffish.

Suppose that you are a lawyer hired by an American electronics company that relies on Japanese parts. Part of your job entails securing a long-term contract to ensure that the company can continue to import the parts it needs for its products. It might help you in your negotiations with the lawyers that represent the Japanese firm to learn about the nonverbal language used by Japanese people in their conversations and to learn how they interpret some of our nonverbal language. What do they consider to be polite standing or sitting distance between people? Are there any American gestures that we

Training Teachers in Cape Verde, *continued*

of Alaska, where fish and fishing is of great importance, the Dena'ina language has particular words to differentiate between dried fish, half-dried fish, a bundle of dried fish, fish dried in one day's wind, fish dried with eggs inside, fish dried ungutted, fish dried flat, smoked fish, and half-smoked fish. To know these words is to be a part of the community, which places great significance on fish and fishing. Each language allows its speakers to talk about what is important to discuss in that society. In Cape Verde, widespread vocabulary exists for the type of food made by corn. This is significant because corn is the staple crop, and there is an important need to talk about it, the planting and cultivation of it, and the dishes made from corn, in detailed ways. When students attempt to translate specific corn words and phrases, they find that no exact translation exists in English, as corn and the planting of it are may not be as important to an English speaking person. This should not be simply disregarded however. Customs and ways of life are expressed in language in this way. Along with analyzing our own values, patterns and rituals are expressed in language and provide a mirror for one attempting to understand another culture."

Katherine Carter is an excellent example of how knowledge of concepts such as culture, and other sociological ideas, are an asset to her work.

tend to use in our communication with others that might be offensive to Japanese people? What are some Japanese gestures that convey warmth, trust, and honesty?

Language influences people's thoughts and experiences to a greater degree than is generally recognized. In 1929, Edward Sapir argued that people see and interpret the world through the grammatical forms, labels, and categories provided by their language. He contended that societies with different languages actually perceive the world differently; that is, they do not just use a different set of labels to describe the same things.

This idea is known as the **Sapir–Whorf hypothesis**. Benjamin Whorf, a student of Sapir, noted while working for an insurance company that workmen handling barrels of gasoline were very careful about matches and cigarettes when the barrels were full, but that they became careless and caused many accidents once the label *empty* had been applied to a barrel. In other words, the application of the word *empty* to a barrel influenced the workers' perception and consequent behavior (Whorf, 1941). Intrigued by this finding, he began to study different cultures to see whether people's behavior was influenced by the language they used. He found that language does influence the way we perceive things and how we behave.

As examples, note how words such as snow or banana create a certain mental image. What do you see when you hear those words? Would you see something different if a precise word or symbol existed for snow, depending on whether it was falling, drifting, frozen, fresh, compacted, in a cone, and so on? Would you behave differently (drive your car, go skiing, eat it, build a snowman), depending on your perception? Is a banana just a banana, or, as to most Filipinos, do bananas differ in their size, colors, and uses and require precise words or symbols to convey the banana desired? Interpreters of languages such as Hebrew, Russian, or German often find that no parallel word exists in English for the word they are trying to translate. Thus, they can only try to convey in English the "reality" of the word they are translating. The Sapir-Whorf hypothesis appears to be valid: Our perceptions of reality are greatly influenced by our language. Languages are learned, shared, and transmitted from one generation to another, and they are a central element of culture.

The Sapir-Whorf hypothesis helps us to realize the necessity of studying foreign languages. Learning a foreign language is important not only because it allows us to speak to non-English-speaking people, but also because it allows us to see their view of reality. For those whose work involves interaction with people from different countries—foreign diplomats, ambassadors, politicians, international businesspeople and lawyers, social workers, or others—being able to speak directly, rather than through an interpreter is essential for complete understanding.

Thinking Sociologically

Relate the Sapir-Whorf hypothesis to your personal life or academic field of study. Show how the language or the specific terminology in your discipline influences your perceptions of reality and your experiences.

Values

Values are ideas shared by the people in a society regarding what is important and worthwhile. Our values are the basis of our judgments about what is desirable, beautiful, correct, and good, as well as what is undesirable, ugly, incorrect, and bad. Most values have both positive and negative counterparts, which are reciprocally related. If you place a high positive value on fighting for your country, for example, you probably place a high negative value on those who refuse to fight. If you value marital sexual exclusiveness, you probably disapprove of those who engage in extramarital sexual relationships. Values are often emotionally charged because they stand for things we believe to be worth defending.

Most of our basic values are learned early in life from family, friends, the mass media, and other sources within society. The value of saving money, for example, may be conveyed directly by parents or others but may be reinforced in more subtle ways as through proverbs. Most of us are familiar with common sayings such as, "A penny saved is a penny earned" or "Waste not, want not" (values that convey frugality or the value of saving money). By whatever manner they are conveyed or learned, the values are generally shared and reinforced by those with whom we interact. Placing a high value on religious faith, honesty, cleanliness, freedom, or on money, children, education, or work serves as a general guide for our behavior and the formation of specific attitudes. Because values indicate what is proper or improper, they tend to justify particular types of behavior and to forbid others.

When basic values are in conflict, we usually place them in a hierarchy of importance and behave in ways consistent with the most important. During a war, for example, the value of patriotism may overcome the value that human life is precious, or vice versa. When it is impossible to place our values in a hierarchy to resolve a conflict, we may feel guilty or suffer mental stress.

To give another example of value conflict, consider the case of a husband who enjoys spending time with his family. If job demands take him away from his family for extended periods, he is likely to feel stress. To avoid stress, he could quit his job, take the family along on job trips, justify the job demands as being in the best interests of the family, compromise on both family and job demands, or leave the family. Some of these choices may be impossible, however. Quitting the job or taking the family along may not be realistic alternatives, and divorce may conflict with social and religious values. Mental stress is likely to result when choices are impossible. The alternative courses of action, as well as the choice selected, will generally be consistent with the values of the society and with those most important to the individual.

Sometimes, our stated values and our behavior are inconsistent. We may place a high value on freedom of the press but want to censor communist writings. We may place a high value on individualism but want to punish people whose behavior is inconsistent with our definition of appropriate behavior. Our true values are often reflected more by what we do than by what we say. If we say we value education but have no interest in attending classes or paying for public schools, or if we say that we value simplicity but spend money conspicuously to display our wealth, our actions expose our real values.

Because values are learned cultural products, they differ from one society to another. Americans, for example, tend to be individualistic, using personal characteristics and achievements to define themselves, while societies such as Japan and the Israeli kibbutzim focus more on group harmony, unity, and loyalty. North Americans tend to see themselves as dominant over nature, while societies such as the Chinese or subcultures such as the Navaho see themselves as living in harmony with nature. Residents of Canada and the United States are more conscious of being "on time" than in Asia and the Middle East.

Most cultures, despite diversity in their populations, tend to share certain value patterns. In American society, Robin M. Williams (1970) described 15 value orientations. These include a belief in achievement and success, stressing personal achievement, especially secular occupational achievement; external conformity, emphasizing the adherence to similarity and uniformity in speech, manners, housing, dress, recreation, politically expressed ideas, and group patterns; and democracy, advocating majority rule, representative institutions, and the rejection of monarchical and aristocratic principles. The extent to which such traditional American value orientations have changed has become a topic of study in recent years, especially in light of the effects of globalization and increased diversity in American society (Brunner, 2003; Coon and Kemmelmeier, 2001; Kester, 2001).

It must be kept in mind that these are general themes in American values, which change constantly. They are often in conflict, and they are not all exhibited in a single person's behavior. Sometimes, they even appear to be inconsistent. How can we value both independence and conformity, or equality and racial differentiation? Some of the explanations for these inconsistencies lie in whether the value is applied generally or specifically. A person might say, for example, "Our society believes strongly in freedom of the press, but I don't want my town library to carry novels with explicit sex in them." Other explanations may reflect the beliefs of different regions of the country.

Williams states that most conflicts between value systems in the United States occur between those centering around individual personalities and those organized around categorical themes or conceptions. Group discrimination and racism, as categorical themes, are contrary to other central values of the society. Each of these values has a historical base and a complexity far greater than is evident in this brief discussion. Evidence does suggest, however, a decline in racist beliefs over several decades: Legislation has forced movements away from enforced segregation and public discrimination, and Congress has passed Civil Rights Acts and a series of laws that forbid discrimination because of race, sex, religion, nationality, place of birth, or place of residence. Thus, while a central value may continue to exist, which grants privilege based on group or racial affiliation, some evidence suggests that this particular theme may be fading.

An understanding of value systems can be useful for many people in their work. In a discussion of how to manage organizational conflict, for example, Hampton, Summer, and Webber (1982) emphasize the importance of being able to recognize that competing value systems are often the source of the conflict. They state:

> Instances of inadequate sharing of values and of competing goals are numerous. Individual self-actualization versus collective will is one value conflict that has been and will be fought on many battlefields. At a business level, salespeople value company responsiveness to the customer, while production personnel value equilibrium and predictability; engineers value ingenuity and quality, while finance values the profit margin; marketing emphasizes gross income, while the credit department values minimum credit loss, and so on. (p. 635)

A way to deal with these competing value systems is to try to create common values. Some experts on how to manage corporations suggest that successful organizations do this by developing stories, slogans, myths, and legends about the corporation (e.g., Kanter, 1983; Peters and Waterman, 1982). These help to decrease conflict and create a greater sense of mutuality. The "human relations school of management" relies heavily on the notion that sharing values is important for members of large corporations.

Thinking Sociologically

1. Values were stated to be learned cultural products. What values do you define as important? Why? Are their differences in values you hold and the behaviors you exhibit (cheating, sexual behavior, weight, etc.)? Do any of these values create stress or conflict in your personal life?
2. To what extent do people have the right (or obligation) to impose their values on others (parents on children, a religious group on those of other religions, a culture on a subculture, etc.)? Illustrate with specific examples.

Norms

Social **norms**, another element of culture, are rules of conduct or social expectations for behavior. These rules and social expectations specify how people should and should not behave in various social situations. They are both *prescriptive* (they tell people what they should do) and *proscriptive* (they tell people what they should not do).

Whereas values are abstract conceptions of what is important and worthwhile, social norms are standards, rules, guides, and expectations for actual behavior. Norms and values are likely to be conceptually consistent, but values are less situation-bound and are more general and abstract. Norms link values with actual events. *Honesty* is a general value; the expectation that students will not cheat on tests is a norm. Most norms permit a range of behaviors; that is, some kinds or degrees of overconformity and underconformity are expected and tolerated, particularly in some settings or situations. We would not criticize a starving man for lying to get food, for example.

An early American sociologist, William G. Sumner (1840–1910), identified two types of norms, which he labeled "folkways" and "mores." They are distinguished not by their content but by the degree to which group members are compelled to conform to them, by their degree of importance, by the severity of punishment if they are violated, or by the intensity of feeling associated with adherence to them. **Folkways** are customs or conventions. They are norms, in that they provide rules for conduct, but violations of folkways bring only mild censure. In the United States, most adults are expected to eat vegetables with a fork rather than a spoon or knife or chopsticks, and most students attend classes in pants or skirts rather than gowns or bathing suits. If you eat vegetables with a spoon or attend class in a gown or bathing suit, the chances are you will not be arrested or beaten, but you may receive some smiles, glances, or occasional comments from others. Why? It may be easier to use a spoon for eating vegetables, and on hot days, a bathing suit may be more comfortable attire. The reason that people would express mild disapproval is that these behaviors violate folkways that exist in the United States.

Like other norms, folkways are learned in interaction with others and are passed down from generation to generation. Folkways change as culture changes or when we enter different situations. Our tendency is to accept the folkways as appropriate without question. Why do suburbanites fertilize lawns and keep them trimmed? Why do people avoid facing one another in elevators? Why are people expected to chew food quietly and with their mouths closed? No written rules are being violated in these situations, and no one is being physically harmed. These are simply the folkways of our culture, the set of norms that specify the way things are usually done, and people who violate these norms are punished only mildly if at all.

Mores are considered more important than folkways, and reactions to their violation are more serious. They are more likely than folkways to involve clear-cut distinctions between right and wrong, and they are more closely associated with the values a society considers important. Violations of mores inspire intense reactions, and some type of punishment inevitably follows. The punishment may involve expulsion from the group, harsh ridicule, imprisonment, or in some cases even death. Why don't people masturbate in public? Why don't physicians end the life of elderly people who have terminal illnesses? Why don't people betray their country's well-being for money? Actions such as these violate cultural mores. Mores that prohibit something, that state "thou shalt not," are **taboos**. To love and care for one's children is a *mos* (the Latin singular of *mores*); to commit incest (marry or have intercourse) with them or neglect them is a taboo. In the United States, people who murder, commit treason, or engage in incest are widely regarded as sinful and wicked. They violate the mores of society by engaging in taboo behaviors.

Because folkways and mores differ only in degree, it is sometimes difficult to tell them apart. Furthermore, because folkways and mores are elements of culture, they vary from one society or subculture to another. The physical punishment of children may be a folkway in some cultures and a taboo in others. Killing may be rewarded in war but condemned in one's local community. Marriage between blacks and whites may be a norm in Hawaii and a strong taboo in some other states. To function effectively in a culture, one must learn the culture's appropriate folkways and mores.

Certain norms that a society feels strongly about may become **laws**, which are formal, standardized expressions of norms enacted by legislative bodies to regulate particular types of behaviors. Laws do not merely state what behaviors are not permitted; they also state the punishment for violating the law. Ideally, the punishment should reflect the seriousness of the crime or civil offense and should be carried out by a judicial system. This system legitimizes physical coercion and is above the control of any individual member of a society. Within the boundaries of their duties, members of a judicial system can use physical force, imprison, or even kill without retaliation. Laws, therefore, are formalized legislated norms that are enforced by a group designated for that purpose. In contrast, folkways and mores (unless they are made into laws) are enforced only by the members of society themselves, not by a separate group designated as enforcers.

When a law does not reflect folkways and mores, its enforcement is likely to be ignored or given low priority. Although certain actions may be formally defined as illegal in certain communities (shopping on Sundays, smoking marijuana, having sex outside of marriage), enforcement is ignored because of changing folkways or mores that grant a degree of social approval to the behavior. This suggests that conformity to the norms of society does not come from formal law-enforcement officials but from the informal interaction of members of society. Most norms are followed by members of society, but adherence is not rigid. Adaptations to changing conditions are possible, and a certain degree of deviation from existing norms is both possible and beneficial for the effective functioning of society.

Indeed, it is important to realize that cultural norms (folkways and mores) are not always beneficial for a society, group, or individual. Some norms may actually be harmful, what Erich Fromm (1965) calls the **"pathology of normalcy."** Thus, we can follow cultural norms when they do not harm us, but we do not always have to follow them. You might be able to improve the quality of your life if you analyze the costs and benefits of the norms you are expected to follow by society or by your peer group. As one clinical sociologist notes,

> Is it part of your peer subculture to take the easy way through school rather than to read, research, study, learn basic skills, and treat teachers and others with respect even while you disagree with them? The benefit of following peer-group norms of little work might be a degree with "no sweat," but the costs may be educationally empty school years, boredom, a bad conscience, a lack of pride in oneself, few solid accomplishments, and lifelong deficits in skills such as reading, writing, and critical thinking. Researching and analyzing the student subculture may show a pathology of normalcy. (Cohen, 1985, p. 46)

In this case, you might decide to deviate from the norms in order to maximize your gains.

The process of violating norms beyond the range of group acceptability is called "deviance," and the process of applying sanctions to obtain social conformity is known as "social control."

Technology and Material Culture

In addition to the nonmaterial aspects of culture—symbols, language, values, norms, and laws—there are certain material techniques and products used by societies to maintain their standards of living and their lifestyles. The practical production and application of these techniques and products is a culture's **technology**. Technology applies the knowledge gained by science in ways that influence all aspects of culture. It includes social customs and practical techniques for converting raw materials to finished products. The production and use of food, shelter, and clothing, as well as commodities and physical structures, are also aspects of a society's technology. These physical products are **artifacts**. A society's artifacts can be very diverse: beer cans, religious objects, pottery, art, pictures, typewriters, computer terminals, buildings and building materials, clothes, books, and even contraceptive devices. Material artifacts reflect the nonmaterial culture—symbols, beliefs, values, norms, and behaviors—shared by the members of a society.

Artifacts provide clues to a society's level of technological development. Americans, especially those of European descent, take great pride in their level of technology. The ability to perform heart transplants, to split atoms, and to produce sophisticated patriotic missiles, supersonic jets, computers, and environmentally controlled living and working conditions leads us to perceive our type of culture as superior, advanced, and progressive. This perception is often accompanied by a belief that cultures with a low level of technological development are inferior and nonprogressive.

These are subjective perceptions, however, not scientific criteria for evaluating cultures. A more objective evaluation of what some call "less-developed" cultures indicates that they possess an amazing degree of skill and ingenuity in dealing with the environment. Many apparently crude techniques are based on fundamental principles of engineering. Today, people marvel at the rice terraces built several thousand years ago on mountainsides in Asia, which included water distribution systems that seem difficult to improve on today. These rice fields produced food for generations of families and communities without the aid of diesel tractors, complex machinery, or hybrid rice plants, and many are still in use. Anthropologists know of countless instances of the survival of people under conditions that few members of "highly developed" cultures could endure. The adobe huts of Native Americans, the igloos of the Eskimos, or the bamboo houses of rural southeast Asia, none of which have indoor plumbing, heating, or air conditioning, would be inadequate homes for most members of more technologically advanced cultures. Yet these people's technology is suited to and perfectly adequate for their particular lifestyles. It could be argued that in more developed nations, the technology is developed by a handful of specialists, so the general population is less technologically proficient than members of so-called primitive groups.

The goals and consequences of technology and the production of material goods are being seriously questioned today. Does a high level of technology increase happiness and improve family life? Do complex technologies bring us clean air and pure water and help us conserve natural resources? All cultures possess a technology so that they can apply knowledge to master the environment and to interact effectively with nature. It is a mistake to dismiss a culture's technological system because it appears less developed or complex than our own.

Thinking Sociologically

The values of a culture are often represented by physical objects. What can you tell about American culture from studying the inside of a refrigerator and of a housing subdivision?

Cultural Lag

Technology and material culture are cumulative; that is, when a more efficient method or tool is found, the old one is replaced. Note how word processors are replacing typewriters, and microcomputers are replacing calculators, for example. The new method or tool must be consistent with the values and beliefs of the culture it is used in, however. Ogburn (1950) wrote that when changes in technology and material culture come more rapidly than changes in nonmaterial culture, we have a phenomenon know as **cultural lag**. Since Ogburn wrote this, it has been recognized that cultural lag occurs not only when material aspects of culture change more rapidly than nonmaterial aspects, but also when two or more aspects of the culture change at different rates. The public acceptance of clean air, for example, has outpaced our governmental interest in forcing companies to eliminate the pouring of pollutants into the air. The desire for the elimination of cancer and AIDS outpaces our cures for them.

In a rapidly changing society, cultural lag is inevitable. Although many effective means of controlling population have been developed, they have not been adopted in some cultures because they are inconsistent with societal beliefs and values. In the United States, for instance, contraceptive devices such as condoms, diaphragms, foams, jellies, and birth control pills are widely used and available to the general population. Yet many adults view their use among adolescents as inappropriate and immoral and believe that they are a cause of high rates of illegitimate births among teenagers. In Latin America, these same contraceptive devices are not suitable to many cultures because of their inconsistency with religious values, even though these devices are available and have proven to be highly effective when properly used. Many other examples can be given: The development of weapons may surpass the techniques of diplomacy and statesmanship within many countries. Medical advances that prolong life may surpass our ability to provide meaningful tasks for the elderly. The production of handguns may surpass our willingness and ability to control their sale, distribution, and use. Cultural lag indicates that various elements of culture change at different rates and shows how the technological and material aspects of culture affect and are affected by the nonmaterial aspects of culture.

Our attention is often focused on material aspects of culture because of their concrete nature. When archaeologists dig up the remains of an ancient civilization, they may find pots, shells, stones, jewelry, building foundations, and bones. When people visit other countries, they notice the goods in the markets, the means of transportation, and the types of housing, whereas the values, beliefs, and meanings associated with symbols and with the language system are less obvious. The material and nonmaterial are both significant elements of culture, however, and they have a strong influence on each other.

INTERPRETING CULTURE: OUR OWN AND OTHERS

An enormous variety of cultural symbols, languages, values, norms, and technologies is available to us. How do members of a society decide which to accept or use? When a society chooses one cultural system, how do its members perceive the systems of other cultures? Answers to such questions can be found by examining such concepts as ethnocentrism, xenocentrism, temporocentrism, and cultural relativism.

Ethnocentrism

Do you know of any culture that is better than your own? Do you think other types of families, religions, races, school systems, athletes, or artists are superior to, or even as good as, those found in your society? If not, you are like most people in assuming that your own culture, group, and behaviors are superior to those of others. The attitude that our own culture is superior to others, that our own beliefs, values, and behaviors are more correct than others, and that other people and cultures can be evaluated in terms of our own culture is known as **ethnocentrism.** Ethnocentrism was defined by Sumner (1906) as "that view of things in which one's own group is the center of everything and all others are scaled and rated with reference to it" (p. 13).

Most groups in any society tend to be ethnocentric. Religious groups believe that they know the "truth" and are more moral than others. Some even send out missionaries to convert the heathens and to change the pagan lifestyles of those whom they consider to be backward and lost. Scientists are equally likely to believe that their methods are the best way to approach problems. Countries spend vast sums to defend their economic and political system, believing that their way of life is worth dying for. Most Americans believe that monogamy is more "proper" than polygamy and that capitalism is far superior to communism. Most of us shudder when we read a headline such as "Restaurant in China Serves Rat 30 Ways" (*Wall Street Journal*, May 31, 1991). Many of us are likely to consider people who scar their bodies to be masochists. We are likely to believe that people who refuse to drink milk are ignorant and that people who walk around half-naked are shameless. Each of these views illustrates ethnocentrism: We judge other cultures according to the perspectives and standards of our own. We think it quite natural that American women paint their lips and hang jewelry from their ears, that men tie a strip of cloth around their necks, and that people eat corn, which is considered chicken food in many cultures.

Most people spend their entire lives in the culture in which they were born, and ethnocentrism is particularly strong among people who have had little contact with other cultures. Yet ethnocentric attitudes are maintained even among people who have considerable formal education, access to the mass media, and extensive experience traveling in other countries. Functionalists might argue that this is so because ethnocentrism is functional for a society's and a group's existence because it promotes group loyalty, cohesiveness, and unity. It also improves morale, encourages conformity, and reinforces nationalism and patriotism. Ethnocentric cultures have confidence in their own traditions; they discourage outsiders and thus protect themselves against change. Cultures that consider themselves superior tend to maintain the status quo—if our culture is already best, why change it?

On the other hand, some aspects of ethnocentrism are dysfunctional and have negative consequences. Ethnocentrism can increase resistance to change and can encourage the exclusion of outsiders who may have something good to contribute. It can encourage racism, discourage integration efforts, increase hostility and conflicts among groups, and prevent changes that could be beneficial to all. Carried to an extreme, ethnocentrism is destructive, as evidenced by the Nazis in Germany, who believed in the absolute superiority of the "white Aryan" race and culture. The result was the death of millions of people who did not fit into this category.

Xenocentrism

The opposite of ethnocentrism is **xenocentrism**, the belief that what is foreign is best, that our own lifestyle, products, or ideas are inferior to those of others. The strange, distant, and exotic are regarded as having special value: cars made in Japan, watches made in Switzerland, beer brewed in Germany, fashions created in France, silks imported from India and Thailand, and gymnasts from eastern European countries are believed to be superior to our own. In some instances, feelings of xenocentrism are so strong that people reject their own group. Thus we find anti-American Americans, anti-Semitic Jews, priests who revolt against the church, blacks who reject a black identity, and family members who scorn their kin network. Xenocentrism may focus on a product, an idea, or a lifestyle. Regardless of the focus, it is assumed that native techniques and concepts are inferior.

Temporocentrism

The temporal equivalent of ethnocentrism is **temporocentrism**, the belief that our own time is more important than the past or future. Accordingly, historical events are judged not in their own context but on the basis of contemporary standards. Our tendency toward temporocentrism leads us to assume that current crises are more crucial than those of other periods, that problems need to be solved now before it is too late. An associated belief is that actions taken now will have an enormous impact on life in the future. This belief could conceivably be warranted—as in the case of nuclear warfare, which could end world civilization—but in most cases, what we do in our time will later be viewed as only a minor ripple on the stream of history.

Just as ethnocentrism is strongest among people with little education or exposure to other nations, temporocentrism is most prevalent among people who lack historical perspective. Even people with extensive educational training and a strong grasp of history tend to focus on the present, however. Politicians and social scientists view today as the critical time. Sermons, newspapers, and teachers stress that we are living in perilous times, that this is the age of transition.

Cultural Relativism

Social scientists who study other cultures tend to be highly temporocentric, but most make special efforts to avoid ethnocentrism and xenocentrism. They attempt to view all behaviors, lifestyles, and ideas in their own context. The belief that cultures must be judged on their own terms rather than by the standards of another culture is **cultural relativism**.

According to the cultural relativistic perspective, an act, idea, form of dress, or other cultural manifestation is not inherently right or wrong, correct or incorrect. These things should be judged only in the context in which they occur; what is appropriate in one culture or context may be inappropriate in another. Nudity in the shower is appropriate, but nudity in the classroom is inappropriate. In some hunting societies, being fat may have survival value and may serve as a source of admiration. In America, however, fatness is regarded as unhealthful and rarely serves as a source of admiration. The practice of abandoning unwanted infants would be viewed as intolerable by most contemporary cultures, but many cultures used to follow this practice, and some still do. The point is that any aspect of a culture must be considered within its larger cultural context. Each aspect may be regarded as good if it is acceptable to the members and helps attain desired goals and bad if it is unacceptable or fails to achieve these goals.

Cultural relativity does *not* mean that a behavior appropriate in one place is appropriate everywhere. It is not a license to do as one wishes. Even though having three wives is acceptable for Moslem men, killing female infants is acceptable in a Brazilian tribe, and wearing loincloths is acceptable to African bushmen, these behaviors are not acceptable to most Americans in New York or Los Angeles. They are appropriate in some societies because they are part of a larger belief and value system and are consistent with other norms appropriate to that cultural setting. Judging other societies on the basis of cultural relativism makes us less likely to ridicule or scorn the beliefs and habits of people from other cultures.

APPLYING CULTURAL RELATIVISM

The worth of cultural relativism goes beyond analyzing or judging other societies. That aspect is important for social scientists, but the cultural relativistic perspective is also important for anyone who comes into contact with people from different cultures. Consider, for example, teachers in the United States who are faced with the growing number of students from minority cultures and the prospect of teaching within bilingual education programs. Many teachers have been taught to judge students by the norms of white, middle-class children (See and Strauss, 1985).

However, norms are different from culture to culture. For example, a Native American student might pause two or three seconds before answering a question out of courtesy. A Hawaiian student might interrupt a questioner because such behavior displays interest. Hispanic and Asian children might not maintain eye contact with the teacher because they were raised in cultures in which it is disrespectful to maintain eye contact with someone of higher status. In these situations, it is possible that the teachers might interpret the child's actions as signs of being unprepared, inattentive, or disrespectful, and might treat them accordingly. This ethnocentrism on the part of the teachers could decrease their effectiveness. Ronald Tharp, a professor at the University of California who studies culture and education among ethnic groups, notes that "Every little classroom is turning into a United Nations ... with all the hazards and complexities that that involves. It's as if every teacher has to be a [former U.N. Secretary General Javier Perez] de Cuellar" (Marklein, 1991, p. 9D).

Cultural relativism is important in any type of situation that involves people with different cultural backgrounds. As sociologists See and Strauss (1985, p. 69) note, "Utilizing the cultural [relativistic] approach in the practice of counseling, education, public administration, and the health-care and service professions means that special attention is placed on how the individual one is dealing with analyzes situations given their particular cultural backgrounds, social characteristics, and group affiliations."

The approach also makes good business sense. The would-be entrepreneur from New York who visits the South and notices the lack of Jewish delicatessens might think she has stumbled upon a "gold mine." Assuming that a commodity that is highly valued in one cultural region will be just as "hot" in another region might lead to a financial disaster.

CULTURAL COMPLEXITY AND DIVERSITY

A culture is not simply an accumulation of isolated symbols, languages, values, norms, behaviors, and technology. It is a complex and diverse system of many interdependent factors influenced by physical circumstances—climate, geography, population, and plant and animal life. Eskimos traditionally eat meat almost exclusively, live in igloos or huts made of skins, and dress in furs. Many societies in tropical rain forests have diets composed primarily of fruits and vegetables, live in shelters made of leaves and branches, and wear few clothes. Physical circumstances, however, may have less influence on a culture's functioning than such social factors as contact with other cultures, the stage of technological development, or the prevailing ideologies—the assertions and theories characteristic of the group. The complexity and diversity of a culture can be better understood by examining various units of a culture, such as subcultures, countercultures, idiocultures, the ideal and real cultures, and social institutions.

Subcultures

It is rare to find a society that has a single culture shared equally by all its members. This could happen only in small, isolated, nonindustrial societies. Most societies include groups who share some of the cultural elements of the larger society yet also have their own distinctive set of norms, values, symbols, and lifestyles. These units of culture are **subcultures**. Subcultures exist within the confines of a larger culture. They often reflect racial or ethnic differences, such as those found among black, Polish, or Chinese Americans. Other subcultures develop around occupations: athletics, the military, medicine, or factory work. The Mormons, Amish, Hutterites, and other groups form religious subcultures; some are based on geography, such as those found in the South and New England; others are based on wealth and age. There are also drinking, drug, reggae, and homosexual subcultures. Every society that has diverse languages, religions, ethnic or racial groups, or varying economic levels has subcultures.

All subcultures participate in the larger, dominant culture but possess their own set of cultural elements: symbols, languages, values, norms, and technologies. In heterogeneous societies, a person may be a member of several subcultures at any one time or at different times in his or her life. In the United States, a black adolescent male living in poverty may speak a black dialect, wear a characteristic style of clothing, enjoy soul food, and obtain money by means considered appropriate to his subculture but unacceptable to the dominant culture. An Amish adolescent male living on a Pennsylvania farm might speak a form of German, wear a black suit and hat, part his hair in the middle, enjoy

POLICY DEBATE

Bilingual Education

One of the most controversial policy debates in the United States concerns bilingual education—education that involves two languages. In the United States, these languages are English and a minority language. This debate has had a long, stormy history in the United States. In the mid-1800s, various states with large immigrant communities passed laws that allowed education in languages other than English—for example, German in Wisconsin and Pennsylvania—but then repealed them after World War I, largely due to nationalistic sentiments (Romaine, 1989). The debate was revived when the federal government passed the Bilingual Education Act of 1968. The legislation recognized that "the use of a child's mother tongue can have a beneficial effect upon his *[sic]* education" (Haugen, 1987, p. 4) and that there are "special education needs of a great many students whose mother tongue is other than English" (Stoller, 1976, p. 50). This spurred many sociologists, educators, and linguists to implement bilingual education programs in communities with large numbers of people with limited English proficiency (LEP). The hope was that bilingual education would reduce the LEP students' sense of alienation in an all-English world (Haugen, 1987). Although some bilingual education programs are designed to maintain the native language and culture of the child ("maintenance programs"), most are aimed at providing a transition to English and to mainstream American culture ("transitional programs") (Hakuta, 1986).

The bilingual education debate continues today. This is due mainly to the rapidly expanding proportion of minorities in this country. In America today, more people speak foreign languages than ever before (Bernstein, 1990). This fact has vast implications for education. For example, in New York, over 40 percent of elementary- and secondary-school children belong to an ethnic minority. In California, white pupils are already a minority (Henry, 1990).

Advocates of bilingual education indicate the increasing number of LEP students as one important reason that bilingual education is needed. They claim that because federal policy has been responsible for the presence of a large part of the LEP population in the United States—for example, through the acquisition of territory (such as Puerto Rico) and through wars (such as Vietnam and the Mexican-American Wars)—there should be continued federal policy for bilingual education (Hakuta, 1986). Proponents also claim that a "white, Anglo" education is demeaning and psychologically harmful to minority groups (Bernstein, 1990). They cite bilingual education as the best chance for LEP students—often, not coincidentally, low-income people—to partake fully

sauerkraut and potatoes, be forbidden to dance or go to movies, and turn all earnings over to his father. Both the black and the Amish adolescent are required to abide by the laws of the dominant society, however.

At times, the dominant culture and the subculture may conflict to such a degree that tremendous stresses occur, and a crisis results. Members of the subculture may be required by the dominant culture to register for the military even though they value pacifism. The subculture may value the use of particular drugs but be forbidden by the dominant culture to obtain them. Also, note how subcultural differences are at the heart of the policy issue se-

Bilingual Education, *continued*

in the opportunities of American life (Bernstein, 1990, p. 48). The National Association for Bilingual Education (NABE), for example, has argued that bilingual education programs have led to "improved academic achievement test scores, reduced rates of school dropout and student absenteeism, increased community involvement in education, and enhanced student self-esteem" for LEP students. NABE suggests that this overall improvement in the effectiveness of education benefits not only minority group members, but also the future economic productivity of the United States as a whole. Additionally, it lays the foundation for improving the linguistic competencies of all Americans and enhances their understanding, tolerance, and appreciation for other cultures (Hakuta, 1986).

On the other side, one of the strongest arguments presented against bilingual education is that English is necessary for economic success in the United States (Hakuta, 1986). Opponents believe that bilingual education inadequately prepares students for more advanced professional education or high-potential careers (Bernstein, 1990). U.S. English, Inc., one of the groups most adamantly opposed to bilingualism, asserts that "bilingual education retards the acquisition of language skills and integration of the student into the American mainstream." Additionally, they feel that teaching students in their native language could lead parents to the conclusion that English may not be necessary after all in order to succeed. The problem is compounded by the segregation of bilingual students from English-speaking students, which decreases the chances for full assimilation into American culture (Hakuta, 1986). Interestingly, some opponents of bilingual education are immigrants who had to learn English and assimilate quickly upon coming to the United States at a young age. They insist that a bilingual education would have impeded their integration into American society (Romaine, 1989). Many opponents feel that the United States is becoming too ethnically diverse at a time when there is a strong need to pull the various parts together, and argue that too much cultural diversity leads to a lack of common ground (Bernstein, 1990). They maintain that bilingual education leads to cultural pluralism rather than assimilation, and thus has negative consequences for members of minority groups and for the nation as a whole.

Clearly, the debate over bilingual education is more than a debate about language. It is a debate about cultural pluralism versus cultural assimilation and the values of each.

lected for this chapter: bilingualism. Can or should Spanish, Japanese, or Arab immigrants to the United States be able to retain their native language in their places of work? Can or should children in the public schools be given reading materials and exams in their native language when that language is not English? Subcultural differences and the rights of specific religious, ethnic, or other minority groups are central to many legal and policy debates. An understanding of subcultures makes us realize the importance of differences not merely among cultures but also in the diversity of thinking and behaving of different people within a culture as well.

Thinking Sociologically

Richard Bernstein (1990, p. 48) wrote the following about bilingual education:

> What's at stake … is nothing less than the cultural identity of the country. Those who argue that bilingual education is a right, make up a kind of informal coalition with those who are pressing for changes in the way the United States is perceived—no longer as a primarily European entity to which all others have to adapt, but as a diverse collection of ethnic groups, each of which deserves more or less equal status and respect. …
>
> Those on the other side insist that diversity is all well and good; but they argue that bilingual education could lead to an erosion of the national unity, a fragmentation of the nation into mutually hostile groups.

Use the knowledge about culture presented in this chapter to discuss why and how the policy debate over bilingual education is much more than a debate about language usage in schools.

Countercultures

A **counterculture** is a subculture that adheres to a set of beliefs and values that "rejects and opposes significant elements of the dominant culture of which it is a part" (Johnson, 2000, p. 65). Because they accept such beliefs and values, members of a counterculture may behave in such radically nonconformist ways that they may drop out of society. *Dropping out* may mean either physically leaving or ideologically and behaviorally leaving, by rejecting the dominant values and working to change them.

Delinquent gangs, the Hare Krishna religious sect, and some extreme right-wing religious groups of the 1980s can all be classified as countercultures. The norms and values of each of these groups contrast sharply with those held by conventional middle-class groups. Often, these values are not merely different from those of the dominant culture, but in opposition to them. Delinquent gangs may grant prestige and social approval for lawbreaking, violence, theft, or the use of drugs to achieve their goals of dominance and material success. The stated goal of the Hare Krishna religious sect is the salvation of the world through its conversion to Krishna Consciousness. The Krishna counterculture entails considerable ritualism, ceremony, shaved heads, chant-ins, proselytizing in airports, and other activities often viewed as countercultural. The youth movement of the 1960s, which included political activists, dropouts, and hippies, actively challenged the dominant cultural norms of hard work, financial success, conformity of dress, sexual restrictiveness, military superiority, and white supremacy. Perhaps the pendulum has swung away from countercultural trends among youth to countercultural trends among extreme right-wing adults. Some right-wing religious groups in the 1980s and 1990s have been behind the bombing of abortion clinics, while less extreme groups have made efforts to legalize corporal punishment, mandate prayer in the public schools, and demand the inclusion of creationism in the school curriculum.

Idiocultures

Gary Fine (1979) has argued that every group forms its own culture to a certain extent and called these created cultures **idiocultures**. An *idioculture* is a system of knowledge, beliefs, behaviors, and customs created through group interactions. Members of a group share particular experiences and recognize that references to a shared experience will be understood by other members. Members of one group, for example, might roar with laughter whenever the word *cashew* is mentioned because it triggers a memory of a shared humorous experience. All small groups have a culture that is unique to themselves but that is nevertheless part of a larger cultural pattern. A group's idioculture is formed by the group itself, so idiocultures do not exist when a group is first formed. They are created from the opening moments of group interaction when people begin to learn names and other information about one another. With time, rules are established, opinions expressed, information exchanged, and events experienced together.

Suppose, for example, that a newspaper has just been established and that the editors, reporters, typesetters, and other employees have come together for the first time. Initially, they will have shared no experiences, but as they work together, they will develop unique ways of interacting. At first, the reporters may go out for coffee individually, but eventually they might decide to delegate one person to get coffee for everyone. "Gathering background information" might become a euphemism for wasting time. When the Johnson Warehouse is destroyed in the biggest fire that ever happened in the town, they might come to refer to any big story as a "Johnson." Similarly, stories dealing with improper behavior by politicians might come to be called "Watergates" and the task of writing the relatively uninteresting daily reports about weddings, funerals, and meetings might come to be called the "trivia." After a few unpleasant arguments, the reporters might agree never to comment on one another's stories. After working together for an extended period, the group would develop its own jargon and set of customs that would not be understood by an outsider.

Ideal and Real Culture

In most cultures, differences exist between what people are supposed to do and what they actually do. The **ideal culture** consists of the norms and values people profess to follow; the **real culture** is the culture they actually do follow. If you were asked to tell a foreign visitor about the norms and values of Americans, for example, you would probably describe the ideal culture, mentioning such topics as freedom, democracy, equal rights, monogamy, marital fidelity, and educational opportunity for all. The actual culture differs considerably from the ideal, however. The very poor are less likely to get a good education, marital infidelity is common, and many people have several spouses during their lives.

This distinction between real and ideal culture is expressed by some anthropologists in terms of "explicit" culture and "implicit" culture. These terms may be more accurate than "real" and "ideal"—both types of culture are real in the sense that they actually exist. The point is that stated cultural norms and values are not always practiced. Students should be sensitive to distinctions of this sort. The speed limit may be 55, but many people drive at speeds of 65 or higher. Honesty in the classroom may be the norm, but cheating may be widespread. Clashes between ideal and actual practices may be avoided through rationalizations or flexibility in social control. A student might defend cheating on a test by arguing that "everyone does it." Police rarely arrest all who exceed the speed limit, concentrating instead on extreme violations.

Although cultures vary in their symbols, language, and behavior, and in their subcultures, countercultures, real and ideal cultures, and so forth, all share some basic concerns known as **cultural universals**. People in all cultures must have food, shelter, and protection. All people face illness and death, and every society has a kinship system with taboos on incest. Like American suburbanites, African bushmen and Mongolian nomads socialize and train their members in the ways of the culture, provide for work and leisure activities, and establish leaders and rulers. Many of these basic social needs are met through social institutions. (See George Murdock.)

Social Institutions

A *social institution* is a system of norms, values, statuses, and roles that develops around a basic social goal. Like the concepts *norm* and *value*, the concept **institution** is abstract. All societies have particular institutions to meet their broad goals; indeed, institutions form the foundation of society and supply the basic prerequisites of group life. The family reproduces and socializes children. Religion affirms values and provides an approach to nonempirical questions. Education transmits cultural heritage, knowledge, and skills from one generation to the next. Economic institutions produce and distribute goods and services. Political institutions provide social leadership and protect individuals from one another and from forces outside the society. Other important institutions include marriage, medicine, transportation, and entertainment.

Social institutions are often confused with social groups and social organizations. They are not the same, however. Like institutions, both groups and organizations exist to meet some goals, but groups and organizations are deliberately constructed bodies of individuals, whereas institutions are systems of norms. Thus, education is an institution; the University of Vermont is an organization. Religion is an institution; the Baptist church is an organization.

The confusion between institutions and organizations stems in part from the fact that the names of institutions can often be used to describe concrete entities as well. In its abstract sense, for example, the word *family* is used to refer to an institution. Using the word in this way, we might say, "During the 1980s, the family in the United States experienced important changes." We can also use the word *family* to refer to an actual group of people, however. Using the word in this concrete sense, we might say, "I am going to spend my vacation with my family." The speaker is referring to an existing group of individuals—mother, father, sisters, and brothers. The two meanings of the word are closely related but nevertheless distinct. The word *institution* is an abstraction; the word *organization* refers to an existing group. The distinction should become clearer as we discuss social structures, social groups, social organizations, and specific institutions in future chapters.

SUMMARY

1. A *culture* is a society's social heritage, the system of ideas, values, beliefs, knowledge, norms, customs, and technology that everyone in a society shares.
2. A *society* is a group of people who share a common culture. Some of the most significant elements of a culture are symbols, language, values, norms, and technology.
3. *Symbols* are arbitrary representations of something. The use of symbols is a human capability that allows us to make sense of reality, transmit messages, store complex information, and deal with an abstract world.
4. Our most important set of symbols is language, which enables us to transmit and store our social heritage. The importance of language to humans is illustrated in studies comparing the development of children and of animals such as chimpanzees.
5. It has been demonstrated that language influences how we perceive and experience the

world. The Sapir-Whorf hypothesis suggests that the use of different languages by different societies causes them to perceive the world very differently. Rather than simply seeing the same world with different labels, they actually perceive different realities.

6. *Values* are conceptions about what is important and of worth. They are learned and shared cultural products that justify particular types of behavior. People in the United States tend to value achievement, success, work, a moral orientation, and humanitarian concerns, among other things.

7. Values indicate what is important, whereas norms are rules of conduct, the standards and expectations of behavior. Norms are of two types: *folkways*, which are customs or conventions that provoke only mild censure if violated; and *mores*, which are far more important and provoke severe punishment if violated. Laws are the formalized and standardized expressions of norms.

8. In addition to the nonmaterial aspects of culture such as these, there are material and technological aspects as well. Cultural lag occurs when different aspects of a society change and adapt at differing rates.

9. Members of a society tend to view their own culture in particular ways. *Ethnocentrism* is the belief that one's own culture is superior to others and that one's own cultural standards can be applied in judging other cultures. *Xenocentrism* is the belief that what is foreign is best, that one's own lifestyle, products, or ideas are inferior to those of others. *Temporocentrism* is the belief that the past should be judged in terms of the present and that one's own time is exceptionally important.

10. The idea of *cultural relativism* suggests that cultures must be judged on their own terms, not by the standards of another culture: Acts, ideas, and products are not inherently good or bad; they must be judged in the cultural context in which they happen.

11. A culture is not simply a collection of isolated ideas and values. It is a complex, organized system in which all components, such as its institutions and its subcultures, are interrelated and interdependent.

12. *Subcultures* are groups within a society that share the common culture but have their own distinctive set of cultural complexes. A *counterculture* is a type of subculture adhering to a set of norms and values that sharply contradict the dominant norms and values of the society of which the group is a part. To a certain extent, all groups possess localized cultures of their own, which are known as *idiocultures*.

13. The culture a society professes to follow (its ideal culture) differs from the culture it actually does follow (its real culture).

14. Many social needs common to all cultures are met through social institutions, which are systems of norms, values, statuses, and roles that develop around basic social goals.

15. Understanding the various elements of cul ture is useful in a variety of occupational settings, including health professions, service organizations, politics, public administration, education, business, and others, as well as in your personal life. Sociologists have come to be used as cultural translators who help to lessen misperceptions and increase understandings among people from diverse cultural settings.

KEY TERMS

artifacts Physical products or objects created through human actions.

counterculture A subculture that adheres to a set of norms and values that sharply contradict the dominant norms and values of the society of which that group is a part.

cultural lag The tendency for changes in nonmaterial culture to occur more slowly than changes in technology and material culture.

cultural relativism The belief that cultures must be judged on their own terms rather than by the standards of another culture.

cultural universals Aspects of culture that are shared by all people, such as symbols, shelter, food, and a belief system.

culture The systems of ideas, values, beliefs, knowledge, norms, customs, and technology shared by almost everyone in a particular society.

elite culture The materials and ideas of wealthy, affluent, or upper classes (in contrast to popular culture).

ethnocentrism The view that one's own culture is superior to others and should be used as the standard against which other cultures are judged.

folkways Norms of conduct of everyday life that bring only mild censure or punishment if they are violated.

ideal culture The norms and values that people profess to follow.

idioculture The system of knowledge, beliefs, behaviors, and customs that is unique to a given group.

institution A stable cluster of values, norms, statuses, and roles that develops around a basic social goal.

language The systematized use of speech and hearing to communicate feelings and ideas.

laws Formal, standardized expressions of norms enacted by legislative bodies to regulate certain types of behaviors.

mores Norms of conduct associated with strong feelings of right or wrong, violations of which bring intense reaction and some type of punishment.

norms Formal and informal rules of conduct and social expectations for behavior.

pathology of normalcy The concept that cultural norms are not always beneficial for a society, group, or individual.

popular culture Trends, social activities, and shared experiences of everyday people (in contrast to elite culture).

real culture The norms and values that people actually follow and practice. The real culture may or may not be the same as the ideal culture, which represents the norms and values people profess to follow.

Sapir-Whorf hypothesis The hypothesis that societies with different languages perceive the world differently because their members interpret the world through the grammatical forms, labels, and categories their language provides.

society A group of interacting people who live in a specific geographical area, who are organized in a cooperative manner, and who share a common culture.

subcultures Groups of persons who share in the main culture of a society but also have their own distinctive values, norms, and lifestyles.

symbol Something that is used to represent something else, such as a word, gesture, or object used to represent some aspect of the world.

taboos Mores that prohibit something.

technology The application of nonmaterial and material knowledge by a society to maintain its standard of living and lifestyle.

temporocentrism The belief that one's own time is more important than the past or future.

values Ideas and beliefs shared by the people in a society about what is important and worthwhile.

xenocentrism The belief that what is foreign is best and that one's own lifestyle, products, or ideas are inferior to those of others.

DISCUSSION QUESTIONS

1. Make a list of leisure activities that might be considered elite culture. Do the same for popular culture. How might you explain why you participate in some of these activities and not in others?

2. How many examples can you give of symbols using only your hand and fingers? Can you think of any that mean different things in different contexts or to people of different cultures? Have any of these changed over time?

3. Discuss the significance or accuracy of the statement, "Societies with different languages actually see or perceive the world differently."

4. How would an understanding of the Sapir-Whorf hypothesis help politicians to evaluate whether the United States should promote bilingual education programs?

5. Describe what is meant by value conflict. Give examples. How are such conflicts resolved?

6. Joe listens to his radio (quietly, with earphones, of course), and Mary reads her New York Times in their sociology class. Is this illegal, forbidden, or harmful behavior? Why is the professor likely to disapprove of such behavior?

7. Discuss ways in which existing student norms may not be beneficial or may even be harmful to themselves.

8. Using the concepts of ethnocentrism and cultural relativism, discuss the impact that a bilingual education might have on understanding other cultures.

9. How might ethnocentrism, xenocentrism, and temporocentrism affect people's attitudes toward bilingual education programs?

10. Think about the subcultures, countercultures, or idiocultures of which you are a member. Differentiate these, and explain the differences.

11. Differentiate between real and ideal cultures. Why are they seldom one and the same?

12. What do you perceive to be basic social institutions? Why do they exist?

Social Structure, Social Groups, and Social Organizations

The Bureaucratization of Society

"Organizations surround us; we are born in them and usually die in them; the space in between is filled with them. They are just about impossible to escape. They are inevitable." So writes Richard Hall (1987, p. 1) in his definitive book, *Organizations: Structure, Processes, and Outcomes.* Because this is so, the bureaucratization of organizations is an issue that has captured the interest of sociologists ever since Max Weber wrote on the topic in the late nineteenth century. *Bureaucratization* refers to the changes within organizations toward improved operating efficiency and more effective attainment of organizational goals (Eitzen and Zinn, 1991).

Bureaucratization remains an important social issue because it is necessary as a means for maintaining our style of life as we know it. Charles Perrow (1986) notes, "We have constructed a society where the satisfaction of our wants as consumers largely depends on restricting the employees who do the producing" (p. 5). Until the 1970s, most social scientists criticized bureaucracy on two grounds: rigidity and employee discipline. Perrow offers a third criticism: Bureaucracy has become a means of centralizing power in society and of legitimating or disguising that centralization. This fact is rarely perceived by most of us because we grow up in and spend our lives surrounded by organizations—government, church, school, clubs, teams, hospitals, and so on. To grasp the impact of bureaucratization on us, it is necessary to stand outside them "to see their effect on what we believe, what we value, and, more important, how we think and reason" (Perrow, 1986, p. 5).

Consider this famous case, first presented by Alvin Gouldner (1954) in his book *Patterns of Bureaucracy*, of a gypsum-mining plant in a small midwestern city. Prior to a change in management, the way the plant was organized reflected the small, traditional environment of the nearby semirural towns. People were hired not because of what they knew but because of who they were. The manager allowed the employees a great deal of freedom, such as trying different jobs until they found one they liked, long lunch hours, slack supervision (especially when they had hangovers), occasional "sick days" during hunting and planting season, personal use of plant materials and services, and so on. Eventually, the parent organization, concerned about the plant's production record and its inability to satisfy clients' needs on time, replaced this traditional form of organization with, in Weber's terms, a "rational–legal bureaucracy, a bureaucracy based on rational principles (in terms of management's interests), backed by legal sanctions, and exists in a legal framework" (Perrow, 1986, p. 3). Think how the lives of the employees and the townspeople were controlled by these changes: their free time and how they spent it, friendships in and out of work, job security, income and job benefits, sense of self-worth, and many other areas of their lives.

This chapter describes how the ways in which society is structured affect us as individuals. The statuses, roles, groups, and organizations that we occupy and belong to—concepts that are discussed in this chapter—affect with whom we interact and how, our ideals, our life chances, and our sense of self. As you read the chapter, think of how these elements of social structure are affected by the bureaucratization of organizations and society. The issue of bureaucratization affords us an opportunity to blend macrosociological and microsociological analyses by focusing on how rational, efficient management of organizations and the centralized power it yields to those who are in control affects the nature of our statuses, roles, and group involvements and, in turn, almost every aspect of our lives.

The people who live and interact in a geographical area and share a common culture make up the basic social structure of society. Anything complex has a structure. The building you live in has a physical structure consisting of a certain number of floors, windows and doors, and other physical features. Your body has a biological structure consisting of a brain, digestive system, cardiovascular system, and other anatomical and physiological features. Though we understand the concept of structure, what does it mean to say that society is socially structured? It means that society is organized in a way that makes human behavior and relationships predictable. It means that human behavior is socially patterned. These social regularities or patterns are composed of many interrelated parts or components, which sociologists give labels such as social statuses, roles, groups, organizations, and institutions. With the exception of institutions, these major social structures are examined in this chapter.

SOCIAL STATUSES

Central to an understanding of social structure is the concept of **status**, a socially defined position that an individual occupies. Some statuses are obtained at birth, such as age or sex; these are *ascribed statuses*. Some statuses are those you choose or attain, such as student or parent; these are *achieved statuses*. Every person occupies statuses, including those of age, sex and gender, race, occupation, religion, nationality, and others.

The combination of all the statuses any individual holds at a given time is a **status set**. You, for example, are a student if you are enrolled in a school, a son or daughter to a parent, a brother or sister if you have a sibling, a friend or acquaintance to your peers, and a citizen of some country. A status set including student, daughter, sister, friend, and citizen guides what you do and enables others to predict much of your behavior. Students behave differently from teachers (and are expected to), just as children behave differently from adults.

Sometimes, a particular status in your status set may be of far greater importance than any of the others in shaping both how you see yourself and how others view you. This position, your **master status**, takes priority over the others. As a well-known athlete, chairman of the board, or child of a famous person, you may have doors opened to you that most of us would not have opened to us. On the other hand, suppose that one of your statuses happens to be ex-prisoner, homosexual, citizen of a country the United States dislikes, or a carrier of the AIDS virus. This status may become a master status and cause people to avoid, criticize, or dislike you. All of the other statuses in your status set (husband, father, choir member, employee) may be ignored or subordinated to your master status. Often, societies determine which status becomes your master status. A person's racial status, for example, is a master status in South Africa today. Race is an ascribed status, but other master statuses, such as criminal, are achieved.

SOCIAL ROLES

Status and role, like structure and function, parent and child, or student and teacher, are reciprocal concepts. Any given status in your status set has a dynamic aspect, a set of expectations and behaviors associated with it in a given group or society; these are **roles**. Different roles (expectations for behavior) are associated with different statuses (positions). A useful way to think about this is that you *occupy* a status, you *play* a role. Multiple roles attached to individual statuses are **role sets**. These role expectations and behaviors are learned through the socialization process. Learning what to expect from others who occupy given statuses and what behaviors are appropriate for our own statuses are basic aspects of life as a social being. We learn to expect different behaviors from persons who occupy different statuses. The roles or expectations of a baseball team manager, for instance, differ from those of the batter, pitcher, and fielder. Similarly, roles or expectations differ for infants and adults, males and females, married and single people, and teachers and students.

Sometimes, confusion exists about a given role, in that differences may exist in what is prescribed, what is perceived, and the actual behavior that occurs. To differentiate these, it may help to define prescribed roles, role perceptions, and actual role performance, to clarify any confusion. A **prescribed role** (or roles) describes what society suggests that we should do. The prescribed roles (expectations) for the status of student generally include attending classes, getting to classes on time, listening, taking notes, studying, and getting passing grades. While a student may understand these prescriptions, the student's **role perception** may be that it really is not necessary to attend every class, take complete notes, or get an A or B grade to pass. As a result, some of us have met students whose **role performance** (what they actually do) differs somewhat from the prescribed role. Perhaps you even know students personally who skip class, arrive late when they do attend, and fail to study.

Role perceptions and role performance may differ from the prescription for a variety of reasons. One is that students (or holders of any status or position) may not be deeply committed to the role or may define it as unimportant. A second is that enough flexibility exists in the role that some prescriptions can be fulfilled (such as passing) without the performance (going to class). A third reason may be that the roles associated with other statuses, such as being a boyfriend or girlfriend, athlete, campus leader, and employee, compete for the student's time.

All of us have experienced role ambiguity, role strain, and role conflict. **Role ambiguity** exists when the expectations associated with particular social statuses are unclear. We may not understand precisely what is expected of us. I want to please my date but am uncertain what she expects. I know my friend is making a mistake in marrying that person, but is it my business to inform him?

Role strain results from a role overload or from contradictory demands and expectations built into a given status. Despite our best efforts, the expectations may exceed the time and energy we have available to fulfill them. There may be no role ambiguity about what is expected, but the demands may exceed our abilities. If your parents expect you to get A or B grades, and you cannot meet their expectations because of other demands on your time or because of the difficulty you have in understanding the material, you are likely to experience role strain. If multiple and/or contradictory expectations from a teacher, date, employer, and friend all demand your time, the result, again, will be role strain. The teacher expects studying, the date expects to go to a ball game, the employer expects you to work, and the friend expects you to listen—and all on Monday night.

Role conflict occurs when the demands or expectations associated with two or more statuses are incompatible; though this may also result in role strain, the difficulty is focused on opposing values and the need to make ethical choices. Parents may expect their children not to be involved with drugs, drinking, or sexual activity, whereas friends or dates may expect involvement in all of them. The student who adopts the role of part-time bartender will be expected by her employer to work in an honest and dutiful manner. At the same time, her friends may expect her to give them free drinks. The result: role conflict.

Role conflict can result not only from differing expectations on the part of several persons, but also from having different expectations built into a single status. Can parents be expected to discipline their children at the same time that they are expected to show them love and affection? Can Christians both love their enemies and shoot them during war?

To sum up, then, role ambiguity results from uncertainty over the expectations of a given role. Role strain results from a role overload or the inability to carry out or live up to the expectations of a given status. Role conflict arises from the need to conform to incompatible expectations of the same or differing roles.

Role ambiguity, role strain, and role conflict seem particularly prevalent in industrialized societies where people assume complex status sets with multiple and often unclear and incompatible role expectations. Yet it would be totally misleading to conclude that roles are a negative and troublesome characteristic of human behavior. On the contrary, the role expectations that accompany social statuses are the means by which behavior is made predictable, human relationships become patterned, and society is organized.

APPLYING KNOWLEDGE OF ROLES

Although strict adherence to prescribed role expectations is rare, the power of roles to shape human behavior should not be underestimated. A heatedly debated issue among sociologists, social psychologists, and psychologists is whether the individual shapes the role or the role shapes the individual. Do we often find corruption in high government positions because corrupt people are elected to those positions, or is it because the nature of the role and the power it bestows lead to corruption? Do people have maternal and paternal instincts by nature, or does the role of parent lead one to become nurturing and authoritarian? Are college students "party animals" by nature, or does one become a member of that species because of expectations that students at a particular college should be that way?

The issue will probably never be resolved once and for all, and it may be that role and personality are both involved, but some researchers have found strong evidence that we take on or accept the role we are playing. For example, Zimbardo's famous prison experiment demonstrates the power of social structure and roles over personality. Recall that he had to cancel his experiment prematurely because of how the students—"the cream of the crop of their generation"—had internalized the roles of guards and prisoners that they were assigned to play.

Zimbardo's research is still relevant today. His conclusions were cited in a *Time Magazine* article as an explanation for the behavior of American soldiers mistreating Iraqi prisoners of war in Abu Ghraib. The Bush Administration had blamed the abusive behavior on a "few bad apples." But a look at the backgrounds of the soldiers implicated suggests otherwise. Israeli psychiatrist Dr. Ilan Kutz notes that, "During actual wars, if there isn't any particular command figure in charge who puts a stop to it, [torture and sadism by prison guards] can spread like a psychological epidemic." In prisons, Zimbardo concluded, that abuse is virtually guaranteed if three key components are not present: clear rules, a staff that is well trained in those rules, and tight management that includes punishment for violations. At Abu Ghraib, the conditions for conforming to the role of abuser were present (McGeary, 2004).

How is the knowledge that role expectations play a powerful part in shaping behavior useful to us? Primarily, it alerts us to the possibility that personal and interpersonal behavior is more than a matter of individual personalities or predispositions. This fact in itself has important practical implications. Clinical sociologists, for example, are often hired to conduct training programs in stress management in hospital, business, and educational settings. Training programs that teach managers how to restructure work environments and role relationships are usually more successful in reducing stress than programs that focus exclusively on dealing with the psychological problems of individuals (Goldman, 1984).

Realizing the importance of role relationships and social structure, applied sociologists have actually helped some industries overcome problematic situations. A classic example is William Foote Whyte's work (1949) in the restaurant industry. Whyte found that role ambiguity among waiters, waitresses, and kitchen workers—not personality conflicts—accounted for the friction, anxiety, and emotional outbursts in many restaurants. His solution relied mainly on creating clear, specific roles for each of the different types of workers in the restaurants. It seems obvious to us now that this is the best way to run a restaurant, but in 1949, Whyte's solution had a major impact on the entire restaurant industry.

All of us—sociologists or not—can use what we know about roles and behavior to our advantage. Administrators and managers might examine how roles are structured—instead of individual personalities—to increase efficiency in their organization. In our personal lives, parents might first try to understand the roles outside the family that their children are expected to play before they try to shape their behavior through a series of rewards and punishments.

Clearly, the way that statuses and roles are structured is as important for the success of an organization as selecting the appropriate personnel.

Thinking Sociologically

1. Why is role performance (behavior) not always consistent with role prescriptions?
2. Using school, dating, or work situations, clarify the meaning of role ambiguity, role strain, and role conflict.

SOCIAL GROUPS

We have just discussed how statuses and roles are key components of social structure. Another major component of social structure is the social group.

Humans are social animals. Even those who think of themselves as loners participate in many groups, and, for most of us, groups are a major source of satisfaction. You may eat with a particular group of friends every day, belong to a drama club, or play tennis every week with your gym class. You probably depend on social groups, social organizations, and social systems for most of your psychological and physical needs. Research indicates that we are influenced not only by the groups we currently belong to and those we identify with but also by those we associated with in the past. In fact, life without groups seems impossible. Without group involvements, infants die, adolescents get depressed, middle-aged people suffer psychologically, and the elderly get lonely and lose their will to live. We learn, eat, work, and worship in groups, and deprivation of group involvement is damaging. To better understand groups, we ask, What do sociologists mean when they use the word *group*?

The answer to this question may seem obvious at first: A *group* is a number of people who have something in common. Like most topics in sociology, however, the problem is not that simple. Although the concept of *group* is one of the key elements of sociology, no single definition is universally accepted. The problem is not that sociologists are unable to decide what a group is; rather, there are many types of groups, and sociologists attach different meanings to their forms, their functions, and their consequences.

In our discussion, we focus chiefly on *social groups*—those in which people physically or socially interact. Several other types are also recognized by most sociologists, however, and deserve to be mentioned.

Statistical groups, or, perhaps more accurately, statistical groupings, are formed not by the group members but by sociologists and statisticians. In 2000, for example, there were 75,580,000 family households in the United States (*Current Population Reports*, Series P-20, No. 537, 2000). In 2003, 68% of households were "family" versus "single" households

(*Current Population Reports*, Series P-20, No. 553, 2003). The group of women between 5 feet 1 inch and 5 feet 5 inches tall would be another statistical group. Some sociologists do not consider groups of this sort to be groups at all because the members are unaware of their membership, and there is no social interaction or social organization (see Table 5-1).

Another type of group is the **categorical group** in which a number of people share a common characteristic. Teenagers, the handicapped, unwed mothers, interracial couples, millionaires, redheads, students, women, senior citizens, and virgins are all categorical groups. Members of groups of this type are likely to be aware that they share a particular characteristic and a common identity. Categorical groups, like statistical groups, share common characteristics but are not social groups, in that they do not interact with other members who share their statistical or categorical grouping. They are important, however, in the common identity they share with others like them.

A third type of group is the **aggregate**. An aggregate is a social group comprising a collection of people who are together in one place. You may join a group of this sort buying an ice cream cone, riding a bus, or waiting to cross a street. Aggregates are basically unstructured, and the participants interact briefly and sporadically. Most members act as if they were alone, except perhaps to comment about the weather, ask the time, or complain about the service. The members of an aggregate need not converse but may do so; they need not know one another but may see familiar faces. Members are generally not concerned with the feelings and attitudes of the others. Most aggregates meet only once.

A fourth type is the **associational** or **organizational** group, which is especially important in complex industrialized societies. Associational groups consist of people who join together in some organized way to pursue a common interest, and they have a formal structure. Most of us belong to a number of them; they can be formed for almost any conceivable purpose. A university, a volleyball team, a Rotary Club, the Democratic Party, General Motors Corporation, Protestant churches—all are associational groups. They share the major characteristics of other types of groups, but in addition they also have a formal structure.

As you can see, a number of different kinds of groups are recognized, and their boundaries are not easy to state clearly. Like other classification schemes, the one we have suggested makes use of some criteria but ignores others that may in some circumstances be equally important. Groups might

TABLE 5-1 A CLASSIFICATION OF NONSOCIAL AND SOCIAL GROUPS

Type of Group	Awareness of Kind	Social Interaction	Social Organization	Example
Statistical	No	No	No	Average family size
Categorical	Yes	No	No	Redheads
Aggregate	Yes	Yes	No	Football crowd
Associational	Yes	Yes	Yes	Rotary club

also be classified on the basis of social boundaries between members and nonmembers, adherence to a special set of norms, awareness not only of kind, as in Table 5-1, but also of membership, or a variety of other factors.

Given this range of definitions and possible classification criteria, what types of collectives can we call social groups? Although sociologists do not accept a single definition, there would be widespread agreement that membership in a **social group** involves (a) some type of interaction; (b) a sense of belonging or membership; (c) shared interests or agreement on values, norms, and goals; and (d) a structure—that is, a definable, recognizable arrangement of parts. Thus, the sociological use of *group* involves interaction, a consciousness of membership, shared interests, and a definable structure.

Social groups are important because they provide us with a social identity, serve as a key to understanding social behavior, link the self with the larger society, and help us understand social structure and societal organization. By studying the individual in a group context, the dynamic interactions within groups, and the organizational network of the larger society, we can improve our understanding of the self, of human interaction, and of the larger social order

TYPES OF SOCIAL GROUPS

Social groups vary widely in their size, purpose, and structure (see Figure 5-1). Some are short-lived, such as a group that gathers at the scene of an accident, whereas others last a lifetime, such as a family group. Membership in one type does not preclude membership in other types; in fact, it is not unusual for a single group to fall into several different categories. Next, we cover the types most often discussed in sociology, including primary and secondary groups, in-groups and out-groups, peer groups, reference groups, and small and large groups, with a brief concluding statement on social networks.

Primary and Secondary Groups

Perhaps the most fundamental distinction is that made between primary and secondary groups. The term **primary group**, coined by Charles H. Cooley (1909), is used to refer to small, informal groups of people who interact in a personal, direct, and intimate way. This category includes such groups as the family and play groups, which Cooley believed were the most important in shaping the human personality. Primary groups involve intimate face-to-face association and interaction, and their members have a sense of "we-ness" involving mutual identification and shared feelings. Their members tend to be emotionally attached to one another and involved with other group members as whole people, not just with those aspects of a person that pertain to work, school, or some other isolated part of one's life. Your family, close friends, and some neighbors and work associates are likely to be members of your primary group.

A **secondary group** is a group whose members interact in an impersonal manner, have few emotional ties, and come together for a specific practical purpose. Like primary groups, they may be small and may involve face-to-face contacts and cordial or friendly interactions. However, they are more formal than primary group interactions. Sociologically, however, they are just as important. Most of our time is spent in secondary groups—committees, professional groups, sales-related groups, classroom groups, or neighborhood groups. The key difference between primary and secondary groups is in the quality of the relationships and the extent of personal intimacy and involvement. Primary groups are person-oriented, whereas secondary groups tend to be goal-oriented. A primary group conversation usually focuses on personal experiences, feelings, and casual, open sharing, whereas a secondary group conversation is more apt to be impersonal and purposeful.

Primary and secondary groups are important both to individuals and to society. Primary groups

FIGURE 5-1 APPLYING SOCIOLOGY TO GROUP RELATIONSHIPS: A SOCIOGRAM

Sociologists can use sociograms to chart communications patterns, friendship linkages, and general interaction patterns among the members of small groups. Compare the sociograms of these two groups of nine boys. Based on the data provided, which group does the most interacting? What conclusions can you draw about these two groups? How might sociograms be useful in actual situations?

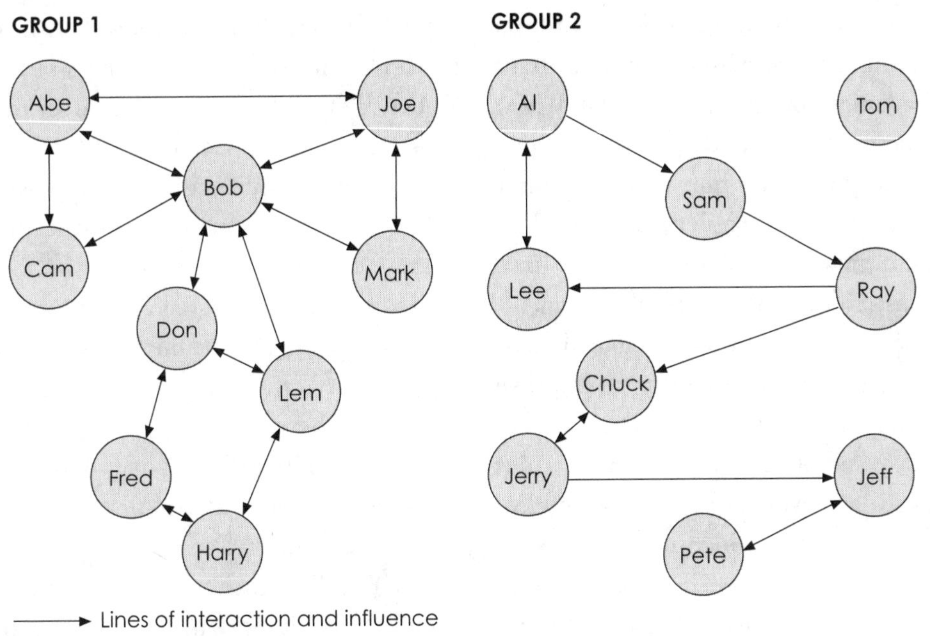

are particularly important in shaping the personality, in formulating self-concepts, in developing a sense of personal worth, and in becoming an accepted member of society. They are also an important source of social control and social cohesion. Such scholars as Erich Fromm (1965) and Lewis Mumford (1962) contend that the strength and vitality of primary groups are the basis of the health of a society. In an increasingly impersonal world, they are sources of openness, trust, and intimacy. People who are not accepted members of some primary group—a marriage, friendship, or work relationship—may have difficulty coping with life or may experience greater health problems.

Although primary groups are vital to the health of both individuals and society, secondary groups are also important because they tend to meet specific goals. They help societies function effectively and permit people who do not know one another intimately to perform their jobs more effectively. Most formal organizations such as schools, corporations, hospitals, and unions comprise many secondary groups and relationships.

It should be recognized that the difference between primary and secondary groups is one of degree. Many formal secondary group situations involve instances of informality and personal openness. In fact, many primary groups develop from secondary groups and organizations. Two students who meet in a formal lecture hall (secondary group) may later marry (primary group); coworkers in a large organization may develop an intimate friendship.

Conversely, two friends who join a corporation may grow apart and ultimately have only a secondary relationship. The composition of an individual's primary and secondary groups shifts frequently.

Nevertheless, understanding the different influences that primary and secondary groups have on the psychological makeup of individuals and on interactions among group members is important and useful. Leaders who do not understand how groups are structured differently along this primary–secondary group continuum may encounter problems. If a leader tries to instill primary ideals—such as warmth, intimacy, and shared feelings—into secondary groups, confusion may result. In an attempt to increase sales, for example, a regional manager of an insurance company might try to improve morale by encouraging the agents to care about and be more expressive and open with one another. This may be difficult to achieve—and may cause confusion—in a formal setting in which people are supposed to relate to one another in a hierarchical, rational, competitive, and efficient manner. Rather than achieve the intended effect of greater productivity, confusion over goals may develop instead.

In-Groups and Out-Groups

As mentioned earlier, one of the key characteristics of a group is the members' sense of belonging. Those who belong think of one another as forming a social unit. This unit has boundaries that separate "us" from "them," that differentiate those who are "in" from those who are "out." An **in-group** is a social category to which persons feel they belong and in which the members have a consciousness or awareness of kind (as in Table 5-1). They feel that they share a common fate, adhere to a common ideology, come from a common background, or otherwise resemble the other members. In-groups may be primary groups but are not necessarily. We can feel "in" with people we have never met or shared personal intimacies with—members of our alumni group, religious group, or veterans group, for example. University of California graduates, Buddhists, or Vietnam veterans may experience feelings of comradeship or a sense of togetherness.

Conversely, an **out-group** is one to which people feel they do not belong. It is made up of those who do not share an awareness of kind. We do not identify or affiliate ourselves with members of out-groups, and we feel little allegiance to them. We treat most members of out-groups with indifference, but at times we may feel hostile toward them because of our tendency toward ethnocentrism—the predisposition to perceive our own in-group as superior to others. The out-group, being inferior, does not deserve the same respect as the in-group. Thus the members of an in-group—friends, classmates, doctors, industrialists—may defend other in-group members even when it does an injustice to those who are "out."

The difference between in- and out-groups is sociologically important for at least two reasons: First, in-group members tend to stereotype out-group members; second, perceived threats from the out-group heightens in-group solidarity. Regarding the first reason, although we may notice individual differences among members of the in-group, most of us notice only similarities in the out-group, and we label them accordingly. Americans may recognize a wide range of variations in appearance, beliefs, and behavior among our fellow citizens but fail to recognize that not all Chinese look alike, not all Germans love sauerkraut, and not all Iranians are revolutionaries. Within the United States, whites (in-group) may label blacks (out-group) as lazy, and blacks (in-group) may label whites (out-group) as racists.

Consider what the consequences of such stereotyping might be in our professional and personal relationships. How, for example, might a college professor communicate with students in class and relate to them outside of class if she assumes that all the students are unmotivated and uninterested in serious academic work? Because of her belief that most students are not serious about academics, she might have a tendency to talk down to them, to discuss difficult course material too quickly, or be unavailable for office hours. If she would recognize that her method of communicating and relating to students is based on a stereotype she holds toward an out-group rather than the qualities of the individual students in her class, she might be able to develop more effective ways of teaching and advising. Thus, we might use the knowledge that people tend to stereotype all members of out-groups to help us improve our interpersonal and communication skills.

A second reason that the two groups are important to sociologists is that any threat or attack, whether imaginary or real, from the out-group tends to increase the cohesion and solidarity of the in-group. Strange as it may seem, a war with a foreign enemy can have a positive effect on a divided nation. After the September 11, 2001, terrorist attack on the World Trade Center, for example, citizens of diverse backgrounds united as "Americans," and ideological, political, and racial differences within the country were diminished. American flags and other displays of support and patriotism were evident everywhere. Similarly, economic hardships may bring the members of a family closer together, just as flood destruction may bring a community closer together.

Knowing that out-group threats often increase the solidarity of members of an in-group is useful for anyone helping a group overcome conflict among its members. A therapist, for example, may try to help the members of a conflict-ridden well-to-do black family feel closer to one another by reminding them about the various ways in which blacks are discriminated against by white people. By focusing the family's attention on out-group threats to their well-being, the individual family members might develop an "us-against-them" attitude and thus recognize a strong common bond. Similarly, in an effort to overcome the conflict among workers in an industrial plant, a labor union leader may call the workers' attention to the common enemy they face in management. If you were a coach of a high school softball team having difficulty with arguments and competition among the team players, how could you use what you know about out-groups to make the players feel closer to one another?

In-groups and out-groups can vary in size. They may be large, like the thousands who attend a football game, or as small as a two-person marriage.

We all have many in-group identities and loyalties, some of which overlap and some of which cause conflict. We may, for example, strongly identify with both the women's movement and the Catholic church but find that our belief that a woman should be able to choose whether to have an abortion is in direct conflict with the position of the Catholic church. To whom should you be loyal when your employer discriminates against your ethnic group? For whom should you cheer when your daughter, who plays on the Michigan tennis team, plays against your alma mater, Ohio State? Our affiliation with a particular in-group may provide us with an identity and a sense of belonging, but it also induces conflict and restricts our relationships and interactions with others.

Peer Groups

One type of group from which in- and out-groups draw their members is the **peer group**, an informal primary group of people who share a similar status and who usually are of a similar age. The unique factor in peer groups is equality. In most groups, even small ones such as marriages or committees, one person or more has a higher status or a position of dominance, but in peer groups, the members are roughly equal in importance.

Although peer groups are most often discussed in connection with young people, they are found in all age groups. Most friendships, regardless of the friends' ages, share the characteristics of a peer group: They are informal, primary relationships, and the participants are of equal rank and often of the same sex.

Reference Groups

Reference groups are the groups we identify with psychologically. They serve as sources of self-evaluation and influence how we think and act and what we believe. People need not belong to a group for it to be a reference group for them; groups we aspire to belong to may also be reference groups. Negative reference groups, those we do not want to be identified with, also serve as sources of self-evaluation. A person might, for example, try to avoid resembling members of a group composed of intellectuals or of football players.

Most attention is focused on positive reference groups. These are the ones we want to be accepted by. Thus, if you want to be an executive, you might carefully observe and imitate the behavior of executives. If you note that they play golf, wear conservative clothes, and read the *Wall Street Journal*, you might do the same.

Reference groups are an important source of information about our performance in a given area. Just as cultures tend to assess themselves on the basis of their own standards (see the discussion on cultural relativity in the Culture and Society chapter), individuals assess themselves in accordance with the standards of their reference group. A grade of B may be a source of pride to students if their peer reference group did worse, but it may be a source of disappointment to a family reference group if they expected an A. A professor's income may be good relative to an assistant professor's income, but it may be poor relative to the income of someone employed in industry. In brief, we tend to judge our worth, accomplishments, and even our morality in comparison with groups of reference.

Reference groups serve not only as sources of current evaluation but also as sources of aspiration and goal attainment. A person who chooses to become a professional baseball player, a lawyer, or a teacher begins to identify with that group and is socialized to have particular goals and expectations associated with that group.

A knowledge of people's reference groups can sometimes help us understand why they behave as they do. It may explain why a teenager who never smokes or drinks at home will do so with a school group, or why politicians may vary their stances on an issue, depending on the audiences they are addressing. Our aim is to please and to conform to the expectations and behaviors of the groups that are important to us.

APPLYING KNOWLEDGE OF REFERENCE GROUPS

The concept of reference groups also helps us understand why some people are unhappy or dissatisfied with their condition. People often feel deprived, not necessarily because of the objective conditions they face, but because they compare themselves to a reference group. This is known as relative deprivation. Sociological research has turned up many instances of groups that have experienced **relative deprivation**. Thomas Pettigrew (1964), for example, found that the economic and social conditions for black Americans improved greatly after World War II (for example, life expectancy increased, civil-service jobs increased, income increased, and college attendance increased), yet blacks became progressively more dissatisfied. Pettigrew pointed out that this was because when compared to whites, a reference group, blacks were and still are considerably behind. Indeed, the economic and social conditions improved much more for whites, so blacks experienced relative deprivation.

Sociologists and economists are finding that employers and administrators would do well to pay attention to relative deprivation when they make decisions about salaries, bonuses, benefits, and other working conditions that affect various groups within an organization (Stark 1990). They could increase their ability to relate to the employees and treat them more fairly if they could understand the reference groups to which their employees compare themselves.

For example, pretend that you are the owner of a construction company, and your staff and your employees are dissatisfied with their wages. Before you consider giving an across-the-board 10-percent raise to all employees, you might first consider the impact of such a raise. The employees making higher salaries to begin with will receive bigger raises in terms of real dollars. So, in effect, you might be giving more money to those who need it the least and less money to those who need it the most. If you do this, do you think that the problem of worker dissatisfaction will be solved? Probably not. Instead, you might consider looking at who the various work groups compare themselves to and try to determine some fair amount that would bring each group more in line with the others or with groups at similar levels in different companies.

On a personal level, the concept of relative deprivation helps us to understand our own feelings of inadequacy and might help us to realize the sources of some of our frustrations. Many of us are happy with our lot in life—or with our car, clothes, stereo equipment, and so on—until we see members of our reference groups with something better. If we could realize that we are experiencing a relative deprivation—not an objective one—we might be able to deal with our feelings of inadequacy.

Small Groups and Large Groups

Categorizing groups according to size is an imprecise way to differentiate them, but numerous consequences or outcomes result from varying the group size:

1. Size has a dramatic effect on member interactions.
2. As size increases, so does the division of labor.
3. As the size of a group increases, its structure becomes more rigid and formal.
4. As the size of a group increases, so does the need for a more formal type of leadership.
5. As the size of a group increases, communication patterns change.
6. As size increases, cohesion decreases.

The remainder of this section explains these consequences. First, it is important to understand how size affects membership interactions. The smallest group, a *dyad*, consists of two people. When just two people are involved, each of them has a special responsibility to interact—if one person withdraws, the group no longer exists. With the addition of a third person, the dyad becomes a *triad*, and the interactions change drastically. If one person drops out, the group can still survive. In a group of three, one person can serve as a mediator in a disagreement, or alternatively side with one person and then the other. A third person, however, can also be a source of conflict or tension. The phrase "two's company, three's a crowd" emphasizes the dramatic shift that takes place when dyads become triads. When a triad adds a fourth or fifth member, two subgroups can emerge. As size increases, it may be more difficult to choose a leader, arrive at an agreement or consensus, or decide who will perform particular tasks.

At what point does a small group become large? Is it small if it has 2, 10, or 20 members? Is it large if it has 25 or 250 or 25,000 members? Determinations of whether a group is large or small may be influenced by the type of group, as well as its goals. In a marriage in many cultures, three would be large. In politics, 30,000 may be small. As you can see, choosing a cutoff point between large and small groups requires that we consider a number of different factors. Even so, such a designation may be largely arbitrary.

Regardless of the distinction between large and small groups, the complexity of group relations increases much more rapidly than the number of members. Two people have only one reciprocal relationship, three people have six reciprocal relationships, four people have 24 relationships, five people have 120 relationships, six people have 720 relationships, and seven people have 5,040 relationships. Beyond that, the number of relationships quickly becomes astronomical. Size *does* make a difference.

A second consequence is that as size increases, so does the division of labor. If the group is small, all the members may engage in the same activities. As size increases, however, activities tend to become specialized. The father of one of the authors, for example, once taught eight grades in a one-room school. He covered the three R's and any other subjects, supervised the playground, did some personal counseling, and occasionally had some transportation responsibilities. As schools got larger, teachers were assigned not only to specific grade levels but also to specific subject areas. They were employed to teach music, art, and other specialized subjects, and a complex system was developed to provide transportation, counseling, lunches, sports, and a wide variety of clubs and other school-related activities. Similar changes in the division of labor occur as churches, families, manufacturing concerns, and other groups grow. Generally, as group size increases, so does the division of labor.

The third consequence is that increases in group size result in an increasingly rigid and formal structure. Whereas small groups are likely to operate informally according to unwritten rules, large groups usually conduct meetings in accordance with Robert's Rules of Order or some other standard formula. Also, small groups are more apt to emphasize personal and primary characteristics. A small grocery store run by a family, for example, may reflect the tastes of the family members. Jobs may be delegated to various people on the basis of their preferences, and work schedules may be drawn up to accommodate one person's going to college or another person's social life. Large groups, on the other hand, emphasize status and secondary characteristics. In a large supermarket chain, decisions are made by committees. Chairpersons, division heads, or managers are selected, and the problems of bureaucratic red tape begin. In contrast to small groups, employees are expected to conform to the demands of their jobs rather than changing their jobs to meet their personal preferences.

The fourth is that as the size of a group increases, so does the need for a more formal type of leadership. With increasing size come complex problems relating to the coordination of activities and decisions, and this leads to the emergence of group leaders, persons who have the authority, the power, or the potential ability to direct or influence the behavior of others.

In all groups, somebody or some collectivity must make the decisions. In small groups, these decisions may be made informally, in a spirit of mutual sharing and agreement, with no designated leader. In large groups, which, as indicated, have more specialized activities and a more rigid and formal structure, the leadership becomes more formal as well, and the decision making is more constraining. When the population of these groups bestows the rights to leadership, authority exists. Authority is legitimized power.

In analyzing leadership in small groups, Bales (1953) found that leaders are of two types, instrumental and expressive. **Instrumental leaders** organize the group around its goals by suggesting ways to achieve them and persuading the members to act appropriately. Thus, the instrumental leader directs activities and helps make group decisions. **Expressive leaders**, on the other hand, resolve conflicts and create group harmony and social cohesion. They make sure that the members can get along with one another and are relatively satisfied and happy. For groups to function effectively, Bales concluded, both types of leaders are needed.

Groups reflect the characteristics of the societies of which they are a part. Suppose, for example, that a neighborhood meeting is called to complain about the garbage collection. Six men and six women show up. What would you guess are the odds that a male will be asked to take the notes or a female will be asked to chair the session or take the formal complaint to the official source? It is unlikely that the group will wait to see who can write most effectively (which might be a male) or who can best serve as leader (which might be a female). Similarly, groups may assign the leadership position to the eldest, the most popular, the one with the most formal training, or the one who called the meeting.

Are there particular traits that distinguish leaders from nonleaders? For several decades, psychologists and social psychologists have tried to compile lists of leadership characteristics, but most results have been disappointing. Why? One explanation is that the attempt has been to find characteristics or traits that reside within individuals rather than seeking characteristics or traits relative to a task environment or a specific interpersonal and social context. Leaders and leadership qualities do not exist in a vacuum. Assigned cultural and social statuses, skills for specific tasks, and prior experience and training will influence the choice of leaders, which suggests that there is no such thing as a "born leader." Inborn characteristics, in combination with training, experience, skills, and social circumstances, determine the likelihood that a given person will occupy leadership positions. This may partially explain why women and blacks seldom become presidents of corporations or top government officials. They may have the leadership characteristics but not the social status characteristics appropriate to these positions in our culture.

A fifth consequence of increase in group size is a change in communication patterns. In large groups, the leaders tend to dominate the discussions. They talk the most and are addressed the most because the discussion and comments of other members are directed toward them. Although similar patterns of communication may exist in small groups, members who never join the discussion in a large group may do so in a small one. Some teachers prefer a large or small class for this very reason. In a large class, the communication is both dominated by them and directed toward them. In a small class, the chances increase that most members will participate and that a communication exchange may take place among the group members. Social psychologists have been especially fascinated with "small-group dynamics." What happens when two, five, or eight people get together? Who sits where, who talks to whom, and how are decisions made?

Sixth, as size increases, cohesion decreases. A group is considered cohesive when members interact frequently, when they talk of "we," when they defend the group from external criticism, when they work together to achieve common goals, and when they are willing to yield their own personal preferences for those of the group. Membership stability is important for cohesion because a high turnover rate has a negative effect. Conformity is

SOCIOLOGY AT WORK

Developing Products and Enhancing the Features of Bank Credit Card Services

Allison Hart has a B.A. in sociology from Elon University and an M.A. in sociology, with a concentration in applied social research, from The University of North Carolina, Charlotte. Her current job title is vice president of New Product Development Manager of Credit Card Services for Bank of America. As part of her job, she develops new and unique products and features and redesigns or enhances existing products for the Consumer Credit Card Services utilizing customer research to identify and validate concept opportunities in order to deliver meaningful points of difference to potential customers. This includes developing business cases, concept/marketing positioning, financial plans, and business requirements.

At first glance, it sounds like she should have a degree in business or marketing. But Hart admits it was sociology that helped her develop the perspective she needs to be a success in her field. "Learning sociological thought opened me to our social surroundings and has allowed me to view the world, the business environment, and the customer with a unique perspective. We are constantly moving into an environment where people's/customer's thoughts and creative genius are more respected and utilized in making business decisions, which gives my degree in sociology value and applicability.

"I started out in marketing research, really applying the social research skills I had learned in both undergraduate and graduate school. Being in the sociological mindset of people's realities, ideals, and the context in which they live, I could translate their survey answers into actionable business decisions that increased revenue for the company by increasing the customer's overall satisfaction. Learning

also important—failure to abide by group norms and decisions lessens cohesiveness. Groups induce conformity by formal means such as fines, not allowing participation, or assigning specific tasks, as well as by informal means such as verbal chides or jokes. Although these informal means become less effective as group size increases, small groups and informal networks exist within the large group or complex organization. The importance of this small group cohesiveness operating in a large group context was evident in World War II; both American and German soldiers admitted to fighting for their buddies, not for the glory and fame of their country.

Social scientists have found that cohesiveness within groups generally improves group performance. Group cohesiveness tends to reduce the anxieties of group members and leads to greater cooperation. A statement such as this suggests that the ability to create cohesion (for example, by reducing group size) can be an important tool for managers and administrators. The adage "many hands make light work" may not apply to all situations.

For example, imagine that you work for an advertising company and are put in charge of forming a committee to develop a new approach to selling a particular product. Considering the findings discussed here, you might be better off putting to-

Developing Products and Enhancing the Features of Bank Credit Card Services, *continued*

that 'perception is reality' was perhaps my most valuable lesson learned, and I applied it in the business world. Just because the business wants it to be a certain way, whatever the perception is is the actual reality—no matter how hard we fight it.

"Not only is this true in dealing with external customers," Hart continues, "but it is very much the case in dealing with coworkers, management, and vendors. Understanding the perception is half the battle in business politics—the other half is creating and molding the perceptions of yourself that will help you advance in your career. In my current role in New Product Development, I am no longer interpreting the perceptions; rather, I am fulfilling them ... creating, developing, and enhancing products that customers want, like, and need. I use these perceptions—i.e., marketing research, both quantitative and qualitative—to help develop ideas and customer needs into viable products and features."

Bank of America is sensitive to the growing bureaucratization of society (the theme of this chapter's opening vignette) and is taking steps to change the way they do business. Hart is instrumental in this culture shift. "We even have a dance called the 'Culture Shift'," Hart says. "We are trying to turn our organization into a customer-focused and customer-friendly one, turning from the mergers and acquisitions culture we once were. It is very interesting to watch a 'forced' shift of culture and be a part of something so grand. We have even added in new cultural elements such as lingo, process, and logo/brand. My sociological knowledge, especially my knowledge of how cultures and social structures interact, is immensely useful for me in helping create this new business environment."

gether a small group of creative people who will become tightly knit and develop a sense of unity, rather than assembling a large team where people do not feel as loyal to one another.

Social Networks

On a daily basis, each of us is involved in numerous groups of the types just described: primary, secondary, large, small, peer, reference, and so forth. Through these groups, we develop linkages or ties to a total set of relationships: a **social network**. Social networks link people. Think, for example, of your social network. It probably includes your family, your friends, your neighbors, classmates, members of social clubs, people you work with, and others.

Social networks do not just happen. Over time, we build and establish ties to others, some strong, some weak. Strong ties may be characterized by emotional involvement and are sustained in a variety of ways, including calls, visits, letters, cards, attendance at particular events, and—as suggested by Cheal (1988)—through gifts. Results from intensive interviews led Cheal to suggest that people use gifts to reinforce relationships already in existence. Strong ties were based on numerous small gifts rather than large expensive ones. Marsden (1987) found that the average individual had only three strong ties with individuals with whom they could discuss important matters. This number increases considerably when other criteria such as with whom you engage in social activities or from whom you would borrow were used.

Unlike the networks just described, many of our social networks include linkages with people with whom we have little in common and only occasional contact. These may be people whom we only know of or who only know of us. These "weak" ties, however, can be extremely important in getting a job or a "good deal" on a purchase. Perhaps this can be illustrated by the frequently heard phrase, "Whom you know is as important as what you know." This is social networking. The "old boy" network seems to be effective in perpetuating social privileges to those who already hold positions of higher rank and prestige.

There is little question of the importance of social networks. Women, for example, whose networks include more relatives than those of men, are paying increasing attention to building networks in the world of work. Many professional women, for example, are finding support in their ties with other women that they find lacking in settings where men both outnumber and overpower them. Social networks do make a difference in professional advancement, as well as in developing a sense of self-worth and integration into the society and culture of which we are a part.

Thinking Sociologically

1. Provide examples of the various types of groups described, and examine the importance of each in your life.
2. How do people establish social networks? Examine how they might differ for selected status categories: women, the wealthy, or college students, for example.

FORMAL ORGANIZATIONS

As stated in the introduction to this chapter, organizations surround us; we are born in them and usually die in them. Many sociologists view the study of social organizations as the key to understanding society, groups, and personal behavior. The organization, they suggest, is different from the sum of the individuals who belong to it. If all the parts of an automobile are put in one pile, we have all the ingredients necessary for a car, but we certainly do not have an operable means of transportation. Only when those parts are properly assembled and interrelated do we get a car that works. Organizations are much the same. The whole is greater than the sum of its parts. In analyzing organizations, we focus not on the individual but on the social structure, the interrelated statuses and accompanying roles, and the norms that specify the rules of conduct and expectations for behavior. (Note the example of the structures of two social organizations in Figure 5-2.)

Used generally, *social organization* refers to the way society is organized: its norms, mores, roles, values, communication patterns, social institutions, and the like. One form of social organization is the **formal organization**, a large social group deliberately constructed and organized to achieve some specific and clearly stated goals. The *Encyclopedia of Associations* (2003) provides details of more than 22,000 national professional societies, labor unions, trade associations, fraternal and patriotic organizations, and other types of structured groups in the United States alone, which consist solely of voluntary members. More than 135,000 entries are listed when international as well as regional, state, and local organizations are included.

Organizations tend to be stable, often keeping the same structure and continuing to exist for many years. Those who belong to an organization generally feel a sense of membership. Industrial corporations, professional sports, country clubs, trade

FIGURE 5-2 THE STRUCTURES OF TWO SOCIAL ORGANIZATIONS

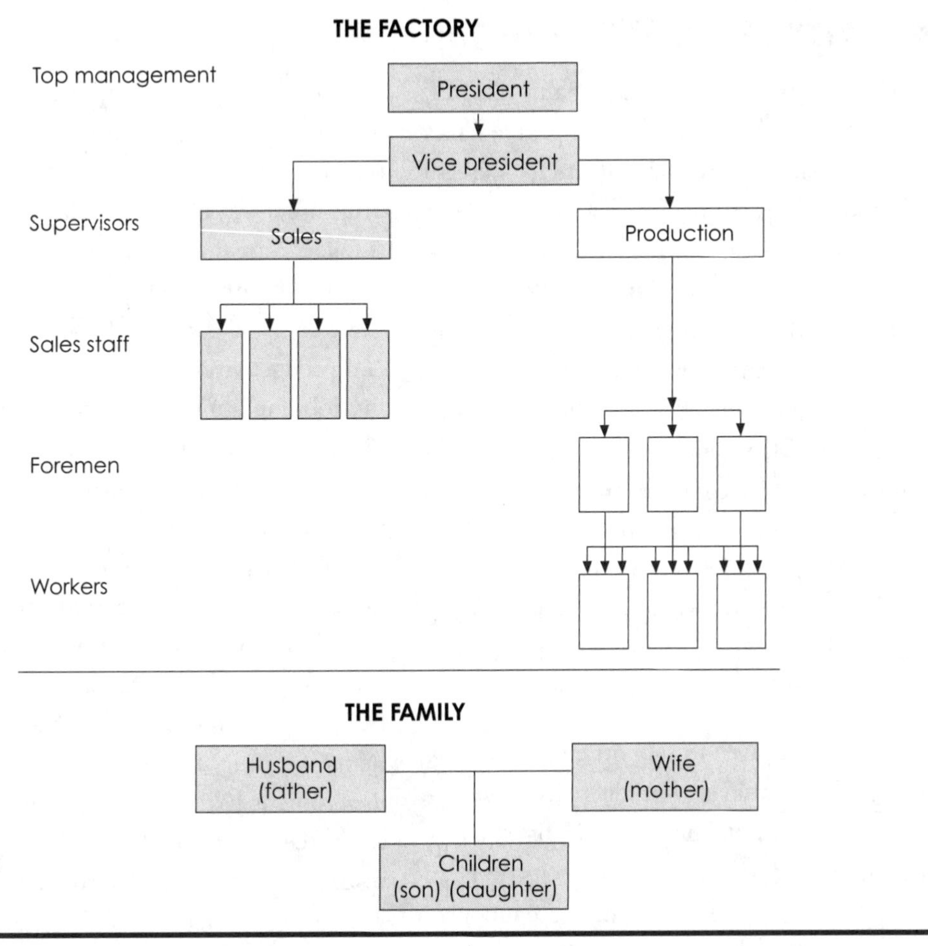

unions, schools, churches, prisons, hospitals, and government agencies are formal organizations created to meet specific goals. All groups have goals of some sort, but they are often latent, unstated, and general. Group members may even have conflicting goals, but in an organization, the goals are specific, clearly stated, and usually understood precisely by the members.

Consider the case of a family and a school. Both have as goals the education of children. The parents in a family may read to the youngest children and provide the older ones with books, magazines, and newspapers. They may also encourage children to play learning games or take them to museums and concerts. In a formal organization such as a school, however, the education program is much more highly structured. The teachers, administrators, and other staff members have been trained to teach a particular subject to a single group or to meet some other specific goal. The overall educational goals of the school, although perhaps subject to disagreement, are stated and understood more clearly than those of the family. The same holds true with factories (see Figure 5-2) and all other formal organizations, including voluntary associations, which are described at the end of this chapter.

POLICY DEBATE

Employee Drug Testing

As discussed in the introductory issue to this chapter, the bureaucratization of society is affecting people's lives in personal ways. Along with their efforts to increase productivity and efficiency, many organizations have deemed it necessary to ensure that their employees are "drug free." According to the National Institute on Drug Abuse (NIDA), more than 8 million working Americans had their urine tested for illegal drugs in 1989. In 1990 the figure jumped to 15 million. According to the American Management Association, 21 percent of companies subjected their employees or job applicants to drug testing in 1986. In 1989, the figure was 50 percent (Horgan, 1990a). And by 1998, 75 percent of America's biggest companies required job applicants to undergo urinalysis (Koch, 1998). The trend is clear. Employee drug testing is on the increase.

Varieties of reasons are given to support employee drug testing; most focus on safety and productivity. The Department of Transportation, one of the strongest advocates of employee drug testing, rationalizes its decision to routinely test 4 million private-industry employees out of concern for the public (Navasky, 1990). Airline pilots, railroad engineers, air traffic controllers, and other mass transportation workers under the influence of drugs obviously pose a severe safety hazard. Corporate legal liability and moral responsibility for the actions of its employees has been given as a compelling reason to allow corporations the right to test its employees for drug use (Moore, 1989).

Lost productivity is another often-cited reason for drug testing. J. Michael Walsh, head of NIDA's applied research division and a supporter of employee drug testing, claimed that the "cost of drug abuse to U.S. industry" was more than about $50 billion a year and that drug users—from crack addicts to weekend marijuana smokers—are more likely to cause accidents, miss work, and use health benefits (Horgan, 1990b). Conversely, some companies report that absenteeism, medical costs, and productivity have improved after they started testing job applicants and workers suspected of drug use (Kupfer, 1988). This evidence is used to suggest that one of the reasons that our economy has suffered in recent years is that many of our workers have drug problems. Accordingly, besides its positive effects on the workplace, drug testing is considered to be an additional weapon in society's overall war on drugs. Because drug use is responsible for lost productivity, absenteeism, on-the-job accidents, medical claims, and thefts, proponents of drug testing feel that employers and the government have a right to insist that workers remain drug free. Interestingly, and in further support of drug testing, the majority of respondents to a 1900s Gallup poll favored random drug testing of all workers (Horgan, 1990a).

In spite of wide public support, this policy has its opponents. One criticism is that much of the evidence that supports drug testing is inaccurate and that the said benefits of drug testing cannot be proven (Koch, 1998). Statistics regarding lost productivity are often based on faulty methodology or interpretation and contain, even according to Walsh of the NIDA, "assumptions that need additional validation" (Horgan, 1990a, p. 22). For example,

Employee Drug Testing, *continued*

- Some of the most often cited statistics are extrapolations based on unwarranted assumptions and are contrived in order to support a drug-testing policy (Horgan, 1990a).

- The discussions of the statistics often mistake correlation for causation, especially when there is an inverse relationship between income level and drug use (Horgan, 1990a).

- Companies that reported increased productivity after the initiation of drug testing also indicate that other variables, such as a raft of managerial incentives, might have been equally responsible (Kupfer, 1988).

Chronic illegal drug use may adversely affect job performance, but critics insist that drug testing is unreasonable because heavy drug users can be easily spotted in the workplace or are not working in the types of jobs that are routinely tested. There is also concern about the unreliability of drug tests and the high rate of both false positives and false negatives. These types of errors could destroy an employee's reputation and chances for advancement or too quickly release a corporation from liability.

These criticisms notwithstanding, most of the debate about drug testing focuses on the right to privacy (Moore, 1989). Drug testing has been mostly criticized on the grounds that it violates the Fourth Amendment, which prohibits unreasonable searches and seizures. Victor Navasky (1990, p. 39), editor of the Nation, suggests that employee drug testing "is just one small part of a vast campaign of control that seeks to examine every aspect of a person's physical, social, and emotional life—down to the genetic core—and subordinate the right of privacy to the imperatives of state power. . . . The enormously expensive, elaborate, totalitarian testing procedures are meant to control consciousness and regulate behavior." While employers have the right to fire or reprehend employees whose drug use hampers their work performance, they should have no right to sanction employees who perform well who use drugs for recreational use, nor do they have a right to interfere in their personal lives.

In our discussions about the bureaucratization of society, we raised the question, To what extent does bureaucracy affect our personal lives? Has the increasing tendency toward bureaucratization and the associated centralization of power cost us some freedom in exchange for increased efficiency and productivity? Policies regarding employee drug testing illustrate the tension between the virtues and evils of bureaucracy. Which position do you agree with? Consider these questions from the perspectives of both organizations and individuals. Should drug testing be allowed or prohibited in all work situations? Should public safety and monetary loss warrant corporations and governments delving into our private lives? If so, where should the line be drawn with regard to control over our private lives? Should any other types of personal behavior be prohibited if they are deemed to be a threat to safety or productivity? Questions such as these are becoming increasingly relevant as advances in technology increasingly enable the examination of our private lives.

The Importance of Formal Organizations

The importance of formal organizations in modern complex societies can hardly be overestimated. Every day, we deal with some sort of formal organization in connection with work, food, travel, health care, police protection, or some other necessity of life. Organizations enable people who are often total strangers to work together toward common goals. They create levels of authority and channels of command that clarify who gives orders, who obeys them, and who does which tasks. They are also a source of continuity and permanence in a society's efforts to meet specific goals. Individual members may come and go, but the organization continues to function. Thus, formal organizations make it possible for highly complex industrialized societies to meet their most fundamental needs and to pursue their collective aspirations.

Formalization is the process by which the norms, roles, or procedures of a group or organization become established, precise, and valid and by which increasing attention is given to structure, detail, and form. The formalization of organizations is the characteristic that distinguishes complex societies from small tribal societies. Herman Turk (1970) went so far as to state that modern societies are "an aggregate of organizations, which appear, disappear, change, merge, and form networks of relations with one another" (p. 1).

The Goals of Formal Organizations

As you can well imagine, the goals of different organizations vary widely. Businesses are interested chiefly in making a profit. Service organizations assist people with problems such as unemployment or illness. Some organizations, such as unions or stamp collectors, exist to promote the interests of their own group; other organizations, such as governments, the military, and prisons, are established to provide services to the general public.

Given this diversity of goals, it is not surprising that some formal organizations are in conflict with each other. The goals of right-to-life organizations and of the National Organization for Women (NOW), for example, are very different, and conflict between the two is evident. Also, note the policy debate in this chapter over employee drug testing. The goals of some organizations, such as the Department of Transportation, favor this activity, while the goals of other organizations focus on the right to privacy and the noninterference into our personal matters.

Conflicts appear both between organizations and within them. Universities must determine whether the primary goal of their faculty is teaching or research. Medical organizations must decide whether their chief function is to aid and protect the physician or to improve the health care given to the public. Sometimes, an organization's apparent primary goal (e.g., service) is used to conceal its actual primary goal (e.g., profit). A private mental institution, for example, may emphasize the quality of the care it gives in its literature, but decisions about whether to provide a particular service to its clients may always be made on the basis of its profitability.

There are often conflicts between the goals of an organization's administration and those of its employees or the clients or public it serves. In a university, for example, the main priority for the administration may be to balance the budget. The aim of the faculty may be to do research and publish papers. The students may be most concerned with receiving a good education through exceptional teaching and the use of outstanding library and laboratory facilities, which may conflict with cost-saving measures and cut into professors' research time. Finally, some influential alumni may consider all these goals less important than having an outstanding football team, which brings the school national recognition.

Formal organizations have a particular type of administrative machinery designed to help them meet their goals. This administrative structure is known as bureaucratic organization, or, more simply, bureaucracy.

BUREAUCRACY

Bureaucratization of society was the issue selected for the opening of this chapter. What does it mean to talk about bureaucracies or bureaucratization? What are its characteristics? What are some functions and dysfunctions of these types of structures and their accompanying processes?

A **bureaucracy** is a formal organizational structure that directs and coordinates the efforts of the people involved in various organizational tasks. It is simply a hierarchical arrangement of an organization's parts, based on the division of labor and authority. A hierarchical structure is like a pyramid—the people at each level have authority over the larger number of people at the level below them. The authority resides in the office, position, or status, not in a particular person. In other words, the responsibilities and authority associated with a particular job in the hierarchy remain essentially the same, regardless of the person occupying the position. Merton (1968) defines bureaucracy as "a formal, rationally organized social structure involving clearly defined patterns of activity in which, ideally, every series of actions is functionally related to the purposes of the organization" (p. 195).

Bureaucracy As an Ideal Type and Its Functions

The classical work on bureaucracy was written by Max Weber (1864–1920), one of the pioneers of sociology. Weber dealt with bureaucracy as an **ideal type**, which is a model of a hypothetical pure form of an existing entity. In other words, he did not concern himself with describing a specific bureaucracy; rather, he examined a great many bureaucracies, in an attempt to discover the general principles that govern how they operate. An ideal type, then, is not to be thought of as a perfect entity in the usual sense of the word ideal. As this chapter later shows, bureaucracies are often far from perfect. Weber, in a work translated by Gerth and Mills (1946), stated that bureaucracies typically have the following characteristics:

- *Division of Labor.* The staff and activities of an organization are divided into units. Each unit has carefully described responsibilities, and each job is designed to meet a specific need.

- *Hierarchy of Authority.* Organizations are ran by a chain of command—a hierarchy of bosses and workers who are, in turn, the bosses of other workers. As indicated earlier, the hierarchy is in the form of a pyramid: All officials are accountable to those at a higher level for their own responsibilities and for those of subordinates. The top of the chain of command is often a board of directors or company officers. Below this level are the middle-level managers, administrators, foremen, and department heads. The largest number of workers is at the bottom of the hierarchy (refer back to Figure 5-2).

- *Public Office.* The office and the organization's written files are in a separate location from the employees' homes and families and are not subject to their influence. The organization's money and equipment belong to the organization, not to individuals, and its activity is separate from the activity of private life. Public office implies impersonality, a separation of person and the organization.

- *Merit Selection.* Organizations select personnel on the basis of merit, using standardized criteria such as civil service examinations or educational training rather than friendship or political or family connections. Those who are hired are expected to have the specialized knowledge or skills necessary to perform their assigned task.

- *Career Pattern.* Employees are expected to devote themselves completely to the business of the organization and to recognize that people work their way to the top. As one moves up in the hierarchy, job security and salaries improve. Seniority is recognized, valued, and rewarded. Whether the organization is the U.S. Army, General Motors, or the Catholic church, increasing time with the organization and adequate job performance are supposed to bring promotions, higher pay and status, and stronger tenure or job security.

- *Objective Rules.* The operation of the organization is governed by a consistent set of rules that define the responsibilities of various positions, assure the coordination of tasks, and encourage the uniform treatment of clients. These rules are quite stable and comprehensive, and they can be readily learned and followed.

Although in any given formal organization, some members are employed for personal reasons rather than merit, the rules are occasionally ignored, and some customers are not treated impartially, most bureaucracies share the characteristics described here. A hierarchical organization, division of labor, and the other attributes of the bureaucratic ideal type are essential to efficient functioning. As we all know, however, bureaucracies have their shortcomings. Most of us associate them with red tape, mountains of forms to complete, and endless lines. How and why do bureaucracies get so bogged down?

Dysfunctions of Bureaucracies

Weber focused on many of the positive accomplishments of bureaucracies: precision, coordination, reliability, efficiency, stability, and continuity. Merton (1957) was the most important writer on the dysfunctions of bureaucracy. He observed that people in bureaucracies tend to develop what Veblen called **trained incapacity**, which occurs when the demands of discipline, rigidity, conformity, and adherence to rules render people unable to perceive the end for which the rules were developed. In Merton's words, "Adherence to the rules, originally conceived as a means, becomes transformed into an end-in-itself" (p. 199). This condition is similar to *ritualism*, which is discussed in another chapter.

We have all had experiences in which an obsessive adherence to procedures and rules kept us from meeting goals. In corporations, for example, employees are often required to routinely send copies of memos and letters to people who do not look at them and perhaps would not know what they meant if they did. It would be much more efficient simply to stop sending them. Often, our training, habits, or traditional ways of behaving blind us to alternatives that might be far more effective than the ones to which we are accustomed.

A second dysfunction comes about when hiring and promotions are based on a rigid set of formal qualifications—five years' experience or a college degree, for example—rather than skill or performance. In one instance, a woman with ten years' experience in her company and an excellent work reputation was passed over for promotion to supervisor because her company's policy dictated that supervisors must have a college degree. There are also instances in which excellent college teachers are denied tenure because they do not have a sufficient number of publishing credits. In bureaucratic organizations, formal qualifications may supersede performance in hiring and promotion.

A third dysfunction of bureaucracy with which we are all familiar is the runaround. Who among us has not called an organization and had our call transferred to two or three other departments, only to be returned to the first person to whom we spoke, with the problem still unresolved? Recall that bureaucracies have rules defining the duties and responsibilities of various offices. The legal department handles legal matters, the personnel office handles recruitment, rank, and salary matters, and the payroll department issues checks, withholds money for benefits, and pays taxes. Other departments handle other matters. Now which one would you get in touch with about a lawsuit concerning the payment of salary? The difficulty is that actual problems do not always fit neatly into the compartments designed to handle them. If a problem does not clearly fall within a department's area of responsibility, or if it involves several departments, the runaround is likely to begin.

Understanding the dysfunctions of bureaucracy may help administrators, managers, and entrepreneurs assess whether the positive aspects of this form of organizational structure outweigh the negative. Bureaucracy as an organizational form is not for every situation. The mom-and-pop grocery store, for example, may attract large numbers of customers precisely because of its friendly, informal, "homey," unbusinesslike atmosphere. Running that business according to bureaucratic principles would probably lead to its demise. Some professional and educational settings where efficiency and production are less important than high-quality interpersonal relationships are also better off without rigid bureaucratic procedures. The large-scale "student-processing" that efficiently pushes students through a university system and hands them a diploma in four years would be dysfunctional in the small liberal arts college. The physician who boasts "family care in a caring way" would probably see a decline in business if she decided that seeing patients without appointments was an inefficient way to run her practice. In situations such as these, the manifest function of the organization might possibly be distorted—and failure might result—if the principles of bureaucracy are applied.

Must Bureaucracies Be Dehumanizing and Impersonal? The Case of Japan

The very impersonality that makes an organization efficient can create problems on the human level. Merton (1957) wrote that bureaucracies stress depersonalization of relationships, categorization, and indifference to individuals. C. Wright Mills (1951) wrote that middle-class, white-collar employees of bureaucratic organizations were enmeshed in a vast impersonal structure of rationalized activity in which their own rationality is lost. Interestingly, www.dictionary.com defines a *bureaucrat* as "an official of a bureaucracy who is rigidly devoted to the details of administrative procedure." Similarly, www.infoplease.com, another Internet information source, defines a bureaucrat as, "an official who works by fixed routine without exercising intelligent judgment." The prevalence of rigidity and formality suggests that bureaucracies will almost inevitably be dehumanized and impersonal.

Do organizations have to be dehumanizing and impersonal, though? Perhaps a brief look at American and Japanese automotive assembly plants can help us answer this question. Richard Florida and Martin Kenney (1991), in studying whether Japanese industrial organization could be transplanted to the United States, describe the U.S. organizational environment as typically characterized in terms of diversity, individualism, and unrestrained market forces. Japan is characterized in terms of homogeneity, familism, paternalism, and/or welfare corporatism. U.S. organization is distinguished by high levels of functional specialization, large numbers of job classifications, and adversarial labor–management relations among others. In contrast, the Japanese manufacturing firm is distinguished by small numbers of job classifications, team-based work organization, and consensual relations between labor and management.

What does this have to do with the issue of dehumanization and impersonality in bureaucracies? It suggests that bureaucracies can be organized in ways that are both more humanizing and personal. Work in Japanese organizations is generally based on teams that are responsible for planning and carrying out production tasks. The teams have team leaders, but unlike U.S. foremen, they do not supervise workers. While they have managerial responsibility, they are themselves members of the work group.

This is related to another feature of Japanese organization, that of minimal status distinction between management and blue-collar workers. In Japan, workers and managers are likely to eat in the same cafeteria and to wear the same uniforms. Generally, managers do not have enclosed offices but sit at desks on a large open floor adjacent to the production facility. Within the production facility, the workers rotate tasks within their teams. This functions both to train workers in multiple tasks and to reduce the incidence of repetitive-motion injuries.

Unlike U.S. companies, a main objective of the Japanese system of work and production organization is to harness the collective intelligence of workers for continuous product and process improvement (Kenney and Florida, 1988). This means that in Japan, workers actively participate in company suggestion programs and quality-control circles, as well as informal, everyday continuous improvement activities. Workers have significant input into the design of their jobs, the production process, and the operation of the organization.

American individualism stands in contrast to Japanese familism in that Japanese workers become "married" to the organization, with guaranteed lifetime employment. Classes of workers receive uniform wages, with raises at regular intervals based on work effort, absenteeism, willingness to work in teams, and willingness to suggest new ideas. Semiannual bonuses are said to often constitute 30 percent of total remuneration (Aoki, 1988). These factors, among others, are related to morale and job security, frequently discussed features of the Japanese system.

Must bureaucracies be dehumanizing and impersonal? Japan provides us with one example of how they can be made less so. Guaranteed lifetime employment, participation in decision making, team-based activities, workers trained and rotated among a variety of specialties, minimal adversarial relationships, and diminished status distinctions between workers and management, all combine to increase the probabilities of greater humanization and personalization within bureaucracies. Other examples of this process may be evident in organizations that people join voluntarily.

Thinking Sociologically

1. Describe how bureaucratization might affect the lives of people in a traditional rural community, such as the one described in the opening issue discussion to this chapter. Consider how the following items might be affected, and, in turn, how people would experience life differently: statuses, roles, group involvements, and organizations.

2. Compare two organizations that you encounter often: one that is very bureaucratic and one that is not. Using your knowledge of social structure, groups, and organizations, discuss how each of these organizations would be different if they became less bureaucratic and more bureaucratic, respectively.

Voluntary Associations

Voluntary associations are organizations that people join because they share their goals and values and voluntarily choose to support them. People join many formal organizations because they are forced to or because they need the income, protection, or training that these organizations offer. Examples include schools, the armed services, insurance companies, and places of work. Voluntary associations, however, are joined out of personal interest, to participate in some social program, or as a channel for political action.

Voluntary associations are instances of associational or organizational groups, which were discussed earlier in this chapter. They typically involve awareness of kind, social interaction, and formal organization. Awareness of kind is central to our voluntary involvement because we share the interests and goals of the membership, whether the group is the League of Women Voters, the Boy Scouts of America, the National Rifle Association (NRA), the National Association for the Advancement of Colored People (NAACP), the Baptist Church, or the American Sociological Association. We enjoy socially interacting with other members because of our common focus of attention and shared interests. Because these associations are formally organized, they have officers and bylaws or a constitution. Some associations are small and highly informal; others are large, formal, bureaucratically organized, and demand dues and conformity to established procedures. Because membership is voluntary rather than by ascription, members can leave if they become dissatisfied.

In studies covering several decades, sociologists have learned a good deal about voluntary associations. We know that they are class-limited—members in any given association usually come from similar socioeconomic levels. Bowling club members are unlikely to join golf clubs; members of a wealthy businessmen's club are unlikely to join the Ku Klux Klan. Churches are voluntary associations that cover the class and wealth spectrum, but those living at a poverty level seldom attend the same church as the affluent. Although people of all ages and socioeconomic levels join voluntary associations, middle-aged people of high social status and education are the most frequent participants. Men are more likely to join than women, but American women are more likely to join associations than women in most other countries.

SUMMARY

1. Society is socially structured. It is composed of many parts, including social statuses, roles, groups, organizations, and institutions. Statuses are socially defined positions that individuals occupy. A combination of statuses held by a person is a *status set*. Sometimes a particular status, a *master status*, takes priority over all the others.

2. All statuses have sets of expectations and behaviors associated with them. These are roles and role sets. What a role prescribes, the perception of it, and the behavior that is actually performed may be very different. Commitment to the role, the flexibility it permits, and competing demands from other roles may clarify these differences.

3. Three difficulties that can result from roles are *role ambiguity*, in which the expectations are not clear, *role strain*, in which contradictory demands or the ability to live up to the expectations of the role produces stress, and *role conflict*, in which inconsistent expectations are associated with the same role. However, roles

are basic to social structure and social behavior, making them predictable, patterned, and organized.

4. Social groups are so fundamental a part of our existence that it is difficult to imagine life without them. Most social groups involve interaction, a sense of belonging or membership, shared interests and values, and some type of structure.

5. Members of statistical and categorical groups, often formed for comparative and research purposes, share common characteristics but are not social groups, in that they do not interact with one another.

6. *Aggregates* are social collections of people who are in physical proximity to one another. They are loosely structured groups that are short-lived and involve little interaction. Members of *associations* and *organizational groups* interact, are aware of their similarity, and, in addition, are organized to pursue a common goal.

7. *Primary groups* are small and informal and emphasize interpersonal cohesion and personal involvement. *Secondary groups* are less personal and intimate, and they are more goal-oriented and purposeful.

8. *In-groups* are those to which people feel they belong. The in-group shares a common allegiance and identity, tends to be ethnocentric, and stereotypes members of the out-group. In-group cohesion is intensified by out-group threats.

9. *Peer groups* are informal primary groups of people who share a similar status and usually are of similar age. *Reference groups* provide self-evaluation and direct aspirations. They are the groups we use to assess our own performance, even if we do not actually belong to them.

10. Groups are also differentiated by size. The addition of even a few people changes group interactions considerably, and, as size increases, there are generally changes in the division of labor, formality, leadership, communication, and cohesion.

11. Formal organizations are deliberately organized to achieve specific goals. They are particularly important in industrialized societies, in which many relationships are impersonal. Formal organizations are sources of authority and of continuity in our efforts to meet basic societal and personal goals, but conflict within and between organizations is common.

12. *Bureaucracy* is a type of administrative structure found in formal organizations. It is a hierarchical arrangement of the parts of an organization, based on a division of labor and authority. Roles in the hierarchy are based on position or office, not on individual characteristics. Bureaucracies operate in a location separate from the homes and families of their employees. They also operate according to objective rules, hire and promote people on the basis of merit, and encourage workers to rise in the hierarchy through hard work. They can have a positive influence on efficiency, precision, coordination, stability, and continuity.

13. Bureaucracies have dysfunctions as well. Trained incapacity, the bureaucratic runaround, dehumanization, and impersonality appear to be negative characteristics of bureaucracies.

14. The case of Japan illustrates how bureaucracies and formal organizations can be made less dehumanizing and impersonal. Participation in decision making, team-based activities, work rotation, and diminution of status distinctions between workers and management all may contribute to humanizing the bureaucratic organization.

15. *Voluntary associations* are organizations that people join because they share the goals and values of these organizations and choose to support them. Because membership is voluntary, members can resign if their interest wanes.

KEY TERMS

aggregate group Any collection of people together in one place; participants interact briefly and sporadically.

associational group A group of people who join together to pursue a common interest in an organized, formally structured way.

bureaucracy A hierarchical, formally organized structural arrangement of an organization based on the division of labor and authority.

categorical group A group of people who share a common characteristic but do not interact or have any social organization.

expressive leader A type of leader that focuses on resolving conflicts and creating group harmony and social cohesion.

formal organization A large social group deliberately organized to achieve certain specific, clearly stated goals.

ideal type A model of a hypothetical pure form of an existing entity.

in-group A social group to which people feel they belong and with which they share a consciousness of kind.

instrumental leader A type of leader that focuses on goals, directing activities, and helping make group decisions.

master status A particular status in one's status set that takes priority over the others.

out-group A group to which people feel they do not belong; they do not share consciousness of kind, and they feel little identity to the group.

peer group An informal primary group of people who share a similar or equal status and who are usually of roughly the same age.

prescribed role The expectations associated with a given status that are based on what society suggests or dictates.

primary group A small, informal group of people who interact in a personal, direct, and intimate way.

reference group A group with which people identify psychologically and to which they refer in evaluating themselves and their behavior.

relative deprivation A feeling of being deprived, not because of objective conditions, but because of comparison to a reference group.

role The social expectations or behaviors associated with a particular status.

role ambiguity A situation in which the expectations associated with a particular social status are unclear.

role conflict A situation that exists when differing expectations are associated with the same role.

role perception The way that expectations for behavior are perceived or defined—which may differ considerably from what is prescribed or actually done.

role performance The actual behavior of a person in a particular role, in contrast to the way that person is expected to behave.

role set The multiple roles attached to statuses.

role strain A situation that occurs when differing and incompatible roles are associated with the same status.

secondary group A group in which the members interact impersonally, have few emotional ties, and come together for a specific, practical purpose.

social group A group in which people physically or socially interact.

social network The linkage or ties to a set of relationships.

statistical group A group formed by sociologists or statisticians; members are unaware of belonging and there is no social interaction or social organization.

status The socially defined position an individual occupies.

status set The combination of all the statuses any individual holds at a given time.

trained incapacity The situation that exists when the demands of discipline, conformity, and adherence to rules render people unable to perceive the end for which the rules were developed.

voluntary association An organization people join because they share the organization's goals and values and voluntarily choose to support them.

DISCUSSION QUESTIONS

1. What is meant by the statement, "society is socially structured"?
2. Answer the question, "Who am I?" in terms of your status set. List several social expectations (roles) that are generally attributed to statuses within the set. From this, discuss the various role conflicts that are part of your life.
3. List some of your primary and secondary groups. Describe the ways you act in each of these. Compare the criterion by which you are judged by others in each of these groups.
4. Discuss some of the most important reference groups in your life. How do they affect how you think about things and about yourself, and how you act?
5. Illustrate how group processes and outcomes or consequences are influenced by the size of the group.
6. In relation to social networks, discuss the statement, "Whom you know is as important as what you know."
7. Must bureaucracies be dehumanizing and impersonal? Contrast Japanese and American corporations in your response.
8. Discuss some problems that primary groups in an organization might encounter when faced with increasing bureaucratization.
9. How are statuses and roles in a group, organization, and community affected by bureaucratization?
10. Why do people join voluntary organizations?

Socialization and Social Interaction

Child Care

The use of substitute child care has increased so quickly that its long-term effects on children when they become adults cannot be known yet. Most of the research to date suggests that extensive nonparental care in the first year of life does have an impact on a child's development. However, the results are contradictory about what the overall effects are, how long they last, and whether they are beneficial or detrimental to the child (cf., e.g., Belsky, 1990; Clarke-Stewart, 1989; Leavitt and Power, 1989; Phillips et al., 1987).

During the past few decades, child care has become a major issue in American society for a number of reasons:

In 2002, preschool age children averaged 32 hours per week. 36% had employed mothers, and 18% of mothers were not employed. (US Census Bureau, October 2005).

23.8 million mothers with school-age children are employed. 9.8 million mothers of preschool age children are also employed. (US Census Bureau, October 2005).

Surveys indicate that more than 50 percent of working parents think that their children suffer from lack of quality care (Browne-Miller, 1990).

Employers now accept that a lack of adequate substitute child care can lead to greater employee absenteeism and less productivity (Browne-Miller, 1990).

Additionally, the prevalence of social problems such as domestic violence, teenage pregnancy, and alcohol and other drug abuse has engendered an increased public interest in strengthening the family (Browne-Miller, 1990). Clearly, the impact of nonparental child care on children has become an issue of much concern for many Americans.

Referring to the widespread use of substitute child care, social critic Charles Siegel (1990) writes that "An entire generation of children is the subject of a risky experiment" (p. 37). While the related political debates focus mostly on who should be responsible for ensuring that there is adequate child care—government, business, or family—the heart of the matter is socialization: How well are children learning to function in society? Is the socialization of children with parental care different than with nonparental care? If so, what are the differences, and are they detrimental or beneficial to the development of the child? Answers to questions such as these will probably have an impact on any national child-care policies that are developed.

Unfortunately, the public and political debate about child-care policies simplifies the issue into a polemic about the role of parents in child rearing and does not consider the social science research about the impact of different socialization settings on children. The debate over the role of parents in child rearing may never be resolved once and for all since it is largely based upon values and beliefs. Research findings, however, can provide a different basis for discussion about child-care policies. Many social scientists have conducted comparative analyses of socialization in parental versus nonparental child care. They have studied children's emotional development (for example, ability to form attachments with parents and others, sense of security, ability to recognize and deal with their emotions), cognitive development (for example, intellectual curiosity, language development, learning potential and academic skills, intellectual self-confidence, intellectual motivation), social development (for example, interpersonal skills, ability to channel or control aggressiveness, respect for rules and authority), and physical development (for example, resistance to and recuperation from illness and disease, sensorimotor coordination), and other areas of development (Belsky et al., 2001). All these aspects of development are part of the socialization of children.

All socialization processes, including child-care socialization, are embedded in a social structure. Many structural factors of the child-care setting shape the socialization process: the ratio of caregivers to children, the personalities of the caregivers, the demographics of the caregiving population, the overall philosophy of the child-care team, the use of unstructured versus structured time, the attention given to discipline and rules, the personal and emotional involvement of the caregivers, the attention given to preventive and recuperative health care, the overall environment in which the care takes place, and many other factors (Browne-Miller, 1990).

Social structure alone, though, does not determine the outcomes of socialization. Children, like all other humans, are not simply molded by their environment. Socialization occurs through an interaction with the environment. For example, how does the ratio of caregivers to children act as a means of socialization? Is it possible that children may perceive themselves differently when they know that they are the object of attention as opposed to when they think that no one is paying attention to them? Does this affect what they think others might expect from them? How do the demographics of the caregiving population (racial, ethnic, age, and so forth) affect the way children think? Do the caregivers hold racial or ethnic stereotypes that may affect children's perceptions of themselves? These are only a few examples. To answer questions like these it is helpful to understand the social theories that explain the processes by which humans develop through social interaction. George Herbert Mead's theory of "role taking" explains the process by which humans learn what others expect from them. Charles Horton Cooley's "looking glass self" theory explains how humans come to define themselves. Erving Goffman's theories about the "presentation of self" explain the processes through which we interact with others. These theories—which you will read about in this chapter—and an understanding of the socialization process offer insights into the way in which humans develop that should be considered when assessing the impact of socialization in different types of child-care settings.

The child-care issue is no longer whether American society needs alternative methods of child care; it is how we devise child-care policies that can ensure the best possible socialization of children, while addressing the realities of American families as they exist today. It is our hope that this chapter will help you to think further about this issue by introducing you to some important ideas about socialization and social interaction.

WHAT IS SOCIALIZATION?

Socialization is the lifelong process through which people are prepared to participate in society (Johnson, 2000). This learning occurs in all interactions from the minute a baby is born. Individuals must learn about their culture, including the rules and expectations of the culture. In the United States, most people learn to speak the English language and to eat with a fork. They learn that cereal, bacon, and eggs are breakfast foods and that sandwiches are appropriate for lunch. They find out that some people do work that is defined as important, and that those who do not or will not work are of less value. They discover that particular countries and people are friendly and others are hostile. Women learn to smile when they are tense and to cry at good news as a release of tension. Men learn that they should not cry at all, although some do so at times.

Sociologists are interested in socialization because by studying how people learn the rules of society, we hope to understand better why people think and act as they do. If we understand why we think and act as we do, we can change our values, our beliefs, our expectations, and our behavior in ways that might otherwise never occur to us. The study of socialization is a very liberating part of a liberal education. In order to understand socialization, however, we must look to our earliest social interaction.

IS HUMAN INTERACTION NECESSARY?

Normal human infants are born with all the muscles, bones, and biological organs needed to live. They are utterly helpless, however, and cannot survive without human interaction. Babies not only need food and warmth to survive physically, but they also need physical stimulation to grow. When they are handled physically by an adult, they are stimulated by touch, tones of voice, and facial expressions, which make them aware of their environment and which stimulate them to respond to it. Observations of infants who were comparatively isolated from human contact have shown that a lack of social interaction can have very serious consequences.

Children in Institutions

Rene Spitz (1946) observed children who had apparently been healthy when they were born and who had been living in a foundling home for about two years. Nutrition, clothing, bedding, and room temperatures in the home were suitable, and every child was seen by a physician at least once a day. A small staff of nurses took care of the physical needs of the children, but other interaction was very limited.

Despite their excellent physical care, 34 percent of the 91 children in the home died within two years of the study, and 21 other children (23 percent) showed slow physical and social development. They were small, and some could not walk or even sit up. Those who could talk could say only a few words, and some could not talk at all.

Spitz compared these children with infants brought up in another institution, where their mothers were being held for delinquency. Physical care was basically the same as in the foundling home, but their mothers, who had little else to occupy them, enjoyed playing with their children for hours. The infants received a great deal of social stimulation, and their development was normal. Spitz concluded that the difference between the foundling home and the home for delinquent mothers was the amount of attention the children received, which illustrates the crucial importance of social interactions in child development.

Isolated and Feral Children

Children who have been isolated from others in their own homes also show a lack of development. Kingsley Davis (1940, 1947) described two girls found in the 1930s who had been hidden in the attics of their family homes because they were illegitimate and unwanted.

One child, Isabelle, had been kept in seclusion until age 6 1/2 years. Her mother was deaf and mute, and because Isabelle had been confined in a dark room with her mother, she had no chance to develop speech. She communicated with her mother by gestures and could make only a strange croaking sound.

Although it was established that Isabelle could hear, specialists working with her believed that she was retarded because she had not developed any social skills. They thought that she could not be educated and that any attempt to teach her to speak would fail after so long a period of silence. Nevertheless, the people in charge of Isabelle launched a systematic and skillful program of training that involved pantomime and dramatization. After one week of intensive effort, she made her first attempt to speak, and in two months, she was putting sentences together.

Eighteen months after her discovery, she spoke well, walked, ran, and sang with gusto. Once she learned speech, she developed rapidly, and at age 14 years, she had completed the sixth grade in public school.

The importance of social interaction is also evident in studies of feral children, those who have grown up in the wild. Several feral children were reportedly found in Europe during the past few centuries. Probably the most famous was the wild boy of Aveyron, found in the wilderness in France in 1800 (Shattuck, 1980). It is not known when the boy was separated from other humans or how he survived in the wilderness until he reached puberty, but he did not know any language, so he might have been separated from humans while very young.

The boy's behavior seemed very strange to those who found him. When given a choice of food to eat, he rejected most of it. He liked potatoes, which he threw into a fire and then picked out with his bare hands, eating them while they were very hot. He could tolerate cold as well as heat, and he was happy to be outdoors in the winter without clothes. He could swing from tree to tree easily, and he was excited by the wind and the moon.

A young doctor took an interest in the boy and taught him to eat a wider variety of foods, to sleep at regular hours, and to wear clothes. It was determined that he could hear noises and make sounds, so an effort was made to teach him to talk. He learned to say a word for milk, but only after he had been given milk—he never learned to use the word to ask for it. After five years of training he had not learned to talk. He did, however, learn to cry occasionally and to hug his teacher. He survived for 22 years after the training stopped, living a quiet life in a cottage with a housekeeper, but he never advanced his learning. Those who studied him were interested to note that he never showed any interest in sexual behavior.

Why do children develop so little when they are isolated from others? Sociologists believe that even physically healthy children could not develop normal social behavior without social interaction. The controversy over the extent to which behavior results from predetermined biological characteristics or from socialization is known as the **nature–nurture debate**. This debate has continued for centuries, but it has drawn more interest recently as a result of the new science of sociobiology.

Sociobiology and the Nature–Nurture Debate

Sociobiology is the study of the biological and genetic determinants of social behavior (Wilson, 1975). Sociobiologists are biologists by training, although some sociologists and other social scientists support their views. Sociobiologists believe that social behavior is determined by inborn genetic traits, which influence human behavior in much the same way that animals are influenced by their genetic inheritance. An example in sociology would be that sexual preference is determined genetically and that humans have a genetic tendency to have only one or a very few mates (Van den Berghe, 1979). Sociobiologists also think that homosexuality is genetically determined, although temporary homosexual behavior (occurring, for example, when opposite-sex partners are not available) may be environmental. They also believe, for example, that altruistic behavior (behavior performed to benefit others without regard for oneself) and warlike behavior are biologically based, although these and other behaviors may be modified by social experience.

Most sociologists criticize the sociobiological viewpoint on the grounds that behavior varies greatly from culture to culture. Sexual behavior, for example, whether with the same sex or the opposite sex, varies enormously. Altruistic behavior also varies widely and is entirely lacking in humans and monkeys who have been raised in isolation. As for warlike behavior, it is completely absent in many societies. According to Hoffman (1985), a specialist in the study of socialization, geneticists do not pay enough attention to environmental and socialization factors in their studies. Thus, when they draw conclusions from their studies, they do not know what effects the environment or socialization might have had.

In addition to the doubts of sociologists, many physiologists believe that there is no genetic basis for human behavior. Biological drives or **instincts**, which are patterns of reflexes that occur in animals, are very powerful. Insects and birds perform many complex behaviors even when they have been reared in isolation. Honeybees perform complicated dances to show other bees where food is located, and birds build intricate nests in the same manner as others of their species, each without having had any environmental opportunities for learning. So far no powerful, fixed drives or instincts have been discovered in human beings. Humans who have been raised in isolation do almost nothing, as the Spitz study indicated.

Sexual behavior in human beings, long thought to be a biological drive, varies so much from society to society and from time to time that researchers are now convinced that it is greatly shaped by social learning. Lauer and Handel (1983), for example, report some of the following variations: In the Victorian age, it was assumed that women did not enjoy sexual intercourse, and men were sometimes advised not to have intercourse more than 12 times per year. Today, women who were studied in an Irish community expressed no sexual desire and engaged in intercourse only as a duty. Men in the community avoided intercourse before hard work because they thought it sapped them of their energy. On the other hand, young men in some South Pacific cultures have intercourse several times a night. Appropriate sexual behavior, then, is learned in the context of a particular culture.

Yet there is a resurgence of interest among a growing faction of sociologists in the sociobiological approach. Arcaro (2002), for example, argues that incorporating sociobiology with traditional sociological perspectives is essential for developing a unified body of sociological theory. Sanderson (2001), a contemporary social theorist, feels that if sociologists ignore the importance of biology as an explanation of behavior, "they are going to look increasingly foolish both within the academy and to the larger educated public."

Money (1980), a physiologist and a psychologist, believes that the nature–nurture controversy is based on an illusion. He believes that environmental factors become part of our biology when we perceive them. When a piece of information enters our minds, it is translated into a biochemical form. Although we do not fully understand the workings of the brain, we do know both that the brain stores information permanently and that information in the brain can cause physiological changes in other parts of our bodies. Money contends that the information in our brains shapes our behavior and that distinctions between nature and nurture are irrelevant.

Although a few sociologists emphasize the sociobiological perspective, most believe that human behavior can be limited by our physiology: We can tolerate just so much heat, cold, or hunger. However, the way in which we respond to our physical limits—or how we behave under any other circumstances—is learned from interacting with other people. This interaction occurs in a manner different from any other animals because humans use language and other symbols.

SYMBOLIC INTERACTION

All animals interact, but we humans are unique in our ability to create societies, cultures, and social institutions. We are also unique in our capacity to use language. George Herbert Mead (1863–1931) was the first to describe why language makes humans different from all other animals.

George Herbert Mead: Mind, Self, and Society

The students of George Herbert Mead were so impressed with his insights about human interaction that after his death, they compiled his lectures and published his book, *Mind, Self and Society from the Standpoint of a Social Behaviorist* (1934). Mead demonstrated that the unique feature of the human mind is its capacity to use symbols, and he discussed how human development proceeds because of this ability. Language is a symbol system. The words in a language have meaning, and when we know the meanings of words and the grammatical syntax in which they function, we can communicate with others who share the same language.

We use language symbols when we think or talk to ourselves and when we talk to other people. When we see another person in the street, we do not simply react to the person instinctively. We interpret the situation by giving meaning to the other person's behavior. We think, "Is this someone I know, or a stranger? Do I want to know this person, ignore her, say hello to her?" If we say "hello" to the other person, we are using a symbol that means, "I wish to greet you in a friendly manner." The other person knows the meaning of the symbol. This is an example of **symbolic interaction**, the social process that occurs within and among individuals as a result of the internalization of meanings and the use of language.

Mead recognized how important it is for people to interact with others in the development of the self. When infants are born, they cannot differentiate among all the objects they see. The world appears as a kaleidoscope of color and movement. Very soon, however, they learn to distinguish important objects, such as the source of nourishment and the parent who brings it. Infants also eventually learn to differentiate themselves from their surroundings and from other persons. For example, as a father repeatedly brings a bottle to his daughter, she becomes aware that she is the object of her father's attention. She learns to differentiate herself from the crib and other objects. She learns that she is a separate object receiving both the bottle and her father's attention. Infants also develop expectations about their parents' behavior and about their parents' role. They expect their parents to bring the bottle.

Mead used the term **role taking** to describe the process of figuring out how others will act. The ability to take a role is extremely important to children. In fact, **play** is a way of practicing role-taking. Children often play "house" or "school," taking the role of **significant others**—mother, father, or any other person important to them. By taking the roles of these significant others, children can better understand their own roles as children, students, sons, or daughters. By practicing the roles of others in play, they learn to understand what others expect of them and how to behave to meet those expectations. As adults, when we take roles, we figure out what others are thinking and how others will act, and then we can act accordingly. Often, however, we do not have the opportunity to play out the role of others, except in our imagination.

APPLYING MEAD'S ROLE-TAKING

Although many of Mead's theories are useful in providing an understanding of how our self develops, his concept of role-taking is particularly helpful. Role-taking is important not only for self-development but also for our personal and professional relationships. For clinical sociologists, therapists, and other counselors who help people deal with problems, role-taking is an important *verstehen* technique. *Verstehen* is Max Weber's concept referring to a deep imagining of how things might be and feel for others. For example, a client undergoing drug counseling may explain his or her fears and feelings of inadequacy to the therapist, but unless the therapist can see things from a drug user's point of view, the therapy might be cold and meaningless to the client.

Clinicians, counselors, and therapists may also ask their clients to engage in role-taking as part of their treatment. Marriage counselors sometimes help husbands and wives confront their marital problems by having them switch roles temporarily so that they can feel what it is like to be in the other's position. By having the husband take the role of wife and the wife take the role of husband, each spouse may learn to see himself or herself the way the other spouse does. Each spouse's role-taking might help in developing more sensitivity to the partner's needs.

How can you use role-taking in your career or occupation? By engaging in role-taking, you will probably improve how you relate to, organize, and lead other people. As a teacher, you might find examples that students can relate to better if you can imagine how the students see the subject matter. For example, teachers sometimes show movies explaining serious topics, but if a particular movie is old, the students may find the fashions dated and the movie quaint, thus missing the point of the movie. As a physician, you might develop a better "bedside manner" if you can put yourself in the place of the cancer patient you are treating. Novels, movies, and even jokes make fun of doctors who become patients and are shocked because they had never previously understood how the patient felt. All of us find it difficult to understand the feelings, attitudes, and ideas of every person with whom we interact, so we find more efficient ways to deal with people. We develop a sense of self and a generalized other.

A child who responded differently to each person in his or her life would never develop a sense of **self**, an identity, a way of behaving in routine situations. In order to develop this sense of self, a child learns to see others not as individuals but as a **generalized other**, distinguishing among the expectations for different roles, but blurring the distinctions among individuals filling these roles. Mead's famous example is that of a baseball team. A child playing baseball develops generalized expectations of each position on the team; pitchers throw, fielders catch, batters hit and run, regardless of the individuals playing those positions. These generalized expectations become incorporated into the child's sense of self.

Once a child has an idea of the generalized other, he or she can begin to develop a personality, an individual way of behaving. The child learns to meet the expectation of the group in some situations but may argue with the group on other occasions. The child interprets the situation and then decides how to act. That is what makes each person unique.

To analyze each person's unique ability to respond to the generalized other, Mead theoretically divided the person into two parts, the **I** and the **me**. The *I* represents the acting person, as in "I attend class." The *I* is not self-conscious. When taking a test in class, the *I* concentrates on the test, not on the self.

The *me* represents the part of self that sees self as object, the part that is concerned with society's expectations of self, such as, "Society expects me to go to class." It is the *me*, seeing self as an object, who says after class, "You really did great on the exam!" or after the party says, "You really made a fool of yourself!" The *me* spends a good deal of time talking to the I.

We use the generalized other to shape our own personality throughout life. We may decide, for example, that attending class is a waste of time or that multiple-choice tests are unfair. We may choose to go along with the norms, or we may choose to argue against them. To do either, however, we must understand the expectations of the generalized other—the school, in this case. We develop our own **mind**, our own ability to think, based on the expectations of the generalized other.

Mead believed that the human mind is entirely social and develops in interaction. Although we are born with a brain, Mead argued, we do not learn to use our mind to think and develop ideas until we have learned the expectations of our society. We learn these expectations mostly through language, and then we use language to talk to ourselves and to develop our own ideas. We get ideas about the usefulness of class attendance and multiple-choice tests. We also get ideas about what we are like, what we want to become in the future, or the relative attractiveness of the persons sitting next to us. It is easy to understand that we would not think about class attendance if there were no classes to attend. It is not as obvious, but just as true, that the relative attractiveness of the persons sitting next to us is based on what we have learned from society about attractiveness. We have learned what color of hair and skin, what size of nose, and what height and weight are valued by society. Based on this, we establish our own definition of attractiveness in others and in ourselves.

Charles Horton Cooley: The Looking-Glass Self

Charles Horton Cooley (1864–1929), like Mead, theorized that the idea of the self develops in a process that requires reference to other people, a process he called the **looking-glass self**. According to Cooley, the looking-glass self has three components: (1) how we think our behavior appears to others, (2) how we think others judge our behavior, and (3) how we feel about their judgments. We know that we exist, that we are beautiful or ugly, serious or funny, lively or dull, intelligent or stupid, through the way other people treat us. We never know exactly what other people think of us, of course, but we can imagine how we appear to them and how they evaluate our appearance.

Our imagination about our own looking-glass self may or may not be accurate. If it is not accurate, we may think we are clumsy when other people think we move very gracefully. We may think we speak clearly when others think we mumble. We may think we are shy even when others admire our confidence. Whether our ideas about ourselves are accurate or not, we believe them, and we often respond to these imagined evaluations with some feeling, such as pride, mortification, or humiliation.

Cooley noted that when we refer to ourselves, we are usually referring to our looking-glass self, not to our physical being, our heart, lungs, arms, and legs. We usually refer to our opinions, desires, ideas, or feelings (I think, I feel, I want), or we associate the idea of the self with roles (I am a student, an athlete, a friend). This sense of self exists in relation to other people. We compare and contrast ourselves with others; our own sense of uniqueness is based on that comparison. Even the language we use to refer to ourselves must be learned from other people.

In sum, both Mead and Cooley pointed out that the major difference between social theories of the self and psychological theories of the self is that social theories emphasize that society exists first and that the individual is shaped by society. Psychological theories emphasize individual development apart from social processes; that is, the individual develops and then responds to society based on preexisting tendencies to behave in particular ways. (See Jean Piaget, Sigmund Freud, Lawrence Kohlberg.)

APPLYING COOLEY'S "LOOKING-GLASS SELF"

One common manifestation of Cooley's theory is the **self-fulfilling prophecy**, a concept developed by Robert Merton. A self-fulfilling prophecy is a prediction that causes us to act as if a particular definition of ourselves, others, or a situation were true (even if it is not true), and as a result, it becomes true because of our actions. A classic example of a self-fulfilling prophecy is a bank failure. Banks operate under the reasonable assumption that all the depositors will not want all of their money back at the same time. Banks do not merely keep our money in a vault; rather, they invest it so that they can pay us interest and also make a profit. However, if all the depositors at the First Intranational Bank believe a rumor (or a prediction) that the bank does not have enough money to give back to them, they might all rush to get their money from the bank at the same time. The resultant bank failure would not be due to any economic or management problems, but solely to a sociological self-fulfilling prophecy.

We now look at the self-fulfilling prophecy and see how it relates to the looking-glass self. If we imagine that others think we are a particular kind of person or have a particular characteristic (even if we are not), we may believe that their perceptions are true, and as a result, we may act in a manner that results in our becoming that way. Suppose, for example, that you imagine that others think you are a funny person. (It does not matter whether they really think you are funny; what matters is that you imagine that they think you are funny.) Because you believe that you are a funny person, you may make an extra effort to become funny by learning and telling new jokes, doing amusing things at parties, and generally cultivating your sense of humor. ("Because I am a funny person, I am the kind of person who knows a lot of good jokes, so I had better be prepared.")

The knowledge that the looking-glass self often becomes a self-fulfilling prophecy may be useful in a variety of ways. First, it might be applied in some occupational settings. How, for example, could this knowledge improve your effectiveness as a teacher? If you are aware that people see themselves as they think others (especially significant others) see them, you might try to be especially sensitive to how you react to students when they ask questions in class, when you speak to them in your office, or when you make comments on their papers. If students think that they are being put down or are perceived as unintelligent, they may prematurely give up on learning a subject. Conversely, if students develop positive views of themselves because they think you as the teacher see them as intuitive, creative, and interesting, they may strive to cultivate those qualities even further, and it may play an important part in their interaction with others.

Erving Goffman: The Presentation of Self

Throughout life, our socialization influences the way we interact with each other. Erving Goffman (1959) was interested in the process of interaction once a self has been developed. Every interaction, Goffman believed, begins with a **presentation of self**. The way we present ourselves gives other people cues about the type of interaction we expect. In formal situations, we usually greet friends with a handshake or a remark, whereas in informal situations, we may greet friends with a hug or a kiss. If we are with friends, we talk and laugh, but on a bus or in an elevator, we do not speak to strangers, and we keep a social distance even when space is crowded and we cannot keep physically distant. Psychologists refer to our manner of presentation as "body language." We give cues about ourselves in the way we present and use our bodies in interaction.

In an attempt to analyze how interaction takes place, Goffman (1959) compared social interaction to a drama on stage—a comparison known as the **dramaturgical approach**. Whenever we interact, we prepare ourselves backstage and then present ourselves as if onstage, according to what we have learned in the socialization process. Goffman believed that all behavior, even the most routine, is neither instinctual nor habitual; it is a presentation. Most Americans prepare to present themselves by showering, washing their hair, and using deodorant—in our society, cleanliness and a lack of odor are important. Complexions must be smooth, so men shave, women put on makeup, and adolescents use cosmetics to cover up acne. Suitable clothing is selected so that we can present ourselves formally in formal situations and casually in casual situations. A formal setting such as a church, a more informal setting such as a classroom, and a casual setting such as a basketball arena require very different presentations. In some settings, one can race for a front-row seat, talk loudly, wave to friends, and eat and drink. In other settings, these behaviors would be quite inappropriate.

In illustrating the dramaturgical approach, Goffman described a character, called "Preedy," as he presented himself on a beach on the Riviera. Preedy very consciously tried to make an impression on the people around him. It was his first day on vacation, and he knew no one. He wanted to meet some people, but he did not want to appear too lonely or too eager, so he presented himself as perfectly content in his solitary state.

The following excerpt from Goffman (1959) describes Preedy's behavior:

> If by chance a ball was thrown his way, he looked surprised; then let a smile of amusement lighten his face (Kindly Preedy), looked round dazed to see that there were people on the beach, tossed it back with a smile to himself and not a smile at the people, and then resumed carelessly his nonchalant survey of space.
>
> But it was time to institute a little parade, the parade of the Ideal Preedy. By devious handlings he gave any who wanted to look a chance to see the title of his book—a Spanish translation of Homer, classic thus, but not daring, cosmopolitan too—and then gathered together his beach-wrap and bag into a neat sand-resistant pile (Methodical and Sensible Preedy), rose slowly to stretch at ease his huge frame (Big-Cat Preedy), and tossed aside his sandals (Carefree Preedy, after all).
>
> The marriage of Preedy and the sea! There were alternative rituals. The first involved the stroll that turns into a run and a dive straight into the water, thereafter smoothing into a strong splashless crawl towards the horizon. But of course not really on the horizon. Quite suddenly he would turn on to his back and thrash great white splashes with his legs, somehow thus showing that he could have swum further had he wanted to, and then would stand up a quarter out of water for all to see who it was.
>
> The alternative course was simpler, it avoided the cold-water shock and it avoided the risk of appearing too high-spirited. The point was to appear to be so used to the sea, the Mediterranean, and this particular beach, that one might as well be in the sea as out of it. It involved a slow stroll down and into the edge of the water—not even noticing his toes were wet, land and water all the same to him—with his eyes up at the sky gravely surveying

portents, invisible to others, of the weather (Local Fisherman Preedy). (p. 5)

Notice how much Preedy could tell about himself without saying a word. Whether anyone enters the water in as calculated a manner as Preedy is questionable, but whoever watches someone like Preedy will form an opinion of him from his presentation. The dramaturgical approach helps us understand that how one appears is at least as important as what one actually does or says—and often, it is more important.

Maintaining the Self

Once we have presented ourselves in a particular role and have begun to interact, we must maintain our presentation. In class, students cannot begin to shake hands with fellow students, wander around the room, or write on the blackboard. It would not only disrupt the class, but it would also spoil the presentation of the student, who would be considered disruptive, strange, or worse. If students or others want to maintain the definitions others have of them, they must maintain a performance in accord with the definition.

Sometimes we inadvertently do not maintain our performance, so we try to **account** for or to **excuse** our behavior (Scott and Lyman, 1968; Simon and Manstead, 1983). If we are late and want to avoid giving the impression that we are always late, we make excuses: "I am usually very prompt, but my car ran out of gas," or "I thought the meeting was at eight o'clock, not seven o'clock."

We also try to maintain our presentations by **disclaimers**—that is, disclaiming a role even while we are acting in that role. "I usually don't drink, but this punch is so good" disclaims the role of drinker. "I'm not prejudiced, but ...," followed by a racist remark, or "I'm no expert, but ...," followed by a remark only an expert could make, are phrases that tell the audience that the self is not what it appears to be.

Often, the audience accepts a person's accounts or disclaimers, and the interaction proceeds smoothly, but sometimes, the drama does not work out so well. We may present ourselves in the role of someone who knows how to act in social situations but not live up to those claims. We may fall down a flight of stairs as we make our grand entrance. We may stand up at a meeting to give a report, claiming to be an expert, but our trembling hands and factual errors will not support these claims. The speaker and those in the audience may attempt to ignore the errors, but at some point, the speaker may get too flustered to continue the pretense of living up to the role or may become embarrassed and laugh, cry, faint, or blush. When a group can no longer support the claims made by an individual, the whole group may become embarrassed or angry (Goffman, 1967).

Implicit in interactions is the assumption that presentations will be maintained. Each person agrees to maintain the self and to support the presentations of others. If people's presentations are not supported by the people themselves or by others, they may be followed by an emotional response. For example, in some situations, I may become embarrassed, and if my presentation is ridiculed, I may get angry. In another situation, if someone seems to fill your image of the ideal romantic love, you may fall in love with that individual; if the person then is cruel, unfaithful, or behaves in some other way that tarnishes your image of him or her, you may grow angry and eventually fall out of love.

Not only do we learn behavior in the process of socialization and interaction, but we also learn appropriate feelings about ourselves and others. We learn self-esteem by understanding how others evaluate us; we learn when to be embarrassed, when to be angry, and both when to fall in love and with what type of person. If we are angry at someone who deserves our respect, we feel guilty about our feelings. If we love someone whom others define as entirely inappropriate, we become confused. Again, we have expectations about maintaining these performances of self—both our own and others'—and we respond emotionally when these expectations are not met. This happens in all of our roles and in whatever groups we act.

Thinking Sociologically

1. Think of times you have done some inaccurate role-taking. What were the results of your interaction?

2. Think of times you have seen your looking-glass self inaccurately. How has this shaped your actions?

3. Think of a time when your presentation of self was not maintained. How did you respond emotionally?

AGENCIES OF SOCIALIZATION

Socialization is found in all interaction, but the most influential interaction occurs in particular groups referred to as "agencies of socialization." Among the most important are the family, the schools, peer groups, and the mass media.

The Family

The family is considered the primary agency of socialization. It is within the family that the first socializing influence is encountered by most children, and this influence affects them for the rest of their lives. For example, families give children their geographical location, as easterners or westerners, and their urban or rural background. The family also determines the child's social class, race, religious background, and ethnic group. Each of these factors can have a profound influence on children. They may learn to speak a particular dialect, to prefer particular foods, and to pursue some types of leisure activities.

Families also teach children values that they will hold throughout life. Children frequently adopt their parents' attitudes about the importance of education, work, patriotism, and religion. Even a child's sense of worth is determined, at least in part, by the child's parents.

One of the values instilled in the children of most American families concerns the worth of the unique individual. We are taught that we possess a set of talents, personality characteristics, strengths, and weaknesses peculiar to ourselves, and that we are responsible for developing these traits. This view of the value of the individual is not found in all cultures, however. Many people who emigrated from southern Europe, for example, believe that one's primary responsibility is to the family, not to oneself. The son of a European farm family, for example, is expected to be loyal and obedient to the family, to work for its benefit, and eventually, to take over the management of the farm when the parents are old. In our culture, however, staying with the family is often regarded as a sign of weakness or of lack of ambition on the part of young adults, and when adult children return home to live, both they and their parents often feel uncomfortable (Clemens and Axelsen, 1985; Schnaiberg and Goldenberg, 1989). These beliefs are just two of the many values that people learn primarily through the family.

As more and more children spend time in child care instead of in the family, the question of what type of socialization will take place in these organizations is of major concern. Can nonfamilial child care really replace family care, and will the quality of socialization be maintained in these organizations? Note the introduction to this chapter and its discussion of child care, and also note the discussion in this chapter on policies about what kinds of child-care programs work best.

Thinking Sociologically

1. Use the theories of Mead, Cooley, and Goffman discussed in this chapter to speculate how different structural factors in child care settings might affect a child's development.
2. How could theories about socialization and social interaction be useful in deciding what types of child-care policies should be implemented?

The Schools

In some societies, socialization takes place almost entirely within the family, but in highly technical societies, children are also socialized by the educational system. Schools in the United States teach more than reading, writing, arithmetic, and other basic academic skills. They also teach students to develop themselves, to test their achievements through competition, to discipline themselves, to cooperate with others, and to obey rules, all of which are necessary if a youngster is to achieve success in a society dominated by large organizations.

Schools teach sets of expectations about the work children will do when they mature. The children begin by learning about the work roles of community helpers such as firefighters and doctors, and later, they learn about occupations more formally. They take aptitude tests to discover their unique talents, and with the help of teachers and guidance counselors, they set occupational goals.

Schools also teach citizenship in countless ways: They encourage children to take pride in their communities; to feel patriotic about their nation; to learn about their country's geography, history, and national holidays; to study government, explain the role of good citizens, urge their parents to vote, and pledge allegiance to the U.S. flag; to become informed about community and school leaders; and to respect school property.

Most school administrators and teachers reinforce our cultural emphasis on the uniqueness of individuals. Thus, they try to identify the unique talents of students through comparison and competition with other students and then attempt to develop these talents so that they will become useful to the larger society. Japanese schools, operating in a less individualistic society, assume that all students will be able to meet whatever standards the schools set.

Peer Groups

Young people spend considerable time in school, and their **peer group** of people their own age is an important influence on their socialization. Peer-group socialization has been increasing in this century because young people have been attending school for longer periods of time. They no longer drop out at age 14 years—most finish high school, and 61.9% go on to college (EVS Beyond Test Scores; Kevin Bushweller 1995).

Young people today also spend more time with one another outside of school. Unlike young people of earlier decades, few are isolated on farms. Most live in cities or suburbs, and increasingly, they have access to automobiles so that they can spend time together away from their families. Teenagers' most intimate relationships are often those they have with their peers, not with parents or siblings, and they influence one another greatly. In fact, some young people create their own unique subcultures. Coleman et al. (1974), who refer to these groups simply as "cultures," list as examples the culture of athletic groups in high schools, the college campus culture, the drug culture, motorcycle cultures, the culture of surfers, and religious cultures. In part because teenagers are often unsure of themselves, they may prize the sense of belonging that they get from their subculture, although the pressures to conform to group expectations can be quite severe.

The Mass Media

The American **mass media**—television, popular magazines, and other forms of communication intended for a large audience—play a major role in teaching Americans to consume goods. They devise programs that attract a particular audience and then sell products to that audience. American children watch 1500 hours per year of television by the time they are 18 years old (Source Book for Teaching Science, 2001). Thus, younger children, who watch an average of almost four hours of television a day, urge their parents to buy the cereals, snack foods, and toys they see advertised. An average 200 junk food adds are shown in four hours of children's Saturday morning cartoon programming (Source Book for Teaching Science 2001). Teenagers listen to their favorite music on radio or MTV and buy the products advertised there. At the very least, the mass media teach people what products are available. In addition, by the age of 18 the average American has seen 200,000 acts of violence on television, 40,000 of these being murders (Source Book for Teaching Science 2001).

The mass media also teach values and needs. An advertisement may teach you, for example, that thoughtful, sensitive children send their parents Hallmark cards on special occasions or just to say "I love you." You may learn that "people on the go," like you, drink Pepsi "uh-huh"; or you may learn that intelligent, frequent travelers should not leave home without their American Express cards.

The mass media also teach viewers something about what life is like, although the view presented may be an idealized version. For example, people learn from television comedy shows that the American family is very happy. Everyday problems of living, such as dented automobiles, lackluster sex lives, occupational failures, trouble juggling two careers and child care, or a shortage of money, all are treated as abnormalities on television. In these media, rich people are often miserable, and poor people, who usually appear in comedies, have a wonderful time and never seem to worry about money. After watching this, viewers may develop unrealistic expectations about the quality of their own lives, becoming unnecessarily frustrated and discontent. If we can understand that our conception of what is normal is one that we have been socialized to accept by the media, perhaps we would not have such unrealistic expectations of ourselves, our spouses, and our children. With more realistic expectations, perhaps we could become more tolerant of ourselves and of others.

Researchers now believe that television shapes not only what we think, but how we think. Healy (1990) believes that television prevents thinking, at least in characteristic ways. Before television, children spent much more time learning about things by talking or reading. This required more use of the imagination. When learning through conversation, a person has to formulate ideas and respond to what is being said in order to maintain the conversation. When learning through reading, a child has to imagine what things look like and how things sound in order to grasp the meaning of the written word. When watching television, children are provided with pictures and sounds and are not required to formulate ideas and respond. As a result, Healy (1990) argues that children who have grown up watching a great deal of television do not think unless the pictures and sounds are provided for them.

Undoubtedly, many more theories about how the mass media shape our thoughts will be forthcoming. Nevertheless, the fact that the mass media play a part in socialization is widely accepted.

SOCIALIZATION OF GENDER ROLES

Socialization plays an especially important part in determining what children believe to be acceptable behaviors for members of their own sex. Even though the situation has begun to change, our environment bombards both men and women with subtle and not-so-subtle suggestions that some types of behavior are acceptable for women and other types of behavior are acceptable for men. People who diverge significantly from expected gender roles often meet with resistance from individuals and from the social system. The same sources of socialization that influence people in other areas of their lives—home, school, the mass media, and interactions with others—also affect the socialization of gender roles.

Infant and Childhood Experiences

Gender-role socialization in our society begins at birth. When a baby is born, he or she is wrapped in a blue or a pink blanket, and from that moment on, parents respond to the infant on the basis of its gender (Bem and Bem, 1976). In decades past, parents could predict the future role expectations of their infants. Boys were expected to grow up to play **instrumental roles**, performing tasks that lead to goals they have set for themselves. Girls were expected to be more verbal, more expressive, more emotional, and when they grew up, more interested in interpersonal relationships, characteristics that have been labeled the **expressive role** by sociologists (Zelditch, 1955).

Research has shown that infants are viewed differently, depending on these future role expectations. Infant boys are often described as big, athletic, strong, or alert, but girls are usually described as tiny, dainty, sweet, pretty, delicate, inattentive, or weak. Parents tend to notice the dainty fingernails of the baby girl, even though those of the baby boy look identical. Boy and girl infants are also treated differently. Boys are handled roughly and tossed around playfully, but girls are held more, cuddled, talked to, and treated as if they were very fragile. Even the tone of voice used is different. Boys are talked to in loud voices, whereas girls are spoken to gently. Parents also give their children different surroundings, toys, and games, based on gender.

Infants respond differently to these very early variations in treatment (Pridham, Becker, and Brown, 2000). Children who are touched and talked to cling to their mothers and talk to them more, regardless of their gender, and because girls are held and talked to more than boys, they tend to reciprocate with this kind of behavior (Goldberg and Lewis, 1969; Moss, 1967).

Parents teach their boys and girls different techniques for solving problems. When doing a puzzle, for example, parents give girls specific advice, but they try to help boys learn problem-solving techniques (Frankel and Rollins, 1983). Toys selected for boys are either constructive (pieces are added to build or change the toy, such as railroads) or aggressive (such as guns), while toys for girls are more nurturant or attractive (such as dolls) (Lorber, 2003).

Today, parents are beginning to have different role expectations for their daughters. More and more parents realize that their daughters will have to compete in the work force. In Sweden, where the government has long been active in discouraging differential treatment of boys and girls, Lamb et al. (1982) found that parents treated their infant sons and daughters alike. However, the two parents differed from one another. They treated their children the way they were treated as children. Mothers smiled, cooed, and cuddled their infants more than fathers did, and fathers were more playful. These children experienced both types of socialization.

Gender-Role Socialization in Schools

Children continue to learn gender-role behavior in nursery school (Ornstein, 1994). Classroom observations of 15 nursery schools showed that the teachers (all women) treated boys and girls differently. Teachers responded three times more often to disruptive behavior by boys than by girls. The boys usually got a loud public reprimand, whereas the girls were given a quiet rebuke that others could not hear. Disruptive behavior is often an attempt to gain attention, and because the boys received the attention they were seeking, they continued to behave disruptively. When the teacher paid less attention to the boys, this behavior diminished. Teachers were also more willing to help the boys find something to do. The girls who were not doing anything were ignored and received attention only when they were literally clinging to the teacher's skirts.

The teachers spent more time teaching boys. In one instance, the teacher showed boys how to use a stapler, but when a girl did not know how to use it, the teacher took the materials, stapled them herself, and handed them back to the girl. Both problem-solving and analytical abilities are related to active participation, but girls were not given the opportunity to try things as often as boys were. Boys are also praised more for good work and are encouraged to keep trying. Girls are praised for appearance but left in the dark about their academic performance (Sadker and Sadker, 1994).

Teachers also evaluate boys differently from girls. If the preschool child is a boy, the teacher evaluates him no differently whether he is compliant or not. However, compliance is a significant factor in evaluating girls. Less compliant girls are viewed as less intellectually competent (Gold, Crombie, and Noble, 1987).

Schools teach gender roles in other ways as well. Most teachers are women, but principals and superintendents are men. Women teachers are more likely to teach young children, but as subject matter becomes more sophisticated and specialized, more men are found teaching. Children receive subtle messages about the capability of men and women as they observe the jobs they hold. School counselors also encourage children to follow expected gender roles. Girls who want to enter masculine occupations or boys who want to enter traditionally feminine occupations will be defined by career counselors as in need of more extensive guidance. Efforts are sometimes made to steer them into more "appropriate" occupations.

Gender-Role Socialization in Peer Groups

Children play mainly in same-sex groups, and this contributes to their socialization. Maccoby (1998) notes that children segregate themselves into same-sex play groups whenever they have a choice of playmates. This tendency begins at the preschool ages and increases until the children reach puberty. Furthermore, this tendency to segregate is stronger when adults do not interfere—in other words, children are more segregated in the cafeteria than they are in the classroom.

Although it is not clear why children segregate themselves in play groups, at least part of the explanation is that children in mixed groups will be teased for liking or loving a member of the opposite sex (Maccoby, 1998). Children who have ongoing friendships with members of the opposite sex often go into hiding about these friendships by age 7 years. They will not acknowledge each other in public but only play together in the privacy of their own homes. To the extent that children segregate themselves to avoid teasing, they are responding to the behavior of older members of the society. They are being socialized to play in same-sex groups.

The result of playing in same-sex groups is that girls are socialized to act like girls and boys are socialized to act like boys (Greenwald, 1996; Lawson, 1992). Maccoby (1998) found that the children did not form groups based on like interests. Whether the girls were passive or aggressive, they played with other girls, and the same was true of boys. Once in the play group, however, girls learn to act in socially binding ways while boys act competitively. In conversation, for example, girls acknowledge each other, agree with each other, and pause frequently to give others a chance to speak. Boys more often use commands, interrupt, boast, heckle each other, tell jokes, and engage in name-calling. When engaged in taking turns, boys use physical means to get a turn, such as pushing and shoving, while girls use conversational means, persuading others to let them have a turn. As they learn how to get along with others of the same sex, girls especially are less interested in playing with those of the opposite sex because their socially binding norms are less influential and powerful than the competitive norms of boys (Maccoby, 1988), and when girls do play with boys, girls become passive.

Mass Media and Socialization of Gender Roles

From childhood on, Americans spend thousands of hours watching television, which has a strong tendency to portray gender-role stereotypes. In children's television programming, male characters are more often portrayed as aggressive, constructive, and helpful, whereas female characters are more often passive and defer to males. Adult programs, especially the situation comedies, are watched by many children and adults. *I Love Lucy*, which was originally produced in the 1950s and is still seen in reruns, featured Lucille Ball as a consistently inept housewife who had to be rescued by her harassed but tolerant husband. Every episode revolved around Lucy's getting into some sort of trouble. Current situation comedies are a little more subtle.

Music videos, however, are usually not at all subtle. They show men acting rough, tough, even violent. "Their" women follow or even crawl after the men, waiting, competing, even suffering for a bit of attention.

Advertising on television and in the press also tends to stereotype both men and women or to portray roles that are impossible to live up to. Career women are portrayed as superwomen who combine a successful career, motherhood, and a terrific marriage while cooking a gourmet meal for a small dinner party of ten. At the other extreme, women are portrayed as beautiful, bewildered homemakers, even when they work outside the home. These ads show the woman arriving home from work to cook the family meal or do the family wash but apparently overwhelmed by indecision about what to serve or how to get shirt collars really clean. A male voice heard in the background tells the woman how to solve her problem. Men in ads are stereotyped as forceful, athletic, involved in business of some kind, or at least actively watching a ball game, but always knowing exactly what they want or which beer has more gusto.

APPLYING GENDER-ROLE SOCIALIZATION

Understanding that gender-role stereotypes are a product of socialization is important for you in your work life and in your personal life. One important problem in the workplace that results from gender-role stereotypes is discrimination against women. This has taken a variety of forms, including unfair hiring practices, lower wages, sexual harassment, and many others.

Some companies hire consultants to develop training programs to help employees at all levels understand the sources of these gender-related tensions in the workplace. Employees can be made aware of how stereotypes are generated through media and other agents of socialization. Also, exercises may be used to help men and women employees understand each other's work experience a little better. One way is to have the men and women engage in role-reversal role-playing. This can help them to see situations from the other gender's point of view and to become more sensitive to each other's needs and attitudes.

The key theme that runs through the training is to get beyond the gender stereotypes that people have learned in their previous socialization.

Stereotypes generated through gender-role socialization may also create problems in your intimate relationships. In her book Intimate Strangers, Lillian Rubin (1983) discusses how our **gender identity** as males or females often prevents people of the opposite sex (husbands and wives, boyfriends and girlfriends, or just close friends) from developing true intimacy. That is, as a result of gender-role socialization, males often learn to see themselves in terms of stereotypical instrumental traits (aggressive, unemotional, dominant, career-oriented, and so forth), and females often learn to see themselves in terms of stereotypical expressive traits (passive, emotional, subordinate, relationship-oriented, and so forth). Think of how these perceptions of ourselves might interfere with the ability of men and women to develop close emotional bonds. Because you see yourself as a "real man," for example, you may find it difficult to express your emotions openly, to cry in front of others, or to be sensitive, even if these feelings tend to emerge. Because you see yourself as a "real woman," you may find it difficult or confusing to have an equal say in your relationship, to take charge of a situation, or to be aggressive, even though you may want to. The realization that gender roles and gender identities are learned through socialization and are not an inherent part of our biological makeup can help both sexes to overcome many barriers to intimacy and to relate to each other as whole individuals.

Thinking Sociologically

Think of characteristics you have in your personality that no one intended to socialize you to have. What events in your life socialized you to learn these characteristics?

SOCIALIZATION IN ADULTHOOD

The knowledge we acquire as children shapes the meanings we give to ourselves and to the world, and it can continue to influence us for the rest of our lives. We never stop learning new things, however; every day, we have new experiences, learn new information, and add the meanings of these new facts to what we already know. Although new knowledge may be different from knowledge acquired as children, the same agencies of socialization are at work.

Types of Adult Socialization

Like children, adults are socialized by their families. Single people must be socialized when they marry in order to live intimately with their spouses and to share living arrangements. If they have children, they learn the role of parent and will probably rely on the knowledge of child care they acquired from their own parents. Because the two parents were themselves brought up by different sets of parents, they will have learned different child-rearing techniques and therefore will have to socialize each other to reach agreement about child-care practices. As the children grow up, the parents must be socialized to allow their children to become independent after years of dependency. All of this learning is a part of adult socialization.

Children themselves are often very active socializers of their parents. As infants, they let their parents know when they need attention. Beginning at about age 2 years, they become aware of themselves, learn to say "no," and begin to let their parents know when they need some independence. This process of demanding both attention and independence continues as long as the children are at home. It can result in serious conflicts in some youths, particularly those who rebel, fight, take drugs, or run away from home. The socialization of parents can be quite dramatic, but it is often successful. A questionnaire given to mothers and fathers of college students (Peters, 1985) found that the parents had learned different attitudes and behaviors about sports, leisure, minority groups, drug use, and sexuality from their children.

Adult socialization also occurs in schools. Colleges teach adults of all ages, and the move from home to college can be a period of intense socialization. College freshmen must adapt to their new independence from the family and make their own decisions about health, food, sleep, class attendance, study habits, exercise, and social relationships. They must learn to live in crowded situations and to compete with peers. Some avoid these decisions by going along with the crowd. Others drop the values they learned in the family and adopt a new set of values, whereas some continue to maintain family values in the new setting. Each choice entails some socialization.

Another type of adult socialization is occupational training, which teaches the attitudes and values associated with an occupation, as well as skills. A new employee in an office has to learn how to conform to the expectations of the other workers and to the business's written and unwritten rules. During this socialization, the employee will discover the answers to questions such as these: Are men and women expected to wear suits, or is less formal clothing acceptable? Do employees address one another by their first names? Is rigid adherence to established procedures expected? Are some department heads more accommodating than others?

Resocialization

Major adaptations to new situations in adulthood may sometimes require **resocialization**. The changes people undergo during this period are much more pervasive than the gradual adaptations characteristic of regular socialization. Resocialization usually follows a major break in a person's customary life; this break requires that the person adopt an entirely new set of meanings to understand his or her new life. **Mortification of self** (Goffman, 1961), the most dramatic type of resocialization, occurs in such institutions as the armed forces, prisons, and mental hospitals. People entering these institutions are totally stripped of their old selves. Physically, they are required to strip, shower, and don institutional clothing. All personal possessions are taken away, and they must leave behind family, friends, and work roles. They must live in a new environment under a new set of rules and adopt a new role as a military person, prisoner, or mental patient. Their previous learning must be completely reorganized.

Retirement from work is sometimes an easy process of socialization to a new situation, but it often requires a great deal of resocialization. Retired people often lose at least part of their income, so they may have to adapt to a new standard of living. With the loss of work, new sources of self-esteem may have to be developed, but society may help in this process by providing education on financial management, health, and housing. Counseling services and support groups for retired persons may also be provided, often by employers, especially when they want employees to retire.

Besides loss of income and self-esteem, retirement creates another resocialization problem. Most roles involve social expectations and provide rewards for meeting those expectations. However, there are few social expectations associated with retirement other than the loss of a previous role; as a result, the satisfactory performance of the retirement role goes unrecognized. To compound the problem, the retired person's spouse often dies during this period, so he or she must relinquish the family role, as well as the work role. Nonetheless, if the retired person has enough money to buy nice clothes, enjoy hobbies, and afford travel for social events or volunteer work, then he or she can create a new role that is rewarding.

Whether dealing with socialization or with resocialization, the human mind is very complex. People learn a varied set of meanings during their lives, and they interpret each situation on the basis of their own biography and their own definition of the situation. How a person presents the self and maintains interactions depends on his or her unique interpretation of self, others, and the situation. It is this ability to interpret that makes socialization and social interaction such a varied, interesting, and challenging area of study.

SUMMARY

1. Socialization is the process of learning how to interact in society. Infants must interact in order to survive, and as they interact, they learn about society.

2. Children who have been isolated or who received little attention when very young do not learn to walk, talk, or otherwise respond to people because early social interactions are crucial to development.

3. Sociobiologists believe that inborn genetic traits direct human behavior just as they direct the behavior of animals. They contend that sexual, altruistic, and warlike behaviors occur in humans because we are predisposed to them in our genetic makeup. Most biologists and social scientists, however, sidestep the nature–nurture debate by believing that people's behavior is determined by their biological capacity to learn socially.

4. Human beings are unique because they learn a symbol system—language. Through linguistic interaction, we develop an idea of who we are.

5. Mead used the term *role-taking* to describe the process of figuring out how others think and perceive us. According to Mead, children take the role of only one other person at a time at first. Children *practice* role-taking in play and learn to generalize in team games. The I acts, but the *me* sees the self as an object. The interplay between the two allows the self to act freely while aware of social reactions.

6. Charles Horton Cooley used the term *looking-glass self* to describe how people learn about themselves; he argued that our identities are heavily influenced by our perceptions of how others view us. We see ourselves not as we are, and not as others see us, but as we think others see us.

7. Goffman compared interaction to a drama on stage. We present ourselves as we want other people to define us. Once we have presented ourselves, everyone involved in the interaction is expected to maintain that presentation. We justify our discrepant behavior by making excuses or disclaimers. If we cannot maintain our presentations, we will respond to our failure with emotion, often embarrassment or anger.

8. Some of the important agencies of socialization are the family, schools, peer groups, and mass media.

9. From birth, males and females are socialized differently. Men are expected to be instrumental, active, and task-oriented, whereas women are expected to be expressive, nurturing, and people-oriented.
10. Resocialization may be necessary when a person's life changes dramatically and abruptly, such as when he or she goes to prison or retires.

KEY TERMS

account of behavior An effort at maintaining the self by explaining the reasons for or facts surrounding the behavior.

disclaimers An aspect of maintaining our presentation of self in which we deny behavior that contradicts how we wish to be viewed.

dramaturgical approach An approach to the study of interaction in which interaction is compared to a drama on stage; the importance of setting and presentation of self are emphasized.

excuse of behavior An effort at maintaining the self by justifying or making an apology for the behavior.

expressive role A role that emphasizes warmth and understanding rather than action or leadership; traditionally associated more with women than with men.

gender identity The social construction of boys and girls, men and women, as opposed to their biological characteristics.

generalized other The assumption that other people have similar attitudes, values, beliefs, and expectations. It is therefore not necessary to know a specific individual in order to know how to behave toward that individual.

I The acting, unselfconscious person.

instinct Biological or hereditary impulses, drives, or behaviors that require no learning or reasoning.

instrumental role A role that emphasizes accomplishment of tasks, such as earning a living to provide food and shelter; traditionally associated more with men than with women.

looking-glass self A process occurring in social interaction. It has three components: (1) how we think our behavior appears to others, (2) how we think others judge our behavior, and (3) how we feel about their judgments.

mass media Forms of communication, such as television, popular magazines, and radio, intended for a large audience.

me The part of self that sees self as object, evaluates self, and is aware of society's expectations of self.

mind The process of using a language and thinking.

mortification of self Stripping the self of all the characteristics of a past identity, including clothing, personal possessions, friends, roles and routines, and so on.

nature–nurture debate A longstanding debate over whether behavior results from predetermined biological characteristics or from socialization.

peer group An informal primary group of people who share a similar or equal status and who are usually of roughly the same age.

play According to Mead, a way of practicing role taking.

presentation of self The way we present ourselves to others and how our presentation influences others.

resocialization Socialization to a new role or position in life that requires a dramatic shift in the attitudes, values, behaviors, and expectations learned in the past.

role taking Assuming the roles of others and seeing the world from their perspective.

self The sense of one's own identity as a person.

self-fulfilling prophecy A prediction that comes true because people believe it and act as though it were true.

significant others Persons that one identifies with psychologically and whose opinions are considered important.

socialization The process of learning how to interact in society by learning the rules and expectations of society.

sociobiology The study of the biological and genetic determinants of social behavior.

symbolic interaction theory The social theory stressing interactions between people and the social processes that occur within the individual that are made possible by language and internalized meanings.

DISCUSSION QUESTIONS

1. How could the ideas of Mead and Cooley be used to discuss your own gender-role socialization?
2. Discuss ways you could become a better student if you changed your looking-glass self.
3. Discuss things you do in college that you believe are important because your peers tell you they are important. Are these messages from your peers making you a better student?
4. Discuss things you do in college that you believe are important because the mass media tell you they are important. Are these messages from the mass media making you a better student?
5. Imagine that you are putting on a skit about getting ready to go to class (or put on such a skit, if possible). What impression are you going to make on professors? On classmates?
6. How does your backstage preparation for class differ from your performance onstage?
7. Think back to your most recent casual conversation, perhaps at lunch. What disclaimers were used in the course of this conversation?
8. Use Goffman's ideas about social interaction to develop an explanation of socialization.
9. List ten answers to the question, "What kind of person are you?" Explore how Cooley's looking-glass self can be applied to explaining these aspects of yourself.

Deviance and Social Control

Drug Use

Drug abuse remains one of America's most important domestic- and foreign-policy issues. However, many misconceptions still surround this issue—misconceptions that can cloud the policies that are meant to solve the drug problem. (Note that when we use the term drug, we refer to psychoactive drugs—that is, drugs that alter the user's mood or mental state, not antibiotic, metabolic, or other nonpsychoactive drugs.)

One common misconception is that the word *drugs* (and even psychoactive drugs) refers only to illegal drugs, such as marijuana, cocaine (and cocaine derivatives, such as "crack"), heroin, phencyclidine (PCP), methylenedioxymethamphetamine (MDMA—"ecstasy"), lysergic acid diethylamide (LSD), and other hallucinogens (Coleman and Cressey, 1990). However, alcohol and tobacco are also psychoactive drugs, and they can be more dangerous than illegal drugs and are readily accepted in many, if not most, social circles. Alcoholic beverages and cigarettes seem to flow freely without any negative sanction. Indeed, the expectation at many types of social events is that guests will indulge themselves in such socially acceptable behaviors in order to "loosen up" and to help create a festive and relaxed atmosphere. Over the past decade, though, the efforts of groups such as MADD (Mothers Against Drunk Driving) have begun to pay off. In 1999, deaths due to drunken driving reached a record low, down from 57 percent in 1982 to 38 percent in 1999. By 2003 the percentage had declined to about 30 percent. But there are still 43 alcohol-related fatalities each day in the United States, the equivalent to two airplane crashes a week. Further, progress in reducing drunk driving fatalities has slowed (Koch, 2000).

According to the latest statistics, in 2005, 62 percent of college students reported drinking alcohol in the last month (National Survey on Drug and Health). In 2004, the percentage of college students one to four years beyond high school reported the use of the following drugs:

Alcohol=85%
Marijuana/Hashish=49%
Inhalants=8%
Amphetamines=13%
Hallucinogens=12%
Cocain (except crack)=10%
Crack=2%
Source: Ksir, Hart, Ray, 2007).

The other commonly accepted drug, tobacco, contains nicotine, which is at least as addictive as heroin and other illegal drugs (Coleman and Cressey, 1990). There is overwhelming evidence that cigarette smoking causes various types of cancer, bronchitis, emphysema, ulcers, and heart and circulatory disorders; it also reduces the life span, causes damage to babies of mothers who smoke, and kills more people than all other drugs combined (Colson, 1990; Coleman and Cressey, 1990). Tobacco caused 435,000 deaths in 2000, up by 35,000 annually since 1990. By 2004, the total "smoking attributable mortality" reached over 440,000 pre-mature deaths annually in the United States (Ray et al., 2007). Smoking is also a social and medical problem worldwide with 3 million people dying from its use every year. It is the leading preventable cause of death in the United States (Ritter, 2000). Clearly, the problem of drug abuse goes beyond their legality. Focusing solely on illegal drugs ignores a major aspect of the drug problem.

Another common misconception is that drug abuse is primarily a problem of the African-American and Hispanic-American underclass. While illicit drug use occurs less often among the affluent, drug abuse is a problem for all social, economic, and ethnic groups (Falco, 1989). For example, nearly 70 percent of all cocaine users are white, and two-thirds of drug users are employed. The widespread use of cocaine started in the upper middle class in the 1970s and spread to the poor in the mid-1980s with the development of crack, a much lower-priced form of cocaine (Shannon, 1990). In a national poll conducted by *The Washington Post*, about half of all Americans said they had a relative or close friend who has a problem with illicit drugs. Further, this statistic does not include problems stemming from legal drugs, such as alcohol, prescribed psychoactive drugs, or tobacco (Melville, 1989). Teen drug use bottomed out to less than 30 percent in 1992, from its peak of over 60 percent in the 1970s, but it began rising again in 1993. Today more than half of all teenagers try an illicit drug before they finish high school, and use is occurring at increasingly early ages (Masci, 2002). More than 23 million Americans use drugs regularly. As many as 4 million use them daily. The United States still has the highest rate of illegal drug use of any industrialized country in the world (Falco, 1989). The myth that drug abuse is primarily associated with the lower class can lead both the general public and policy-makers to ignore the problem. Also, they may ascribe the problems of the lower class to involvement with drugs and thus avoid considering other possible causes of their problems, such as unemployment and lack of education (Shannon, 1990).

Sociology does not focus on individual blame to understand social problems, but rather explores the structural and cultural factors that create problems. For example, while it does not deny that some people may be more or less biologically or psychologically prone to drug abuse, it is more concerned with understanding the social nature of the drug world and the ways it can affect people's tendencies toward drug use. The issue of drug abuse illustrates how sociological theories of deviance can be used to reconceptualize social problems in ways that might help to solve them.

Deviance is universal because people everywhere violate social norms. It exists in all societies, wherever people interact and live in groups. It is found in complex, industrialized, urban areas, as well as in tribal, folk, and agrarian regions. Although it is sometimes claimed that people in some societies cooperate in complete harmony and peace, anthropologists claim that no society or culture, large or small, rural or urban, has complete behavioral conformity and a total absence of deviance.

WHAT IS DEVIANCE?

Deviance means different things to different people. The definition we use influences our explanations of its causes and our attempts to control it. Does deviance reside in the individual? Is it a particular type of act or behavior? Is it defined socially? Are some groups of people immune from being labeled deviants? Our answers to questions such as these will influence how we analyze deviance and whether we ultimately understand it.

We define **deviance** as variation from a set of norms or shared social expectations and deviants as the people who violate these shared expectations. Deviance involves a social audience that defines particular people and behaviors as going beyond the tolerance limits of social norms. Social norms, rules, and expectations about appropriate and inappropriate behavior exist in all societies. People everywhere have social controls to enforce the rules and to punish those who do not conform.

Norms rarely state exactly which behaviors are acceptable and which are unacceptable, and universal adherence to norms is unknown. All societies permit variations in the behavior demanded by the norms. Where variations are possible, people will test their range, and some will inevitably exceed the boundaries of permissible and approved behavior. People's perceptions of deviance rarely correspond to its reality, however, as is shown in the following discussion of some traditional views of deviance and of deviants.

TRADITIONAL VIEWS OF DEVIANCE AND OF DEVIANTS

Who and what is deviant involves a range of perspectives. Sociologists are likely to focus on social aspects of deviance (and of deviants), including how it is formally and informally controlled. As you might guess, there are also biological, psychological, legal, religious, and other perspectives, including views by those who counsel, treat, punish, or work with those defined as deviant. We begin by noting some traditional views of deviance that are widely held today.

The Absolutist and Moral Views

One common traditional view of deviance, often found in conservative political and religious contexts, is that deviance is both **absolute** and **immoral**. That is, particular behaviors, be they extramarital sexual relationships, homosexuality, criminal acts, dishonesty, or the use of psychoactive drugs, are *always* deviant (*absolutism*) and bad or wrong (*immoral*). Black is black, and white is white, and no theory, teaching, or argument will make it otherwise. From this perspective, the social rules are clear, and people should adhere to them. Those who do not are labeled as "bad" people, people who lack proper moral codes, and people who need to be punished.

The Medical and Social-Pathological Views

A second traditional approach is the **medical view** of deviance, in which deviance is assumed to be essentially pathological—evidence that deviants are "sick" people and that society is unhealthy. Just as healthy humans function efficiently without pain or the need for drugs or criminal activities, healthy societies are thought to function smoothly without social problems such as deviance. The prevalence of child abuse, rape, robbery, mental disorders, and alcoholism are thought to indicate that the society in which these occur has a sickness, and the people who do these things or who behave in these ways need to be "cured." Like the absolutist and moral view, the medical view assumes that people are either deviant or not deviant—there is no gray area—but this polarity is expressed in terms of health or illness, not good or evil. The "Medicalization of Deviance" is a relatively new term in the world of Sociology. Over the last 50 years society has watched certain conditions such as AIDS and alcoholism transform from deviant and moral issues into medical conditions (Kimberlin et al., 2006).

The Statistical View

A third traditional view of deviance relies on statistics. Any behavior that is atypical—that varies from the average or the mode—is considered deviant. This view is not absolutist: Deviance is assumed to be a variable characteristic that increases the further a behavior is removed from the average. Deviants are viewed not as sick people, as in the medical view, but simply as being different. According to the **statistical view**, any variation from a statistical norm is deviant. Thus, a person who is left-handed, who has red hair, or who belongs to a minority group is defined as a deviant. Everyone fails to conform to the average in some respect, however, so according to this definition, we are all deviants.

THE RELATIVE NATURE OF DEVIANCE

More recently, sociologists have begun to advocate a relativistic model. Cultural relativism is the assumption that behaviors, ideas, and products can be understood or evaluated only within the context of the culture and society of which they are a part. In the same way, a **relativistic view** suggests that deviance can be interpreted only in the sociocultural context in which it happens. Is a person who is 7 feet tall a deviant in the context of professional basketball? Is a person without a bathing suit a deviant at a nudist beach? Is taking opiate drugs to treat excruciating pain deviant? Is killing deviant in the context of war? Context influences all of these determinations.

If deviance is relative rather than absolute, an act that is deviant in one context may not be deviant in another. A behavior considered "sick" in one society could be thought of as healthy in a different society. An act that might be statistically deviant in one culture might not be in another. Thus, as is generally true of cultural relativism, acts that are defined as deviant in some places are not defined as such everywhere. By the same token, however, the fact that an act is defined as nondeviant in one situation does not mean that it is nondeviant everywhere. Deviance does not consist merely of acts or behaviors, but of the group responses, definitions, and meanings attached to behaviors, and we therefore can expect definitions of deviance to vary with differing circumstances. Some of the most important variations that affect these definitions concern time, place, situation, and social status.

Variation by Time

An act considered deviant in one time period may be considered nondeviant in another. Cigarette smoking, for example, has a long history of changing normative definitions. Nuehring and Markle (1974) note that in the United States, between 1895 and 1921, 14 states completely banned cigarette smoking, and all other states except Texas passed laws regulating the sale of cigarettes to minors. In the early years of this century, stop-smoking clinics were opened in several cities, and antismoking campaigns were widespread. Following World War I, however, cigarette sales increased, and public attitudes toward smoking changed. Through the mass media, the tobacco industry appealed to women, weight-watchers, and even to health seekers. States began to realize that tobacco could be a rich source of revenue, and by 1927, the 14 states that had banned cigarettes had repealed their laws. By the end of World War II, smoking had become acceptable, and in many contexts, it was considered to be socially desirable.

In the 1950s, scientists found that smoking could cause a variety of diseases, including lung cancer and heart disease. In 1964, the Surgeon General published a landmark report on smoking and health, and soon thereafter, some states began passing anticigarette legislation again. Laws were passed requiring a health warning on cigarette packages, and in 1973, the National Association of Broadcasters agreed to phase out cigarette advertising on television (Markle and Troyer, 1979). Another Surgeon General's report in 1986 crystallized the push of this public health concern to a new level; smoking not only harms the health of those who choose to smoke, but it is also hazardous to those who must breathe residual smoke while in physical proximity of someone who is smoking.

The result was that by the 1990s, airlines, restaurants, and other public places either prohibited smoking totally or designated segregated sections for smokers and nonsmokers. Many states have completely prohibited smoking in such places as elevators, concert halls, museums, and physicians' offices. In 2006, the State of Ohio enacted the statewide law banning all smoking in any public place including private clubs, which suggests that smoking is again increasingly considered a deviant behavior. Many other examples could be given to illustrate how behaviors

TABLE 7-1 LEGAL PROHIBITION OF VARIOUS ACTS: VIEWS IN SIX COUNTRIES

	India (N = 509)		Indonesia (N = 500)		Iran (N = 475)		Italy (Sardinia) (N = 200)		U.S.A. (N = 169)		Yugoslavia (N = 500)	
	Yes	No	Yes	No	Yes	No	Yes	No	Yes	No	Yes	No
Incest	94.3	5.7	98.0	0.6	98.1	1.9	97.5	2.0	71.0	20.7	95.0	0.8
Robbery	97.3	2.7	99.2	0.0	97.9	2.1	100.0	0.0	100.0	0.0	98.4	0.4
Appropriation[a]	96.6	1.2	99.8	0.2	97.1	2.9	100.0	0.0	92.3	7.1	98.0	0.0
Homosexuality	74.1	25.0	85.9	7.2	90.3	9.7	86.5	12.5	18.3	66.9	71.6	13.6
Abortion	40.9	58.7	95.3	3.0	83.9	16.1	76.5	21.5	21.9	74.5	24.8	63.2
Taking drugs	74.9	24.6	93.3	2.4	89.8	10.2	92.0	3.0	89.6	11.8	89.2	4.2
Factory pollution	98.8	1.2	94.9	1.0	97.7	2.3	96.0	3.5	96.4	3.0	92.8	1.6
Public protest	33.3	65.8	72.3	20.9	77.0	23.0	34.5	64.5	5.9	91.1	46.2	38.4
Not helping	44.5	53.9	67.7	24.4	56.4	43.6	79.5	20.0	27.8	52.7	76.6	12.2

Note: "Do you think this act should be prohibited by law?" (percentage distribution: "Don't know" category excluded)

[a] Taking over someone else's property for your own use.

Source: *Comparative Deviance: Perception and Law in Six Cultures,* p. 116. New York: Elsevier Science Publishing Company, Inc., 1976. Reprinted by permission of the author.

defined as deviant change over time: the use of various other psychoactive drugs, appropriate bathing attire, nonmarital sexual behavior, and so forth.

Variation by Place

Behaviors viewed as deviant in one location, society, or culture may be considered nondeviant in others. In most African cultures, having more than one wife is a sign of wealth, prestige, and high status. In the United States, however, having more than one wife at once is a punishable offense. Topless bathing is common on certain public beaches in Southern Europe, but is defined as immoral, criminal, or delinquent in American society. Bullfighting in Spain and Mexico and cockfighting in the Philippines are festive, legal gambling activities that produce income, but they are forbidden in the United States. On the other hand, American dating practices, divorce rates, crime rates, and the widespread acceptance of and practice of capital punishment are considered shocking by much of both the Western and non-Western world. Table 7-1 provides the result of research in six countries in which the people were asked how they felt about the legal prohibition of specific acts. Note the extent to which the people in the United States differed from other countries in their response to the issues, particularly in regard to incest, homosexuality, and public protest.

There are variations in definitions of deviance within cultures as well as among them. Take, for example, the smoking issue, used in illustrating variation of deviance over time. Ferraro (1990) showed that although Illinois and North Carolina (a major tobacco-growing and cigarette-producing state) show a similar prevalence of smoking, Illinois residents are more likely to consider smoking harmful to the individual engaged in the act and are more likely to support legal controls of public smoking.

Variation by Situation

Behavior that is defined as deviant in one situation may not be in another, even in the same time period and geographical area. A man who dresses in women's clothes to act in a play would be considered normal, but a man who dresses in women's clothes in the audience would not. Sex between husband and wife in the home is granted social approval, but sex by the same husband and wife at a public beach or on the church altar might land them in jail or in a mental hospital.

Cheating by college students was found to vary by situation as well (LaBeff et al., 1990). Although most students included in this study stated that cheating was wrong, more than half admitted to cheating during the previous six-month period and felt that in some special circumstances, cheating is not only acceptable but actually necessary. Circumstances or situations that they considered to have justified their behavior included blame directed toward the faculty or the testing procedures, missed classes, pressure from parents for good grades, accidental observation of the answers given by others, and so forth.

While many might argue and agree that cheating is always wrong, the social relativity of deviance reminds us that we must carefully select the time, place, and situation in which to behave in particular ways. The identical behavior by the same individual may be appropriate at one time, place, or situation yet not at others.

Variation by Social Status

Deviance also varies with social status, as was illustrated in the introductory issue to this chapter on drug use. Ascribed statuses are those acquired at birth: age, sex, race, and so on. Achieved statuses are those that people gain on their own: marital status, educational status, occupational status, and so on. Until recently, a woman or a black person who aspired to be a bank president might have been considered deviant, but such an aspiration might have been encouraged in a white male. Similarly, members of a country club might try to encourage a rich Mafia member to join, but may treat the drug dealers and prostitutes who provided the Mafia's money with contempt. The status associated with a person's sex, race, age, and income will influence which of his or her behaviors are considered deviant.

We can examine how deviance varies by social status by noting differences in appropriate behaviors for males and females. There are variations by time, place, and situation, but some behaviors are generally given greater approval for women than for men, whereas others are given greater approval for men than for women. It is generally considered acceptable for women to wear high heels, panty hose, and lipstick, but in our society, such behaviors in men would be considered deviant. Men can go topless to any beach, but women who do so would be considered deviant.

The relativistic perspective acknowledges the diversity of behaviors, convictions, and sanctions that can be found in society, as well as the variety of meanings and definitions attributed to behaviors and sanctions. This view also recognizes the potential for conflict, both in a large society and in a single person who attempts to conform to the norms of different groups. A teenager may be encouraged to drink alcohol by peers but not by parents. A Catholic couple may wish to use only what are considered "natural" contraceptive methods to conform to church norms, yet want to use more artificial methods to conform to their own norms and those of their friends and society.

From the relativistic perspective, deviance is not assumed to reside exclusively either in people or in actions. It is, rather, an interactive process involving people's behavior, an audience, societal norms or subgroup norms and definitions, and society as a whole. To understand deviance, we must focus not only on people or acts but also on the time, place, situation, and social status of the deviance and the deviants, on the reactions of others to both, and on the means by which the deviants are controlled or punished.

APPLYING THE RELATIVISTIC VIEW OF DEVIANCE

The view that deviance can be interpreted only in the sociocultural context in which it occurs has important implications for the creation, implementation, and evaluation of many social policies. Social policies and programs often deal with social problems such as poverty, teen pregnancies, the spread of disease, homelessness, drug addiction, and alcoholism, among many others. Although people's lifestyles and choices sometimes do cause their problems, it is incorrect to categorically explain the existence of particular social problems (for example, poverty) as the result of people's failure to conform with societal norms. That type of explanation is based on the absolutist, social-pathological, or statistical views of deviance described earlier in this chapter.

If we do not use the relativistic view of deviance that looks at people's lifestyles in terms of their sociocultural context, it is easy for us to say that people have problems because their behavior is atypical. This type of reasoning, known as **blaming the victim**, implies that social problems are caused by the people facing them. The way that policymakers (politicians, legislators, and the people who vote for them) explain social problems directly influences how they propose to deal with them. If you feel that a group is to blame for its situation, you may try to change the group rather than to search for other causes of the problem or to examine the social context or circumstances in which the problems take place.

Policies are not formulated exclusively by governments. You probably will formulate policies in your job and even in your personal life, so you, too, may benefit from using the relativistic view of deviance. For example, the value of this view may help you if you are or decide to become a parent. As a parent, you will find yourself constantly making policies that you want your children to obey. Will you forbid your daughter to ask a boy out on a date because that type of behavior might have been considered immoral in your grandparents' day? Will you prohibit your son from growing his hair long or from wearing an earring because that was considered a sign of rebellion at one time? Both of these behaviors, considered deviant at one time, are acceptable behaviors in contemporary society. You run the risk of alienating your children and breaking down the channels of communication if you judge their behavior by standards of acceptability that no longer apply. Parents may improve their relationship with their children if they keep in mind the relativistic view of deviance. One way of doing that might be for parents to think of some of the things they did as adolescents that they thought were perfectly justifiable but were abhorrent to their parents.

Thinking Sociologically

1. Is there such a thing as an immoral society, a sick society, or a deviant society?

2. Select a behavior, such as drug use, sexual behavior, or homosexuality. Using the views of deviance just described, think how this or these behaviors have been defined traditionally. Then, examine ways in which these behaviors may or may not be considered deviant, according to the dimensions of time, place, situation, and social status.

THEORIES EXPLAINING DEVIANCE

As we have illustrated, deviance varies by time, place, situation, and social status. Given the wide variations in deviance, how can it be explained? What causes deviance? Why do people violate social norms? Equally important, why do people conform to and obey social norms? Most people do conform, and conformity is granted greater social approval in most circumstances; thus, theories have tended to focus more on the deviant than the nondeviant. The two are not easily separated, however, and explanations of one are equally applicable to the other.

Scientists have developed a variety of theories to explain deviance, but the fact that many theories exist does not mean that one is correct and the others incorrect. Theories often reflect the discipline from which they were developed. Biological theories tend to focus on genetic, anatomical, or physiological factors. Psychological theories tend to emphasize personality, motives, aggression, frustration, or ego strength. Sociologists usually emphasize sociocultural, organizational, environmental, or group factors. Although some theories have more empirical support than others, all can increase our understanding of the complexities of human behavior—whether deviant or nondeviant—and of the social order.

Biological Theories of Deviance

Several of the traditional views discussed earlier in this chapter involved biological factors. The view that deviance is a sickness adheres to a medical model, which assumes not just a social pathology or mental illness but an unhealthy biological organism as well. Similarly, the moral model implies that some people possess a biologically based resistance to conformity. These views share the assumption that particular defects or weaknesses in an individual's physical constitution produce deviant behaviors.

Biological theories of deviance are often traced back to the Italian physician-psychiatrist Cesare Lombroso (1835–1909). Lombroso, sometimes referred to as the "father of modern criminology," was interested in the scientific study of crime. He believed that attention should be shifted from the criminal act to the criminal—specifically, to the physical characteristics of the criminal. He was convinced that the major determinants of crime (or deviance) were biological—that there was a "born criminal type." While Lombroso's ideas were influential for many years, research has basically ruled out this notion.

Other research on biological explanations of crime and deviance followed. In the 1930s, the American anthropologist Ernest Hooton claimed that criminals were organically inferior to those he called "normal" people (Vold, 1958). In the 1940s, William Sheldon attempted to link body type to behavior. He classified people into three categories—*endomorphs*, who are soft, round, and usually fat; *mesomorphs*, who are muscular, stocky, and athletic; and *ectomorphs*, who are skinny and fragile. A disproportionate percentage of criminals were found to be mesomorphs, but the reasons for this remained unclear.

In the 1970s and 1980s, considerable excitement was generated by claims that a specific genetic condition, in combination with social influences, may be associated with crimes of physical violence (Jencks, 1987; Rowe and Osgood, 1984; and Suchar, 1978). Some violent criminals were found to have an extra Y chromosome: They had XYY chromosomes rather than the usual XY. Other findings, however, indicate that the great majority of XYY males have never been convicted of any crime, which suggests that the XYY factor is not a specific cause of deviance.

As you may have guessed, there are many problems with biological theories of crime, delinquency, and deviance, but the recent interest in the new science of sociobiology testifies to the continuing appeal of biological approaches. There are theories suggesting that sexual behaviors, both deviant and nondeviant, are biologically rooted, and that alcohol and other drug abuse is caused by some chromosome component or genetic deficiency. Most of these explanations fail to explain, however, why others with a similar biological makeup do not exhibit the same forms of behaviors. In other words, biological explanations do not clearly differentiate the deviant from the nondeviant, and they fail to explain the tremendous variation in deviance, as well as its relative nature. Today, most sociologists reject the notion that biology, heredity, or constitutional factors cause deviance, but a number accept the idea that genetic or biological factors, in combination with social factors, may be predisposing conditions or may increase the likelihood of some types of behaviors that are socially defined as deviant.

Psychological Theories of Deviance

Like biological explanations, psychological theories tend to focus on the person who engages in deviant behavior. Some psychological theories share with biological approaches the notion that the causes of behavior are rooted in a person's physiological or genetic makeup: instincts, needs, drives, and impulses. In psychological theories, however, the emphasis is on the mind rather than the body. Social psychologists often consider the social context of behavior in addition to these factors.

Psychological theories are often tied to the medical model, associating deviance with a sickness, arguing that deviance results from a psychological abnormality, a psychopathic personality, or a mental illness. This explanation assumes that deviant behaviors such as alcoholism, child abuse, and crime are the consequences of mental illness. It is certainly true that mentally ill people may commit deviant acts, but this theory does not account for deviance among people who are not otherwise considered mentally ill, nor does it explain why some mentally ill people do not engage in deviant behaviors.

Some psychological explanations suggest that deviance results from frustration and aggression. When needs are not fulfilled, frustration results, which in turn leads to aggression and often to antisocial, deviant behaviors. The greater the frustration, the more extreme the aggression. Frustration over the lack of money, the loss of a job, or a failure in love can lead to aggressive acts: speeding, child abuse, robbery, or even murder. One difficulty with this explanation is that frustration is defined so broadly that it includes almost any behavior. Another problem is that it does not account for people who are frustrated but do not act deviantly.

In general, psychological explanations based on frustration, aggression, unconscious needs, instincts, guilt, weak egos, personality traits, and so forth have generated much research but have resulted in very inconclusive results. Many theories or ideas, such as those involving instinct and unconscious needs, are extremely difficult—if not impossible—to test empirically. Explanations based on frustration and aggression or on illness fail to differentiate the deviant from the nondeviant. Another major difficulty with most biological and psychological theories is that they ignore the relative nature of deviance: the influence of social context, variations in rates of deviance, and social responses to deviance. Several sociological theories, some of which incorporate psychological components, consider factors other than acts and actors.

SOCIOLOGICAL THEORIES EXPLAINING DEVIANCE

Sociological theories attempt to explain deviance by looking at sociocultural processes and organizational structures, although acts and actors are considered as well. *Strain and anomie theory*, a structural functional theory, focuses on value conflicts among culturally prescribed goals and socially approved ways of achieving them. *Conflict theory* contends that groups in power define the acts of the weaker groups as deviant in order to exploit them. *Sociocultural learning theories* are concerned with how people interact and learn deviance. *Labeling theory* regards deviance as a process of symbolic interaction and focuses on the meanings, definitions, and interpretations applied to people and acts. *Control theories* concentrate heavily on conformity; they ask why people choose not to be deviant, and they deal with internal and external social controls that inhibit people's involvement in deviance.

Strain and Anomie Theory

A number of traditional sociological theories are collectively referred to as **strain theories** because they suggest that in one way or another the experience of socially induced strain forces people to engage in deviant activities (Agnew, 1997; Thornberry, 1997). To some theorists, the strain is the inability to realize a success goal. To others, the strain is the failure to achieve high status. For our purposes, we focus on what is perhaps the best-known example of strain theory—namely, anomie theory.

Emile Durkheim concluded that suicide is a social phenomenon related to a person's involvement in group life and membership in a cohesive social unit. Anomic suicide, he said, happens because of social and personal disorganization. People feel lost when the values of a society or group are confused or norms break down. Under most conditions, norms are clear, and most people adhere to them, but during times of social turmoil, people find themselves in unfamiliar situations. Making distinctions between the possible and the impossible, between desires and the fulfillment of those desires, becomes impossible. This condition of social normlessness is termed *anomie*.

Merton (1957) extended Durkheim's explanation of anomie. His **anomie theory** suggests that deviance arises from the incongruence between a society's emphasis on attaining particular goals and the availability of legitimate, institutionalized means of reaching these goals. Such groups as the poor, teenagers, racial minorities, and blue-collar workers are constantly informed through education, the media, and friends that material success is an important goal, but legitimate means for achieving it are often unavailable. Thus, deviance is the result of a strain between a society's culture and its social structure, between culturally prescribed goals and the socially approved ways of achieving them.

Merton listed five ways in which people adapt to the goals of a culture and the institutionalized means of achieving them (see Table 7-2). Only *conformity* to both the goals and the means is nondeviant. The other

TABLE 7-2 MERTON'S TYPOLOGY OF MODES OF INDIVIDUAL ADAPTATION

Modes of Adaptation	Culture Goals	Institutionalized Means
I. Conformity	+	+
II. Innovation	+	–
III. Ritualism	–	+
IV. Retreatism	–	–
V. Rebellion	±	±

Note: In this typology, Merton used the symbol **+** to signify "acceptance," **–** to signify "rejection," and **±** to signify "rejection of prevailing values and substitution of new values."

Source: *Social Theory and Social Structure* by Robert K. Merton. Copyright © 1957, by The Free Press; copyright renewed 1985 by Robert K. Merton. Reprinted with the permission of The Free Press, a division of Macmillan, Inc.

SOCIOLOGY AT WORK

Redirecting Juvenile Offenders

Linda Myers has a bachelor's degree with a concentration in sociology and psychology from Lake Erie College and a master's degree in sociology from Kent State University. After completing her baccalaureate, Myers was hired as an intake officer with the Geauga County Juvenile Court. As intake officer, she screened incoming complaints against juveniles, conducted home and school investigations, and provided the judge with a social history of the juvenile, as well as a recommendation on the handling of the case. Myers's sociological background in family systems and relationships helped her objectively assess home environments and their effect on the adolescents brought to court.

Although Myers's bachelor's degree also qualified her for her next job as juvenile probation officer with the Geauga County Juvenile Court in Chardon, Ohio, she decided to pursue a master's degree in sociology at Kent State. She credits the program with giving her a greater understanding of social systems and social agencies, how they work and interact—invaluable knowledge for her job as probation officer. Although her official job description was to ensure that juvenile offenders placed on probation followed the orders of the court, her job involved much more than that. Myers worked with not only her probationers but also their families and teachers, to gain insights into how the probationers interact with those around them—from authority figures to peers—and to formulate the most effective programs for helping the offenders overcome their deviant behavior. While studying for her master's degree, she explored the "diversity of programs offered by the human services along with the organizational framework of such institutions and the numerous roles available to sociologists within the social services." This training was particularly useful to her in directing her proba-

four methods of adaptations are all varieties of deviant behavior, including Merton's second mode of adaptation: innovation. *Innovators* accept social goals but reject the normatively prescribed means of achieving them. Students who want to get good grades are adhering to widely held values, but if they cheat, they are violating a norm for achieving that goal.

A third mode of adaptation is ritualism. *Ritualists* follow rules rigidly without regard for the ends for which they are designed. The office manager who spends all his or her time making sure employees come to work on time, do not drink coffee at their desks, and do not make personal phone calls is a ritualist. By focusing on petty rules, he or she loses sight of the real goal of the office. Ritualists conform to traditions and never take chances. Merton suggests that lower-middle-class Americans are likely to be ritualists, because parents in this group pressure their children to compulsively abide by the moral mandates and mores of society. This form of adaptation is not generally considered a serious form of deviant behavior. People cling to safe routines and institutional norms, thereby avoiding dangers and frustrations that they feel are inherent in the competition for major cultural goals.

Retreatism is a more drastic mode of adaptation. *Retreatists*, such as tramps, alcoholics, and drug addicts, reject both the cultural goals and the institutional means. These people are truly aliens: They are in the society but not of it. They are members of

Redirecting Juvenile Offenders, *continued*

tioners to the community services and agencies that best fit their needs.

As part of her master's program, Myers undertook an internship in which she investigated one of her main concerns—the relationship between substance abuse and the variety of offenses for which juveniles are brought to court. Geauga County's high recidivism rate—48 percent of juvenile offenders end up in court two or more times—convinced her that treatment was often misdirected toward an obvious offense such as truancy while ignoring a more serious cause—drug abuse. Her study revealed that indeed 69 percent of juvenile offenses were drug-related. One 13-year-old girl, for example, was found guilty of unruliness, as charged by her parents who could not control her, and placed on probation. According to her social history, she had been involved in increasingly serious offenses since the age of 10—running away, truancy, shoplifting, and assault and battery. Prior to Myers's review of the case, no one had recognized the possibility of drug abuse as the problem. The girl had denied it vehemently, and her parents had agreed, pointing out that she did not even smoke cigarettes. At one point, however, the girl asked Myers, "Do you think I'm insane?" "No," was Myers's response, "but I'm convinced you're on drugs." Shocked by Myers's detection of the problem, the girl admitted she'd been taking drugs for three years. Subsequent testing revealed that she was chemically addicted, and only then did she begin receiving treatment.

Myers's case is particularly instructive because it not only demonstrates the value of sociological knowledge in a job, but also the value of an internship. It is important to note that internships are undertaken at the undergraduate level, as well as at graduate levels of sociological training.

their society only in that they live in the same place. Retreatism is probably the least common form of adaptation, and it is heartily condemned by conventional representatives of society. Retreatist deviants are widely regarded as a social liability. According to Merton (1957), this fourth mode of adaptation "is that of the socially disinherited who, if they have none of the rewards held out by society, also have few of the frustrations attendant upon continuing to seek these rewards" (p. 155).

The fifth and final mode of adaptation is rebellion. *Rebels*, such as members of revolutionary movements, withdraw their allegiance to a society they feel is unjust and seek to bring into being a new, greatly modified social structure. Most social movements, such as the gay rights or women's liberation movements, fall short of what Merton considered rebellion because these activists do not reject most societal goals. These movements do advocate substituting new values in some parts of society, however. Merton suggests that it is typically members of a rising class rather than the most depressed strata who organize the resentful and the rebellious into a revolutionary group.

Merton's theory has been criticized on a number of different grounds (Thio, 1988). Some critics argue that it erroneously assumes that a single system of cultural goals is shared by the entire society. It has also been faulted for failing to explain why some people choose one response while others choose a different one. Another weakness is that some types of deviance—rape, the behavior of hippies in the 1960s—do not neatly fall into any of his five modes of adaptation. Other critics argue that Merton's theory ignores the influence of societal reactions in the shaping of deviance and the fact that much perceived deviance involves collective rather than individual action. Finally, much criticism has been leveled at Merton's underlying assumption that deviance is disproportionately concentrated in the lower socioeconomic levels.

Anomie theory does have some strengths, however. It provides a framework for examining a wide range of social behavior, it has stimulated many research studies, and it has raised the social consciousness of deviance analysts. This last-mentioned point is particularly true of some members of the new generation of sociologists. These theorists have devised conflict theories of deviance that emphasize the widespread social oppression and basic contradictions found at the heart of our socioeconomic system.

Conflict Theory

Conflict theorists are the major critics of the assumption of the functionalist and anomie theories that a society shares a single set of values. **Conflict theory** contends that most societies contain many groups that have different, often conflicting, values and that the strongest groups in a society have the power to define the values of weaker groups as deviant. Conflict theorists emphasize the repression of the weak by the powerful, the exploitation of the masses by strong interest groups, and the influential and often wealthy groups who use laws, courts, and other agencies to oppose the interests and activities of lower socioeconomic groups and minorities.

Most businesses exist to make a profit; if, in making a profit, they also (intentionally or unintentionally) provide jobs, raise the level of personal gratification, and improve the community, little conflict may result. If, however, high taxes, high wages, fringe benefits, safety requirements, or pollution controls disrupt profits, then lobbying groups, political contributions, and media campaigns are used to influence legislation, taxation, and controls. Part-time workers may be used extensively, to eliminate fringe benefits. Women and blacks may be hired at lower wages than those paid to men and whites. Community tax incentives may be granted to sustain businesses or industries at the expense of the individual. The powerful exploit those with less power, and this exploitation by the elite produces inequality and institutionalized violence. The conflict between the powerful and the weak, therefore, influences both the creation of deviance and our response to it.

People tend to assume that the law is based on the consensus of its citizens, that it represents the public interest, and that it treats citizens as equals and serves the best interests of society. Conflict theorists, however, argue that the law means that legal authorities *ought* to be fair and just but are actually unfair and unjust, favoring the rich and powerful over the poor and weak. This condition exists, they say, not because law enforcement officials are cruel or evil, but because they would antagonize members of the middle and upper classes if they arrested them for their white-collar offenses. These classes might then withdraw their support from law-enforcement agencies, thus leading to loss of law-enforcement jobs.

Quinney (1979) and Spitzer (1975), who agree that deviance and deviants are defined and controlled by the powerful, go a step further and blame the lack of justice directly on the capitalist system. Drawing heavily from Karl Marx, Spitzer contends that populations are considered deviant by capitalists when they disturb, hinder, or question any of the following: (1) capitalist modes of appropriating the products of human labor; (2) the social conditions under which capitalist production takes place; (3)

patterns of distribution and consumption in capitalist society; (4) the socialization of productive and nonproductive roles; or (5) the ideology that supports capitalist society.

According to the conflict perspective, definitions of deviance are determined largely by the dominant class, rates of deviance are determined primarily by the extent to which the potentially deviant behaviors threaten dominant class interests, and control of deviance is largely determined by the extent to which the powerful can socialize and reward those who follow their demands. Many conflict theorists perceive their theory as a call for political action to raise a revolutionary consciousness and end the oppression of the powerless by the powerful.

Like other theories, conflict theory has its critics, who fault it for not searching for the causes of deviant behavior. They also say it does not explain the crimes and deviances that are basically nonpolitical (vices or trivial deviations such as outlandish forms of dress or goldfish-swallowing contests). In addition, conflict theorists have been criticized for assuming that in the utopian communist society murder, robbery, rape, and other crimes will disappear after the power to criminalize them is abolished.

Sociocultural Learning Theories

Sociocultural learning theories deal with the processes through which deviant acts are learned and the conditions under which learning takes place. Deviant behaviors are learned through essentially the same processes as other behaviors. Unlike anomie and conflict theories, sociocultural learning theories emphasize the groups to which people belong and the ways in which they learn the norms prescribed by those groups. In other words, people grow up in groups and situations in which deviance is the norm and is learned. Three of these theories focus specifically on deviance: cultural transmission theory, differential association theory, and social learning theory.

Cultural transmission theory, sometimes called "subculture theory," stems from the Chicago school of sociology. This theory suggests that when deviance is part of a subculture's cultural pattern, it is transmitted to newcomers through socialization. Shaw and McKay (1929) noted that high crime rates persisted in some Chicago neighborhoods over several decades even though the areas changed in ethnic composition and in other ways. When there is a tradition of deviance in a subculture, they suggested, the norms of that subculture are passed on by the gang, peer group, or play group during interaction with newcomers. As a result, they too become deviant, not by violating norms but by conforming to the norms of the subculture.

Other sociologists quickly picked up on the idea that deviance is transmitted culturally through learning and socialization. These scientists extended the theory, suggesting that people learn not only from gangs or peer groups but also from other agents of socialization: parents, teachers, church leaders, business colleagues, and others. A person could learn deviant attitudes by observing that people throw away parking tickets, keep incorrect change in a supermarket, or find ways to avoid paying taxes. One primary source of learning about deviance may be institutions designed to correct deviance, such as juvenile homes, detention centers, reformatories, prisons, and mental hospitals. Even people within these subcultures, however, are exposed to and learn conforming behaviors. So why are some people attracted to deviant behaviors while others are not?

To answer this question and explain how deviance and crime are culturally transmitted, differential association theory was devised by Sutherland (1939; Sutherland and Cressey, 1970). Sutherland attempted to determine why crime rates vary among different groups of people. Why is the crime rate higher in the city than in the country, and higher in impoverished areas than in other areas? Why do more males than females and more young people than older people commit crimes? Sutherland also wanted to explain why some individuals become criminals and others do not.

Differential association theory suggests that deviance results when individuals have more contact with groups that define deviance favorably than with groups that define it unfavorably. Sutherland contended that criminal behavior is learned rather than inherited or invented and that it takes place through verbal and nonverbal communications, primarily in intimate groups. Learning a criminal behavior involves acquiring a set of motives, drives, rationalizations, and attitudes, as well as specific techniques for committing the act itself. Sutherland did not believe that contact with criminals was necessary for a person to become deviant—exposure to definitions favoring deviance was sufficient, and the influence and frequency of these exposures vary from person to person. According to this theory, deviance is a learned behavior, a set of behaviors transmitted to people through their interactions with others.

Social learning theory is a revision of Sutherland's differential association theory, in accordance with the principles of behavioral theory (Akers, 1977; Akers et al., 1979). Social learning theory suggests that deviant and conforming behaviors are determined by the consequences—rewards or punishment—that follow them. This is known as operant or instrumental conditioning, whereby behavior is acquired through direct conditioning or through imitating the modeled behavior of others. A behavior is strengthened by rewards (positive reinforcement) or the avoidance of punishment (negative reinforcement) and weakened by aversive stimuli (positive punishment) or loss of rewards (negative punishment). Akers et al. (1979) state that the acquisition and persistence of either deviant or conforming behavior are a function of what particular behaviors have been rewarded or punished, which is known as **differential reinforcement**. The norms and attitudes people learn from others, especially peers and family, are also influential.

Suppose, for example, that a 15-year-old, John, has just moved to a new neighborhood. Initially, he has no friends. One day, unhappy and lonely, he defies a teacher and gets into a violent argument with him. After class, several of his peers comment admiringly on the way he told the teacher off. The attention serves as positive reinforcement: John needs friends. He tells his mother what happened, but she says only that she wishes she could tell her boss to go to hell once in a while, which encourages John to think that his behavior is acceptable. He begins to deliberately provoke arguments with teachers, and gradually he gets a reputation as a rebel. Girls begin to pay attention to him (more positive reinforcement). Eventually, however, he is suspended from school for two weeks, which then deprives him of the attention of his friends (negative punishment). When he returns, he finds that his teachers have collectively decided to ask him to leave the room whenever he acts up, so he learns to be more cautious (negative reinforcement). He is also required to clean the bathrooms after school every time he gets into trouble (positive punishment). The positive reinforcement encouraged him to act in a mildly deviant fashion, but the negative punishment, negative reinforcement, and positive punishment encouraged him to conform to school standards. Eventually, he finds a level of disruption that maintains his reputation without forcing his teachers to try to change his behavior.

Akers et al. (1979) assessed their social learning theory of deviant behavior with data on factors that influenced the drinking (alcohol) and other drug use of 3,000 adolescents. They found that alcohol and other drug use were both positively correlated with exposure to users and association with users. They also found that the use of drugs such as alcohol increased when it was reinforced more than punished and when use was defined positively or neutrally. Although differential association accounted for most of the adolescents' variations in alcohol and other drug use, differential reinforcement, definitions, and imitation were also influential.

Sociocultural learning theories focus on how deviance is learned. Critics argue that these theories do not explain how deviance originated or how some behaviors came to be defined as deviant. It has also been argued that they do not deal adequately with those who commit deviant acts in isolation rather than as part of a group. Furthermore, these theories are often difficult to test empirically without engaging in circular reasoning: Deviance is caused by a tradition of deviance, caused by earlier deviance. Another weakness is that it is very difficult to determine precisely what stimuli or learning experiences cause a person initially to commit a deviant instead of a conforming act. Nevertheless, sociocultural learning theories have contributed to our understanding of the nature of deviance.

Labeling Theory

The theories of deviance discussed so far have focused on deviant people, deviant acts, the process of learning deviance, and the causes of deviance. **Labeling theory** is concerned primarily with how some behaviors are labeled "deviant" and how being given such a label influences a person's behavior.

Most labeling theorists interpret deviance in terms of symbolic interaction processes . Like other behaviors, deviant behavior is not regarded as a particular type of act undertaken by a person in isolation. It is, rather, a result of human interactions, as well as people's interpretations and definitions of their own actions and those of others. As Kitsuse (1962) stated it, "Forms of behavior *per se* do not differentiate deviants from nondeviants; it is the responses of the conventional and conforming members of the society who identify and interpret behavior as deviant which sociologically transform persons into deviants" (p. 253).

Note that, according to this perspective, deviance is a relative condition. It is not a specific type of act; rather, it is the consequence of applying a particular label. As noted several decades ago by Becker (1963), "Social groups create deviance by making the rules whose infraction constitutes deviance and by applying those rules to particular people and labeling them as outsiders" (p. 9). Thus, if two people commit the same act, one might be labeled a deviant and the other might not, depending on the meaning given to the act by their social groups.

Edwin Lemert (1951), one of the first labeling theorists, identified two categories of deviance. *Primary deviance* involves behavior that violates social norms but is temporary and sporadic. Individuals who are involved in primary deviance do not regard themselves as deviant, nor are they regarded as such by those around them. Secondary deviance involves habitual violation of norms by individuals who not only consider themselves deviant but also are labeled as deviant by others. *Secondary deviance* becomes a routine, resulting in a label that leads to further deviance. The behavior, for example, of a student who buys one term paper to turn in to a history professor might be primary deviance. However, if this student consistently cheated on tests and turned in papers that she had not written herself, her behavior would be considered deviant by her peers, her professors, and herself, and it would therefore constitute secondary deviance.

What are the consequences of labeling? According to this theory, being labeled as deviant has negative consequences because labeled people tend to see themselves as deviant, which leads them to continue their so-called deviant behavior. Thus, we have the development of a deviant career and a label that becomes a master status: cheat, prostitute, liar, and so on. Getting so labeled leads others to view one in terms of that deviant status, overlooking other qualities or statuses. Beyond that, labeled people may no longer be treated as respectable parents, teachers, or community members; they may lose their jobs, be rejected by friends, or be sent to a prison or a mental hospital. Responses of this sort often push labeled people further into the deviant activity. Ex-convicts who cannot get legitimate jobs may return to robbery or drug dealing. Those labeled as mentally ill lose many of the social supports necessary for mental health. Drug addicts, alcoholics, and prostitutes may turn to others who share the same label for support and companionship, which leads them to organize their lives around their deviance.

Who labels whom? Of labeling, Becker (1974) says, "A major element in every aspect of the drama of deviance is the imposition of definitions—of situations, acts, and people—by those powerful enough or legitimated to be able to do so" (p. 62). The labelers, therefore, would include such social control agents as police, judges, prison guards, and psychiatrists, whereas the labeled would include criminals, delinquents, drug addicts, prostitutes, mental patients, and others. Consistent with the conflict theory described earlier, rich, white, or powerful people are more likely to apply the labels, and poor, black, and otherwise powerless people are more likely to be labeled. A poor or black person is more apt to be arrested, prosecuted, and convicted than a rich or a white person for committing the same act.

Data from the Bureau of Justice Statistics, for example, show that in 2005, over 7 million people were on probation, in jail or prison, or on parole. Blacks constituted 12.3 percent of the U.S. population, but their lifetime likelihood of going to prison was 18.6 percent, compared to 10 percent for Hispanics, and 3.4 percent for whites. Similar statistics show a higher arrest, prosecution, and conviction rate among men, the young, the less educated, and the poor. For example, about 93 percent of all state prison inmates are male, 57 percent are under 35 years of age, 43 percent have less than 12 years of schooling, and more than one-third (36 percent) were not employed at the time of their arrest (*Bureau of Justice Statistics*, 2005).

Although it is accepted by many sociologists, labeling theory has its critics. It does not explain the causes of deviance, nor can it be used to predict who will be labeled and in what contexts. Like other symbolic interaction theories, labeling theory is difficult to test empirically. Another criticism is one that also applies to conflict theory: If the powerful create and impose the deviant label, how is it possible that powerful people are also sometimes labeled as deviant? Critics have also questioned the extent to which the labeling of deviance encourages rather than deters deviant behavior. Finally, are all persons in prisons or mental hospitals there simply because someone chose to label them, or are some behaviors so disruptive that severe sanctions such as institutionalization must be imposed to maintain social order? Other social consequences of deviance are discussed in the next section.

Thinking Sociologically

1. Pretend that you are in a position to shape a public policy that is designed to help combat drug abuse in your community. Prepare a well-rounded policy by integrating all of the sociological theories of deviance discussed in this chapter:

strain and anomie theory, conflict theory, the sociocultural learning theories, and labeling theory.

2. Most parents have some fears that their child or children will become involved in some form of deviant behavior. What is one type of deviant behavior that you most fear for you children? Use specific theories, concepts, and ideas contained in this chapter:

   a. to determine whether and why your fears are justified

   b. to help you understand the nature of that behavior, why it is considered deviant, and whether it is actually harmful

   c. to help you better understand why that type of deviance might occur

   d. to help you decide what you might do to lessen the possibilities of your child engaging in that type of behavior

   e. to help you decide what you might do if your child or children do become involved in such behavior.

THE SOCIAL CONSEQUENCES OF DEVIANCE

Social systems are composed of many parts, which exist because they perform some function in the maintenance of the system. Any part of a social system may be dysfunctional in some respects, but the part continues to exist because it performs a function that leads to the maintenance and stability of the system. Also, as we stated earlier in this chapter, deviance is universal—it exists in all societies—and therefore it seems plausible to argue that deviance continues to exist because it serves some functions in the maintenance of societies.

Social Functions of Deviance

The notion that deviance may have positive effects runs counter to the traditional views described earlier. According to these views, deviance is harmful, immoral, antisocial, a sickness in society. Deviance is not merely a sickness, however; it is part of the nature of all social systems. It has also been traditionally regarded as evidence of social disorganization, but many deviant subcultures, such as gangs, organized crime, prostitution, or police corruption, may be found in highly organized societies and may be highly organized themselves. As early as 1894, Durkheim pointed out that deviations should be regarded as a normal part of a society (Kelly, 1979). It appears that deviance performs various social functions, some of which are described next.

Deviance helps to *define the limits of social tolerance*. By indicating the extent to which norms can be violated without provoking a reaction, it helps to clarify the boundaries of social norms and the limits of behavioral diversity. Methods of social control, such as arrests, psychiatric counseling, criminal trials, and social ostracism, help to define these limits. Arrests and trials indicate to the public the seriousness of some deviations and the extent to which violations of norms are tolerated. Driving 57 miles per hour when the speed limit is 55, for example, is tolerated by police, and driving 60 is usually tolerated, but driving 80 or 100 is likely to lead to punishment. Spanking a child may be acceptable, but a parent who physically injures a child can be arrested. By observing societal reactions to deviance, members learn the limits of acceptable variation from norms.

Deviance can *increase the solidarity and integration of a group*. Such a label can unite the people who share it. Some deviants find emotional support and a sense of community among others who share their values and behavior patterns. Student protesters, homosexuals, and members of religious cults and other subcultures tend to defend and protect one another and derive their identities from their deviant group. By the same token, highly integrated groups may form in an attempt to defeat or eliminate deviants—having a common enemy tends to unite group members.

Deviance can *serve as a "safety valve" for social discontent.* When people desire things that the social norms do not permit them to have, they may become frustrated and angry and attack norms or even attempt to destroy the social system. Some types of deviance permit people to escape from conventional norms and rid themselves of frustration without disrupting the social system as a whole. Cheating on paying income tax may be an outlet for frustration with government spending on wasteful projects or with being underpaid. The use of illegal drugs may be a safety valve against job frustrations or an unhappy marriage. Income-tax cheating and drug use involve risk to individuals, but they may prevent expressions of frustration more injurious to society. Thus, they tend indirectly to support such basic institutions as marriage, the economy, and the government. By funneling off anger and discontent, deviance may remove some of the strain produced by social mores.

Deviance can *indicate defects or inadequacies in the existing social organization.* High rates of some kinds of deviance may expose problems in the social order. Large numbers of parking violations may indicate that there is not enough parking space. Outbreaks of violence in prison serve as a warning that the system is inadequate. Activities such as freedom marches by blacks in the South, the burning of draft cards by young men in the 1960s, and the hunger strikes of IRA members in Ireland were organized acts of defiance (and deviance), intended to force leaders and the public to address perceived problems in the social system.

Another functional aspect of deviance, therefore, is that it can *set in motion steps that lead to social change.* Such change can occur in many different forms. It can involve modifications in the existing structure, modifications in behavior, or changes in the definitions of deviance. Until the early 1960s, a black person who tried to sit in the front of a bus in Alabama was regarded as deviant. Following court cases and rulings against segregation, this behavior is no longer considered deviant. As social norms change, so do their definitions, and folkways and mores may be modified as a consequence of deviant acts.

Social Dysfunctions of Deviance

Some consequences of deviance are dysfunctional: They can disrupt, destabilize, or even lead to the complete breakdown of a social system. Given the range of tolerance of norm violations, isolated instances of deviance generally have little effect on the stability of systems. Widespread, long-term, and more extreme norm violations can impair the functioning of groups or of entire systems.

Deviance can *disrupt the social order.* Violations of norms can disturb the status quo, make social life unpredictable, and create tension and conflict. Teachers who refuse to teach, parents who ignore their children, or workers who fail to perform their appointed tasks can keep the system from functioning smoothly. The effect of an alcoholic father on a family system is a good example. The family's income may decrease, the wife may have to assume full responsibility for raising the children, and the children may be ashamed to bring friends home. All routines and social expectations are subject to being disturbed by him. Deviance is often dysfunctional because it disrupts the order and predictability of life.

Deviance can *disrupt the will of others to conform.* If norm violations are unpunished or if members of society refuse to obey established rules, the desire to conform is decreased. Studying for an exam may seem pointless if you know that other students are going to cheat. Obeying the speed limit can be frustrating if other drivers blow their horns to get you out of the way so that they can speed by. To work hard when others are lazy, to be honest when others are dishonest, or to obey the rules when others ignore them can make these efforts seem pointless. When deviance and conformity are not differentiated, deviance disappears. If they receive the same response or reward, what is the motivation to conform? Conformity to a given norm, rule, or law makes sense only if (1) others conform as well, (2) those who conform are differentiated from those who do not in some way, or (3) norm violators receive some type of punishment. Deviance that erodes the desire to follow rules and conform to social norms is dysfunctional.

Deviance can *destroy trust.* Social life is based in part on the assumption that other people are honest and trustworthy. When interpersonal trust decreases, people become more dependent on the legal system to define, interpret, support, and enforce the law. If all car dealers (or car buyers) were honest, written contracts would not be necessary, and a few judges and lawyers would be out of work. In this sense, deviance is functional for the legal system, but it is dysfunctional to the society as a whole. Widespread deviance destroys our confidence and trust in others, just as it disrupts the will to conform.

Deviance can *divert resources* into social rehabilitation and control efforts, which otherwise could be used elsewhere. It may be functional in that it provides thousands of jobs for those who rehabilitate and control criminals, drug addicts, the mentally ill, and others, but it is dysfunctional in that the money and other resources used to deal with deviance cannot be used for other constructive and productive purposes. Criminal activities alone cost billions of dollars every year. Most would agree that these funds could be used more profitably elsewhere.

Clearly, deviance is neither all good nor all bad. Some of its consequences lead to the stability and maintenance of the system, others tend to disrupt it. Whatever the case, it is here to stay, an inevitable part of every society.

Deviance and Crime

We have defined deviance as variations from a set of norms or shared social expectations. A **crime** is a violation of criminal statutory law, and a specific punishment applied by some governmental authority generally accompanies the violation. Many types of deviance, such as rape, robbery, and murder, are criminal acts in most states; other types of deviance, such as bizarre behaviors related to mental disorders, wearing unusual clothes, and shouting at strangers passing by, are not. Just as definitions of deviance differ from group to group, criminal activities and crime rates vary in different legal jurisdictions, with accompanying differences in rates of enforcement. For example, prostitution, illegal in most states, is legal in Nevada. A decade ago, it was legally impossible for a man to rape his wife. Today, many states have amended their rape laws to make the relationship between the rapist and the victim irrelevant.

Accurate estimates of crime rates are difficult to make because a high percentage of most crimes go undetected and unreported. Even crimes such as murder in which the body of a victim can serve as evidence present classification problems. Official data on crime in the United States are collected by the Federal Bureau of Investigation (FBI) and reported in a yearly volume entitled *Uniform Crime Reports (UCR).* The statistics are gathered from more than 16,000 city, county, and state law-enforcement agencies that voluntarily report data on criminal offenses. The crimes recorded in the FBI reports are divided into two categories: One includes *violent crimes,* such as murder, forcible rape, robbery, and aggravated assault; the other category includes *property crimes,* such as burglary, larceny of $50 or more, motor vehicle theft, and arson. Approximately 13 million of these crimes are known to be committed each year. The famous FBI "Crime Clock" for 2005, shown in Figure 7-1, is one dramatic way of illustrating how frequently some offenses are committed.

It is estimated that more than half of all serious crimes do not show up in official statistics, and a much higher percentage of the less serious ones go both undetected and unreported. Surveys asking people whether they have been victims of crimes or asking them whether they have committed various criminal acts show the incidence of crime to be much higher than the officially reported incidence.

Surveys also reveal what conflict and labeling theorists contend: a discriminatory bias in the legal system. Some groups of people are far more likely to be caught and punished for their crimes than others. Young people, blacks, persons from a lower socioeco-

FIGURE 7-1 CRIME CLOCK, 2005

The crime clock should be viewed with care. Because it is the most aggregate representation of *Uniform Crime Reports (UCR)* data, it is designed to convey the annual reported crime experience by showing the relative frequency of occurrence of the index offenses. This mode of display should not be taken to imply a regularity in the commission of offenses; rather, it represents the annual ratio of crime to fixed time intervals.

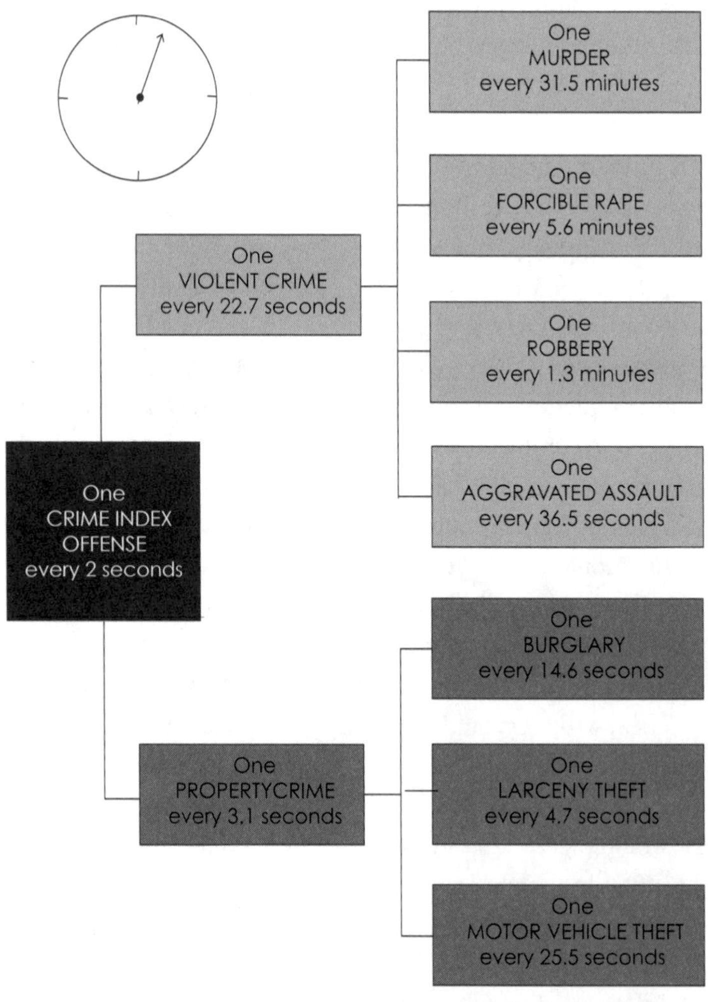

nomic status, and disadvantaged groups in general are more likely to be picked up by the police, to have their cases reported, to be arrested, and to be punished.

Biases in the legal system are also evident in the way the legal system handles some types of crime. The term "white-collar crime" was coined by Edwin H. Sutherland (1940, 1983), who noted that some crimes are committed in the course of the occupations and daily business activities of persons who are otherwise deemed to be "respectable" and of high social status. The savings-and-loan scandal of the early 1990s is, in part, a contemporary example of white-collar crime. In addition to poor management and risky business deals, it sometimes involved collective embezzlement—that is, the siphoning off of billions of dollars of other people's money for personal use by the top management of savings-and-loan institutions (Calavita and Pontell, 1991). Other examples of these kinds of criminals include lawyers who defraud their clients of securities and physicians who illegally sell and use narcotics. Recently, white-collar crime has come to include offenses by businesses and corporations, as well as by individuals. Crimes of this nature include consumer fraud, stock manipulation and insider trading, income-tax evasion, misrepresentation in advertising, and bribery. These types of offenses, although they cost billions of dollars yearly, are usually dealt with by federal and state regulatory agencies rather than criminal courts, and the offenders are more likely to receive fines than prison sentences.

Organized crime consists of groups expressly organized to carry out illegal activities such as the distribution of drugs, the operation of a gambling business, or loan sharking (lending money at excessively high rates), for example. Some consider organized crime to be the tightly knit national organization variously called the "Mafia," the "Cosa Nostra," the "syndicate," or the "mob"; others use the term more loosely to cover any group of organized professional criminals who maintain control of a large-scale illegal business enterprise.

In either case, the organization has a strict hierarchy, ranging from the "lords of the underworld" (who make the important decisions and direct the activities) to those at the lower levels (who follow the orders). Those at the lower levels, who deal directly with the public, are the ones who get caught, but some may get released through the leader's connections with the police, judges, or relevant professionals. Organized crime groups maintain control within their group or organization through threats, intimidation, bribery, and, when they deem it necessary, violence. Most deviance is not controlled by such severe means, however. It should also be noted that some types of formal and informal means of social control exist in all societies in order to encourage people to conform to social norms.

DEVIANCE AND SOCIAL CONTROL

The fact that deviance is universal and sometimes has positive social functions does not eliminate the need to control it. If societies are to survive, they must have ways of making people conform to social norms. Control is maintained both by encouraging conformity and by discouraging deviance through means such as a variety of punishments.

Conformity to social norms is generally explained in terms of two social control processes: (1) **Internal controls** cause members of society themselves to want to conform to the norms of society; (2) **external controls** are pressures or sanctions that are applied to members by others. The two types of control tend to operate interactively.

Internal Controls of Deviance

Internal controls are those that exist within the particular individual's moral and social codes of behavior. They include a wide range of factors: positive self-image, self-control, ego strength, high frustration tolerance, and a sense of social responsibility, among others. The workings of internal controls can be explained in part by socialization theories. These theories explain how we internalize norms, learn what others expect of us, and develop a desire to conform to those expectations. Some types of deviance, such as criminality and mental illness, are widely believed to be caused by inadequate socialization, especially in the years of early childhood.

Most social control is directly related to a person's *social self*—our definitions of who we are in relation to the society we live in. Internal motivations to conform result not from a fear of being caught or a fear of punishment, but because people have been socialized to see themselves in a certain way and to believe that stealing, cheating, murder, and some other behaviors are wrong. In a study of deterrents to shoplifting, for example, Kraut (1976) concluded, "People's definitions of themselves and of deviant behavior seem to act as internal constraints on shoplifting. When respondents explained why they hadn't stolen the last time they bought an item in a store, the two most important reasons they gave were their own honesty and their belief that shoplifting was unacceptable behavior" (p. 365).

Again, the looking-glass self and the self-fulfilling prophecy are relevant here and could be used in personal and professional relationships. The manager of a large department store, for example, might have a problem with employee theft of goods in the store. Instead of dealing with the problem by threats of punishment, the manager might try to get the employees to see themselves as part of a team working together toward a common goal. College teachers who have a problem with students cutting classes or not doing their reading assignments might treat the students as if they are mature, responsible individuals and commend their positive actions. It is true that rewards or punishments might work at times. However, when people act only out of fear of punishment or desire for a reward, and the reward or punishment is the only reason for conforming to the desired behavior, people may no longer conform if the reward or punishment is removed.

Parents might use the knowledge that people tend to act in a manner consistent with their view of themselves in a positive way to influence and socialize children. Instead of trying to control their behavior with rewards or punishments, parents might try to instill a sense of high self-esteem and self-respect in their children by the way they act toward them. If children are constantly ridiculed and put down, they may come to have a low self-esteem and low self-respect, and thus may act accordingly. On the other hand, if children are often praised or corrected in a more positive way, their positive self-images may motivate them to adopt more positive social values and to act in accordance with these values.

Feelings about right and wrong are sometimes referred to as "conscience." The saying, "Let your conscience be your guide," assumes that you have internalized some notions about deviant and nondeviant behavior. For most people, the conscience develops as a direct result of socialization experiences in early childhood and later in life. Social institutions such as the family and religion significantly aid in the internalization of social norms. Once social norms are internalized, deviations produce feelings of guilt, remorse, or conflict. The relatively high prevalence of conformity in comparison to deviance is largely due to internal controls.

External Controls of Deviance

External controls are those that come from outside an individual. They can be either informal or formal. **Informal external controls** involve peers, friends, parents, or the other people with whom we associate regularly; these people apply pressure to encourage us to obey the rules and conform to social expectations. The same techniques can be used to encourage conformity to deviant norms. In the shoplifting study just mentioned, Kraut (1976) found that external constraints are also very important and that informal sanctions are a stronger deterrent than formal sanctions. Shoplifting was strongly correlated with the subjects' perception of their friends' involvement in and approval of shoplifting. In other words, subjects whose friends either shoplifted or approved of it were more apt to shoplift than subjects whose friends disapproved of it, which suggests that friends have a powerful influence on the acceptance or rejection of deviant behavior.

Informal social controls have been found to be the major cause of the low rates of alcoholism found among Jews. Glassner and Berg (1980) found that American Jews avoid alcohol problems through four protective social processes: (1) They associate alcohol abuse with non-Jews; (2) they learn moderate drinking norms, practices, and symbolism during childhood, through religious and secular rituals; (3) they form adult relationships primarily with other moderate drinkers; and (4) they use a repertoire of techniques to avoid excessive drinking under social pressure. These techniques included reprimands by the spouse, developing reputations as nondrinkers by making jokes, avoiding many drinking situations, and finding rationalizations for not drinking. Alcoholism is a common form of deviance, but the low rate of alcoholism among Jews indicates that informal social controls can exert a powerful influence in controlling it.

Formal external controls, the systems created by society specifically to control deviance, are probably the least influential. Courts, police officers, and prisons are formal external controls. Unlike internal controls and informal external controls, formal controls are supposed to be impersonal and just. In actuality, however, the legal system tends to favor some groups of people, just as conflict theory suggests. Even in prisons, guards tend to overlook rule violations by some prisoners and to enforce rules with others. The discretionary power of police officers, prosecutors, judges, and other officials in arresting, prosecuting, and convicting people is often used arbitrarily. It may be highly dependent on factors other than deviance per se. Age, race, sex, social status, known prior deviations, and other factors all have been shown to affect the nature and outcome of formal control mechanisms.

SUMMARY

1. Deviance is universal, and every society has people who commit acts defined as exceeding the tolerance limits of social norms.

2. There are several traditional views of deviance. The *absolutist and moral view* assumes that particular acts or people are deviant in all contexts and that these acts and people are bad and immoral. The *medical model* of deviance suggests that deviants are sick people and that deviance is unhealthy. A *statistical model* defines deviance as any behavior that varies from the average or the mode.

3. The *relativistic view*, a more sociological perspective, assumes that deviance can be defined only in the context of the society or group in which it takes place. Deviance is not thought to be a particular type of act. It is, rather, a relative condition that varies according to time,

place, situation, and social status. This view takes into account the great diversity of meanings that can be associated with people or acts in different situations.

4. Many theories have been developed to explain who is deviant, the causes of deviance, and how it can be controlled or modified. Biological theories have attempted to associate it with body type, physical abnormalities, and chromosome aberrations. Psychological theories emphasize such factors as personality, motivation, willpower, frustration, aggression, and ego strength.

5. Sociological theorists do not ignore biological and psychological factors, but they tend to view theories based on these factors as insufficient. Sociological theories focus on the interactional, organizational, and social normative factors through which people learn definitions of deviance. These factors also determine people's behavior, which a social audience labels as either deviant or nondeviant.

6. *Strain* and *anomie theories* link deviance to conflicts between culturally valued goals and institutionalized means of achieving them. Innovation, ritualism, retreatism, and rebellion are deviant modes of adaptation.

7. *Conflict theories* contend that definitions of deviance are devised by the powerful to repress and exploit the weak. An influential, wealthy elite is assumed to oppose and control the powerless, the poor, and minorities.

8. *Sociocultural learning theories*, which are basically both social and psychological in nature, emphasize the processes through which deviant acts are learned and the types of conditions under which they are learned. *Cultural transmission theory*, sometimes called "subculture theory," explains the continuity of crime and deviance in some geographical areas as the result of the transmission of deviant norms from one generation to the next.

9. *Differential association theory* contends that deviance is learned through verbal and nonverbal communication, by associating differentially with deviant or nondeviant individuals or groups. The social learning theory of deviance, which draws heavily on differential association theory, suggests that operant (instrumental) conditioning and imitation play important roles in the learning of behaviors. Differential rewards and punishments, as well as exposure to conforming or deviant models, greatly influence whether we develop deviant or conforming attitudes and behaviors.

10. *Labeling theory*, rather than emphasizing acts or individuals in isolation, focuses on why some people and acts are singled out as deviant and also on the effects of being labeled deviant. This approach, which is based on the principles of symbolic interaction, assumes that the definition of deviance and other behaviors is a collective process. People in social contexts define and interpret their own behavior and that of others and apply labels on the basis of their definitions. These labels have a significant effect on the continuation of deviant behavior for both those defined as deviant and the audience who labels them.

11. Deviance can influence social systems in several different ways. Some of the consequences are *functional:* They can help to define the limits of social tolerance, increase the solidarity and integration of groups, indicate inadequacies in the system, and bring about constructive change. Other consequences are *dysfunctional:* Deviance

can disrupt the social order, decrease the will of others to conform, destroy trust, and divert resources that otherwise could be used elsewhere into social rehabilitation and control efforts.

12. Deviance differs from crime, in that *crimes* are violations of criminal statutory law. Rates of criminal activity are published annually by the FBI, in its UCR, but offenses are widely underreported.

13. Two types of crime that are generally not reported are white-collar crime and organized crime. The former is committed by higher-status persons or by businesses and organizations in the course of their daily activities. The latter involves a group organized with the expressed intent of carrying out illegal activities.

14. The control of deviance is generally explained in terms of two factors: internal controls and external controls. *Internal controls*, which are exerted by individuals on themselves, involve such factors as self-concept, ego strength, high frustration tolerance, and conscience. These controls are believed to be acquired through socialization. *External controls* include both informal interactions with people, such as family and friends, and formal controls, which are carried out by the agencies designated by society to maintain law and order.

KEY TERMS

absolutist view The view that there is wide agreement about social norms and that certain behaviors are deviant regardless of the social context in which they occur.

anomie theory The view that deviance arises from the incongruences between a society's emphasis on attaining certain goals and the availability of legitimate, institutionalized means of reaching those goals.

blaming the victim A type of reasoning that implies that social problems are caused by the people facing them.

conflict theory A social theory that views conflict as inevitable and natural and as a significant cause of social change.

crime A violation of a criminal statutory law accompanied by a specific punishment applied by some governmental authority.

cultural transmission theory The theory that a community's deviance may be transmitted to newcomers through learning and socialization.

deviance Variation from a set of norms or shared social expectations.

differential association theory The theory that deviance results when individuals have more contact with groups that define deviance favorably than with groups that define it unfavorably.

differential reinforcement The view that the acquisition and persistence of either deviant or conforming behavior is a function of what behaviors have been rewarded or punished.

external controls Pressures or sanctions applied to members of society by others.

formal external controls Formal systems of social control applied to the individual by others; examples include courts, police, and prisons.

immoral view The view that deviance is immoral and antisocial.

informal external controls Pressure applied by peers, friends, parents, and other people with whom one associates regularly that are intended to encourage one to obey rules and conform to social expectations.

internal controls Learned patterns of control that exist in the minds of individuals and make them want to conform to social norms.

labeling theory A theory that emphasizes how certain behaviors are labeled "deviant" and how being given such a label influences a person's behavior.

medical view The view that deviance is essentially pathological evidence that a society is unhealthy.

"medicalization of deviance" The transformation of moral and legal deviance into a medical condition.

organized crime Groups expressly organized to carry out illegal activities.

relativistic view The view that deviance can be interpreted only in the sociocultural context in which it occurs.

social learning theory The view that deviant and conforming behaviors are strongly influenced by the consequences that follow them.

sociocultural learning theories Theories that deal with the processes through which deviant acts are learned and the conditions under which learning takes place.

statistical view A perspective on deviance that defines deviant as any variation from a statistical norm.

strain theories Theories of deviance suggesting that the experience of socially induced strain, such as anomie, forces people to engage in deviant activities.

DISCUSSION QUESTIONS

1. How do you define deviance? Explain what it means to say that deviance is socially defined.
2. Evaluate the debate about the legalization of drugs in terms of the traditional and relativist views of deviance.
3. How would you explain the variation in types of deviant behavior between males and females? Can it be explained genetically or biologically? How do social responses differ?
4. What are the similarities and differences among the anomie, conflict, sociocultural, and labeling theories of deviance?
5. How can the definition of some types of behavior as deviant regardless of their sociocultural context result in misguided social policies? Give some examples other than the ones shown in this chapter.
6. What are some types of behavior that are commonly explained in terms of biological and psychological theories of deviance? Is it possible to explain these in terms of sociological theories? If so, how?
7. Compare the usefulness of the biological and psychological theories of deviance with the sociological theories of deviance.
8. How does being labeled a "deviant" influence interaction patterns? Does "truth" (i.e., accuracy, correctness) matter?
9. Discuss some ways in which deviance has positive functions for society. Give examples.
10. Use the sociological theories of deviance to discuss the internal and external controls of deviance.

PART THREE

Social Inequality

All animals are equal, but some animals are more equal than others.

George Orwell

Social Differentiation and Stratification

The Growth of Income Inequality

Private security in upper-income communities is common in the United States. These communities exemplify the increasing economic segregation between upper- and lower-income Americans. It is ironic that people who live in upper-income communities often depend on people from whom they wish to live apart to perform services that are vital to maintaining their lifestyle.

The "fortunate fifth," as Harvard political economist Robert B. Reich refers to the upper 20 percent of income earners in America, "is quietly seceding from the rest of the nation" (1991, p. 42). This is not simply in terms of residence. Wealthier Americans have chosen to be economically segregated for generations. More important, Reich argues, many have withdrawn their financial support from public spaces and institutions and have redirected it to private services. For example, members of condominiums and affluent residential communities must pay for private maintenance, security, and recreational services that local governments can no longer afford. Many cities lose the benefits of the taxes paid by higher income Americans when they move into separate communities. Thus, while public parks and playgrounds in poorer communities deteriorate, private clubs and recreational facilities in wealthier neighborhoods proliferate. Even though many successful Americans generously help their communities through volunteer work and financial support, not much of this goes to enhance social services for the poor—to improve schools, health clinics or recreational centers, and so on—but goes instead to the places and institutions used by wealthier Americans, such as art museums, theaters, orchestras, private hospitals, elite universities, and private schools (Reich, 1991).

The secession of wealthier Americans is part of a wider social issue: increased income inequality. *Income inequality*—specifically, the gap between "rich" and "poor" (most commonly defined as the upper and lower 20 percent of income earners)—is widening rapidly in the United States (Goffman, 1990). Between 1990 and 2001, according to the U.S. Census Bureau, the average income for the richest fifth of American families increased from $94,404 to $159,644, but less dramatically for the poorest fifth, shifting only from $9,833 to $14, 021. In 2001, the top 5 percent took home $280,312—the highest portion in post–World War II history (U.S. Census Bureau, Historical Income Tables, F-3, 2001). Although these statistics are oversimplifications in that they do not distinguish among different income-earning groups—such as families with a male or female as primary breadwinner, dual-income families, single-parent families, various age groups, black families, and white families—they do indicate that income polarization is increasing in the United States and that the trend is likely to continue (Maxwell, 1990).

More recent studies illuminate some specific effects of economic segregation. For example, Ovadia (2003) has shown that the racial gap in men's employment rates is affected by the level of economic segregation in a metropolitan area. That is, black men are less likely to be employed than white men in cities with high levels of economic segregation. Additionally, the odds of employment for black men in economically segregated cities *decline* with each additional year, while the odds of employment for white men in economically segregated cities *increase* over time, thus widening the racial gap. On the other hand, black men in economically integrated cities have employment chances that are virtually equal to white men, and there is no racial gap in employment odds increases over time in economically integrated cities.

Furthermore, Swanstrom, Dreier, and Mollenkopf (2002) contend that rising economic segregation is a cause of rising economic inequality and subsequently produces effects in ways that do not show up in the income statistics. They suggest that economic segregation not only undermines equal opportunity, it also damages American democracy.

This is an important sociological issue because it indicates that there are significant changes occurring in our *system of social stratification*—that is, our system of ranking people in society. Although social inequality exists to a certain degree in every society, some societies—such as the United States—have a system of stratification in which people can achieve higher or lower social positions. As this chapter shows, a variety of social factors affect different groups' chances for achieving a higher social position. Nevertheless, it has been possible—

possible, not necessarily easy—for most people to improve somewhat their overall lot in life. However, the widening gap between the upper- and lower-income groups suggests that we may be moving, willingly or unwillingly, toward a stratification system in which the chances for lower-income groups to achieve a higher social position are becoming less and less possible. While some people have all or most of their needs and desires met, enjoy a high quality of life, and have most of their dreams come true, those at the other end of the stratification system do not have even their most basic needs met and stand little chance of ever having their dreams fulfilled. Thus, while life improves for those at the top, the widening gap between the rich and the poor suggests that it is becoming worse for those at the bottom and that it is increasingly unlikely that their conditions will change within the near future.

SOCIAL STRATIFICATION

Americans emphasize a commitment to equality and a belief in the American middle-class lifestyle. The belief is that people are basically equal and that most are middle class. There is a tendency to believe that a few people are rich because they worked extra hard. A select few were creative enough to build a better mousetrap, develop a more sophisticated transistor, or cook a better hamburger. On the other hand, the tendency is to believe that only a few Americans are poor, mostly as a result of not taking advantage of the opportunities the country has to offer.

What Americans seldom realize is how incredibly wealthy a few are and how extremely poor others are. A relatively few people control great wealth and power. Most of them have not worked hard for their money—they inherited it. They live in luxury in summer and winter mansions. Meanwhile, as many as 2 or 3 million Americans eat in soup kitchens (when they eat), have no homes at all, and without a home are not qualified to vote. Some of these people work hard for a living, and many are only children. In reality, people are not created equal, nor do they experience equality in their lives.

Inequality—the unequal distribution of scarce goods or resources—is found in most, if not all, societies. Some goods and resources are hard to come by in every society. In some countries, meat is scarce; in others, it is plentiful. Land is a scarce resource in some areas of the world; in others, it is so plentiful that no one bothers to claim ownership. In societies where there are not enough workers, children become a valuable resource. From their youth, they work on the family farm, and they later provide for their elderly parents. Some commodities are universally scarce; for example, mansions and luxury cars are scarce commodities in nearly every society.

Of course, people differ in other ways as well. Some people have blue eyes, and some have brown eyes. Some people live and work on the east coast and some on the west coast. Some people travel in their work, and others prefer to work at a desk. Some people like to work with people, and others prefer solitary work. This is **social differentiation**—how people vary according to social characteristics. Usually, we do not rank people as high or low based on these differences.

Rather, people are ranked according to the scarce resources they control. Money and property are two types of scarce resources. Other scarce resources are social status—or prestige in the community, such as professional prestige—and high rank in a political or philanthropic organization. The ranking of people according to their wealth or prestige is known as **social stratification**. Stratification, then, is a hierarchical structure of society.

Our ranking in the stratification system influences every part of our lives: where we live, go to school, and work; what we eat; how we vote; and whom we marry. Our sexual behavior, sports, hobbies, and health are all affected by the rank society gives us. This chapter examines the ways in which stratification affects people's lives and explores how to use this knowledge in our work and in our personal lives. We begin by noting social differentiation in selected types of societies.

TYPES OF SOCIETIES AND SOCIAL DIFFERENTIATION

In simple societies, there is little division of labor, and all people perform similar tasks and possess similar wealth. As a result, there is little social differentiation. In complex societies, there are wide divisions of labor, with a wide array of social positions. Stratification develops as we rank these positions in order of importance. Lenski (1966) has shown that stratification generally increases as societies grow in wealth and become more complex. He discerned five basic types of societies:

1. Hunting-and-gathering societies
2. Simple horticultural societies
3. Advanced horticultural societies
4. Agrarian societies
5. Industrial societies

Hunting-and-gathering societies consist of about 50 people, or even fewer, who live on what they can find to eat. They are often nomadic, moving from place to place in search of food. They are usually very poor and must share what they find to eat in order to survive. No one can be excused from work. Surpluses of food or supplies are not accumulated, so no one can become wealthy. Some people may gain special respect because of their age, wisdom, skill in hunting, or magical abilities, but they do not derive any power from their status because there is no area to exercise their authority and little to do except work. With so little differentiation in these societies, there is little stratification.

In **simple horticultural societies**, the people farm using a digging stick as their basic tool. They have a fairly reliable source of food and may even have a surplus from time to time. Thus, they can remain in one location, build shelters, and make tools. A surplus of food and supplies allows them some leisure time, which they use in sports and ceremonial activities. They also occasionally fight wars to protect their land. A **division of labor** develops when some people do certain specialized occupations: warriors and ceremonial and political leaders, for example. Ceremonial leaders are sometimes paid for performing ceremonies, especially those involving healing, and they may become wealthy. Political leaders, with the assistance of warriors, can capture slaves and enforce their edicts. As labor is divided among different groups and wealth and status accumulate, a stratification system develops.

Advanced horticultural societies farm with irrigation, terracing, and fertilization. These techniques increase the food supply, so the size of the population can grow. Societies at this level have learned how to work metals. This increases the variety of material goods and also the variety of occupations. As the size and wealth of the populations increase and a greater variety of occupations develops, stratification increases, and the political leader becomes a very wealthy and powerful person who can raise a large army and can use it to capture more slaves and force them to do whatever the leader chooses. Social differentiation and stratification are much greater in these societies than in simple horticultural societies.

Agrarian societies, such as those found in Europe during the Middle Ages, have far more sophisticated technology than horticultural societies. This advanced technology increases the development of centralized power in two ways: First, as defenses and weapons are improved, arming a warrior with the materials needed to win battles becomes an expensive proposition. By supplying the weapons, the rich are able to develop armies, which they use to conquer land and slaves and to control farmers, who become the serfs of the society. Second, as the variety of goods grows, a merchant class develops to trade those goods. The more powerful rulers tax the wealth accumulated by the merchant class and become extremely rich.

As wealth and power become concentrated in the hands of very few people, society becomes severely stratified. During the Middle Ages, the ruler and governing classes in agrarian societies probably received income of about a quarter to a half of the national income (Lenski, 1966).

Industrial societies, such as the United States and western European countries, have the greatest division of labor, the most wealth, and therefore the most stratification, at least at the beginnings of industrial revolutions. Industrialization, which is structured on the factory system of production and the assembly line, requires workers to perform very specialized tasks. Workers specialize in operating a particular piece of equipment, packing a manufactured product, driving a truck to market, advertising the product, selling the product, and so on. Workers do not produce goods for personal consumption. Instead, they do a specific job in exchange for money and then buy personal goods with that money.

Durkheim (1933) argued that in preindustrial times the division of labor created **mechanical solidarity**, a situation in which people do similar work but they are not very dependent on each other. Most people farmed and were self-sufficient. He believed that the division of labor could create **organic solidarity** because as each person specializes in one phase of production, he or she becomes dependent on others to produce other products. As a result, Durkheim believed, society would become more integrated and people would become more equal. However, Durkheim's predictions did not come about. Industrial societies have developed a wide gap between those at the top and those at the bottom. The surplus of goods produced, when accumulated in the hands of just a few people, make those people very wealthy compared with others.

TYPES OF STRATIFICATION

There are two basic types of stratification in the world today: caste and class. In a **caste system**, caste is ascribed at birth. An individual's worth is judged on the basis of religious or traditional beliefs about the person or the person's family. The caste system is very rigid: it is a **closed system**. No one can move into another caste.

This system is found in India, where there are some 3,000 castes. Caste determines status, identity, education, occupation, and trade union. The caste into which people are born affects what kind of food they eat, where they live, what kind of medical care they receive, how they are supported in old age, and how they are buried. Although economic or social success does not change an individual's caste, the caste as a whole can raise its status by changing its customs and rituals to imitate a higher caste. This process takes several generations, however.

In the purest form of a **class system**, social level is defined in terms of wealth and income. There are no legal definitions of class, so the system is an **open system**. Classes are fluid—that is, there is no boundary between one class and another. Anyone can move to a higher or lower ranking by either gaining or losing wealth; as a result, class societies are highly competitive, and power has become increasingly important to maintain a high position in the stratification system.

SOURCES OF POWER IN A CLASS SYSTEM

As mentioned, in the purest form of a class system, wealth determines class. Weber (1946) pointed out that as the class system developed in industrial societies, there actually developed three closely related scarce resources that are sources of **power**: class, status, and party. While these sources of power are closely related, they can be analyzed separately.

Social Class

Social class is based on several closely related factors: wealth, the power derived from wealth, and the "life chances" to acquire wealth. **Life chances** are the opportunities people have to improve their income. A woman from the upper-middle class, for example, has a better opportunity to get a good education and thus a good job than a woman from the lower classes. A man who inherits an income from a rich uncle has a better chance to invest in the stock market than one who has no such source of income. A person who associates with educated people in the suburbs has a better chance to become well spoken and well dressed than a person who lives in an urban ghetto. A person's use of language and style of dress also increases the chances of being successful in business.

People who have a scarce resource other than wealth, such as an advanced education, a special skill, or a talent or service to sell, have power in the marketplace. They can sell when the price is right or sell to the highest bidder, and they can refuse to sell when the price is too low. Social class, then, is determined by life chances to acquire wealth as well as by wealth itself.

The French sociologist Pierre Bourdieu made a classic distinction between material wealth and cultural assets when he coined the term cultural capital. The term cultural capital represents the collection of noneconomic forces such as family background, social class, varying investments in and commitments to education, different resources, etc., that influence academic success (Bourdieu, 1983). The objectified state of cultural capital is represented by cultural goods, material objects such as books, paintings, instruments, or machines.

Social Status

Social status, according to Weber, is the amount of honor and prestige a person receives from others in the community. Prestige is acquired by being born into a highly respected family, living in a high-status neighborhood, attending prestigious schools, or joining high-status groups or clubs. People also gain prestige by being able to buy consumer goods that others admire, such as expensive houses, yachts, or airplanes. Status can also be acquired by holding respected positions in the community, such as clergy or professors. In short, status is acquired by doing things and buying things that others admire. Thus, people's status is very closely related to their wealth. Some people use their wealth to buy status, while other wealthy people are content to live quietly, relatively unknown in the community.

Parties

A **party** is an organization in which decisions are made to reach the group's goals, such as to win an election, change a law, revise the banking system, educate children, or any other goal. A person can gain power in the community by being politically active in national, state, or local politics; in special interest groups; in influential clubs; or in any other type of organization in which decisions are made to reach broad-based societal goals. By developing power in parties, people can increase their social status through winning respect and can increase their social class through reaching goals that are profitable to them.

Class, status, and party are often closely interrelated. Status and party can be used to increase wealth. Wealth can be used to buy consumer goods and increase status or to join prestigious clubs and increase political power. These three sources of power do not always go together, however. Wealthy people who are criminals, who live reclusive lives, or who are otherwise atypical have low status if no one respects them. Priests, ministers, college professors, and community leaders may be poor but still have a high status. Party leaders who use their position to increase their wealth sometimes do so in such a way that they lose status and the respect of others.

You may better understand characteristics of stratification—class, social status, party—if you think back to your high school days and the ways in which students could gain recognition. Some students gained recognition in dimensions of class, others gained recognition in dimensions of status, and still others in dimensions of political activities. Table 8-1 provides examples of these dimensions of stratification.

TABLE 8-1 DIMENSIONS OF STRATIFICATION IN A HIGH SCHOOL ELITE

Class (wealth or skills for the marketplace)
Wealthy students
Most likely to succeed
Valedictorian
Best athletes
Honor Society members
Best actors and actresses
Status (honor and respect)
Most popular
Best dressed
Best looking
Members of sororities and fraternities
Most poised
Prom queens
Parties (political activity)
Student body officers and delegates
Club officers
Newspaper editors
Class officers
Sorority and fraternity officers

Thinking Sociologically

1. Think of ways in which you could gain power if you had great wealth.
2. Think of how you could gain power if you had a high position in a corporation.
3. If you had more power, how would you use it to increase your life chances to gain wealth?

Socioeconomic Status

It is difficult to place individuals in a particular social stratum because class, status, and party affiliations can all influence where they might be placed. Is the widower of a distinguished scholar who lives on a small retirement income in the same class as a mail carrier or a shoplifter who has the same income? Does a rural doctor who serves the poor and receives a small income have the same class position as a suburban doctor who serves the rich and has a large income? As you can see, class boundaries can be difficult to determine. A person who has a high position in one category may have a low position in a different category. Where, then, should that person be placed?

To resolve this problem, sociologists have developed the concept of **socioeconomic status (SES)**. This concept considers income, education, and occupation when assessing a person's status. Someone who earns $50,000 will be ranked higher than a person earning $10,000, a college graduate will be ranked higher than a high school graduate, and anybody in a

SOCIOLOGY AT WORK

Helping Disabled Drug Addicts

Alexander Boros received his Ph.D. in sociology from Case Western Reserve University in 1969. He is the director of Addiction Intervention with the Disabled (AID) in Cleveland, Ohio. Currently, two groups on which AID focuses much of its attention are deaf people and people who are reading limited.

Boros notes how a sociological perspective is quite different than other approaches that try to help the disabled with alcohol and other drug problems. "Human services people tend to have a very individualistic orientation," he says. "Whether they're doctors or therapists or counselors, they deal with the problem as an individual's problem. Sociologists try to understand the social and cultural conditions in which the problem arises. Most deaf people, for example, live out their lives as members of a closed community. They have their own language and their own culture. They read at, on the average, a third-grade level. The rate of intermarriage within the group is about 90 percent. Deaf people represent a different community with different needs. As a sociologist, I am able to see the social context in which members of this group act out their problems through alcohol and [other] drug abuse."

Boros, who has been known for his work in the area of rehabilitation for more than 30 years, began his work on AID when he was approached by a group of deaf people who wanted sign-language interpreters at local meetings of Alcoholics Anonymous. AID organized a national conference on treating deaf alcoholics. It also conducted workshops for people already involved in the treatment of addiction to alcohol and other drugs, regarding the unique needs of the deaf. However, Boros began to perceive a larger need. "About 16 percent of the population is disabled—deaf, blind, retarded, spinal

professional or management occupation will be ranked higher than a laborer. Usually there is a consistent pattern among these three rankings of status. People with many years of education tend to hold occupations that afford high status and high incomes. One of the more interesting problems sociologists study is how to categorize people who have "status inconsistency"—an advanced education but a very low income, for example.

THEORIES OF SOCIAL STRATIFICATION

Why are societies stratified? How is it that some people have more of the scarce resources society has to offer? This question was widely debated by early sociologists. Spencer believed that superior people would educate themselves and become leaders, whereas inferior people would remain in the bottom ranks of society. Society, he said, developed through an evolutionary process, and those who profited from natural selection—"survival of the fittest"—came out on top. This process of natural selection was good for social progress, he argued, and society should not interfere with it.

The opposing view was formulated by Marx, who argued that stratification would eventually cause revolution. The upper class in industrial society hired the proletariat to work in their factories, exploited them for profit, and drove them

Helping Disabled Drug Addicts, *continued*

cord-injured, and so on. We have been able to determine that the rate of alcohol and [other] drug addiction among the deaf is about the same as among the general population. But the other disabled lack the kind of cohesive community the deaf have developed. They probably experience a much higher rate—some of us estimate twice as high. But in the standard treatment programs, the rate of participation by the disabled is about 1 percent. So it's not just that the need was being met badly. It wasn't being met at all."

The solution: Set up special services for the deaf and multidisabled, find the alcohol and other drug abusers in that population, and refer them to those services. "The rehabilitation agencies for the disabled tend not to understand alcohol and [other] drug addiction. They see it as a self-inflicted problem. They prefer to work with what they call the 'true disabled.' The people who work in alcohol addiction treatment, on the other hand, are people whose expertise is life experience: They tend to be recovering alcoholics themselves. Many do not have the time or the desire to learn about what the special needs of the deaf or the disabled. So we needed something new."

To meet the need, Boros, his staff, and their volunteer assistants train alcohol- and other drug-abuse counselors to work in educational programs with the deaf and the disabled. Boros and his staff continue to come up with new ideas. A recent byproduct of their early work is a new "picture-idea methodology" for communicating material about alcohol and other drug abuse to people who are reading-limited. This methodology uses a picture format with a sentence above each picture, simplified to a fourth-grade reading level. "With help," Boros says, "this methodology enables people that are reading-limited to have access to material about drug … abuse."

into poverty. As the proletariat became poorer, Marx contended, they would become aware of their plight and would revolt. The theories of these early European writers have had a strong influence on modern theories of stratification, and have resulted in the structural functional theory and the conflict theory.

Structural Functional Theory

Structural functionalists have refined Spencer's notion that society, like any other organism, is self-regulating and self-maintaining. It consists of interrelated parts that serve a function in maintaining the system as a whole. When they recognized that stratification was a persistent force in society, they argued that it must be serving some function. They hypothesized that because modern society is so complex, people with strong leadership skills are needed to organize and run the complex businesses and industries. People with strong leadership abilities need advanced training and must be willing to work very hard and assume a great deal of responsibility. Society must encourage these efforts by rewarding leaders with wealth and status—scarce resources that in turn can be used to gain power.

In terms of inherent worth as a human being, Davis and Moore (1945) acknowledged that an artist or a teacher might be equal to a corporate executive. The talents of artists and teachers, however, are not as scarce and therefore not as valuable to the society, according to Davis and Moore. Thus, corporate executives who have the talent to lead business and industry are more highly rewarded, not because they are more worthwhile human beings but because they are making greater contributions to the functioning of society. This theoretical perspective permits a belief in human equality at the same time that it explains inequality. If society had an equal need for all types of work, then all its members would be equal in the stratification system.

Conflict Theory

Conflict theorists reject the functional viewpoint (Duberman, 1976), arguing that inequality develops as a result of people's desire for power and that close-knit groups compete with one another to gain possession of the scarce resources that are a source of power. According to this view, resources are not rewards for talent or for assuming difficult tasks but are acquired through inheritance, coercion, or exploitation. Inequality results when one group acquires more resources than other groups.

Once a dominant group gets power, according to conflict theorists, the group **legitimates** its power and makes it acceptable by appealing to the values of the masses. Politicians often use democratic values, a mandate from the people, to legitimate their stands on issues. The powerful may point to progress as a value, to gain support for everything from expenditures for scientific research to acceptance of a polluted environment. Corporations may appeal directly to patriotic values to justify their opposition to a raise in corporate taxes—what is good for the corporation is good for the nation—or they may appeal to the value of equal opportunity, arguing that such a raise would cost jobs. These beliefs and perceptions, when accepted by the masses, become the prevailing **ideology**. *Ideology* refers to a set of cultural beliefs, values, and attitudes that legitimate the status quo as well as attempts to change it

If the masses are influenced by elite ideology, they are said to have **false consciousness**, a lack of awareness of their own interests and an acceptance of elite rule. If, on the other hand, the masses are aware that people's fates are tied to the fate of their own class, they are said to have **class consciousness**. For example, if people realize that which neighborhood school they attend is determined by how much money they have, they have class consciousness.

Theories of social stratification are important not only because they help us to understand why some basic social inequalities exist, but also because they provide a basis on which politicians and legislators may develop social policies. For example, whether a politician favors increased government spending on social services (such as welfare, Medicaid, food stamps, and shelters for the homeless) may have to do with his or her understanding of why people need such services. A politician who believes that poverty exists because of individuals' unwillingness or lack of motivation to work hard may oppose government spending. Conversely, a politician who believes that poverty exists because of basic inequities in the system may support government spending. Issues such as these often have no clear answers, but theories of social stratification can offer politicians important insights for dealing with them and can prevent them from relying solely on their own values and beliefs.

Attempts at Synthesis

Some sociologists have tried to reconcile the functional and conflict theories of stratification (Dahrendorf, 1951; Lenski, 1966; Tumin, 1963). Accumulating research suggests that stratification has a wide variety of causes, some based on conflict, some on cooperation. A stratification system based on religion, for example, may emphasize feelings of community and selflessness. Others, based on land ownership or accumulation of money, may emphasize competition and the efforts of individuals. As our understanding of the nature and development of stratification improves, it is becoming increasingly apparent that stratification is influenced by a great many different factors: how food is grown, how supplies are manufactured and distributed, how much wealth accumulates, and how people use their leisure time, to name a few. Neither functional nor conflict theory offers us a full understanding of how stratification systems develop.

There is, however, widespread agreement that all stratification systems are based on the consensus among members of the society that inequality is good, fair, and just. People may accept stratification because they value the achievements of the wealthy or because they have been misled by the media. Whatever the reason, acceptance of the stratification system confers power on those of high rank.

INEQUALITY IN THE UNITED STATES

Social inequality in the United States is based on family background, wealth, education, occupation, and a variety of other characteristics. The best way to understand the class system is to look at its various dimensions separately.

The Distribution of Income

In 2005, the median income in the United States for people with full-time jobs was $33,083 for men and $22,594 for women (*Current Population Reports*, Series P-60, 2005). (The median is the amount at which half of a given population falls above and half falls below.) The median household income was $46,326 (U.S. Bureau of the Census,2005).

Another way to look at income distribution is to consider the share of the total U.S. income received by each 20 percent of the U.S. population, referred

TABLE 8-2 PERCENTAGE OF HOUSEHOLD INCOME FOR EACH FIFTH OF U.S. POPULATION

Total Population	Total Available Income 1980	1990
Highest fifth	46.6	50.1
Second highest fifth	24.0	23.0
Middle fifth	15.9	14.6
Second lowest fifth	19.6	8.7
Lowest fifth	3.9	3.5

Source: U.S. Department of Commerce, Bureau of the Census, *Historical Income Tables*, Table IE-3. U.S. Government Printing Office, Washington, D.C., 2001.

to as quintiles. Table 8-2 shows that the poorest 20 percent of households received only 3.9 percent of the total available income in 1990, but by 2001, that had decreased to 3.5 percent. The richest 20 percent of households received 46.6 percent of the available income in 1990, and that increased to 50.1 percent in 2001. As of 2005, no measurable statistical change had occurred.

The Distribution of Wealth

Wealth consists of personal property. *Personal property* includes liquid assets (cash in bank accounts), real estate, stocks, bonds, and other owned assets. The introduction to this chapter talks about the wealth of the top 20 percent of the population. This wealth is not evenly distributed within this group. The 13,000 richest families in the U.S. now have almost as much income as the 20 million poorest (Lewis, 2003). Even this wealth is not distributed evenly. Since 1977, the richest 1% of American households have doubled their share of our nation's wealth. The richest 1% of the population now owns as much wealth as the bottom 95% of all Americans combined. The richest 5%

of American households own more than 60% of our nation's household wealth (Sanders, 2003).

Moreover, the very wealthy actually *control* even more money than they *possess*. By owning many shares of the major corporations, they influence not just their own fortunes but also those of many others. The Rockefeller family, for example, dominates key banks and corporations and has been known to control assets of more than 15 times their personal wealth.

Social Status in American Society

The earliest studies of stratification in America were based on the concept of status—people's opinions of other people. Status can be conferred on others for any reason a person chooses—mystical or religious powers, athletic ability, youth or beauty, good deeds—whatever seems appropriate to the person doing the ranking. It was found that in this country, status was conferred on others on the basis of their wealth. However, wealth used to be more obvious than it is today.

A study done in Middletown during the Great Depression (Lynd and Lynd, 1929, 1937) found status differences between the business class and the working class. When the study was originally done, the business class lived in larger and better quality housing than did the working class. The very wealthy had elaborate mansions with indoor plumbing and central heating, whereas working-class homes were much smaller and often lacked indoor plumbing; water had to be carried in from an outdoor well. Heating was provided by a wood or coal stove.

A more recent study of Middletown (Caplow et al., 1982) found that it had become more difficult to identify classes among the population. The working class now lives in houses that are only slightly smaller than those of the business class, and they contain all of the amenities that modern society provides—not only indoor plumbing and central heating but also self-cleaning ovens, dishwashers, and other labor-saving devices. The wealthy, while living relatively modestly in town, spend more of their money less conspicuously out of town, buying condominiums and yachts in Florida, for example. Today, then, it is more difficult to assign status on the basis of wealth.

Class Consciousness

Class consciousness, the awareness that different classes exist in society and that people's fates are tied to the fate of their whole class, was studied in a national survey by Jackman and Jackman (1983). They found that respondents throughout the country defined classes in much the same way. When questioned and given a free choice, most respondents assigned themselves to one of five classes, as follows:

1. *Poor*—7.6 percent considered themselves poor.
2. *Working Class*—36.6 percent considered themselves working class.
3. *Middle Class*—3.3 percent considered themselves middle class, just as the majority of Americans have done for many decades (Centers, 1949).
4. *Upper Middle Class*—8.2 percent put themselves in this category.
5. *Upper Class*—1 percent assigned themselves to this class.

Like Weber, respondents in this study used both class and status variables to determine social class. Occupation was a primary consideration, and education was also important, but the amount of money a person had was not given major consideration by this sample. Status issues such as a person's values, beliefs, and style of life were very important in this sample's rankings.

Members of the different classes were aware of others in their class, and when asked how they felt about people in the different classes, they responded that they felt warmest toward people in their own class. They were also very aware of political issues that affected their class. The poor, for example, would like the government to guarantee good jobs for all, and they would like a higher minimum wage. The upper middle class does not support these programs. The poor would like there to be smaller income differences between occupations, whereas the upper middle class thinks large income differences between occupations are quite proper.

Overall, the majority of Americans believe that government should do nothing to create greater equality, even when tax policy changes by government cause greater inequality. People believe our system of inequality is justified and promises to be a productive system for the United States (Dionne, 1990). This is a change from American attitudes in the past. During the depression of the 1930s, for example, Americans thought that the differences in what the wealthy earned from their investments and what the worker earned in wages was unjust, and workers wanted the government to do something to reduce this inequality. During the decade of the 1960s, Americans seemed to forget about the difference between the wealthy and the worker, but they became concerned about poverty and wanted government to increase opportunities for the poor. During the 1980s, Americans appeared to be uninterested in any action by government to reduce inequality. As a result, the rich continued to get richer, and those living in poverty continued to suffer from lack of food, shelter, and other basic necessities. In 2003, social inequality continues to be a major social problem.

Poverty

Poverty is defined as having fewer resources than necessary to meet the basic necessities of life—food, shelter, and medical care. The U.S. government has developed a measure of poverty that takes into account the size of the family, the number of children, and whether the family lives on a farm. They assume that living on a farm costs less than living in the city. The income level considered impoverished varies with these factors. For a family of four not living on a farm, the poverty line in 2005 was $19,874. The government reports that in 2005, 12.6 percent of the population, or 37 million people, were living in poverty (U.S. Census Bureau, 2005). In that same year, 17.6 percent of people under age 18 lived in poverty.

Jobs for poor people would not solve the problems of poverty. Of the adult poor, about 40 percent work at jobs that pay so little that they fall below the poverty line even though they work. The adults who are poor and not working are either retired, ill or disabled, going to school, or keeping house. Approximately one-third of the poor in the United States are children. Only about 5 percent of poor people are adults who could be working but are not, and most of these people do not work because they cannot find work (Eitzen and Zinn, 2004).

TABLE 8-3 COMPARATIVE POVERTY RATES

Survey Year	Country	% Population Below Poverty Line
1997	Philippines	40.6
1997	Cambodia	36.1
1994	India	35.0
1994	Romania	21.5
1990	Brazil	17.4
1992	Thailand	13.1
2001	United States	11.1
1990	Hungary	8.6

Source: *World Development Report,* Table 4: Poverty, 2000/2001.

The level of poverty in the United States is generally higher than in other countries. Table 8-3, however, illustrates other countries' high levels of poverty compared to the United States. These rates are computed somewhat differently from the way the census computes rates, but they allow comparison with other countries.

INEQUALITY AND LIFE CHANCES

Occupations

For most people, the most important life chance in a society such as the United States is the opportunity to have a successful and respectable occupation or career that provides an adequate income. The majority of professional positions, including doctors, lawyers, business managers, and other high-ranking workers in large organizations, are held by the upper middle class. Many people think of the professional person as the typical American worker—educated, earning a comfortable living, owning a home, and sending children to college. Most people in the ordinary ranks of business management, however, need a second worker in the family to afford this higher standard of living.

The majority of people in the United States are considered working class by sociologists because they work in blue-collar jobs—skilled laborers, labor supervisors, and unskilled laborers in industry, or service workers who provide cleaning, maintenance, and other services to those industries. Some sociologists argue that clerical workers, most of whom are women with routine jobs and low pay, should also be considered part of the working class. Strictly speaking, they are not blue-collar workers because they do not wear work clothes or spend their days in a factory or plant, but they have much in common with working-class people—low wages and strict supervision.

Other working-class occupations pay considerably less than either manufacturing or clerical positions. For one thing, many blue-collar workers, especially construction workers, typically are laid off at some point during the year, which reduces their total annual income. Also, these workers make less than the median income even when there are no layoffs. Many low-paid, working-class people fall below the poverty line and enter the class that has come to be called the "working poor." Most of these people work at jobs that do not pay enough money to bring them out of poverty. The minimum wage in the United States provides income to one person working full-time year-round that is well below the poverty line for a family of four people.

In the recent, widely read work, *Nickel and Dimed: On (Not) Getting By in America* (2001), Barbara Ehrenreich lends a first-hand look at the plight of the working poor in America. Ehrenreich highlights deplorable working conditions, lack of access to affordable housing, and the social isolation endured by those attempting to live on pitifully poor wages.

Housing and Lifestyle

The rich often own several homes: a family estate, an estate in an exclusive resort area, and a large apartment in an exclusive apartment building in the center of a major city. They spend their leisure time with their wealthy friends and neighbors, and they work together on the boards of banks and corporations. They manage their business affairs with much mutual respect and close cooperation (Domhoff, 2001). Their children usually marry the children of other wealthy families, so that rich families are often related to other rich families, and their wealth remains in the same group. Their housing provides a lifestyle that enables them to know other wealthy people, thereby giving them numerous opportunities to increase their wealth further.

Upper-middle-class managers and professionals, who are near the top 20 percent of earners, are more likely to own homes in the suburbs. In addition to having a nice place to live, owning a home has proved to be a good investment because homes increase in value with inflation. The mortgage interest on homes also provides income tax deductions.

Working-class people are also likely to live in the suburbs, but they are less apt to own their own homes. Those who rent houses or apartments do not have financial buffers from inflation or benefit from home-owner tax deductions. Instead, as prices go up, their rents go up, and they may find it very difficult to maintain their standard of living.

Poor people find it very difficult to get adequate housing. They may live in substandard housing in rural areas or in urban slums, and they often pay high rents for it. Sometimes two or more families share the same overcrowded apartment, in order to meet the rent payments.

The poorest people in the United States do not even have homes or apartments. They live in shelters or on the street. The number of street people is not known, but it is estimated that there are as many as 3 million homeless in the United States. The homeless have either lost contact with their families or have no families. Some of these people work, but they do not earn enough money to rent a place to live. Others have no income. They sleep in subways, doorways, or on park benches. They are often raped or assaulted, and in winter, they sometimes freeze to death. In addition to the homeless adults and children on the streets, one-half million children live in hospitals, foster homes, mental health facilities, and detention centers because they have no homes or families who can take care of them (Rich, 1989).

Furthermore, children with the most extensive experiences with homelessness exhibit high degrees of social isolation which is, in turn, related to emotional health concerns such as depression and social anxiety (Anooshian, 2003). Measures of social isolation, rejection, and withdrawal are reliably correlated with general estimates of educational achievement, particularly for children who had experienced extensive homelessness.

Unfortunately, children who live in homeless shelters fare little better than the homeless. Shelter children between kindergarten and 6th grade report feeling that their chances of academic success are virtually unattainable. A recurring theme among shelter parents and children is that their lower social status negatively influences the attitude of school officials toward them (Marcus, 2002).

Education

The children of the rich are the group most likely to go to private preparatory schools and elite colleges, regardless of their grades. Not only do they earn credentials that are useful in business, but also they make more valuable contacts with influential people who can help them get high-paying positions. Middle-class children ordinarily graduate from public or parochial high schools, and they have an excellent chance of going to college. Working-class children usually complete high school, but only those who achieve very high grades are likely to attend college. Poor children tend to drop out of high school and often live in neighborhoods with poor schools, in which they may not even learn to read and write. Moreover, when they see that high school graduates often have trouble getting jobs, they become discouraged and quit as soon as they are old enough because there is no apparent advantage to staying in school. Education is thus a life chance very closely associated with family wealth.

Medical Care

Medical care is not distributed equally. The rich and the middle classes are usually covered by medical insurance through their employers. Insurance covers most medical expenses, and members of these classes generally receive good medical care.

Some estimates are that one-third of Americans do not have health insurance and do not obtain the same medical care as the rich. According to the U.S Bureau of the Census, 2005, there were 46.6 million people in the United States without medical insurance. In the United States, children have low rates of immunization for diseases, compared to other nations. For example, 24 percent of children are not vaccinated against measles/ polio/ tetanus; vaccines for these illnesses are necessary for entry into most schools (Federal Interagency Forum on Child and Family Statistics, 2002). One of eight children under age 12 suffers from hunger and is at risk for disease resulting from malnourishment. The poor of all ages suffer from malnourishment, assaults, rat and dog bites, and other hazards of living in poverty, and they are more likely to commit suicide.

The very poor and homeless see doctors only when they are picked up by the police and brought to public hospitals. Among the most unfortunate cases seen in emergency rooms are homeless people who are frostbite victims; they may have to have a toe or a foot amputated, only to return to the streets to suffer frostbite again.

In all modern industrialized societies except the United States and South Africa, everyone in the society is covered by a national health system that meets their health needs. As a result, infants are born with full medical care, children are immunized from childhood diseases, and the diseases of adults are treated promptly, usually at no cost to the patient.

Thinking Sociologically

1. Explore the city in which you live, to see whether you can determine where different income groups reside, work, play, attend school, attend church, receive medical care, and so on. Use specific examples from your city to illustrate the inequality and life chances of different classes, as discussed in this chapter.
2. Develop explanations for the inequality found in your city, using structural functional theory and conflict theory. Again, use specific examples.
3. Using theories, concepts, facts, and discussions found in this chapter, as well as your observations, write a proposal for a long-term plan that would reduce income inequality in the city in which you live. Write your proposal as if you were going to present it to the local government (such as the city council) or some other community organization.

APPLYING KNOWLEDGE OF INEQUALITY AND LIFE CHANCES

Knowledge of the different life chances available to members of different social classes can be used in a number of practical ways. Clinical sociologists and other therapists may use this knowledge to gain a greater understanding of clients from different social classes. As we have seen, people from different social classes have different types of problems and different perspectives on those problems.

Politicians and legislators may rely on this information to help them develop meaningful, relevant, and workable social policies to help the underprivileged. The differential occupational opportunities, living arrangements, education, and medical treatment may strongly influence their psychological makeup. This fact has important implications for what type of policies will or will not succeed. Consider, for example, policies regarding welfare. A welfare program that increases the number of jobs for the poor may look very attractive to someone in the middle or upper class. However, to assume that the mere availability of jobs will enable the downtrodden to compete in the same manner that members of the middle class do is to assume that people from all classes are the same. A welfare program may need to include some type of counseling for recipients to help them gain the confidence and self-esteem necessary for success in a competitive market. Other measures might include education and career training, housing reforms, and improved medical care.

Teachers may also benefit from knowledge of different life chances. The crowded living conditions of some lower-class families may inhibit lower-class students from spending the necessary amount of solitary homework time it takes to understand some subjects. Because their parents may not have experienced the rewards that a good education can bring, lower-class students may not receive the same reinforcement about the importance of studying and achieving good grades that middle-class students do. Lower-class students may not have role models who have achieved upward mobility due to a good education and, as a result, may have a difficult time seeing the value in schoolwork.

Teaching upper-middle-class students and lower-class students, therefore, may require very different teaching strategies. Teachers of lower-class students may need to spend as much time helping their students understand the value and importance of an education as they do with the course material itself, and they may need to explain difficult material more slowly, more intensively, and in more ways during class time rather than expect students to master the material at home.

They might also spend time teaching student about workplace culture and behavioral expectations that might differ from the expectations of their daily lives. Jay McLeod (1995) in his classic ethnography, *Ain't No Makin' It: Aspirations and Attainment in a Low-income Neighborhood*, points out that students adapt to their living conditions by exhibiting behaviors that are not appropriate for the workplace. Therefore, they are unprepared for the social demands and expectations that accompany working in and for the public.

These examples are only a few ways in which knowledge of how life chances relate to position in the stratification system can he used. Consider how you could use this knowledge in a career that you are thinking about entering. Also consider how you can use this knowledge to understand how to get ahead. Are people more or less stuck in their social strata, or can they get ahead?

SOCIAL MOBILITY IN THE UNITED STATES

Social mobility—changing social position—can occur in a variety of ways. A change to a job of higher rank or marriage to a person of higher rank is **upward mobility**, and a movement to a job of lower rank is **downward mobility**. Sometimes, marrying someone of a lower rank can produce downward mobility.

Persons who change class or status within their own lifetimes experience **intragenerational mobility**. Mobility between generations, or **intergenerational mobility**, is traditionally measured by comparing the social positions of parents and children. If sons or daughters have higher positions than their parents had, they are upwardly mobile; if the younger generation's position is lower, they are downwardly mobile. Both the social structure and individual characteristics influence upward and downward mobility.

Structural Characteristics of Mobility in the United States

Mobility in this country is influenced by numerous factors, including (a) growth of large corporations; (b) increased standard of living; (c) growth of urban areas; (d) maintenance of a split labor market, which splinters the labor pool in ways that minimize mobility; and (e) advanced technology, such as reliance on computers and robots.

The growth of large corporations has influenced the wages people are paid. Those who work in large organizations often earn more than those who work in small firms. People in supervisory positions earn a percentage more than the people they supervise, and their earnings generally increase as the number of people they supervise increases. Thus, as corporations grow larger, supervisors earn more. Many qualified people in large organizations never have the opportunity to be supervisors, however, and despite their high qualifications, they will never be able to earn the income of the supervisor.

The increasing standard of living over the past century has improved the lives of most workers in the United States, even though their relative class or status remains unchanged. This improvement is especially true of factory workers, whose wages and living conditions have improved dramatically since the turn of the century.

The growth of urban areas, in which the cost of living is higher, has led to higher wages for city dwellers. Equally qualified people doing the same work are apt to earn more money in the city than in the country. Doctors, for example, earn considerably more in large metropolitan areas than in rural areas.

A split labor market is one in which some jobs afford upward mobility and others do not. The job market is split between manual and nonmanual work, and is further segmented within these spheres. White-collar workers cannot move into higher-level manual work or into the professions, which normally require extensive educational certification. Manual workers cannot be promoted into the skilled crafts or into white-collar positions. Farmers are completely outside the main sphere of upward mobility.

The **split labor market** provides even greater obstacles for women, the poor, and minority groups, most of whom work in the lowest ranks of manual and nonmanual occupations. Their jobs often have no career paths at all, and the poor rarely get the opportunity for professional training or apprenticeships in the skilled crafts. In recent years, more and more manual jobs are done by robots (or corporations have moved such jobs overseas where labor is cheaper). Not only is there no mobility in manual work, but also the number of manual-labor jobs is shrinking. Thus, increased technology has eliminated some jobs involving manual labor and has increased the number of white-collar clerical and service jobs.

Furthermore, even if a move from a low-paying assembly-line job to a low-paying desk job were likely, should it be considered upward mobility, or is it movement that does not bring with it any real advantages? Some sociologists argue that white-collar work has a higher status, but others contend that this shift merely changes the nature of work, not the class or status of the worker.

Individual Characteristics and Upward Mobility

A basic assumption of structural functional theory is that society rewards people who develop leadership skills through education and hard work. Researchers have conducted many studies to learn about the characteristics of individuals who succeed. These studies, most of which were concerned with men, have examined the influence of such factors as family background, grades in school, years of education, and attitudes.

The attitudes of young men from Wisconsin were thoroughly studied by William Sewell (Sewell et al., 1975), who found no relationship between attitude and success. The research did show that those Wisconsin boys whose attitudes were ambitious (i.e., who desired an occupation of a higher status than that of their fathers) often found it necessary to change their attitudes when they did not have the opportunity to reach their goals. In most cases, people get discouraged when they cannot obtain the training required for a particular occupation and then adjust their attitudes to suit what they can attain.

Family background is the factor that most accurately predicts the future earnings of men, not upward mobility. Anywhere from 15 to 50 percent of the variation in men's earnings appears to be related to family background. Men from families with high incomes generally make more money than those from families with low incomes. The studies do not, however, explain why family income is related to a son's future earnings. Structural functionalists argue that sons from families with high incomes usually have all of the advantages believed to contribute to future money-making ability. Their parents can teach their sons important skills, and they live in neighborhoods in which their friends have the same advantages. Because of family advantages, they are likely to do well in high school and to attend college.

Structural functionalists believe that the best way to increase upward mobility in the U.S. is to increase the opportunities available to children from poor families. Such a move would involve providing better preschool education, better public school education (including the opportunity to attend schools with young people from wealthier backgrounds), and the opportunity to go on to college or technical schools.

Conflict theorists criticize the notion that sons from high-income families succeed because they are better educated, or that the poor can enter the upper class through increased education. Women and blacks have demonstrated that advanced education does not guarantee upward mobility. This fact may discourage members of minority groups, who may find it difficult to spend the time and money required to receive a higher education if they believe they will not be rewarded for their efforts. Conflict theorists contend that opportunity and equality for the poor will be brought about only through changes in the stratification system and in the distribution of wealth.

SUMMARY

1. Inequality develops as a result of the unequal distribution of scarce resources. People are differentiated, but not usually ranked, on the basis of many criteria: hair color, height, hobbies, or region of the country in which they live.
2. People are ranked, or stratified, on the basis of their possession of or access to scarce resources.
3. Very simple societies have little division of labor and little stratification. Agrarian and industrial societies have more wealth, greater division of labor, and more stratification.
4. There are two types of stratification systems in the world today: (1) In *caste systems*, positions are assigned at birth, according to the position of the caste, and a person's caste is fixed for life; (2) in *class systems*, found in industrial societies, a person may be able to move into higher or lower strata. Sources of power in a class-based society include class position, status, and party position.

5. Structural functionalists believe that systems of stratification develop because societies need scarce leadership skills and reward those who are willing to assume the responsibility of leadership.
6. Conflict theorists contend that stratification develops because some groups gain a monopoly of the scarce resources, through either inheritance or conflict, and they use those resources to maintain their high positions.
7. Most people identify themselves as middle class, but lifestyles of Americans vary widely, most importantly in terms of occupation, housing, health care, and educational opportunity.
8. Life chances for occupations, housing, education, and medical care vary, in relation to a person's place in the stratification system.
9. Upward mobility is most influenced by structural changes in the workplace. The proliferation and increasing size of large corporations has improved the standard of living for many workers. The segmented or split labor market has limited upward mobility for lower-class people.
10. The important determinant of class position in this country is family background.

KEY TERMS

advanced horticultural societies Societies with irrigation systems and other advanced farming practices.

agrarian societies Complex societies with farming, armies, merchants, and a concentration of wealth in the hands of a few people.

caste system A system of stratification in which one's social position is ascribed at birth, one's value is assessed in terms of religious or traditional beliefs, and in which upward social mobility is impossible.

class consciousness Awareness among members of a society that the society is stratified.

class system A system of stratification found in industrial societies in which one's class is determined by one's wealth and in which vertical social mobility is possible.

closed system A system of stratification in which there is no movement from one rank to another.

division of labor A situation in which some people do certain specialized occupations.

downward mobility A move to a position of lower rank in the stratification system.

false consciousness Lack of awareness of class differences and acceptance of upper-class rule.

hunting-and-gathering societies Small, often nomadic societies that have no agriculture and live on food that is found.

ideology A set of ideas about what society is like, how it functions, whether it is good or bad, and how it should be changed.

industrial societies Societies with great division of labor, highly specialized work, and a great concentration of wealth.

inequality Differences between groups in wealth, status, or power.

intergenerational mobility A change of social position or rank, up or down, from one generation to the next, such as when children have a higher status than their parents.

intragenerational mobility A change of social position or rank, up or down, within one's own lifetime.

legitimate To make the power of the dominant group acceptable to the masses so they let the dominant group rule without question.

life chances The opportunities a person has to improve his or her income and lifestyle.

mechanical solidarity The idea of Durkheim in which people do similar work but are not very dependent on one another (in contrast to organic solidarity, in which people are very dependent on others).

open system A system of stratification in which it is possible to move to a higher or lower position.

organic solidarity Durkheim's term for the integration of society that results from the division of labor.

party An organization in which decisions are made to reach certain goals, the achievement of which affects society.

poverty Having fewer resources than are required to meet the basic necessities of life. Rates are usually based on a government index of income relative to size of family and farm/nonfarm residence.

power The ability to control or influence the behavior of others, even without their consent.

simple horticultural societies Societies that grow food using very simple tools, such as digging sticks.

social class A category of people who have approximately the same amount of power and wealth and the same life chances to acquire wealth.

social differentiation The difference or variation of people based on selected social characteristics such as class, gender, race, or age.

social status The amount of honor and prestige a person receives from others in the community; also, the position one occupies in the stratification system.

social stratification The ranking of people according to their wealth, prestige, or party position.

socioeconomic status (SES) An assessment of status that takes into account a person's income, education, and occupation.

split labor market A labor market in which some jobs afford upward mobility and others do not.

upward mobility Movement in the stratification system to a position of greater wealth, status, and power.

DISCUSSION QUESTIONS

1. Discuss the functions of the stratification system in American society. Discuss its dysfunctions.
2. Look through your campus newspaper, and find ways that groups legitimate their political positions.
3. Discuss the extent of class consciousness you would expect to find on your campus and in your community. Do you think people are very aware of class? Would the people you know use the same categories of class used in the Jackman and Jackman study?
4. What people have the most power in your community? Do they have power because of their wealth, their status, or their position in an organization?
5. Has the quality of your education been influenced by the amount of money your family has?

6. How do you think that your family's position in the stratification system has affected your attitudes, norms, roles, ambitions, and identity?

7. How does the split labor market lead to further separation between the rich and the poor?

Racial and Ethnic Differentiation

Ethnic and Racial Inequality

It is ironic that while one of America's greatest attractions for its immigrants is its ideal of equality, racial and ethnic minorities disproportionately occupy the lower rungs of the social ladder in American society. Historically, Americans have professed the belief that people of all races are created equal and that all should have an equal chance to obtain society's benefits. In fact, according to the National Opinion Research Center (2001), most U.S. adults believe that a qualified woman could be president. In November of 2004, we elected the forty-third white, male president of the United States. Therefore, as John Macionis (2004) points out, some of our most dominant cultural beliefs actually contradict one another, an observation that echoes the arguments in the early mid-twentieth century advanced in the classic work by Gunnar Myrdal, An American Dilemma (1944). More specifically, according to sociologists Elliot Currie and Jerome Skolnick, "American history is also the history of the conquest, enslavement, and exclusion of racial minorities. The vision of racial equality and the harsh reality of unequal treatment have coexisted uneasily from the beginning" (1988, p. 136).

In 2007 the media proved just how sensitive society can be towards members of minority, ethnic, and racial groups in the United States. It started with MSNBC/CBS radio and television host Don Imus and his derogatory remarks made towards the women's basketball team of Rutgers University. What followed was a gigantic wave of support for not only the women of Rutgers University but for all minorities, ethnic, and racial groups throughout this country. Many religious leaders and public officials called for the termination of Mr. Imus and MSNBC/CBS listened to those voices. Many thought that after Don Imus made his personal apology to the women of Reutgers everything would go back to the way it was, however, those same leaders and officials decided to persuade the music industry to also commit to the banning of many of the same words used by Mr. Imus and others throughout history that depicted the minorities in this country. This has set off a huge debate among citizens throughout the U.S. with the biggest argument leaning towards the right to free speech. It is too early to say if this newest step towards equality in America will continue in the direction it is going, but we can say that this was a giant leap in a different direction.

The Civil Rights Memorial located in Montgomery, Alabama, along with the civil rights museum housed in Memphis, Tennessee where Dr. King was assassinated, are tributes to the lasting impact of the 40 people killed in the cause of racial equality between 1955 and 1968. Their dedication to the pursuit of racial equality is symbolized in the statement by Martin Luther King, Jr., found on the wall in the Alabama memorial: "until justice rolls down like waters and righteousness like a mighty stream."

Regardless of the social and economic gains achieved by African-Americans and other minorities in the 1960s and 1970s, many of these achievements have been halted or reversed. The economic gap between African-Americans and European-Americans is widening, as we saw in Chapter 8, in large part due to economic segregation, and the situation is not much better for other ethnic minorities. With the exception of some Asian-American groups, most minority groups lag far behind European-Americans in terms of median family incomes. Native Americans, African-Americans, and Hispanic-Americans are much more likely than European-Americans to be unemployed, sporadically employed, or underemployed—that is, to be overqualified for the jobs they hold; thus, they are more likely to occupy positions with the lowest income, benefits, security, and status (Neubeck, 1991, p. 257). In a more recent study, De Jong and Madamba (2001) show that Blacks and Hispanics have higher unemployment and working-poverty rates compared to non-Hispanic whites and Asians. Interestingly, they also found that minority group status and effects were stronger than immigrant status in predicting underemployment. Not surprisingly, they also point out that females are more likely to suffer underemployment than males. Inequality is not just confined to income and occupation. Minorities are also more likely to be illiterate and are less likely to complete high school and to go to college. Additionally, nonwhite families are more likely to experience divorce and are more likely to be headed by single women than white families. Furthermore, according to an October, 2004 *Washington Post* article, the gap between white wealth and the wealth of non-whites is growing due to a downturn in home ownership for minority members. The article contends that while minority members earn about two-thirds the income of whites, black and Hispanic households tend to have disproportionately smaller share of assets in the form of savings accounts, stocks, and perhaps, most importantly, homes. Homeownership provides a two-dimensional advantage. For one, the homes appreciate in value giving the homeowners equity to secure loans, cover emergencies, or a number of other things. Second, homeownership suggests an air of stability, or at least the perception of stability (*Washington Post*, Witte and Henderson, 2004). These facts do not mean that every white American is necessarily better off than every member of an ethnic minority group. However, when looked at as a whole, there is a great deal of inequality between whites and nonwhites. These facts do not mean that every white American is necessarily better off than every member of an ethnic minority group. However, when looked at as a whole, there is a great deal of inequality between whites and nonwhites.

Scholars widely agree that racial and ethnic inequality in America exists. The statistical evidence is overwhelming. What they disagree about is *why* racial and ethnic groups suffer from so much inequality. There are two contrasting perspectives. One is that the problems faced by minorities are the result of discrimination. The second is that they are due to social class and to what are called "culture-specific" factors. In 1978, University of Chicago sociologist William Julius Wilson wrote a book elaborating the latter view, in which he suggested that race had declined in importance in America as a source of discrimination. In *The Declining Significance of Race*, one of the most important and controversial books on race published in the past 25 years, Wilson stated, "Race relations in the United States have undergone fundamental changes in recent years, so much so that now the life chances of individual blacks have more to do with their economic class position than with their day-to-day encounters with whites" (Wilson 1978, in Finsterbusch and McKenna, 1990, p. 134). Wilson has argued that while racism and discrimination originally forced minorities into a lower socioeconomic position, today's problems are due to the consequences of being in the lower class, to cultural deficiencies, and to the effects of past—not present—discrimination. This viewpoint created much controversy because it implies that affirmative action programs that give preference to minorities are not necessarily needed to help minorities overcome their problems. More recent studies support Wilson's hypothesis, such as the research published by Sakamoto and Kim (2001) that shows class to be a greater disadvantage than race in explaining the wage differences in black men versus white men.

Others, such as Harvard University educator and sociologist Charles V. Willie, disagree with Wilson's explanation; Willie argues that racial inequality still results primarily from discrimination. "It is all a matter of perspective," says Willie. "From the perspective of the dominant people of power, inequality exists because of the personal inadequacies of those who are less fortunate. ... Moreover, they assert that poverty is not a function of institutional arrangements but a matter of individual capacities. ... this orientation toward individual mobility tends to deny the presence of opposition and oppression that are connected with institutions" (Willie, 1978, in Finsterbusch and McKenna, 1990, p. 141). Willie and others who share his perspective contend that the "opposition and oppression that are connected with institutions" continue to give privileges to the white majority, who have a greater chance of attending the "right" schools, of living in the "right" neighborhoods, and of being employed with the "right" companies. The result is that institutional discrimination increases the chances of racial minorities for upward mobility. This view maintains that while racial and ethnic discrimination may not always be blatant or overtly visible, the institutional discrimination and segregation that exist provide continued advantage to the white majority.

Understanding the subtleties and intricacies of race and ethnicity and of racism and discrimination is extremely important today, as American society experiences heightened racial tensions and as the proportion of minorities in this country continues to increase. It is our hope that this chapter will provide you with knowledge to help you reach your own conclusions about the reasons for racial and ethnic inequality, and to help you to make informed decisions that might have an impact on the future of racial and ethnic equality.

The United States is aptly called "a nation of nations." The diversity of the country's social and cultural life is a result of the many different groups who have migrated here. Can you imagine how monotonous life would be if people were all the same? Almost everyone enjoys the exotic sights, sounds, and smells of Chinatown. Greek, Italian, or Japanese cuisine is a welcome change from the usual American diet of hamburger and french fries. We also benefit from our diverse cultural heritage in many more important ways as well.

Racial and ethnic relations in the United States, however, are far from smooth. Our history has been marked by conflict, competition, prejudice, and discrimination. In this chapter, we identify the major minority groups in North America and discuss some of the causes and consequences of stereotyping, racism, prejudice, discrimination, and racial inequality. We also consider two approaches, the pluralistic and integrationist perspectives, that may help to reduce racial and ethnic inequality.

RACIAL, ETHNIC, AND MINORITY GROUPS

The terms *racial, ethnic,* and *minority* are often used rather loosely. Although they may be treated as equivalent or overlapping concepts, it is important to differentiate these terms before we discuss the more substantive issues of race and ethnic relations.

Racial Groups

A **racial group** is a socially defined group distinguished by selected inherited physical characteristics. Frequently, definitions of race focus exclusively on physical and biological characteristics, overlooking the "socially defined" and "selected" aspects of the definition. As Schaeffer (2005) points out, the term racial group is "reserved for minorities and the corresponding majorities that are socially set apart because of obvious physical differences." He further addresses the concern in defining racial groups by posing the question, "What is obvious?" In short, racial groups emphasize physical differences whereas ethnic groups focus upon cultural distinctions. Not surprisingly, however, even anthropologists and biologists remain deadlocked over the issue of whether race is a meaningful biological concept.

The essential question is whether there are significant variations in the physical traits of different populations of humans. The focus of investigation has ranged from obvious characteristics, such as skin and hair coloring, to less obvious traits, such as blood type and genetically transmitted diseases. In pursuing their research, scientists have measured heads, examined eye color, and even examined earwax. (A wet type of earwax was found to be common among East Asian groups, especially among the Chinese and Japanese, whereas a drier type was found among European and black populations.)

Classification of peoples by skin color has been complicated by the effects of climate. It has been found that variations in skin shading are caused by varying degrees of exposure to sunlight. Asians and Africans have darker coloring because they live in more tropical climates. Classification by skin color is further complicated by biological mixing—for example, the Creoles of Alabama and Mississippi, the Red Bones of Louisiana, the Croatians of North Carolina, and the Mestizos of South America. Whether members of these groups have Native American or African-American ancestors is a matter of dispute.

In reality, truly objective criteria of racial groups based strictly on physical or biological characteristics do not seem to exist. When persons are defined by others and present themselves as a member of a given race, their physical characteristics matter little.

Evidence of the importance of social definitions exists both in the United States and around the world. For example, in Latin American countries such as Brazil, many individuals are listed in the census as white and may be considered by others as white even if a grandparent was of pure African descent. In South Africa, the "Cape colored," who have mixed black and white ancestry, are accorded privileges denied to black natives irrespective of skin coloring. In the United States, a self-definition of racial classification is used in the 2000 census and respondents were asked to place themselves in 1 or more of 19 possible groups listed (with the option to write in an additional racial category). The 2010 Census will be offered in at least five other languages. This concept of race comes close to being equated with national origin; hence "Filipino," "Korean," and "Vietnamese" are treated as racial classifications. There are no legal or generic rules to use in determining which category to check on the census definition.

In review, social definitions far outweigh biological definitions of race, but these social definitions are based on some combination of some inherited physical traits. Thus, some physical traits—such as hair color, height, and size of feet—may be inherited, but these are rarely used to differentiate people into one racial category or another; however, other physical traits—such as skin color—may be used. Taking these considerations into account, biological differences per se do not constitute racial differences. Rather, a racial group is a socially defined group distinguished by selected inherited physical characteristics.

Ethnic Groups

The word *ethnic* is derived from the Greek word ethnikos, which translates to mean "nations" in English. The word was initially applied to European immigrants such as the Italians, Germans, Poles, and other national groups who came to the United States in large numbers, especially between 1900 and 1925. Today, ethnicity is given a wider definition and may also refer to group membership based on religion, language, or region. Using the word in this sense, Jews, Mormons, Latinos, and white Southerners can be considered ethnic groups.

Again, whereas race is based on social definitions of selected physical characteristics such as skin color, hair texture, or eye shape, ethnicity is based on cultural traits that reflect national origin, religion, and language. Cultural traits may be apparent in manner of dress, speech patterns, and modes of emotional expression. Other cultural traits are less obvious but still vital to the group's heritage—characteristics such as ethical values, folklore, and literature.

Some authors prefer to focus on "sense of peoplehood" or "consciousness of kind" as the defining characteristic of ethnicity. We include in our definition of ethnicity the "sense of peoplehood" criterion, as expressed by Milton M. Gordon. According to Gordon (1964), an ethnic group is

> any group that is defined or set off by race, religion, or national origin, or some combination of these categories. ... All of these categories have a common social-psychological referent, in that all of them serve to create, through historical circumstances, a sense of peoplehood. (p. 27)

Minority Groups

A **minority group** is a group that is subordinate to the majority in terms of power and privilege. Such groups are usually but not always smaller than the dominant group; however, it is erroneous to think of minority groups in terms of numerical size. Women, for example, are a numerical majority in American society, yet they have a minority status. In the Republic of South Africa, whites comprise less than one-fifth of the total population, but they are in a position of dominance. In a similar fashion, Schaeffer (2005) defines a *minority group* as a subordinate group whose members have significantly less control or power over their own lives than do the members of a dominant or majority group. Schaeffer says that minorities, as subordinated members of a society, experience more than a loss of control or power over their own lives: they also experience a narrowing of life's opportunities for success, education, wealth, and the pursuit of happiness. In other words, a minority group does not share, in proportion to its numbers, what a given society defines as valuable (Schaeffer, 2005).

In the United States, the most highly valued norms have historically been those of the white, Anglo-Saxon Protestant (WASP) middle classes. Even today, WASP norms, values, cultural patterns, standards of beauty, and laws are widely observed and enforced. Minority groups are distinguished on the basis of the extent of their departure from these norms. They are also set apart on the basis of power and size. Using all three criteria—social norms, power, and size—Newman (1973, p. 20) defined minority groups as those

> that vary from the social norms or archetypes in some manner, are subordinate with regard to the distribution of social power, and rarely constitute more than one-half of the population of the society in which they are found.

According to this definition, aged poor people, poor people in Appalachia, southern whites, handicapped persons, and homosexuals are minority groups. Prior to discussing any specific racial, ethnic, or minority groups, we examine various types of attitudes, behaviors, and patterns of group interaction.

Thinking Sociologically

1. To what extent is race, based solely on biological criteria, a meaningful concept or way in which people are identified, differentiated, or treated?
2. Using the ideas of interactionist theory, explain the social significance of groups as racial, ethnic, or minority categories.

ATTITUDES, BEHAVIORS, AND THEIR INFLUENCE

One of the most serious problems faced by most racial and ethnic groups in America and around the world concerns how they are perceived and treated by others. For a number of reasons, people tend to treat those they perceive to be different in ways that they would not treat members of their own group. Not infrequently, this has led to inequalities and has increased societal strains and tensions. To pursue ideals of equality, we must understand how the attitudes underlying unfair practices are formed.

Prejudice

A **prejudice** is a negative attitude that rejects an entire group (Schaefer, 2005). It involves thoughts and beliefs that exist inside people's heads. These beliefs can lead to categorical rejection and the disliking of an entire racial or ethnic group, even if the prejudiced person has had little or no contact with them. Note that this is very different from disliking someone you meet because you find their behavior objectionable.

In the United States, prejudice is frequently expressed through the use of ethnic slurs such as "redskin," "honkie," "wetback," "eagle beaks," or "nigger." According to Allen (1990), these ethnic labels are "unkind words" and usually express negative feelings. A recent example of the controversy that ethnic slurs and stereotypes create is the battle between Dream Works SKG and Italian-American groups over Don Lino, a character in the 2004 movie *Shark Tale*. Don Lino is the godfather of great white sharks. The voice is that of Robert DeNiro. The Italian-American groups who are protesting say that the movie's gangster-like shark characters foster ethnic stereotypes. In particular, they say that "The movie introduces young minds to the idea that people with Italian names—like millions of Americans across the country— are gangsters" (Reuters, 2004).

A variety of theories have been offered to explain prejudice. Early theories were often based on the premise that prejudiced attitudes are innate or biological, but more recent explanations tend to attribute the development of prejudices to the social environment. Locating the source of prejudice in the social environment, rather than in innate or biological traits, means that measures can be taken to curtail prejudice. Some examples of such measures are discussed later in this chapter.

Economic theories of prejudice are based on the supposition that both competition and conflict among groups are inevitable when different groups desire commodities that are in short supply. These theories explain why racial prejudice is most salient during periods of depression and economic turmoil. In California, for example, from the 1840s through the depression of the 1930s, economic relations between European- and Chinese-Americans were tolerant and amiable as long as the Chinese confined themselves to occupations such as laundry and curio shops. When the Chinese-Americans began to compete with European-Americans in gold mining and other business enterprises, however, violent racial conflicts erupted. Japanese-Americans had a similar experience.

The exploitation variant of economic theory argues that prejudice is used to stigmatize a group as inferior, to put its members in a subordinate position, and to justify their exploitation. The exploitation theme explains how systems under capitalism have traditionally justified exploiting recent immigrants who had little money, few skills, and difficulties with English.

Psychological theories of prejudice suggest that prejudice satisfies psychic needs or compensates for some defect in the personality. When people use **scapegoating**, they blame other persons or groups for their own problems. Another psychological strategy involves **projection**, in which people attribute their own unacceptable traits or behaviors to another person. In this way, people transfer responsibility for their own failures to a vulnerable group, often a racial or ethnic group. **Frustration-aggression theory** involves a form of projection (Dollard et al., 1939). In this view, groups who strive repeatedly to achieve their goals become frustrated after failing a number of times. When the frustration reaches a high intensity, the group seeks an outlet for its frustration by displacing its aggressive behavior to a socially approved target, a racial or ethnic group. Thus, it has been argued that the Germans, frustrated by runaway inflation and the failure of their nationalist ambitions, vented their aggressive feelings by persecuting the Jews. Poor whites, frustrated by their unproductive lands and financial problems, drained off their hostilities through anti-black prejudices. Schaeffer (2005) adds a theory called *normative theory* that emphasizes socialization as an explanation for prejudice. The theory maintains that peers and social influences either encourage tolerance or intolerance toward others. In other words, a person from an intolerant household is more likely to be openly prejudiced than someone from a tolerant household.

The **authoritarian personality theory** argues that some people are more inclined to prejudice than others, due to differences in personality. According to the authors of the theory (Adorno et al., 1950), prejudiced individuals are characterized by rigidity of outlook, intolerance, suggestibility, dislike for ambiguity, and irrational attitudes. They tend to be authoritarian, preferring stability and orderliness to the indefiniteness that accompanies social change. Simpson and Yinger (1972) questioned whether these traits cause prejudice and suggested that they may in fact be an effect of prejudice or even completely unrelated to it.

Regardless of what theory is believed to explain prejudice, it is sustained through **stereotypes**, which are widely held beliefs about the character and behavior of all members of a group. They are usually based on readily discernible characteristics, such as physical appearance, and are oversimplifications that seldom correspond to the facts. A prejudiced person might say of one group, "They breed like rabbits," of another, "They are a bunch of hoodlums," overlooking the great range of individual differences found within every group.

Stereotypes of the majority are usually more favorable than those of minorities. Whites may be portrayed as industrious, intelligent, ambitious, and progressive, whereas blacks may be described as lazy, happy-go-lucky, and ignorant. There are several stereotypes associated with Native Americans. One image often projected to the public by the movies and television advertising is of the Native American who is strong and stoic, who has a special relationship to nature. A stereotype more common in the past was of the ruthless, bloodthirsty savage cruelly murdering innocent white settlers. A third suggests that all Native Americans are alcoholics who live in self-induced poverty. Needless to say, none of these stereotypes even begins to reflect the great diversity of behavior that exists now and that has always existed among Native Americans, as among other groups.

Stereotyping is not entirely dysfunctional. Albrecht et al. (1980) have argued that "stereotypes afford us the comfort of recognition and save us the time and effort of interpreting masses of new stimuli hourly" (p. 254). They help us mentally sort people into predictable categories and make social interaction easier. Most of our encounters are dominated by stereotyped conceptions of how we should act and how others should respond, whether we are dealing with bank tellers, employers, or family members.

Most would agree, however, that the dysfunctional aspects of stereotyping far outweigh the functional aspects. In addition to pointing out how stereotyping is functional, Albrecht et al. (1980) cited several harmful consequences. First, stereotypes are often based on inaccurate information, and these distortions of reality could very well interfere with a person's adjustment to his or her social environment. Second, they are used to justify discrimination against members of various ethnic and racial groups. The stereotype that blacks are lazy and unintelligent, for example, could be used as a basis for categorically barring blacks from highly paid executive and managerial positions.

A third damaging effect of stereotyping is that it may contribute to the development of an inferior self-concept. The *symbolic interaction viewpoint* tells us that self-perceptions are created through internalizing the attitudes, responses, and definitions one believes are held by others. An inferior self-concept may be developed because stereotyped predictions about behavior influence behavior in such a way that those predictions come true. The outcome is then used to confirm the original prediction. This is another example of the self-fulfilling prophecy discussed elsewhere in the text.

Radke and Trager's (1950) early studies of black children support the idea that members of a stereotyped minority tend to internalize the definitions attached to them. In these studies, the children were asked to evaluate black and white dolls and to tell stories about black and white persons in photographs. The children overwhelmingly preferred the white dolls to the black ones; the white dolls were described as good, the black dolls as bad. The black individuals in the photographs were given inferior roles as servants, maids, or gardeners.

Later studies of self-esteem, however, tended to find little or no difference between blacks and whites. Zirkel (1971) reviewed over a dozen studies of black and white students attending grammar and secondary schools and concluded that black and white children have similar levels of self-esteem. Simmons et al. (1978) found that minority students have even stronger self-concepts than majority students. This change in attitudes can be linked to the civil rights movements of the late 1960s and early 1970s, when emerging ethnic pride began to be expressed in such slogans as "Red Power" and "Black is beautiful."

APPLYING THEORIES OF PREJUDICE

Gordon Allport (1954), in *The Nature of Prejudice*, noted that interracial interaction will reduce prejudice only when the groups are of equal status, they have common goals, and their interaction is sanctioned by authorities. Allport's notion is congruent with the economic theory that says that competition and conflict can heighten prejudice. Using these ideas, a classroom program known as the "jigsaw technique" was developed by Aronson and his associates. Weyant (1995) offers a description of that technique:

> The jigsaw technique involves dividing the class into small groups of usually about five to six students each. Each child in a group is given information about one part of a total lesson. For example, a lesson on Spanish and Portuguese explorers might be divided such that one child in the group is given information about Magellan, another student receives information about Balboa, another about Ponce de Leon, etc. The members of the group then proceed to teach their part to the group. Afterward, the students are tested individually on the entire lesson. Just as all the pieces of a jigsaw puzzle must be put into place to get the whole picture, the only way any one student can master the entire lesson is to learn all the pieces of

information from his or her peers. Equal status is attained because every student has an equally important part. The common goal is to put together the entire lesson. (pp. 108–109)

Evaluation studies of the jigsaw technique found very positive results, including increased attraction of classmates for one another and higher self-esteem. These results also helped alleviate some of the causes of prejudice suggested by psychological theories. Furthermore, the results were obtained with only a few hours of "jigsawing" a week, so the goals of desegregation were met without a major restructuring of the schools.

Techniques to reduce prejudice do not have to be confined to the classroom. Community leaders such as local politicians, businesspeople, and ministers might help eliminate racial tensions in a neighborhood by developing programs that require citizen participation. A church, for example, might sponsor a food drive to help the needy. In organizing a committee to run such a drive, the pastor or director could create racially and ethnically integrated committees to handle the various responsibilities necessary to make the drive a success. These might include committees for advertising and publicizing, collection, distribution, setup, and cleanup. Like the classroom, people of different minority groups would come to work with and to depend on each other in a cooperative rather than a competitive situation and thus have an opportunity to overcome some of their prejudices.

Your knowledge of how prejudice occurs could lead to many other programs to help eliminate this serious social problem. For example, as a parent, how do you think you could use what you have learned in this chapter to prevent your children and their friends from developing prejudice against minority groups?

Thinking Sociologically

1. What are some dysfunctional aspects of prejudices and stereotyping? What are some functional aspects?
2. How could the information contained in the section "Applying Theories of Prejudice" be used to make social action programs more effective?

Discrimination

Prejudice is a judgment, an attitude. **Discrimination**, on the other hand, is overt behavior or actions. It is the categorical exclusion of members of a specific group from certain rights, opportunities, and/or privileges (Schaefer, 2005). According to the conflict perspective, the dominant group in a society practices discrimination to protect its advantages, privileges, and interests.

Most of us can understand discrimination at the individual level. A person may engage in behavior that excludes another individual from rights, opportunities, or privileges simply on the basis of that person's racial, ethnic, or minority status. For example, if I refuse to hire a particular Japanese-American to type this manuscript because he or she does not does not read English, I am not engaging in prejudicially determined discrimination. On the other hand, if I refuse to hire a highly qualified typist of English because he or she is Japanese-American, that is discrimination.

Discrimination does not operate solely at the individual level. Rothman (2005) defines the institutionalization of inequality as the structural dimension: the collection of laws, customs, and social practices that combine to create and sustain the unequal distribution of rewards based on class, minority status, and gender (Rothman, 2005). Therefore, institutional discrimination occurs as well. **Institu-**

tional discrimination is the continuing exclusion or oppression of a group as a result of criteria established by an institution. In this form of discrimination, individual prejudice is not a factor, nor are laws or rules applied with the intent of excluding any person or group from particular rights, opportunities, or privileges; however, the outcome has discriminatory consequences.

Suppose, for example, that a school requires for admission a particular minimum score on a standardized national exam based on European-American culture, or that a club requires a $10,000 annual membership fee. In such cases, no bias against any particular racial or ethnic group may be intended—anyone who meets the criteria can be admitted. However, the result is the same as if the discrimination were by design. Few members of minority or ethnic groups could meet the requirements for admittance to the school or club, and the benefits of belonging would accrue only to those groups that already belonged. This would tend to continue existing patterns of educational and occupational deprivation from one generation to the next.

A similar process operates in our criminal justice system. Suppose that individuals from two different ethnic groups are arrested for identical offenses and given the same fine. If one can pay the fine but the other cannot, their fates may be quite different. The one who cannot pay will go to jail while the other one goes home. The result is institutional discrimination against the poor. Once a person has been imprisoned and has probably lost her or his job, that individual may find that other jobs are harder to find. Blacks and other minority groups do spend more time in prison, which disrupts family and work life and can continue the cycle of poverty.

Racism

Racism is the belief that one racial group or category is inherently superior to others. It includes prejudices and discriminatory behaviors based on this belief. Racism can be regarded as having three major components. First, the racist believes that her or his own race is superior to other racial groups. This component may involve racial prejudice, but it is not synonymous with it. Racial prejudice is an attitude, usually negative, toward the members of other racial groups. The belief in the superiority of one's own group may also involve *ethnocentrism*, which is the belief in the superiority of one's own group on the basis of cultural criteria. A person's own group may be an ethnic group, but it need not be. Thus, racial prejudice and ethnocentrism can be regarded as properties of racism, not synonyms for it.

The second property of racism is that it has an ideology, or set of beliefs, that justifies the subjugation and exploitation of another group. According to Rothman (1978, p. 51), a racist ideology serves five functions:

1. It provides a moral rationale for systematic deprivation.
2. It allows the dominant group to reconcile values and behavior.
3. It discourages the subordinate group from challenging the system.
4. It rallies adherence in support of a "just" cause.
5. It defends the existing division of labor.

Perpetuators of racist ideologies claim that they are based on scientific evidence. One pseudoscientific theory, for example, held that the various races evolved at different times. Blacks, who presumably evolved first, were regarded as the most primitive race. As such, they were believed to be incapable of creating a superior culture or carrying on the culture of the higher, white races, and the theory further argued that some benefits could accrue to the blacks by serving members of the white race. This theory is obviously self-serving and completely without scientific foundation.

Richard Schaeffer points out six ways that racism is dysfunctional, or disruptive to the stability of a social system, even to the dominant members of the society (Schaeffer, 2005). These are:

1. A society that practices discrimination fails to use the resources of all individuals. Discrimination limits the search for talent and leadership to the dominant group.
2. Discrimination aggravates social problems such as poverty, delinquency, and crime and places the financial burden of alleviating these problems on the dominant group.
3. Society must invest a good deal of time and money to defend the barriers that prevent the full participation of all members.
4. Racial prejudice and discrimination undercut goodwill and friendly diplomatic relations between nations.
5. Social change is inhibited because change may assist a subordinate group.
6. Discrimination promotes disrespect for law enforcement and for the peaceful settlement of disputes.

The third of the three elements in racism is that the beliefs are acted upon. Many examples of racist actions in this country could be given. The lynching of blacks in the U.S. South and the destruction of entire tribes of Native Americans who were regarded as little more than animals are two of the more extreme instances.

Racism, like discrimination, can be of two types. Individual racism originates in the racist beliefs of a single person. Racist store owners, for example, might refuse to hire black employees because they regard them as inferior beings. **Institutional racism** occurs when racist ideas and practices are embodied in the folkways, mores, or legal structures of various institutions.

The policy of apartheid in the Republic of South Africa was, and in many ways is, one of the most notorious examples of institutional racism. This policy calls for biological, territorial, social, educational, economic, and political separation of the various racial groups that compose the nation. Only in the past few years have the media brought the South African racial situation to the conscious attention of most Americans. As a result, many schools, foundations, and industries have removed from their investment portfolios companies that have a major investment in that country. Others have taken public stands against the institutionalized racism that supports different rules, opportunities, and activities based on the color of one's skin.

Racism can take many different forms—separatism, segregation, subjugation, exploitation, expulsion, and others. We focus next on two forms considered the most extreme: genocide and mass expulsion.

Genocide is the practice of deliberately destroying a whole race or ethnic group. The term was coined by Raphael Lemkin to describe the heinous crimes committed by the Nazis during World War II against the Jewish people, which is the supreme example of racism. Of the 9,600,000 Jews who lived in Nazi-dominated Europe between 1933 and 1945, 60 percent died in concentration camps. The British also solved race problems through annihilation during their colonization campaigns overseas. Between 1803 and 1876, for example, they almost wiped out the native population of Tasmania. The aborigines were believed by the British to be a degenerate race, wild beasts to be hunted and killed. One colonist regularly hunted natives to feed his dogs. However, we do not have to go to Australia for illustrations nor do we need to go back in time to see this occurring. As early as 1717, the U.S. government was giving incentives to private citizens for exterminating the so-called troublesome (American) Indians, and Americans were paid generous bounties for natives' scalps. In the 1990's the world got to witness the genocide in Rwanda that left over a million men, women, and children dead and many more displaced from their homeland. Today, we are once again witnessing the tragic events of genocide taking place in the Darfur region of Sudan. Tens of thousands of people are being raped and killed based only on their ethnicity.

Mass expulsion is the practice of expelling racial or ethnic groups from their homeland. The United States routinely used expulsion to solve conflicts with Native Americans. In an incident known as "the trail of tears," the Cherokees were forced out of their homeland in the region where Georgia meets Tennessee and North Carolina. The removal was triggered by the discovery of gold in the Georgia mountains and the determination of European-Americans to take possession of it. The exodus went to the Ohio River and then to the Mississippi, ending in what is now Oklahoma. Of the 10,000 Cherokees rounded up, about 4,000 perished during the exodus.

Racist thinking and racist doctrine were rampant between 1850 and 1950, which is aptly called "the century of racism." Since 1950, it has declined in many parts of the world, but there is no question that it still exists.

PATTERNS OF GROUP INTERACTION

When different racial and ethnic groups live in the same area, widespread and continuous contact among groups is inevitable, but it rarely results in equality. Generally, one group holds more power and dominates the other groups. In some cases, the group in power attempts mass expulsion or genocide, but integration, assimilation, and pluralism are more common. Whatever the form of group interaction, relations among groups are strongly influenced by their rankings in the stratification system.

The rankings of people because of race, nationality, religious, or other ethnic or minority affiliation is clearly not unique to the United States. Descendants of slavery in Brazil are bound by second-class status. Great Britain is described as a country with a long history as a colonizer but was not colonized. Thus, blacks born in Britain are classified by white Britons as immigrants; Asians, even those who speak fluent English, are automatically expected to have language problems; and the peoples of India, Pakistan, and the West Indies are forced to occupy a subordinate role in Britain. Over the past decade, Northern Ireland has had numerous incidents and reports of armed conflict between Protestants and Catholics. The strife between Jews and Muslims in Israel and other Middle-Eastern countries is well known. In the early 1990s, Yugoslavia was faced with an ethnic war between Croats and Serbs. Numerous other examples could be given to illustrate racial, ethnic, or minority stratification within a particular country. An examination of ethnic stratification follows.

Ethnic Stratification: Inequality and Interaction

Stratification is the structured ranking of entire groups of people that perpetuates unequal rewards and power in a society (Schaeffer, 2005). Stratification in a society takes a variety of forms. Sometimes, it is based on a status ascribed at birth, as in a caste system; and sometimes, it is based on an acquired status, such as income or occupation, as in many industrialized countries. Some societies, including our own, stratify people on the basis of ascribed statuses such as race and ethnic heritage, in addition to the achieved statuses of education and income.

In America, the predominant norms, values, beliefs, ideas, and character traits are those of the WASP majority—described more fully later in this chapter. The more a group diverges from the economic status and norms of the majority, the lower its rank in the social hierarchy. Thus, it may be less advantageous to be Chinese or Mexican than to be Polish or Irish, as well as less desirable to be Polish or Irish than to be a WASP.

The consequences of allocating status on the basis of ethnic or racial membership are most evident in the different lifestyles and opportunities of different groups. When social inequality is based on racial lines, the majority holds the more desirable positions and minorities hold the less desirable ones.

Donald L. Noel (1975) contends that three conditions are necessary for ethnic stratification to occur in a society: ethnocentrism, which is the tendency to assume that one's culture and way of life are superior to all others (Schaeffer, 2005); competition for resources; and inequalities in power. The inevitable outcome of ethnocentrism is that other groups are disparaged to a greater or lesser degree, depending on the extent of their difference from the majority. Competition among groups occurs when they must vie for the same scarce resources or goals, but it need not lead to ethnic stratification if values concerning freedom and equality are held and enforced. According to Noel, it is the third condition, inequality in power that enables one group to impose its will upon the others. Power permits the dominant group to render the subordinate groups ineffectual as competitors and to institutionalize the distribution of rewards and the opportunities to consolidate their position.

This view of inequality is central to the conflict perspective on racial and ethnic relations. Conflict theories assume that the relative powerlessness of minority groups provides a basis for exploitation and a pool of cheap labor for the ruling class. It is argued that racial or ethnic minorities who are willing to accept jobs at very low wages restrict the wages of all workers because workers from majority groups who demand higher wages can be replaced by low-status, relatively powerless minority members. This idea is described more fully in the upcoming sections on ethnic antagonism and the split labor market.

What positions do ethnic and racial groups occupy in the stratification system of the United States? Table 9-1 lists the income, education, and labor force status of selected groupings of racial and ethnic groups in America, as of 2004. Unfortunately, complete statistics on Native Americans are not available, and groups such as Japanese-Americans, Chinese-Americans, Filipino-Americans, Hawaiians, and Samoans are all grouped together under "Asian and Pacific Islanders." Nevertheless, major differences remain.

In our society, income and education are important indicators of a group's place in the stratification system. As the table indicates, African-Americans, Native Americans, and Hispanic-Americans had the lowest median family incomes and lowest levels of education in 2004. One-half of all Asian-Americans had attended or completed college, compared with one-third of the European-American population, one-fourth of the Native American and Eskimo population, and one-fifth of the African-American and Hispanic-American populations. The percentages of persons in the labor force did not differ dramatically, but the percentage of those unemployed did. African-American and Hispanic-American males and females had about twice the rate of unemployment as European-Americans and Asian-Americans. The results shown in table 9-1 are statistically the same as in 2002.

The high income and education levels of Asian-Americans reflect the emphasis placed on education by those groups. It probably also reflects the changes in immigration policy in the mid-1960s, which gave priority to highly skilled and professional immigrants. The low incomes of African- and Hispanic-American families reflect their overrepresentation in less prestigious, less skilled, and lower-paying occupational categories. Native Americans would be in similar lower-level occupational groupings. One common consequence of these income, education, and employment differentials is antagonism among ethnic groups and between the less powerful and the more powerful.

TABLE 9-1 INCOME, EDUCATION, AND LABOR FORCE STATUS OF EUROPEAN-, AFRICAN-, ASIAN-, HISPANIC-, AND NATIVE AMERICANS

Characteristics	White	Black	Asian/ Pacific Islanders	Hispanic	American Indian, Eskimo
Median family income (2004)	55,389	38,758	—	39,311	—
Less than $10,000	2 %	11.3%	—	6.7%	—
More than $25,000	27.0%	37.5%	—	34.6%	—
More than $50,000	38.2%	37.4%	—	37.7%	—
Years of school completed (2004)					
Elementary 0–8	6%	7%	6.8%	25.6%	—
High school 1–4	30.6%	32.7%	19.9%	26.5%	—
College 1–4 or more	28.3%	17.3%	40.0%	12.1%	—
Labor force status (2004)					
Labor force, age 15 and over	77.9%	69.1%	71.7%	67.4%	68.2%
Unemployed	3.0	6.9	3.2	5.5	7.6
Not in labor force	22.1	30.9	28.3	32.6	31.8

Source: U.S. Bureau of the Census, *Statistical Abstracts of the United States,* 2003, Washington , DC: U.S. Government Printing Office, 2005. (1) "Money Income" Series P-60, No 213; (2) Educational Attainment" C2KBR-27.

Ethnic Antagonism

Ethnic antagonism is mutual opposition, conflict, or hostility among different ethnic groups. In the broadest sense, the term encompasses all levels of intergroup conflict—ideologies and beliefs such as racism and prejudice, behaviors such as discrimination and riots, and institutions such as the legal and economic systems. Ethnic antagonism is closely linked to the racial and ethnic stratification system. The best-known theory of ethnic antagonism is that of the split labor market, as formulated by Edna Bonacich in a series of articles in the 1970s (1972, 1975, and 1976).

A central tenet of split-labor-market theory is that when the price of labor for the same work differs by ethnic group, a three-way conflict develops among business managers and owners, higher-priced labor, and cheaper labor. Business—that is, the employer—aims at having as cheap and docile a labor force as possible. Higher-priced labor may include current employees or a dominant ethnic group that demands higher wages, a share of the profits, or fringe benefits that increase the employer's costs. Cheaper labor refers to any ethnic group that can do the work done by the higher-priced laborers at a lower cost to the employer.

Antagonism results when the higher-paid labor groups, who want to keep both their jobs and their wages (including benefits), are threatened by the introduction of cheaper labor into the market. The fear is that the cheaper labor group will either replace them or force them to lower their wage level. This basic class conflict then becomes an ethnic and racial conflict. If the higher-paid labor groups are strong enough, they may try to exclude the lower-paid group. **Exclusion** is the attempt to keep out the cheaper labor (or the product they produce). Thus, laws may be passed that make it illegal for Mexicans, Cubans, Haitians, Chinese, Filipinos, or other immigrants to enter the country; taxes may be imposed on Japanese automobiles, foreign steel, or clothes made in Taiwan. Another technique used by higher-paid labor is the imposition of a caste system, in which the cheaper labor can get jobs only in low-paying, low-prestige occupations. As a result, the higher-paid group controls the prestigious jobs that pay well. In one sense, it can be argued that a sort of caste system exists today for women and blacks. Both groups hold jobs of lower status and power and receive lower wages.

Bonacich claims that another process, **displacement**, is also likely to arise in split labor markets. Capitalists who want to reduce labor costs may simply displace the higher-paid employees with cheaper labor. They can replace workers at their present location or move their factories and businesses to states or countries where the costs are lower. This is evident in auto parts, clothes, and other products with tags or labels such as "made in Mexico," or "made in Korea," or made in any other country where labor costs are considerably lower than in the United States. Within the United States, the early 1980s witnessed many examples of strike-breaking by powerful business managers and government officials, who replaced union and higher-paid workers with nonunion and lower-paid employees. The steel, airline, and automobile industries are three cases in point.

An alternative to the split labor market is what Bonacich terms **radicalism**, in which labor groups join together in a coalition against the capitalist class and present a united front. When this occurs, Bonacich claims, no one is displaced or excluded, and no caste system is established. Anyone who gets hired comes in under the conditions of the higher-priced labor. Bonacich believes that as long as there is cheap labor anywhere in the world, there may not be a solution to a split labor market within a capitalist system.

Thinking Sociologically

1. Can you identify five ethnic groups in the United States and stratify them? What criteria do you use? What social significance can you attach to the ranking you have given a particular group?
2. A member of an ethnic or other minority group is capable of doing your job and willing to do it for less money. How might this affect your feelings or behavior toward that person or the group she or he represents?

Integration and Assimilation

Integration occurs when ethnicity becomes insignificant and everyone can freely and fully participate in the social, economic, and political mainstream. All groups are brought together. **Assimilation** occurs when individuals and groups forsake their own cultural tradition to become part of a different group and tradition. With complete assimilation, the minority group loses its identity as a subordinate group and becomes fully integrated into the institutions, groups, and activities of society. The extent to which integration and assimilation has occurred represents what sociologists call **social distance**, meaning the degree of intimacy and equality between two groups. It is measured by asking questions as to whether one would be willing to have members of a particular ethnic group live in one's neighborhood, have them as friends, or be willing to marry them.

Assimilation in the United States appears to focus on one of two models: the **melting pot** and **Anglo conformity**. The following formulations differentiate these two terms (Newman, 1973).

Melting pot: A + B + C = D
Anglo conformity: A + B + C = A

In melting-pot assimilation, each group contributes a bit of its own culture and absorbs aspects of other cultures such that the whole is a combination of all the groups. Many sociologists in the United States view the melting-pot model as a popular myth, with reality better illustrated by the Anglo conformity model. *Anglo conformity* is equated with "Americanization," whereby the minority completely loses its identity to the dominant WASP culture.

Integration is a two-way process: The immigrants must want to assimilate, and the host society must be willing to have them assimilate. The immigrant must undergo *cultural assimilation*, learning the day-to-day norms of the WASP culture pertaining to dress, language, food, and sports. This process also involves internalizing the more crucial aspects of the culture, such as values, ideas, beliefs, and attitudes. **Structural assimilation** involves developing patterns of intimate contact between the guest and host groups in the clubs, organizations, and institutions of the host society. Cultural assimilation generally precedes structural assimilation, although the two sometimes happen simultaneously.

Cultural assimilation has occurred on a large scale in American society, although the various minorities differed in the pace at which they were assimilated. With white ethnics of European origin, cultural assimilation went hand in hand with **amalgamation** (biological mixing through large-scale intermarriage). Among Asian ethnics, Japanese-Americans seem to have assimilated most completely and are being rewarded with high socioeconomic status. In contrast, Chinese-Americans, particularly first-generation migrants, have resisted assimilation and have retained strong ties to their cultural traditions. The existence of Chinatowns in many cities reflects this desire for cultural continuity.

Assimilation involves more than just culture borrowing because immigrants want access to the host's institutional privileges. The issue of integration is particularly relevant in three areas: housing, schooling, and employment.

Segregation

Segregation is the physical and social separation of groups or categories or people. It results in ethnic enclaves such as Little Italies, black ghettos, and Hispanic barrios. The most significant division, however, is between the whites in the suburbs and the blacks and other minorities in the inner cities. At the institutional level, segregation can be attributed to discriminatory practices and policies of the federal housing agencies and of mortgage-lending institutions. Suburban zoning patterns that tend to keep out poorer families are also influential. At the individual level, segregation is the result of some whites' refusal to sell their houses to nonwhites or the desire of minorities themselves to live in ethnic communities.

The city-suburb polarization of blacks and whites continues through the early part of this millennium. This pattern of segregation continues in spite of a 1965 federal law that prohibits discrimination in the rental, sale, or financing of suburban housing. Based on this law, all banks and savings and loan associations bidding for deposits of federal funds were requested to sign antiredlining pledges. *Redlining* is the practice among mortgage-lending institutions of imposing artificial restrictions on housing loans for areas where minorities have started to buy. Despite these and other advances, American society has a long way to go in desegregating housing patterns.

School segregation was brought to national attention with the 1954 decision in Brown v. Board of Education, in which the U.S. Supreme Court ruled that the assignment of children to schools solely because of race—called **de jure segregation** (meaning segregation by law)—violates the U.S. Constitution and that the schools involved must desegregate. For decades prior to the Brown decision, particularly in the South, busing was used to keep the races apart even when they lived in the same neighborhoods and communities.

In the past few decades, attention has shifted to the North and West, where school segregation resulted from blacks and whites living in separate neighborhoods, with school assignment based on residence boundaries. This pattern, which is called **de facto segregation** (meaning segregation in fact), led to legislation in many cities that bused blacks and whites out of their neighborhood schools for purposes of achieving racial balance. Defenders of the legislation argue that minority students who are exposed to high-achieving white middle-class students will do better academically. They also contend that desegregation by busing is a way for whites and minority groups to learn about each other, which may diminish stereotypes and racist attitudes.

It is not always clear whether segregation is de facto or de jure. School districts may follow neighborhood boundaries and define a neighborhood school so that it minimizes contact between black and white children. Is that de facto segregation (resulting from black and white neighborhoods) or de jure segregation (resulting from legally sanctioned assignment of children to schools based on race)? Regardless of what it is, the vast majority of black children in Atlanta, Baltimore, Chicago, Cleveland, Detroit, Los Angeles, Memphis, Philadelphia, and many other cities today attend schools that are predominantly black.

Pluralism

Are the elimination of segregation and the achievement of integration the only choices of societies with racial and ethnic diversity, or can diverse racial and ethnic groups coexist side by side and maintain their distinctive heritages and cultures? This issue is what Lambert and Taylor (1990) address as "the American challenge: assimilation or multiculturalism" and what Lieberson and Waters (1988) state as "melting pot versus cultural pluralism."

Multiculturalism or **cultural pluralism** can be defined as a situation in which the various racial, ethnic, or other minority groups in a society maintain their distinctive cultural patterns, subsystems, and institutions. Perhaps this can be illustrated by the following formula:

$$\text{Cultural pluralism: } A + B + C = A + B + C$$

Whereas those who support assimilation and integration seek to eliminate ethnic boundaries, a pluralist wants to retain them. Pluralists argue that groups can coexist by accepting their differences. Basic to cultural pluralism are beliefs that individuals never forget or escape their social origin, that all groups bring positive contributions that enrich the larger society, and that groups have the right to be different yet equal.

Several authorities believe that assimilation and pluralism are happening simultaneously in American society. Glazer and Moynihan (1970) perceive the process of becoming what they call "hyphenated" Americans as involving cultural assimilation. Thus, a Russian-American is different from a Russian in Russia, and an African-American is not the same as an African in Africa. On the other hand, they perceive the emergence of minority groups as political interest groups as a pluralistic trend. Gordon (1978) contends that assimilation of minorities is the prevailing trend in economic, political, and educational institutions, whereas cultural pluralism prevails in religion, the family, and recreation.

Cultural pluralism results in separate ethnic communities, many of which are characterized by a high degree of institutional completeness; that is, they include institutions and services that meet the needs of the group, such as ethnic churches, newspapers, mutual aid societies, and recreational groups. These ethnic enclaves are particularly attractive to recent immigrants who have language problems and few skills. Schaefer (2003) compared ethnic communities to decompression chambers. "Just as divers use such chambers to adjust to the rapid change in water pressure, immigrants use the communities to adjust to cultural change they are forced to make upon arriving in a new country" (p. 48).

Today, we are witnessing a resurgence of interest by various ethnic groups in almost forgotten languages, customs, and traditions. This is characterized by people's increased interest in the culture of their ethnic group, visits to ancestral homes, their increased use of ethnic names, and their renewed interest in the native language of their own group.

The general rule has been for American minorities to assimilate, however. Most ethnic groups are oriented toward the future, not toward the past. American ethnics are far more interested in shaping their future within the American structure than in maintaining cultural ties with the past. However, as Rothman (2005) contends, the importance of a mulitcultural model is accelerated by the recognition that whites will probably be a numerical minority sometime after the year 2050. The concluding section of this chapter examines the major racial, ethnic, and other minority groups in the United States.

MAJOR RACIAL, ETHNIC, AND OTHER MINORITY GROUPS IN THE UNITED STATES

The Hispanic-American population is the largest racial, ethnic minority group in the U.S., constituting approximately 12.5 percent of the population. The Hispanic-American classification, however, is very difficult to measure for many reasons, including overlap with other categories and illegal immigration. The African-American population is the second largest racial, ethnic, minority group in (see Table 9-2), constituting 12.3 percent of the total population. On October 17th, 2007 the total population in the United States reached 300 million people for the first time. Since the U.S. Census is only taken every 10 years, we can only give the figures up to the year 2000. The U.S. Census can project certain populations in the United States yearly and those that are published were taken from the latest report in 2006. (White: 198,460,626. Black: 39,784,136. Hispanic: 42,687,224. Asian: 14,376,658.

TABLE 9-2 RESIDENT POPULATION OF VARIOUS RACIAL, ETHNIC, AND MINORITY GROUPS IN THE UNITED STATES

	1990		2000	
Race	**Number**	**Percentage**	**Number**	**Percentage**
White	199,686,000	80.30	211,460,626	75.00
Black	29,986,000	12.10	34,658,190	12.30
Hispanic	22,354,000	9.00	35,305,818	12.50
Asian	7,274,000	2.90	10,242,998	3.60
Pacific Islander			398,835	.01
American Indian/ Alaskan Native	1,959,000	.08	2,475,956	.09
Two or more races			6,826,228	2.40
All others	6,999,200	3.10	15,359,073	5.50
Total	**268,258,200**	**100.00**	**281,421,906**	**100.00**

The third largest group, the Asian-American community, includes Americans whose historical roots are Chinese, Filipinos, Japanese, Asian Indians (from India), Koreans, Vietnamese, and people in other Asian nations. The number of Asians in the United States increased by 3.3 million between 1990 and 2000, bringing the Asian-American population count to 10,242,998 or 3.6 percent of the entire United States population. This increase is in large part due to the influx of immigrants (discussed more later in this chapter) and is evidenced in Table 9-2.

Following the Asian-Americans in size are the Native Americans, categorized in the U.S. census as "American Indians" and grouped with the Eskimos and Aleuts (native Eskimoan tribes from the Aleutian Islands, which is a chain of volcanic islands extending some 1,100 miles from the tip of the Alaskan Peninsula). These Native American groups included about 2.4 million people in 2000, slightly less than 1 percent of the U.S. population.

FIGURE 9-1 HISPANIC HOUSEHOLDERS, BY COUNTRY OR REGION OF ORIGIN: MARCH 2000

Source: U.S. Bureau of the Census. *Current Population Reports,* "The Hispanic Population of the United States, May 2001," Washington, DC: U.S. Government Printing Office.

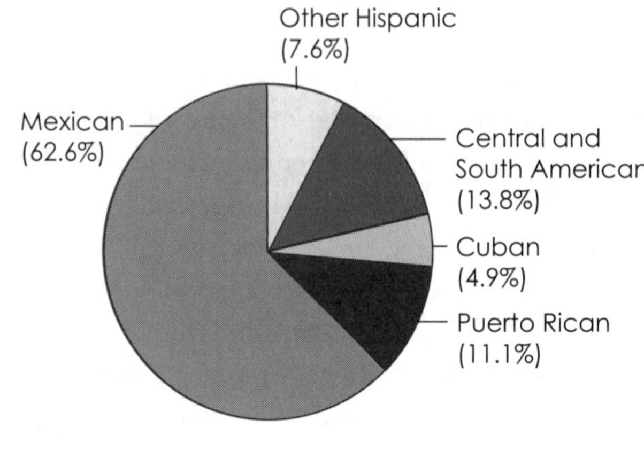

Hispanic-Americans

As of 2000, there were about 35.3 million people in the United States who claimed Hispanic origins (see Table 9-2). This category includes those who classify themselves as Mexican-American (58.5 percent), Puerto Rican (9.6 percent), Cuban (3.5 percent), Central American (4.8 percent), South American (3.8 percent), Dominican (2.2 percent), and other Hispanics (17.6 percent) from Spain or other Spanish-speaking countries (see Figure 9-1). These also include those who simply identify themselves as "Spanish-American," "Hispanic," or "Latino." Our discussion focuses on Mexican-Americans, who constitute approximately 58 percent of the Hispanic-American group.

Mexican-Americans are also identified as Chicanos, a contraction of Mexicanos (pronounced "meschicanos" in the ancient Nahuatl language of Mexico). Over 1 million Mexican-Americans are descendants of the native Mexicans who lived in the Southwest before it became part of the United States, following the Mexican-American war. They became Americans in 1848, when Texas, California, New Mexico, and most of Arizona became U.S. territory. These four states plus Colorado contain the largest concentrations of this group today. Most urban Mexican-Americans live in California, especially in Los Angeles.

Other Mexican-Americans came from Mexico since 1848. They can be classified into three types: (1) legal immigrants; (2) *braceros,* or temporary workers; and (3) illegal aliens. Large-scale migration in the early 1900s was caused by the Mexican Revolution and unsettled economic conditions in Mexico and by the demand for labor on cotton farms and railroads in California. Before the minimum wage law was passed, agricultural employers preferred braceros to local workers because they could be paid less, and the braceros were not a burden to the federal government inasmuch as they returned to Mexico when their services were no longer needed.

The number of illegal aliens from Mexico is not known; estimates range from 1 to 10 million. Immigration policy concerning legal and illegal Mexican immigrants generally varies with the need for labor, which in turn depends on economic conditions. When the demand for Mexican labor was high, immigration was encouraged. When times were bad, illegal aliens were tracked down, rounded up, and deported. They were scapegoats in the depression of the 1930s and again in the recession of the early 1980s.

Traditional Mexican-American culture is characterized by strong family ties and large families. The extended family is the most important institution in the Chicano community. The theme of family honor and unity occurs throughout Mexican-American society, irrespective of social class or geographical location. This theme extends beyond the nuclear family unit of husband, wife, and children to relatives on both sides and persists even when the dominance of the male becomes weakened. It is a primary source of emotional and economic support and the primary focus of obligations.

Most American families have two or three children, but it is not unusual for Mexican-American families to have five or more. In 2001, for example, Hispanic families had an average of 3.52 persons (compared to 2.48 in non-Hispanic families). About twice as many Hispanic families had five or more members compared to non-Hispanics. Families of this size, when linked with minimal skills and low levels of income, make it difficult for the Mexican-American to enjoy life at a level equal to the dominant groups in American society. For example, the median family income for non-Hispanic families in 2006 was $50,784 compared to $38,067 for Hispanic Families. Combining a large family size with a low income makes life very hard for most Hispanic-Americans.

To improve the educational and income level of the Mexican-American family, several Mexican-American social movements have emerged over the past three decades. One movement was directed at having bilingual instruction introduced at the elementary level. Bilingualism emerged into such a politically controversial issue that in 1986 California passed a resolution (joining six other states) making English the state's official language.

Another movement was led by Cesar Chavez, one of the best-known Chicano leaders. In 1962, he formed the National Farm Workers Association (later the United Farm Workers Union) and organized Mexican migrant farm workers first to strike against grape growers and later against lettuce growers. The strikes included boycotts against these products, which carried the struggles of low-paid Chicano laborers into the kitchens of homes throughout America. Primary goals of Chicano agricultural and political movements, in addition to increasing wages and benefits for migrant workers, included increasing the rights of all workers and restoring pride in Mexican-American heritage.

African-Americans

As noted, African-Americans comprise the second largest racial minority in the United States. Because of such unique historical experiences as slavery, legal and social segregation, and economic discrimination, many African-Americans have lifestyles and value patterns that differ from those of the European-American majority. The relations between whites and blacks have been the source of a number of major social issues in the past several decades: busing, segregation, job discrimination, and interracial marriage, to mention a few.

Perhaps these issues can be understood more fully by examining five major social transitions that have affected or will affect African-Americans (Eshleman, 1991). The first transition was the movement from Africa to America, which is significant because of three factors: color, cultural discontinuity, and slavery. *Color* is the most obvious characteristic that sets whites and blacks apart. *Cultural discontinuity* was the abrupt shift from the culture learned and accepted in Africa to the cultural system of America. Rarely has any ethnic or racial group faced such a severe disruption of cultural patterns. *Slavery* was the unique circumstance that brought many Africans to America. Unlike almost all other groups, Africans did not come to this country by choice. Most were brought as slaves to work on southern U.S. plantations. Unlike many free African-Americans in the North, slaves in the South had few legal rights. Southern blacks were considered the property of their white owners, who had complete control over every aspect of their lives. Furthermore, there were no established groups of blacks to welcome and aid the newly-arrived Africans, as was the case with other immigrant groups.

A second major transition was from slavery to emancipation. In 1863, a proclamation issued by President Lincoln freed the slaves in the Union and in all territories still at war with the Union. Although the slaves were legally free, emancipation presented a major crisis for many African-Americans because most were faced with the difficult choice of either remaining on the plantations as tenants with low wages or none at all for their labor, or searching beyond the plantation for jobs, food, and housing. Many men left to search for jobs, so women became the major source of family stability. The shift to emancipation from slavery contributed to the third and fourth transitions.

The third transition was from rural to urban and from southern to northern communities. For many African-Americans, this shift had both good and bad effects. Cities were much more impersonal than the rural areas most blacks moved from, but they also provided more jobs, better schools, improved health facilities, a greater tolerance of racial minorities, and a greater chance for vertical social mobility. As of 2001, 23 million African-Americans lived in a metropolitan area and 13.5 million lived within a central city (*Current Population Reports*, Annual Demographic Survey, March 2002).

The job opportunities created by World War I and World War II were the major impetus for the exodus of African-Americans from the South to the North, a trend that continued through the 1960s. In 1900, 90 percent of all African-Americans lived in the South. By 1980, this figure had dropped to 53 percent, but increased to 55.3 percent by 2002 (*Current Population Reports*, Series P-20, No. 541, 2003). Today, there are more African-Americans in New York City and Chicago than in any other cities in the world, including African cities, and these cities have retained their top rankings for 30 years. Detroit and Philadelphia are the cities with the third and fourth largest African-American population.

The fourth transition was from negative to positive social status. The African-American middle class has been growing in recent years and resembles the European-American middle class in terms of education, job level, and other factors. A high proportion of African-Americans remain in the lower income brackets, however, because of the prejudice, segregation, and discriminatory practices endured by them throughout most of their time in this country; only in the past 30 years have they achieved a measure of equality. Previously, they were routinely denied equal protection under the law, equal access to schools and housing, and equal wages.

The final transition was from negative to positive self-image. A basic tenet of the symbolic interaction approach is that we develop ourselves, our identities, and our feelings of self-worth through our interactions with others. Throughout most of our history, African-Americans have been the last to be hired and the first to be fired. It would be understandable if black self-esteem were lower than white, but studies have shown that blacks' self-evaluations are equal to or higher than those of whites, and their rate of suicide is about one-half that of whites. Unfortunately, one major consequence of cuts in social programs that took place under the Reagan and George H. Bush administrations is that the cuts may have conveyed a message to all minority groups in the United States that they are of little importance, compared with the interests of the dominant white middle and upper classes.

Asian-Americans

The Asian-American community in the United States is a highly diverse group. The most numerous groups within it are those with Chinese, Filipino, and Japanese heritages. Also included in the Asian-American category are Asian Indians, Koreans, Hawaiians, and Guamanians. In the past decade, more immigrants have come from the Philippines, China, Vietnam, Korea, and India, than from any country outside of North and South America (see Table 9-2). Other groups represented in the large amounts of immigrants to America come from Africa, Iran, Cambodia, and the United Kingdom, with recent increases from Poland and Laos.

The Chinese were the first Asians to enter this country in large numbers. Unlike the Japanese, the Chinese resist assimilation and tend to uphold traditional values, such as filial duty, veneration of the aged and of deceased ancestors, and arranged marriages. Chinese-American families tend to be male-dominated, and an extended family pattern is the rule.

Today, most Chinese-Americans live in large urban enclaves in Hawaii, San Francisco, Los Angeles, and New York. A tourist visiting a Chinatown is likely to notice only the exotic sights, smells, and sounds; the problems prevalent in Chinatowns are less evident. There is often overcrowding, poverty, poor health, rundown housing, and inadequate care for the elderly. Not all Chinese live in Chinatowns, however. Those who have "made it" live in the suburbs.

Like the Chinese, most early Japanese immigrants were males imported for their labor. For both groups, employment was at physically difficult, low-prestige, and low-paying jobs. Both groups were victims of prejudice, discrimination, and racism. Most Americans did not or could not tell them apart, and both were denied entrance into the mainstream of American life.

Kitano (1991) notes, however, a number of important differences between the Chinese and Japanese that resulted in diverse outcomes. For example, the Japanese came from a nation that was moving toward modernization and an industrial economy, while China (during the time of major emigration) was an agricultural nation that was weak and growing weaker. This meant that the Japanese had the backing of a growing international power, while the Chinese were more dependent on local resources. Another difference focused on marriage and family life. The Japanese men sent for their wives and families almost immediately. In contrast, many Chinese men left their wives in China or remained as bachelors primarily as a result of the Chinese Exclusion Act of 1882, which closed the door to Chinese immigrants. One consequence of this was the birth and presence of children for the Japanese, which meant facing issues of acculturation and a permanent place in the larger community. This process was delayed among the Chinese because they had so few children. Japanese-Americans are today more fully integrated into American culture and have higher incomes than the Chinese or other Asian groups.

During World War II, European-Americans feared that there might be Japanese-Americans working against the American war effort, so the federal government moved most of them to what they called "relocation camps." Regardless of their political views or how long they had been in this country, families were forced to pack up whatever possessions they could and to move to camps in Utah, Arizona, California, Idaho, Wyoming, Colorado, and Arkansas, abandoning or selling at nominal prices their land and their homes, severely disrupting their lives. Many were incensed at the suggestion that they were not loyal Americans capable of making valuable contributions to the American war effort.

Many also noted that German-Americans were not similarly relocated. Also, some of the relocated families even had sons serving in the U.S. armed forces. Altogether, more than 110,000 people of Japanese ancestry, 70,000 of them U.S. citizens by birth, were moved. After the war, the Japanese were allowed to return to their homes, but even with the token monetary compensation recently awarded them, they have never been compensated adequately for the time, businesses, or property that they lost.

Native Americans

The Native American population is actually a varied group of tribes having different languages and cultures. At the time of the European invasion of America, there were perhaps 200 distinct groups that traditionally have been grouped into seven major geographical areas (Feagin and Feagin, 2002):

1. the Eastern tribes, who hunted, farmed, and fished
2. the Great Plains hunters and agriculturists
3. the fishing societies of the Pacific Northwest
4. the seed gatherers of California and neighboring areas
5. the Navaho shepherds and Pueblo farmers of the Arizona and New Mexico area
6. the desert societies (e.g., Hopi) of Southern Arizona and New Mexico
7. the Alaskan groups, including the Eskimos

Estimates of the number of Native Americans in the United States at the time of the European settlement range from 1 to 10 million. By 1800, the native population had declined to 600,000, and by 1850, it had dwindled to 250,000, as a result of starvation, deliberate massacre, and diseases such as smallpox, measles, and the common cold. Since the turn of the century, however, their numbers have increased dramatically. In the 1970s, the Native American population exceeded the 1 million mark for the first time since the period of European expansion, and by 2000, it reached approximately 2.4 million (including Eskimos and Aleuts), according to U.S. Bureau of the Census data, and by July 1, 2005 the population was estimated to be 4,453,660 (see Table 9-2).

By the 1960s, Native Americans were no longer regarded as nations to be dealt with through treaties. Most tribes were treated as wards of the U.S. government and lived isolated lives on reservations. Today, about half of all Native Americans live on or near reservations administered fully or partly by the Bureau of Indian Affairs (BIA). Many other Native Americans have moved to urban areas or have been relocated there by the BIA to help in their search for jobs and improved living conditions.

Native Americans are among the most deprived of American minority groups. Their unemployment rate is twice that of European-Americans (Feagin and Feagin, 2002). Most hold jobs at lower occupational levels and have incomes far below the median for American families. Housing is often severely crowded, and two-thirds of their houses in rural areas have no plumbing facilities. The life expectancy is about two-thirds the national average. It appears that teenage suicide, alcoholism, and adult diabetes are more common among reservation-dwelling Native Americans than among any other group in the country. Studies suggest that Native Americans have the lowest school enrollment rates of any racial or ethnic group in the United States (Feagin and Feagin, 2002). The norms, practices, and even materials within public schools often are at variance with those of Native American groups. In the Southwest, at least, many of these public schools are actually boarding schools, removing children entirely from their families and homes. In either type of school, children are often pressured not to speak their native language or to practice their native traditions.

One area in which Native Americans differ from the mainstream culture is in family structure. The

Native American equivalent to the family is the band, which includes a number of related families who live in close proximity. The band is composed of kinspeople who share property, jointly organize rituals and festivals, and provide mutual support and assistance. Bands are egalitarian and arrive at decisions collectively.

Since the 1960s, many Native American tribes united and formed organized collectives to demand a better life for their people. Several tribes have banded together to bargain more effectively with the federal government, and they have sometimes used militant tactics to get results. Nonetheless, Native Americans—the only group that did not immigrate to the United States—remain a subordinate group. Stereotyped as inferior, they have suffered exploitation and discrimination in all of our basic social institutions.

WASPs and White Ethnic Americans

Most of the white population in the United States today emigrated as a result of European expansionist policies of the past 350 years. Earlier immigrants were WASPs, who came mainly from northern and western European countries such as Britain, Ireland, Scotland, Sweden, Norway, Germany, France, and Switzerland. Although within the U.S. population they are a minority group in terms of numbers, they are not a minority in terms of political and economic power. Thus, they have pressured African-Americans, Hispanic-Americans, Native Americans, and other racial, ethnic, and other minority groups to assimilate or acculturate to the ideal of Anglo conformity, the ideal of Americanization, or the model of A + B + C = A.

Historically, WASP immigrants displayed what became known as the "Protestant ethic." This was an ethic of a strong belief in God, honesty, frugality, piety, abstinence, and hard work. As the majority group in terms of power, they were not subject to the prejudices and discrimination experienced by other, and later, immigrants. The pressure on these other groups to be assimilated and integrated into American society meant basically to think and behave like the WASP.

These more recent European immigrants are today's white ethnics. They came largely from southern and eastern European countries, such as Italy, Greece, Yugoslavia, Russia and other formerly Soviet republics, and Poland. Schaefer (2003) states that white ethnics separate themselves from WASPs and make it clear that they were not responsible for the oppression of Native Americans, African-Americans, and Mexican-Americans that took place before their ancestors had left Europe.

The majority of these immigrants, although they did not totally discard their roots, adopted American norms and values. Many dropped their European names in favor of names that sounded more "American," and most white ethnics have successfully assimilated. Michael Novak (1975), who is of Slovak ancestry, wrote the following about his experiences:

> Under challenge in grammar school concerning my nationality, I had been instructed by my father to announce proudly: "American." When my family moved from the Slovak ghetto of Johnston to the WASP suburb on the hill, my mother impressed upon us how well we must be dressed, and show good manners, and behave—people think of us as "different" and we mustn't give them any cause. (p. 593)

The emerging assertiveness of African-Americans and other nonwhites in the 1960s induced many white ethnics to reexamine their positions. Today, many American ethnic communities emphasize more than their folk culture, native food, dance, costume, and religious traditions in establishing their ethnic identities. They have sought a more structured means of expressing, preserving, and expanding their cultures, and many have formed fraternal organizations, museums, and native-language newspapers in an effort to preserve their heritage (Lopata, 1976).

Jewish-Americans

One of the predominant religious ethnic groups is the Jewish-American. America has the largest Jewish population in the world, its estimated 6.5 million exceeding the approximately 4 million Jews in Israel. They are heavily concentrated in the New York City metropolitan area and other urban areas.

Jewish-Americans are basically ethnic in nature, in that they share cultural traits to a greater extent than physical features or religious beliefs. As a minority group, they have a strong sense of group solidarity, tend to marry one another, and experience unequal treatment from non-Jews in the form of prejudice, discrimination, and segregation. Although Jews are generally perceived to be affiliated with one of the three Jewish religious groups—Orthodox, Reform, or Conservative—many, if not the majority of Jews, do not participate as adults in religious services or belong to a temple or synagogue; yet, they do not cease to think of themselves as Jews. The trend in the United States seems to be the substitution of cultural traditions for religion as the binding and solidifying force among Jewish-Americans.

Injustices to Jewish people have continued for centuries all over the world. The most tragic example of anti-Semitism occurred during World War II, when Adolf Hitler succeeded in having 6 million Jewish civilians exterminated—the terrifying event that has become known as the "Holocaust." Anti-Semitism in the United States never reached the extreme of Germany, but it did exist. As early as the 1870s, some colleges excluded Jewish-Americans. In the 1920s and 1930s, a myth of international Jewry emerged that suggested Jews were going to conquer all governments throughout the world by using the vehicle of communism, which was believed by anti-Semites to be a Jewish movement. At that time, Henry Ford, Catholic priest Charles E. Coughlin, and groups such as the Ku Klux Klan published, preached, and spoke about a Jewish conspiracy as if it were fact. Unlike in Germany or Italy, however, the United States government never publicly promoted anti-Semitism, and Jewish-Americans were more likely to face questions concerning how to assimilate than how to survive.

Concern about anti-Semitism seemed to decrease drastically following World War II through the 1960s, but in the 1970s and continuing today, anti-Semitic sentiments and behaviors appear to be on the increase. Whatever the cause, racial or ethnic hostility tends to unify the victims against attackers, and Jewish-Americans are no exception.

Thinking Sociologically

1. Using information found in this chapter (and other relevant chapters, if necessary), discuss why you think there is such a great deal of racial and ethnic inequality in American society.

2. Compare and contrast experiences of African-, Hispanic-, and Asian-Americans, as well as Native and white-ethnic Americans. How would you explain the differences?

THE FUTURE

What does the future hold for ethnic groups and integration in the United States? Most observers agree that serious problems remain to be overcome. Racism continues to powerfully influence individual lives and the interactions of different ethnic groups, and each step in the integrative process presents new problems. One recent twist, for example, involves Supreme Court shifts that are predicted to weaken affirmative action. Another involves the attempt to instill racial fears in the minds of voters, as was done successfully with Willie Horton, an African-American prisoner, in the first George H. Bush presidential campaign and again successfully by Jessie Helms in the 1990 U.S. Senate race in North Carolina, by showing an African-American, under an imaginary quota system, taking a job that perhaps could have been *yours.*

Despite the new problems that crop up and the frequent news stories of racial and racist incidents, there is reason for optimism. Just as few would argue that race relations are not everything they should be in this country, few would refute the fact that progress has been made during the past three decades. A number of barriers to equality have been eliminated. Civil rights activism during the 1960s and 1970s brought about reforms in laws and government policies. In 1963, affirmative action policies were established (again, note this chapter's policy debate), and President Kennedy issued an executive order calling for the disregard of race, creed, color, or national origin in hiring procedures, as well as in the treatment of employees. Affirmative action has since become a principal government instrument in eradicating institutional racism (Feagin and Feagin, 2002); its laws were later amended to include women, so that today, the laws also prohibit discrimination on the basis of sex.

The reduction of institutional racism has had both indirect and direct effects. According to the "contact hypothesis," interracial contact leads to reductions in prejudice if at least the following conditions exist: (1) The parties involved are of equal status, and (2) the situation in which the contact occurs is pleasant or harmonious. This hypothesis, reflecting an interactionist perspective, claims that these conditions cause people to become less prejudiced and to abandon previously held stereotypes. The importance of both equal status and pleasant contact cannot be overlooked. For example, a black employee being abused by a white employer (unequal status) or two people of equal status from different ethnic or minority groups competing for the same job opening (unpleasant contact) do little to promote interracial harmony and, in fact, may lead to greater hostility.

Changes in the way that minorities are portrayed in the mass media have also influenced levels of prejudice. During the 1950s and 1960s, when blacks and other minorities were portrayed at all, it was usually in stereotyped roles as servants or other low-status workers. Today, although it could be argued that portrayals of minorities in the media still tend to reflect stereotypes, the situation has improved considerably.

Another cause for optimism is the frequent finding of research studies that better-educated people are more likely to express liking for groups other than their own. It may be that the educated have a more cosmopolitan outlook and are more likely to question the accuracy of racial stereotypes. It is to be hoped that the trend in this country toward a more-educated population, along with the other advances that have been made, will contribute to a reduction in prejudice and the more complete realization of the American ideals of freedom and equal opportunity.

Lastly, one needs to look no further than the 2008 presidential election and the forum of candidates who seek this office. There has never been a time of such diversity within the political spectrum for President of the United States. This appears to be the first time that the predicted front runners in the election are from such diverse backgrounds. Hillary Clinton is a strong female candidate for the Democratic Party and along side of her is Barack Obama another strong contender who happens to be African-American. The field of candidates also includes Mitt Romney who is a very strong prospect in the Republican Party who happens to be Mormon. While it may be hard to say who gets elected for what reason, we should realize that these are truly positive steps in recognizing the changes that are currently under way towards making the United States of America a land where "All Men Are Created Equal."

SUMMARY

1. A *race* is a socially defined group or category of people distinguished by selected inherited physical characteristics. An *ethnic group* is a collection of individuals who feel they are one people because they have a common race, religion, national origin, and/or language.

2. Racial and ethnic groups are considered minorities when they are subordinate to another group in terms of power, social status, and privilege, and when their norms, values, and other characteristics differ from those that prevail in a society.

3. A *prejudice* is a negative attitude toward an entire category of people. A variety of theories have been offered to explain prejudice, including economic and psychological ones. Prejudice often involves acceptance of ethnic *stereotypes*, widely held beliefs about the character and behavior of all members of a group.

4. Whereas prejudice is an attitude, *discrimination* is overt behavior on the part of individuals or institutions. It is the categorical exclusion of all members of a group from particular rights, opportunities, or privileges.

5. *Racism* includes prejudices and discriminatory behaviors based on three distinguishing characteristics: (1) the belief that one's own race is superior to any other race, (2) an ideology, and (3) actions based on racist beliefs. Genocide and mass expulsion are consequences of extreme forms of racism.

6. *Ethnic stratification* allocates status on the basis of ethnic or racial membership and is most evident in the different lifestyles and opportunities of different groups. Three conditions necessary for ethnic stratification to occur include ethnocentrism, competition, and inequalities in power.

7. Inequality may lead to ethnic antagonism. A leading theory of ethnic antagonism, the split-labor-market theory, suggests that conflict results among business ownership and management, higher-priced labor, and lower-priced labor. The basic fear of those in higher-priced labor is of being displaced by the lower-priced labor, which business owners view as one way of reducing costs.

8. Racial and ethnic inequalities can be resolved through either integration or pluralism. Integration involves assimilation, an event that occurs when individuals and groups forsake their own cultural traditions to become part of a different group or tradition. The extent to which integration and assimilation has or has not occurred represents *social distance.*

9. Two models of assimilation include the *melting pot* and *Anglo conformity*. The former means that different groups contribute something of their own culture and absorb aspects of other cultures, with an outcome different from any former groups. The latter, equated with Americanization, means that the minority loses its identity to the dominant WASP culture.

10. *Segregation* is the physical and social separation of groups or categories of people. It may be de jure, segregation by law, or *de facto*, segregation in fact.

11. *Cultural pluralism* refers to a situation in which various racial, ethnic, or minority groups exist side by side but maintain their distinctive cultural patterns, subsystems, and institutions. A resurgence in this idea is evident in the ethnic

and other minority emphasis on their native language, customs, and traditions.

12. The major racial or ethnic groups in the United States are African-Americans, Hispanic-Americans, Asian-Americans, Native Americans, and European ethnics. The largest of these groups is the African-American. African-Americans, with the unique historical fact of slavery, have long been in the process of going through a number of social transitions. Today, most live in metropolitan areas with high population concentrations in northern cities.

13. Hispanic-Americans include those who classify themselves as Mexican, Puerto Rican, Cuban, Central and South American, and other Hispanics from Spain or other Spanish-speaking countries. Mexican-Americans, or Chicanos, are the largest Hispanic-American group and are characterized by strong family ties and large families. A number of social movements have emerged over the past few decades to improve the status and living conditions of this group.

14. Numerous other ethnic and other minority groups exist in the United States today. Asian-Americans include those with ties to China, Japan, the Philippines, India, Korea, Vietnam, and other Asian countries. Native Americans, the only nonimmigrant group, are often grouped into seven major geographical areas with distinct language patterns and tribal customs.

15. White Anglo-Saxon Protestant (WASP) groups came predominantly from northern and western European countries, while white ethnic groups came predominantly from southern and eastern European countries. Jewish-Americans are basically ethnic in nature, in that they share cultural traits to a greater extent than physical features or religious beliefs.

16. Although relations among ethnic groups are far from perfect in this country, some progress has been made during the past few decades. Government regulations have made discriminatory action illegal, and numerous affirmative action programs have been instituted in political, educational, and economic agencies throughout the country. Changes in the portrayal of minorities in the media and the trend toward a better-educated population may lead to further progress in this area.

KEY TERMS

amalgamation The process by which different racial or ethnic groups form a new group through interbreeding or intermarriage.

Anglo conformity A form of assimilation in which the minority loses its identity completely and adopts the norms and practices of the dominant WASP culture.

assimilation The process through which individuals and groups forsake their own cultural tradition to become part of a different group and tradition.

authoritarian personality theory The view that people with an authoritarian type of personality are more likely to be prejudiced than those who have other personality types.

cultural pluralism The situation in which the various ethnic groups in a society maintain their distinctive cultural patterns, subsystems, and institutions.

de facto segregation School assignment based on residence boundaries in which blacks and whites live in separate neighborhoods.

de jure segregation The legal assignment of children to schools solely because of race.

discrimination Overt unequal and unfair treatment of people on the basis of their membership in a particular group.

displacement A process occurring in split labor markets in which higher-paid workers are replaced with cheaper labor.

ethnic antagonism Mutual opposition, conflict, or hostility among different ethnic groups.

ethnic group A group set apart from others because of its national origin or distinctive cultural patterns, such as religion, language, or region of the country.

exclusion Attempts to keep cheaper labor from taking jobs from groups that receive higher pay.

frustration-aggression theory The theory that prejudice results when personal frustrations are displaced to a socially approved racial or ethnic target.

genocide The deliberate destruction of an entire racial or ethnic group.

institutional discrimination The continuing exclusion or oppression of a group as a result of criteria established by an institution.

institutional racism Racism that is embodied in the folkways, mores, or legal structures of a social institution.

institutionalism of inequality The collection of laws, customs, and social practices that combine to create and sustain the unequal distribution of rewards based on class, minority status, and gender

integration The situation that exists when ethnicity becomes insignificant and everyone can freely and fully participate in the social, economic, and political mainstream.

mass expulsion Expelling racial or ethnic groups from their homeland.

melting pot A form of assimilation in which each group contributes aspects of its own culture and absorbs aspects of other cultures, such that the whole is a combination of all the groups.

minority group A group subordinate to the dominant group in terms of the distribution of social power; such groups are defined by some physical or cultural characteristic and are usually but not always smaller than the dominant group.

prejudice A preconceived attitude or judgment, either good or bad, about another group; prejudices usually involve negative stereotypes.

projection A psychological explanation of prejudice that suggests that people transfer responsibility for their own failures to a vulnerable group, usually a racial or ethnic group.

racial group A socially defined group distinguished by selected inherited physical characteristics.

racism Discrimination based on racial characteristics.

radicalism Labor groups joining together in a coalition against the capitalist class.

scapegoating A psychological explanation of prejudice that involves blaming another person or group for one's own problems.

segregation The separation of a group from the main body; it usually involves separating a minority group from the dominant group.

social distance The degree of intimacy and equality between groups of people.

stereotypes Widely held and oversimplified beliefs about the character and behavior of all members of a group that seldom correspond to the facts.

structural assimilation One aspect of assimilation in which patterns of intimate contact between the guest and host groups are developed in the clubs, organizations, and institutions of the host society.

stratification The structured ranking of entire groups of people that perpetuates unequal rewards and power in a society.

DISCUSSION QUESTIONS

1. Discuss the differences between the sociological concepts of racial, ethnic, and minority groups.
2. Do you feel that "race" is a legitimate and useful biological or sociological concept? Why or why not?
3. Select a racial, ethnic, or minority group other than your own, and compare it with your own.
4. Identify a prejudice that you hold, and use the theories of prejudice to discuss why you might have this prejudice.
5. Do you think that anyone has ever held a prejudice or discriminated against you? Why do you think so? Was this prejudice accurate?
6. What is the difference between de jure and de facto segregation? Can you identify either in your local community or state?
7. Differentiate between individual and institutional racism. Give specific examples.
8. Discuss the melting-pot, Anglo conformity, and pluralism models described in the chapter. Show how your community or city would be different, depending on which model was most prevalent.
9. What is the significance of any of the social transitions that have occurred or are occurring for African-Americans? For example, is the demographic shift from the rural South to the urban North significant? How?
10. Based on the increases in the African-American, Hispanic-American, and Asian-American population in the United States, social demographers suggest that within the next quarter century, the number of these groups will surpass the number of white-ethnic and WASP Americans. Will white Americans then be the minority?

Gender Differentiation

Women in the Workplace

In 1983, women who had full-time occupations out of the home had median weekly earnings of $252, compared to $379 for men. In 2001, median earnings for female, full-time workers were $511, just 76 percent of the $672 median weekly earners for men. In 2005, women were earning $585 or 81 percent of the $722 median income of their male counterparts. In addition:

Between 1979 and 2005, earnings for white women rose by 30 percent; they rose 18 percent for black women, and 9 percent for Hispanic women.

In 1979, there was a 30 percent increase in male college graduates' median income, compared to a 20 percent increase for female college graduates. By 2005, the median weekly earnings still varied significantly by levels of education. Women with less than a high school diploma earned $341 per week compared to $883 for those with a college degree. Men earned $435 with less than a high school diploma compared to $1,167 for college graduates (U.S. Department of Labor and Statistics, September 2006, Report #995).

In 1983, 41 percent of professional and middle management jobs were held by women. In 2001, 49.5 percent of these positions were occupied by women (U.S. Department of Labor Statistics, *Highlights of Women's Earnings in 2001*, Report 960, May 2002).

In spite of the fact that the majority of women have entered the work force and that nearly 50 percent of the work force consists of women, women's earning power has not increased commensurately, and still lags noticeably behind men's. In the mid-1970s, women earned 61 cents for every dollar men earned. In 2001, it was 76 cents—an increase of only 15 cents. In 2005, women who were paid an hourly rate had a median hourly earnings of $10.31 compared to the median hourly earnings of men at $12.16. One reason for this is that women in the workplace continue to be constrained by powerful gender-role traditions that make some employment opportunities more accessible to men. Women are still underrepresented and only on the fringe of equality in many of the higher-salaried occupations and professions that traditionally have been dominated by males. These traditions are most clearly evident at the highest levels of employment. Women still hold a very small amount of most senior management jobs. According to Jaclyn Fierman (1990), "The cool reception women once got at the door has followed them up the organizational hierarchy. For all but an exceptional few, the corner office still looks as remote as it did to Rosie the Riveter."

It appears that the final frontier for gender equality in the labor force—and perhaps the most formidable one—is senior management. The "glass ceiling"—a barrier that enables women to glimpse the upper management positions, but not attain them—is still very much a reality, and, according to many researchers on this subject, it is likely to remain so until well into the twenty-first century. Most research on the topic demonstrates that the glass ceiling bars women from the top not because they lack the technical skills to make it to the top, but because of their gender, women are denied positions largely as a result of male traditions, prejudices, stereotypes, and preconceptions of women. In 2006, just 6 percent of women earned $1,500 or more per week compared to 14 percent of men.

Nevertheless, most researchers agree that the glass ceiling for women will disappear some day. However, equality in the workplace, as in almost every area of social life, will not occur automatically; rather, it must be achieved. Tradition is a powerful force that often acts to keep things the way they are, enhancing the positions of those who already have it on their side. Until now, the labor force in America has been guided strictly by male traditions that are rooted in hierarchical organizations, rituals of dominance and masculine competition, and status differentiation (Jardim and Hennig, 1990). For women to make it through a barrier that men have shaped and earnestly control, both men and women will have to reach greater understanding about the complex and subtle differences between the genders. The material in this chapter explores some of these differences.

SEX AND GENDER DIFFERENTIATION

Sex refers to biological characteristics—the genetic, hormonal, and anatomical differences between males and females. **Gender**, on the other hand, is a social status. It refers to social differences between the sexes, specifically to the cultural concepts of masculinity and femininity. Our culture traditionally defines masculinity to mean strong, competent, rational, unemotional, and competitive. It defines femininity to mean nurturant, caring, and able to deal with the emotional side of relationships.

Gender roles refer to the behaviors that are expected of men and women. For example, men are supposed to work hard to get ahead, run the nation's industries, make tough political and economic decisions, and—of course—earn a living for their families. Women are expected to cook, clean, and care for their families, as well as earn additional income if their families require it. Gender roles, in other words, are behaviors assigned on the basis of the assumed characteristics of masculinity and femininity. They are roles required to fill the needs of the society.

Very often, these two concepts—gender and sex—are linked together without good reason. Our biology, or our sex, is often seen as the cause of our gender roles, even when our biology has little or no importance in the performance of these roles. In order to understand the difference between biological sex and socially defined gender roles, we review some of the basic biological differences between men and women.

Biological Bases of Gender Differentiation

Males and females differ from the moment of conception, when sex is determined. The ovum of the mother always carries an X chromosome, one of which is needed to bear the genetic material to develop either a male or a female. The father's sperm may carry either an X or a Y chromosome. If the sperm carries a second X chromosome, the fetus will develop into a female. If the sperm carries a Y chromosome, on the other hand, testes develop that secrete a hormone that causes the embryo to develop as a male. Between birth and puberty, the hormones produced by males and females are the same, so other than the development of either male or female sex organs, these chromosome differences cause very few physical differences between boys and girls.

Physiologists and psychologists have been more interested in behavioral differences between males and females. They ask whether the sex hormones in the fetus affect the central nervous system and therefore influence how males and females behave. In order to find answers to this question, they study infants and children.

The research literature is extensive on this point, but it gives no clear indication that boys and girls are born with a predisposition toward different behaviors. In a recent cross-cultural study, researchers observed aggression in 192 children between the ages of 3 and 9 years. They observed children in naturalistic settings in Belize, Kenya, Nepal, and American Samoa. Results showed that boys exhibited aggression in approximately 10% of their social behaviors, girls in 6%, and in all four cultures the aggression of boys was more frequent than that of girls (Munroe, et al., 2000). These differences could be explained as differences in socialization.

Social Bases of Gender Differentiation

Most people in nurturing roles—such as teachers, counselors, and parents—are unaware that they have a tendency to treat males and females in gender-biased ways in nurturing, counseling, and educational situations (Sadker and Sadker, 1985, 1986). It is a profoundly important fact for people in these roles to understand that a person's gender characteristics may be determined as much by social conditions as by heredity. The concept of the self-fulfilling prophecy comes into play here. If children are treated as if they have (or do not have) particular characteristics, they may well develop (or fail to develop) those traits. Teachers play a significant role in shaping the potential of males and females treating students—from kindergarten to graduate school—in terms of stereotypical gender traits. This occurs both in and out of the classroom.

If parents assume, for example, that females are by nature non-aggressive, they might directly discourage—or indirectly discourage by lack of attention or praise—their daughter from engaging in rough-and-tumble activities or contact games. As a result, the girl may not develop aggressive or competitive qualities—not because of her genetic makeup, but because she was never encouraged to develop them.

On the other hand, if parents assume that their son, because he is male, necessarily has good physical dexterity or analytical ability, they might encourage him to play with puzzles and to figure them out on his own. As a result, he may become adept at tasks that require physical coordination and analytical ability. The point is that children often develop the traits that we assume that they have by nature, as a result of the activities we provide for them.

One study, for example, found that in classrooms, boys were more likely than girls to get individual instruction on a task when they asked for it, and they got more tangible and verbal rewards for academic work (Serbin and O'Leary, 1975). Girls were responded to less than the boys—usually only when they were physically close to the teacher—and were rarely encouraged to work on their own. Boys received more attention whether they were close to the teacher or not, and they were encouraged to do independent work.

By keeping in mind that we often unintentionally send hidden messages to males and females regarding their capabilities, teachers, counselors, and parents might develop more effective ways to give both genders an equal opportunity to excel in all academic areas and to develop ways to advise students (in terms of careers, choice of major, and other areas related to academics) based on their qualities and characteristics as individuals, and not on whether they are male or female.

Adult Sex Differentiation

When children reach adolescence, they begin to produce sex hormones again, and the secondary sex characteristics develop—facial hair on men and breasts on women, for example. Most of these secondary sex characteristics are of little importance in behavior. Men do develop more muscular builds than women, especially in the upper part of their body. As a result, men have more muscle strength, greater spurts of energy, and are able to lift heavier objects. Women have a larger proportion of fat on their bodies, particularly through the breast and hip areas. This enables them to have more endurance than men over long periods of time. Women also have greater finger dexterity and should tend to be better able to do fine work with their hands, such as surgery, needlework, or dentistry.

However, socialization to gender roles rather than physical differences shape adult behavior. In our society, for example, even though women have greater finger dexterity, most dentists and surgeons are men. Women's finger dexterity is valued primarily in low-paying factory work, where sewing or electronics work is assigned to women. Cross-cultural studies show that the variety of gender roles men and women play in societies depend on the norms of the society and not on any physical characteristics.

Thinking Sociologically

Do you think any gender roles might really be sex roles—in other words, based on biological characteristics rather than social experiences? Explain why or why not.

CROSS-CULTURAL GENDER DIFFERENTIATION

In some cultures, men and women occupy roles in ways very unlike those typically found in the United States. In the Chambri (formerly called "Tchambuli") society of New Guinea, for example, the women are the workers. They do the fishing, weaving, planting, harvesting, and cooking, all the while they are carrying and caring for their children. They are generally confident, laughing, brisk, good-natured, and efficient. They have a jolly comradeship that involves much rough joking. The men, on the other hand, are more involved in producing arts and crafts and in planning ceremonies. They tend to be more emotional than the women and also more responsive to the needs of others. The women typically have an attitude of kindly toleration toward the men, enjoying the men's games and parties but remaining rather remote emotionally (Mead, 1935).

In many African societies, the women have traditionally owned much of the land. Europeans have often tried to impose their own system of ownership on these tribes, sometimes with dire consequences. When Europeans introduced modern farming methods to the Ibo tribe of Nigeria, they took the land from the women and gave it to the men. The men raised cash crops, which they sold, and the women were left without their traditional means of subsistence. In 1923, the Ibo women rioted; 10,000 women looted shops and released prisoners from jail. In two days of intense rioting, 50 people were killed and another 50 were injured. Later, the women became more organized and continued their revolt against land reforms and taxation with more riots, strikes, cursing, and ridicule (Leavitt, 1971).

THEORIES OF GENDER DIFFERENTIATION

The gender-role socialization of members of a society seems to differ with the type of society. In hunting-and-gathering societies, in which survival depends on the constant search for food, both males and females must be responsible for finding food, and therefore both are socialized to be assertive and independent. As societies grow wealthier and more complex, and as the division of labor increases and hunting is no longer necessary to provide food for people, gender-role differentiation increases. If both men and women are capable of meeting the demands of almost all positions or statuses without being constrained by biological factors, why does role differentiation increase? Why do women have lower status in modern society than men? Sociologists have explored these questions from several theoretical perspectives, including structural functionalism and conflict theory.

Structural Functional Theory

As mentioned previously, structural functionalists believe that society consists of interrelated parts, each of which performs functions in maintaining the whole system. They assume, accordingly, that women have traditionally made important contributions to society. They raised children, maintained the home, and provided food, clean clothing, and other necessities of daily living. They played an expressive role, nurturing and providing emotional support for husbands and children returning home from work or school. The woman in the family created the atmosphere of close interpersonal relationships necessary to a worthwhile human existence, relationships lacking in the competitive workplace (Parsons and Bales,

1955). Although these skills are vital to society, they do not command a salary outside of the marketplace. According to this perspective, the traditional function of the male was to play the instrumental role of protecting and providing for his wife and children. He was the head of the household, controlling where the family lived, how money was spent, and making other decisions important to the survival of the family. He also made the political and economic decisions in the community by serving in powerful decision-making positions.

Structural functionalists might argue that many traditional family functions have moved from the family to other social institutions. Most families no longer find support through work at home. Instead, work is more likely to take place in the factory or office. Recreation has also moved away from the family and is sponsored by Little Leagues, tennis clubs, and other organizations at recreation centers. Structural functional theorists believe that because of changing socialization practices and changing beliefs about work, play, and other functions of the family, the complementary roles of husbands and wives are changing to parallel roles, where roles of husbands and wives are similar. The change has been gradual, but both husbands and wives are now likely to work outside the home, and both are increasingly sharing household duties. Most functionalists believe that the family will benefit as equality increases between men and women.

Conflict Theory

A conflict theory of gender differentiation focuses on the power and authority discrepancies between men and women. The conflict perspective views women's relative social status, domestic violence, rape, and disparities in wages as resulting from degradation and exploitation by men. Very early in the development of horticultural societies, military force was used to protect land and other valuable private property and also to capture women from other tribes. Women were prized possessions who could work for their captors to increase wealth, provide children who would grow into future workers, and increase the prestige of the men who owned them. It was not just as future workers that children were important. Men needed children to look after the property when they grew old and to inherit it when they died. To know who his children were, a man needed to isolate his women from other men. Thus, women became the protected property of men, so that men could accumulate wealth and have children to inherit it. According to this perspective, from earliest times, women were exploited by men for the work they did and for the children they bore and reared.

The process of industrialization removed work from the family, but, conflict theorists argue, men were not willing to lose their control over the labor of women. They either tried to keep women out of the work force entirely or used them as a surplus labor force, moving them in and out of the lowest-paying jobs as the economy required. They passed laws regulating the kind of work that women could do and the hours they could work. They also passed laws regulating women's rights to income, property ownership, and birth control, and they made women exclusively responsible for domestic tasks. Men forbade women from joining unions and from entering professions. Legally and by tradition, they prevented women from gaining high positions in the work force. Men increased their position of power and dominance and sustained the dependence of women on them. Less powerful men were also hurt by the practice of keeping women in positions with low pay. The existence of a labor force of poorly paid women meant that men who asked for higher wages could easily be replaced by lower-paid women.

As can be seen, these two theories of gender differentiation lead sociologists to diverse approaches in the study and understanding of the behavior and roles of men and women. According to a structural functional perspective, as industrial society develops, women should move into the work force and attain equality with men. According to a conflict perspective, as industrial society creates more wealth and power for men, men will use their wealth and power to improve their own position, and women will lag farther and farther behind. We now turn our attention to gender differentiation in the workplace and more specifically to women in the workplace.

GENDER DIFFERENTIATION AND THE WORKPLACE

Women in the Workplace

The status of women in the workplace is often treated as if it were a new issue, but women have always played an important economic role in society, moving in and out of the work force as the economy required. Throughout much of history, women produced much of what was needed in the home and also made items for sale in the marketplace. With the growth of large cities during the Middle Ages, new options became available to them. They became traders and innkeepers and occasionally ran breweries and blacksmith shops. They often joined guilds (Bernard, 1981), which were a type of medieval trade union. Those who did not wish to marry could become **Beguines**, members of urban communes of seven or eight women who pursued such occupations as sewing, baking, spinning, and weaving.

Women from the upper class could join convents and become nuns. At that time, some convents had great wealth and beautiful furnishings, and nuns wore beautiful embroidered robes. Some convents also had great scholarly reputations and were political forces to be reckoned with.

When the plagues swept Europe and devastated the population, the powerful Catholic Church and the states of that time wanted women to stay home and have babies to increase the population. The states passed laws banning the Beguine communes, and the Church closed most of the nunneries. In those nunneries that remained open, the nuns were required to wear black habits and to serve the poor. Otherwise, family life was the only secure option for women, and their income was from the goods, particularly textiles, that they could produce in the home.

The textile and other goods traditionally produced by women in the home were the first to be manufactured in factories at the beginning of the Industrial Revolution. Many women who were poor, young, and single went to work in the mills under deplorable working conditions, for very little pay. Married women could seldom leave the home for the 12-hour workdays required in the mills and still maintain their homes, so they lost their ability to earn income.

With increased population growth and industrialization, good farmland became increasingly scarce, so men also became available for factory work. Protective labor laws were passed that limited both the number of hours that women and children could work and the types of work they could do. By the nineteenth century, then, women had lost the few work options that had existed for them in earlier centuries. The only source of economic well-being was marriage.

In the United States at the beginning of the twentieth century, many upper-class women received an education, and some worked in the professions. Poor women who worked were usually employed as servants. The vast majority of women, however, were married and worked in the home to meet the needs of their families. In fact, during the Great Depression in the 1930s, married women who took jobs were considered selfish and unpatriotic. Jobs were scarce, the unemployment rate rose to 25 percent, and if a woman worked, she was seen as taking a job away from a man who needed it to support his family.

In 1941, the country went to war. Men were sent overseas, and women were told that it was now their patriotic duty to help out in the war effort by going to work. Women held every conceivable job, and for many of them, it was their first opportunity to earn a good salary. They not only worked at white-collar jobs, but they also did factory work, building the planes and ships needed for war. In fact, so many women went to work in defense plants that they were often nicknamed "Rosie the Riveter."

After the war was over, men returned to their jobs, and many women were seen as dispensable and were fired. Because many of these women had supported themselves and families on their salaries, it was a hardship to give up work. However, as the economy shifted from the needs of wartime to peace, it had become their patriotic duty to go home and have babies. The country had experienced very low birth rates throughout the depression and World War II, and it needed to build its population of future workers. Thus began the "baby boom," which continued until 1960, when the birth rate began to decline.

In the 1960s, there was a labor shortage because of the low birth rates during the depression and World War II. Unemployment was low, and salaries were high. Women were once again welcomed into the labor force, at least to fill low-paying jobs. From that time to the present, wages did not keep up with inflation, and more and more women were required to work to help pay family expenses. As of 1988, 57.5 percent of women were in the work force, and they composed 45 percent of workers.

Income

The median income for women working full-time year round in 2005 was $30,420 compared to men's median of $37,544. In 1960, women earned 61 percent of what men made, but during the 1960s and 1970s, the gap between men and women widened as more women moved into the work force and took low-paying jobs. By the late 1970s, women made only 59 percent of what men made. This wage differential is now narrowing, largely because the mean income of men is decreasing. There are several reasons for the continuing gap in earnings:

1. More women than men are entering the work force in low-paying occupations, such as clerical, service, or blue-collar work. Often, these jobs have no career lines, so women cannot advance to higher positions.
2. Women are sometimes paid less than men, even though they hold equivalent jobs.
3. People with low salaries receive smaller raises. A 10 percent raise on $20,000 is smaller than a 10 percent raise on $30,000, with the result that income differentials increase even as percentage increases remain equal.

Women have been steadily returning to work for three decades. Surely, many women have gained considerable education and work experience during this time, and the gap in earnings between men and women should be closing more rapidly than it is. The question, then, is this: Why do women remain in low-paying occupations?

The Split Labor Market

One reason that women are not advancing is the split labor market. In a split labor market there are two distinct and unequal groups of workers (Bonacich, 1972). The **primary labor market** is reserved for elites, people who will advance to high-level positions. Primary-labor-market jobs offer job security, on-the-job training, high wages, and frequent promotions. Corporate managers, professionals, and engineers belong to this labor market.

In the **secondary labor market**, jobs pay poorly, and there is little job security. There are many layoffs but few promotions or salary increases. Most women work in the secondary labor force in secretarial, typing, and clerical jobs, or as sales clerks or waitresses, or in manufacturing jobs. This inequality caused by the split labor market accounts for much of the inequality in earnings between women and men (Bose and Rossi, 1983; Marshall and Paulin, 1985).

The secondary labor market is growing in size, both in the United States and throughout the world. During the decade of the 1980s, unions worldwide lost power. As a result, there has been increasing pressure to weaken job security and to reduce or eliminate minimum-wage regulations. It is now easier for employers to dismiss midlevel managers or highly skilled manufacturing workers. The employer then can automate the job with robotic or other machinery or can divide it into simple, repetitive tasks, which can be done by temporary workers at very low wages. Such workers do not develop complex skills; they have no route into the primary labor force and they are not promoted; they do not receive any company benefits such as child care, health insurance, or pensions, and often are not eligible for social security.

According to the United Nations (1996), women account for 70 percent of the world's poor. Many of the jobs in the secondary labor force are being moved from industrialized countries to Third World countries, where labor is even cheaper. There, many rural women are being recruited to leave their homes and take jobs in the new urban industries. Leaving home to go to work is a greater sacrifice in Asian countries than it is in Western countries because in Asia, the women are traditionally very sheltered. Often, once they leave home, they are no longer respectable, they are not welcome to return home, and they also lose their opportunity to marry. In some countries, the women compose almost half the work force. Globally, women earn on average about three-fourths what men earn for the same work (U.N. Fourth World Conference on Women, 1995).

Comparable Worth

Some jobs are low paying simply because they are held by women, not because the job does not require considerable skill. For example, some office work requires many skills but is often paid less than maintenance work, a position traditionally held by men. Many women argue that pay scales should be based on **comparable worth**—work of equal value, requiring the same level of skills—should earn equal pay, even when the work is not identical. If clerical work, for example, is as necessary to an organization and requires the same level of skills as maintenance work, workers in these two occupations should receive equal pay. If the sale of women's clothing is of equal value and requires the same skills as the sale of men's clothing, it is argued that these two occupations should receive equal pay. Currently, they do not.

The idea of comparable worth has met with a great deal of resistance because companies resist increasing salaries, and women have little bargaining power (O'Donnell, 1984). Legally, it is discriminatory to pay women less for their low-status jobs if the low status is conferred solely because of the gender of the worker. It is not considered discriminatory to pay a worker less if the job has low prestige.

Upward Mobility

As was noted in the beginning of this chapter, women who reach management-level positions seem to confront a glass ceiling. Only 5 percent of all senior executives in Fortune 500 companies are women (U.S. Department of Labor). At the level of vice president or above in major companies, there has been no significant increase in the number of women in these positions during recent years.

Research has shown that in order to increase earnings and to get promoted into executive positions, a person needs experience in two areas: authority and autonomy (Spaeth, 1985). **Authority** consists of supervisory experience and experience in a decision-making position. Autonomy on the job means having the ability to decide how work will be done. People who decide for themselves how they will do a job are more committed to their work than people who are told what to do (Spaeth, 1985).

Women have less authority and less autonomy in their work than do men (Jaffee, 1989). The major reason is that most women work in female-dominated jobs—they are nurses, teachers, and bank tellers—and these jobs do not generally offer either authority or autonomy. However, discrimination also plays a role in why women do not achieve these more powerful positions. When men enter a female-dominated work field, they often quickly move into one of the few jobs that have authority and autonomy. For example, the majority of elementary school teachers are women, but most school superintendents are male.

When women work in occupations in which the work force is mixed—male and female—women are still less likely than men to get the jobs with authority and autonomy. This lack of opportunity has been shown to occur even when education and work experience are equal and regardless of whether the woman has family responsibilities (Jaffee, 1989).

Thinking Sociologically

1. How could the material in this chapter be used to develop a strategy for parents, teachers, employers, and politicians that would help lead to greater equality for women and men in the workplace?
2. Use material (including theories, concepts, and facts) in this chapter to discuss why the glass ceiling exists for women.

Women's Work in the Family

It is generally recognized that women carry the greatest burden in the family, doing the unpaid but necessary labor of housework and child care (Berk, 1985). As women enter the work force, they continue to carry this family burden. Working women spend less time on housework than women who do not work, but working women spend more time on housework than their husbands, even when the wife works 40 hours a week and the husband is unemployed (Hochschild, 2003). When household chores increase, such as when a child is ill, women are more likely than men to increase their hours of work at home. (One study in 2007 completed by workers and women's organizations determined that if "stay at home mothers" were actually paid for their services, they would earn approximately $114,000 per year).

Women who would like more equality in their marriages have been waiting for the time when it would be acceptable for men to share more of the workload. She does most of the unpleasant chores, he makes decisions. When he does household chores, *he is helping her*. The day-to-day activities in the household are rituals that reinforce the ideas that women are different and are subservient to men. Seeing women's and men's work as "different" is one way structural functionalists describe this phenomenon. Viewing disparate roles where women are subservient to men makes is best explained from the conflict perspective.

When women try to manage work, housework, and children, their health suffers under the strain (Arber, Nigel, and Dale, 1985). As a group, they are less healthy than working childless women and than women over 40. Also, if they are dominated by their husbands, doing more than their share of work but having less than a fair share in decision-making processes, they are likely to suffer from depression (Davies and Doyle, 2002). Just as women face a glass ceiling in the workplace, they also face one at home.

THE WOMEN'S MOVEMENT

Efforts by women to gain political and economic power—known collectively as the **women's movement**—have taken place for more than a century in both Europe and the United States. However, these movements have had different emphases on either side of the Atlantic.

The Women's Movement in the United States

The women's movement in the United States, instead of seeking special privileges for women, has emphasized equal rights. In an attempt to unite all women behind the cause of equality, the movement has remained separate from any particular political party or union, for fear that such an alignment would divide women.

In fact, however, the cause of equality has divided women. The movement wants equality for women in the workplace and thereby plays down the importance of special treatment for women as homemakers. This has served to alienate women who give primary importance to their roles as homemakers and who want special support and protection in their homemaking roles. In general, the level of benefits that working mothers in this country can expect falls far below the norm for their European counterparts, and they continue to have difficulty being recognized as fully committed workers.

The women's movement has succeeded in gaining many rights for women. Through the women's suffrage movement, women first gained the right to vote in the 1920s, and they can now hold many jobs from which they previously were barred. Today, there are female bartenders, construction workers, and bus drivers, to mention just a few. Laws have been passed guaranteeing them equal pay for equal work, and they have gained the right to practice birth control and to obtain abortions. Except for the right to vote, however, these rights are not guaranteed under the U.S. Constitution, and the laws that grant these rights could be changed at any time by Congress (or their constitutional legitimacy could be changed through new U.S. Supreme Court rulings).

The women's movement supported the **Equal Rights Amendment (ERA)**, a proposed amendment that would have guaranteed women equal rights under the Constitution. The ERA states simply, "Equality of rights under the law shall not be denied or abridged by the United States or any state on account of sex." The amendment was approved by Congress in 1972, and although 60 percent of Americans support the ERA (Lansing, 1986), it was not ratified by the required number of states to become a part of the U.S. Constitution. The women's movement thus failed to gain guaranteed equal rights.

This was a major disappointment to the American women's movement. Their attempts to gain equal rights in the workplace and in the law met with only partial success, but American women gained even less as homemakers and mothers. Without adequate pay, American women who are widowed, divorced, or never married often find themselves and their children living in poverty. The benefits that European women received as a result of their movement assures them that they and their children are not as likely to be poor as they would be if they lived in the United States.

The Women's Movement in Europe

In Europe, the women's movement focused on special privileges for women (Hewlett, 1986). Those involved in the movement believe that women have special problems because they assume most of the responsibility for child rearing and therefore need better pay when they work, time off for childbearing, and help from the community in providing child rearing. The movement in European countries has aligned itself with political parties and labor unions who support the programs women need, and this political support has been successful in gaining benefits. Swedish women, for example, have recently been earning more than 80 percent of what men earn (Hewlett, 1986). When a child is born in Sweden, either parent may take leave for one year and still receive 90 percent of salary for 38 weeks of that year. In addition, state-supported child care, noted for its excellence, is usually available for children when the parent returns to work. In Austria, women in manufacturing earn 82 percent of what men earn, and women receive 100 percent of their salaries while on leave for the birth of a child, although the leave granted is shorter than it is in Sweden. Although Sweden has the best benefits for women, almost all European nations pay women a higher proportion of men's earnings than women earn in the United States. In addition, these countries offer both child care and paid leaves-of-absence for parenting.

THE CONSEQUENCES OF INEQUALITY

The most obvious result of gender inequality in the United States is the high level of poverty among women. However, the stratification system results in other notable gender differences as well. In this section, we discuss the problems of poverty, women's self-esteem, medical care, sexual harassment in the workplace, family violence, and rape.

Gender and Poverty

Given the many problems women face in the workplace, it is not surprising that 32.6 percent of those who are heads of families with no husband present have incomes below the poverty line (U.S. Census, 2000). (Women are said to be *heads of families* if they have children to support.) Persons in female-householder families are the most likely demographic group to be chronically poor. U.S. Census and Labor Statistics show a steady trend of poverty, which primarily affects women and children in their care. This increase in the number of women who head families suffering in poverty continues and has been called the **feminization of poverty**. Black and Hispanic women have a much greater likelihood of living in poverty than white women.

In the older population, the increase in poor women is partly due to their longevity because men die at an earlier age than do women (McLanahan et al., 1989). Also, the death of a man can throw his widow into poverty by reducing the amounts of Social Security and pension she receives and also by reducing any savings she might have had, which were used to pay for medical and nursing care prior to his death.

Those most severely affected by poverty are women who are responsible for both the care and the financial support of children, as well as the children in their care. Children either reduce the hours that a mother can work or increase her child-care costs. Available new jobs tend to be low-paying and frequently do not provide the basics for mother and children. Also, since the mid-1970s, public benefits in the form of welfare to single mothers with children have declined in terms of the actual dollar amounts paid (McLanahan et al., 1989); when inflationary factors are also considered, it is clear that single mothers and their children are far poorer now than they were two decades ago. A dramatic cause of the increase of the feminization of poverty relates to single-parent families, often resulting from no-fault divorce and the rising divorce rate.

No-fault divorce laws, first passed in California in 1970 and since adopted in some form by most states, do not require that anyone be blamed for the breakdown of the marriage (Weitzman, 1985) and do not allow punitive payments to be paid by one spouse to the other. This is in sharp contrast to traditional divorce laws, in which one spouse, usually the husband, was considered to be at fault. As punishment, he was sometimes required to pay alimony to his wife and sometimes the family home was awarded to her. This could support her for the rest of her life. Under no-fault divorce, both husband and wife are expected to assume equal responsibility for themselves and for their children after the divorce. Alimony, if awarded, is usually awarded as a temporary measure to give the wife time to find a job and adjust to a new life. The family home is usually ordered to be sold so that the proceeds can be divided equally. The child-support payments required of the husband are usually low because the courts assume that the wife will help to support the children. Little consideration is given to the fact that she may not be able to earn much money.

As a result of the no-fault divorce laws, a man who divorces his wife can expect a 42 percent rise in his standard of living (Weitzman, 1985). He is allowed to keep half of the family assets and most of his income. He is free from the burden of supporting his wife and needs only to contribute a small portion of his paycheck to his children while they are under the age of 18 years. In contrast, a woman who is divorced will experience a 73 percent decline in her standard of living (as will her children, if she has custody). The woman must provide a home, support herself, and support her children on what is usually a very small paycheck.

In addition, if a father sues for custody, the low earnings of a woman may be taken into account by the courts. In 70 percent of the cases where the father sues for custody, he will win because he has the financial means to support his children (Weitzman, 1985). Often, men threaten to sue for custody even when they do not want it, to get women to negotiate smaller child-support payments (Weitzman, 1985); some women so fear losing their children that they will sacrifice future income rather than risk a custody battle. Thus, many women are receiving even smaller settlements than they are entitled to under the law, which increases the number of women (and their children) who have incomes below the poverty line.

Women's Self-Esteem

Most women are, sooner or later, housewives and mothers, at least for a time. Because our society gives so little respect and esteem to these roles, it is not surprising that women tend to give themselves little respect for accomplishments in these areas, and they often find the demands of the role stressful. Gove and Geerken (1977), in trying to develop a theory to explain stress, argued that married women experience high rates of stress because the role of a married woman is not respected in American society. To test this theory, a study was conducted comparing American women of European descent with Mexican women (Ross et al., 1983b). Because previous research had shown that the family is more highly valued in Mexico than it is in the United States, this research hypothesized that Mexican women would feel less stress because they were more valued as family members. It was found that Mexican women did in fact suffer less stress and receive more support for their role in the family.

In America, some evidence supports the idea that many women have low self-esteem regarding their personal appearance. They are expected to be thin and beautiful, and as a result, women spend more time, energy, and money than men do on cosmetics, diet, and exercise products. Numerous examples exist of women who are extremely critical of their bodies and diet, to the point of malnutrition. In extreme cases, excessive dieting results in anorexia or bulimia, illnesses most often seen in women, which sometimes result in death from starvation.

Medical Care

When men go to their physicians with complaints, they are likely to receive a very thorough physical. When women go to their physician with complaints, they are likely to receive a prescription for tranquilizers or antidepressants instead of a physical (Ehrenreich and English, 1979). Even when their symptoms are severe, women receive fewer diagnostic tests for heart disease and receive less treatment; although post-menopausal women have comparable rates of heart disease to men's rates, only half as many women receive heart bypass operations as men, for example. Women also receive only half the number of diagnostic tests for lung cancer (despite women's increasing rates of lung cancer) and are only half as likely to receive a kidney transplant (Trafford, 1991). According to Trafford, this indicates negligent health care for women.

While women receive less care for the major diseases that kill people in this country, physicians have a tendency to interfere with and over treat the normal reproductive process (Schur, 1984), and as a result, the following procedures are done routinely and are unnecessary in 90 percent of cases: fetal monitoring during labor; use of drugs to induce early labor; use of anesthesia, forceps, and related techniques in delivery; performance of *episiotomy* (surgical incision at the opening of the vagina during the birth process); and surgical delivery through cesarean section. Cesarean sections have risen from 5 percent to 30 percent of births in the past three decades.

Women also have an excessive number of *hysterectomies*, the removal of the uterus and sometimes of the other female reproductive organs. Physicians have argued that the female reproductive organs are not useful except to have children, and they perform this major abdominal surgery for any number of reasons, sometimes as minor as for the relief of menstruation. However, many women who have had hysterectomies report serious depression and difficulty in adjusting to sexual activity (Stokes, 1986).

In recent years, there has been increasing interest in new reproductive technologies. Although research continues to investigate the causes of infertility and birth defects, most research has concentrated on amniocentesis and artificial reproduction. Amniocentesis is early testing of the fetus, and the fetus is usually aborted if defective. The mother often feels little choice in whether to abort (Rothman, 1986) because the social pressure to abort a defective baby is so strong. Reproductive technologies also include the work associated with so-called test-tube babies. Some hope that women eventually will be freed of the reproductive role, but others fear that women's status would be lowered further, and their bodies would become no more than a source of spare parts (Corea, 1985; Rowland, 1985).

Sexual Harassment

Women in all types of jobs suffer from **sexual harassment**, unwelcome sexual advances made by coworkers or superiors at work. Women who reject sexual advances may be denied a job, intimidated, given poor work evaluations, denied raises or promotions, or fired.

Sexual harassment is much more widespread than is generally realized. The first questionnaire ever devoted solely to this topic surveyed working women in 1975 (Farley, 1978). The results were startling: 92 percent of respondents cited sexual harassment as a serious problem, and 70 percent reported that they had personally experienced some form of harassment. Other more recent studies indicate that sexual harassment is also a major problem in colleges and universities, in offices of the United Nations, in the United States military, in civil service jobs, and in private industry.

In deciding how to respond to sexual harassment, the victim must consider the economic necessity of keeping the job, opportunities for getting another job, the likelihood of obtaining decent work evaluations and future promotions, the possibility of being fired, and the attitudes of family and friends to her situation. The victim usually decides to quit, transfer to another job within the organization, or simply to do nothing and to suffer in silence because probably no one will believe her if she makes a complaint.

Family Violence

Family violence is a widespread problem in the United States. While exact statistics cannot be known, it has been estimated that each year, more than 4 million women are battered by their husbands or lovers, and more than 4,000 women are beaten to death. Battery causes more injury to women than rape (including rape with battery), auto accidents, and muggings combined (Cleage, 1993).

When a wife or child is being abused, the wife often does not leave the home or remove the child from the home. Sometimes, the wife believes she deserves to be beaten, but women frequently have no money of their own and no safe place to go. It is likewise difficult for a woman to take her children out of her home when she has no means of support, no food, and no shelter. Thus, while the reasons for family violence are complex, one of the major reasons it continues is that women are unable to support themselves and their children and are therefore unwilling to leave home.

Rape

Rape is another form of violence that results in part from gender inequality. The FBI's Uniform Crime Reports show that 78,770 rapes were reported in 1982 and increased significantly to 109,593 one decade later. The number of reported rapes decreased in 2001 to 90,491. but once again increased 3.4 percent to 93,934 in 2006. These numbers are estimates of actual rapes, which are likely two to three times higher than the number reported to authorities.

To obtain a measure of the incidence of rape other than what is reported to the police, **victimization surveys** have been done, asking random samples of people if they have been victims of rape or attempted rape. Results from these surveys indicate that in the United States, 3 out of 10,000 people have been raped and 7 out of 10,000 people have been victims of attempted rape.

One myth about rape often believed by the public is that rape usually occurs between strangers. However, very often men know the women they rape. In the typical incidence of **acquaintance rape** or *date rape*, the man and woman have been dating for a long time, perhaps a year. In one study of rape on a college campus, 21 percent of female college students reported having been raped (Muehlenhard and Linton, 1987).

Another myth about rape is that rape is sexually motivated. However, when men rape women, it is often an act of aggressiveness. Men may rape because they hate women, they wish to be cruel or violent, or they seek revenge (Henslin, 1990). Nonetheless, because society believes that rape is a sexual act, they believe that women involved in rape have done something sexual to invite rape. Perhaps the women wore enticing clothing, appeared in public at late hours, drank too much, or did not resist the advances of men. Efforts are being made to reduce the tendency to blame the victim of the rape for her victimization. Nevertheless, should the rapist be caught and brought to trial, the reputation of the victim will come under scrutiny. It will be assumed that if she is sexually active, the rapist may have interpreted her behavior as an invitation to him to attack her (Hamlin, 2001).

Some feminists have argued that rape and other forms of violence are the end result of the norms of aggressiveness that men learn to display toward women. Pornography, or erotic literature, has been severely criticized, not because it is sexual but because in this society, most pornography depicts women as passive victims of violent men. The message to readers of this type of pornographic literature is that the violent abuse of women is both masculine and normal (Lederer, 1980). A society that differentiates the sexes, gives one sex a lower status than the other, and provides little opportunity for mutual respect between the sexes is likely to continue to see violence against one sex by the other.

THE FUTURE OF GENDER INEQUALITY

Will gender differentiation decrease? Will women become economically and occupationally equal to men? If the structural functionalists are correct, women will gradually win promotions and pay increases that will move them into the upper echelons of the bureaucratic work world and that will win them equality with men. According to the U.S. Department of Labor and Statistics in its 2006 report, "At all levels of education women have fared better than men with respect to earnings."

A third alternative is also possible, one that combines aspects of the functionalist and conflict views. Upper-class women may use a college education as a stepping-stone into the primary labor market. Their educational credentials and their family background will help them get good positions, where, like upper-class men, they will be groomed for greater responsibility and will achieve higher and higher positions. Working-class women, without family connections and educational opportunity, are likely to remain in the secondary labor market and to fall farther and farther behind. In such a scenario, gender differentiation could diminish considerably even while class differences remained great. Complete equality between men and women requires an end to class, as well as gender, differentiation.

Thinking Sociologically

1. Do you believe that women will progress through the glass ceiling? What factors explain why they may or may not?
2. If women made it through the glass ceiling, which of the consequences of inequality would disappear?

SUMMARY

1. Modern societies differentiate people on the basis of gender, gender roles, and our concepts of masculinity and femininity.
2. Males and females differ in anatomy, chromosomes, and hormones, but research does not show important differences in behavior because of these sex differences. In fact, where one might expect to find differences in behavior based on physical characteristics, such as females having the most important jobs requiring finger dexterity, the opposite is true. Men have the jobs defined as most important, regardless of physical attributes.
3. In other cultures, the definitions of masculinity and femininity differ, so that men and women occupy roles very different from those found in the United States.
4. According to structural functionalists, women play an expressive role in society, nurturing the family, and men play an instrumental role, providing financially for the family. These roles are changing rapidly, and men and women are sharing roles more often now.
5. According to conflict theorists, women have been exploited by men throughout history, kept out of the paid work force, or moved in and out of the lowest-paying jobs, as needed by the economy.
6. Women have been pushed out of the work force when birth rates were low, so their only alternative would be to get married and have babies.

Women have also been encouraged to enter the work force when there was a shortage of workers.

7. When women enter the work force, it is often to take positions in the growing secondary labor market, where salaries are low, work is often part-time or temporary, and fringe benefits are practically nonexistent.

8. Even when women have jobs requiring skills equal to men's jobs, they are not paid for comparable worth.

9. Upward mobility for women is limited first by the inability to move from the secondary work force to the primary work force, and then by the inability to move above the glass ceiling to executive positions. Women are not given positions that provide experience in authority and autonomy and therefore are not eligible for promotion.

10. Women who have families do most of the work at home, whether they are married or not. Their physical and mental health often suffers.

11. The women's movement in Europe fought for special privileges for women and made significant gains in women's salaries, child care, and maternity leaves.

12. The women's movement in the United States fought for equality and gained the right to vote and to work at a wider variety of jobs, but it divided women because there was no support for women's family responsibilities.

13. As a result of all of these discriminating conditions, 34 percent of women in the United States suffer from poverty when they have children to support.

14. *In no-fault divorce*, the father is required to pay only a small portion of the cost of caring for his children because it is assumed that the mother will pay a share, even if she has custody of the children and a low-paying job.

15. Women in the United States suffer low self-esteem because they get little respect for their family responsibilities.

16. Women get less than adequate health care because women's reproductive organs are seen as problematic when they are not, and women's complaints about other organs are not taken seriously enough.

17. Women are subjected to a great deal of violence. They are harassed at work, treated violently at home, and raped by acquaintances and strangers.

18. It is possible that women may gradually win promotions and get ahead, or they may be trapped in the secondary labor market. It is also possible that women of the upper classes will move ahead while women of the lower classes remain in the secondary work force, reinforcing two classes of women.

KEY TERMS

acquaintance rape Rape by someone who is known to the person being raped (such as in date rape).

authority Power accepted as legitimate by those it affects.

Beguines Communes of peasant women who did not choose to marry and who took vows of celibacy; these communes existed during the Middle Ages.

comparable worth Evaluating and rewarding different occupations equally if the work in each occupation requires the same level of skill and is of equal value to the employer.

Equal Rights Amendment (ERA) A proposed amendment to the Constitution of the United States giving equal rights to women; it was not ratified.

feminization of poverty The increase in the number of persons who are below the level of poverty being predominantly women, particularly as found in female headed families.

gender A social status that refers to differences between the sexes, specifically to differences in masculinity and femininity.

gender roles The cultural concepts of masculinity and femininity that society creates around gender.

primary labor market The labor market reserved for people who will advance to high-level positions.

secondary labor market The labor market in which jobs pay poorly, there is little job security, and there are few promotions or salary increases.

sex The biological and anatomical characteristics that differentiate males and females.

sexual harassment Sexual advances made by coworkers or superiors at work.

victimization surveys Asking samples of people if they have been victims of a particular behavior, such as rape.

women's movement The social movements led by women to gain political and economic equality.

DISCUSSION QUESTIONS

1. Discuss the relationships among sex, gender, and gender roles.
2. Discuss how various explanations of gender differentiation can be used to account for the way that you have developed. In doing so, identify some experiences in your life in which you were treated in a particular way primarily because of your gender.
3. Use the knowledge of cross-cultural gender differentiation to evaluate the merits of social and biological explanations of gender differentiation.
4. How do structural functionalism and conflict theory account for the persistence of traditional gender roles? Use personal examples to illustrate each approach.
5. Why do you think that the status of women in the workplace is often treated as if it were a new issue? What are some factors that have affected women's status and role in the workplace throughout history?
6. Why is there a wage differential between women and men in the workplace?
7. How has the split labor market affected men and women differently?
8. Discuss some structural factors that make upward mobility easier for men than for women.
9. Compare the impact of the women's movement in Europe with the women's movement in the United States. Where do you think that women have the best chance for equality? Why?
10. What are some consequences of gender inequality for men and women in families and at work?
11. How are such issues as sexual harassment, family violence, and rape a result of gender inequality?

Age Differentiation and the Aged

When Does Life End?

When is a person's life over? The answer seems simple enough, and a few decades ago, the question probably would have been dismissed as absurd. Traditionally, a person's life was considered over when his or her heart stopped beating or lungs could no longer breathe. However, over the past few decades, medical technology has made the question about when life ends vastly complex. Consider what people might be thinking and feeling regarding someone who is being kept alive by the life-support system. Is a person whose vital organs function only with the help of life-sustaining machinery really alive? Is a person in an irreversible coma or in a vegetative state really alive? In addition, is there a specific physical quality of life—other than the ability to sustain life functions on one's own—that now needs to be considered in deciding when life is over? The answers to these questions are not at all simple, as evidenced by highly publicized court battles—such as the cases of Karen Ann Quinlan and Nancy Cruzan and more recently the highly charged case of Terri Schiavo—in which relatives of patients in irreversible comas or kept alive through life-support systems had fought to allow their loved ones to die. Although the questions about when life ends are not confined to any one age group, they are more relevant to the elderly as a group precisely because they are in their later stages of life and are more likely to face such questions than members of other age groups.

While court battles such as those faced by the relatives of Karen Ann Quinlan, Nancy Cruzan, and Terri Schiavo still take place, there is evidence that most adults in the United States would prefer death for themselves or others to living in permanent pain or on life-support systems. Reports from the Harris Poll (2001) affirm this evidence. Consider the following results:

> By approximately two-to-one, most adults continue to favor the right to euthanasia and physician-assisted suicide.
>
> By 65 percent to 29 percent, a substantial majority thinks "the law should allow doctors to comply with the wishes of a dying patient in severe distress who asks to have his or her life ended."
>
> In a recent 2005 Journal review of euthanasia, nearly 70 percent of Americans favored or would support legislation that would allow terminally ill patients experiencing extreme distress and wish to shorten their lives with the assistance of their physician.
>
> A 61 percent to 34 percent majority (when read a detailed description of it) favors the Oregon proposition that would allow doctor-assisted suicide for patients with six months to live, if all three of the following conditions were met:
>
> a. The patient requests it three times.
> b. There is a second physician's opinion.
> c. There is a 15-day waiting period for the patient to change his or her mind.

Globally, there is support for euthanasia as well. Consider the following:

> *The British public supports legalization of euthanasia.* Even though surveys of public opinion are notoriously fickle, findings about euthanasia have been remarkably consistent. Nationwide polls have been consistently unanimous in showing a majority to be in favor of legalized voluntary euthanasia, with support as high as 82 percent (British Social Attitudes Report, 1996). As recent as 2005, British doctors were still calling for more relaxed laws to assist the terminally ill in death.
>
> *No nationwide poll has ever shown a majority against voluntary euthanasia.* Opponents of voluntary euthanasia have found similar results in their own research. A MORI poll commissioned by the antivoluntary euthanasia group Doctors Who Respect Human Life in 1987 found 72 percent of respondents in favor of legalized euthanasia. Antivoluntary euthanasia groups have been unable to produce a single survey of U.K. opinion which did not show a majority in favor of legalization.
>
> *This support for voluntary euthanasia is mirrored across the globe.* Consider the poll that found 78 percent of Australians affirm the doctor's right to end the patient's life (Roy Morgan Research Centre poll, 1995).
>
> Interestingly enough, *support for voluntary euthanasia is even stronger among the elderly.* Those who oppose voluntary euthanasia often base their opposition upon the notion that legalization of euthanasia would pose a

threat to the most vulnerable in society—in particular, the elderly and the disabled. Support among members of such groups is actually higher than among those not deemed to be at special risk. In what is believed to be the first such poll specifically targeted at pensioners, 92 percent of those surveyed replied that doctors should be allowed to end the life of terminally ill patients who want to die. Only 29 percent agreed with the statement that legalizing euthanasia posed a realistic risk of allowing the unscrupulous to end a patient's life without consent (Yours magazine, November 1994).

Support for voluntary euthanasia is actually growing. Opinion polls show that not only do euthanasia and assisted suicide already enjoy the support of a substantial majority of the U.K. population, but also that this support is actually growing. The percentages of those favoring euthanasia increased from 75 percent in 1984 to 79 percent in 1989 and to 82 percent in 1996 (British Social Attitudes Report, 1996).

However, a 1991 Gallup poll also found that only a third of Americans feel that people have the right to end their own lives if they place extremely heavy burdens on their families. Even fewer—only 16 percent—would be willing to condone the suicide of an otherwise healthy person. "Thus," as the report from which these findings were taken notes, "while Americans certainly are not supportive of a culture in which suicide is condoned under any and all circumstances, they are strongly in favor of societal norms which allow for and support the idea that patients nearing the end of their lives—with incurable diseases and great pain—should be allowed to choose to die, and that doctors should be encouraged to aid and abet in these decisions" (*The Gallup Poll Monthly*, January, 1991).

What do the results of this poll suggest that individuals and societies believe about when life ends? Do we feel that life ends only when a person's heart has stopped or a person can no longer breathe independently? Do we feel that life ends when a person can no longer live naturally without support from a life-sustaining system? Do we feel that life ends when a person is in intolerable pain that cannot be alleviated? We cannot infer answers to these questions based on the poll results that have been cited. However, it is reasonable to conclude that many societies are at least beginning to include quality of life among the criteria used to determine when life ends.

While the questions associated with when life ends or should end seem to be more suited to philosophy or biology courses than to sociology, they are significant questions for sociologists as well. We live within a society that has the technological capabilities to sustain physical life well beyond when a person might naturally die, yet we have not yet fully answered the questions about the social implications involved in these life-and-death decisions. Who has the power to decide when a person's life is really over: individuals, families, medical institutions, religious institutions, the government? How will the meanings that we attach to illness and death change if euthanasia becomes adopted as one of our cultural norms? How will the social meanings of being elderly or terminally ill change? What types of social expectations will be placed upon the elderly and the terminally ill? Clearly, a cultural lag exists because of a rapidly advancing medical technology and a society that has not yet learned to deal with such questions. The questions are particularly relevant in light of the fact that the number of elderly in our society is becoming larger than ever. In terms of functional theory, this cultural lag represents the manifest functions of medical technology while exposing the latent consequences produced by the aging population in our society.

All societies expect different behaviors from people who are of a different age. In dress, music, leisure, sex, work, and so forth, what may be expected and appropriate for the young might not be expected or appropriate for the elderly. In many countries, including the United States, people are living longer than ever before, and an aging population creates new concerns for both individuals and societies. Many individuals do not look forward to growing old because they associate attractiveness, health, and productivity with the young. For the society as a whole, an increasing aged population arouses concerns about financial support, health care, housing, productivity, and other issues.

An example of how an aging society presents new concerns has been cited in Sweden (Ekman, 2001) where bicycling has almost doubled between 1980 and 1992–93 among persons aged 25 to 64. For the elderly (65 or older) the bicycle is a common means of transport, in both Sweden and a number of other countries. The risk of dying due to bicycling was about 3.7 times greater among the elderly than among children aged 14 or under. The elderly face a greater risk of being injured or killed than their younger counterparts. For all ages the risk is 7.4 times higher for a bicyclist than for a car driver. The risk for the elderly is about 3 times greater than for the average bicyclist, and as much as 6 times higher for the age group 75 to 84 years. The author states, "With some few exceptions, there is no doubt that society has neglected the problem." He attributes the neglect to the fact that decision-makers have a tendency to focus on the relatively young. But people are living longer today and the elderly are healthier, which indicates the need for greater interest and more intervention. "We have signs of an epidemic, but one that can be ameliorated or prevented" (Ekman, 2001).

AGE, AGING, AND THE AGED

The introductory paragraph uses terms such as *young, old, growing old, age, aging, aged,* and the *elderly.* Although most of us use and understand these terms in everyday language, they refer to different phenomena and have different meanings attached to them at different times and places. Have you noticed personally the fact that *who or what* is old changes as you grow older? Have you ever wished you were of a different age so that you could do things that you could not do at your own age? The former question alerts us to the relative nature of what is young or old. The latter question suggests that the changes are related to chronological time.

Age generally refers to the number of years since birth. It is an ascribed status over which we have no choice or control. As such, each age status includes different social expectations about the appropriate behavior for different age groups. We expect babies to suck their thumbs and crawl on the floor, but we do not expect adults to do these things. We expect children to skip down the sidewalk, teenagers to attend school, and middle-aged executives to wear suits. Expectations about the behavior considered appropriate for people of a given age are called **age norms**. Because these particular expected behaviors are associated with particular ages, we ask people, according to their age, whether they have finished high school, are married, have children or grandchildren, or are retired. These social timetables tell people whether their lives are on schedule. There seems to be wide agreement among adults about age norms within societies, but age norms vary widely among different societies. One society may agree that the aged should be accorded deference, respect, and reverence; another may agree that they should retire and become less productive. One society may expect old people to live with and be cared for by their families; another may expect them to join other elderly persons in retirement communities or be cared for by the government.

A concept related to age but one that implies something different is **aging**, which suggests process and change. This broad concept includes biological or physical changes in our bodies; psychological changes in our mental capacities; and social changes in how we are defined, what is expected of us, and what we expect from others. *Biological aging* is the result of many processes, but includes changes in our physical appearance (such as wrinkled skin, gray hair, and midriff bulge), physiological changes (such as puberty and menopause), and other changes in bodily systems (such as the nervous, endocrine, or immune systems). *Psychological aging*, also the result of many factors, includes changes in our mental functioning (such as learning, thinking, memory, or emotions).

Social aging, while greatly influenced by chronological age, deals with social roles, the life course, and age norms. In family terms, we speak of the family life cycle for heterosexuals in terms of progressive stages, which may include marriage, having children, raising preschool and then school-age children, dealing with adolescents, launching the children and entering an empty-nest stage, and progressing through middle age into old age, with its accompanying events of retirement, widowhood, and death. In general sociological terms, frequent reference is made to the **life course**, an age-related progression or sequence of roles and group memberships that people are expected to follow as they mature and move through life. Thus, there is an age or time to go to school, get a job, get married, have children and grandchildren, retire, and so forth. What sociologists make real is an awareness of the wide diversity of paths in the life course, depending on culture, ethnicity, gender, social class, sexuality, and so forth. Life-course events, while related to chronological age, occur over a wide range of years. Both 15- and 35-year-old women get pregnant and have children, and both 55- and 75-year-old workers retire. However, to retire at 15 or get pregnant at 55 is highly inconsistent with expected behaviors for those ages.

The **aged** refers to one specific age grouping and to a particular stage or point in the life cycle or life course. This is the group we define as old, elderly, or as senior citizens; it occupies the later part of the aging process or the life span. This age segment of our population is the central focus of this chapter.

The systematic study of the aging process is known as **gerontology**, an interdisciplinary field of study that draws heavily on the biological and social sciences. One biological branch of gerontology is **geriatrics**, the medical care of the aged. **Social gerontology** focuses on the social and cultural factors related to age and the aging process.

Many age norms, particularly those concerning the aged in the United States, are inaccurate. Based upon false assumptions, the enforcement of these age norms tends to restrict the lifestyles and limit the personal fulfillment of elderly persons. Many definitions and perceptions of old people or the aging process are *stereotypes*—conventional mental images applied universally to all old people. Although widely held, many of these stereotypes are not supported by empirical evidence. Unfortunately, these misinformed, negative stereotypes can lead to **ageism:** prejudice and discrimination based on age. Like racism and sexism, ageism involves beliefs about the inherent inferiority of a group that are used to justify individual or institutionalized discrimination. We examine a few of these prejudices, stereotypes, and myths in the next section of this chapter.

MYTHS ABOUT OLD AGE

The development of gerontology as a field of study and our increasing body of research on the aging process show that many traditional beliefs about the aged are inaccurate. It is important to understand that many of these beliefs about the aged are, in fact, myths. These beliefs influence (a) the way in which the aged are treated by family and employers, (b) the nature of social policies that are designed with the aged in mind, and (c) the self-esteem of old people. Kart (2000) lists ten misconceptions about old people and the aging process

1. Old age is inevitably accompanied by senility, a mental infirmity associated with the aging process.
2. In general, old people are miserable.
3. Most old people are lonely.
4. The majority of old people have health problems.
5. Old people are more likely than younger people to be victimized by crime.
6. The majority of old people live in poverty.
7. Most old people are unable to manage a household.
8. Old people who retire usually suffer a decline in health.
9. Most old people have no interest in or capacity for sexual relations.
10. Most old people end up in nursing homes and other long-term care institutions.

Some of these myths are discussed later in this chapter. At this point, we briefly summarize why each of these statements is false:

1. Senility. Senility does not inevitably accompany old age; many people, including a number of the world's leaders and other famous figures, make significant contributions in their seventh and eighth decades of life. In the absence of disease, age-related changes in learning ability appear to be small, even after the keenness of the senses has begun to decline. Dispelling this myth about the elderly could have enormous social consequences. If the elderly are treated as if they are still vibrant and alert human beings, they may be encouraged to see themselves as such. (Remember Cooley's "looking-glass self.") If old people believe that they still have the potential for personal growth, they may make the effort to remain mentally and physically active. However, they will probably not make that effort if they believe they have no potential for growth, and thus mental and physical deterioration may become a self-fulfilling prophecy. It is also essential that policymakers understand that age-related changes in learning ability are relatively small, so that they can strengthen their efforts to combat age discrimination in the workplace.

2. Despondence. Most old people are not miserable and lonely; the evidence consistently indicates that old people are satisfied with their lives. Among

Americans aged 65 to 69, 49 percent said "these are the best years of my life." Many people in their seventies (44 percent) and eighties (33 percent) agreed. (Among Americans of all ages, 66 percent described the present as their best years.) Sixty percent of older black and 57 percent of older Hispanic respondents said these are their best years. In 2002, 58 percent of 70 year olds and older stated they would be "very happy" to live another 10 years. ("Myths & Realities of Aging Study," NCOA, 2002). Nearly half of older Americans consider themselves to be middle aged or young. Only 15 percent of those 75-plus consider themselves "very old" ("American Perceptions on Aging in the 21st Century," NCOA, 2002).

*3. **Loneliness.*** Although many old people are alone, they are not necessarily lonely. The meaning of loneliness appears to change with age, and except for widows who miss their husbands and express higher degrees of loneliness, other groups of older people do not find loneliness to be problematic.

*4. **Health Problems.*** Although many old people do have some health problems, the majority of those over age 65 do not have problems that limit their ability to work, keep house, or engage in routine daily activities. This myth—like the first one mentioned—has enormous implications concerning discrimination in the workplace. If all elderly are stereotyped as having health problems, employers may not hire them or may create policies that force them to take early retirement.

In 2005, 4.2 million (12.8 percent) older Americans made up 3 percent of the labor force (working or actively seeking work), including 2.4 million men (19.5 percent) and 1.8 million women (11.5 percent). The majority of mature workers (those over 55)—more than 70 percent in 2001—are employed full time and are doing so by choice. (Bureau of Labor Statistics, 2005). The average unemployment rate for mature workers was 3 percent in 2001, up from 2.6 percent in 2000. It is important to note that it typically takes those 55 and over some 18 weeks to find a job versus an average of 12.7 weeks for those under age 55 (EEOC, 2001). Although some accommodations must be made, and some forms of discrimination do exist, the elderly are active and employed.

*5. **Victimization.*** Crime against older people is an area of increasing study, and surveys show that the elderly are more fearful of crime than the young. However, the popular belief that elderly persons are victimized more often is false. The victimization rate of old people for assault and robbery, for example, is much lower than it is for others. The one exception may be personal larceny, such as purse- and wallet-snatchings, in which the victimization rates are about equal.

*6. **Poverty.*** Most old people do not live in poverty. Admittedly, many of the elderly are poor, but taking into account their Social Security benefits, private pension plans, tax relief laws, and income from sources such as rents, annuities, retirement plans, savings, dividends, and so on, plus the high percentage of older people who own their own homes and automobiles, the vast majority are not at the poverty level. In 2005, 12.9 percent of all householders age 65 and over were below the poverty level (*Current Population Reports*, 2005). These figures, by contrast, are considerably lower than the 11.7 million or 16.3 percent of children under age 18 who were below the poverty level the same year (*Statistical Abstract*, 2005).

*7. **Dependence and Incompetence.*** Most old people can manage a household; in 2000, 89 percent of men and 81 percent of women over age 75 lived alone or with their spouse in their own household. Most aged people prefer to live close to their adult children but in separate households from them.

8. Postretirement Decline. Not all old people suffer a decline in health when they retire. Although some people do retire because of health problems, the widespread tale of the individual who retired and "went downhill fast" appears to have little empirical support.

9. Sexual Disinterest or Incapacity. Although sexual interests, capacities, and functions do change with age, detailed clinical studies of sexuality in late life have demonstrated the lifelong potential for sexual response and the reversibility of sexual disorders occurring later in life (Masters and Johnson, 1981). Ade-Ridder (1990) joins others (e.g., Janus and Janus, 1994) in dispelling the myth that old people have no interest in or capacity for sexual relations. She studied the sexual behavior of 488 married men and women (244 couples) with a mean age of 72 years and found that two-thirds of the couples were still sexually active. While the data concur with other reports of a decline in sexual interest with advancing age, it is clear that sexual expression continues late in life and that sexual intimacy, including but not restricted to intercourse, is important to older persons. More recently, the National Council on Aging (1998) found that among sexually active seniors, most (74 percent of the men and 70 percent of the women) said they were as satisfied or more satisfied with their sex lives, compared to when they were in their 40s ("Healthy Sexuality and Vital Aging," NCOA, 1998).

10. Institutionalization. Most old people are not in nursing homes or other long-term care institutions; U.S. Bureau of the Census data indicate that only about 5 percent of the elderly are in old-age institutions of one kind or another. The vast majority of them live alone or with their spouse in their own household. It is clearly not the case that the elderly are predominantly institutionalized. According to the U.S. Bureau of the Census (2002), most people aged 65-plus live with family members, with over half (55 percent) of noninstitutionalized persons living with their spouses. In 2000, approximately 10.1 million or 73 percent of older men, and 7.7 million or 41 percent of older women, lived with their spouses. Only 1.56 million (4.5 percent) of the 65-plus population lived in nursing homes in 2000.

In general, blind acceptance of these myths can impair the way that the elderly are treated by family, government, health care personnel, social workers, employers, and even themselves. By understanding that the lifestyles, mental and physical health, sexual attitudes and capabilities, and learning potential of the aged are not markedly different from those of younger people, we might be more sensitive to our treatment of them and learn to overcome our ageist attitudes. It is commonplace to say that people have difficulty overcoming their prejudices against minority groups because they are not members of that minority themselves. However, keep in mind that barring any major illness or accident, some day you will be among the elderly. Eliminating discrimination and prejudice against the aged clearly concerns all of us.

Thinking Sociologically

1. State two or three ideas or perceptions you hold about old people. Are any of them likely to be myths?
2. Many myths exist about old age and the elderly: (a) Consider the extent to which the myths just presented may not be myths in societies outside of North America; and (b) if such myths differ by culture, how many can be attributed solely or even primarily to the biological effects of aging?
3. Since sociological findings can be used to empower individuals and groups while debunking myths and misinformation, how could educating old people about their actual versus perceived chances of victimization change the quality of their lives?

DEMOGRAPHIC ASPECTS OF AGING

The study of population is a central concern of sociologists. A number of questions tend to arise in examining any population: How many people are there? Has the number of people changed in the past? How is it likely to change in the future? What are the characteristics of the population? How do these numbers compare with other groups in society and with the numbers of similar groups in other societies? The answers to questions such as these alert us to the increasing significance of aging in most industrialized nations, because the large number of elderly people is unprecedented in world history. Never have so many people lived so long.

One key question in investigations of an aged population concerns the age at which people are considered elderly. Most of us know of men and women over age 70 years who look, think, and act young and others who seem old at age 35 or 45. Nevertheless, social policy and much of the available data in the United States define the elderly population as those 65 years of age and over. This cutoff point is somewhat arbitrary, but it is widely used by gerontologists, and we follow it in this chapter. It is not universal, however, and today many gerontologists distinguish between the "young-old" (those ages 55 to 74) and the "old-old" (those 75 years old and over). You should recognize that numbers such as these are statistical generalizations and that wide variations exist in people's life expectancy, income, activity, and so forth.

Numbers of the Elderly: The Graying of America

The population aged 65 and older is projected to double over the next three decades from 35.3 million to nearly 70 million. In 2030, people 65-plus are expected to make up 20 percent of the population. The Census Bureau projects the 65-plus population to be 39.7 million in 2010, 53.7 million in 2020 and 70.3 million in 2030. The U.S. will rank third in the world in population of those 65 and older.

The population aged 85 and older is the fastest growing segment of the older population. In 2000, it was estimated that persons 85-plus made up 2 percent of the population, and by 2050, the percentage of this age group is projected to grow to be 5 percent of the population. The 4 million 85-plus population in 2000 will grow to 19 million in 2050. The U.S. will rank second in the world in this population sector. (U.S. Bureau of the Census, 2002).

These numbers are not wild speculation: these people have already been born, and—barring any major wars or diseases—nearly three-fourths of those currently living can expect to reach old age. These numbers can, of course, be influenced by migrations of people into or out of the United States, in addition to the unexpected death factor.

This pattern of growth raises many questions relating to work, leisure, health, housing, family life, and other matters. One approach gerontologists have taken in considering how changes in these areas will affect society involves examining the relationship between the elderly and the rest of the population.

One way to examine the relationship between the old and the young is by calculating the **dependency ratio**—the ratio between the number of people in the dependent population and the number of people in the supportive or working population. The dependent population includes both the aged and children.

A figure that excludes children is an *old-age dependency ratio,* which can be determined by dividing the number of persons over a specific age by the number of those in the supportive or working population. Using data provided by the U.S. Bureau of the Census, we can compute this ratio by noting the number of nonworkers 60 years old and over per 100 workers ages 20 to 59 and get a figure of about

31 (*Statistical Abstract*, 1991). This means that there were about three workers under age 60 to support each nonworker 60 years old or more.

Today's lower birth rate will result in fewer workers to support each elderly non-working person. Thus, we can expect issues such as Social Security, health care costs, and support services to become increasingly serious concerns. Shifts in dependency ratios will create problems of familial and societal support of the aged throughout this century, and such problems will become even more serious after the turn of the century, at about the time most of you will be considering retirement. According to the U.S. Bureau of the Census, there were 50,545 centenarians in 2000, a 35 percent increase from 1990. This number is expected to further increase to 324,000 by 2030 and to 834,000 in 2050 (U.S. Census, 2002).

TABLE 11-1 LIFE EXPECTANCY AT BIRTH FOR SELECTED COUNTRIES, 2000

Country	Life Expectancy
Japan	80.8
Singapore	80.1
Sweden	79.6
Italy	79.0
Sweden	79.6
France	78.8
United Kingdom	77.7
United States	77.1
Mexico	71.5
China (mainland)	71.4
Philippines	67.5
Brazil	62.9
India	62.5
Bangladesh	60.2
Liberia	51.0
Kenya	48.0
Zimbabwe	37.8

Source: U.S. Bureau of the Census, *An Aging World: 2001*, P95/01-1. Washington, DC: U.S. Government Printing Office, 2001, p. 24.

Life Expectancy

Life expectancy is the average years of life remaining for people who attain a given age. The most commonly cited life expectancy figure is based on birth. In other words, how many years, on average, can infants born in a given year expect to live? A glimpse at Table 11-1 shows these figures for selected countries. In most countries of North America and western Europe, life expectancy at birth as of 2000 was greater than 70 years. However, for many countries in Africa and selected countries in southeast Asia, life expectancy at birth was less than 60 and for some countries less than 50. You may want to take a moment to consider some reasons as to why these figures vary so extensively. However, at this point, we focus on the United States and the life expectancy of older persons here.

Within the United States, in 2005 the expectation of longevity was 77.5 years, but this figure varies considerably by sex and race. White females had a life expectancy of 80.1 years, (white females have the highest level of life expectancy of all races and genders) compared with 74.8 for white males; black females had a life expectancy of 76.1, compared with 69 for black males (*National Vital Statistics*, 2005). Instead of dealing with life expectancy at birth, what about the life expectancy of older persons? Suppose that we consider life expectancy at age 65 rather than life expectancy at birth. In 1988, the life expectancy at age 65 was 16.9 more years (*Statistical Abstract*, 1991:74), which means that those who lived to age 65 could expect on average to live to age 81.9. Surprisingly, in 1900, the life expectancy of those who reached 65 was 11.9 additional years, which means that they could expect to live until age 76.9. Thus, although many more people are living longer, there has been relatively little increase (5.0 years) in the life expectancy of older persons since the turn of the century.

This finding is related to the notion of **life span**, the biological age limit beyond which no one can expect to live. Gerontologists estimate the life span to be slightly over a hundred years, and many believe it has remained basically unchanged throughout recorded history. Therefore, while life expectancy has increased dramatically, and more people are reaching old age than ever before, the life span is virtually unchanged. Despite frequent efforts to find a "fountain of youth," most biologists see no major scientific breakthrough in the near future that will extend the life span. Some time ago, there were reports of many persons in the Ural Mountains who lived to be 130 and individuals who lived to be 150 years old, but according to the Russian gerontologist Medvedev (1974, 1975), these reports were without scientific foundation.

Thinking Sociologically

1. What are some implications of a changing dependency ratio in terms of (a) Social Security, (b) labor force demands, (c) health care, and (d) intergenerational relationships?

2. Recognizing the difference in life expectancy and life span, why has life expectancy increased in the United States and many other countries while the life span has remained virtually unchanged? What possibilities do you see for changes in either life expectancy or the life span over the next several decades?

3. Pretend you are going to take an elderly person on a tour of your university campus. What are things you would consider as you plan your tour? What does this tell you about your own beliefs concerning the elderly?

TABLE 11-2 MARITAL STATUS OF WOMEN AND MEN AGE 65 AND OVER, 2001 (PERCENTAGE DISTRIBUTION)

Marital Status	Men	Women
Never married	4	4
Married	41	73
Separated/Divorced	9	10
Widowed	46	14
Total	100.0	100.0

Source: United States Administration of Aging. September, 2003 (www.aoa.gov).

Social Characteristics of the Elderly

The elderly population, like the rest of the population, varies in terms of sex (male or female), marital status, living arrangements, geographical distribution, labor force participation, and other characteristics. Many characteristics are related in some way to the fact that women greatly outnumber men. The *sex ratio* (number of males per 100 females) is about 69 men per 100 women ages 65 and over. This factor has a major impact on conditions such as marital status and living arrangements.

Elderly men and women differ sharply in their marital status (see Table 11-2). About three-fourths of all older men are married and living with their spouse, compared with less than half of the women. The most dramatic difference in marital status between the sexes is shown under the category "Widowed." In 2003, of people over 65, 14 percent of the men and 46 percent of the women were widowed. These differences are due to the fact that men tend to marry younger women and die at younger ages. Also, elderly widowed men have remarriage rates about seven times higher than those of women.

Living arrangements differ as well. Most elderly men are married, and 74.3 percent live in their own household with their spouse, while only 40.1 percent of the women have this arrangement. About 41 percent of the women live alone, compared with 16 percent of the men. Also, as noted earlier, the notion that most old people end up in nursing homes and other long-term care institutions is a myth: Only about 5 percent, or 1 in 20, is institutionalized.

Geographically, the elderly are heavily concentrated in metropolitan areas and in a few states. Compared with those under age 65, elderly persons are less likely to live in the suburbs. In the early 1990s, as was true a decade earlier, about two-thirds lived in metropolitan areas. Black and Hispanic elderly are especially concentrated in central cities, whereas whites are more likely to live outside the central city. In 2000, there were nine states with more than 1 million people age 65 and over: California (3.5 million), Florida (2.8 million), New York (2.4 million), Pennsylvania (1.9 million), Texas (2 million), Illinois (1.5 million), Ohio (1.5 million), Michigan (1.2 million), and New Jersey (1.1 million). More than half of the total elderly population of the United States is found in these nine states. Alaska has the smallest number of elderly persons—only 35,699 or 5.7 percent of its population. Florida is the state with the highest proportion of persons over age 65—18.9 percent. During the past decade, the largest increases in the elderly population were in the southern and western states.

Applying Demographic Aspects of Aging

The demographic aspects of aging are useful in a number of ways. Politicians and other policymakers are discovering that they need to understand the demographics of this growing constituency, such as knowing how many people will be over age 65 years and identifying their social characteristics. This understanding is important in determining the nature and form of policies and laws regarding mandatory retirement, pension plans, Social Security, Medicaid, Medicare, disability provisions, and so forth. Effective politicians realize that millions of older persons are active in special interest groups that can wield strong political pressure and support, such as the Gray Panthers, the National Retired Teachers Association, the National Council of Senior Citizens, and the American Association of Retired Persons (AARP). The AARP alone has more than 35 million members and more than 4,000 local chapters. Organizations such as these often apply their efforts toward improving the lives of older Americans by offering travel possibilities and insurance plans, as well as through selective lobbying efforts at the state and local level. To be politically effective, politicians cannot ignore the needs of this substantial and increasingly powerful group of Americans.

Business leaders and advertisers also need to be aware of the various demographic characteristics of the elderly. How will the needs of consumers change as the population grows older? What kinds of products should research-and-development (R&D) departments of corporations be concerned with when planning for future corporate growth? Advertisers particularly must be concerned with elderly demographics. No longer can advertising campaigns focus exclusively on the young; as the median age of the population climbs, so does the age of consumers who have a large disposable income. In fact, if you pay close attention to television commercials and magazine ads, you will notice that more and more middle-aged and elderly models, actors, and actresses are being used.

Considering that the percentage of the population over 65 years of age is steadily increasing, community planners need to consider this age group in many aspects of their plans for the near future. For example, are there enough municipal parks? Are they conveniently located? Do they contain the facilities that will be needed by the elderly? If the number of elderly people in the population is increasing, it might make more sense to include park facilities that the aged are more likely to use (such as picnic areas, walking paths, botanical areas, and so forth) rather than increasing the number of basketball courts or bicycle paths. Planners also need to ensure that there will be adequate nursing home facilities and retirement villages, increased availability of low-cost housing and apartments, and adequate medical facilities that specialize in the health care of the elderly.

Awareness of the demographics of aging can also be useful for you personally. As you formulate your career plans, you may want to consider what types of services will be needed by the growing population of elderly. Will some careers or occupations be more highly rewarded because of increased demand? How will the increased population of elderly people affect your family planning, finances, and investments? There may be investment opportunities that you can take advantage of by knowing that the population of the United States is getting older. Knowing that there will be increased competition—and thus, rising costs—for retirement homes, cemetery plots, and so forth, may affect the way you plan for your future.

THEORIES OF AGING AND OF AGE DIFFERENTIATION

Tremendous emphasis is given to children and youth in the literature, but the socialization and resocialization needs of the elderly are more likely to be ignored. For the socialization of young people, we have families, schools, peers, jobs, and the community, but what socialization agents exist to direct the aging process, to train people for retirement, widowhood, illness, or death? How can we explain differences among age groups in income, status, prestige, usefulness, and similar characteristics?

Aging is a biological as well as a social process, and many theories of aging focus on genetic or physiological changes. As we age, our skin wrinkles, our posture becomes stooped, our muscle reflexes become less efficient, and our responses to sexual stimuli are slower. These biological changes are important to note, but they do not explain what happens to humans socially as we grow older. For these explanations, we turn to social-psychological and sociological theories.

Structural Functional Theory

Structural functional theories assess aging in terms of social changes, such as population shifts and industrialization, attempting to determine how they influence social organization. According to the functionalist perspective, societies should be able to provide rewards and meaningful lives for all their citizens, including the elderly. Yet some observers argue that changes in the extended family structure have stripped the elderly of their respected positions as leaders and authorities. With today's rapid changes in industry and high technology, the elderly often lack the skills and training needed to fulfill beneficial economic roles. Today, there are more old people and fewer productive roles for them to fulfill. It could be said that there is an imbalance between the age structures and the role-performance structures of our basic social institutions. This view is reflected in two structural functional perspectives: modernization theory and disengagement theory.

Modernization theory (Cowgill, 1974; Cowgill and Holmes, 1972) states that with increasing modernization, the status of older people declines, which is reflected in diminished power and influence for the elderly and fewer leadership roles for them in community life. This lower status is a consequence of the processes of modernization: scientific technology, urbanization, literacy and mass education, and health technology. *Scientific technology* creates new jobs primarily for the young, with the elderly more likely to remain in traditional occupations that become obsolete. One illustration of this phenomenon is the gap between generations in the use of computers. *Urbanization* and urban life, unlike farm life, involves a good deal of mobility, especially among the young, and this mobility tends to separate the youthful generation from the older one. *Mass education* is targeted at the young, so younger people rapidly gain a higher level of literacy and greater contemporary skills than their parents. They occupy higher-status positions, and the elderly experience reduced leadership roles and influence. *Health technology* has led to declining birth rates and longer lives. Considering all four factors together, early retirement is encouraged, and the elderly are often denied a chance to participate in the labor market, which reduces their income, prestige, honor, and status.

Modernization theory has received some empirical support in cross-cultural studies, which reveal that as technology, education, and the like increased, and the importance of agriculture declined, the elderly population's control of important information and the esteem and deference accorded to them decreased. However, critics of this theory say that *modernization* is a vague term often used to describe development, progress, and, more specifically, westernization. They note that whatever modernization may be, it is not necessarily a linear process, and the elderly and other age groups may be affected differently by different stages in the process.

For example, as societies move beyond an initial stage of modernization, status differences between generations may decrease and the status of the elderly may rise, particularly when reinforced by social policies such as Social Security and more positive media images of the elderly. Critics also note exceptions, such as the treatment of the elderly in Japan. Keefer (1990), for example, states that in Japan, the prestige and power of the elderly was maintained at fairly high levels throughout the industrialization process. In other words, a decline in status of the elderly did not accompany modernization, and respect for the elderly still remains.

Disengagement theory (Cumming and Henry, 1961) states that as people grow older, they go through a period of disengagement or withdrawal. This theory has been widely discussed since the 1960s, but the available evidence lends it little support. Consistent with aspects of structural functionalism, disengagement theory suggests that gradual withdrawal or disengagement of the elderly from jobs and some other roles is functional both for the elderly and for society. It prepares them for the end of life and also opens up opportunities for the younger generations, whereas a sudden withdrawal of the elderly would lead to social disruption.

Implicit in this theory is the idea that society should help older people to disengage themselves from their accustomed roles by separating them residentially (having them retire to the Sunbelt or to retirement communities), educating them about new activities designed for the elderly, and providing recreational alternatives such as social centers for senior citizens. These steps, which are often initiated by aging individuals themselves, are believed to help the old surrender their roles to a younger segment of the population. This disengagement process also prepares people for their death, with minimal disruption to society.

Disengagement theory did contribute to the view that old age is a normal stage of life. It differentiated this stage of life from middle age and emphasized that a lower level of social involvement and activity can still be highly rewarding. Critics, however, argue that elderly people do not want to be disengaged, do not want to be "put away," and do not want to withdraw from the mainstream of society. Robert Atchley (1991) suggests that disengagement is not a mutually satisfying process but one that is imposed on older people by the withdrawal of opportunities to participate and by circumstances such as ill health. In other words, although disengagement is not what most older people want, it is what many get.

Symbolic Interaction Theory

Symbolic interaction theory focuses on how people define themselves and others, what meanings they give to events, and how they relate to their reference groups. When applied to the elderly, the theory emphasizes how people define the aging process and the status of the aged. Interaction patterns that bring satisfaction to the elderly are also noted. For many older persons, marital and family relationships are primary sources of social involvement, companionship, fulfillment, and happiness. Lee (1978), for example, found that marital satisfaction has a positive effect on morale, which supports the basic tenet of symbolic interaction theory: Interactions with significant others in primary types of group relationships are crucial to personal satisfaction and psychological well-being.

Symbolic interaction theory provides the context for what Lemon and his colleagues (1977) have termed the **activity theory** of aging. In contrast to the disengagement theory, which suggests that aging people go through a process of mutual withdrawal and a severance of relationships, the activity theory argues that the best-adjusted elderly persons are those who remain actively engaged. Many older people may not have the desire or the ability to perform the roles they performed at age 30 or 40, but they have essentially the same need for social interaction that they had years earlier. Activity theory contends that in order to achieve a satisfying adjustment to the aging process, avocations, part-time jobs, and hobbies should replace full-time employment, and friends or loved ones who move away or die should be replaced by new friends and associates.

In an attempt to test activity theory, Lemon and his colleagues investigated a sample of more than 400 potential joiners of a retirement community in southern California. His findings were mixed. He discovered that *informal activity* such as interaction with friends, relatives, and neighbors was significantly related to life satisfaction, whereas solitary activities such as housework and *formal activities* such as involvement in voluntary organizations were not.

This theory, however, presents problems as well. The basic idea of involvement in activities with primary networks of people has merit, but it is not safe to assume that elderly persons have full control over their social lives and ready access to intimate relationships. Widows who see loved ones die or retirees who have too much leisure time and lower incomes may find it extremely difficult to replace loved ones and to fill their time with meaningful activities. Furthermore, the economic resources needed to reconstruct their lives may be lacking. Another questionable assumption is whether activity of any kind can always substitute for the loss of a spouse, job, child, or friend, or particularly of one's health. Psychologists and sociologists would agree that merely knowing a large number of people and being involved in many activities is not enough for a satisfactory life.

In brief, the relationship between aging and life satisfaction or well-being is one of the oldest and most persistently investigated issues in studies of aging. The issue took the form of a debate regarding disengagement versus activity. The disengagement theorists held that withdrawal from major social roles would optimize life satisfaction in old age. The activity theorists held that involvement and activity would maximize well-being. While this debate is still given some attention, it is now widely viewed as *specious*—that is, attractively plausible but having a deceptive or false sense of truth. Other theories of aging have emerged, including the application of variants of exchange and conflict theories.

Social Exchange Theory

Social exchange theory, as discussed elsewhere in this book, assumes that people try to maximize rewards and minimize costs. It suggests that voluntary social interactions are contingent on rewarding reactions from others. Each person receives in the exchange something perceived as equivalent to what is given. If the reciprocal exchanges are not fair, one person is at a disadvantage, and the other controls the relationship.

Dowd (1975, 1980) drew on exchange theory to offer an alternative to the disengagement and activity theories of aging. He believes that the problems of the aged in twentieth-century industrial societies are really problems of decreasing power. The low status of the elderly relative to younger people limits their bargaining power. Their economic and social dependence means that they have less power than those in the rest of society, and with the gradual loss of power comes the need to comply. The elderly, who once could exchange their labor and skills for wages, must now exchange compliance for a Social Security pension or for health-care benefits. According to Dowd, the withdrawal from social roles that disengagement theorists view as satisfying to the elderly is the result of a series of exchange relationships in which the aged lose power.

Even those who have financial resources, skills, and good health are often at a disadvantage in an exchange relationship. Their ability to gain new skills, more resources, or better health is limited. Stereotypes about the aged, rules forcing them to retire at a specific age, and declining physical capacities all hinder their ability to compete with their younger counterparts.

Conflict theorists might suggest that the elderly form coalitions to increase their power, but for the majority this has not taken place because the aged lack a shared awareness of common social and economic circumstances. Others might suggest that the AARP, which admits members at age 50 who are not necessarily retired, is one example of a rapidly growing coalition that (a) provides a collective consciousness about issues central to the elderly, (b) presses for legislative changes, and (c) uses its large membership size as bargaining power for obtaining favorable rates for insurance, travel, and the like.

Conflict Theory

The conflict theory of the aged emphasizes the inequality and discrimination that occur among all subordinate groups that have little power. According to this view, the aged are a minority group in a youth-oriented society. Because they are less powerful than the younger group, they are treated unfairly, especially in the job market. The corporate elite prefers to hire younger people, who are stronger, healthier, and work for less pay than older, more experienced employees. Younger workers, concerned about the scarcity of jobs, support laws that force the elderly to vacate jobs that the younger workers need. Faced with the opposition of these two powerful groups, the elderly are forced to retire. Because younger workers do not want to pay high taxes to support large numbers of older people, the elderly are often left with no work and little or no income.

Without income, conflict theorists contend, the elderly have little power. As a result, they are unable to combat the negative stereotypes assigned to them. The aged may often be perceived as unattractive, poor, neglected, sickly, depressed, and senile, and these perceptions are used in turn to justify denying them an equitable share of society's resources. Like other minority groups, they are discriminated against in jobs, wages, housing, and many other areas.

According to conflict theorists, the controversies that result from this inequality are beneficial, insofar as they emphasize aging as a social problem and alert increasing numbers of people to the plight of the elderly. Recognizing the problem is the first step toward organizing for political action. Just as the National Organization for Women (NOW) was established to fight for equal rights for women, the Gray Panthers was founded in 1971 by Margaret Kuhn, a retired church worker, to promote the rights of the elderly. Conflict theorists suggest that groups such as the Gray Panthers or the AARP are essential to bringing inequalities to public awareness, to campaigning for social reform, and to forcing social-policy changes.

Thinking Sociologically

Review the theories of aging just presented. Using that presentation as a starting point, discuss the following:

1. How is the modernization of societies likely to affect older people?
2. How may the activity theory lead to different results for widows or married people, those having differing degrees of health, or those with different levels of skills or financial resources?
3. Why are older people often at a disadvantage in terms of bargaining and social exchange? In light of the growing numbers of elderly citizens, are there possible advantages to being old?
4. In terms of conflict theory, how are the aged, as a minority group, likely to experience discrimination?

PROBLEMS OF THE AGED

The problems faced by the elderly in the United States resemble those that some other groups face, but they are compounded by old age. These problems are often magnified among ethnic and minority group members. Here, we discuss just four of these areas of concern: retirement, lifestyles and income, health, and abuse.

Retirement

Retirement is basically a phenomenon of modern industrialized nations. In agrarian societies, there is little paid employment from which to retire. In many areas of the world, the life expectancy is such that too few people live to old age to make retirement an issue of social concern. In Japan, on the other hand, people traditionally retired at age 55 years. When life expectancy was relatively short (50 years in 1945), this allowed Japanese companies to maintain a tradition of "lifetime employment." This tradition of lifetime employment has been threatened, however, by the increased life expectancy to 80 in Japan (see Table 11-1). If retirement was maintained at age 55, the typical Japanese worker could expect to live 25 years or more in retirement, which would mean a substantial increase in the ratio of retirees to workers (old-age dependency ratio).

To address this labor and retirement problem, Japan, in contrast to many other industrialized countries that eliminated or lowered a mandatory retirement age for most workers, increased the retirement age to 60. In a nation with a fairly strict seniority system where age and length of service meant higher pay, discontent resulted when some companies attempted to cut the pay of older workers. Government joined businesses in attempts to encourage part-time employment for older workers (Martin, 1989). The Japanese government also created "Silver

Talent Centers" (Conner, 1992), to provide the retired Japanese worker with an opportunity to make a contribution to society, as well as to continue their productivity. Through these government-funded centers, retired Japanese workers were reemployed in public-service jobs, such as tutors, translators, and advisers to selected businesses. Such opportunities for making positive contributions to societies or to communities may be an important ingredient for self-worth, dignity, and satisfaction in old age, for elderly persons in any location.

Retirement is likely to be increasingly problematic when it is nonvoluntary or when it is associated with loss of status, productivity, usefulness, income, or life itself. Voluntary retirement, which appears to be increasing in the United States, is often viewed as an opportunity to travel, enjoy greater freedom and leisure, and work at self-chosen occupations and avocations. When retirement is mandatory, on the other hand, the person involved does not have control over the decision. Retirement of both types involves resocialization to accommodate new roles, new definitions of self, and modified lifestyles.

Mandatory retirement has been the subject of a long and heated debate. According to Harris and Cole (1980), the issue goes back to 1777, when the first American mandatory-retirement laws were enacted in New York. By 1820, six other states had passed laws requiring the mandatory retirement of judges at ages ranging from 60 to 70 years. The decision to begin retirement at age 65 dates back to the Social Security Act of 1935. This cutoff point was the standard mandatory retirement age until 1978, when Congress raised it to 70, and the issue is still not settled today. It is argued that mandatory retirement is discriminatory, fails to consider the abilities of older people, and leads to resentment among those who want to keep working. Others argue that mandatory retirement is not discriminatory because it ensures that everyone is treated equally and serves as a face-saving device when it is necessary to ease out ineffective workers. It also opens up job and promotional opportunities for younger workers.

Having a set retirement age places the emphasis on retirement as an event rather than a process. As an event, we note the age, the year, or the date at which we leave work. There may be an announcement in the company or community newspaper and a ceremony with a token gift and speech making. The process of retirement, however, may cover a span of many years.

Robert Atchley (1982) believes that the retirement process involves three major periods: preretirement, the retirement transition, and postretirement. Preretirement is the period of looking ahead to retirement: determining when to retire, wondering what to expect, and the like. The *retirement transition* requires leaving a job, ending a career role, and taking up the role of a retired person. The *postretirement* period involves life without the job that was a major focus of time and attention in the preceding years.

To investigate the retirement process, Atchley mailed questionnaires to men and women in a small town near a large metropolitan area in 1975, 1977, 1979, and 1981. Of the 1,100 respondents, about 350 were in the preretirement period and employed full-time. About 50 of the respondents did not plan to retire because they were self-employed and in good health or were unmarried women too poor to retire. The average retirement age for those who planned to retire was 64. Women were much more likely than men to plan to retire before age 60 or after age 70 years. The early retirees tended to have high social status and to be married, whereas the late retirees tended to have low social status and to be unmarried. Thus, there appear to be important class differences in retirement, but general statements about women's retirement should be viewed with caution. Less than 1 percent of either sex in this preretirement period had negative attitudes toward retirement.

Between 1975 and 1979, 170 of the persons surveyed went through the retirement transition. Those who had a negative attitude toward retirement (17 percent of the women and 11 percent of the men) were more apt to have poorer health, lower social status, and incomes they regarded as inadequate. Retirement turned out better than they expected, however, and attitude scores went up significantly following retirement. For both men and women in the total sample, retirement tended to improve life satisfaction slightly, regardless of marital status, health, income adequacy, social status, or living arrangements. It also reduced the activity level for both sexes, but the reduction was much greater for women than for men because their level of activity was much higher before retirement. These activities included visiting with friends, being with children or grandchildren, going for walks, attending church, and so on.

About 300 respondents were in the postretirement period in 1975. This group had very positive attitudes toward their retirement, relatively high activity levels, and positive life satisfaction scores for both sexes. Activity level was a strong predictor of morale among retired men; health was more important among retired women. Interestingly, the older the women, the more positive their attitudes toward retirement were likely to be. It should be noted that the findings in this study were for generally healthy people in one small community, who had many opportunities for participation. In this context, people look forward to retirement, go through the transition smoothly, and find life in retirement to be satisfying.

Lifestyles and Income

The lifestyles of the elderly resemble those of other adult age groups (see Table 11-3). The very wealthy have access to the best care available, can vacation when and where they choose (influenced by health conditions), and can choose to have a second home in a resort area. The wealthy are better able than others to live with their families and to continue the activities they previously enjoyed.

The middle classes often leave their suburban homes when they retire because their income is reduced to the point where they cannot continue to maintain a house. They may move from urban to rural areas, where the cost of living is lower, or to the warmer climates of the South. Some have enough money to move to retirement villages, where they can enjoy a variety of activities and the companionship of other elderly people. Others do not like the age segregation and retire to small towns or rural areas.

People who have always been poor usually continue to live in the same poor areas when they grow old. They may live in subsidized housing for the elderly, in cheap hotels or rooming houses in the city, or in rural housing. The rural poor occasionally migrate to the city because of the shortage of affordable housing and adequate services in rural areas. The elderly poor in general are most likely to suffer from social isolation. They often have no network of friends for socializing and no money to spend on activities. They frequently live in crime-ridden areas and are afraid to venture out into the streets. Their nutrition may be inadequate, so they are more apt to be ill than wealthier people. Thus, the elderly poor suffer from poverty in much the same way that younger groups suffer from poverty.

The aged comprise a large but rapidly decreasing group of the nation's poor. As was mentioned previously, 9.98 percent of family householders age 65 and over in 2000 were below the poverty level. Of those below the poverty level, 8.75 percent were white and 22.5 percent were black. In 2001, the median income of all households with a householder age 65 or over was $23,118, compared with a total median income of $49,227 for all families and $58,045 for householders age 45 to 54. As might be expected, the figures differed considerably by race or Hispanic origin. For non-Hispanic whites over age 65, the mean income was $23,769; for Hispanics, it was $16,870; but for blacks, it was only $16,761 (*Current Population*

TABLE 11-3 THE LIFESTYLES OF OLDER PEOPLE, BY SOCIAL CLASS

	Upper Class	Middle Class	Lower Class
Vacation	Mediterranean cruise	Group bus tour	Visit sister Dora in Detroit
Place for Social Life	Country club	Senior citizens center	Park bench
Recreation	Golf	Shuffleboard	Checkers
Rejuvenation Aids	Spas in Switzerland and Romania	Vitamins	Patent medicines
Retirement Rite	Guest of honor at banquet	Gold watch and group dinner	Handshake and a beer with the boys
Retirement Residence	Condominiums or age-segregated apartment buildings	Retirement communities	Public housing or living with children
Gifts to Grandchildren Under 18	Money	Toys	Cookies and pies
Gifts to Grandchildren Over 18	Checking accounts and cars	Clothes	Cookies and pies

Source: Adaptation of chart from Diane K. Harris and William E. Cole, *Sociology of Aging*. Copyright © 1980 by Harper & Row Publishers, Inc. Reprinted by permission of the publisher.

Survey, 2001). Based on current statistical figures, these figures have not changed significantly.

Despite these figures and the sharp decline in income among the elderly, David Cheal (1983) reminds us that, overall, old people in North America are not as poor as the stereotypes may suggest. Average incomes decline sharply, but so do average expenditures. The ownership of domestic assets such as the family home makes it possible to enjoy a higher standard of living with a lower income than would otherwise be required. In fact, Cheal says that gift-giving by old people is more significant than might be expected and that the elderly give more financial aid to relatives than they receive.

The most common source of income for the aged is **Social Security**. If people work to earn additional income, their Social Security may be reduced or eliminated. If retirees are not eligible for Social Security and have no other income, they are eligible for Supplemental Security Income (SSI), which in 2000 paid an aged person an average of $882 a month. In 2005, the amount increased slightly to $1,002 a month (*Statistical Abstract*, 2000, 2005).

The United States began the Social Security program during the depression of 1930s, when millions of people were out of work and unable to support themselves. The Social Security Act, signed in 1935, was designed such that working citizens covered by the program paid a part of their wages into the program and at age 65 became eligible to receive income based on the amount they had contributed. It was not intended to provide an adequate income, however. It was assumed that savings or pensions that had been accumulated during the working years would also be used during retirement and that Social Security would just provide a secure base on which to build a retirement income.

Social Security benefits have increased steadily since the program began in order to reduce the number of people living in poverty. Whether these benefits will continue to increase is a serious concern to the elderly. As the number of older people increases, the costs of paying benefits may put pressure on the Social Security system, and many expect to see benefits reduced drastically.

Millions of workers in the lowest-paying jobs have never even been covered by Social Security. Either they have been employed by companies that did not have pensions, or they have lost their pensions when they were laid off or their companies went out of business. The meager wages earned during their working years have not permitted them to save money. Today, many of these people live in poverty even when they are assisted by the small SSI payments.

A married woman receives her husband's Social Security benefits after he dies, but forfeits the additional 50 percent share she received while married. The company pensions of husbands are often stopped when the husband dies. Working women often receive low benefits or none at all because they earned low wages or worked in occupations not covered by Social Security. Thus, on the average, women collect much lower benefits than men.

Health

As mentioned, one of the myths discussed earlier in this chapter is that most old people have health problems. No one denies that organs deteriorate and gradually diminish in function over time, but diminishing function alone is not a real threat to the health of most older people. As the U.S. Census Special Report on Aging states (Statistical Briefs, 1995), the older population is healthier than is commonly assumed. In 1992, three in every four noninstitutionalized elderly persons 65 to 74 described their own health as "fair" to "good," as compared with others of their own age. Only 8 percent said that their health was poor. About 40 percent reported that, for health reasons, a major activity had been limited (compared with 20 percent between ages 45 and 64), but 54 percent reported no limitations of any kind in their activities. It is not until age 85 and older that about half of the population report being unable to carry on a major activity because of a chronic illness. Good health among the elderly is highly associated with higher income levels, which probably reflects different opportunities for leisure activities and different eating and nutritional habits.

Health is one area in which differentiating the old-old from the young-old reveals significant differences. The very old need more assistance in eating (4 percent of those over 85 compared with 1 percent of those under), in toileting (7 percent versus 2 percent), in dressing (11 percent), and in bathing (18 percent). The report indicates that, on the basis of these types of activities, more than 80 percent of the noninstitutionalized very old can take care of their own daily needs.

As mentioned earlier, among Americans aged 65 to 69, 49 percent said "these are the best years of my life." Many people in their seventies (44 percent) and eighties (33 percent) agreed. (Among Americans of all ages, 66 percent described the present as their best years.) Sixty percent of older black and 57 percent of older Hispanic respondents said these are their best years ("Myths & Realities of Aging Study," NCOA, 2001).

Nearly half of older Americans consider themselves to be middle aged or young. Only 15 percent of those 75-plus consider themselves "very old" ("American Perceptions on Aging in the 21st Century," NCOA, 2002).

Why, then, is there so much concern about health as a social problem among the elderly? There

SOCIOLOGY AT WORK

Using Sociology in Nursing Care of the Elderly

Drucilla Tiliakos combines the skills of a registered nurse in psychiatric nursing with the advanced training she received from her graduate studies in sociology at Kent State University. In her doctoral work, she specialized in the study of complex organizations and medical sociology. While she was pursuing her Ph.D., she worked as an independent consultant in applied sociology, helping organizations to identify, understand, and resolve problems in which patterns of social interaction play an important role.

In several settings, Tiliakos has used her skills to help elderly patients who were victims of Alzheimer's disease and other chronic brain syndromes involving progressive mental and physical deterioration. Tiliakos explains that it is important to understand the sociological aspects of Alzheimer's disease, as well as the psychological and physiological ones. "Alzheimer's disease, apart from being a tragic condition for the victim and his or her family, is sociologically interesting because of the role changes and social stress that occur among the victim and his or her family constellation. It is of further sociological interest because of the demographic trends in our population, in which a growing proportion consists of persons over the age of sixty-five years. The increasing 'graying' of America is expected to place great strains on our health care facilities and social agencies in terms of their capabilities to provide reasonable care and assistance. Most frequently, sufferers eventually require nursing home care because families, when present, are hard pressed to cope with the scope of the patient's mental and physical deterioration. Since full recovery such as we might expect in acute diseases like pneumonia is not yet possible, a setting which emphasizes a rehabilitation philosophy is most appropriate."

are several reasons. One is chronic disease. The principal diagnoses made by doctors for the elderly in 1980 and 1981 were for hypertension, diabetes, chronic heart disease, cataracts, and osteoarthritis. The diseases predominant among older men are likely to cause death, whereas those that predominate among older women cause only illness.

A second major concern is medical care. The census report on aging indicates that persons 65 and over average only six doctor visits for every five made by the general population. However, the elderly are hospitalized approximately twice as often, stay twice as long, and use twice as many prescription drugs, all of which are very expensive. At the same time, the cost of drugs, hospital care, and physician care has increased at a rate far exceeding that of inflation. Medicaid and Medicare, although widely believed to cover these bills, actually pay for only about half. In addition, both medical programs totally exclude such items as hearing aids, eyeglasses, and some dental services. The problem is compounded by the fact that (1) the American medical profession has a general lack of interest in the problems of the elderly, who are less likely to be cured; (2) the income of the elderly decreases after retirement and becomes fixed, which means that they cannot keep pace with increasing costs; and (3) qualifying for Medicaid requires *pauperization*—people are eligible only after they have drained their resources and literally have joined the aged poor.

Using Sociology in Nursing Care of the Elderly, *continued*

The goals of a rehabilitation center differ from those of acute-care facilities such as hospitals, Tiliakos explains. The treatment of acute illness focuses on curing the disease, whereas rehabilitation focuses on "restoration, adjustment, motivation, and training in the skills needed in daily life. As staff in rehabilitation facilities struggle to care for patients, they need support and training in skills to help them manage distressing patient behaviors and provide support systems for victims and their families."

In her work as an independent consultant for rehabilitation centers, then, Tiliakos has relied on a broad range of sociological information. She has applied her knowledge of the changing roles of the aging, of research methods, and of therapeutic techniques. Her eclectic approach reflects her reasons for pursuing the field of medical sociology and the study of complex organizations. "Essentially, I wanted specialties that would complement my considerable experience and training in psychiatric nursing and that would allow me to develop additional skills that would be useful in organizational development, human relations, and health promotion consultation. I am especially interested in the process of change in organizations as they attempt to adapt to increasingly complex technologies. This trend has affected hospitals, home health care, and nursing homes as well, where we are seeing increases in the [intensity] of patient care and, as a result, the level of knowledge, skills, and technology needed to adequately care for patients and their families. The rapidity of change, while bringing progress in treatment methods, often is accompanied by a considerable degree of organizational and personal stress and strain."

A third problem, one that is often overlooked, is mental health. A destructive stereotype suggests that senility is inevitable in old age and that aged individuals who are not in some state of mental deterioration are rare. However, **senility**—mental infirmity due to old age—is not inevitable. It is estimated that 15–25 percent of the elderly have significant symptoms of mental illness, with about 10 percent due to depression and 5–6 percent to senile dementia (Current Population Reports, Series P-20, No. 128, 1983). The number of elderly mentally ill is projected to swell from about four million in 1970 to 15 million in 2030 (Sanderson, 1999). Psychiatrists and gerontologists are increasingly reporting that even patients who have senile dementia can be helped if the disability is deemphasized and the general quality of their life is improved.

A closely related mental health problem among the aged is **Alzheimer's disease**. According to the Alzheimer's Association, about 4.5 million persons in the United States have this disease, which causes the brain to gradually atrophy (shrink in both size and weight). Affected individuals gradually lose their memories. Their thought processes slow, their judgment is impaired, communication disturbances develop, and disorientation occurs. Those familiar with this incurable disease recognize the tragedy of watching a healthy, able-bodied person gradually deteriorate, come to no longer recognize his or her own children or best friends, and eventually die. By

2050, the estimated range of Alzheimer's disease prevalence will be 11.3 million to 16 million Americans, with a middle estimate of 13.2 million unless a cure or prevention is found. In a 1993 national survey, 19 million Americans said they had a family member with Alzheimer's, and 37 million said they knew someone with Alzheimer's. One in 10 persons over 65 and nearly half of those over 85 have Alzheimer's. A small percentage of people as young as their 30's and 40's get the disease.

A final mental health concern among the elderly is suicide. The annual suicide rate for all ages in the United States is between 11.3 per 100,000 population. However, for white males ages 65 years and older, the rate is about 37 per 100,000, and for black males, 11.6 per 100,000. Interestingly, similar increases do not occur among women. The rate for elderly white women is 5.0 per 100,000 and 1.2 for black women.

The following possible reasons for these dramatically higher rates for men have been suggested: Men may be more adversely affected by retirement; may be less willing to endure illness and inactive status; may be more action-oriented, combative, and aggressive; may feel diminished by not being in charge in the home as they were in the workplace; and may be less integrated into an intimate network of friends. In contrast, women are said to be more intimately involved in a circle of supportive friends, better able to handle poverty, and more accustomed to a secondary status in a male dominated society. Clearly, Durkheim's propositions relating the degree of social integration to levels of mental health and suicide seem as applicable to the elderly as to other groups.

Abuse

One problem that has only recently received major research and policy attention is the abuse, exploitation, and neglect of the elderly by the people upon whom they depend. This is one of our newest social problems, and little information about it was available until the late 1970s. Since then, a number of investigations have been conducted, and they show an estimated 293,000 reports of domestic elder abuse nationwide (Tatara and Kuzmeskus, 1997).

The severity of mistreatment of older people ranges from reasonably benign neglect to severe emotional and physical abuse. The most common form of neglect is *passive*, such as when an elderly dependent is left alone without essential medical care, food, or clothing. Passive neglect may also happen because a caregiver is inept or unable to provide for the needs of the elderly person. *Active neglect*, which is less common, occurs when needed goods or services are intentionally withheld, and social contacts are forbidden. Caregivers have been known to tie older people to a bed or chair or to lock them in a room while they go out, give them alcohol or excessive medication to make them more manageable, to threaten violence to force them to sign over a Social Security check, and to deceive them into changing their wills. Many of these examples of passive and active neglect result in severe emotional pain and abuse.

A commonly cited cause of such abuses is that the caregiver is being overtaxed by the requirements of looking after a dependent adult. Pillemer (1985), however, found no support for the hypothesis that the dependency of the elderly leads to abuse. His research suggests that the typical abused elder, rather than being a dependent, may be an older woman supporting a dependent child or, to a lesser extent, a physically or mentally disabled spouse. From an exchange perspective, the victims perceived themselves as being on the losing end, or as giving much and receiving little. Most did not leave the situation but felt trapped by a sense of family obligation.

In addition to benign neglect or emotional abuse is physical abuse. *Physical abuse* may involve beating, hitting, pushing, burning, cutting, mugging, sexually molesting, or otherwise injuring an elderly person. This type of abuse, more than neglect, is likely to come to the attention of police, physicians, community social service workers (caseworkers), or clergy. The professionals involved in such instances are also likely to observe various other forms of emotional abuse, such as threats, fraud or financial exploitation, and intimidation.

With all types of abuse, women are victims more often than men. Victims also tend to be the older elderly (75 or older), people who are frail and mentally or physically disabled. The abuser is usually a son or a daughter of the victim and is often experiencing great stress brought about by alcoholism, drug addiction, marital problems, or chronic financial difficulties, in addition to the burden of caring for an aging parent.

Parallels can be drawn between the abuse and neglect of children. In both cases, the victims are heavily if not totally dependent on others for basic survival needs. They both lack resources such as strength, speed, and independent finances to protect themselves. The family or intimate group network is the source of abuse far more often than strangers are. In both cases, the abuse generally occurs in the home. In fact, for all citizens, young or old, rich or poor, the most dangerous place is the home.

It is unlikely that major government-supported programs at a federal, state, or local level will be created to combat neglect and abuse of the elderly, even though governments have taken action to prevent child and spouse abuse. Today's political climate, economic support for social programs, and conservative orientation toward social concerns all tend to place the emphasis on voluntary responses to human needs. Some local and voluntary agencies have joined together to organize reporting and referral systems and temporary shelters for elderly victims. Other services are needed, however—laws mandating that physicians and others who work with the elderly report their suspicions of abuse, free or low-cost legal service systems, and increased support services, such as transportation, meal preparation, and chore and homemaker services. Many of these services now exist at a minimal level, but the need is too great, and voluntary services alone cannot solve the problem.

Thinking Sociologically

What factors do you consider important in influential in preparation for (a) retirement, (b) a particular lifestyle in old age, (c) a high level of physical and mental health, and (d) the prevention of elder abuse?

DEATH AND DYING

All humans die. Therefore, for most persons, the awareness and the anticipation of death is an important aspect of living. While death may occur at any age, it is most expected, accepted, and understood among the elderly. As a result, groups and societies develop patterns of behavior and institutional arrangements to manage death and its impact (see Marshall and Levy, 1990).

The aged must confront two difficult facts—their own death and the death of their friends and loved ones. Surprising though it may seem, socialization plays a role in preparing people for death. As with other types of social behavior, our social institutions, norms, and practices largely determine how we think about dying. Symbolic interaction theory, for example, would suggest that the definitions and meanings we attach to illness and death greatly influence our ability to cope with it. An understanding of reference groups may help us understand the functioning of the church, friends, or a kin network as support systems in facing death. How we mourn, what we do with the physical remains of the dead, how we behave after the death of a family member, how we prepare for our own death—all are influenced by cultural, class, and other social factors.

In the United States and most other cultures, the family and kin network is the major social support in times of illness. Among the elderly, the presence of relatives may make it possible for bedridden persons to live outside of institutions. Elderly people turn first to their families for help, then to neighbors, and finally—only as a last resort—to bureaucratic replacements for families. This sequence is consistent with survey findings that show that most people would like to die at home. Nevertheless, medical attention, nursing care, and social workers for the dying are based in hospitals. Four people wish to die at home for every one who would like to die in a hospital, but in actual practice, the ratio is reversed (Hine, 1979–1980). More recently from the BBC News, a survey found two-thirds of those sampled would want to die at home if they were terminally ill. But a lack of funding for palliative care means only 25 percent of cancer patients can currently do so (BBC News, U.K. Edition, March 2004).

An alternative to hospital care, the hospice movement is intended to make family interaction with the terminally ill or dying patient easier. A **hospice** is a therapeutic environment designed from the patients' point of view. Unlike a regular hospital with its emphasis on privacy, a hospice provides space for interaction with staff, family, and friends. Instead of subordinating the patient to the needs of the institution, hospice programs are designed to provide as much care in the patient's home as possible; when medical facilities are required, they include a team of medical, nursing, psychiatric, religious, and social workers, as needed, plus family members. The concern is to increase the quality of the last days or months of life and to provide humane care. The family of the institutionalized patient is encouraged to be involved: They can bring in "home cooking," bathe the patient, supply medication, or even bring along the family dog. Hours for visits are unlimited, and patients are allowed to interact with young children or grandchildren. The program is innovative, but it is very expensive as well, and few hospices care for chronically ill people who are expected to live for a year or more.

A controversial issue concerning the terminally ill is **euthanasia**. Euthanasia, sometimes called "mercy killing" or "elective death," is the deliberate ending of a person's life, to spare him or her from the suffering that goes with an incurable and agonizing disease. Euthanasia can be passive (not preventing death) or active (causing death).

In *passive euthanasia*, treatment is terminated, and nothing is done to prolong the person's life artificially. In *active euthanasia*, actions are deliberately taken to end a person's life. The person who takes the action may be a physician, a husband or wife who shoots or strangles a terminally ill spouse because the loved one's suffering is unbearable or because the loved one has asked that it be done, or other persons who have been asked by the dying to assist in their deciding their own destiny. A Michigan doctor, Jack Kevorkian, brought the physician-assisted suicide issue to national attention in 1991 when he consented to instruct and assist three women in using his suicide machine to end their lives. As this textbook goes into print, societal and legal responses to his actions are continuing. Thus, in contrast to passive euthanasia, where the decision is made to let a person die without medical intervention, active euthanasia includes the decision to assist in the termination of life.

As noted in this chapter, the growth of the aged population and the increased numbers who will survive to age 85 years and beyond will provide major challenges to societies in providing economic assistance and social services to this segment of the population. One of our great challenges will be to devise social structures that will allow the elderly to lead active lives for as long as possible and to live graciously and with dignity even when they can no longer be active.

Thinking Sociologically

While euthanasia is not just relevant to elderly patients, it is clear that it is an issue that is more likely to concern the elderly because they are closer to the point at which life would naturally end, and they are more likely to encounter illness or enter a state of health in which euthanasia might be considered. Using theories of aging and age differentiation—and other material in this chapter—evaluate the pros and cons of both passive and active euthanasia. After you evaluate each side of the debate, take a position as to whether active euthanasia should be allowed.

SUMMARY

1. All societies differentiate behavior by age. *Age*, an ascribed status, includes social expectations about appropriate behaviors for persons who have lived a certain number of years. *Aging*, the process of growing older, is accompanied by biological, psychological, and social changes as people move through the life course.

2. The systematic study of the aging process is known as *gerontology*. *Social gerontology*, a subfield of gerontology, focuses on the social and cultural aspects of age and of the aging process.

3. Expectations about the behavior considered appropriate for people of a given age are *age norms*. Many such norms reflect inaccurate stereotypes and may lead to ageism, which is prejudice and discrimination based on age.

4. Myths about the aged suggest that they are senile, miserable, lonely, unhealthy, frequent victims of crime, poor, unable to manage households, incapable of and disinterested in sexual relations, and probably live in nursing homes. All of these stereotypes are basically false.

5. The elderly are considered to be those age 65 and over. Some gerontologists differentiate between the young-old (55–74) and the *old-old* (75 and over). Demographically, the percentage of elderly people in the total population is increasing, as is life expectancy, although there are considerable variations due to sex and race. Interestingly, the life expectancy of those who reach old age has increased very little and the life span is basically unchanged. The proportion of older people who do not work is increasing in comparison to the younger working population; this proportion is known as the old-age *dependency ratio*.

6. The social characteristics of the elderly vary widely according to sex, marital status, living arrangements, geographical distribution, labor force participation, and other factors. Women greatly outnumber men, and many women are widows, but most of the elderly live in their own homes or with their families. Geographically, they tend to live in metropolitan areas, and they are heavily concentrated in some states. The proportion of the elderly in the labor force has dropped considerably over the past several decades.

7. There are a number of theories on aging and age differentiation. Theories based on the structural functional perspective include modernization and disengagement theory. *Modernization theory* assumes that the status of old people declines with increasing modernization.

Disengagement theory, which is less widely accepted, contends that as people grow older, they go through a period of mutual disengagement or withdrawal from the rest of society.

8. A symbolic interaction perspective, *activity theory*, states that those who remain active, particularly with avocations, part-time jobs, and interaction in primary networks, will be better adjusted than those who do not.

9. *Social exchange theory* suggests that both withdrawal and activity can be best explained in terms of the decreasing power of the elderly. Having less to exchange and a greater dependency on others forces the elderly into social compliance. Finally, *conflict theory*, drawing on exchange theory, assumes that inequalities in areas such as jobs, wages, and housing permit the elderly to be exploited.

10. The aged share many of the problems of the rest of society, but their problems are often compounded because they have fewer resources and less power. Nevertheless, most people look forward to retirement.

11. The lifestyles of the elderly vary greatly, depending on their social class and income. Women and blacks are the groups most likely to live in poverty. The most common source of income for the aged is Social Security. A minimal income is available to those not on Social Security through the Supplemental Security Income (SSI) program.

12. Income and class level greatly influence the health of the elderly. Most say that their health is fair or good, but those whose health is poor often face chronic disease, high medical costs, and prolonged hospitalization. A relatively small proportion of the aged suffer from mental problems such as those related to Alzheimer's disease.

13. The abuse of the elderly has come to be recognized recently as a widespread problem. Like dependent children, the elderly are often neglected or physically abused. They have few resources to protect themselves. In most cases, they are abused in their homes by their caregivers.

14. A *hospice* is a therapeutic environment for terminally ill patients, designed to permit interaction with family and friends and to combine good medical care with humane treatment. Euthanasia, sometimes called "mercy killing," is a controversial issue concerning those who have terminal illnesses.

KEY TERMS

activity theory The theory of aging that suggests that elderly persons who remain active will be the best adjusted.

age The number of years since birth.

aged The age group that occupies the later part of the life span, generally meaning the old, elderly, or senior citizens.

ageism Prejudice and discrimination based on age.

age norms Expectations about the behavior considered appropriate for people of a given age.

aging The biological, psychological, or social processes that occur with growing older.

Alzheimer's disease A disease affecting primarily older persons in which the brain gradually atrophies, resulting in loss of memory and impairment of thought processes.

dependency ratio The ratio between the number of persons in the dependent population and the number of people in the supportive or working population.

disengagement theory The theory of aging that suggests that as people get older, they and the younger people around them go through a period of mutual withdrawal.

euthanasia Sometimes called mercy killing; deliberately ending a person's life to spare him or her suffering from an incurable and agonizing disease.

geriatrics The subfield of gerontological practice that deals with the medical care of the aging.

gerontology The systematic study of the aging process.

hospice A home for terminally ill patients in which the emphasis is on providing a comfortable, supportive environment for the patient and the patient's family.

life course An age-related progression or sequence of roles and group memberships that people go through as they mature and move through life.

life expectancy The average years of life remaining for persons who attain a given age.

life span The biological age limit beyond which no one can expect to live.

modernization theory The view that the status of older people declines with modernization.

senility A mental infirmity associated with the aging process.

social gerontology A branch of gerontology that focuses on the social and cultural factors related to age and the aging process.

Social Security The federal program that provides financial support for the elderly.

DISCUSSION QUESTIONS

1. List a number of age norms that exist for teenagers or those in their early 20s. How would you explain their existence and differentiation from those existing for younger or older persons?
2. How do myths about old age lead to prejudice against the elderly?
3. Discuss some ways in which shifts in the dependency ratio might effect family life. How have changes in the dependency ratio affected life in your family over the past two or three generations?
4. What types of social changes, social problems, and social benefits might occur from the increase in life expectancy?
5. Discuss changes in marital status and living arrangements by age. What types of factors other than widowhood affect marital status and living arrangements?
6. It was stated that the elderly are heavily concentrated in a few states. Why? What are some social implications (recreation, transportation, consumer spending, health care, etc.) of this geographical distribution?
7. Briefly discuss how structural functional theory, conflict theory, symbolic interaction theory, and social exchange theory could be used to explore the role of elderly people in your family and how they are treated.
8. People are retiring at earlier ages than in the past. Why? What benefits and costs, for society

as well as for the individuals themselves, are associated with this change?

9. Examine the lifestyles of the elderly by ethnicity. What differences exist? Why do these differences exist? Is there any need to establish different policies for Hispanic-Americans, Native Americans, African-Americans, or white Appalachian Americans?

10. Describe various health needs that are most prevalent among the elderly, and discuss issues related to them: care, cost, curability, and the like.

PART FOUR

Social Institutions

The aim of education is the knowledge not of fact, but of values.

DEAN WILLIAM R. INGE

Family Groups and Systems

Same-Sex Relationships in the United States

The United States is experiencing an unprecedented debate over the definitions and consequences of marriage, appropriate sexual behaviors, acceptable parents, sex education, and same-sex partnerships. In our history as a society, never has there been such unrest and urgency about the morals and values attached to these particular issues—all related to home and family. We have been able to record and study the consequences of divorce and its effects on the individuals involved. However, many topics that are currently debated have not been a part of official research long enough for us to know the effects.

Perhaps the fear of the unknown is a major part of the urgency felt by many Americans. However, there is also a battle being waged around moral values. Many Americans fear the collapse of family if new forms are accepted and socially sanctioned as appropriate. These debates give us much information as to how social structures are created and maintained.

Without doubt, the current source of national contention, for those with strong opinions or personal interest, is the attempts being made and the possibility for same-sex marriages. In early March of 2004, President George W. Bush called on Congress "to promptly pass" and send to the states for ratification an amendment to the Constitution that would ban gay marriage anywhere in the United States (Powe, Jr., 2004). Although the proposal was defeated in the Senate as most predicted, the suggestion of an amendment stirred strong sentiment in many organizations, groups, and individuals on both sides of the same-sex debate. More politically important, the suggestion of an amendment led eleven states to pass amendments to their constitutions outlawing marriage between same-sex couples. The amendments were passed in these eleven states by mostly overwhelming majorities. The following states passed amendments: Arkansas, Georgia, Kentucky, Michigan, Mississippi, Montana, North Dakota, Oklahoma, Ohio, Oregon, and Utah. To date no act or agency of the U.S. Federal Government recognizes same sex marriages. Among the two major political parties in the United States the Republican Party opposes gay rights more so than the Democratic Party.

Although eleven states have passed amendments, the larger issue of same-sex rights related to marriage is much more complex. According to poll results published in the *Washington Times*, most Americans say homosexual sexual relations are morally wrong. Additionally, after two decades of tracking, results also show that a majority of Americans oppose homosexual marriage (Wetzstein, 2003). However, majorities of people in such polls say homosexual relations between consenting adults should not be against the law.

Data from the National Opinion Research Center at the University of Chicago depict the following characteristics of those most accepting of homosexual relationships. They are likely to be Americans in their 20s who rarely attend religious services and live in the northeastern states. Furthermore, Americans generally support some sort of domestic benefits to homosexual couples, says Karlyn Bowman, a scholar at American Enterprise Institute (AEI), "but they draw the line at gay marriage" (Wetzstein, 2003). The same article reports that a recent Gallup Poll found that 55 percent of Americans said "marriages" between homosexuals "should not be recognized as valid." This however is a smaller majority than in 1996, when 68 percent of Americans said homosexual "marriages" shouldn't be valid.

Although the numbers against same-sex marriage are greater than those who favor, the trend seems to be pointing in a direction of greater understanding, with a substantial increase in the last several years of voters who agree that same-sex couples deserve the same legal protections and benefits as heterosexual couples (National Gallup Poll, May 2003). With the numbers and public sentiment shifting in the direction of equality, another idea, civil unions, has been discussed and debated as well. What is the difference between a marriage and a civil union?

A civil union is a legal status created by the state of Vermont in 2000, the State of California in 2003, and the State of Massachusetts in 2004. It provides legal protection to couples at the state law level, but omits federal protections as well as the dignity, clarity, security and power of the word "marriage" (GLAD, 2004). Those who support marriage over civil unions argue that even if there were no substantive differences in the way the law treated marriages and civil unions, the fact that a civil union remains a separate status just for gay people represents real and powerful inequality.

This chapter is particularly useful for helping us learn to look at new family forms with "fresh eyes," because it examines the family as an institution. That is, it shows how families within different societies and cultures are structured to meet the associated differing needs. In this light, we can begin to explore the new family forms that result from the societal needs that are emerging in a society where uncertainty about family, marriage, and partnering is becoming more prevalent.

If we want to understand society and social life, it is impossible to ignore the family. Most of us spend a major portion of our lives in one form of family or another. It is unlikely that any society has ever existed without some social arrangement that could be termed "family," and we cannot overestimate its importance to the individual and to society as a whole.

This chapter considers the family as a group, as a social system, and as a social institution. For most of us, the family serves as a primary social group; it is the first agency of socialization. Sociologists consider the family to be a *social system* because it is composed of interdependent parts, it has a characteristic organization and pattern of functioning, and it has subsystems that are part of the larger system. The family is considered a *social institution* because it is an area of social life that is organized into discernible patterns and because it helps to meet crucial societal goals.

Families do not exist in isolation, of course. They are an interdependent unit of the larger society. If families have many children, for example, schools may become crowded and unemployment may become a problem. If, on the other hand, they have few children, over several generations Social Security, the care of the aged, and an adequate work force may become important issues. It also makes a difference whether one spouse is employed or both are. Do newlyweds live with one set of parents or establish independent residences? Is divorce frequent or infrequent? Do people select their own mates or have them selected for them? Family practices have a profound influence on many aspects of social life.

We begin our discussion by clarifying what we mean by the term *family*. Although the answer may appear quite obvious to most of us, it becomes less obvious to judges who must make decisions on property settlements with cohabiting couples, social service workers who get adoption requests from unmarried persons or same-sex couples, or government agencies who must decide who is eligible for various benefits. Some definitions result in informal stigmatization and discrimination against families who do not meet the qualifications, such as a mother and her child, two men, or an unmarried man and woman.

WHAT IS FAMILY?

The **family** has traditionally been defined as a group of kin united by blood, marriage, or adoption, who share a common residence for some part of their lives, and who assume reciprocal rights and obligations with regard to one another. Today, however, an increasing number of writers are defining *families* differently. They recognize the reality of childless marriages, step-parents, one-parent households, same-sex unions, and cohabiting couples. Currently, we can think about families in terms of intimate relationships, sexual bonds, and family realms.

The traditional definition of *family* suggests ideas of legal unions, permanence, children, intergenerational continuity, and a perceived ideal of what families should be. The nontraditional definition suggests a broader and more comprehensive portrayal of intimate relationships that often fall outside of fixed legal boundaries. Thus, a same-sex (lesbian or gay) couple or a heterosexual cohabiting couple, with or without children, would not be a family in traditional terms of blood, marriage, or adoptive ties. However, in terms of family-like relationships based on what families do (engage in intimate interactions, share household expenses and a division of labor, recognize other members as part of a primary intimate bonded unit), some same-sex or cohabiting partners are being viewed as families for purposes of property settlements, housing regulations for "families only," or employee benefit plans. Up to this point, however, few numbers or figures have existed that include these types of families.

This is not to deny the tremendous variations in traditional family structures and processes that exist in our own culture and in others around the world. There exists a recognition of differentiating families as conjugal, nuclear, families of orientation and procreation, as well as extended or modifications of an extended structure. The smallest units are called **conjugal families**, which must include a husband and wife but may or may not include children. **Nuclear families** may or may not include a husband and wife—they consist of any two or more persons related to one another by blood, marriage, or adoption who share a common residence. Thus, a brother and sister or a single parent and child would be nuclear families but not conjugal families. These terms are sometimes used interchangeably, and some families fall under both categories.

The definition used in census reporting in the United States is the nuclear family. Family households are identified when the members of a household are related to the householder. The count of family units, regardless of whether the householder is in that family, is considered a family group. In 2000, there were 72 million family households and 76 million family groups in this country. Of these, 56.5 million were husband-and-wife family households (*Current Population Reports*, Series P-20, No. 537, 2001). Traditionally, family households made up the majority of all households. In 1970, 81 percent were family households; by 2000, family households made up 69 percent of all households.

Approximately 95 percent of all Americans marry at some time in their lives. In so doing, they become members of two different but overlapping nuclear families. The nuclear family into which a person is born and reared (consisting of the person, brothers, sisters, and parents) is termed the **family of orientation**. This is the family in which most basic early childhood socialization occurs. When a person marries, a new nuclear (and conjugal) family is formed, which is called the **family of procreation**. This family consists of the person, a spouse, and children. These relations are diagrammed in Figure 12-1.

In the world as a whole, conjugal and nuclear families as isolated and independent units are rare. In most societies, the norm is the **extended family**, which goes beyond the nuclear family to include other nuclear families and relatives, such as grandparents, aunts, uncles, and cousins.

Is the typical family in the United States nuclear or extended? Actually, it is both. It is not an isolated nuclear unit that is separate from extended kin contacts and support, nor is it an extended family in the traditional sense that extended family members share the same household. American families typically have what is called a **modified-extended family structure**, in which individual nuclear families retain considerable autonomy and yet maintain connections with other nuclear families through visits,

FIGURE 12-1 FAMILIES OF ORIENTATION AND OF PROCREATION

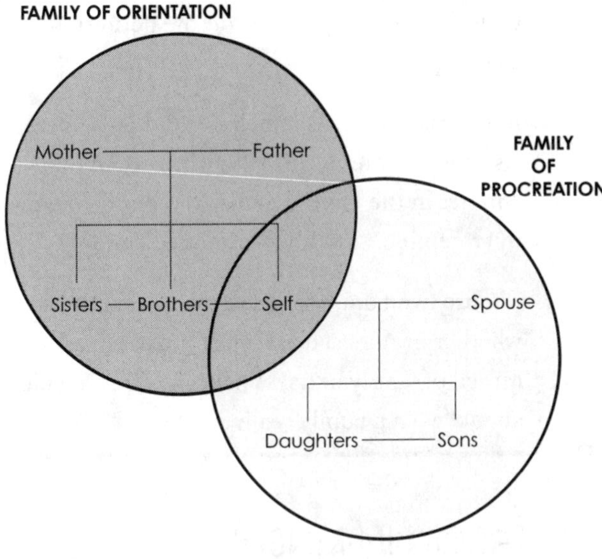

calls, or the exchange of goods, services, or affective greetings. This type of family differs from the traditional extended family, in that its members may live in different parts of the country and may choose their occupations independently rather than following the parent's occupation.

APPLYING DEFINITIONS OF FAMILY

It is important for many reasons, therefore, to realize that there may be more than one acceptable definition of what a family is. Social scientist Arlene Skolnick (1992) points out that one of the major obstacles to social scientists in studying and understanding the family is the temptation to use our own experience as a basis for generalizations and comparisons. Everyone has a great deal of experience with families—their own—and there is a tendency to use our own family as a basis for insights and theories about families in general. Recognizing that there is a tremendous variety of types of family patterns is an essential part of helping social scientists to overcome their own ethnocentrism, stereotypes, and prejudices, which might get in the way of doing their objective research.

As suggested earlier, it is important for politicians who make policies that affect families to understand that because there are variations in types of families, strict definitions may be problematic. As Skolnick (1997) and many others who have explored the impact of policies upon the family have noted, how a family is defined has important consequences for the nature of policies and how they are carried out. Zoning laws, tax laws, welfare regulations, federally funded student loan guidelines, and many other policies often employ a particular definition of a family. Limiting the definition of what a family is to one type—or even a few—can have serious consequences for people's lives. Suppose there is a zoning ordinance that stipulates that only single families can occupy homes in a particular area. Are two unmarried people of the opposite or same sex who live together considered a family? Are two spouses and their children who live together with both of one spouse's parents and the brother of one of the spouses a single family or two families? How that zoning ordinance defines what a family is would determine whether either of these groups would be allowed to live in the area in question. Policymakers need to understand that families may not necessarily be limited to the middle-class norm of mother, father, and their children residing together in a male-dominated household.

In a clinical setting, the therapeutic and counseling techniques used by marriage and family counselors may be determined largely by how the family is defined. Assuming that there is only one definition of the family could lead some therapists to look at families that fall outside that definition as pathological or troubled. Certainly, some families are in trouble, but not necessarily because they do not fit the norm of the white, middle-class nuclear family. In recognizing that there are many possible ways to live as a family, marriage counselors might be able to be more creative and flexible in what they have to offer their clients.

Finally, and perhaps most important for you, the recognition that there is more than one acceptable definition of a family can lead to more choices and freedom in your own life. This does not mean, however, that you have complete freedom to live the way you want to or that every family pattern will necessarily work. As this chapter shows later, many family and kinship patterns may be workable only in a particular social context that emphasizes the social creation and construction of family and kinship patterns. However, the options that are workable in a particular social context may not be as limited as they were once thought to be.

Family groups and systems are only one type of kinship association. **Kinship** is the web of relationships among people linked by common ancestry, adoption, or marriage. All societies have general norms for defining family and kin groups and how these relationships are organized. These norms concern such matters as who lives together, who is the head of the group, who marries whom, how mates are selected, which relatives in family and kin groups are most important, and how and by whom children are to be raised. Although some general norms tend to determine the statuses and roles of family members, other norms and the kinship systems they govern vary greatly. These variations are discussed in the next section.

Thinking Sociologically

1. Examine both traditional and nontraditional definitions of the family. How might family policies differ, depending on the definition used?

2. In terms of patterns of helping and assistance, visiting, or letter writing, to what extent do families in the United States (or your own family) resemble a modified-extended family?

3. Choose two family forms to compare. Discuss whether or not each can meet the basic tasks required of family units. What can you conclude about "what a family really is"?

VARIATION IN KINSHIP AND FAMILY ORGANIZATION

Each society defines particular patterns of marriage, family, and kinship as correct and proper. Because we tend to be ethnocentric and to favor the family structure found in our own society, we may overlook the wide range of variations that exist. We may also tend to assume that if our current family forms change too drastically, the institution of the family will collapse. It is important to recognize that a tremendous variety of marriage, family, and kinship patterns exist and that any of these patterns may be both appropriate and workable in a particular social context. One fundamental variation concerns marriage and the number of spouses considered acceptable.

Marriage and Number of Spouses

Marital status (single, married, separated, widowed, divorced) and number of spouses (none, one, more than one) are two major variations in family organization. Every society permits some form of marriage, although some groups, such as the Catholic Church, take the position that nuns and priests, to devote their lives fully to God, must take vows of chastity and remain unmarried. Totally apart from religious reasons, in the United States today, it seems that remaining single may be emerging as an acceptable lifestyle. It is unclear, however, whether this is a permanent alternative to marriage or just a delay in marriage.

To most Americans, the most "proper" form of marriage is monogamy, in which one man is married to one woman at a time. Throughout the world, this form of marriage is the only one universally recognized; it is the predominant form even in societies where other forms exist. However, only about 20 percent of the world's societies are strictly monogamous, considering monogamy the only acceptable form of marriage.

Although the United States is considered strictly monogamous, it is possible to have more than one husband or one wife. An increasing number of married people end their relationship with one spouse and remarry another. This pattern of marrying is called **serial** or **sequential monogamy**. It is both legally and socially accepted to have more than one wife or husband as long as it is done sequentially and not simultaneously. It is completely illegal in every state in the United States to be married to more than one person at any given time.

There are a variety of alternatives to monogamy. Murdock (1957) investigated the frequency of **polygamy**, marriage to more than one spouse, in a sample of 554 societies from around the world. He found that **polygyny**, in which a man has more than one wife, was the norm in 77 percent of these societies, whereas **polyandry**, in which a woman has more than one husband, was culturally favored in less than 1 percent. **Group marriage**, in which several or many men are married to several or many women, has been practiced among selected groups in some societies, but nowhere is it the dominant form.

One example of group marriage in the United States was that of the Oneida Community, the founding group of Oneida Corporation that is listed today on the New York Stock Exchange. For about 30 years in the mid-1800s, John Humphrey Noyes preached that people were capable of living sinless lives based on a spiritual equality of all persons: materially, socially, and sexually. The outcome of this teaching was a group marriage structure where all adults were recognized as married to each other, all adults were parents to all children, and the total emphasis was on "we" rather than "I."

In discussing polygamy or any family structure with a plural number of spouses, several words of caution are in order. First, a distinction must be made between ideology and actual occurrence. The fact that a society permits one to have several spouses does not necessarily mean that a large proportion of all marriages are polygamous. Second, except for group marriage, multiple spouses are possible on a large scale only when the ratio of the sexes is unbalanced. Third, when polygamy is practiced, it is controlled by societal norms like any other form of marriage. Rather than resulting from strictly personal or psychological motives, it is supported by the values and norms of both sexes and is closely linked to the economic conditions and belief systems of the wider society. Fourth, polygamy itself may take a variety of forms. The multiple husbands may all be brothers or the multiple wives may all be sisters, for example.

The most common form of polygamy is polygyny. In many societies, having several wives is a mark of prestige and high status. The wealthy, the leaders, and the best hunters may get a second or third wife. Multiple wives may also be desired as a source of children, especially sons. Polygyny is very common in Africa, among Muslim groups in the Middle East and Asia, and in many tribal groups in South America and throughout the world. In Ibadan, Nigeria, for example, a study of more than 6,600 women (Ware, 1979) found that nearly one wife in two was living in a polygamous marriage; the proportion rose to two out of three for wives age 40 years and above. The Muslim religion permits men to have up to four wives. In the United States, despite its illegality, some Mormon fundamentalists living in Utah and neighboring states practice polygyny.

The Web site Absolam, http://www.absalom.com/mormon/polygamy/faq.htm, reports that 70 percent of Utah is Mormon and of those Mormons, 5 percent or 60,000 people practice polygamy. (Even though the Mormon Church has not recognized the practice of polygamy for over a hundred years). A (1998) poll by the Salt Lake tribune found that 35 percent of Utah's population thinks that polygamists should not be prosecuted.

Polyandry is quite rare. Where it is practiced, the co-husbands are usually brothers, either blood brothers or clan brothers who belong to the same clan and are of the same generation. Among the Todas, for example, a non-Hindu tribe in India, it is understood that when a woman marries a man, she becomes the wife of his brothers at the same time. This type of polyandry, where brothers are co-husbands, may also be referred to as **fraternal polyandry**.

Norms of Residence

When people marry, they must decide where to live. Decisions about place of residence are typically dictated by societal norms and conform to one of three patterns. In Western societies, the residence norm is **neolocal**—the couple lives alone wherever they wish—but this pattern is rare in the rest of the world. Of the societies Murdock (1949) examined, only about 10 percent considered it appropriate for newlywed couples to move to a place of residence separate from both the husband's and the wife's families. This type of residence pattern seems to be linked with norms of monogamy and individualism. Nearly three-fourths of the societies studied by Murdock were **patrilocal**—the newlywed couple lived not just in the groom's community, but usually in his parents' home or compound. This type of residence is most common in polygamous hunting-and-gathering societies throughout Asia, Africa, and Latin America. In the United States, the Amish communities represent one example of a patrilocal system. A **matrilocal** residence pattern, in which the newly married couple lives with the wife's family, was the norm in about 15 percent of the societies Murdock studied and was generally found where women held title to the land.

Norms of Descent and Inheritance

Children inherit two separate bloodlines at birth, the mother's and the father's. Most societies place more importance on one lineage or the other. In much of the Western world, particularly in the United States, lineage is of small importance. It determines surname but little else. In most societies, however, explicit rules indicate that one bloodline is more important than the other. These rules are known as the "norms of descent and inheritance."

The most common norms of descent are **patrilineal**, in which kinship is traced through the male kin, the father's lineage. In this type of descent system, offspring owe a special allegiance and loyalty to the father and his kin, who in turn protect and socialize the children and eventually pass to the sons their authority, property, and wealth. Under this system, the key ties are those among father, sons, and grandsons. The wife may maintain ties to her kin, and she contributes her genes to her children, but she and her children are considered members of her husband's family.

In a **matrilineal** system of descent, descent and inheritance are traced through the mother's line. The mother's kin assume the important role among offspring. Matrilineal norms of descent are uncommon, but they do exist. Among the Trobriand Islanders, for example, kinship, wealth, and responsibility for support are traced through the female line.

In the United States, the norm is to assign influence, wealth, and power to both sides of the family. This system is referred to as **bilateral lineage**. Kinship lines are traced equally through the biological relatives of both the mother and the father, and inheritance is passed on in equal proportions to all children regardless of sex. One consequence of this descent system is that, although the kin of both parents are equally recognized and respected, neither kin group exerts much power and influence over the children, which has a significant effect on social change: a newlywed couple coming from families with different values and lifestyles may choose to conform to neither and establish a lifestyle of their own. In addition, the likelihood of marrying someone with different values increases because the parents and kin groups in bilateral systems have relatively little influence over whom their sons or daughters marry.

Norms of Authority

All families and kinship systems have norms concerning who makes important decisions. These norms follow the pattern of other norm variations in that they are aligned with gender. Most societies are **patriarchal**—the men have the power and authority and are dominant. In Iran, Thailand, and Japan, the male position of dominance is even reflected in the law. In matriarchal societies, the authority rests with the females, especially wives and mothers. **Matriarchal** systems are rare, even among matrilineal societies such as that of the Trobriand Islanders, where the wives do not have authority over their husbands.

It is important to recognize that although authority in most families rests with the males, other family members have a strong influence on the decision-making process. Male family members are generally most influential, but wives and mothers often have a strong impact on decisions as well.

The least common pattern of authority is the **egalitarian** model, in which decisions are equally divided between husband and wife. Some have argued that the United States is egalitarian because husbands and wives either make decisions jointly or assume responsibility for different areas of concern. The husband might make decisions related to his job, the automobile, or home repairs, whereas the wife might make decisions related to her job, the home, food, clothing, or the children. Many would argue that the family system in the United States is more patriarchal than egalitarian, however, because males generally control income and other family resources.

Norms for Choice of Marriage Partner

Every society, including the United States, has norms concerning the appropriateness or unacceptability of some types of marriage partners. These norms can be divided into two categories: **exogamy**, in which people must marry outside of their own group, and **endogamy**, which requires that people considering marriage share particular group characteristics, such as age, race, religion, or socioeconomic status.

Some exogamous norms are almost universal. **Incest**—sexual relations or marriage with close relatives—is forbidden in almost every society. One cannot marry one's mother, father, brother, sister, son, or daughter. Isolated exceptions to this taboo are said to have existed among Egyptian and Inca royalty. Most societies also forbid marriage between first cousins and between members of the same sex. The Netherlands, Belgium, Canada, and most recently Spain in 2005 and South Africa in 2006, and the state of Massachusetts in the United States now allow same-sex marriages.

Endogamous norms of one sort or another are also very widespread, although they vary greatly from one society to another. In this country, for example, marriages between members of different racial groups were considered improper or even forbidden by law at different times.

Why have norms concerning endogamy and exogamy evolved? It seems clear from their universality that they perform an important social function, but the nature of that function is widely debated. A number of authorities have suggested that the incest taboo, for instance, is a result of the dangers of inbreeding. Others contend that the taboo is instinctive, that prolonged associations with people during childhood precludes viewing them as a marriage partner, or that marriage within a kinship group would lead to intense conflicts and jealousy. Each of these explanations has its shortcomings, however. Murdock (1949) suggests that a complete explanation of the incest taboo must synthesize theories from the different disciplines that deal with human behavior.

There are also a number of explanations for endogamy. It is widely believed that members of similar groups share similar values, role expectations, and attitudes, which results in fewer marital or kinship conflicts. For example, some suggest that people from similar age groups share similar developmental tasks and interests. Marriage within the race maintains what the race considers to be its pure genetic traits. Marriages between people of the same socioeconomic status keep the wealth and power within the social class. Marriages within the same religious orientation are likely to agree on child-rearing practices, family rituals, and beliefs relating to the sacred. Although the norms of endogamy—and of what determines being in the same social group—vary among and within societies such as the United States, all societies foster suspicion and dislike of groups whose values, behaviors, and customs are unfamiliar or seem strange. This is a manifestation of Merton's in-group virtues to out-group vices. Both exogamy and endogamy, therefore, restrict the eligibility of available marriage partners for both sexes.

Thinking Sociologically

1. Polygyny is known to exist as a legitimate form of marriage in many societies around the world. Why does (or should) the United States not legally permit either polygyny or polyandry?
2. What are some consequences of a particular type of lineage system? Think of examples that illustrate whether families are patrilineal, matrilineal, or bilateral, and what difference it makes.
3. What factors aid in determining "appropriate" societal norms around marriage and family? How does determining these factors help us understand societal unrest around marriage and family in the United States?

A FUNCTIONALIST PERSPECTIVE ON THE FAMILY

The functionalist perspective emphasizes the structures of social systems and the functions of these parts in maintaining the society. Despite the many variations that exist in family structure around the world, families everywhere perform many of the same functions. Among the more important are socialization, affection and emotional support, sexual regulation, reproduction, and social placement.

Socialization

As discussed elsewhere, the family is one of the most important agents of socialization because it teaches its members the rules and expectations for behavior in the society. Reiss (1965) argues that although families perform many functions, only the function of nurturant socialization of children is universal. It is doubtful whether infants could even survive, much less develop into mentally, physically, and socially healthy human beings, outside of the intimate network of the family.

The family is not only more permanent than other social institutions, but also provides the care, protection, and love best suited to teaching children the knowledge, skills, values, and norms of the society and subculture. However excellent hospitals, child-care centers, and nursery or elementary schools may be, none seems to perform the socialization and learning functions as well as the family (Elkin and Handel, 1989; Spitz, 1945). This emphasis on the infant and young child should not cause us to overlook the socialization function of the family on adults, however. Parents learn from each other, from their children, and from other kin as they interact in the intimate network bound by blood and marriage ties. This affective support is a second function provided by the family.

Affection and Emotional Support

More than 35 years ago, Parsons and Bales (1955) suggested that the family has two essential functions: (1) the primary socialization of children so that they can become true members of the society they were born in, and (2) the stabilization of the adult personalities of the society. This second function, although often ignored, seems to be just as important as the first. Although some individuals enjoy living alone, most people need others who care, show affection, share joys and sorrows, and give support in times of need. Humans are social animals who depend on their families at every stage of the life cycle, and although social support is also provided by friends, neighbors, co-workers, and government agencies, none is as effective as the family at providing warm, supportive relationships.

The importance of this family function is evidenced in many different ways. Aging persons particularly exemplify this idea: in studies, they often indicated that good relationships with their children are a major source of gratification. In fact, people who have a network of family connections live longer than those who are single, widowed, or divorced.

Sexual Regulation

All societies approve of some sexual behaviors and disapprove of others. As mentioned earlier, there is an almost universal taboo against incest, whereas marriage is the most universally approved outlet for sexual behavior. Both are linked to the family system.

Societies control sexual activity in a number of ways. The chief means is by socializing sexual norms and attempting to enforce them. Secluding single women, for example, might enforce the norm of chastity. Society also differentiates sexual rights in accordance with various roles and statuses (male, female, single, married, priest, teacher) and places taboos on intercourse at some times in the reproductive cycle, such as during menstruation, pregnancy, or immediately following childbirth. The norms of most societies discourage practices such as rape, child molesting, voyeurism, and the like. Sexual norms are concerned with more than just sexual intercourse; they also cover such behaviors as kissing and touching, as well as appropriate attitudes and values.

In the United States, the most pervasive socially approved sexual interest is heterosexual. Sexual relationships are generally defined in terms of the family and marriage, as premarital or extramarital relationships, for example. Other institutions—religion, education, economics, or politics—may also regulate sexual behaviors and attitudes, but it is not one of their primary tasks. Families have the chief responsibility in this area, and because they regulate sexual activity, it seems logical that they also control the function of reproduction.

Reproduction

The family is the most widely approved social context for having children. Children are sometimes born outside the family, of course, but if it is common, it is considered a social problem. According to the functionalist perspective, a society's reproductive practices should conform to institutional patterns and should be integrated with other societal functions, such as sexual regulation, physical and emotional support, and socialization. This view reflects the **principle of legitimacy**, formulated by Bronislaw Malinowski (1930) more than 70 years ago. The principle states that every society has a rule that every child should have a legitimate father to act as the child's protector, guardian, and representative in the society.

Those who are not functionalists may be disturbed at this explanation of the role of the family. It suggests that children born outside of the family are stigmatized in some way, that they are illegitimate. Even functionalists would concede that there are functional alternatives to a biological father; father substitutes can fulfill the essential social tasks and roles of a father. Interactionists would also argue that the biological link between parent and child is less significant than the social links—what is important to the child are role models, social support, and patterns of interaction that will enable the child to develop adequately and to function effectively in society.

Clinicians often deal with problems of adjustment between adopted children and their parents, who may have fears of rejection or inadequacy because they are not biologically related to their child. Counselors can help parents to realize the overriding significance of the social ties between parent and child, and thus help to allay the parents' fears. With today's high divorce rate (discussed later in this chapter), many of you will remarry and perhaps be involved in **blended families**—families composed of at least one formerly married spouse, the children of the previous marriage or marriages, and new offspring. Sometimes, stepparents feel guilty about not being able to instantly love their stepchildren. Other tensions may develop between biologically unrelated children. Realizing the essential significance of the social links between family members may help family members to overcome some of those tensions. Further, a more active approach by family members and counselors working with such families could involve finding ways to strengthen those links through activities that provide close interaction and communication.

Although it is true that children born outside the family can develop into functioning members of society, it is undeniably the family that universally fulfills the function of giving legal status and social approval to parenthood and reproduction. This function is related to another family function, that of social placement.

Social Placement

The social placement of children is a family function closely associated with socialization and reproduction. Social placement involves determining what roles and statuses the child will occupy in society. As discussed elsewhere, some of the statuses that a person will occupy arc ascribed at birth, such as age, sex, and social class position. Children generally assume the legal, religious, and political status of their family as well. Even statuses that are achieved, such as marriage, occupation, and education, are greatly influenced by one's membership in a particular family or kin network.

The family also performs functions other than the five mentioned (i.e., socialization, affection and emotional support, sexual regulation, reproduction, and social placement). It fulfills basic economic, protective, educational, recreational, and religious functions, as well.

A CONFLICT PERSPECTIVE ON THE FAMILY

Conflict theorists, like functionalists, recognize variations in family structure and accept the idea that the family provides basic social needs and goals. The two approaches are fundamentally very different, however. Conflict theorists contend that social systems, including the family, are not static structures that maintain equilibrium and harmony among the parts. They argue, rather, that social systems are constantly in a state of conflict and change. They contend that conflict is natural and inevitable in all human interactions, including those between male and female, husband and wife, and parent and child, and that these conflicts are the result of a continual struggle for power and control. Marriage is one of many contexts in which each person seeks his or her rights. The struggles of parenthood involve not just rivalries among siblings but also between parents and children.

Conflict stems from the unequal distribution of scarce resources. In all systems, some have more resources than others, which gives them dominance and power over others. Feminist theories, like conflict theories, argue that inequalities exist not only in the economic and occupational realm but also in the family. Friedrich Engels (1902) claimed that the family, the basic unit in a capitalist society, serves as the chief means of oppressing women. The husband is the bourgeois and the wife the proletariat. As general Marxist–feminist theory suggests, when women become aware of their collective interests, they will question the legitimacy of the existing patterns of inequality and will join together against men to bring about changes and the redistribution of resources: power, money, education, job opportunities, and the like. Conflict is as inevitable in the family as it is in society, and it leads to change.

Conflict theory assumes that economic organization, especially the ownership of property, generates revolutionary class conflict. In families, property ownership involves not just one's home and possessions, but people as well. Collins and Coltrane (2000) argue that basic to the institution of sexual stratification is the notion of sexual property, the belief that one has permanent exclusive sexual rights to a particular person. In societies operating under a system of patriarchy that is dominated by males, the principal form of sexual property is male ownership of females, husband ownership of wives.

This pattern of male ownership and male dominance has a long history, stemming from laws in ancient Hebrew society and continuing through the twentieth century. The Hebrew laws stated, among other things, that if a man had sexual intercourse with an *unbetrothed* (not contracted for marriage) virgin, he was required to marry her and to pay her father the bride price. In many societies, women are closely guarded so they will not attract other men and lose their market value. These practices are reflected in such customs as wearing a veil and strict chaperonage. Even in the United States, women could not legally make contracts or obtain credit until recently, and women are still not guaranteed equal rights under the U.S. Constitution. The status of women is also evident in many wedding ceremonies, in which the father "gives away" some of his property—the bride—and the bride vows not just to love but also to honor and obey her new owner (the groom).

How can this inequality and the prevalence of male domination be explained? The most common theory relates power and domination to available resources. Men gain power over women through their physical strength and their freedom from the biological limitations of childbirth. The traditional resource of women, on the other hand, is their sexuality. Before and during marriage, women traditionally control men by giving or withholding sexual "favors."

Conflict theory suggests that the structure of domination shifts as resources shift. In general, those with greater occupational prestige, higher income, or more education have more power. Women who bear children, it could be argued, gain status, prestige, and power because they are fulfilling the important role of mother. However, realistically, exactly the opposite happens. A woman's power declines with the birth of a child and goes down even more with additional children. Why? Women with children are more likely to be confined to the home, with the primary responsibilities of child care, and do not have the time or the liberty to acquire resources such as education, income, or the type of job that would increase their power. Logically, we can argue and might expect women today to be in better bargaining positions relative to men because they are having fewer children and are more likely hold jobs. Being free from unwanted pregnancies and from childbirth, combined with an increased education and income, lessens their economic dependence on husbands. The result today is that there seems to be a major trend, at least in the more industrialized nations, toward greater equality between the sexes, both within and outside of marriage and the family.

Conflict in families also occurs over issues other than inequality between men and women. It can arise over a variety of issues: place of residence, inheritance rights, decision making, selection of mates, violence (especially rape), sexual relationships, and marital adjustment, to mention a few. In every instance, the issue is likely to involve an inequality of power, authority, or resources, which will lead to conflict. This means that these marital conflicts are not necessarily due to personality clashes but, rather, to inequality, a power imbalance in the relationship.

It is important for married people and marriage counselors to understand this in trying to work out troubled relationships. It may be more important to try to adjust the balance of power between spouses than to try to adjust personalities that are thought to be incompatible. These ideas may be useful for you even if you are not currently married. Consider your relationship with your boyfriend or girlfriend. Can you think of any ways in which an imbalance of power sometimes leads to disagreements? The disagreements do not necessarily mean that there is a loss of affection for one another—although there may be—but may instead reflect inequality in the relationship.

OTHER PERSPECTIVES ON THE FAMILY

An Exchange Perspective

All human interactions, including those between husbands and wives or parents and children, can be viewed in terms of social exchange. Social exchange theory assumes that people weigh rewards and costs in their social interactions. If the exchange is unequal or is perceived as unequal, one person will be at a disadvantage, and the other will control the relationship. In this regard, exchange theory parallels the conflict perspective. If people in a relationship give a great deal and receive little in return, they will perceive the relationship as unsatisfactory. These ideas can be illustrated with mate selection.

Everywhere in the world, selecting a mate involves trying to get the best spouse for what one has to offer. As you know from our earlier discussion of the endogamous and exogamous rules of marriage, selecting a mate is never a matter of completely free and independent choice. One must conform to societal norms.

Marriages may be arranged in several ways. At one extreme, they may be organized by the families of the people to be married; the prospective spouses may have no say in the matter at all. When this practice is followed, the criteria of the exchange involve such factors as money, prestige, family position, or power. When, on the other hand, the people to be married choose their mates themselves, the exchange criteria involve factors such as love, affection, emotional support, beauty, fulfillment of needs, prestige, or personality. The latter procedure is rare in the world as a whole, the United States being one of the few countries that practices it.

One of the most widely researched exchange theories of mate selection is the theory of **complementary needs**. Robert Winch (1954, 1958) believed that although mates tend to resemble each other in such social characteristics as age, race, religion, ethnic origin, socioeconomic status, and education, they are usually complementary rather than similar in respect to needs, psychic fulfillment, and individual motivation. Rather than seeking a mate with a similar personality, one seeks a person who will satisfy one's needs. If both people are dominant, for example, the relationship will not succeed, but if one is dominant and the other submissive, the relationship is complementary, and the needs of both parties are met. A great deal of research was instigated by this theory of complementary needs, but the results did not provide empirical support for the notion that people choose mates whose needs complement their own.

An earlier exchange theory of mate selection was Willard Waller's (1938) analysis of courtship conduct as a process of bargaining, exploitation, or both. In his words, "When one marries he makes a number of different bargains. Everyone knows this and this knowledge affects the sentiment of love and the process of falling in love" (p. 239). Although it is doubtful that only "he makes bargains" or that "everyone knows this," the fact that bargaining and exchanges take place for both males and females in the mate-selection process is today widely recognized and accepted. Good looks, athletic stardom, a sense of humor, clothes, or money are resources commonly perceived as valuable in the exchange process. In mate selection, as in other interaction processes, people rarely get something for nothing, although each person, either consciously or unconsciously, tries to maximize gains and minimize costs. Over the long run, however, actual exchanges tend to be about equal, and if they are not, the relationship is likely to end.

Like conflict theory, exchange theory helps us to recognize the importance of equality in a marriage and may be a useful perspective in dealing with troubled marriages. If a relationship is in trouble, counselors or therapists might try to evaluate the balance of exchange that exists in a marriage. They might find that there is more of a balanced exchange than appears and, if this is the case, they could explain to the couple the resources that each partner provides. If there were, indeed, an imbalance, the clinician would recognize that this is likely to be a major source of trouble and may help the couple to find ways to attain a balanced exchange. Here, again, is a perspective that you can use to examine some of your relationships even if you are not married.

An Interactionist Perspective

An interactionist perspective on the family uses a social-psychological approach to examine interaction patterns, socialization processes, role expectations and behaviors, and the definitions or meanings given to various family issues. This approach considers not just structural variations but also the interactional patterns and covert definitions associated with structural arrangements.

Few relationships are more enduring or more intense than marriage, and few reflect the principles of interactionism so comprehensively. Marriage exemplifies the central ideas of symbolic interaction: shared meanings, significant others, role expectations, role-taking, definitions of situations, symbolic communication, and so on.

Marriage is dynamic—the needs of the married individuals and their role relationships change frequently. According to the interactionist perspective, husband and wife have a reciprocal influence on each other. Each partner continually affects the other, so adjustment is a process, not an end result. Good adjustment means "the individual or the pair has a good working arrangement with reality, adulthood, and expectations of others" (Waller and Hill, 1951, p. 362).

Each of us brings to a marriage certain ideas about what is proper behavior for our spouses and ourselves. Inevitably, people find as they interact that some behaviors do not fit their preconceived definitions. Unless the definitions or the behaviors change, one spouse or both may be frustrated in attempting to fulfill their roles. Some argue that these frustrations are increasing because the roles of husband and wife are more flexible and diverse than they were in the past. Others maintain that today's increased flexibility and diversity decrease marital strain by allowing partners a greater range of options. In either case, what the interactionist considers important is that the couple share definitions, perceptions, and meanings. Also, disagreements may not lead to conflict if they involve issues considered unimportant. Suppose, for example, that a wife likes football but her husband does not. The situation will not lead to conflict if the husband defines football as important to his wife and accepts her behavior. In the same way, a husband's desire for only part-time employment or his wish to avoid cooking is a source of conflict only if the wife has different expectations. Adjustment is a result of shared expectations.

To maintain a satisfactory relationship, married couples must continually redefine themselves in relation to each other, which is often an unconscious process. When problems arise, marriage counseling may help by bringing unconscious definitions into consciousness, thus allowing the couple to examine how they influence the relationship.

The interactionist perspective stresses the importance of analyzing marriages and other relationships in the context in which they occur. A definition, role expectation, or behavior that is appropriate in one setting may be inappropriate in another. This perspective also emphasizes the notion that a successful marriage involves a process of adjustment, or continual adaptation to shifts in shared meaning.

Interactionism, thus, is a particularly useful perspective for marital therapy. The family is not simply a group of separate people performing separate functions independently. The interactionist perspective helps us to realize that family members act largely on the basis of how they interpret one another's actions. Using the interactionist perspective, clinicians may come to understand that each family has its own context that provides the basis for interaction and for interpretation of each family member's actions. This being the case, a clinician using this perspective might work on making sure that the individual family members understand clearly what the other family members intentions are, and might also help to clarify how each person defines the actions of the others.

A Developmental Perspective

The developmental perspective on the family suggests that families pass through a family life cycle, a series of different responsibilities and tasks. This perspective suggests that successful achievement at one point in the developmental process is essential to effectively accomplishing later tasks, whereas failure in earlier tasks leads to increased difficulty with later tasks. Just as individuals must learn to crawl and walk before they can run, new families must be able to perform various financial, sexual, and interpersonal tasks to maintain the family unit and meet later developmental goals.

During its life cycle, the family passes through a sequence of stages that require different interaction patterns, roles, and responsibilities. The number of stages identified depends on the intent of the researcher. There may be as few as two, but the most typical division is of seven stages. The transition points between stages most often center around the age of the oldest child.

The first stage typically begins with marriage and extends to the birth of the first child. For most couples, this stage involves defining the marital relationship, learning to communicate effectively and resolve conflicts, working out mutually satisfying and realistic systems for getting and spending the family income, and deciding about parenthood. Obviously, not all newlyweds face the same tasks. If the woman is pregnant before the marriage, if it is a teenage, interracial, or second marriage, or if the couple lived together before marriage, their concerns may differ. Nevertheless, the first stage of the family life cycle typically focuses on the married couple and their adjustment to life as a married pair.

Stage two may include families with a preschool child, or be subdivided into families with an infant (birth to age 2 or 3 years) and families with an older preschool child (ages 2 or 3 to 6 years). During this stage, the couple changes from a dyad of husband and wife to a triad of parents and offspring. The central tasks are adjusting to parenthood, dealing with the needs and development of the infant and young children, relating to parents and in-laws who are grandparents to the child, assuming and managing the additional housing and space needs, and continuing the communicative, sexual, and financial responsibilities described in stage one.

Stage three may extend from the time the oldest child begins school until he or she reaches the teens. When children enter school, both parents and children face new relationships and responsibilities. In this stage, the family focuses on the education and socialization of children. The increasing significance of peer relationships, children's changing interests and activities, and the management of parent–child conflicts are added to the ongoing marital, work, and other responsibilities. A second or third child, the loss of a job, or the dissolution of the marriage modifies the responsibilities generally associated with this stage.

Stage four is the family with adolescents or teenagers. Data suggest that at the adolescent stage, the family often undergoes economic problems. Medical and dental costs, food, clothing, transportation, entertainment, education, and other expenses often place a strain on the budget. For many families, such issues as drinking, drugs, and sex become additional sources of strain. New types of adolescent dance, music, dress, and jargon must also be accommodated. In addition, families in this stage begin to prepare their teenager to be launched from the home.

Stage five begins when the oldest child leaves home and is frequently called the launching stage. The young person's departure—to marry, to attend college, or to take a full-time job—creates a significant transition for both parent and child. This stage may be very brief, as with a one-child family in which the child marries upon graduation from high school, or it may extend over many years, as happens when there are several children or when an unmarried child remains in the home for many years, dependent on parents for support. When the children have been launched, the family returns to the original two-person conjugal unit; at the same time, however, it may expand to include sons- or daughters-in-law and grandchildren.

Stage six is the period when all the children have left home; this is called the "empty-nest" stage. It starts with the departure of the last child from the home and continues until the retirement or death of one spouse. Again, it may be very brief because of one or more children who remain in the home through their 20s or because of an early death of a parent, or it may cover many years, as when the last child departs when the parents are in their late 30s or early 40s and when the parents remain employed until age 70 or later. At this stage, the interpersonal focus is on the married couple, yet intergenerational family responsibilities can arise. The husband and wife in the middle years may have some responsibility for their retired and elderly parents and also for their married children and grandchildren, who may seek emotional and financial support from the middle generation from time to time.

The seventh and final stage generally begins with retirement and extends until the marriage ends with the death of one spouse. Because women live longer than men and are usually younger than their husbands, they are widowed more often than men. With the death of both spouses, the family life span for that family has ended, and the cycle continues with each successive generation.

Family life-cycle stages can be used to analyze a wide range of behaviors and interaction patterns. Frequency of sexual relations, income patterns, recreational activities, and interactions with children have been found to differ by the stage of the family life cycle. Olson and McCubbin (1983), for example, used a seven-stage family life-cycle model to study how 1,140 families managed their lives and why they succeeded in some areas better than in others. One finding consistent with other studies was that adults' satisfaction with marriage and family tends to decline between the birth of the first child and that child's adolescence, and to rise as the children are launched from the nest. One explanation for the dramatic increase in satisfaction following the launching stage concerns the relaxation of sex roles between the parents. Women see themselves as more free to look for work and organizational roles outside the home, and men find themselves with decreased financial responsibilities and allow themselves to be more passive and dependent.

Thinking Sociologically

1. Apply an exchange perspective to several close relationships in your life. What did you have to offer, and in turn, what did you receive? Can you identify instances in which an unequal relationship led to the termination of the relationship?

2. Suppose that you are a sociologist who is called upon to testify as an expert witness in a child custody case. This is a case in which the father wants a joint custody arrangement, but the mother objects and wants sole custody of the child. Assume that there is no violence or any other urgent reason to keep the child away from the father. Develop an argument for or against joint custody, using any or all of the theories just covered.

THE AMERICAN FAMILY SYSTEM

As indicated earlier in this chapter, the American family system emphasizes monogamy, neolocal residence, a modified-extended kinship linkage, bilateral descent and inheritance, egalitarian decision making, endogamous marriage, and relatively free choice of mate. A number of other structural characteristics have also been described: American families tend to be small and, compared with other countries, rather isolated; marital and family roles for women and men are becoming increasingly ambiguous; we tend to emphasize love in mate selection; we are often sexually permissive prior to or outside of marriage; and divorce is granted easily.

Table 12-1 shows the marital status of the population by sex and age. You can see that as of 2000, the population of the United States included 103 million males and 110.6 million females age 15 years and over. Approximately 31.3 percent of the men and 25.1 percent of the women were never married. A relatively small number (2.6 million) of the men were widowers, compared with 11 million of the women who were widows. Such publicity is given to the breakup of marriages through divorce, but only 7.0 percent of the men and 9.1 percent of the women had a divorced status in 1989. Note how these figures vary by age. Very few older people are single, and very few young and middle-aged people are widowed. The divorced population is concentrated most heavily in the 35–54 age group.

TABLE 12-1 MARITAL STATUS OF PEOPLE 15 YEARS AND OVER: MARCH 1970 AND MARCH 2000 (IN THOUSANDS)

Characteristic	March 2000								March 1970
	Number								
	Total	Married Spouse Present	Married Spouse Absent	Separated	Divorced	Widowed	Never Married	Percent Never Married	Percent Never Married†
Both sexes									
Total 15 years old+	213,773	113,002	2,730	4,479	19,881	13,885	60,016	28.1	24.9
15 to 19 years old	20,102	345	36	103	64	13	19,541	97.2	93.9
20 to 24 years old	18,440	3,362	134	234	269	11	14,430	78.3	44.5
25 to 29 years old	18,269	8,334	280	459	917	27	8,252	45.2	14.7
30 to 34 years old	19,519	11,930	278	546	1,616	78	5,071	26.0	7.8
35 to 44 years old	44,804	29,353	717	1,436	5,987	399	8,932	15.5	5.9
45 to 54 years old	36,633	24,460	492	399	5,597	882	3,303	9.0	6.1
55 to 64 years old	23,388	16,393	308	441	3,258	1,770	1,218	5.2	7.2
65 years+	32,920	17,827	485	361	2,193	10,484	1,270	3.9	7.6
Males									
Total 15 years old+	103,113	56,501	1,365	1,818	8,572	2,604	32,253	31.3	28.1
15 to 19 years old	10,295	69	3	51	29	3	10,140	98.5	97.4
20 to 24 years old	9,208	1,252	75	70	101	*	7,710	83.7	54.7
25 to 29 years old	8,943	3,658	139	170	342	9	4,825	51.7	19.1
30 to 34 years old	9,622	5,640	151	205	712	15	2,899	30.1	9.4
35 to 44 years old	22,134	14,310	387	585	2,775	96	3,981	18.0	6.7
45 to 54 years old	17,891	13,027	255	378	2,377	157	1,897	9.5	7.5
55 to 64 years old	11,137	8,463	155	188	1,387	329	812	5.5	7.8
65 years+	13,885	10,084	197	171	849	1,994	590	4.2	7.5
Females									
Total 15 years old+	110,660	58,501	1,365	2,681	11,309	11,061	27,763	25.1	22.1
15 to 19 years old	9,807	276	33	52	35	10	9,401	98.9	90.3
20 to 24 years old	9,232	2,110	59	164	163	11	6,720	72.8	35.8
25 to 29 years old	9,326	4,676	141	289	575	18	3,627	38.9	10.5
30 to 34 years old	9,898	6,290	127	341	904	63	2,172	21.9	6.2
35 to 44 years old	22,670	15,043	330	851	3,192	303	2,951	13.0	5.2
45 to 54 years old	18,742	12,433	237	521	3,220	725	1,606	8.6	4.9
55 to 64 years old	12,251	7,830	150	263	1,871	1,441	606	4.9	8.8
65 years old+	15,736	7,743	288	190	1,344	8,490	680	3.6	7.7

*Represents zero or rounds to zero.

†The 1970 percentages include 14-year-olds, and thus are for 14+ and 14–19.

Source: U.S. Census Bureau. Current Population Survey, March 2000.

Broad profiles of the sort given in the preceding paragraph, however, do not indicate the frequency or range of specific trends in the evolution of the family. In the following sections, we examine some of these trends in more detail.

Marriage Rates and Age at Marriage

Rates of marriage (the number of people who marry in a given year per 1,000 people [or per 1,000 unmarried women age 15 and over]) are influenced by a variety of factors. The rate characteristically falls during periods of economic recession and rises during periods of prosperity. The rate also tends to rise at the beginning of a war and after a war has ended. Variations in the age of the population are also influential.

In the United States prior to 1900, the rate was relatively stable, varying between 8.6 and 9.6 marriages per 1,000 population per year. Shortly after the turn of the century, the rate rose, until the depression of the early 1930s, when it dropped to a low of 7.9. Marriage rates rose dramatically at the outset of World War II, as young men sought to avail themselves of the deferred status granted to married men or simply wanted to marry before going overseas. The end of the war and the return of men to civilian life precipitated another upsurge in marriages. In 1946, the marriage rate reached 16.4, an unprecedented and to-date unsurpassed peak. Subsequently, it dropped. Over the past 30 years, the rate has fluctuated between 8.5 and 11.0 per 1,000, with the marriage rate in 1997 at 7.2 per 1,000 population, and the rate in 1998 at 8.3 per 1,000 population (U.S. National Center for Health Statistics, Vital Statistics of the United States, annual; and National Vital Statistics Reports).

In the United States, marriage rates have distinct seasonal and geographic variations. More marriages take place in June than in any other month, followed by August, May, and September. The fewest marriages are in January, February, and March. Interestingly, the favorite month for marriage varies by age group: teenage brides and grooms prefer June; brides ages 30–34 and grooms ages 45–54 most often choose December; and brides 35–54 and grooms 55–64 tend to select July. Most marriages take place on Saturday. Friday is next in popularity, and Tuesdays, Wednesdays, and Thursdays are the least popular.

As an example of a use of sociological statistics, put yourself in the position of a business that has to do with marriage—a florist, bridal boutique, tuxedo rental store, caterer, limousine service, or travel agent. Knowing the times of year that people prefer to get married and what the specific age group preferences are could vastly help these businesses increase their success. This information could help them to plan when and where to advertise, when to have the most personnel available to help potential customers, how to decorate the showrooms and arrange displays to appeal to the age groups most likely to shop at a particular time of year, and so forth.

Suppose that you are a travel agent and you know not only that June is the most popular time to get married, but also that young people prefer it most. You might decorate your showroom with travel posters with young rather than middle-aged people in them, have a large number of low-priced packages available, perhaps have a young travel agent on duty, and advertise during the preceding months in the magazines that young people are most likely to read.

Statistics about when people get married could also be very useful to you in planning your own marriage. If most marriages occur in June, for example, it will be more difficult to reserve the specific time and place you want for your ceremony, and the rates for caterers, limousines, travel, flowers, and tuxedo rentals are likely to be higher then. Knowing this, you may want to start making your plans as early as possible; or, you might decide to change the date of your marriage to a less popular time.

Most marriages in the United States are between people of roughly the same age, although people are free to marry someone considerably older or younger, within the legal limits determined by each state. *Current Population Reports*, published by the U.S. Bureau of the Census, shows the median age at first marriage in 2000 to be 26.8 for men and 25.1 for women, a difference of 1.7 years (Figure 12-2).

The median age at first marriage and the age difference between males and females have varied considerably since the turn of the century. In 1900, these figures were 25.9 for males and 21.9 for females, a difference of 4 years. Recently, people have been postponing marriage until they are older, which reflects a decision on the part of young people to live independently as they pursue higher education or job opportunities. In the past two decades, there has been a rapid increase in the percentage of men and women who have never married. In 1970, one in every ten women (10.5 percent) ages 25–29 years had never married, but by 2000, this proportion had increased to 31.3 percent for men and 25.1 percent for women (*Current Population Reports*, Series P-20, No. 537, 2001).

FIGURE 12-2 MEDIAN AGE AT FIRST MARRIAGE OF THE POPULATION 15 YEARS AND OVER BY SEX: SELECTED YEARS, 1970 TO 2000 (AGE IN YEARS)

Source: U.S. Census Bureau, *Current Population Surveys*, March Supplements: 1970 to 2000.

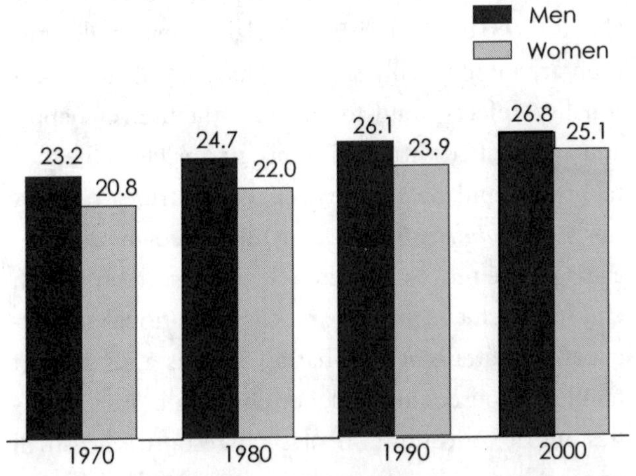

Teenage marriages are an issue of special concern in the United States. Married teenagers have an increased high school dropout rate and a high unemployment rate. The divorce rate for teenagers is estimated to be from two to four times the rate for marriages that begin after age 20. Many teenage marriages involve a pregnancy at the time of marriage, and data consistently show a higher divorce rate among marriages begun with a pregnancy (Teachman, 1983). In reference to his research on economically disadvantaged couples, Fein (2004) states: "Whereas the vast bulk of first transitions to parenthood among upper middle class couples *follow* first marriages, first births among disadvantaged newlyweds are far more likely to *precede* marriage." Furthermore, among couples who married in 1990, one-third of those in the bottom education category had their first child before marriage, compared with one-tenth of those in the top education category. Among African Americans, the fraction is even higher: over half (51 percent) married after their first transition to parenthood (Fein, 2004). Studies indicate that people who marry young, for a variety of reasons, are unprepared for the process of selecting a mate and assuming a marital role and are disproportionately represented in divorce statistics.

Family Size

In this country, as in the rest of the world, most married couples have or want to have children. Voluntarily childless marriages are uncommon, although as the next section describes, a pattern of childless marriages does exist. In the United States in 2000, 34.6 million married couples were without children. In 2003, there were 4.0 million births, a rate of 13.3 per 1,000 population (*National Vital Statistics*, 2003). Like marriage rates, birth rates fluctuate with wars, socioeconomic conditions, and other variables. At the turn of the century, the birth rate was over 30 per 1,000 population. Decreasing to 18.7 in 1935, it increased to 25 by the mid-1950s. It subsequently declined until it reached a rate of 14.6 in 1975. As of January 2003, the live birth rate was 13.9 per 1,000 people in the United States.

The "baby boom" period of the late 1940s and the 1950s produced an unanticipated but significant rise in the United States birth rate. It may have been caused by increases in the normative pressures on women to have children, the end of the disruption brought about by war, postwar economic prosperity, or the long-term psychological effects of growing up during the Great Depression. Bean (1983) states that while social and cultural conditions during the era supported having families, increased costs tended to discourage couples from having large families. Thus, only a minor part of the baby boom can be attributed to families deciding to have three or more children.

In 2000, 19.5 million married couples had four or more children under age 18 (*Current Population Reports*, 2001). Improved methods of birth control, liberalized abortion laws, and a widespread acceptance of family planning measures have decreased the number of unplanned and unwanted births and have enabled couples to have the number of children they want. It remains to be seen just what impact, if any, the political and legal moves toward restricting abortion that are currently taking place will have on the number of births. Analysis of newly released Census Bureau figures emphasize that over the last decades of the twentieth century, the size of U.S. families has declined very rapidly. Since 1970 the percentage of households containing five or more people has fallen by half. On the other hand, the number of single and two-person households has soared. One group of single households that has increased particularly fast is single women between the ages of 30 and 35 (Grier and Miller, 2004).

Does family size make a difference in interactions among siblings or between children and their parents? Because families are groups and the number of people in a group influences the behavior of its members, the answer is "yes." Specifically, how does family size make a difference? Perhaps the greatest difference in family interaction patterns comes with the birth of the first child, because the transition to parenthood involves a major shift in parental role expectations and behaviors. A number of writers have called the early stages of parenthood a "crisis," a traumatic change that forces couples to drastically reorganize their lives (Hobbs, 1965; LeMasters, 1957). Later studies concluded, however, that for most couples, beginning parenthood is a period of transition but not a period of change so dramatic that it should be termed a crisis.

With the birth of the first child, the expectation exists that a second and third child should follow. One-child families have generally been viewed as unhealthy for parents and child alike. The "only" child has been described as spoiled, selfish, overly dependent, maladjusted, and lonely. Parents of a single child have been described as selfish, self-centered, immature, cold, and abnormal. Research findings, however, do not support these descriptions.

Findings generally tend to support those of Blake (1981a, 1981b, and 1989), who claims that single children are intellectually superior, have no obvious personality defects, tend to consider themselves happy, and are satisfied with the important aspects of life, notably jobs and health. In fact, Blake's research supports the *dilution hypothesis*, which predicts that, on average, the more children a family has, the less each child will achieve in such areas as educational and occupational attainment. That is, there is a dilution of familial resources available for children in large families and a concentration of such resources in small ones. These diluted resources include the parents' time, emotional and physical energy (including that of a mother who is frequently pregnant), attention, personal interaction, and material resources that allow for personal living space and privacy within the home, better neighborhoods surrounding the home, specialized medical and dental care, travel, and specialized instruction, such as music lessons.

These findings are extremely important for you to consider in planning your own families. Would you be more receptive to having just one child, knowing that "only" children do as well as or better than children with siblings? Would you be less willing to have a large number of children, knowing about the dilution hypothesis? Clearly, many factors enter into the decision as to how many children you may personally want or actually have: age at marriage, religious orientation, effective use of contraception, career pattern, and so forth. Nonetheless, what is known about the consequences of having few or many children has important implications for personal decision making and social policy as well.

Although people may agree that a one-child family is small, there is less agreement about the number of children required to make a family be considered "large." Perceptions of a family as small or large are relative. A family with four children in the United States at the turn of the century would not have been perceived as large. However, today, it generally would be. The more central issue in reference to family size, however, concerns the consequences of having more children in a given family.

It is known that family size increases with factors such as younger ages at marriage, lower educational and socioeconomic levels, and rural residence. Certain religious groups, such as the Amish and the Mormons, place a major value on having children and tend to have large families. It is known that as families increase in size, the chances increase that some children will be unplanned and unwanted. One review of family size effects (Wagner et al., 1985) showed that in larger families, child-rearing becomes more rule-ridden and less individualized. There is more corporal punishment and fewer resources to invest per child. Smaller families tend to result in higher IQ, academic achievement, and occupational performance. Large families produce more delinquents and alcoholics. In regard to health, in large families, *perinatal* (surrounding birth) *morbidity* (injury and illness) and *mortality* (death) rates are higher, and mothers are at higher risk from several physical diseases.

Although a number of studies revealed no effect, positive or negative, to be associated with family size, very few exist that associate positive consequences with large families. It is not family size per se, however, that creates health problems or family difficulties. Large families heighten the complexity of intragroup relations, pose problems in fulfilling family needs, and influence how much money and attention can be devoted to each child.

Divorce

Whenever two people interact, conflicts may arise, and one person or both may want to end the relationship. This is true not only of marriage but of other relationships as well. Unlike most relationships, however, marriage involves civil, legal, or religious ties that specify if and how the relationship can end. In countries such as Spain, Brazil, and Peru, in conformity with the doctrine of the Roman Catholic Church, marriage is indissoluble except by death. In Switzerland, the Scandinavian countries, Poland, Russia, and several other countries, a divorce is granted if it is shown that the marriage has failed. The laws of Islam and Judaism give a husband the power to terminate his marriage by simply renouncing his wife or wives. In this country, most states, traditionally at least, grant a divorce if it is shown that one party has gravely violated his or her marital obligations. Since 1970, however, many states have

SOCIOLOGY AT WORK

Family Counseling

Marie Witkin Kargman, who considers herself a clinical sociologist, has both a law degree and a Ph.D. in sociology. She has been a family disputes mediator, a marriage counselor, a divorce counselor, and a family counselor. Kargman feels that her law degree and sociology degree offer a variable combination of skills for the type of work that she does.

Kargman tells of a realization that she came to early in her career. "Before I trained in sociology at graduate school [Department of Social Relations, Harvard University], I was a practicing lawyer in the juvenile and family courts of Chicago. I discovered that the law is in a very real sense applied sociology: It deals with institutionalized patterns of behavior legitimized by the legal system, and with the sanctions applied when people deviate. I felt I needed to know more about the family, its structure, and its functions to be a better lawyer. Most lawyers rearrange the family, writing divorce and separation agreements that create new family structures, without knowing much about the sociology of the family. I was not comfortable rearranging family relationships when I knew so little theory in the field. But by the time I got my sociology degree I knew that I wanted to be a marriage counselor who worked with lawyers, helping them do a better job."

Using her knowledge gained from her experience as a family counselor, disputes mediator, and sociologist, Kargman wrote a book called *How to Manage a Marriage*. In it, she explains that the family system must be viewed as a combination of subsystems: a political, economic, and kinship system. If a marriage is in trouble, she explains, people have a tendency to blame one another. The advice she offers is, "Attack the problematic subsystem within the family; attack the problem, not the person."

Kargman explains how she is able to apply her sociological knowledge. "In my family disputes mediation, and

moved to a no-fault divorce system, in which marriages can be ended on the basis of what are commonly called "irreconcilable differences." Why are our divorce rates so high in this county? Experts agree that there are (6) main reasons why this is so today:

1) Individualism. Families are spending less and less time together and are more concerned with personal happiness.
2) Romantic love subsides. The excitement goes away.
3) Women are less dependant on men. They now have careers of their own.
4) Stressful relationships. Especially since both work outside of the home.
5) Divorce is now more socially acceptable.
6) Divorce is now easier to legally obtain. (Macionis,2005).

The United States has one of the highest divorce rates in the world. According to the Summary of Vital Statistics, the U.S. rate of divorce per 1,000 persons per year in 2000 was 4.1, compared with 3.2 in Germany, 2.4 in Sweden, 2.27 in Japan, 2.0 in France, and 0.6 in Italy.

Why, then, do we so often hear that one marriage in two ends in divorce? Because the divorce

Family Counseling, *continued*

particularly in child custody disputes, I am apt to say to the divorced parents who have a child custody problem, 'What we are trying to do here is to get two parents and their children to come together to carry out the family functions without the foundation of living in a joint household. Each household is a family group with a political system, an economic system, and a kinship system. The child must now live in two households, juggle two different sets of systems, integrate them, or deal with them as unrelated parts of his or her life.' We then look at the similarities of expectation of the child's two separate households, and try to decide what is in the best interests of the child."

Kargman gives an example of one particular case in which she was appointed by the court to represent a child in a custody case. The mother had asked the court for permission to take the child out of Massachusetts; she had remarried, and there were two additional children in the second marriage. This meant that there was an additional family involved besides the child's original one. Because the mother wanted to move across the country with her new family, the question of reasonable visitation for the child's father was in dispute. "Before I got into the dispute, the only persons discussed by the lawyers were the natural father, the natural mother, and the child. That the child was part of many different family relationships was never discussed. From a legal point of view, the family before the court was the original family of procreation. But this child was a member of three families: his original family, the step-family, and the family of his half-sisters. The child wanted to spend holidays with 'his family' and the natural father wanted the holidays on a strict two-parent division. All of the child's social systems were described in my report to the judge, whose decision was made based on the child's multi-family expectations."

rate is figured by dividing the number of divorces in a given year by the number of marriages in the same year. For example, the *National Vital Statistics Report* (Vol. 39, No. 13, 1991) showed that in 1997, there were 2,384,000 marriages and 1,163,000 divorces. Dividing the number of divorces in 1997 by the number of marriages in 1997 gives a rate of 48, or nearly one in two. This is the rate used to illustrate the "breakdown in the American family." It does not, however, provide proof that half of all marriages end in divorce any more than saying that a community that had 100 marriages and 100 divorces in a given year would prove that all marriages end in divorce. Few of the divorces that take place in a given year are of the marriages that took place that same year. Rather, they were probably from marriages that occurred 2, 5, or 15 years earlier. According to Current Population Reports, 2002, approximately 10% of marriages end in divorce after 5 years of marriage while another 10% (or 20% cumulatively) are divorced by the 10th year. There is, nevertheless, a great deal of concern about the frequency of divorce in the United States.

Divorce rates take on a very different perspective when based on the number per 1,000 population. As just indicated, there were approximately 1,163,000 divorces in the United States in 1997, a rate of 4.5 per 1,000 population. This figure is a decrease from the 1981 figure of 1,213,000 divorces and the rate of 5.3 per 1,000, the highest ever for the United States.

Like marriage rates, divorce rates tend to decline in times of economic depression and rise during periods of prosperity. They also vary by geographic and social characteristics. Geographically, the general trend in the United States is for divorce rates to increase as one moves from east to west. Demographic figures show that more than one-half of all divorces are among persons in their late 20s and early 30s. While the numbers are fewer, the divorce rate is exceptionally high among teenagers. Divorce is also most frequent in the first three years after marriage, and the incidence is higher among the lower socioeconomic levels. Whether education, occupation, or income is used as an index of socioeconomic level, the divorce rate goes up as the socioeconomic level goes down.

The National Center for Policy Analysis reported in 1999 that states in the "Bible belt" lead the United States in divorces. In the southern states included, the divorce rates are roughly 50 percent above the national average (Crary, 1999). According to the article, nationally there were about 4.2 divorces for every thousand people in 1998. The rate was 8.5 per thousand in Nevada, 6.4 in Tennessee, 6.1 in Arkansas, and 6.0 in Alabama and Oklahoma. In fact, of southeastern states, only South Carolina's rate of 3.8 was below the national average. Do southern people just have a harder time getting along? A true sociological explanation will look for trends and patterns. Experts cite low household incomes, the tendency to marry at a younger age, and religious belief systems that allow divorce as major factors in producing such a high divorce rate. After 1999, the Center for Disease Control and the National Center for Health Statistics ceased to publish aggregated divorce counts for all 50 states due to 4 major states failing to report their statistics. The findings will continue in the U.S.Census Reports.

These variations in rate of divorce give us clues about its causes. The fact that rates are higher in the western United States indicates that divorce may be related to the liberality of the laws and the degree of cultural mixing. Financial problems and emotional immaturity may be factors in the high rates found among teenagers. Difficulties in adjusting to new relationships or discrepancies in role expectations may contribute to the divorce rates in the first three years after marriage. Money problems, lack of education, and working at a low-status job may account for the rates found in the lower socioeconomic levels. Although other factors are involved, and there are some exceptions to these general patterns, divorce is not merely a result of personal characteristics. These variations illustrate how social and cultural factors can influence the chances that a marriage will end in divorce.

Thinking Sociologically

1. The research suggests many advantages of small families over large ones. Can you think of ways that large families may be advantageous over small ones?
2. How would you explain the tremendous variation in divorce rates (a) from one country or society to another; (b) between religious and ethnic groups in a given country such as the United States or Canada; and (c) over time?

NONTRADITIONAL MARITAL AND FAMILY LIFESTYLES

In the United States today, many people are choosing alternatives to the *traditional family*, which consisted of a husband, a wife, and two or more children. The husband was the authority and primary if not sole wage earner, whereas the wife was submissive to the husband and served as primary child caregiver and homemaker. Now, however, the diversity of families in this country is greater than ever before, and changes are occurring rapidly. Four nontraditional approaches to family life are discussed in more detail next: (1) nonmarital cohabitation, (2) childless marriage, (3) one-parent families, and (4) dual-career marriages.

Nonmarital Cohabitation

Nonmarital cohabitation, or living together, occurs when two adults who are not related or married to each other occupy the same dwelling as a couple in an intimate relationship or partnership. As mentioned earlier in this chapter, in relation to, "What is a family?" reference was made to defining families in nontraditional ways. Examples used to illustrate families defined in terms of intimate relationships, sexual bonds, and family realms included examples of both heterosexual and homosexual (lesbian and gay) cohabitation.

Both heterosexual and same-sex unions are attracting increasing attention among social researchers, as well as policymakers. A number of churches are recognizing the legitimacy of gay/lesbian unions. A number of businesses are extending spousal benefits to both heterosexual and homosexual cohabitants. A number of communities are accepting the civil registration of such relationships. State and national legislators are being forced to reexamine who is to be included or excluded from social policies covering a range of issues (family/parent benefits, adoption, surrogate parenting, housing, and others).

Most census data on unmarried couples have tended to focus on the heterosexual union. As stated previously, about 3.8 million unmarried couples lived together in 2000, more than five times the number in 1970. Contrary to a widely held assumption, nonmarital heterosexual cohabitation is not just a college-student phenomenon, nor is it confined to the generation under age 25. Despite these findings, most research on cohabitation has involved college student populations. In a review of this research, (Waite et al., 2000) found that non-married cohabitants are significantly less committed to each other than married couples. With regard to the division of labor, cohabiting couples tended to mirror the society around them and accept gender roles characteristic of other couples their age. The same was true for sexual exclusivity. Most believed in sexual freedom within their nonmarried relationship, but most voluntarily limited their sexual activity with outsiders.

Nonmarital heterosexual cohabitation does not appear to be a substitute for marriage, a cure-all for marital problems, or a solution to the problem of frequent divorce. Most cohabitating relationships are short-term and last only a few months, but the longer that couples cohabit, the more likely they are to eventually marry. However, according to the National Marriage Project completed by Rutgers University in 2005 titled, "The State of Our Unions", while the divorce rates in the U.S. may be declining, more men and women are cohabitating, many with children, rather than marrying. In cohabiting heterosexual couples, as in married couples, women do most of the housework.

Unmarried couples, whether of the same or the opposite sex, experience problems quite similar to those of married couples: concern over financial matters, the division of labor, and relationships with extended family members. Although unmarried cohabitation does not fall within acceptable value limits for everyone, it does appear to have functional value for an increasing number of adults of all ages. For many couples, it provides a financially practical situation (two together can live more cheaply than two separately); a warm, homelike atmosphere; ready access to a sexual partner; an intimate interpersonal relationship; and for some, a highly exclusive, long-term partnership.

Childless Marriage

Most unmarried couples are childless. Among these couples, a desire for children, a pregnancy, or the birth of a child often leads to marriage. On the other hand, what of the legally married couples who have no children and who desire none? In recent years, the subject of the voluntarily childless marriage as an acceptable marital lifestyle has gained increased attention for a number of reasons. First, it is inconsistent with myths about the existence of a maternal instinct, the notion that all women want to have, love, and care for a child or children. Second, it changes the functions of marriage and the family that deal with reproduction, nurturant socialization, and social placement. Third, the availability and reliability of contraceptives and of abortion make it possible for women and couples to have no children if they so choose.

Veevers (1975) conducted in-depth interviews with childless wives living with their husbands and found that they held a number of uncommon beliefs about parenting. Most of these women were married to husbands who agreed that children were not desirable. The wives defined parenthood in negative rather than positive terms and denied the existence of a maternal instinct. They dismissed the accusation that childlessness was abnormal. Pregnancy and childbirth were perceived to be at best unpleasant and at worst difficult and dangerous. They regarded child care as excessively burdensome and unrewarding and as having a deleterious effect on a woman's life chances. Finally, they defined parenthood as a trap that interfered with personal happiness.

The child-free alternative may be an acceptable family form and lifestyle for a small proportion of families. Under some conditions, as in the dual-career marriages discussed later, childlessness may be conducive to both personal and marital satisfaction and adjustment.

One-Parent Families

One-parent families are those in which the mother or more commonly the father does not share the household with the children and the remaining parent. As shown in Table 12-2, 84 percent of Asian American, 79 percent of white non-Hispanic, 68 percent of Hispanic origin, 62 percent of American Indian, and 38 percent of black children under age 18 years were living with both parents in 1996. In the traditional view, this is the way families "should be," the most appropriate family structure for the socialization of children. However, 13 percent of Asian American, 16 percent of white non-Hispanic children, 26 percent of Hispanic-origin children, 30 percent of American Indian, and 52 percent of black children were living with the mother only. About 3 percent of all children were living with the father only, with an additional 2 percent of Asian American children, 3 percent of white children, 4 percent of Hispanic-origin children, 6 percent of American Indian children, and 8 percent of black children were living with neither parent.

Families below the poverty level, (3.6 million), particularly one-parent, fatherless families (3.3 million) are those who receive Medicare, school lunches, and food stamps, and who live in subsidized housing. These are the families affected most harshly by middle-class efforts to cut welfare, by religious group efforts to forbid abortion, and by government policies that demand what is called "workfare" (i.e., programs requiring welfare recipients to work full- or part-time in order to receive their below-poverty-level income). Members of such families often have disproportionate school dropout rates, few job-related skills, high unemployment rates, irregular incomes, little dental or other health care, and little control over their own fates.

In a cross-cultural study, Bilge and Kaufman (1983) contend that one-parent families are neither pathological nor inferior. Stigmatizing them in this way, they claim, is a refusal to recognize the economic inequalities of our society. They say that in combination with an extended network of concerned kin (grandparents, siblings, uncles, aunts, etc.) single-parent families can offer emotional support and that they are a suitable alternative to the traditional family. Bilge and Kaufman also note that around the world, one-parent female-headed families are able to bring up children and provide emotional support.

What happens to children in American female-headed families? Cashion (1982) reviewed the social-psychological research pertaining to female-headed families published between 1970 and 1980. She concluded that children in these families are likely to have good emotional adjustment, good self-esteem (except when they are stigmatized), comparable intellectual development to others of the same socioeconomic status, and rates of juvenile delinquency comparable to other children of the same socioeconomic standing. The major problems in these families stem from *poverty* and from *stigmatization.* Poverty is associated with problems in school and juvenile delinquency. It

TABLE 12-2 LIVING ARRANGEMENTS OF CHILDREN BY RACE AND ETHNICITY: FALL 1996 (IN THOUSANDS)

Living Arrangements	All races	White	White Non-Hispanic	Black	American Indian and Alaska Native	Asian and Pacific Islander	Hispanic[1]
Children	71,494	56,212	46,657	11,631	1,073	2,578	10,428
Living with:							
Two parents[2]	50,885	43,466	36,837	4,397	667	2,156	7,112
Both married to each other	49,186	42,333	36,110	4,126	605	2,123	6,627
In a traditional nuclear family[3]	39,746	34,859	30,132	2,985	395	1,507	5,024
One Parent	16,165	11,131	8,632	6,320	345	369	2,870
Mother only	18,340	9,599	7,274	6,088	320	333	2,689
Father only	1,825	1,533	1,358	232	25	36	181
Neither parent	2,644	1,615	1,188	915	62	54	445
Grandparents only	1,266	837	501	571	34	24	143
Other relatives only	588	447	272	199	19	22	183
Nonrelatives only	522	822	383	122	9	8	105
Other arrangement	69	48	32	22	–	1	14
At least 1 stepparent	4,902	4,066	3,556	849	94	93	563
At least 1 foster parent	313	224	153	86	2	2	75

– Represents zero or rounds to zero.

[1] People of Hispanic origin may be of any race.

[2] In the SIPP data, children identify both of their parents regardless of their marital status. This means that both married and unmarried parents are included in this category in this table. This represents a difference from the CPS because only married parents are recorded in two-parent households. Correspondingly, there are more children in two-parent households in the SIPP, and more in single-parent households in the CPS.

[3] Children in a traditional nuclear family live with both biological parents and, if siblings are present, with full brothers and sisters. No other household members are present.

Source: U.S. Census Bureau, 1996 Survey of Income and Program Participation, Wave 2.

also contributes to poor attitudes among mothers about their situations and impairs a mother's sense of being in control. Stigmatization is associated with low self-esteem in children. It results in defining children as problems even when they do not have problems. Cashion's general conclusion is that the majority of female-headed families, when not plagued by poverty, have children who are as successful and well-adjusted as those of two-parent families.

About 8 percent of American households can be categorized as female-headed households with children, but there is significant variation in the share of female-headed households by race and ethnicity. In 2002, about 5 percent of non-Hispanic women headed white and Asian households with children. In contrast, single mothers with kids accounted for 22 percent of all black households. The percentage of Hispanic households headed by women with kids falls in between these two estimates, at about 14 percent. Over the past 25 years, the percentage of female-headed households with children has increased particularly rapidly among blacks, but this trend appears to have slowed during the last five years (Ameristat, 2003).

Dual-Career Marriages

One of the important social changes since World War II has been the increase of women generally and of married women more specifically in the labor force. In 1940, despite a sharp increase in the number of working wives during the depression of the 1930s, only 15 percent of all married women living with their husbands held an outside job. By 1960, the proportion had risen to 32 percent, and by 1990, to close to 60 percent (*Statistical Abstract*, 1991: 390). Today, about three of every five married women hold jobs in the civilian labor force.

Women who have children are less likely to hold jobs than those who do not, although with each decade, the presence of children decreases in importance as a factor in whether women are employed. The proportion of married women in the labor force is highest among those who have no children under age 6 years to take care of at home. However, even among the women who have one or more children under the age of six, more than half are employed. Most of these employed women are in clerical or service work, with earnings well below those of their male counterparts. Arrangements of this type are called "dual-employed marriages." (It is assumed, sometimes incorrectly, that the husband is also employed.)

Although women have been taking jobs in increasing numbers, the "dual-career" marriage is a relatively recent development. The word career is used to designate jobs that are not taken just to produce additional income, but also for the satisfaction involved. Careers typically involve a higher level of commitment than just "paid employment," and they progress through a developmental sequence of increasing responsibility. One study (Burke and Weir, 1976) of one- and two-career families found that women in two-career families reported fewer pressures and worries, more communication with husbands, more happiness with their marriages, and better physical and mental health than women who did not work outside the home. In contrast, the men in the two-career families, as opposed to one-career families, were in poorer health and less content with marriage, work, and life in general. It seems that the husband of a career wife loses part of his support system when his wife no longer functions as a servant, homemaker, and mother. Wives who have careers, on the other hand, are able to expand into roles that have a more positive value for them.

Despite these rewards for women, most studies of dual-career marriages suggest that they involve certain strains. One of these strains, particularly for women, is brought on by what Fox and Nichols (1983) call a "time crunch." Wives are often expected to perform the majority of household tasks whether they have careers outside the home or not. In addition, wives usually accommodate more to the husband's career than vice versa, and husbands and wives have differential gains and losses when both have a career. Although the professional employment of women is gaining increasing acceptance, sexual equality in marriage has not yet been achieved. Wives are generally expected to give up their own jobs for the sake of their husbands and to consider their families their first duty.

Thinking Sociologically

1. Does an increase in nontraditional marital and family lifestyles signify a breakdown of the family?
2. In regard to one-parent families, discuss:
   (a) the adoption of children by single persons,
   (b) the feminization of poverty, and
   (c) the need for children to have two parents.

SUMMARY

1. The family serves a number of different purposes. It is the primary social group, a system of interdependent statuses and structures, and a social institution organized to meet certain essential societal goals.
2. The smallest family units—nuclear and conjugal families—consist of persons related by blood, marriage, or adoption who share a common residence. Sociologists also distinguish families of orientation, families of procreation, extended families, and modified-extended families.
3. Families throughout the world vary in many different ways, such as in number of spouses. A person may have one spouse (*monogamy*) or two or more (*polygamy*). In group *marriages*, there are several people of each sex. *Sequential monogamy* involves having several wives or husbands in succession but just one at any given time. *Polygyny*, in which one man is married to more than one woman, is the most common form of polygamy; *polyandry*, in which one woman has several husbands, is very rare.
4. Families vary in their norms of residence. Most cultures adhere to one of three patterns: *neolocal*, in which the couple is free to choose its own place of residence; *patrilocal*, in which the couple lives in the groom's community; and *matrilocal*, in which the couple lives in the bride's community. Worldwide, the patrilocal pattern is the most common.
5. Families have different norms of descent and inheritance. The *patrilineal* pattern, in which lineage is traced through the father's kin, is the most common, but there are also matrilineal and bilateral patterns.
6. Families vary in their norms of authority and decision making. Sociologists recognize systems of three types: patriarchal, matriarchal, and egalitarian. The *patriarchal* pattern of male dominance, power, and authority is the most widespread.
7. Norms vary with regard to the marriage partner considered appropriate. *Endogamous rules* state that a marriage partner should be from a similar group. *Exogamous rules* state that marriage partners should be from a different group.

Incest and same-sex marriages are almost universally forbidden, whereas marriage to a person of the same race, religion, and socioeconomic status is widely encouraged.

8. Several theoretical perspectives are widely used to explain family structures, interaction patterns, and behaviors. *Functionalists* examine variations in family structures, such as those just described, in terms of the functions they perform. According to this perspective, the family has many major functions: socialization, affection and emotional support, sexual regulation, reproduction, and social placement.

9. According to the *conflict perspective*, family members continually struggle for power and control. Conflict, which stems from the unequal distribution of scarce resources, is a major force behind social change.

10. The *exchange perspective* assumes that there are rewards and costs in all relationships, including those in marriage and the family. This view suggests that when selecting a spouse, people try to get the best they can with what they have to offer. The *complementary needs theory* proposes that people seek mates who will meet their needs without causing conflicts.

11. The *interactionist perspective* emphasizes the influence of role expectations and how people define situations. In this view, marriage, like other relationships, is a dynamic process of reciprocal interactions.

12. The d*evelopmental perspective* focuses on the time dimension. Change is analyzed in terms of the family life cycle, a series of stages that families go through from their inception at marriage through their dissolution by death or divorce.

13. The American family system emphasizes norms of monogamy, neolocal residence, modified-extended kinship, bilateral descent and inheritance, egalitarian decision making, endogamous marriage, and relatively free choice of mate. In a number of respects, however, the American family is quite variable.

14. Rates of marriage vary widely in terms of time period, geographical location, economic conditions, and other factors. The number of marriages also varies by season and by day of the week. The age at marriage in the United States, which declined from the turn of the century until the mid-1950s, has since increased, and marriages among teenagers are unlikely to last.

15. Norms concerning family size and parent-child relations are influenced by such variables as socioeconomic status, religion, education, urbanization, and female participation in the labor force. Although most married couples have or want to have children, younger women today generally plan to have small families, compared with earlier generations.

16. The United States has one of the highest divorce rates in the world. Like birth rates, rates of divorce vary with time period, geographical location, and socioeconomic level, and differing techniques of computing the divorce rate yield different figures about the rate of divorce. Variations in these rates illustrate how social and cultural factors influence the chances of marital dissolution.

17. Many marital and family lifestyles exist today that do not conform to the traditional model of two parents, two or more children, with the husband and wife performing fixed roles. The number of unmarried couples of all ages

who live together, for example, is increasing dramatically.

18. Childless marriages are increasingly common, in part because of the availability and reliability of contraceptives and abortion.

19. The number of one-parent families is increasing sharply, and many of these families are below the poverty level.

20. Marriages in which both spouses work have been common for a long time, but the dual-career marriage is a relatively recent development. There are many strains in these marriages, but women who have careers report fewer life pressures and worries and more happiness in their marriages. The men involved in two-career marriages tend to be relatively discontent, however.

KEY TERMS

bilateral lineage A descent system in which influence, wealth, and power are assigned to both sides of the family.

blended families Families composed of at least one formerly married spouse, the children of the previous marriage or marriages, and new offspring.

complementary needs A theory of mate selection based on the idea that people marry those who provide the maximum need gratification. Needs tend to be complementary rather than similar.

conjugal families Families consisting of a husband and wife, with or without children.

egalitarian The norm of authority in the family in which decisions are equally divided between husband and wife.

endogamy A marriage norm requiring a person to marry someone from his or her own group.

exogamy A marriage norm requiring a person to marry someone from outside his or her own group.

extended family A family that goes beyond the nuclear family to include other nuclear families and relatives such as grandparents, aunts, uncles, and cousins.

family A group of kin united by blood, marriage, or adoption who share a common residence for some part of their lives and assume reciprocal rights and obligations with regard to one another.

family of orientation The nuclear family into which one was born and in which one was reared.

family of procreation The nuclear family formed by marriage.

fraternal polyandry A form of polyandry where brothers are co-husbands.

group marriage A form of marriage in which several or many men are married to several or many women.

incest Socially forbidden sexual relationships or marriage with certain close relatives.

kinship The web of relationships among people linked by common ancestry, adoption, or marriage.

matriarchal A family structure in which the wife dominates the husband.

matrilineal A family structure in which descent and inheritance are traced through the mother's line.

matrilocal A family norm that newly married couples should live with the wife's family.

modified-extended family structure The family structure in which individual nuclear families retain considerable autonomy yet maintain connections with other nuclear families in the extended family structure.

monogamy The marriage of one man to one woman.

neolocal A family norm that newly married couples should establish residences separate from those of both sets of parents.

nonmarital cohabitation An arrangement in which two unmarried and unrelated adults share a common household or dwelling.

nuclear families Families in which two or more persons are related by blood, marriage, or adoption and who share a common residence.

patriarchal A family structure in which the husband dominates the wife.

patrilineal A family system in which descent and inheritance are traced through the father's line.

patrilocal A family norm that newly married couples should live with the husband's family.

polyandry The marriage of one woman to more than one husband at the same time.

polygamy The marriage of one man or woman to more than one person of the opposite sex at the same time.

polygyny The marriage of one man to more than one wife at the same time.

principle of legitimacy Malinowski's idea that every society has a rule that every child should have a legitimate father to act as the child's protector, guardian, and representative in society.

serial or sequential monogamy Marriage to a number of different spouses in succession, but only one at any given time.

DISCUSSION QUESTIONS

1. Discuss the importance of definitions of the family with regard to child custody policies.
2. What types of norms for choice of marriage partner—endogamy or exogamy—exist for you? In what ways are these norms encouraged and enforced?
3. Why does the United States insist on monogamy when many countries of the world permit polygamy? Why is polygyny very common and polyandry very rare?
4. How have norms of residence, descent and inheritance, authority, and choice of marriage partner changed in the United States over the past century? What do you think has led to these changes?
5. What types of questions would you ask about parent-child relations, using functionalist, conflict, interactionist, exchange, and developmental perspectives?
6. How do you explain the rapid increase in the median age at first marriage over the past two decades in the United States?
7. What types of social conditions are likely to affect the size of families in the United States and around the world? How does size affect family interaction patterns, educational systems, or the economy?
8. Should divorce be made more difficult to obtain? Why or why not? Discuss the consequences of divorce for men, women, children, and the society at large.
9. Discuss the pros and cons of nonmarital cohabitation. How are these types of relationships similar to or different from marriages?

10. What kinds of problems are encountered in dual-career marriages that do not occur in marriages where only one spouse is employed?

Religious Groups and Systems

The Increasing Role of Fundamentalism in Society

Although the First Amendment of the U.S. Constitution requires the separation of church and state, religious groups are increasingly exercising their influence and control over American political life. This is occurring primarily through alliances between right-wing religious and political groups. One of the most powerful religious forces that has of late been influencing the course of American politics is a faction of the Southern Baptist Convention known as "fundamentalists." *Fundamentalism* is the belief that the teachings of the Bible must be taken literally—that is, the Bible is not open to interpretation—and a belief in the inerrancy of the Bible. For example, fundamentalism accepts as absolute truth the literal account of the creation of the universe found in Genesis, and it rejects any form of evolutionary theory. Fundamentalism is a growing religious force in society, and its impact is being felt in many areas of social life, especially in politics. President George W. Bush has supported prayer in schools and opposes abortion. In return for sharing these views, he has won the overwhelming support of the most politically powerful religious group in the country.

One of the strongest indicators of the increasing role of fundamentalism in society is illustrated by the "holy war" that has been taking place during the past decade among Southern Baptists, the largest Protestant denomination in the United States—15.7 million people in 41,000 congregations, 7,600 missionaries in the United States and 116 in foreign countries, and more than $4.6 billion in receipts annually. Although there are over 130 different Baptist groups in the world with somewhat different perspectives, one thing they have in common is a strong belief in freedom; each church decides for itself in matters of faith and practice. Traditionally, Baptists have adhered to the belief that people should use the Bible as their guide to living as it speaks to them personally. For Baptists, there has not been a set creed—other than that the Bible is the word of God—and the Bible, even though it should be used as a prescription for living and moral guidance, has been open to interpretation. According to Bill Moyers—a lifelong Southern Baptist himself—in a multi-award-winning documentary on religion and politics, the heart of Baptist practice is "the priesthood of the believer: every Christian is competent to deal directly with God and no institution comes between you. What's important is your own experience, not what anyone says but what the Bible says to you." The inherent freedom and democracy contained within the Baptist religion largely accounts for its popularity in America. Historically, it has been a highly democratic religion, with no interference from any organizations, and it has embraced the belief that all are equal, with no one having the power to force interpretation about any particular piece of Scripture.

Within the past ten years, however, a significant rift has occurred among Southern Baptists. "Something is happening to Southern Baptists," notes Moyers. "Something alien—not quite Baptist. A sizable number of Fundamentalists, feeling disenfranchised, set out to take over the denomination. … The stakes of this 'holy war' are not only theological. They are political. The fundamentalist party wants to make one view of the Bible—their view—the test of religious and political truth. For Baptists, that's radical. For America, it's political dynamite, because how Baptists read the Bible affects how they vote." Their impact is felt on many political issues. For example, fundamentalists have lobbied to oppose abortion, the ERA, and gay rights, and to favor prayer in schools, corporal punishment (this chapter's policy debate), and many forms of legislation that support traditional gender roles. Additionally, they have been appointed to the boards of directors and trustees in Baptist schools and organizations, thus being able to control what Baptist colleges can teach and what their organizations can support.

Conservative religion and politics coalesced in the early 1980s with the fundamentalist support of Ronald Reagan for president, and, in turn, his support of them. In a speech made at the Dallas Religious Roundtable in 1980, Reagan said of the Bible: "It is an incontrovertible fact that all the complex and horrendous questions confronting us at home and worldwide have their answers in that single book." When Reagan received the nomination for president at the 1984 Republican Convention, the alliance between the Republican party and religious conservatism was firmly established symbolically when Dr. W. A. Criswell—the father figure of the fundamentalist movement—gave a blessing in support of Reagan. This alliance continued and grew during President Bush's administration.

At the same time that fundamentalism was gaining ground politically, it continued to gain strength in the religious world. In June 1990, Reverend Morris Chapman, a fundamentalist, was voted in as the president of the Southern Baptist Convention, thus giving fundamentalists the control they had been seeking for more than a decade. Many Southern Baptist leaders believe that fundamentalism will now come to dominate the Baptist religion around the world.

Moyers feels that fundamentalist control over the largest Protestant denomination in America is highly significant because fundamentalist leaders can now decide what the appropriate beliefs are for all Baptists. "As part of a political campaign with a specific agenda for America" notes Moyers, "they will be able to enroll God in partisan politics and make one party the sole party of truth."

The increasing role of fundamentalism in society is relevant to sociology because it demonstrates how religion is organized, how it gets its power, and how it affects society. As this chapter shows, religious groups and systems have implications for society that go well beyond our involvement in spiritual life.

Throughout the world, people meditate, pray, join communes, worry about "being saved," partake in rituals, bow to statues, burn incense, chant, offer sacrifices, torture themselves, and proclaim their allegiance to many gods or to a particular god. Anthropologists suggest that events, acts, and beliefs such as these are part of every society, both today and throughout history. Together, these behaviors constitute a society's religious system.

Religion has always been the anchor of identity for human beings. Religious beliefs give meaning to life, and the experiences associated with them provide personal gratification, as well as a release from the frustrations and anxieties of daily life. Ceremonies, formal acts, or rituals are essential for both personal identity and social cohesion. We have ceremonies to rejoice about the birth of an infant, to initiate a young person into adult society, to celebrate a new marriage, to bury the dead, and to fortify our belief that life goes on. Most of these ceremonies are linked to religion.

It may make you uneasy to examine these events and rituals objectively, but the goal of sociological investigations of religion is not to criticize anyone's faith or to compare the validity of different religions. Sociologists are interested, rather, in studying how religion is organized and how it affects the members of a given society. They study how people organize in groups in regard to religious beliefs and how these belief systems affect their behavior in other areas, such as family life and economic achievement. Sociologists also examine the kinds of belief systems developed by people in different circumstances and how religious beliefs change over time as external circumstances change.

A SOCIOLOGICAL APPROACH TO RELIGION

What Is Religion?

One of the earliest writers on the sociology of religion was the French sociologist Emile Durkheim. In *The Elementary Forms of the Religious Life* (1915), Durkheim defined *religion* as "a unified system of beliefs and practices relative to sacred things, that is to say, things set apart and forbidden—beliefs and practices which unite into one single moral community called a Church, all those who adhere to them" (p. 47).

In this definition, Durkheim identified several elements that he believed to be common to all religions. The first element, *a system of beliefs and practices*, he saw as the cultural component of religion. The *beliefs* are states of opinion, and the practices, which Durkheim termed "rites," are modes of action. These beliefs and practices exist within a social context, consistent with the values and norms of the culture.

The second element, *a community or church*, he saw as the social organizational component. A *church* in this sense is not a building or even a local group that gathers together to worship. Rather it is a collective of persons who share similar beliefs and practices. He claimed that in all history, we do not find a single religion without a community of believers. Sometimes, this community is strictly national, it sometimes is directed by a corps of priests, and it sometimes lacks any official directing body, but it always has a definite group at its foundation. Even the so-called cults satisfy this condition, for they are always celebrated by a group or a family. What the community does is to translate the beliefs and practices into something shared, which led Durkheim to think of these first two elements—the cultural and social components of religion—as being linked. Contemporary sociologists of religion do recognize a functional difference between the two, in that a person may accept a set of religious beliefs without being affiliated with a particular church.

The third element, *sacred things*, he saw as existing only in relation to the profane. The **profane** is the realm of the everyday world: food, clothes, work, play, or anything generally considered mundane and unspiritual. In contrast, the **sacred** consists of objects or ideas that are treated with reverence and awe: an altar, bible, prayer, or rosary is sacred. A hamburger, rock song, football, or sociology text is profane. However, Durkheim believed that anything could become sacred. Sacredness is not a property inherent in an object. It exists in the mind of the beholder. Thus, a tree, a pebble, a ring, a scarf worn by Elvis Presley, or a baseball bat used by Babe Ruth may be considered sacred.

Durkheim hypothesized that religion developed out of group experiences, as primitive tribes came to believe that feelings about sacredness were derived from some supernatural power. As people perform certain rituals, they develop feelings of awe, which reinforce the moral norms of society. When they no longer feel in awe of moral norms, society is in a state of anomie or normlessness. Informal social control is possible largely because people have strong feelings that they should or should not do certain things. When they no longer have such feelings, social control breaks down. We see an example of this in some of our cities, where church doors are locked to prevent robberies. In many societies, nobody steals from churches because they believe they will be punished or suffer some form of retribution from their god(s).

Other sociologists present somewhat different views of religion, but most would agree that a **religion** has the following elements:

1. Things considered sacred, such as gods, spirits, special persons, or any object or thought defined as being sacred
2. A group or community of believers who make religion a social, as well as a personal, experience because members of a religion share goals, norms, and beliefs
3. A set of rituals, ceremonies, or behaviors that take on religious meaning when they express a relationship to the sacred—in Christian ceremonies, for example, bread and wine are sacred components of communion that symbolize the body and the blood of Christ
4. A set of beliefs, such as a creed, doctrine, or holy book, which may define what is to be emphasized, how people should relate to society, or what happens to persons after their death
5. A form of organization that reinforces the sacred, unites the community of believers, carries out the rituals, teaches the creeds and doctrines, initiates new members, and so on

THE ORGANIZATION OF RELIGION

People have tried to understand the world around them throughout history, but we do not know exactly how or why they began to believe in supernatural beings or powers. Societies such as the Bushmen of Africa, who rely on hunting and gathering as their primary means of subsistence, often explain things in naturalistic terms. This type of religion is known as **animism**, which is the belief that spirits inhabit virtually everything in nature—rocks, trees, lakes, animals, and humans alike—and that these spirits influence all aspects of life and destiny. Sometimes they help, perhaps causing an arrow to strike and kill a wild pig for food. At other times, they are harmful, as when they make a child get sick and die. These spirits can sometimes be influenced by specific rituals or behaviors, however, and pleasing them results in favorable treatment.

Some groups, such as the Tapajos of Brazil, practice a form of religion known as **shamanism**, which revolves around the belief that certain individuals, called "shamans," have special skill or knowledge in influencing the spirits that influence processes and events in their environment. Shamans (spiritual leaders), most of whom are men, are called upon to heal the sick and wounded, to make hunting expeditions successful, to protect the group against evil spirits, and to generally ensure the group's well-being. Shamans receive their power through ecstatic experiences, which might originate from a psychotic episode, the use of a hallucinogen such as peyote, or deprivation such as fasting or lack of sleep. More than 10 million people in the world are identified as shamanists. All but about 250,000 of these are located in Asia.

Within the United States, Native Americans of the Pacific Northwest who live on reservations hold that ancestral spirits work for the good or ill of the tribe through shamans. The shaman is a very powerful spiritual leader among most of the 176 Native American tribes recognized by the federal government. According to Joe Therrien from Michigan, a Chippewa leader, sociologist, and friend of one of the authors of this textbook, this form of religion is more ceremonial than a daily practice. He cautions us that we should not be misled into believing that all Native Americans follow the shaman or tribal spiritual leader. Most (70 percent) are urban, and most are Christian, primarily Roman Catholic. Many have gotten involved in The Native American Church Movement, started in the late 1960s, which serves as a compromise between traditional ceremonial practices and Christian beliefs.

A third form of religion among selected groups is **totemism**, the worship of plants, animals, or other natural objects, both as gods and ancestors. The totem itself is the plant or animal believed to be ancestrally related to a person, tribe, or clan. Totems usually represent something important to the community, such as a food source or a dangerous predator, and the people often wear costumes and perform dances to mimic the totem object. Most readers are probably familiar with the totem poles used by North American Indians in Ketchikan, Alaska, often depicted in photographs, illustrations, or artifacts purchased by tourists. These tall posts, carved or painted with totemic symbols, were erected as a memorial to the dead. Totemism is still practiced today by some New Guinea tribes and by Australian aborigines. Durkheim believed that totemism was one of the earliest forms of religion and that other forms of religious organization evolved from it.

Religions may be organized in terms of the number of gods their adherents worship. **Polytheism** is belief in and worship of more than one god. Hinduism, which is practiced mainly in India, has a special god for each village and caste. People believe that these gods have special powers or control a significant life event, such as harvest or childbirth. Monotheism, on the other hand, is belief in only one god. **Monotheism** is familiar to most Americans because the three major religious groups in this country—Protestants, Catholics, and Jews—all believe in one god.

Most Westerners are less familiar with such major religions as Buddhism, Confucianism, Shintoism, and Taoism. These religions are neither monotheistic nor polytheistic, because they do not involve a god figure. They are based, rather, on sets of moral, ethical, or philosophical principles. Most are dedicated to achieving some form of moral or spiritual excellence. Some groups, such as the Confucianists, have no priesthood. Shintoism and Confucianism both place heavy emphasis on honoring one's ancestors, particularly one's parents, who gave the greatest of all gifts, life itself.

Churches, Sects, and Cults

Religious systems differ in many ways, and sociologists have devised numerous ways for classifying them. We have already seen how Durkheim divided the world into the sacred and the profane. We have noted how the religious practices of some hunting-and-gathering societies were described in terms of animism, shamanism, and totemism. Can Christianity be understood in terms of the profane or of shamanism? Most contemporary religious scholars think not. Thus, another scheme of classification is used—that of churches, sects, and cults. This scheme focuses directly on the relationship between the type of religious organization and the world surrounding it.

Max Weber (1905) was one of the first sociologists to clarify the interrelationships between people's beliefs and their surroundings. In his classic essay, *The Protestant Ethic and the Spirit of Capitalism*, he argued that capitalism would not have been possible without Protestantism because Protestantism stressed the importance of work as an end in itself, of personal frugality, and of worldly success as a means of confirming one's salvation and as evidence of God's favor. In dealing with this relationship between religion and the economy, he identified two major types of religious leaders. One, the **priest**, owes authority to the power of the office. By contrast, the **prophet** holds authority on the basis of charismatic qualities. Priestly and prophetic leaders are often in conflict, for the priest defends and represents the institution or society in question and supports the status quo. The prophet, not bound to a given institution, is more likely to criticize both the institutions and the general society.

This contrast led Weber to suggest that different sectors of society would develop different types of organizations to accompany their different belief systems. The ruling class or leaders, the better educated, and the more wealthy would need a more formalized type of religion that accepts modern science and the existing social world. The laboring class, the less educated, and the poor would need a type of religion that emphasizes another world or life and an emotional, spontaneous experience to console them for the deprivation in this life.

A German theologian and student of Weber, Ernst Troeltsch (1931), continued this line of thinking. Troeltsch divided religions into three categories: mysticism, churches, and sects. **Mysticism** is the belief that spiritual or divine truths come to us through intuition and meditation, not through the use of reason or the ordinary range of human experience and senses. *Mystics*, persons who believe in mysticism, practice their beliefs outside of organized religion. They often pose problems for other religious groups because they purport to be in direct contact with divine power. Evelyn Underhill, a Christian mystic, defines mysticism in the following way: "Mysticism, according to its historical and psychological definitions, is the direct intuition or experience of God; a mystic is a person who has, to a greater or less degree, such a direct experience—one whose religion and life are centered, not merely on an accepted belief or practice, but on that which the person regards as first-hand personal knowledge."

The church and the sect are differentiated in many ways but in particular by their relationships with the world around them (see Table 13-1). A **church** is an institutionalized organization of people who share common religious beliefs. The membership of churches is fairly stable. Most have formal bureaucratic structures with trained clergy and other officials, and they are closely linked to the larger society and seek to work within it. The majority of the religious organizations in the United States would be considered churches. The Roman Catholic church is the largest religious group in the United States, with more than 62 million members. When combined, more than half (55 percent) of all church members in this country are Protestants, however. Protestants belong to such churches as the National and Southern Baptist conventions, the Assemblies of God, the United Methodist church, and the Lutheran church, to mention just a few. The Church of Jesus Christ of Latter-Day Saints (Mormons) with 5.0 million members, the Greek Orthodox church with 1.95 million members, and the Jewish congregations with 6.1 million members are the largest non-Protestant churches (*Statistical Abstract*, 2000).

Two categories of churches that are sometimes differentiated are the ecclesia and the denomination. An **ecclesia** is an official state religion that includes all or most of the members of society. As a state church, it accepts state support and sanctions the basic cultural values and norms of the society. Sometimes, it administers the educational system as well. The Church of England in Great Britain and the Lutheran churches in the Scandinavian countries are two contemporary examples of national churches. The contemporary power of these churches, however, is not as great as was the power of the Roman Catholic church in Western Europe during the Middle Ages or even its power today in Spain, Italy, and many Latin American countries.

Churches in the United States are termed **denominations**. They are not officially linked to state or national governments. In fact, various denominations may be at odds with state positions on war, abortion, taxes, pornography, alcohol, equal rights, and other issues, and no nation has more denominations than the United States. The U.S. Bureau of the Census lists approximately 80 denominations with memberships of 60,000 or more (Statistical Abstract, 2000), but the list would probably exceed several hundred if all of the small or independent denominations were added.

Whereas churches (ecclesia and denominations) are well established and highly institutionalized, **sects** are small groups that have broken away from a parent church and that call for a return to the old

TABLE 13-1 CHARACTERISTICS OF CHURCHES, SECTS, AND CULTS

Characteristic	Church	Sect	Cult
Membership based on:	Faith	Conversion	Emotional commitment
Membership is:	Inclusive, regional/ national boundaries	Closely guarded and protected	Closely guarded and protected
Size is:	Large	Small	Small
Class/wealth is:	Middle/higher	Lower, limited	Varies by recruit
Organization is:	Bureaucratic	Informal organization of faithful	Loose, organization around leader
Authority is:	Traditional	Charismatic	Single leader
Emphasis is on:	Brother/sisterhood of all humanity	The select and faithful	New and unusual lifestyle
Clergy are:	Highly trained, professional	Deemphasized, high lay participation	Divinely chosen, individualized
Salvation is through:	Grace of God	Moral purity and being born again	Adherence to leader/cult demands
Relationship to state is:	Compromising, closely aligned	Hostile	Ignored and avoided
Theology is:	Modernistic	Fundamentalistic	Innovative, unique, pathbreaking
Worship is:	Formal, orderly	Informal and spontaneous	Innovative, often radical

ways. They follow rigid doctrines and emphasize fundamentalist teachings. As suggested in this chapter's introduction, **fundamentalism** is the belief that the Bible is the divine word of God and that all statements in it are to be taken literally, word for word. Incidentally, this is a position taken by about one-third of the United States population (Wood, 1990, p. 361), most of whom are *not* members of sects but are affiliated with institutionalized churches that take very conservative views toward social issues (note the introductory issue in this chapter). The size of this group depends on how fundamentalism is defined. Conservatively estimated, there are at least 30 million Christian fundamentalists in the United States alone. Fundamentalism stands with Pentecostalism as one of the most successful religious movements of the 20th century (2000; Religious Movements Homepage at the University of Virginia http://religious movements.lib.virginia.edu/.)

The creationism controversy, for example, stems from the fundamentalist position that the world was literally created in six days. Sect groups follow this type of literal interpretation of the Bible, although different groups focus their attention on different Bible scriptures. Their religious services often involve extensive member participation, with an emphasis on emotional expression.

The clergy of sects, who frequently preach part-time, often have little professional training and no seminary degrees. Members of sects tend to emphasize other-worldly rewards and are more likely to be of lower occupational and educational status than members of churches. Most of them are dissatisfied with their position in life and believe that the world is evil and sinful. As a result, their degree of commitment to the sect is often far greater than the commitment found among church members. Unwilling to compromise their beliefs, they are often in conflict with the government, the schools, and other social institutions. Although most sects are short-lived, some acquire a stable membership and a formal organizational structure and gradually become denominations.

There are many sects in the United States today including the Jehovah's Witnesses, Jews for Jesus, and a number of fundamentalist, evangelical, and Pentecostal groups. Although evangelical groups, like fundamentalist groups, maintain that the Bible is the only rule of faith, they focus their attention on preaching that salvation comes through faith as described in the four New Testament Gospels: Matthew, Mark, Luke, and John. Pentecostal groups, though usually both evangelical and fundamentalist, are Christian sects with a highly emotional form of worship experience. Some contrasting characteristics of churches, sects, and cults are shown in Table 13-1. You may want to place your religious group or affiliation, if any, on this church-sect-cult continuum.

Another form, some would say "extreme form," of religious organization is the **cult**, the most loosely organized and most temporary of all religious groups. Unlike sects, cults call for a totally new, unique, and frequently unusual lifestyle, often under the direction of a charismatic leader. Jim Jones and Father Divine, for example, believed that they were divinely chosen to lead humanity, as does the Reverend Sun Myung Moon today. In cults, the emphasis is on the individual rather than on society. Because cults operate outside the mainstream of society and are focused around one leader or prophet, their existence depends on the life and health of their leader. In some cases, they have given up their more radical teachings and, accepting more mainstream beliefs, have become churches. The Seventh-Day Adventists, for example, began as a cult group that proclaimed the end of the world on a specific date, but when that date passed, it maintained many of its other beliefs. Today, it is a church with a trained clergy, a stable membership, and a formal organizational structure.

Thinking Sociologically

Select your own religion or one with which you are well familiar. Can you identify for this religion (a) things that are considered sacred, (b) selected characteristics of the membership or its adherents, (c) selected rituals or ceremonies in which the adherents participate, (d) key beliefs of the religion, and (e) the form of social organization that exists?

THEORIES OF RELIGION

A Functionalist Approach

The universality of religion suggests to the functionalist that religion is a requirement of group life and that it serves both manifest and latent functions. Durkheim's classic study of religion, *The Elementary Forms of the Religious Life* (1915), posed two basic questions: (1) what is religion? and (2) what are the functions of religion for human society? In answering the first question, he noted that religion is a unified system of beliefs and practices relative to sacred things. He answered the second question by focusing on religion's social function of promoting solidarity within a society.

Unlike most people today, who view religion as primarily a private and personal experience, Durkheim believed that the primary function of religion was *to preserve and solidify society.* Noting that worship, God, and society are inseparable, he paid little attention to the other functions of religion.

This perspective assumes that religion is the central focus for integrating the social system. By developing the awe that members of society feel for moral norms, religion functions to hold society together. This social solidarity is developed through rituals such as church or synagogue services, baptisms, bar (or bas) mitzvahs, Christmas caroling and gift-giving, and the multitude of observances and ceremonies practiced by specific religious groups.

A second function, related to promoting social solidarity, is to *create a community of believers.* A religion provides a system of beliefs around which people may gather to belong to something greater than themselves and to have their personal beliefs reinforced by the group and its rituals. Those who share a common ideology develop a collective identity and a sense of fellowship.

A third function is to *provide social control.* Religion reinforces social norms, providing sanctions for violations of norms and reinforcing basic values, such as property rights and respect for others. Society's existence depends on its members' willingness to abide by folkways and mores and to interact with one another in a spirit of cooperation and trust.

Religion also serves to *provide answers to ultimate questions.* Why are we here? Is there a supreme being? What happens after death? Religions provide systems of belief based on the faith that life has a purpose, that someone or something is in control of the universe. They make the world seem comprehensible, often by attributing familiar, human motives to supernatural forces.

Religion also provides *rites of passage, ceremonies, and rituals* designed to give sacred meaning and a social significance to birth, the attainment of adulthood, marriage, death, and other momentous events.

Religion helps to *reconcile people to hardship.* All societies have inequality, poverty, and oppression, and everyone experiences pain, crises, prejudice, and sorrow. By belonging to a religion, people may come to feel that they are special in some way, that they will be rewarded in the future for having suffered today. Many religions call for caring, mercy, charity, kindness, and other prosocial behaviors. They may provide moral, ethical, social, and even financial support to those in need.

Religion can also *cultivate social change.* Many religious groups criticize social injustice, existing social morality, and community or government actions. Some take action to change unfavorable conditions. The churches have been a major force in the civil rights movement, for example. Many protests against the Vietnam War were a result of religious teachings about love and peace. Other major protests have been mounted by religious groups to oppose social reforms, such as opposition to the right to have an abortion, equal rights for homosexuals, and the women's rights movement.

This list of *manifest functions* performed by religion could be continued. Some latent functions of religion concern mate selection, experience in public speaking, and psychic rewards for donating funds or labor to worthy causes. Other groups and systems may be able to fulfill some of these manifest or latent functions, but many social scientists argue that particular functions provided by religion cannot be adequately met by other means; others might suggest that some of the functions of religion may not be needed by society.

A functionalist approach to religion reminds us that while it performs many basic functions for society and individuals, it is likely to have dysfunctions as well.

If it serves to preserve and solidify society, to create a community of believers, to reinforce social norms, and to reconcile people to hardship, it also can serve to divide society, create bias against the nonbeliever, exclude nonmembers of the group, and maintain the status quo. Religion can be dysfunctional in forcing people to accept inequities and in inhibiting its members from acting to change them. It can be dysfunctional in convincing its followers to reject this world for a future life in which rewards are guaranteed, and it can often inhibit the search for and acceptance of new truths, new ideas, and additional knowledge.

Examples of religion as both a source of integration and conflict are evident throughout the world. In Iran, the religious teachings of Islam formed the basis for convincing youth that it was honorable to die for their country in their war with Iraq. In Northern Ireland, protests and violence abound between Catholics and Protestants. In the Middle East, the conflicts between Jews and Moslems are intense. In India and Pakistan, caste and class conflicts linked to religious traditions cause death and destruction. In many countries, Jews are persecuted. Overpopulation and wars can be justified in the name of religion. As mentioned elsewhere, to have in-groups is to have out-groups. To believe that there is only one *Truth* is to reject all ideas that challenge prejudices.

APPLYING THE FUNCTIONALIST APPROACH TO RELIGION

Some useful insights provided by the functionalist approach are that religion serves a variety of essential social functions and that an understanding of religion is closely linked to an understanding of an entire culture. For example, can we understand Israel without knowing about Judaism, Saudi Arabia without knowing about Islam, or the United States without knowing about Christianity? Judeo-Christian religions penetrate most of our lives—even though we may be unaware of it and may not subscribe to any particular religion. This is exemplified even by our legal tender, on every piece of which is the phrase, "In God We Trust." Our entire economic system is imbued with religious overtones.

The knowledge that religion serves basic social functions may be useful in a number of careers. Notably, people whose jobs lead them to deal with foreign cultures might benefit from a thorough understanding of the major religions in those countries. Consider, for example, the difficulties that politicians, diplomats, and military personnel from the United States might have in dealing with the governments in the Middle East if they do not first understand the basic religions in these countries, their influence on Middle Eastern culture, and how they contrast with the Protestant ethic, one of the mainstays of U.S. culture. In the war with Iraq in 2003, many Americans came to realize just how important it is to understand the impact of a country's religious traditions on its culture. Many American soldiers, other military personnel, medical personnel, news reporters, and others who observed the war had to adjust to what they thought were the odd attitudes that the Arab world has toward such things as gender roles, alcohol use, and the female body. Imagine what it must be like for someone from the Middle East who comes to the United States, where many religious viewpoints are tolerated.

Because religion plays such a key part in a society's values, norms, roles, and beliefs, people involved in international business may benefit by fully understanding a country's religious traditions. This could be especially true in the advertising of products. Even though most advertisements in the

United States are still geared toward traditional gender roles, for example, much of it is beginning to cater to the changing roles of women and men in American society. Considering again the example of Islam, we see that using this type of advertising would be a serious mistake in Middle eastern countries, where religion plays a central role in keeping marriage and homemaking the central occupations of women.

A Conflict Approach

As discussed in previous chapters, the conflict approach focuses on the exploitation of the poor by the elite. The classical Marxist perspective suggests that religion, like other social structures, can be understood only in the context of its role in the economic system.

In sharp contrast to the functionalist approach, conflict theorists view religion as a tool that the elite uses to get the poor to obey authority and to follow the rules established by the privileged. Religion counsels the masses to be humble and to accept their condition. In the words of Karl Marx, religion "is the opiate of the masses" because it distracts them from finding practical political solutions to their problems. The powerless find an illusion of happiness through religion and look forward to future life after death, where the streets will be paved with gold, and life will be joyful and everlasting. Marx urged revolution so that people could experience during life the joy and freedom that religion postpones until after death. In American society, we supplement that illusion of happiness by focusing upon individualism and meritocracy. Loosely, meritocracy advocates that "you get what you deserve and you deserve what you get." These two belief systems shore up the religious ideas that help to hold the inequality and lack of action in place.

Most theorists today would agree that religion serves interests other than those of the ruling class, but it is unquestionably true that there are strong relationships between religion and social class. Churches are highly segregated along racial and economic lines. In the United States, a number of denominations are largely or wholly black. Although the ideals faith are supposed unite people across the great chasms carved by race and ethnicity, social scientists have long noted the in a manner of speaking "Sunday morning service is the most segregated hour in America."

Within the white population, different religious groups tend to attract people of similar educational and occupational levels. Few factory workers are Episcopalians, for example, and few professional people and company executives are Baptists or members of Pentecostal groups. Some groups, such as the Roman Catholic church, have working-class as well as wealthy members, but the data generally show that occupation and income vary with religious affiliation.

Is religion related to class conflict? In a general way, yes. Religious affiliation is related to class, and many social controversies result from perceptions that differ according to social class. Opinions on such issues as prayer in the schools, the teaching of creationism, abortion, women as clergy, the Equal Rights Amendment, and homosexuality vary both by class and by religion. The conservative positions are generally supported both by fundamentalist and Pentecostal churches and by people who have lower incomes and less education.

APPLYING THE CONFLICT APPROACH TO RELIGION

In pointing out how religion is related to class conflict, the conflict approach yields some other useful findings. One is that occupation and income vary with religious affiliation. This is an important fact for church leaders to consider. By knowing that the members of a particular religious congregation are likely to be from a particular social class, ministers, priests, deacons, rabbis, and others could address the relevant needs of that congregation and might formulate examples to which the people can relate.

> In Latin America, a branch of religious teaching known as "liberation theology" has been gaining wide acceptance. Liberation theology directly applies church policy and intervention to the social and class conflicts that plague Latin American society. Church leaders who support this approach speak out against repressive government policies, promote land reform, and generally act as advocates for the peasant population. Although not condoned by Catholic leadership in Rome, many priests praise liberation theology as an example of the applicability of religion to social welfare.

Understanding the relationship between social class and religious affiliation could be useful for you personally. You can learn a great deal about a community, for instance, by noticing its variety of churches. If you see a fairly broad representation of Baptist, Methodist, Catholic, and Episcopalian churches and Jewish synagogues, you know that the community has a fairly wide range of income and educational levels and probably a diversity of political attitudes. However, a preponderance of one type of church or temple might be a reflection of a community with less cultural diversity and less tolerance for differences.

Thinking Sociologically

1. Evaluate the major social functions of religion provided in this chapter. Can you give examples to illustrate each function? Do each of these functions exist for all religions?
2. From the conflict perspective, how does religion serve the elite?

RELIGIONS OF THE WORLD

The world population is more than 6 billion. About 14 percent of these people are listed as nonreligious (see Figure 13-1). Thus, whether we refer to Asia, to Russia and other countries in the Commonwealth of Independent States, to North America, or to Africa, the vast majority of people in the world adhere to or profess adherence to some religion.

It is difficult to obtain accurate counts of the number of adherents to the world's religions. The procedures used by different countries and groups to measure religious membership vary widely. Some assessments include only adults, others include everyone who attends services. Some people may be included in several different religious groups, such as Confucianism, Taoism, and Shintoism. Some religions forbid counts of their members. In countries where a particular religion has prevailed for many centuries (such as Christianity in Europe and Hinduism in India), the entire population may be reported as adherents. While most of us are likely to be familiar with one or two specific religions we may be less familiar with others. We now briefly examine some major ones.

Christianity and Judaism

More than 2 billion people adhere to Christianity, and more than 17.4 million adhere to Judaism in the world today. **Christians**, who comprise about one third of the world's population (see Figure 13-1) profess faith in the teachings of Jesus Christ, as found in the New Testament of the Bible, whereas adherents to **Judaism** find the source of their beliefs in the Hebrew Bible (called the "Old Testament" by Christians), especially in its first five books, which are called the "Torah." The Torah was traditionally regarded as the primary revelation of God, originally passed on orally and eventually written.

FIGURE 13-1 RELIGIONS OF THE WORLD, PERCENTAGES

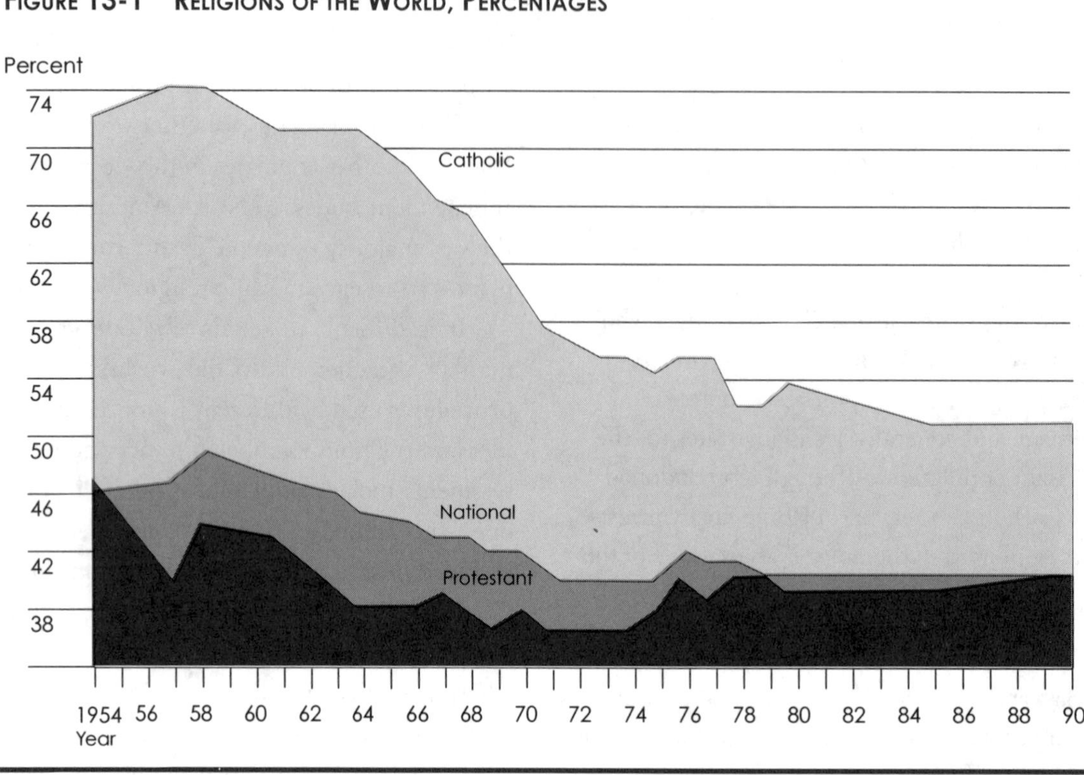

Judaism is the oldest religion in the Western world. It comprises both a religious and an ethnic community. It was the first religion to teach monotheism, which was based on the Old Testament verse "Hear O Israel, the Lord our God, the Lord is one" (Deuteronomy 6:4). Jews, the people who identify with and practice Judaism, believe that God's providence extends into a special covenant with the ancient Israelites: to bring God's message to humanity by their example. As a result, the emphasis is on conduct rather than on doctrinal correctness. Adherents to Judaism have a considerable measure of latitude in matters of belief because their beliefs have never been formulated in an official creed. This lack of an official creed also meant that Judaism did not stop developing after the Bible was completed. One result of this development was the traditional Jewish prayer book, which reflects the basic beliefs of Judaism as well as changes in emphasis in response to changing conditions.

Judaism has a system of law that regulates civil and criminal justice, family relationships, personal ethics and manners, and social responsibilities to the community, as well as worship and other religious observances. Individual practice of these laws varies greatly. Some widely observed practices concern strict adherence to kosher foods, daily prayer and study, the marital relationship, and the meaning of the yarmulke (skullcap) and tefillin (worn on the forehead and left arm during morning prayers).

The Jewish religious calendar, which is of Babylonian origin, consists of 12 lunar months, amounting to approximately 354 days. Six times over a 19-year cycle, a thirteenth month is added, to adjust the calendar to the solar year. The Sabbath is from sunset Friday to sunset Saturday.

Male children are circumcised on the eighth day after birth as a sign of the covenant with Abraham. At age 13, Jewish boys undergo the rite of becoming a bar mitzvah, to signify adult status and a responsibility for performing the commandments. A similar ceremony for girls, the bas mitzvah, is a more recent innovation.

Christianity diverged from Judaism in ancient Israel. Christians considered Jesus to be the Jewish savior, or Messiah, and incorporated the traditional Hebrew writings of Christ's followers into the canon of their faith, the Bible. After Christ's death (and, as Christians believe, his resurrection), his teachings spread to Rome and many other centers of the Roman Empire. When the Roman Empire split in a.d. 1054, so did the Christian church; it came to be called the Orthodox church in the East and the Roman Catholic church in the West. The Roman Catholic church was united under popes until the sixteenth century. Today, of the estimated 2 billion plus Christians, nearly 57 percent are Roman Catholic. Slightly more than one-third are Protestant, and the rest are Eastern Orthodox.

Christians, like Jews, believe in one god (monotheism), but for most Christians, their God takes the form of a Holy Trinity: Father, Son, and Holy Spirit. Christians experience God as the Father, Jesus Christ as the son of God, and the Holy Spirit as the continuing presence of God. Also, most Christians worship on Sunday instead of Saturday, which is the Jewish Sabbath. They also practice baptism by water when they become adherents or give a public testimony of their acceptance of Christ and of Christ's divinity. Christians also take the Eucharist, a sacred meal recalling the last supper that Jesus had with his disciples. The breaking of bread, symbolizing the body of Christ, and the drinking of wine, symbolizing the blood of Christ, are sacred acts (sacraments) to most Christians. Prayer and preaching are also important Christian functions.

Islam

There are nearly 1 billion Islamic adherents in the world. Followers of **Islam** follow the teachings of the Koran and of Muhammad, a prophet. Islam means "surrender, resignation," and "submission." A person who submits to the will of Allah, the one and only God, is called a Muslim (sometimes spelled "Moslem"). This surrender involves a total commitment in faith, obedience, and trust to this one God. The insistence that no one but God be worshiped has led many Muslims to object to the term "Muhammadanism," a designation widely used in the West but thought to suggest that Muhammad, a great prophet of Islam, is worshiped in a manner that parallels the worship of Christ by Christians.

It is sometimes assumed that Islam originated during the lifetime of Muhammad (a.d. 570–630), specifically during the years in which he received the divine revelations recorded in the Muslim sacred book, the Qur'an (Koran). Many Muslims, however, believe that the prophet Muhammad simply restored the original religion of Abraham.

Islam encompasses a code of ethics, a distinctive culture, a system of laws, and a set of guidelines and rules for other aspects of life. The Muslim place of worship is the mosque, and the chief gathering of the congregation takes place on Fridays. Muslims profess their faith by repeating that "there is no God but God, and Muhammad is the messenger of God." The Muslims also have a deep awareness of the importance of a fellowship of faith and a community of believers.

The Koran includes rules for ordering social relationships. It is especially explicit about matters pertaining to the family, marriage, divorce, and inheritance. The family is basically authoritarian, patriarchal, polygamous, patrilineal, and largely patrilocal. Women are clearly subordinate to men and receive only half the inheritance that male heirs receive. Muslim males may marry non-Muslim women, and in countries where the Muslim holy law is the law of the state, Muslim women may not marry outside their faith. A Muslim male may take up to four wives (polygyny) and traditionally can divorce a wife by simple pronouncement and dowry repayment. Children, especially sons, are perceived as desirable.

Although laws are changing in many Islamic countries, and the education of women has increased dramatically, fewer females than males attend school, and even fewer women receive a higher education. Marriage and housekeeping are considered the proper occupations of women. It is not surprising, therefore, that Islam is finding it difficult to come to terms with the scientific ideas and the technology of the Western world. and since it is very difficult to accurately report the number of Muslims in the U.S. due to the U.S. Census not reporting religious identification, we have to estimate the members to be from 1.1 million to 2.98 million based on recent studies.

Hinduism

The great majority of the 786 million Hindus in the world live in India and Pakistan. In India, approximately 85 percent of the population is Hindu. **Hinduism** has evolved over about 4,000 years and comprises an enormous variety of beliefs and practices. It hardly corresponds to most Western conceptions of religion because organization is minimal, and there is no religious hierarchy.

Hinduism is so closely intertwined with other aspects of the society that it is difficult to describe it clearly, especially in regard to castes. Hindus sometimes refer to the ideal way of life as fulfilling the duties of one's class and station, which means obeying the rules of the four great castes of India: the Brahmans, or priests; the Kshatriyas, warriors and rulers; the Vaisyas, merchants and farmers; and the Sudras, peasants and laborers. A fifth class, the Untouchables, includes those whose occupations require them to handle "unclean" objects.

These classes encompass males only. The position of women is ambiguous. In some respects, they are treated as symbols of the divine, yet in other ways, they are considered inferior beings. Traditionally, women have been expected to serve their husbands and to have no independent interests, but this is rapidly changing.

Although caste is a powerful influence in Hindu religious behavior, a person's village community and family are important as well. Every village has gods and goddesses who ward off epidemics and drought. Hindu belief holds that the universe is populated by a multitude of gods (polytheism) who behave much as humans do, and worship of these gods takes many forms. Some are thought to require sacrifices, others are worshiped at shrines or temples, and shrines devoted to several gods associated with a family deity are often erected in private homes.

To Hindus, the word *dharma* means the cosmos, or the social order. Hindus practice rituals that uphold the great cosmic order. They believe that to be righteous, a person must strive to behave in accordance with the way things are. In a sense, the Hindu sees life as a ritual. The world is regarded as a great dance determined by one's karma, or personal destiny, and the final goal of the believer is liberation from this cosmic dance. Hindus also believe in *transmigration of souls:* After an individual dies, that individual's soul is born again in another form, as either a higher or a lower being, depending on whether the person was righteous or evil in the previous life. If an individual becomes righteous enough, the soul will be liberated and will cease to be reborn into an earthly form and will exist only as spirit.

A fundamental principle of Hinduism is that our perceptions of the external world are limitations. When we think about one thing, we are cut off from the infinite number of things we are not thinking about but could be. If we think of nothing, we become in tune with the universe and freed of these limitations. One means of doing this is through meditation.

The actual belief systems of India are extremely confusing to Westerners, because so many different tribal religions have been assimilated into Hinduism, but the basic nature of polytheism in general and of Hinduism in particular permits new gods to be admitted.

Buddhism

Buddhism has about 362 million adherents. It is impossible to precisely determine the number of Buddhists because many people accept Buddhist beliefs and engage in Buddhist rites while practicing other religions, such as Shintoism, Confucianism, Taoism, or Hinduism.

Buddhism is thought to have originated as a reaction against the Brahmanic tradition of Hinduism in the fifth century b.c. At this time, a prince named Siddhartha Gautama was born in northern India to a prosperous ruling family. As he grew older, he was distressed by the suffering he witnessed among the people. At the age of 29, he left his wife and family to go on a religious quest. One day, sitting under a giant fig tree, he passed through several stages of awareness and became the first Buddha, the enlightened one. He decided to share his experience with others and became a wandering teacher, preaching his doctrine of the "Four Noble Truths": (1) this life is suffering and pain; (2) the source of suffering is desire and craving; (3) suffering can cease; and (4) the practice of an "eightfold path" can end suffering. The eightfold path consisted of right views, right intentions, right speech, right conduct, right livelihood, right effort, right mindfulness, and right concentration. It combined ethical and disciplinary practices, training in concentration and meditation, and the development of enlightened wisdom. This doctrine was Buddha's message until the age of 80, when he passed into final nirvana, a state of transcendence forever free from the cycle of suffering and rebirth.

After Buddha's death, legends of his great deeds and supernatural powers emerged. Stories were told of his heroism in past lives, and speculations arose about his true nature. Some groups viewed him as a historical figure, whereas others placed him in a succession of several Buddhas of the past and a Buddha yet to come. Differing views eventually led to a diversity of Buddhist sects in different countries. Some remained householders who set up Buddha images and established many holy sites that became centers of pilgrimage. Others became monks, living in monastic communities and depending on the laity for food and material support. Many monks became beggars, and in several Southeast Asian countries, they still go on daily alms rounds. They spend their days in rituals, devotions, meditation, study, and preaching. Flowers, incense, and praise are offered to the image of the Buddha. These acts are thought to ensure that the monks will be reborn in one of the heavens or in a better place in life, from which they may be able to attain the goal of enlightenment.

In every society where Buddhism is widespread, people combine Buddhist thought with a native religion, supporting the monks and paying for rituals in the temples. These societies are also organized around other religions, however.

Today, the integration of Buddhism into many cultures has resulted in different interpretations of the way to Buddhahood. Yet we can supposedly reach Nirvana by seeing with complete detachment, by seeing things as they really are without being attached to any theoretical concept or doctrine.

Confucianism

Confucianism, which has about 5.8 million adherents, is associated primarily with China, the home of nearly 180 million adherents to Chinese folk religions. Confucianism has influenced the civilizations of Korea, Japan, and Vietnam, as well as China. Confucianism is the philosophical and religious system based on the teachings of Confucius, who was born to a poor family in 551 b.c., in what is today Shantung Province in China, and was orphaned at an early age. As a young man, he held several minor government positions, but he became best known as a teacher, philosopher, and scholar. Distressed by the misery and oppression that surrounded him, he dedicated his life to attempting to relieve the suffering of the people.

By talking with younger men about his ideas to reform government to serve the people rather than the rulers, Confucius attracted many disciples. He emphasized the total person, sincerity, ethics, and the right of individuals to make decisions for themselves. Although Confucius was not a religious leader in the usual sense of the word, he believed that there was a righteous force in the universe, and yet his philosophy was founded not on supernaturalism but on humanity. He said that virtue is to love people, and wisdom is to understand them.

The basic philosophy of Confucius is found in his many sayings: "All people are brothers." "Sincerity and reciprocity should be one's guiding principles." "The truly virtuous person, desiring to be established personally, seeks to establish others; desiring success for oneself can help others to succeed." "The superior person stands in awe of three things: the ordinances of heaven, great persons, and the words of sages." The ideals of Confucius were motivated not by the desire for rewards or an afterlife but simply by the satisfaction of acting in accordance with the divine order.

Confucius had a pervasive influence on all aspects of Chinese life, so much so that every county in China built a temple to him. Everyone tried to live in accordance with the Confucian code of conduct. His values guided human relations at all levels—among individuals, communities, and nations. His thought guided conduct in work and in the family. Even today, the Chinese who profess to be Taoists, Buddhists, or Christians still generally act in accordance with Confucian ideals.

One of the books in the classical literature of Confucius is the *Book of Changes*, or the I Ching. This book is familiar to many Americans and is used to guide a person's behavior and attitude toward the future.

Thinking Sociologically

Given the tremendous variability in religious beliefs and practices around the world, consider statements such as these:

1. Religious truth is only found in a literal interpretation of the Bible.
2. Religion is a social creation.
3. Whether there is no god, one god, or many gods is only relevant in terms of what people believe.

RELIGION IN THE UNITED STATES

Of the religions of the world just described, most readers of this text are well aware that Christianity predominates in the United States. The General Social Survey conducted annually by the National Opinion Research Center (NORC) affiliated with the University of Chicago indicates that more than half of the U.S. population state their religious preference to be Protestant, 25 percent Catholic, 2 percent Jewish, 8 percent "none," and 2 percent "other" (NORC, 1999:124). Although the numbers vary, most Americans identify with some religion. In 1990, ninety percent of the adult population identified with one or another religion group. In 2001, the American Religious Identity Survey reported: 81% Christian, 1.4% Jewish, 15% (none), and .07% (other).

The United States, which has no state church, has more than 200 denominations and is greatly influenced by a variety of religious groups and belief systems. In addition to churches and denominations, revivalists preach on TV and radio, and religious leaders such as Billy Graham give spiritual advice and seek converts to Christianity. Bumper stickers tell us that "Jesus Saves" or to "Honk if you love Jesus."

Williams (1980) conceptualizes American religion as an interplay between two forces, the structured and the unstructured, the major religious communities and the informal groups that he calls "popular religions." These two trends developed, he says, in response to the demands of life in a new country. Faced with a diverse population, a new political system, and rapid technological change, Americans sometimes have found organized religions too limited, and in response to the demands of a new nation, they have developed new religious movements.

The Development of Religious Movements

Religion in American society has become increasingly rationalized and centralized. Some so-called liberal religious groups have downplayed the supernatural aspects of Christianity and have emphasized the importance of ethical conduct and a remote, depersonalized God. Others worship a personal god and express their beliefs emotionally. Those who worship in this way seek signs of divine intervention in their daily lives.

Another religious movement is the development of sects (review Table 13-1). The proliferation of these groups accompanied the breakdown of the feudal structure and the development of industrialization. One wave of groups, known as the Pietist sects, rejected worldliness in favor of pacifism, communal living, and aspiration toward perfection. The Amish and the Hutterites are American groups descended from these sects.

Another sect is the Religious Society of Friends (Quakers), who came to Pennsylvania from England. Quakers believe in an "inner light," that people mystically partake of the nature of God. Thus, they see no need for a religious structure (e.g., clergy or churches) interceding between God and human beings.

Another theme in American religious life is **millennialism**, the belief that a dramatic transformation of the earth will occur and that Christ will rule the world for a thousand years of prosperity and happiness. One millennial movement took place among the Millerites in the 1830s. William Miller, the founder, was convinced that the Second Coming of Christ would happen in 1843. When it did not, he changed the date to 1844. Again nothing happened. Some of his followers, who believed that the Second Coming had occurred invisibly and spiritually, founded the *Seventh-Day Adventists.*

Other religious movements have been based on divine revelation. One American prophet who received a divine revelation was Joseph Smith, who founded the *Church of Jesus Christ of Latter-Day Saints* (Mormons) in 1830. His following was recruited from the rural people of upstate New York. About 30 years later, Mary Baker Eddy began a movement in the urban middle class, known as the Christian Science movement. Ms. Eddy's revelation was that illness could be controlled by the mind. This sect developed into a denomination when people of wealth and status became adherents.

Pentecostalism involves a practice similar to divine revelation. Pentecostal Christians hold highly emotional services that resemble revivals. Participants also "speak in tongues" (*glossolalia*), in which they go into ecstatic seizures and utter a rapid flow of apparently meaningless syllables that are claimed to be a direct gift of the Holy Spirit.

An offshoot of Pentecostalism is *faith healing*, which experienced a rapid growth after World War II. In faith healing, the fundamentalist preacher asks members of the congregation who are sick or disabled

SOCIOLOGY AT WORK

Helping Religious Refugees Readjust

Baila Miller received a doctorate in sociology at the University of Illinois at Chicago Circle. She has used her sociological training in a variety of ways. She has been a member of the faculty doing applied research in gerontology in the Department of Medical Social Work at the University of Illinois at Chicago since 1988. Prior to that, she handled publications and training for SPSS, a computer software company, and before that, she was the assistant director of research at the Jewish Federation of Metropolitan Chicago.

It was at the Jewish Federation where Miller first used her sociological training to earn a living. When Miller was asked how she used her sociological training in her work at the Jewish Federation, she responded, "The federation raises charitable funds and allocates them to Jewish causes in Israel and overseas and to local Jewish social welfare, health, and educational institutions. The office of research and planning where I worked was a small department—just three people. We were responsible for analyzing the budgets of some of the agencies we supported, for preparing service statistics for submission to the United Way, for collecting and analyzing data needed by our volunteer committees, and for carrying out special research projects."

It was in these special research projects that Miller found the fullest application of her training. "In one project we completed a survey of the Jewish population of greater Chicago," she says—a survey that presented unique problems among population studies because the U.S. Bureau of the Census does not collect data on religious affiliations in its decennial census. "We wanted to determine many things about the Jewish community: How many people were there? Where did they live? How did they maintain their Jewish identity? Did they participate

to come forward. The preacher asks the disabled person and the rest of the congregation to call upon the power of the Lord to heal: "In the name of Jesus, heal." If their faith in Christ is strong enough, the blind will see, the lame can throw away their crutches, and so on. Followers of faith healers come primarily from the poor or working classes, who often do not have health insurance, adequate financial resources, or sometimes an awareness of what is available or where to go for adequate medical treatment.

A recent manifestation of the interplay between churches or denominations and fundamentalist groups of the sect type concerns the teaching of evolution in the public schools. Most educated people in the United States accept Darwin's theory of biological evolution. Many fundamentalist Christians, however, interpret the Bible literally and believe that God created heaven and earth in exactly the six days it specifies. The creationists are urging that creationism be given "equal time" with evolution in school science classes. The basic assumptions of scientists and religious fundamentalists are in direct conflict: Science is based on deductions drawn from empirical reality, whereas creationism is based on divine revelation and denounces empirical evidence that contradicts Biblical accounts. The issue of whether creationism should be taught in the public schools was temporarily muted in 1982 when a federal district judge in Arkansas ruled that the two-model approach of the creationists is simply a

Helping Religious Refugees Readjust, *continued*

in religious observances and in Jewish education? What were their service needs and how could a Jewish agency meet [these needs]? Should we have concentrated on services for the elderly or on child care for two-career families? Who were the Jewish poor?"

Clearly, many areas of Miller's sociological training came into play with this one study alone. In addition to needing a knowledge of various types of quantitative and qualitative research techniques, she needed to know about substantive areas in sociology, such as minority groups, religious groups, population, community, families, and social psychology, which were invaluable to her research.

Another project with which Miller was involved at the Jewish Federation was a study of the adjustment of Soviet Jewish émigrés to life in various communities in the United States. Miller analyzed data about Soviet Jewish émigrés in a number of ways. First, at the individual level, she studied how these people adjusted to American life in terms of occupational achievement, language acquisition, social and cultural involvement in the Jewish community, and maintenance of Jewish identity. She looked at the effects of *background characteristics*—social and economic status and place of origin in the former Soviet Union; and *of mediating factors*—the type of resettlement services that were offered in various communities in this country. Second, on the community level, she looked at *aggregate measures* of differences in adjustment in various cities in the United States. This included an investigation of comparable studies that were done in 13 U.S. cities and a cross-cultural analysis of the similarities and differences with other large refugee or émigré groups, particularly Asians and Mexicans. Finally, she did a policy analysis of different programs offered by Jewish agencies and national refugee organizations in order to determine their effectiveness.

contrived dualism that has no scientific factual basis or legitimate educational purpose. The ruling contended that because creationism is not science, the conclusion is inescapable that the only real effect of teaching creation theory is the advancement of religion. What the creation law does, in effect, is to make the teaching of creationism in the public schools unconstitutional.

A ruling in the opposite direction that illustrates the impact of fundamentalism on our judicial system took place in 1987. A federal district judge in Alabama ruled that about 40 social studies books be removed from the public schools because they taught what creationists called "secular humanism." The judge ruled that secular humanism was a religion that gave credit to humans rather than to God.

Current Trends in Religion

The use of computers and sophisticated statistical techniques have brought about significant changes in social science research in general and in the scientific study of religion in particular. Researchers can now deal efficiently with large samples of the population and can test some of the theories developed by Durkheim and Weber.

One such study was published in 1961 by Gerhard Lenski, whose book, *The Religious Factor*, is now considered a pioneering quantitative study of religion. Using survey techniques on a probability sample of males in the Detroit area, Lenski tried to test Weber's notions about the Protestant ethic. Lenski reasoned that if Protestants were more oriented toward the Protestant ethic than Catholics, they should show more upward mobility. He found that more white Protestant men than Catholic men rose into the upper middle class or retained that status and that Catholic men were more likely to move into or remain in the lower half of the working class.

Subsequent studies (Greeley, 1989) have contradicted Lenski's findings and show no direct relationship between Protestant or Catholic religious beliefs and socioeconomic status. Nevertheless, quantitative research on religion became much more popular following Lenski's publication. We now have a profile of American religious beliefs and their relation to social class, race, age, and other factors. One important finding of this research has been that a sizable part of the population has no conventional religious commitment, although they are concerned with ethical and moral beliefs and practices that often have their roots in Judeo-Christian teachings. This movement away from the church is known as "secularization."

Secularization

It is widely accepted by social scientists that the dominant trend in modern religion is secularization. **Secularization** means to focus on this world and on worldly things such as science, reason and technology, as distinguished from the church, religious affairs, and faith. It means that problems are solved by humans through their own efforts (the essence of so-called secular humanism), as opposed to unquestioned faith in supernatural powers and a focus on the next world or an afterlife. It means a trend toward the declining influence of religion in the lives of people and in the institutions of society. Today, for example, marriages are assumed to be decided between humans, not foreordained by a god. Tragedies such as automobile accidents are explained in terms of human interactions and the laws of science, not as manifestations of divine will.

This secular way of thinking is extremely disturbing to fundamentalists and to right-wing evangelicals. To them, the idea that human beings are in control of their own destiny and that individuals themselves can change the condition of their lives without divine providence or intervention is unimaginable and unbelievable, if not evil and sinful. To emphasize materialism, consumption, and the here and now runs counter to giving up your "sinful ways," trusting in God, and focusing on salvation and the hereafter.

Stark and Bainbridge (1981) argue that secularization is a major trend but that it is not a new or modern development and does not presage the demise of religion. It is a process that goes on in all societies while countervailing intensification of religion goes on in other parts. The dominant religious organizations are always becoming more *secularized* (worldly) but are supplanted by more vigorous and less worldly religions.

Researchers from the Religious Movements Homepage at the University of Virginia (2000) found that women are more likely than men to describe their outlook as "religious" versus secular. They also found that older Americans are less likely than younger Americans to describe their outlook as religious, and African-Americans are the least likely to describe themselves as secular. Asian Americans are most likely to describe their outlook as secular (Religious Movements Homepage at the University of Virginia, http://religious-movements.lib.virginia.edu/).

The authors demonstrate that secularization is one of three interrelated processes that constantly occur in all societies. Secularization itself generates two countervailing processes: revival and religious innovation. *Revival* is born out of secularization, as protest groups and sect movements form to meet the demand for a less worldly religion and to restore vigorous otherworldliness to a conventional faith. *Religious innovation*, also stimulated by secularization, leads to new faiths and new religious traditions. The birth of these new faiths will not be found in the directories of major church listings but will be found in lists of obscure cult movements.

Cults flourish where conventional churches are weakest. Stark and Bainbridge provide evidence that in America, there are very robust *negative* correlations between church membership rates and cult activity rates. The states and cities that have low church membership rates have the highest rates of membership in cults. Centuries ago, Christianity, Judaism, Islam, and Buddhism began as cults that rose to power because of the weaknesses in the dominant religions of their time. Stark and Bainbridge argue that the same process is happening today. Thus, in America, as in most societies, the history of religion is not only a pattern of secularization and decline but equally one of birth and growth. While the sources of religion are shifting constantly, the amount of religion remains fairly constant.

Religiosity and Church Attendance

Religiosity, intensity of religious feeling, is a qualitative factor that is difficult to assess accurately. While very difficult to measure, church attendance is one indication of the importance of religion. Beginning in the late 1950s, weekly church attendance in the United States declined steadily for 15 years, but since the early 1970s, it has remained stable at about 40 percent. According to a 2004 March Gallup Poll, 40% of Americans say they go to religious services at least once a week. Nearly half of all Southerners attend services weekly, and 44 percent of women, compared to 32 percent of men, attend weekly services. Additionally, 47 percent of Republicans attend church regularly, compared to 38 percent of Democrats and 29 percent of independents. Catholic women are almost twice as likely to attend as Catholic men.

Yet church attendance may not be an accurate measure of religiosity because people go to churches, synagogues, temples, or mosques for many reasons: to worship God, see friends, enjoy music, meet social expectations, and so on. Public opinion polls consistently indicate that a high percentage of people believe in God (more than 90 percent) and a life after death (about 75 percent) and overwhelmingly want their children to have religious training. The discrepancy between church attendance figures and religious beliefs indicates that factors other than formal religious organizations influence religious thought.

The Electronic Church

Through television, many people in the United States "attend church" without ever leaving their homes. Evangelists such as Robert Schuller, Pat Robertson, Jerry Falwell, Oral Roberts, Bob Jones, Jimmy Swaggart, and Jim and Tammy Bakker became national celebrities in the 1980s through this medium. Each of them created a huge financial empire through a variety of marketing techniques.

The notoriety of some of these TV evangelists increased by unusual activities that the press picked up and sensationalized. Oral Roberts announced that God had told him that he would die unless he raised millions of dollars by a certain date. The Bakkers used Praise the Lord (PTL) funds for a Christian theme park, several expensive homes for their personal use, a new Corvette and houseboat, and a luxurious air-conditioned doghouse. Both Jim Bakker and Jimmy Swaggart were caught in indiscrete sexual relationships. Pat Robertson, who "speaks in tongues" and receives prophecies directly from God, ran for President of the United States. Jerry Falwell started the Moral Majority and became actively involved in supporting conservative political candidates and right-wing social causes, before passing away in May of 2007. Several, such

POLICY DEBATE

Should Corporal Punishment of Children Be Allowed?

The concept of corporal punishment is an example of the linkage between religion and other institutions—specifically the family and education—and how religious beliefs have played an important part in shaping cultural practices. Corporal punishment is broadly defined as the infliction of physical pain, loss, or confinement in response to an offense or an occurrence of misbehavior. Typical forms of corporal punishment against children are slapping, spanking, and paddling, but corporal punishment has included other much more abusive practices as well, such as vigorous shaking (often causing concussion), grabbing, dragging, kicking, washing a child's mouth with noxious substances, not allowing a child to use the bathroom, denying a child normal movement, forcing a child to do pushups or run laps, denying adequate free time for recess and lunch, and many others. Corporal punishment usually is discussed primarily in connection with children in schools, but it is also important to consider it in relation to disciplining children at home and in nonparental child-care settings (Clark and Clark, 1989; Vockell, 1991).

The religious roots of corporal punishment are traceable from ancient Greece, Rome, and Egypt, through medieval Europe and then early colonial America to the present in America. As was true in the past, religious groups still maintain considerable influence over corporal-punishment legislation. For example, in 1991, legislation in North Carolina banned corporal punishment in public-run child-care centers, but not in church-operated ones. Many religious groups—especially fundamentalist, evangelical, and Pentecostal Protestants—argue that corporal punishment is positively sanctioned in the Bible in the books of Proverbs, Chronicles, Joshua, and Kings in the Old Testament. The key text that is cited in support of corporal punishment is Proverbs 23:14—"Thou shalt beat him with the rod, / And shalt deliver his soul from hell." The more common contemporary expression of this, with which you are probably familiar, is "Spare the rod and spoil the child." The rationale for corporal punishment from the New Testament, although Jesus never urges punishment for children, is derived from the belief that wickedness will be punished in hell, which is taken to imply the need to inflict pain on children in the present to prevent them from evil (Clark and Clark, 1989; Silverman, 1991). This reasoning prevails in many contemporary fundamentalist child-rearing manuals, some of which offer detailed advice on the discipline ritual, what instruments to use, and where to position children when hitting them (Greven, 1991). The religious basis of corporal punishment has had a strong influence on its acceptance among groups that continue to use it in the United States.

From its inception, American law viewed corporal punishment as an effective and acceptable method of maintaining order both at home and in school. Nevertheless, its morality (or immorality) and long-term effects on children have long been debated by parents, educators, and legislators. In 1867, New Jersey banned corporal punishment in public schools. However, not until more than 100 years later did another state, Massachusetts, make corporal punishment illegal. In 1977, the United States Supreme Court upheld the constitutionality of corporal punishment in Ingraham v. Wright, a case that involved a student whose physical injuries resulted in hospitalization from injuries inflicted by a paddling from school authorities. In Baker v. Owen, the Supreme Court ruled that the school has authority over parents

Should Corporal Punishment of Children Be Allowed?, *continued*

in issues involving discipline. These cases upheld corporal punishment as an acceptable means of maintaining discipline in schools, even over a parent's objection to corporal punishment, and the court ruled that the Eighth Amendment—which prohibits cruel and unusual punishment—does not apply to the paddling of children in school (Clark and Clark, 1989). Thus, as of 1988, corporal punishment was still legal in 41 states.

While suitable punishment of children is sometimes necessary, justifiable, and effective as a means of maintaining order and for the proper socialization of children, the debate over the use of corporal punishment continues. Besides the religious arguments, there are other important aspects of the debate. In a 1991 article, Edward L. Vockell, professor of education at Purdue University Calumet, discusses some the pros and cons of corporal punishment in education.

One advantage of corporal punishment—because it involves physical pain—is that it is very likely to be perceived by the recipient as unpleasant. Nonphysical forms of punishment, such as being sent to the principal's office or writing an essay on "Why I Should Not Talk in Class," may be thought by the teacher to be unpleasant, but may not necessarily be perceived as particularly painful by the child. On the other hand, when a child receives physical punishment (i.e., corporal punishment), the message is unequivocal.

Second, corporal punishment can be administered quickly and can be over with quickly. If a student commits a major offense and receives, for example, three afternoons of detention, the prolonged punishment may affect other interactions between the student and teacher during those three days. As a result, the learning situation may be compromised during that time. Additionally, because the punishment takes up time, the student may not be able to use this time in productive behavior. With corporal punishment, however, the teacher could paddle the student, get it over with, and get back to the business of education more quickly.

Third, corporal punishment has very clear, specific, and obvious consequences. In classrooms where corporal punishment is used, students know exactly what will happen if they misbehave. In settings where corporal punishment is not used as a disciplinary practice, students may not be able to clearly anticipate the consequences for misbehavior, and thus, the teacher may have less control over the class.

The disadvantages of corporal punishment, Vockell suggests, are both theoretical and practical. One theoretical disadvantage is that the punishment is not likely to be logically related to the misbehavior. For example, being paddled is not logically related to smoking in the washroom, talking in class, or failing to turn in homework. As adults, we sometimes engage in similar indiscretions—being late for work, failing to obey the speed limit, inadequately performing our jobs—but we certainly do not expect to be struck or hit violently for doing so. In fact, laws prevent it. In other words, corporal punishment is likely to be an *artificial* form of punishment—a punishment not related directly to the behavior such as paddling someone for not doing a homework assignment—rather than a *natural* form of reinforcement and punishment—punishment directly related to the misbehavior, such as making a student

(continues)

Should Corporal Punishment of Children Be Allowed?, *continued*

stay after school to complete an assignment. While artificial punishment is sometimes necessary when there are no logical forms of natural punishment available, most theorists feel that natural forms of punishment should be used whenever possible.

A second disadvantage is that it is usually very difficult for the recipient of corporal punishment to behave in a desirable way in order to end the punishment (that is, "time off for good behavior"), whereas for many other forms of punishment, engaging in good behavior is often possible. For example, if a child's television privileges are suspended because he or she fails to complete homework assignments, privileges might be reinstated if the child demonstrates that his or her study habits have changed. If, instead, corporal punishment is used, there is nothing the child can do once the punishment has commenced.

Third, physical punishment affirms the value of physical assault as a means of effecting change and models socially inappropriate behaviors to children. Many studies have clearly shown that children who are spanked more often are more likely to hit other children and to behave aggressively as they grow up. On the other hand, if parents and teachers reason with children and use more natural forms of punishment, children are more likely to learn these behaviors and to use them in their interactions with others.

Fourth, corporal punishment may inflict real injury or may easily escalate into child abuse. This does not mean that corporal punishment is child abuse. Theoretically, corporal punishment is carried out dispassionately, with the goal of correcting a child's behavior. However, corporal punishment can escalate into child abuse when the punishment is not directly related to a specific misbehavior of a child and instead may be employed because the parent or teacher is irritated, frustrated, or angry about past behaviors or about unrelated events.

Fifth, corporal punishment is often perceived by the recipients as embarrassing and demeaning to their dignity. While this can be an advantage in helping to bring about a change in behavior, it often has the reverse effect. Some children harbor resentment and feel the need to retaliate, thus creating interference with the punisher's future attempts at discipline and instruction.

A final disadvantage of corporal punishment is the practical problem of accidents and lawsuits. A teacher may have the best of intentions and may not be acting abusively. Nevertheless, the child may be hit too hard, may move to block a blow, or something else unexpected may occur that results in serious injury. Aside from the possible physical damage that could occur to the student, lawsuits may also follow. Even in states where corporal punishment is not prohibited, teachers are often prosecuted in such instances.

as Jerry Falwell and Bob Jones, established universities that only accept "born-again" instructors and that serve as bastions of fundamentalist Christian teachings. Some, such as Robert Schuller, who has a congregation of 10,000 at his "Crystal Cathedral" in California as well as international members worldwide, have established worldwide ministries while retaining a direct affiliation with a church or denomination (Reformed Church of America) rather than becoming sectlike.

With some exceptions, such as Robert Schuller just mentioned, it might be asked why television religious shows appear to be dominated be right-wing and fundamentalist ministers rather than preachers of mainstream denominations? Although no simple answers are available, some clues may lie in their message and in their organization. The message is simple, clear, precise, and based on a literal interpretation of the Bible. In a pluralistic society with social and moral ambiguities over the role of women, freedom of speech and expression, sexual norms, family planning, abortion and the like, it is comforting to believe that social as well as personal problems can be solved by a doctrinaire return to traditional gender roles and social values and a faith in God. The claim can be made that television is not friendly to intellectual discussions of ambiguous moral issues that are more commonly expressed by seminary graduates and the leadership in more established denominations.

The *organization* is often established around the charismatic quality of a single person (almost always male). These persons select their advisors and boards to back them and to establish an independent media network that is seldom accountable to other organizations or institutions. The leaders understand the value of showmanship and make appeals (often highly emotional) in the name of God to save souls, cleanse an immoral nation, and support their ministry. Unless an organization becomes established and institutionalized to provide continuity of the television program, the ministry is likely to die with the removal or death of the charismatic leader.

In functional terms, the success of the electronic church is explained in terms of what it does for people: that is, its religious functions. Among others, it may provide answers to ultimate questions, reconcile people to hardship, and advocate the return to less complex and more traditional ways. The extent to which it facilitates social integration, creates a community of believers, and provides rituals is questionable, however. It is unlikely that many people kneel for prayer or join hands with others in front of a TV set. On the other hand, the millions of dollars sent to television preachers indicate that they are important to many Americans and fill various needs.

Ecumenism

One response to the current trend toward secularization has been for different denominations to join together in pursuit of common interests. This trend, known as **ecumenism** or the ecumenical movement, calls for worldwide Christian unity. Interdenominational organizations such as the National Council of Churches are attempting to reconcile the beliefs and practices of different religious groups.

Thinking Sociologically

1. Is religion a key factor in maintaining the status quo, a key factor in stimulating social change, both, or neither?
2. What types of variables influence the involvement of religious groups in politics? Do the variables change depending on the sociological theory you are using? Describe and explain.
3. How is secularization related to or caused by changes such as industrialization, urbanization, an increasingly educated population, political conservatism or liberalism, changing roles of women, and so forth?

A New Religious Consciousness

A number of new religious groups have sprung up in the United States over the past few decades. Many of them emphasize the personal religious experience rather than a rational, bureaucratic religious organization. The ideas of many of these new groups, such as the Moral Majority, Children of God, Messianic Jews, and the Christian World Liberation Front, have roots in the Christian tradition. The Reverend Sun Myung Moon's Unification Church (popularly known as "Moonies") is a combination of Protestantism and anticommunism. Others, like Synanon, Erhart Seminars Training (est), Church of Scientology, and Silva Mind Control, grew out of the "human potential" movement of the 1960s and 1970s. Still others, such as Zen Buddhism, Yoga, and ISKCON (the organization of Hare Krishnas), are rooted in Eastern religions such as Buddhism, Hinduism, and Confucianism. Many of these religious movements demand of their members total conformity to the practices of the group and are generally often rigid in their teachings.

Why have these groups and religious movements arisen? A number of factors may be responsible. Durkheim believed that as societies become more complex and diversified, so do the forms of religious belief and practice. Some see the new religious consciousness as a search for identity and meaning. Some see these movements as a reaction against the militaristic and capitalistic values that are emphasized by contemporary American society. Others contend that the new religions have arisen in response to the climate of moral ambiguity in the United States. The decline of the established churches has undoubtedly been influential as well. In all probability, each of these factors has had an effect.

Religion and Other Institutions

The relationship between the church and other institutions is a complex one. The institutions and the functions they perform are not always easy to differentiate. As was mentioned earlier, Max Weber argued shortly after the turn of the century that capitalism was enhanced by the work ethic of Protestantism. In the 1980s, the entry of television evangelists such as Jerry Falwell and Pat Robertson into the political arena reflected the linkage between religion and politics. Other interinstitutional linkages include the influence of religion on school curricula and prayer, the impact of religious teachings on family size and use of contraceptives or abortion, and the influence of religion on the economy through the ownership or control of many businesses and the endorsement or nonendorsement by religious groups of various products.

There is also a strong link between religion and marital status. Those who identify with one of the main religious groups (twenty-two classifications account for 98 percent of the sample) are considerably more likely to be married than those who claim no religion. In particular, individuals in the "no religion" group were far more likely to be either single, never married, or single and living with a partner than any other group. Indeed, the "no religion" group shows the lowest incidence of marriage (just 19 percent) of all twenty-two (identified religious) groups. In sharp contrast, those identifying with the Assemblies of God or Evangelical/Born Again Christians show the highest incidence of marriage, 73 percent and 74 percent, respectively (http://religious movements.lib.virginia.edu/. 2000)

Emile Durkheim noted the key linkage between the sacred and the secular or profane when he stated that anything can be made sacred. Political rituals such as those that accompany the election of a president, family behaviors such as eating dinner together, economic goods such as automobiles, or educational events such as a graduation can all be considered sacred. These interrelationships and religious influences extend beyond the basic institutions. Note, for example, how religious principles have served as the foundation for opposition to war, restrictions on alcohol, or the disciplining of children (note policy debate). In today's society, although the church as a social institution has come under attack, religion and religious values continue to exert a major influence on societies, on all the institutions within them, and on the lives of individuals throughout the world.

Thinking Sociologically

1. How might you define "being religious"? Can you be religious without attending some church or synagogue or participating in some social group of like-minded persons?
2. Using theories and facts about religious groups and systems, discuss how and why religious groups become involved in political activities, both domestically and internationally. Provide specific examples of the types of policies with which religious groups would be concerned.

SUMMARY

1. A religion is a ritualized system of beliefs and practices related to things defined as sacred by an organized community of believers.
2. People have believed in supernatural powers throughout history. Some societies have believed that supernatural powers inhabit objects such as rocks and trees, which is known as animism. Others have assumed that supernatural powers reside in a shaman, who could be called upon to protect the group or to bring success. A third form of belief is totemism, in which a plant or animal is thought to be ancestrally related to a person or tribe.
3. Sometimes, religions are differentiated by the number of gods that adherents worship: Monotheistic religions believe in one god, and polytheistic religions believe in a number of gods.
4. Religion may take a variety of forms. Mysticism is based on the belief in powers that are mysterious, secret, and hidden from human understanding. Churches are institutional organizations with formal bureaucratic structures; they are sometimes differentiated into ecclesia, which are official state religions, and denominations, which are independent of the state.
5. Sects are small separatist groups that follow rigid doctrines and emphasize fundamentalist teachings. Cults are loosely organized religious organizations whose members adopt a new, unique, and unusual lifestyle. Rather than attempting to change society, cults generally focus on the spiritual lives of the individual participants.
6. There are a number of theories about religion. The functionalist perspective examines what religion does for society. Religion is generally perceived as fulfilling social functions, such as preserving and solidifying society, creating a community of believers, cultivating social change, and providing a means of social control. It also fulfills personal functions such as answering ultimate questions, providing rites of passage, and reconciling people to hardship.
7. The conflict perspective views religion as a tool used by the dominant individuals and groups to justify their position and to keep the less privileged in subordinate positions.
8. More than 5 billion people are believed to be identified with or have an affiliation with one of

the world's major religions. About 2 billion are Christians, who profess faith in the teachings of Jesus Christ. Another billion believe in Islam and surrender their wills to Allah, following the teachings of the prophet Muhammad.

9. Excluding the nonreligious, the third largest religious group is the followers of Hinduism, which is closely linked to the traditional caste system of India. Hindus have a vast array of religious practices and beliefs.

10. Followers of Buddhism believe that they can avoid human suffering by following an eightfold path of appropriate behavior. Confucianism, based on the life and teachings of Confucius, is both a philosophy and a religion and is closely linked to Taoism and Shintoism, as well as to Buddhism.

11. The United States has no state church, and a wide variety of religious groups exist in this country. There are two contrasting trends in contemporary religious practice: One type of group emphasizes formal religious organization, whereas the other emphasizes an informal, personalized, emotional belief system. Throughout American history, religious life has been influenced by folk religions, sects, Pentecostal groups, and groups that believe in millennialism, divine revelation, and faith healing.

12. Currently, religion is being studied in new ways, as a result of developments in qualitative and quantitative research techniques and computer technology. The use of these and other techniques has revealed a trend toward secularization, which is counterintuitively believed to contribute to the emergence of cult activities.

13. U.S. church attendance has leveled off at an estimated 40 percent, but a large majority of the population still profess a belief in God and in life after death.

14. Televised religious programs reach millions of persons in their homes. Along with these developments have come increased ecumenicalism and a new religious consciousness. This new consciousness is professed by many new religious sects and movements, some derived from the Christian tradition, others from the human potential movement and Eastern religions.

15. Several explanations for the creation of these groups have been offered. It has been suggested that they have arisen in response to our diverse culture, search for identity, and need for precise, simplistic answers, or as a protest against secularization and materialism. The institution of religion in America and around the world is closely linked with the family, as well as with economic, political, and educational institutions. These institutions both influence religious beliefs and practices and in turn are influenced by religion.

KEY TERMS

animism The religious belief that spirits inhabit virtually everything in nature and control all aspects of life and destiny.

Buddhism One of the world's principal religions; adherents follow the teachings of Buddha, the enlightened one, who preached a doctrine of "Four Noble Truths."

Christianity One of the principal religions of the world, followers of which profess faith in the teachings of Jesus Christ.

church An institutionalized organization of people who share common religious beliefs.

Confucianism One of the world's principal religions, found mainly in China, adherents of which follow the teachings of Confucius.

cults Extreme forms of sects that call for a totally new and unique lifestyle, often under the direction of a charismatic leader.

denominations Well-established and highly institutionalized churches.

ecclesia An official state religion that includes all or most members of society.

ecumenism The trend for different denominations to join together in pursuit of common interests in a spirit of worldwide Christian unity.

fundamentalism The belief that the Bible is the divine word of God and that all statements in it are to be taken literally, word for word.

Hinduism One of the world's principal polytheistic religions, with no religious hierarchy but a close involvement with society and the cosmic order; it is practiced mainly in India and Pakistan.

Islam One of the world's principal religions, followers of which adhere to the teachings of the Koran and of Muhammad, a prophet.

Judaism The oldest religion in the Western world and the first to teach monotheism; today, the Jews are both an ethnic community and a religious group.

millennialism The belief prevalent among certain sects that there will be a dramatic transformation of life on earth and that Christ will rule the world for a thousand years of prosperity and happiness.

monotheism The belief in one god.

mysticism The belief that spiritual or divine truths come to us through intuition and meditation, not through the use of reason or via the ordinary range of human experience and senses.

polytheism The belief in and worship of more than one god.

priests Religious leaders who owe their authority to the power of their office.

profane That which belongs to the realm of the everyday world; anything considered mundane and unspiritual.

prophets Religious leaders who have authority on the basis of their charismatic qualities.

religion An organized community of believers who hold certain things sacred and follow a set of beliefs, ceremonies, or special behaviors.

sacred Involving objects and ideas that are treated with reverence and awe.

sects Religious groups that have broken away from a parent church, follow rigid doctrines and fundamentalist teachings, and emphasize "otherworldly" rewards, rejecting or deemphasizing contemporary society.

secularization The process through which beliefs concerning the supernatural and religious institutions lose social influence.

shamanism The religious belief that certain persons (shamans) have special charm, skill, or knowledge in influencing spirits.

totemism The worship of plants, animals, and other natural objects as gods and ancestors.

DISCUSSION QUESTIONS

1. Discuss some ways in which religion affects our identity and our behavior.
2. How do you think life in America would be different if our culture was based on polytheism rather than monotheism?
3. How would you explain why some people are attracted to churches, others to sects, some to cults, and still others to no religious groups at all?
4. Regardless of an American's specific religious beliefs, we are all affected by the Protestant ethic. Explain how Protestantism has helped to shape our cultural beliefs and values, and how it may have affected you.
5. Compare the functionalist and conflict approaches to religion, and discuss how these views are different from or similar to views that you may have been socialized to believe about religion.
6. Discuss some ways in which religion effects the outcomes of peace, gender roles, politics, and so forth in the Middle East, Ireland, or southern U.S. states, for example.
7. Select one of the religions discussed in the text other than your own (if you do not have a religion, then select any one). Explore how your involvement in family and in political, economic, and educational institutions might be different if you were a member of that religion.
8. Make a list of selected trends in religion. How would you explain them? How can they be changed?
9. Explain the appeal of TV preachers or evangelists. What accounts for their appeal, popularity, fund-raising success, and longevity?
10. Discuss the linkage between religion and life in other institutions, such as the family or school.

Educational Groups and Systems

The Quality of Education

The employment market in the United States requires higher educational skills than ever before. The availability of lower-level blue-collar jobs—such as in manufacturing—in the United States has declined. Concurrently, more U.S. jobs require the skills needed to process information, to manage, and to provide services. Many people who previously might have been able to secure employment in the blue-collar job market face a job market for which they are unprepared. Thus, these people are at a distinct disadvantage when they compete for jobs that require skills different from those needed to perform adequately in blue-collar employment. According to sociologist John Kasarda, the demand for higher skills, coupled with an ineffectiveness of educational systems to meet this demand, has led to an "education–job opportunities mismatch" (Kasarda, 1990).

This "mismatch" reflects a larger issue that has plagued the nation for decades: the quality of education. Twenty years ago, the National Commission on Excellence in Education issued a scathing report—*A Nation at Risk*—that claimed that "a rising tide of mediocrity" had devastated public education. Some of the problems it identified were teacher incompetence, a less challenging curriculum, and low student achievement (cited in Parillo et al., 1989). Underlying the Commission's concern was then–Secretary of Education Terrell Bell's belief that unless public schools were improved, middle-class Americans would shift their support from public to private schools, leaving only the poor and a disproportionate share of minorities in poorly supported public schools. This would create such inequality that the future of the nation's economic, social, and political strength would be in jeopardy (Gardner, 1990). The "jobs–skills mismatch" that this country now faces seems to verify Bell's forecast.

While some improvements have occurred in education since *A Nation at Risk* was issued in 1983, the situation is still critical. Jeanne Allen, current President of The Center for Education Reform said, "Much about America is flourishing, at least for now, at least for a lot of people. Yet the state of our children's education is still far, very far, from what it ought to be (Former Secretary of Education Bell agrees and reaffirms his concerns of a decade ago.

According to research published in 2003 by the Hoover Institution at Stanford University, American K–12 education remains mired in mediocrity and will require enormous changes "at its core" in order to become more effective (Hoover Institution, 2003). The report adds that despite many earnest reform efforts and steadily-climbing school expenditures, there is little evidence that students are learning more.

This data indicates (2003) indicates that students do no more homework now than they did in 1982—less than one hour per day.

Science scores of 17-year-olds taking the National Assessment of Educational Progress remain below levels reached in 1970, and their math and reading scores have hardly budged.

On international tests of math and science, the U.S. remains roughly at the international average—right where it was in 1970—and still trails high-flyers such as Japan, Korea, and the Netherlands.

In addition, *A Nation at Risk* called for higher standards for teachers as well as students. It also urged that more time be spent on learning. Research shows that the situation has actually worsened over the past twenty years:

> The share of teachers with a master's degree in a subject area (rather than education) has fallen, from 17 percent in 1982 to 5 percent now.
>
> Teachers with a B.A. in a subject area fell from 28 percent to 23 percent.
>
> The school year is about seven days shorter today than it was in the early 1970s.

Clearly America's education system is failing to meet our societal needs. Some progress has been made during the 1990s, as a result of increased national attention on our education system, but the need to improve the quality of American education continues well into 2005. This issue concerns sociologists because of the deep implications it has for creating equality or inequality within society.

Children in the United States are required to go to school. They sometimes begin at age 2 or 3 years, long before the required age of 6 or 7, and often stay in school long past age 16 years, when they could legally drop out. Thus, education dominates the lives of children, and it also plays an important role in adult life, as adult students, parents, taxpayers, school employees, government officials, and voters participate in the school system. At the same time, education in the United States produces (a) high school graduates who cannot read and write and are not prepared for college, (b) Scholastic Aptitude (SAT) scores below scores of 30 years ago, and (c) examination scores in mathematics below other industrial societies, as mentioned in the introduction to this chapter.

Why is education so important? We all know some of the reasons we believe in the value of education. We learn science, the arts, and skills for employment, and we learn to make informed judgments about our leisure activities, our political involvement, and our everyday lives.

Is this all that we get from education? What else does it accomplish for society? What part does our education system play in creating a literate population and in selecting people for occupations that match their talents? What part does it play in maintaining the stratification system and in justifying the unequal distribution of wealth in society? Much of the debate about whether schools are doing the job they are supposed to do is really a debate about the proper function of schools. The goal of this chapter is to help you understand how education functions in society today.

STRUCTURAL FUNCTIONAL THEORY OF EDUCATION

Structural functional theory recognizes the family as an important agency of socialization. It is in the family that the child learns the culture's values, norms, and language—how to be a social person. By the age of 5 or 6 years, the child has developed a unique social personality, and in a properly functioning family, the child is socialized to adjust to the routines and disciplines of the school system. How does education in the schools differ from education in the home?

The Manifest Functions of Education

The *manifest*, or intended, function of the educational system, according to structural functionalists, is to supplement family socialization. The schools use experts (teachers) to teach children the knowledge, skills, and values necessary to function in the world outside the family (Parsons, 1959).

The most obvious teaching in school is the teaching of *skills*. Students today are expected to learn to read, write, and do arithmetic; these skills are taught by specially trained experts. Schools also teach students *knowledge* about the larger world, through such courses as history, geography, and science. In addition, students learn the *values* of the larger society, including those that pertain to large organizations. They learn to tell time and to be punctual, to cooperate with others to achieve group goals, and to obey the rules necessary for a smooth-running organization.

Another function of education is to select and develop, through evaluation and testing, those young people who have especially useful talents so that each individual will be as productive as his or her abilities permit. Schools give I.Q. tests to determine students' capabilities, and they give grades and achievement tests to find out how much students have learned. They also give psychological tests, to help determine which occupations suit the students so that they can then guide them into vocational lines appropriate to their abilities. Some students are guided into vocational courses and the work force;

others go to academic high schools and then into two- or four-year colleges. A few of the most talented go to elite colleges and graduate schools and then on to the professions.

A third function of the education system is to transmit new behaviors, skills, ideas, discoveries, and inventions resulting from research. Today, for example, schools teach typing and place less emphasis on penmanship. In some school systems, elementary school students are taught to use a computer terminal before they have mastered their multiplication tables.

The creation of new knowledge is another function of education. Our medical technology is one outstanding example of the knowledge developed in universities. Attempts have also been made to use the educational system to decrease poverty. Education develops the skills necessary to earn income, and special programs have been devised to help the poor to develop these skills. Some high schools and colleges, for example, offer students training in specific vocational skills, such as car repair, computer programming, or restaurant management. Early educational programs such as Head Start are designed to teach disadvantaged children the skills they need to keep up with their peers.

The Latent Functions of Education

The functions so far discussed are manifest, or intentional functions, but the educational system also operates in ways that are latent, or unintentional, and these functions are also influential. Some latent functions include the prolonging of adolescence, age segregation, and child care.

Prolonged adolescence is a unique feature of modern industrial society. In other societies, the transition from childhood to adulthood is clearly marked. The Kpelle of Liberia in West Africa, for example, mark the passage of boy into manhood by a circumcision ritual. After this ceremony, the young man is regarded as having the same responsibilities as the other men of his tribe. In our society, children have been relieved of work roles for increasingly long periods so that they can acquire an education. The age of mandatory school attendance was raised from 12 to 14 and then to 16 years, so students today have to remain in school for a longer time than they once did. Another factor that has increased the number of years they spend in school is that many jobs require a high school or college diploma. Students stay in school longer when unemployment rates are high and jobs are not available, and parents have to continue to support and assume responsibility for their children during this extended education. As a result, in the United States, the period of dependency on parental support sometimes continues for two decades or even longer.

A report out of the Joint Center for Housing Studies at Harvard University examined the literature of young American adults (25–34) living at home with their parents. Using the *Current Population* Survey they determined that as of March 2001, 2.3 million men and 1.5 million women between the ages of 25–34 still lived in their parents' houses. These numbers comprise 12.5 percent of men in the age category and 7.9 percent of women. After considering several variables, the researchers concluded that young adults' personal income is the major constraining factor when considering independent living (Zhu, 2002).

Age segregation is the separation of some age groups from the larger population. Children in schools spend their time with children of the same age—their peers. The peer group is an important agency of socialization. Peer groups sometimes develop into distinct subcultures, whose members dress alike, listen to the same music, eat the same foods, wear similar hairstyles and makeup, and develop code words and slang—a language of their own. One such age-segregated subculture evolved in the late 1960s. During that decade, adolescents and college students were often in conflict with families, schools, and businesses. Fathers and sons stopped speaking over the length of the sons' hair, and students were expelled from schools and colleges and denied jobs because they wore long hair and blue jeans. The plethora of bare-chested young men and barefooted youths prompted signs to appear on storefronts, announcing "Shirts and shoes required." Students in the late 1960s learned values of equality and individual worth in school but found that the larger society did not reflect these values.

Our education system has also developed other latent functions, such as child care. This function has become increasingly important in American society because in many families, both parents must work simply to make ends meet. Although the hours that children are in school—9 to 3—are often not convenient for working parents, they could not even consider working if their children were not in school. Some school systems are so attuned to their supervisory, child-care function that they offer after-school play groups—at a nominal fee—to take care of children until a parent gets off work and can take the child home.

In sum, structural functionalists believe that the educational system fulfills both manifest and latent functions. It reinforces the socialization process that started with the family, prepares children for work in a complex industrial society, and guides them into the occupations most appropriate to their abilities and to society's needs. Some latent functions of education include the segregation of age groups, the extension of adolescence, and supervisory child care.

APPLYING THE FUNCTIONS OF EDUCATION

Understanding the functions of education is important for teachers, counselors, school administrators, parents, students, and employers. If teachers, for example, concentrate their efforts exclusively on providing specific academic skills to students, the schools may fail to teach values and norms such as honesty, punctuality, respect, trust, civic responsibility, competition, and cooperation. As a result, undue pressure on students by parents and counselors to succeed academically might turn some students into scholars who lack competence in social skills, and academically poor students might become alienated from the entire educational process. By no means are we suggesting that high academic achievement should not be emphasized. However, it may not be the only measure of a successful education for every student.

Understanding the many functions of education is especially important for college students. One of the most difficult decisions you and other students must make early in your college career is your choice of a major. Most often, students lose sight of the many functions of education and focus exclusively—understandably so—on the types of jobs that are available to a graduate with a particular major. It is true that for some career fields, such as accounting, computer programming, architecture, or engineering, students must acquire specific career-related skills and knowledge during their college careers. For the most part, however, the specific occupational skills that people need to do their jobs are learned in some form of on-the-job training or in graduate or other professional schools. Therefore, unless you are pursuing one of the fields that requires a specific major—especially in a liberal arts college—you might do just as well to select a major that interests you. Unfortunately, the functions of a college education are not understood by many parents and students. The common question asked by parents is, What kind of a job can you get with a major in English (sociology, history, political science, biology, psychology, and so forth)? By mistakenly believing that the sole function of college is to learn specific job skills, students may be pressured to select majors in which they have little interest. However, if you (and just as important, your parents) understand that the functions of a college education include learning social and cultural norms as well as the development of basic communicative, critical thinking, and interpersonal skills, you might select a major that better suits your needs and desires.

College students and their parents are not the only ones who misunderstand the various functions of a college education. Personnel in college placement offices and employers who are hiring college graduates often make similar mistakes in associating careers only with particular major fields. Business majors will not necessarily be better as sales representatives, sociology majors will not necessarily be better as city planners, and English majors will not necessarily be better as journalists. By not understanding the many ways a college education serves a student, college graduates may be channeled into careers for which they are not particularly suited and not considered for jobs in which they might excel.

CONFLICT THEORY OF EDUCATION

Conflict theorists might argue that educational systems help sustain inequalities between the haves and have nots in a society. Thus, the school system, through a **hidden curriculum**, teaches values and norms that are necessary to maintain the stratification system in society. The educational system is also used to justify giving higher-status jobs to the children of elites and lower-status jobs to children of the poor.

The Hidden Curriculum

Schools require students to learn, albeit subtly, how to behave appropriately for their position in society. This learning is not a part of the stated curriculum—the acknowledged subjects, such as reading, writing, or arithmetic. It is a part of a hidden curriculum, in which students learn such things as obedience, competition, and patriotism. No one ever announces that these qualities are being taught. Nevertheless, if students are to be educated for a job, they must learn to obey rules, to do whatever a superior orders them to do, to work as hard as they can—or at least harder than their coworkers—and to be loyal to the superior, the organization, and the nation in which they work. Both the values and the norms of the elite are a part of the hidden curriculum.

The Teaching of Values

Conflict theorists believe that schools teach children the values of the group in power. Children are taught patriotism by saying the "Pledge of Allegiance" and by studying the history and geography of the United States and of their own states and communities. They learn that the United States is a great country founded by prominent leaders who believed in freedom for all. Students learn about the democratic system of government, the fairness of representation, and the importance of the vote. They are taught to value the capitalist system, in which everyone has the right to accumulate as much private property as possible and to pass it on to their children.

The importance of teaching values can be appreciated by looking at the conflicts that sometimes arise in schools. Teachers may be fired if they teach high school students the advantages of socialism or the disadvantages of capitalism. The topics omitted from school curricula also shed light on the teaching of values. Students are seldom instructed on the family systems or sexual practices of people in other cultures. They are rarely taught about great philosophers who have criticized the United States' political or economic systems, nor are they generally made aware of the people who have suffered under these systems. Students who reach a college sociology course that attempts to analyze both strengths and weaknesses of social systems are often shocked by what they learn.

The Learning of Norms

According to conflict theorists, students learn to conform to the standards of behavior of those in power through the educational process. For example, students are told when to stand in line, when to take turns, when to talk, when to be quiet, when to read, when to listen, when to hang up their coats—the list goes on and on. Students are not taught when to complain, when their rights are being infringed upon, when their time is being wasted, or when to use their freedom of speech. Rules are an important part of the complex organization of a school, and acceptance of certain rules is vital to the maintenance of the social order.

Students are also expected to compete with other students in school. They are taught that they must do better than others to receive attention, good grades, and privileges. Those who do not compete, who pursue the activities they enjoy, may fail, be separated from their peer group, and be labeled as slow, hyperactive, disabled, or otherwise deviant. In short, they are punished.

The competition, however, is unfair because it is based on the norms of the middle class, not those of working-class ethnics or inner-city blacks. Some ethnic groups, for example, find it embarrassing to compete scholastically, to display that they know more than someone else, and do not enter into the competition.

Most teachers come from the middle class and teach students their own values and norms. They tend to teach middle-class literature rather than the literature that might be more germane to their students. When stories about middle-class children in the suburbs with a house, a lawn, a pet dog, and a car are used to teach reading to 5-year-old inner-city children who have never had houses to live in, lawns to play on, pet dogs, or cars to ride in, the meaning of the story is as incomprehensible as if the story were written in a foreign language.

Credentialism

Conflict theorists argue that the credentials, diplomas, and degrees given by schools represent learning that is not essential to doing most jobs (Collins, 1979). Nevertheless, some jobs afford wealth and prestige to those who hold these credentials. Because such jobs are scarce and so many people want them and compete for them, those who control these jobs can require qualifications of their applicants that have little to do with the skills needed for the job. Instead, the qualifications can serve to place upper-class persons in higher-status or elite jobs, middle-class people in middle-class jobs, working-class people in blue-collar or lower-paying service jobs, and the poor in the lowest-status, lowest-paying jobs society has to offer.

Credentialism is the practice of requiring degrees for jobs whether or not the degrees actually teach skills necessary to accomplish the jobs. Everyone—from assembly-line workers to physicians—learns much more than is necessary to do his or her work. Physicians, for example, must complete four years of college, four years of medical school, and a one-year internship to become general practitioners. Those who want to specialize need an additional three or more years of training. Communist societies such as China and Cuba successfully train people in a much shorter time to take care of most of the health needs of the society. The system in the United States perpetuates the prestige of physicians by demanding credentials that can be obtained only by those who have the time and money to enter this high-prestige profession. In addition, physicians come to form their own subculture of shared values and beliefs during their years of training.

Collins (1979) also argues that the jobs requiring a great deal of education do not necessarily require the skills people learn in school, but the jobs do require the cultural norms learned in school. When college-educated people enter management positions, the elite can rest assured that the managers will make decisions consistent with the cultural norms.

In sum, conflict theorists believe that the educational system is run by the group in power, to legitimate their position. They teach values and norms useful in maintaining their position, use an unfair competitive system to legitimate upper-middle-class success, and insist on certification of skills beyond those necessary to do a job. The upper-middle class has the competitive advantage, but everyone learns the values and norms that maintain the system.

HISTORICAL PERSPECTIVES ON EDUCATION

When sociologists study education, they ask whether it functions to teach a body of knowledge to students, to select the students most capable to perform work in society, or to generate new knowledge. They also ask whether education reflects the conflicts in society by maintaining the stratification system. When we look at historical evidence to analyze how the system functions, we find that from the beginning, education was focused on serving a select group of powerful higher-status persons and was related to occupational training.

Occupational Training

The Puritans, who considered education important, founded Harvard College in Massachusetts in 1636, to educate ministers. Initially, only male students between the ages of 12 and 20 were accepted. The subject matter was morals and ethics, and learning was accomplished through rote memorization. William and Mary (1693), Yale (1701), and Princeton (1746) colleges were founded in quick succession and for the same purpose as Harvard.

The University of Virginia, founded by Thomas Jefferson in 1819, had a somewhat broader goal than many earlier universities. Aware of the need to train national leaders, Jefferson wanted to form an institution to educate a "natural aristocracy" in a wide range of subjects, including modern languages, science, and mathematics. This curriculum was widely adopted later in the century (Seely, 1970).

After about 1850, emphasis on occupational training increased and reached a broader segment of the population. The federal government began to encourage states to begin colleges that would teach agriculture and mechanics (A&M schools). They were provided with *land grants* (i.e., gifts of land) to build the colleges. These land-grant colleges developed into today's public state universities.

During the same period, universities such as Johns Hopkins (1876), which emphasized a scientific curriculum, were founded. Johns Hopkins was also one of the first to systematically support advanced research and the publishing of research findings. Prior to the founding of schools with advanced scientific programs, professions such as medicine, law, and dentistry were learned through the apprenticeship system or were practiced without formal education. Once scientific programs were developed, professionals were required to go to school to be accepted into the profession.

Compulsory public education is public-funded education that is mandatory for all children until a certain age. It developed during the eighteenth and nineteenth centuries, to educate immigrants. The immigrant children who attended public schools learned English and were assimilated into American society. Some then became ashamed of their parents, who often did not learn the new culture (Novak, 1972).

More current data show that learning to speak English and working hard to achieve are two traits of immigrant children. Statistics show that children of immigrants are adapting rapidly, surpassing their parents, and utilizing the opportunities that the United States has to offer. Studies also indicate that immigrant children prefer English to the native languages of their parents and that speaking education is linked to their achieving success. Not surprisingly then, studies show that millions of immigrant children have higher grades and sharply lower dropout rates than native-born American children—about one-third the rate. They also do far more homework compared to other children their age—spending an average of two hours per day, in contrast to the national average of about 30 minutes—reflecting their belief that hard work and accomplishment can triumph over any prejudice they've experienced (Immigration Policy Report, 2001).

Public schooling met with resistance from a variety of groups. Some religious leaders believed that education should include training in morals and ethics. Catholic religious leaders were afraid that public education would be Protestant education. Landowners did not want to pay taxes for other people's education because they felt that this was socialism. Farmers did not want to lose their sons' labor to the schoolroom, even though concessions were made by giving students summers off to work on the farm. In spite of the objections of these groups, however, local educational systems were developed and run by local leaders, which reflected the strong commitment to local governance in the United States.

Beliefs About Children

The goals and structure of an education system both shape and are shaped by the society's views of the nature and role of children. Are children good or evil, impulsive or rational? Are they fundamentally different from adults in some ways? Are they naturally curious or naturally passive and indolent? The ways in which a society answers questions such as these are manifested in the structure of its education system.

The Puritans believed that children were possessed by the devil. Their education involved memorizing parts of the Bible, catechisms, and other sources of moral wisdom until the evil nature of children was overcome. This process was hurried along by the schoolmaster's liberal use of the switch, stick, whip, or dunce cap to make the children behave (Johnson et al., 1985). Rather than being isolated from adults, children were encouraged to emulate the adults' good examples because it was assumed that adults had already learned right from wrong.

Early in this century, education became more student centered. Children were not thought to be controlled by the devil, but they were thought to be impulsive, and thus strict discipline was still necessary. Children were required to sit in rows, to memorize their spelling and mathematics, and to raise their hands to recite.

Since 1960, some important changes have taken place. The moral issue of whether children are good or evil has lost importance, but it has come to be believed that children have a natural curiosity—they want to learn. In schools based on this belief, discipline has decreased, rows of chairs have been rearranged to allow freedom of movement, and *learning centers* have been developed and placed around the room so that children can move from center to center as their interests dictate. Under this system, students who fail to learn are likely to be blamed for their failure. It is assumed that they lack curiosity or a desire to learn.

Many parents would like to see a return to an emphasis on basic skills and strict discipline in the schools. They believe that an education is necessary in order to acquire a good job, and they want to be sure their children learn the necessary skills rather than relying on their natural curiosity. Parents may not approve of the way schools are run now, but their power to bring about changes is limited.

WHO RULES THE SCHOOLS?

Most American education is public—the schools are open to everyone. They are funded by local and federal governments, so there are strong ties between the educational system and the political system. Education is paid for through tax dollars, and although it is controlled locally, it complies with all the laws of the land. These laws are interpreted by those who head federal, state, and local school bureaucracies. Students, parents, and teachers have little opportunity to influence decisions in the bureaucracy.

The bureaucracy of a local school system is headed by a local school board, which adopts a budget, sets policies, and directs the supervisor of schools. The supervisor develops guidelines based on the policies of the school board and directs the principals of the schools in the area. The principals make rules for the local schools, based on the guidelines of the supervisor, and they direct the teachers to carry out the rules. The teacher establishes rules for the classroom in accordance with the principal's direction and teaches the students.

The Center for Public Education lists five reasons that school boards matter (http://www.nsba.org). These are:

1. School boards look out for children, first and foremost. Education is not a line item in a school board's budget—it is the ONLY item.
2. School boards are advocates for their communities when decisions are made about its children's education.
3. School boards set the standards for achievement in their communities, incorporating their community's view of what students should know and be able to do at each grade level.
4. School boards are the public link to public schools. They are accessible to the public and accountable for the performance of their schools.
5. School boards are the education watchdog for their communities, ensuring that taxpayers get the most for their tax dollars.

Although the United States emphasizes local control of schools, it is somewhat misleading to suggest that school boards operate independently because the federal government passes many laws that affect the educational system. Schools must respect the rights protected by the U.S. Constitution; they must allow religious freedom and offer equal opportunity. The federal government influences such issues as prayer in school, the teaching of evolution, equal opportunity for minorities, and the education of the handicapped, including provisions for children with special educational needs. School boards must comply with federal laws regarding these and other concerns.

States also have constitutions, which cannot contradict federal law. Within the restrictions of federal law and the state constitution, the states pass laws that set standards for the schools. They certify teachers, set the number of days that students must attend school, determine school holidays, and establish minimum requirements for the curriculum and for graduation.

Within the limits set by the state and federal governments, local school boards set policy to be carried out by school principals and teachers, who must teach course content and follow schedules set by higher authorities (Scimecca, 1980). The evaluation of teachers is heavily based on cooperation with the principal and local school board, rather than on creativity or teaching skills. Furthermore, teachers today are overwhelmed with the paperwork of the bureaucracy—seating charts, report cards, attendance records, schedules, lesson plans—which takes considerable time away from teaching (Ballantine, 1983). The National Education Association (NEA) reports that teachers spend an average of 50 hours per week on instructional duties, including an average of 12 hours each week on non-compensated school-related activities such as grading papers, bus duty, and club advising. Furthermore, teachers spend an average of $443 of their own money each year to meet the needs of their students (http://www.chiff.com/a/EC803LoveTe htm), and in 2005 the IRS started allowing teachers to deduct $250.00 of those expenses from their yearly tax returns. Also, as with any bureaucracy, the school-system bureaucracy denotes a stratification system.

STRATIFICATION IN THE SCHOOL SYSTEM

Like other social systems, schools reflect stratification and can promote still further stratification. The school that children attend can have an enormous influence on their life chances. Those who attend first-rate elementary and high schools can go on to prestigious colleges and can obtain high-paying jobs. At the other end of the spectrum, those who receive a poor education may become so frustrated that they quit without graduating. Some critics contend that schools are biased in favor of middle- and upper-class students at all levels, from the federal education bureaucracy to the local school board.

School Boards

Local school boards are usually elected by the people of the school district, although in about 10 percent of the districts, they are appointed by the mayor. They have traditionally consisted primarily of white, male business or professional people, although in the past decades, more women and minorities have won elections to school boards. Sometimes, board members come into conflict with groups in their school districts. Disagreements have ranged from hairstyles to vocational training, from discipline to teaching the basics of reading, writing, and arithmetic.

Some critics argue that school boards would represent their communities better if they consisted of a greater variety of people, including members from ethnic and other minority groups, labor, faculty, and the student body.

Faculty

Faculty in public schools are predominantly middle class. The majority of the faculty in elementary schools are women, 74 percent of whom are from the middle class. In high schools, there are more male faculty, many of whom are from the lower socioeconomic class. White males in the public school system often move rather rapidly into administration, normally to vice-principal and then on to more responsible positions in the hierarchy. Women and blacks move into administration much more slowly, and when they do, it is often in special assignments, such as in programs specifically for women and blacks. These moves out of the mainstream then make future promotions for them even more difficult (Ortiz, 1982). Although the number of women in the superintendency has increased dramatically since 1970, historical data indicate that women are on the margin of the profession and held fewer chief executive office positions in 1992 than they did in 1910! In sum, 96 percent of superintendents in the United States are male, and the census bureau has reported this position as being the most male-dominated executive position of any profession in the United States (Glass, 1992).

In colleges and universities, the majority of faculty members are white males, although the number of females has increased. Women are found mostly in the lower ranks and in spite of laws requiring equal pay for equal work, they are often paid less than their male colleagues of equal rank. Women in some schools have filed complaints to raise their salaries to the level of the men on the faculty, but to date, full equality has not been achieved. Also significant is the fact that blacks are underrepresented in college and university teaching.

Students

Traditionally, schools have been segregated by socioeconomic status in the United States because children go to neighborhood schools, and neighborhoods are segregated. Students of different races often attend different schools for the same reason. Many African- and Hispanic-Americans live in inner-city neighborhoods and go to predominantly African- and Hispanic-American schools. They also traditionally finish fewer years of school (see Table 14-1).

Lower-class students do not learn to read and write as well as those from higher-class backgrounds. As a result, they may come to believe that they are not capable of accomplishing what their contemporaries at other schools can accomplish. This lowers their achievement motivation, and they may become apathetic or alienated from the system.

Bowles and Gintis (1976) have theorized that the wealthy, powerful class benefits from neighborhood school systems that segregate students. In segregated school systems, students learn their place in the stratification system. Upper-class students learn about the hierarchy and the need to follow the rules of a hierarchy. They also learn that they too can someday take their rightful place among the wealthy and powerful. They are actively socialized into the social system. Lower-class students also come to believe that upper-class people have a legitimate right to rule (Oakes, 1982). Intelligence tests have been shown to perpetuate the beliefs of all classes that the wealthy have a right to rule.

Biased Intelligence Tests

In 1916, Lewis M. Terman designed a test to measure what was called an "intelligence quotient," or "I.Q." The test was used for assessing a person's attainment of skills used in upper-middle-class occupations that involved manipulating numbers and words. The purpose of the test was to select students who were good at such manipulations to go on to advanced training. Terman and others believed that it measured an inherited genetic trait called "intelligence." They assumed that those who scored low on the test lacked intelligence and were less capable of learning than those who did well. It was argued that those who did poorly should be assigned to lower-class jobs.

TABLE 14-1 COMPARATIVE LEVELS OF EDUCATION OF THE POPULATION AGE 25 AND OVER, MARCH 2002

Education	Percentage of Hispanic Origin	Percentage of African Origin	Percentage of European Origin	Percentage of Asian Origin
Not high school graduate	46.5	27.3	16.4	17.7
High school graduate	53.5	72.7	83.6	82.3
Bachelor's degree or higher	8.7	14.0	25.8	40.1

Source: Data from U.S. Bureau of the Census, *Current Population Reports,* Series PPL-169, 2002.

Critics have argued that I.Q. tests measure not an inherited characteristic but a person's knowledge of upper-middle-class culture, which is why immigrants, the working class, the poor, and blacks score low while upper-middle-class Americans score high. For example, many I.Q. tests are mostly vocabulary tests, and the words that separate the average from the high scorers are words such as "amanuensis," "moiety," and "traduce." Critics say that the test serves the stratification system by creating a myth that convinces the lower classes that their station in life is part of the natural order of things (Karier, 1986). They come to believe that they are not capable of advancing in society to the higher positions, partly because they are not capable of attending prestigious private schools.

AMERICAN PRIVATE SCHOOLS

As of 2007, there were 30,000 private schools listed in the National Center for Educational Statistics. The most common private schools in the United States, those serving a broad segment of the population, are the **parochial schools** run by the Catholic church and founded to serve Catholics who want both an academic and a religious education for their children.

A newer phenomenon in American society is the growth of private religious schools not associated with the Catholic church. These schools are sometimes referred to as "Christian schools," even though most private schools in the United States already have a Christian tradition. Some of the newer schools are affiliated with Protestant churches, and some have no formal link to traditional religion. Some of these schools developed to provide an alternative to racially integrated schools, and some to provide a place to teach an alternative set of values to students from those taught in the public schools. Currently, the number of students that these schools serve is about one-third the number of parochial-school students.

Other private preparatory schools have a very long history in this country, they are more expensive and they serve a wealthier student body. Finally, private schools of higher education offer an expensive education and serve only a small segment of society. Private systems are generally recognized as providing an education that is superior to those provided by the public schools.

In the following sections, we discuss parochial schools, the traditional private preparatory schools, and private colleges. We are not able to discuss the newer private Christian schools because they are a diverse group with a variety of characteristics, and their impact on society has not yet been adequately studied.

Parochial Schools

Researchers (Lee, Bryk, and Holland, 1995; *Financing Schools*, 1997) have found that Catholic-school students perform better than public high school students. They also found that school performance was not as closely linked to socioeconomic background in the Catholic high schools as it was in public schools. There are many reasons for the stronger performance of students in Catholic schools, including effective discipline, more monitoring of students' work, and higher expectations of the teachers for all students. For example, students in Catholic schools are more likely to take academic courses than they are in public schools, regardless of their ability or socioeconomic background. Students in Catholic schools are more likely to be groomed for college, whether they are financially able to go or not (Lee, et al., 1995). In public schools, on the other hand, students from lower socioeconomic backgrounds are more likely to be steered into general or vocational curricula, they are less likely to see a future connected with academic performance, and so quite naturally, they will not work hard at academics.

Private Preparatory Schools

The wealthy in America do not usually send their children to public schools, but rather to private **preparatory ("prep") schools** and then to private universities. Most of the elite private preparatory schools were founded in the late 1800s, as the American public school system developed. These private schools stated that their goals were more than intellectual development. For example, Groton, founded in 1884 in Massachusetts, stated in its opening announcement the following: "Every endeavor will be made to cultivate manly, Christian character, having regard to moral and physical as well as intellectual development." (McLachlan, 1970, p. 256). These prep schools offer a very intensive education, both in academics and in sports and cultural activities. It is generally accepted that these students receive an education superior to most if not all public high schools. The cost of tuition at Groton in the 2006-07 school year was $39,850 per year.

Furthermore, students learn to see themselves as a select, exclusive group. In a study of administrators and faculty of 20 prestigious prep schools, as well as freshmen and seniors at those schools, Cookson and Persell (1989) found that students believed that they belonged to an exclusive, elite group. They also believed that because family and school provided all the friends they needed, they had no interest in meeting other people.

The exclusive nature of preparatory schools bothered both outside critics and the schools themselves, and efforts have been made to admit some students who would normally not be able to finance such an education. One such program was "A Better Chance," also known as the "ABC" program (Zweigenhaft and Domhoff, 1993). ABC enabled talented, inner-city minority students to attend some of the most prestigious prep schools with children of some of the wealthiest families in the United States. The minority students flourished both academically and socially, and well over 90 percent continued their education at highly selective colleges and universities. In spite of these accomplishments, these minority students still tended to be limited in their careers to middle-management positions. According to the National Center for Educational Statistics, the average cost for a year at a private school ranged from $9,000 to $36,000 per student in 2006.

Selective Private Colleges

Admittance to selective colleges and universities is no simple task, as many college students know by the time they read this text. The most prestigious colleges do not select students on the basis of intelligence and achievement alone. Studies of how Harvard University (2006-07 tuition $46,655) selects its students (Karen, 1990; Klitgaard, 1985) demonstrate how selection for college works against the student from a middle-class background who has little to offer except good grades. Harvard does not select only students of high scholastic aptitude. They believe that the quality of their educational program would suffer because those who entered Harvard with very high grades but who found themselves in the bottom 25 percent of the class at Harvard would be unhappy (Klitgaard, 1985). Harvard would rather select some students who were not outstanding academically who would be happy to be in the bottom 25 percent of the class. Though Harvard does choose applicants with truly outstanding academic records on the basis of intelligence alone, it also tries to choose students based on other criteria.

Harvard's Admissions Committee includes a few faculty members, but it comprises primarily professional admissions officers who specialize in searching for students who would add a "well-rounded" dimension to the student body. They sort applications according to a variety of criteria, such as scholastic aptitude, whether the student is the child of a Harvard graduate, an athlete, a public or private school graduate, from what area of the country the student comes, or whether the student is a foreign candidate.

The outcome of this selection process is, according to Karen (1990), that those from prep schools have an advantage over those from public schools, and those from elite prep schools have the best advantage. Children of alumni and athletes have a great advantage, minority groups have an advantage if they went to elite prep schools, and Asians are at a disadvantage.

Harvard, like many elite institutions, hopes to improve the lives of young people, but it also wants its educational program to have impact on the society as a whole. It attempts to select young people on the basis of what they will be able to contribute to society. A young person who has been educated in one of the best private schools and whose family has important connections in business or government is more likely eventually to hold a key position in society. Education will probably have a greater added value in that person's career than educating a person with no such contacts. Most selective American colleges are believed to have similar procedures.

Although our prestigious colleges are respected worldwide for providing a high-quality education, most of the American educational system has come under attack in the past two decades.

In 2003-04: The average total price of attendance (tuition plus room and board) for full time students at a public 2 year college was $10,500 per year, $15,200 per year at a public 4 year college, and $28,300 at a private 4 year private institution per year. Studies show no sign of college tuition rates slowing down their rising pace. (NCED, #8, 2006).

THE FAILURE OF AMERICAN SCHOOLS

Americans and foreign nations alike have been increasingly concerned about the failure of American public schools to educate its young people. As mentioned in the introduction, comparisons with other countries reveal that Americans do poorly on test scores.

Performance in reading was equally poor. Only 5 percent of 17-year-olds could understand the meaning of an article about as difficult as an editorial in a good newspaper. Writing scores were even worse, and learning in history has been described as "sketchy." (Prowse, 1990). The Digest of Education Statistics (2002) report that between 1971 and 1999 reading proficiency scores for middle school children increased, but that significant gaps in performance continue to exist between ethnic groups and between females and males. Additionally, math and verbal SAT scores differ greatly between males and females, as shown in Figures 14-1a and 14-1b.

WHY STUDENTS DO NOT LEARN

A variety of reasons are given to explain why American students do not learn in school. They include low socioeconomic statuses of families and pupils, poor resources in school facilities, inadequate curricula, students discouraged from striving toward success, and high dropout rates.

Financial Problems

Whatever the problems are in our educational system, they probably are not due simply to the lack of money. Money spent per pupil on public school education has risen sharply, especially in the past two decades, as shown in Figure 14-2. The increase has been more rapid than could be explained by a rising

FIGURE 14-1 SAT SCORES, 1985–2005

Source: The College Board, Summary Reporting Service, 2006.

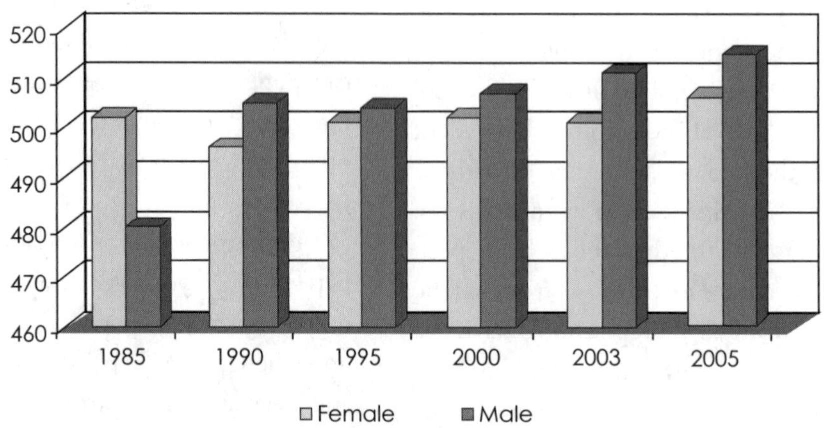

FIGURE 14-1A VERBAL SAT SCORES, 1985–2005

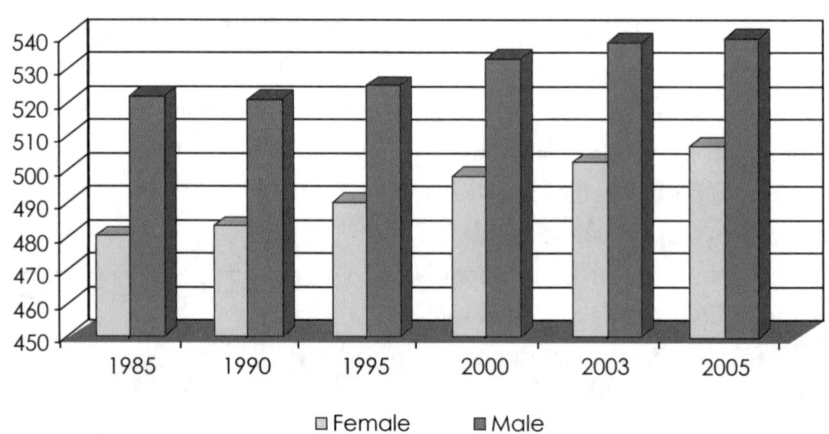

FIGURE 14-1B MATH SAT SCORES, 1985–2005

cost of living. Some of this money has been used to increase the number of teachers and staff, with the result being a steady decrease in the number of students per instructional staff member (Figure 14-3).

School Facilities

James Coleman and a team of sociologists have done a series of studies (1993, 1997) to compare the facilities of schools in black and white neighborhoods. Coleman found that the schools were the same age, spent the same amount of money per pupil, and had equivalent library and laboratory facilities. Teacher qualifications and class size were also the same. He concluded that the differences in achievement were related to the students' socioeconomic backgrounds, not to differences in the school plants. Coleman also found that black students performed better in white schools and recommended

FIGURE 14-2 CURRENT EXPENDITURE PER PUPIL IN PUBLIC ELEMENTARY AND SECONDARY SCHOOL, 1960–2002

Source: *Digest of Education Statistics*, Elementary and Secondary Education, 2002 (data in unadjusted dollar

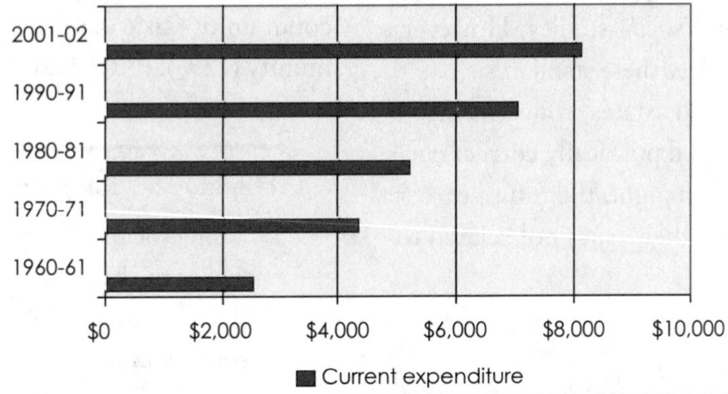

FIGURE 14-3 PUBLIC AND PRIVATE ELEMENTARY AND SECONDARY TEACHERS, PUPIL/TEACHER RATIOS, FALL 1970–FALL 2001

Source: *Digest of Education Statistics*, Elementary and Secondary Education, 2002.

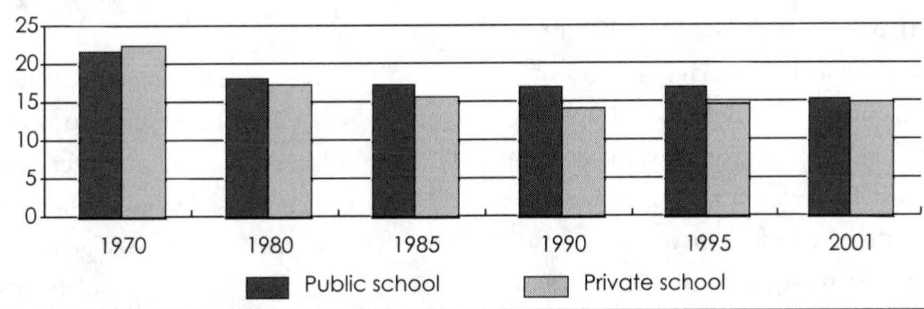

busing students to promote integration. Busing was carried out in many localities, but both black and white citizens disliked busing children to schools in other neighborhoods. Many argued that it interfered with the concept of neighborhood schools and local control.

Inadequate Curricula

Much of the problem in why students do not learn, according to the National Commission on Excellence in Education, is deteriorating school curricula in the public schools. Today, about half of all students in high school take a general studies course, compared to only 12 percent in 1964. While most of the courses in a general studies program are traditional academic studies such as English, history, or science, 25 percent of the credits earned in general studies are in physical and health education, work experience, remedial courses, and electives such as bachelor living. Only 31 percent of high school students take intermediate algebra, only 6 percent take calculus, and total homework assignments require an average of less than one hour a night. It has already been noted that parochial schools have an advantage over public schools, in part because they continue to emphasize academic subjects. The National Commission urged a greater emphasis on academic subjects in the public schools, recommending four years of English and three years each of math, science, and social studies. However, most states have failed to meet these standards.

Meanwhile, the United States concerns itself with issues such as a so-called politically correct curriculum, the values that are taught, the future career potential of students, and other issues not related to academic subjects.

The Self-Fulfilling Prophecy

There are many ways to discourage students from achieving in the classroom. One way is to discourage students from believing that learning and achievement are possible. Rosenthal and Jacobson (1968) found that students do not learn as well when their teachers believe that they are not very bright. If teachers have learned that lower-class and minority students do not perform well on I.Q. and achievement tests, they will have lower expectations of them in class. Even if they do perform well, teachers may fail to recognize their talents, give them lower grades, and confuse and frustrate them. Thus, a **self-fulfilling prophecy** is at work.

This self-fulfilling prophecy was evident in a study of pupil-teacher interaction, where it was found that teachers asked black students simpler questions than they asked white students. If a black pupil could not answer a question, the teacher asked somebody else. If a white pupil could not answer a question, however, the teacher gave an explanation. Teachers also praised andcomplimented white students more than black students when they gave correct answers (Weinberg, 1977).

High Dropout Rate

Worse than the students who finish without adequate preparation are those who do not finish at all. Dropout rates of young people ages 16-24 has declined between 1972-2004 from 15 percent to 10 percent. However, these rates are still considered high and are even higher in the Hispanic-American community (24%) and the African-American community (12%). (NCES,2006).

Thinking Sociologically

1. Using sociological perspectives about education as the basis for your ideas, what types of changes in your college's curriculum would you recommend to the administration at your school?
2. Discuss the extent to which the curriculum in your college is guided by a traditional Western intellectual perspective or a multicultural perspective. In light of this, what are the functions of your school's curriculum?
3. If you were to become a high school teacher, what personal assumptions would you have to address? Do you hold stereotypes about particular groups? Do you believe that children learn differently because of gender? Social class? How would being an observant sociologist guide your work as a teacher?

IMPROVING THE SCHOOLS

A variety of changes to the public school system are being tested in order to improve the schools in the United States. Some of these changes are discussed in the following sections.

Magnet Schools

In recent years, magnet schools have been developed in segregated school districts. **Magnet schools** are schools with special programs designed to attract exceptional students. These students voluntarily travel outside of their neighborhoods to go to the magnet schools. The hope is that white students will be attracted to schools with heavy black enrollment, to achieve integration. One fear of magnet school programs is that tax dollars and the best students in a district will be concentrated in magnet schools, and other schools will be left with mediocre programs and students. Most magnet schools are new, so it is too early to judge their success.

Decentralized Bureaucracies

Another approach to improving the schools is to **decentralize** the **bureaucracy**; in other words, put more of the decision-making processes in the local schools instead of in the school boards. This approach is being attempted in the Chicago school system (Muwakkil, 1990), with considerable debate and conflict. Chicago is a very large school system, where the relatively elite central Board of Education has been distant from the less aristocratic local schools over which it rules. Chicago has worked very hard to recruit ethnic and racial minorities onto the school board of this mostly minority school system. Now that they have succeeded in getting minority representation on the school board, critics want to decentralize, and some believe the real intent is to take power away from the now-integrated school board. In other words, the intent is to reinstitute discrimination through a new mechanism.

Instead of the school board running the schools, the schools in Chicago are now to be run by parent-controlled local school councils (LSCs). The LSCs have the right to hire and fire principals, select textbooks, and develop curricula. Many have chosen to fire the principals and are under attack for discrimination and other unfair practices. Some critics argue that parents, especially in the poorest districts, are not equipped to carry out the responsibilities of the LSCs. Whether these changes actually will improve Chicago's schools remains to be seen.

Vouchers

A third approach to improving our educational system is to give parents the choice of a school to which to send their children. If they choose a private school, they will receive a **voucher** for state funds to pay the tuition. The Supreme Court of the state of Wisconsin ruled on June 10th, 1998, that the Milwaukee voucher program, which will allow up to 15,000 children to attend any religious or private school, does not violate the state or federal constitution. This decision was appealed all the way to the United States Supreme Court. The high court ruled 8-1 not to hear the appeal and thus allowed the verdict in Wisconsin to stand. Government-run voucher programs are very controversial, and have been heavily criticized. Those who support the idea of choosing a school believe that parents will choose the best schools for their children. Schools will have to upgrade in order to compete for students, or they will not be able to stay open. Critics of the system argue, however, that parents may not be in the best position to choose a school and may be offered a shoddy product. Furthermore, the number of good schools is limited, and most students will have to remain in the Milwaukee school system, which has admittedly been doing a poor job of educating its students.

New Management

Chelsea, Massachusetts, has turned over the management of the city schools to Boston University (Ribadeneira, 1990), and those educators now run the local schools. This approach has also met with criticism. Critics argue that the university is authoritarian and patronizing. Teachers complain that they are left out of the decision-making process. Hispanic leaders complain that the university has failed to consider bilingual education. This, like other experiments in reform, has met with considerable conflict from the community.

SOCIOLOGY AT WORK

Developing Strategies in the Classroom

Victor Gibson has a B.A. in sociology from Wayne State University (in Michigan), and he currently works as an educational technician for the Detroit Board of Education and as an elementary school teacher. One of his jobs as educational technician is to identify students within third- and fourth-grade classes who need remedial help in language arts—that is, reading, spelling, syntax, grammar, and other areas related to the English language. He works with these students to help them develop the skills they need to proceed at a normal pace with their education. Gibson points out that in addition to providing remedial help in the language arts, he helps these students by helping them raise their level of self-esteem. His sociological training has taught him not only how stereotypes lead people to be treated in a way that might hold them back, but also how people come to believe certain things about themselves. In situations like this, a self-fulfilling prophecy results when particular types of students believe that they are not capable of doing the work.

The movie Stand and Deliver is especially meaningful to Gibson. In that movie, a teacher of predominantly lower-class Hispanic-Americans in a southern California school faced the challenge of getting teachers, parents, and the students to overcome the stereotype that these students were not capable of advanced mathematical learning. The teacher in that movie succeeded in both helping to reinforce the students' self-esteem and teaching them calculus. Gibson's task is similar to this. A sociological concept that Gibson relies upon often in helping him raise his students' self-esteem is Cooley's "looking-glass self." He knows that the way in which he and others react toward students plays a significant part in how they see themselves. Thus, he is very careful to say and do things that will help students to see themselves in a positive light.

Other approaches being considered or attempted include paying teachers on the basis of merit, involving business and industry more extensively in the educational system, having children begin school at age 4 years, and increasing the length of the school day and the school year. A wholesale increase in schooling is a risky proposition at best, however, when we do not know why students are not performing well. If schools, however subtly, are encouraging our lower classes and minority students to fail, as would be indicated by the high dropout rate among these students, increasing the school day, the school year, and the number of requirements might also increase the apathy and discouragement felt by these students. Likewise, if school is too strongly oriented toward middle-class occupations and is therefore discouraging to people from the lower classes, and if job opportunities are not increased, might the involvement of the business community in the schools make matters worse? Simple solutions to remedy our very complex problems in education and stratification will probably not work.

Creating Future Goals

Although differences in achievement have been related to family background and to the quality of the schools, one variable—future opportunity—has

Developing Strategies in the Classroom, *continued*

Besides using sociology in his specific task of identifying and helping students who need special attention with language arts, Gibson points out that his sociological knowledge has helped him to become a better teacher. "My classroom control is exceptional," he says, "because I understand group dynamics and social theories like social exchange and symbolic interactionism. Cultural sensitivity also plays a major role with transmitting knowledge in terms that the children can readily accept and decode at their level."

Gibson emphasizes that learning the sociological perspective in general has had a significant impact on his teaching style. "In general, sociology has helped me develop a 'holistic' point of view to gaining knowledge. I don't see myself as being a math teacher or a science teacher or social studies teacher. As I'm teaching one subject I'm also placing the subject in perspective to other subjects. I am constantly thinking about and telling students how each subject relates and interacts with others. No one subject can stand alone in reality. Why teach it in an isolated perspective?"

Additionally, Gibson feels that the continual emphasis on current issues that took place in his sociology classes helps him with his own approach to teaching. "Collectively, understanding today's and tomorrow's demands on future generations was very helpful in preparing me to help children. Understanding how political issues affect program development gives me insight on possible directions of future policy making. This helps me focus students' minds on everyday issues and how these issues might affect their lives. That is something that even young students find very important and can relate to."

been given little consideration. However, a program begun almost accidentally may demonstrate that future opportunity is most important when considering achievement. In 1981, multimillionaire Eugene Lang returned to his old school in East Harlem to speak to the sixth-grade graduating class, a group of minority students living in one of the poorest neighborhoods in the country (Bickford, 2002). He told them that he would pay for the college education of everyone in the class if they would stay in school. He also changed their poor environment by giving them his friendship and moral support, through tutoring, career counseling, and other advantages that wealth can bring. In a school where typically only half graduate and where only one or two in a hundred have grades high enough for college admissions, 90 percent of Lang's group of hopeful sixth-graders stayed in school through high school, and more than half had grades that would enable them to attend college. Perhaps a promising future is necessary for success in school, especially if teachers as well as students believe that success is possible. Perhaps a belief that the students can and will attend college is as necessary in public high schools as it is in parochial high schools. Perhaps the United States should look at a different system of rewards for work accomplished in school.

CONTEST AND SPONSORED MOBILITY

In the United States, students can get as much education as they are willing and able to pay for, as long as they maintain the grades necessary for acceptance at the next higher level. This system has been labeled **contest mobility** (Turner, 1960) because students can continue as long as they meet the standards of each level. The high school graduate can apply to college, the two-year college graduate can apply to a four-year institution, and the college graduate can apply to a graduate school. Once out of school, the contest continues, as students compete with each other for jobs.

However, the contest is not based entirely on performance. As was stressed earlier, the most prestigious schools in America do choose students who have good grades, but they also choose students with lower grades who are likely to make outstanding contributions to society (Klitgaard, 1985). These students are often children of people in powerful government or business positions. Education is also limited by the ability to pay. Poor students in the United States have been able to get grants and loans to help pay college costs, but middle-income families in the United States must pay thousands of dollars a year, on average, to attend a public or private college.

By contrast, Japan and most European countries have a system known as **sponsored mobility**. In these countries, students must pass qualifying examinations to gain admittance into different types of high schools and colleges. Once they pass the exams, however, their education is sponsored, and furthermore, if they do their work, they are assured of success both in school and upon completion of their studies. They do not pay any tuition for their higher education (Johnstone, 1986). In Britain and in Sweden, students receive grants and loans for living expenses and are discouraged from working while in school. Of course, students in these countries who do not earn good grades cannot further their education.

Within these systems, educational tracks vary. Students may receive a classical education leading to a university degree, a business education, or engineering and technical training. Once they enter a particular track, they rarely change to another type of education. A student in business school, for example, is unlikely to switch to a university.

IS ALL THIS EDUCATION NECESSARY?

In spite of the unequal education received by various groups in the United States, most people have had great faith in education as a means to upward mobility. It is this faith that is largely responsible for the phenomenal growth of our educational institutions, especially public institutions. Community and junior (two-year) colleges have been built, and loan programs have been established to assist those who could not otherwise afford a college education. The women's movement has stressed education as a means of upward mobility for women, and poverty programs have focused on training and educating the poor to help them rise out of poverty. Underlying all these steps is the assumption that education leads to upward mobility.

In the past, most sociologists supported this view. Blau and Duncan (1967), for example, argued that if children from large families could get as much education as children from small families, their existing occupational disadvantages would largely disappear. The belief among sociologists that education leads to upward mobility is so widespread that each year presenters at the American Sociological Association conference focus on inequalities in education.

There is, however, reason to doubt that education has much impact on social mobility. Sociologist Ivar Berg (2003) has argued that increasing the educational demands on the disadvantaged creates a hardship for them. They are encouraged to spend more money on education, but when they complete their education, they do not necessarily have additional earning power. Berg refers to this low return on educational investment as "the great training robbery."

The fact that increased education does not necessarily lead to better jobs may come as a surprise. The truth is, however, that factors other than education have a powerful influence on what jobs people take and what salaries they earn. Family background, for example, is more closely related to future occupation than level of education (Jencks, 1979). A son from a working-class family is more likely to enter a working-class occupation than a son from a middle-class family, even if they have the same amount of education (Jencks, 1979; Lipset and Bendix, 1967).

Occupational choice for today's generation is more complicated than in the past. Although the occupation of the parent(s) is still important in predicting occupational choice, other factors appear in the research. For example, Badgett and Folber (2003) propose and support the theory that occupational segregation is perpetuated along gender lines because women (and men) may be penalized in the marriage market for making nontraditional occupational choices. Holding all else equal, their empirical research supports the fact that having a gender-nonconforming occupation reduced the attractiveness of both men and women (Badgett and Folbre, 2003). Lupart and Cannon (2002) found significant gender differences in the future career interests of boys and girls, in particular in the career interests of girls, which are falling along traditional paths. What seems to have remained constant is that "the correlation between parents' education and socioeconomic status and the educational outcomes of their offspring remains a rather universal phenomenon" (Schnabel, 2002).

As the level of education for everyone in the society increases, members of the upper class get more education than others, go to the most prestigious schools, and use their influential family and friends to help them find the best jobs. On the other hand, the children of the working class, although they get more education than their parents had, find that working-class jobs now require at least a high school diploma, and many jobs in corporations that used to require only a high school diploma now require a college degree or even an M.B.A. Furthermore, even as educational requirements increase, all credentials are not equal. An M.B.A. from a prestigious university opens doors to jobs that are not available to an M.B.A. from a small public university.

Thinking Sociologically

1. How would you change job qualifications or credentials so that students would be more eager to perform?
2. Do you think that guaranteed jobs for top performers would increase school performance?
3. How would you change the school system so that it would be less costly?

SUMMARY

1. Structural functional theory argues that education in a complex industrial society supplements what families can teach their children, that it helps children to acquire both the complex skills and the knowledge necessary to function in the world. The educational system also selects students on the basis of their talents and abilities to meet the needs of society, directing the most talented into advanced education and training for positions of leadership and directing those with less talent to the positions in which they will serve society best. Educational institutions also create new knowledge and new technology, which they teach to the next generation. They create innovation and change so that society can advance.

2. Conflict theory argues that education is a means by which powerful groups prevent change; powerful groups use the educational system to teach children their values and norms so that everyone will believe that the position of the powerful is justified. Powerful groups promote children and give diplomas and degrees on the basis of how well students know their culture. Children of the wealthy usually receive prestigious credentials from prestigious schools and move into high-paying, prestigious jobs, while those from the lower classes tend to remain in lower-class jobs.

3. The American educational system was begun by the Puritans and developed into our modern system of elementary schools, secondary schools, colleges, and universities.

4. Schools are complicated bureaucracies, directed and financed by local, state, and federal boards, which determine curricula, testing procedures, and other requirements for certification. Supervisors, principals, and teachers implement the various rules and standards, and students, upon meeting the standards, receive the appropriate diplomas and degrees.

5. Stratification is pervasive in the educational system. School board members are likely to be business leaders and teachers are likely to be from the middle or working classes. Students are segregated into rich or poor neighborhood schools. Intelligence tests are biased toward upper-middle-class culture.

6. Private schools in the United States include Catholic parochial schools, private preparatory schools, and private colleges. Select private colleges have a complicated admissions system that does not select exclusively on the basis of grades, thereby allowing class-based differences to play a stronger role in selection.

7. Education in the United States has been criticized because tests show that American students perform well below those in other industrialized countries. Schools have been criticized for lacking funding, strong curricula, and good facilities.

8. School systems are trying solutions such as magnet schools, decentralized bureaucracies, vouchers, and management by universities.

9. European school systems differ from the American system not only by providing a better education but also by sponsoring students who academically qualify for further education. College tuition is provided by the national governments.

10. Some critics argue that too much education is required now and that this requirement is detrimental to the working class, who cannot afford it when, at the end of their courses of

study, they do not experience the upward mobility in occupations that they had hoped to gain.

KEY TERMS

age segregation The separation of groups by age such as occurs in our education system.

bureaucracy A hierarchical, formally organized structural arrangement of an organization based on the division of labor and authority.

compulsory public education Publicly funded education that is mandatory until a certain age.

contest mobility A competitive system of education in which those who do best at each level are able to move on to the next level.

credentialism The practice of requiring degrees for most high-paying jobs, whether or not the degrees actually signify skills necessary to accomplish the jobs.

decentralized bureaucracies Putting the decision-making processes in the hands of the people or local units rather than in the hands of a centralized few.

hidden curriculum The teaching and learning of things such as obedience, competition, and patriotism that are not part of the stated curriculum.

magnet schools Schools with special programs designed to attract exceptional students.

parochial schools Schools run and maintained by a religious body or organization rather than the public at large.

preparatory schools Private schools, usually of a select and elite nature, that are intended to offer an intensive education in both academic as well as social/cultural activities.

prolonged adolescence A latent function of education that serves to maintain parental dependency and keep young people out of the job market.

self-fulfilling prophecy A prediction that comes true because people believe it and act as though it were true.

sponsored mobility A system of education in which certain students are selected at an early age to receive advanced education and training.

vouchers Giving parents the choice of a private school for their children to attend and using state funds to pay for the tuition.

DISCUSSION QUESTIONS

1. What do you see as some specific latent and manifest functions of education in your college?
2. To what extent does your school emphasize credentialism in your selection of courses and major?
3. Discuss ways in which your own educational experience has served to maintain your socioeconomic position in society.
4. If you believed that children were naturally lethargic, how would you structure schools? If you believed that children were naturally geniuses, how would you structure schools? Given the nature of your own school experience, what assumptions about children do you suppose have been made?
5. How might your school experience have been different if you had gone to a more integrated school? A less integrated school? Be specific.
6. How might your school experience have been different if you had gone to a school with more money? A school with less money? Be specific.

7. If there were less opportunity to go to college in the United States, but tuition were free, would this improve your chances of finishing college, or would it diminish your chances? Does your answer have anything to do with your socioeconomic status?

8. If there were fewer educational credentials for jobs and more emphasis on job experiences, would this improve your chances for a good career or make your chances more difficult? Does your answer have anything to do with your socioeconomic status?

9. Discuss the positive and negative functions of contest and of sponsored mobility for individuals and for society.

10. Make up a list of issues for the board of trustees of your college to consider, in order to improve education where you are.

Political Groups and Systems

Influence Peddling

The practice of trying to influence government legislation and decision making has always been an important part of the American political process. Governmental influence commonly takes one or more of three forms: lobbying, consulting, and public relations.

1. Lobbyists, described in more detail later in this chapter, support and promote an interest group's positions on specific issues—such as abortion, gun control, affirmative action, environmental regulation, and many other issues—to Congress and federal agencies. Lobbyists muster support for the groups they represent in many ways, such as making telephone calls, writing letters, or sending petitions to members of Congress, organizing rallies about a specific political issue, and especially through developing alliances with lawmakers. You will typically find lobbyists mingling with lawmakers in the hallways of government office buildings, particularly at times when lawmakers are passing judgment on legislation opposed or supported by one or more groups of lobbyists.

2. Consultants advise clients seeking government funds—for example, a building contractor who seeks HUD funding—how best to apply for them in a way that will give them an advantage over other applicants and how to get through governmental bureaucratic hurdles. They may also try to influence government officials to accept their clients' applications by pointing out specific merits of the group that has applied.

3. Public relations experts try to influence the government to make the desired decisions by shaping public opinion on an issue. Government officials are more likely to support a policy that will win them votes. Because of the knowledge they possess, consultants and public relations experts can demand very high fees for their services, thus giving those who can afford them an advantage in obtaining the influence they need.

The attempts of these three groups—lobbyists, consultants, and public relations experts—to influence governmental legislation by providing knowledge and information to governmental officials, clients, or the public constitute a legitimate part of the American democratic political process. However, the legitimacy of "influence peddlers" who try to win governmental support for groups by using their political contacts rather than their knowledge of a subject is questionable (Glazer, 1989).

Although influence peddling has always been a social and political issue in America, the increasing size and complexity of the government has blurred even further the distinction between influence that is based on knowledge and influence that is based on political contacts, thus making it increasingly difficult to distinguish legitimate from illegitimate types of influence. As Susanne Garment, a Fellow at the American Enterprise Institute in Washington, D.C., sees it, "As the government has grown, so has influence peddling, because there are more dollars there and government affects more people's lives. More people have to go to government for what they need or at least to keep government from doing something bad to them. When you have the demand, and the official channels are not adequate to meet the demand, you're going to have to have growth in the number of middlemen" (Glazer, 1989, p. 699).

The perception that influence peddling is essential to achieving success when dealing with the government has resulted in a self-fulfilling prophecy. Groups interested in obtaining something from the government—such as funding for a project or passage of legislation that would benefit them—often feel that because competing groups probably have intermediaries working on behalf of the competing groups' interests, it is necessary for them to do so also. A danger of this, according to James Madison University political scientist Robert N. Roberts, is that the public will become cynical about the integrity of their government and about government's ability to make fair decisions without expensive intermediaries (Glazer, 1989).

Sociologists, and other social scientists, are interested in the issue of influence peddling because it goes to the heart of a number of other important sociological ideas about political groups and systems. Do political systems reflect the common values and interests of a society, or do they reflect the values and interests of those who have the most power and wealth? Do all the people have a say in the policies that govern people, or does a ruling elite determine policy? If it is a ruling elite, who are they, and how do they maintain their power? Stated simply, sociologists are interested in explaining who rules, how, and why.

The United States is a nation of many laws. We register our births, go to school, marry, and divorce according to the law. We paint our houses, mow our grass, shovel our sidewalks, take our driving tests, and park our cars when and where we are supposed to, and we refrain from spitting and other socially unacceptable behaviors in public places. We may get a summons if we do not behave as the law states that we should, but often, we are not even aware that there are laws dictating these activities.

Some laws are not obeyed, however. Prohibition of liquor consumption and sales did not stop people from drinking, banning abortions did not stop people from having them, and making marijuana illegal does not stop people from smoking it.

In large, complex societies, many decisions must be made about the duties and responsibilities of citizens and also about their rights and privileges. If the society is to be orderly, people must obey the rules that are made.

Power is generally viewed as the ability to control the behavior of others, to make the decisions about their rights and privileges, to see to it that people obey the rules or other expectations of the powerful. **Politics** is the use of power to determine who gets what in society. The political institution establishes and enforces the laws and punishes those who disobey them. It can levy taxes, distribute scarce resources, sponsor education, plan the economy, encourage or ban religion, determine who can marry and who is responsible for children, and otherwise influence behavior. The study of political groups and systems, then, is the study of power.

TYPES OF POWER

Weber (1958) pointed out that there are several types of power. **Physical force** is one obvious type. An individual or an army can be captured and put into handcuffs or prison by a stronger individual or army. Often, however, sheer force accomplishes little. Although people can be physically restrained, they cannot be made to perform complicated tasks by force alone.

Latent force, or the threat of force, is more powerful than force alone. Kidnappers can get what they want by demanding ransom in exchange for the victim's life. The kidnappers want the money and hope that the threat of murder will produce it—a dead victim does not do the kidnapper any good. Similarly, a ruler can say, "Either perform your duty or you will go to jail," hoping that the threat of jail will make the citizen perform the desired duty. Putting the citizen in jail, however, does not really help the ruler. In fact, latent force can sometimes produce results in situations in which direct force would not.

Controlling a society through force, whether actual or latent, is expensive and inefficient. It does not bring about the cooperation necessary for society to function productively. A group that relies on force to maintain its power faces a constant threat of being overthrown by its citizens, whereas more reliable types of power do not rely on force for their effectiveness. **Legitimate power**, for example, is power that is accepted by the people in a society as being necessary and beneficial, such as the power to make and enforce rules that benefit all.

Authority is power accepted as legitimate by those it affects. The people give the ruler the authority to rule, and they obey willingly without the need or threat of force. Weber, who was a master at classifying the abstract concepts needed to understand society, identified three types of authority: (1) traditional authority, (2) charismatic authority, and (3) legal authority. In **traditional authority**, the leader of the group leads by tradition or custom. In a patriarchal society, the father is the ruler and is obeyed because this practice is accepted by those ruled. When the father dies, his eldest son becomes ruler and has authority based on the nation's customs. Rulers who have traditional authority are usually born into their positions, and their competence to rule is not usually at issue. Also, the bounds of authority for traditional rulers are fairly broad—their power can range from settling minor disagreements to dictating who can marry whom.

The second type of authority, **charismatic authority**, is based on the personal attributes of the leader. Sometimes, a person can win the confidence, support, and trust of a group of people who then give the leader the authority to make decisions and set down rules. A charismatic leader attracts followers because they judge him or her to be particularly wise or capable.

Martin Luther King, Jr., was this kind of leader. King gained followers because he was a moving speaker who addressed people with sincerity and a sense of mission, and he won their respect. With their support, he was able to lead a political fight to improve the position of blacks in the United States.

Another charismatic leader is the Reverend Sun Myung Moon of the Unification Church. Moon has built a following on the basis of his own conviction that he was chosen by God to spread the word of Christianity throughout the world, and to rebuild God's kingdom on earth. Moon, who has gained followers in his native Korea and in Japan, Europe, and America, instructs his people to work hard and live a simple life of poverty. When they join the church, they sacrifice their worldly goods and the pleasures they consider evil, such as alcohol, tobacco, and drugs.

The third type of authority, **legal authority**, is based on a system of rules and regulations that determine how the society will be governed. In the United States, the U.S. Constitution sets down the bases for the government's authority, the Congress has the legal authority to enact laws, and the president has the legal authority to carry them out. The president also directs the military when it is needed to enforce the law and brings before courts or pardons those who break it. The courts interpret the laws and make judgments about whether the laws have been broken.

Weber was extremely concerned about some of the characteristics of legal authority. The power granted by legal authority is based on the rules and regulations governing the office. The power of the individual officeholder is limited by those rules, and the individual has power only as long as he or she adheres to those rules. Legal authority rests in the organization, and the organization attempts to serve its own interests and to meet its own goals. Thus, power in the United States rests in organizations and not in the will of the individual citizens.

The federal bureaucracy in the United States, for example, has grown so much in recent years that its size has become an issue in presidential elections. Candidates routinely promise to cut back on the number of federal employees. Once in office, however, they find that the bureaucracy has ways of resisting major cutbacks, and it is almost impossible to make substantial reductions—even in the president's own executive branch. Because presidents cannot afford to antagonize the people they rely on to implement their policies, the bureaucracy often continues from administration to administration without significant reduction in size.

APPLYING POWER AND AUTHORITY

Power is not something that is used only by political leaders or army officers. Most of us use it at one time or another in our daily personal and professional lives. If you know the various types of power and authority, you may be able to increase your effectiveness as a parent, employer, business executive, teacher, doctor, politician, police officer, and in many other roles. Although Weber probably did not have these roles in mind when he was developing his ideas regarding power and authority, we can extrapolate how these concepts might be applied to everyday roles. (As you have probably noticed after reading much of this book, the application of sociological concepts and theories often requires thinking about them in ways that extend or go beyond their original meaning.)

As a parent, for example, you have the ability to control your children through traditional authority, for the most part. Typically, you would have little need to justify your demands, and you would not have to rely on latent or physical force when you want them to clean their rooms or to be home by midnight. "Because I said so" is a sufficient explanation for parents to give for demands they make on their children. However, a teacher who uses the same type of explanation to get students to complete a reading assignment will probably suffer a loss of students' respect and diminished overall effectiveness. Often, teachers are more effective when they rely on legal authority, in which the students are firmly reminded that to learn the material and get a passing grade, they must comply with the rules. In some instances, talented teachers can inspire their students to work hard through their charismatic personalities, but charismatic authority would be unlikely to work in most classrooms. However, charismatic authority could be an extremely effective form of control and leadership for political leaders, ministers, or even managers of sports teams. Generally, then, a more effective way of leading people is to be aware of the different forms of power and authority and to be sensitive to what works best in various situations, rather than merely to rely on one method that worked well in one situation.

THE DEVELOPMENT OF POLITICAL SYSTEMS

As societies become wealthier and more complex, political systems grow more powerful. In very primitive and simple societies, there was no ruler and decisions were made as a group. As societies evolved from uncomplicated bands, they grew wealthier, and their rulers were able to control larger areas with their armies. States developed—**states** are institutions organized around a set of social functions, including political regulation (government and laws), military defense, and support for the welfare of the population (Johnson, 2000). At first, controlled areas were small, but later, cities and the surrounding areas came under the power of individual rulers. These territories were called city-states. Today, most of the world is organized into nation-states, large territories ruled by a single institution. Nation-states developed in Europe several centuries ago, but they arose in Africa only during the past century.

When does a nation-state become a cohesive society? How does a country develop laws that will unite the population, create an orderly society, give authority to the governed, and eliminate the need for force? These are two of the oldest questions in political history, but the modern ideas of particular concern to sociologists fall within the basic theoretical approaches discussed throughout this text.

Structural Functional Theory

Structural functionalists believe that a society is built on a common set of values. Our society believes in work, achievement, equal opportunity, and the freedom to run our own lives, to name just a few of our predominant values. These values are learned by young children in the family and passed on to subsequent generations.

In a legal system of authority, a society's values shape its laws and political policies. If people value achievement, the law will protect the right to achieve. If people value freedom, the law will protect freedom, and social policy will encourage freedom—no one will be forced to practice a particular religion, for example, and marriage will be a matter of personal choice. Political institutions pass laws and develop policies that reflect the values of the population. Often, the political institution must extend itself into international affairs to protect the society's values. It may limit the import of foreign goods, to protect its own workers, and negotiate with other nations in order to allow trade for the benefit of its own citizens. It protects its citizens from aggressive acts and maintains armed forces to carry out its international functions.

Sometimes, however, the values of a society are not mutually consistent. Our views about work and achievement may come into conflict with our view about the freedom to run our own lives: If some people do not want to work, forcing them to do so would impinge on their freedom. Even when values are shared, it is not always easy to determine which values should be translated into laws and which laws will be obeyed. The abortion issue involves two basically conflicting values, one involving the rights of the embryo or fetus and one involving the rights of the mother. Legislatures must decide which rights to protect, and individuals must choose whether to abide by the law or to act according to their own values if they conflict with the law. Predicting which laws will be obeyed becomes even more difficult when different subcultures have conflicting values. Youth groups who do not register for the draft and religious groups who practice polygamy are subcultures with values that conflict with the dominant culture.

Structural functionalists believe that the political institution holds the values of the dominant society and arbitrates conflicts when they arise. One person may act on a value of freedom by marrying more than one spouse, or members of a subculture may feel free to use illegal drugs. It is the political system that decides which values must be upheld and which must be limited, to maintain social order. In the United States, where freedom is a value, constant arbitration is necessary to protect the freedoms of the individual without impinging on the other values of society.

Conflict Theory

Conflict theory differs radically from structural functional theory. It assumes not that societies are based on a set of values, but that they are drawn together by people's need for resources: food, shelter, and other necessities. Some groups get a larger share of the resources, and they use these resources to gain power. Just as they hire people to work for their financial interests in the economic sphere, they use their resources to hire people to protect their power interests in the political sphere. They use their wealth to influence political leaders to support their economic interests, and they bring about the downfall of individuals or governments who oppose their interests.

The history of Europe provides many examples of how economic groups have used legal power to protect their own interests (Pirenne, 1914). European merchants in the Middle Ages at first sold their goods at strategic points along heavily traveled highways. Eventually, however, they built towns at those points and passed laws restricting others from trading, thus using their political power to create a monopoly of trade. These merchants dominated the cities of Europe for several centuries by passing laws to protect their interests.

In the fifteenth and sixteenth centuries, as worldwide shipping increased, nation-states became powerful and used their political power to protect their shippers. When machinery came into use and manufacturing grew, the manufacturers initially required no political support. They preferred a laissez-faire economy, a free and competitive market. Workers were plentiful, and industry could hire them for very low wages and could fire them at will. The workers, who suffered greatly under this system, eventually caused serious civil disturbances, and the industrialists had to develop a legal system to protect their own interests. Conflict theorists believe that in every age, the wealthy have used both laws and force to protect their wealth.

Why, then, do the great majority of people support the laws of the wealthy? According to conflict theorists, it is because the rich use their wealth and power to control the mass media. They teach their values to the majority of people by controlling the schools, the press, radio, television, and other means of communication. They try to legitimate their power by convincing the population that the rich have a right to their wealth and that they should have the power to restrict trade, hire and fire workers, and otherwise restrict the behavior of the majority to maintain their own position. Unlike the structural functionalists, who believe that the values of the society shape the political system, conflict theorists believe that the political systems shape the values of society.

POLITICAL STRUCTURES IN MODERN SOCIETIES

There are two types of legal political rule in modern societies: democracy, in which the people control the government, and *totalitarianism*, in which the state rules the people. Neither of these types is found in a pure form, and many countries have a mixed power structure. In analyzing modern societies, however, it is useful to describe power structures in terms of their ideal types.

The Democratic State

In its ideal form, a **democracy** is a power structure in which people govern themselves. Philosophers such as Jean Jacques Rousseau, John Locke, John Stuart Mill, and John Dewey believed that people knew what was in their own best interests and could learn how to protect these interests within the political system. They also believed that the experience of being politically involved would develop better citizens (Orum, 1978). One major problem with democracies, however, is the likelihood that **oligarchies**, or ruling elites, will develop (Michels, 1911). As a result, instead of all people sharing in their own governance, a few people have a monopoly of power and rule for everyone. Michels (1911) believed that in nation-states and other large organizations, the rise of a few to dominate power was inevitable. He called this the **iron law of oligarchy**.

An early attempt to practice democracy was made by the Greek city-state of Athens, but it was actually an oligarchy. Leadership was rotated, and all government responsibility was shared among the citizens. This system is evident in the Greek use of the term citizen to refer to those who were considered members of the city-state and who were entitled to the freedoms and privileges granted to members of the state. Only a small percentage of the population of Athens were citizens, and because there were so few, every citizen could participate directly in the political process. However, the great majority of the city's inhabitants—the slaves, women, and foreigners—were not considered citizens and had no political standing.

Changes in social attitudes have raised women, the lower socioeconomic classes, and other groups from the low status they occupied in ancient Greece to the status of citizens in modern Western civilization. Nonetheless, true democracy continues to be impossible because of the unwieldy size of modern political populations. As a result, modern democracies have chosen a system of representation by which the population elects officials to act as their agents. The elected officials in turn appoint the upper-level civil servants and justices of the court. Therefore, when we refer today to "democratic" power structures, we mean those in which people are allowed to vote for elected representatives. It is assumed that the elected representatives will be removed from office if they are not responsive to the desires of the people. Although representative governments of this sort have laws to limit the power of officials and to protect the rights of individuals, especially their rights to equality and to dissent, there is no question that the elected officials and the people they appoint have a great deal of power.

Even in modern democracies, elites may use their power to form an oligarchy. They maintain power by manipulating the electorate. They may, for example, stuff ballot boxes and miscount votes. They may use the mass media to distribute information selectively, advertising favorable information and covering up information that the electorate may not favor. When an oligarchy develops in large bureaucratic governments, the elite sets policy, the bureaucracy carries out that policy, and the citizens believe that the rule is still legitimate, as long as they are allowed to vote (Etzioni-Halevy, 1997).

The Totalitarian State

Totalitarianism is a system of rule in which the government has total control. The government dictates the society's values, ideology, and rules. It controls the educational system and plans education based on the skills and technology the rulers believe that the society needs. It also controls economic development, which is planned in advance, and production is based on the needs of the society, as determined by the leaders.

Totalitarian societies do not permit dissent. Their goal is to develop a unified population, one that is not divided by differing religious loyalties or political views. They eliminate dissenters through violence, imprisonment, or expulsion, especially when the societies are just developing.

Democratic and totalitarian societies have several characteristics in common, and they often have similar ideologies. Both types of government may believe in freedom and equality for their citizens; for example, in both types of societies, citizens may be free to vote on some issues. Another ideological similarity is that each considers its own system superior to the other. The most conspicuous similarity, however, is their bureaucratic organization. Both systems are run by bureaucracies of enormous complexity and power, and political parties play an important role in shaping and unifying the organizational structures under each system.

Political Parties

Political parties are groups of citizens formed with the express intent of gaining control of the political body of the state. They exist in both democratic and totalitarian states. Parties nominate candidates to run for office, provide personnel for bureaucratic posts, and make public policy. Their goal is not just to influence government but to manage it.

Political party systems differ in structure, organization, and reasons for existence. Some parties form around a particular person, such as Charles de Gaulle's Gaullist party in France, which was a strong force in French politics even after the death of its founder. Other parties exist to promote a specific issue. The Green party of West Germany was created to support environmental and antinuclear legislation. The National Woman's party was founded at the beginning of this century in the United States to represent the interests of a particular minority. Most powerful parties, however, are not organized around a single issue. They concern themselves with managing the entire government and the many issues that government addresses.

A party's role in government is strongly influenced by the number of parties in a particular governmental system. Totalitarian states have only one party, so there is no competition for control of the government. Nevertheless, unless the party is run by the military and order is maintained by force, the political party must react to public opinion while encouraging support for the government. The party also selects candidates for public office and then presents them to the general public. There are no competing candidates in one-party systems, however, so nomination ensures election. In addition, the party defines issues and must convince the electorate to support their stand on these issues. The issues not brought up by the party are not debated, but every effort is made to win support from the public for the activities that the party does undertake.

Two or more political parties are found in democratic countries. This allows competition between candidates and debate over competing issues. In a two-party system, such as in the United States, one party must gain a majority of the votes, so each party tries to attract the voters in the moderate center. Because they have to avoid taking any stand that would alienate this central group of moderate voters, both parties have to be moderate and they dare not offer creative solutions to problems. They can only support the status quo. The voter has little real choice.

In governments with more than two political parties, the parties do not have to seek moderation or win a majority of votes. Instead, they take a definite stand and offer creative solutions to problems in order to satisfy a group of people who are committed to a particular issue—a labor issue, an antiwar issue, or an environmental issue. They then nominate a candidate who will take a strong stand on the chosen one or two issues. Because it is very difficult for such a candidate to get a majority of votes, parties compromise with each other and form coalitions even when they hold opposing positions on a variety of issues. Government policies can change dramatically with each election, depending on which party or coalition of parties gains power. Nevertheless, the voters have a clear choice on a variety of issues when they cast their ballots.

APPLYING KNOWLEDGE OF POLITICAL SYSTEMS

Knowledge of the different types of political structures and systems in modern societies is useful in a number of ways. First, academic sociologists can learn a great deal about a culture by understanding its political systems. By knowing how close a country is to being democratic or totalitarian and knowing the nature of its political parties, sociologists can gain insight into some of the values and behaviors of a people.

Certainly, politicians and diplomats need to know about the nature of the various political systems. A U.S. diplomat could not effectively negotiate with a foreign diplomat without first thoroughly understanding that the rules, policies, and decision-making processes are likely to be very different from those of the United States. Even similar types of political systems do not all operate in the same way. Both France and the United States are democracies, for example, but, as noted in the discussion of France, it is not entirely clear who in the French government is in charge of it.

Corporations involved in international business also need to have a thorough knowledge of foreign political structures. The policies that offer a great deal of freedom to American businesses are not found in all countries. Tax laws, tariffs, import and export laws, and other regulations greatly affect the way a business operates. Before making massive investments in an international business, then, corporate executives need to scrupulously study how the politics of a country will affect their ability to make a profit.

On the clinical side, understanding the nature of various political systems might help therapists and social workers to counsel immigrants who are having problems of adjustment. For someone who is used to being overtly controlled, the freedom offered by some democracies could be difficult to handle. New responsibilities, expectations, and rules about making personal decisions might be disorienting. For immigrants who seek education, teachers and school counselors may also find themselves in a position where they have to help foreign students adjust.

The issue of helping people adjust to new political systems is especially relevant today, considering the sweeping political changes that have been occurring in Eastern Europe. Imagine the psychological and sociological turmoil that could envelop people who have lived within very controlled political environments when their country democratizes almost overnight, or so it seems to have happened in many cases. The classical sociologist Emile Durkheim said that when people are faced with sudden changes in their lives (either positive or negative), they may experience anomie—a condition in which their old goals, values, and norms lose their meaning, and people are left with unclear guidelines for their lives. Perhaps private therapists, teachers, counselors, journalists, politicians, and other public speakers could use a sociological knowledge of political groups and systems to help people adjust to their new situations brought about by rapid political change.

Finally, anyone who travels abroad would benefit by understanding the political systems of foreign countries. Suppose that you decide to visit, work, or attend school in a European or Asian country. Do you know the rights you would have in, say, Greece, Italy, France, or China? If you happened to be accused of a crime, would you have the same rights as a U.S. citizen? Do you know, for example, that possession of marijuana is a more serious crime in many other countries than it is in the United States? To protect yourself and avoid unnecessary expenses or delays in time, you might carefully study the ways in which other political systems operate in such countries before you travel.

THE POLITICAL SYSTEM IN THE UNITED STATES

The United States, like France, has a democratic political system. Citizens are expected to rule the country by participating in the political process—debating issues, joining one of the two major political parties or remaining independent, voting for officials, and then expressing their opinions to officeholders.

The elected officials serve in a diverse, decentralized system of federal, state, and local governments. Each level of government has a system of checks and balances: The legislative branch makes the laws, the executive branch carries out the laws, and the judicial branch interprets the laws. Our system of government is representative, but how representative is it in practice? Who holds the power? Which groups influence government the most? There are two opposing perspectives on power in America. The first is that a powerful elite holds all of the power, and the second is that power is divided among many diversified groups.

The Power Elite

C. Wright Mills (1958) argued that the United States is run by a **power elite**, consisting of leaders in the upper echelons of business, the military, and the government. These leaders, Mills contended, are likely to come from similar backgrounds and have similar beliefs and values. There is no actual conspiracy among these leaders to promote the interests of their own high social stratum, but they nevertheless tend to support the same policies, as these policies support their common interests. Recent research, especially by Domhoff (2001, 2003) supports the theory that there is a power elite who holds power in United States political affairs.

One example of the operation of a power elite is what has come to be known as the "military–industrial complex." This complex evolved during World War II, when some of the checks and balances regulating the defense department were dismantled. The absence of these checks and balances meant that the American defense industry was producing for a consumer, the American taxpayer, for whom price was not negotiable. As a result, unprecedented profits were made. In this way, United States military actions in foreign countries such as Korea and Vietnam kept the defense industry employed, and the industry became a decisive force in governmental policy.

Political Pluralism

Many sociologists believe that numerous groups in the United States play a significant role in political decision making. David Riesman et al. (1950) described the power system of the United States as one of **political pluralism**—rule by many different groups. A variety of special interest groups try to influence legislation. They form lobbies that represent various industries, labor, religions, educational groups, and other special interests. These groups try to protect their own interests by pressuring politicians for favorable legislation and fighting against legislation they dislike. Thus, Riesman et al. believed, no single group had absolute power because different groups would balance one another's actions when they had competing interests.

There is little question that a variety of interest groups exist in the United States today. The issue for critics of pluralism is whether these various groups have any real power. Political pluralists believe that many groups are equally powerful and balance the power of other groups. Those who believe that a governing class or a military–industrial complex is most powerful fear that other groups are not strong enough to counteract the power of the elite, no matter how active and well organized they are.

Two types of groups are frequently in the news in American politics: *political action committees*, which contribute money to political campaigns, and lobbies, which attempt to influence legislation. Both types clearly have more power than individuals who do not belong to such groups. Questions remain about whether either type of group has enough power to counteract the power of elites or whether these groups actually tend to represent and extend the power of elite groups.

Political Action Committees (PACs)

Political action committees (PACs) are organizations formed to raise money for political campaigns. Candidates running for office need a great deal of money for political advertising, office overhead, transportation, and other needs. The expenses can reach millions of dollars per campaign. As a rule, the people who are elected to political office spend more money than their opponents, and PACs help to pay these election expenses. In the 2004 Presidential election, PACs contributed 384 million dollars to the candidates, (Center for Responsive Politics, Oct., 2005).

PACs represent many special interest groups—often groups that are at variance with one another. Business groups, labor groups, and professional groups all sponsor PACs. Some of the largest are the National Conservative PAC, Fund for a Conservative Majority, National Congressional Club, Realtors Political Action Committee, National Rifle Association (NRA), Political Victory Fund, Republican Majority Fund, American Medical Association (AMA), and the Fund for a Democratic Majority. Many of the most powerful favor the Republican party, but others favor the Democratic party. Those that have business interests often split their contributions, giving money to members of both parties. Nonetheless, although PACs support both parties and a variety of candidates, they do not represent a cross-section of American voters. Only groups with moneyed connections can possibly raise the sums needed to be influential in funding candidates.

A few PACs, particularly very conservative groups, have used PAC money to try to defeat **incumbents**, the elected officials who already hold office and are trying to be reelected. Most PAC money, however, goes to incumbents and therefore tends to maintain the power structure as it is. Currently there exists a very high rate of reelection of incumbents to the U.S. Congress, partly because they have access to PAC money.

Each PAC is allowed to contribute up to $5,000 to each politician per election unless it is a presidential campaign, in which case up to $10,000 is allowed. PACs are not permitted to persuade politicians to take a particular stand, but of course, they support only politicians who will support their cause. Oil and gas PACs, for example, support those members of Congress who vote for bills that will help the oil and gas industry; real estate PACs support only members who vote for bills that will help the real estate industry; and so on.

Although PACs are not technically allowed to persuade politicians to take political stands, thousands of associations and groups are permitted to try to influence both politicians and civil servants. These groups are commonly called "lobbies."

Lobbies

Lobbies are organizations of people who wish to influence the political process on specific issues. Unlike political parties, lobbies do not nominate candidates or hope to manage the government. Their goal, rather, is to persuade elected and appointed officials to vote for or against a particular regulation or piece of legislation, as discussed in the introduction to this chapter. Groups of people with a common interest often form an association with the express purpose of influencing the legislative process. Thousands of such associations are based within blocks of the United States Capitol, where they monitor the legislation being considered. They maintain close contact with government officials and scrutinize the work of bureaucrats when budgets are being prepared or hearings are being held, so that they can influence the government to their own best interest. Because most national associations are federations of state and local associations, they have influence at every level of government, from the smallest town to the federal government.

Some of the largest and best-known associations are those involved in manufacturing, such as the National Association of Manufacturers (NAM), the Chamber of Commerce of the United States, the Chemical Specialties Manufacturers Association, the National Asphalt Pavement Association, the Evaporated Milk Association, the National Association of Retail Druggists, and the National Cemetery Association; the list is endless. Who these organizations hire to lobby for them is a subject of serious debate, as discussed in the policy debate in this chapter.

It is estimated that as many as one in ten Americans depends on defense spending for their livelihood, and these individuals, the corporations for whom they work, and the military are well organized to lobby Congress for money for defense spending. The National Defense Industrial Association, founded in 1997, has 1,100 corporate members who are defense contractors and 27,000 additional members from industry, universities, and the Pentagon; the Aerospace Industries Association has 154 associate member companies and 83 member companies. There are also the Navy League, the Air Force Association, the Association of the U.S. Army, the Armed Forces Communications and Electronics Association, the Shipbuilders Council of America, the Electronic Industries Association, and the Society of Naval Architects and Marine Engineers.

There are also some lobby groups who are concerned with issues unrelated to business. They are supported by donations from the public, and they lobby for issues related to the public good. Such groups include Common Cause, the National Wildlife Federation, the Center for Science in the Public Interest, and the ACLU.

The workings of the powerful automobile lobby show how much time, energy, and money are involved in influencing the political process. During the early 1960s, Ralph Nader, a public interest lobbyist, launched an attack on the faulty design of American automobiles in his book *Unsafe at Any Speed.* After the book was published, Nader continued to work for improved auto safety. In response, Congress considered passing legislation to set safety standards for cars, when the auto lobby, led by Henry Ford, moved in to stop the legislation (Dowie, 1977). Ford went to Washington and spoke to the Business Council, an organization of 100 executives of large organizations who come to Washington from time to time to advise government. He visited members of Congress, held press conferences, and recruited business support, but he still failed to stop the passage of the Motor Vehicle Safety Act, which was signed into law in 1966. Ralph Nader ran for president of the United States in 2000.

A regulatory agency was then made responsible for setting guidelines for auto safety. The Ford Motor Company responded by sending representatives to the agency to argue that poor drivers, unsafe guard rail designs, poor visibility, and a variety of other highway and driving hazards were responsible for accidents. They contended that not only was the automobile safe, but also the regulations requiring improvements would increase the cost of cars and would save few lives.

Despite these lobbying efforts, in 1968 the regulatory agency issued new safety standards designed to reduce the risk of fire in automobiles after a rear-end crash. As required by law, the agency scheduled hearings on the regulation. Ford responded with a report stating that automobile fires were not a problem. The agency then had to conduct several studies to determine whether fire was a problem. It found that 400,000 cars burned up every year and that 3,000 people burned to death. It again proposed safety standards, and Ford again responded, arguing that although burning accidents do happen, rear-end collisions were not the cause. The agency researched this question and found that rear-end collisions were in fact the cause in most cases. Again, regulations were proposed, again Ford responded, and again research was conducted. The total delay in developing regulations was eight years. The regulations eventually did pass; however, during those eight years, the company managed to defeat regulations requiring other safety measures. For example, it was 20 more years before air bags were finally installed in automobiles.

This account of one corporation's reluctance to comply with a safety regulation shows that big business has enormous but not absolute power over government. It also shows how time-consuming and expensive the business of lobbying is. It can be practiced only by organizations with much wealth and power, and bureaucratic organizations have much more power than any individual citizen.

Thinking Sociologically

1. Use the knowledge of political groups and systems provided in this chapter to discuss whether the government should further limit the amount of money that PACs can contribute to political campaigns.

2. Reconstruct the debate about whether there should be restrictions on lobbying by former government officials (see the policy debate) in terms of structural functionalism and conflict theory.

3. Using the information about lobbies and PACs, develop arguments to support and oppose the two views of political power groups offered in this chapter—the power elite and political pluralism.

THE ROLE OF THE INDIVIDUAL

Special interest groups can use their power to try to influence political decisions, but what is the role of the individual? As stated earlier in this chapter, American citizens are expected to participate in the political process by voting, debating issues, either joining one of the two major political parties or remaining independent, and expressing their views to their elected officials. People learn these and other responsibilities through the process of political socialization.

Political Socialization

In most American communities, many children watch the mayor lead the Fourth of July parade and learn that the mayor is a good and benevolent leader. Most youngsters also learn that other leaders likewise give time and money to make the community a better place to live. During elections, children often learn about political parties as their families discuss candidates, and frequently they identify with a political party on an emotional level long before they can understand political issues. To a child, the president of the United States is to the country what the father is to the family: a leader, provider, and protector.

Political socialization of this sort continues when children enter school. Through formal courses in history, literature, and government, they learn to respect society's norms and political systems. Leaders are presented in history books as role models for society's norms. In an interesting study of how history books portray George Washington, Schwartz (1991) found that in the early part of the nineteenth century, when the United States believed that our leaders should be genteel, Washington was described in biographies as remote, of flawless virtue, refined, with a dignified air. After the Civil War, Americans wanted their leaders to be more populist, so historians were criticized for making Washington sound cold, harsh, stern and soulless—a human iceberg. Historians described him at this point as one who loved life, children, flashy clothes, good wine, good houses, cards, and dirty jokes. After 1920, in order to fit into the growth of business, historians began to describe Washington as a good businessman, a captain of industry. Thus, whatever characteristics were considered admirable in a given period, those were the characteristics emphasized when discussing our first president.

Not all children emerge from their family and school socialization with the idea that political leaders are benevolent, caring, achieving people, of course. They may accumulate contradictory evidence along the way, perhaps having experiences with parents, teachers, or others who indicate that leaders are not to be trusted. They may also acquire a distrust of the political system by listening to parental complaints about lack of jobs or other conditions that result from political decisions and that cause family hardship. Schools teaching middle-class values may fail to convince a child living in poverty that the political system is fair and benevolent; realities in the child's environment may provide harsh evidence that not everyone can move from a log cabin to the White House. Children from Appalachia and urban ghettos have been much less apt to support the American political system than middle-class American children (Dowse and Hughes, 1972).

Political Socialization in the Mass Media

By the time that children finish school, they have developed political attitudes that will shape their political behavior in adult life, but political socialization still continues, especially through the mass media, which reinforce childhood socialization. Much mass media socialization presents political issues in emotional terms. Slogans that promise a better America without offering data about how this is to be done are seeking an emotional response from voters, a response resembling the one a child feels for the mayor leading the Fourth of July parade. Although these emotional appeals for voter support are routinely criticized as "flag waving," emotion is believed to play a very large role in voter choice.

The price one pays to run for president: In the 2000 Presidential election, the candidates spent a total of 3 billion dollars. This increased by 30 percent in the 2004 presidential election where the candidates spent 3.9 billion dollars. It appears that there is no slowing down in the spending trend. So far for the 2008 Presidential race, (as of May, 2007) all of the records for raising money to run for the position have already been broken. It is estimated that each Primary candidate will need to raise at least 500 million dollars just to compete in the election. As of May, 2007, there were already 18 candidates running for the position. (Center for Responsive Politics, 2004).

APPLYING POLITICAL SOCIALIZATION

By being aware that this emotional ploy is used often by some politicians, you can increase your ability to critically evaluate their political statements, positions, and campaign platforms. Some politicians—particularly those who have training in acting or public speaking—have mastered this ability to manipulate people's emotions. This skill provides them with a great deal of charismatic authority, which affords them considerable political clout. Often, politicians can muster overwhelming public support for policies that are devoid of any meaningful substance or even—at times—not in the best interests of the population. However, emotion can also be used by politicians to sway the population to accept meaningful and beneficial policies. As voters, you need to be particularly critical of political proposals that are directed more to your hearts to than your minds. The most effective way for the mass media to influence people is to present information in such a way that there is only one obvious conclusion (Goodin, 1980). The media often give only one side of an issue, and if the so-called obvious solution is heard frequently enough, it will seem to make sense to most people. Often, for a year or two before an election, we hear a candidate mentioned as the obvious choice for the party. The candidate might even say that if people do not have jobs, they obviously do not want jobs. If people do not vote, they are obviously not interested. These statements are not obvious at all, but unless contradictory information is provided, they may seem obvious enough and will probably be accepted by the majority of the public.

In the United States, there is concern that the mass media express only the views of the large

POLICY DEBATE

Should Former Members of Congress or Congressional Staff Be Restricted from Lobbying?

Lobbying has long been a tradition in American politics. In many instances, lobbying has not only been legitimate but also necessary. For example, after the Civil War, many veterans and widows seeking pensions hired lobbyists to help them because the official qualifications for pensions required documents that many eligible citizens did not possess. The lobbyists asked Congress to pass private bills granting pensions to those who could not produce the necessary documents. In The *Spider Web*, a history of lobbying in President Ulysses S. Grant's administration, Syracuse University historian Margaret Thompson writes, "Establishing access, particularly if one's demand was individual and basically indistinguishable from hordes of others, was time-consuming, debilitating, and practically impossible unless someone was continuously on the scene to oversee it. Obviously one's chances were improved if one could afford to hire an advocate—and the better the advocate's record was, the higher his or her fees ... were likely to be" (Thompson, 1985, p. 165). In principle, using experts to influence what goes on in the government is a legitimate part of a representative democracy.

However, whether it is legitimate and fair for top government officials to trade their government positions for jobs in which they lobby their former congressional colleagues and use their political contacts to help win favors for private organizations is debatable. As mentioned in the introduction to this chapter, this practice of giving up a government position for a position as a lobbyist is known as the "revolving-door" phenomenon. This phenomenon, although not new, received much public attention during the mid-1980s when White House aide Michael K. Deaver left his position in the Reagan administration to set up a high-priced lobbying firm. The political connections, friends, and expertise that Deaver gained as a White House aide provided him with a tremendous potential to influence government legislation. His inside knowledge of the governmental bureaucracy—such as knowing the mechanics about how legislation really gets accepted, the types of policies that Congress might be willing to accept, the specific members of Congress who might be sympathetic to a particular cause, how the president and cabinet secretaries feel about certain matters, and so on—make him highly valuable to private organizations and groups that could benefit from having particular legislation passed. Because of this, private organizations and groups are willing to pay Deaver and his associates enormous salaries—a great deal more money than he was paid in his government job—to counsel them and to help lobby for their cause in Congress. This type of activity has led to a debate over whether revolving-door restrictions should be placed on former members of Congress, the congressional staff, and other White House officials.

Opponents to revolving-door restrictions believe that lobbying is an activity that is sanctioned by the Constitution's First Amendment right "to petition the government for redress of grievances" and that it is protected by the Constitutional right to free speech. According to Morton H. Halperin, Director of the American Civil Liberties Union's Washington, D.C., office and Leslie A. Harris, the ACLU's legislative counsel, "Lobbying, at bottom, is political speech entitled to the full protection of the First Amendment. To justify any restriction on that speech, [one] must show that the restrictions serve a compelling state interest and that they are narrowly tailored to serve

Should Former Members of Congress or Congressional Staff Be Restricted from Lobbying?, *continued*

that interest. We do not believe such a showing can be made with respect to members of Congress." Stated simply, everyone has a constitutional right to lobby.

Those who favor restrictions on revolving-door lobbying feel that revolving-door abuses overstep the boundaries of free political speech guaranteed by the First Amendment, thus disqualifying some people from acting as lobbyists. Archibald Cox, chairperson of a government watchdog group called Common Cause, says "Nothing in the constitution or judicial precedents supports the view that any individual has an absolute right to speak about government business *in a representative capacity* to a member or agent of the legislative or executive branch. One may well doubt whether the First Amendment gives any right to act in a representative capacity. … Speaking for another, with or without compensation, involves association—a relationship sometimes protected by the First Amendment but not as absolutely pure speech. … Ample Supreme Court precedent upholds … restrictions when designed to preserve the integrity of our political processes and public confidence therein."

A second point of contention is whether the type of lobbying that the revolving door promotes is democratic. Opponents of revolving-door restrictions contend that all citizens have somebody to represent them and, therefore, lobbying that is connected to the revolving door is democratic. A multitude of associations in Washington represent various age, sex, ethnic, and professional groups. It would therefore be undemocratic to disqualify some people from lobbying or to deny some groups access to people who have the influence that they may need to have their interests served.

The problem, according to advocates of restrictions, is that the revolving door grants some lobbyists greater power to influence legislation, thus enabling them to charge a very high fee for their services. What's undemocratic, say advocates of revolving-door restrictions, is that those at the upper end of the income scale can afford the very influential revolving-door lobbyists—such as Michael Deaver or James Watt—while those with lower incomes cannot. David Luban, a research scholar at the University of Maryland's Institute for Philosophy and Public Policy, feels that "the idea that everyone's represented [by lobbying groups] is pretty illusory. … The more diffuse a group is, the harder it is to represent all the interests of that group." Thus, the less-diffuse wealthy groups have a better chance of being served than lower-income, more-diffuse groups.

Luban and other supporters of lobbying restrictions feel that the revolving-door phenomenon also carries the potential for being undemocratic because many revolving-door veterans—with their influence—may, in effect, run the country while no one really knows it and while there is no way to control it. This can have a very corrupting and unhealthy effect on government.

In contrast, opponents of revolving-door restrictions feel that the revolving door is healthy because it helps attract talented people to government service. In order to serve in government, talented lawyers and businesspeople may give up lucrative positions in law firms or businesses. If there was no possibility of economically benefiting from their expertise gained while in government, the most talented might not be interested in serving in government.

(continues)

Should Former Members of Congress or Congressional Staff Be Restricted from Lobbying?, *continued*

Thus, they deserve to sell their expertise and their influence to organizations that can afford to pay them once they give up their government service.

Furthermore, the turnover created by revolving-door opportunities is healthy because it enables more talented people to become involved in government at the executive branch. Advocates of revolving-door restrictions counter this by arguing that it is not the government's responsibility to oversee the economic well-being of former officials, nor is it the government's obligation to let former officials profit economically from the expertise they gained at government expense.

This debate is summarized from Sarah Glazer's "Getting a Grip on Influence Peddling," Congressional Quarterly's Editorial Research Reports, 2(22) (December 15, 1989): 698–711. Reprinted by permission.

corporations that generally own them. Few newspapers, for example, are still locally owned and compete with other locally owned newspapers. Gannett Company dominates the newspaper business, owning a national newspaper, USA Today, plus local newspapers, radio and television stations, and even most of the nation's billboards. There are only a few major television networks, including ABC, CBS, NBC, and FOX. Thus, information about politics may be severely limited, and the information presented may represent only the viewpoint of the mass-media owners.

The federal government also provides information to its citizens regarding health, agriculture, education, labor, housing, and population statistics. This information is dispensed in a variety of ways, through county agricultural agents, public health centers, libraries, newspapers, radio, and television. Many of the statistics used by sociologists are collected and published by government agencies. Sociologists are well aware, however, that the government also attempts to shape public opinion, and it sometimes reports information that presents a misleading description of a problem. Government unemployment figures, for example, count only those unemployed persons who are still known to be actively seeking work; they do not report the number of people who have given up the search for a job. This practice artificially lowers the statistics on unemployment in the country.

Political Participation

The United States has one of the lowest voter turnouts in the democratic world. In 1996, 82.3 percent (105 million) of registered voters chose to vote (see Figure 15-1). Of those registered to vote in the 2000 presidential election, 18.7 million (14.5 percent) chose not to vote. Voter turnout hurts the Democratic party because the blocks of people who do not vote—the young, the poor, and blacks—are statistically more apt to be Democratic. When voter turnout is low, the Republican party is more likely to win elections, and social programs that help the poor and minority groups are more likely to be ignored.

A variety of explanations for the lack of voter participation have been proposed: One set of explanations

FIGURE 15-1 PARTICIPATION IN PRESIDENTIAL ELECTIONS, 1968–2000

Source: U.S. Census Bureau, *Current Population Reports*. "Voting and Registration in the Election of November 2000." Series P20-542, February 2002.

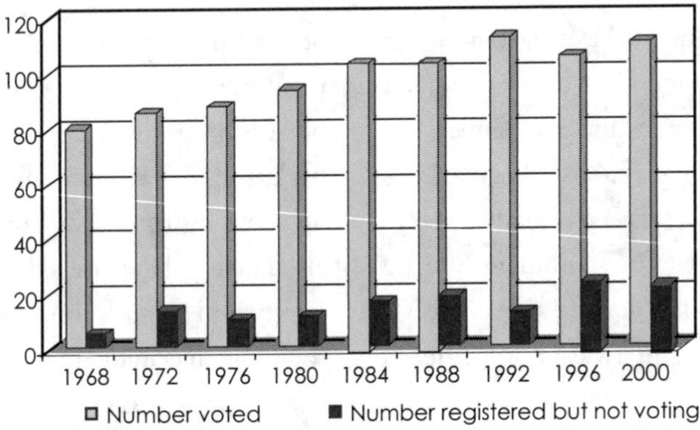

attributes the lack of voter participation to social-psychological reasons, the attitude of the voter. For example, potential voters stay away from the polls because they may believe that their vote does not make a difference, or because they do not feel any civic obligation to participate, or they do not like either party's candidates, or they are satisfied with both parties' candidates, or they lack the education to know either the importance of voting or the issues being considered, or they are too young or too poor to care—in a word, they are *apathetic*. Those who believe that social-psychological reasons are the reasons that people do not vote also tend to believe that if government is less than perfect, the voters have no one to blame but themselves. If they seek change, they should give politics more attention.

However, critics of this theory argue that people are not staying away from the polls because of apathy. In this nation, before the twentieth century, and in other nations currently, people have participated at much greater rates than they do in the United States now (see Table 15-1). The young, the poor, and the less educated all vote as often as the old, the rich, and the more educated in most European nations. If apathy and social-psychological attitudes

TABLE 15-1 RANKING OF VOTER TURNOUT PERCENTAGES IN DEMOCRATIC NATIONS

Country	Percentage
1. Belgium	93
2. Italy	89
3. Luxembourg	87
4. Sweden	86
5. Austria	86
6. Iceland	86
7. Denmark	83
8. Norway	83
9. Germany	78
10. Greece	77
11. United Kingdom	76
12. Finland	72
13. Spain	70
14. Portugal	68
15. Ireland	69
16. France	65
17. United States	38

Source: *The Almanac of European Politics Congressional Quarterly*, 1995.

SOCIOLOGY AT WORK

Sociology and Municipal Politics

Karen George earned her B.A. and M.A. in sociology at Wayne State University. George has been a councilwoman in the city of Southgate, Michigan, since 1983. Besides serving as councilwoman, she is a licensed cosmetologist and has worked as a secretary, matron, police cadet, and part-time instructor in sociology. She decided to major in sociology after having been involved with the public for many years in a variety of different roles. "I have always been a people watcher and can just sit and watch different groups in a mall," George says. "Having worked with people in such a variety of settings led me to wonder why different groups dressed and acted in the manner in which they did. Sociology gave me some of the answers."

George feels that sociology has been particularly useful to her in her position as city council-woman. "In my present position as an elected official, I am accountable to all the citizens of the city of Southgate and not to one person or employer. However, I feel that my sociology background has made me much more sensitive to understanding the needs of different groups and individuals. Having been raised in a very traditional religious family and white suburban middle class neighborhood, sociology has made me remove my blinders of prejudice and be more tolerant to those whose lifestyles differ from mine.

"Being in a political position, I could at times take advantage of my position. I must admit that it has opened doors that would not have been opened otherwise. I have experienced first-hand discrimination that went on in me 'before' and 'after' holding public office. My sociological background has helped me to

are to explain a lack of voter participation, such explanations ought to hold in other twentieth-century democratic, industrialized societies, as they do in the United States.

Critics of social-psychological theories argue that the reasons for a lack of voter participation are found in the social structure of voting procedures. Piven and Cloward (1989), for example, argue that voter participation in this country was high before 1880, and many of the issues in elections were populist issues that stimulated the participation of farmers and of the working class. However, after the election of 1880, powerful business leaders formed oligarchies in both parties, and as both parties then supported business issues almost exclusively, competition between the parties collapsed. The populists were shut out of party politics.

The business leaders of both parties were concerned about the waves of immigrants flowing into this country and wanted to restrict their power to influence elections, and they were concerned about the power that black people had been developing since the Civil War. In order to restrict these groups, they instituted reforms dealing with registration and voting procedures. They instituted poll taxes, official ballots, registration lists that required a worker to be away from work in order to get on the list, literacy tests, residency requirements, and other complicated voting procedures. While many of these restrictions have been declared illegal, the procedures for registering and voting are still burdensome in this country (Piven and Cloward, 1989). Registration sometimes requires traveling to the county seat or even to the state capital. In addition to the diffi-

Sociology and Municipal Politics, *continued*

realize that groups will always be in competition with one another. In the political arena, one gets used to a constant power struggle. Conflict theory has helped me understand that politics is much more than a matter of individual personalities. I have come to understand the ways in which groups can use their respective power in order to attempt to obtain what they want."

George notes that sociology has given her more than just an overall perspective that she takes to her political career. Specific sociological knowledge also helps her to serve her constituency better. "My sociology background has made me aware of many aspects of the socialization process. This has made me especially sensitive to the needs of the youth in our cities. I am also keenly sensitive to the needs of single-parent households. The traditional two-parent family is 'history' even in my small homogenous community. The course in the family that I took helped me to view the traditional family and newer family forms in proper perspective. This knowledge has been invaluable to me when dealing with matters that affect children and single-parent households."

Finally, George says that sociology has helped her get beyond simply using common sense. "Sociology as a science has helped me to examine the facts and not to simply see things as they may appear. Many times our common sense leads us to believe one way, while the facts point in another direction." George believes that having this perspective is essential for someone who is in a position to influence the way in which a municipality operates.

culties of registering to vote, there are too many elections, too many elected officials, and too many **referenda**—that is, questions on the ballot concerning everything from building roads to changing the qualifications of elected officials. In some countries, registration is automatic when the voter reaches an eligible age. In other countries, voting is mandatory, and people who do not vote are fined.

The people in the United States who do vote tend to remain very loyal to either the Republican or the Democratic party, a loyalty based primarily on emotional ties formed during the earlier socialization process. Approximately 90 percent of both parties voted for their own party affiliation in the 2004 election(CNN Election Poll, 2004). Most people do not choose a party on the basis of political opinions, usually because they are not well informed about political issues, and the parties do not differ significantly on most issues. Instead, they affiliate with a party and then are educated by the party's stand on the issues. Because they are loyal to their party, they accept the stand of the party. In an interesting study, Heritage and Greatbatch (1986) found that people interrupt political speeches with applause after emotion-laden slogans, not after informative analyses of domestic or foreign affairs.

While on most issues, the voters will accept the stand taken by their party, this is not true of the so-called moral issues, such as race, sexual behavior, and religion. People usually have a strong opinion on moral issues, and they will leave their party and either will not vote or else will vote for the other party if they disagree with their own party's stand. As a result, political parties generally try to avoid

TABLE 15-2 WHO VOTED IN THE LAST PRESIDENTIAL ELECTION?

Voted by Race:	Percentage
White	77%
African-American	11%
Latino	2%
Voted by Age:	**Percentage**
18-29 year olds	17%
30-44 year olds	29%
45-59 year olds	30%
60-older	24%
Voted by Income:	**Percentage**
Under $15,000	8%
$15,000-30,000	15%
$30,000-50,000	22%
$50,000-75,000	23%
Voted by Education:	**Percentage**
No high school diploma	4%
High school graduate	22%
Some college	32%
College graduate	26%

Source: *CNN Election Poll, 2004.*

moral issues altogether and take a middle-of-the-road stand on other issues, to attract the largest number of voters.

Some groups outside of the major political parties have attempted to bring moral issues into politics. They recognize that a large minority of people often can be easily influenced by emotional issues, and they have used these issues to attract followers. They cannot, however, attract the majority of voters. If the majority of the voters agreed, for example, that abortions should be outlawed, the major political parties would also express that belief, and the issue would cease to be divisive.

Thinking Sociologically

1. What features of the United States political system increase legitimate authority?
2. Given our low voter turnout, is legitimate authority decreasing?
3. Are the social values reflected in the United States political system the values of all the people or the values only of more powerful people?

SUMMARY

1. A society's *political institution* is the structure that has the power to rule in a society. Power is the ability to control the behavior of others. Politics is the use of power to determine who gets what in society.
2. Two types of power are physical force and latent force. Physical force is an inefficient way to control a society. *Latent force,* making people comply by threatening them with punishment, is more effective.
3. *Authority* is the most effective means of power and is considered legitimate because the people believe that the ruler has a right to rule, so they comply voluntarily. *Traditional authority* is derived from accepted practices or customs. *Legal authority* is based on a system of legislated rules and regulations. *Charismatic authority* comes from the personal traits of the leader.
4. Structural functionalists believe that political systems reflect societal values. If a society values freedom, monogamy, hard work, and achieve-

ment, laws will be passed to enforce these values, and members of the society will comply with the law because it reflects their own beliefs.

5. Structural functionalists also believe that the political system must try to resolve conflicts in values. The value of freedom, for example, may come into conflict with the value of hard work, and the government must arbitrate to ensure that behavior does not infringe on either value. Some subcultures teach values that conflict with those of the larger society, but the government must protect the values of the dominant society.

6. Conflict theorists believe that some groups gain power because they possess a large share of society's resources. They use these resources to acquire power and use the law and the political system to protect their own wealth. The rich teach the population through the schools and the mass media that their wealth, power, and laws are legitimate. In other words, they shape the values of the society to serve their own interests.

7. Modern societies have two types of legal power structures: democratic systems and totalitarian systems. *Democratic systems* allow citizens to participate in their own governance. *Totalitarian systems* have powerful governments that control the society.

8. The French government is a democracy with elected officials and appointed civil servants. The French bureaucracy is very complex and powerful, and the civil servants often play very important roles in both government and business.

9. The Union of Soviet Socialist Republics (USSR) had been a totalitarian society with a very powerful single political party, the members of which played the most powerful roles in the government. Changes are now being made in their political system, to dissolve the union and create various independent republics.

10. Debate about how power is distributed in the United States has continued for many years. Theorists have argued on the one hand that a power elite made up of business and government officials controls the power, and on the other hand that there are a variety of diversified groups that protect their own interests.

11. In the United States, socialization legitimates legal authority, and political socialization begins early. Youngsters learn about political leaders and political parties at home and in the community. Socialization continues in school, and most children learn to respect the political system, although poor children are more likely to question government and its practices.

12. Voter participation is low in this country. Social-psychological explanations do not fully explain why voters do not vote. Instead, the structure of our political parties and our registration and voting procedures explains much of our low voter participation.

13. Most Americans remain loyal to one political party and permit it to guide them on important issues. On moral issues, however, voters tend to act more independently.

KEY TERMS

authority Power accepted as legitimate by those it affects.

charismatic authority Authority granted to someone on the bases of his or her personality characteristics.

citizen One who is considered a member of a state and who is entitled to the privileges and freedoms granted to members of the state.

city-state A city and the surrounding area ruled independently of other areas.

democracy A power structure in which people govern themselves, either directly or through elected representatives.

incumbent One holding an elected office.

iron law of oligarchy In democratic societies, the inevitable rise of a few elite leaders who dominate power.

latent force A type of power in which force is threatened.

legal authority Authority based on a system of rules and regulations that determine how a society will be governed.

legitimate power Controlling the behavior of others through having people accept the authority as necessary and beneficial to all.

lobby An organization of people who want to influence the political process on a specific issue.

nation-states Large territories ruled by a single political institution.

oligarchy Government by a small elite group.

physical force A type of power backed by sheer force such as an army or physical might.

political action committees (PACs) Organizations formed to raise money for a political campaign.

political parties Groups of citizens formed with the express intent of gaining control of the political body of the state.

political pluralism A political system in which many diverse groups have a share of the power.

politics The use of power to determine who gets what in society.

power The ability to control or influence the behavior of others, even without their consent.

power elite A small group of people who hold all of the powerful positions and cooperate to maintain their social positions.

referenda Questions on a ballot to be decided by the electorate.

states Societies with institutional government and laws as a means of political regulation, a military defense, and a way to finance these activities.

totalitarianism A power structure in which the government has total power to dictate the values, rules, ideology, and economic development of a society.

traditional authority The right to rule granted to someone on the basis of tradition, as with a patriarch or king.

DISCUSSION QUESTIONS

1. Discuss how knowledge of different types of power could be useful in your everyday life. Use examples of specific social situations in which you are routinely involved.
2. Discuss the advantages of authority as a source of power.
3. Select a policy or a piece of legislation currently in the news, and examine it from the structural functional and conflict perspectives on political systems.
4. Discuss which would be a more efficient form of government—democracy or totalitarianism.

5. Has the bureaucracy played similar roles in the French, Soviet, and United States governments? Does it make these governments more or less democratic?

6. Discuss whether you think that power in the United States is monopolized by a few—as in the military–industrial complex—or is broadly distributed, as in a pluralistic model.

7. Discuss the advantages and disadvantages of a one-party political system, a two-party political system, and a political system with multiple parties.

8. What kinds of abuses might result from PACs and lobbies?

9. Examine your own political attitudes and how they have been developed through socialization.

10. Do you believe that a political party educates voters who have chosen the party, or do voters choose a party after educating themselves on issues? Discuss how this difference shapes the nature of authority.

Economic Groups and Systems

Multinational Corporations

Chapter 8 examined the growing income gap between the rich and the poor. Significantly, the growth of inequality in the United States is most prevalent among people who are employed. That is, the growing gap between rich and poor is not necessarily the result of unemployment but can be explained as a function of the type of employment that is available in America. "The American economy," according to political economist Robert B. Reich, "is creating a wider range of earnings than at any other time in the postwar era. The most basic reason, put simply, is that America itself is ceasing to exist as a system of production and exchange separate from the rest of the world" (Reich, 1989, p. 23). What Reich is alluding to is that an increase in the number of multinational corporations—corporations that do not confine their operation to their own country—is dramatically affecting the labor market in the United States.

Briefly, new technologies that enable almost instant communication and rapid transportation around the world—such as advanced telecommunications and computer networks, fax communications, and even the Concorde—have helped restructure corporations, particularly in America. American industries are no longer solely American, nor are Japanese industries solely Japanese, and so on. A company may have its headquarters in the United States; its production facilities in a less developed country where it can procure cheaper labor, pay less taxes, and have fewer environmental regulations, and have its marketing divisions spread across a number of countries. The result is that in their efforts to increase profits, many U.S. multinational corporations that have their production facilities abroad—such as the Chrysler facility in Tolucan, Mexico—have eliminated many of their production jobs at home. "So," as Reich (1989) comments, "when General Motors, say, is doing well, that probably is good news for a lot of executives in Detroit, and for GM shareholders across the globe, but it isn't necessarily good news for a lot of assembly-line workers in Detroit, because there may, in fact, be very few GM assembly-line workers in Detroit, or anywhere else in America" (p. 26).

A *New York Times* article (2004) confirms this trend of an earnings gap between the highest paid employees and the rest of the workforce over a period of 30 years. "The trend is most striking in factories, which accounted for the bulk of job losses in the last three years and tended to pay above-average wages" (Andrews, 2004). A recent survey conducted by the Labor Department determined that 57 percent of displaced workers who had found another job were earning less than they did in their old jobs (Andrews, 2004). Therefore, the impact might in fact be much harder for factory workers when adjusting to unemployment or a new job.

Translated into employment opportunities, this means that people who have the higher level communication, research, and problem-solving skills that are valuable and useful to the operation of a corporation—managers, accountants, consultants, lawyers, advertisers, investment bankers, research scientists, public relations executives, and many other such professionals—are in more demand and thus paid more, while those with routine production skills—for example, assembly-line workers, equipment operators, skilled craftspeople—are in less demand and thus paid less.

Sociologists are interested in studying the growth of multinational corporations for a variety of reasons. Specifically, the issue can be used to examine the functions and dysfunctions of some types of economic systems, such as capitalism. On a general level, the issue calls attention to some of the ways in which social institutions are shaped, and it demonstrates the impact of social institutions and social systems on individuals. Do social systems reflect the values of a society and work to meet basic social needs, or do they reflect the values and work to meet the needs of those who have the power to shape them? Insights into how economic systems are shaped, their affect on labor markets, their impact on individual job opportunities and wages, and other such matters can be gained by examining multinational corporations.

To survive, people need food, shelter, and health care. Except for those who live in the tropics, people also need clothing and a source of heat. To be accepted in modern American society, however, we need a great deal more—soap, deodorant, toothpaste, shoes, and various types of clothes for different occasions. We also enjoy the luxuries our society provides: plates, knives, forks, furniture, cars, sporting equipment, radios, televisions, the internet, I-pods, palm pilots, and so on. All these things, from the most basic necessities to the most expensive luxuries, are produced by our economic system.

The **economic system** is the social system that provides for the production, distribution, and consumption of goods and services. Sociologists study the economic system because it is a major social institution that influences every aspect of society. Sociologists are not economists, however. Economists study the internal workings of the economic system: supply and demand, how much industry is producing, how much consumers are buying, how much government is taxing, borrowing, and spending, and so on. Sociologists, on the other hand, study how the economic system interacts with other social institutions. They study types of economic systems, the size and power of corporations, the occupations of the people in economic systems, how work affects the rest of our lives, and similar issues.

Although sociologists and economists do not study the economy in the same way, they actually cover much of the same material. Economists cannot understand the success or failure of an economic system without considering how it interacts with the rest of society. Sociologists cannot understand how social systems interact unless they understand the internal functioning of each system. Nevertheless, the disciplines have different goals. Economists specialize in studying the economic system as one of society's important interacting parts. Sociologists study the whole of society, including the economic system.

APPLYING SOCIOLOGICAL PERSPECTIVES ON ECONOMIC GROUPS AND SYSTEMS

Developing a sociological perspective about the nature of economic groups and systems is useful in a variety of ways. For example, all of us can learn a great deal about different societies by understanding their economic systems. In addition, sociological perspectives can aid individuals who have specialized interests. For example, politicians can gain important insights because an important aspect of international politics concerns the economic relationships among countries (for example, trade agreements regarding goods, such as oil, wheat, or other natural resources). International business executives need to understand the relationship between social systems and economic systems, to make prudent business decisions. In addition, on a personal level, individual investors in stocks, bonds, mutual funds, and so on can benefit from insights that may help them understand and predict trends in foreign markets. The world of business and investments is no longer limited to the country of residence or of origin. The practical need to understand the relationship between social systems and economic systems has never been greater and is likely to continue to grow.

TYPES OF ECONOMIC SYSTEMS

To produce goods and services for a society, an economic system requires land on which to produce food and to build factories. It also needs raw materials, tools, and machinery to process them, and it needs labor. Economic systems in modern societies vary according to who owns the land, the factories, the raw materials, and the equipment. These *means of production* may be *privately owned*—that is, owned by individuals, or they may be *publicly owned* by the state. **Capitalism** is a system based on private ownership. **Socialism** is a system based on state ownership of the means of production. Once again, these pure economic systems are only ideal types. In practice, in capitalist societies, some property is owned by the state, and in socialist societies, some property is privately owned, such as small plots of land used to grow food for the local market. No society is purely capitalist or purely socialist. *Mixed economies*, in which private and public ownership are both practiced extensively, are called **welfare capitalism or democratic socialism**.

Although all existing economic systems are based on capitalism, socialism, or some combination of the two, one other system deserves mention, even though it has never been developed in a major nation. **Communism** is an economic system that is the goal of communist political parties throughout the world. It is a system in which the ownership of the means of production is held in common by all citizens. A society's economic system has a powerful influence on how it produces and distributes goods.

Capitalism

The United States has a capitalist economic system; that is, the means of production, the land and the factories, are owned by one or more individuals. Most large corporations are owned by the many groups and individuals who own stock, stock being shares of the corporation. Many small businesses are owned by one person, a family, or a few individuals. Individuals who own the means of production are *capitalists*. In this sense, most Americans are not capitalists because they do not derive income from owning a business. They may own cars, clothes, and television sets, but these are consumer goods. They do not provide profit to the owner. Even homes that increase in value over the years and that produce a profit when sold do not produce income when they are used by the owners as a personal residence. Capitalists earn income from what they own; consumers spend income for what they own.

Capitalism is a **market economy**—that is, the goods sold and the price at which they are sold are determined by the people who buy them and the people who sell them. Products no one wants to buy or sell are not traded. If everyone needs a product—fuel, for example—the product will be sold for as much money as people will pay for it. In a **free-market** system, all people are theoretically free to buy, sell, and make a profit if they can, although there are prohibitions against selling some things, such as illegal drugs, and some services, such as sexual favors. The free-market system is the reason that capitalism is so strongly associated with freedom.

Socialism

Socialism differs from capitalism, in that the means of production are owned by the state. Socialist systems are designed to ensure that all members of the society have some share of its wealth. Ownership is social rather than private. So-called communist systems, such as in Cuba, are actually socialist systems because the government owns all of the industries in the country.

Socialism also differs from capitalism in that the economy is not controlled by the marketplace. It has a **planned economy**—the government first decides what goods the society needs, what are luxuries, and what can be done without altogether; then it controls what will be produced and consumed and sets prices for these goods. Thus, there is no free market. The Soviet Union, for example, faced with a severe housing shortage after World War II, gave high priority to building low-cost housing for its population but gave very low priority to building automobiles.

Welfare Capitalism

Welfare capitalism, sometimes called "democratic socialism," is found in most western European countries. In Sweden and Great Britain, some industries are privately owned, and others are state owned. Generally, the state owns the industries most vital to the country's well-being, such as the railroads and the communications industry. The most crucial needs—medical care, education, and old-age benefits—are paid for by the government with tax dollars. As a result, the taxes in welfare capitalist countries are quite high in order to pay for these benefits.

Whether a country is more or less capitalistic can sometimes be determined by comparing the taxes collected to the **gross national product (GNP)**, the total value of the goods and the services that the country produces in a year. Often, the greater the proportion of the GNP that goes to taxes, the more social programs the country has. The GNP includes all necessities, luxuries, and military supplies produced for a price. It does not include anything not produced for profit. The worth of the work of housewives, for example, is the largest item not included in the GNP. As you can see from Table 16-1 (Scaruffi, 2000), GNP in the United States is high compared to other countries.

The GNP does not indicate what the various countries produce, nor does it show what tax dollars are spent for. The United States, which spends much of its tax money on the armed forces, includes military spending in its GNP. Many other countries, on the other hand, spend little of their tax revenue on the military and spend a great deal on health, social planning, and the reduction of poverty. As a result, these countries—such as Canada, France, the Netherlands, Norway, Spain, Sweden, and Switzerland—all have populations with longer life expectancies than are found in the United States (*The World Factbook*, 2004). These countries have combined capitalism with social programs paid for through taxation and government spending programs.

The United States ranks 49 in life expectancy at birth among a comparison of international countries (see Table 16-2).

TABLE 16-1 INTERNATIONAL COMPARISONS, PER CAPITA (IN THOUSAND DOLLARS) AND GROSS NATIONAL PRODUCT

Country	Per Capita	GNP
United States	$38	$10,533
Japan	$38	$4,852
Sweden	$31	$275
Netherlands	$27	$429
Britain	$26	$1,544
Canada	$24	$760
Italy	$22	$1,260
Spain	$16	$651
Argentina	$8	$300
Mexico	$6	$578
China	$1	$1,329

TABLE 16-2 LIFE EXPECTANCY AT BIRTH, 2004

Country	World Rank	Expectancy in Years
Switzerland	7	80.31
Sweden	8	80.30
Canada	12	79.96
France	16	79.44
Spain	19	79.37
Norway	20	79.25
Netherlands	30	78.68
United States	49	77.43

For a complete list of life expectancies at birth, refer to (www.worldbank.org/data/) and *The World Factbook* (2004).

Communism—A Utopian Idea

Communism is an economic system that does not exist in any of the world's larger societies. The basic premise of communism is that all property should be held in common and that distribution of goods and services should be based on the principle developed by Marx (1964, p. 258), "From each according to his ability, to each according to his needs!" Thus, in the ideal communist society, workers would do their best to serve the needs of the society and would be assured of receiving whatever they needed.

Communism has been achieved in some small communities. It was especially popular in the nineteenth century in the United States, when there were an estimated 100 communes with a total of more than 100,000 members (Etzioni-Halevy, 1997). Most were formed by religious sects, such as the Shakers, Rappists, Zoarites, Amana Communists, and Perfectionists. One notable example was the Oneida community in Oneida, New York. All members of this religious society shared the property, buildings, and industries of the community. They also shared the work, rotating in their jobs so that no one would long suffer the burden of the heaviest or the least pleasant work, and no one would become attached to a particular job. Work was done by groups, so that fellowship was a part of cooking, cleaning, farming, and whatever else had to be done. There was no monogamous marriage, which they believed would have implied the ownership of another person. The birth of children was planned by the community, and when children were born, they were members of the community, not possessions of their parents. The Oneida community was very successful in carrying out its ideal of communism, and its members were very happy with their fellowship and security. However, neighbors of the commune did not approve of their practices, especially their lack of marriage, and the community was forced to disband.

Communist communities have also been popular in the twentieth century—especially in Europe in the 1930s and in the United States in the 1970s. Most of the recent communes were not religious groups. They did not put a strong emphasis on work, and they failed because they could not sustain themselves.

Communism, like socialism, requires a major redistribution of wealth. Individuals would no longer own the farms, factories, and other means of production. Many capitalists, in fact, confuse socialist systems with communist systems and use these words almost interchangeably. They are, however, very different systems. In socialism, the government controls the economy. In communism, the people themselves control the economy.

THEORIES OF ECONOMIC DEVELOPMENT

Historically, capitalism became the dominant economic system in Europe during the Industrial Revolution. How did this system develop, and why does it persist? Theorists have been considering this question for several centuries. As in so many areas of sociological inquiry, two basic perspectives have evolved—structural functionalism and conflict theory.

Structural Functional Theory

As discussed previously, structural functional theory suggests that social systems reflect the values of a society and work to meet basic social needs. According to this perspective, the capitalist economic system reflects the social values a society places on the freedom of the individual to accumulate and own private property. Especially in the United States, capitalism is highly valued, and welfare programs are hotly debated. The capitalist system has evolved because immigrants coming to this country brought with them the desire to be free to determine their own economic welfare.

Functionalists argue that capitalism succeeds so well because it meets basic needs. Conservative economists have been describing capitalism as a vast cooperative system for centuries. In *The Wealth of Nations*, written in 1776, Adam Smith pointed out the beautiful balance that is achieved in the ideal functioning of the capitalist economy. This balance, which we know as the "law of supply and demand," ensures that social needs will be met because it is profitable to meet them. When there is a demand, someone will profit from supplying it. People need food, clothing, and medical care, for example, and huge industries have developed to meet these needs. By tending to their self-interests, this theory suggests, everyone who produces a necessary product or service will profit and will thereby benefit both themselves and society.

In recent years, structural functionalists have been concerned about the large number of people who seem unable to find profitable means of supporting themselves. Most structural functionalists do not fault the capitalistic system, but they do recognize that some dysfunctions make it difficult for some individuals and groups to have an equal opportunity in the marketplace. A child raised in an urban ghetto or on an impoverished Indian reservation is unlikely to get the education needed to land jobs that pay well. Even when members of minority groups do manage to get a good education, racism and stereotyping may prevent them from finding a profitable occupation. As a result, the benefits of a capitalistic system are not equally available to all. Another dysfunction concerns the development of monopolies, which limit competition and thereby narrow the range of opportunities available in the marketplace. When one corporation dominates the sale of a good or service, it disrupts the market economy and can set its own price.

APPLYING STRUCTURAL FUNCTIONAL PERSPECTIVES OF ECONOMIC SYSTEMS

According to the structural functional perspective, because capitalism reflects our primary American value of individualism, capitalist policies assume that the individual alone is solely responsible for his or her life chances. Understanding the functions and dysfunctions of such capitalist policies—or those of any economic system, for that matter—is essential for policymakers. To create effective economic policies that benefit all people in a society, policymakers would do well to consider both the functions and dysfunctions of particular economic systems, regardless of their reflection of social values. Unfortunately, values—not rationality—form the basis of most public policy (and politicians risk losing public support and reelection when they lose sight of this). Rice (1985) suggests, for example, that it would be rational to have an economic policy in which the government regulates the cost and supply of oil, to prevent the oil market from being monopolized by a few giant corporations, but the American value of individualism—as reflected in free enterprise—prohibits this.

Most of you will not be in a position to affect national economic policies, but many of you will be involved in work or business situations that may be arranged to reflect individualism. For example, suppose that you are the manager or owner of a retail clothing store, and you hope to achieve high sales by basing your employees' salaries on the number of sales each makes. Although individual competition might stimulate them to work harder initially, the store might eventually suffer from this policy. The competition for sales could lead to a lack of trust and lower morale among the sales personnel, and thus to a weakened work team. Some employees might quit because they are dissatisfied with working conditions. Time and money would then be lost to hiring and training new personnel. What seems like a good idea theoretically might turn out, in reality, to contain some serious dysfunctions that could undermine your original goals. By realizing that business and economic policies contain dysfunctions as well as functions and by trying to anticipate what they might be, you might be able to avoid some problems before they arise.

Conflict Theory

In the *Communist Manifesto,* Marx described the development of both capitalism and communism as historical events. When most people produced needed goods directly from farming, there was an agricultural economic system. As industrialization developed and trading of manufactured articles increased, however, the economy came to be based on money, or capital. Marx realized that as some people increased their store of capital, they would be able to buy more and more factories and other means of production. Those who did not own any means of production would be forced to sell their only asset—their labor—to the factory owners. As the owners grew richer and more powerful, they would buy up more and more of the means of production and would force still more people to rely on their labor for subsistence. Eventually, Marx believed, the number of workers would grow so large that competition would reduce wages to a minimum, and an entire class of impoverished workers would develop. He felt that conditions among the working class would ultimately deteriorate to the point that they would revolt, overthrow the owners, and develop a system in which the means of production would be owned communally and would be operated for the benefit of all.

Max Weber (1946) agreed with Marx's fundamental view of the economic order, but he differed slightly in his assessment of the means and outcome of oppression. Weber was concerned with the growth of bureaucracy. Bureaucracies operate in accordance with rational rules and procedures rather than humanitarian principles. With the compartmentalization of responsibility, it would be possible for a company to become extremely ruthless in the pursuit of profit, even if it meant that thousands of workers and the population at large would suffer. Those who made the decisions would be far removed from those who actually carried them out and who were in a position to observe their consequences. Weber was less optimistic than Marx, believing that eventually bureaucracies would grow so rich and powerful that no human effort could dislodge them. Even today, some conflict theorists contend that giant multinational corporations are too powerful to be controlled by individuals—or even nations—and that the world will come under progressively greater corporate control.

THE AMERICAN ECONOMIC SYSTEM

Most American citizens are convinced that the capitalist system is good and cherish the freedom of the marketplace, the freedom to buy, sell, and earn a living in any way they can. We value these freedoms as much as we value our religious freedom, and in fact, the two systems arise out of the same tradition.

In *The Protestant Ethic and the Spirit of Capitalism* (1905), Weber discussed the Puritans' influence on the American desire for profit. He noted that capitalism, the exchange of goods for profit, has existed at one time or another in all societies. In the United States, however, profit became a major goal, desired not simply to provide for one's daily needs, but to accumulate wealth.

The Puritans were *Protestant Calvinists:* Their doctrine stated that most people lived in sin but that a few had been predestined for everlasting life by the grace of God. No one on this earth could affect that predestination; people's fates were sealed by God. The chosen were on earth to build God's kingdom as God intended.

How did people know whether they were among the elect? They could not know, but it was believed that those who were involved in the work of the world, who appeared to be building God's kingdom, must be among the elect. Those who spent their lives in idleness, carousing, drinking, and card-playing were obviously not doing God's work and obviously not among the chosen. The Calvinists feared death and sought confirmation that they were among the chosen. They worked to produce goods, taking wealth as a sign that they were among the chosen. They did not spend time or money on comforts, play, or anything else that might indicate that they were not chosen, nor did they associate with people whom they believed to be outside the elect. They worked, and they accumulated wealth, believing it to be an indication of self-worth. We now know this perspective as the **Protestant ethic**.

There is strong evidence that religious values play a role in present day economics as well. "Religion is an important factor in wealth accumulation . . . (it) keeps coming up in any model you run to explain wealth" (Keister, 2003). Even after considering other ways of accumulating wealth associated with particular denominations, such as inheritance, levels of education, and other factors, the effect of religion is still significant. According to the study, Keister found that families have a powerful influence on how people learn to save, and religion has a powerful impact on shaping family life. The religious beliefs children learn in their families translate into educational attainment, adult occupations, financial literacy, social connections, and other factors that influence adult wealth ownership, according to Keister. For example, conservative Protestants often emphasize prayer and trust in God to meet their needs, which may reduce their desire to invest. These same groups also look forward to the rewards of the afterlife and don't promote acquiring wealth as good for this life. Jews, on the other hand, don't have a strong orientation to the afterlife, but encourage pursuits that will lead to wealth accumulation, such as high-income careers and investing in this life.

Overall, the median net worth of Jewish people in the survey was $150,890, more than three times the median for the entire sample ($48,200); for conservative Protestants (which included Baptists, Jehovah's Witnesses, Seventh-Day Adventists, Christian Scientists, among others), the median net worth was $26,200, or about half the overall average; and median net worth of mainstream Protestants (including Episcopalians, Methodists, Presbyterians, Lutherans, Unitarians, and others) and Catholics were similar to each other, and fell at about the average for the whole sample (Keister, 2003).

Keister also found that people who regularly attended religious services tended to be wealthier. Going to religious services may provide another opportunity to be indoctrinated with beliefs that help build wealth. Also, attending services provides a social network of like others where one may meet contacts or learn investment tips.

Overall, the results of Keister's study demonstrate the importance of family socialization and processes in shaping wealth accumulation. Furthermore, the results underscore the importance of culture in shaping economic behavior and ultimately in creating social inequality.

The Growth of Large Corporations

The almost religious fervor with which we work for profit has contributed to the growth of large corporations. **Mass production** has also contributed to the growth of corporations. Building one car by hand is very expensive. Obviously, workers on an assembly line, using machinery, can assemble many identical parts and produce many cars in less time, at a lower cost per car. Robots cost even less than workers, and the cars can be sold at a much greater profit. Factories and mass production have replaced the shoemaker, the spinner, the weaver, the dressmaker, the furniture maker, the cigar maker, the glass blower, the potter, the butcher, the baker, and the candlestick maker. Factories, the specialized division of labor, and automation make it possible to mass produce goods that can be sold at low prices and still bring profit to the manufacturer.

Profits have also been increased by **vertical expansion** of businesses, in which a business owns everything from its raw materials to its retail outlets. If a business owns not only the factory that produces the goods but also the source of the raw materials purchased by the factory, the trucks that take the goods to market, and the stores that sell the products, the business can cut its costs at every step of the operation. It does not have to pay part of its profits to the owner of the raw material, the trucker, and the store owner. A business that owns all related businesses, from the raw material to the retailer can increase its profits at every stage of its operation.

American corporations have expanded their operations to control the entire process from raw material to retail sales (Zwerdling, 1976). A large food store chain, for example, may own thousands of food stores and more than a hundred manufacturing and processing plants, including bakeries, milk plants, ice cream plants, soft drink plants, meat processors, and coffee roasting plants. It may manufacture its own soap, peanut butter, and salad oil, and it might own a fleet of thousands of trucks to ship these products to its stores. Members of the board of directors of the chain would also sit on the boards of banks and corporations involved in agriculture, food production, food processing, food packaging, gas and electric power, and fuel oil. By owning or influencing every stage of production from the land on which the food is grown on to the retail sales outlets, such a chain becomes a very large corporation.

Horizontal expansion, another way to increase profits, refers to the practice of taking over similar businesses in order to gain a monopoly and reduce competition in the field. For example, a company that makes soup may buy all of the competing soup-making companies. Then, when a customer enters the grocery store, most of the soup available to buy is made by the same company, which can define the quality standards, set the price of soup, and not worry about losing sales to competition. That company controls the market.

Another form of expansion that assures continued profits is **diversification**—entering a variety of businesses in an attempt to ensure a stable rate of profit. Investors might buy a variety of stocks so that if one went down, another might remain stable or go up, and they would be protected from losing their entire investment. In the same way, corporations buy a variety of businesses so that those that are not highly profitable can be supported by those that are. Great Western United owns sugar companies, Shakey's Pizza, and large real estate holdings. The real estate is extremely valuable, but it does not provide income. By diversifying, Great Western United can support its real estate holdings with income from other sources. United States Steel Corporation, when the demand for steel fell, diversified by buying other companies and changing its name to USX.

The legally structured size of corporations tells only half the story of their tremendous power. Corporate links may join corporations that appear to be unrelated. When IBM was developing computers in a highly competitive market, IBM officers and directors were on the boards of Bankers Trust Company of New York, the Rockefeller Foundation, First National City Bank of New York, Chemical Bank, Federal Reserve Bank of New York, Morgan Guaranty Trust Company of New York, the J. P. Morgan Bank, and the United States Trust Company (DeLamarter, 1986). According to DeLamarter, these banks made it difficult for competitors of IBM to finance the development of their own computer products, thus aiding IBM in its domination of the field. As corporations grow larger and more powerful, they do not confine their operations to their own country, but instead expand internationally.

Multinational Corporations

Very large corporations own companies in one or more foreign nations, where they employ workers and produce and sell their products. These companies, as mentioned in the introduction, are known as **multinational corporations**. Ford Motor Company is a major example of a multinational corporation. In 1980, one-third of Ford employees were foreigners. In 2002, out of 280,000 workers and 108 plants worldwide, more than half of Ford's employees were foreigners, and 38 percent of Ford sales were in foreign countries (www.ford.com).

Most multinational corporations are owned by Americans. These companies often become involved in political arrangements made between the United States and other countries. They affect the economies of this country and those countries in which they have holdings in several ways: (a) They can buy foreign materials even when the United States would like to reduce overseas spending and would prefer that they "Buy American." (b) They can play one country against another, offering to build a plant in the one that gives them the greatest advantages in taxes, cheap labor, and freedom from regulation. (c) By closing plants, they can create unemployment problems. (d) In a sense, multinational corporations are above the laws of any nation because they can use their vast wealth and power to dominate a nation's economy or evade its laws. The annual sales of either General Motors or Exxon are greater than the GNP of countries such as Austria, Denmark, Norway, Greece, Portugal, and the smaller nations of the world. Corporations can borrow vast amounts of money on the basis of their sales; countries can tax only their GNP. As corporations increase in size, they gain progressively more power to dominate the economies of entire nations.

While the major increase in multinational business has been in the developed nations of the world, Third World nations have also been powerfully influenced by multinationals. Large agricultural corporations, for example, have converted large tracts of farmland into huge plantations, cultivated by modern machinery to produce cash crops for worldwide shipment. Del Monte and Dole grow pineapples in the Philippines and Thailand, where there is an abundance of cheap labor, and they then ship the pineapples to United States and Japanese markets. The Gulf and Western corporation controls land in the Dominican Republic, which is used to grow sugar for Gulf and Western's sugar mill. The large corporations often do not own the land, but enter into agreements with local landowners to grow what they need for their processing plants, and the local landowners and governments usually cooperate—even when the nutrition of their own local people suffers.

Multinational corporations have such a great impact on the nations in which they do business and are so influential in international relations that some observers believe that nations as we know them today will eventually vanish and that affairs of state will come to be run by the boards of directors of huge corporations. Whether this will happen and whether it would create a more peaceful and orderly world or more poverty for workers is still a matter of speculation, for now. In any case, as corporations change and grow, the nature of work also changes.

Thinking Sociologically

1. Evaluate the structural functional view that capitalism is efficient for a society, especially as corporations grow larger.

2. Evaluate Weber's stance that corporations are becoming so large that they could become ruthless in search of profits and have no regard for people.

3. If you were running a large organization, what would you consider the best way to manage your employees? Incorporating interactionist

principles, why would employers benefit by creating primary and in-group feelings among their employees? If you were a lower-level employee, would you agree?

THE CHANGING NATURE OF WORK

In simple agricultural societies, most people are **primary workers**. Those who grow food, who fish, who mine, or who otherwise produce raw materials are referred to as "primary workers" because their work is so essential to their country. In an industrial society such as our own, where most farming is done by machine, only a small portion of the population farms for a living. Most of the population works to produce manufactured goods; these workers are called **secondary workers**. They are the wage earners, the people on the assembly line, the construction workers, and the laborers in industry. The fastest-growing segment of the labor force consists of **tertiary** (or **service**) **workers**, which includes such people as police officers, doctors, lawyers, maids, and plumbers. The following sections describe the nature of secondary and tertiary work in modern society and discuss some important issues for these workers.

Factory Work and Alienation

In an earlier era, the cobbler or the candlestick maker developed a product from start to finish, sold it to the customer, took pride in the finished goods, and stood by his or her reputation as a skilled producer. The factory worker has none of these satisfactions, which has been a continuous problem for worker and manager alike.

Alienation is a term Marx used in describing the working conditions of the factory worker. Factory workers are alienated from their work because they have no control over it and derive no satisfaction from it. Their work involves only a part of the finished product, and they see neither the beginning nor the end of the process. They have no satisfaction in creating a product and no pride in selling it to the customer. They perform one routine task over and over again, and in return they receive money, which may or may not be enough to provide them with a satisfactory lifestyle outside of work.

Factory workers have been studied extensively since the turn of the century. Initially, most studies were designed to improve worker efficiency through scientific management, and this remains an important focus of research in the workplace. More recently, however, the human relations school of management has gained prominence; this perspective suggests that increasing worker satisfaction and decreasing alienation could also increase production.

SCIENTIFIC MANAGEMENT

Scientific management, a term coined by Frederick W. Taylor (1911), is management designed to improve worker efficiency. In an entrepreneurial setting, the workers own the business and are responsible for knowing the best way to do their own job. In companies that practice scientific management, the manager is assumed to know how to accomplish a task most efficiently. By keeping records and using a stopwatch, the manager determines rules for the most efficient work routine and then selects and trains workers to follow directions. The division of labor requires the manager to do the thinking and the worker to do the labor.

Taylor developed his program at Bethlehem Steel Company to improve the efficiency of workers loading pig iron (crude iron) into railroad cars. A crude casting of pig iron, often just called a "pig," weighed about 92 pounds; workers lifted a pig, carried it up a plank, and dropped it into a car. Before Taylor designed his scientific management plan, each worker loaded an average of 121/2 tons of pig iron a day. By carefully controlling the pace at which the workers lifted, walked up the plank, rested, and lifted again, Taylor found that he could get the workers to load 47 tons of pig iron a day, almost four times as much as they had been loading. The workers were rewarded with a pay increase of 60 percent, and the profit to the company was enormous.

Taylor (1911) described the best type of worker to handle pig iron as follows: "He shall be so stupid and so phlegmatic that he more nearly resembles in his mental make-up the ox than any other type" (p. 51). A man who was alert and intelligent would quickly be dissatisfied and bored with routine labor and the way it was scientifically managed. Nevertheless, scientific management played an important role in increasing the efficient use of workers; the fact that most workers were not as dumb as an ox was overlooked. The intelligence of human workers, however, eventually had to be considered, and it was at that point that the human relations school of management developed.

The Human Relations School

The **human relations school** of management considers the psychological makeup of workers, their attitudes toward management, peer pressures, and similar factors, in an attempt to promote worker efficiency. A scientific management study discovered the importance of human relations in the workplace by accident. In the now famous Hawthorne studies, experiments were done to improve the productivity of assembly-line workers making telephone equipment. As indicated by the Hawthorne effect, worker productivity did not increase as scientific management had expected—the workers responded to the attention they received from the researchers. More important, the study found that worker productivity depended on the informal group structure of the workers. When they were allowed to form their own working relationships and develop some of their own rules, they were much more cooperative with management, and their productivity increased. When they felt uneasy about changes handed down by management, they resisted these changes, and productivity did not increase. The findings of the Hawthorne studies made management aware of the importance of informal groups, worker attitudes toward management, and the effects of these factors on productivity.

The human relations school of worker management developed to probe these issues further. Its researchers studied the formal organization of the workplace, company rules and working conditions, and informal organization among the workers themselves, including their customs, traditions, routines, values, and beliefs (Roethlisberger and Dickson, 1939). The goal of these studies was to find the best type of person for the job and the best type of environment for maintaining and improving worker attitudes.

A classic study of employee values and their effect on productivity was done by Gouldner (1954), in a gypsum factory. Initially, the workers had been quite happy with their management, and management had been flexible with the workers. They were occasionally allowed to leave early for personal reasons, and they were sometimes allowed to take supplies for their personal use. They were also encouraged to discuss work problems with management and to make suggestions for improving working conditions. Managers and workers cooperated well together, and neither took advantage of the other.

Then, however, a new management team came to the company. To increase production, they adhered strictly to the rules. Workers were not allowed to leave early or to take supplies, nor were they given a chance to discuss problems with management. The workers, who valued the flexibility of the earlier managers, resented the enforcement of the rules. They believed that they were being treated with less respect, and they no longer cooperated with and supported the company.

APPLYING THE HUMAN RELATIONS MODEL

If you are involved in a management position, you might have the opportunity to apply the human relations model. Schrank (1979), an expert on the human relations style of management, is skeptical about the possibility of making routine work interesting, but he does feel that it is possible to encourage employees to work for you rather than against you and, thus, to increase productivity. Some fairly easy ways to accomplish this could be by having clean restrooms, pleasant dining areas, and an improved social atmosphere in the workplace. Telephones, vending machines, and lounges could be made available.

You may also find ways to apply this management technique in areas other than the office or the factory. You might, for example, become more effective as a teacher if you could encourage your students to work for you instead of against you. This might be achieved by creating an informal atmosphere in the classroom, having students call you by your first name, having an open-door policy with regard to your office hours, having lunch with students, attending campus events with students, or perhaps just by spending a few minutes a day in informal conversations with students. You already may have thought of other ways to encourage employees (or students) to work with you instead of against you.

Although there have been some gains in the area of human relations research during the past few decades, many workers in the United States are still frustrated in their jobs, and management continues to be frustrated with low productivity. In recent years, American managers have turned their attention to Japanese workers to try to understand why they are more productive than American workers.

Modern Trends in Management

The Japanese work force has proven itself to be exceptional in production and efficiency. This efficiency and productivity is attributed to two Japanese employee policies—lifetime jobs and quality control circles.

An article called "Unstoppable Canon" features Fujio Mitarai, president of Canon Corporation, who has succeeded in making the company one of the most profitable in the world (*Japan Today*, 2004). In Mitarai's seven years as president, Canon's total assets at the current market value increased to 4,400 billion yen, three times as much as when he took over. He maintains the life-time employment system, but has eliminated the seniority system from it. He sees speed of promotion as being important in American management, whereas in Japanese corporations, many retain the seniority system. Presidents of those companies reward employees who have worked the longest for their companies. Because many have life-time employment plans, Japanese corporations can pursue their businesses based on long-term plans. Furthermore, they have a system for consensus management, which eliminates the need for employees to take responsibility.

Lifetime jobs are held by only a third of Japanese men and by no women, and they are held only until age 55 or 60, which creates a hardship for workers when they are older. Nevertheless, a guaranteed job for even this short a "lifetime" creates security for the Japanese man—a security most American workers do not have because they can be fired or laid off at any time. The Japanese man is also encouraged to have close personal relationships with other workers, and to care about those in his work group just as he cares about his family. The group takes pride in its work, and its members do not need to compete as individuals. They are paid a low base pay and then receive a bonus, often 50 percent of base pay, on the basis of their productivity. The provision of lifetime jobs, commitment to the group, and high productivity works to everyone's advantage.

Knowing that long-term employment leads to efficient, high-quality production may be useful for you someday as an employer. You might not be able to guarantee your employees a lifetime job, but you might be able to provide an atmosphere and benefits that give employees a sense of security and belonging. This could entail having informal employer-employee interactions, discussing long-term company plans with employees, and in general soliciting feedback from your employees.

Quality control circles are meetings held by the group to improve its productivity. Orders do not come down from the manager, as they do in American bureaucracies; instead, the groups meet regularly to decide how their work can best be accomplished. They consider such problems as production, flow of work, work roles, worker-management relations, production schedules, improvements in the work environment, innovations in jobs, and ways of enhancing worker profitability, and then they make recommendations to management. If management approves the recommendations, the work group is allowed to change its procedures.

Although these management techniques seem quite revolutionary to American managers, who still value scientific management, efficiency experts, and stopwatches, quality control groups are being tried in a few American companies, with reported success.

Unionization

Workers have for years tried to improve their own working conditions and economic benefits through **unionization**, organizing workers to improve wages and working conditions. Unions can be traced back to the guilds of the Middle Ages, which protected skilled workers in the arts and crafts. As factories developed, workers formed unions to better their work environments. In the United States, skilled artisans were unionized before 1800, and women textile workers united in the early 1800s to protest working conditions in factories.

The later part of the nineteenth century was a period of intense labor-union struggle and conflict, and the result of this struggle continues to shape labor unions today. There was a strong and popular socialist movement in the United States during this period, which was influenced by Marx's theory and his conception of alienation. Workers in various industries saw that they had much in common with one another and wanted to build a strong union covering all workers. They did not expect to cooperate with industry. They wanted, rather, to fight for collective ownership of industry so that they would own the companies they worked in and reap the profits of their own labor. Removing industry from private ownership and placing it in collective ownership would cause a radical redistribution of wealth, of course. The owners of American business, with the aid of federal, state, and local police and military power, forced these more radical labor unions out of existence, deported any of their foreign-born members, tried citizens for treason, and passed laws preventing such unions from forming in the future.

The more conservative unions of the period worked to protect their jobs through legislation. Tariff laws were passed to prevent competition from cheap imported goods, and immigration laws prevented cheap foreign labor from entering the country. Protective labor laws kept women and children out of the labor force, thereby eliminating another source of cheap labor. In addition, the unions tried to maintain a cooperative relationship with their employers. They wanted work contracts and preferred to settle disputes by mediation and compromise. Strikes were used only as a last resort.

The owners of American industry put up a fierce struggle against the conservative unions, however (Griffin, Wallace, and Rubin, 1986). Manufacturers subdivided tasks into simple units, for example, so that skilled artisans and workers could then be replaced with unskilled workers. They hired workers from different ethnic groups so that the workers could not talk to each other and unionize, and they created antagonism among ethnic groups by discriminating against them. One week, an industry would hire only Swedes, the next week only Slavs, and then they would sometimes fire all workers of one ethnic group, building further resentment among groups. Manufacturers also organized themselves into large associations, most notably the National Association of Manufacturers (NAM), to crusade against unionism so that unions would not have the support of the general public. On a more positive note, some industries improved their working conditions and employee benefits so that workers would not want to unionize.

Some small, conservative unions developed, but they were quite powerless to negotiate with large industries. In the 1930s, unions united into large federations, the American Federation of Labor (AFL) and the Congress of Industrial Organizations (CIO), and eventually these two giant federations united to form the AFL-CIO. The federations included all workers, skilled and unskilled, and they practiced conservative policies. The unions were not structured according to class, so that workers would protect the interests of all workers. Instead, they were organized by industry. Steelworkers, for example, acted in unison when negotiating with the steel industry, and autoworkers acted in unison when negotiating with the auto industry; but other than refusing to cross a picket line, workers could do little to support the efforts of those outside of their own industry.

Unions have weakened considerably in the past decades, partly because corporations have provided employee benefits (Cornfield, 1986) and partly as a result of corporate expansion (Compa, 1986). When a major corporation buys other corporations, it acquires the unions associated with its new acquisition. The owning corporation is then in a position to negotiate with several unions separately. When steelworkers struck against USX, the old U.S. Steel Corporation, the unions representing the newly acquired oil and chemical interests of USX continued to work, and USX could operate very profitable segments of its business even during the steel strike. The other unions were forbidden to strike in support of the steelworkers because of their separate union contracts and because of regulations imposed by the National Labor Relations Board (NLRB), the government agency that regulates the activities of unions.

Through acquisitions, the airline industry has developed a maze of unions serving pilots, mechanics, transport workers, flight attendants, and other specialized workers. For example, a major airline that has acquired several other lines may have several different unions serving just their mechanics. As a result, each of the unions is ineffective in negotiations. Through acquisitions, General Electric was at one point negotiating with a dozen different unions, and until those unions formed their own federation, each was quite powerless. Increasingly, these unions are also covering the lower-paid workers in the service sector.

When the University of California/San Francisco contracted out twenty custodial positions, workers were given a pay decrease from $15.65 to $11.71 per hour, their pensions were eliminated, and health care benefits were reduced by the privateers who were awarded the contract. After holding weekly pickets and joining a local union, the workers were able to regain their positions with full pay and benefits. (AFSCME, 2003).

Service Work

The increase in the size of corporations has increased the number of tertiary (service) workers, who are not directly involved in producing goods. These are the employees who answer the telephones, keep the records, file the papers, pay the taxes, clean the buildings, and do a host of other jobs necessary to keep large corporations functioning. Another class of service workers meets community rather than corporate needs, and this class has also been growing. As people have moved to urban areas to work, more police officers, firefighters, teachers, doctors, lawyers, and accountants have been needed to serve them.

Service workers are an expense to a corporation, part of its fixed overhead costs. They increase the costs of products, but they do not directly increase the production of products. Similarly, in a community, they are a necessary expense to taxpayers, but they do not produce any tangible wealth. Service workers such as filing clerks, typists, police officers, and teachers typically have more education and training than blue-collar workers, but they do not necessarily receive more pay.

Technology has greatly increased the efficiency of service workers. For example, in 1950, it took several thousand switchboard operators to handle 1 million long-distance telephone calls; today, it takes only a few dozen. This efficiency has not reduced the work of the workers (Howard, 2000). Instead, in many ways, it has increased the work they do. Telephone operators' work is less demanding physically now that switchboards are computerized and calls are connected with the touch of a button, and the work is also simpler because computers time the calls and make the necessary computations. However, computers attached to switchboards now keep track of the time that telephone operators spend on each call. These measurements are in seconds.

Each operator can now handle 100 calls per hour. If one operator is particularly fast, other operators are expected to match that time, so there is always pressure for greater speed. Users of long-distance operators may observe this speed when the operator announces that the party does not answer after only four or five rings. A request to please let the phone ring longer may cause the operator to show stress when being timed, because waiting for the phone to be answered uses precious seconds.

Like operators, postal workers are timed as to how rapidly they read and sort zip codes, all done on modern computerized sorters. Typists are also timed as they work on word processors. There are no daily quotas that permanently satisfy work requirements. Employers are always looking for faster workers and replacing their slower workers, so quotas tend to creep higher and higher. Many lower-paid service workers are joining unions to improve their working conditions.

Professions

The professions are widely regarded as rewarding service occupations. Professional jobs share five characteristics that set them apart from other types of service work:

1. *A body of knowledge.* The professions are based on knowledge not generally available to the public. Because only professionals fully understand this knowledge, they can control how it is applied.
2. *A code of ethics.* Professionals gain the confidence of the public by adhering to a code of ethics, promising a specific level of service.
3. *Licensing.* Licensing demonstrates to the community that the licensed individuals have in fact mastered the body of knowledge associated with their profession.
4. *Peer control.* Because the body of knowledge is specialized, only professionals can judge one another's work. Outsiders do not have the knowledge necessary to make such judgments.
5. *A professional association.* The association devises and maintains the profession's educational standards, licensing requirements, peer review procedures, and code of ethics.

Two of the most important professions in the United States are law and medicine. Professionals in these fields are well paid and have some autonomy in their work. The proportion of professionals employed by large bureaucracies, both profit and nonprofit organizations—hospitals, pharmaceutical companies, medical and legal clinics, and large companies in other fields—has been increasing in recent years. Professionals lose some autonomy in these organizations, and their workloads can be increased by the organization. Their workloads are also increased by modern technology—especially car phones and beepers, which keep them constantly in touch with the office. The first major strike by physicians occurred in 1986, when physicians working for a large corporation, Group Health Association, protested increased workloads.

POLITICS AND THE DISTRIBUTION OF WEALTH

The economic system in our society produces wealth, but it has no responsibility to distribute wealth to all of the citizens. It is the political system that determines how the wealth is distributed. The government levies taxes and use its funds to support programs for its citizens. In recent years, there has been much debate regarding the extent to which government should support the less privileged in society. Critics contend that the country must not drop programs that aid those unable to work because they are too young, too old, or too ill, or simply because no jobs are available. They believe that as long as the needs of society are met only when they provide profits to capitalists, the society will continue to have unemployment and poverty, and human needs will go unmet simply because it is not profitable to meet them. One such debate about government support of the low-income worker centers on the issue of the minimum wage.

Those who encourage government action to help redistribute wealth argue that a more equitable redistribution of money would permit everyone to benefit from the wealth generated by society. Today, most government effort to help those who cannot manage financially takes the form of some type of welfare payment.

Welfare

Welfare consists of government payments to people who have an inadequate income. The United States Federal Government spends more than $400 billion dollars per year to fund welfare programs. Welfare programs include:

1. One of the oldest alleviative poverty programs at the national level is Temporary Assistance for Needy Families (TANF), first enacted (under the name Aid to Families with Dependent Children) as part of the landmark Social Security Act of 1935.TANF is jointly funded with state and federal revenues.
2. Medicaid, the medical insurance program for the poor
3. Supplemental Security Income (SSI), part of the Social Security system, which is designed to aid the poorest of the aged, blind, and disabled
4. General Assistance, a program to help poor people not covered by other programs

Piven and Cloward (1993) have shown that historically, welfare payments increase when unemployment is high and discontent is widespread, but decrease when workers are scarce and unemployment is low. They argue that welfare payments are used to keep the unemployed from expressing their discontentment in hard times.

Gans (1996) lists some advantages that the middle and upper classes derive by keeping people poor:

1. They are a source of cheap labor.
2. They can be sold goods of inferior quality that otherwise could not be sold at all.
3. They serve as examples of deviance, thereby motivating others to support the norms of the dominant group.
4. They make mobility easier for others, because they are out of the competition.
5. They do the most unpleasant jobs.
6. They absorb the costs of change because they suffer the unemployment when technological advances are made by industry.
7. They create jobs in social work and related fields for the middle class.
8. They create distinctive cultural forms of music and art, which the middle class adopts.

Welfare payments to the poor comprise only a small part of the federal government's efforts to improve living conditions, but most programs are designed to assist classes other than the poor.

Welfare for the Well-Off

There are more government programs to help the middle and upper classes than to help the poor. Following is a partial list:

1. Veterans' benefits, such as life insurance, health care, educational support, housing loans, and burial grounds
2. Housing loans, available to higher-income groups, offering lower interest rates and reduced down payments
3. Business loans on favorable terms, available to owners of both small and large businesses
4. Farming subsidies to landowners who agree not to farm some of their lands or who grow products for which there are powerful lobbies, such as tobacco
5. Social Security, which is not available to the unemployed or to those who work in jobs the program does not cover, and which is not taxed on incomes above a certain level
6. Medical care in hospitals built with government funds, staffed by doctors educated with government support, who use treatments developed with the help of government grants
7. College classrooms and dormitories built with government funds and financial assistance for college students

Even in the face of programs such as these, it is the programs for the poor that generally come under attack when the government tries to cut the domestic budget. Programs that benefit the middle class, especially veterans' and housing benefits, are considered sacred and are never reduced. The next section describes a society that has improved the living conditions of the poor under a very different economic system.

THE CHINESE SYSTEM: AN EXAMPLE OF SOCIALISM

Economic systems, whether capitalist or socialist, are strongly influenced by the societies of which they are a part. We cannot discuss adequately in this chapter all of the variations that exist in the world. However, we do describe one socialist system, that of the Chinese, to provide a comparison with capitalism.

In 1920, China was a nation ruled by local warlords and populated by millions of poor peasants. More than half the peasants owned no land whatsoever, and many who did have land owned so little that they could not support themselves. Chinese

SOCIOLOGY AT WORK

Counseling Investors: Sociology and the Stock Market

T. Dale Whitsit has worked in two very different fields—the restaurant business and financial services. The two fields, he says, have more in common than one might imagine, however, and restaurant work was good training for brokering. In both areas, his B.A. in sociology, which he obtained from the State University of New York at Stony Brook, has proven useful. Since 1980, he has worked as a financial consultant at Merrill Lynch, Pierce, Fenner & Smith, where he is currently an assistant vice president.

"After college, I worked for six years as a bartender at a bar and disco called Tuey's. That experience taught me how to deal with every kind of person imaginable." One of the secrets of being a good bartender, of maintaining control, Whitsit says, is developing the ability to establish a common bond with anybody. "If somebody's getting rowdy, for example, you relate to him, you become his friend. You highlight your similarities, not your differences, and you make him feel important. Once you've established that empathy, that bond, he doesn't want to create problems because he's your friend." Whitsit says that he gained many insights about what creates a sense of cohesion among people from some of the sociology courses he took. "Sometimes I could develop a rapport with a person by letting him or her know that we have similar reference groups, that we might be members of the same in-group, or have some out-groups in common. There are lots of things I learned in sociology about what makes people think in similar ways. Of course, I don't use the sociological jargon when I talk to them."

The ability to interact with people from all different backgrounds is one of the skills that led Whitsit to become a financial consultant. "I wanted a career that would pay me the most money for my ability to communicate one to one with people of any group or back-

workers in the cities were equally poor. Women and children who worked in the silk mills made 12 cents for a 15-hour workday. The average wage for male workers was $10 a month (Freeman, 1979).

Two groups of Chinese organized to fight the warlords and to modernize the Chinese nation. One group, the Kuomintang, was made up of middle-class people, merchants, nationalists, and intellectuals. This group had the support of the United States in their efforts to organize labor and to make China a modern industrial nation. The other group, the Chinese Communist party, developed around a small number of radicals from the middle class. This group had the support of the Soviet Union.

For almost 30 years, these two groups fought the warlords, Japanese invaders, and each other. The Japanese invasion of China did much to turn peasant support to the Communist party. In their response to the Japanese, the Kuomintang leaders treated the peasants cruelly, forcibly drafting them into their army and bringing them to training camps in chains. When the Kuomintang fought the Japanese in open battle, they generally lost, and then they taxed the peasants heavily to rebuild their army. Inflation and corruption were rampant.

Counseling Investors: Sociology and the Stock Market, *continued*

ground," he says. "I believe my training in sociology has aided me greatly in my field by helping me realize that people, because of their different demographic, ethnic, and financial backgrounds, have uniquely different ideas of how to invest their money and plan for the future."

When he sees new clients, Whitsit's first task is to develop a financial profile. Although he cautions that there are no hard-and-fast rules, he has found that "people who have similar demographics, upbringing, and family situations have similar ideas about how to increase their financial well-being. Young investors, for example, tend to be more aggressive in their investments than older individuals. Younger people feel that they can make up any losses, whereas older people feel that their ability to recover losses is hindered by their age, that their best earnings are behind them. Doctors seem to trust their investment counselors more—they want someone to guide them, perhaps because most successful doctors don't have time to monitor their investments. Teachers, on the other hand, tend to be much more conservative. Furthermore, 'old money' tends to be more confident—and more conservative—than 'new money,' because they're used to having money and they know how the system works."

In addition to using his sociology skills to understand people's backgrounds and investment needs, Whitsit makes use of another aspect of sociology—social statistics. "Merrill Lynch has a large research staff that produces information that can be used to spot trends and guide investment," he says. "One of the factors they take into account is demographic changes." For example, he notes that many members of the baby-boom generation who are having babies themselves are dual-income couples. "Now might be a good time to buy stock in companies that provide day-care centers."

When World War II ended, the Kuomintang controlled most of Chinese industry and had the support of most of the world's nations. The United States sent them $1.1 billion in aid in 1945 alone. They had no social programs; they specialized in graft and corruption and treated the peasants with contempt.

The peasants, unhappy under Kuomintang rule, turned to the Communist party, which treated them well. The Communists gave the peasants guns, fought the Japanese in guerrilla warfare, and were better able to protect themselves and the peasants. They preached mutual love and assistance and instructed their army to behave as follows (Freeman, 1979, p. 210):

1. Obey orders in all your actions.
2. Do not take a single needle or piece of thread from the masses.
3. Turn in everything captured.
4. Speak politely.
5. Pay fairly for what you buy.
6. Return everything you borrow.
7. Pay for anything you damage.
8. Do not hit or swear at people.
9. Do not damage crops.

10. Do not take liberties with women.
11. Do not ill-treat captives.

Through these policies and practices, the Communists gained the support of the peasants—2 million in the army and 10 million in village self-defense squads. They eventually won the civil war and created the People's Republic of China on October 1, 1949.

In a matter of months, the Communists made dramatic changes in support of their theme of mutual love and assistance. They outlawed opium-growing, gambling, *female infanticide* (the killing of girl infants), dowries, arranged marriages, the selling of wives and concubines, and many other practices that had existed for centuries. The benefits were great to everyone except the wealthy landowners.

The primary workers were formed into thousands of agricultural communes. The communes of today average 15,000 members, each divided into brigades averaging 1,000 members each. Brigades are further divided into teams of 150 persons. The peasants were slow to adapt to communes after centuries of working their own plots, but the Communists brought much new land under cultivation by terracing hillsides, digging wells for irrigation, improving the soil, and using new seed strains. They also introduced modern farming equipment, such as machines for planting and transplanting rice. As improvements in farming developed, crop yields increased enormously. The life of the peasants improved, and they have now adapted to communal living.

The Chinese Communists developed successful industries rather quickly. Industries such as iron, steel, machinery, coal, petroleum, electric power, and chemicals were developed in moderate-size factories and plants spread about the country. An effort was also made to keep industry in small-scale plants so that the secondary workers would not feel lost or alienated. In addition, workers were encouraged to feel pride in their individual contribution to the functioning of the plant and to the commune the plant served.

The Communists also made remarkable strides in service (tertiary) areas, such as education and health care. To facilitate education of their people, the Chinese language was simplified, schools and colleges were opened, and teachers were trained. In the ten years after the Communist takeover, enrollment in middle schools, comparable to our junior high and high schools, jumped from 1 million to 12 million students. The schools emphasize the teaching of Communist doctrine, equality, mutual love and assistance, and pride in the ability to contribute to the good of society.

The Chinese system developed in a very poor nation that now has more than 1 billion people. China is still poor by U.S. standards, but the planning and setting of priorities required by the socialist system allowed the Chinese to make the most use of their people and their resources. Now that the socialist system has been well established, the system in China is slowly changing to allow more capitalism.

In China, people are expected to put the welfare of the group above their own interests; such cultural norms leave little room for individual self-expression. In fact, reformers who want to increase democracy in China have been treated harshly. The average Chinese worker has sacrificed many of the freedoms that Americans take for granted in the process of developing a socialist economic system.

Thinking Sociologically

1. Carefully go through this chapter, and list all of the topics that could provide insight into the policy debate about raising the minimum wage.

2. How are each of the topics selected in Question 1 useful in evaluating each side of the debate?

3. How are the Japanese models of quality control circles and lifetime jobs at odds with a capitalistic system? In what ways could capitalists benefit from the Japanese models?

4. Although they may be far more subtle, are there employee practices in place today that mirror the tactics of industry owners in their attempts to discourage unionization?

SUMMARY

1. A society's economic system provides for the production and distribution of the goods and services the society uses. Sociologists study economic systems to better understand how the production of goods influences social life.

2. There are currently two basic types of economic systems: capitalism and socialism. In *capitalism*, the property needed to produce resources and goods is privately owned, and goods are sold for a profit. The United States is the most capitalistic of modern nations, but even in this country, some property is not privately owned.

3. In *socialism*, the property needed to produce goods and resources is owned by the state, and production is planned by the state.

4. In a *welfare capitalism* system, some property is private, and some is owned by the state.

5. *Communism* is a system in which the members of the society own the means of production in common. Communism has had some success in small communities, but has not been developed on a national scale.

6. Structural functional theorists point out that capitalism reflects social values favoring private property and the freedom to determine one's own economic course. Functionalists believe that capitalism persists because it functions well, providing profit to whoever supplies any needed goods.

7. Conflict theorists argue that capitalism both creates a monopoly of wealth and alienates workers.

8. The American economic system reflects values held by its people. These values were strongly influenced by the Puritans, who believed that those who accumulated wealth were chosen by God. Americans value *growth*, the individual right to accumulate wealth. In considering the influence of different denominations of religion, there appears to be a correlation between religion, family values, and the accumulation of wealth.

9. Through *vertical expansion*, American corporations have grown from large factories to giant corporations that control every step in the manufacturing process, from raw materials to retail sales. Some corporations have grown, through *horizontal expansion*, to monopolize most of the sales in a field; and others have grown, through *diversification*, to own a number of different types of unrelated businesses. Businesses may also be linked by being owned or controlled by the same bank or wealthy individual.

10. Many very large multinational corporations do business in many countries.

11. Work in large factories is said to be alienating when employees cannot control their work or create a product from start to finish.

12. Research has been done to increase productivity, but the scientific management and human relations perspectives offer different views on how to improve efficiency. The Japanese emphasize lifetime jobs and quality control circles to improve efficiency.

13. Employees have formed unions to improve their working conditions. American unions have been conservative, cooperating with management and striking only as a last resort. More radical labor unions, which wanted workers to own the means of production, were outlawed in America.

14. Large corporations and urban areas need many service workers. Most of them are poorly paid, and technology is increasing both their productivity and the stress in their work. Many are forming unions.

15. Professionals are highly trained workers familiar with some specialized bodies of knowledge, who have codes of ethics, licensing procedures, peer controls, and professional organizations. Through legislation, they can limit the practice of their profession and can demand high fees. More and more professionals now work for large corporations.

16. China has a socialist economic system. Through their planned economy, the Chinese have been able to improve the standard of living of a very poor nation. The Chinese Communist party organized workers into communes, built industries, and provided for the country's other basic needs. They are now developing more capitalism.

KEY TERMS

alienation A feeling of estrangement or dissociation, such as Marx's idea of feeling alienated from work because of no control over it or satisfaction from it.

capitalism An economic system in which all of the means of production are privately owned.

communism An economic system in which members of the society own the means of production in common.

democratic socialism An economic system in which the means of production are owned primarily by individuals or groups of individuals; goods and services vital to the society, such as transportation systems and medical care, are owned and run by the state.

diversification The corporate practice of entering business in a variety of areas of manufacturing in order to protect profits; a decrease in profits in one type of business might be made up by an increase in profits in another type, for example.

economic system The social institution that provides for the production, distribution, and consumption of goods and services.

free market An economic system in which all people are theoretically free to buy, sell, and make a profit.

gross national product (GNP) The total value of the goods and services a nation produces in a year.

horizontal expansion Corporations taking over similar businesses in order to gain a monopoly and reduce competition.

human relations school A form of industrial management in which the workers' psychology, peer pressures, and attitudes toward management are taken into account.

lifetime jobs An employment practice in which workers are guaranteed a job for a lengthy period of time.

market economy An economy in which the price and production of goods are determined by what people are willing to pay in the marketplace.

mass production The production of many items of a product, which lowers the cost per item and reduces the time needed to make it.

multinational corporation Corporations that do business in a number of nations.

planned economy An economy in which the production and prices of goods are planned by the government.

primary workers Workers who produce raw materials, such as food or minerals.

Protestant ethic The view associated with the Puritans that hard work is valuable for its own sake; according to Weber, the Protestant ethic is responsible for the high value placed on capitalism in the United States.

quality control circles Meetings at which workers discuss ways of improving production and set policy to reach their goals.

scientific management A method of managing assembly-line workers such that their every movement is efficient.

secondary workers Workers who produce manufactured goods from raw materials.

socialism An economic system in which the means of production are owned by all the people through the state.

tertiary workers Workers who provide a service, such as doctors, lawyers, politicians, police officers, and secretaries.

unionization The process of organizing workers to improve their wages and working conditions.

vertical expansion Business expansion in order to own everything related to a business, from raw materials to sales outlets.

welfare capitalism A mixed economy in which private and public ownership are both practiced extensively.

DISCUSSION QUESTIONS

1. Make a list of the socialistic programs that exist in the United States. Which of these programs should be eliminated? What programs do you think should be added to the list?
2. Discuss the traditional values of American society that spur our economy. What values are changing, and what new values are evolving that spur the economy?
3. Consider the advantages and the disadvantages of Sweden's system of having large tax bills and more social programs, compared to the United States having lower taxes and fewer programs.
4. Compare how structural functional theory and conflict theory would explain the growth of multinational corporations.
5. What are some of the positive and negative functions of the scientific management and the human relations school of management?
6. What are the advantages and disadvantages of very meager welfare payments? What would they be for very generous welfare payments?
7. What are some of the reasons for providing government programs to improve the standard of living of the middle class and the wealthy?

8. Discuss how China might have developed under a capitalist system. What would have been the advantages and disadvantages?

9. Discuss the advantages and disadvantages to China's development as a socialist system.

Health-Care Groups and Systems

AIDS

The AIDS quilt, a project that began in the 1980's, is a collective effort by those infected and affected by HIV and AIDS. The quilt has been displayed annually since the late 1980s in Washington, D.C. Each section of the quilt has been constructed by the family or friends of a person who has died of AIDS (acquired immunodeficiency syndrome). The quilt is displayed by activists who feel that there is a need for increased government funding for AIDS research and legislation that could help AIDS patients, such as making treatment more accessible and affordable to AIDS patients. It is also displayed to memorialize those who have died of AIDS. As of this writing, there have been more than 524,060 AIDS deaths and over 929,985diagnosed cases of AIDS in the United States since 1981 when on June 6th of that same year, the first documented case of AIDS was discovered. In 2002, more than 41,300 cases in the U.S. and 5 million cases worldwide were diagnosed.

According to statistics from UNAIDS/WHO, 2006 (AVERT.org, 2006), the following were true concerning AIDS worldwide:

- Total number of AIDS deaths between 1981 and the end of 2006: 25 million.
- Nearly 40 million people living with HIV/AIDS today.
- Number of children orphaned by AIDS living in sub-Saharan Africa at the end of 2003: 12 million.
- By December 2004 women accounted for 47 percent of all people living with HIV

worldwide, and for 57 percent in sub-Saharan Africa.

- In 2003, young people (15–24 years old) accounted for half of all new HIV infections worldwide; more than 6,000 became infected with HIV every day.
- An estimated five million people in low- and middle-income countries (80%) do not have the AIDS drugs that could save their lives.

Those same statistics provide us with information concerning the AIDS crisis in the United States (AVERT, 2004). Of those in the United States living with AIDS:

- 36 percent were white
- 42 percent were black
- 20 percent were Hispanic
- 2 percent were of other race/ethnicity

Of the adults and adolescents with AIDS, 77% were men. Of these men:

- 58 percent were men who had sex with men (MSM)
- 22 percent were injection drug users (IDU)
- 11 percent were exposed through heterosexual contact
- 8 percent were both MSM and IDU.

Of the 88,815 adult and adolescent women with AIDS:

- 63 percent were exposed through heterosexual contact
- 35 percent were exposed through injection drug use.

An estimated 1,998 children were living with AIDS at the end of 2003 (AVERT.org, 2004).

As indicated by the numbers above, the magnitude of the AIDS epidemic has raised important issues concerning the health-care systems in the United States and around the world. Some of the most significant issues relate to cost—both for individuals and for society. AIDS is a very expensive illness, often requiring lengthy hospital stays and prolonged usage of prescribed drugs. Because the number of AIDS cases is increasing at such a rapid rate—particularly among nonaffluent segments of the population, such as inner-city drug abusers who are likely to have limited or no health insurance—public hospitals will require increased space, staffing, and other resources to meet these demands (Neubeck, 1991). Where will the money come from to accommodate these needs? What kind of responsibility, if any, does society have to care for people with AIDS? How will the quality of care for all patients be affected as a result of hospitals being overburdened with AIDS patients? If AIDS continues to spread at the rate that it has, will the cost of medical insurance rise so much that more people will not be able to afford it?

The health-care system is also facing AIDS-related social issues other than cost. Should medical workers—such as doctors, nurses, laboratory technicians, dentists, and others—be required to be tested for AIDS or for HIV? If they test positive, should they be allowed to continue to work in health care? Should physicians be allowed not to treat AIDS patients? Should health insurance companies test prospective policyholders for AIDS or for HIV? Should they be required to provide insurance—and at an affordable cost—to those infected?

Besides issues that pertain directly to health-care systems, AIDS has raised a number of other important social issues. Should the government provide free needles to drug addicts in order to help curtail the spread of AIDS caused by intravenous drug addicts sharing needles? Should colleges, and perhaps high schools, install condom machines in restrooms and dormitories? At what point should sex education begin in schools? Can employers require that prospective employees be tested for AIDS or for HIV? Should employers be allowed to discriminate in job hiring against those carrying the disease? Should people be tested for AIDS when applying for a marriage license? Should immigrants who have AIDS be allowed to enter the country? These are only a few of the issues generated by the AIDS epidemic. Many others currently exist, and others are likely to arise in the coming years.

The AIDS crisis is an important area of study for sociology because it raises many issues that we will continue to confront in the years to come. In particular, however, it is relevant to the sociological study of health-care groups and systems. The crisis is leading sociologists to carefully examine the current systems of health care, to determine whether they can adequately function to meet the needs of all members of society. As this chapter shows, health-care systems do not exist apart from society but are interconnected with other social systems and institutions. The AIDS issue directs our attention to some of the interconnections that we must come to understand if we wish to understand the ways in which our health systems operate.

Every society must give serious attention to the health of its population if it is to survive. Illness disrupts society inasmuch as members who are ill cannot fulfill their social roles, they use scarce resources such as medicines, and they require the time and attention of healthy persons to take care of them. In extreme instances, illness has even destroyed entire societies, sometimes even killing everyone. Because of these factors, every society has developed ways of coping with illness.

We often think of health and illness in strictly biological terms, and believe that the diagnosis and treatment of illness are based on a scientific analysis of a biological problem. Social factors, however, play a major role in defining who is well and who is ill, and they also influence how illness is treated. This chapter discusses health and illness from a sociological perspective.

THE SOCIAL NATURE OF HEALTH AND ILLNESS

The World Health Organization has defined health to be, in the most idealistic terms, the "complete physical, mental and social well being and not merely the absence of disease and infirmity.". It is difficult to estimate how many people would be considered totally healthy according to this glowing definition. Does anyone ever have complete physical, mental, and social well-being all at the same time? Rather than use such an all-encompassing definition, others in the health field prefer to define *health* as the body in a state of equilibrium. Our biological systems should function in a particular way, and we are healthy when they function as they should.

Others prefer to define *health* as the absence of illness—but illness is an equally difficult term to define. **Pathological illnesses** are those in which the body is clearly diseased or malfunctioning in some way, as when viruses cause measles and chicken pox, cancer cells develop and grow, or an artery to the heart is blocked. These conditions are either obvious when examining the patient, or they are detected in laboratory tests involving X-rays, microscopes, or the more advanced technology available today. Not all biological abnormalities are considered illnesses, however. Herpes simplex, for example, was not considered an illness until venereal herpes became widespread and life-threatening to newborn infants.

Statistical illnesses are those in which a person's health varies from the norm. For example, high blood pressure is a statistical illness indicating that the person's blood pressure is considerably higher than is deemed normal. The trouble with defining statistical illnesses is knowing whether the norm is actually healthy. In the case of high blood pressure, the norm in the United States (140/95) is probably too high for optimal health. A much lower blood pressure is probably desirable, say 100/60, but that level is so abnormally low in the United States that if it were used as a standard, everyone would be classified as ill.

Iron-deficiency anemia is another example of a statistical disease. How much below the norm does a person have to be before being considered anemic and needing to take iron supplements? The answer is determined by the norm for the majority of the population.

Mental illnesses are even more difficult to define than physical ones. Manic-depressives have more extreme mood swings than normal, but everyone has some mood swings. We are all depressed sometimes, so how depressed must a person be before being labeled as having the illness called "depression"? The diagnosis is made by comparing an individual's behavior and verbalizations to the norm. Medical researchers are searching diligently for biological causes of depression and other behaviors, and they may in time find biological bases for some of these problems. Behavior is social, nevertheless, in that it is learned in social interaction, and whether our behavior is considered healthy or ill will continue to be determined by social criteria.

THEORETICAL PERSPECTIVES ON ILLNESS

How does society handle illness? Who decides when we are ill and when we are well? Why is it that we can sometimes miss school or work while at other times when we feel just as bad we are not excused? Should illness be decided objectively on the basis of biological criteria? Sociologists do not believe that an objective view of illness can ever be achieved, because illness is social as well as biological.

A Functional Explanation of Illness

Talcott Parsons (1951) pointed out that people are classified as ill not on the basis of their physical condition, but on the basis of how they are functioning in society. If people do not function well in their social roles, especially in family and work roles, they are considered deviant and disruptive to society. To maintain social order, such people are labeled "ill" and are placed in a **sick role**—a set of expectations, privileges, and obligations related to their illness. The expectations of the sick role vary somewhat, depending on the person and the illness, but they generally involve three assumptions:

1. Sick people are expected to reduce their performance in other roles. Those with a serious case of the flu who have a high temperature and other symptoms may be excused from all other roles. Those suffering from a mild case of flu may be expected to perform work or student roles as usual, but they will be expected to reduce social and recreational roles. The sick role reflects a society's need to have members participate in the work of that society. The first roles relinquished are those that are for pleasure. The last ones relinquished are work roles.
2. Sick people are expected to try to get better. They should do whatever they can to improve their health and not linger in their illness.
3. They are expected to take the advice of others. Children must take the advice of parents, and adults must listen to their doctor or to the family members who are caring for them. Sometimes, children take care of their parents, and although they would not usually tell their parents how to behave, in the event of illness, they give extensive advice. Furthermore, if the advice is not accepted, the advice-giver often becomes very hurt or angry.

Society places the power to declare who is sick in the hands of physicians. Only the physician has the legal right to diagnose and treat illness. The physician can excuse you from work or school, admit you to a hospital, or have you declared disabled or too ill to stand trial in a court of law. A person's self-diagnosis is not adequate. He or she must go to a doctor to be seriously considered ill. If the doctor does not agree with the patient's diagnosis, the individual is labeled "well." If the patient disagrees with the diagnosis as well, the individual may be called a **hypochondriac**, a well person who believes that he or she is ill. If people believe they are healthy but a physician declares them ill, they can be declared mentally ill, as well as physically ill. A person diagnosed as having cancer who refused to accept such a diagnosis might be sent for psychiatric evaluation, for example.

The sick role varies, depending on a variety of social circumstances such as age, gender, and the influence of caregivers. Elderly people are expected to be ill and are easily placed in the sick role. It is also acceptable for women to be ill unless they have responsibility for young children—women are rarely excused from child-care duties. The caregiver also influences the sick role. If he or she accepts the illness, the sick person will play the role more fully, but if the caregiver is someone who works staunchly under all but the most dire circumstances, the sick person may be required to perform work roles. Some mothers are happy to bring soup and tender loving care to their children for long periods of time. Other mothers believe that their children should be up and about as soon as possible. Although the sick role expectations may vary, it does place a person in the social order with a set of both responsibilities and privileges to guide behavior, so that the social order can be kept integrated and functioning.

APPLYING THE SICK ROLE

At one time or another, everyone will become sick or be required to care for someone who is sick. It is therefore important to acknowledge the existence and implications of the sick role. If, by being placed in a sick role, a person is expected to reduce his or her performance in other roles, is expected to try to get better, and is expected to take the advice of others, then labeling someone as "sick" becomes a useful device in their treatment and path to recovery.

People often have ailments that require them to suspend their routine roles in order to return to proper health. Sometimes, though, people are unable to do this, either because they feel compelled to continue to function in their role as worker, parent, or student, or because they are unable to be excused. Have you ever, for example, felt sick yet continued your routine of play or work, and later, when diagnosed as sick by a parent or a doctor, decided that resting was the proper thing to do? The label "sick" serves the important function of not only allowing, but requiring, that the sick role become the predominant one, at least temporarily.

It is also important to understand the social consequences of such a label and how they might work to a person's disadvantage. Suppose that a person with a physical limitation is labeled as "sick." This can be negative in a few ways. First, although that person might be able to perform adequately in a job, he or she might not be given an opportunity because of the expectation that sick people reduce their performance in other roles. Similarly, some people who are "sick" may be stigmatized or feared. AIDS victims, for example, are often shunned, even though AIDS cannot be transmitted through casual contact. Second, a person with a physical limitation who is labeled "sick" may come to conform to the expectations associated with the sick role. Clearly, the sick role is a powerful social phenomenon that can be applied to the detriment or advantage of people's physical and mental health.

While various factors affect sick role performances, playing the sick role produces various consequences for the sick person. Dr. Christine Laine (1997) found that patients who are active and engaged with regard to their own health care fare better than patients who are less active or adopt the sick role. Although there may be perceived advantages to letting the professionals do the work, the end result is that those who adopt the sick role may lessen their chances of attaining "optimal outcomes" (Laine, 1997). As stated earlier, older, sicker, and lesser educated patients are more likely to adopt the sick role.

The Conflict Perspective of Illness

Conflict theorists believe that the health-care system is an elite system intent on maintaining its power. The health-care system legitimates its power by claiming a specialized body of knowledge and uses its power to gain wealth and maintain the status quo. Conflict theorists contend, for example, that the system of giving birth in hospitals rather than at home or in birthing centers persists because it is convenient for doctors and profitable for hospitals (Rothman, 2000). Deliveries are made by doctors rather than by midwives because it provides employment for doctors, not because it is necessary or better for women and babies. Conflict theorists also note that insurance programs such as *Medicare*, the federal health insurance program for the elderly, are structured such that wealthy people receive more benefits than the poor (Davis, 1975).

In the United States, from 1998 to 2002, the cost of health care rose markedly by 35 percent and the costs of prescription drugs by 37 percent (cnn.com, 2004). One idea being proposed by the current administration to help with Medicare costs is a private medical savings account in which individuals could open tax-free accounts to offset medical bills. Critics of this idea maintain that the plan does nothing to help those who cannot afford to open savings, but favors the wealthy with tax-free savings opportunities.

Conflict theorists argue that much of the diagnosis and treatment of diseases benefits the large medical corporations more than the patients. Although drug companies sell drugs of questionable safety and effectiveness for the common cold, they do not like to manufacture **orphan drugs** that are valuable in the treatment of rare diseases but not profitable to the manufacturer. Manufacturers of high-technology medical equipment may sell rarely used, expensive devices to many hospitals within a locality, when one device could be shared by several hospitals (Waitzkin, 2000); this raises hospital costs by encouraging physicians to engage in more testing and procedures that must be paid for by the patient, in order to justify the expensive device.

Physicians, who usually represent the upper middle class, may use their power to control patients and to maintain the status quo. Physicians have the power to excuse people from work or to refuse to excuse them. Availability of adequate health insurance often plays a role in patient care. For example, well-paid specialists can put well-insured business executives with back pain into a hospital for days or weeks of treatment. On the other hand, for a similar back condition, public health clinic physicians may give inadequately insured laborers painkillers and send them back to work. Physicians declare who is eligible for insurance payments for illness and disability and who must return to work. Physicians can declare criminals insane and unable to stand trial. Elite criminals are more likely to obtain the services of prestigious psychiatrists, who declare the accused to be insane, whereas lower-class criminals cannot afford such services, and if they receive any psychiatric attention, such services are likely to be publicly funded, which makes it probable that the criminal will stand trial and go to prison. Thus, the sick role and illness are used to perpetuate the existing social system.

Symbolic Interaction and Illness Behavior

Because illness is social, symbolic interaction has played a major role in the study of medical groups and systems. For example, researchers who study symbolic interaction explore the meanings that patients give to symptoms and illness. Patients are the first to recognize their own illness and to decide to visit a doctor, who then takes a medical history. How the patient describes symptoms influences the diagnosis, and patients describe their illness based on what society teaches them. They learn that nausea and dizziness are signs of illness (unless they are smoking their first cigarette, in which case they ignore it). They learn that headaches or stomach pains require a drugstore remedy, but chest pains require a visit to the doctor. They learn that if they are tired at night, they need to go to bed, but if they are tired in the morning, they must ignore it and go to class or to work, as expected. These experience-based facts and hearsay knowledge are not necessarily good diagnoses, however; pains in the head or stomach, as well as nausea, dizziness, and fatigue, are symptoms that may indicate serious as well as mild diseases.

Children learn about the causes of disease as they grow up. They learn that if they do not wear a sweater, boots, or a coat, they will catch cold. If they do not eat right or get enough sleep, they will get sick. If they go outdoors for fresh air and exercise, they will be healthier. Then, when they get sick, they wonder what they did wrong. As adults, we tend to blame sick people when they develop heart disease or cancer. Did they eat too much or drink too much? Did they live stressful lives? Surely, they must have done something wrong. We accept a great deal of guilt and blame for our health in this society, even though there is no evidence that we can prevent death, little evidence that we can even forestall death significantly, and a great deal of evidence that the environment influences our health more than our own behavior does.

We also learn medical theories of illness as we grow up. We learn that viruses, germs, or other enemies of the body attack us from outside and that we must ward off attack, if not with boots and sweaters, then with drugs, food, vitamin C, rest, exercise, prayer, or whatever else is fashionable at the time. The approach of the Native Americans was more peaceful.

They believed that illness occurred when there was an imbalance with nature, and treatments were designed to bring the ill person back into harmony with nature. These treatments were often successful.

Other societies, and our own in an earlier age, placed illness in a religious context. Lepers and alcoholics were sinners. The ill were disfavored by the gods or possessed by a devil who had to be exorcised. Exorcists, priests, shamans, or religious leaders of other types were called upon to treat the ill person. Ceremonies were performed, gods were called upon to remove the illness, and the shaman was well paid for these talents.

Today, we have great faith in medical science and believe our current good health is the result of good medicine. History shows that in fact, improved nutrition and sanitation played the most important role in eradicating diseases in the past and that poorer nutrition and a polluted environment are important factors causing today's illnesses.

Smog has been a problem for various reasons, but it is being increasingly linked to asthma. Asthma appears to be on the rise in the United States. Since 1980, the prevalence of the disease has increased by more than 75 percent. In 2002, the results of a 10-year study of children funded by the California Environmental Protection Agency's Air Resources Board (ARB) and conducted by the University of Southern California (USC) produced strong evidence that ozone, commonly know as smog, can cause asthma in children (California Environmental Protection Agency (2002). It is widely accepted that smog can trigger or aggravate asthma, but representatives maintain that ozone can also cause asthma.

THE CHANGE IN ILLNESS OVER TIME

Prior to industrialization in Europe, the major killing diseases were **infectious diseases** caused by germs and viruses. Infectious diseases such as tuberculosis, influenza, pneumonia, and the plague were the most common, and they often killed children. This pattern continued until the twentieth century and then changed, according to **epidemiologists**, the people who study the social distribution of disease and illness. Today, the diseases that kill the most people are heart disease, cancer, and stroke, which are called **degenerative diseases** because they slowly disable the body as we get older. Both infectious diseases and degenerative diseases have proven to be related to environmental conditions.

The Age of Infectious Diseases

In the Middle Ages, diseases were widespread. Whenever crops failed, there was a food shortage. Transportation was not good enough to bring in large supplies of food, so the population became undernourished, weak, and increasingly susceptible to infection. Devastating plagues swept Europe from 1370 on. In some areas, one-third to one-half the population died. Often, when the plague hit a city, people fled to the countryside, dying on the way or carrying the plague deep into rural areas.

The causes of the plague and other diseases were not understood. In the cities, human waste was thrown into the streets. People did not concern themselves with cleanliness and did not use soap and water. It was considered immoral to concern oneself with the flesh and immodest to wash below the waist (Thomlinson, 1976).

When it was discovered that rats carry the plague and that germs cause infections, urban sanitation systems were developed. Supplies of water were brought to cities, and sewage systems were built. The improvement of sanitation may have added more to the average life expectancy than all modern medical advances.

Improvements in nutrition played an even more dramatic role in reducing the death rate. It is believed that nutrition improved in Europe when the potato came into widespread use, in about the middle of the eighteenth century. The potato is rich in nutrients and easy to store and ship from place to place. Until the development of potato crops, infectious diseases were rampant and the average life expectancy was probably less than 40 years.

Modern medicine may have helped to reduce the death rate from infectious diseases in two important ways: *Antibiotics*, such as penicillin, were developed to cure infections; and *vaccines*, such as for measles, were developed to prevent diseases. There is no question that antibiotics save lives, but researchers McKinlay and McKinlay (1981) argue that vaccines actually affected the death rate only slightly, reducing it by 3.5 percent at most. The infectious diseases that were the major causes of death in 1900—influenza, pneumonia, tuberculosis, diphtheria, typhoid, scarlet fever, measles, and whooping cough—were declining steadily as causes of death long before modern vaccines were discovered. They continued to fall after the vaccines were introduced, but not appreciably. Poliomyelitis, commonly called "polio," is an exception. It showed a very noticeable decline soon after the vaccine came into widespread use. Otherwise, the reduction in infectious diseases was largely a result of better nutrition, better sanitation, and better housing.

Current Causes of Death

Poor nutrition is still widespread among the poor of most nations, and starvation and infectious diseases are persistent problems. However, the causes of death in industrial societies are dramatically different. Currently, the major causes of death in the United States and most other industrial nations have been heart disease, cancer, and stroke (see Table 17-1). Although heart disease and strokes have been declining slightly, these and other rarer diseases that damage the heart and blood vessels cause more deaths in the United States than any other disease.

TABLE 17-1 TEN LEADING CAUSES OF DEATH IN THE UNITED STATES, 2006

Cause	Deaths
Heart disease	685,089
Cancer	556,902
Stroke	157,689
Chronic Lower Respiratory Disease	126,382
Accidents	109,277
Diabetes	74,219
Pneumonia and influenza	65,163
Alzheimer's Disease	63,457
Nephritis, nephritic syndrome, and nephrosis	42,453
Septicemia	34,069

Source: Adapted from the *National Vital Statistics Report*, Vol. 55, No. 10, 2007.

The American diet is believed to contribute significantly to these diseases.

The American diet, along with pollution, is also blamed for the increasing cancer rate. Cancer caused 556,902 deaths in 2003 (*National Vital Statistics Report*, 2003). Most experts in the field estimate that 80–90 percent of all cancer cases are environmentally induced. The risk of *carcinogens* (cancer-causing products) in the environment has been known since 1942, when publications urged that measures be taken to minimize cancer hazards on the job (Agran, 1975), but little effective action has been taken. Rubber-workers die of cancer of the stomach and prostate, leukemia, and other cancers of the blood and lymphatic systems. Steelworkers have excessive rates of lung cancer. Workers who produce dyestuffs have high rates of bladder cancer. Miners have a wide range of cancers, and half of them die from some form of cancer. Dry cleaners, painters, printers, petroleum workers, and others who are exposed to benzene have high rates of leukemia. The 1.5 million workers who are exposed to insecticides, copper, lead, and arsenic have high rates of lung and lymphatic cancer. Machinists, chemical workers, woodworkers, roofers, and countless others suffer from cancer risks of one kind or another.

Cancer rates are also higher in neighborhoods where these industries are located, thereby shortening the lives of people who never even enter the plant. If these problems are not successfully checked, increasing cancer rates may shorten life expectancy and cause genetic defects in the next generation.

Accidents, the fifth most common cause of death, are the leading cause of death for persons under age 35 years. Motor vehicle accidents, which account for half of these deaths, have declined as speed limits were reduced to 55 miles per hour and the use of seat belts increased. White males between the ages of 15 and 25 have the highest death rate from automobile accidents.

Alcoholism: Moral Failure or Major Disease?

Alcoholism is a major killer of Americans and would probably appear on the list of major killers if all deaths due to alcoholism were listed on death certificates. By some estimates, there are 14 million alcoholics in the United States. Among children ages 13–17 years, there are 3 million alcoholics. Untold numbers of heart attack victims are probably victims of alcoholism. Many cancer victims, especially of the mouth, throat, larynx, esophagus, pancreas and liver, are really victims of alcoholism. In 2001, more than 17,000 were killed in alcohol-related motor accidents. Today, 25,000 people are killed each year in alcohol related accidents and another 70,000 are injured.

In recent decades, experts in the field of alcoholism have found more and more evidence that alcoholism is a physical disease that cannot be cured by willpower any more than could heart disease or cancer. In 1956, the American Medical Association (AMA) declared that **alcoholism** is a disease with identifiable and progressive symptoms, and that if it is untreated, it leads to mental damage, physical incapacity, and early death. The physical nature of the disease was described shortly thereafter by Jellineck (1960). It was demonstrated that alcoholism occurs in people who have inherited a body chemistry that fails to metabolize alcohol the way normal people do. Instead, the body produces toxic substances that cause widespread damage in the body and changes that cause the body to require more alcohol to function. Thus, the victim is addicted to alcohol, because once having introduced alcohol into the body, the victim must continue to drink in order to continue to function. Sooner or later, however, the body will be poisoned to the extent that the victim cannot function with or without alcohol.

Yet alcoholism is not often listed as the cause of death when a patient dies of an alcohol-related disease, and thus it does not appear on the list of common causes of death. Because alcoholism has historically been viewed as a sin, a crime, a moral lapse, or a psychological illness, physicians prefer not to use it as a cause of death in order to protect the reputation of the family.

Thinking Sociologically

1. Because we give personal meanings to health and illness, we do not always recognize the threat of illness objectively. Have you ever thought you were well when you were ill? Have you ever not noticed one of your own symptoms of a disease?

2. At any time, have you learned anything about alcoholism to lead you to believe that alcoholics are weak-willed people rather than people who are ill?

3. What are some possible short-term consequences of assigning someone the "sick role"? Long-term consequences? The older, sicker, and less educated are more likely to take on the sick role. Sociologically, how do you explain this?

THE AMERICAN HEALTH-CARE SYSTEM

The American health-care system consists of physicians, nurses, and other health-care workers who treat illness primarily as a biological event, to be prevented or cured on an individual basis. Illness, however, can be viewed as a social phenomenon and can often be eliminated in society before many individuals are stricken.

The Social Model of Illness

Historically, the greatest strides in reducing illness have been changes in lifestyle, particularly in nutrition, sanitation, and shelter. The **social model of illness** suggests that much disease is caused by social conditions and that it can be cured by changing those conditions. Some observers believe that death rates from modern causes, such as heart disease, cancer, and automobile accidents, also could be reduced by taking a social approach. Food supplies, for example, could be improved by having a more varied assortment of whole-grain foods on the market, as well as foods that do not contain sugar or excessive amounts of fat or salt. Vegetables and fruits could be improved by practicing farming methods that put nutrients into the soil and keeping pesticides out of the fruit. More efficient water systems could reduce waste and provide more pure drinking water. A modern transportation system could reduce air pollution and accidents. Early detection of AIDS and safe sex practices could reduce the spread of this disease. All of these improvements would need to be accomplished through social reorganization and social change, however.

The Medical Model of Illness

Currently, almost all of our research and health care are based on a **medical model of illness**, in which sickness is viewed as an individual problem requiring individual treatment. Cures for heart attacks and cancer are applied after the patient is sick. People are taken to shock trauma centers after the automobile accident occurs. Even when preventive measures are considered, the responsibility rests with the individual. People must seek good food to eat by searching for stores that sell sugar-free and pesticide-free foods, for example, and they must treat their own water if they want pure water to drink. They must find ways to get proper exercise individually.

The American health-care system is designed to maintain the medical model of illness, with a full complement of physicians, nurses, and other staff, plus hospitals, the pharmaceutical industry, and modern medical technology. Ninety-three cents of every health-care dollar is spent trying to cure people after they get sick. Physicians played a major role in building the health-care system we have today.

The Profession of Medicine

The profession of medicine, for which an M.D. degree is required, is now one of the most prestigious professions in the United States—but this has not always been true. In the early years of United States history, there were very few doctors. Women took care of the ill members of the family and community and also delivered babies. Older women often gained considerable experience in these activities and would be consulted whenever someone was particularly ill or a baby was born. Many of the women of the community would gather for births, so younger women observed and understood the birthing process before they had their own children. A doctor was rarely needed.

There were only a few physicians in this country at the time of the American Revolution, and they were trained in Europe, where they studied Latin or Greek. There was little science taught in universities in those days, and no medical science. Most physicians learned to practice medicine by being an apprentice to a physician, taking on more and more responsibility until they were able to venture out on their own, often to the frontier to seek patients who needed their services. The medicine practiced was often **heroic medicine**, a dramatic intervention by the physician. Patients were bled, blistered, and given poisonous laxatives in an attempt to kill the disease. Often, the treatment killed the patient. Most people went to doctors only when they were desperate. Doctors were often poor and had little work to do. They sometimes had to beg in the streets to survive (Rothstein, 1992).

By the early 1800s, many physicians were entering the profession, some of whom had been trained in Europe, some trained in apprenticeships, and some not trained at all. There was also a populist health movement at this time, when many groups formed health clubs, started to eat health foods, and learned the best healing remedies from the women in the community. Some populists even set up medical schools to train and graduate physicians in one or another favorite type of remedy. This situation concerned the physicians who had been educated in Europe and who knew that in Europe, the profession was held in high esteem. They felt that it was necessary to create the same respect for medical authority here in the United States (Starr, 1984).

In about 1800, European-educated physicians were able to get state legislatures to pass laws forbidding healers without formal education from practicing medicine, but the laws were unpopular and were soon repealed. In 1847, physicians formed the AMA and adopted the Hippocratic Oath as a vow to practice good and ethical medicine. They lobbied states to ban abortion, which was widely practiced until that time and had been an important source of income to women healers who were not physicians. By this method, the AMA effectively made it impossible for these women to earn a living in the practice of medicine.

In 1910, another major move limited the practice of medicine to wealthy males. Abraham Flexner published the "Flexner Report," which stated that most existing medical schools were inadequate. Congress responded to the "Flexner Report" by giving the AMA the right to determine which schools were qualified to train physicians, an important power in controlling the profession. All seven medical schools for women and most medical schools for blacks were closed, eliminating women and most blacks from the practice of medicine. Part-time schools were also closed, eliminating those who could not afford full-time study. The medical field remained open only to white males of the upper classes, and a shortage of physicians developed, which made medicine a very lucrative profession.

Today, medical care has become a huge industry in the United States, with 600,000 physicians supported by the pharmaceutical industry, the medical technology industry, the health insurance industry, and more than 7,000 hospitals. The AMA has power and influence over hospitals, medical education, prescription drugs, the use of medical technology, and the qualifications for receiving insurance payments.

The most common type of medical practice is private practice on a **fee-for-service** basis, in which the physician is paid for each visit and each service rendered. In this type of practice, the physician is self-employed and must establish an office with expensive equipment. In the office, the physician provides **primary medical care**, which is the first general, overall care the patient requires. It may include a medical history, checkup, and treatment of minor cuts, colds, sore throats, and other ailments. The primary care physician usually has privileges at a nearby hospital (i.e., the hospital permits the physician's patients to be treated there, under the physician's supervision and care). There, patients may go to have surgery, deliver babies, and receive tests or other services.

Hospitals

Hospitals provide **secondary medical care**, which is more specialized than the general practitioner provides, and **secondary caregivers** are those who deliver the specialized care. Hospitals were once poorhouses or places where people went to die. When there was little specialized knowledge of complex treatment procedures, there was no advantage to putting people in the hospital for treatment. Babies were born at home, and tonsils were removed using the kitchen table as an operating table. As medical knowledge increased and hospitals came to be better equipped and more convenient places for doctors to treat patients, hospitals and their specialized staffs of physicians, nurses, and technicians drew large numbers of patients needing short-term specialized care.

There are now many types of hospitals. The most common is the community **voluntary hospital**, a nonprofit facility that treats patients who need short-term care. Most of these hospitals are in the suburbs, and money to build some of them was provided by the Hill-Burton Act of 1954. The only restriction made by Congress was that such hospitals should do some charity work. Otherwise, physicians had complete control over the new buildings and where they were built. As a result of the Hill-Burton Act, many more hospitals than necessary were built, and many have now been closed.

A second type is the **municipal hospital**, which is built by a city or county. These hospitals are often the only ones available to treat the poor and often have names such as "City General" or "County General." They are noted for their busy emergency rooms, which serve as primary care centers for the urban poor, who do not have personal physicians. This method of providing primary care is far more expensive than it would be if health clinics were more widely available. Unfortunately, when government budgets are strained, rather than provide more cost-effective clinic care, hospital funding may be cut, emergency rooms may be closed, and sometimes the hospitals themselves are closed, eliminating a vital source of health care for many, especially poor people. As mentioned in the introduction to this chapter, this has special impact on people with AIDS.

A third type is the **proprietary hospital**. These are privately owned, usually by physicians or by hospital corporations. Such hospitals have been growing rapidly. They can control costs by refusing patients who cannot pay, by specializing in less expensive short-term procedures, and by not investing in the variety of equipment and services that are costly but not profitable, so they can treat their patients at lower costs than nonprofit hospitals.

A fourth type of hospital, developed with federal funds after World War II, is the **medical center**, which trains new physicians, conducts research, and gives **tertiary medical care**—long-term care requiring complex technology, usually at great expense. It uses specialized modern equipment—such as artificial kidneys, heart-lung machines, computed axial tomography (CAT) scanners, as well as 3-D computed tomography (CT) scanners, magnetic resonance imaging (MRI), positron emission tomography (PET), single photon emission computed tomography (SPECT), coronary care units, electronic fetal-monitoring machines, radioisotopes, ultrasound, and fiber optics. This equipment may or may not be safe or effective, and much of it is not regulated by the federal government. It is also extremely expensive. An MRI scanner can cost 1 million to 3 million to buy, and each scan costs the patient or the insurance company about $1,000 (Levy, 2003).

In a well-planned medical system, the very expensive technology used in tertiary care is centrally located in medical centers, to which patients are referred from their community hospitals. In a free economy such as ours, corporations are eager to sell their very expensive equipment to all hospitals, and hospitals, competing to fill their beds, have bought high technology regardless of the community need. Every hospital wants to have its own coronary care unit, CT scanner, fetal monitors, and all of the other technology. Tertiary health care, which theoretically should be limited to a few medical centers, is now hardly distinguishable from secondary health care.

This extension of the secondary health-care system to provide tertiary services has the obvious disadvantage of being very costly. Almost 40 cents of every medical care dollar is spent in hospitals, much of it to buy and operate equipment. Having spent so much on costly equipment, hospitals and doctors feel pressured to use it. Ordinary head injuries get CT scans, and almost every baby being born is subject to **fetal monitoring**, which measures the heart rate of the infant being born and is not an exact science. Changes in the patterns measured are often treated with alarm, and the mother may be unnecessarily subjected to a cesarean section, which involves surgically opening the womb. Cesarean sections, considered major abdominal surgery, have increased from less than 5 percent to more than 30 percent of all births since the introduction of fetal monitoring. Technology, then, is expensive to buy and use, and it requires teams of medical technicians to operate the equipment. The largest staff in the hospital, however, is the people who actually take care of the patients—the nurses.

Nurses

In the early days of medicine, nurses were considered gentle and caring people who wiped fevered brows and otherwise tenderly cared for patients. Nurses played the roles of wife to the doctor and mother to the patient. In the days before advanced scientific knowledge, nursing duties were not very different from what was done at home. As medicine has changed, the role of the nurse has changed. However, the nursing profession has had difficulty changing its image, partly because of the way in which nurses are educated. Today, there are approximately 2.4million registered nurses in the United States and they make up the largest healthcare occupation (U.S. Dept. of Labor and Statisitics, 2007).

To be a nurse, one must get certification as a registered nurse (RN). The educational requirements for RNs vary. Originally, they were trained in hospitals in a three-year program with some classroom work to supplement their on-the-job training. Hospitals gained their labor for three years, and the nurses paid only room, board, and sometimes a modest fee for tuition. Most nurses were from the working class and the low-cost training gave them entree to a profession that was far superior in salary and working conditions to the typical kind of factory job they might otherwise obtain.

Advances in medical technology brought changes to this educational system. As scientific knowledge accumulated in the 1950s and 1960s, nurses needed more time in the classroom. This was expensive for hospitals, however. During these same two decades, two-year community colleges, four-year colleges, and universities were expanding, and these schools wanted students to prepare for occupations. At that point, the needs of the schools matched the needs of hospitals, so the latter continued to train nurses in the hospital but turned the classroom education over to schools. The two-year colleges awarded the RN after two years of school, and the four-year colleges awarded the RN after four years. Two-year colleges served the working classes, and four-year colleges served upper-middle-class women. In addition, some nurses were still trained entirely by hospitals.

As a result of this change in education, some nurses have two years of college training, some have four years, and some have no formal college training but more practical hospital training. The goals of the different groups vary. Nurses with four years of college training would like to change the image of nursing to an upper-class profession with more autonomy, more respect, and better salaries. The four-year nurses have not won the support of many less-educated nurses because the new standards would require several more years of education for them. Nurses have not won the support of physicians either. Physicians now have authority over them and do not want to relinquish it.

To date, nurses work at inconvenient hours, such as evenings, nights, and weekends. They work under the strict supervision of the physician, and even though they spend more time with patients, they must follow the physician's directions at all times. They also are not paid as well as many other professionals with four-year degrees. Hospitals, suffering under increasing budgetary pressures, resist the efforts of nurses to improve their professional standing.

Even those who specialize in a field such as nurse midwifery have difficulty in finding autonomous ways to practice their profession. Nurse midwives are trained to deliver babies, and they use methods that are, in the opinion of many, safer than the drugs and surgical procedures used by physicians. At present, nurse midwives also have difficulty obtaining hospital privileges and must practice under the supervision of a physician.

Other Health-Care Workers

Although physicians, hospitals, and nurses make up the core of the American health-care system, many other professionals are involved in health care. Hospital administrators are sometimes physicians, but in recent years, they are more likely to have been trained in business administration or health-care administration (Sager, 1986). "A growing recognition among many hospital boards is that the best way to keep physicians happy in times of crisis is to make one of them the boss" (Modern Healthcare, 2002). They have a staff working with them who have a variety of special skills, such as keeping medical records, purchasing medical supplies, and performing all of the tasks necessary to keep a hospital running.

Medical research is conducted by physicians or by researchers trained in other sciences, such as biology and chemistry. Research takes place at hospitals, in centers devoted to research, or in corporations that produce pharmaceuticals (drugs) or medical equipment.

Registered dietitians (RDs), important members of the hospital staff, plan regular meals and special diets for patients. Registered dietitians are licensed by their own association of dietitians. **Nutritionists** have similar concerns, but their education, theories, and licenses are quite different from those of dietitians. Dietitians more and more refer to themselves as nutritionists, and in many states, dietitians are lobbying legislatures to ban nutritionists who lack RD certification from advising people on what to eat. Neither group is allowed to diagnose or treat diseases; they can only recommend proper eating programs.

Dentists, who have earned a Doctor of Dental Science (D.D.S.) degree, do not normally work in a hospital setting. They are not allowed to diagnose or treat diseases other than those defined as a part of dentistry, such as gum diseases. Many other diseases, such as oral cancer, are easily detected in the mouth, and dentists are expected to be able to detect them and refer patients to a physician.

Chiropractors have been outside of the health-care system for the most part. *Chiropractic* healing is a Greek term for healing by manipulating the body with the hands. Today, chiropractors are primarily concerned with manipulating the spine, but they also use X-rays and other modern technologies, and they educate their patients about nutrition and a healthy lifestyle as preventive measures. Physicians generally do not recognize chiropractic healing as a legitimate form of medicine, and during the nineteenth century, when physicians were building their profession, they lobbied legislatures to have chiropractors outlawed. Chiropractors, who had their own professional association, managed to survive, and today many people recognize that their work is beneficial. Using data from a 1991 Gallup Poll and numbers from the 2000 U.S. Census Bureau, the Mississippi chiropractic Association (2004) estimates that around 28 million people in the United States see a chiropractor each year.

Many other health workers are even farther from the mainstream of American medicine. Acupuncture and acupressure are not now generally recognized as legitimate forms of healing in the United States, although recent research is bringing new attention to these methods. Rolfing and other forms of massage are also outside of the mainstream, as are herbal medicines, yoga, relaxation techniques, and a wide variety of other techniques used elsewhere in the world. The American health-care system is dominated by physicians and hospitals, who favor expensive modern technologies and pharmaceuticals.

APPLYING SOCIOLOGY TO HEALTH CARE

Although health care is typically thought to be the sole domain of the medical profession, social science can provide important clues to help diagnose and treat much physical and mental illness. Social scientists can help point out the interplay between social, environmental, and psychological factors in both illness and disease and in their treatment and prevention.

Using a social model of illness in connection with a medical model, health-care workers might be encouraged to explore how the values and norms of a society might help or hinder the development of disease, or how the beliefs and attitudes about a specific illness might affect a return to good health. For example, if alcoholism is still viewed as a moral failure or a lack of willpower, how might this interfere with the prevention of disease in people who are genetically at high risk, or how might this hinder a person from admitting to having the disease, being willing to seek help, or gaining the support of friends and family while receiving treatment? If AIDS is seen as a disease caused by males' sexual preferences or by intravenous drug use, how might this interfere with prevention, diagnosis, or treatment of this disease in a heterosexual teenager who does not use intravenous drugs?

PAYING FOR MEDICAL CARE

Government-based insurance such as Medicare, Medicaid, or military health care accounted for more than 25 percent of all insurance health coverage. Employment-based coverage accounted for more than 61 percent Americans' health insurance (U.S. Census, 2003). Between 2004 and 2005, the percentage of Americans with no coverage increased from 15.6 percent to 15.9 percent (see Figure 17-1). Government costs are expected to rise dramatically as the AIDS epidemic spreads, as mentioned in the introduction to this chapter.

Health Insurance

Private health insurance began during the Great Depression, when physicians had to wait months or even years to get paid for their services (Starr, 1982). Physicians developed *Blue Cross*, a nonprofit insurance system, to be sold to groups of workers. Employers offered to pay part of the insurance premium for workers instead of giving them raises, and the

FIGURE 17-1 TYPE OF HEALTH INSURANCE AND COVERAGE STATUS: 2004 AND 2005

Source: U.S. Census Bureau, *Current Population Statistics*, "Health Insurance Coverage in the United States: 2005," Series P60-231, 2005.

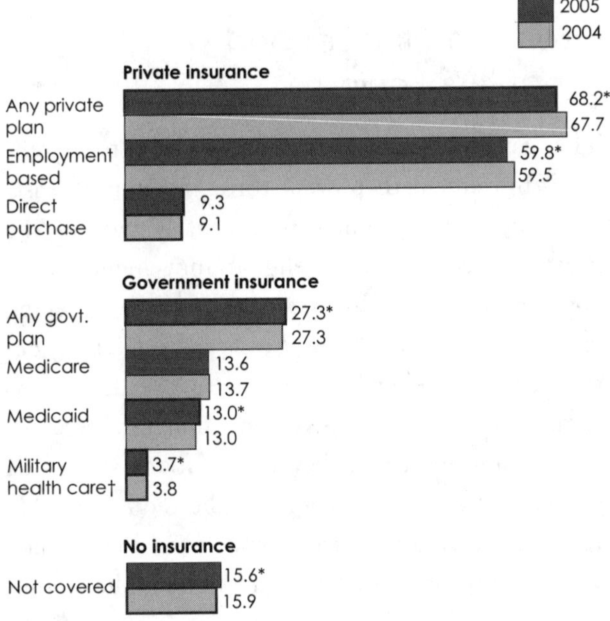

*Change is statistically different from zero at the 90-percent confidence level.

†Military health care includes: CHAMPUS (Comprehensive Health and Medical Plan for Uniformed Services)/Tricare and CHAMPVA (Civilian Health and Medical Program of the Department of Veterans Affairs), as well as care provided by the Veterans Administration and the military.

Note: The estimates by types of coverage are not mutually exclusive: people can be covered by more than one type of health insurance during the year.

program was such a success that in the 1950s, private insurance companies began to offer health insurance. The benefits of health insurance were many. Workers were insured, companies could show their concern for the workers, and there was a large flow of money into the health-care system. The income of physicians increased dramatically, and hospitals were able to afford high-technology medical equipment, which benefited the industries that produced it.

Those who did not benefit from health insurance were the retired, the unemployed, part-time workers, and workers in jobs without fringe benefits. They saw health costs rise and found physicians and hospitals less interested in charity work. To help these people, the United States began the **Medicare** program for retired workers and the **Medicaid** program for the poor. All of these insurance systems paid whatever the physician and hospital charged, and prices soared.

Some people would like to have the federal government provide a national health insurance program that would cover everyone, but others fear that a further infusion of money into the health-care system would cause further cost increases. History has shown us that as more money is available for health care, the costs of health care increase. The medical profession vigorously opposes cost control, considering it an interference with their right to practice medicine as they see fit.

Nevertheless, actions have been taken to resist the rising cost of insurance. In 1983, the federal government began to limit the amount of money it would pay through Medicare and Medicaid. The government devised **diagnostic related groups (DRGs)**, which set a maximum payment for any treatment, and hospitals have had to limit the length of stay and the number of tests given to Medicare and Medicaid patients in order to treat them within the limits of the DRGs. Corporations have responded to rising insurance costs by eliminating insurance as a fringe benefit. Instead, corporations are hiring physicians to run clinics for the specific purpose of providing health care for workers. They find that they are able to contain costs and provide cheaper care directly, rather than through insurance. More and more workers have also responded to the high costs of health insurance by turning to prepaid health care.

Prepaid Health Care

In the United States, the emphasis has been on fee-for-service care, in which the doctor charges a fee for each visit. However, another type of health-care provider, the **health maintenance organization (HMO)**, is growing rapidly. HMOs are prepaid plans in which a fee is paid in advance, and most—if not all—necessary health care is provided at no additional cost.

HMOs have four goals: (1) to provide preventive medicine and early detection of disease; (2) to practice the best scientific medicine possible when a disease is detected; (3) to reduce hospitalization through the use of preventive medicine and early detection of disease; and (4) to reduce medical costs through better use of tests, procedures, and hospitalization.

Because their health care is prepaid, HMO members do not hesitate to have regular checkups and to visit their doctors when illness occurs. Because HMO physicians now practice in large groups, they can communicate with one another easily, they have access to all the necessary equipment and other services, and they have resources and schedules that allow ongoing educational programs. Medical testing can be done knowledgeably, reducing the use of unnecessary tests. Preventive medicine and good medical care reduce hospitalization and medical costs. HMOs also trim costs by using auxiliary medical personnel, such as nurses and physicians' assistants whenever possible. Physicians are motivated to keep costs down because HMOs share cost savings with them in the form of bonuses. Some HMOs even have their own hospitals and are motivated to run these efficiently for further cost savings.

HEALTH MOVEMENTS

In the past, lack of trust in physicians and reliance on home treatment meant that people took responsibility for their own health. Because health was linked to religious values, people considered slovenliness, gluttony, and neglect of one's health to be sinful. It is not surprising, then, that the most notable health movement was inspired by religion.

Health and the Second Great Awakening

The "Second Great Awakening" was a popular religious movement that swept through the northeastern part of the country in the early part of the nineteenth century. This religious movement was accompanied by a health movement, where sweeping changes in attitudes about the care of one's body accompanied concern for one's soul. A leader in this health movement was Sylvester Graham, a Presbyterian minister who believed that foods should be simple, not concocted from complicated recipes. He recommended eating fruits and vegetables, which were unpopular at the time, and although he did not know about vitamins or other scientific nutritional matters, he recommended eating the whole kernel of wheat (Root and de Rochemont, 1976). Graham developed a wheat cracker and traveled through the Northeast preaching his dietary religion and gaining many followers. Boarding houses were set up to serve the Graham crackers and other foods recommended by Graham. Oberlin College reserved part of its cafeteria for those following the Graham diet.

The health movement developed an ecumenical spirit when Seventh-Day Adventists became followers of Dr. Graham. Mother Ellen Harmon White, a Seventh-Day Adventist, founded the Western Health Reform Institute in Battle Creek, Michigan, a sanitarium to restore health to the ailing. She hired Dr. John Harvey Kellogg to manage it. Kellogg thought that chewing on dried, crispy foods would benefit the teeth, and he added them to the menu. One patient, Charles Post, was treated for ulcers at the sanitarium for nine months. Although not cured of ulcers, he believed that the food business might be profitable and developed a drink called Postum and later a cereal, Post Toasties. Kellogg soon followed suit, and the development of packaged foods began. While Americans are still concerned about the food they eat, the more dynamic health movement today is centered around drinking habits.

Alcoholics Anonymous (AA)

Millions of people every day attend AA meetings for the treatment of their alcoholism, a disease that has found no cure within established medical circles. AA is not organized with a bureaucratic structure; it has no membership lists, no dues, no fees, and no hierarchy. It was founded in the 1930s by two alcoholics who found that they could stay sober by talking to each other and by following a 12-step program. Today, AA is the major source of help for one of the most serious diseases in modern society.

Furthermore, this movement is spreading, so that now there are groups reaching people who live or have lived with alcoholics, such as Al-Anon, Al-Ateen, Codependents Anonymous (CoDA), and Adult Children of Alcoholics (ACOA). There are also programs for other addicts, such as overeaters in Overeaters Anonymous (OA), narcotics addicts in Narcotics Anonymous (NA), and smokers in Smokers Anonymous (SA). These groups also have no fees, no dues, and no hierarchy, but all practice a series of 12 steps, which each member works individually.

Modern Concerns About Diet and Exercise

Recent concerns about diet and exercise are not religiously motivated and do not have the strength of movements with a religious or spiritual motivation. Modern concerns about diet began with the peace movement of the late 1960s, which also opposed pollution and rejected both chemically filled foods and food packaging that added to litter and pollution. Health food stores sprang up to serve foods without chemicals, such as dyes, hormones, antibiotics, pesticides, and other nonfood ingredients. Foods were sold in bulk and used a minimum of packaging. Food additives account for $1.5 billion in sales for American chemical companies, who assure us that they are safe, and most Americans are satisfied with that assurance.

This is probably the first time in history that exercise could be classified as a social movement. In the past, people got a good deal of exercise quite naturally. Heavy labor had not been replaced by automation, and everyone knows that Abraham Lincoln walked miles to school, as did our grandparents and some of our parents. Today, heavy labor has been replaced by automation, and the automobile has replaced walking. In order to get exercise, a special time of the day must be set aside for such activity, as it no longer occurs naturally in the course of the day.

Americans are showing some concern about diet and exercise in order to reduce their chances of contracting heart disease and cancer. While there may be some improvement in this area, the percentage of overweight people in the United States has not been reduced over the past 20 years. In fact, the incidence of obesity in the United States has risen dramatically over the past 20 years, and research shows the situation may be worsening. According to data from the 1999–2002 National Health and Nutrition Examination Survey, nearly one-third of all adults are obese. Obesity is defined by the CDC as having an excessively high amount of body fat or adipose tissue in relation to lean body mass (CDC 2004).

Furthermore, according to the same data, the numbers of children who are overweight continues to increase as well which, in turn, means that these children have an increased chance of being overweight adults. Among children and teens ages 6–19, 16 percent (over 9 million) are overweight.

SOCIOLOGY AT WORK

Monitoring Medical Billing Practices

Henry Pontell has a B.A., an M.A, and a Ph.D., all in sociology, from the State University of New York at Stony Brook. He now teaches courses and does research in criminology at the University of California. In addition, he is a general partner in his own consulting firm, Pontell, Jesilow and Associates. One of his most significant projects was to help insurance companies and corporations prevent and detect incorrect billings by health-care providers.

The cost effectiveness of health care is very much an issue today, with health care consuming more than 11 percent of the GNP It is a major concern of the government, which administers the Medicare and Medicaid Systems; of individual consumers, who must pay ever-increasing insurance premiums or risk having to pay enormous medical bills out of their own pockets; and of businesses, which have traditionally offered health insurance for their employees.

"In many companies," Pontell explains, "health care is the fastest growing operating expense, and they're looking for ways to hold down costs. Some are making greater use of prepaid plans such as HMOs. Others are going to copayment, in which the company requires employees to pay part of the cost of insurance themselves. In effect, they're reducing employees' benefits. Another approach is simply to offer plans that provide less extensive coverage."

Pontell's company attacked the problem from a different angle—cutting down the incidence of fraud and abuse on the part of medical practitioners. Improper billing is a sizeable problem. In the Medicare and Medicaid systems, Pontell says, between 10 and 20 percent of all resources are lost to fraud and abuse. *Fraud* occurs when a health-care practitioner knowingly exploits the system, perhaps billing an insurer for services he or she did not actually provide. *Abuse* is unintentionally profit-

Overall, there are a variety of factors that play a role in obesity. In general, behavior, environment, and genetic factors have a part in causing people to be overweight and obese. "Despite obesity having strong genetic determinants, the genetic composition of the population does not change rapidly. Therefore, the large increase in ... [obesity] must reflect major changes in nongenetic factors" (Hill and Trowbridge, 1998). Behavior and environment are most readily manipulated and are the greatest areas in which prevention could occur.

While our culture has succeeded in producing fast and convenient food, more and more options, and super-size portions, we have not succeeded in getting off the sofa. Furthermore, because of technological innovations, our need to exert actual physical energy is diminished so that we increasingly are taking in more calories than we burn. According to the Behavioral Risk Factor Surveillance System, in 2000 more than 26 percent of adults reported no leisure time physical activity (CDC, 2004).

HEALTH CARE IN OTHER COUNTRIES

Most modern countries spend a great deal of money on health care, but unlike the American health-care system, where up to one third of the population gets

Monitoring Medical Billing Practices, *continued*

ing unfairly, perhaps by mistakenly sending two bills for the same medical procedure.

In essence, the Pontell system is quite simple. Some companies run their own health insurance programs; others contract with insurance companies, in effect paying them to administer the program for their employees. Most companies have some staff dedicated to investigating cases of potential fraud, but they rarely have the resources to do comprehensive investigations of thousands, or sometimes millions, of claims. Pontell's objective was to help them use their resources more effectively. "Through my research, I've developed a program for reviewing a company's records of claims filed by different physicians." What it yields is a list of names of physicians whose billing of the company is aberrant in some way. It is then up to the company to investigate these practitioners further.

"To conduct this work successfully," Pontell says, "I drew on my training in research methods, human relations, criminological theories relating to white-collar crime, criminal deterrence, medical sociology, law, and the professions. My sociological background is also helpful in two other ways: First, in relating the value of my service to executives in many different industries, and second, in interacting with and coordinating the efforts of corporate executives, insurance investigators, computer analysts, health care personnel, and my research staff."

Besides doing his consulting on medical billing practices, Pontell and his associates have written a book, *Prescriptions for Profit*, which fully describes the ways in which abuses can and have occurred within the health field. Pontell is a prime example of a sociologist who has blended an academic and an applied sociological career. He not only conducts criminological research, but also puts to use the knowledge he uncovers.

less than the care they need (Basch, 1999), other countries have found ways to distribute health care to all. The health-care systems of Great Britain and China illustrate how health-care planning can work. Also, health care in Third World nations, such as those in Africa, is traditional and does not involve expensive technological medicine.

The British Health-Care System

At the beginning of the Industrial Revolution, Great Britain had a **laissez-faire** economy—an economy with little government planning and intervention. Health care depended on **noblesse oblige**, the moral obligation of the rich to give to the poor and the suffering. Unfortunately, the economy produced a great many poor and suffering people whom the rich did not take care of. The British economic system gradually progressed from laissez-faire to welfare capitalism, in which the government takes a major responsibility for the welfare of its people within the capitalist system. The move to welfare capitalism was inspired in part by the need for an adequate health-care system.

In the nineteenth century, Great Britain was forced to use government money to provide some medical care for its people, and since 1911, Great Britain has had national health insurance, which has covered the medical expenses of workers (Denton, 1986, Brown 2000). Their wives and children were not insured, however, and they either did not go to doctors or else postponed treatment until it was too late. After World War II, the poor health of the people and the large number of elderly in the population created a serious problem, and the British developed the National Health Service (NHS), which provides health care for everyone and is funded by tax revenues.

The NHS has three branches, which are patterned after the health-care system that already existed in Great Britain. General practitioners deliver primary health care, treating the sick in their communities. *Consultants*, physician specialists in hospitals, provide secondary health care. The third sector is the public health sector, consisting of nursing homes, home nursing services, vaccination services, health inspections, and other community health services.

Physicians lost their autonomy when the government took control. General practitioners are now paid according to the number of patients for whom they provide care. This system does not provide the independence of a fee-for-service practice, but it does allow physicians more control over their income than working for straight salaries. Physicians are also allowed to see private patients and to charge them whatever they are willing to pay. This dual setup has been criticized for creating a two-class medical system, but very few patients want private care.

The working class is especially pleased with the NHS. Any citizen can go to a general practitioner without paying a fee; if hospitalization is required, the general practitioner refers the patient to a hospital consultant, again without charge. To control the costs of such a system, patients who do not have serious problems may have to wait for weeks or months for a consultation, as those who do have serious problems are seen first. The citizens of Great Britain have been very happy with the system.

Health Care in the People's Republic of China

The most dramatic development of a health-care system occurred in China after the Communist takeover in 1949. Before that time, the huge Chinese population suffered from malnutrition, poor sanitation, and poor health. Medical care was almost totally lacking. When the Communists came into power, disease and starvation were rampant (Denton, 1978). There was a shortage of doctors, and the few doctors available were divided between Eastern and Western medical practices. Because the Communists had few resources, they had to make efficient use of what little they had.

They did not try to develop scientific medicine after the model set by Western physicians. They combined Western medicine with traditional Chinese medicine, using acupuncture and herbs, along with some Western drugs and technology. The Communists also trained enormous numbers of so-called **barefoot doctors** to serve as unpaid health workers. The peasants in the communes selected commune members for training to become barefoot doctors. Trainees are not chosen on the basis of their academic or intellectual achievements, but on the basis of their political attitudes and their attitudes toward people, and they are required to support the political system, as well as the communes they serve.

To become barefoot doctors, the trainees receive 3–18 months of training in both Eastern and Western medical techniques. They then serve in their communes, emphasizing preventive medicine by developing sanitary systems and practices in the community, by teaching peasants proper hygiene and health care, and by vaccinating the population. As volunteers, they also work at ordinary jobs, side by side with the peasants for whom they provide care, and they can thereby easily recognize those who have poor health habits or illnesses. They treat simple illnesses and emergencies and direct the more seriously ill to better-trained doctors and nurses.

Urban areas have *Red Guard doctors*, who are not as well trained as the barefoot doctors. In addition, there are *worker doctors*, who work in factories. These doctors receive less training because highly trained full-time physicians and nurses are available in urban areas. The Red Guard and worker doctors serve the same grass-roots function as the barefoot doctors, serving without pay, stressing preventive medicine such as sanitation and inoculations, and generally looking after the health of members of their communes.

When hospitalization is necessary for an illness, individuals must pay for it. A variety of insurance plans are available to cover the costs of hospital care, but the costs are not high. Open heart surgery, the most expensive procedure, costs about two weeks' wages for the average worker—far less than in the United States.

The Chinese Communists emphasize equality. Although most doctors work in urban areas, they are transferred to rural areas if the need develops. They are not free to practice where they wish. They are expected to help nurses to care for patients, and differentiating the various types of doctors and nurses along class lines is forbidden.

When the Communists began their health-care system, the number of educated people needed to administer the large bureaucracy was inadequate. Because physicians were the most educated and capable people in the society, they became the leaders of the health-care system regardless of their political leanings. As the Communists increased their power, they became concerned about the independence of the Ministry of Public Health and its practices. They felt that this group did not place enough emphasis on treating rural populations and that this group focused on curative rather than preventive medicine (Maykovich, 1980). By 1955, the Communists had developed more political leaders to rule the Ministry of Public Health, along with physicians. Conflicts developed, and some errors were made because the politicians were not trained in medicine, but the conflicts generally broadened the work of the ministry because the politicians insisted on emphasizing areas that do not ordinarily interest physicians. The conflict between the interests of physicians and political interests has continued. Currently, the emphasis is on what interests the physicians—developing better technology and more sophisticated procedures for treating complicated illnesses.

Along with their interest in technology, the Chinese are doing more than any other country to develop the ancient art of herbal medicine, the use of plants in natural health-care systems (Ayensu, 1981). Beijing (formerly called "Peking" by Westerners) has an Institute of Medical Materials, and Guangzhou (formerly called "Canton") has the Provincial Institute of Botany for the study of herbal medicines. Thousands of medicinal plants are under cultivation for use in biological evaluations and chemical studies, and every year thousands of barefoot doctors are taught about the use of these herbs in health care. Medicinal plants have been used to treat venereal diseases, leukemia, high blood pressure, ulcers, poor digestion, skin cancer, and countless other diseases. They can be used as heart stimulants, diuretics, sedatives, and to induce abortion. The value of herbs is widely known throughout the world; for example, 25 percent of prescription drugs in the United States are based on flowering plants.

The Herbalist in Underdeveloped Nations

The WHO estimates that between 75 and 90 percent of the world's rural populations have herbalists as their only health-care practitioners. Cultural tradition gives the herbalist an important role, not only as a leading health practitioner but also as an influential spiritual leader who uses magic and religion, as well as herbs, to heal.

There are three types of healers in the African rural tradition, according to Ayensu (1981). The herbalists have the most prestige, but there are also *divine healers*, who cure through religious ceremonies, and *witch doctors*, who intercede against the evil deeds of witches who have possessed a patient. These three types of doctors have kept the native population reasonably healthy throughout history.

Herbalists traditionally have a three-year educational program. The first year often consists of ritual training and ceremony, including abstinence from sex and a ritual bath in a cemetery to make contact with ancestors. Alcohol, quarreling, and either cutting or combing the hair are forbidden. The first year's training serves to set the trainee apart from the rest of the community, in order to develop a distinctive personality.

The second year may begin with practical training in the gathering, identification, and use of herbs. The herbalist is also trained to carefully observe the natural habitats of herbs. Animals have been known to use plants in a medicinal fashion, and they can provide clues to the herbalist in the various uses of plants. Herbalists also learn to be sensitive to any spiritual messages that may increase their knowledge.

After the training program is completed at the end of the third year, herbalists pass through many ceremonies and rituals. They take an oath of allegiance to the trainer and have a graduation ceremony, much as physicians in the United States take an oath and are graduated so that the community will recognize their new status.

Many natives of Third World cultures who are trained in modern medicine in other countries resume using herbs for treatment when they return to their native cultures. The herbs are not only beneficial in themselves, but the tradition and ceremony involved in their use probably provide a **placebo effect** for the patient, a benefit arising from the belief that the medicine will work. It is widely known in our culture that if one believes that a medicine will help, the medicine is very likely to make the patient feel better.

However, some Third World physicians trained in modern medicine and the use of modern chemical pharmaceuticals do not use herbal medicines when they return to their native lands, probably because they are ignorant of the herbs' benefits. This is especially unfortunate, because pharmaceutical companies often go to underdeveloped countries and export the very plants that the modern physicians ignore. In fact, the export of medicinal plants to Western pharmaceutical companies is becoming so widespread that some plants—for example, a type of yam used as the foundation material in birth control pills—are becoming rare. After the plants are exported and manufactured into pharmaceuticals, they are then sold back to the country of origin at prices considered by many to be exorbitant.

Thinking Sociologically

1. How could we reduce U.S. health-care costs?
2. How could we provide health care efficiently to all of those who do not have insurance and cannot afford to pay for health care?
3. Why doesn't the United States have a national health service similar to Great Britain?
4. How can the conflict theory of health and illness help to explain the high cost of health care?

SUMMARY

1. Health and illness are of interest to sociologists because they are defined socially, as well as biologically, and because society needs a healthy population to survive.

2. *Pathological illnesses* are those in which the body is diseased or malfunctioning.

3. *Statistical illnesses* are those in which a person's health deviates from the norm.

4. Structural functionalists, who emphasize the integrative, functional characteristics of society, note that a sick role exists to integrate ill people into the social structure. This sick role involves certain expectations—for example, sick people are expected to get better and to resume their major roles, thereby ensuring the smooth functioning of society.

5. Conflict theorists contend that physicians share the viewpoint of elite classes in society and use their power over patients to maintain the social system.

6. Symbolic interactionists study the learned meanings associated with illness. In many societies, illness has been associated with sin or demons, and treatment often has had religious overtones.

7. In preindustrial days, when nutrition and sanitation were poor, infectious diseases were the greatest health hazard. The major health hazards now are heart disease, cancer, stroke, and accidents. Many of the occurrences of these diseases are caused by alcoholism.

8. AIDS, an infectious disease, could reach epidemic proportions.

9. Changing social structures often cause changes in prevailing illnesses—for example, industrialization and its accompanying pollutants are a major cause of cancer.

10. In the American health-care system, the medical model of illness prevails. The individual is considered responsible for prevention, and the health-care system becomes involved only when a person is already sick. The social causes of illness receive little attention.

11. Physicians developed their profession through the nineteenth and twentieth centuries to be powerful and prestigious. Most physicians provide primary health care.

12. Secondary care is provided by hospitals, which have specialized equipment and staff. There are several kinds of hospitals: nonprofit voluntary hospitals, tax-supported municipal hospitals, and privately owned proprietary hospitals.

13. Tertiary health care, the very highly specialized care developed with modern technology, is given in medical centers, which also conduct research and train physicians. Since specialized technology has been purchased by the other types of hospitals as well, the cost of medical care has greatly increased.

14. Most nurses work in hospitals. Nursing is still a relatively low-paying profession that reflects its origins as an occupation for working-class women.

15. A wide variety of other health-care workers work in hospitals, including technicians, administrators, and dietitians. Many others work outside of traditional medical settings.

Dentists are well-respected health-care workers, but nutritionists, chiropractors, and acupuncturists still struggle to have their practices accepted.

16. Health care, with its emphasis on expensive technology, has become very costly. Health insurance—such as Blue Cross/Blue Shield, insurance issued by private companies, and Medicare and Medicaid issued by the federal government—were first designed to help pay costs, but as more money became available, costs rose further.
17. The major departure in health-care delivery from the fee-for-service system and health insurance is the HMO. By using resources more efficiently, HMOs may provide a better, less costly system.
18. Health movements have called for improved diets and have provided treatment for alcoholism and related diseases. These movements typically have a religious or spiritual motivation.
19. Medical care in other countries reflects practices in their social systems. Great Britain's health-care system has evolved from the laissez-faire economic system with its belief in noblesse oblige to a welfare system within the capitalist framework.
20. China has developed a health-care system using both Eastern and Western medical knowledge. It has been able to integrate the system with its political system, and it has developed a corps of barefoot doctors who provide preventive health care in rural areas. China has also done research on the more sophisticated use of traditional medicines.
21. Underdeveloped nations continue to depend on herbalists, as they have for centuries. Herbalists go through an extensive training period, which both sets them apart from other members of their society and teaches them how to use herbs. Herbalists have been successful because their medicines cure illness.

KEY TERMS

alcoholism A disease related to the drinking of alcohol that has identifiable and progressive symptoms; if untreated, alcoholism can lead to mental damage, physical incapacity, and early death.

barefoot doctors People chosen by the peasants in the communes in Communist China to provide medicine and treat simple illnesses and emergencies. They receive three to eighteen months of training.

chiropractors Those who practice healing by manipulating the body, especially the spine.

degenerative diseases Those diseases that slowly disable the body as one gets older, such as heart disease and cancer.

diagnostic related groups (DRGs) The schedule of payment limits set by the federal government for Medicaid and Medicare recipients.

epidemiology The study of the spread of diseases.

fee-for-service A medical payment system in which the physician is paid for each visit and each service rendered.

fetal monitoring Measuring the vital signs of the infant as it is being born.

health maintenance organization (HMO) A prepaid health care plan in which a fee is paid in advance for all necessary health care.

heroic medicine Dramatic medical treatments such as bleeding, blistering, or administering poisonous laxatives.

hypochondriac A healthy person who believes he or she is ill.

infectious diseases Diseases caused by germs and viruses that can be spread from one person to another.

laissez faire An economy in which there is no government planning or intervention.

Medicaid Federally sponsored health insurance for the poor.

medical center A major hospital that trains new physicians, conducts research, and provides tertiary medical care.

medical model of illness A model of illness in which sickness is viewed as an individual problem requiring individual treatment.

Medicare Federally sponsored health insurance for people age 65 or older.

municipal hospital A hospital built and operated by a city or county.

noblesse oblige The obligation of the rich to give to the poor and suffering.

nutritionist A person who specializes in proper eating programs.

orphan drugs Drugs that are valuable in the treatment of rare diseases but are not profitable to manufacture.

pathological illness An illness in which the body is clearly diseased or malfunctioning in some way.

placebo effect A benefit arising from a patient's belief that a medicine will have a beneficial effect.

primary medical care The first general, overall care the patient needs.

proprietary hospital A hospital that is privately owned, usually by physicians or hospital corporations.

registered dietitian (RD) Licensed members of hospital staffs that plan regular meals and special diets for patients.

secondary care givers Those who provide more specialized care than that provided by a general practitioner.

secondary medical care Care that is more specialized than the care that a general practitioner provides.

sick role A set of expectations, privileges, and obligations related to illness.

social model of illness The view that much disease is caused by social conditions and that it can be cured by changing social conditions.

statistical illness An illness in which one's health varies from the norm.

tertiary medical care Long-term care requiring complex technology.

voluntary hospital A nonprofit hospital that treats patients who need short-term care.

DISCUSSION QUESTIONS

1. Discuss why it is important to understand the difference between pathological and statistical illness.
2. What are some positive and negative functions of the sick role for people with pathological illness and for people with statistical illness?
3. If you had the power to set social norms, when would you put people in the sick role, and when would you insist they perform their normal roles?
4. Does your definition of illness match current norms?

5. What are some advantages and disadvantages of the social model of illness and of the medical model of illness? Has the social model of illness become more valued in recent years? Explain and illustrate your answer.
6. Who benefits financially from the current health-care system?
7. Who would lose financially if the United States were to change to a plan similar to the National Health Service in Great Britain?
8. Discuss the relative merits and disadvantages of voluntary hospitals, proprietary hospitals, and medical centers.
9. How does the medical care in various countries reflect their social systems?
10. If you had the power to set social norms, what changes would you make, based on a social model of illness, to end the AIDS epidemic?
11. Discuss your thoughts as to why successful health movements are related to religious or spiritual movements.
12. Compare the training of a physician in this country with that of the herbalist in other societies. Is there a similarity in the way each is learning social roles?

PART FIVE

Human Ecology and Change

We have come to a turning point in the human habitation of the earth.

BARRY COMMONER

Collective Behaviors and Social Movements

Censorship

After having read much of this book, you probably realize that one of the central themes of sociology—and, some would argue, one of the central themes of a liberal arts education—is the notion that many aspects of social reality are not defined absolutely. For example, political and religious beliefs, standards of morality, and the cultural value of specific works of art and literature are often open to interpretation. Simply stated, people often disagree about what is true, false, good, or bad. When this is the case, competing groups often attempt—through censorship—to manipulate public opinion to accept their respective interpretations. Understanding how public opinion is shaped is an important topic in the study of collective behavior.

One of the most famous cases of censorship in the past few decades resulted in the death warrant issued by the Iranian leader Ayatolla Khomeini against author Salman Rushdie for his book Satanic Verses. Khomeini and his followers regarded the book as blasphemy against the Muslim religion, the belief system that lies at the heart of Iranian social and political life (Long, 1990). *Censorship*—the prohibition of some types of information—is deeply rooted and openly espoused in many cultures of the Middle East and Asia, and in countries with repressive governments. However, censorship also occurs in free countries, including the United States.

Censorship has long been a controversial issue in America, even though the First Amendment to the U.S. Constitution decrees that,

"Congress should make no law … abridging the freedom of speech, or of the press." For example, in 1798, John Adams, second president of the United States signed into law the Alien and Sedition Acts, which made it a crime to speak, write, or publish materials "with intent to defame … or bring into contempt or disrepute" members of the government. Under this law, some newspapers were shut down and their editors imprisoned. (It is interesting to note that in 1991, the leaders of the reform movement for democracy in the Soviet Union temporarily shut down *Pravda*, a major newspaper in the Soviet Union, because of its overtly communistic orientation.) The Alien and Sedition Acts expired in 1801 under President Thomas Jefferson. Jefferson believed that people should have free access to all information because, he argued, they would be able to recognize falsehood from the truth (Orr, 1990). Jefferson felt that Americans should be free to voice any opinion or to express themselves in any way, as long as it does not directly cause harm to any individual or to society. The rationale for this position is that censorship would be a greater harm to America's ideals than the expression itself.

In spite of the dysfunctions of censorship, recent controversies demonstrate that censorship is still a major issue in the United States. Robert Mapplethorpe's artwork calls attention to one such controversy—whether so-called offensive artworks should be censored. In 1990, many members of the U.S. Congress demanded that the National Endowment of the Arts (NEA) cease its funding of offensive art after Mapplethorpe—a recipient of NEA funding—displayed photographs depicting acts of homosexuality and other sexual behavior.

More recently, the issue of censorship has been in the news surrounding protest songs written in protest to the Iraqi invasion. Many country stations in much of the United States pulled recording artists the Dixie Chicks from their play lists because of a statement made by the group's lead singer, Natalie Maines. Maines expressed embarrassment and shame that the president of the United States is from Texas, the state that is also home to the country trio. *The New York Times* describes an event called a CD-smashing rally that took place in Louisiana, where a 33,000-pound tractor smashed collection of Dixie Chicks CDs, tapes, and other paraphernalia (Krugman, 2003).

Gumbel (2004) in the *Independent*, a newspaper published in the United Kingdom, noted that the comment might have been a "non-event" except for the actions of some ardent supporters of the president and some politically sympathetic stations. He goes on to describe the atmosphere in the U.S. as "not one of systematic censorship so much as extreme volatility" (Gumbel 2004). Brent Staples in the *New York Times* links the power of corporate monopolies to the near elimination of protest songs (Staples, 2003). Staples writes:

… independent radio stations that once would have played edgy, political music have been gobbled up by corporations that control hundreds of stations and have no wish to rock the boat. Corporate ownership has changed what gets played—and who plays it. With a few exceptions, the disc jockeys who once existed to discover provocative new music have long since been put out to pasture (Staples, 2003).

In April of 2007, television stations and radio stations all over the United States once again were faced with the issue of censorship. This time it was radio and television host Don Imus who was pushing it to the limits and was forced off of the air by NBC/MSNBC for making comments about a female college basketball team. After the efforts of many political and community leaders calling for the firing of Mr. Imus were heard by the networks (and their advertisers), he was terminated from his hosting position. Everyone was thinking that it would end there; however, what happened was once again a battle over censorship and the freedom of speech. A battle that still goes on even today. Should opinions be protected? Is freedom of speech being taken away? How far is too far when speaking over the public airwaves?

Perhaps now more than ever, the issue of censorship raises a number of important sociological questions: How are definitions of social reality created and maintained? Who benefits from censorship—society, or the groups that are attempting to prohibit the dissemination of some information? What part does censorship play in accelerating or inhibiting social movements? This chapter addresses these and other questions about collective behavior and social movements.

Most facets of social life follow patterns of rules and norms. People generally have a daily routine and conform to the roles expected of them. In the same way, such organizations as schools, churches, factories, and governments are highly structured institutions that tend to be stable and relatively static. In these organizations, decisions are made through some semblance of logical, rational discussion.

There is, however, another dimension of social life in which the activities are relatively spontaneous, unstructured, and unstable. This category includes such group activities as panics, demonstrations, riots, fads and fashions, disasters, and social movements. These actions, which may also follow certain patterns and established norms and rules, are instances of what sociologists call "collective behavior."

WHAT IS COLLECTIVE BEHAVIOR?

Sociologists use the term **collective behavior** to refer to spontaneous, unstructured, and transitory behavior of a group of people in response to a specific event. If the term were taken literally, it would incorporate all behaviors involving more than one person—that is, all of sociology—but sociologists use it in a more restrictive sense. The difference between the literal and the sociological definition can be clarified with an example. Take an event such as automobile crashes. To conduct safety tests, car manufacturers have a group of employees perform tests repeatedly and then collect data in an organized fashion about what happens when a car moving 35 miles per hour hits something. Compare this with the behavior of a group of people gathered at the site of a highway accident. Although both groups gathered to observe car crashes and are thus behaving collectively in the literal sense, only the second group is engaged in collective behavior in the sociological sense. The car company employees are reacting to a carefully controlled event in which the action is both expected and repeated. The group observing the highway accident reacts to a spontaneous, unstructured, unexpected, nonrecurring event. Panics, riots, crowds, fads, and fashions can all be viewed as spontaneous collective responses to transitory and loosely structured circumstances.

Collective behavior can be contrasted with **institutionalized behavior**, which is recurrent and follows an orderly pattern with a relatively stable set of goals, expectations, and values. In the preceding example, the autoworkers are involved in institutionalized behavior. Other examples of routine, predictable behavior would be going to class, commuting on a train, and going to church. If some unusual event takes place—an earthquake, train wreck, or fire, for example—collective behavior takes over. When people are confronted with an unfamiliar event for which no norms or rules have been established, they may behave in ways that differ radically from their normal conduct. People generally leave a theater in a calm, orderly fashion without pushing or shouting. However, if a fire breaks out, their conventional behavior would change to screams, shoving, and a rush for the exits. The ordinary norms break down and are replaced by new ones. Such actions occur infrequently, however, and only under special conditions.

Sociological theories and perspectives on collective behavior are useful to those whose occupations lead them to deal with large numbers of people. These include police, religious leaders, politicians, organizers of sports events, concert organizers, and others. Others who do not deal directly with large numbers of people but whose work may affect a large population could also use sociological insights into collective behavior. By understanding, for example, the preconditions of collective behavior or how spatial proximity affects crowds—both of which are discussed in this chapter—architects, designers, and city planners might be able to create more effective ways to channel large numbers of people. Concert halls, sports arenas, convention halls, apartment complexes, subways, airports, and other places that hold large numbers of people could be designed in ways that impede the formation of collective behavior. This chapter explores some theories and perspectives on collective behavior and suggests some ways that they might be used to promote social order in some situations involving large numbers of people.

PRECONDITION OF COLLECTIVE BEHAVIOR

Some specific conditions in contemporary societies tend to increase the likelihood of collective behavior. Rapid social change creates tensions and conflicts that sometimes lead to collective actions and violence. Social diversity and the associated inequalities in the distribution of wealth and of opportunities have produced many social movements—the women's movement, the Gray Panthers, the civil rights movement, and the labor movement. The mass media also play an important role in the dissemination of information of all types, from the trends in fashion and trends in music to prison riots. Some critics have suggested that the riots of the 1960s occurred in part because information on riots in other cities was transmitted through the media.

In addition to rapid social change, social diversity, and mass communications, some other preconditions encourage collective behavior. Neil Smelser, in his *Theory of Collective Behavior* (1962), identified six factors that, when they exist simultaneously, will produce collective behavior: (1) structural conduciveness, (2) structural strain, (3) generalized belief, (4) precipitating factors, (5) mobilization for action, and (6) operation of social control.

Structural conduciveness, the most general precondition, is the extent to which a society's organization makes collective behavior possible. A society that has no stock market cannot have a stock market crash. A country that has only one race or religion will not have race or religious riots. Note that structural conduciveness—the existence of banks, stock markets, or different religious or racial groups, for example—does not cause collective behavior. Rather, it is a measure of the existence of conditions in which it can occur. The fact that some aspect of a society is structurally conducive does not mean that collective behavior will happen; it means that, given certain other conditions, it can.

A **structural strain** is any kind of conflict or ambiguity that causes frustration and stress. Structural strains may be caused by conflicts between real and ideal norms, by conflicts between goals and the available means to reach them (anomie), or by the gap between social ideals (full employment, wealth, equality) and social realities (unemployment, poverty, and discrimination by age, race, and gender). Widespread unemployment among teenage blacks is an example of a structural strain.

A third determinant of collective behavior is **generalized belief**. Given structural conduciveness and structural strain, people must identify a problem and share a common interpretation of it for collective action to occur. People develop generalized beliefs about the conditions causing the strain. The women's movement, for example, began to grow only after the belief became widespread that women were discriminated against in employment, education, and other areas. Mobs form and riots take place only when people share a perception of some injustice or unfair treatment. Generalized beliefs may be based on known facts, shared attitudes, or a common ideology. The truth or accuracy of the beliefs is unimportant—the important thing is that they are shared.

Precipitating factors are the fourth determinant. Structural conduciveness, structural strain, and generalized belief alone do not inevitably cause collective behavior. A precipitating event must trigger a collective response. The precipitating event itself is sometimes fairly insignificant. An unwarranted search may start a collective protest in an overcrowded prison. Commodity trading may proceed quietly until a rumor arises that frost has severely damaged the expected orange harvest. The precipitating event can also be a more serious incident, of course. News that a police officer has shot a black youth can inflame a tense racial situation. As was true of generalized beliefs, a precipitating event need not be true or accurately communicated to exert an influence. Even an unfounded rumor can lend focus and support to a belief and can increase the likelihood of a collective response.

Mobilization for action is the fifth determinant of collective behavior. Once a precipitating event has taken place, people have to be persuaded to join the movement. Sometimes, an event mobilizes a group spontaneously, as when the crowd boos the umpire for making a bad call or when a crowd panics if someone yells "Fire!" Sometimes leaders emerge from within the group to encourage participation, which is what occurred during the formation of the Solidarity labor movement in Poland in 1980, when Lech Walesa, an unemployed electrician, quickly became the leader and spokesperson for the group. In other cases, outside leadership steps in to organize the people and push them into action, which is what often happened during the era when labor unions were being formed in this country. Collective behavior begins when mobilization for action takes place.

The **operation of social control** is the sixth and final determinant of collective behavior. Social control consists of the actions of the mass media, government, and other groups when they try to suppress or influence collective behavior. In the case of a potential strike, management might agree to listen to grievances, make a few changes, or raise wages slightly. If the strike takes place, it might fire striking workers and hire new ones. If social control cannot prevent collective action before it starts or halt it once it has begun, the collective behavior continues.

Smelser's approach, then, suggests that a series of six preconditions is necessary to produce collective action. The preconditions are closely interrelated—structural strains will not appear unless the society is structurally conducive to them, for example. This approach has been widely criticized, but it remains the most systematic and important theory of collective behavior.

Smelser's model should be applicable to a wide variety of collective behaviors. As an example, we use the 1991 police assault of a black motorist, Rodney King, in Los Angeles. The incident, shown many times on national television and reported in most newspapers in the country, involved four white baton-wielding police officers striking Rodney King more than 50 times after he was pulled over in his car for speeding. What caused this event to make national headlines and led thousands of citizens to demand the resignation of Los Angeles Police Chief Daryl Gates?

First, the circumstances were structurally conducive to a hostile outburst. It involved issues of race differences (black versus white) and power differences (police officers versus a motorist). Second, structural strains in the United States between blacks and whites, as well as between criminals and victims, are common. Note for example, how politicians often exploit fears over racial quotas, affirmative action, the early release of prisoners, and so forth to win elections. Concerns over the rights of the criminal exceeding the rights of the victim are widespread. These and many other structural strains were present in the Los Angeles police incident. Third, a shared generalized belief existed about inequalities, injustices, and unfair treatment of whites toward blacks, as well as of officers toward selected violators of the law. It is likely that most people are aware of instances of racism and brutality in police departments. Nonetheless, the existence of these three conditions, all quite common, seldom leads to collective action. What was different about this event?

A key factor differentiating this event from others was the videotaping of the brutal beating of an unarmed single black man by a group of white police officers. This videotaped film, frequently aired over national television, was a precipitating factor (our fourth precondition) that triggered a collective response. Denial was no longer a possible police or community response. The fifth determinant of collective behavior was the mobilization of people to take action. The action suggested was not merely toward the police officers, but toward the person in charge of them: police chief Daryl Gates. Social control, the sixth determinant, came with a commission report recommending that the chief step down, the involvement of Los Angeles Mayor Bradley in demanding police reform, and other measures to convince the public that corrective actions would follow.

APPLYING KNOWLEDGE OF PRECONDITIONS OF COLLECTIVE BEHAVIOR

One of the preconditions of collective behavior mentioned earlier is the failure of social control to halt collective behavior. Turner and Killian (1987) discuss four ways that the members of the "power structure"—the police, the courts, religious authorities, community leaders, and so forth—attempt to control collective behavior. We now briefly examine these social control measures and discuss their effectiveness in terms of the preconditions of collective behavior.

Repressive measures are used to control collective behavior through such means as banning public assemblies, forbidding the publication of subversive views, and punishing individuals who challenge the authorities. This form of social control is likely to be employed in repressive societies. For example, in the 1980s, the South African government outlawed the African National Congress (ANC) when the ANC tried to mobilize black South Africans to overthrow the established order of racial segregation known as "apartheid." In 1989, the Chinese government relied on military force to suppress an impending democratic revolution by its citizens. As is evident from such societies that attempt to use repressive measures, this is neither a practical nor a civil means of social control. Denying the civil liberties of some citizens is likely to be perceived by the populace as reducing freedom for the society in general. This may lead to structural strain and a generalized belief that groups are being treated unfairly.

Ironically, the very measures that some governments use to control collective behavior may function as preconditions for collective behavior. For example, in 1991, there was an attempted coup d'etat in what was then the Soviet Union, in which Mikhail Gorbachev was temporarily ousted from power. At the same time, military tanks filled the streets of Moscow to demonstrate the forceful intentions of those who attempted to take over. Many social scientists and journalists felt that the overt use of the military to suppress the democratic reform movement in the Soviet Union was a very significant factor that generated further public support for reform. Since then, of course, Gorbachev resigned as the Soviet Union disbanded into independent states.

Another means of controlling collective behavior is through the **role of police**, the military, the National Guard, or other formal agents. This type of control is self-explanatory: police force is used to restrain or break up situations in which large numbers of people pose a threat to an existing social order. This differs from the aforementioned repressive measures, however, in that it does not necessarily represent a repressive political or social policy, but can be purely situational. Such force may indeed be a part of repressive measures, however. Perhaps the major problem of using police force to control collective behavior is that it may actually heighten the potential for collective behavior rather than eliminate it. In the preceding section, for example, we called your attention to how the police in Los Angeles provided all of the preconditions for collective behavior.

Hidden repression—a means of controlling collective behavior that is not obviously or overtly repressive—is usually a more effective measure of social control. Typically, this occurs when governments manipulate the news through press releases, staged press conferences, and news "leaks." We mentioned earlier that some critics suggested that the ghetto riots of the 1960s were provoked because the media presented news of riots in other cities throughout the country. In the same way, governments can defuse collective social unrest by manipulating the media. The knowledge that the media have the power to help mobilize people to action is important not only because it can be a means of social control, but because it helps define the limits of responsible journalism. Because journalists and other members of the news media have the power to play a decisive role in creating social conflict or harmony, they need to seriously consider the perspectives they take on news events.

The final technique mentioned by Turner and Killian is **social control through amelioration**. This refers to the elimination of the source of strain that lies behind the collective behavior through the creation of specific policies. If high unemployment among black youths creates the potential for disruptive collective behavior, the government might create a policy that helps to create more jobs for black youths. If CIA recruitment on college campuses appears to cause stress among large numbers of college students, the CIA could change their recruitment policy and look elsewhere for potential employees. This method of social control might function to eliminate the structural strain that serves as a precondition for collective behavior.

Knowledge of collective behavior is useful not only to government policymakers and other members of the power structure, but to anyone who deals with large crowds—police, concert promoters, sports event organizers, religious leaders, and others. In the following section, we direct our attention to specific types of collective behavior and demonstrate how that information may be useful in some occupational settings.

Thinking Sociologically

1. Select an example of collective behavior that took place in your state or community. Can you identify preconditions that encouraged it?
2. Assess how social control measures (overt repressive measures, the police, hidden repression, or amelioration) could be or have been effective in controlling the example you used in the first question.
3. Can you cite an example during your lifetime in which collective behavior has produced positive social change?

SPATIALLY PROXIMATE COLLECTIVE BEHAVIORS: CROWDS

Characteristics of Crowds

A **spatially proximate collective** exists when people are geographically close and physically visible to one another. The most common type of spatially proximate collective is the **crowd**, a temporary group of people in face-to-face contact who share a common interest or focus of attention. This common interest may be unexpected and unusual, but it is not necessarily so. Although people in a crowd interact a good deal, the crowd as a whole is organized poorly if at all. According to Spencer and Turner (2000), crowds have four features that make them a unique area for study: anonymity, suggestibility, contagion, and emotional arousability.

Most types of collective behavior involve *anonymity*. People who do not know those around them may behave in ways that they would consider unacceptable if they were alone or with their family or neighbors. During a riot, the anonymity of crowd members makes it easier for people to loot and steal. In a lynch mob, brutal acts can be committed without feelings of shame or responsibility. Whatever the type of crowd, the anonymity of the individuals involved shifts the responsibility to the crowd as a whole.

Because crowds are relatively unstructured and often unpredictable, crowd members are often highly *suggestible*. People who are seeking direction in an uncertain situation are highly responsive to the suggestions of others and become very willing to do what a leader or group of individuals suggests, especially given the crowd's anonymity.

The characteristic of *contagion* is closely linked to anonymity and suggestibility. As people interact, the crowd's response to the common event or situation increases in intensity. If they are clapping or screaming, their behavior is likely to move others to clap or scream, and contagion increases when people are packed close together. An alert evangelist, comedian, or rock singer will try to get the audience to move close to one another to increase the likelihood of contagion and to encourage the listeners to get caught up in the mood, spirit, and activity of the crowd.

A fourth characteristic is *emotional arousal.* Anonymity, suggestibility, and contagion tend to arouse emotions. Inhibitions are forgotten, and people become emotionally charged to act. In some cases, their emotional involvement encourages them to act in uncharacteristic ways. During the Beatles concerts in the early 1960s, for example, teenage girls who were presumably quite conventional most of the time tried to rush on stage and had to be carried away by police. The combination of the four characteristics of crowds makes their behavior extremely volatile and frightening.

Although these four aspects of crowd behavior may be seen in almost any crowd, their intensity varies. Some crowds permit greater anonymity than others, and some have higher levels of suggestibility and contagion, yet one or more of these characteristics may not appear at all. The presence or absence of certain crowd features can be used to organize crowds into different categories.

Types of Crowds

All crowds are spatially proximate and temporary, and every crowd shares a common focus. However, some crowds are very low in emotional arousal and are highly unstructured, whereas others are quite emotional, aggressive, and even dangerous to one's safety.

The literature on collective behavior, following the lead of Herbert Blumer (1939), tends to label the nonemotional, unstructured crowd as a **casual crowd.** People who stop to look at an animated holiday display or who gather to watch a street musician would be of this type. Another type of crowd, sometimes called a **conventional crowd,** is more highly structured and occurs, for example, when spectators gather at a baseball game, attend a concert, or ride on an airplane. Although the participants are generally unknown to one another (anonymous), they have a specific goal or common purpose and are expected to follow established norms and procedures. At symphony concerts, for example, people applaud at the end of the music (an established procedure). When the music is being played, however, they do not run up and down the aisles or call out to a friend at the opposite side of the concert hall (not an established procedure).

The type of crowds that attract the most public attention are called **acting crowds,** the behavior of which is centered around and typifies aroused impulses. The two most dramatic forms of acting crowds are mobs and riots.

Mobs are groups that are emotionally aroused and ready to engage in violent behavior. They are generally short-lived and highly unstable. Their violent actions often stem from strong dissatisfaction with existing government policies or social circumstances; extreme discontentment with prevailing conditions is used to justify immediate and direct action. Disdainful of regular institutional channels and legal approaches, mobs take matters into their own hands.

Most mobs are predisposed to violence before their actions are triggered by a specific event. When feelings of frustration and hostility are widespread, leaders can easily recruit and command members. With aggressive leadership, an angry, frustrated mob in an atmosphere of hostility can be readily motivated to riot, commit lynchings, throw firebombs, hang people in effigy, or engage in destructive orgies.

Mob violence has erupted in many different circumstances. During the French Revolution of the 1780s and 1790s, angry mobs stormed through Paris, breaking into the Bastille prison for arms and calling for the execution of Louis XVI. In nineteenth-century England, enraged workers burned the factories in which they worked. Lynchings of blacks in the United States for real or imagined offenses continued into the twentieth century, often with little or no opposition from the formal agencies of control—police, courts, and public officials. Although lynch mobs are uncommon today, occasional instances of mob behavior take place over civil rights issues such as busing or housing, during political conventions and rallies, and among student or labor groups angry about perceived injustices. In 1987, for example, mob violence erupted in all-white Forsyth County, Georgia, when a white mob disrupted a march by whites and blacks protesting discriminatory antiblack housing policy.

A report in the *Seattle Times* called "Smart Mobs: The Next Social Revolution" examines Howard Rheingold's proposal that cyberspace and the coming generation of fast wireless devices and its experienced users could change the way mobs are created. Rheingold states that "the coming generation of fast wireless devices will make ad hoc 'swarming' a potent force for cultural transformation" (Andrews, 2002). Social protesters have managed to use technology effectively in part because it is still largely unregulated. However, with national security changes taking place, it remains to be seen whether or not technology will change the way action is mobilized.

Riots are collective actions involving mass violence and mob actions. The targets of their hostility and violence are less specific than those of mobs, and the groups involved are more diffuse. Most riots result from an intense hatred of a particular group with no specific person or property in mind. Destruction, burning, or looting may be indiscriminate, and unfocused anger can lead to violent acts against any object or person who happens to be in the wrong area at the wrong time. Like mobs, rioters take actions into their own hands when they feel that institutional reactions to their concerns about war, poverty, racial injustices, or other problems are inadequate.

The race riots of the 1960s in Watts in Los Angeles, Harlem in New York, and many other cities are the most commonly cited examples of rioting. These riots, which generally occurred in black ghettos, involved widespread destruction of property followed by extensive looting. The National Advisory Commission on Civil Disorders (Kerner, 1968) found that riots are associated with a number of factors, including discrimination, prejudice, disadvantaged living conditions, and frustration over the inability to bring about change. The incident that triggers a riot can be relatively trivial. In Detroit, for example, riots began after police raided social clubs suspected of permitting illegal gambling and the sale of liquor after hours. The riots of the 1960s, however, took place almost without exception in communities long frustrated by high unemployment, poverty, police harassment, and other factors. In the riots of the summer of 1967, tensions were increased by the sweltering weather. The riots that resulted from the 1991, post–Rodney King verdict are a similar example.

These findings are highly consistent with those of Lieberson and Silverman (1965), who studied conditions underlying 76 race riots in the United States between 1913 and 1963. They found that only four of them started without a precipitating event, such as a rape, murder, arrest, or holdup. They also found that race riots are most probable in communities with a history of being unable to resolve racial problems. The characteristics of crowd behavior—anonymity, suggestibility, contagion, and emotional arousal—were present in all the riots studied by Lieberson and Silverman.

THEORIES OF ACTING-CROWD BEHAVIOR

Students of crowd behavior have historically focused on acting crowds. How do acting crowds diminish individualism and encourage people to accept the attitudes and behaviors of the group? We have already examined Smelser's theory about the preconditions of collective behavior. Four additional perspectives are representative of the various other interpretations prevalent today. These include Le Bon's classical perspective, Blumer's interactionist perspective, Turner and Killian's emergent norm perspective, and Berk's game perspective.

The Classical Perspective

The **classical perspective** of acting-crowd behavior suggests that people in a crowd lose their conscious personalities and act impulsively on the basis of their instincts rather than reason. This perspective was articulated in what is probably the most influential single book ever written on collective behavior, The Crowd: *A Study of the Popular Mind* (1895), by the French sociologist Gustave Le Bon (1841–1931). During Le Bon's life, France was experiencing rapid social change, and earlier, mobs and riots had brought about the French Revolution. Le Bon, who considered crowds pathological, violent, threatening groups, believed that their destructive potential stemmed from "the psychological law of the mental unity of the crowd." According to Le Bon (1895, p. 2),

> The sentiments and ideas of all the persons in the gathering take one and the same direction, and their conscious personality vanishes. A collective mind is formed, doubtless transitory, but presenting very clearly defined characteristics. The gathering has thus become what, in the absence of a better expression, I will call an organised crowd, or, if the term is considered preferable, a psychological crowd. It forms a single being, and is subjected to the law of the mental unity of crowds.

This quote mentions two key concepts in the classical view of crowds: "collective mind" and "mental unity." Le Bon, the originator of the group-mind concept, believed that crowds cause people to regress. According to this view, crowds are guided by instinct, not by rational decisions. Under the influence of crowds, even conventional, law-abiding citizens may act impulsively and be guided by unconscious influences. Crowds do not reason, they respond instantly to the immediate situation. Why? (a) The anonymity of the collective gives each person in a crowd a feeling of power. (b) A contagion sweeps through the crowd like a virus passing from one person to another. (c) The participants become as suggestible as if they had been hypnotized. The result is the unquestioned acceptance of and obedience to the leaders.

The Interactionist Perspective

The **interactionist perspective** assumes that people in crowds reinforce and heighten one another's reactions. Often referred to as the *contagion model*, it was developed by Herbert Blumer (1939), who—like Le Bon—believed that crowd behavior is often irrational and emotional. Blumer, however, rejected the idea that it stems from a group or collective mind. Rather, he believed that crowd behavior results from what he called "circular reactions" operating in a situation of social unrest. In Blumer's words, a *circular reaction* is

> a type of interstimulation wherein the response of one individual reproduces the stimulation that has come from another individual and in being reflected back to this individual reinforces the stimulation. Thus, the interstimulation assumes a circular form in which individuals reflect one another's states of feeling and in so doing intensify this feeling. (p. 170)

In other words, in a situation of social unrest, interactions reinforce and heighten the unrest. If one group, for example, shouts "Let's get him," others model this behavior and usually adopt the same feelings and ways of expressing them. The reactions of these others increase the fervor of the original group, which in turn excites the rest of the crowd even further. In the absence of widespread unrest, such a reaction would never begin. Three types of circular reactions are milling, collective excitement, and social contagion.

In a milling crowd, people move about aimlessly. **Milling** tends to make people preoccupied with one another and less responsive to the usual sources of stimulation. Like hypnotic subjects who become increasingly preoccupied with the hypnotist, milling individuals grow more preoccupied with others in the crowd and become increasingly inclined to respond quickly, directly, and without thinking.

Collective excitement takes place when milling reaches a high level of agitation. People in the grip of collective excitement are emotionally aroused. They respond on the basis of their impulses, they are likely to feel little personal responsibility for their actions, and under the influence of collective excitement they may behave in an uncharacteristic manner (Blumer, 1939).

Social contagion comes about wherever milling and collective excitement are intense and widespread. What is fascinating about social contagion is that it can attract people who were initially just indifferent spectators. They get caught up in the excitement and grow more inclined to become involved. Unlike Le Bon's theory, this theory does not suggest the existence of a group mind. Rather, people's interactions tend to heighten in intensity until the group is capable of spontaneous behavior.

The Emergent-Norm Perspective

The **emergent-norm perspective**, first proposed by Turner and Killian (1957), emphasizes how norms influence crowd behavior and how new norms emerge and are maintained. Whereas Le Bon and Blumer stress similarities in the behavior of crowd members, the emergent-norm perspective focuses on differences in crowd members' behavior. As Turner and Killian (1957, p. 22) state,

> An emergent norm approach reflects the empirical observation that the crowd is characterized not by unanimity but by differential expression, with different individuals in the crowd feeling differently, participating because of diverse motives, and even acting differently.

According to this view, crowds do not behave as a homogeneous unit. Observers may think they act as a unit, but divergent views and behaviors may go unrecognized or be dismissed as unimportant. When attention is focused on the acting crowd, people frequently overlook those who remain silently on the sidelines, those who passively lend their support, and those who express little excitement. People behave differently because they act in accordance with different norms. Norms influence all social conduct, and new norms arise during novel situations such as mob actions or riots. Some may accept norms that make violence and looting acceptable. Others may define the situation differently and choose to leave or remain uninvolved.

The process by which norms emerge occurs daily in any context of human social interaction and communication. All of us are dependent on those around us to define and determine what a given event means. When others in the group shout, run, or express fear, we are likely to feel tremendous pressure to conform to their behavior. An untrained observer may note the one dominant behavior and describe the group members as unanimous in their definition, mood, and behavior. More careful observation, as emergent norm theory suggests, would reveal that unanimity is an illusion and that differential expression does take place.

The Game Perspective

The **game perspective** on crowd behavior suggests that crowd members think about their actions and consciously try to act in ways that will produce rewards (Berk, 1974). Unlike other theories, which assume that crowds behave irrationally, game theory stresses the importance of rational decisions. People weigh the rewards and costs of various actions and choose the course that is most likely to lead to a desired end. Looting, for example, may yield a reward such as a television set. If few people are looting, the chances of arrest may be fairly great, and a potential looter may choose not to take the risk. If, on the other hand, there are thousands of people looting stores, the chances of arrest are quite low, and the person may decide to join in. Milling about before engaging in violent action may be used as a time for assessing various courses of action and for evaluating the strength of support. According to this perspective, violence is not necessarily irrational. It may be the result of a conscious decision that it will be useful in acquiring a desired end: civil rights, jobs, housing, new leaders, or something else. When many people desire the same goal, collective action can increase their chances of achieving it.

APPLYING THEORIES OF ACTING-CROWD BEHAVIOR

Knowledge of crowd behavior, especially what causes crowds to become volatile, could be used by organizers of mass events—sports contests, rock concerts, political conventions—to help protect against potential disaster. We now look at one example—a stampede in a Chicago nightclub in 2003, in which over 70 people were killed or critically injured—to see how knowledge of crowd behavior could have been used to avert this catastrophe.

MSN news (February 3, 2003) gave the following account of what happened:

> More than 20 people have died and dozens more have been injured following a stampede in a U.S. nightclub. It is believed up to 1,500 people fled in panic after security staff at the Chicago club used capsicum spray to stop a fight. The nightclub was still packed at 3 a.m. when a fight broke out. Security guards forced their way through the crowd and in a decision that's already being questioned by police, they used pepper spray and mace to break it up. That had an immediate and deadly effect on the crush of humanity. The gas started to spread, affecting hundreds of club patrons who started to panic. Many were gagging for breath, others were vomiting. The rush for the one stairway turned into a stampede, and people tripped and were crushed trying to find the exit. So many people tried to get out through the front door that they formed a human wedge. As more clubbers started pushing from behind, few could break out of the crush. "I was pushed down the stairs, then everybody started piling down on my leg and I couldn't move my legs at all," said a victim. Rescuers were confronted with a chaotic scene with emotional survivors looking for partners and screaming at police to arrest the security guards who started the panic. Police in Chicago say at least 21 people are confirmed dead and another 50 are injured. Ambulance officers say 19 people were in cardiac arrest when they arrived but many were eventually revived. Five hospitals were deluged with victims, some critically injured with crushed chests and broken bones, others suffering from asthma-like symptoms. At this early stage, the police say they've already discovered that the club's owners had broken several safety regula-

tions. There were more than 1,500 people in the club—way over the permitted number. The emergency exits were also locked.

We now look carefully at the preceding account to see whether there are some precautions that could have been taken, based on knowledge of the theories of acting crowd behavior, that might have prevented the stampede. Three organizational facts leading to the collective behavior that occurred that evening are apparent. First, the club was over capacity. Second, the security officers sprayed mace into the crowd. Third, there were insufficient emergency exits for club participants. Had an interactionist perspective been used beforehand, it could have been deduced that people would begin to become preoccupied with one another (as a result of milling) and would become aroused by any central event such as a fight or start performer (leading to collective excitement), and that this excitement would spread to even the most mild-tempered party-goers (social contagion).

Although it is always easier to understand events in retrospect, knowledge of the theories of crowd behavior could have spurred the club owners to handle the situation differently. First, the club owners could have limited the number of people they admitted. Second, perhaps the club security could have found used alternate means to break up the disturbance, a method that would not have caused partygoers to panic, gag for breath, or vomit. Third, a greater number of exits could have been available, so that in the event of an emergency, they would have been able to quickly disperse. Using the characteristics of crowd behavior and the theories of crowd behavior discussed so far in this chapter, what would you do to lower the probability of catastrophic collective behavior at a night club, concert, or sports event?

Thinking Sociologically

1. How might the emergent-norm and game perspectives be applied to explain the acting-crowd behavior of the Chicago night club event?

2. The rock group the Grateful Dead, which came into existence in the late 1960s, is still popular, especially among its faithful fans, known as "Dead Heads." The band has ceased touring since the death of Jerry Garcia. Even though they attracted large crowds, the Grateful Dead concerts were notably peaceful and orderly. This is ironic because the group seemed to represent very free, liberal, nontraditional, antiestablishment values. Use the knowledge of collective behavior found in this chapter to examine why Grateful Dead concerts were usually orderly and devoid of dangerous outbreaks of collective behavior.

3. Use knowledge contained within this chapter, including insights that you have gained from the preceding example of Grateful Dead concerts, to develop a strategy that concert and sporting-event organizers could use to try to protect against the potentially dangerous outbreaks of collective behavior.

SPATIALLY DIFFUSE COLLECTIVE BEHAVIORS

Spatially diffuse collectives are collectives that form among people spread over a wide geographical area. The most common types are known as masses and publics.

Masses and Mass Behavior

A **mass** is a collective of geographically dispersed individuals who react to or focus on some common event. We often hear the term *mass* in speech: mass media, mass communication, mass hysteria. The millions of people who watch the Super Bowl or World Series on television or who listen to these on radio constitute a mass. The thousands of people who rush to the store to buy an item rumored to be in short supply constitute a mass. Although dispersed over a large geographical area, they are reacting to a common event.

Members of a mass come from all educational and socioeconomic levels. They are anonymous, and they interact little or not at all. A mass has no established rules or rituals, no shared or common ideology, no hierarchy of statuses or roles, and no established leadership (Blumer, 1939).

Fads and fashions are specific types of diffuse collective mass behaviors. Generally, they arrive suddenly and disappear quickly, but they may attract great interest from large numbers of people during their tenure. A **fad** is a superficial or trivial behavior that is very popular for a short time. Some examples of fads are flagpole sitting; crowding into telephone booths; using hula hoops; dancing the jitterbug, twist, or frug; swallowing goldfish; streaking; and buying pet rocks, Trivial Pursuit, "Cabbage Patch" dolls, or more recently Bart Simpson shirts, cups, and other paraphernalia. Most of these fads were or are harmless and have no long-range social consequences.

Aguirre and others (1988) examined the characteristics and effects of fads and tested them with data on over 1,000 incidents of streaking—running nude through a public area— at colleges and universities. They reviewed some characteristics of fads listed in the literature, which included their homogeneity, their novelty, their oddness when examined by existing social norms, their nonutilitarian behavior that lacks serious consequences for the participants, their suddenness in appearance, their rapid spread, as well as their quick acceptance and short-lived nature. Contrary to conventional wisdom, their analysis of streaking as a fad revealed that streaking events had clearly identifiable social structures. They suggest that the oddness, impulsivity, inconsequentiability, and novelty of fads has been exaggerated in the literature. To those participating in streaking, the behavior was meaningful and consequential.

Their results conform to the emergent-norm framework of collective behavior that was described earlier. The fad of streaking was made up of compact and diffuse crowds, and was greatly influenced by mass media coverage of previous events; it had a division of labor and clear normative limits and, in the words of Aguirre et al., "was spawned by social organization; it was a product of group life."

In contrast to a fad, **fashions** are more enduring, widespread, and socially significant. A fashion is a temporary trend in some aspect of appearance or behavior. Fashions resemble fads, but they tend to be more cyclical. They are generally thought of as influencing styles of dress, but there are also fashions in music, art, literature, and even sociological theories. To be "in fashion" is to wear the style of hair and the types of clothes that advertisers are pushing and that are currently in vogue. At any given time, hemlines may be long or short, neckties may be wide or narrow, and hairstyles may be straight or curly. Designer clothing, blue jeans, or rap may reveal important information about who is "in" and other important information about social status.

Fads and fashions provide many people with a sense of excitement, feelings of belonging, or a source of identification and self-esteem. Fads and fashions, however, are also big business. Packaging pet rocks, opening a hip-hop club, and selling the latest clothes are ways of making money. Although fads and fashions may seem trivial to the average consumer, they can bring large profits to those who take advantage of them.

SOCIOLOGY AT WORK

Market Research

A. Emerson Smith is the president of Metromark Market Research, Inc., in Columbia, South Carolina. The firm helps hospitals, utility companies, financial institutions, newspapers, and other businesses identify marketing problems, and it uses opinion and attitude surveys as tools to find solutions to those problems.

Smith began doing market research in 1974 when he was an assistant professor in sociology at the University of South Carolina in Columbia. He and a colleague discovered that marketing researchers were using the methods of sociology and social psychology. "In fact," he says, "we saw other areas in market research where the methods and theory of sociology could be used but weren't. We found that many people in marketing research had business or marketing backgrounds but little training in social theory and research methods."

Smith's job is to help clients identify problems in their business and in marketing, decide on the most appropriate research tools, do the research, interpret the findings, make recommendations to the client on the best ways to solve the problem, and then see that those recommendations are tested and implemented. "The bulk of my time," he says, "is spent talking with clients about problems they have in running their companies and in marketing products and services to their customers."

Smith tells of a particular problem he had to help a client solve. "The marketing director of an investor-owned electric and gas utility came to us with this problem: How can we satisfy the needs of our engineers for investment in equipment, the needs of our customers for a continual improvement in the quality of service, and the needs of our stockholders for a return on investment? The utility's residential customers don't have a choice over their supplier of electricity. To many, a utility is seen as a monopoly, able to take advantage of that situation by raising rates without having to improve services. Yet, the utility is regulated by a state power commission that can either allow or

Mass hysteria and panic are two other types of diffuse collective mass behaviors. **Mass hysteria** is a widespread, highly emotional fear of a potentially threatening situation. A **panic** occurs when people try to escape from a perceived danger. An example of mass hysteria and panic took place at Three Mile Island beginning on Wednesday, March 28, 1979, and it continued for several weeks. The incident involved a series of events at the nuclear power plant at Middletown, Pennsylvania. The fear was that a total meltdown of a power unit would cause serious radiation contamination of all people in the area and the destruction of all plant life over a vast land area. When news of the event first broke, commercial telephone lines were jammed with calls to and from people living near the Three Mile Island area. Newspapers around the country carried maps of the area that showed 5-, 10-, and 20-mile concentric circles of danger and reported that evacuation would be the only hope of avoiding contamination. By noon Friday, just two days after the event, the governor of Pennsylvania recommended the immediate evacuation of all pregnant women and preschool children living within 5 miles of the area. By evening that plan was expanded to include everyone within a 20-mile radius. By this time, vast numbers (the actual percentages and numbers are unknown) had already departed, many going to stay with relatives

Market Research, *continued*

disallow requests for rate increases. Unless the utility gets the support of its customers and improves services, these customers and consumer advocates can argue in front of the power commission to disallow rate increases needed for equipment and stockholder dividends."

How did Smith use his sociological training to help his client? "First, we did library research on studies that had been published on customer satisfaction in power companies and other service industries. Next, we used U.S. census data to describe the customer base, which included rural and urban residents. Our training in demography was helpful here. The problem called for us to do explanatory research. We expected to find that customers with higher incomes would have different evaluations and expectations than would customers with the lowest incomes, whose expenditures on electric bills would constitute a greater proportion of their household income. Here we used our knowledge of social stratification and status, both basic sociological concepts. Our training in research methods helped us design high return mail survey samples that were representative of all customers. We then presented the client with our recommendations on how they could satisfy the needs of customers and, thereby, the needs of their engineers and stockholders."

Smith emphasizes that the skills he learned from sociology courses are very valuable to people in business, and he encourages more sociology students to seek work with companies like his. "All those hours sitting through sociology and social statistics courses really pay off when I have to analyze the impact of social variables on the attitudes and behaviors of utility customers, hospital patients, physicians, or bank customers. Sociology students are not destined to work only in nonprofit or social welfare settings. Sociology students have perspectives and skills that are useful to businesses. Business executives want consultants to help them understand the behavior and lifestyle of consumers. Sociologists can do that."

and friends in neighboring states or in other areas. To lessen the extent of mass hysteria and panic and to convey an impression that all was "safe and under control," President Carter visited the reactor site on Saturday, March 31.

A more recent example of mass hysteria might be the public reaction to AIDS after basketball star "Magic" Johnson announced in November 1991 that he had HIV. This disease was first reported in 1981, but for ten years was assumed by the major media to be confined to homosexuals and intravenous (IV) drug users. There seemed to be a widespread belief that "I am neither gay nor a user of IV drugs, so it can't happen to me." Public opinion polls (described in the next section) showed that almost everyone knew about AIDS, but about 10 percent thought it could be spread from simply being in the presence of an infected person. These beliefs resulted in instances of children being kept home from school, people refusing to work with AIDS victims, and police being given masks and gloves for protection, responses which, given current medical knowledge about the disease, seem to be overreactions.

With Magic Johnson's announcement that he had contracted the AIDS virus through heterosexual intercourse and his plea to practice "safe sex," the world reacted with surprise and shock. Discussions of condoms became more frequent and more public than ever before in U.S. history. The lack of an existing coherent educational program about AIDS and the lack of a widespread distribution system and an open discussion of condoms helped fuel mass hysteria about the disease. As of this writing, AIDS is still an incurable disease, but the public is now widely aware of it, and AIDS awareness is likely to have a significant impact on sexual behavior in nonmarital as well as marital relationships.

Thinking Sociologically

1. In what ways and in what contexts over the past decade might an example of AIDS be considered mass hysteria? Can you identify ways in which the emotional fear of this threatening situation could have or can be lessened?

2. Consider the recent anthrax scares in our society. Could public reactions to this perceived threat constitute mass hysteria? Why/why not?

Publics and Public Opinion

A public is another type of spatially diffuse collective; Blumer (1939) defines a **public** as a group of people who are confronted with an issue, who do not agree on how to address the issue, and who discuss the issue. Publics have no culture and no consciousness of themselves as a group. Voters, consumers, magazine subscribers, and stockholders are separate publics. Although these people are geographically dispersed, they share a concern about an issue. As they discuss the issue to resolve their differences about it, a generalized public opinion begins to prevail.

Public opinion is defined variously as any opinion held by a substantial number of people or as the dominant opinion in a given population. Public opinion is especially complex in mass cultures, in which many publics have differing viewpoints. Some publics want their tax money to go to defense; others would prefer to see it spent on social programs. Some publics favor abortion; others oppose it. These conflicts of interest multiply as cultures become more complex. In simpler cultures, most decisions about new issues can be made on the basis of traditional folkways and mores.

The formation of public opinion is influenced by a wide range of factors. Organizations such as the political parties, the National Organization for Women (NOW), and the National Rifle Association (NRA) have a profound effect on public opinion. The mass media are also influential. They do not merely report the news; they can also create it. By choosing to discuss a particular issue, the media focus people's attention on it. The frequency with which an issue is reported often depends entirely on the discretion of the media, particularly with issues that seldom have events, such as homelessness, illiteracy, common crimes such as rape or murder, or child abuse. If their reporting tends to favor one side of the issue, they may succeed in shifting public opinion in that direction. Opinion is further influenced by a population's cultural values and ethnic and social makeup. Leaders from business, government, or religion also shape public opinion, and it is interesting that elected leaders, who were put in office by the public, often try to use their office to influence those who elected them. Because public opinion is so important in contemporary social life, there is considerable interest in how it is measured.

Knowledge of public opinion is generally obtained through the use of polls, which are a form of survey research. A *public opinion poll* is a sampling of a population representative of a geographical area, of a group of interest to the pollster, or of a society as a whole. The pollster asks the sample population a series of questions about the issue of concern. In most polls, the responses are provided in advance, and the respondents simply state whether they agree or disagree with a statement or answer a yes-no question.

These responses are then tabulated and reported to the sponsoring agency.

In recent elections, pollsters have been criticized for announcing results before the voting is completed, but in most cases, increasingly refined polling techniques enable pollsters to make very accurate predictions. There are a number of potential problems in taking accurate polls, however. The sample to be polled and the questions to be asked must be carefully selected, because answers to ambiguous or loaded questions may not reflect true opinions. For example, even those who support a woman's right to abortion might find it difficult to answer "yes" to a question such as, "Do you favor a mother's right to murder her helpless unborn children?" A question phrased in this way will not yield representative responses. Polls may also force people to express opinions on subjects they know nothing about. Another problem is that they do not attempt to assess a person's reasons for giving a "yes" or no response.

Those who sponsor polls often use the results to influence public opinion, which may be done through the use of **propaganda**—attempts to manipulate ideas or opinions by presenting limited, selective, or false information. The purpose is to induce the public to accept a particular view. Propagandists rarely present opposing or alternative views, and when they do present those views, the presentations are usually distorted. Propaganda tries to influence people by playing on their emotions rather than by discussing the merits of the various positions. However, if it diverges too far from known facts or personal beliefs, the public may simply dismiss it as nonsense.

The use of propaganda in the early 1980s was evident in the controversy over requiring that both biblical and evolutionary versions of human life on earth be taught in the public schools. Each side issued statements that played on emotions, diverged from known facts, and contained limited and selected information. Each side had the goal of inducing people to accept its own point of view. Those who believe in the literal biblical interpretation that God created all matter and energy in exactly six solar days are not swayed by those who present fossil evidence of evolution covering a time period of millions of years. On the other hand, those who believe in the separation of church and state are not swayed by the argument that evolution and the scientific method is based as much on belief as creation theory is. If propaganda is to be successful, it must not conflict too strongly with a person's existing values and beliefs.

Another way to manipulate public opinion is through **censorship**, prohibiting the dissemination of some types of information. A community may try to prohibit sex education, X-rated movies, or the sale of pornographic magazines. A car manufacturer may refuse to release information about a potential danger in a car's construction. Government officials may withhold controversial information, as the United States government did when it kept secret the bombing of Cambodia during the Vietnam War and kept secret the diversion of funds to the Nicaraguan Contras. Censorship manipulates public opinion not by presenting distorted or incomplete information, as propaganda does, but by withholding information that might influence public opinion.

Thinking Sociologically

1. Select a controversial censorship issue that currently exists in your community. Use the material in this chapter to examine the following: (a) Why is there an attempt to censor the information? (b) Who are the groups that are the force behind the censorship attempts? (c) What are the definitions of social reality that are at stake? (d) Who would benefit from censorship of this information? (e) What would be the individual and social costs, if any, if the information were censored? and (f) Is censorship justified in this particular case?

2. We have been witnessing social movements toward freedom and democracy around the world. Is censorship justifiable if the intention is to bring about social reforms that would provide people with more democratic social systems and government?

SOCIAL MOVEMENTS

A social movement is a collective effort to bring about social change and to establish a new order of social thought and action. Movements involve more than a single event or community; they begin during periods of unrest and dissatisfaction with some aspect of society, and they are motivated by the hope that the society can be changed.

Initially, social movements are poorly organized. They have no identity, and their actions are often spontaneous. As they develop, however, they acquire an established leadership, a body of customs and traditions, divisions of labor, social rules and values, and new ways of thinking. This process of institutionalization leads to the development of formal organizations and, ultimately, to new social systems.

Types of Social Movements

In the United States, a number of new movements have developed during the past few decades, including the civil rights movement, the women's liberation movement, the ecology movement, the peace movement, the gay liberation movement, and the nuclear freeze movement. Each one involves a collective effort to bring about social change and to establish a new social order. Various authorities have used different schemes to classify such movements.

Turner and Killian (1987) organize these movements in terms of their orientation: *Value-oriented movements* advocate social changes concerning various groups, which result in broader adherence to the central values of the larger society. The civil rights, gay liberation, and women's movements, for example, are efforts to fulfill the American values of equality, freedom, and justice. *Power-oriented movements* aim to achieve power, recognition, or status. The Nazi movement in Germany and the Bolshevik Revolution in Russia are extreme examples of this type of movement. *Participant-oriented movements* focus on personal rewards and fulfillment for their participants. Back-to-nature and evangelical movements are of this type.

Actually, there are as many different kinds of movements as there are goals. *Reactionary movements* advocate the restoration of the values and behaviors of previous times. *Conservative movements* attempt to protect the status quo and resist change. *Resistance movements* are aimed at preventing or reversing changes that have already occurred. *Reformist movements* try to modify some aspect of society without destroying or changing the entire system. *Revolutionary movements* believe in the overthrow of the existing social order as a means of creating a new one. *Nationalistic movements* hope to instill national pride and a sense of identity with one's country. The goal of *utopian movements* is to create the perfect community. *Religious movements* want to convert or modify the existing belief system in accordance with a religious principle. *Expressive movements* would like to change people's emotional reactions to help them cope with prevailing social conditions. Some movements have several purposes or combine the features of several types of movements. Regardless of the way they are categorized, they all involve collective efforts to initiate (or sometimes resist) a new order of social thought and action.

The Development and Life Cycle of Social Movements

Social movements develop most frequently in complex, nontotalitarian societies. They evolve through a series of stages that closely parallel those suggested by Smelser as preconditions of the development of any type of collective behavior. Blumer (1939) divided the development of movements into four steps: social unrest, popular excitement, formalization, and institutionalization. These stages are idealized types, of course, because development varies considerably from one movement to another.

The stage of **social unrest** parallels Smelser's stages of conduciveness and structural strain. This stage is characterized by unfocused restlessness and increasing disorder. Often, people are unaware that others share the same feelings and concerns. Rumors abound, and persons become increasingly susceptible to the appeals of agitators. These agitators do not advocate any particular ideology or course of action; rather, they make people more aware of their discontentment and raise issues and questions to get people thinking.

Social unrest is followed by the stage of **popular excitement**. During this period, unrest is brought into the open. People with similar concerns begin to establish a rapport with one another, and they openly express their anger and restlessness. Then the group begins to acquire a collective identity, and more definite ideas emerge about the causes of the group's condition and how the situation can be changed. Leaders help define and justify feelings, identify the opposition, and point out obstacles that must be overcome. They also offer a vision of what things could be like after the movement succeeds. In the past, movements such as these have been led by social reformers such as Martin Luther King, Jr., charismatic leaders such as Gandhi, and prophets such as Christ. In other instances, a *group* of individuals clarifies the issues, provides direction, and stirs up excitement. In these cases, the movement becomes increasingly better organized.

During the third stage, **formalization**, a formal structure is developed, and rules, policies, and tactics are laid out. The movement becomes a disciplined organization capable of securing member commitment to stable goals and strategies. At this stage, movements make concerted efforts to influence centers of power (Turner and Killian, 1972). The stable organization of the movement and the establishment of various programs and committees serve to keep members involved after the initial urgency has died down. The leadership shifts from agitators, reformers, or prophets to statespersons or intellectual leaders and administrators. The intellectual leaders develop the ideology, symbols, and slogans that keep the movement alive. The administrators work on procedures, tactics, and organization. It is at this stage that movements often split into factions or break down completely due to differences of opinion over such questions as how the movement should proceed, how radical its tactics should be, and what types of concessions should be granted.

In the formalization stage, it becomes clear that the success of social movements requires more than just successful leadership. A group of committed followers is also needed. It has traditionally been assumed that followers are drawn from the ranks of the discontented, the deprived, the frustrated, and the angry. A more recent perspective, **resource mobilization theory**, suggests that the success of a social movement depends not only on those who benefit from it directly but also on their ability to mobilize other individuals and groups to contribute time, money, and influence to the cause even though they may not directly benefit.

Oberschall (1973) argues that mobilization results not from the recruitment of large numbers of isolated individuals, but from the recruitment of blocs that are already highly organized and politically active. Gamson (1975) agrees, maintaining that collective resources are more important than personal goals in shaping a movement, and that one of the most important resources is groups that are already organized. The success of the civil rights movement, for example, depended on the effective mobilization of churches, state and federal agencies, and government leaders, as well as white sympathizers. Martin Luther King, Jr., and his followers could not have been as successful alone. Likewise, the women's movement, to be effective, needed the support of legislation, the mass media, political leaders, men, and existing groups that supported feminist goals.

If adequate resource mobilization takes place, social movements reach the final stage in the life cycle of social movements, **institutionalization**. During this stage, the movement becomes integrated into society. It may have a permanent office and personnel hired to continue its efforts. At this point, it may also have accomplished its primary purpose and may disappear into the network of institutions that already exists. In other instances, the success of a movement leads to the development of new social movements. Some movements never reach this stage—they are suppressed by formal or informal powers and disappear or go underground. At the institutional stage, the unrest, discontent, and popular excitement have largely ceased and are replaced by formal offices, organized groups, and structured activities.

Thinking Sociologically

Using Blumer's and Smelser's ideas concerning social movements, what role might the Internet play in developing and shaping future social movements? What sort of role, if any, do you currently see the Internet playing in the development of social movements?

SUMMARY

1. Collective behavior is spontaneous, loosely structured, and transitory. Institutionalized behavior, by contrast, is more orderly and has stable goals, expectations, and values.

2. There are two types of collective behavior: *spatially proximate*, in which people are in face-to-face contact or geographical proximity, and *spatially diffuse*, in which people are dispersed over a wide geographical area.

3. Certain conditions increase the likelihood of collective behavior. Smelser described six of them: (1) *structural conduciveness*, the existence of conditions or situations in which collective behavior is possible; (2) *structural strain*, some type of frustration, stress, conflict, or dissatisfaction in society; (3) *generalized belief*, a shared understanding of the reasons for the strain and stress; (4) *precipitating factors*, events that trigger a collective response; (5) *mobilization for action*, in which individuals or groups encourage participation in collective behavior; and (6) *the initiation of social controls*, in order to counter the conditions just listed.

4. The most common type of spatially proximate collective behavior is the *crowd*. The characteristics of crowds are anonymity, suggestibility, contagion, and emotional arousability.

5. Crowds vary in type, ranging from very unemotional and highly unstructured crowds to very emotional, active crowds, such as mobs or rioting crowds.

6. There are four major theories of acting-crowd behavior. The classical theory of Le Bon posited the existence of a collective or group mind that

has a regressive influence on behavior, which tends to be irrational, irritable, and impulsive.

7. Blumer's interactionist theory focused on social interactions and a circular reaction process that generates milling, collective excitement, and social contagion.

8. The emergent-norm theory of Turner and Killian emphasized how norms influence crowd behavior and how the emergence of new norms causes a divergence of crowd views and behaviors.

9. Berk's game theory stressed the rational decision-making process involved in crowd behavior and suggested that people consciously weigh the rewards and costs associated with various kinds of collective activity.

10. In spatially diffuse collectives, people who are widely dispersed focus on a common event. The groups who watch a particular television show or buy a given item are considered masses—although they are geographically separate, they participate in a common behavior.

11. Fads and fashions are mass behaviors in which a large number of people participate for a brief period.

12. Mass hysteria takes place when a potentially destructive or threatening event causes a widespread, highly emotional fear. Sometimes, these fears are accompanied by panic, mass flight, or attempts to escape.

13. A public is a spatially dispersed group confronted with a common issue but divided about how to address it. As the issue is debated or discussed, a variety of public opinions develop, which vary from one public to another.

14. Opinions are influenced by such factors as dominant cultural values, the mass media, group affiliations, and social backgrounds. They can be measured by a type of survey research known as "polling." Propaganda and censorship are two ways of manipulating public opinion.

15. Social movements are organized collective efforts to bring about social change and establish a new order of social thought and action. Turner and Killian classify movements in terms of their orientation, whereas other authorities use different classification schemes.

16. As social movements develop, they generally go through four distinct stages: social unrest, popular excitement, formalization, and institutionalization. Although all social movements grow through roughly the same process, the goals of different movements can vary considerably. Their success depends heavily on their ability to effectively mobilize resources.

KEY TERMS

acting crowd A crowd that acts on the basis of aroused impulse and thus one that may be volatile, aggressive, and dangerous.

casual crowd A crowd that is high in anonymity but low in suggestibility, contagion, emotional arousal, and unity.

censorship Prohibiting the availability of some type of information.

classical perspective A view of acting crowd behavior that suggests that people in a crowd lose their conscious personalities and act impulsively on the basis of their instincts rather than reason.

collective behavior The spontaneous, unstructured, and transitory behavior of a group of people in reaction to a specific event.

collective excitement In the interactionist perspective on crowd behavior, the stage during which milling reaches a high level of agitation.

conventional crowd A crowd, such as the spectators at a baseball game, whose members are anonymous but share a common focus and follow established social norms and rules.

crowd A temporary group of people in face-to-face contact who share a common interest or focus of attention.

emergent norm perspective A view of collective behavior that emphasizes how new norms emerge and influence the behavior of crowds.

fad Superficial or trivial behavior that is very popular for a short time.

fashion Temporary trend in some aspect of appearance or behavior. Fashions resemble fads but tend to be more cyclical.

formalization The stage in the development of social movements in which a formal structure is developed, and rules, policies, and tactics are laid out.

game perspective A view of crowd behavior that suggests that members think about their actions and consciously try to act in ways that will produce rewards.

generalized belief A stage in the development of collective behavior in which people share a common identification and interpretation of a problem.

hidden repression A means of controlling collective behavior that is not obviously or overtly repressive.

institutionalization The process by which orderly, stable, structured, and increasingly predictable forms of behavior and interaction are developed.

institutionalized behavior Recurrent behavior that follows an orderly pattern with a relatively stable set of goals, expectations, and values.

interactionist perspective A view of crowd behavior that emphasizes how people in crowds reinforce and heighten one another's reactions.

mass A spatially diffuse collective in which geographically dispersed persons react to or focus upon some common event.

mass hysteria A form of diffuse collective behavior involving a widespread, highly emotional fear of a potentially threatening situation.

milling The stage in the development of crowd behavior during which people move about aimlessly, grow increasingly preoccupied with others, and become increasingly inclined to respond without thinking.

mobilization for action A stage in the development of collective behavior during which people are persuaded to join the movement.

mobs Emotionally aroused groups ready to engage in violent behavior.

operation of social controls A stage in the development of collective behavior in which the mass media, government, and other groups try to suppress or influence collective behavior.

panic An attempt to rapidly escape from a perceived danger.

popular excitement The stage in the development of a social movement during which social unrest is brought into the open and people with similar concerns begin to organize.

precipitating factors A stage in the development of collective behavior during which an event triggers a collective response.

propaganda An attempt to manipulate the ideas or opinions of the public by presenting limited, selective, or false information.

public A group of people who are confronted with an issue, who do not agree on how to address the issue, and who discuss the issue.

public opinion Any opinion held by a substantial number of people; or, the dominant opinion in a given population.

repressive measures Measures, such as banning public assemblies, used to control collective behavior.

resource mobilization theory The theory that the success of a social movement depends not only on those who benefit from it directly but also on its ability to mobilize other individuals and groups to contribute time, money, and influence.

riot A form of collective behavior involving mass violence and mob action.

role of the police A means of controlling collective behavior through the use of police force.

social contagion A stage in the development of crowd behavior during which the crowd's response to a common event increases in intensity and the crowd's behavior moves others to behave in the same way.

social control through amelioration The creation of specific policies to eliminate the source of strain that lies behind the collective behavior.

social movements Collective noninstitutionalized efforts to bring about social change and establish a new order of social thought and action.

social unrest The stage in the development of social unrest that is characterized by unfocused restlessness and increasing disorder.

spatially diffuse collectives Collectives that form among people spread over a wide geographical area.

spatially proximate collectives Collectives in which people are geographically close and physically visible to one another.

structural conduciveness The extent to which a society's organization has the conditions that make a particular form of collective behavior possible.

structural strain Any conflict or ambiguity in a society's organization that causes frustration and stress; often seen as a precondition for collective behavior.

DISCUSSION QUESTIONS

1. How does collective behavior differ from institutionalized behavior? Give examples of each type of behavior.
2. Select an incident of collective behavior that has occurred recently, and discuss the preconditions that might have led to it.
3. Explore the different types of crowds and crowd behavior that tend to exist or have existed in your college campus, community, or city where you live.
4. How do mobs and riots differ? Are either or both less likely when and where people know one another?
5. Select examples not provided in the text that illustrate each of the theories of acting-crowd behavior. Discuss how the theories can be used to explain each of the respective examples you have selected.
6. Mass behaviors include fads and fashions. Can you identify any fads that exist at present? What is currently in fashion in terms of hairstyle or clothes among your peer group?

7. Public opinion poll results appear daily in newspapers and magazines. Find one, and discuss: (a) Who was the public that was polled? (b) What issue was raised? and (c) Of what use are the results, and to whom?

8. How does propaganda differ from censorship? Provide examples of each.

9. Propaganda was described as the use of limited or selective information. In what contexts is this useful? Is it ethical or dishonest to not "present the truth, the whole truth, and nothing but the truth"?

10. Examine the development and life cycle of a contemporary social movement or any other social movement in which you might be interested.

Population and Ecology

Environment

Environmental pollution has been a prominent public issue for more than two decades. While the major threats to the environment are now commonplace knowledge—our natural resources are being depleted while our air, land, and water are becoming polluted—people in the United States and many other countries have a history of taking natural resources and the environment for granted. As a result, the environmental damage can be catastrophic. In Romania, decades of industrial pollution have made it nearly impossible for children to play outside without becoming covered with soot, which should serve as a warning to the rest of the world the type of damage that can occur when there is a lack of concern for the environment.

In the prosperous decades following World War II—the 1950s and 1960s—cultural values in the United States did not include high regard for the environment or concern for energy conservation. For example, Eliott Currie and Jerome Skolnick (1997) cite evidence that American energy consumption has doubled between the years 1950 and 1972, increasing as much during that time as it had in the entire 175 previous years of American history. The table on the following pages shows the 65 countries that account for virtually 100 percent of the oil consumption in the world.

The early 1970s, however, marked the end of this "state of environmental unconsciousness." In 1970, President Richard Nixon created the Environmental Protection Agency (EPA), thus demonstrating the federal government's concern about the environment and bringing environmental issues to the fore of national

Major Oil Consumers
(Oil Consumption in Millions of Tons)

Rank	Country	1980	1990	2000	2003	Percent of Total
1.	United States	794.1	781.8	897.6	914.3	25.14%
2.	China	88.0	110.3	230.1	275.2	7.57%
3.	Japan	237.7	247.7	255.5	248.7	6.84%
4.	Germany	147.3	127.3	129.8	125.1	3.44%
5.	Russian Federation	na	249.7	123.5	124.7	3.43%
6.	India	31.6	57.9	106.1	113.3	3.12%
7.	South Korea	24.1	49.5	103.2	105.7	2.91%
8.	Canada	90.1	79.8	88.1	96.4	2.65%
9.	France	109.9	89.4	94.9	94.2	2.59%
10.	Italy	97.9	93.6	93.5	92.1	2.53%
11.	Brazil	55.0	58.4	85.8	84.1	2.31%
12.	Mexico	48.7	67.7	85.7	82.6	2.27%
13.	United Kingdom	80.8	82.9	78.6	76.8	2.11%
14.	Spain	52.2	48.7	70.0	75.5	2.08%
15.	Saudi Arabia	29.9	51.2	62.4	67.0	1.84%
16.	Iran	31.0	47.1	56.1	54.0	1.48%
17.	Indonesia	19.7	29.8	50.2	53.9	1.48%
18.	Netherlands	38.6	35.0	41.7	44.5	1.22%
19.	Taiwan	19.7	26.8	39.8	41.7	1.15%
20.	Thailand	11.6	19.6	34.8	38.7	1.06%
21.	Australia	29.7	31.6	37.7	38.1	1.05%
22.	Belgium & Luxembourg	26.6	24.8	33.9	34.8	0.96%
23.	Singapore	9.5	23.3	33.5	34.1	0.94%
24.	Turkey	14.8	22.1	31.6	31.9	0.88%
25.	Egypt	13.2	23.8	27.2	25.9	0.71%
26.	South Africa	12.0	16.6	22.5	24.2	0.67%
27.	Venezuela	19.5	18.4	22.5	23.9	0.66%
28.	Malaysia	8.1	13.0	20.4	23.9	0.66%
29.	Greece	12.4	15.7	19.9	20.9	0.57%
30.	Poland	17.1	15.8	20.0	20.5	0.56%
31.	Argentina	22.9	18.3	20.3	17.5	0.48%
32.	Pakistan	5.1	10.7	18.8	17.0	0.47%
33.	Portugal	8.5	11.1	15.5	16.6	0.46%
34.	Sweden	24.8	16.4	15.2	15.8	0.43%
35.	Philippines	10.9	11.5	16.6	15.6	0.43%
36.	United Arab Emirates	5.4	12.7	12.2	15.0	0.41%
37.	Austria	12.2	10.8	11.8	14.3	0.39%
38.	Kuwait	4.3	5.5	10.4	13.7	0.38%

(continues)

Rank	Country	1980	1990	2000	2003	Percent of Total
39.	Ukraine	na	63.0	12.0	13.1	0.36%
40.	China Hong Kong SAR	6.5	6.3	9.7	13.1	0.36%
41.	Switzerland	12.8	12.8	12.2	12.1	0.33%
42.	Finland	12.8	11.0	10.7	11.4	0.31%
43.	Romania	18.6	18.7	10.0	11.0	0.30%
44.	Chile	5.1	6.6	10.9	10.4	0.29%
45.	Colombia	7.8	9.5	10.5	10.0	0.27%
46.	Algeria	5.5	9.2	8.5	10.0	0.27%
47.	Norway	9.3	9.2	9.4	9.6	0.26%
48.	Kazakhstan	na	21.5	7.4	9.5	0.26%
49.	Denmark	13.6	9.0	10.4	9.3	0.26%
50.	Czech Republic	11.6	8.4	7.9	8.6	0.24%
51.	Republic of Ireland	5.7	4.4	8.2	8.4	0.23%
52.	Peru	6.6	5.8	7.4	7.4	0.20%
53.	New Zealand	4.2	4.9	6.3	6.9	0.19%
54.	Uzbekistan	na	12.6	6.8	6.5	0.18%
55.	Hungary	11.3	9.3	6.8	6.2	0.17%
56.	Ecuador	3.0	4.2	5.8	6.1	0.17%
57.	Belarus	na	24.8	6.6	6.1	0.17%
58.	Azerbaijan	na	8.5	6.2	4.4	0.12%
59.	Bulgaria	14.0	8.8	3.9	4.3	0.12%
60.	Bangladesh	1.6	1.9	3.2	4.2	0.12%
61.	Slovakia	6.7	5.0	3.4	3.7	0.10%
62.	Turkmenistan	na	4.4	3.1	3.7	0.10%
63.	Lithuania	na	7.5	2.4	2.5	0.07%
64.	Qatar	0.5	1.1	1.2	1.7	0.05%
65.	Iceland	0.6	0.6	0.9	0.9	0.02%
	World	2,974.7	3,138.0	3,526.1	3,636.6	100%

Source: "Statistical Review of World Energy 2004."

Although the US ranks first in consumption, it ranks third in production with 9.23% of production (Statistical Review of World Energy 2004).

attention, where they have remained since (Melville, 1989). Although there has been some success in environmental protection since the 1970s—for example, the phasing out of leaded gasoline has curtailed *some* forms of air pollution, regulations about dumping of toxic wastes and raw sewage have improved the water quality in some lakes and streams—the pressures of a growing population and an expanding economy have led to increased environmental pollution and, in the words of EPA head William K. Reilly, to "an array of environmental problems even more daunting than the pollution crises of the past generation" (Melville, 1988, p. 4).

Keith Melville identifies three reasons why environmental issues are more difficult to address today then they were when they first came to the fore of public attention. First, many of today's pressing environmental hazards are less visible, and thus more difficult to call to the public's attention. It is much easier to mobilize public support for problems that are readily apparent, such as polluted water, air, and land. However, it is difficult to reach consensus about problems that cannot be seen easily, such as acid rain, contaminated groundwater, carbon-dioxide emissions and their resultant greenhouse effect, or ozone-layer depletion.

Second, responsibility for environmental pollution is widespread. When attention was first called to environmental pollution, individual sources were identified and forced to take remedial action. However, today's knowledge about pollution makes it clear that we are all partially responsible for environmental protection. Melville states, "Virtually everyone who owns a car, operates a power lawn-mower, or uses electricity generated by burning fossil fuels contributes to the build-up of ozone near ground level and carbon dioxide and other greenhouse gases in the atmosphere. While major toxic air emissions from industrial sources are fairly well controlled, many of the current emissions come from relatively small sources, such as dry cleaners and wood stoves."

Third, environmental problems are global in scope. Most of our environmental problems are not truly local, but result from worldwide industrial and consumer behavior. For example, air pollution is not only the result of fossil fuel use in the United States, but because of its use worldwide as well. Because the source of the problem is global rather than local—that is, the result of the habits of 6.4 billion inhabitants of the planet—many people feel that it makes little difference what they do, as individuals or perhaps even as a nation. However, this belief took a turn in 2006/2007 when the phrase "Going Green" was introduced to the public. The concept of going green, which was started in order to gain the public's interest in cutting back on the usage of oil, electricity, and those machines that require these types of energy to operate has seen a tremendous boost over the last year. From Hollywood to Washington, DC, the public is becoming more aware of the need for the United States to take the lead in this ecological battle. It has been the platform for many presidential candidates for the 2008 election and in the early part of 2007, past Vice-President and perhaps future Presidential candidate Al Gore won an Academy Award for his documentary film on Global Warming. This cemented the gap between the film industry and politics and created a platform for the majority of society to be able to not only relate to but also to weigh in on.

Although the environment seems to be a topic more suited to engineers, chemists, biologists, and geologists, it is important to sociologists as well because of the interrelationships that exist between population and the environment. The rapid population growth and increased social needs that have occurred during the twentieth century have led to increased industrialization. From the structural functional perspective, the social well-being and high standard of living that industry functions to provide are accompanied by the latent dysfunction of environmental pollution. At first glance, this gives the impression that industry itself is to blame for environmental problems. However, as James Coleman and Donald Cressey suggest, "The origins of the environmental crisis are not to be found in a few polluting industries but in the basic social organization and cultural outlook of the modern world" (1990, p. 538). In other words, industry in and of itself is not to blame for environmental pollution. Rather, the key to understanding environmental pollution lies in understanding our cultural ideals and the ways in which our social life is organized. Natural scientists study and explain the physical ways in which the balance of nature is disturbed; sociologists and social scientists study and explain the intricacies of society and culture that often lead to practices that disturb the balance of nature.

If you are like [illegible] you worry about the population a gr[illegible]gh you may not realize it. By [illegible] number of people in [illegible]cts your chances [illegible] If you do marry, [illegible] your spouse, whether you [illegible] many you will have. It may also [illegible]ces of being promoted, your taxes, the [illegible]hich you will retire, and your income after retire[illegible]ent.

Sometimes, we also worry about population problems in the larger world. Poverty, disease, accident and death rates, world hunger, the problems of crowded cities, vanishing farmlands—all are population problems. To avoid sounding all too gloomy, we should point out that some of the most practical things we can do to resolve these problems involve studying the population in hopes of influencing it. We may be able to better understand our own lives, plan sensible social policies to shape the world's future, and develop sound business, investment, and economic strategies by understanding the size, age, sex ratios, and movements of the population. The study of these various characteristics of society is called "demography."

DEMOGRAPHY AND THE STUDY OF POPULATION

Demography is the study of the size and makeup of the human population and how it changes. Demographers want to know how many babies are being born, what diseases are in the population, how long people live, whether they stay in the same place or move about, and whether they live in remote regions or crowded urban areas.

Collecting the Data

Demographers use many statistics in their work. After all, their main concern is counting people. In fact, the word *demography* is often used to refer to the study of population statistics. Societies have always realized how important it is to know about their members, and since early times have kept some form of **census**—a count of the population—usually with a record of the age and sex of its members. From such records, estimates of early populations can be made and studied. For hundreds and sometimes thousands of years, family lineages have been recorded and passed on orally, to keep track of who was born to whom. Written records of deaths can be found in early Greek and Egyptian accounts. The Bible says that Mary and Joseph were on their way to be counted in a Roman census when Jesus was born.

Modern nations keep much more reliable records of their populations. The first census in the United States was carried out in 1790, and censuses are still carried out once every ten years, with questionnaires mailed to all known households. In addition, interviewers search door to door for those who are not contacted or do not respond by mail. These large attempts to gather data are very difficult to accomplish.

The 2000 census has been seriously criticized for underreporting people, especially the poor and homeless. Some people do not receive the questionnaires or do not bother to return them. Interviewers do not find some people, sometimes because the job is not organized or done properly, sometimes because people avoid being found. State and local governments are quick to complain that their populations have been undercounted because these governments receive federal funds based on their population counts.

A smaller census is made every year and is more accurate than the ten-year census because it is based on a carefully chosen random sample of the population rather than trying to count everyone in the population. A random sample has the advantage of assuring that everyone in the population is represented in the sample without the necessity of finding everyone in the population. The smaller yearly census also has the advantage of being done by more highly experienced interviewers, and there is less need to hire many temporary, inexperienced people, as is required for the ten-year census.

In addition to population counts, **vital statistics**—records of all births, deaths and their causes, marriages, divorces, some diseases, and similar data—are recorded in each state and reported to the National Center for Health Statistics. Most modern nations keep records as accurate as those of the United States. Underdeveloped nations also attempt to record their populations, and although data from these countries may be relatively inaccurate, they provide enough information to assess world population trends.

Three variables can cause the size of the population in a given region to change: (1) births, (2) deaths, and (3) migrations. Demographers measure these factors in terms of their rates. **Fertility** is a measure of the rate at which people are born. **Mortality** is a measure of the rate at which people die. **Migration** is the movement of people into or out of a geographical area. To understand how populations change, it is necessary to understand how demographers measure these factors.

Fertility

Fertility data indicate the rate at which babies are born. The crude birth rate is simply the number of births per 1,000 population, but if we want to predict how many babies will actually be born, more information is needed. We must know the **age-sex composition** of the society, and the number of males and females in the population, along with their ages. A population with few women will have few children. The ages of the females are especially important because children and older women do not have babies.

In most societies, the number of men and women is about equal. About 105 males are born for each 100 females, but women live longer than men. Thus, there may be more men at younger ages, but there are more women in older groups. During the childbearing years, the number of men and women is usually about equal, except in societies suffering from wars in which large numbers of men are killed, or in societies experiencing a great deal of migration. Areas that men move out of have a surplus of women, whereas the areas they move into have a surplus of men; and a society with unequal numbers of men and women will have a low birth rate. There was an imbalance of this sort in the Soviet Union because so many men were killed during World War I, the Civil War of 1917–1921, World War II, and the repressive era following World War II. As a result, many women were left without husbands and did not have children, and the birth rate dropped dramatically. For years, the Soviets kept secret their great loss of population and low birth rates, but the latest available information indicates that they are now comparable to the United States in birth rates and population size.

Demographers generally assume that women are fertile from age 15 to age 49. They also know that more children are born to women in the middle of their childbearing years, but some women in their childbearing years choose not to have children, and few have as many as they potentially could. An individual woman's potential for bearing children is called her **fecundity**. Although women can potentially have 20–25 children, very few have this many. Developed countries have experienced some unprecedented declines in fertility rates during the last half of the twentieth century where the mean fecundity rate has been falling since the 1920s (*Human Reproduction*. 2001).

Fertility varies greatly among societies and among subcultures within societies. The number of children born in a society is affected by three major factors: wealth, environment, and societal norms about marriage and children. Generally, richer nations have lower birth rates, and poorer nations have higher birth rates. The same relationship between wealth and birth rates holds within nations: the upper classes usually have lower birth rates than the poor classes.

Fertility rates are also different in rural and urban areas. Women in rural areas usually have more children than those in cities. In rural areas, children are needed to help with farm labor, but in modern urban areas, children are not productive. Rather, they are an expense to house, feed, clothe, and educate. They may also decrease a family's income when a parent must either pay for child care or stay home to care for them. Many demographers believe that the birth rate of the world will decline and perhaps drop sharply as underdeveloped nations become more industrialized and urban.

A society's norms regarding the value of children and the age at which marriage is considered acceptable have a strong effect on fertility rates. In countries in which women marry young, the birth rates are higher than those in which they marry later ,because of differences in the number of childbearing years. Norms about the number of children a family should have and about the acceptability of birth control and abortion also affect the birth rate. Separation by war, working away from home, and conflicts between spouses also reduce the birth rate, whereas a cultural practice of abstaining from intercourse during menstruation may make intercourse more likely during fertile periods and may result in an increased birth rate.

A low or high fertility rate will of course affect the number of people born into the population, but this is only one of several factors that influence population size. Mortality and migration rates are also influential.

Mortality

Mortality, the rate of death in a population, can be measured very simply. The crude death rate is the number of deaths in a given year per 1,000 population. Like the crude birth rate, however, the crude death rate does not provide enough information to predict how many people will die or to compare death rates among populations. For a more accurate estimate of the death rate, demographers consider age and gender. A population with many old people will have a higher death rate than a comparatively young population, and because women live longer than men, a population with many women will have a lower death rate. Demographers often use an **age-adjusted death rate**, a measure of the number of deaths at each age for each sex, usually per 100,000 living at that age. Demographers can also compute life expectancy by predicting how many of each age cohort, or age group, will die at each age.

Mortality, like fertility, varies with wealth. When people, especially infants, have adequate food, housing, and medical care, they are less likely to die of disease. The rate of *infant mortality*, death in the first year of life, was very high in the Middle Ages, but now it is lower, and the average life expectancy has been greatly increased. Infant mortality is low and life expectancy high in more developed nations, such as the United States, Canada, and European countries.

Researchers have uncovered what they hope to be a one-time blip in infant mortality rates in the United States. Infant mortality rates rose in 2002 for the first time in decades. Our nation's infant mortality rate edged upward from 6.8 deaths per 1,000 live births in 2001 to 7.0 deaths per 1,000 in 2002 (Stein, 2004; CDC, 2004). In explaining the higher infant mortality rate, researchers point to the surge in older women having babies; the popularity of fertility treatments; and, paradoxically, advancements in identifying and saving fetuses in distress. Because we have the ability to identify fetuses in distress and deliver them early, they are dying at higher rates in early infancy (Stein, 2004; CDC, 2004).

An increase in infant mortality is cause for attention, because the infant mortality rate usually reflects the general well-being of the larger society. However, life expectancy in the United States continues to rise because of our ability to prevent, detect, and treat cancer, accidents, stroke, and heart disease.

TABLE 19-1 2003 CRUDE BIRTH RATES AND DEATH RATES FOR SELECTED COUNTRIES

Country	Birth Rates	Death Rates
Australia	12.6	7.32
Austria	9.4	9.7
Denmark	11.5	10.7
Finland	10.5	9.9
France	12.5	9.1
Greece	9.8	9.9
Italy	9.2	10.1
Japan	9.6	8.6
Netherlands	11.3	8.7
Panama	20.8	6.2
Romania	10.8	12.2
Sweden	9.7	10.6
United States	14.1	8.4

Source: Data from *The 2003 Information Please Almanac.*

People in Norway, Sweden, and the Netherlands have the longest life expectancy. An infant boy in these countries can expect to live 72 years, an infant girl 78 years. The death rate is higher and the life expectancy shorter in India, Africa, South America, and Southeast Asia, where poverty is widespread (see Table 19-1).

Death rates also vary by class within nations. In the United States, for example, poor people have a higher rate of infant mortality and a shorter life expectancy than the rich; blacks have a larger proportion of poor people, higher rates of infant mortality, and shorter life expectancies than whites (CDC, 2004). The more important factor in infant mortality, however, is poverty, not race. Black infants born to parents living in predominantly white neighborhoods, indicating higher income, have lower infant mortality rates than white infants living in predominantly black neighborhoods, where poverty is greater (Yankauer, 1990).

Migration

Migration includes both **immigration**, movement into an area, and **emigration**, movement out of an area. Migration is harder to define and measure than birth or death rates. To be considered a migrant, how far must a person move, and how long should the person remain in the new place? In the United States, moving within a county is not considered migration, but moving from one county to another is. *Migrant workers*, who travel about the country doing farm labor, are not technically considered migrants because rather than remaining in a new location after the work season is over, they return to their original starting point and take up jobs in that area.

Why do people move? Demographers speak in terms of push factors and pull factors. **Push factors** are those that push people away from their homes: famines, wars, political oppression, loss of jobs, or bad climate. Some eastern Europeans, for example, have migrated to the west where jobs are more plentiful. **Pull factors** are those that make a new place seem more inviting: the chance to acquire land or jobs, the discovery of riches such as gold or oil, or the chance to live in a more desirable climate. Discoveries of gold in California, for example, drew fortune seekers from all over the world.

In prehistoric times, waves of migrants moved out of Africa and Asia into the Middle East and eastern Europe. Later, tribes moved further into Europe, spreading their culture as they moved. It is assumed that these waves of migration were caused by push factors, such as changes in climate, changes in food supply, or pressure from increasing populations in Asia, as well as pull factors, such as Europe's more favorable climate.

The population of Europe increased slowly throughout the Middle Ages. When Columbus first came to America, a new wave of migration began. It started slowly, but it is estimated that more than 60 million Europeans eventually left Europe. Many later returned, so the net migration—the actual population change—was much lower (Heer, 1975).

Between 1820 and 1970, 46 million migrants entered the United States (Thomlinson, 1976). In a single peak year, 1854, a total of 428,000 immigrants came to this country. This group consisted mainly of Irish leaving their country because of the potato famine and Germans leaving because of political turmoil in their country. A second peak was reached around the turn of the century, when immigrants averaged a million per year. Most of the Europeans who entered the United States at that time were from Italy or other southern and eastern European countries.

A more long-term great migration occurred between 1619 and 1808, when 400,000 Africans were forced to migrate to the United States as slaves. Considering all the Americas, between 10 and 20 million Africans were brought to the Western Hemisphere (Thomlinson, 1976).

Immigration restrictions were first imposed in the United States in 1921 and again in 1924 in order to slow the rate of immigration. During this period, most immigrants were from Canada, Mexico, Germany, the United Kingdom, or Italy. After 1965, immigration quotas were relaxed, and a new wave of immigrants entered the country, changing dramatically the origins of American immigrants at that time. About 2.4 million Asians entered the United States in the decade of the 1980s, or about 46 percent of all immigrants. Another 2 million, or 38 percent of immigrants, came from Mexico and from Central and South America (*Information Please Almanac*, 1991). Over half of all new legal immigrants arrived from just 10 countries, and 63 percent live in six states. The 10 countries of origin were Mexico (116,000), India (50,000), the Philippines (45,000), China (41,000), El Salvador (28,000), the Dominican Republic (26,000), Vietnam (22,000), Colombia

FIGURE 19-1 TEMPORARY ADMISSIONS BY REGION OF ORIGIN, 1999–2003

Source: Meyers and Yau, 2004.

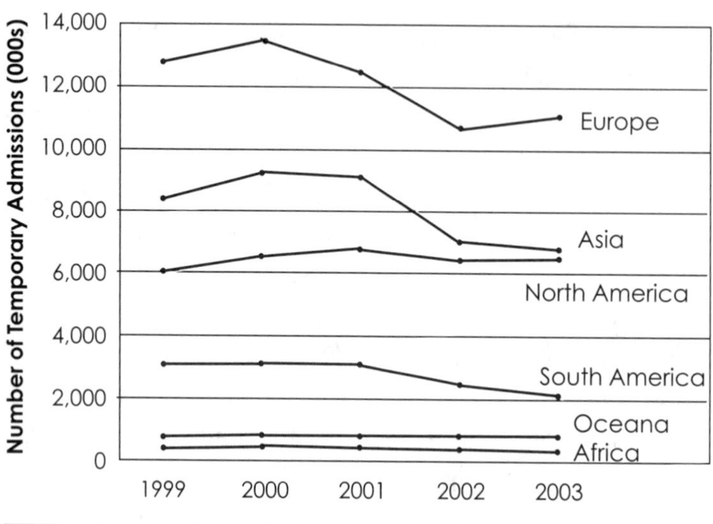

(15,000), Guatemala (14,000), and Russia (14,000) (Meyers and Yau, 2004). See Figure 19-1.

The vast majority of these immigrants have settled in cities. Over a third of the immigrants have settled in California, and New York has received the second largest number. They congregate in neighborhoods such as Garden Grove in Los Angeles or Flushing in Queens. The top six states of residence are California, New York, Texas, Florida, New Jersey, and Illinois (Meyers and Yau, 2004).

Immigrants work at very low-paying jobs when they arrive in the United States, such as in clothing factories or as doormen. Some are able to begin small businesses of their own. Many immigrants are better off than they were in their country of origin, but others who are more highly educated and trained for professions are unable to find work to match their qualifications, and they too must work at the very low-paying jobs available to them. There is some research evidence that the influx of low-wage immigrant workers into the Los Angeles area has kept wages there from rising for the population as a whole (Vernez and Ronfeldt, 1991). Because of recent restrictions however, admissions for categories such as temporary agricultural workers and holders of NAFTA visas for professionals declined to 650,000 in 2003, a continued decline from 2002 levels of 688,000 (UNFPA, 2004).

Migration within the United States has also been extensive. Throughout this country's history, people have moved predominantly from east to west and from rural to urban areas. After World War I, when immigration was restricted and the supply of laborers entering the country was limited, northern cities recruited southern blacks to fill labor jobs. Many blacks moved to northern cities, far exceeding the number of jobs or the housing available. The migrants could not return to the South because they had neither money to make the return trip nor a home waiting for their return. Even today, we can see the pattern of inadequate jobs and housing for blacks living in northern cities.

FIGURE 19-2 AGE-SEX POPULATION PYRAMID, UNITED STATES, FOR THE YEAR 2000

Source: Population Reference Bureau. *Statistical Abstract of the United States: 1991*, p. 16. Washington DC: U.S. Government Printing Office, 1992.

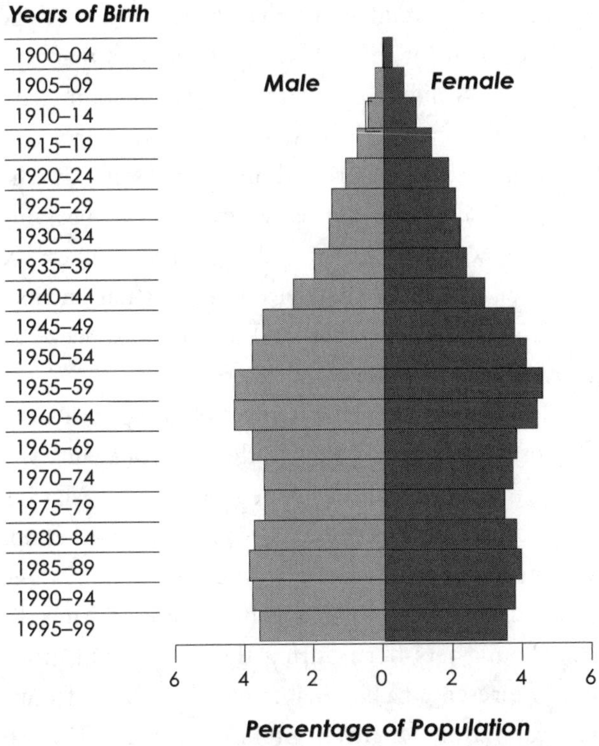

Years of Birth

1900–04
1905–09
1910–14
1915–19
1920–24
1925–29
1930–34
1935–39
1940–44
1945–49
1950–54
1955–59
1960–64
1965–69
1970–74
1975–79
1980–84
1985–89
1990–94
1995–99

Male ***Female***

6 4 2 0 2 4 6

Percentage of Population

The rate of population change is determined by all the foregoing factors. If the birth rate is high and the mortality rate is low, the population increases. If the mortality rate is high compared with the birth rate, the population will decline. Where migration enters the picture, the population can grow or decrease very rapidly. Even relatively small changes in demographic patterns can make long-term, sweeping changes in the lives of people in the population. For example, people born when birth rates are high in the United States have many different experiences from people born when birth rates are low.

POPULATION TRENDS AND LIFE EXPERIENCES

Figure 19-2 is a **population pyramid**, a graph that shows how many males and females from each age category there are in the United States today. Find in the left-hand column the category containing the year you were born, noting that the bars extending to the left and right represent the males and females born in those years. By looking at the bottom of the graph, you can determine the percentage of people of your age and sex in the population. If one were born between 1975 and 1979, the bottom line tells us that about 7 percent of the population consists of people in that age range—about 3.5 percent male and about 3.5 percent female. Notice also how the pyramid curves in for these years, especially compared to the way it bulges out for the years between 1955 and 1964. The bulge represents the people born during what is called the "baby boom."

Why were so many people born during those baby boom years? During the depression of the 1930s and World War II in the 1940s, many people postponed having children. After the war, the country was both peaceful and affluent. Those who had postponed having children began families, and those who were just entering their 20s began having children, too. The result was a disproportionate number of babies born in the 1950s and 1960s, compared to other decades.

How has the baby boom affected the lives of people born during those years? First, it may have affected their education. Children might not have gone to nursery school because the schools were full. Schools were crowded because there were not enough schools to take care of so many children, and many children attended schools in temporary classroom buildings. When students reached college age, they faced strong competition to gain entrance to colleges, which were overcrowded trying to deal with the surge in population. At the end of the baby boom, schools closed because there were fewer students to fill all the space that had been created. Some students, especially those in suburban areas, watched their elementary schools close when they left them, went to a junior high school that was closed while they were there, moved to a second junior high, and saw that one close before they had finished senior high school.

Students born between 1975 and 1979 have had a very different educational experience. Their experience is similar to those who were born in the 1930s and followed the baby boom of the 1920s. Harter (1987) describes the generation of the 1930s as the "good-time" cohort. When they went to school, there was plenty of space in school, plus a full complement of athletic teams, glee clubs, debating societies, and other extracurricular activities. The cohort of the 1930s could participate without facing much competition. So it has been with those born between 1975 and 1979. There has been plenty of room in school for them throughout their educational years, and there has not been the extreme competition for a place in college. In fact, colleges have been competing for students to attend their schools and have made every effort to recruit students and provide them with scholarships and loans so that they are able to attend. The lack of competition may also have reduced the amount of studying and learning that has taken place in school.

When baby boom children completed their education, unemployment rates were high. Many people were competing for jobs, and only a small part of the work force was retiring to create more job openings. About a generation later, the drop in the unemployment rate in 1984 was largely a result of a drop in the number of young people entering the job market.

When the people born between 1975 and 1979 enter the job market, there will be fewer of them, and unless the economy is weak, they should have an easier time finding jobs. Furthermore, the bulge of people born between 1920 and 1929 will have retired, and there should be some room for upward mobility in corporations.

Population trends also affect marriage rates. Women born during the baby boom were more likely to marry at an older age or to stay single than was true in earlier generations. Why? Because of what is referred to as the **marriage squeeze**. Women traditionally marry older men, and a look at the population pyramid shows that there was a shortage of older men for these women to marry (a marriage squeeze). Women born after the baby boom have many older men to marry, so they may marry at a younger age. Men born late in the baby boom who want to follow the normative practice of marrying younger women face a shortage (also a marriage squeeze), and so far they have not shown an inclination to start a new trend and avoid the squeeze by marrying slightly older women.

Population trends also affect clothing styles and fashions. After World War II, the mark of beauty was to have a more well-developed figure, like Marilyn Monroe or Betty Grable, because the market for clothes was found among women in their 20s and 30s, who had been unable to buy clothes during the war. Youngsters born during the baby boom, however, represented a big, new market, and manufacturers catered to them beginning in the 1960s. It became stylish to be thin because adolescents tend to be thin during their period of rapid growth, and a whole nation dieted to look like adolescents. When the baby boom generation grew older, clothing manufacturers changed styles to meet the market for clothes for more mature figures, and low-cut jeans were replaced by stretch blue jeans with a fuller-cut thigh and an elastic waist. Also, the health club business began to boom because this age group wanted to stay thin and look young. Ski resorts suffered a slump, however, because as members of the baby boom got older, they began staying home, having children, and watching their budgets, and there were not enough younger people to replace them on the slopes. Golf, a gentler sport, began to increase in popularity.

Housing costs are also affected by population trends. Housing prices increased dramatically when baby boom young adults bought houses, but then dropped as demand eased. Retirement homes also saw a boom when those born in the 1920s retired, but prices fell when those born in the 1930s retired. Through studying population trends, we can see that consumer interests become very predictable.

Population trends may also determine government policies that affect you in your old age. In the year 2020, most of the baby boom will have reached age 60, and many will be collecting Social Security, while others will still hold powerful positions in business and government. Moreover, because they will be a large voting bloc, they may be able to control decisions about continuing the support of Social Security benefits. Because the smaller population just younger than the baby boom may have a large tax burden to help support all the people in retirement, it is to be hoped that the younger population will be fully employed.

Knowledge of this population trend can help us do more than merely hope for the best, however. Because policymakers today know with certainty that there will be massive numbers of people in need of Social Security through 2025, they can take the necessary steps now to avert a future break-down in the Social Security system. By studying population and predicting how it will affect our lives, we can tailor public policy planning to accommodate these shifts in population trends.

Population trends may affect business and investment decisions, both on the personal and corporate levels. Consider, for example, how corporations that provide services for the elderly will prosper when the baby boom reaches retirement age. Nursing homes, retirement villages, and pharmaceutical products for the aged are likely to experience explosive growth as a result of this population trend. Other services, such as automated car washes, house cleaning and yard services, and restaurants may also develop due to the increased numbers of the elderly. Think of how this knowledge can help businesses plan for those needs. New businesses in new fields may open up and may offer opportunities to those shrewd enough to anticipate the future needs of the population.

Different nations have different population pyramids and therefore must plan for very different future needs of the population. As shown in the hypothetical pyramid in Figure 19-3, countries in which a large proportion of the population is very young, such as Mexico, can be expected to grow rapidly as children mature and have children of their own. Here the care and education of the young will be of primary importance. In Sweden, where the proportion of young people is smaller, the population cannot be expected to grow. However, they have a larger proportion of elderly and will need to plan for their care.

Thinking Sociologically

1. If the United States were a very young population, such as Mexico, what social problems would probably be more prevalent than they are today? What social problems would probably be less prevalent?

2. If the United States were an older population, such as Sweden, what social problems would probably be more prevalent than they are today? What social problems would be less prevalent?

THE WORLD POPULATION EXPLOSION AND THE DEMOGRAPHIC TRANSITION

Until about 200 years ago, both birth and death rates were very high. As a result, the size of the world population remained stable. For every person who was born, someone died. Then a dramatic change took

FIGURE 19-3 POPULATION PYRAMIDS OF A YOUNG POPULATION (MEXICO) AND AN OLDER POPULATION (SWEDEN)

Source: Reprinted from U.S. Census Bureau, IDB Population Pyramids, 2003.

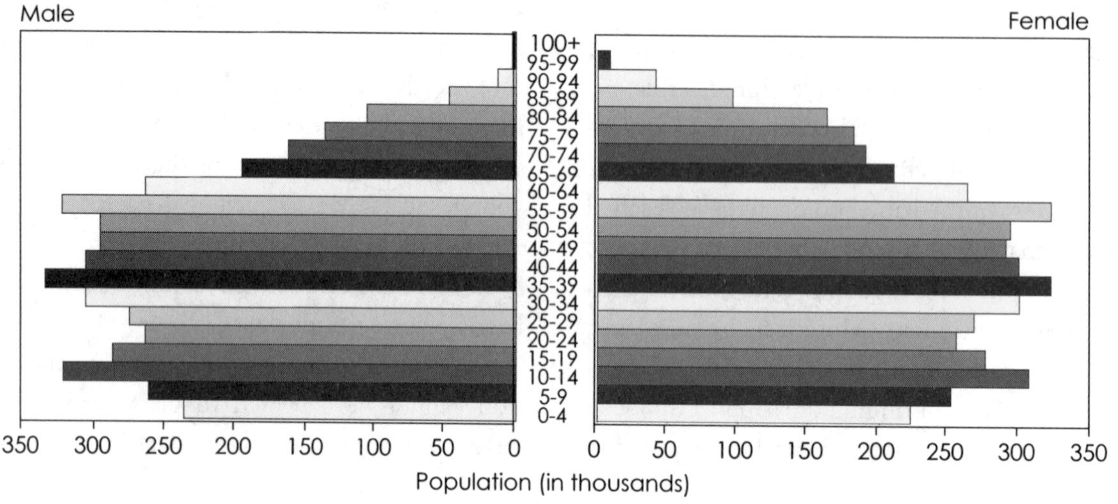

Source: U.S. Census Bureau, International Data Base.

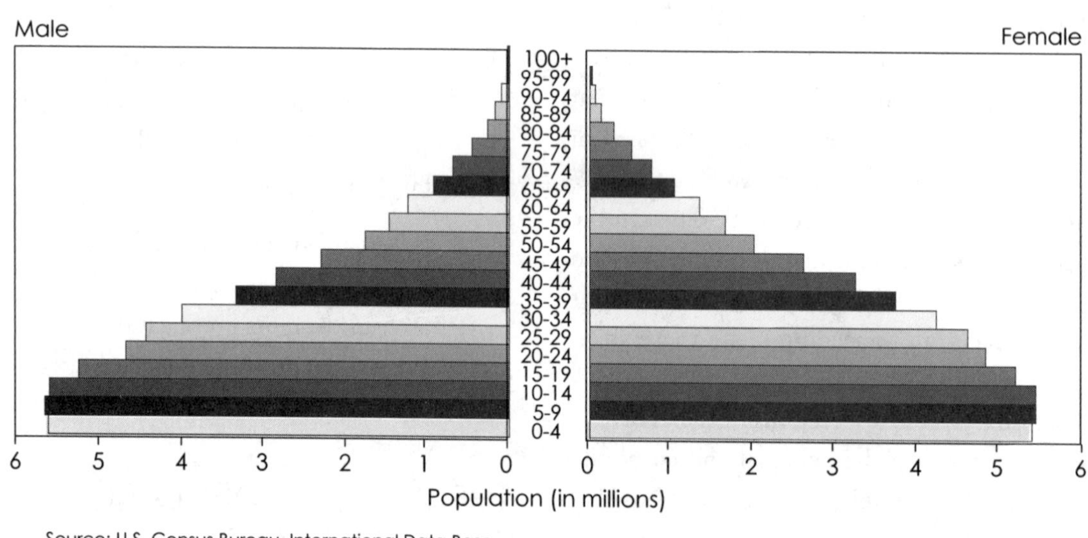

Source: U.S. Census Bureau, International Data Base.

place. First, in industrial nations in the early part of the nineteenth century, the death rate dropped because of improvements in nutrition and sanitation. For several generations, however, the birth rate remained high. (This is the period when what we now refer to as the "population explosion" began.) Then, in about 1850, the birth rate began to decrease also and the rate of population increase slowed. This

FIGURE 19-4 WORLD POPULATION GROWTH

Source: UN Population Division ; UNFPA, "State of World Population 2004," www.unfpa.org.

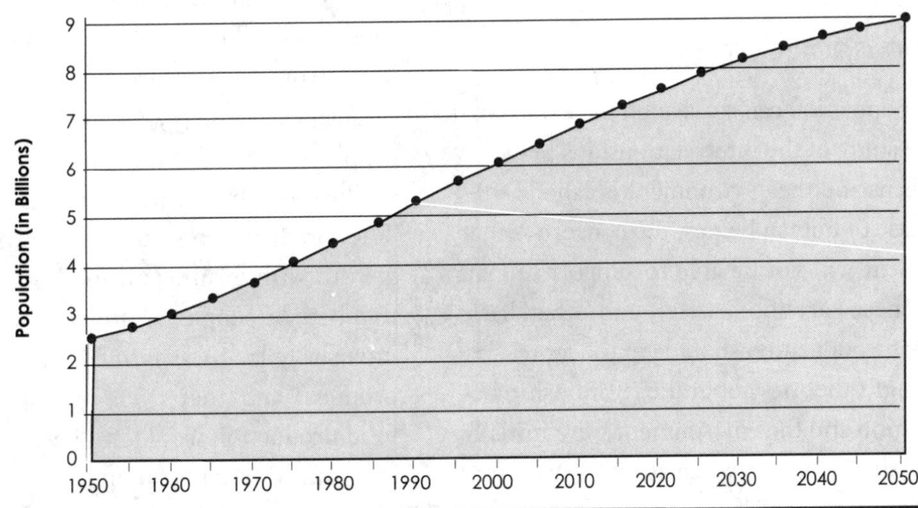

change from high birth and death rates to low birth and death rates with a period of rapid population growth in between is known as the **demographic transition** It occurs as a society evolves from a traditional premodern stage to a modern industrial stage; most European nations and other industrial countries have already passed through it. Other countries, particularly those in the Third World, still have very high birth rates in rural areas because children are highly valued for the tasks they do and for the security they provide when their parents reach old age. It is in these countries that population growth continues at very high rates. It took the human race from the beginning of history until 1850 to reach a population of 1 billion people, it took only an additional 100 years to reach 2 billion, and only 35 more years to reach 4.8 billion. Currently, the world is populated with more than 6 billion people (see Figure 19-4).

Population Density

The population explosion has dramatically increased the number of people in the world, but migrations have not distributed people evenly over the face of the earth. Whereas the population is sparse in many areas of the world, in some regions it is extremely dense. Such areas cannot provide the natural resources needed to maintain their population.

The United States, although it has absorbed millions of immigrants, has a relatively low population density. In some remote areas, the density is only 5 people per square mile. In major cities during the business day, on the other hand, the population density is as high as 100,000 people per square mile. For the entire United States, the density is 76 people per square mile (*World Almanac and Book of Facts*, 2002).

The other highly industrialized nations of the world have a higher population density than the United States. In Europe, it is very high. The developing nations are less densely populated than European countries, but they are not highly industrialized and therefore have less wealth to support themselves. China, the largest nation in the world, now has a population of more than 1 billion people, but its area is so great that its population density is only 306 people per square mile. There are places in the Third

World where the population density is so very high that the land cannot begin to support the human life in the area, and the poverty is devastating.

Population and Ecology

How large a population can survive on the earth's resources? The study of the interrelationships between living organisms and the environment is called **ecology**. In the case of human beings, the concern is that the environment will not be able to support human life with the necessary food, water, and other basic necessities if the population should get too large.

Interestingly, theories about the relationship between population and the environment were initially developed during a period when it was feared that there were too few people to produce what society needed. Between 1450 and 1750, European traders were exporting Europe's products in exchange for gold and silver. In some areas, however, one-third to one-half of the population had been killed by the plague. Many writers argued that if the population were larger, there would be a better ecological balance. More products could be produced and exported, which would bring more gold and silver to the merchants. If the population were large enough, labor would be cheap, wages could be kept low, the people would have little to spend, and increases in imports would not be needed. Thus, all increased production could be traded for gold, silver, or merchandise valuable to the traders.

The political activity of this period was designed to encourage a high birth rate. The birth rate did increase, and by 1750, writers had begun to worry about overpopulation. The most famous of this second group of writers was Thomas Malthus.

Malthus's Theory of Population

Thomas Robert Malthus (1766–1834) argued in his *Essay on the Principle of Population* that because of the strong attraction between the two sexes, the population could increase by multiples, doubling every 25 years. According to **Malthusian theory**, the population would increase much more rapidly than the food supply. That is, the population would increase in a geometric progression, as illustrated by the numbers 2, 4, 8, 16, 32, and so on, while the food supply would increase in an arithmetical progression as illustrated by the numbers 1, 2, 3, 4, 5, and so on. The predicted result was a runaway population growth with insufficient food to feed the exploding numbers of people. Malthus believed that the more intensively land was farmed, the less the land would produce, and that even by expanding farmlands, food production would not keep up with population growth. Malthus contended that the population would eventually grow so large that food production would be insufficient, and famine and crowding would cause widespread suffering and would increase the death rate—acting as nature's check on overpopulation. Malthus suggested as an alternative that the birth rate be decreased, especially through postponing marriage until a later age.

Malthusian theory created much debate. Writers such as John Stuart Mill and the economist John Maynard Keynes supported his theory. Others have argued against it. Karl Marx, for example, contended that starvation was caused by the unequal distribution of the wealth and its accumulation by capitalists.

During the depression of the 1930s, the debate changed because the birth rate fell sharply in industrial nations. Some predicted that the human species would die out—first the Caucasians, then other races. Schemes were proposed to encourage families to have more children by giving them allowances for each child born. Many economists, however, believed that even in societies with smaller populations, people could prosper and industry could grow if the wealth were redistributed to increase consumption by poor families. Government spending on programs for the poor and unemployed could be increased, and low interest rates could be used to encourage spending on houses, cars, and other consumer goods.

The birth rate rose sharply after World War II, especially in the underdeveloped nations; people starved in Bangladesh, Africa, and India. Birth control programs were instituted, and it was argued that the only way to eliminate starvation was to reduce the birth rate. Malthusian theory became popular once again. Malthus's contention that food production could not increase rapidly was much debated when new technology began to give farmers much greater yields. Malthus's contentions were revised, and **neo-Malthusian theory** developed, revising his theory to include more information—such as taking into account the effects of technology—but still predicting the fact that population cannot grow indefinitely without dire consequences.

The debate nevertheless continues, and some social thinkers continue to believe that population explosion is not necessarily a threat. The French sociologist Dupreel (1977) argued that an increasing population would spur rapid innovation and development to solve problems, whereas a stable population would be complacent and less likely to progress.

World Food Distribution Today

Before World War II, Africa, India, and Asia exported grain to other nations, primarily to the industrial nations of Europe (George, 1977). Why, then, are people in these underdeveloped nations starving today?

Some analysts argue that the land in overpopulated areas has been farmed too intensively to provide food for large populations and thus has been ruined. Even the United States, with its comparatively low population density, has lost 10–15 percent of its farmland through soil erosion since the time of the European immigration (Humphrey and Buttel, 1982). In parts of Asia, Latin America, and Africa, the problem is much worse because overuse of the land is causing it to deteriorate very rapidly. In Africa, the size of the Sahara Desert is estimated to be decreasing by 30 miles a year because the land cannot sustain the population using it.

Other observers of the world food situation have criticized American corporations for creating the world food shortage. They contend that because we had a surplus of grain, we encouraged underdeveloped nations to grow nonfood cash crops, such as cotton and rubber, or nonnutritious foods, such as coffee, tea, and sugar. The United States would lend money and supply fertilizer and farm equipment only to nations that agreed to grow products needed in the United States. In Brazil, for example, the United States encouraged soybean production, while American corporations own all the soybean processing plants and receive most of the profit from soybean production.

In the past few decades, many underdeveloped nations have become increasingly dependent on American grain imports because they use their own land for nonfood products. In the 1970s, the price of grains rose dramatically, and critics argue that the United States, having acquired a monopoly of the food supply, increased prices to make enormous profits. Today, the cash crops grown by other nations cannot be sold at prices high enough to buy all the grain needed from the United States. Thus, poor people everywhere starve because they do not have land on which to grow food or the money to buy food, even when enough food is produced in the world to feed all its people. U.S. grain exports are projected to rise by 34 percent between 1995 and 2020 (Study: 1999).

Population and Other Natural Resources

Food production and distribution is only one of the problems that occurs as the world population increases. As was noted in the introduction to this

SOCIOLOGY AT WORK

Monitoring Population Trends

Mathew Greenwald received his Ph.D. in sociology from Rutgers University. Prior to opening up his own consulting firm—Mathew Greenwald and Associates, Inc.—he was the director of the social research services department of the American Council of Life Insurance (ACLI). While with the ACLI, he supervised a ten-person staff, designated to monitor past social changes and to predict future social change. The results of this type of work are used by insurance companies to construct policies and to prepare for the future.

Greenwald explains that because whole-life insurance policies can ran for 50 or 60 years, insurance companies have an interest in the long view. "Of course, some aspects of the social world are so volatile that it's difficult to say what will be happening fifteen years from now," Greenwald says. However, it is still possible to make predictions. "For example, we know that Social Security will be in trouble in 2011. That's when the first year of the baby-boom generation, those born in 1946, will be retiring. We also expect important medical breakthroughs in such areas as cancer research. Certain trends in computerization and global economics will probably also continue. Thus, while there's a lot we can't know, some trends can be accurately predicted, and the more we know the easier it is to make decisions."

Here is where his sociological training comes in. "The sociological perspective is of crucial importance," Greenwald says. "It's really a certain type of logic, a guide for analysis. It provides a structure for assessing situations. I might approach a family-related problem by looking at it in terms of statuses and roles, for example. More concretely, my training is useful in developing questionnaires and doing survey research. Besides my coursework in methods and statistics being useful, my work in theory, health, population, and the family also has been very valuable."

Greenwald provides an example of how sociological knowledge is useful in making predictions for insurance

chapter, environmental problems are serious in nature and global in scope. Humans need water just as we need food, and the earth's large human population is rapidly polluting the available water. Waste from modern life, including the many chemicals that are now produced each year, find their way into small streams and large seas, making the water unfit for human consumption. It also makes water unfit for fish, thereby reducing the hope of turning to the sea for a source of additional food.

The increased population also affects the air we breathe. As the population increases, more and more rural areas become densely settled, and atmospheric pollution is exacerbated by the toxic elements emanating from cars, planes, industrial smoke, and other sources. Almost every human activity generates dust; when these particles become airborne, they seed the clouds and increase the rainfall. On the east coast, especially in Canada and New England in recent years, pollution from midwestern industries has caused acid rain to fall, killing fish and changing the composition of the land on which it falls. Another pollution-related problem is that as the cloud cover increases with airborne pollutants it has a *greenhouse effect*, holding warmth from the sun close to the earth rather than

Monitoring Population Trends, *continued*

companies. "The primary purpose of life insurance is to replace income if a family breadwinner dies or is disabled, so the insurance business is bound up with many basic social institutions. We use survey research to keep track of a number of trends on an ongoing basis, including attitudes toward death, retirement, and family responsibility. We also use demographic data about factors such as health, birth rates, death rates, divorce rates, and the number of women working." As you might expect, major social developments influence the sales of life-insurance policies. "Now that families are more dependent on wives' income, women are buying much more insurance than they did previously. We're also finding that sales among Afro-Americans and Hispanics are increasing as these groups become more affluent."

In addition to following demographic trends, Greenwald and his department often undertook special projects. For example, one study concerned the public's sense of control over key aspects of their lives. Their findings? "Sadly, we found that people feel they have less control than they did a few decades ago, especially over the long term." This is probably the result of a number of factors, such as a volatile economic system, political turmoil at home and abroad, terrorism, and wars. "It's unfortunate," he says. "People who don't feel that they have much control are less likely to take a stand and try to change the situation—they don't take advantage of the control they do have. As concerns the insurance business, there's evidence that feelings of lack of control are associated with ill health."

Although Greenwald is no longer with ACLI, he still maintains his ties to the life-insurance industry; his own company mostly does surveys that focus on market research for life-insurance companies. These surveys are used to develop new products, assess the effectiveness of advertising, enhance client relationships, and anticipate how to respond to changes in the social environment.

---

letting it escape into the upper atmosphere. As a result, some scientists suggest that the climate of the earth will become warmer and icebergs may even begin to melt, which could raise the sea level and flood coastal areas.

Our forests are also being rapidly depleted. Trees are cut down to make room for people, to provide fuel, and to provide wood for houses, furniture, and other products. The loss of forests not only means the loss of these wood products, but also affects the ecological balance between the earth and the atmosphere. In particular, plants consume an excess of carbon dioxide and give off an excess of oxygen; this crucially affects the ratio of oxygen to carbon dioxide in the air we breathe.

As these natural resources are lost—and the loss will be rapid if we do not use resources wisely—conflict will occur. People who lack the necessary resources to survive will fight those who do have resources. Although conflict in the world is usually expressed in political terms, these conflicts are not based on political ideology. They are conflicts over scarce resources. The United States involvement in the Middle East is motivated largely by our desire to safeguard our supplies of oil. Latin American countries such as El Salvador and Nicaragua cannot provide for the

POLICY DEBATE

Should Stricter Environmental Protection Measures Be Enacted?

As noted in the introduction to this chapter, measures to protect the environment through the regulation of consumer and industrial behavior have accomplished a great deal over the past few decades, but many feel that a great deal more is needed. A variety of environmental protection groups, scientists, and politicians have suggested that further regulatory steps be taken, such as

Ban chlorofluorocarbons (CFCs) and other ozone-depleting chemicals.

Enforce air-quality standards established by the Clean Air Act.

Insist upon stringent vehicle emission standards, and require auto manufacturers to produce cars that can yield at least 40 miles per gallon of gasoline.

Reduce the number of miles people drive by requiring carpooling.

Ban, highly restrict, or reformulate products that are environmentally unsound, such as gasoline-powered lawnmowers, charcoal lighter fluid, some kinds of deodorants, polystyrene foam (StyrofoamTM), varnishes, adhesives, and hundreds of other products.

Require rapid reductions in sulfur emissions.

There are many other regulatory measures like these that many consider to be necessary to prevent further environmental destruction (Melville, 1988). Yet, despite Americans' heightened environmental consciousness, there still is considerable debate as to whether the government should impose stricter environmental regulations on consumer and industrial behavior. Perhaps this is because many of the proposed environmental regulations would significantly affect both consumer and industrial behavior.

Opponents of strict environmental regulation believe that the aforementioned types of measures would seriously damage the economy and, thus, lead to a decline in our standard of living. It would be very costly in terms of money, time, and reorganization for industries to meet some of the stricter environmental regulations. Opponents therefore contend that the cost and complexity of complying with stricter environmental regulations would discourage investment, hinder the construction of new plants, cut into profits, create unemployment, lead to a loss of production, and generally curtail economic growth (Currie and Skolnick, 1997).

Advocates of strict environmental regulation argue that putting short-term corporate profits ahead of a cleaner environment is dangerously shortsighted. For example, in 1974, scientists warned of the dangers to the ozone layer that result from the chemicals—such as CFCs—used in aerosol sprays and other products. For many years, manufacturers of CFCs dismissed the warnings as speculative and fought proposed government legislation to restrict their usage on the grounds that eliminating them would lead to serious economic losses. In 1985, however, when a hole in the ozone layer was discovered over Antarctica, the public took notice. CFCs began being phased out of production, nearly two decades after scientists' warnings. The re-

Should Stricter Environmental Protection Measures Be Enacted?, *continued*

sult of acting nearly two decades too late, according to advocates of stricter environmental regulations, is that humans are exposed to higher levels of dangerous ultraviolet rays (Melville, 1988).

While most opponents of environmental regulation would probably agree that we would all be better off with a cleaner environment, they contend that a certain amount of pollution and environmental destruction is an unavoidable by-product of industrial society. This is part of the price that must be paid for a high standard of living. Opponents feel that the economic dislocation that would be caused by strict environmental regulation would have negative consequences not just for industry, but for all of society. For example, the taxes that large corporations pay help to support public schools, public hospitals, fire departments, police departments, and many other services. In many communities, most of the tax base to support these services is provided by large corporations. Decreased profits for industry mean that less tax money would be paid by them and, thus, less money would be available for public services. In order to maintain the same level of service, the tax burden would have to be passed on to the citizens. Opponents of stricter regulation contend that the problem would be even worse for poor people in underdeveloped nations that now can benefit from the economic and technological growth associated with industrialization.

Advocates maintain that while environmental regulation may involve short-range costs to the economy, the long-range economic impact actually is positive. A study conducted by the Council on Environmental Quality found that environmental controls would lower industrial productivity by only a minuscule amount and would entail one-time expenses (Currie and Skolnick, 1997). While the cost of stricter environmental regulation could be significant, advocates say that there is no evidence that there would be substantial negative effects on investment. On the contrary, they suggest that environmental regulations carry the potential for increased economic growth. For example, an EPA study projected that unemployment would decrease slightly as a result of newly created jobs in antipollution-equipment industries and services. Another study, conducted by the Conservation Foundation, found no evidence that environmental regulations had caused industries to avoid locating in states with stricter regulations. As Currie and Skolnick note, "California, for example, which has very stringent environmental regulations, also had the largest gain in manufacturing jobs of any state during the 1970s" (1988, p. 345).

Finally, some opponents of stricter environmental regulation feel that this type of control is an unwarranted intrusion of the government into our lives and contradicts our free-market economy. They feel that government should not control individual behavior or private producers unless it is absolutely necessary (Melville, 1988). Advocates of environmental regulation, however, say that it is absolutely necessary for the government to step in because it is unrealistic to trust the free market and consumers to make prudent decisions about environmental effects.

peasants who have been driven off their land by the larger agriculturalists—a dilemma that induces revolution. As suggested by conflict theory, if revolutions and inequalities are to be eliminated, increasing population must be accompanied by an end to the unregulated freedom to pursue wealth and a more equitable rationing of the world's scarce resources.

Note the discussion of environmental protection measures in the policy debate.

Thinking Sociologically

Suppose that you were hired by an environmental protection group to help lobby for stricter environmental regulation. How could you use knowledge of demography and population to help in gathering public support for environmental protection?

Political Policies Regarding Population

Although a more even distribution of resources would solve some of the world's hunger problems, and careful planning would help us to preserve what resources we still have, ultimately, our population must be controlled. The current policies of most governments are now aimed at reducing the birth rate to improve the standard of living. After World War II, Japan initiated a program legalizing abortion and encouraging contraception. Soon afterward, India and most other Asian nations began such programs. In spite of programs to discourage births, however, many nations still experienced a population explosion. China toughened its policies most severely, limiting Chinese families to having only one child.

In the 1960s, the United States began to offer millions of dollars worth of contraceptive aids, especially intrauterine devices and birth control pills, to underdeveloped countries, requesting help in controlling their populations. The federal government also provided funds to states to open family-planning clinics and disseminate information about contraceptives in this country. These programs have succeeded in reducing birth rates in many nations, but they have also been severely criticized, for several reasons.

First, some of the contraceptive methods used in underdeveloped nations are those considered unsafe and banned in the United States. Users in other countries, not warned of the dangers, unknowingly risk infection, heart attacks, strokes, and death when they use these contraceptives. Second, lowering the birth rate in underdeveloped nations deprives parents of children, who are an asset in rural areas. They can help carry water and grow food on family plots and care for their parents in illness and old age. Thus, the policies implemented to reduce poverty in industrial nations could well increase poverty for families living in some rural areas. When planning policy, it is crucial to consider all the factors at work in the countries that will be affected.

Zero Population Growth

The goal of current world population policy is zero **population growth**, which is achieved when parents have only two children, just enough to replace themselves. If this practice were followed, the population would remain the same generation after generation. In reality, of course, some people do not have children, and some children die before reaching adulthood, so zero population growth could be attained if couples averaged slightly more than two children each. Given current rates of infant mortality and the number of women who actually have children, the population would remain stable if couples averaged 2.1 children. In the United States, the rate has been steady at 1.9, below the zero growth rate. Many underdeveloped nations have much higher birth rates, however, so the world population explosion is continuing. Increasing population and associated ecological problems will continue to be crucial issues in the future. A more equal and careful distribution of resources is essential to preventing starvation and pollution. This relationship between population and ecology illustrates the need for a sociological understanding of the interrelationships between population size and social institutions.

Thinking Sociologically

1. Predict what the future would be like, both the good and the bad, if all birth control and abortion were eliminated from the world.
2. Predict what the future would be like, both the good and the bad, if the entire world achieved zero population growth.

SUMMARY

1. *Demography* is the study of population statistics. Demographers study census data on the number of people in the population and records of births and deaths to compute the birth and death rates.
2. The crude birth and death rates are computed by determining the number of births and deaths per 1,000 people. Neither of these measures takes age or sex into account, but these factors also influence the number of births and deaths.
3. Populations remain stable when people are born at the same rate at which they die. Population increases when the birth rate exceeds the death rate and decreases when the death rate exceeds the birth rate.
4. Populations may also change through migration. Push factors are conditions that encourage people to move out of an area; pull factors encourage people to move into an area.
5. The size of the population affects each of us quite personally. Whether we are born into a growing or a shrinking population has a bearing on our education, the age at which we marry, our ability to get a job, the taxes we pay, and many other aspects of our lives.
6. The population explosion of the past 200 years occurred because of improvements in nutrition and sanitation, which lowered the death rate. In industrial nations, the birth rate has also dropped, but rapid population growth continues in many Third World countries.
7. Population densities vary greatly in different parts of the world. Generally, the most densely populated countries are industrialized nations of Europe and Japan.
8. *Ecology* is the interrelationship between organisms and their environment.
9. Malthusian theory states that because the population grows faster than the food supply, starvation is inevitable if population growth is not controlled. Although his arguments have received much support through the years, critics contend that the world produces enough food to feed everyone but the problem arises because food is distributed unequally.
10. Some underdeveloped nations raise cash crops that neither feed the people nor bring in

enough money to buy food. Some observers believe that the United States, which is the world's largest food exporter, encouraged other countries to grow nonfood cash crops and then, having cornered the grain market, raised prices to increase profits.

11. Other problems affecting food production vis-à-vis population stem from pollution of the air and water and the destruction of forests.
12. Most nations are now attempting to reduce their birth rates, and contraceptives have been distributed throughout the world for this purpose.
13. The goal of world population policy is zero population growth, calculated to be an average of 2.1 children per family.

KEY TERMS

age-adjusted death rate The number of deaths occurring at each age for each sex, per 100,000 people of that age who are living.

age-sex composition The number of men and women in the population, along with their ages.

census An official count of the number of people in a given area.

demographic transition The change from high birth and death rates to low birth and death rates with a period of rapid population growth in between; this transition occurs as a society evolves from a traditional premodern stage to a modern industrial stage.

demography The statistical study of population, especially data on birth rates, death rates, marriage rates, health, and migration.

ecology The study of the interrelationships between living organisms and the environment.

emigration Movement of people out of an area.

fecundity A woman's potential for bearing children.

fertility A measure of the rate at which people are being born.

Going green The phrase that defines people who are mindful of what they consume, mindful of others, and who are working towards protecting the ecology both nationally and internationally.

immigration Movement of people into an area.

Malthusian theory The theory proposed by Thomas Malthus stating that population expands much faster than the food supply, resulting in starvation for much of the population when it grows too large.

marriage squeeze The effects of an imbalance between the number of males and females in the prime marriage ages due to rising or falling birth rates and the median age differences at marriage.

migration Movement of people into or out of an area.

mortality A measure of the rate at which people die.

neo-Malthusian theory Revisions of Malthusian theory about food production and population growth that include more information, such as taking into account the effects of technology.

pull factors Natural or social factors that cause people to move into an area.

push factors Natural or social factors that cause people to move out of an area.

vital statistics Records of all births, deaths and their causes, marriages, divorces, and certain diseases in a society.

zero population growth A population policy that encourages parents to have no more than two children to limit the growth of the population.

DISCUSSION QUESTIONS

1. Discuss how the age and sex of a population can affect its fertility and mortality rates.
2. Based on the conflict perspective, discuss how migration can maintain the position of elites in a society.
3. Based on a functionalist viewpoint, describe when a high fertility rate would be functional and when it would not be.
4. What are some factors that could lead to rapid changes in the rate of population change? Using this information, what kinds of changes do you predict in the rate of population change in your lifetime?
5. Assume that because of increasing rates of cancer and AIDS, the life expectancy of the United States declines dramatically. How would that change society when you reach age 60?
6. If the world were purely capitalist, what would happen to the rates of starvation in the world? Why? What if it were purely socialist?
7. Discuss all of the ways in which your life has been shaped by the year of your birth and the number of people your age.
8. Discuss how the relationship between population and ecology is evident today.

The Changing Community

Homelessness

Homelessness can occur anywhere—in any section of the country, in any city, in any neighborhood. Although a great deal of media attention has focused on homelessness in recent years, it is not a new social issue. It has been traced as far back as the Middle Ages in Europe and at least to the colonial era in America (Schutt, 1990; Wright, 1989). What is relatively new, however, is the character of homelessness.

According to sociologists who have studied homelessness in twentieth-century America extensively, the nature and the magnitude of homelessness in America have changed dramatically during the past few decades:

1. Overall, 14.4 million families have critical housing needs.

2. Between 1973 and 1993, 2.2 million low-rent units disappeared from the market. These low-rent units were either abandoned, demolished, converted into condominiums or expensive apartments, or became unaffordable because of cost increases (Daskal, 1998).

3. In 1997, 3 million low to moderate income working families spent more than one half of their income on housing. By 2001 this number had jumped to 4.8 million—a 67 percent increase.

4. From 2000 to 2002, the national housing wage for a two bedroom home increased by 18 percent. By comparison, the inflation rate for 2001 was 1.6 percent (Out of Reach, 2002).

5. In 2002, families comprised 41 percent of the urban homeless population, an increase of 5 percent in just two years (U.S. Conference of Mayors, 2002).

6. In rural areas, research indicates that families, single mothers, and children make up the largest group of people who are homeless (Vissing, 1996). Nationally, children make up approximately 39 percent of the homeless population (Urban Institute 2000).

Sociologists are particularly interested in explaining the growth of homelessness and in debunking the myths about the homeless. Some of the more common myths are that people are homeless because they are mentally impaired, alcoholics and/or other drug abusers, and lazy, and that they have a choice about their homeless condition. As James Wright states, "Some of the homeless *are* broken-down alcoholics, but most are not. Some *are* mentally impaired, but most are not. Some *are* living off the benefit programs made available through the social welfare system, but most are not" (Wright, 1989, p. 46). There are a number of interrelated and complex reasons for homelessness today that go beyond the popular stereotypes about the homeless and that have been addressed in many books and articles written by sociologists and other social scientists. (For an excellent bibliography, see Schutt, 1990.) Most agree that the most basic reasons for homelessness today include an insufficient supply of affordable housing, an increase in the poverty rate, a deterioration of the purchasing power of welfare benefits, and a decrease in social supports to help the poor establish themselves (Schutt, 1990; Wright, 1989).

The issue of homelessness is relevant to many areas of sociology—for example, stratification, political systems, economic systems, and minority groups. It is particularly relevant to this chapter because the growth and change of urban communities are partially responsible for homelessness. In order to help overcome the myths about homelessness and to help address the homelessness issue, it is important to understand the structure and process of the community; as well as other areas of sociological concern.

The towns and cities of the United States and the rest of the world have been changing rapidly for many years. The communities in which many of you were brought up have probably undergone dramatic changes during your lifetime, or even since you entered college. Some of these changes are readily apparent: one of your favorite old buildings may have been razed to make way for a new office complex, or perhaps a new park has been created near your home. Other changes, although less tangible, are equally important. The streets you played on as a child may now be considered unsafe after dark. You may have trouble finding a summer job because several large businesses have left your city.

The reasons for changes such as these are many. We touched on a number of them in earlier chapters. Form of government, the family, changing gender roles, bureaucracies, ethnicity—the list of factors that influence the communities we live in is endless. Past and present trends in community living, their causes, and the problems they have brought are the subject of this chapter.

THE ORIGIN AND DEVELOPMENT OF COMMUNITIES

A **community** is a collection of people within a geographic area among whom there is some degree of mutual identification, interdependence, or organized activity. This term is applied by sociologists to a variety of social groups, including small North American Indian tribes, towns, communes, and large urban centers. As this chapter shows, urban communities have become larger and more diverse throughout the course of human history.

Early Community and Urban Development

The first communities, which originated more than 35,000 years ago, were small bands that hunted and foraged for food. Their means of subsistence dictated the size and activity of the group: they were *nomadic*, moving frequently to new areas as food ran out. There were few status distinctions among members of these communities, although males and older persons had somewhat higher status and more power than others. Apparently, there were few conflicts among hunting-and-gathering bands, and there was little evidence of war-making tools or group attacks. This rather idyllic form of community predominated for about 25,000 years.

Roughly 10,000 years ago, humans learned to produce and store their food. This "Neolithic revolution," as it is called, ushered in the era of horticultural communities. **Horticulture** was essentially small-scale farming that relied on tools such as the hoe to till the soil. Though horticulture was tedious, back-breaking work, it doubled the number of people the land could support—from one to nearly two persons per square mile (Davis, 1973). Stable communities developed around fertile agricultural regions, and in the more fertile areas, a surplus of food was produced, which freed some members of the community from agricultural activities. As agricultural techniques improved, horticultural communities became larger and more diverse. Artisans who produced the tools and implements necessary for survival were the first specialists in history (Childe, 1951). It was during this era, which lasted about 7,000 years, that the first urban communities emerged.

Defining what constitutes an urban community is no simple task. Demographic definitions today are likely to use criteria such as a permanent settlement with a single name that is occupied by a specific minimum of residents. Other definitions, and one that we can use in this context of early urban development, is to define an urban community as one in which people are not primarily engaged in the collection or production of food. In terms of numbers or residents, the earliest cities, which developed along the fertile banks of the Tigris and Euphrates rivers, in what is today known as Iraq, were small by modern standards. Cities could grow only as large as the food surplus allowed; that is, the release of a number of people from agriculture required that the remaining members produce more than before. Ancient Babylon, for example, had a population of 25,000 and covered roughly 3 square miles; Ur, one of the oldest known cities, had about 5,000 people and covered less than a square mile (Davis, 1970). Urban communities grew slowly for the next several thousand years because of the inefficiency of horticultural techniques—it took about 50 horticulturists to produce enough surplus to support 1 urban resident—and also because of the primitive political and social organization (Davis, 1973).

Preindustrial Urban Communities

The introduction of metals, the invention of the plow, the use of animals for transportation and farming, and the refinement of irrigation techniques helped usher in a new era in human history around 3000 b.c.—the Agrarian Age (Lenski, 1966). The development of writing and counting and the evolution of political and social organizations were also essential to the spread of agrarian society. These technological advances increased surpluses, so still more people were freed from agriculture. Cities grew larger and their activities became more diverse. Around 1600 b.c., Thebes, the capital of Egypt, had a population of over 200,000. Athens had a population of 150,000 or so during the same period (Childe, 1951). By a.d. 100, Rome had an estimated population of over 500,000.

This trend of urban growth was not to continue, however. Rome fell in the fifth century a.d., and subsequent wars and plagues reduced the size of cities. The rate of agricultural innovation was slow because human energies were redirected toward the technology of war. The social system became more rigid: status and occupations were determined on the basis of heredity rather than achievement or ability.

In the eleventh century, cities, especially those along natural routes and junctures, began to flourish after feudal wars subsided. As the food surplus increased, the population in the cities became more specialized. In fourteenth-century Paris, for example, tax rolls listed 157 different trades (Russell, 1972). In addition to artisans, cities also had specialists in other areas, such as government, military service, education, and religion. Each major urban activity led to the development of an institution devoted to its performance, and churches, shops, marketplaces, city halls, and palaces became the prominent features of medieval cities.

Community Development in the Industrial Era

It was not until the end of the eighteenth century that cities began to grow rapidly, due largely to the effects of the Industrial Revolution. The social and economic forces that converged at this time eventually changed Western Europe and later the United States from rural to urban societies. The growth of the number of people who live in urban rather than rural areas and the subsequent development of different values and lifestyles are referred to as **urbanization** Agricultural innovations—crop rotation, soil fertilization, and the selective breeding of animals—brought larger and larger surpluses.

At the same time, the development of manufacturing in the cities attracted many people. As the nineteenth century progressed, cities became much larger and grew into centers of commerce and production, but at the same time, they were the locus of poverty and disease. Also, as migration from rural areas increased, the city population became more heterogeneous. The variety of occupations, ethnic backgrounds, dialects, and lifestyles in these urban areas stood in sharp contrast to the relatively homogeneous populations of small towns and rural communities.

Population diversity, poverty, cramped living quarters, inadequate garbage disposal and sewage facilities, and other social and economic problems placed a tremendous strain on the urban political order. Cities became centers of unrest. Riots and revolutions, strikes by workers, and numerous clashes among members of different social groups were a significant part of nineteenth-century urban history. Many of the problems that arose in European cities during this era persist to some degree in all Western nations and in a different way in Third World nations.

Third World Urbanization

Prior to 1900, urbanization outside of Western Europe and North America was limited in both scale and extent to colonial expansion. Throughout this century; however, the situation has been changing dramatically. During the past 50 years, while the urban population increased in the more developed regions of the world, the increase was most dramatic in Third World countries, the least developed countries. In Latin America and Africa, for example, the urban population increased eightfold.

By the end of World War II, the colonial powers had relinquished control to the local governments of the colonies they had created. In each developing nation, one city became the focus of change and progress. Because these cities had improved health conditions and facilities, more jobs, and better education, they drew masses of people. The newly created governments, usually controlled by military juntas or other totalitarian regimes, were unable to keep pace with this rapid growth, however, and those who had moved from the country found that they had exchanged lives of rural poverty for lives of urban poverty.

Much of this Third World urban growth became concentrated in what are called "squatter" settlements; people would settle temporarily—*squat*—along railways, highways, the banks of streams, or on vacant government land. Most major cities in developing countries have squatter areas: Manila in the Philippines; Calcutta, India; Lima, Peru; and Saigon, Vietnam. These areas (a) lacked all the basic amenities; (b) were physically decrepit and highly disorganized; and (c) became centers of squalor, illiteracy, sickness, and human depravity. However, they played an important role in solving the housing shortage and the other complex problems associated with migration from rural to urban centers. On closer examination, they were found to provide access to the jobs and services of the central city. Many squatter areas developed highly organized self-help efforts over a period of a few years. The residents gave shelter, security, and assistance to one another, and many of these settlements provided opportunities to continue rural values and ways of living, thereby easing the transition to the density and fast pace of the city.

To Western observers, the solution to these problem areas was to relocate them and provide housing, usually outside the central city limits. These solutions rarely solved the problems of most squatters, however, for they involved heavy costs for investment (and interest), maintenance, and transportation and did not originate in the self-help efforts of the squatters themselves. Often funded by developed nations, these efforts tended to follow patterns established in the Western world, ignoring the values and priorities of the Third World residents themselves. They also tended to overlook the importance of urban community services and failed to follow through on a long-term basis with a commitment to the residents themselves. In most Third World countries, one of the residents' high priorities is to own or have a secure right to the land they occupy. These problems, which have existed in most Third World countries throughout this century, are more severe today than ever before because of rapid population growth.

Table 20-1 represents one attempt at comparing the world's largest cities. The cities are defined as population clusters of continuous built-up areas with a population density of at least 5,000 persons per square mile. The boundary of the city was determined by examining detailed maps of each city in conjunction with the most recent official population statistics. Exclaves of areas exceeding the minimum population density were added to the city if the intervening gap was less than 1 mile. To the extent practical, nonresidential areas such parks, airports,

TABLE 20-1 20 MOST POPULOUS CITIES OF THE WORLD: 2006

Rank	City	Population
1.	Mumbai (Bombay), India	11,914,398
2.	São Paulo, Brazil	11,016,703
3.	Shanghai, China	10,996,500
4.	Moscow, Russia	10,101,500
5.	Seoul, South Korea	9,820,171
6.	Delhi, India	9,817,439
7.	Karachi, Pakistan	9,339,023
8.	Istanbul, Turkey	8,831,805
9.	Beijing, China	8,689,000
10.	Mexico City, Mexico	8,591,309
11.	Tokyo, Japan	8,483,050
12.	Jakarta, Indonesia	8,389,443
13.	Shenzhen, China	8,227,500
14.	New York City, U.S.	8,143,197
15.	Teheran, Iran	7,796,257
16.	Cairo, Egypt	7,629,866
17.	London, UK	7,429,200
18.	Lima, Peru	7,029,928
19.	Bogota, Colombia	6,776,009
20.	Bangkok, Thailand	6,320,174

Source: www.xist.org/charts/cynotagg.aspx 2007

industrial complexes, and water were excluded from the area reported for each city, thus making the population density reflective of the concentrations in the residential portions of the city. By using a consistent definition for the city, it is possible to make comparisons of the cities on the basis of total population, area, and population density.

This rapid urban population growth in the Third World and elsewhere shows no sign of abating. By 2000, there were more than 250 cities in the world with a population of 1 million or more, and the largest metropolises had in excess of 15 million inhabitants. While the New York City—Northern New Jersey metropolitan area is the largest in the United States, this region falls behind Tokyo in Japan (the world's largest, with more than 28 million people) (see Table 20-1). Given the extreme levels of poverty found in many of these large and densely populated areas, one may question whether solutions are available to deal with the enormous problems and whether living conditions can be made humane and livable. Topics related to this issue are addressed later in this chapter.

Thinking Sociologically

1. The introductory issue described homelessness, and the chapter text described squatter settlements. What similarities or differences exist between the homeless in the United States and squatters in Third World countries?
2. How can living conditions be made humane in cities with 10, 20, or 30 million people or in areas with a population density of more than 100,000 people in 1 square mile?

TABLE 20-2 TEN LARGEST CITIES IN THE UNITED STATES, 2005

Rank	City	Population
1.	New York, N.Y.	8,143,197
2.	Los Angeles, Calif.	3,844,829
3.	Chicago, Ill.	2,842,518
4.	Houston, Texas	2,016,582
5.	Philadelphia, Pa.	1,463,281
6.	Phoenix, Ariz.	1,461,575
7.	San Antonio, Texas	1,256,509
8.	San Diego, Calif.	1,255,540
9.	Dallas, Texas	1,213,825
10.	San Jose, Calif.	912,332

Source: U.S. Census Bureau, Statistical Abstract of the United States, 2005, www.infoplease.com.

URBANIZATION IN THE UNITED STATES

Population Trends

The Industrial Revolution began approximately half a century later in the United States than it did in Western Europe. The major population shift from rural to urban areas did not begin here until the Civil War. An *urban area*, according to the United States Bureau of the Census, is a city or town that has at least 2500 inhabitants. In 1800, 6 percent of the population of the United States lived in urban areas. This figure rose to 20 percent by 1860. The period of greatest urban development took place during the 60-year period between 1860 and 1920; by 1920, slightly more than half the population lived in urban areas. This figure has continued to increase; as of the 2000 decennial census, 80.3 percent of Americans (226 million people) live in an urban area. Table 20-2 shows the size of the 9 largest cities in the United States and the percentage of the total U.S. population they share.

Why do people live in cities? The answer is that an increasing number of jobs in our society are nonagricultural. Thus, the shift of the population from rural to urban areas has paralleled the growth of jobs and opportunities in the industrial and service sectors of the economy. Because of their early industrial and commercial development, northeastern states such as New York and Pennsylvania were among the first to urbanize. A few years later, midwestern cities such as Chicago and Detroit became large urban centers. The western states experienced strong urban growth only after World War II, as a result of the growth of the defense industries.

As of 2000, the West coast and the South were our fastest-growing regions. In the past decade the population of 15 states increased 15 percent or more. There was a 66.3 percent growth in Nevada and 40 percent growth in Arizona (see Figure 20-1). An increasingly aging population in the United

FIGURE 20-1 FIFTEEN MOST POPULATED STATES, PERCENTAGE OF POPULATION CHANGE, 1990–2000

Source: U.S. Bureau of the Census. Population Change and Distribution: 1990-2000.

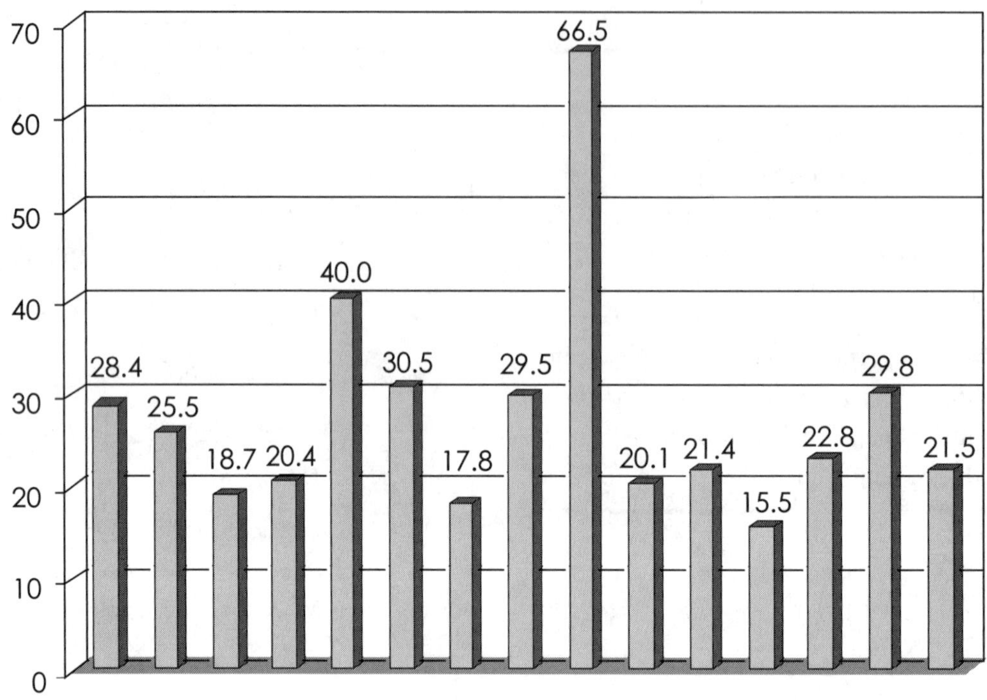

States has led many older residents to seek a retirement community in states with warmer climates. In addition, a number of businesses have relocated in the Sunbelt because of the economic advantages this area offers: primarily low wage scales, few problems with unions, cheap land and energy, and low taxes.

One recent example of this shift was the decision of General Motors to locate their new Saturn automobile plant in Tennessee rather than in one of the northern midwestern industrial urban centers. As history demonstrates, people want to move to areas that provide, or at least are perceived as providing, good employment opportunities. A number of Sunbelt businesses have attracted many skilled specialists to Sunbelt areas. This loss of industry and commerce in Snowbelt cities has decreased the tax base of numerous northern cities and states and has magnified their social and economic problems.

The Metropolitan Community

The large, densely populated cities of the early 1900s have given way to the growth of metropolitan areas. The U.S. Bureau of the Census describes a **metropolitan statistical area (MSA)** as a large population nucleus, together with adjacent communities that have a high degree of social and economic integration with that nucleus. The metropolitan community is the organization of people and institutions that performs the routine functions necessary to sustain the existence of both the city and the area around it.

The growth of metropolitan areas has been rapid and dramatic. Because of new developments in technology, in transportation, and in social structures, the concentration of large numbers of people has become possible. These same developments have also enabled a population dispersed over a wide area to become part of a larger, integrated community.

Metropolitan growth was caused initially by a shortage of space for industrial development, new housing, and new highways. Businesses were forced to design their facilities to fit the space that was available. Because streets were narrow and heavily congested, the transportation of goods was tedious and costly. Room for storage and loading was scarce. The land adjacent to the cities was ideal: It was inexpensive, property taxes were low, and businesses could design their facilities to suit their needs. The development of the steam engine and, later, the electric trolley facilitated the transportation of goods and employees over a wider area. After the 1920s, the increase in motor vehicles and the accompanying growth of highway systems stimulated unprecedented metropolitan development. Trucking became an important method of moving goods and supplies. As manufacturing and industry moved to the suburbs, so did the people and a variety of small businesses and stores. After World War II, hundreds of suburbs developed, each of which had its own government, school system, and public services. The suburban growth paralleled a slower growth and a recent decline in the population of central cities.

A metropolitan area that extends beyond the city and the MSA is the **megalopolis**, which is a continuous strip of urban and suburban development that may stretch for hundreds of miles. One example exists between Boston and Washington, D.C., on the east coast. This megalopolis covers ten states, includes hundreds of local governments, and

TABLE 20-3 POPULATION CHANGE FOR THE TEN FASTEST GROWING METROPOLITAN AREAS: 1990–2000

Highest Growth	1990 Population	2000 Population	% Growth 1990–2000
Metropolitan statistical area			
Las Vegas, NV	252,737	1,563,282	83.3
Naples, FL	152,099	251,377	65.3
Yuma, AZ	106,895	160,026	49.7
McAllen-Edinburg-Mission, TX	383,545	569,463	48.5
Austin-San Marcos, TX	846,227	1,249,763	47.7
Fayetteville-Springdale-Rogers, AZ	210,908	311,121	47.5
Boise City, ID	295,851	432,345	46.1
Phoenix-Mesa, AZ	2,238,480	3,251,876	45.3
Laredo, TX	133,239	193,117	44.9
Provo-Orem, UT	263,590	368,536	39.8

Source: U.S. Bureau of the Census. *Population Change and Distribution: 1990–2000*.

has a population of nearly 50 million. Other megalopolis areas are forming between San Francisco and San Diego on the west coast and between Chicago and Pittsburgh in the Midwest. Sometime in the next 50 years, half of the United States population may live in one of these three enormous population conglomerations.

URBAN ECOLOGY

In recent years, *ecology* has come to be associated with the biological and natural world of plants and animals and how they are affected by pollution and other environmental influences, but the term is also concerned with populations and communities. In this context, it is the study of the interrelationships of people and the environment in which they live. **Urban ecology** is concerned not only with urban spatial arrangements but also with the processes that create and reinforce these arrangements.

Urban Processes

Urban areas are not static; they change continually. The urban environment is formed and transformed by three processes: (1) concentration and deconcentration, (2) ecological specialization, and (3) invasion and succession.

The term **concentration** refers to increasing density of population, services, and institutions in a region. As people migrate to the city to find jobs, living quarters become scarce and the institutions that serve the people become strained. This starts an outward trend, called **deconcentration**, as land values and property taxes increase, and the services and public facilities decline. As a result, the core of the city—the central business district—eventually comes to consist of businesses that use space intensively and can afford to pay the economic costs. These consist of prestigious department and retail stores, financial institutions, high-rise luxury apartments, and other highly profitable ventures.

People, institutions, and services are not randomly distributed in the city. Different groups and activities tend to be concentrated in different areas. This phenomenon is called **ecological specialization**. Commercial and retail trade concerns are generally found in a different part of the city than are manufacturing and production. Similarly, public housing and low-rent tenements are seldom located near suburban residences. The basic principle at work is that people and institutions usually sort themselves into spatially homogeneous groups. As we have indicated, this homogeneity may result from economic factors: people gravitate toward places they can afford. Personal preference is also influential, as is evident from the existence of ethnic communities and areas that attract people with a particular lifestyle, such as Greenwich Village and Chicago's Gold Coast.

Changes in community membership or land use result from **invasion** by other social groups or land users, which leads to **succession**, as the old occupants and institutions are replaced by the new. One example of invasion and succession is evident when a major industry buys a sizable tract of urban land, destroys the single-family dwellings, and converts the land to commercial or industrial use. In metropolitan Detroit, for example, the residents of an ethnic community called "Poletown" were displaced by a huge automobile assembly complex.

Perhaps the most notable case of invasion and succession is reflected in the changing racial composition of central cities. The "white flight" of the 1960s, 1970s, and 1980s changed the racial composition of large cities such as Detroit, Atlanta, and Washington, D.C., from predominantly white to predominantly black. A related development is the "ghettoization" of inner cities, which occurs as minorities become trapped in central cities that have diminishing tax bases, deteriorating housing, and inefficient public services.

Urban Structure

The three ecological processes just described are the basis for several different models of urban structure. One of the most influential models during the early development of ecological theory was the **concentric zone model**, developed by Ernest W. Burgess (Burgess, 1925) in the 1920s (see Figure 20-2). According to this theory, a city spreads out equally in all directions from its original center to produce uniform circles of growth. Each zone has its own characteristic land use, population, activities, and institutions. At the center of the city is the business district, which consists of retail stores, civil activity centers, banks, hotels, and institutional administrative offices. Zone 2, the transitional zone, contains older factories, wholesale and light manufacturing businesses, and low-rent tenements. It is in this zone that immigrants or migrants are likely to live when they first arrive in the city. At the turn of the century, first-generation European immigrants made their home in this zone, but today it is populated by minorities: African-Americans, Hispanic-Americans, and other ethnic groups. Zone 3 marks the edge of the residential areas and consists of progressively more expensive houses and apartments, ending finally with the commuter zone.

Since its formulation, Burgess's zone theory has come under considerable attack. Many cities do not fit the concentric zone pattern, which is more characteristic of commercial–industrial cities than of administrative cities. *Commercial–industrial cities* are those built around industry, such as Detroit, Cleveland, and Pittsburgh. These cities have a high proportion of blue-collar workers. *Administrative cities*, such as Washington, D.C., and New York City, rely heavily on government, education, and nonindustrial businesses. Also, it seems to more accurately describe cities such as Chicago that developed at the turn of the century than cities such as Houston, Phoenix, and San Diego that are developing today.

There are two major alternatives to Burgess's theory. One is the **sector model**, formulated by Hoyt (1939). According to Hoyt, the city is organized into pie-shaped wedges radiating from the central business district. Patterns of land use—industrial, high-income residential, and low-income tenements—tend to extend outward from the city core in internally consistent sectors or wedges. An industrial zone might radiate from the core in one wedge and spread into the suburbs, whereas high-income housing might push outward from the core in another wedge. Hoyt noticed this pattern in several large cities, notably Minneapolis and San Francisco.

The third theory of spatial growth rejects the idea of a single urban core or center, maintaining instead that areas of different land use have different centers. This is the **multiple-nuclei model** formulated by Harris and Ullman (1945). In their view, each area expands from its center, and the form of expansion may fit either the concentric or the sector zone models. In many ways, the multiple-nuclei model describes the growth of metropolitan areas better than the growth of central cities.

These three models do not reflect every possible variety or pattern of growth. Urban expansion is influenced by a variety of factors, including rate of migration into the city, cultural and historical precedents for urban development, and the physical characteristics of the land. As a result of these and other factors, Latin American cities, for example, do not fit American growth patterns, and cities built near major waterways grow differently from other cities. Sociologists today are developing more complex models of urban development that take into account a wide variety of factors, including social, economic, and cultural variables.

FIGURE 20-2 ECOLOGICAL MODELS OF URBAN STRUCTURE

Source: Reprinted from "The Nature of Cities" by Chauncy D. Harris and Edward L. Ullman in Vol. 242 of *The Annals of the American Academy of Political and Social Science,* November 1945.

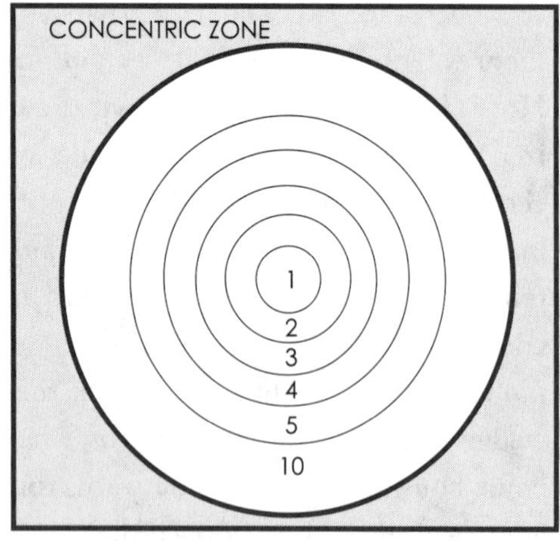

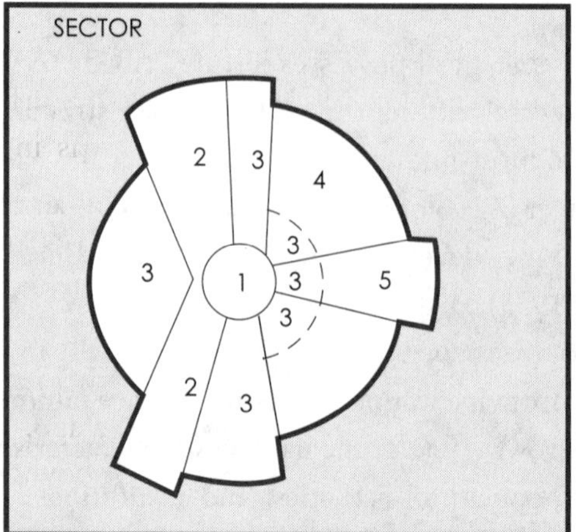

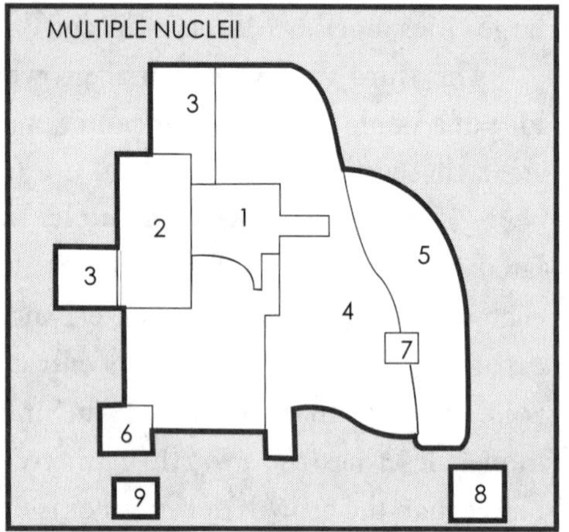

Three generalizations of the internal structure of cities:

DISTRICT

1. Central business district
2. Wholesale light Manufacturing
3. Low-class residential
4. Middle class residential
5. High class residential
6. Heavy manufacturing
7. Outlying business district
8. Residential suburb
9. Industrial suburb
10. Commuters zone

Thinking Sociologically

1. Get a map of the city in which you live or a nearby city with which you are familiar. Using the map and what you know about the city, determine which, if any, of the ecological models of urban structure discussed in this chapter it seems to follow. If it does not seem to fit any of these models, try to develop a model that it does fit.

2. Using the same city as in the preceding question, discuss what processes and growth factors might have contributed to the structure of the city. What does the city's structure help you discern and explain about some of the specific problems that the city faces?

LIFE IN CITIES AND SUBURBS

Metropolitan areas, urban areas, cities, and towns are generally defined and described in terms of population. However, the term *community* suggests some degree of interdependence, mutual identification, or organization of activities. The emergence of urban communities has altered human lifestyles and values. The size, complexity, and density of urban communities have given rise to new forms of social organization, new behaviors, and new attitudes. One of the major questions with which sociologists have grappled is why urban communities are different from rural areas in so many ways, rather than just the fact that they are larger and more densely populated. Sociologists have long recognized that there are qualitative differences between urban and rural life, and Ferdinand Tönnies (1887), a German sociologist, made a distinction in this regard over a century ago. He called the small, rural villages of his boyhood gemeinschaft (communities) and the centers of activity *gesellschaft* (associations).

A **gemeinschaft** community is characterized by a sense of solidarity and a common identity. It is a primary community rooted in tradition. Relationships among neighbors are intimate and personal, and there is a strong emphasis on shared values and sentiments, a "we" feeling. People frequently interact with one another and tend to establish deep, long-term relationships. Many small towns and communes have these characteristics.

A **gesellschaft** community, in contrast, is based on diverse economic, political, and social interrelationships. It is characterized by individualism, mobility, impersonality, the pursuit of self-interest, and an emphasis on progress rather than tradition. Shared values and total personal involvement become secondary. People live and work together because it is necessary or convenient, and people are viewed more in terms of their roles than as unique individuals. In a large city, for example, one is likely to interact with a police officer as a public servant or authority figure who has stereotyped characteristics and obligations. In a small town, on the other hand, residents would be likely to know a police officer personally. Rather than viewing the officer as a manifestation of a certain form of authority, one would know the officer as an individual with unique character traits. Historically, there has been a shift from gemeinschaft to gesellschaft relationships as a result of role specialization and, more generally, of bureaucratization. In the nineteenth century, Weber labeled this as a change from a "traditional" to a "rational" society. In the twentieth century, American sociologists have used these ideas as a springboard for their own theories. In the next two sections, we examine some of these theories about the quality of life in cities and suburbs.

City Life

Robert Redfield (1941), an American sociologist, developed a typology similar to those formulated by nineteenth-century scholars. He distinguished a **folk society**, which is small, isolated, homogeneous, and kin oriented, from an urban society, which is large, impersonal, heterogeneous, and fast-paced. Around the same time, Louis Wirth, a colleague of Redfield's at the University of Chicago, described the effects of large numbers, density, and heterogeneity on urban life. In "Urbanism as a Way of Life" (1938), Wirth argued that as the population in an area becomes denser, lifestyles diversify, new opportunities arise, and institutions develop. At the same time, density increases the number of short-term, impersonal, and utilitarian social relationships that a person is likely to have.

According to Wirth, these three factors—large numbers, density, and heterogeneity—create a distinctive way of life, called "urbanism." The distinctive characteristics of urbanism are an extensive and complex division of labor; an emphasis on success, achievement, and social mobility, along with a behavioral orientation that includes rationality and utilitarianism; a decline of the family and kinship bonds and a concurrent rise of specialized agencies that assume roles previously taken by kin; a breakdown of primary relationships and the substitution of secondary group-control mechanisms; the replacement of deep, long-term relationships with superficial, short-term relationships; a decline of shared values and homogeneity and an increase in diversity; and finally, segregation on the basis of achieved and ascribed status characteristics.

Milgram (1970) has focused on the effects of urbanism. In midtown Manhattan, for example, someone can meet 220,000 people within a 10-minute walking radius of his or her office and not recognize a single person. Such experiences, says Milgram, may cause "psychic overload" and result in the detached, "don't get involved" attitude that is frequently cited as a part of big-city life. There have been a number of recorded incidents, for instance, in which people have been mugged, raped, or beaten in plain view of pedestrians who refused to help the victim.

These views of urban life give the impression that it is cold, violent, and alienating. City living conditions have been viewed by scholars as the cause of crime, mental illness, aggression, and other serious problems, but recent studies by sociologists have questioned the validity of this assessment. Certainly, these negative aspects of city life do exist; the real question is how typical or widespread they are. Several studies have found that there is considerable cohesion and solidarity in the city, particularly in neighborhoods where the residents are relatively homogeneous in terms of social or demographic characteristics. The findings of early sociologists may have accurately described the central core of American cities such as Chicago during periods of rapid growth. Contemporary research illustrates that a variety of lifestyles and adaptations can be found in cities.

Several decades ago, Herbert Gans (1962) presented research showing the diversity of urban lifestyles that are likely to remain true today. He argues that there are at least five types of residents in the city: cosmopolites, singles, ethnic villagers, the deprived, and the trapped.

Cosmopolites usually choose to remain in the city because of its convenience and cultural benefits. This group includes artists, intellectuals, and professionals who are drawn by the opportunities and activities generally found only in large urban centers. They are typically young, married, and involved in upper-middle-class occupations.

Singles like to live in the city because it is close to their jobs and permits a suitable lifestyle. The central city, with its nightclubs and singles-only apartments, offers a basis for social interaction. It gives singles opportunities to make friends, develop a social identity, and eventually find a mate. Many of these people are not permanent urban residents; they live in the city only until they marry or have children, at which time they move to the suburbs.

The third group identified by Gans, *ethnic villagers*, generally consists of working-class people who have chosen to reside in specific areas of the city. Their neighborhoods often develop a distinctive ethnic color as shops, restaurants, and organizations spring up. The Chinatowns in New York and San Francisco, the Hispanic areas of San Antonio and San Diego, and the Polish communities of Chicago and Detroit are neighborhoods of this type. Because of their strong ethnic ties, they usually do not identify as strongly with the city, nor do they engage in many of the cultural, social, or political activities that take place beyond their ethnic community. Their identity and allegiance are tied to the ethnic group and local community to a far greater extent than to the city. A strong emphasis is placed on kinship and primary group relationships, and members of other groups are often perceived as intruders or outsiders.

The fourth group, the *deprived*, is composed of the poor, the handicapped, and racial minorities who have fallen victim to class inequality, prejudice, or personal misfortune. They live in the city because it offers inexpensive housing and holds the promise of future job opportunities that will enable them to move to a better environment.

Finally, *the trapped* are those who cannot afford to move to a newer community and must remain in their deteriorating neighborhoods. The elderly who live on pensions make up much of this group, and because many have lived in the city all their lives, they tend to identify strongly with their neighborhoods. The deprived and the trapped are the most frequent victims of the problems of the city. They are more likely to be the targets of assault, mugging, extortion, and other crimes than other city residents. In high-crime areas, many of these people live isolated lives and are terrified by the ongoing violence in their neighborhoods.

Suburban Life

The dominance of **suburbs**, communities surrounding and dependent on urban areas, is a recent phenomenon, although the population movement to the suburbs began at the end of the nineteenth century. Suburbs grew as a result of both push and pull factors. The problems of the city drove residents to the suburbs, and the positive aspects of suburban life—cleaner air, lower property taxes, larger lots, and a chance to own a home—attracted people. Because the move involved a substantial capital investment, this transition was made primarily by the more affluent.

The growth of the suburbs was also influenced by technological developments, especially those in transportation. Before the 1920s, trains and electric trolleys were the major means of mass transportation to and from the central city. Accordingly, the first pattern of suburban growth was star-shaped, as communities sprang up along the railway and trolley corridors radiating from the center of the city. The automobile gave the suburban movement a significant boost by permitting the development of land not located near a railway or trolley corridor.

After World War II, the suburbs took on a different appearance. The increased affluence of American workers and the mass production of relatively inexpensive housing enabled many lower-middle-class and blue-collar families to become suburbanites (i.e., residents of the suburbs). The type of housing that emerged in the post-World War II suburbs, called "tract housing," was based on mass-production techniques. Neighborhoods and sometimes whole communities of similar houses were constructed. As the population began to shift to the suburbs, so did the retail trade and small businesses. The result was an unprecedented growth of suburban shopping centers.

The rapid growth of suburbs in the 1950s and early 1960s caused a great deal of concern among many social commentators. Suburban life was characterized as a "rat race" dominated by a preoccupation with "keeping up with the Joneses." Suburbanites were seen as anxious, child-oriented, status-seeking people who led empty, frustrating lives (Bell, 1958; Gordon et al., 1961; Mills, 1951). The typical suburbanites were viewed as more concerned with household gadgets, status symbols, and getting into what they consider to be the right organizations than with understanding the world around them or achieving individuality. These views generated what sociologists call the "myth of suburbia." Recent research has given us reason to doubt that the patterns of behavior found in the suburbs are due to suburban residence and even that there is a distinctively suburban way of life.

The suburbs and the people who live there are actually quite diverse. Most of you can differentiate suburbs by the types of housing and land areas that accompany it. Most cities have one or two identifiable suburban communities of the affluent, which are occupied by white, upper-middle class executives and professionals. Other identifiable communities consist of white-collar and upper-working-class residents with their three-bedroom, two-and-one-half-bathroom homes with an attached two-car garage. A third type of suburban community is that of the blue-collar, less educated and less affluent resident.

These homes, without garages, are small and are the least expensive type of suburban housing. In all categories, a primary reason cited for moving to the suburbs is the desire to own a home. A second important reason is to find a suitable environment in which to raise children. Other factors common to most suburbanites are a desire for open spaces and for a less hectic pace.

Do people change when they move from the city to the suburbs? Is there evidence of a **conversion effect**, a radical shift of interest and lifestyle? Research from the 1960s by Berger (1960) and by Cohen and Hodges (1963) found that blue-collar families had similar values, behavior patterns, and psychological orientations whether they lived in the city or in the suburbs. Similarly, Gans (1967) found that middle-class suburbanites in Levittown were not plagued by the stereotypical problems of boredom, unhappiness, and frustrated status-seeking. He found instead that they were generally happy, well-adjusted, and involved in family and social activities. In short, there was little evidence of a conversion effect.

In recent years, the number of blacks who live in the suburbs has increased sharply. There is little evidence, however, that many suburbs are becoming racially integrated. Because the median income of blacks is still considerably lower than that of whites, many blacks cannot afford to move into the suburbs where most whites reside. Instead, they are moving into the older suburbs with lower property values, which whites are leaving behind in their search for better suburban communities. Though whites often react strongly to blacks who move into their suburban communities because they are perceived as being different, research shows that blacks who move to the suburbs have values and lifestyles similar to those of their white neighbors (Austin, 1976).

Hispanics, blacks, and Asians are more likely than non-Hispanic whites to live in central cities (*Changing America*, 1998). In 1996 more than half of blacks and Hispanics and nearly half of Asians lived in central cities, compared with less than a quarter of non-Hispanic whites. By contrast, over half of all non-Hispanic whites lived in the suburbs in 1996, as did 48 percent of Asians. Native Americans are by far most likely to live outside cities and suburbs; in 1990 nearly half of the American Indian population lived outside of metropolitan areas (*Changing America*, 1998).

Thinking Sociologically

1. Would you say that the town in which you live could be characterized as a gemeinschaft or a gesellschaft? Why? Discuss some features and qualities of the town that lead you to characterize it in this way.

2. Discuss the accuracy of the statement, "People who live in cities are different from people who live in suburban or rural areas."

3. How accurate do you find Gan's classification and description of the five types of urban residents? As you reflect, can you identify these types from your own experiences?

Urban Problems

The most severe problems in urban areas are found in the central cities: poverty, unemployment, crime, noise and air pollution, waste disposal, water purity, transportation, housing, population congestion, and so on. Although the suburbs are by no means immune to these problems, they generally do not experience them to the same degree as central cities. The central cities are beset by a number of crises, some of which are becoming worse. In this section, three problems are discussed: poverty and unemployment, crime, and schooling.

Among the most serious issues facing cities today are the related problems of poverty and unemployment. The economic vitality of central cities has diminished over the years, as industry, affluent taxpayers, and jobs have moved out. The result has been a steady deterioration of housing and public services and the loss of high-paying jobs. The least fortunate of city residents are forced to live in slums and ghettos.

Slums are overcrowded streets or sections of a city marked by poverty and poor living conditions, which result from the dirt, disease, rodents, and other health hazards that accompany concentrations of housing with poor plumbing, garbage disposal, and sanitation facilities. Slum residents are often victims of social injustice and personal misfortune: racial minorities, the elderly, women who head large families, and addicts. Over the years, research has shown that slum living has a number of detrimental effects on health: residents of slums are more likely than others to contract diseases and to become seriously ill; they have poorer overall health and shorter life spans; and they are more apt to have poorer self-images and experience psychological problems such as depression and alienation.

The most serious poverty and its accompanying social problems occur in ghettos. A **ghetto** is an area, usually a deteriorating one, in which members of a racial or ethnic minority are forcibly segregated. Urban areas that are no longer of interest to the more affluent majority tend to become ghettos. A ghetto is a social and economic trap that keeps members of the minority group within a controllable geographic area. Crane (1991) describes ghettos as neighborhoods that have experienced epidemics of social problems: epidemics of crack, gang violence, teenage childbearing, and so forth. His assumption is that social problems are contagious and are spread through peer influence within ghetto neighborhoods. He found that the neighborhood effect on the pattern of dropping out of school and of childbearing—the two variables he studied among teenagers—was precisely the one implied by an epidemic hypothesis. Urban ghettos, the worst areas of large cities, produced sharp jumps, that is epidemics, in both dimensions.

Wilson (1987) argues that the problems of inner-city ghettos indicate the existence of a growing, largely black underclass. In his words,

> Inner-city neighborhoods have undergone a profound social transformation in the last several years as reflected not only in their increasing rates of social dislocation (including crime, joblessness, out-of-wedlock births, female-headed families, and welfare dependency) but also in the changing economic class structure of ghetto neighborhoods. ... The movement of middle-class professionals from the inner city, followed in increasing numbers by working class blacks, has left behind a much larger concentration of the most disadvantaged segments of the black urban population to which I refer when I speak of the ghetto underclass. (p. 49)

There is evidence that black ghettoization is increasing today. In 2002, 52 percent of all African Americans lived in an urban area, compared to 21 percent whites (*Current Population Reports*, 2003).

The jobs that the less affluent central-city residents are qualified for are usually low-paying and scarce, and the unemployment rate is twice as high as the rate in the suburbs. The departure of industry and manufacturing jobs has left inner-city residents with jobs characterized by high turnover, low wages, and few opportunities for advancement. It is not unusual to find a person who heads a family and works full-time but barely earns enough to stay above the poverty line. With recent cuts in federal aid to job-training programs, it is unlikely that the situation of these city residents will improve in the near future.

Crime is another serious urban problem. In fact, *The Gallup Poll Monthly* (September 1990, p. 40) reported that Americans have an overwhelmingly negative perception of the safety of many of America's largest cities. Results from a randomly selected national sample of adults revealed that New

York, leading the list, was seen as an unsafe place to live in or visit by 85 percent of the respondents. New York was followed by Miami (76 percent), Washington, D.C. (71 percent), Detroit (68 percent), and Chicago (65 percent). The picture of cities was not entirely dismal, however. Minneapolis and Seaule were only viewed as unsafe by 11 and 16 percent, respectively, with less than 30 percent viewing Houston, Dallas, San Diego, and Boston similarly.

Data shows that household perceptions of crime as a problem rose during the late 1980s and early 1990s as the actual crime rate rose. On the other hand, this is not always a predictable correlation. Differences in perception of crime and actual victimization are found because as crime dropped sharply from 1994 to 1995, perceptions that crime was a neighborhood problem remained relatively stable. Black households were much more likely than white households to indicate crime was a neighborhood problem. In 1995, 2.5 times as many black households indicated crime was a problem; but the difference was not nearly as large for actual victimization: 27 percent of black households experienced one or more crimes, compared to 23 percent of white households (Bureau of Justice Statistics, 1998).

Furthermore, urban households have historically been and continue to be the most vulnerable to property crime, burglary, motor vehicle theft and theft in the United States (Bureau of Justice Statistics, 2003).

Crime is at the heart of viewing cities as unsafe places in which to live, visit, and work, and with some justification. Theft, arson, violence, illegal vice activities (such as prostitution, gambling), and the use and sale of narcotics are generally found more in large cities, where there is greater anonymity. In addition, the methods of control are different in large cities and small towns. Whereas towns rely on internalized values and primary-group pressure for enforcement, cities depend on abstract laws and impersonal, bureaucratic agencies such as the police (Dinitz, 1973). When high density, heterogeneity, and anonymity are combined with poverty, a physically decayed environment, and other characteristics of inner-city living, there is great potential for social deviance and violence.

Not all areas of a city experience the same crime rate or the same types of crimes. The highest crime rates are found in the inner-city sectors; the rate decreases as one moves toward the fringes of the urban area. Zonal differences in crime tend to persist, however, even when the physical characteristics and the occupants of a zone change.

Using sociological research as a guide, one might argue that there are several ways of reducing urban crime. Increased police surveillance is often an important political issue in cities, but there is some evidence that it has little if any effect on the crime rate. Furthermore, research shows that despite the apparent popularity of the community policing approach, community residents may not want closer interaction with the police nor the responsibility for maintaining social control (Grinc, 1994). Because high-crime areas are located in similar areas in different cities—generally the most poverty-stricken areas—one might argue that providing the people in these areas with decent living conditions and meaningful jobs would have a greater impact on crime than increasing the size of the police force. One could also argue that voluntary neighborhood organizations in high crime areas might not only provide role models of lawful behavior but also create a sense of community that is frequently lacking in these areas.

A third urban problem area is schooling. Today, city schools are faced with a variety of major problems, two of which are inadequate financing and social disorder, including violence. Many cities have a very difficult time keeping pace with the accelerating costs. This difficulty is accentuated by inequalities in school funding: Urban schools generally have a much lower per-student expenditure allowance than schools in the suburbs. City schools have reacted to this funding problem in several ways. In some areas, school bond increases have been used to retain financial solvency. In recent years, however, an increasing percentage of school bond proposals are being rejected by irate taxpayers. As a result of the fiscal crisis, many schools are forced to use outdated or damaged curricular material. Reductions in staff and salary are another means of dealing with the financial woes. These responses to funding cuts have been a factor in recent teacher strikes and walkouts. Staff and salary cutbacks also seem to be related to the morale problems found in many inner-city schools.

School disorder, especially violence, is widespread in many city schools. Incidents that rarely occurred a generation ago happen today on a fairly routine basis: theft, extortion, physical attacks on fellow students and on teachers, and vandalism. In some schools, the halls are routinely patrolled by police officers; in others, the doors of classrooms are locked during class hours to prevent intruders from entering; still other schools have unannounced locker checks to confiscate drugs and weapons, an activity strongly opposed by the American Civil Liberties Union (ACLU). One explanation for the increase in crime in the schools is that schools are no longer immune to the day-to-day problems of the city. Solving some of the problems that cause crime on the streets would therefore probably reduce crime in the schools. Another explanation is that the schools themselves are responsible for disorder. Deteriorating buildings, prejudiced or inadequately trained teachers, inequalities in the curriculum (known as "tracking"), and pessimism about the future may all produce an atmosphere of despair and anger. Without adequate funds to buy better equipment and to hire and train more qualified teachers, this problem is likely to persist.

URBAN REJUVENATION: PROBLEMS AND PROSPECTS

What can be done to help our cities survive? Has the central city outlived its usefulness? These are a couple of the serious questions addressed by scholars concerned about the future of our cities. Some feel that the future of cities is dim as the tax base continues to erode, buildings and homes continue to deteriorate, tax rebellions become more frequent, and the people who remain in inner cities constitute the ghetto underclass of racial and class exclusion, single mothers and absent fathers, homeless and unemployed, and so forth (see Wilson, 1997). Others, such as Feagin and Parke (1990), write about rebuilding American cities, with the developers, bankers, and speculators as shapers of cities being joined by protesters of urban redevelopment who want to reinvigorate democracy in urban cities. These protesters are citizens who are demanding more popular control over home and neighborhood spaces and over the quality of life in their communities.

Downtown Revitalization

A person's perspective on and attitude toward the problems and prospects of the city depends greatly on whether the central business district or residential areas are being considered, and on who is doing the considering. The business districts of many cities are being revitalized and are experiencing significant new business construction. Because the downtown areas of our cities are a major center of white-collar employment, financial firms, insurance companies, and private and government services, the future of these areas is relatively secure.

Downtown revitalization programs tend to have a greater impact on white-collar jobs than on blue-collar ones, however. The number of white-collar jobs in cities is increasing, but the number of blue-collar jobs continues to decline. Because the revitalization of the central business district creates a need for well-educated, highly skilled employees, many inner-city residents who have weaker credentials do not directly benefit from these types of economic programs. This has made many city residents angry because they feel that their problems and concerns are secondary to the plans of affluent city and suburban developers and residents. Those who advocate downtown revitalization do not fully acknowledge the dislocating and segregative effects of urban renewal and public housing on central city neighborhoods (Gotham, 2001). Feagin and Parke (1990 [Chapter 10]) describe the actions of some citizen protest groups that have voiced their concerns about affordable rental housing, highway projects, shopping malls, high-rise construction, and urban renewal. There is a concern that urban rejuvenation must include residential neighborhoods, as well as the business district, and must create jobs for all city residents, regardless of their levels of skill or education.

Urban Renewal

Urban renewal is, at least in theory, the residential counterpart of downtown revitalization. According to the Urban Renewal Act of 1954, the major goal is to rebuild and renovate the ghettos and slums of American cities, but urban-renewal projects have had several shortcomings. First, local urban renewal agencies were given the power by the federal government to define which areas were considered to be "blighted" and therefore qualified for renewal. Generally, the better areas of the slums were developed, while the worst were allowed to remain. Sometimes, the reason for this selection was the perception that one area was more likely to produce income than the other. Shopping centers and high-rise apartments for the middle class, for example, often replaced low-income housing. Ironically, many of the residents whose homes were razed did not benefit at all from the structures that were erected, though exactly the opposite effect was intended in the 1954 act. Second, the act specified that the people displaced by urban renewal should be relocated in "decent, safe, and sanitary" housing in other areas of the city. In a number of instances, the new neighborhoods were just as bad as the old ones, and the relocation often destroyed an existing sense of community with friends and neighbors.

The case of the Pruitt-Igoe Housing Project in St. Louis several decades back exemplifies some of the problems associated with urban renewal projects (Newman, 1972). The project, which had cleared some of the city's slum dwellings by 1955, consisted of 33 buildings, each 11 stories high. It was lauded as a model for all future public housing projects because of its design and use of innovative structures. By 1970, however, the project had become a symbol of all the negative aspects of public housing. The physical deterioration and destruction of elevators, laundry rooms, and stairways were considerable. Residents were afraid to leave their apartments because of the frequency of robbery and rape. The absence of public bathrooms on the ground floors resulted in foul-smelling hallways. Gradually, most of the occupants fled the project, and even the most desperate welfare recipients were unwilling to tolerate the living conditions. The government finally closed down the entire project and later razed it. The basic problem was that human values and lifestyles were not fully considered in the project's design. The high-rise construction isolated residents from one another; the architectural design left too much open space (halls, elevators, laundry rooms) that no one felt responsible for and that made surveillance of children and adolescents very difficult.

Other means of housing the poor were legislated after the problems with urban-renewal projects were publicized in the 1960s. Most of them received mixed reviews. One form of legislation included the Housing and Urban Redevelopment Act, which provided direct subsidies to low-income families so that they could either buy their own homes or rent apartments of their own choosing. The Experimental Housing Allowance Program was implemented in the early 1970s, to help low-income tenants pay their rent. In both cases, part of the rent was paid by the government, either to the tenant or directly to the landlord.

Another federal plan that has been implemented is **urban homesteading**. Homesteading programs sell abandoned and foreclosed homes to private families for between 1 and 100 dollars if they agree to live in the house for at least 3 years and to bring the house up to housing code standards within 18 months. Though the program has limited funds, it has had a significant effect on a number of cities, but there have been pitfalls. Individuals and lending institutions are reluctant to invest in houses surrounded by vandalized, rundown buildings, and despite the low purchase price, repairs may be quite expensive. The Department of Housing and Urban Development (HUD) has acted to alleviate these problems by buying up and making modest repairs on entire neighborhoods. If the federal government were to continue its commitment to urban homesteading in the 1990s, some of our deteriorating neighborhoods could probably be transformed. At the time of this writing, however, this type of commitment by the federal government appears highly unlikely.

A growing number of urban neighborhoods are being rejuvenated by **gentrification**: the movement of middle-class people into old rundown homes that they repair at their own expense. Notable examples of this are found in Chicago's Newtown, the Mission District of San Francisco, and Atlanta's Ansley Park. These people are generally young, white, childless couples who work in the city; They tend to have different values than their suburban counterparts. Many do not want to have families and are turned off by the sameness and the Tack of charm of suburban housing. This trend may continue in the future, with the increasing costs of transportation and suburban housing.

Urban Planning

Most of our urban development has occurred without a long-term commitment to community living or a strong theoretical understanding of it. Urban planning is a field of study concerned with urban physical structures and spatial configurations and their effects on human attitudes and behavior. Two traditional goals of this field are the reduction of population density and the creation of appealing community structures.

Urban planning became a concern in the nineteenth century when many large cities in Europe and the United States were experiencing severe problems because of rapid industrial and population growth. One early influential figure was Ebenezer Howard. In his *Garden Cities of Tomorrow* (1902), Howard argued that the ideal was to develop cities that combined the benefits of both rural and urban living. All new towns, or "garden cities as he called them, would be built on undeveloped land, in accordance with scientific principles. Population density, a factor he felt was responsible for urban blight, would be carefully controlled. Cities were also to be surrounded by a **greenbelt**, an area preserved for farming and recreation, thus limiting the outward growth of the city. Howard's ideas have had a significant impact on the theoretical orientations of several generations of urban planners, whose major focus has been the construction of new towns, which have a careful mixture of houses, entertainment areas, businesses, and industries.

A number of modern new towns have been carefully designed and monitored. Columbia, Maryland, located between Washington, D.C., and Baltimore, is an example of a city developed with human needs and lifestyles in mind. The city is divided into what are called "villages" and "neighborhoods." Each neighborhood has its own elementary school and recreational facilities, and the villages form a circle around a plaza with a shopping center, office buildings, and medical facilities. The community has also made a conscious attempt to achieve racial balance.

Other, more recent new towns have not been as successful as Columbia, and federal cutbacks in funding for development have led to the demise of more than half a dozen new towns. The lesson to be learned from these experiences is that the successful development of planned communities requires a long-term investment of money, perhaps as long as 15 or 20 years, by the federal government. With its present economic woes, our government is unlikely to make such a commitment in the near future.

Diversity of Values

Urban planners must be sensitive to the diverse values and lifestyles of the people who live in urban communities if they are to achieve their goals, but they have not been completely successful in this area. They have been criticized as having a distinctly middle-class bias. This point can be illustrated with findings about the design and use of space.

Most planners assume that people like a considerable amount of open public space and clearly demarcated areas of private space. Among members of many blue-collar and minority groups, however, the distinction between public and private space is blurred, and social interactions tend to flow more freely across private and public regions than they do in middle-class environments.

That urban planners and the less affluent have different spatial preferences has been noted with regard to the structure of individual apartments. An experiment in which Hispanic residents of a New York tenement conferred with an architect about the redesign of their apartments revealed that the residents did not like the large areas of open space in an apartment that middle-class couples prefer; they also wanted an apartment entrance that did not open directly into the living room, and they liked an apartment in which the kitchen was isolated from the rest of the house by a wall or a door (Zeisel, 1973).

As suggested, the development of attractive, functional physical surroundings cannot be accomplished without a long-term commitment by the government to aid our ailing cities. The rejuvenation of the city also requires the creation of jobs and opportunities for inner-city residents. In the past few decades, major steps have been taken toward the realization of these goals, but many look with despair at the discrepancy between where we are today and where we need to go.

Thinking Sociologically

1. Make a list of urban problems and a list of rural problems. (a) Is the list different? (b) What are key factors that contribute to both? (c) Who holds primary responsibility (private citizens, private business, local government, federal government, or others) for changing them?

2. Discuss what urban planners or politicians mean when they talk about downtown revitalization and urban renewal. What are some consequences of programs or actions such as the razing of blighted areas, homesteading, and gentrification?

APPLYING SOCIOLOGY TO URBAN PLANNING

Sociological knowledge plays an important part in urban planning. Some professional sociologists have jobs in urban planning as consultants and researchers for state, city, and local governments and for engineers, architects, lawyers, and others involved in planning cities and communities. Before engineers design a new road going through a neighborhood, for example, they might want to know how the increased traffic flow will influence the social organization of the community. Municipal governments might need to know how a neighborhood renewal project might influence the social organization of a particular community before they begin the project. Will the residents' networks of cooperation and exchange be disrupted? How will leisure time and work roles be affected? Will the project impose middle-class values on a lower-class culture? Recall the discussion of how the Pruitt-Igoe Housing Project in St. Louis failed partially because the values and lifestyles of the people who lived there were not considered in the project's design.

Andrew Collver (1983), in an article on housing and environmental planning, suggests six ways in which sociology can contribute to urban planning:

1. Regional data collection and analysis
2. Neighborhood life-cycle analysis
3. Preparation of long-range community plans
4. Critical review and evaluation of alternative courses of action
5. Project evaluation
6. Creation of social inventions or alternate structures

Regional Data Collection and Analysis. To plan a workable community or neighborhood, the planners—policymakers, engineers, architects, lawyers, and others—should understand the developmental trends of the larger region in which it is located and how its location both serves and is served by the larger metropolitan system. Is the population of the region growing? How much migration in and out of the area is there? How are the age patterns of the population changing? What are the various types of income, religious, and ethnic groups within the community, and how well integrated are they? Answers to questions such as these require some knowledge of social stratification, minority groups, and demography, as well as knowledge of sociological research methods.

Neighborhood Life-Cycle Analysis. This entails examining the history of the neighborhood and its trend of growth or decline, rather than just examining the neighborhood at a single point in time. Is the average income level of the residents rising or declining? Are new businesses opening, or are old businesses closing, or both? Is the middle class moving in or out? As Collver (1983, p. 281) points out, "to try to attract middle-class homeowners back to an inner-city neighborhood that lacks such essential elements as architectural charm, good schools, and convenient access to work and recreation would be an exercise in frustration." A sociological analysis of a community can help to create plans that are more in line with the natural tendencies of the community.

Preparation of Long-Range Community Plans. Long-range plans are not always effectively carried out, but they are a useful way for urban planners to reach common understandings and assumptions about what should be done. This increases the level of communication among the planners and helps to make them of one mind. Sociological knowledge can be a helpful way to create workable plans from the stated goals of community leaders. Suppose, for example, that one of the stated goals of the community government is to create an ethnically and racially diverse neighborhood of middle-income people. Knowledge of prejudice, minority groups, values, norms, roles, culture, and so forth would be useful in devising a means to achieve the community's goals.

Critical Review and Evaluation of Alternative Courses of Action. What kind of impact will the proposed urban plan have? What are some possible alternatives to the plan? If they are inferior to the plan chosen, why are they inferior? How can architectural and environmental impact be assessed and managed? Knowledge of people's lifestyles and the effects of spatial arrangement, density, crowding, heterogeneity, and other factors offers insight into the impact of a plan. Field experiments are a means of testing policies before they are actually implemented. Similarly, field experiments can be conducted to assess the impact of various alternative planning measures before selecting one. Collver notes also that impact analysis is required by federal and state regulations.

Project Evaluation. Once a project has been completed, planners must determine whether it met its goals. Outcome evaluation would be one way of assessing the results of an urban planning project. A knowledge of the methodology of outcome evaluation research could be used to help fine-tune the plan being evaluated. There are four steps in evaluation research: specification (defining or identifying the goals of the project), measurement (the information needed to evaluate the goal), analysis (the use of the information to draw conclusions), and recommendation (the advice given regarding what should be done, based on the analysis).

Creation of Social Inventions or Alternative Structures. How can the necessary functions of a community be met in new and better ways? Developing such inventions might require changes in basic ideologies and institutions. Could a neighborhood or community, for example, share the use and maintenance of common property rather than having individual property owners? This would require a restructuring of our basic ideology of private ownership, but this seemingly revolutionary idea is what lies behind the movement toward condominiums and cooperative apartments. A sociological analysis of our basic ideologies and institutions may help free us from some confinements that are not practical or beneficial in every situation.

SUMMARY

1. Urban communities can exist only when there is a group of people to grow and process food for the urbanites. A degree of social organization is also necessary to transform a crowded group of people into a social group that behaves in an orderly and predictable manner.
2. The first urban communities developed approximately 10,000 years ago, during the horticultural era. This development was possible because of increased food production and the creation of regular surpluses. Several thousand years later, technological advances—the plow, metallurgy, the use of animals, counting, and writing—and the increasing complexity of

social and political organization-enabled cities to grow to unprecedented sizes.

3. The fall of Rome in the fifth century a.d. marked the beginning of a precipitous decline in city size and complexity that lasted for nearly 600 years. Urban communities did not begin to grow substantially again until the late eighteenth century, with the dawn of the industrial age. Urban populations then increased dramatically, and within a few decades, more people lived in cities than in rural areas.

4. The most dramatic increase in urban population is in Third World countries, the least developed countries. Some of this urban growth became concentrated in squatter settlements. Today, there are about 250 cities in the world with increasing populations of more than 1 million people, and there is little hope of this trend abating.

5. In the United States today, three-fourths of our population live in urban areas, which have increased in size as well as in number. The rapid industrial and population growth in large cities during the early part of this century caused people and industries to move from central cities to the sparsely populated areas outside of them. This process resulted in the modern metropolis.

6. *A metropolitan statistical area (MSA)* is a large population nucleus, together with adjacent communities that have a high degree of social and economic integration with that nucleus. A *megalopolis* results from the overlap of two or more metropolitan areas.

7. Urban ecology is the study of the interrelationships of people and the environment in which they live. It includes urban processes of (a) concentration and deconcentration as people move into and out of geographical areas, (b) ecological specialization, and (c) invasion of and succession by new and different social groups and land areas.

8. Various models of urban structure and spatial growth include the *concentric zone model of cities*, spreading out equally in all directions producing uniform circles of growth; the *sector model of cities*, as organized into pie-shaped wedges radiating from the central business district; and the *multiple nuclei zone models of cities*, as having various centers as well as duplicate areas of business, industrial, shopping, and residential locations.

9. Cities and suburbs, while often described in terms of population, also involve a sense of community. *Gemeinschaft* communities are characterized by a sense of intimacy, common identity, and tradition, in contrast to *gesellschaft* communities, which are characterized by impersonality, self-interest, and an emphasis on progress.

10. In contrast to popular stereotypes, cities and suburbs have quite diverse populations. Early sociologists believed that city living was unhealthy and encouraged family breakdown, violence, and depersonalization. Recent research, however, shows that a variety of people and lifestyles are found in the city. A number of people prefer the city because of its social and economic advantages.

11. Suburban life is also quite diverse, and suburbanites do not differ in lifestyle or values from city residents with similar demographic and social characteristics.

12. Our cities face a number of problems today, notably poverty and unemployment, crime, and inadequate schools. Slum areas and ghetto areas experience the most serious social problems. Attempts to remedy these problems are not likely to succeed without a considerable influx of money and the creation of social and economic opportunities.

13. The downtown areas of many cities are being revitalized, and a number of residential neighborhoods are being given a new appearance as a result of urban renewal and urban homesteading projects. Some urban neighborhoods are being rejuvenated by gentrification efforts.

14. The field of urban planning may play an important role in the future of our cities and can have a significant impact on the quality of urban social and cultural life if it is sensitive to the needs and values of different groups of city residents.

KEY TERMS

community A collection of people within a geographic area among whom there is some degree of mutual identification, interdependence, or organization of activities.

concentration An urban ecological process in which population, services, and institutions come to be gathered most densely in the areas in which conditions are advantageous.

concentric zone model A model of urban structure showing that cities grow out equally in all directions from their original centers, producing uniform circles of growth that have their own distinctive land use, population, activities, and institutions.

conversion effect A radical shift of interests and lifestyle that occurs when people move from one type of area to another, as from an urban area to a suburb.

deconcentration Movement outward from the city because of increases in land values and taxes and declines in services and public facilities.

ecological specialization The concentration of homogeneous groups and activities into different sections or urban areas.

folk society A community described by Redfield as small, isolated, homogeneous, and kin-oriented.

gemeinschaft A traditional community characterized by a sense of solidarity and common identity and emphasizing intimate and personal relationships.

gentrification The rejuvenation of urban neighborhoods by middle-class people who move into and repair run-down houses.

gesellschaft A modern community characterized by individualism, mobility, and impersonality, with an emphasis on progress rather than tradition.

ghetto An area in a city in which members of a racial or ethnic minority are forcibly segregated.

greenbelt An area surrounding cities that is preserved for farming and recreation and that limits the growth of cities.

horticulture Small-scale farming that relies on tools such as the hoe to till the soil.

invasion An ecological process in which new types of people, organizations, or activities move into an area occupied by a different type.

megalopolis A continuous strip of urban and suburban development that may stretch for hundreds of miles.

metropolitan statistical area (MSA) A county or group of counties with a central city with a population of at least 50,000, a density of at least 1,000 persons per square mile, and outlying areas that are socially and economically integrated with the central city.

multiple-nuclei model The model of urban development showing that cities have areas of different types of land use, each of which has its own center or nucleus.

sector model An explanation of the ecology of cities as a series of pie-shaped wedges radiating from the central business district, each with its own characteristics and uses.

slums Sections of a city marked by poverty, overcrowding, substandard housing, and poor living conditions.

suburbs The communities that surround a central city and are dependent on it.

succession An urban process of replacing old occupants and institutions with new ones.

urban ecology The study of the interrelationships between people in urban settings and the social and physical environment in which they live.

urban homesteading A federal plan in which abandoned and foreclosed homes are sold to private families at extremely low prices if they agree to live in the house and bring it up to code standards.

urbanization The growth of the number of people who live in urban rather than rural areas and the process of taking on organizational patterns and lifestyles characteristic of urban areas.

DISCUSSION QUESTIONS

1. Discuss the types of factors that historically led to the location and growth of urban areas.

2. What are some of the problems associated with Third World urbanization?

3. What are some factors that have led to urbanization in different areas of the United States?

4. Why are southern and southwestern states and cities the fastest-growing areas of the United States? Why have numerous midwestern and eastern cities lost population during the past decade?

5. Compare the reasons for the growth of metropolitan statistical areas and of nonmetropolitan areas.

6. Discuss how the urban processes of concentration and deconcentration, ecological specialization, and invasion and succession form the basis of different models of urban structure.

7. Does your city, or one with which you are familiar, fit any one of the three models of urban structure described in this chapter? Why or why not?

8. Why is it argued that relationships and communities shift from gemeinschaft to gesellschaft characteristics with increasing urbanization?

9. Describe conditions that characterize a slum and a ghetto. Why do either exist?

10. Identify two urban problems in the city in which you live or a nearby city, and discuss them, using a sociological perspective.

11. What is meant by urban renewal? Discuss the impact on families of tearing down houses in

blighted areas to build new apartments or housing units.

12. Examine the pros and cons of such activities as downtown revitalization, homesteading, and gentrification.

The Nature of Social Change

Changes in Eastern Europe

Since the late 1980s, rapid changes have been taking place in Eastern Europe. Dramatic shifts in political, economic, and social systems have occurred in Hungary, Poland, Germany, Czechoslovakia, Yugoslavia, and in almost every country in Eastern Europe. Perhaps the most notable change that has occurred has been the demise of the communist political party in the Soviet Union.

To many Westerners and observers of Soviet society, the ever-present Soviet secret police—also known as the KGB—represented the oppression associated with the communist party. Many longstanding symbols of communism in the Soviet Union were dismantled during the 1991 revolution. Perhaps most significant were the representations of Vladimir Lenin. Lenin was the driving force behind the 1917 Russian Revolution and the ruler under whom communism, as the world has come to know it, was established. Until 1991, Lenin's presence in the Soviet Union, as well as in other communist countries, was overwhelming. Statues, photographs, and other icons of him were present in almost every arena of public life—in schools, in government buildings, on billboards, in parks, and so on—in much the same way that the American flag and many of our Judeo-Christian symbols are present in the United States. People in the Soviet Union and Eastern bloc nations revered Lenin as a figure to whom all communists should pay their allegiance. After the revolutionary changes in the Soviet Union in 1991, these icons were removed from display because Lenin's views were no longer accepted as the ruling ideology.

Unsurprisingly, much of the Western world reacted positively to the changes in Eastern Europe and especially the demise of the party in the Soviet Union. What many Westerners perceived as an oppressive system appeared to give way to a free system. However positive these changes may appear, people often overlook their full impact on individuals, society, and culture. As this chapter shows, sociologists have always been interested in studying how social change affects individuals and interpersonal relationships. Classic social theorists such as Durkheim, Marx, Tönnies, Weber, and others studied how changes from simple to complex societies affect human relationships. They wrote during the Industrial Revolution—a time when many societies of the world were rapidly changing from agrarian to industrial. Now—and for years to come—sociologists will study the impact of the sudden changes in Eastern Europe.

How will the sudden changes in Eastern Europe affect social institutions such as the economy, religion, education, and the family in these countries? How will such changes affect the individuals whose lives are rooted in these social institutions? Will the sudden changes result in anomie—a condition in which the norms and values that guide people's lives lose their meaning? Will there be different expectations about the way people should practice their religion? Will changes in the institutions of marriage and the family affect the ways that husbands and wives interact with each other? Will parents have different expectations of success for their children? Will the relationship between parents and children change? Will gender roles and relationships between men and women change? What will be the impact on family stability and the divorce rate?

Besides institutional changes, the undoing of the communists is likely to bring sweeping cultural changes. The cultures of many European countries developed around an ideology that shapes people's values, beliefs, attitudes, norms, roles, and worldviews, just as democracy shapes Americans' lives. For many, a communist culture permeated their family and community for generations. What will be the impact of the loss of this cultural heritage? How will people be affected by the loss of national figures in whom they can no longer believe? How will people come to define themselves culturally? Will people who identified with being communists their whole lives suffer an identity crisis? How will the children whose beliefs and values were informed by communist culture reconcile the idea that these beliefs and values no longer hold true? How would you feel if you were taught one set of truths as you were growing up and then suddenly you were told to disregard them and substitute an opposite set of beliefs? How would it affect your confidence in authority figures, your sense of self, your self-confidence, your emotional and psychological security?

Consider some other possibilities. Although the party has generally been associated with oppression and lack of freedom for individuals and groups, there was an element of certainty about it. People living under communists may not have been free to choose any occupation or to leave the country at will, but there was some degree of certainty about what life held in store for them. Freedom and social mobility were limited, but people knew their place in society and in the world. With the end of socialism, people will and must be able to make more decisions about their own lives and to accept more responsibility for their fate. How will people who have not lived and grown within a capitalist culture now understand the full implications of free enterprise and competition? While this may be a way of life that Americans and other Westerners understand and embrace, it is a new concept for people who know little about freedom and who are accustomed to living under strict government control.

Understand that the changes in Eastern Europe go well beyond changes in political, economic, and social systems. As mentioned, it is possible that these changes will bring benefits in the long run, but the sudden demise of an ideology needs to be understood in terms of the larger social and cultural implications for individuals, groups, and institutions within these countries.

In our rapidly changing society, sociology is largely the study of **social change**, change in the structure of society and in its institutions. This chapter discusses some approaches used to understand social change, with an emphasis on changes in social structures and social institutions.

Sociologists have tried to answer three basic questions about social change. The earlier sociologists wanted to know whether social change was good or bad. As societies change, do they get better, or do they deteriorate? Because they were writing at the beginning of the Industrial Revolution, they saw their traditional family-oriented society vanish and watched it being replaced by urbanization and factory work.

Today, we are more likely to accept social change, but we are still interested in the reasons for it. Thus, the second basic question is, What causes the change? Also, like the early sociologists, we are still concerned with the third question: What happens to the people in a society when their society changes?

THEORIES OF SOCIAL CHANGE

Evolutionary Theory of Change

During more optimistic periods of our history, social change was regarded as progress. When society changed, it was assumed to be getting better. Evolutionary theory suggests that societies evolved from the simple and primitive to the more complex and advanced, just as animal life progressed from the simplest one-celled organisms to the most complex animal, the human being. Herbert Spencer, a classic evolutionary theorist, believed that as a society grows, the functions of its members become more specialized and better coordinated into the larger system, and thus, there is progress. Spencer was very influential for many years, especially in the United States, where growth was equated with progress.

Evolutionary theory is less popular today. Change may create social problems rather than social progress, and Spencer's optimistic theory is regarded with some skepticism. Conflict theorists are among those who do not believe in the continuous evolution of progress.

Conflict Theory of Social Change

Conflict theorists are in many ways as optimistic as evolutionary theorists, but they do not assume that societies smoothly evolve to higher levels. Instead, change comes about as oppressed groups struggle to improve their lot. Thus, change is a result of conflict and struggle; however, the result still is generally an improvement in society. Each stage of conflict leads to a higher order. As oppressed groups are able to work their way out of oppression, society is able to provide more justice and equality for all. This is a positive view and very optimistic, especially compared with the views of some cyclical theorists.

Cyclical Theories of Change

The most pessimistic cyclical theorists think that decay is inevitable. One such theorist was the historian Oswald Spengler (1918), whose **cyclical change theory** suggests that every society is born, matures, decays, and eventually dies. The Roman Empire rose to power and then gradually collapsed, just as the British Empire grew strong and then deteriorated. Spengler contended that social change may take the form of progress or of decay but that no society lives forever.

Most sociologists believe this view is too rigid and that although societies may have cycles of change, the cycles are not preordained. Pitirim Sorokin (1889–1968), a Russian social theorist who lived through the Russian Revolution of 1917, did not equate change with progress, but neither did he believe that all societies are inevitably destined to decay. He noted, rather, that societies go through various stages. At different stages, he suggested, they emphasize religious beliefs, scientific beliefs, or the pleasures of art, music, and the beauty of nature. They shift from one cycle to another, moving first in one direction, then in another, as the needs of the society demand. Sorokin is still respected for these ideas and has greatly influenced the attempts of structural functionalists to explain social change.

Structural Functionalism and Social Change

Structural functionalists, who believe that society is a balanced system of institutions, each of which serves a function in maintaining society, suggest that when events outside or inside the society disrupt the equilibrium, social institutions make adjustments to restore stability. An influx of immigrants can bring new ideas into a community that then spread throughout the society. A natural disaster, a famine, or a war may disrupt the social order and force the social institutions to make adjustments. Like Sorokin, the structural functionalists do not necessarily consider social change per se to be good or bad—rather, it is the process through which societies lose and regain their equilibrium.

The term *cultural lag* is often used to describe the state of disequilibrium. When an event such as an increase in population or a depletion of natural resources causes a strain in a society, it takes some time for the society to understand the strain and to alter its values and institutions to adapt to the change. Just as the human body must adjust its functioning to adapt to changes, societies adjust to maintain and restore themselves.

Social Change Theory: A Synthesis

Few theorists today are so optimistic that they believe societies inevitably improve, and few are so pessimistic that they believe that societies inevitably decay. Most integrate the ideas of Sorokin, the structural functionalists, and the conflict theorists. Societies do change, but the changes are not necessarily good or bad. Societies attempt to remain stable, and although a stable one is usually better than a chaotic one, stability sometimes causes harsh conditions, injustice, and oppression. When this happens, conflicts arise, and society is forced to change, perhaps for the better, but not necessarily so.

Change and stability, then, are processes that can take place simultaneously in any society. At any given time, one or the other will dominate, depending on the society's needs. Change is inevitable, and it is often beneficial.

Thinking Sociologically

1. Which theory or combination of theories do you think best describes how society changes?
2. Is your own understanding of social change described adequately by theories in this chapter?

WHAT CAUSES SOCIAL CHANGE?

Sociologists believe that social systems change when powerful internal or external forces influence them such that the previous social order can no longer be maintained. However, societies are complex, interdependent systems of values, norms, and institutions; they are often amazingly resistant to change and rarely transformed by the ideas or behavior of a single person. When a major change does occur, however, it influences the entire society, and each social institution must adapt to the new order.

Sociologists have determined that **ecological changes**—variations in the relationship between population and geography—are a powerful source of social change. They can shape the ideology and political arrangements of a society and can also bring about other innovations.

Population, Geography, and Political Power

Chirot (1994) described the nature of the social changes that brought about the industrialization of western Europe. He began by comparing the influence of geography on early civilizations in tropical regions with its influence on civilizations in the temperate zones of northwestern Europe. The first civilizations developed in tropical areas of the Middle East, India, and northern Africa, where parasitic diseases were rampant (Boserup, 1981). The favorite places to settle in these tropical areas were fertile valleys surrounded by arid lands. As the populations grew, irrigation was developed to make use of the arid lands, but these populations could grow only while the water supply lasted. When the population grew too large to be supported by the natural resources, the people became weak and sickly, and disease reduced their numbers. As a result, the size of these populations remained stable.

Later civilizations developed in northwestern Europe, where the cold winters controlled parasitic diseases and abundant rainfall produced plenty of food without the need for irrigation. Agriculture in northern Europe could potentially support a large population. Furthermore, the geography of northern Europe protected the inhabitants from invasion. Recall that great waves of Asians migrated to the Middle East and to eastern and southern Europe long before written history began. It is assumed that this migration was largely the result of changes in the Asian climate, perhaps increasing cold weather or severe droughts. The waves of migration continued until the Middle Ages.

The migrants were warring nomads who raided the civilizations in the warmer climates, destroying their irrigation systems and plundering the wealth of the people. They did not enter northwestern Europe, however; the geography was not suitable for their nomadic lifestyle because it lacked grazing lands and room to maneuver.

The Europeans, free from disease, drought, and war, were left to accumulate wealth in the form of animals and improved farmlands. The animals provided food, fertilizer, and labor, pulling the plows that improved the farmland.

Chirot (1994) describes how European geography also played an important role in the type of political system that developed. Europe has many river valleys, and settlements were scattered everywhere along these rivers, making the region difficult to conquer. In contrast, it is easier to conquer a civilization if its people are dependent on one river; China, which has only two major rivers, had fewer centers of power that needed to be conquered, to gain control of the entire population. Once in control, the conquerors generally imposed excessive taxes and repressive policies. With the tax money, the government in power could build a powerful kingdom.

In Europe, however, because the people were spread about, it was more difficult for conquerors to gain control and to collect taxes. Without the ability to tax, it became impossible to build a strong state, and the kingdoms that developed were not very powerful. Instead, feudal estates developed to provide some security for farmers against invaders. Eventually, cities grew, where merchants and artisans could escape the feudal lords. Later, the Catholic Church gained power and challenged the kingdoms, further dividing power. The kings, the Church, the feudal lords, and the merchants finally agreed to share power, and their parliaments gave each group a voice in the rule of the various countries. In England, this turn of events was marked by the Magna Carta of 1215.

The effect of this division of power was a change from authoritarian to rational rule. Whereas elsewhere in the world, powerful rulers could dictate at whim, in western Europe, rights and obligations were debated and negotiated and finally set down as law. The powerful elites, especially the merchants in the cities, eventually developed a rational way to deal with disagreements.

Changing Ideology

Chirot (1994) argues that the rational political system of northwestern Europe led eventually to a rational ideology, an ideology based on reason rather than on magic or mystical beliefs. Most of the great early civilizations had *rational legal systems*, laws that stated what could or could not be done, but those systems were religious in nature and not very flexible in their outlook. Islamic or Christian laws, for example, did not rationally negotiate the day-to-day needs of peasants. The peasants, who worked the land, depended on magic, mysticism, and the whims of nature for sun, rain, successful crops, and good health.

In northwestern Europe, the political practice of negotiating law made rational rule the predominant ideology. It was especially important to the city dwellers, who were traders and whose livelihood depended on the buying and selling of goods. Their lives were regulated by ledgers and accounts, and they could predict rational outcomes. They carried this rational ideology into their religion. No longer settling for mystical explanations, they developed a practical explanation for personal salvation, which eventually led to the Protestant Reformation.

Max Weber, in *The Protestant Ethic and the Spirit of Capitalism*, describes how this rational ideology, which is reflected in both religion and business practices, motivated businesspersons to develop the Industrial Revolution. The Protestant ethic promised its believers that they would be rewarded in heaven for an honest, hard-working, disciplined lifestyle, and these rewards would be apparent in this life. The Protestant businessmen who led the Industrial Revolution did work hard, did not indulge in sins such as gambling or extravagant living, saved their money, and accumulated wealth, which they believed to be visible proof of their Christian lifestyle. Furthermore, because of the power they had in European parliaments, they were able to keep that wealth and continue to operate with considerable freedom.

The rational ideology also made scientific inquiry acceptable; before the Reformation, science had been frowned upon, especially when it led to discoveries that went against the teachings of the church. The new acceptance of scientific inquiry then led to discoveries and inventions, new sources of social change.

Discoveries and Inventions

Discoveries and inventions have caused far-reaching changes in modern societies, which are becoming increasingly technological. Discoveries and inventions are called innovations, changes that offer something new to society and that alter its norms or institutions. A **discovery** is the act of finding something that has always existed but that no one previously knew about. The discovery that the world was round opened new possibilities in exploration and navigation. The discovery of America led to the great migrations from Europe and the creation of new countries. The discovery of gold and other scarce resources in the American West led Americans to continue their migration. The discovery of oil today leads to great social changes in the areas where it is found.

An **invention** is a device constructed by putting two or more things together in a new way. Navigational equipment, factories, and the assembly line were all invented by putting together in new ways materials already discovered and available.

Inventions can be social as well as technological. An example of a social invention is bureaucratic organization. Weber noted that bureaucracies were rational organizations based on rules, not on the word of rulers, such as emperors, queens, or other regents. By the time that Weber wrote, in the nineteenth century, rational systems of organization were rapidly replacing the traditional patriarchal systems throughout Europe, in business as well as in government. Modern societies would not be able to function without them because bureaucracies can organize highly complex groups of people and highly complex tasks into a working whole. No one can deny that modern societies have developed complex bureaucratic organization.

Discoveries and inventions must be acceptable to a society, however, if they are to create social change, and they are not always accepted, no matter how worthwhile they may be.

Diffusion

Diffusion is the process by which an innovation is spread throughout a social system. The rate at which diffusion occurs depends on the values and beliefs of a society. Rogers (2003) points out that after the British navy discovered that citrus fruits (e.g., lemons, limes, and oranges) could cure scurvy, the biggest killer of the world's sailors, it was 200 years before they began to supply sailors with oranges and lemons. Other remedies were more popular, even though they did not work.

We can be just as slow today in accepting new innovations. The current typewriter keyboard was carefully designed to slow down the typist's speed so that touch typists would not jam up the keys on the first mechanical typewriters. Now, typewriters are more efficient, and computer keyboards could accommodate very rapid speeds. A more efficient arrangement of the keyboard that allows for more speed was designed in 1932, but it has yet to be adopted (Rogers, 1983).

Innovations are sometimes most rapidly adopted when an authority enforces their use. For example, laws requiring installation and use of seatbelts made them acceptable to many people. The automobile itself, however, did not need the force of law to become widely adopted.

The Automobile: Impact of an Innovation

Perhaps no single development has changed the United States more than the invention and diffusion of the automobile. The automobile is considered by many historians to have played a major role in the social changes of the Progressive era in American history.

The Automobile and Economic Growth

Progressive reformers used the automobile to help create a more stable system in which capitalism might grow and flourish, according to Ling (1992). One action necessary to create this better environment for capitalism was to open rural areas by improved methods of transportation. At first, railroads and trolleys—and later, the widespread adoption of the automobile—brought rural areas into the mainstream of American life and brought rural people into the influence of centralized social institutions—educational, religious, and economic.

A second action taken to create an environment better for capitalism was to encourage consumerism. As assembly lines developed and became an alienating work experience, reformers wished to create a compensating culture of consumerism. Even while the work itself was not rewarding, the fruits of the work, the goods that money could buy, could become the reward for work. The most promising consumer item was the automobile (Ling, 1992).

While railroad and trolley systems opened rural areas to urban markets, the automobile was immediately successful as a consumer product. By the end of the 1920s, mass production of the automobile brought the price down to the point where the majority of middle-class families in the United States who wanted an automobile had bought one. Demand decreased, and General Motors needed new markets (Snell, 1976), so they began to produce buses. They bought interurban electric railways and urban trolley systems, dismantled them, and replaced them with buses. By 1949, General Motors, working with companies such as Greyhound, Standard Oil of California, and Firestone Tire, had replaced more than 100 relatively clean electric transit systems with buses.

Buses were slow, inefficient, dirty, and expensive to operate. People did not enjoy riding in them. Furthermore, when people were bombarded with advertisements encouraging them to buy cars not just as a means of transportation but as status symbols, they turned from using public transportation and bought more automobiles. In the meantime, the automotive industry lobbied to have the federal interstate highway system constructed. Between 1945 and 1970, state and local governments spent $156 billion to build hundreds of thousands of miles of roads. Only 16 miles of subway were built during the same period. Thus, the automobile became a necessity as a means of transportation, and Americans bought them in ever-increasing numbers.

Ironically, the road system that was built to accommodate the widespread use of the automobile is itself on the verge of disintegration from neglect, and while the present road system verges on collapse, few new roads are being built. As the population continues to increase, the use of the automobile grows, and all these cars must compete for space on the deteriorating road system. Major traffic jams are more and more common as roadways approach their capacity for handling traffic.

The Automobile and the Environment

The heavy use of automobiles and diesel buses causes pollution, and smog from automobile emissions has become a serious problem in American cities. The bad urban air burns the eyes, damages lung tissues, and increases the levels of poisons in the human body and in food products. The automobile has also vastly increased our need for oil. The United States, even though it has huge supplies of oil, uses so much oil that it imports more than half of what is used in this country.

Oil is the major pollutant of the ocean, and huge tankers routinely leak, spill, or purposely dump oil into the sea. In addition, hundreds of accidents involving tankers take place at sea each year. This issue was brought to international attention in 1989 when an Exxon oil tanker dumped 11 million gallons of oil into Prince William Sound, oil that spread over 3,000 square miles of Alaskan waters. Spilled oil poisons, smothers, burns, or coats sea plants and animals, thus killing them. The oceans of the world from the Arctic to the Antarctic are slowly being covered with oil slicks, and to date, there is no effective way to clean them up.

The demand for oil as a fuel is so substantial that the United States is willing to go to war to protect its supply from foreign oil fields. Since World War II, this country has built up a vast military force, and the government has vowed to use it to protect oil-producing nations that sell to the United States, such as Kuwait.

Thus, we see that the United States has become so economically dependent on the automobile and on oil that it is willing to pollute land and sea, and go to war to prevent risk to our oil supply. Steps to diminish this dependence have not been and are not being taken, however. It is obvious that these factors have serious worldwide consequences.

Thinking Sociologically

Evaluate the advantages and disadvantages of the development of the automobile in this country.

SOCIAL CHANGE IN UNDERDEVELOPED NATIONS

Although Europe (and later the United States) industrialized, other nations did not. Attempts to explain this lack of development have evolved around two different theoretical points of view—modernization, which has its roots in evolutionary theory, and dependency theory, which is also known as world systems theory.

Modernization in Underdeveloped Nations

Evolutionary theorists tend to assume that today's underdeveloped nations in Africa, South America, and other areas that do not have modern industry, such as is found in Europe and North America, will pass through the same stages that industrialized nations passed through in their quest for modernization. **Modernization** is the process whereby preindustrial countries emerge as urban societies with lower birth rates, more goods and services, better nutrition and health care, improved housing, and some luxuries.

A closer comparison, however, suggests that contemporary nations may not be able to take the same course as those that are already industrialized. The United States developed into an industrial society due to its work ethic, its lack of competition from other countries, and its vast supply of natural resources, including its excellent land for agriculture and its minerals, such as iron and coal. The United States can also bring in the labor it requires through immigration and can stop immigration when no more workers are needed.

Many underdeveloped nations simply lack this abundance of natural resources. Tropical forests and arid deserts cannot easily be developed to produce grain. Oil, coal, iron, and lumber are unavailable in many countries. Many of these items must be purchased from other countries to meet the needs of the ever-growing native population. To purchase these necessities, Third World countries have borrowed enormous sums and now have huge debts to Western banks, especially to the large banks in the United States.

To pay these debts, Third World countries have tried to develop cash crops that can be exported to pay for the goods the country must buy. These agricultural products are usually not foods, but such products as coffee, cotton, and flowers; unfortunately, because the land has been taken over for cash crops, the native population no longer has land on which to grow food for themselves. They do not have jobs in agriculture either, because most of the work is done with farm machinery. Part of the rural population has moved into the already crowded cities hoping to find work, but work is scarce, and pay is poor. Often the poor live in the streets or in makeshift homes that provide little shelter. Dysentery and pneumonia are common, especially among children. The need for medical care puts further strain on the resources of the population.

Inasmuch as undeveloped nations cannot compete with the large multinational industries, they sometimes invite those industries to come into their countries to do business, hoping that these industries will provide employment for the natives and income for the country. This is rarely successful. Employment opportunities are usually too few and are limited to the lowest-paying jobs. When the goods are exported, the profits go to the multinational corporation and not to the host country.

Thus, while the United States developed its industry with control over its population, abundant natural resources, and no competition from other world industries, developing nations have tried to modernize with too large a population, too few natural resources, and too much competition from worldwide industries. Not surprisingly, they have been unable to support their people. In trying to do so, they have gone into debt to such an extent that the world banking system is threatened by bankruptcy from the unpaid debts of these nations.

Dependency theorists agree that underdeveloped nations are suffering. However, their understanding of the cause of the problems is very different.

Dependency or World Systems Theory

Dependency theory was inspired by Marx and has been developed by conflict theorists, who believe that underdeveloped nations cannot industrialize as the Western world did because they have been made dependent on the Western world. One must look at the entire world system, and not just at individual regions, if one is to understand social change. **World systems theory** states that **core nations** (those that are already industrialized) dominate the economies of **peripheral nations** (underdeveloped nations), taking wealth from the peripheral nations to further their own development.

Wallerstein (2000) argues that the northwestern European core nations first exploited the eastern and southern European nations and when exploration opened trade in the sixteenth century, they went on to exploit North and South America, Africa, and India. The Europeans took raw materials from the rest of the world, used them to produce manufactured goods, and then sold manufactured goods to the peripheral nations at high cost, driving these nations into poverty.

This exploitation is still common. Del Monte and Dole, multinational corporations, grow pineapples in the Philippines and Thailand and ship them to the United States, now a core nation. The Gulf and Western Corporation grows sugar in Central America for sale in the United States. Coffee and bananas are other major products taken exploitatively from Latin American nations. The pharmaceutical industry also takes raw materials from peripheral countries, manufactures medicines, and sells them back to these countries at high prices (Gereffi, 1983). The profits from these diverse ventures go to the core nations' stockholders, not to the peripheral nations that provided the raw materials.

Gereffi (1983) suggests that these exploited countries could begin to remedy this situation by putting a ban on the purchase of all but the most essential manufactured products until they develop their own industries, and they could nationalize the industries of foreign corporations in their own countries. However, this would require a revolutionary change in ideology in many cases. As long as the elites in peripheral nations cooperate with business from the core nations, such changes are not possible.

Wallerstein (2000) believes that there are worldwide forces uniting to change this ideology and to oppose such extreme inequality. He believes that these movements are growing in strength and, over the next two centuries, will bring an end to capitalistic exploitation and the powerful national systems we know today.

As mentioned in the introduction to this chapter, the totalitarian nations of Eastern Europe saw dramatic social changes in the past decade. These are clearly conflicts over extreme inequality. Many of the people involved in these changes see capitalism as a means to greater equality, but others may not be willing to give up the personal security of socialism in exchange for the economic insecurity of capitalism. It will be interesting to watch what solutions the countries of Eastern Europe find to solve their problems and how the rest of the world responds to the needs of these countries. World systems theory has done a great deal to alter our perception of the world, and it has generated a great deal of scholarly research by viewing the world as one large, complex system. It will be interesting to see whether world systems theory will influence ongoing political actions of nations.

SOCIAL CHANGE AND THE INDIVIDUAL

How does social change affect the individual? In developing nations, increasing population and the removal of people from their land have had a devastating effect on the individual. Whenever social change is so disruptive to the social order that individuals cannot obtain the basic necessities of life, change can be terrifying. However, when the social change is generally perceived as progress, what are its effects? This question has always been of interest to sociologists.

Most early sociologists believed that industrialization alienates people from their work and from one another. Durkheim was one of the few who believed that complex industrial societies would have a positive effect on human relationships. Noting that peasants were moving to European cities in large numbers, he recognized that this changed the nature of their labor. Peasants had been self-sufficient and performed all of the work necessary to meet their personal needs, but in the city, work was specialized, and workers were not self-sufficient. Each person specialized in a particular product and then traded that product for money to meet personal needs. Thus, the cobbler sold shoes and bought food and clothing. In *The Division of Labor* (1893), Durkheim endorsed the move toward specialization, arguing

SOCIOLOGY AT WORK

Societal Analysis in the Auto Industry

Carroll DeWeese has worked as a staff research scientist in the Societal Analysis Department of General Motors (GM) Research Laboratories. The objectives of GM Research Laboratories are to generate new technical knowledge of commercial interest to GM, to evaluate outside technical advances for possible application to GM products and processes, to anticipate future technological needs and develop the expertise to meet those needs, and to assist in the analysis of corporate priorities, policies, and programs. The Societal Analysis Department is an interdisciplinary department, the mission of which is to study the impact of GM on society and vice versa. DeWeese led a group with degrees in applied mathematics, economics, operations research, psychology, and sociology.

Research in the department is generally interdisciplinary, problem oriented, and quantitative. Researchers have worked on a variety of topics, including air pollution, auto safety, auto service, customer satisfaction, energy usage and efficiency, product quality, diesel odor, and other areas of public concern.

DeWeese studied sociology at the University of Houston and at Purdue. He joined GM Research Laboratories immediately on completing his Ph.D. at Purdue. DeWeese talks about what makes researchers successful in an environment such as this. He has been able to identify several characteristics. "They must be pragmatic, not ideological—interested in doing whatever is necessary to solve a problem. They are persons looking for tools to solve problems, not persons with some particular tool trying to find problems to solve. They must be able to communicate, to excite and convince others about their ideas. Brevity is a virtue here. After a year's work, they should be able to convince a deci-

that this interdependence would create a more integrated society.

Marx, on the other hand, was concerned that the move from agrarian to industrial societies would alienate people from their work. The goods produced would be owned by the factory owner, not the worker. Marx believed that this arrangement was so unfair that it would not survive. Workers would rebel and a more equitable system of work would be developed.

Tönnies (1887) was also concerned that interpersonal relationships would suffer in industrial society. Peasant society, he contended, was characterized by *gemeinschaft relationships*, in which people knew one another totally, whereas in urban society, they would be strangers. Those who worked together would know nothing about their coworkers' families or religious or political views, for example. Tönnies referred to these impersonal relationships as *gesellschaft*.

Weber was concerned about the increasing rationalization of society. The traditional beliefs of the family were rapidly disappearing, and in Weber's day, society was becoming more bureaucratic. Decisions were no longer being based on traditional family concerns. The system in which people performed tasks according to their capabilities and were taken care of when they were unable to be productive gave

Societal Analysis in the Auto Industry, *continued*

sion maker of the importance of the problem studied and the results found on a single sheet of paper or in five minutes of conversation. They must know how to identify critical problems—the more critical the problem the more attention any actionable results will receive. They must know how to work as part of a team, to secure the cooperation and support of their colleagues. And they must have quantitative ability combined with qualitative flexibility. That's where the interdisciplinary arrangement, the variety of perspectives, pays off." In sum, to be successful in this type of setting, people should have research skills, critical-thinking and problem-solving skills, communication skills, and interpersonal skills.

Interestingly, DeWeese's list of characteristics of the successful researcher in his department does not include specific substantive knowledge. This does not mean that substantive knowledge is not important in this type of work. Instead, he says, "People are expected to acquire whatever substantive knowledge is needed to solve the problems they are working on. On the other hand, use of the sociological imagination is critical for identifying, studying, and solving problems. The strength of sociology is the perspective it gives a person. I am not saying substantive knowledge is unimportant. When we hire people, we have problem areas in mind and we look for people with substantive backgrounds in those problem areas. But that substantive knowledge is a given. It is not a characteristic of success." The important thing that a person needs to come to this type of job, DeWeese suggests, is to be able to look at situations and problems from a variety of different perspectives and to be able to recognize the relative merit of each perspective. The sociological imagination enables a person to do this.

way to one in which decisions about employment were made on the basis of the employer's needs. Employees were hired or fired regardless of their own needs for work, income, or self-respect.

Sociologists realize that modern socialization encourages individuals to behave in a fashion compatible with industrial society. In the nineteenth century, when frontiers were being conquered and industries were being built, people were encouraged to be highly innovative, and even the most ruthless could find a place in society taming the frontier or building new industries. Also, people on the frontier far from neighbors did not have to worry about being popular, getting along with others, cooperating, or making a good impression. They did, however, need the skill and wit to stay alive. These people were described as **inner-directed** by Riesman (1950).

The same skills were needed in the business world. Businesses were small, and whether one owned a store or began a small factory, survival depended on one's own skill and hard work. The most successful industrial leaders of the nineteenth century, the so-called robber barons, were noted for their extreme ruthlessness.

Today, the nature of work has changed dramatically. Most people work in corporations with many other individuals. In a large corporation, a competitive person who lives by skill and wit and is concerned exclusively with his or her own survival makes many enemies and can create chaos rather than cooperation. Many jobs in corporations today require cooperation, teamwork, and a concern for others. Riesman described the cooperative person, the person who is concerned with the reaction of others, as **other-directed**. Maccoby (1977), has called this other-directed person the **gamesman**, the person who is highly competitive and innovative but who prefers to function as the leader of a team. The gamesman thus occupies a position similar to that of a quarterback on a football team. Interestingly, football surpassed baseball as the most popular American sport in the mid-1960s. The more individualistic sport of baseball has given way to a type of sport requiring a team effort and cooperation. It seems that changes in the way we spend our leisure correspond to changes in the types of managers sought in the job market.

The economic prosperity of a country can affect the generation of young people growing up at the time, as has been shown by Elder (1974), who studied children of the Great Depression, and by Jones (1980), who studied children of the prosperous baby-boom generation. Generally speaking, children raised during periods of prosperity and whose families are economically secure develop fairly positive views of the world and are interested in self-development. Children raised during hard times, especially if their families suffered, are more pessimistic and assume that life will be a struggle. They come to value independence, hard work, and security (Stewart and Healy, 1989).

Television and the other mass media have also affected individual lifestyles. The media encourage us to buy consumer products such as cosmetics and designer clothes, and we watch programs depicting middle-class lifestyles. We listen to news broadcasts that tell us what is important in the world. If we have learned to be good team players, we buy our products and let the politicians worry about the state of the world.

Thinking Sociologically

How have social changes in the past decade shaped your personal development?

APPLYING SOCIOLOGY TO THE FUTURE

Futurists, people who attempt to describe what the future will be like, range from the most pessimistic doomsayers to the greatest optimists. The doomsayers predict an economic depression far worse than the depression of the 1930s. The wisest investment, they say, is to buy a piece of land in a very remote part of the country, build a substantial shelter that will be well hidden from the hordes of the poor and starving who will be roaming the countryside when the economy collapses, and bury near the shelter a supply of dehydrated food, guns, and other basic equipment needed to survive alone in the wilderness.

The optimists predict an end to poverty and drudgery and believe that human innovation will solve our problems. For example, computers may make a more individualistic society possible. People may be able to remain at home and earn their livings by telecommunications, engendering for themselves and their children a more unique and creative individual lifestyle.

Sociologists are more hesitant to make predictions. One realistic method of determining what the future will be like is to analyze the possibilities and problems that it might hold and to use social planning to strive for future goals and to avoid future disasters.

Etzioni (1980) followed this course in making his predictions. He argues that society should make choices and should plan for a future that will provide a satisfactory lifestyle to its members. Our economy is currently based on the consumption of vast amounts of goods, and we are using up our natural and economic resources. Meanwhile, our factories, transportation systems, roads, railroads, and bridges are deteriorating rapidly. We must choose either to continue to spend money on goods or to spend hundreds of billions of dollars to modernize our factories and to build an efficient transportation system. This rebuilding would reduce the hazards of pollution and would improve the quality of life for all, but it might mean we would have to cut back on our consumption of goods.

Etzioni used the typical approach of sociologists in his study of social change, which is to try to understand the social system. Our social system is based on a profit-oriented economy, and we manufacture products that can be sold for a profit. Our system functions to support a cycle of production and consumption, but it does not support modernization of factories or an efficient use of resources unless such actions provide a profit. By understanding that our system now functions only when profits are made, it is possible to predict what will happen if we continue to function as we have in the past. We will use up all our resources.

Nonetheless, innovations can be made, institutions can be changed, and values and goals can be altered: A society can change its course and move in a new direction. We cannot today optimistically assume that progress will be inevitable and that we do not have to plan to reach our goals. Neither is there reason to be so pessimistic that we resign ourselves to becoming victims of a social system in decline. Furthermore, we cannot blithely assume that society will run its course from good times to bad and then bounce back to good times again; we could in the meantime destroy all life on earth. By understanding how societies function, we can make choices, alter our social institutions, and develop lifestyles that will reduce conflict, avoid ecological devastation, and support human life in the ever-increasing numbers that seem inevitable. We can plan to use our resources wisely.

Sociologists who study society from a historical perspective, observing the relationship between social changes and social problems—for example, increased automobile use and today's energy problems—are likely to be frustrated by the practice of solving problems as they arise rather than trying to find long-range solutions. These solutions might require better technology—to control auto emissions or clean up oil spills. In any case, more effective solutions can be developed if we understand the social basis of the problems.

Our problems are caused in part by a cultural lag in our awareness of future needs. Social planning could help us to change our social systems and to improve the situation. Those who have a vested interest in our current system might resist change, which would create a certain amount of conflict, but such conflict might be beneficial to society. Sociology, by helping us to understand social change, can help us to direct it. Academic sociologists will continue to study how changes affect our social institutions and will help us to predict future trends; professional sociologists in the workplace may use knowledge of sociology to help policymakers and social planners design long-range solutions to social and technological problems; nonprofessional sociologists in the workplace may use knowledge of social change to help them foresee and plan for business trends and consumer needs; and you may use knowledge of social change and other sociological theories to plan for your family's future.

Sociology originally grew out of an attempt to understand and do something about the social problems related to changes brought about by modernization. Thus, as Shostak (1985, p. 172) notes, "it was conceived as a way of managing social change and helping humankind stay in charge of events." Although it may be impossible to predict with certainty the impact of technological or institutional changes on the whole social system, sociology does alert us to the important fact that a change in one part of the system will continue to reverberate throughout the system long into the future. Armed with this knowledge and with the knowledge of the other theories, perspectives, and concepts sociology offers, humankind may be better equipped to shape its social institutions, and you may be better equipped to shape your own life. The authors hope that this introduction to the study of sociology has sparked your own sociological imagination so that you can think about the good life for you in terms of social as well as individual accomplishments.

SUMMARY

1. Society is changing so rapidly that sociology has become in many respects the study of social change.
2. Evolutionary theory proposes the optimistic view that change is progress, that growth is always good, and that stagnation leads to decay.
3. Conflict theorists are also optimistic about social change, but they believe that conflict will occasionally arise to correct adverse social developments. The outcome of such conflict, they say, will be better social systems.
4. Cyclical theorists can be very pessimistic. They assume that societies grow, reach a peak, and then inevitably decay. Some cyclical theorists, however, do not assume that change is always for the better or the worse. Societies move back and forth, they contend, emphasizing first one value, then another, as the needs of the society change.
5. Structural functionalists have been concerned primarily with stability, but they recognize that society changes occasionally. Often, a change that affects one social institution will be followed by cultural lag, a disruption in the functioning of society until other institutions adjust to the change.
6. Most sociologists agree that society is orderly and that social institutions function to maintain order. They also agree that conflicts may arise when the existing social order causes hardship for the members of a society but that such conflicts can be beneficial.
7. Some major causes of social change and conflict are population changes, geographic changes, political arrangements, and ideology. In northwestern Europe, the geography allowed many small communities to grow, develop political systems through negotiation, and develop a rational ideology that led to the age of exploration. The migration that followed brought

different cultures into contact with one another, spreading the ideas of one culture to another.

8. Discoveries, inventions, and the diffusion of these innovations also cause social change. The automobile has had enormous impact on life in industrial nations.

9. Modernization theorists believe that underdeveloped nations have different natural resources, different values, and a different work ethic, all of which have caused their patterns of growth to differ from those of the developed, or core, nations.

10. Dependency or world systems theorists believe that less developed nations are exploited by the nations that developed first.

11. Changes in modern industrial societies have changed the nature of human relationships. From the peasant's concern for family and community, we moved to a period of competitive individualism, and we are now moving into an era of competitive team play.

12. In the future, it is hoped that we will be able to plan innovations that will improve our ecology and our ways of relating to one another.

KEY TERMS

core nations Industrial nations that exploit underdeveloped, peripheral nations.

cyclical change theory The view that societies go through a cycle of birth, maturation, decline, and death.

dependency theory Conflict theory stating that underdeveloped nations cannot industrialize because they are dependent on the nations already industrialized.

discovery The act of finding something that has always existed but that no one previously knew about.

ecological change Change brought about by the way a population uses the natural resources available to it.

gamesman The type of manager sought by corporations today: a person who is highly competitive and innovative but who prefers to function as the leader of a team.

inner-directed A description by David Riesman of people who are independent, innovative, and focused on their own survival with little concern with what others think.

invention A device constructed by putting two or more things together in a new way.

modernization The process whereby preindustrial countries emerge as urban societies with lower birth rates, more goods and services, and better nutrition and health care.

other-directed A description by David Riesman of people who focus on making a good impression, being popular, getting along with others, and being cooperative.

peripheral nations Underdeveloped nations who are exploited by core nations.

social change Changes in the structure of a society or in its social institutions.

world systems theory Conflict theory stating core nations dominate the economics of peripheral nations.

DISCUSSION QUESTIONS

1. Discuss how the geography of the United States led to its development as a modern industrial nation.
2. Discuss how closely linked American ideology is to what Weber called "rationalism," as opposed to an ideology linked to traditionalism.
3. Discuss how the American political system developed as a result of geography and of rationalism.
4. Why does the United States have a less developed railroad system than Europe and Japan?
5. Discuss ways in which the United States could change its transportation system and the advantages and disadvantages to such changes.
6. Discuss the reasons why Third World nations cannot develop industries the way the United States did.
7. Predict the future. Are you an optimist or a pessimist?

Glossary

absolutist view The view that there is wide agreement about social norms and that certain behaviors are deviant regardless of the social context in which they occur.

account of behavior An effort at maintaining the self by explaining the reasons for or facts surrounding the behavior.

achieved status A social position, such as teacher, graduate, or wife, obtained through one's own efforts.

acquaintance rape Rape by someone who is known to the person being raped (such as in date rape).

acting crowd A crowd that acts on the basis of aroused impulse and thus one that may be volatile, aggressive, and dangerous.

activity theory The theory of aging that suggests that elderly persons who remain active will be the best adjusted.

advanced horticultural societies Societies with irrigation systems and other advanced farming practices.

age The number of years since birth.

age-adjusted death rate The number of deaths occurring at each age for each sex, per 100,000 people of that age who are living.

aged The age group that occupies the later part of the life span, generally meaning the old, elderly, or senior citizens.

ageism Prejudice and discrimination based on age.

age norms Expectations about the behavior considered appropriate for people of a given age.

age segregation The separation of groups by age such as occurs in our education system.

age-sex composition The number of men and women in the population, along with their ages.

aggregate group Any collection of people together in one place; participants interact briefly and sporadically.

aging The biological, psychological, or social processes that occur with growing older.

agrarian societies Complex societies with farming, armies, merchants, and a concentration of wealth in the hands of a few people.

alcoholism A disease related to the drinking of alcohol that has identifiable and progressive symptoms; if untreated, alcoholism can lead to mental damage, physical incapacity, and early death.

alienation A feeling of estrangement or dissociation, such as Marx's idea of feeling alienated from work because of no control over it or satisfaction from it.

Alzheimer's disease A disease affecting primarily older persons in which the brain gradually atrophies, resulting in loss of memory and impairment of thought processes.

amalgamation The process by which different racial or ethnic groups form a new group through interbreeding or intermarriage.

analytical or explanatory studies The studies used to help explain what causes certain events or problems.

Anglo conformity A form of assimilation in which the minority loses its identity completely and adopts the norms and practices of the dominant WASP culture.

animism The religious belief that spirits inhabit virtually everything in nature and control all aspects of life and destiny.

anomie theory The view that deviance arises from the incongruences between a society's emphasis on attaining certain goals and the availability of legitimate, institutionalized means of reaching those goals.

anthropology The study of the physical, biological, social, and cultural development of humans, often on a comparative basis.

applied science The area of science in which the knowledge gained from the "pure" sciences is put into practice.

applied social research The use of sociological knowledge and research skills to obtain information for groups and organizations.

artifacts Physical products or objects created through human actions.

ascribed status A social position assigned to a person on the basis of a characteristic over which he or she has no control, such as age, sex, or race.

assimilation The process through which individuals and groups forsake their own cultural tradition to become part of a different group and tradition.

associational group A group of people who join together to pursue a common interest in an organized, formally structured way.

authoritarian personality theory The view that people with an authoritarian type of personality are more likely to be prejudiced than those who have other personality types.

authority Power accepted as legitimate by those it affects.

barefoot doctors People chosen by the peasants in the communes in Communist China to provide medicine and treat simple illnesses and emergencies. They receive three to eighteen months of training.

blaming the victim A type of reasoning that implies that social problems are caused by the people facing them.

Beguines Communes of peasant women who did not choose to marry and who took vows of celibacy; these communes existed during the Middle Ages.

bilateral lineage A descent system in which influence, wealth, and power are assigned to both sides of the family.

blended families Families composed of at least one formerly married spouse, the children of the previous marriage or marriages, and new offspring.

bourgeoisie The class of people who own the means of production.

Buddhism One of the world's principal religions; adherents follow the teachings of Buddha, the enlightened one, who preached a doctrine of "Four Noble Truths."

bureaucracy A hierarchical, formally organized structural arrangement of an organization based on the division of labor and authority.

capitalism An economic system in which all of the means of production are privately owned.

caste system A system of stratification in which one's social position is ascribed at birth, one's value is assessed in terms of religious or traditional beliefs, and in which upward social mobility is impossible.

casual crowd A crowd that is high in anonymity but low in suggestibility, contagion, emotional arousal, and unity.

categorical group A group of people who share a common characteristic but do not interact or have any social organization.

censorship Prohibiting the availability of some type of information.

census An official count of the number of people in a given area.

charismatic authority Authority granted to someone on the bases of his or her personality characteristics.

Chicago School An approach developed by Cooley, Mead, Thomas, and others in the 1920s that emphasized the importance of social interactions in the development of human thought and action.

chiropractors Those who practice healing by manipulating the body, especially the spine.

Christianity One of the principal religions of the world, followers of which profess faith in the teachings of Jesus Christ.

church An institutionalized organization of people who share common religious beliefs.

citizen One who is considered a member of a state and who is entitled to the privileges and freedoms granted to members of the state.

city-state A city and the surrounding area ruled independently of other areas.

class consciousness Awareness among members of a society that the society is stratified.

classical perspective A view of acting crowd behavior that suggests that people in a crowd lose their conscious personalities and act impulsively on the basis of their instincts rather than reason.

class system A system of stratification found in industrial societies in which one's class is determined by one's wealth and in which vertical social mobility is possible.

clinical sociology The use of sociological perspectives, theories, concepts, research, and methods for consulting and providing technical assistance to individuals or organizations.

closed system A system of stratification in which there is no movement from one rank to another.

collective behavior The spontaneous, unstructured, and transitory behavior of a group of people in reaction to a specific event.

collective conscience A collective psyche that results from the blending of many individual mentalities, but exists above any one individual.

collective excitement In the interactionist perspective on crowd behavior, the stage during which milling reaches a high level of agitation.

community A collection of people within a geographic area among whom there is some degree of mutual identification, interdependence, or organization of activities.

comparable worth Evaluating and rewarding different occupations equally if the work in each occupation requires the same level of skill and is of equal value to the employer.

complementary needs A theory of mate selection based on the idea that people marry those who provide the maximum need gratification. Needs tend to be complementary rather than similar.

compulsory public education Publicly funded education that is mandatory until a certain age.

communism An economic system in which members of the society own the means of production in common.

concentration An urban ecological process in which population, services, and institutions come to be gathered most densely in the areas in which conditions are advantageous.

concentric zone model A model of urban structure showing that cities grow out equally in all directions from their original centers, producing uniform circles of growth that have their own distinctive land use, population, activities, and institutions.

concept An abstract system of meaning that enables us to perceive a phenomenon in a certain way.

conflict theory A social theory that views conflict as inevitable and natural and as a significant cause of social change.

Confucianism One of the world's principal religions, found mainly in China, adherents of which follow the teachings of Confucius.

conjugal families Families consisting of a husband and wife, with or without children.

content analysis The procedure of systematically extracting thematic data from a wide range of communications.

contest mobility A competitive system of education in which those who do best at each level are able to move on to the next level.

control group In an experiment, the group not exposed to the independent variable that is introduced to the experimental group.

conventional crowd A crowd, such as the spectators at a baseball game, whose members are anonymous but share a common focus and follow established social norms and rules.

conversion effect A radical shift of interests and lifestyle that occurs when people move from one type of area to another, as from an urban area to a suburb.

core nations Industrial nations that exploit underdeveloped, peripheral nations.

counterculture A subculture that adheres to a set of norms and values that sharply contradict the dominant norms and values of the society of which that group is a part.

credentialism The practice of requiring degrees for most high-paying jobs, whether or not the degrees actually signify skills necessary to accomplish the jobs.

crime A violation of a criminal statutory law accompanied by a specific punishment applied by some governmental authority.

crowd A temporary group of people in face-to-face contact who share a common interest or focus of attention.

cults Extreme forms of sects that call for a totally new and unique lifestyle, often under the direction of a charismatic leader.

cultural lag The tendency for changes in nonmaterial culture to occur more slowly than changes in technology and material culture.

cultural pluralism The situation in which the various ethnic groups in a society maintain their distinctive cultural patterns, subsystems, and institutions.

cultural relativism The belief that cultures must be judged on their own terms rather than by the standards of another culture.

cultural transmission theory The theory that a community's deviance may be transmitted to newcomers through learning and socialization.

cultural universals Aspects of culture that are shared by all people, such as symbols, shelter, food, and a belief system.

culture The systems of ideas, values, beliefs, knowledge, norms, customs, and technology shared by almost everyone in a particular society.

cyclical change theory The view that societies go through a cycle of birth, maturation, decline, and death.

decentralized bureaucracies Putting the decision-making processes in the hands of the people or local units rather than in the hands of a centralized few.

deconcentration Movement outward from the city because of increases in land values and taxes and declines in services and public facilities.

de facto segregation School assignment based on residence boundaries in which blacks and whites live in separate neighborhoods.

degenerative diseases Those diseases that slowly disable the body as one gets older, such as heart disease and cancer.

de jure segregation The legal assignment of children to schools solely because of race.

democracy A power structure in which people govern themselves, either directly or through elected representatives.

democratic socialism An economic system in which the means of production are owned primarily by individuals or groups of individuals; goods and services vital to the society, such as transportation systems and medical care, are owned and run by the state.

demographic transition The change from high birth and death rates to low birth and death rates with a period of rapid population growth in between; this transition occurs as a society evolves from a traditional premodern stage to a modern industrial stage.

demography The statistical study of population, especially data on birth rates, death rates, marriage rates, health, and migration.

denominations Well-established and highly institutionalized churches.

dependency ratio The ratio between the number of persons in the dependent population and the number of people in the supportive or working population.

dependency theory Conflict theory stating that underdeveloped nations cannot industrialize because they are dependent on the nations already industrialized.

dependent variable A variable that is changed or influenced by another variable.

descriptive research Research that describes social reality or provides facts about the social world.

descriptive studies Studies used primarily to obtain information about a particular social problem, event, or population.

deviance Variation from a set of norms or shared social expectations.

diagnostic related groups (DRGs) The schedule of payment limits set by the federal government for Medicaid and Medicare recipients.

differential association theory The theory that deviance results when individuals have more contact with groups that define deviance favorably than with groups that define it unfavorably.

differential reinforcement The view that the acquisition and persistence of either deviant or conforming behavior is a function of what behaviors have been rewarded or punished.

direct relationship A relationship between two variables in which an increase in one variable is accompanied by an increase in the other; compare with *inverse relationship*.

disclaimers An aspect of maintaining our presentation of self in which we deny behavior that contradicts how we wish to be viewed.

discovery The act of finding something that has always existed but that no one previously knew about.

discrimination Overt unequal and unfair treatment of people on the basis of their membership in a particular group.

disengagement theory The theory of aging that suggests that as people get older, they and the younger people around them go through a period of mutual withdrawal.

displacement A process occurring in split labor markets in which higher-paid workers are replaced with cheaper labor.

diversification The corporate practice of entering business in a variety of areas of manufacturing in order to protect profits; a decrease in profits in one type of business might be made up by an increase in profits in another type, for example.

division of labor A situation in which some people do certain specialized occupations.

downward mobility A move to a position of lower rank in the stratification system.

dramaturgical approach An approach to the study of interaction in which interaction is compared to a drama on stage; the importance of setting and presentation of self are emphasized.

dysfunction In structural functional theory, factors that lead to the disruption or breakdown of the social system.

ecclesia An official state religion that includes all or most members of society.

ecological change Change brought about by the way a population uses the natural resources available to it.

ecological specialization The concentration of homogeneous groups and activities into different sections or urban areas.

ecology The study of the interrelationships between living organisms and the environment.

economic determinism The idea that economic factors are responsible for most social change and for the nature of social conditions, activities, and institutions.

economics The study of how goods, services, and wealth are produced, consumed, and distributed.

economic system The social institution that provides for the production, distribution, and consumption of goods and services.

ecumenism The trend for different denominations to join together in pursuit of common interests in a spirit of worldwide Christian unity.

egalitarian The norm of authority in the family in which decisions are equally divided between husband and wife.

elite culture The materials and ideas of wealthy, affluent, or upper classes (in contrast to popular culture).

emergent norm perspective A view of collective behavior that emphasizes how new norms emerge and influence the behavior of crowds.

emigration Movement of people out of an area.

endogamy A marriage norm requiring a person to marry someone from his or her own group.

epidemiology The study of the spread of diseases.

Equal Rights Amendment (ERA) A proposed amendment to the Constitution of the United States giving equal rights to women; it was not ratified.

ethnic antagonism Mutual opposition, conflict, or hostility among different ethnic groups.

ethnic group A group set apart from others because of its national origin or distinctive cultural patterns, such as religion, language, or region of the country.

ethnocentrism The view that one's own culture is superior to others and should be used as the standard against which other cultures are judged.

ethnographic research A form of descriptive research focusing on the sociology of meaning through close observation of sociocultural phenomena

euthanasia Sometimes called mercy killing; deliberately ending a person's life to spare him or her suffering from an incurable and agonizing disease.

evaluation research Research that measures how well a program or project works in relation to its goals.

evaluative studies Studies used to estimate the effects of specific social programs or policies.

evolutionary theory A theory of social development that suggests that societies, like biological organisms, progress through stages of increasing complexity.

exchange theory A theory of interaction that attempts to explain social behavior in terms of reciprocity of costs and rewards.

exclusion Attempts to keep cheaper labor from taking jobs from groups that receive higher pay.

excuse of behavior An effort at maintaining the self by justifying or making an apology for the behavior.

exogamy A marriage norm requiring a person to marry someone from outside his or her own group.

experimental design A scientific procedure in which at least two matched groups, differing only in the variable being studied, are used to collect and compare data.

experimental group In an experiment, the group to which an independent variable is introduced; this variable is not introduced in the control group.

explanatory research Research that attempts to explain why things do or do not happen by examining the relationship between social variables.

expressive leader A type of leader that focuses on resolving conflicts and creating group harmony and social cohesion.

expressive role A role that emphasizes warmth and understanding rather than action or leadership; traditionally associated more with women than with men.

extended family A family that goes beyond the nuclear family to include other nuclear families and relatives such as grandparents, aunts, uncles, and cousins.

external controls Pressures or sanctions applied to members of society by others.

fad Superficial or trivial behavior that is very popular for a short time.

false consciousness Lack of awareness of class differences and acceptance of upper-class rule.

family A group of kin united by blood, marriage, or adoption who share a common residence for some part of their lives and assume reciprocal rights and obligations with regard to one another.

family of orientation The nuclear family into which one was born and in which one was reared.

family of procreation The nuclear family formed by marriage.

fashion Temporary trend in some aspect of appearance or behavior. Fashions resemble fads but tend to be more cyclical.

fecundity A woman's potential for bearing children.

fee-for-service A medical payment system in which the physician is paid for each visit and each service rendered.

feminization of poverty The increase in the number of persons who are below the level of poverty being predominantly women, particularly as found in female headed families.

fertility A measure of the rate at which people are being born.

fetal monitoring Measuring the vital signs of the infant as it is being born.

folk society A community described by Redfield as small, isolated, homogeneous, and kin-oriented.

folkways Norms of conduct of everyday life that bring only mild censure or punishment if they are violated.

formal external controls Formal systems of social control applied to the individual by others; examples include courts, police, and prisons.

formalization The stage in the development of social movements in which a formal structure is developed, and rules, policies, and tactics are laid out.

formal organization A large social group deliberately organized to achieve certain specific, clearly stated goals.

fraternal polyandry A form of polyandry where brothers are co-husbands.

free market An economic system in which all people are theoretically free to buy, sell, and make a profit.

functional alternatives Alternate ways to achieve an intended goal in order to avoid dysfunctions.

frustration-aggression theory The theory that prejudice results when personal frustrations are displaced to a socially approved racial or ethnic target.

fundamentalism The belief that the Bible is the divine word of God and that all statements in it are to be taken literally, word for word.

game perspective A view of crowd behavior that suggests that members think about their actions and consciously try to act in ways that will produce rewards.

gamesman The type of manager sought by corporations today: a person who is highly competitive and innovative but who prefers to function as the leader of a team.

gemeinschaft A traditional community characterized by a sense of solidarity and common identity and emphasizing intimate and personal relationships.

gender A social status that refers to differences between the sexes, specifically to differences in masculinity and femininity.

gender identity The social construction of boys and girls, men and women, as opposed to their biological characteristics.

gender roles The cultural concepts of masculinity and femininity that society creates around gender.

generalized belief A stage in the development of collective behavior in which people share a common identification and interpretation of a problem.

generalized other The assumption that other people have similar attitudes, values, beliefs, and expectations. It is therefore not necessary to know a specific individual in order to know how to behave toward that individual.

genocide The deliberate destruction of an entire racial or ethnic group.

gentrification The rejuvenation of urban neighborhoods by middle-class people who move into and repair run-down houses.

geography The study of the physical environment and the distribution of plants and animals, including humans.

geriatrics The subfield of gerontological practice that deals with the medical care of the aging.

gerontology The systematic study of the aging process.

gesellschaft A modern community characterized by individualism, mobility, and impersonality, with an emphasis on progress rather than tradition.

ghetto An area in a city in which members of a racial or ethnic minority are forcibly segregated.

greenbelt An area surrounding cities that is preserved for farming and recreation and that limits the growth of cities.

gross national product (GNP) The total value of the goods and services a nation produces in a year.

group marriage A form of marriage in which several or many men are married to several or many women.

health maintenance organization (HMO) A prepaid health care plan in which a fee is paid in advance for all necessary health care.

heroic medicine Dramatic medical treatments such as bleeding, blistering, or administering poisonous laxatives.

hidden curriculum The teaching and learning of things such as obedience, competition, and patriotism that are not part of the stated curriculum.

hidden repression A means of controlling collective behavior that is not obviously or overtly repressive.

Hinduism One of the world's principal polytheistic religions, with no religious hierarchy but a close involvement with society and the cosmic order; it is practiced mainly in India and Pakistan.

history The study of the past; social history is concerned with past human social events.

horizontal expansion Corporations taking over similar businesses in order to gain a monopoly and reduce competition.

horticulture Small-scale farming that relies on tools such as the hoe to till the soil.

hospice A home for terminally ill patients in which the emphasis is on providing a comfortable, supportive environment for the patient and the patient's family.

human relations school A form of industrial management in which the workers' psychology, peer pressures, and attitudes toward management are taken into account.

hunting-and-gathering societies Small, often nomadic societies that have no agriculture and live on food that is found.

hypochondriac A healthy person who believes he or she is ill.

hypothesis A statement about the relationship between variables that can be put to an empirical test.

I The acting, unselfconscious person.

ideal culture The norms and values that people profess to follow.

ideal type A model of a hypothetical pure form of an existing entity.

ideology A set of ideas about what society is like, how it functions, whether it is good or bad, and how it should be changed.

idioculture The system of knowledge, beliefs, behaviors, and customs that is unique to a given group.

immigration Movement of people into an area.

immoral view The view that deviance is immoral and antisocial.

incest Socially forbidden sexual relationships or marriage with certain close relatives.

incumbent One holding an elected office.

independent variable A variable that causes a change or variation in a dependent variable.

industrial societies Societies with great division of labor, highly specialized work, and a great concentration of wealth.

inequality Differences between groups in wealth, status, or power.

infectious diseases Diseases caused by germs and viruses that can be spread from one person to another.

informal external controls Pressure applied by peers, friends, parents, and other people with whom one associates regularly that are intended to encourage one to obey rules and conform to social expectations.

in-group A social group to which people feel they belong and with which they share a consciousness of kind.

inner-directed A description by David Riesman of people who are independent, innovative, and focused on their own survival with little concern with what others think.

instinct Biological or hereditary impulses, drives, or behaviors that require no learning or reasoning.

institution A stable cluster of values, norms, statuses, and roles that develops around a basic social goal.

institutional discrimination The continuing exclusion or oppression of a group as a result of criteria established by an institution.

Institutional Review Boards (IRBs) Committees on college/university campuses and in research organizations that provide oversight of research that is conducted on human subjects.

institutionalization The process by which orderly, stable, structured, and increasingly predictable forms of behavior and interaction are developed.

institutionalized behavior Recurrent behavior that follows an orderly pattern with a relatively stable set of goals, expectations, and values.

institutionalism of inequality The collection of laws, customs, and social practices that combine to create and sustain the unequal distribution of rewards based on class, minority status, and gender.

institutional racism Racism that is embodied in the folkways, mores, or legal structures of a social institution.

instrumental leader A type of leader that focuses on goals, directing activities, and helping make group decisions.

instrumental role A role that emphasizes accomplishment of tasks, such as earning a living to provide food and shelter; traditionally associated more with men than with women.

interactionist perspective A view of crowd behavior that emphasizes how people in crowds reinforce and heighten one another's reactions.

integration The situation that exists when ethnicity becomes insignificant and everyone can freely and fully participate in the social, economic, and political mainstream.

intergenerational mobility A change of social position or rank, up or down, from one generation to the next, such as when children have a higher status than their parents.

internal controls Learned patterns of control that exist in the minds of individuals and make them want to conform to social norms.

intragenerational mobility A change of social position or rank, up or down, within one's own lifetime.

invasion An ecological process in which new types of people, organizations, or activities move into an area occupied by a different type.

invention A device constructed by putting two or more things together in a new way.

inverse relationship A relationship between two variables such that an increase in one variable is accompanied by a decrease in the other; compare with *direct relationship*.

iron law of oligarchy In democratic societies, the inevitable rise of a few elite leaders who dominate power.

Islam One of the world's principal religions, followers of which adhere to the teachings of the Koran and of Muhammad, a prophet.

Judaism The oldest religion in the Western world and the first to teach monotheism; today, the Jews are both an ethnic community and a religious group.

kinship The web of relationships among people linked by common ancestry, adoption, or marriage.

labeling theory A theory that emphasizes how certain behaviors are labeled "deviant" and how being given such a label influences a person's behavior.

language The systematized use of speech and hearing to communicate feelings and ideas.

laissez faire An economy in which there is no government planning or intervention.

latent force A type of power in which force is threatened.

latent functions The unintended consequences of a social system.

law of human progress Comte's notion that all knowledge passes through three successive theoretical conditions: the theological, the metaphysical, and the scientific.

laws Formal, standardized expressions of norms enacted by legislative bodies to regulate certain types of behaviors.

legal authority Authority based on a system of rules and regulations that determine how a society will be governed.

legitimate To make the power of the dominant group acceptable to the masses so they let the dominant group rule without question.

legitimate power Controlling the behavior of others through having people accept the authority as necessary and beneficial to all.

life chances The opportunities a person has to improve his or her income and lifestyle.

life course An age-related progression or sequence of roles and group memberships that people go through as they mature and move through life.

life expectancy The average years of life remaining for persons who attain a given age.

life span The biological age limit beyond which no one can expect to live.

lifetime jobs An employment practice in which workers are guaranteed a job for a lengthy period of time.

lobby An organization of people who want to influence the political process on a specific issue.

looking-glass self A process occurring in social interaction. It has three components: (1) how we think our behavior appears to others, (2) how we think others judge our behavior, and (3) how we feel about their judgments.

macrosociology A level of sociological analysis concerned with large-scale units such as institutions, social categories, and social systems.

magnet schools Schools with special programs designed to attract exceptional students.

Malthusian theory The theory proposed by Thomas Malthus stating that population expands much faster than the food supply, resulting in starvation for much of the population when it grows too large.

manifest functions The intended consequences of a social system.

market economy An economy in which the price and production of goods are determined by what people are willing to pay in the marketplace.

marriage squeeze The effects of an imbalance between the number of males and females in the prime marriage ages due to rising or falling birth rates and the median age differences at marriage.

mass A spatially diffuse collective in which geographically dispersed persons react to or focus upon some common event.

mass expulsion Expelling racial or ethnic groups from their homeland.

mass hysteria A form of diffuse collective behavior involving a widespread, highly emotional fear of a potentially threatening situation.

mass media Forms of communication, such as television, popular magazines, and radio, intended for a large audience.

mass production The production of many items of a product, which lowers the cost per item and reduces the time needed to make it.

master status A particular status in one's status set that takes priority over the others.

matriarchal A family structure in which the wife dominates the husband.

matrilineal A family structure in which descent and inheritance are traced through the mother's line.

matrilocal A family norm that newly married couples should live with the wife's family.

me The part of self that sees self as object, evaluates self, and is aware of society's expectations of self.

mean A measure of central tendency computed by adding the figures and dividing by the number of figures; also known as the average.

mechanical solidarity The idea of Durkheim in which people do similar work but are not very dependent on one another (in contrast to organic solidarity, in which people are very dependent on others).

median A measure of central tendency in which half the figures fall above and half the figures fall below; also known as the midpoint.

Medicaid Federally sponsored health insurance for the poor.

medical center A major hospital that trains new physicians, conducts research, and provides tertiary medical care.

medical model of illness A model of illness in which sickness is viewed as an individual problem requiring individual treatment.

medical view The view that deviance is essentially pathological evidence that a society is unhealthy.

Medicare Federally sponsored health insurance for people age 65 or older.

megalopolis A continuous strip of urban and suburban development that may stretch for hundreds of miles.

melting pot A form of assimilation in which each group contributes aspects of its own culture and absorbs aspects of other cultures, such that the whole is a combination of all the groups.

metropolitan statistical area (MSA) A county or group of counties with a central city with a population of at least 50,000, a density of at least 1,000 persons per square mile, and outlying areas that are socially and economically integrated with the central city.

microsociology The level of sociological analysis concerned with small-scale units such as individuals in small group interactions.

middle-range theory A set of propositions designed to link abstract propositions with empirical testing.

migration Movement of people into or out of an area.

millennialism The belief prevalent among certain sects that there will be a dramatic transformation of life on earth and that Christ will rule the world for a thousand years of prosperity and happiness.

milling The stage in the development of crowd behavior during which people move about aimlessly, grow increasingly preoccupied with others, and become increasingly inclined to respond without thinking.

mind The process of using a language and thinking.

minority group A group subordinate to the dominant group in terms of the distribution of social power; such groups are defined by some physical or cultural characteristic and are usually but not always smaller than the dominant group.

mobilization for action A stage in the development of collective behavior during which people are persuaded to join the movement.

mobs Emotionally aroused groups ready to engage in violent behavior.

mode The most frequent response in a body of data.

modernization The process whereby preindustrial countries emerge as urban societies with lower birth rates, more goods and services, and better nutrition and health care.

modernization theory The view that the status of older people declines with modernization.

modified-extended family structure The family structure in which individual nuclear families retain considerable autonomy yet maintain connections with other nuclear families in the extended family structure.

monogamy The marriage of one man to one woman.

monotheism The belief in one god.

mores Norms of conduct associated with strong feelings of right or wrong, violations of which bring intense reaction and some type of punishment.

mortality A measure of the rate at which people die.

mortification of self Stripping the self of all the characteristics of a past identity, including clothing, personal possessions, friends, roles and routines, and so on.

multinational corporation Corporations that do business in a number of nations.

multiple-nuclei model The model of urban development showing that cities have areas of different types of land use, each of which has its own center or nucleus.

municipal hospital A hospital built and operated by a city or county.

mysticism The belief that spiritual or divine truths come to us through intuition and meditation, not through the use of reason or via the ordinary range of human experience and senses.

nation-states Large territories ruled by a single political institution.

nature–nurture debate A longstanding debate over whether behavior results from predetermined biological characteristics or from socialization.

neolocal A family norm that newly married couples should establish residences separate from those of both sets of parents.

neo-Malthusian theory Revisions of Malthusian theory about food production and population growth that include more information, such as taking into account the effects of technology.

noblesse oblige The obligation of the rich to give to the poor and suffering.

nonmarital cohabitation An arrangement in which two unmarried and unrelated adults share a common household or dwelling.

norms Formal and informal rules of conduct and social expectations for behavior.

nuclear families Families in which two or more persons are related by blood, marriage, or adoption and who share a common residence.

nutritionist A person who specializes in proper eating programs.

observational research Research in which the researcher watches what is happening and makes no attempt to control or modify the activity being observed.

oligarchy Government by a small elite group.

open system A system of stratification in which it is possible to move to a higher or lower position.

operational definition A definition of a concept or variable such that it can be measured.

operation of social controls A stage in the development of collective behavior in which the mass media, government, and other groups try to suppress or influence collective behavior.

organic solidarity Durkheim's term for the integration of society that results from the division of labor.

organized crime Groups expressly organized to carry out illegal activities.

orphan drugs Drugs that are valuable in the treatment of rare diseases but are not profitable to manufacture.

other-directed A description by David Riesman of people who focus on making a good impression, being popular, getting along with others, and being cooperative.

out-group A group to which people feel they do not belong; they do not share consciousness of kind, and they feel little identity to the group.

panic An attempt to rapidly escape from a perceived danger.

parochial schools Schools run and maintained by a religious body or organization rather than the public at large.

party An organization in which decisions are made to reach certain goals, the achievement of which affects society.

pathological illness An illness in which the body is clearly diseased or malfunctioning in some way.

pathology of normalcy The concept that cultural norms are not always beneficial for a society, group, or individual.

patriarchal A family structure in which the husband dominates the wife.

patrilineal A family system in which descent and inheritance are traced through the father's line.

patrilocal A family norm that newly married couples should live with the husband's family.

peer group An informal primary group of people who share a similar or equal status and who are usually of roughly the same age.

peripheral nations Underdeveloped nations who are exploited by core nations.

physical force A type of power backed by sheer force such as an army or physical might.

placebo effect A benefit arising from a patient's belief that a medicine will have a beneficial effect.

planned economy An economy in which the production and prices of goods are planned by the government.

play According to Mead, a way of practicing role taking.

political action committees (PACs) Organizations formed to raise money for a political campaign.

political parties Groups of citizens formed with the express intent of gaining control of the political body of the state.

political pluralism A political system in which many diverse groups have a share of the power.

politics The use of power to determine who gets what in society.

political science The study of power, government, and the political process.

polyandry The marriage of one woman to more than one husband at the same time.

polygamy The marriage of one man or woman to more than one person of the opposite sex at the same time.

polygyny The marriage of one man to more than one wife at the same time.

polytheism The belief in and worship of more than one god.

popular culture Trends, social activities, and shared experiences of everyday people (in contrast to elite culture).

popular excitement The stage in the development of a social movement during which social unrest is brought into the open and people with similar concerns begin to organize.

poverty Having fewer resources than are required to meet the basic necessities of life. Rates are usually based on a government index of income relative to size of family and farm/nonfarm residence.

power The ability to control or influence the behavior of others, even without their consent.

power elite A small group of people who hold all of the powerful positions and cooperate to maintain their social positions.

precipitating factors A stage in the development of collective behavior during which an event triggers a collective response.

prejudice A preconceived attitude or judgment, either good or bad, about another group; prejudices usually involve negative stereotypes.

preparatory schools Private schools, usually of a select and elite nature, that are intended to offer an intensive education in both academic as well as social/cultural activities.

prescribed role The expectations associated with a given status that are based on what society suggests or dictates.

presentation of self The way we present ourselves to others and how our presentation influences others.

priests Religious leaders who owe their authority to the power of their office.

primary group A small, informal group of people who interact in a personal, direct, and intimate way.

primary labor market The labor market reserved for people who will advance to high-level positions.

primary medical care The first general, overall care the patient needs.

primary workers Workers who produce raw materials, such as food or minerals.

principle of legitimacy Malinowski's idea that every society has a rule that every child should have a legitimate father to act as the child's protector, guardian, and representative in society.

profane That which belongs to the realm of the everyday world; anything considered mundane and unspiritual.

projection A psychological explanation of prejudice that suggests that people transfer responsibility for their own failures to a vulnerable group, usually a racial or ethnic group.

proletariat The group in capitalist societies that does not own the means of production and has only labor to sell.

prolonged adolescence A latent function of education that serves to maintain parental dependency and keep young people out of the job market.

propaganda An attempt to manipulate the ideas or opinions of the public by presenting limited, selective, or false information.

prophets Religious leaders who have authority on the basis of their charismatic qualities.

proposition A statement of the relationship between two or more concepts or variables.

proprietary hospital A hospital that is privately owned, usually by physicians or hospital corporations.

Protestant ethic The view associated with the Puritans that hard work is valuable for its own sake; according to Weber, the Protestant ethic is responsible for the high value placed on capitalism in the United States.

psychology The study of human mental processes and individual human behavior.

public A group of people who are confronted with an issue, who do not agree on how to address the issue, and who discuss the issue.

public opinion Any opinion held by a substantial number of people; or, the dominant opinion in a given population.

pull factors Natural or social factors that cause people to move into an area.

pure science The area of science in which knowledge is sought for its own sake with little emphasis on how the knowledge might be applied.

push factors Natural or social factors that cause people to move out of an area.

qualitative methods The gathering and reporting of non-numerical data used to determine the essential characteristics, properties, or processes of something or someone.

quality control circles Meetings at which workers discuss ways of improving production and set policy to reach their goals.

quantitative methods The gathering and reporting of data based on numbers or amounts of something.

racial group A socially defined group distinguished by selected inherited physical characteristics.

racism Discrimination based on racial characteristics.

radicalism Labor groups joining together in a coalition against the capitalist class.

random sample A sample selected in such a way that every member of a population has an equal chance of being chosen.

range The span between the largest and smallest amount of a variable.

real culture The norms and values that people actually follow and practice. The real culture may or may not be the same as the ideal culture, which represents the norms and values people profess to follow.

reference group A group with which people identify psychologically and to which they refer in evaluating themselves and their behavior.

referenda Questions on a ballot to be decided by the electorate.

registered dietitian (RD) Licensed members of hospital staffs that plan regular meals and special diets for patients.

relative deprivation A feeling of being deprived, not because of objective conditions, but because of comparison to a reference group.

relativistic view The view that deviance can be interpreted only in the sociocultural context in which it occurs.

reliability The extent to which repeated observations of the same phenomena yield similar results.

religion An organized community of believers who hold certain things sacred and follow a set of beliefs, ceremonies, or special behaviors.

repressive measures Measures, such as banning public assemblies, used to control collective behavior.

resocialization Socialization to a new role or position in life that requires a dramatic shift in the attitudes, values, behaviors, and expectations learned in the past.

resource mobilization theory The theory that the success of a social movement depends not only on those who benefit from it directly but also on its ability to mobilize other individuals and groups to contribute time, money, and influence.

riot A form of collective behavior involving mass violence and mob action.

role The social expectations or behaviors associated with a particular status.

role ambiguity A situation in which the expectations associated with a particular social status are unclear.

role conflict A situation that exists when differing expectations are associated with the same role.

role of the police A means of controlling collective behavior through the use of police force.

role perception The way that expectations for behavior are perceived or defined—which may differ considerably from what is prescribed or actually done.

role performance The actual behavior of a person in a particular role, in contrast to the way that person is expected to behave.

role set The multiple roles attached to statuses.

role strain A situation that occurs when differing and incompatible roles are associated with the same status.

role taking Assuming the roles of others and seeing the world from their perspective.

sacred Involving objects and ideas that are treated with reverence and awe.

sample A number of individuals or cases drawn from a larger population.

Sapir-Whorf Hypothesis The hypothesis that societies with different languages perceive the world differently because their members interpret the world through the grammatical forms, labels, and categories their language provides.

scapegoating A psychological explanation of prejudice that involves blaming another person or group for one's own problems.

scientific management A method of managing assembly-line workers such that their every movement is efficient.

scientific method A procedure that involves systematically formulating problems, collecting data through observation and experiment, and devising and testing hypotheses.

secondary analysis The use of existing information that was gathered or exists independently of one's own research.

secondary care givers Those who provide more specialized care than that provided by a general practitioner.

secondary group A group in which the members interact impersonally, have few emotional ties, and come together for a specific, practical purpose.

secondary labor market The labor market in which jobs pay poorly, there is little job security, and there are few promotions or salary increases.

secondary medical care Care that is more specialized than the care that a general practitioner provides.

secondary workers Workers who produce manufactured goods from raw materials.

sector model An explanation of the ecology of cities as a series of pie-shaped wedges radiating from the central business district, each with its own characteristics and uses.

sects Religious groups that have broken away from a parent church, follow rigid doctrines and fundamentalist teachings, and emphasize "otherworldly" rewards, rejecting or deemphasizing contemporary society.

secularization The process through which beliefs concerning the supernatural and religious institutions lose social influence.

segregation The separation of a group from the main body; it usually involves separating a minority group from the dominant group.

self The sense of one's own identity as a person.

self-fulfilling prophecy A prediction that comes true because people believe it and act as though it were true.

senility A mental infirmity associated with the aging process.

serial or sequential monogamy Marriage to a number of different spouses in succession, but only one at any given time.

sex The biological and anatomical characteristics that differentiate males and females.

sexual harassment Sexual advances made by coworkers or superiors at work.

shamanism The religious belief that certain persons (shamans) have special charm, skill, or knowledge in influencing spirits.

sick role A set of expectations, privileges, and obligations related to illness.

significant others Persons that one identifies with psychologically and whose opinions are considered important.

simple horticultural societies Societies that grow food using very simple tools, such as digging sticks.

slums Sections of a city marked by poverty, overcrowding, substandard housing, and poor living conditions.

social change Changes in the structure of a society or in its social institutions.

social class A category of people who have approximately the same amount of power and wealth and the same life chances to acquire wealth.

social conflict A view of Karl Marx that social conflict—class struggle due to economic inequality—is at the core of society and the key source of social change.

social contagion A stage in the development of crowd behavior during which the crowd's response to a common event increases in intensity and the crowd's behavior moves others to behave in the same way.

social control through amelioration The creation of specific policies to eliminate the source of strain that lies behind the collective behavior.

social differentiation The difference or variation of people based on selected social characteristics such as class, gender, race, or age.

social distance The degree of intimacy and equality between groups of people.

social dynamics Comte's term for social processes and forms of change.

social engineering Attempting to change the way a society, community, organization, institution, or group is arranged so that a particular goal may be achieved.

social facts Reliable and valid items of information about society.

social gerontology A branch of gerontology that focuses on the social and cultural factors related to age and the aging process.

social group A group in which people physically or socially interact.

socialism An economic system in which the means of production are owned by all the people through the state.

socialization The process of learning how to interact in society by learning the rules and expectations of society.

social learning theory The view that deviant and conforming behaviors are strongly influenced by the consequences that follow them.

social model of illness The view that much disease is caused by social conditions and that it can be cured by changing social conditions.

social movements Collective noninstitutionalized efforts to bring about social change and establish a new order of social thought and action.

social network The linkage or ties to a set of relationships.

social psychology The study of how individuals interact with other individuals or groups and how groups influence the individual.

social science A science that has as its subject matter human behavior, social organizations, or society.

Social Security The federal program that provides financial support for the elderly.

social statics Comte's term for the stable structure of a society.

social status The amount of honor and prestige a person receives from others in the community; also, the position one occupies in the stratification system.

social stratification The ranking of people according to their wealth, prestige, or party position.

social system A set of interrelated social statuses and the expectations that accompany them.

social unrest The stage in the development of social unrest that is characterized by unfocused restlessness and increasing disorder.

social work The field in which the principles of the social sciences are applied to actual social problems.

society A group of interacting people who live in a specific geographical area, who are organized in a cooperative manner, and who share a common culture.

sociobiology The study of the biological and genetic determinants of social behavior.

sociocultural learning theories Theories that deal with the processes through which deviant acts are learned and the conditions under which learning takes place.

socioeconomic status (SES) An assessment of status that takes into account a person's income, education, and occupation.

sociological perspective A way of looking at society and social behavior that involves questioning the obvious, seeking patterns, and looking beyond the individual in an attempt to discern social processes.

sociology The study of human society and social life and the social causes and consequences of human behavior.

spatially diffuse collectives Collectives that form among people spread over a wide geographical area.

spatially proximate collectives Collectives in which people are geographically close and physically visible to one another.

split labor market A labor market in which some jobs afford upward mobility and others do not.

sponsored mobility A system of education in which certain students are selected at an early age to receive advanced education and training.

statistical group A group formed by sociologists or statisticians; members are unaware of belonging and there is no social interaction or social organization.

states Societies with institutional government and laws as a means of political regulation, a military defense, and a way to finance these activities.

statistical illness An illness in which one's health varies from the norm.

statistical view A perspective on deviance that defines deviant as any variation from a statistical norm.

stereotypes Widely held and oversimplified beliefs about the character and behavior of all members of a group that seldom correspond to the facts.

stratification The structured ranking of entire groups of people that perpetuates unequal rewards and power in a society.

stratified sampling Sampling in which a population is divided into groups and then subjects are chosen at random from within those groups.

status The socially defined position an individual occupies.

status set The combination of all the statuses any individual holds at a given time.

strain theories Theories of deviance suggesting that the experience of socially induced strain, such as anomie, forces people to engage in deviant activities.

structural assimilation One aspect of assimilation in which patterns of intimate contact between the guest and host groups are developed in the clubs, organizations, and institutions of the host society.

structural conduciveness The extent to which a society's organization has the conditions that make a particular form of collective behavior possible.

structural functionalism The theory that societies contain certain interdependent structures, each of which performs certain functions for the maintenance of society.

structural strain Any conflict or ambiguity in a society's organization that causes frustration and stress; often seen as a precondition for collective behavior.

subcultures Groups of persons who share in the main culture of a society but also have their own distinctive values, norms, and lifestyles.

suburbs The communities that surround a central city and are dependent on it.

succession An urban process of replacing old occupants and institutions with new ones.

survey research A quantitative research technique that involves asking people questions about the subject being surveyed.

symbolic interaction theory The social theory stressing interactions between people and the social processes that occur within the individual that are made possible by language and internalized meanings.

symbol Something that is used to represent something else, such as a word, gesture, or object used to represent some aspect of the world.

systematic sampling Obtaining a sample from a population by following a specific pattern of selection, such as choosing every tenth person.

taboos Mores that prohibit something.

technology The application of nonmaterial and material knowledge by a society to maintain its standard of living and lifestyle.

temporocentrism The belief that one's own time is more important than the past or future.

tertiary medical care Long-term care requiring complex technology.

tertiary workers Workers who provide a service, such as doctors, lawyers, politicians, police officers, and secretaries.

theory A set of logically and systematically interrelated propositions that explain a particular process or phenomenon.

totalitarianism A power structure in which the government has total power to dictate the values, rules, ideology, and economic development of a society.

traditional authority The right to rule granted to someone on the basis of tradition, as with a patriarch or king.

totemism The worship of plants, animals, and other natural objects as gods and ancestors.

trained incapacity The situation that exists when the demands of discipline, conformity, and adherence to rules render people unable to perceive the end for which the rules were developed.

unionization The process of organizing workers to improve their wages and working conditions.

upward mobility Movement in the stratification system to a position of greater wealth, status, and power.

urban ecology The study of the interrelationships between people in urban settings and the social and physical environment in which they live.

urban homesteading A federal plan in which abandoned and foreclosed homes are sold to private families at extremely low prices if they agree to live in the house and bring it up to code standards.

urbanization The growth of the number of people who live in urban rather than rural areas and the process of taking on organizational patterns and lifestyles characteristic of urban areas.

validity The extent to which observations actually measure what they are supposed to measure.

values Ideas and beliefs shared by the people in a society about what is important and worthwhile.

variable A characteristic such as age, class, or income that can vary from one person to another; a concept that can have two or more values.

variance A descriptive statistic that tells how the data are spread over the range.

verstehen Understanding human action by examining the subjective meanings that people attach to their own behavior and the behavior of others.

vertical expansion Business expansion in order to own everything related to a business, from raw materials to sales outlets.

victimization surveys Asking samples of people if they have been victims of a particular behavior, such as rape.

vital statistics Records of all births, deaths and their causes, marriages, divorces, and certain diseases in a society.

voluntary association An organization people join because they share the organization's goals and values and voluntarily choose to support them.

voluntary hospital A nonprofit hospital that treats patients who need short-term care.

vouchers Giving parents the choice of a private school for their children to attend and using state funds to pay for the tuition.

welfare capitalism A mixed economy in which private and public ownership are both practiced extensively.

women's movement The social movements led by women to gain political and economic equality.

world systems theory Conflict theory stating core nations dominate the economics of peripheral nations.

xenocentrism The belief that what is foreign is best and that one's own lifestyle, products, or ideas are inferior to those of others.

zero population growth A population policy that encourages parents to have no more than two children to limit the growth of the population.

References

Abrahamson, Mark. *Sociological Theory: An Introduction to Concepts, Issues, and Research*, 2nd ed. Englewood Cliffs, NJ: Prentice Hall, 1990.

Abu-Lughod, Janet. *Changing Cities.* New York: Harper Collins, 1991.

Ade-Ridder, Linda. "Sexuality and Marital Quality Among Older Married Couples," in Timothy H. Brubaker, ed., *Family Relationships in Later Life*, 2nd ed. Newbury Park, CA: Sage Publications, 1990.

Adler, Jerry, Mark Starr, Farai Chideya, Lynda Wright, Pat Wingert, and Linda Haac. "Taking Offense: Is This the New Enlightenment on Campus or the New McCarthyism?" *Newsweek*, December 24, 1990, pp. 48–54.

Adorno, T. W., Else Frenkel-Brunswik, Daniel J. Levinson, and R. Nevitt Sanford. *The Authoritarian Personality.* New York: Wiley, 1950.

Agnew, Robert. "A Revised Strain Theory of Delinquency," *Social Forces 64* (September 1985): 151–167.

Agran, Larry. "Getting Cancer on the Job," *The Nation*, April 12, 1975, pp. 433–437.

Aguirre, B. E., E. L. Quarantelli, and Jorge L. Mendoza. "The Collective Behavior of Fads: The Characteristics, Effects, and Career of Streaking," *American Sociological Review 53* (August 1988): 569–584.

Akers, Ronald L. *Deviant Behavior: A Social Learning Approach*, 2nd ed. Belmont, CA: Wadsworth, 1977.

Akers, R. L., M. D. Krohn, L. Lonza Kaduce, and M. Radosevich. "Social Learning and Deviant Behavior: A Specific Test of a General Theory," *American Sociological Review 44* (August 1979): 636–655.

Albrecht, Stanley L., Darwin L. Thomas, and Bruce A. Chadwick. *Social Psychology.* Englewood Cliffs, NJ: Prentice-Hall, 1980.

Allen, Irving Lewis. *Unkind Words: Ethnic Labeling from Redskin to WASP.* New York: Bergin and Garvey, 1990.

Allport, Gordon. *The Nature of Prejudice.* Boston: Beacon Press, 1954.

American Sociological Association. *Careers in Sociology.* Washington, DC: American Sociological Association, 1977.

AmeriStat. "Diversity, Poverty Characterize Female-Headed Households. Tabulations from the Census Bureau's Current Population Survey," (March 2003).

Andrews, Edmund L. "It's Not Just the Jobs Lost, but the Pay in the New Ones," *New York Times*, August 9, 2004.

Anooshian, Linda J. "Social Isolation and Rejection of Homeless Children," *Journal of Children and Poverty* 9, no.2 (September 2003): 115–134.

Aoki, Masahiko. *Information, Incentives and Bargaining in the Japanese Economy.* Cambridge, England: Cambridge University Press, 1988.

Arber, Sara, Gilbert G. Nigel, and Angela Dale. "Paid Employment and Women's Health: A Benefit or a Source of Role Strain?" *Sociology of Health and Illness* 7 (November 1985): 375–400.

Aronson, E., C. Stephan, J. Sikes, N. Blaney, and M. Snapp. *The Jigsaw Classroom.* Beverly Hills, CA: Sage Publications, 1978.

Atchley, Robert C. "The Process of Retirement: Comparing Men and Women," in Maximiliane Szinovacz, ed., *Women's Retirement: Policy Implications of Recent Research.* Beverly Hills, CA: Sage Publications, 1982, pp. 153–168.

Atchley, Robert. *Social Forces and Aging: An Introduction to Social Gerontology*, 6th ed. Belmont, CA: Wadsworth, 1991.

Atkinson, A. B. *The Economics of Inequality*, 2nd ed. Oxford, England: Clarendon Press, 1983.

Austin, Sarah. "Crisis in New York City," *New York Times*, January 4, 1976, p. 40.

Ayensu, Edward S. "A Worldwide Role for the Healing Powers of Plants," *Smithsonian 12* (November 1981): 86–97.

Badgett, M. V. Lee, and Nancy Folbre. "Job Gendering: Occupational Choice and the Marriage Market," *Industrial Relations* 42, no. 2 (2003).

Bakanic, Von, Clark McPhail, and Rita J. Simon. "The Manuscript Review and Decision-Making Process," *American Sociological Review 52* (October 1987): 631–642.

Bales, Robert F. "The Equilibrium Problem in Small Groups," in Talcott Parsons, Robert F. Bales, and Edward A. Shils, *Working Papers in the Theory of Action.* Glencoe, IL: Free Press, 1953.

Ballantine, Jeanne H. *The Sociology of Education.* Englewood Cliffs, NJ: Prentice-Hall, 1983.

Bart, Pauline B. "Rape as a Paradigm of Sexism in Society—Victimization and Its Discontents," *Women's Studies International Quarterly 2* (1979): 347–357.

Basirico, Laurence A. "The Art and Craft Fair: A New Institution in an Old Art World," *Qualitative Sociology 9*(4) (Winter 1986): 339–353.

Basirico, Laurence A. *Glass Consciousness: Social Organization and Social Interaction in the Stained Glass World.* Ph.D.

dissertation, Department of Sociology, State University of New York at Stony Brook. Ann Arbor, MI: University Microfilms International, 1983.

Basirico, L., Cashion, B., Eshleman, J., Kimberlin, W., *Understanding Sociology.* Horizon Textbook Publishing, Redding, Ca 2006.

Bayles, Fred. "First a Puzzle, Then a Plague: A Decade of AIDS," *Greensboro News and Record* [Associated Press], June 2, 1991, pp. 1, 8.

Bean, Frank D. "The Baby Boom and Its Explanations," *Sociological Quarterly 24* (Summer 1983): 353–365.

Becker, Howard S. "The Labeling Theory Reconsidered," in Paul Rock and Mary McIntosh, eds., *Deviance and Social Control.* London: Tavistock, 1974.

Becker, Howard S. *Outsiders: Studies in the Sociology of Deviance.* New York: Free Press, 1963.

Becker, Howard. "Whose Side Are We On?" *Social Problems 14* (Winter 1967): 239–249.

Bell, Terrell. "Key to Education Problem: More Government. . . ," *New Perspectives Quarterly,* Winter, 1991, pp. 70–71.

Bell, Wendell. "Social Choice, Life Styles, and Suburban Residences," in W. Dobriner, ed., *The Suburban Community.* New York: Putnam, 1958.

Belsky, Jay. "Infant Day Care, Child Development, and Family Policy," *Society* 27 (July/August 1990): 10–12.

Bem, S., and D. Bem. "Training the Woman to Know Her Place: The Power of a Nonconscious Ideology," in S. Cox, ed., *Female Psychology: The Emerging Self.* Chicago: SRA, 1976, pp. 180–191.

Berg, Ivar. *Education and Jobs: The Great Training Robbery.* New York: Praeger, 1970.

Berger, Bennett. *Working Class Suburbs.* Berkeley, CA: University of California Press, 1960.

Berk, Richard A. *Collective Behavior.* Dubuque, IA: Brown, 1974.

Berk, Sarah Fenstermaker. *The Gender Factory: The Apportionment of Work in American Households.* New York: Plenum Press, 1985.

Bernard, Jessie. *The Female World.* New York: Free Press, 1981.

Bernard, Thomas J. "Control Criticisms of Strain Theories: An Assessment of Theoretical and Empirical Adequacy," *Journal of Research in Crime and Delinquency 21* (November 1984): 353–372.

Bernstein, Richard. "In U.S. Schools: A War of Words," *New York Times Magazine,* October 14, 1990, p. 34.

Beutler, Ivan F., Wesley R. Burr, Kathleen S. Bahr, and Donald A. Herrin, "The Family Realm: Theoretical Contributions for Understanding its Uniqueness," *Journal of Marriage and the Family 51* (August 1989): 805–816.

Bilge, Barbara, and Gladis Kaufman. "Children of Divorce and One-Parent Families: Cross-Cultural Perspectives," *Family Relations 32* (January 1983): 59–71.

Blake, Judith. *Family Size and Achievement.* Berkeley: University of California Press, 1989.

Blake, Judith. "Family Size and the Quality of Children," *Demography 18* (1981a): 421–442.

Blake, Judith. "The Only Child in America: Prejudice Versus Performance," *Population and Development Review* 7 (March 1981b): 43–54.

Blau, Peter. *Exchange and Power in Social Life.* New York: Wiley, 1964.

Blau, Peter M., and Otis Dudley Duncan. *The American Occupational Structure.* New York: Wiley, 1967.

Blits, Jan H., and Linda S. Gottfredson. "Equality of Lasting Inequality?" *Society 27* (March/April 1990): 4–12.

Blumer, Herbert. "Collective Behavior," in Alfred McClung Lee, ed., *Principles of Sociology.* New York: Barnes and Noble, 1939.

Blumstein, Philip, and Pepper Schwartz. *American Couples: Money, Work and Sex.* New York: William Morrow, 1983.

Bonacich, Edna. "Abolition, the Extension of Slavery, and the Position of Free Blacks: A Study of Split Labor Markets in the United States, 1830–1863," *American Journal of Sociology 81* November 1975): 601–628.

Bonacich, Edna. "Advanced Capitalism and Black/White Race Relations in the United States: A Split Labor Market Interpretation," *American Sociological Review 41* (February 1976): 34–51.

Bonacich, Edna. "A Theory of Ethnic Antagonism: The Split Labor Market," *American Sociological Review 37* (October 1972): 547–559.

Bose, Christine E., and Peter H. Rossi. "Prestige Standings of Occupations as Affected by Gender," *American Sociological Review 48* (June 1983): 316–330.

Boserup, Ester. *Population and Technological Change.* Chicago: University of Chicago Press, 1981.

Bourdieu, Pierre. *The Forms of Capital.* In John Richardson, ed., *Handbook of Theory and Research for the Sociology of Education.* New York: Greenwood Press, 1986, pp. 241–258.

Bowles, Samuel, and Herbert Gintis. *Schooling in Capitalist America.* New York: Basic Books, 1976.

Bowman, Madonna E., and Constance R. Ahrons. "Impact of Legal Custody Status on Fathers' Parenting Postdivorce," *Journal of Marriage and the Family 47* (May 1985): 481–488.

Boyer, Ernest. "College: The Undergraduate Experience in America," *Chronicle of Higher Education, 33*(10) November 5, 1986): 16.

Bradbard, Marilyn R. "Sex Differences in Adults' Gifts and Children's Toy Requests at Christmas," *Psychological Reports 56* (1985): 969–970.

Brockway, George P. "Minimum Wage vs. Maximum Confusion," *The New Leader* 7 (April 3, 1989): 14–15.

Brown, Cynthia Stokes. "No Amen for School Prayer," *Learning*, August, 1983, pp. 42–43.

Brown, Henry Phelps. *Egalitarianism and the Generation of Inequality.* New York: Oxford University Press, 1988.

Browne-Miller, Angela. *The Day Care Dilemma: Critical Concerns for American Families.* New York: Plenum Press, 1990.

Bureau of Justice Statistics, U.S. Department of Justice (May 11, 1998). www.ojp.usdoj.gov/bjs

Burgess, Ernest W. "The Growth of the City," in Robert E. Park and Ernest W. Burgess, eds., *The City.* Chicago: University of Chicago Press, 1925, pp. 47–62.

Burke, Ronald J., and Tamara Weir. "Relationship of Wives' Employment Status to Husband, Wife and Pair Satisfaction and Performance," *Journal of Marriage and the Family 38* (May 1976): 279–287.

Calavita, Kitty, and Henry N. Pontell. "Other's People's Money Revisited: Collective Embezzlement in the Savings and Loan Industries," *Social Problems 38* (February 1991): 94–112.

Caldecott, Helen. *Missile Envy: The Arms Race and Nuclear War.* New York: Bantam Books, 1986.

California Environmnental Protection Agency Air Resources Board. "Study Links Air Pollution and Asthma," January 31, 2002.

Callahan, Daniel. In Robert Landers, "Right to Die: Medical, Legal & Moral Issues," *Congressional Quarterly's Editorial Research Reports*, September 28, 1990, pp. 554–567.

Caplow, Theodore, Howard M. Bahr, Bruce A. Chadwick, Reuben Hill, and Margaret Holmes Williamson. *Middletown Families: Fifty Years of Change and Continuity.* Minneapolis: University of Minnesota Press, 1982.

Carison, Margaret. "Only English Spoken Here," *Time*, December 5, 1988, p. 29.

Cashion, Barbara G. "Female-Headed Families: Effects on Children and Clinical Implications," *Journal of Marital and Family Therapy* (April 1982): 77–85.

"Catholic Schools Serving Disadvantaged Students," *Financing Schools* 7, no. 3 (Winter 1997).

Centers, Richard. *The Psychology of Social Classes.* Princeton, NJ: Princeton University Press, 1949.

Centers for Disease Control and Prevention (CDC). "Births: Preliminary Data for 2003," *NVSR* 53, no. 9 (2004): 18.

"Changing America: Indicators of Social and Economic Well-Being by Race and Hispanic Origin," Council of Economic Advisers for the Presidentís Initiative on Race, September 1998.

Cheal, David. *The Gift Economy.* Boston: Routledge & Kegan Paul, 1988.

Cheal, David J. "Intergenerational Family Transfers," *Journal of Marriage and the Family 45* (November 1983): 805–813.

Chesler, Mark A., and William M. Cave. *A Sociology of Education: Access to Power and Privilege.* New York: Macmillan, 1981.

Childe, V. Gordon. "The Urban Revolution," *Town Planning Review 21* (April 1951): 3–17.

Chirot, Daniel. "The Rise of the West," *American Sociological Review 50* (April 1985): 181–195.

Church, George. "Thinking the Unthinkable," *Time*, May 30, 1988, pp. 12–19.

Clark, Robin E., and Judith Freeman Clark. *The Encyclopedia of Child Abuse.* New York: Facts on File, 1989.

Clarke-Stewart, K. Alison. "Infant Day Care: Maligned or Malignant?" *American Psychologist 44* (February 1989): 266–273.

Clemens, Audra W., and Leland J. Axelsen. "The Not-So-Empty Nest: The Return of the Fledgling Adult," *Family Relations 34* (April 1985): 259–264.

Cohen, Albert K., and Harold M. Hodges, Jr. "Characteristics of Lower Blue-Collar Class," *Social Problems 10* (Winter 1963): 307–321.

Cohen, Harry S. "Sociology and You: Good Living," in Roger A. Strauss, ed., *Using Sociology: An Introduction from the Clinical Perspective.* New York: General Hall, 1985.

Coleman, James W., and Donald R. Cressey. *Social Problems*, 4th ed. New York: HarperCollins Publishers, 1990.

Coleman, James, Thomas Hoffer, and Sally Kilgore. *Public and Private High Schools: An Analysis of High Schools and Beyond.* Washington, DC: National Center for Education Statistics, 1982.

Coleman, James S., et al. *Equality of Educational Opportunity.* Washington, DC: U.S. Government Printing Office, 1966.

Coleman, James S., et al. *Youth: Transition to Adulthood. Report of the Panel on Youth of the President's Science Advisory Committee.* Chicago: University of Chicago Press, 1974.

Collver, Andrew. "Housing and Environmental Planning," in Howard Freeman, Russel R. Dynes, Peter H. Rossi, and William Foote Whyte, eds., *Applied Sociology.* San Francisco: Jossey-Bass, 1983, pp. 275–286.

Collins, Randall. *The Credential Society: An Historical Sociology of Education and Stratification.* New York: Academic Press, 1979.

Collins, Randall, and Scott Coltrane. *Sociology of Marriage and the Family: Gender, Love, and Property*, 3rd ed. Chicago: Nelson-Hall, 1991.

Colson, Charles. "Half-Stoned Logic," *Christianity Today*, March 5, 1990, p. 64.

Compa, Lance. "To Cure Labor's Ills: Bigger Unions, Fewer of Them," *Washington Post*, November 16, 1986, p. H1.

Connelly, Julie. "How Dual-Income Couples Cope," *Fortune*, September 24, 1990, pp. 129–130, 133–134, 136.

Conner, Karen A. *Aging America: Issues Facing an Aging Society.* Englewood Cliffs, NJ: Prentice Hall, 1992.

Cookson, Peter W., Jr., and Caroline Hodges Persell. *Preparing for Power: America's Elite Boarding Schools.* New York: Basic Books, 1985.

Cooley, Charles H. *Social Organization.* New York: Scribner's, 1909.

Corea, Genoveffa. "How the New Reproductive Technologies Could Be Used to Apply the Brothel Model of Social Control over Women," *Women's Studies International Forum 8* (1985): 299–305.

Cornfield, Daniel B. "Declining Union Membership in the Post–World War II Era: The United Furniture Workers of America, 1939–1982," *American Journal of Sociology 91* (March 1986): 1112–1153.

Cose, Ellis. "Are Quotas Really the Problem?" *Time*, June 24, 1991, p. 70.

Coser, Lewis. *Masters of Sociological Thought.* New York: Harcourt Brace Jovanovich, 1977.

Cowgill, Donald. "Aging and Modernization: A Revision of the Theory," in J. Gubrium, ed., *Late Life Communities and Environmental Policy.* Springfield, IL: Charles C. Thomas, 1974.

Cowgill, Donald, and Lowell Holmes. *Aging and Modernization.* New York: Appleton-Century-Crofts, 1972.

Coyne, William J. "Pro: Should the House-Passed Wage Proposal Be Enacted?" *Congressional Digest 68(5)* (May 1989): 154, 156.

Crane, Jonathan. "The Epidemic Theory of Ghettos and Neighborhood Effects on Dropping Out and Teenage Childbearing," *American Journal of Sociology 96* (March 1991): 1226–1259.

Crary, David. "Bible Belt Leads U.S. in Divorces," Associated Press, November 12, 1999.

Cumming, E., and W. Henry. *Growing Old: The Process of Disengagement.* New York: Basic Books, 1961.

Current Population Reports (see U.S. Bureau of the Census, *Current Population Reports).*

Currie, Elliott. *Confronting Crime: An American Challenge.* New York: Pantheon Books, 1985.

Currie, Elliott, and Jerome H. Skolnick. *America's Problems: Social Issues and Public Policy.* Glenview, IL: Scott, Foresman/Little, Brown, 1988.

Cuzzort, R. P., and E. W. King. *20th Century Social Thought*, 3rd ed. New York: Holt, Rinehart and Winston. 1980.

Dahrendorf, Raif. *Class and Class Conflict in Industrial Society.* Palo Alto, CA: Stanford University Press, 1951.

Davis, Karen. "Equal Treatment and Unequal Benefits: The Medicare Program," *Milbank Memorial Fund Quarterly 53*(4) (1975): 449–458.

Davis, Kingsley. "Extreme Social Isolation of a Child," *American Journal of Sociology 45* (1940): 554–565.

Davis, Kingsley. "Final Note on a Case of Extreme Isolation," *American Journal of Sociology 50* (1947): 432–437.

Davis, Kingsley. "The First Cities: How and Why Did They Arise?" in K. Davis, ed., *Cities: Their Origin, Growth, and Human Impact.* San Francisco: W. H. Freeman, 1973.

Davis, Kingsley, and Wilbert E. Moore. "Some Principles of Stratification," *American Sociological Review 10* (April 1945): 242–249.

Davis, Wayne H. "Overpopulated America," *New Republic*, January 10, 1970, pp. 13–15.

DeJong, G. F. and A. B. Madamba. "A Double Disadvantage? Minority Group, Immigrant Status, and Underemployment in the United States," *Social Science Quarterly*, 82, no. 1 (2001):117–130.

DeLamarter, Richard Thomas. *Big Blue: IBM's Use and Abuse of Power.* New York: Dodd, Mead, 1986.

Demo, David H., and Alan C. Acock. "The Impact of Divorce on Children," *Journal of Marriage and the Family 50* (August 1988): 619–648.

Dennis, Richard J. "Bill Bennett Won't You Please Come Home," *New Perspectives Quarterly* (Winter 1991): 69.

Denton, John A. *Medical Sociology.* Boston: Houghton Mifflin, 1978.

Dentzer, Susan, and Tom Hughes. "Going After the Rich," *U.S. News and World Report*, August 19, 1990, pp. 49–50.

Diamond, Milton. "Sexual Identity, Monozygotic Twins Reared in Discordant Sex Roles and a BBC Follow-up," *Archives of Sexual Behavior 11*(2) (April 1982): 181–186.

Dinitz, Simon. "Progress, Crime, and the Folk Ethic," *Criminology 11* (May 1973): 3–21.

Dionne, E. J., Jr. "Loss of Faith in Egalitarianism Alters U.S. Social Vision," *Washington Post*, April 30, 1990, p. 1.

Dobson, James C. *Attorney General's Commission on Pornography, Final Report.* Washington, DC: U.S. Government Printing Office, June 1986, pp. 71–87.

Dollard, John, Neal E. Miller, Leonard W. Doob, O. H. Mowrer, and Robert R. Sears. *Frustration and Aggression.* New Haven, CT: Yale University Press, 1939.

Domhoff, G. William. *The Higher Circles: The Governing Class in America.* New York: Vintage (Random House), 1971.

Domhoff, G. William. *The Power Elite and the State: How Policy Is Made in America.* Hawthorne, NY: Aldine de Gruyter, 1990.

Domhoff, G. William. *The Powers That Be: Process of Ruling Class Domination in America.* New York: Vintage (Random House), 1979.

Domhoff, G. William. *Who Rules America Now? A View for the Eighties.* Englewood Cliffs, NJ: Prentice-Hall, 1983.

Dority, Barbara. "Feminist Moralism, 'Pornography,' and Censorship," *The Humanist* (November/December 1989): 8–9, 46.

Douglas, Richard L. "Domestic Neglect and Abuse of the Elderly: Implications for Research and Service," *Family Relations 32* (July 1983): 395–402.

Dowd, James. "Aging as Exchange: A Preface to Theory," *Journal of Gerontology 30* (September 1975): 584–594.

Dowd, James. *Stratification Among the Aged.* Monterey, CA: Brooks/Cole, 1980.

Dowie, Mark. "Pinto Madness," *Mother Jones, 2*(8) (September–October 1977): 43–47.

Dowse, Robert E., and John A. Hughes. *Political Sociology.* New York: Wiley, 1972.

D'Souza, Dinesh. "Illiberal Education," *Atlantic Monthly,* March, 1991a, pp. 51–79.

D'Souza, Dinesh. "In the Name of Academic Freedom, Colleges Should Back Professors Against Students' Demands for 'Correct' Views," *The Chronicles of Higher Education* 37 (April 24, 1991b): B1, B3.

Duberman, Lucile. *Social Inequality: Class and Caste in America.* Philadelphia: Lippincott, 1976.

Dupreel, Eugene G. "Demographic Change and Progress," in Johannes Overbeek, ed., *The Evolution of Population Theory.* Westport, CT: Greenwood Press, 1977, pp. 80–85. (Originally published in 1922)

Durkheim, Emile. *The Division of Labor in Society.* New York: Free Press, 1933. (Originally published in 1893)

Durkheim, Emile. *The Elementary Forms of the Religious Life.* New York: Free Press, 1926. (Originally published in 1915)

Eccles, Jacquelynne. "Sex Differences in Math Achievement and Course Enrollment." Paper presented at the annual meeting of the American Educational Research Association, New York, March, 1982.

Ehrenreich, Barbara. "A Conservative Tax Proposal," *Time,* August 27, 1990, p. 70.

Ehrenreich, Barbara. *Nickel and Dimed: On (Not) Getting By in America.* New York: Metropolitan Books, 2001.

Ehrenreich, B., and D. English. *For Her Own Good: 150 Years of the Experts' Advice to Women.* Garden City, NY: Anchor Books, 1979.

Ehrlich, Elizabeth. "The Mommy Track," in Kurt Finsterbusch, ed., *Annual Editions.* Guilford, CT: Dushkin, 1991, pp. 83–85.

Eitzen, Stanley, and Maxine Baca Zinn. *In Conflict and Order: Understanding Society,* 5th ed. Boston: Allyn and Bacon, 1991.

Eitzen, D. Stanley, and Maxine Baca Zinn. *Social Problems,* 4th ed. Needham Heights, MA: Allyn and Bacon, 1989.

Ekman, R., et al. "Bicycle-Related Injuries Among the Elderly—A New Epidemic?" *Public Health* 115, no. 1 (January 2001): 38–43. Karolinska Institutet, Department of Public Health Sciences, Division of Social Medicine, Stockholm, Sweden.

Elder, Glenn. *Children of the Great Depression.* Chicago: University of Chicago Press, 1974.

Elkin, Frederick, and Gerald Handel. *The Child and Society: The Process of Socialization,* 5th ed. New York: Random House, 1989.

Encyclopedia of Associations, Vol. 1, 25th ed., "National Organizations of the U.S." Detroit: Gale Research, 1991.

Engels, Friedrich. *The Origin of the Family, Private Property and the State.* Chicago: Charles H. Ken, 1902.

Erikson, Kai J. *Everything in Its Path: Destruction of Community in the Buffalo Creek Flood.* New York: Simon and Schuster, 1976.

Eshleman, J. Ross. *The Family: An Introduction,* 6th ed. Boston: Allyn and Bacon, 1991.

Etzioni, Amitai. *A Sociological Reader on Complex Organizations,* 3rd ed. New York: Holt, Rinehart and Winston, 1980.

Etzioni-Halevy, Eva. *Social Change.* Boston: Routledge and Kegan Paul, 1981.

Facts on File. World News Digest with Index 46 (August 1, 1986): 622C2.

Falco, Mathea. *Winning the Drug War: A National Strategy.* New York: Priority Press, 1989.

Farley, Lin. *Sexual Shakedown.* New York: Warner Books, 1978.

Farmer, Rod. "The School Prayer Issue," *Education,* Spring, 1984, pp. 248–249.

Feagin, Joe R. *Racial and Ethnic Relations.* Englewood Cliffs, NJ: Prentice-Hall, 2nd ed., 1984; 3rd ed., 1989.

Feagin, Joe R., and Robert Parke. *Building American Cities: The Urban Real Estate Game,* 2nd ed. Englewood Cliffs, NJ: Prentice Hall, 1990.

Fein, David J. "Married and Poor: Basic Characteristics of Economically Disadvantaged Couples in the U.S." ABT Associates (2004). www.mdrc.org/publications/393/workpaper.html.

Feldman-Summers, Shirley, and Gayle C. Palmer. "Rape as Viewed by Judges, Prosecutors and Police Officers," *Criminal Justice and Behavior* 7 (March 1980): 19–40.

Ferraro, Kenneth F., "Health Beliefs and Proscriptions on Public Smoking," *Sociological Inquiry 60* (August 1990): 244–255.

Fierman, Jaclyn. "Why Women Still Don't Hit the Top," *Fortune 122* (July 30, 1990): 40.

Finkelstein, E. A., I. C. Fiebelkorn, and G. Wang. "National Medical Spending Attributable to Overweight and Obesity: How Much, and Whoís Paying?" *Health Affairs* W3 (2003): 219–226.

Fine, Gary Alan. "Small Groups and Culture Creation: The Ideoculture of Little League Baseball Teams," *American Sociological Review 44* (October 1979): 733–745.

Finsterbusch, Kurt, and Annabelle Bender Mars. *Social Research for Policy Decisions.* Belmont, CA: Wadsworth, 1980.

Finsterbusch, Kurt, and George McKenna, eds. *Taking Sides: Clashing Views on Controversial Social Issues*, 4th ed. Guilford, CT: Dushkin Publishing, 1986; 6th ed., 1990.

FitzGerald, Kathleen Whalen. *Alcoholism: The Genetic Inheritance.* New York: Doubleday, 1988.

Florida, Richard, and Martin Kenney. "Transplanted Organizations: The Transfer of Japanese Industrial Organization to the U.S." *American Sociological Review 56* (June 1991): 381–398.

Foster, George M. "Relationships Between Theoretical and Applied Anthropology," in Alvin W. Gouldner and S. M. Miller, eds., *Applied Sociology: Opportunities and Problems.* New York: Free Press, 1965.

Fox, Karen D., and Sharon Y. Nichols. "The Time Crunch: Wife's Employment and Family Work," *Journal of Family Issues 4* (March 1983): 61–82.

Frankel, Marc T., and Rollins, Howard A., Jr. "Does Mother Know Best? Mothers and Fathers Interacting with Preschool Sons and Daughters," *Developmental Psychology 19* (1983): 694–702.

Freeman, Harold. *Toward Socialism in America.* Cambridge, MA: Schenkman, 1979.

Freeman, Howard E., and Peter H. Rossi. "Furthering the Applied Side of Sociology," *American Sociological Review 49* (1984): 571–580.

Frenzel, Bill. "Con: Should the House-Passed Wage Proposal Be Enacted?" *Congressional Digest 68*(5) (May 1989): 151,153.

Fromm, Erich. *The Sane Society.* New York: Holt, Rinehart and Winston, 1965.

Fullerton, Howard N., Jr. "Labor Force Participation: 75 Years of Change, 1950–98 and 1998–2025," *Monthly Labor Review* (December 1999).

Galbraith, John Kenneth. "Why Arms Makers Must Be Checked," *Scholastic Update*, April 29, 1983, pp. 19–20.

Gallup, George Jr., and Frank Newport. "Major U.S. Cities Seen as Unsafe Places to Live and Work," *The Gallup Poll Monthly 300* (September 1990): 40–41.

The Gallop Poll Monthly, June, 1990, p. 36; January, 1991, p. 52.

Gamson, William A. *The Strategy of Social Protest.* Homewood, IL: Dorsey Press, 1975.

Gans, Herbert J. *The Levittowners: Ways of Life and Politics in a New Suburb.* New York: Random House, 1967.

Gans, Herbert J. *More Equality.* New York: Pantheon Books, 1972.

Gans, Herbert J. *The Urban Villagers.* New York: Free Press, 1962.

Garcia, Robert. "Pro: Should the House-Passed Wage Proposal Be Enacted?" *Congressional Digest 68*(5) (May 1989): 152, 154.

Gardner, David Pierpont. "If We Stand, They Will Deliver," *New Perspectives Quarterly* 7 (Fall 1990): 4–6.

Gelfand, Donald E. *Aging: The Ethnic Factor.* Boston: Little, Brown, 1982.

George, Susan. *How the Other Half Dies: The Real Reasons for World Hunger.* Montclair, NJ: Allanheld, Osmun, 1977.

Gereffi, Gary. *The Pharmaceutical Industry and Dependency in the Third World.* Princeton, NJ: Princeton University Press, 1983.

Glass, T. *The 1992 Study of the American School Superintendency: Americaís Education Leaders in a Time of Reform.* Arlington, VA: American Association of School Administrators, 1992.

Glassner, Barry, and Bruce Berg. "How Jews Avoid Alcohol Problems," *American Sociological Review 45* (August 1980): 647–664.

Glazer, Nathan, and Daniel P. Moynihan. *Beyond the Melting Pot*, 2nd ed. Cambridge, MA: Massachusetts Institute of Technology Press, 1970.

Glazer, Sarah. "Getting a Grip on Influence Peddling," *Congressional Quarterly's Editorial Research Reports 22* (December 15,1989): 697–711.

Glazer, Sarah. "Joint Custody: Is it Good for the Children?" *Congressional Quarterly's Editorial Research Reports 1* (February 3, 1989): 58–71.

Goering, John M. "The Emergence of Ethnic Interests: A Case of Serendipity," *Social Forces 48* (March 1971): 379–384.

Goetz, Harriet. "Euthanasia Should Be Considered for Terminally Ill Patients," in *Opposing Viewpoints Sources: Death/Dying, 1990 Annual.* San Diego: Greenhaven Press, 1990, pp. 1–3. (Originally published by Harriet Goetz as "Euthanasia: A Bedside View," *The Christian Century* [June 21, 1989])

Goffman, Erving. *Asylums: Essays on the Situation of Mental Patients and Other Inmates.* Garden City, NY: Anchor/ Doubleday, 1961.

Goffman, Erving. *Encounters.* Indianapolis, IN: Bobbs-Merrill, 1961.

Goffman, Erving. *Interaction Ritual: Essays on Face-to-Face Behavior.* Garden City, NY: Doubleday/Anchor, 1967.

Goffman, Erving. *The Presentation of Self in Everyday Life.* Garden City, NY: Doubleday/Anchor, 1959.

Goffman, Ethan. "The Income Gap and Its Causes," *Dissent*, Winter, 1990, p. 8.

Gold, Dolores, Gail Crombie, and Sally Noble. "Relations between teachers' judgments of girls' and boys' compliance and intellectual competence," *Sex Roles 16* (1987): 351–358.

Gold, Mark S. "Legalize Drugs: Just Say Never," *National Review*, April 1, 1990, pp. 42–43.

Goldberg, S., and M. Lewis. "Play Behavior in the Year-Old Infant: Early Sex Differences," *Child Development 40* (1969): 21–30.

Goldman, Kathryn L. "Stress Management: The Importance of Organizational Context," *Clinical Sociology Review 2* (1984): 133–136.

Goodin, Robert E. *Manipulatory Politics.* New Haven, CT: Yale University Press, 1980.

Gordon, Milton. *Assimilation in American Life.* New York: Oxford University Press, 1964.

Gordon, Milton M. *Human Nature, Class and Ethnicity.* New York: Oxford University Press, 1978.

Gordon, Richard, Katherine Gordon, and Max Gunther. *The Split Level Trap.* New York: Bernard Geis Associates, 1961.

Gouldner, Alvin W. *Patterns of Industrial Bureaucracy.* New York: Free Press, 1954.

Gove, Walter R., and Michael R. Geerken. "The Effect of Children and Employment on the Mental Health of Married Men and Women," *Social Forces 56* (February 1977): 66–76.

Grant, Linda, Kathryn B. Ward, and Xue Lan Rong. "Is There an Association Between Gender and Methods in Sociological Research?" *American Sociological Research 52* (December 1987): 856–862.

Greeley, Andrew. *Religious Change in America.* Cambridge, MA: Harvard University Press, 1989.

Greven, Phillip. *Spare the Child: The Religious Roots of Punishment and the Psychological Impact of Child Abuse.* New York: Knopf, 1991.

Griffin, Larry J., Michael E. Wallace, and Beth A. Rubin. "Capitalist Resistance to the Organization of Labor Before the New Deal: Why? How? Success?" *American Sociological Review 51* (April 1986): 147–167.

Grossman, Richard. *The Other Medicines: An Invitation to Understanding and Using Them for Health and Healing.* Garden City, NY: Doubleday, 1985.

Grzelkowski, Kathryn, and Jim Mitchell. "Applied Curriculum Can Enhance Liberal Arts Learning," *ASA Footnotes, 13*(9) (December 1985): 5–6.

Guillemin, Jeanne Harley, and Lynda Lythe Holmstrom. "The Business of Childbirth," *Society 23* (July/August 1986): 48–53.

Guterman, Stanley S., ed. *Black Psyche: Modal Personality Patterns of Black Americans.* Berkeley, CA: Glendessary Press, 1972, p. 87.

Hakuta, Kenji. *Mirror of Language: The Debate on Bilingualism.* New York: Basic Books, 1986.

Hall, Douglas T. "Promoting Work/Family Balance: An Organization- Change Approach," *Organizational Dynamics,* Winter, 1990, pp. 5–18.

Hall, Richard H. *Organizations: Structures, Processes, and Outcomes,* 4th ed. Englewood Cliffs, NJ: Prentice Hall, 1987.

Hall, Thomas D. "Incorporation in the World System: Toward a Critique," *American Sociological Review 51* (June 1986): 390–402.

Hampton, David R., Charles E. Summer, and Ross A. Webber. *Organizational Behavior and the Practice of Management,* 4th ed. Glenview, IL: Scott, Foresman, 1982.

Harris, Chauncy, and Edward L. Ullman. "The Nature of Cities," *Annals of the American Academy of Political and Social Science 242* (November 1945): 7–17.

Harris, Diana K., and William E. Cole. *Sociology of Aging.* Boston: Houghton Mifflin, 1980.

Harter, Carl L. "The 'Good Times' Cohort of the 1930s: Sometimes Less Means More (and More Means Less)," in Scott W. Menard and Elizabeth W. Moen, *Perspectives on Population: An Introduction to Concepts and Issues.* New York: Oxford University Press, 1987, pp. 372–376.

Hartmann, Heidi. "Capitalism, Patriarchy, and Job Segregation by Sex," in Nona Glazer and Helen Youngelson Waehaer, eds., *Woman in a Man-Made World,* 2nd ed. Chicago: Rand McNally, 1977, pp. 71–84.

Haseltine, Robert W. "The Minimum Wage: Help or Hindrance?" *USA Today Magazine,* July, 1989, p. 31.

Haugen, Emar. *Blessings of Babel: Bilingualism and Language Planning.* Berlin: Mouton de Gruyter, 1987.

Hayes, C. *The Ape in Our House.* New York: Harper and Row, 1951.

Healy, Jane M. *Endangered Minds: Why Our Children Don't Think.* New York: Simon and Schuster, 1990.

Heer, David M. *Society and Population.* Englewood Cliffs, NJ: Prentice-Hall, 1975.

Hefley, Joel. "Con: Should the House-Passed Wage Proposal Be Enacted?" *Congressional Digest 68*(5) (May 1989): 159.

Heilbroner, Robert L. *The Making of Economic Society.* Englewood Cliffs, NJ: Prentice-Hall, 1980.

Henry, William A. "Upside Down in the Groves of Academe," *Time,* April 1, 1991, pp. 66–69.

Henry, William A. "Beyond the Melting Pot," *Time,* April 9, 1990, p. 28.

Henslin, James M. *Social Problems,* 2nd ed. Englewood Cliffs, NJ: Prentice Hall, 1990.

Heritage, John, and David Greatbatch. "Generating Applause: A Study of Rhetoric and Response at Party Political Conferences," *American Journal of Sociology 92* (July 1986): 110–157.

Hewlett, Sylvia Ann. *A Lesser Life: The Myth of Women's Liberation in America.* New York: William Morrow, 1986.

Heyzer, Noeleen. "Asian Women Wage-Earners: Their Situation and Possibilities for Donor Intervention," *World Development 17*(7) (1989): 1109–1123.

Hill, James O., and Frederick L. Trowbridge. "Childhood Obesity: Future Directions and Research Priorities," *Pediatrics* (1998 supplement): 571.

Hine, Virginia H. "Dying at Home: Can Families Cope?" *Omega 10* (1979–1980).

Hobbs, Daniel F., Jr. "Parenthood as Crisis: A Third Study," *Journal of Marriage and the Family 27* (August 1965): 367–372.

Hoffman, Lois Wladis. "The Changing Genetics/Socialization Balance," *Journal of Social Issues 41* (Spring 1985): 127–148.

Homans, George C. *Social Behavior: Its Elementary Forms.* New York: Harcourt, Brace and World, 1961; 2nd ed., Harcourt Brace Jovanovich, 1974.

Horgan, John. "Test Negative: A Look at the 'Evidence' Justifying Illicit-Drug Tests," *Scientific American 262* (March 1990a): 18–19.

Horgan, John. "Your Analysis Is Faulty," *The New Republic,* April 2, 1990b, pp. 22–24.

Howard, Ebenezer. *Garden Cities of Tomorrow.* London: Faber and Faber, 1902.

Howard, Robert. "Brave New Workplace," in Jerome H. Skolnick and Elliott Currie, eds., *Crisis in American Institutions,* 7th ed. Glenview, IL: Scott, Foresman, 1988.

Hoyer, Steny H. "Con: Should President Bush's Minimum Wage Proposals Be Adopted?" *Congressional Digest 68*(5) (May 1989): 145, 147.

Hoyt, Homer. *The Structure of Residential Neighborhoods in American Cities.* Washington, DC: Federal Housing Administration, 1939.

Humphrey, Craig, R., and Frederick R. Buttel. *Environment, Energy and Society.* Belmont, CA: Wadsworth, 1982.

Hunt, J. G., and L. L. Hunt: "Race, Daughters and Father-Loss: Does Absence Make the Girl Grow Stronger?" *Social Problems 25* (February 1977a): 90–102.

Hunt, Janet G., and Larry C. Hunt. "Racial Inequality and Self-image: Identity Maintenance as Identity Confusion," *Sociology and Social Research 61* (July 1977b): 539–559.

"Immigrant Children Exceed Expectations. Studies Show That Immigrant Children Are Assimilating," *Immigration Policy Report (2001).* www.ailf.org/ipc/policy_reports_2001_childre.asp.

Information Please Almanac Atlas & Yearbook, 1991, 44th ed. Boston: Houghton Mifflin, 1991.

Jackman, Mary R., and Robert W. Jackman. *Class Awareness in the United States.* Berkeley: University of California Press, 1983.

Jacob, John E. "Racism Denies Minorities Equal Opportunities," in Carol Wekesser, ed., *Social Justice: Opposing Viewpoints.* San Diego: Greenhaven Press, 1990, pp. 107–114.

Jaffee, David. "Gender Inequality in Workplace Autonomy and Authority," *Social Science Quarterly 70*(2) (June 1989): 375–388.

Jardim, Anne, and Margaret Hennig. "The Last Barrier: Breaking into the Boys' Club at the Top," *Working Woman 15* (November 1990): 130.

Jellinek, E. M. *The Disease Concept of Alcoholism.* New Haven, CT: Yale University Press, 1960.

Jencks, Christopher. "Genes and Crime," *The New York Review,* February 12, 1987, pp. 33–41.

Jencks, Christopher. *Who Gets Ahead? The Determinant of Economic Success in America.* New York: Basic Books, 1979.

Johnson, Doyle Paul. "Using Sociology to Analyze Human and Organizational Problems: A Humanistic Perspective to Link Theory and Practice," *Clinical Sociology Review 4* (1986): 57–71.

Johnson, James A., Harold W. Collins, Victor L. Dupuis, and John H. Johansen. *Introduction to the Foundations of American Education,* 6th ed. Boston: Allyn and Bacon, 1985.

Johnstone, D. Bruce. *Sharing the Costs of Higher Education.* New York: College Board Publications, 1986.

Jones, Charles O. *An Introduction to the Study of Public Policy,* 3rd ed. Monterey, CA: Brooks/Cole, 1984.

Jones, L. Y. *Great Expectations: America and the Baby Boom Generation.* New York: Coward, McCann & Geohegan, 1980.

Kagan, Sharon Lynn, and James W. Newton. "For-Profit and Nonprofit Child Care: Similarities and Differences," *Young Children,* November, 1989, pp. 4–10.

Kanter, Rosabeth Moss. *The Change Masters.* New York: Simon and Schuster, 1983.

Karen, David. "Toward a Political-Organizational Model of Gatekeeping: The Case of Elite Colleges," *Sociology of Education 63* (October 1990): 227–239.

Karier, Clarence J. "Testing for Order and Control in the Corporate Liberal State," in NJ Block and Gerald Dworkin, eds., *The I.Q. Controversy: Critical Readings.* New York: Pantheon, 1976, pp. 339–373.

Kart, Cary S. *The Realities of Aging: An Introduction to Gerontology.* Boston: Allyn and Bacon, 1981.

Kasarda, John. "The Changing Occupational Structure of the American Metropolis," in Barry Schwartz, ed., *The Changing Face of the Suburbs.* Chicago: University of Chicago Press, 1976, pp. 113–136.

Kasarda, John D. "The Jobs-Skills Mismatch," *New Perspectives Quarterly* 7 (Fall 1990): 34–37.

Kass, Leon R. "Active Euthanasia Is Inhumane," in *Opposing Viewpoints Sources: Death/Dying, 1990 Annual.* San Diego: Greenhaven Press, 1990, pp. 1–3. (Originally published as "Neither for Love nor Money: Why Doctors Must Not Kill." *The Public Interest 94* (Winter 1989): 25–46.

Kathan, Boardman W. "Prayer and the Public Schools: The Issue in Historical Perspective and Implications for Religious Education Today," *Religious Education 84*(2) (Spring 1989): 232–248.

Keister, Lisa A. "Religion and Wealth: The Role of Religious Affiliation and Participation in Early Adult Asset Accumulation," *Social Forces* 82, no. 1 (September 2003): 175–207.

Kellogg, W. N., and L. A. Kellogg. *The Ape and the Child.* New York: McGraw-Hill, 1933.

Kelly, Delos H. *Deviant Behavior: Readings in the Sociology of Deviance.* New York: St. Martin's Press, 1979.

Kennedy, Robert E., Jr. *Life Choices: Applying Sociology.* New York: Holt, Rinehart and Winston, 1986.

Kenney, Martin, and Richard Florida. "Beyond Mass Production: Production and the Labor Process in Japan," *Politics and Society 16* (1988): 121–158.

King, Rufus. "A Worthless Crusade," *Newsweek*, January 1, 1990, pp. 4–5.

Kinsley, Michael. "Stat Wars," *The New Republic*, March 26, 1990, p. 4.

Kitano, Harry H. L. *Race Relations*, 4th ed. Englewood Cliffs, NJ: Prentice-Hall, 1991.

Kitsuse, John I. "Societal Reaction to Deviant Behavior: Problems of Theory and Method," *Social Problems 9* (Winter 1962): 247–256.

Klitgaard, Robert. *Choosing Elites: Selecting the "Best and Brightest" at Top Universities and Elsewhere.* New York: Basic Books, 1985.

Konos, Susan. "For-Profit Programs in the Child Care Delivery System: Bane or Benefit?" *Child and Youth Care Quarterly 19* (Winter 1990): 211–213.

Kozol, Jonathan. "Distancing the Homeless," *The Yale Review*, Winter, 1988, p. 158.

Kraut, Robert E. "Deterrent and Definitional Influences on Shoplifting," *Social Problems 23* (February 1976): 358–368.

Ksir, C., Hart, C., Ray, O., *Drugs, Society, and Human Behavior.* 12th. Edition. McGraw Hill, Boston. 2007

Kupfer, Andrew. "Is Drug Testing Good or Bad?" *Fortune 118* (December 19, 1988): 133–140.

LaBeff, Emily E., Robert E. Clark, Valerie J. Haines, and George M. Dickhoff. "Situational Ethics and College Student Cheating," *Sociological Inquiry 60* (May 1990): 190–198.

Lamanna, Mary Ann, and Agnes Riedmann. *Marriages and Families: Making Choices and Facing Change*, 4th ed. Belmont, CA: Wadsworth, 1991.

Lamb, Michael E., Ann M. Frodi, Carl Philip Hwang, Majt Frodi, and Jamie Steinberg. "Mother- and Father-Infant Interaction Involving Play and Holding in Traditional and Nontraditional Swedish Families," *Developmental Psychology 18* (1982): 215–221.

Lambert, Wallace E., and Donald M. Taylor. *Coping with Cultural and Racial Diversity in Urban America.* New York: Praeger, 1990.

Landers, Robert K. "Benefits and Dangers of Opinion Polls," *Congressional Quarterly's Editorial Research Reports*, October, 1988, pp. 454–463.

Landers, Robert K. "Is Affirmative Action Still the Answer?" *Congressional Quarterly's Editorial Research Reports*, April, 1989, pp. 198–211.

Landers, Robert K. "Right to Die: Medical, Legal & Moral Issues," *Congressional Quarterly's Editorial Research Reports*, September 28, 1990, pp. 551–567.

Landers, Robert K. "Why Homeless Need More Than Shelter," *Congressional Quarterly's Editorial Research Reports*, March 30, 1990, pp. 173–187.

Lane, Charles. "To Help or Not to Help," *Newsweek*, September 2, 1991, pp. 54–56.

Lansing, Marjorie. "The Gender Gap in American Politics," in Lynne B. Igletzin and Ruth Ross, eds., *Women in the World, 1975–1985.* Santa Barbara, CA: ABC-CLIO, 1986.

Lapinski, Susan. "Now, They Have a Dream," *Parade Magazine*, September 7, 1986, pp. 8–11.

Larson, Calvin J. "Applied/Practical Sociological Theory: Problems and Issues," *Sociological Practice Review 1*(1) (June 1990): 8–18.

Lauer, Robert H., and Warren H. Handel. *Social Psychology: The Theory and Application of Symbolic Interactionism*, 2nd ed. Englewood Cliffs, NJ: Prentice-Hall, 1983.

Le Bon, Gustave. *The Crowd: A Study of the Popular Mind.* London: Ernest Benn, 1895; 2nd ed., Dunwoody, GA: Norman S. Berg, 1968.

Leavitt, Fred. Research Methods for Behavioral Scientists. Dubuque, IA: Brown, 1991.

Leavitt, Robin Lynn, and Martha Bauman Power. "Emotional Socialization in the Postmodern Era: Children in Day Care," *Social Psychology Quarterly 52* (1989): 35–43.

Leavitt, Ruby R. "Women of Other Cultures," in Vivian Gornick and Barbara K. Moran, eds., *Women in Sexist Society: Studies in Power and Powerlessness.* New York: New American Library, 1971.

Lederer, Laura, ed. *Take Back the Night: Women on Pornography.* New York: Morrow, 1980.

Lee, Alfred McClung. *Sociology for People: Toward a Caring Profession.* Syracuse, NY: Syracuse University Press, 1988.

Lee, Gary R. "Marriage and Morale in Later Life," *Journal of Marriage and the Family 40* (February 1978): 131–139.

Lee, Valerie E., and Anthony S. Bryk. "A Multilevel Model of the Social Distribution of High School Achievement," *Sociology of Education 62* (July 1989): 172–192.

LeMasters, E. E. "Parenthood as Crisis," *Marriage and Family Living 19* (November 1957): 352–355.

Lemert, Edwin. *Social Pathology.* New York: McGraw-Hill, 1951.

Lemon, B. L., V. L. Bengtson, and J. A. Peterson. "An Exploration of Activity Theory of Aging: Activity Types and Life Satisfaction Among In-Movers to a Retirement Community," *Journal of Gerontology* 27 (1977): 511–523.

Lengermann, Patricia M. "The Founding of the American Sociological Review: The Anatomy of a Rebellion," *American Sociological Review 44* (April 1979): 185–198.

Lengermann, Patricia Madoo, and Jill Niebrugge-Brantley. "Contemporary Feminist Theory," in George Ritzer, ed., *Contemporary Sociological Theory.* New York: Knopf, 1988, pp. 282–325.

Lenski, Gerhard. "Hungary in April," *Society 26* (January/February 1989): 11–12.

Lenski, Gerhard. *Power and Privilege.* New York: McGraw-Hill, 1966.

Lenski, Gerhard. *The Religious Factor.* New York: Doubleday, 1961.

Levison, Andrew. *The Working-Class Majority.* New York: Coward, McCann and Geohegan, 1974.

Lieberson, Stanley, and Arnold R. Silverman. "The Precipitants and Underlying Conditions of Race Riots," *American Sociological Review 30* (December 1965): 887–898.

Laine, Christine. "Should Physicians Discourage Patients from Playing the Sick Role?" *CMAJ* 157 (1997): 393ñ394

Lieberson, Stanley, and Mary C. Waters. *From Many Strands: Ethnic and Racial Groups in Contemporary America.* New York: Russell Sage Foundation, 1988.

Lin, Nan, Walter M. Ensel, and John C. Vaughn. "Social Resources and Strength of Ties: Structural Factors in Occupational Status Attainment," *American Sociological Review 46* (August 1981): 393–405.

Ling, Peter J. *America and the Automobile: Technology, Reform and Social Change, 1893–1923.* Manchester, England: Manchester University Press, 1990.

Lipset, S. M., and Reinhard Bendix. *Social Mobility in Industrial Society.* Berkeley: University of California Press, 1967.

Long, Theodore E., and Jeffrey K. Hadden. "A Reconception of Socialization," *Sociological Theory 3* (Spring 1985): 39–49.

Lopata, Helena Z. *Polish Americans: Status Competition in an Ethnic Community.* Englewood Cliffs, NJ: Prentice-Hall, 1976.

Lueptow, Lloyd B. "Social Structure, Social Change and Parental Influence in Adolescent Sex-Role Socialization: 1964–1975," *Journal of Marriage and the Family 42* (June 1980): 93–104.

Lundberg, George. *Can Science Save Us?* 2nd ed. New York: David McKay, 1961.

Lupart, Judy, and Elizabeth Cannon. "Computers and Career Choices: Gender Differences in Grades 7 and 10 Students," *Gender, Technology and Development* (May–August 2002): 233–248.

Lynd, Robert S., and Helen Merrell Lynd. *Middletown.* New York: Harcourt, Brace and World, 1929.

Lynd, Robert S., and Helen Merrell Lynd. *Middletown in Transition.* New York: Harcourt, Brace and World, 1937.

Maccoby, Eleanor E. "Gender As a Social Category," *Developmental Psychology 24* (1988): 755–765.

Maccoby, Eleanor and Carol N. Jacklin. *The Psychology of Sex Differences.* Stanford, CA: Stanford University Press, 1974.

Maccoby, Michael. "The Changing Corporate Character," in Gordon J. DiRenzo, ed., *We, The People: American Character and Social Change.* Westport, CT: Greenwood Press, 1977.

Macklin, Eleanor D. "Nonmarital Heterosexual Cohabitation: An Overview," in Eleanor D. Macklin and Roger H. Rubin, eds., *Contemporary Families and Alternative Lifestyles.* Beverly Hills, CA: Sage Publications, 1983, pp. 49–74.

MacLeod, Jay. *Ain't No Makin' It: Aspirations and Attainment in a Low-income Neighborhood.* Boulder, CO: Westview Press, 1995.

Magner, Denise. "Piercing the 'Posturing and Taboo' of Debate on Campus Reforms. *The Chronicles of Higher Education 37* (April 10, 1991): A3.

Malinowski, Bronislaw. "Parenthood: The Basis of Social Structure," in V. F. Calverton and Samuel D. Schmalhausen, eds., *The New Generation.* New York: Macaulay, 1930.

Marcus, Warren Stewart. "Tracing the Bitter Roots of Personal Violation and Social Displacement: A Comparative Phenomenological Study of the Life Histories of Homeless Mothers and Their Dependent Children," *Dissertation Abstracts International, A: The Humanities and Social Sciences*, 2002, 63, 1, July, 137-A–138-A.

Markle, Gerald E., and Ronald J. Troyer. "Smoke Gets in Your Eyes: Cigarette Smoking as Deviant Behavior," *Social Problems 26* (June 1979): 611–625.

Marklein, Mary Beth. "Learning Despite Language Differences," *USA Today*, February 20, 1991, p. 9D.

Marsden, Peter V. "Core Discussion Networks of Americans," *American Sociological Review 52* (February 1987): 122–131.

Marshall, Ray, and Beth Paulin. "The Wages of Women's Work," *Society 22* (July–August 1985): 28–38.

Marshall, Victor W., and Judith Levy. "Aging and Dying," in Robert H. Binstock and Linda K. George, eds., *Handbook of Aging and the Social Sciences*, 3rd ed. New York: Academic Press, 1990, pp. 245–260.

Martin, Linda G., "The Graying of Japan," *Population Bulletin 44* (July 1989): (Washington, DC: Population Reference Bureau).

Marx, Karl. *Selected Writings in Sociology and Social Philosophy;* T. B. Bottomore, trans. New York: McGraw-Hill, 1964.

Marx, Karl, and Friedrich Engels. *Communist Manifesto.* Baltimore: Penguin Books, 1969. (Originally published in 1847)

Masters, William H., and Virginia E. Johnson. *Human Sexual Inadequacy.* Boston: Little, Brown, 1970.

Masters, William H., and Virginia E. Johnson. *Human Sexual Response.* Boston: Little, Brown, 1966.

Maxwell, Nan L. *Income Inequality in the United States: 1947–1985.* New York: Greenwood Press, 1990.

Maykovich, Minako K. *Medical Sociology.* Palo Alto, CA: Mayfield Publishing, 1980.

McIntyre, Robert S., Douglas P. Kelly, Michael P. Ettlinger, and Elizabeth A. Fray. *A Far Cry from Fair: CTJ's Guide to State Tax Reform,* Washington, DC: Citizens for Tax Justice, April, 1991.

McKinlay, John B., and Sonja M. McKinlay. "Medical Measures and the Decline of Mortality," in Peter Conrad and Rochelle Kern, eds., *The Sociology of Health and Illness: Critical Perspectives.* New York: St. Martin's Press, 1981, pp. 12–30.

McLachlan, James. *American Boarding Schools: A Historical Study.* New York: Charles Scribner's Sons, 1970.

McLanahan, Sara S., Annemette Sorensen, and Dorothy Watson. "Sex Differences in Poverty, 1950–1980," *Signs: Journal of Women in Culture and Society 15*(1) (1989): 102–122.

McNeely, D. L., and John L. Calen, eds. *Aging in Minority Groups.* Beverly Hills, CA: Sage Publications, 1983.

Mead, George Herbert. *Mind, Self and Society from the Standpoint of a Social Behaviorist.* Charles Morris, ed. Chicago: University of Chicago Press, 1934.

Mead, Margaret. *Sex and Temperament in Three Primitive Societies.* New York: Morrow, 1935.

Mechanic, David. *Medical Sociology,* 2nd ed. New York: Free Press, 1978.

Medvedev, Zhores A. "Aging and Longevity: New Approaches and New Perspectives," *Gerontologist 15* (1975): 196–201.

Medvedev, Zhores A. "Caucasus and Altay Longevity: A Biological or Social Problem?" *Gerontologist 14* (1974): 381–387.

Melville, Keith. *The Drug Crisis: Public Strategies for Breaking the Habit* (National Issues Forum Series). Dayton, OH: The Kettering Foundation and the Kendall/Hunt Publishing Company, 1989.

Melville, Keith. *The Environment at Risk: Responding to Growing Dangers* (National Issues Forum Series). Dayton, OH: The Kettering Foundation and the Kendall/Hunt Publishing Company, 1989.

Merton, Robert K. *Social Theory and Social Structure.* New York: Free Press, 1949; rev. eds., 1957 and 1968.

Meyers, Deborah, and Jennifer Yau. "U.S. Immigration Statistics in 2003," *Migration Policy Institute* (2004).

Michels, Robert. *Political Parties.* New York: Free Press, 1911.

Milgram, Stanley. "The Experience of Living in Cities," *Science 167* (March 13, 1970): 1461–1468.

Miller, Cynthia L. "Qualitative Differences Among Gender-Stereotyped Toys: Implications for Cognitive and Social Development in Girls and Boys," *Sex Roles 16* (1987): 473–487.

Mills, C. Wright. *The Power Elite.* New York: Oxford University Press, 1958.

Mills, C. Wright. *The Sociological Imagination.* New York: Oxford University Press, 1959.

Mills, Charles W. *White Collar: American Middle Classes.* New York: Oxford University Press, 1951.

Mirowsky, John. "Depression and Marital Power: An Equity Model," *American Journal of Sociology 91* (November 1985): 557–592.

Money, John. *Love and Love Sickness: The Science of Sex, Gender Difference, and Pair-Bonding.* Baltimore: Johns Hopkins University Press, 1980.

Monroe, Sylvester. "Does Affirmative Action Help or Hurt?" *Time,* May 27, 1991, pp. 22–23.

Moore, Jennifer. "Drug Testing and Corporate Responsibility: The 'Ought Implies Can' Argument," *Journal of Business Ethics 8* (1989): 270–287.

Morriss, Frank. "Euthanasia Is Never Justified," in *Death and Dying: Opposing Viewpoints.* San Diego: Greenhaven Press, 1987, pp. 146–149.

Moss, H. "Sex, Age and State as Determinants of Mother–Infant Interaction," *Merrill-Palmer Quarterly 13* (1967): 19–36.

Mostert, Noel. "Supership," in Jerome H. Skolnick and Elliott Currie, eds., *Crisis in American Institutions,* 3rd ed. Boston: Little, Brown, 1976, pp. 286–304.

Muehlenhard, Charlene L., and Melaney A. Linton. "Date Rape: Familiar Strangers," *Journal of Counseling Psychology 34* (1987): 186–196.

Mumford, Lewis. *The Transformation of Man.* New York: Collier, 1962.

Murdock, George P. *Social Structure.* New York: Macmillan, 1949.

Murdock, George P. "World Ethnographic Sample," *American Anthropologist 59* (August 1957): 664–687.

Muwakkil, Salim. "Schools in Transition," *The Washington Post Education Review,* August 5, 1990, p. 1.

National Advisory Commission on Civil Disorders. *Kerner Report.* New York: Bantam Books, 1968.

National Center for Health Statistics. "Annual Summary of Births, Marriages, Divorces, and Deaths: United States, 1990," *Monthly Vital Statistics Report 39*(13) (August 28, 1991): 4 (Public Health Service, Hyattsville, MD).

National Commission on Excellence in Education. *A Nation at Risk: The Imperative for Educational Reform.* Washington, DC: U.S. Government Printing Office, 1983.

National Opinion Research Center. *General Social Surveys, 1972–1982: Cumulative Codebook.* Chicago: National Opinion Research Center, 1982.

Navasky, Victor. "Body Invaders," *The Nation 250* (January 8, 1990): 39–40.

Nelson, Margaret K. *Negotiated Care: The Experience of Family Day Care Providers.* Philadelphia: Temple University Press, 1990.

Neubeck, Kenneth J. *Social Problems: A Critical Approach*, 3rd ed. New York: McGraw-Hill, 1991.

Newman, Oscar. *Defensible Space.* New York: Macmillan, 1972.

Newman, William M. *American Pluralism: A Study of Social Groups and Social Theory.* New York: Harper and Row, 1973.

Nicholson, David. "Schools in Transition," *The Washington Post Education Review*, August 5, 1990, p. 1.

Noel, Donald L. "A Theory of the Origin of Ethnic Stratification," in Norman R. Yetman and C. Hoy Steele, eds., *Majority and Minority: The Dynamics of Racial and Ethnic Relations.* Boston: Allyn and Bacon, 1975.

Novak, M. *The Rise of the Unmeltable Ethnics.* New York: Macmillan, 1972.

Novak, Michael. "White Ethnic," in Norman R. Yetman and C. Hoy Steele, eds., *Majority and Minority: The Dynamics of Racial and Ethnic Relations.* Boston: Allyn and Bacon, 1975.

Nuehring, Elane, and Gerald E. Markle. "Nicotine and Norms: The Reemergence of a Deviant Behavior," *Social Problems 21* (April 1974): 513–526.

Oakes, Jeannie. "Classroom Social Relationships: Exploring the Bowles and Gintis Hypothesis," *Sociology of Education 55* (October 1982): 197–212.

Oberschall, Anthony. *Social Conflict and Social Movements.* Englewood Cliffs, NJ: Prentice-Hall, 1973.

O'Donnell, Carol. "Major Theories of the Labour Market and Women's Place Within It," *Journal of Industrial Relations 26* (June 1984): 147–165.

Ogburn, William F. *Social Change.* New York: Viking, 1950.

Okin, Susan Joller. *Justice, Gender and the Family.* New York: Basic Books, 1989.

Olson, David H., and Hamilton I. McCubbin. *Families: What Makes Them Work.* Beverly Hills, CA: Sage Publications, 1983.

Orr, Lisa (ed.). *Censorship: Opposing Viewpoints.* San Diego, CA: Greenhaven Press, 1990.

Ortiz, Flora Ida. *Career Patterns in Education: Women, Men and Minorities in Public School Administration.* New York: Praeger, 1982.

Orum, Anthony M. *Introduction to Political Sociology: The Social Anatomy of the Body Politic.* Englewood Cliffs, NJ: Prentice-Hall, 1978.

Ouchi, William G. *Theory Z: How American Business Can Meet the Japanese Challenge.* Reading, MA: Addison-Wesley, 1981.

Ovadia, Seth Alan. "Urban Structure and Individual Outcomes: The Effects of Economic and Racial Segregation on the Black-White Gap in Employment Rates," *Dissertation Abstracts International, A: The Humanities and Social Sciences* 64, no. 6 (December 2003), 2270-A.

Parillo, Vincent N., John Stimson, and Ardyth Stimson. *Contemporary Social Problems*, 2nd ed. New York: Macmillan, 1989.

Park, Robert E., and Ernest W. Burgess. *Introduction to the Science of Sociology.* Chicago: University of Chicago Press, 1921.

Park, Robert E., Ernest W. Burgess, and Roderick D. McKenzie. *The City.* Chicago: University of Chicago Press, 1925.

Parsons, Talcott. "The School Class as Social System: Some of Its Functions in American Society," *Harvard Educational Review 29*(4) (1959): 297–318.

Parsons, Talcott. *The Social System.* Glencoe, IL: Free Press, 1951.

Parsons, Talcott, and Robert F. Bales. *Family, Socialization and Interaction Process.* New York: Free Press, 1955.

Parsons, Talcott, and Edward A. Shils, eds. *Toward a General Theory of Action.* New York: Harper and Row, 1951.

Pearce, Diana M. "The Feminization of Ghetto Poverty," *Society 21* (November–December 1983): 70–74.

Perrow, Charles. *Complex Organizations: A Critical Essay*, 3rd ed. New York: Random House, 1986.

Peters, John F. "Adolescents as Socialization Agents to Parents," *Adolescence 20* (Winter 1985): 921–933.

Peters, Thomas J., and Robert H. Waterman. *In Search of Excellence.* New York: Harper and Row, 1982.

Pettigrew, Thomas F. *A Profile of the Negro American.* Princeton, NJ: Van Nostrand, 1964.

Phillips, Deborah, Kathleen McCartney, and Sandra Scarr. "Child-Care Quality and Children's Social Development," *Developmental Psychology 23* (1987): 537–543.

Pifer, Alan, and Lydia Bronte. *Our Aging Society: Paradox and Promise.* New York: Norton, 1986.

Pillemer, Karl. "The Dangers of Dependency: New Findings on Domestic Violence Against the Elderly," *Social Problems 33* (December 1985): 146–158.

Pillemer, Karl, and David Finkelhor. "The Prevalence of Elder Abuse: A Random Sample Survey," *The Gerontologist 28* (1988): 51–57.

Pirenne, Henri. "Stages in the Social History of Capitalism," *American Historical Review 19* (July 1914): 494–515.

Piven, Frances Fox, and Richard A. Cloward. *Regulating the Poor: The Functions of Public Welfare.* New York: Vintage Books, 1971.

Piven, Frances Fox, and Richard A. Cloward. *Why Americans Don't Vote.* New York: Pantheon Books, 1989.

Pogrebin, Letty Cottin. *Family Politics: Love and Power on an Intimate Frontier.* New York: McGraw-Hill, 1983.

"Polygamy: Frequently Asked Questions." Statistical data provided by numerous organizations from 1998–2002. www.absalom.com/mormon/polygamy/faq.htm. Provenzo, Eugene F. *Religious Fundamentalism and American Education: The Battle for the Public Schools.* New York: State University of New York Press, 1990.

Powe, L. A. Scot, Jr. "Alter Calls: Constitutional Amendments: The Winners And Losers," *Village Voice* (March 3–9, 2004). www.villagevoice.com/issues/0409/powe.php.

Prowse, Michael. "U.S. Schools: Nearly Bottom of the Class," *Financial Times,* May 4, 1990, p. 18.

Quinney, Richard. *Criminology.* Boston: Little, Brown, 1979.

Radke, Marian J., and Helen G. Trager. "Children's Perceptions of the Social Roles of Negroes and Whites," *Journal of Psychology 29* (1950): 3–33.

Redfield, Robert. *The Folk Culture of Yucatan.* Chicago: University of Chicago Press, 1941.

Reich, Robert B. "As the World Turns," *The New Republic,* May 21, 1989, pp. 23–28.

Reich, Robert B. "Secession of the Successful," *New York Times Magazine,* March 17, 1991, pp. 16–45.

Reiss, Ira L. "The Universality of the Family: A Conceptual Analysis," *Journal of Marriage and the Family* 27 (November 1965): 443–453.

Religious Movements Homepage at the University of Virginia (2000). http://religiousmovements.lib.virginia.edu.

Ribadeneira, Diego. "Schools in Transition," *Washington Post Education Review,* August 5, 1990, p. 1.

Riccio, James. "Religious Affiliation and Socioeconomic Achievement," in Robert Wuthnow, ed., *The Religious Dimension: New Directions in Quantitative Research.* New York: Academic Press, 1979, pp. 199–231.

Rice, Thomas. "American Public Policy Formation and Implementation," in Roger A. Strauss, ed. *Using Sociology: An Introduction from the Clinical Perspective.* Bayside, New York: General Hall, 1985.

Rich, Spencer. "Hunger Said to Afflict 1 in 8 American Children," *Washington Post,* March 27, 1991b, p. A4.

Rich, Spencer. "Nearly 500,000 Children Rely on Government Care," *Washington Post,* December 12, 1989, p. 1.

Rich, Spencer. "U.S. Poverty Rate up: Median Income Falls," *Washington Post,* September 27, 1991a, p. 1.

Ridley, F. F., ed. *Government and Administration in Western Europe.* New York: St. Martin's Press, 1979.

Riesman, David, with Nathan Glazer and Reuel Denney. *The Lonely Crowd: A Study of the Changing American Character.* New Haven, CT: Yale University Press, 1950.

Risley, Robert L. "Legalizing Euthanasia Would Be Beneficial," in *Opposing Viewpoints Sources: Death/Dying, 1989 Annual.* San Diego: Greenhaven Press, 1989, pp. 49–54. (Originally published by Robert L. Risley as "In Defense of the Humane and Dignified Death Act," *Free Inquiry,* Winter, 1988–1989)

Ritzer, George. *Contemporary Sociological Theory,* 3rd ed. New York: McGraw-Hill, 1991.

Roethlisberger, Fritz J., and William J. Dickson. *Management and the Worker.* Cambridge, MA: Harvard University Press, 1939.

Rogers, Everett M. *Diffusion of Innovations.* New York: Free Press, 1983.

Romaine, Suzanne. *Bilingualism.* Oxford, England: Basil Blackwell, 1989.

Root, Waverley, and Richard de Rochemont. *Eating in America: A History.* New York: Ecco Press, 1976.

Rose, Vicki McNickle, and Susan Carol Randall. "The Impact of Investigator Perceptions of Victim Legitimacy on the Processing of Rape Sexual Assault Cases," *Symbolic Interaction 5* (Spring 1982): 23–36.

Rosenthal, Robert, and Lenore Jacobson. *Pygmalion in the Classroom: Teacher Expectation and Pupil's Intellectual Development.* New York: Holt, Rinehart and Winston, 1968.

Ross, Catherine E., John Mirowsky, and Patricia Ulbrich. "Comparison of Mexicans and Anglos," *American Journal of Sociology 89* (November 1983b): 670–682.

Rossi, Peter. *Down and Out in America: The Origins of Homelessness.* Chicago: University of Chicago Press, 1989.

Rossi, Peter. *Without Shelter: Homelessness in the 1980s.* New York: Priority Press, 1989.

Rossi, Peter H., and William Foote Whyte. "The Applied Side of Sociology," in Howard E. Freeman, Russel R. Dynes, Peter H. Rossi, and William Foote Whyte, eds., *Applied Sociology.* San Francisco: Jossey-Bass, 1983.

Rothenberg, Paula. "Critics of Attempts to Democratize the Curriculum Are Waging a Campaign to Misrepresent the Work of Responsible Professors," *The Chronicles of Higher Education 37* (April 10, 1991): B1, B3.

Rothman, Barbara Katz. "Midwives in Transition: The Structure of a Clinical Revolution," in Peter Conrad and

Rochelle Kern, eds., *The Sociology of Health and Illness: Critical Perspectives*, 2nd ed. New York: St. Martin's Press, 1986a.

Rothman, Barbara Katz. *The Tentative Pregnancy: Prenatal Diagnoses and the Future of Motherhood.* New York: Viking, 1986b.

Rothman, Robert A. *Inequality and Stratification in the United States.* Englewood Cliffs, NJ: Prentice-Hall, 1978.

Rothman, Robert A. *Inequality and Stratification: Race, Class, and Gender*, fifth edition. Englewood Cliffs, NJ: Pearson Prentice Hall, 2005.

Rothstein, William G. *American Physicians in the Nineteenth Century: From Sects to Science.* Baltimore: Johns Hopkins Press, 1970.

Rovner, Sandy. "Battered Wives: Centuries of Silence," *Washington Post Health* [Washington, DC], August 20, 1991, p. 7.

Rowe, David C., and D. Wayne Osgood. "Heredity and Sociological Theories of Delinquency: A Reconsideration," *American Sociological Review 49* (August 1984): 526–540.

Rowland, Robyn. "A Child at Any Price? An Overview of Issues in the Use of the New Reproductive Technologies, and the Threat to Women," *Women's Studies International Forum 8* (1985): 539–546.

Rubin, J., F. Provenzano, and Z. Luria. "The Eye of the Beholder: Parents' Views on Sex of Newborns," *American Journal of Orthopsychiatry 44* (1974): 512–519.

Rubin, Lillian. *Intimate Strangers.* New York: Harper and Row, 1983.

Rubin, Zick. *Liking and Loving.* New York: Holt, Rinehart and Winston, 1973.

Ruopp, R., J. Travers, F. Glantz, and C. Coelen. *Children at the Center: Summary Findings and Their Implications.* Cambridge, MA: Abt Books, 1979.

Russell, John. *British Medieval Population.* Albuquerque: University of New Mexico Press, 1972.

Ryan, William. *Equality.* New York: Pantheon Books, 1981.

Sadker, Myra, and David Sadker. "Sexism in the Classroom: From Grade School to Graduate School," *Phi Delta Kappan*, March, 1986, pp. 512–515.

Sadker, Myra, and David Sadker. "Sexism in the Schoolroom of the '80s," *Psychology Today*, March, 1985, pp. 54–57.

Sager, Alan. "Opiate of the Managers," *Society 23* (July/ August 1986): 65–71.

Sakamoto, Arthur, and Changhwan Kim. "The Declining Significance of Race, the Increasing Significance of Class, and Wilson's Hypothesis," *Working Papers Series.* Austin: Population Research Center, University of Texas, 2001.

Salholz, Eloise. "Say It in English," *Newsweek*, February 20, 1989, pp. 22–23.

Salinger, Lawrence M., Paul Jesilow, Henry N. Pontell, and Gilbert Geiss. "Assaults Against Airline Flight Attendants: A Victimization Study," *Transportation Journal 25* (Fall 1985): 66–71.

Scanzoni, John, Karen Polonko, Jay Teachman, and Linda Thompson. *The Sexual Bond: Rethinking Families and Close Relationships.* Newbury Park, CA: Sage Publications, 1989.

Schaefer, Richard T. *Race and Ethnicity in the United States*, third edition. Englewood Cliffs, NJ: Pearson Prentice Hall, 2005.

Schaefer, Richard T. *Racial and Ethnic Groups*, 4th ed. New York: Harper Collins, 1990.

Schnabel, Kai U., et al. (2002). "Parental Influence on Students' Educational Choices in the United States and Germany: Different Ramifications—Same Effect?" *Journal of Vocational Behavior* 60, no. 2 (April 2002): 178–198.

Schnaiberg, Allan, and Sheldon Goldenberg. "From Empty Nest to Crowded Nest: The Dynamics of Incompletely-Launched Young Adults," *Social Problems 36* (June 1989): 251–267.

"School Prayer Controversy: Pro and Con," *Congressional Digest 63* (May 1984). Washington, DC.

Schrank, Thomas. "Schmoozing with Robert Schrank: An Interview with a Common Sense Sociologist," *Successful Business* (Spring 1979).

Schur, Edwin M. *Labeling Women Deviant: Gender, Stigma, and Social Control.* New York: Random House, 1984.

Schutt, Russell K. "The Quantity and Quality of Homelessness: Research Results and Policy Implications," *Sociological Practice Review 1*(2) (August 1990): 77–87.

Schwartz, Barry. "Social Change and Collective Memory: The Democratization of George Washington," *American Sociological Review 56* (April 1991): 221–236.

Schwartz, Felice. "Management Women and the New Facts of Life," *Harvard Business Review*, January–February, 1989, pp. 66–76.

Schwartz, Herman. "In Defense of Affirmative Action," in Leslie Dunbar, ed., *Minority Report.* New York: Pantheon Books, 1984.

Scimecca, Joseph A. *Education and Society.* New York: Holt, Rinehart and Winston, 1980.

Scott, Marvin, and Stanford Lyman. "Accounts," *American Sociological Review 33* (December 1968): 46–62.

Sears, Alan E. "The Legal Case for Restricting Pornography." In Dale Zillman and Jennings Bryant, eds., *Pornography: Research Advances and Policy Decisions.* Hillsdale, NJ: Erlbaum, 1989.

See, Patricia, and Roger Strauss. "The Sociology of the Individual," in Roger A. Strauss, ed., *Using Sociology: An In-*

troduction from the Clinical Perspective. Bayside, NY: General Hall, 1985.

Seely, Gordon M. *Education and Opportunity: For What and for Whom?* Englewood Cliffs, NJ: Prentice-Hall, 1970.

Serbin, L., and K. O'Leary. "How Nursery Schools Teach Girls to Shut Up," *Psychology Today*, December, 1975, pp. 56–58.

Sewell, William H. "Inequality of Opportunity for Higher Education," *American Sociological Review 36* (October 1971): 793–809.

Sewell, William H., and Robert M. Hauser. *Education, Occupation, and Earnings: Achievement in the Early Career.* New York: Academic Press, 1975.

Shannon, Elaine. "A Losing Battle," *Time*, December 3, 1990, pp. 44–48.

Shattuck, Roger. *The Forbidden Experiment: The Story of the Wild Boy of Aveyron.* New York: Farrar, Straus and Giroux, 1980.

Shaw, Clifford R., and Henry D. McKay. *Delinquency Areas.* Chicago: University of Chicago Press, 1929.

Sheremet, Konstantin. "Law and Social Change in the USSR of the 1990s," *Society* 27 (May/June 1990): 90–97.

Shostak, Arthur. "How Can We All Survive? Managing Social Change," in Roger A. Strauss, ed. *Using Sociology: An Introduction from the Clinical Perspective.* Bayside, New York: General Hall, 1985, pp. 172–182.

Siegel, Charles N. "The Brave New World of Children," *New Perspectives Quarterly* 7 (Winter 1990): 34–45.

Silverman, Kenneth. "Cruel and Usual Punishment" [Review of *Spare the Child: The Religious Roots of Punishment and the Psychological Impact of Physical Abuse* by Phillip Greven], *The New York Times Book Review*, February 17, 1991, pp. 5–6.

Simmons, Roberta G., Leslie Brown, Diane M. Bush, and Dale A. Blyth. "Self-esteem and Achievement of Black and White Adolescents," *Social Problems 26* (October 1978): 86–96.

Simon, G. R., and A. S. R. Manstead. *The Accountability of Conduct: A Social Psychological Analysis.* New York: Academic Press, 1983.

Simpson, George Eaton, and J. Milton Yinger. *Racial and Cultural Minorities: An Analysis of Prejudice and Discrimination.* New York: Harper and Row, 1972.

Skolnick, Arlene. *The Intimate Environment: Exploring Marriage and the Family*, 5th ed. New York: HarperCollins, 1992; 4th ed., Boston: Little, Brown, 1987.

Smart, Carol. "Power and the Politics of Child Custody," in Carol Smart and Selma Sevenhuijsen, eds., *Child Custody and the Politics of Gender.* London: Routledge and Kegan Paul, 1989.

Smart, Carol, and Selma Sevenhuijsen, eds. *Child Custody and the Politics of Gender.* London: Routledge and Kegan Paul, 1989.

Smelser, Neil J. *Theory of Collective Behavior.* New York: Free Press, 1962.

Snell, Bradford. "American Ground Transport," in Jerome H. Skolnick and Elliott Currie, eds., *Crisis in American Institutions*, 3rd ed. Boston: Little, Brown, 1976, pp. 304–326.

Snipp, C. Matthew. "Occupational Mobility and Social Class: Insights from Men's Career Mobility," *American Sociological Review 50* (August 1985): 475–493.

Spaeth, Joe. "Job Power and Earnings," *American Sociological Review 50* (1985): 603–617.

Spengler, Oswald. *The Decline of the West.* New York: Knopf, 1962. (Originally published in 1918)

Spitz, Rene A. "Hospitalism," *The Psychoanalytic Study of the Child 1* (1945): 53–72.

Spitz, Rene A. "Hospitalism: A Follow-Up Report," *The Psychoanalytic Study of the Child 2* (1946): 113–117.

Spitzer, Steven. "Toward a Marxist Theory of Deviance," *Social Problems 22* (June 1975): 638–651.

Squires, Sally. "Million-Dollar Images," *Washington Post Health*, November 6, 1990, pp. 12–13.

Sroka, Stephen R. "Common Sense on Condom Education," *Education Week 10*(5) (March 13, 1991): 39–40.

Standing, Guy. "Global Feminization Through Flexible Labor," *World Development 17* (July 1989): 1077–1095.

Stark, Oded. "A Relative Deprivation Approach to Performance Incentives in Career Games and Other Contests," *Kyklos 43* (1990): 211–227.

Stark, Rodney, and William Sims Bainbridge. "Secularization and Cult Formation in the Jazz Age," *Journal for the Scientific Study of Religion 20* (December 1981): 360–373.

Starr, Paul. *The Social Transformation of American Medicine.* New York: Basic Books, 1982.

Statistical Abstract (see U.S. Bureau of the Census, *Statistical Abstract of the United States*).

Stein, Rob. "U.S. Infant Mortality Rate Rises 3%: First Increase Since '58 Surprises Officials as Other Health Indicators Keep Improving," *Washington Post*, February 12, 2004.

Stewart, Abigail J., and Joseph M. Healy, Jr. " Linking Individual Development and Social Changes," *American Psychologist 44* (January, 1989): 30–42.

Stokes, Naomi Miller. *The Castrated Woman: What Your Doctor Won't Tell You About Hysterectomy.* New York: Franklin Watts, 1986.

Stoller, P. "The Language Planning Activities of the U.S. Office of Bilingual Education," *International Journal of the Sociology of Language 11* (1976): 45–60.

Stone, Geoffrey R. "Repeating Past Mistakes," *Society 24* (1987): 5.

Strauss, Roger A., ed. *Using Sociology: An Introduction from the Clinical Perspective.* Bayside, NY: General Hall, 1985.

"Study: More Grain Needed to Feed World in 2020," *Telegraph Herald* (Dubuque, IA), November 7, 1999.

Suchar, Charles S. *Social Deviance: Perspectives and Prospects.* New York: Holt, Rinehart and Winston, 1978.

Sumner, William G. *Folkways.* New York: New American Library, 1980. (Originally published in 1906)

Sutherland, Edwin H. *Principles of Criminology.* Philadelphia: Lippincort, 1939.

Sutherland, Edwin H. *White Collar Crime: The Uncut Version.* New Haven, CT: Yale University Press, 1983.

Sutherland, Edwin H. "White-Collar Criminality," *American Sociological Review 5* (February 1940): 1–11.

Sutherland, Edwin H., and Donald R. Cressey. *Criminology.* Philadelphia: Lippincott, 1970.

Swan, L. Alex. *The Practice of Clinical Sociology and Sociotherapy.* Cambridge, MA: Schenkman, 1984.

Swanstrom, Todd, Peter Dreier, and John Mollenkopf. "Economic Inequality and Public Policy: The Power of Place," *City & Community* 1, no. 4 (December 2002): 349–372.

Szymanski, Albert. *The Capitalist State and the Politics of Class.* Cambridge, MA: Winthrop, 1978.

Tavris, Carol, and Carole Wade. *The Longest War: Sex Differences in Perspective*, 2nd ed. New York: Harcourt Brace Jovanovich, 1984.

Taylor, Frederick Winslow. *Scientific Management.* New York: Harper and Row, 1911.

Taylor, Humphrey. "2-1 Majorities Continue to Support Rights to Both Euthanasia and Doctor-Assisted Suicide" The Harris Poll, Harris Interactive (January 9, 2002).

Taylor, Steven J. "Observing Abuse: Professional Ethics and Personal Morality," *Qualitative Sociology 10* (1987): 288–302.

Teachman, Jay D. "Early Marriage, Premarital Fertility, and Marital Dissolution," *Journal of Family Issues 4* (March 1983): 105–126.

Thio, Alex. *Deviant Behavior.* Boston: Houghton Mifflin, 1978; 3rd ed., Harper and Row, 1988.

"The 13th British Social Attitudes Report," ed. Roger Jowell, et al. (Dartmouth, 1996).

Thomlinson, Ralph. *Population Dynamics: Causes and Consequences of World Demographic Change.* New York: Random House, 1976.

Thomlinson, Ralph. *Urban Structure.* New York: Random House, 1969.

Thompson, Margaret Susan. *The "Spider Web": Congress and Lobbying in the Age of Grant.* New York: Cornell University Press, 1985.

Thornton, Billy, Michael A. Robbins, and Joel A. Johnson. "Social Perception of a Rape Victim's Culpability: The Influence of Respondents' Personal-Environmental Causal Attribution Tendencies," *Human Relations 34* (March 1981): 225–237.

Tifft, Susan. "Better Safe Than Sorry?" *Time*, January 21, 1991, pp. 66–67.

Tönnies, Ferdinand. *Community and Society;* C. P. Loomis, trans. New York: Harper and Row, 1963. (Originally published in 1887)

Towell, Pat. "Plowshare Plan Beaten," *Congressional Quarterly*, November 16, 1991a, pp. 3393–3395.

Towell, Pat. "Soviet Aid Package May Be Doomed by Calls to Keep Money at Home," *Congressional Quarterly*, November 9, 1991b, pp. 3293–3297.

Trafford, Abigail. "Gender Bias in Health Care Is No Myth," *Washington Post Health*, July 30, 1991, p. 4.

Troeltsch, Ernst. *The Social Teachings of the Christian Churches.* New York: Macmillan, 1931.

Tumin, Melvin. "On Social Inequality," *American Sociological Review 28* (February 1963): 19–26.

Turk, Herman. "Interorganizational Networks in Urban Society: Initial Perspectives and Comparative Research," *American Sociological Review 35* (February 1970): 1–19.

Turner, Castellano B., and Barbara F. Turner. "Gender, Race, Social Class, and Self-evaluations Among College Students," *The Sociological Artery 23* (Autumn 1982): 491–507.

Turner, Jonathan H. *Sociology: The Science of Human Organization.* Chicago: Nelson-Hall, 1985.

Turner R. H. "Sponsored and Contest Mobility and the School System," *American Sociological Review 25* (December 1960): 855–867.

Turner, Ralph H., and Lewis M. Killian, eds. *Collective Behavior.* Englewood Cliffs, NJ: Prentice-Hall, 1957; 2nd ed., 1972; 3rd ed., 1987.

Turner, Stephen P., and Jonathan H. Turner. *The Impossible Science: An Institutional Analysis of American Sociology.* Newbury Park, CA: Sage Publications, 1990.

Underhill, Evelyn. "Christian Mystics: The Site for Christian Mystics, Traditional and Contemporary," (2004). www.christianmystics.com.

UNFPA, "State of World Population 2004," (2004). www.unfpa.org.

United Nations. *Demographic Yearbook, 1989.* New York: 1991.

"Unstoppable Canon," *Shukan Post*, December 24, 2004. www.japantoday.com/e/?content=executive&id=176

U.S. Bureau of the Census. *Current Population Reports* (Series P-20, No. 288, "Fertility History and Prospects of

American Women: June 1975'). Washington, DC: U.S. Government Printing Office, 1976.

U.S. Bureau of the Census. *Current Population Reports* (Series P-20, No. 447, "Household and Family Characteristics: March 1990 and 1989'). Washington, DC: U.S. Government Printing Office, 1990.

U.S. Bureau of the Census. *Current Population Reports* (Series P-20, No. 448, "The Black Population in the United States: March 1990 and 1989"). Washington, DC: U.S. Government Printing Office, 1991.

U.S. Bureau of the Census. *Current Population Reports* (Series P-20, No. 450, "Marital Status and Living Arrangements: March 1990"). Washington, DC: U.S. Government Printing Office, 1991.

U.S. Bureau of the Census. *Current Population Reports* (Series P-20, No. 454, "Fertility of American Women: June 1990"). Washington, DC: U.S. Government Printing Office, 1991.

U.S. Bureau of the Census. *Current Population Reports* (Series P-20, No. 455, "The Hispanic Population in the United States: March 1991"). Washington, DC: U.S. Government Printing Office, 1991.

U.S. Bureau of the Census. *Current Population Reports* (Series P-23, No. 128, "America in Transition: An Aging Society"). Washington, DC: U.S. Government Printing Office, 1983.

U.S. Bureau of the Census. *Current Population Reports* (Series P-60, No. 170. "Money Income and Poverty Status in the United States: 1990"). Washington, DC: U.S. Government Printing Office, 1991.

U.S. Bureau of the Census. *Current Population Reports* (Series P-60, No. 175. "Poverty in the United States: 1990"). Washington, DC: U.S. Government Printing Office, 1991.

U.S. Bureau of the Census. *Statistical Abstract of the United States: 1990*, 110th ed. Washington, DC: U.S. Government Printing Office, 1990.

U.S. Bureau of the Census. *Statistical Abstract of the United States: 1991*, 111th ed. Washington, DC: U.S. Government Printing Office, 1991.

U.S. Department of Justice. "Crime in the United States." *Uniform Crime Reports*. Washington, DC: U.S. Government Printing Office, 1990.

Van den Berghe, Pierre L. *Human Family Systems: An Evolutionary View*. New York: Elsevier, 1979.

van der Sluis, I. "People Should Not Have the Right to Die," in *Opposing Viewpoints Sources: Death/Dying, 1990 Annual*. San Diego: Greenhaven Press, 1990, pp. 13–16. (Originally published by I. van der Sluis as "The Practice of Euthanasia in the Netherlands," *Issues in Law and Medicine 4* [Spring 1989])

Veevers, J. E. "The Moral Careers of Voluntary Childless Wives: Notes on the Defense of a Variant World View," *The Family Coordinator 24* (October 1975): 473–487.

Vernez, Georges, and David Ronfeldt. "The Current Situation in Mexican Immigration," *Science 51* (March 8, 1991): 1189–1193.

Vockell, Edward L. "Corporal Punishment: The Pros and Cons," *Clearing House*, March/April, 1991, pp. 278–283.

Vold, George B. *Theoretical Criminology*. New York: Oxford University Press, 1958.

Wagner, Mazie Earle, Herman J. P. Schubert, and Daniel S. P. Schubert, "Family Size Effects: A Review," *Journal of Genetic Psychology 146* (March 1985): 65–78.

Waitzkin, Howard. "A Marxian Interpretation of the Growth and Development of Coronary Care Technology," in Peter Conrad and Rochelle Kern, eds., *The Sociology of Health and Illness: Critical Perspectives*, 2nd ed. New York: St. Martin's Press, 1986.

Waller, Willard. *The Family: A Dynamic Interpretation*. New York: Cordon, 1938.

Waller, Willard, and Reuben Hill. *The Family*. New York: Dryden Press, 1951.

Wallerstein, Immanuel. *The Capitalist World-Economy*. Cambridge, England: Cambridge University Press, 1979.

Wallerstein, Immanuel. *The Politics of the World Economy: The States, the Movements, and the Civilizations*. New York: Cambridge University Press, 1984.

Wallerstein, Judith S., and Sandra Blakeslee. *Second Chances: Men, Women, and Children a Decade After Divorce*. New York: Ticknor and Fields, 1990.

Walters, Pamela Barnhouse. "Educational Expansion in the United States," *American Sociological Review 49* (October 1984): 659–671.

Wanzer, Sidney H., Daniel D. Federman, S. James Adelstein, Christine K. Cassel, Edwin H. Cassem, Ronald E. Cranford, Edward W. Hook, Bernard Lo, Charles G. Moertel, Peter Safar, Alan Stone, and Jan van Eys. "Doctors Should Sometimes Help Dying Patients Commit Suicide," in *Opposing Viewpoints Sources: Death and Dying 1990 Annual*. San Diego: Greenhaven Press, 1990, pp. 17–19. (Originally published by Wanzer et al. as "The Physician's Responsibility Toward Hopelessly Ill Patients: A Second Look," *The New England Journal of Medicine 13* [March 30, 1989])

Ware, Helen. "Polygyny: Women's Views in a Traditional Society, Nigeria, 1975," *Journal of Marriage and the Family 41* (February 1979): 185–195.

Watson, Russell. "A Death Trap in Sheffield," *Newsweek*, April 24, 1989, p. 54.

Weber, Max. *The City*. New York: Free Press, 1958.

Weber, Max. *From Max Weber: Essays in Sociology;* trans. and eds., H. Gerth and C. Wright Mills. New York: Oxford University Press, 1946.

Weber, Max. *The Protestant Ethic and the Spirit of Capitalism;* trans. Talcott Parsons. New York: Scribner's, 1930. (Originally published in 1905)

Weinberg, M. *Minority Students: A Research Appraisal.* Washington, DC: U.S. Government Printing Office, 1977.

Weinberger, Caspar W. "The State of the Union's Schools," *Forbes,* July 23, 1990, p. 27.

Weiss, Carol H., and Michael J. Bucavalas. *Social Science Research and Decision-Making.* New York: Columbia University Press, 1980.

Weiss, Ted. "Pro: Should the House-Passed Wage Proposal Be Enacted?" *Congressional Digest 68*(5) (May 1989): 150, 152.

Weitzman, Lenore J. *The Divorce Revolution: The Unexpected Social and Economic Consequences for Women and Children in America.* New York: Free Press, 1985.

Weyant, James M. *Applied Social Psychology.* New York: Oxford University Press, 1986.

Whitebook, M., C. Howes, and D. Phillips. *Who Cares? Child Care Teachers and the Quality of Care in America.* Oakland, CA: Child Care Employee Project, 1989.

Whorf, Benjamin L. "The Relation of Habitual Thought and Behavior to Language," in Leslie Spier, A. Irving Hallowell, and Stanley S. Newman (eds.), *Language, Culture and Personality: Essays in Memory of Edward Sapir.* Menasha, WI: Sapir Memorial Publication, 1941.

Whyte, William Foote. *Human Relations in the Restaurant Industry.* New York: McGraw-Hill, 1949.

Wiley, Kim Wright. "Up Against the Ceiling," *Savvy,* June, 1987, pp. 51–52.

Williams, Peter. *Popular Religion in America: Symbolic Change and the Modernization Process in Historical Perspective.* Englewood Cliffs, NJ: Prentice-Hall, 1980.

Williams, Robin M., Jr. *American Society: A Sociological Interpretation,* 3rd ed. New York: Knopf, 1970.

Willie, Charles. V. "The Inclining Significance of Race," *Society 15* (1978).

Wilson, E. O. *Sociobiology.* Cambridge, MA: Harvard University Press, 1975.

Wilson, William Julius. *The Declining Significance of Race.* Chicago: University of Chicago Press, 1978.

Wilson, William Julius. *The Truly Disadvantaged: The Inner City, the Underclass, and Public Policy.* Chicago: University of Chicago Press, 1987.

Wilson, William Julius (ed.). "The Ghetto Underclass: Social Science Perspectives," *Annals of the American Academy of Political and Social Science 50* (January 1989).

Winch, Robert F. *Mate Selection.* New York: Harper, 1958.

Winch, Robert F., Thomas Ktsanes, and Virginia Ktsanes. "The Theory of Complementary Needs in Mate Selection: An Analytic and Descriptive Study," *American Sociological Review 19* (June 1954): 241–249.

Wirth, Louis. "Urbanism as a Way of Life," *American Journal of Sociology 44* (July 1938): 3–24.

Wolf, A. "What Is the Economic Case for Treating Obesity?" *Obesity Research* 6 (1998 supplement): 2S–7S.

Wolf, A. M., and G. A. Colditz. "Current Estimates of the Economic Cost of Obesity in the United States," *Obesity Research* 6, no. 2 (1998): 97–106.

Wood, Floris W., ed. *An American Profile—Opinions and Behavior, 1972–1989.* Detroit: Gale Research, 1990.

World Almanac and Book of Facts, 1992. New York: Pharos Books, 1991.

Wright, James D. "Address Unknown: Homelessness in Contemporary America," *Society 26*(6) (September/ October 1989): 45–53.

Yankauer, Alfred. "What Infant Mortality Tells Us," *American Journal of Public Health 80* (
June 1990): 653–654.

Yinger, J. Milton. "Countercultures and Social Change," *American Sociological Review 42* (December 1977): 833–853.

Zeisel, John. *Sociology and Architectural Design.* New York: Russell Sage Foundation, 1973.

Zelditch, M., Jr. "Role Differentiation in the Nuclear Family," in Talcott Parsons, Robert F. Bales, James Olds, Morris Zelditch, and Philip E. Slater (eds.), *Family, Socialization and Interaction Process.* Glencoe, IL: Free Press, 1955.

Zimbardo, Philip G. "The Pathology of Imprisonment," in James H. Henslin, ed. *Down to Earth Sociology: Introductory Readings,* 6th ed. New York: Free Press, 1991, pp. 287–293.

Zirkel, P. A. "Self-concept and the Disadvantage of Ethnic Group Membership and Mixture," *Review of Educational Research 41* (1971): 211–225.

Zweigenhaft, Richard L., and G. William Domhoff. *Blacks in the White Establishment: A Study of Race and Class in America.* New Haven, CT: Yale University Press, 1991.

Zwerdling, Daniel. "The Food Monopolies," in Jerome H. Skolnick and Elliott Currie, eds., *Crisis in American Institutions,* 3rd ed. Boston: Little, Brown, 1976, pp. 43–51.

Zhu Xiao Di, Yi Yang and Xiaodong Liu. "Young American Adults Living in Parental Homes," *Joint Center for Housing Studies* (Winter 2002– 2003).

Index

A

Achieved statuses 43
Addiction intervention 212-213
Adulthood, socialization in 170-171
Advanced horticultural societies 208
African-American population 245, 248
Age differentiation 277
Aged
  problems of 293-294
  sociology in nursing care of 298-299
Aggregate group 127
Aging
  defined 280-282
  demographics of 285
  myths about 282
  theories of 289
Agrarian societies 209
AIDS 455-456
Amalgamation 243
Amelioration, social control through 492
Anglo conformity 242
Anomonie theory of deviance 185-188
Apartheid 238
Artifacts 106
Ascribed statuses 43
Asian-American population 246, 249
Assimilation 243
Associational or organizational group 127
Authoritarian personality theory 234
Automobile, social impact of 572-573
  societal analysis in 576-577

B

Bilateral lineage 317
Bilingualism 95, 112
Biological theories of deviance 183
Blacks, self-esteem of 10
Blaming the victim 182
Bureaucracy 143-146
  in Japan 145
  dysfunctions of 144
Bureaucratization of society 121-122

C

Caste system 209
Categorical groups 127
Censorship 485, 503
Chicago School 41
Child care research 151
Children
  beliefs about 385
  child care for 151
  gender roles for 166
  human interaction necessary for 154
  in institutions 154
  isolated and feral 154
  socialization of 151
Class consciousness 216-217
  closed 209
  defined 209
  open 209
  sources of power 210
Classical perspective of acting-crowd behavior 495
Cohabitation, nonmarital 335
Collective behavior
  defined 487
  of crowds and mobs 492-498
  of masses and publics 499-501
  preconditions of 488-490
  social movements 504
Collective excitement 496
Community
  changing 537
  development and urbanization of 539
Compulsory public education 384
Concentration, of populations 546
Concentric zone model 547, 548
Concept 67
Conflict theory 46-50
  of aging
  of deviance 188
  of economic development
  of family 321
  of illness 461
  of religion 356
  of social change 568
  of social stratification 214
  on political systems 408-409
Contest mobility 398
Conversion effect 552
Core nation 574
Countercultures 114
Creationism versus evolution 27-28, 48
Creationism versus evolutionism 567-568
Credentialism 383-384
Crime
  organized 197
  rates of 9, 195-196, 553-555
Crowds
  acting 493
  casual 493
  conventional 493
  defined 492
  theories of behavior 494
Cultural capital 210
Cultural complexity and diversity 111-115
Cultural lag 107-108
Cultural relativism 110
Cultural transmission theory 189
Cultural universals 115
Culture
  defined 97
  elements of 98-106
  ideal versus real 115
  interpreting 108
  material 106-107
  society and 95
Cyclical theories of change 568

D

Death and dying 301-303
  fear of 11
Death rates 464
Deconcentration 546
Demography 515-518
  defined 515
Dependency theory 573
Descriptive research 70-72
Developmental perspective of the family 324-326
Deviance
  absolute view 178
  defined 177
  formal external controls 199
  immoral view of 178
  informal external controls 198
  internal controls 197
  medical view 178
  relativistic view 179
  social consequences of 193
  social control and 175
  statistical view 178
  theories of 183
  traditional views of 178
Differential association theory 190
Differential reinforcement 190
Direct relationship 68
Discovery versus invention 571
Discrimination 237
  institutional 236-237
Displacement 242
Division of labor 208
Divorce rates 8, 331-334
Dramaturgical approach 161

Drugs
testing of employees 140
use of 175-177, 212
Dysfunction 44

E

Ecological changes 569
Ecological specialization 546-547
Ecology
population and 511, 569-570
urban 546
Economic groups and systems 429
theories of 434-436
types of 431-433, 436-439, 447-450
Education. See also Schools
historical perspectives on
life chances and 219
necessity of 398-399
occupational choices 399
quality of 377-378
social mobility and 398
theories of 379-382
Educational groups and systems 377
Egalitarian model of authority 317
Elite culture 97
Emergent-norm perspective of crowd behavior 496
Employee drug testing 140-141
Endogamy 317
Environment 511-515
protection measures for 530-531
Ethics in research 63-65
Ethnic antagonism 242
Ethnic groups. See also specific groups 232, 245
Ethnic stratification 240
Ethnocentrism 108
Ethnography 71
Ethnography research 71
Europe
women's movement in 269
Evaluation research 74-75
Evolutionary theory 55-57, 567
Exchange theory 53-55
of family 322
Exclusion 242
Exogamy 317
Experimental designs as sociology research 82-85, 86
Explanatory research 73
Expressive leader 135

F

Fad 499
False consciousness 214
Family
American 326
as agency of socialization 319
blended 320
conjugal 312
functions of 318
nontraditional 335
nuclear 312
organization of 314
perspectives on 320
size of 329
Family counseling career 332-333
Family Groups and Systems 309
Family of orientation 312
Family of procreation 312
Fashions 499
Feminist theories 58
Financial consultant career 448-449
Folk society 549
Folkways 104
Fraternal polyandry 316
Frustration-aggression theory 234
Functional alternatives 45
Fundamentalism, religion 345-347, 352

G

Game perspective of crowd behavior 497
Gamesman 578
Gemeinschaft 549
Gender differentiation 259
adult 262
bases of 261-262
cross-cultural 263
sex and 261
theories of 263-264
workplace and 265-268
Gender roles 165
Generalized belief 489
Generalized other 158
Genocide 238
Gentrification 557
Gesellschaft 549
Ghetto 553
Greenbelt 557
Group interaction, patterns of 239
Group marriage 315
Groups, social 116
in and out 131
peer 132, 164, 168
primary and secondary 129-130
reference 132-133
small and large 133

H

Health movements 472-474
Health-care groups and systems 455
Hidden curriculum 382
Hispanic-American population 246-247
Homelessness 537-538
Horticulture, in early communities 539
Human ecology and change 483
Human interaction, importance of 154
Humanistic theories 58
Hunting-and-gathering societies 208
Hypothesis 67-68

I

Ideal culture 115
Ideal type 143
Ideology 214
Idiocultures 114
Illness
pathological and statistical 458
patterns of 462
theories of 458, 465
In-Groups 130
Incest 317
Income inequality, growth of 205-206
Industrial societies 209
Inequality
and life chances 218
consequences of gender 271-273
ethnic and racial 227
Influence peddling, political 403-405
Inner-directed 577-578
Institutional Review Boards (IRBs) 63
Institutionalization 506
Instrumental leader 135
Integration 242
Interactionist perspective
of crowd behavior 495
of the family 323
Invasion in communities 546
Inventions versus discovery 571
Inverse relationships 68

J

Jewish-Americans 252

K

Kinship 314

L

Labeling theory 191-192
Language in culture 99
Latent functions 45
Laws, in a culture 105
Life
city 549-551, 551-552, 552-553
end of. See also Death rates 277
suburban 551
Life chances 210, 218
Life expectancy 286-287
table of 433
Lobbying restrictions 418-420
Looking-glass self 160

M

Magnet schools 394
Manifest functions 44
Market research career 500-501

Marriage rates and trends 328
Marriage, partners and types of 318
Mass expulsion 239
Mass hysteria 500-501
Mass media
as agency of socialization 165
gender-role socialization in 168
political socialization in 417, 420
Masses and behavior 499
Matriarchal norm of authority 317
Matrilineal line of descent 316
Matrilocal, residence norm 316
Mean 87
Mechanical solidarity 209
Median 87
Medical billing 474-475
Medical care costs 470-472
Megalopolis 545-546
Melting pot 242
Metropolitan statistical area (MSA) 544-546
Middle-range theory 42
Milling of crowds 496
Minority groups 232
Mobility of students, contest and sponsored 398
Mobilization for action 422-423
Mobs 493-494
Mode 87
Modernization 573
Monogamy 315
serial 315
Mores 105
Mortification of self 170
Multinational corporations 429-430, 439
Multiple-nuclei model 547

N

Native American population 246, 250
Nature-nurture debate 155-156
Neolocal, residence norm 316
Nonsociologists, sociological skills of 19-22
Normative theory 234
Norms, cultural 104, 114

O

Observation studies as sociological research 78
Operation of social control 489
Operational definition 70
Organic solidarity 209
Organizations, formal 138
Other-directed 578
Out-Groups 130

P

Panic 500
Party, as a social group 210
Pathology of normalcy 106
Patriarchal norm of authority 317
Patrilineal line of descent 316
Patrilocal, residence norm 316
Peer Group 131
Peer groups
as agency of socialization 164, 167
Peripheral nation 574
Play, as a form of role taking 157
Pluralism, cultural 244
Police, role of 491
Political groups and systems 403
development of 407
Polygamy 315
Polygyny 315
fraternal 316
Popular culture 97
Popular excitement 505
Population
ecology and 511
monitoring population trends 528-529
world 523-529
Population trends 521
Poverty 217
Power and authority 405-407
Prayer in schools 48-50
Precipitating factor 489
Prejudice against category of people 233-236
Prescribed role 123-124
Presentation of self 160-161
Primary group 128
Principle of legitimacy 320
Product development career 136
Projection 234
Prolonged adolescence 380-381
Propaganda 503
Proposition 67
Psychological theories of deviance 184
Public 502
Public opinion 502
Public sociologies 3-4, 19

Q

Qualitative methods 77
Quantitative methods 77

R

Racial and ethnic differentiation 227
Racial groups 231
Racism 237-238
dysfunctionality of 238
institutional 238
Radicalism 242
Random sample 80
Range 88
Real culture 115
Reference groups 132
Relative deprivation 132
Relativistic view of defiance 178
Reliability, in research 71
Religion
schools and 389
Religious
defined 348-349
marital status and 372
other institutions and 372-373
sociological approach to 348
theories of 353-356
trends in 365
types of world 357
Religious groups and systems 345
Religious refugees 364-365
Repressive measures 491
hidden 491
Research analyst career 82
Research process 85-88
Resocialization 170
Resource mobilization theory 505
Role ambiguity 124
Role conflict 124
Role perception 124
Role performance 124
Role set 123
Role strain 124
Role taking 157
Roles social 123

S

Same-sex relationships 310-311, 317, 335
Sampling technique in research
stratified 81
systematic 81
Sapir-Whorf hypothesis 100
Scapegoating 234
School boards 386, 387
Schools. See also Education
as agency of socialization 164, 167
gender-role socialization in 166
improving 394-397
private and parochial, U.S. 390
problems with 391-394
religion and 48-50, 389
Scientific inquiry, standards of 69-70
Scientific method 66
Scientific theory, components of 68
Secondary analysis as sociology research 85, 86
Secondary groups 128
Sector model 547, 548
Segregation 243
de facto 244
de jure 243
Self, symbolic interaction 158-159
Self-fulfilling prophecy 160, 394
Significant others, in role taking 157
Simple horticultural societies, 208

Slums 553
Social inequality 203
  defined 207
  in United States 216-218
  life chances affected by 218
Social Change
  causes of 569
  defined 567
  for individuals 575
  in underdeveloped nations 573
  nature of 565
  theories of 567
Social class 210
Social contagion 496
Social control, deviance and 175
Social differentiation
  defined 207
  social stratification and 205
  types of societies and 208
Social distance 242
Social exchange theory 292
Social groups 126
  types of 126
Social Institutions 116
Social interaction, socialization and 151
Social mobility 221-223
  downward 221
  intergenerational 221
  intragenerational 221
  upward 222
Social movements 504
Social networks 138
Social organizations 116
  formal 138
Social roles 123
Social science, applied versus pure 4-5, 15
Social status 209
  in American society 216
Social stratification
  defined 207-208
  in school system 387-388
  theories of 212-215
  types of 209-211
Social systems 43-44
Social theories 43-58
Social unrest 505
Socialization
  agencies of 163-165
  defined 153
  of gender roles 166-169
  political 416-417
  social interaction and 151
Society
  bureaucratization of 121
  culture and 95
  individuals within 95
  methods of studying 63
  political structures in 409
  types of 208
Sociobiological theories 57, 155
Sociocultural learning theories 189-190
Sociological research, methods and types of 70
Sociological theories of deviance 185
Sociologists, types of 15
Sociology
  as science
  defined 6
  development of 27
  municipal politics and 423
  nature and uses of 3
  occupational and personal uses of 16-23
  relationship of other social sciences to 12-15
Spatially diffuse collectives 498
Spatially proximate collective 492
Split labor market 222
Sponsored mobility 398
Statistical groups 127
Status set 123
Status, social 123
Stereotypes 234
Strain theory of deviance 185
Structural assimilation 243
Structural conduciveness 489
Structural functional theory 43
  of aging 290
  of economic development 434
  of education 379-382
  of illness 458
  of political systems 408
  of religion 353
  of social stratification 214
  of upward mobility 222
Structural strain 489
Subcultures 111-113
Suburbs 548-549
Succession, in communities 546
Survey research in sociology
Symbolic interaction 157
Symbolic interaction theory 51-52
  of family 323
  of aging 291
Symbols, cultural 98-99

T

Tables, steps in reading 13
Taboos 105
Teacher trainer career 101
Technology, material culture and 106
Temporocentrism 109
Theoretical perspectives 42
Theory 43
Trained incapacity 144

U

United States
  aging population of 286
  economic system in 436
  health-care system 465
  political system in
  urbanization in 543-544
  women's movement 269
Urban ecology 546
Urban homesteading 557
Urban revitalization 555
Urbanization
  in the United States 543

V

Validity, in research
Values, cultural 102-104, 115
Variable
Variance
Verstehen 40
Voluntary associations 146-147
Vouchers, school 395

W

Wealth, distribution of 446
Welfare 446
White ethnic Americans 245, 251
Women
  inequality of 270
  self-esteem of 271
  work in family 268
Women's movement 269-270, 398
Work, nature of 440
Workers, management of 440
World systems theory 574-578

X

Xenocentrism 109